CHINA'S ECONOMIC DILEMMAS IN THE 1990s

Studies on Contemporary China

CHINA'S ECONOMIC DILEMMAS IN THE 1990s

THE PROBLEMS OF REFORMS, MODERNIZATION, AND INTERDEPENDENCE

EDITED BY THE JOINT ECONOMIC COMMITTEE, CONGRESS OF THE UNITED STATES

M.E. Sharpe

Armonk, New York
London, England

Library of Congress Cataloging-in-Publication Data

China's economic dilemmas in the 1990s : the problems of reforms,
modernization, and interdependence / edited by the
Joint Economic Committee, Congress of the United States.

p. cm.(Studies in contemporary China)
Includes index.
ISBN 1-56324-158-7.—ISBN 1-56324-159-5 (pbk.)
1. China—Economic conditions—1976–
2. China—Economic policy—1976{
3. China—Foreign economic relations.
I. United States. Congress. Joint Economic Committee.
II. Series.

HC427.92.46469 1992
338.951′009′049—dc20
92-29068
CIP

Printed in the United States of America

The paper used in this publication meets the minimum requirements of
American National Standard for Information Sciences—
Permanence of Paper for Printed Library Materials,
ANSI Z39.48–1984.

BM(c) 10 9 8 7 6 5 4 3 2 1
BM(p) 10 9 8 7 6 5 4 3 2

LETTER OF TRANSMITTAL

APRIL 17, 1991

To the Members of the Joint Economic Committee:

I am hereby transmitting for use by the Joint Economic Committee, Congress, and the public a study assessing the economy of the People's Republic of China entitled, China's Economic Dilemmas in the 1990s: The Problems of Reforms, Modernization, and Interdependence. The study is in two volumes and comprises papers prepared at the committee's request by a large number of government and private experts.

China has made significant gains in the period since economic reforms were introduced more than a decade ago. But in recent years it has experienced serious problems which many experts believe have slowed and perhaps halted the momentum towards liberalization of the economy. The leadership understands that change is necessary to achieve modernization, but fears the instability that might accompany further change. The papers in these volumes examine recent economic performance and policies, and the underlying debate over the basic direction that China should follow.

The study was planned and directed by John P. Hardt, Associate Director of the Congressional Research Service of the Library of Congress, and Richard F Kaufman, General Counsel of the Joint Economic Committee. Leo A. Orleans acted as publications coordinator, assisted by Phillip Kaiser. We are grateful to the Congressional Research Service for making Dr. Hardt and others available to work on the project, and to the many authors who contributed papers.

The views contained in the volumes are those of the authors and not necessarily those of the Joint Economic Committee or its individual members.

Sincerely,

PAUL S. SARBANES,
Chairman.

LETTER OF SUBMITTAL

THE LIBRARY OF CONGRESS,
CONGRESSIONAL RESEARCH SERVICE,
Washington, DC, April 12, 1991.

Hon. PAUL S. SARBANES
Chairman, Joint Economic Committee
Congress of the United States
Washington, DC.

DEAR MR. CHAIRMAN: I am pleased to be able to transmit to you a collection of papers on the economy of the People's Republic of China entitled, "China's Economic Dilemmas in the 1990s: The Problems of Reforms, Modernization, and Interdependence."

The study was directed by John P. Hardt, Associate Director of the Congressional Research Service and Richard F Kaufman, General Counsel of the Joint Economic Committee. Leo A. Orleans served as the coordinator of the publication, assisted by Phillip Kaiser. Many CRS and other Library of Congress personnel, as well as government and private specialists, contributed significantly to the project.

We trust that the analyses and information contained in this study will be of value to the Joint Economic Committee, as well as the Congress in general and the broad audience of students of China.

Sincerely,

JOSEPH E. ROSS,
Director.

CONTENTS

CHINESE MODEL FOR CHANGE: PROSPECTS AND PROBLEMS

By John P. Hardt and Richard F Kaufman *

In his vision for China, Deng Xioping understood that in order to modernize, the country would have to open up to the outside world, and introduce market forces into the economy. The decollectivization of agriculture was followed by a variety of reforms to adjust the Stalinist system of central controls, but the impressive economic performance over the past decade was accomplished without democratization and without rejecting socialism.

Current models of democratization and transition toward a market economy in Central and Eastern Europe and elsewhere raise many questions about China. How applicable is the experience of the East European countries to the People's Republic of China? Will Western corporations, which favor a competitive market, be deterred from investing in a politically stagnant and economically indecisive China? What are the prospects for further reforms? Is China likely to follow in the footsteps of South Korea's Pak Chung-hi, who built that country's "economic miracle" by combining authoritarian control with some market reforms? Although these are difficult questions to answer at this time, many of the chapters in these two volumes provide a basis for considering the various options open to China. There is general agreement, however, that any major changes in the present system will have to wait for the passing of Deng and his octogenarian colleagues.

Continuity and caution are the hallmarks of the 8th Five-Year Plan (1991–95) and the 10-year development program for the 1990s. Official discussion of the plan in January 1991 was cautious in emphasizing a need for greater efficiency but suggesting that for now Chinese party leaders are rejecting any radical changes in their economic system. No mention was made, for example, of any steps which would resolve the problems associated with government subsidies to the large and inefficient state enterprises, to the transportation system, and to the privileged urban population, which pays a fraction of the market value for both food and housing. Instead, the new plan seems to focus on reducing uncertainties and only fine-tuning some of the existing policies with regard to prices, finance, taxation, banking, planning, investment, labor and wages.

---

* John P. Hardt is Associate Director, Congressional Research Service, Library of Congress. Richard F Kaufman is General Counsel, Joint Economic Committee, U.S. Congress.

BLUEPRINT FOR THE FUTURE: CONTINUITY AND CAUTION

Continuity of the political framework for the economy was taken as a given. However, unable to force uniformity throughout the country, the weakened central government is no longer micromanaging output levels and materials allocations in all areas, and is searching for policies that would reduce the huge regional differences that now exist between the Special Economic Zones, the large municipalities, and some of the coastal provinces, on the one hand, and the less developed heartland of China on the other hand. Since 1988 there has been a partial reversal of the more liberal economic policies of the mid-1980s. This trend was reinforced after the Tiananmen incident in 1989, strengthening the hands of China's reactionary faction which had opposed many of Deng's market-oriented reforms.

The experiences of other socialist countries which have attempted to reform their economies suggest that a comprehensive approach is necessary. Eastern European countries which have reformed their political systems by making them more democratic have also made the most progress in reforming their economic systems and show the most promise for the future. These efforts contrast sharply with the failed gradual, partial and ambiguous reform efforts of the past. A recent report by several of the largest multilateral financial and economic institutions urges that the Soviet Union implement a comprehensive program of systemic reforms involving the legal, financial, and trade systems, and other vital sectors of the economy.

How relevant are these verdicts to China? Could and should China combine development of political pluralism with a rapid fundamental transition to the market? As might be noted in these volumes and the broader literature, there is no agreement among the China analysts outside or inside the PRC. Some believe that political reforms must go hand-in-hand with, or even precede, economic reforms; others agree with the Chinese leadership and maintain that given China's level of development and her traditional cultural orientation, economic successes over the past decade required social order and could only have been achieved under strong central authority. However, even those who agree with the past necessity of the unique Deng model would question its continued relevance and potential for improving performance.

PERFORMANCE

China's economic performance in the 1980s was a success by most measures. In this decade of reform, the economy expanded at an annual average rate of about 10 percent, living standards and consumption more than doubled, and for most of the period inflation was kept under control. By the end of the decade, China's foreign trade had more than tripled and the PRC had become an important player on the global economic stage. In 1989 China was the world's 13th largest exporter and total trade was equivalent to about one-fourth of its gross national product.

But in the late 1980s, it began experiencing serious problems. Rapid industrial growth intensified shortages of energy and raw materials, and led to transportation bottlenecks. An austerity program was implemented in 1988 to cool the overheated economy and to control inflation which had been accelerating since 1985. Restrictive policies, including sharp cutbacks of credit and added price controls, were effective in dampening inflation. In the process, reforms were put on hold and in some cases reversed; economic growth slowed to about one-third the average for the earlier part of the decade, and unemployment increased. While sustained hyperinflation was avoided, the underlying causes of inflation remain: weakness of the banking system and a tendency in normal times toward excessive growth of credit, protection of inefficient state enterprises, and the distortions caused by the price system.

Beijing extended the austerity program to the foreign sector. To rein in the growth of trade, trading authority was recentralized and a larger share of exports and imports were subjected to controls. The Tiananmen crisis resulted in reduced resource flows from abroad, accelerating the deterioration in the current account balance and the rise in debt service requirements that were already underway. For example, tourism declined sharply, foreign investors postponed projects, and there was a drop in commercial lending. However, these repercussions may prove to be temporary.

UNDERLYING DILEMMAS IN DENG'S MODERNIZATION FORMULA FOR THE FUTURE

As China enters a new economic planning period, the leadership appears indecisive about its critical economic dilemmas. There is a tug-of-war within the political hierarchy over the basic direction China should pursue; and there are differing opinions at this time among the top economic advisers as to the most promising steps that should be taken in order to improve economic performance and raise living standards. Chinese leaders seem to understand that some more basic economic reforms are a prerequisite to modernization, but want to make sure that such reforms are not accompanied by inflation, inequality, corruption, and disorder. The leadership knows, for example, how important it is to continue price reforms, but seems unsure as to when, how, or how quickly to introduce price revisions and the idea of decontrolling prices has been postponed indefinitely. It knows that the door to the outside world must be kept open, but it also fears creeping foreign intervention and subversion of traditional values by the westernization of Chinese society. The leadership understands the need for substantial change, but also requires political, social, and economic stability and fears change will bring about instability. The difficulty foreign observers have in predicting the direction China is likely to take during the coming decade is simply a reflection of the indecisiveness the Chinese themselves are experiencing as they try to balance forces for change and continuity.

The successes of Deng's modernization from 1978 to date notwithstanding, and no matter what mix of market and planned economy China chooses to adopt in the next decade, there are certain dilemmas and contradictions that will have to be faced and that will be more difficult to resolve than in the past. The fact that most of these problems are familiar and in no sense new does not in any way diminish the difficulties they raise. That is why even many of those who supported Deng's model in the past may have second thoughts about the future. Many Western experts would agree that Beijing will not be able to achieve both rapid economic expansion and price stability under the present economic system.

HUMAN FACTORS: MALTHUS REVISITED, WILL POPULATION EXCEED SUBSISTENCE?

China's population, now well over 1.1 billion, is increasing by almost 15 million every year. Because of increasing difficulties in imposing sanctions on couples exceeding the planned number of births, because a large proportion of the population currently is of prime reproductive age, and because of low mortality, the rate of population growth is not likely to decline during the 1990s. By the year 2000, China's total population is expected to be close to 1.3 billion.

China faces serious employment problems as it moves from a labor-intensive society to one that is more capital-intensive. This has been especially true in the most recent years, with some 20 million people being added to the labor force every year. Jobs were created during the boom years of the 1980s for the growing working age population, but economic retrenchment, which has reduced the labor absorption capacity of cities and rural industries, has caused unemployment and a large "floating population" of migrant workers. Also, China's aged population is expanding, and that will create an additional burden on the country's productive labor force to provide a safety net for the old and less employable.

While modernization will require an ever better educated labor force, China's per-capita expenditure on education has been decreasing. The illiteracy rate is still holding at over 20 percent. Even more distressing to the authorities is that the attendance rate of school-age children has been going down and the dropout rate has been rising.

MODERNIZATION OF AGRICULTURE

China has 22 percent of the world's population and only 7 percent of the world's farmland. For three decades, agricultural production has fluctuated widely due to natural disasters, faulty national policies, and local mismangaement, but in the period of reform, Chinese agriculture has demonstrated major achievements. By reducing the role of administrative controls and increasing the role of market forces during the 1980s, the gross value of agriculutral prodcution nearly doubled, and productivity and farm incomes rose sharply.

Understandably, agriculture, which must annually produce more just to keep up with the population growth, continues to be listed as one of China's top national priorities. However, because of its much higher level of productivity, it is unrealistic to expect the agricultural sector to continue its rapid increase into the 1990s. Moreover, it will be facing some serious problems: (1) lacking adequate legal protection and unsure of their land tenure rights, peasants have felt insecure and unwilling to invest in their land, thus inhibiting development; (2) it is difficult to introduce modern technology and improve efficiency when peasants operate "stamp-size" plots—

a condition that is not likely to change soon; (3) too much money and labor have been diverted from agriculture to rural enterprises, which now account for over one-quarter of China's industrial production. Some Chinese officials propose consolidating farms and reassessing administrative controls, but the consensus abroad is that agricultural success can only come if China stays with market-oriented reforms.

INDUSTRIAL MODERNIZATION

Industry made significant progress in the 1980s, especially in areas where foreign investment and joint ventures have been encouraged, such as civil aviation. Industrial production has also increased greatly in township enterprises and collective factories. Nevertheless, serious problems remain and progress may be at a standstill unless more resources are allocated to infrastructure improvements and unless the path of market oriented reforms in manufacturing is resumed.

One obvious problem is that industrial reforms have not been extended to the large state-owned enterprises which are managed in about the same way they always have been under central planning. A growing proportion of these enterprises depend on government subsidies. Elsewhere in industry there has been a suspension of efforts at economic liberalization and deregulation. The trend since 1988 has been toward greater centralized control. In addition, limited budget resources and scarce hard currency hold back efforts to modernize the infrastructure.

There was a significant expansion and upgrading of equipment and facilities in transportation and telecommunications, but railroad and highway transportation have been unable to keep up with demand and telephone service is among the poorest in the world. These problems, together with shortfalls in energy production, may constrain the future expansion of industry and, in turn, the overall economy.

MODERNIZATION OF SCIENCE AND TECHNOLOGY

Science and technology continue to receive top priority from Chinese leaders who have long hoped that advances in this area would lead to accelerated economic and military modernization. China has many accomplishments in fields of technology including biotechnology, space, lasers, energy, and advanced materials. But a variety of bureaucratic, ideological, and cultural attitudes among conservatives and the old guard, and the rigidities of central planning, impedes progress especially with regards to innovation and commercial application. As a consequence, investments in science and technology have produced large numbers of scientists and engineers, but disappointing economic benefits.

The control of science and technology by the state has led to the bottling up of research results in ways that have deprived the civilian economy and the military from more productive sources of innovation. For now, the leadership understands that China must utilize foreign technology to avoid falling further behind the West. Its acquisition, however, has not been matched by an effective program of diffusion and assimilation.

MILITARY MODERNIZATION

Beijing reduced defense spending during the 1980s, along with the size of the Army. While some streamlining in military organization took place, weapons modernization, logistical support and combat capabilities fell and are not on a par with some of China's neighbors much less the West. But defense strategy and policy have recently changed, and for the first time in many years defense spending increased in real terms in 1990. Because of the tradeoffs between modernizing the defense sector and the rest of the economy, such a shift is bound to increase budget deficits, and make it more difficult to finance other activities.

OPENNESS AND MODERNIZATION

Foreign trade and investment from abroad made important contributions to China's modernization in the 1980s. Despite a halting start, China has greatly improved its commercial relations with the outside world. There is still interference by the bureaucracy, and there are still many concerns about legal restrictions imposed on traders and investors, but Beijing is making efforts to enhance the commercial climate and there are no signs that China's policy of modest opening to the world is likely to change. At this time, China's greatest worry regarding foreign economic relations may well be Western concerns about the uncertainty of post-Tiananmen policies, and the competition from Eastern Europe, the Soviet Union, and other areas for foreign investment, credits, and tourism.

Over the years there have been numerous heated arguments among both scholars and bureaucrats studying China not only about where China is going, but also where China has been. The most common assessment, and one that caused little past debate, is that China has been able to "muddle through." It is impossible to summarize the views of almost 60 scholars who have contributed to these volumes, and yet it is safe to say that they all would agree that despite China's innumerable problems, she may continue to "muddle through." In fact, the great majority of the contributors would be more optimistic than that. As long as the current leadership is in power, China will seek the impossible: a market-based system within a socialist planned economy in a one-party state. But before the decade is out the leadership will change and the desire for modernization, competition from her market-oriented neighbors, and pressures by a populace with new ambitions and expectations will force China to find a more efficient system. What precisely the new model will be no one can predict, but it is more than likely that the trend toward a market economy will continue, albeit with Chinese characteristics.

CHINA'S ECONOMIC
DILEMMAS
IN THE 1990s

I. THE CONTEXT FOR ANALYZING CHINA

CHINA'S TRANSITION TO THE POST-DENG ERA

By Christopher M. Clarke *

CONTENTS

INTRODUCTION

China in mid-1990 stands at the edge of an uncertain future. Not since the death of Mao Zedong in 1976 have Chinese leaders faced such serious economic, social, and political challenges. China's economic problems in the 1990s will become increasingly complex, and their management will require the involvement and active support of new actors spawned by Deng Xiaoping's decade economic reform. These actors will demand greater participation in the political process—and fundamental reforms of the political system—as part of the cost of their support.

At the same time, the average Chinese expects more of the government—in terms of economic growth, employment, and consumer goods—than at any time in the past. Rising expectations already have led to increased pressure for change in the political system, a trend likely to continue, and even accelerate, in the 1990s. These rising expectations will place rather narrow limits on any leadership's ability to address such key economic issues as price reform and the state subsidy burden.

Rapid changes in the international environment in 1989 and 1990—most notably the loss of Western goodwill toward China as a

---

* Intelligence Research Specialist, Bureau of Intelligence and Research, U.S. Department of State. The views contained in this paper are solely those of the author and do not necessarily represent those of the U.S. Department of State or any other agency.

result of the Tiananmen massacre of June 1989, as well as the rapid disintegration of the socialist world—also will complicate significantly Beijing's ability to respond to its challenges. For at least the next several years, China probably will face an outside world less willing to grant China special dispensation, whether in terms of foreign investment, favorable trade status, or human rights policies. Changes in the socialist world and in neighboring Asia will present special challenges for China.

Over the short to mid-term, the most likely leadership response to these pressures will be continued efforts to assure "stability" through coercion and central control. Neither party elders who regained influence as a result of quashing the pro-democracy protests of 1989 nor the younger leaders they promoted as successors show the willingness to take the steps needed to accommodate rising demands and pressures for change.

Notwithstanding Deng's frequent and impassioned statements espousing stability as the greatest desideratum, however, the political system Deng inherited and will pass along to the next generation institutionalizes instability at the top. Because the system has no rational and predictable procedures for leadership entry, exit, and popular evaluation, high-level politics will continue to revolve around jockeying for position by sniping at other leaders' ideas, performance, and proteges. The effect of continued high-level internecine struggle and ineffectiveness at dealing with China's problems will be continued erosion of public confidence and support, cynicism, alienation, and corruption.

The combination of falling public morale, rising popular pressures, and instability in the leadership virtually assures continued political conflict and uncertainty for at least the next several years. Periodic outbreaks of violence are a strong possibility.

Over the mid-term, it is difficult to predict exactly how the system will adapt to mounting pressure for change. Several extremes seem improbably, however: China does not seem likely in the foreseeable future to adopt a Western-style multi-party system of competition for power; it lacks most of the historical, cultural, and socio-economic conditions normally associated with such a transition. Nor is China likely to revert to the Maoist anarchy of the Cultural Revolution or disintegrate into local warlordism. China's octogenarian Long March veterans and their designated successors share with more reformist thinkers and politicians—and with most of the Chinese populace—a deep-seated fear of "luan" (chaos) that stems not only from the experience of the Cultural Revolution but from the past 100 years of Chinese history.

In the mid-term, however, China's central governing apparatus—whether more "reformist" or "hardline" in orientation—probably will be weaker and less capable of sustaining a coherent policy line than during the 1980s. Provincial and municipal officials will find the political vacuum. As a result, inequalities between and within areas are likely to worsen, leading to increased inter-regional conflict and social tension. Beijing's principal role may be to referee these disputes and broker deals between relatively autonomous localities rather than pursue a consistent national development strategy.

Over the long-term, old command-style solutions and intimidation cannot solve China's dilemmas or achieve the widely shared and time-honored goal of wealth and power. To succeed at these objectives, successors will need to bolster their legitimacy by accommodating at least some of the new economic, social, and political forces unleashed by a decade of "reform and opening to the outside." The resulting "Chinese-style" solution likely will be less coercive and more inclusive, but still basically authoritarian and centralized, at least in aspiration. At the grassroots, however,great diversity in implementation will remain, and the regime's aspirations will continue to fall short of its capabilities.

II. Increasing Demands of the System

During the coming decade, economic problems, social evolution, pressure for political reform, and the need to respond to a rapidly changing international environment will place new and intensified demands on China's political system. Exacerbating the difficulty of managing these problems will be increasing strains from population growth, which will add more than 15 million new mouths to feed each year.

A. ECONOMIC PRESSURES

That China will face serious economic problems in the 1990s is well known and will be discussed elsewhere in this volume. Energy and transport bottlenecks, outdated industrial plant and equipment, a poorly educated and ill-trained work force, and worsening environmental pollution are only a few of the more difficult economic problems with which the post-Deng leadership will have to wrestle.

Worrisome though they may be, however, China's economic problems are neither inherently intractable nor the most serious challenges the leadership will face. Indeed, for a number of reasons, China's economy in the 1990s could prove to be one of the brighter spots on an otherwise cloudy horizon. China is blessed with a relative abundance of most of the natural resources needed to modernize; it has a huge potential internal market, and a population that, properly motivated, is willing to work and anxious to get ahead. Furthermore, the Chinese economy still has ample room for improvements in efficiency that could sustain impressive growth rates through the decade.

Moreover, even in the economic sectors where China has the most serious problems, a combination of relatively wise policy, judicious application of money and other resources, and a little time could produce substantial benefits. Throughout the 1980s, for example, China sustained double-digit rates of industrial growth on single-digit growth in energy output and transport facilities. Such a pattern probably could continue if China made even moderate gains in eliminating remaining inefficiencies in the energy and transportation sectors and in energy-consuming industries, and achieved relatively modest increases in energy output and transport infrastructure. Similarly, significant improvements in environmental degradation could be accomplished with moderate investment. Factors that could significantly alleviate problems include adjustments of prices for raw materials, energy, and transportation; a continued shift of macro-economic priorities toward light and consumer goods industry and services; and changes in incentive patterns for workers, farmers, managers, and intellectuals.

Even under the relatively favorable conditions of the 1980s, however, China's leaders have been unable to sustain wise policies and judicious application of resources over a sufficient period of time to make breakthroughs in the worst economic bottlenecks. Deng and his colleagues elected to take on the easiest problems first by tackling agriculture; efforts since 1984 to shift attention to the more difficult problems of the urban economy have faltered. The immediate post-Deng leaders probably will be no more successful in addressing these problems than were their predecessors.

B. SOCIAL PRESSURES

More serious than the economic problems China's future leadership will face are the socio-economic and socio-political pressures that have developed during the reform decade. At least two sets of such problems are intractable—demanding management and defying solution—and will seriously exacerbate strains on China's political system in the 1990s.

Expanding population. Arguably, Mao Zedong's most damaging legacy was not the Cultural Revolution, the Great Leap Forward, the collectivization of agriculture, or even the adoption of communism. It was to ignore, and then silence, Ma Yinchu and other economists and demographers who warned in the 1950s that unrestrained population growth would bring disaster to China. The post-Deng leadership is now stuck with a problem not of its own making.

China's population at the end of 1989 surpassed 1.11 billion and is increasing at a rate of over 15 million each year. By the end of the century, the population will grow to around 1.3 billion, topping out at 1.6 to 1.88 billion by the middle of the next century. These projections, considered too low by some demographers, assume continuation of a fairly effective population control program.

China has to feed one-fifth of the world's population on 7 percent of its arable land. Urbanization, construction of housing, rural industrialization, road development, and the impact of sub-dividing land to family-based farming have cut deeply into cultivable land. Unlike energy resources, China has already reached the limit of its finite, and shrinking, available arable land.

It will take 50–70 years before China's population peaks and begins to decline. In the meantime, China will have to wrestle with the impact of both the size and age structure of the population on such issues as the population-to-farmland ratio, urbanization and the need for housing, environmental pollution, employment, education, and old-age insurance. Moreover, efforts to manage the problem—through population control programs and migration to less-populated parts of China—engender new socio-political tensions.

Rising expectations. A second intractable set of socio-political issues China will face inthe1990s stems from the very nature of Deng Xiaoping's reform program. Deng's shift in 1978 from "class struggle as the key link" to the "four modernizations" legitimized the displacement of idealism with self-interest, and substituted consumerism for deferred gratification. Belatedly, Deng and other leaders recognized that this left Chinese society drifting without a spiritual rudder. Their consequent, feeble attempts to revive Marxist orthodoxy and "educate the masses" about the need for "arduous struggle" and austerity through campaigns to "emulate Lei Feng" ring hollow and seem only to foster cynicism among most young people.

Moreover, by replacing ideology with economics as the touchstone of his program, Deng made *performance* the basis of regime legitimacy, and performance increasingly is measured by most Chinese almost exclusively in personal terms. After several generations of being told to defer self-gratification in the greater interest of unifying China, defeating the Japanese, overthrowing the "feudal" system represented by the Kuomintang, and establishing first socialism and then communism, most urban Chinese have decided that it is now their turn to benefit from China's decades of struggle. Widespread knowledge of the living standards of the rest of the world have reinforced Chinese demand for personal betterment and gratification. Chinese under 40 constitute a "me generation," and their self-interest is not likely to disappear during the coming decade.

Short of a national or international cataclysm, there is probably no way to put this genie of heightened expectations back into the bottle. The result is a population that is harder to lead, less forgiving of leadership mistakes, and less willing to accept slogans and ideological cant in place of performance. It may also be quicker to explode in anger.

C. POLITICAL PRESSURES

New players at home. Deng Xiaoping's reforms have resulted in a proliferation of economic interests that did not exist before 1978—or existed only in muted or latent form. These range from individual entrepreneurs to local industries, specialized agricultural households, migrant workers, and export-oriented firms. Such new forces have had a significant, although often obscure, impact on the leadership's decisions about economic policy, particularly on implementation.

New players abroad. In addition, China's growing integration with the outside world has brought into play a new set of foreign and international actors, including international financial institutions, foreign traders and investors, tourists, and bilateral trade associations. Each of these new actors has affected to some degree Chinese leaders' decisions about policy and personnel. For example, the World Bank and International Monetary Fund, along with foreign development assistance loans, have had a profound effect on Chinese development planning. The GATT accession process also has had a major influence on Chinese leaders' thinking about economic reform. And throughout the 1980s, awareness of the way China is perceived by foreign investors has influenced Chinese leaders' decisions not only about economic policy, but about the atmospherics and timing of high-level personnel changes. Foreign human rights groups and international criticism over such issues as population control methods have contributed to some adjustments of Chinese policy, notably a significant easing of Chinese family planning policy in the early 1980s. Finally, considerations about reunification with Hong Kong and Taiwan have shaped Chinese foreign and economic policy Deng created the Special Economic Zones in large part to show that "one country" could house at least "two systems" and have influenced such areas as minority relations and provincial affairs.

A new power elite. At the same time that new domestic and international influences have come into play, Deng's reforms have "pluralized" China's traditional power structure. In the 1980s, provincial and local governments received expanded authority and control over resources, which significantly altered the existing relations between center and locality. Central leaders were unsuccessful—despite strong and repeated efforts in 1989–90 in returning some of this authority to Beijing. In addition, the process of reform not only legitimized the individual pursuit of self-interest, but the pursuit of corporate and regional interests as well. Under the Maoist system, arguments for local interests had to be couched in terms of the national good or ideological purity. Under Deng, overt pursuit of advantage based on bureaucratic, provincial, local, corporate, or other affiliations has become both acceptable and expected.

Peripheral pressures. Internal reforms and examples from abroad have led to increasing ethnic assertiveness among the more than 80 million Chinese citizens who are not members of the Han majority. Tensions between Hans and Tibetans have created continuing difficulties for the Beijing government and have attracted negative international attention. Ethnic, and possibly religious, assertiveness can be expected to grow during the 1990s, not only in Tibet but in other areas on China's periphery, under the increasing pressure of such outside influences as Moslem fundamentalism and contact with fractious relatives across the Soviet border. Dramatic political change in Mongolia could also exacerbate tensions between Hans and Mongols in the PRC. Although such ethnic tensions probably will not come to threaten the central regime, they will demand careful and sensitive management to avoid serious or prolonged bloodshed, expense, and international recrimination.

These forces have led, and will continue to lead, to demands for greater participation in decisionmaking. During the mid-1980s, party chiefs Hu Yaobang and Zhao Ziyang—with at least the tacit approval of Deng—sought ways to incorporate new actors into the political process without ceding the principle of Community Party control. The dramatic and successful popular calls for political pluralization in Eastern Europe and the Soviet Union, along with China's own bloody suppression of the overt demand for wider political participation in June 1989 suggest that such pressures cannot be contained indefinitely.

D. INTERNATIONAL PRESSURES

China is also likely to face increasing demands from external forces in the 1990s. These will come from at least three directions, west, north, and east.

For at least the next several years, the West will be less friendly, forgiving, and forthcoming to China as a result of the Tiananmen Square crackdown. Throughout the 1980s, because China appeared to be headed in the "right" direction, it was accorded the benefit of the doubt on issues ranging from trade relations to human rights. In the Western public's eye, China forfeited the right to the benefit of the doubt on June 4, 1989, and is unlikely to regain its favored public position without undertaking major reforms. The West will be less willing to make exceptions on issues such as GATT accession, bilateral trade frictions, and human rights abuses. Moreover, if the world economy takes a downturn in the 1990s, as some economists predict, China's trade frictions with the West will worsen, hindering Beijing's plans to modernize its economy by means of foreign technology imports and a major export drive.

No matter what Gorbachev's fate, China will probably face a prolonged period of uncertainty along its northern border with the Soviet Union. Certain byproducts of glasnost—such as ethnic tensions—are probably irreversible and may have serious implications for Beijing. As Eastern Europe pulls farther and farther away from Communist Party rule and socialist economics—and as pressures mount for similar changes in the Soviet Union—China's leadership could face an increasingly strong political and ideological challenge and an increasingly attractive alternative for Western investors and lenders.

China could also face problems in the east from its Asian neighbors, possibly including mounting pressures in Japan for converting Japanese economic supremacy into political, and even military influence; a succession struggle in North Korea that could destabilize a 45-year status quo; increasingly strong independence sentiment on Taiwan; and a modernizing Southeast Asia presenting ever-stronger challenges to China as a trading rival and alternative location for foreign investment.

III. DECREASING SYSTEM CAPABILITIES

For at least three interrelated reasons, China's political system in the immediate post-Deng era will be less capable of dealing with the demands placed upon it than it has been during the 1980s, unless major changes are made.

A. THE NATURE OF AUTHORITY

Deng reforms shifted the basis of authority and legitimacy to successful economic performance, and the time frame within which leadership performance is measured has been shortened by the imperatives of power politics, the need to retain popular support to assure compliance with policies, technological developments such as the information revolution, and heightened public awareness in China of external developments. During the early 1980s, leaders could sustain a program for two to three years, making marginal adjustments and improvements, without losing public support or jeopardizing elite consensus. By the mid-1980s, the timeframe had telescoped to about a year, and by the late-1980s, Chinese leaders were increasingly impelled to assess performance on a quarterly or biannual basis. Elite and masses alike are demanding, "What have you done for me lately?" As a result, significant shifts in policy occur relatively rapidly, even as leaders try to reassure domestic and foreign audiences of policy continuity.

This process is likely to continue—even intensify—as leaders jockey for position in the succession by attempting to discredit one another. For at least several years, post-Deng leaders are likely to have a distressingly short time in which to produce results, shift policies and personnel, or be pushed aside. This does not suggest that the system will be capable of considered or sustained approaches to the mounting demands and problems it will face.

B. LEADERSHIP: INSTITUTIONALIZED INSTABILITY

In spite of his effort to replace Mao's "cult of personality" with rational/legal norms of bureaucratic behavior and consensual intra-elite politics, Deng has enjoyed the tremendous advantage of undergirding his performance-based authority with considerable personal prestige and charisma. His successors will enjoy no such advantage, because Deng failed in one of the central goals of his reform program: institutionalizing the succession process. None of Deng's candidates for the top party slot—Hu Yaobang, Zhao Ziyang, and Jiang Zemin—emerged from the rough and tumble of political competition. Each was plucked from relative obscurity and promoted at least as much because of personal ties as performance. Because Jiang, and for that matter, other leaders like Premier Li Peng, were selected through a process that differed little from Mao's selection of Hua, their prospects for political survival after their patrons are gone seem slim.

China's current political system and Deng's own ambivalence in confronting the tradeoffs between the long term benefits of yielding personal authority and the short term costs of doing so to his programs, personnel, and prestige—has militated against the promotion of younger leaders with vision and the development of their personal authority and charisma. Both Hu Yaobang and Zhao Ziyang fell, in part, because they began to assert their own ideas and programs in ways that threatened Deng's personal authority, and in part because they sought to push Deng's own program for political reform to its logical conclusions, which would have eclipsed Deng and other elders.

Neither Jiang Zemin nor Li Peng is likely to make the mistake of challenging Deng and the other elders. As a result, it probably will take several years for new leaders to emerge and develop programs and public support. During the post-Deng transition, China almost certainly will face continued, possibly worsening, problems with corruption, local despotism, fragmented bureaucratic and regional authority, and patron-client politics. Such a system will necessarily be more preoccupied with adjudicating minor problems and disputes than with addressing major demands.

IV. An Uncertain Future

Chinese history since 1949 has been characterized by a major upheaval every five to ten years, including the Great Leap Forward (1958–60), the Cultural Revolution (1966–69), the Lin Biao affair (1971), and the fall of the Gang of Four (1976). In retrospect, the

1980s decade of relative stability, continuity, and prosperity stands out as the exception rather than the rule. As of mid-1990, social, economic, and political conditions in China suggest that the transition to the post-Deng era will not be smooth or easy.

It is impossible to predict with any degree of confidence exactly how events will unfold during this transition period. Too much remains unknown about the inner workings of the leadership and the public mood. Much depends on the order and timing with which a handful of still-influential party elders leave the scene. But the 1989 crackdown on pro-democracy demonstrators and the continuing repression of dissent virtually assure that whichever leaders emerge in the immediate post-Deng period will labor under the handicap of a serious lack of legitimacy and public support at a time when economic, social, political, and international pressures on the regime are mounting.

A. SHORT-TERM: ELDERS TAKING TURNS

As long as Deng Xiaoping is alive and able to function, he will almost certainly remain *primus inter pares*, the final arbiter of leadership disputes, architect of leadership consensus and coalitions, and broker of deals. But in recent years, Deng has shown signs of frail health, and he suffered a severe political setback as a result of the Tiananmen crisis and his loss of two hand-picked successors within a period of two years. These events eroded his power and strengthened that of other remaining elders. When Deng dies, one or more of these elders almost certainly will succeed to his position as the power "behind the screen."

The most likely candidate to succeed Deng in the short term is President and Central Military Commission Vice Chairman Yang Shangkun. Despite his seniority and influence, especially in the military, however, Yang lacks Deng's breadth of experience and network of personal ties. Even more than Deng, Yang will have to share power with such other octogenarians as Chen Yun, Li Xiannian, Peng Zhen, Bo Yibo, and Wang Zhen. To an extent, he will also be dependent on younger leaders to carry out his bidding. But until the passing of the entire generation of veteran "proletarian revolutionaries," younger leaders probably will defer to their elders while jockeying for position and seeking to eliminate rivals.

Over the short term, the leaders and their designated successors are likely to continue to respond to the challenges they face not with offers of conciliation and accommodation or new and imaginative solutions, but with the same tired, outdated slogans and programs they have trumpeted since June 1989. Economically, this means strengthened central planning, a visceral aversion to inflation, and an inclination toward egalitarianism. Politically, they will prescribe rigid adherence to party rule under the "four cardinal principles," with heavy emphasis on the instruments of the "dictatorship of the proletariat": control, coercion and repression. In foreign policy, they combine a grudging and resentful recognition of China's technological backwardness and need for commerce with the West with a prickly nationalism.

The one issue on which almost all top Chinese officials—elders or successors—seem most united is the need for stability. Current leaders drew profound lessons from the fate of fellow communist officials from East Germany to Mongolia who sought to accommodate and manage public pressure for reform of their unpopular regimes. Their conclusion was that such efforts are the first step down a slippery slope into oblivion. Perversely, however, the Chinese leadership's very efforts to assure stability in the short-term through coercion and reversion to failed policies of the past will only strengthen the pressures for change over the mid- to long term.

B. MID-TERM: A RANGE OF POSSIBILITIES

How these pressures will play out over the longer term is even more hazardous to predict than the likely courser of events over the short term. It seems virtually certain, however, that public alienation and antipathy toward the regime will increase under the current repression and economic stagnation. If, as seems likely, intense leadership infighting follows the passing of the elders and continues for a prolonged period with no decisive outcome, dissatisfied and alienated citizens will be quick to take advantage of leadership disarray to press their demands. Under such revolutionary conditions, angry citizens with diverse aims could rally around a common cause of overthrowing the regime.

Democratization. Such a coalition, however, would probably be temporary and fragile, and unlikely to result in a relatively rapid or stable transition to democratic politics. Aside from the communist party, China has no semi-autonomous loci of potential political loyalty, such as the Catholic Church in Poland. Even its intellectual dissident community is highly fragmented and disorganized and lacks coherent, well-considered goals or programs for how to replace the current political system.

Moreover, support for adoption of Western-style parliamentary forms of government is probably neither broad nor deep in China. Chinese political culture lacks a tradition of free competition and coalition-building among equal and independent political groups. Indeed, few Chinese appear to desire the "chaos" of political competition or to believe that China is ready for "one man, one vote." Rather, a "democratic" solution to China's crisis of legitimacy would likely be an almost exclusively urban phenomenon characterized by the existence of numerous groups articulating a wide range of particularistic demands and programs with little penchant for cooperation. Advocates of systemic change in China will be watching closely developments in Eastern Europe and the USSR; if experiments with peaceful transition to democracy succeed there, pro-democracy activists in China will be emboldened and armed with a model to emulate.

Descent into chaos. A situation in which a weak and divided leadership confronts an angry and divided public would be inherently dangerous and unpredictable, especially if competing leaders resorted to the kind of demagogic appeals to mass hysteria and particularistic interests that characterized the Cultural Revolution. Such a situation could lead to a breakdown of social order, at least in many urban areas of China, with considerable violence and bloodshed. The most likely fault lines would pit beneficiaries of reform and most intellectuals against China's growing lumpen proletariat and disadvantaged groups. In some areas, social conflict could also take on ethnic overtones.

Such outbreaks of localized, even intense, violence and unrest are possible in the atmosphere of crisis that could follow the death of Deng Xiaoping or Yang Shangkun. But several factors militate against such a situation persisting or becoming widespread. Most Chinese harbor a deep aversion to "luan" (chaos); many remember the frightening days of the Cultural Revolution and the social, economic, and personal costs it exacted. Although many supported the goals of the 1989 prodemocracy movement such as curbing corruption and nepotism and opposing inflation, many also disapproved of its tactics of street politics. Perhaps an equally compelling argument against the descent into chaos is the strong desire of most Chinese to improve their material well-being. Most probably agree with the current leadership that such improvements can take place only under conditions of relative stability. If chaos threatened, public support for reassertion of order, even by force, would be widespread.

Continued "dictatorship of the proletariat." Political paralysis and succession infighting in Beijing, especially if accompanied by an imminent disintegration of social order, might allow at least a temporary consolidation in power of a post-elder regime dominated by younger hardliners. An entrenchment for several years of leaders committed to economic central planning, political coercion, and social intimidation could result in a Brezhnev-style stagnation. To be sure, such an approach cannot address China's basic problems, but it probably could suppress pressures for change temporarily, albeit at a high cost.

If maintained over a longer term, such a program could doom to failure China's plans for modernization and achieving the status of a world power as the rest of the world continues to outpace China's economic modernization efforts. Moreover, indefinite suppression of pressures for peaceful reform of the existing system is likely to result in increased restiveness, declining worker productivity, and acts of sabotage and terrorism, transforming disaffection into demands to overthrow the system.

The ability of younger hardliners to consolidate control would depend in large part of the extent and depth of divisions within the security apparatus. Rifts in the coercive apparatus were central to the high-level politics surrounding Mao's death and the removal of the Gang of Four, and are likely to be so in the aftermath of Deng's death as well. In this context, there have been clear signs that China's security forces were seriously divided by the Tiananmen crackdown and that hardliners were uncertain of their loyalty.

Resentful military. Many professional military officers deeply resented being drawn once again into civilian politics after almost a decade of efforts to recover from the politicization of the People's Liberation Army during the Cultural Revolution. They probably resent efforts to elevate the propagandists and commissars of the General Political Department to preeminent status in the military, the implicit doubts about their loyalty implied by leadership statements on the need to retain absolute party control over the military, the incessant political browbeating and campaigns to "emulate Lei Feng" since June 1989, and the reorientation of training from military tasks to political education.

Since the crackdown, there have been indications that the civilian security apparatus—comprised of the People's Armed Police and ministries of public security and state security—may be similarly divided and that hardliners suspect its loyalty. Many local police reportedly opposed the use of force to end prodemocracy activity in 1989, recognizing that they must continue to live in close proximity with the protesters and remembering the "reversal of verdicts" that followed the 1976 Tiananmen incident after Zhou Enlai's death. Since June 1989, there have been rumors of continuing poor morale and opposition among rank-and-file police and intelligence cadres. The replacement in March 1990 of the entire top leadership of the PAP and persistent rumors of further impending leadership shakeups suggest leadership concern about the loyalty of the security apparatus.

Despite divisions and reservations, military and security officials probably would not sit on the sidelines if social order began to disintegrate. Although the human cost might be high, China retains sufficient coercive force to reestablish order, and is somewhat better prepared to do so professionally than it was in 1989. However, if some elements of the leadership were to try to stage a coup against rivals, or to order the use of force against civilian protesters in a way that some security officials perceived as illegitimate, existing divisions within the security apparatus could result in armed clashes and street violence such as occurred in Romania in December 1989.

Rising regionalism. Over the longer term, the net effect of the succession struggle probably will be a significant weakening of central authority regardless of whether hardliners or moderates prevail. Beijing's ability to intervene and enforce its will on local authorities—for good or ill—will be diminished.

As a result, local party and government leaders will move to fill the political vacuum and assert local interests and autonomy on such issues as social order, economic development strategy, and budgetary control. Such a trend had already become apparent during the latter half of the 1980s, well before the Tiananmen incident. Having devolved authority and control over resources to the localities in the late 1970s and early 1980s, Beijing was unable to reassert effective control over the economy despite increasing signals through the mid-1980s that to do so was in the urgent national interest.

One result of a situation in which the center is unable to articulate or enforce a consistent national development policy or compel inter-regional cooperation has been increasingly wide variability among provinces and regions in China. Those areas most favored in terms of natural resources, trained manpower, technological level, and access to the outside world—that is, much of coastal China and a few sections of the interior—have been pulling ahead of their less favored counterparts at an accelerating rate. This, in turn, has exacerbated strains between regions—and within regions—resulting in sometimes sharp conflicts over resources, mounting trade wars and inter-provincial protectionism, and increased social conflict.

Beijing to a large extent has been reduced to playing broker between regions, a role that even hardliners in Beijing seem to have recognized by the spring of 1990. From late 1989 to early 1990, the central government appears to have cut a deal under which such revenue-producing areas as Guangdong and Shanghai would be guaranteed a continued large measure of autonomy in economic and even social policy, in exchange for a greater financial contribution to the center. Beijing, in turn, will redistribute the increased revenues as subsidies to urban consumers and loss-producing state enterprises, and to national priority projects. Such a program, in effect, recognizes "two Chinas": a more rapidly growing coastal region, increasingly tied into the international economy and responsive to market forces, and a largely centrally planned and heavy industry oriented "socialist" economy located mainly in the interior.

Such a trend toward increased regional authority would not resemble traditional "warlordism" in the sense of regional-based military dictatorships like those that existed in China in the 1920s. The center would not be likely to lose control of such key issue areas as foreign and defense policy, nor would greater regional autonomy be based on military strength. A severe and prolonged weakening of central authority could, however, result in stepped-up efforts by disaffected minorities in such peripheral areas as Tibet and Xinjiang to pull away from China. A weak center in an uneasy truce with powerful localities would seriously exacerbate the difficulty of absorbing Hong Kong and undermine, if not kill, efforts toward reunification with Taiwan.

C. LONG-TERM: BUILDING A NEW SOCIAL COMPACT

Over the longer term, mounting economic problems and socio-political pressures are likely to force future Chinese leaders to accommodate demands for greater pluralism and wider political participation by groups spawned or strengthened by reforms, including individual entrepreneurs, intellectuals, scientists and technicians, local officials, and urban workers. Indeed, such a trend was already underway before the Tiananmen incident and the ouster of party chief Zhao Ziyang. Zhao and his reformist associates, for example, sought to incorporate specialists into the decision-making process, strengthen the role and independence of trade unions, and make elections more competitive and reflective of the popular will.

Prescriptions for political reform before the Beijing massacre generally had a strong elitist, authoritarian, and centralist flavor. Commentators in 1987–88, for example, debated extensively the lessons of the four "little dragons" and the benefits of "neo-authoritarianism," pointing to the economic successes of Taiwan, South Korea, Hong Kong and Singapore under systems which combined "benevolent" authoritarian political rule with capitalist economics. Such regimes, according to Chinese analysts, incorporated the newly emerging middle classes into the political process without ceding real political authority.

Apparently motivated by hopes to bolster Zhao Ziyang's political-position—and their own influence—against both hardline conservatives and meddling elders (including Deng), advocates of neo-authoritarianism argued that China needed to follow the same path, thereby assuring more, not less, central authority to enable Beijing to make the changes needed to modernize the economy and pave the way for eventual democracy.

Constructing a stable new "social compact" after the leadership's breach of faith in June 1989, however, probably will be a difficult and protracted process of accommodation between the need for central authority, the pressures for local autonomy, and public demands for institutional checks and balances against arbitrary abuse of power by individuals or institutions. Reformers within the system may hope to resume a process of top-down political reform in which political supremacy is retained by China's educated elite and many aspects of central political control are strengthened, while control over the economy is loosened.

Others will demand more than a return to the mid-1980s program of Zhao and Hu Yaobang, however, They will argue that legitimation of the marketplace of ideas and broadening of political participation must be accompanied by a restructuring of political relationships, including at least limited competition for power. Opposition groups will face a strenuous up-hill struggle to present a real challenge to political control by the communist party, at least at the national level, and are unlikely to do so for the foreseeable future. China has little experience in the sorts of cooperation and coalition building among free and equal political groups needed to build a viable opposition.

THE DYNAMICS OF INTERNAL POLICIES

By Kenneth Lieberthal *

CONTENTS

SUMMARY

China, like many third world states, confronts enormous demographic, environmental, economic, and social challenges. Given the magnitude of these challenges, instability would threaten any government in Beijing during the 1990s.

Major current weaknesses stem from four basic sources. First, problematic legacies from the imperial past, especially from the late Qing period (1644–1911), continue to affect the system. Five late Qing failures and their legacies are of particular contemporary importance: failure to develop a concept of federalism that could lend legal and regulatory stability to central-provincial relations; failure to develop an effective system for the central government to collect taxes; failure to establish a stable role for the military in the polity; failure to protect political institutions against personal factional struggles; and failure, in the face of foreign pressure, to achieve a consensus regarding either core values or the types of relations China should have with the outside world.

The second basic source of contemporary system weakness is China's adoption of a Leninist type system. leninist political systems have several key flaws: they are "top-down" polities that too easily lose touch with domestic realities; they suffer from poor flows of information; they have systemic problems with political succession; and they have acute economic difficulties and problems in coping with the social consequences of development once they have passed an early "extensive" economic growth stage. China suffers from all these difficulties.

Third, China's reforms since the late 1970s produced enormous successes but, especially since 1985, they have also generated sys-

---

* Professor of Political Science Center for Chinese Studies University of Michigan.

(15)

temic problems of considerable magnitude. These problems include inflation, corruption, malaise over values, fragmentation of domestic markets, bureaucratic opposition, and expectations that have risen more rapidly than performance.

Finally, the democracy movement of 1989 made Chinese citizens aware of the breadth and depth of the government's unpopularity. The crisis played out in a way that further undermined the prospects for a smooth post-Deng political succession.

Despite the above vulnerabilities and problems, it is still possible that the Chinese polity can avoid serious disruption during the coming years. Part of the explanation for this is cultural: Chinese tend to fear both disruption and the power of a seemingly united top leadership. If the succession can be managed in a fashion that prevents open divisions at the top, therefore, social order may be maintained.

In addition, the political system may have entered a moderately stable period of a standoff between central and local authorities, where the locales de facto have considerable flexibility and the Center retains enough resources to be an active player in the system. Indeed, for all its weaknesses, the Chinese political system retains considerable capacity to act vis-a-vis the society.

In view of the above considerations, China's political future during the 1990s is quite uncertain. Several possibilities are realistic, although as of 1990 no single one of them is highly probable. These include: s structural stalemate between Beijing and the more entrepreneurial provinces and cities; a coup by reformers, followed by a resurgence of the reform agenda; a military coup (or military "king making") during a protracted political stalemate over the succession; a mass political upheaval sparked by elite disunity in the wake of Deng's death; or a fundamental collapse of central authority, reminiscent of the 1911 "revolution" that brought down the Qing. These possibilities are not completely mutually exclusive—e.g., a mass political upheaval could lead to a coup of one sort or another. As these various scenarios highlight, however, the Chinese political system as of 1990 shows every sign of being less capable of coping flexibly and creatively with its demographic, environmental, economic, and social problems than it was only a half decade ago.

I. CHALLENGES OF THE 1990s

The Chinese face a number of formidable challenges in the next decade. Population growth, for example, adds one new mouth to feed roughly every two seconds. Environmental insults such as air pollution, contamination of water resources, and decertification are reaching critical and constraining dimensions. And fundamental processes such as urbanization and the revolution in telecommunications are changing the attitudes and escalating the demands of the country's citizens. Given the magnitude of these challenges, instability would threaten any government in Beijing during the 1990s.

The present Chinese system is very powerful compared with those of most other third world polities. Nevertheless, a combination of factors discussed in this essay has produced weaknesses that are so great that it is appropriate to talk in terms of a "systemic crisis." Analysis of sources of vulnerability rather than of sources of stability, therefore, take up the major part of the following analysis.

II. SYSTEMIC PROBLEMS

If the Chinese political system experiences either major upheaval or fundamental collapse over the coming few years, the reasons for the vulnerability of the system will not be heard to pinpoint. The structural weaknesses of the People's Republic of China (PRC) stem from four sources, which are outlined in this section.

A. LEGACIES FROM THE QING

In it last decades the Qing dynasty (1644–1911) suffered from various systemic maladies, five of which continue to plague the current Chinese government. Some of these problems have deep roots in earlier history, but all were especially prominent during the final years of the imperial system.

First, China's leaders remained wedded to the notion of a unitary state, and they thus failed to do serious work on laws and regulations that might provide this huge country with a federal system that would provide a needed combination of decentralization and stability. China was then and is now too large to govern uniformly and effectively from the capital. But instead of conscious efforts to create a federal system, the actual roles of provinces and other units have been determined by their economic strength, military power, and the political skills of their leaders. The assumption that China should be a unitary (as versus federal) state is an important and deleterious legacy of the imperial past that still robs the country of needed flexibility.

Second, the Qing dynasty in its later years lacked an effective system of central taxation. It depended for revenues on a foreign-administered customs apparatus and on a domestic tax farming system. The PRC as of 1990 still does not directly collect central taxes from individuals and units. Instead it farms out tax collection to the country's 30 provinces and autonomous regions and negotiates revenue agreements with each of them.

Third, the late Qing suffered from a blurring of civil-military relations. The armies that were called into being to suppress the huge mid-nineteenth century rebellions created systemic uncertainties about civil-military relations that in some ways continue to have salience. The Chinese army of 1990 is under the leadership of the ruling political party—not the national government, and the boundaries of the military's role in both elite politics and national governance remain unclear and potentially very changeable.

Fourth, in the late Qing personal politics and factionalism overwhelmed the institutional discipline of the vaunted Chinese civil service. There had always been tensions between court politics and the formal civil service, but toward the end of the dynasty (as in the final stages of previous dynasties) institutional considerations were determined by personal power. The problem of personal power and lack of institutional constraints remains severe in the PRC. While this had its origins in the Qing system, the dynamics of the Leninist political system adopted in 1949 have exacerbated the issue, as explained below.

Finally, foreign pressures in the late Qing contributed to a breakdown in the consensus in China over the country's core values and over the types of relations it should have with the external world. The ripple effects of the subsequent debates extended to disagreement about the roles of Chinese who had been exposed to foreign values, the basis of unity that the government should seek, the type of foreign policy to pursue, and other equally fundamental issues. One of the startling aspects of the political discourse in China during 1988–1990 is that it included in fairly prominent fashion virtually every basic perspective that was being hotly contested at the end of the Qing. No national closure on these fundamental issues has been reached.

B. FLAWS IN LENINIST SYSTEMS

Following a decade of reforms and opening to the outside world, it is easy to forget that the Chinese Communist system still retains the core structural features of a Leninist system. There is an ample literature that details the general capabilities of and flaws in Leninist-type systems, and China's experience fits well within the scope of this general analysis. Overall, strengths of Leninist-type systems include their ability to control the information available to the population, their enormous coercive capability, their mobilizational style that can produce rapid economic development, their ability to extract high levels of savings from the population for state directed use (typically, in concentrated development of heavy industry and related defense expenditures), and their relatively effective control over income distribution. All these characterized the Chinese system until the beginning of the reform decade.

Leninist systems, though, also have key weaknesses, and these have been central to the experience of the PRC since 1949. The major weaknesses are as follows.

These systems are almost wholly "top-down" polities. Each official's career depends on the favor of higher level officials, and thus for every official there is an overriding need to look "up" rather than "down" in considering decisions to make and actions to take. There is thus startling potential in this type of system to ignore the realities of the real world of actual events in favor of responding to the wishes of higher level officials who control one's fate.

This tendency to look "up" is only one of a number of elements that combine to produce seriously flawed information flows in this type of system. In broad terms, the strongly propagandistic nature of these systems encourages development of a generally low information regime. In addition, bureaucrats generally fear producing data and insights that might incur the wrath of a key, powerful leader, and most bureaucracies hoard information as a core resource in itself. The results include lack of coordination among different bureaucratic actors and inadequate consideration of policy externalities during the decision making process. The fact that final policy decisions are thus often flawed by poor data is itself masked by the very secretiveness of the system.

Leninist systems are also notorious for the difficulty of effecting a smooth political succession at the top. Essentially, the coercive, mobilizational nature of the system tends to lead to the development of personalized, charismatic leadership at the apex, with few institutional restraints on the power of the key leader. The general desire to mobilize the population also produces a tendency to avoid constraining the political leadership by a legal system that stands above politics. The result of these various tendencies is personalized rule that is not highly institutionalized. Few top rulers in the history of world communism, moreover, have voluntarily stepped down from power.

The problems for political succession posed by this situation are well known to all students of autocratic political systems of both the Left and the Right. While top leaders may recognize the importance of assuring a smooth succession, they in the final analysis make it impossible for such a succession to occur. Time and again they groom potential successors, only to decide eventually that the heir apparent has become too anxious to take over before the right time has come. As a result, few heirs apparent survive politically long enough to inherit power. Those that do outlive their patrons, moreover, often fail nevertheless to secure the succession because the subservient behavior required to survive while the patron was alive typically tarnishes the heir apparent once the patron is no longer there to provide protection. Succession thus tends to be a time of political upheaval, sharp policy swings, and great uncertainty in Leninist systems.

Finally, Leninist systems have proven effective in producing rapid growth in the early stages of industrial development, but they have been shown to be systematically weak in sustaining that growth and coping with its socio-political consequences. The "extensive" growth characteristic of the early stages of industrial development is well suited to the concentrated power and mobilizational skills of the Leninist polity. But even this type of growth requires technical expertise and increasingly high levels of mass education. As the population becomes more knowledgeable and the economy becomes more complex, there is a need for greater openness with regard to information and for more effective means of dealing with an emerging intelligentsia. But Leninist systems have shown themselves generally incapable of the flexibility required to maintain the loyalty of the intelligentsia and of the emerging middle class.

China has fully exhibited the above rigidities and pathologies. Information distortions have plagued the Chinese leadership from the beginning. At their most extreme, they produced tragically inaccurate understanding of the real conditions of the country with regard to food supplies in the latter years of the Great Leap Forward, with the result that tens of millions of Chinese starved to death. Succession politics have also been core to the experience of the PRC. Arguably, much of the political turmoil at the top in China from 1958 through 1979 revolved around succession dynamics and, as detailed below, from around 1986 to the present political succession has again been a driving (and destabilizing) force in Chinese politics.

Finally, the Chinese reform effort begun in the late 1970s came in part because urban China could no longer develop according to the closed, mobilizational forms that were core to the traditional Leninist (Maoist) system. China needed the contributions of her intellectuals, but relations between the political authorities and the intelligentsia had been sundered by Maoist radicalism. More broadly, intensive economic development required greater exposure to the international arena and freer flows of information within China than could be accommodated in the traditional Leninist framework. The Chinese leaders realized at the end of the decade of the 1970s that the economy as a whole was experiencing a long-term rise in capital-output ratios that boded ill for future development. Recognition of this problem provided major impetus for the reforms that characterized the ensuing decade.

Overall, then, important weaknesses in the polity of the PRC arose from its Leninist structure and operational character. The reforms of the 1980s were directed, in part, at resolving some of these issues. However, the fundamental Leninist structure of the Chinese polity remained in place. While the reforms produced some major improvements, in the final analysis they also created additional structural flaws that exacerbated some of the problems of the underlying system.

C. EFFECTS OF THE REFORMS

By the late 1970s Deng Xiaoping, among others, recognized some of the above weaknesses in the Chinese political system and initiated a major effort to address them and ameliorate their consequences. While the ensuing changes did not proceed according to a detailed, long-term plan, from an early point reformers tried to push the system in four broad directions: toward greater institutionalization and less vulnerability to destabilization because of problems with political succession; toward less detailed management of the economy by the government; toward greater availability of information to both the government and the populace; and toward more personal freedom to enjoy the material rewards from one's labors.

Deng adopted a wide array of measures to increase the chances of a smooth political succession. He personally eschewed holding the top post in either the party or the government so that he could put his successors (Hu Yaobang and Zhao Ziyang) in place and give them time to build up sufficient prestige to hold their own.[1] He also tried to clarify the allocation of authority at the apex of the system and to regularize the procedures by which the top organs functioned. He therefore abolished the post of Chairman of the Chinese Communist Party (CCP) in 1982. This position had provided Mao with a position *above* the party apparatus, and Deng sought instead to have the party led by a General Secretary, as are virtually all other ruling communist parties.[2]

---

[1] Deng did, however, retain direct control of the military through his position as head of the Military Commission of the Communist Party. He finally relinquished this post only in 1990.

[2] The General Secretary heads the party apparatus. Under Mao, the CCP had *both* a General Secretary (Deng himself most of the time) *and* a Chairman (Mao) until the General Secretary position was abolished during the Cultural Revolution.

Deng also encouraged his elderly colleagues to retire from politics, and he created transitional bodies—most notably the Central Advisory Commission—to provide a graceful exit from power for these individuals. In addition, Deng encouraged a regularization of the decision making process, including holding meetings of top government and party bodies on a fairly regular schedule. In these ways and others, Deng launched a multifaceted effort to overcome the Leninist system's structural weakness regarding political succession.

Unfortunately, Deng did not go far enough, and the limitations he placed on his reforms in this area eventually undermined the effectiveness of the important measures he took. Most fundamentally, Deng never developed sufficient confidence in his chosen successors to remove himself completely from power. Rather, he retained his informal position as the "core leader" in the system, thus effectively robbing Hu Yaobang and Zhao Ziyang of independent decision making authority. This put both younger men in an untenable position, and as a result as of 1990 there is no clear successor to this 85-year-old leader.[3]

Deng and his reformist colleagues adopted an impressive array of measures to reduce government micromanagement of the economy. In the rural areas, they reinstated a family farming system, with families being given control over land (on a contract basis) and obtaining considerable discretion over crops to plant. Rural families also gained the right to shift some members out of agricultural production altogether. Externally, the regime opened the country to the international economy. Beijing encouraged foreign investment and adopted numerous laws and regulations to make such investment attractive to foreign firms. China also greatly increased its foreign trade, which grew at a faster rate than did GNP throughout the reform decade. The PRC elected to become a member of the World Bank, the Asian Development Bank, and the International Monetary Fund—all as part of the effort to increase the country's integration into the world economy.

Within China's urban economy, Beijing sought to decentralize control over economic decision making and to enhance the role of market forces in structuring economic outcomes. To promote this effort, in the 1980s China formally adopted a multiple price system for key urban commodities. This system stipulated that goods produced "on the plan" would sell at fixed "plan" prices, while all additional production of the same items would sell at higher, market-influenced prices. The basic idea was to wean the economy off the plan gradually, while avoiding the ruinous inflation that a one-step abandonment of "plan" prices would have produced. The administrative decentralization sought to tap the enthusiasm of local entrepreneurs in order to enliven the economy through material incentives and the energy that competition generates.

These various economic measures promoted rapid economic growth, with impressive increases in the standard of living. But they also created problems that by 1988–89 had become politically very damaging. The family farming system in the countryside pro-

---

[3] Hu was removed as General Secretary in January 1987, and Zhao fell as a consequence of the student movement and its suppression in June 1989.

duced extremely high rates of growth in grain output through 1984, as the increased incentives and more rational crop distribution worked their magic. The flaw in this approach, though, was that peasants did not feel they had secured ownership of their land, and they thus proved very reluctant to invest in basic land improvement. The state, for its part, also cut back on agricultural investment, throwing this burden onto the peasantry. The net result was land deterioration, inadequate infrastructure investment, and disappointing yields, especially in grains. Indeed, the 1984 grain harvest remained China's largest during the 1980s, even though the population grew by nearly 70 million people during the remainder of the decade.

The urban economic reforms also produced many unanticipated and unwanted outcomes. Basically, the decentralization placed economic decision-making power more at the level of large municipalities than in the hands of enterprise directors. These large municipalities tended to adopt a proprietary approach to the firms in "their" economy. Municipal governments thus became increasingly protectionist, establishing trade barriers to shield their own firms from "outside" competition. They also assumed great importance in allocating vital credit, and they used this to promote overly rapid expansion of local industrial facilities (the tax base of the municipality consists primarily of local industry). As a result, Beijing lost much of its ability to control the allocation of credit and the levels of production, but local governmental interference in the operations of the market remained extremely high.

Under this system the gap between living standards in the richer coastal areas and those in the interior grew rapidly. These regional differentials in turn sparked growing resentment from the interior provinces and raised the prospect of increasing pressures for migration from poor interior areas to the richer coastal cities. China by early 1989 estimated that illegal "floating" residents of major cities already totaled more than 50 million people.

The dual price approach produced a situation in which identical items (such as tons of steel could sell for prices that differed by more than 200 percent. Many officials developed ways to acquire items at "plan" prices, sell them at "market" prices, and then use a part of the phenomenal profit to make payoffs to cover up their deeds. Corruption spread rapidly under these conditions, and by the late 1980s reached such an extent that it produced very widespread popular resentment.

Local market protectionism and official corruption also affected foreign investment. Essentially, it became extremely difficult either to realize economies of scale in industrial production or to hold down transaction costs in an environment in which corruption and particularism affected almost all transactions. As a consequence, foreign investment in manufacturing industries remained low, and the typical foreign invested manufacturing enterprise had capital income of only about $1 million. By the late 1980s, foreign firms increasingly turned to Southeast Asia and other areas for industrial investment, at considerable opportunity cost to China.

The reformers sought to improve economic decision making by, inter alia, greatly enhancing the volume and reliability of the information available in the system. At the top of the system, Zhao

Ziyang established policy think tanks that developed extensive information-gathering and processing capabilities. In the scramble to attract foreign investment, moreover, numerous provinces and municipalities began to publish extensive statistics on their local situations, thus vastly enhancing the available information on the Chinese economy.

The above and many related efforts were basically helpful for the system. Greater information provided at least an enhanced possibility for better informed decision making. But the information explosion went beyond economic data for specialists, and in this larger sphere the results proved less uniformly beneficial.

China's leaders decided at the end of the 1970s to increase fundamentally the information available to the country's citizens and officials by making the mass media more diverse and informative. As part of this policy, Beijing multiplied the availability of television to the populace throughout the country. But exposure to the outside world via television produced a revolution of rising expectations. Over time, the gap between economic performance and rising expectations regarding standards of living contributed to a diminution in the authority of the communist leadership. The telecommunications revolution linked up with China's greater openness to the outside world, moreover, to make clear that the Communist party had previously misled the populace when it had declared that China was a model to which other countries looked. Rather, China now stood out clearly as a nation that was comparatively poor and that, moreover, had seen the gap between it and its East Asian neighbors widen considerably since the communist revolution in 1949.

Finally, enhancement of personal freedom to enjoy the fruits of one's labors, like the other measures discussed above, initially produced a surge of support for the leaders but eventually created serious problems. Indeed, this shift away from the values of egalitarianism, ideological commitment, and asceticism that had been promoted during the Maoist era produced considerable malaise in China of the 1980s. One part of this change was generational—there are very marked differences in personal preferences and attitudes toward national issues that differentiate those Chinese raised during different periods: the reform era, the Cultural Revolution decade, the Great Leap Forward, the early 1950s, and various periods in pre-1949 society. In short, Chinese society to a striking degree lacks an integrated value system, and generational cleavages are exceptionally sharp.

In addition, the tremendous stress on making money as an honorable personal goal under the reforms produced pervasive jealousies, as many people felt (often mistakenly) that they were being shortchanged in comparison with other groups. The one thing on which all groups could agree was that they resented the special privileges of the relatives of high officials, who could use their connections to engage in both legitimate and corrupt transactions and to live a good life.

In bureaucratic terms, moreover, the reforms considerably weakened the authority of the national bureaucracies that were in charge of propaganda (with the decline in ideology, these bureaucracies became unclear as to what values they should propagate, and the population's vastly expanded exposure to heterodox ideas put the propaganda apparatus on the defensive), civilian coercion (as material incentives partially replaced brute force in guiding people's behavior and the reforms in their early phases entailed bringing back into authority individuals who had been held by the police organs), and personnel assignments (as discipline broke down through "back door" arrangements and as new priorities encouraged appointments based on skill levels rather than political attitudes). At least initially, bureaucracies in charge of managing the economy experienced a bureaucratic resurgence, but subsequent decentralization measures threatened the positions and clout of many of these, too.

The major bureaucratic winners in the reforms were, therefore, territorial governing bodies, especially those of the large municipalities and some provinces. This mounted to a significant shift in the distribution of power and created numerous disgruntled officeholders. These in turn formed a potential reservoir of support for leaders who might seek to roll back part of the reforms.

The reforms thus brought profound changes. A number of these, such as reducing the regime's ability to use propaganda and coercion to mobilize the population around regime-held goals, weakened the Leninist political system. The reforms produced not only impressive economic growth but also rapidly rising dissatisfaction over increasing regional inequalities, a growing gap between rising expectations and actual economic rewards, and rising concerns about corruption and inflation. Furthermore, while the reforms moved China a significant step away from the centralized control over the economy characteristic of Leninist systems, they left the economy far short of the type of market-driven system envisioned by many reform advocates. The Chinese system continued to be one in which the government dominates the economy, but "the government" by 1988–89 in reality referred largely to major municipalities and provinces, each acting to a significant extent in its own immediate interests. In addition, the reforms undermined any consensus on values to hold the society together. They also produced a large number of bureaucratic losers among Chinese officialdom.

Perhaps most fundamentally, the development of private and collective economic sectors, the reversion to family farming, and the opening to the international economy, among other reform efforts, began to create the basis for a more self-conscious citizenry. Citizens who were better off financially and more knowledgeable about political and economic matters beyond their immediate environment grew in number around the country, especially in the cities. These citizens began to search for ways to gain effective input into the political and economic matters beyond their immediate environment grew in number around the country, especially in the cities. These citizens began to search for ways to gain effective input into the political system that governed them, and they experienced tremendous frustration in their inability to gain legitimate, institutionalized access to this system.

The reforms overall changed and strengthened the Chinese system until around 1984–1985, but since 1986 the problems have mounted more rapidly than the improvements. Popular dissatisfaction reached very high levels by the winter of 1988–1989, to the extent that the top political leaders lost all support among large portions of the urban populace and among many lower level officials during this time. Although aware of the difficulties, these leaders proved unable to agree on appropriate remedies and instead projected a beleaguered image domestically. With rising expectations, a decline in shared values, bitter resentments and jealousies, and a national sense of drift, the Chinese system by early 1989 had entered a crisis. The students who took to the streets to demonstrate in the wake of Hu Yaobang's death on 15 April 1989 sparked nationwide support [4] precisely because the general levels of frustration and dissatisfaction had already grown so great over the issues raised above.

D. SUPPRESSION AND DEEPENING CRISIS

The popular movement in the spring of 1989 and its brutal suppression in Beijing in early June dealt additional blows to the political system. The crisis itself breached the normal boundaries that make it almost impossible for Chinese citizens to know the political views of large numbers of other citizens. At the height of the crisis, numerous groups took to the streets with banners proclaiming their unit identifications and their major grievances/demands. In addition, for a short period the Chinese media gave the movement full and sympathetic coverage, thereby rapidly spreading the news that many millions of citizens (including many Communist party members) shared a sense of profound dissatisfaction with the Chinese polity. This knowledge, once known, cannot be erased by the suppression that began in June, 1989.

Substantively, the crisis greatly exacerbated underlying divisions in the leadership, and in the final analysis it led to the purge of Zhao Ziyang, thus completing the undoing of Deng Xiaoping's initial succession scheme. But the damage at an elite level extended beyond particular personnel changes, even though these were very important.

During the course of the crisis, Deng Xiaoping, Yang Shangkun, and the octogenarian leaders who formally had retired form politics made all the key decisions. Even people who formally held the highest level party, government, and military positions essentially served during this period only as staff to these older individuals. This pattern of decision making made clear that the numerous efforts during the 1980s to invest power in offices and procedures rather than in individuals had failed. When core decisions had to be made, those who had retired dictated to those who purportedly held the most powerful official posts in the land. In the aftermath of this situation, the Chinese political system at its apex lacks the ability to legitimize political power by virtue of appointment to office via formal procedures. There are now thus no specific procedures that can legitimize the transfer of power to a particular successor in a way that will impart some stability to the succession by marking its clear end point.

---

[4] The foreign news media concentrated their coverage of the popular movement in April-June 1989 on events in Beijing. In reality, though, huge demonstrations occurred in scores of cities across the length and breadth of the country. The challenge to the basic political system posed by the popular movement was thus far greater than most Americans realized at the time.

Given the fact that octogenarians now play a crucial role in governing China at the apex, moreover, the issue of succession is constantly on the agenda. Also, because the elderly patrons have significant policy disagreements among themselves and each has his followers among the contenders for the succession, the political system as of 1990 is experiencing a kind of inherent uncertainty and instability that cannot be expunged until he succession has fully worked itself out, which will probably take years.

The 1989 crisis left in its wake, therefore, a deeply wounded polity. Political divisions are fundamental at the very highest levels, while the system is dominated by octogenarians, and formal procedures for allocating power have been shown to be without merit. Large portions of the population not only are deeply frustrated but also for the first time realize that their disillusionment is widely shared. The measures adopted by a greatly frightened top leadership to reassert control and build authority—measures that include launching propaganda campaigns built around blatantly untrue assertions, arresting dissidents, reducing contacts with the outside world, and recentralizing domestic decision making—are, moreover, both very unlikely to reduce popular dissatisfaction and very likely to reduce the reliable information available to the leadership on the real situation in the country. The Chinese polity is, in sum, in systemic crisis, with widespread disagreement on values, rules, and priorities and a striking loss of legitimacy even among many officials themselves.

III. COUNTERVAILING FORCES FOR STABILITY

Political systems can remain in a state of crisis for long periods without experiencing an explosion. Despite the above vulnerabilities and problems, it is still possible that the Chinese polity can avoid serious disruption during the coming years. The stresses in China as of 1990 are very severe, but there are also strong forces that provide some basis for future stability. Four in particular warrant mention.

First, many Chinese citizens and high officials believe that the Chinese urban populations is cowed by an appearance of unity among the leading officials. The top people need not actually agree on major issues. Rather, they must present a relatively united front to populace as a whole. Chinese leaders themselves believe that when they are visibly split over key issues, the country rapidly degenerates into chaos. Popular shows of disaffection can, of course, erupt even in the face of elite unity, but the leaders believe these can be contained by normal political and coercive measures. A major falling out among the elite, though, would be seen by elites and masses alike as an opportunity for political action to spill over into the streets and spread very quickly.

The popular movement and its suppression in 1989 probably strengthened the belief of all concerned in the validity of this relationship between social order and the appearance of elite unity. The movement gained tremendous momentum as disagreements among the leaders stymied their ability to adopt effective measures to contain it. Once the elite closed ranks (by purging Zhao Ziyang and some of his followers), the winners took forceful action to seize back control over Beijing, and disorders elsewhere around the country rather quickly quieted down once the elite had demonstrated its unity (and thus its resolve and ruthlessness) in the capital.

This would suggest that if the political succession can be handled at the top in a way that maintains the appearance of basic unity among the leaders, this succession might unfold without provoking popular unrest. A key moment in this development is likely to come in the wade of Deng Xiaoping's demise. His passing from the scene will greatly heighten tensions, and some small scale acts of public protest will probably occur. A critical test will come with the ability of the top leaders to respond to these acts in a way that conveys their agreement on how to handle matters. Signs of serious disagreement at this stage could provoke major instability or the collapse of all central authority.

Second, there is a palpable fear of disorder in China and a strong belief that chaos lurks just below the surface order at all times. This widely held concept by Chinese (one that allows very little "room" between extraordinary order and extraordinary chaos) provides a basis for supporting social order even in the face of severe disillusionment with the political system. It also, however, means that, once social order begins to break down, the disorder can cascade through the society with exceptional speed. Chinese leaders, well aware of the fine line between chaos and order, will loose few opportunities to remind the population of the potentially enormous social costs of breading ranks and fostering disorder. This same mind set makes it unlikely that even losers in the succession struggle will attempt to mobilize popular action to bolster their position.

Third, the Chinese political system may have entered a moderately stable period of a standoff between central and local authorities. Corruption in the system is so pervasive (one leading Chinese economist estimated in 1990 that rent-seeking behavior by officials involved some 300 billion yuan per year) that it is hard to see what means Beijing can use effectively to discipline provincial and municipal apparatuses. While some individual leaders in various localities may run great risks if they defy the center, ingrained localism became a structurally integral part of the system during the 1980s and will be extremely difficult to root out. At the same time, Beijing retains sufficient resources and authority—especially over the military—to remain a powerful force in the country. In this situation, the Center may for a prolonged period call for greater centralization, especially of budget authority, and the provinces may effectively resist recentralization and pursue quite diverse economic strategies. While fully satisfying nobody, this type of situation could conceivably last for a period of years so long as the other requisites for avoiding social instability mentioned above continue to be met.

Finally, despite its numerous weaknesses, the national political apparatus itself remains extremely powerful. This is an apparatus with tremendous experience in interfering massively in the levels of the populace, and it has exceptional capabilities in terms of cynical political manipulation and ruthless suppression of dissent. No laws or values effectively constrain the political authorities from preserving their dominance, and China's citizens are acutely aware of this fact. The very ruthlessness of the political system in the past.[5] and the sheer size of the career party and security networks are elements of strength in calculations of the current system's ability to weather its crisis. This calculation would, of course, change if the security forces were to turn against the civilian leadership.

IV. CONCLUSIONS

This essay has argued that the PRC inherited some systemic maladies from China's late imperial period, that the Leninist-type system the country initially adopted in the 1950s contained structural weaknesses that have plagued the Chinese polity, that the reforms of the 1980s, despite major successes, contributed additional problems for the political system, and that the dynamics and denouement of the popular movement in 1989 further exacerbated what must be considered to be a profound, systemic crisis in the PRC. At the same time, the decentralization measures of the 1980s have left in their wake considerable "give" in actual policy development and implementation, and it is possible that the underlying crisis will not produce either a political explosion or a complete collapse of authority if the critical succession issue can be managed in a fashion that preserves at least a facade of basic elite unity. Such a facade does not mean the substantive policies cannot change, perhaps dramatically. It suggests, rather, that any major changes are handled in a fashion that keeps the populace convinced that the leaders can band together to contain fundamental challenges to the system.

Although China's political future is uncertain, this paper presented some of the more realistic possibilities which are not necessarily mutually exclusive. There are, in addition, very disturbing changes that will continue to occur under almost any of the scenarios discussed. Specifically, China will face increasing migratory pressures as people from the interior try to share the bounty of the richer coastal regions, and this could produce deeply unsettling demographic changes. In addition, China confronts environmental pressures that are becoming acute and that will produce escalating social and economic strains. The very process of urbanization (regardless of population shifts toward the eastern parts of the country) will also generate tremendous social tensions, as such changes have produced in all other countries.

China during the 1990s, in sum, will confront domestic political pressures on its political system of fundamental magnitude. The party and government will likely be hampered in managing these issues by structural weaknesses and by power struggles that absorb the attention of the elite. In addition, China's leader during the 1990s will be called upon to more than simply maintain themselves in power and preserve surface social order. They should also meet the enormous challenges the country will face in substantive areas like demographic pressures, environmental demand, and urbanization. As of 1990, the Chinese leadership and political system show every sign of being less capable of coping flexibly and creatively with its problems than they were only a half decade ago.

---

[5] Past ruthlessness is, of course, two-edged. It increases both popular disillusionment and the perceived cost of open expression of that disillusionment.

POWER STRUCTURE AND KEY POLITICAL PLAYERS IN CHINA

By Chi Wang *

CONTENTS

I. INTRODUCTION

It is a difficult task to present a full and up-to-date picture of key leadership in China, since there are so many events, personages, unexpected changes of political developments and policies involved. However, it is hoped that from the following analysis, one can obtain a better understanding of the subject through an outline of essential facts and information.

II. EARLY COMMUNIST HISTORY AND LEADERS

The Chinese Communist Party (CCP) was officially founded in July 1921 at the First National Congress in Shanghai by 12 Chinese and two representatives of the Comintern (Communist International) in Moscow. The founding members, including Mao Zedong and other young students, elected Chen Duxiu as chairman, in absentia. From 1921 to 1927, the CCP cooperated with the Kuo Min Tang (KMT), led by Chiang Kai-shek. With the Shanghai Coup of April 12, 1927 Chiang attempted to wipe out the Communists. Mao Zedong and Zhu De engaged in guerrilla tactics, supporting various strategies between 1928 and 1934, but finding themselves encircled by Chiang Kai-shek in October of that year, the Communists began the "Long March", which culminated at Yan'an in Shaanxi Province, where in 1935, the CCP Politburo accepted Mao as leader. From that time until his death in 1976, Mao was the CCP's dominant figure.

By 1945, the CCP reported a membership of 1.2 million, with another 900,000 in the military. On October 1, 1949, the People's Republic of China was established, with Mao as chairman of both the

---

Head, Chinese Section, Library of Congress, and Professor of History, Georgetown University.

CCP and PRC. In 1958, he proposed the Great Leap Forward as an attempt to achieve Communism, but this disrupted the economy and caused 20 million people to die of starvation. In 1959, Mao stepped down in favor of Liu Shaoqi as Chairman of the PRC, who, however, was toppled after Mao launched the Cultural Revolution in 1966. Rising leader Deng Xiaoping and the popular Zhou Enlai managed to ride out the storm of criticism of the ensuing decade. When Mao died in 1976, the Cultural Revolution was brought to a halt. Hua Guofeng became head of the CCP, with Deng Xiaoping returning to power in 1977 as deputy premier, and becoming the dominant figure in both the CCP and PRC, which he has remained ever since.

III. THE PRC'S POWER STRUCTURE TODAY

The current power structure in the PRC is based on the constitution approved by the 12th CCP National Party Congress held in September 1982. The central leading organs are:

- *Central Committee.* Elected by the National Party Congress. When the National Congress is not in session, the Central Committee carries out its decisions, directs the entire work of the Party, and represents the Party in its external relations.
- *Political Bureau (Politburo)* and its *Standing Committee.* Elected by the Central Committee in plenary session. When the Central Committee is not in session, these entities exercise its functions and powers.
- *Secretariat of the Central Committee.* Elected by the Central Committee in plenary session; attends to the day-to-day work of the Central Committee under the direction of the Political Bureau and its Standing Committee.
- *General Secretary.* A member of the Standing Committee of the Political Bureau; elected by the Central Committee in plenary session. Responsible for convening the meetings of the Political Bureau and its Standing Committee and presides over the work of the Secretariat.
- *Central Military Commission.* Selected by the Central Committee.
- *Central Advisory Commission.* A new organ first elected at the 12th National Party Congress as a means of replacing aged leaders with younger people. Acts as political assistant and consultant to the Central Committee and works under the leadership of the Central Committee. Members of the Commission must have Party standing of 40 years or more, have rendered considerable service to the Party, have fairly rich leadership experience and enjoy high prestige inside and outside the Party.
- *Central Commission for Discipline Inspection.* Also a new entity established by the 12th National Party Congress. Elected by the National Party Congress; functions under the leadership of the Central Committee. Main tasks are to uphold the Constitution and other important rules and regulations of the Party and check up on the implementation of the Party's line, principles, policies and decisions.

This theoretical division of authority is quite different in practice, however. For example, according to the CCP constitution, the Central Committee is the highest authority between party congresses. The Politburo and its Standing Committee are elected by the Central Committee to carry out day-to-day work in its name. In actuality, however, convening plenary sessions of the Central Committee has been difficult because of the compromise necessary between the different factions so that its responsibility and power has existed only in name. In fact, the Standing Committee commands the Politburo; and the Politburo commands the Central Committee. In 1956, the Secretariat was established to handle the general management of the party, leaving the Politburo to concentrate on key policy questions. By 1985, the power of the Politburo had diminished, and the Secretariat assumed much of its decision-making power. However, in October 1987, the 13th Party Congress addressed the problem of institutionalization of power at the apex, and restored power to the Politburo, downgrading that of the Secretariat.

The government administrative arm of the party is the State Council, headed by the premier. When the power of the Politburo had temporarily eroded, the state council's power greatly expanded, especially in the management of economic affairs and particularly under Zhao Ziyang (1987–1989). Originally, after 1956, the Politburo for the most part exercised administered control through three channels (the Secretariat for party management); the State Council (for government administration and policy implementation); and the Central Military Commission (for the People's Liberation Army). Before the 13th Party Congress in 1987, the leadership consensus, with the Politburo at the core, split apart as each of the three powerful institutional hierarchies went its own way, resulting in a lack of institutional procedures for the regulation and coordination of the political power held by the general secretary, the premier, and the army. The 13th Party Congress tried to address the problem by restoring decision-making power to the Politburo, composed largely of first line leaders, and downgrading the Secretariat, but this still does not seem to have solved the problem.

In theory, the Central Military Commission (CMC) is responsible to the Central Committee and the Politburo in the conduct of military affairs; after 1985, however, PLA representation on the Politburo was reduced to an all-time low, and military work increasingly came under the CMC (with Deng Xiaoping as chairman). As to the Central Advisory Commission (CAC), under the 1982 constitution, its members had power to oversee the work of the Secretariat, but after the 13th Party Congress, the members of the CAC could no longer give orders to the Politburo, but only advise.

The experience of the past decades thus clearly reveals that the institutions of both party and government authority in China are neither stable nor static vis-a-vis one another and are repeatedly brought into new relationships by external directive rather than by structural balancing mechanisms.

IV. Leadership by Seniority

The CCP has long accepted the concept of leadership by seniority, sometimes also known as leadership by "lines", which has influenced all efforts to devise procedures for an orderly leadership succession. The top leadership group is divided into the "first line" leaders, of average age between 50 to 70, who manage the day-to-day work of the party, including some policy formulation, and the "second line" leaders, average age from 70 to 80, who are involved only in major issues of strategy and policy. In 1962, for example, when all three were in their late 50s and 60s, Liu Shaoqi presided over the Politburo, and Deng Xiaoping headed the Secretariat, to form the "first line"; while Mao Zedong, retreated to the "second line". In 1980, Deng retired from the "first line" by relinquishing his post as first vice premier, and other posts including chairmanship of the CMC; while Hu Yaobang and Zhao Ziyang, and later Zhao Ziyang and Li Peng, formed the "first line" to develop their own bases of support. By August 1989, the "first line" and "second line" leaders were as shown in the following chart:

TABLE 1. Leadership Lineup of the CCP Politburo as of August 1990

First Line Leaders

Name	Age	Key Posts
Yang Shangkun	83	President, PRC and vice chairman of Central Military Commission (CMC)
Wan Li	74	Chairman, National People's Congress
Qin Jiwei	75	Minister of Defense
Jiang Zemin	64	General secretary, CCP; chairman, Central Military Commission
Li Peng	63	Premier; member, CCP Politburo
Qiao Shi	66	Member, Standing Committee, CCP Politburo
Yao Yilin	73	Member, Standing Committee, CCP Politburo; vice premier
Li Ruihuan	56	Member, Standing Committee, CCP Politburo
Song Ping	73	Member, Standing Committee, CCP Politburo
Ding Guangen	62	Member, CCP Secretariat
Tian Jiyun	61	Vice premier
Wu Xueqian	69	Vice premier
Li Tieying	54	State counselor; member, CCP Politburo
Li Ximing	67	Party secretary, Beijing Municipal Government, member, CCP Politburo
Yang Rudai	64	Member, CCP Politburo Sichuan Provincial Party secretary

Second-Line Leaders

Name	Age	Key Posts
Deng Xiaoping	86	Chairman, Central Advisory Commission
Chen Yun	85	First secretary, Central Advisory Commission
Li Xiannian	85	President of the People's Consultative Conference
Peng Zhen	87	
Deng Yingchao	85	
Nie Rongzhen	90	Marshal, PLA
Wang Zhen	81	Vice President, PRC
Fang Yi	83	Vice chairman, National Political Consultative Conference
Bo Yibo	81	Vice chairman, CCP Central Advisory Commission

SOURCES: Official publications and numerous issues of Renmin ribao (Beijing).

V. Tiers and Echelons

During the past 40 years, the Chinese Communists' plan for succession has been generally based on the so-called three-echelon system. The first echelon, or tier, trains and passes power along to the second echelon, which in turn does the same with the third echelon, and so on down the line. At present, the Chinese Communist Party's self-determined echelons may be generally grouped as follows:

The *first echelon* consists of Deng Xiaoping, Chen Yun, Li Xiannian, Peng Zhen, Nie Rongzhen, Yang Shangkun, Deng Yingchao and so on, the so-called older generation of proletarian revolutionaries, most of whom are around eighty years old and all of whom are Long March Veterans.

The *second echelon* consists of Zhao Ziyang—removed from the general secretary post in June 1989—Wan Li, Yao Yilin, Deng Liqun and so on. These are the second generation party members, aged sixty to seventy years old, most of whom joined the Party during the war of resistance against Japan.

The *third echelon* consists of Jiang Zemin, Qiao Shi, Ding Guangen, Yan Mingfu, Li Ruihuan, Li Tieying, Li Peng, Tian Jiyun, and so on, 50–60 years old, some of whom entered the Party just on the eve of the Communist takeover of power, and most of whom were active in the 1950s era of close cooperation with the USSR. Most of those over forty years of age graduated from college before the Cultural Revolution.

The three echelon idea is said to have started with Chen Yun; but in 1981, Deng Xiaoping also repeatedly underscored his intention to ensure policy continuity through the promotion of successors whose personal interests were tied to the reform policy. In 1983, he flatly declared that it was necessary to build up the third echelon, referring not only to the younger generation, but to cadres on reserve and the young and better-educated people in leadership positions. These people will eventually become key political players in China.

From September 1986, criticism of the third echelon started to appear in newspapers, and there has been some indication that conflicts between third echelon cadres and the old veterans are on the rise. The sudden dismissal of Hu Yaobang in January 1987 apparently indicates that some senior leaders are disenchanted with their handpicked successors. However, the third echelon cadres are bound to take over the leadership when the first generation of revolutionaries pass away. The big question is whether the new generation of leaders will be able to manage their differences and achieve unity among themselves in the coming years.

VI. Factions and Struggles

Two contending major factions have emerged since Mao's passing in September 1976, headed apparently by Deng Xiaoping and Chen Yun as respective leaders of the groups in opposition, the "Reform" and "Conservative" factions.

Deng Xiaoping is leader of the reform faction, as well as mediator between the reform and Chen Yun factions. Hu Yaobang and

Zhao Ziyang were in some respects even more reform-minded than Deng.

The Reform Faction has been the most popular, with Deng rising to power as the Party's leading guide during the past 10 years. However, its theories are inconsistent and its military basis is not stable. The Reform Faction is divided into Hu Yaobang's Communist Youth League—the most powerful reform group and Zhao Ziyang's Technical Officers League, promoting economic reform.

Among the Conservative faction are the "Rigid Ideologies" group, including Hu Qiaomu, and Deng Liqun, etc.; the ousted military leaders' group, such as Geng Biao, etc.; the Zhou Enlai faction, including Deng Yingchao (Zhou's wife), protected by Zhou Enlai during the Cultural Revolution and remaining loyal to his memory; and the Soviet Faction of Li Peng and Song Jian, ideologically proponents of the Soviet system, held in high favor by Chen Yun, Li Xiannian, and Deng Yingchao. At the present time, Li Xiannian, 85, seems to be the most influential figure in this conservative faction.

The Conservative Faction has a relatively strong military background, a large body of middle-level cadres as its power base, and a theory of a centrally planned economy. They believe that China's basic economic system should return to that of the 1950s and 1960s.

A very small neutral faction includes those who have not demonstrated a preference for either the Deng or Chen faction; those who respect Deng but not Hu Yaobang; Wan Li who has been known to be very liberal, and to have an open mind towards capitalism; and Qiao Shi who has had strong ties to Hu Yaobang, but has tried to establish his own independence during recent years. Deng Xiaoping had again taken a balancing role between the diverse elements and at the present time is shifting more towards further consolidation of the Reform Faction.

The differences in ideology and sources of support for the two major factions may be analyzed as follows:

With regard to ideology, Chen Yun's faction adheres closely to orthodox Marxism-Leninism, while Deng's faction clearly considers some elements of Marxism-Leninism outmoded. Deng's followers, however, have been wary of making specific criticisms of established Marxist principles.

Chen Yun and his followers promote the strengthening of Communist Party control in all areas. Deng Xiaoping's faction favors the separation of Party and state functions in the administration of economic enterprise, and a more prominent role for "technocrats". Deng has even proposed eliminating the Party's role in economic enterprise, an idea immediately quashed by Chen Yun and Li Xiannian.

Concerning economic policies, Chen Yun's faction would like to restore the policies in effect before the Cultural Revolution. Because they promote and defend the idea of a disciplined, centrally planned economy, they are known as the "Restoration Faction" or the "Small Birdcage Faction". Deng favors a "socialist-market" economy, in which large enterprises remain nationalized but allowed to respond to market forces. Deng's faction is thus known as the "Large Birdcage Faction".

Chen Yun's base of support lies in China's immense bureaucratic machine, which extends its reach from Beijing to every nook and cranny of the land. The machine's functionaries tend to be consciously or unconsciously against reform. The Deng faction's support comes largely from those who stand to benefit from his policies, including "10,000-yuan families", newly-rich farmers, "briefcase" merchants, individual entrepreneurs in both urban and rural areas, "agricultural specialty" families, cooperative enterprises, and young officers who have recently been promoted. All of these terms describe groups who have profitably branched out in some way from the centrally planned economy.

The bureaucratic machine that provides the social base for Chen's faction is very powerful. The social base of the reform faction lacks the organizational cohesiveness to bring its elements together as a unified force. Society is not static, however, and popular support for the reformers will increase day by day as reforms are implemented, while the "old guard" becomes more and more isolated.

VII. PRC LEADERSHIP ROSTERS

The following section lists the names of Beijing leaders as of August, 1990:

- Members of the Central Committee Politburo (listed in the order of the number of strokes in their surnames):

Wan Li	Tian Jiyun	Qiao Shi
Jiang Zemin	Li Peng	Li Tieying
Li Ruihuan	Li Ximing	Yang Rudai
Yang Shangkun	Wu Xueqian	Song Ping
Yao Yilin	Qin Jiwei	

Alternate Member:

Ding Guangen

Members of the Politburo Standing Committee:

Jiang Zemin (Gen. Sec.)	Li Ruihuan	Yao Yilin
Li Peng	Qiao Shi	Song Ping

Military Commission Leaders:

Chairman: Jiang Zemin
First vice chairman: Yang Shangkun
Secretary general: Yang Baibing (younger brother of Yang Shangkun)

The party conference approved the Chairman, Vice chairmen and Standing Committee members of the Central Advisory Commission elected at the Commission's first plenary meeting.

- Central Advisory Commission

Chairman: Chen Yun
Vice chairmen: Bo Yibo, Song Renqiong

- Standing Committee Members (listed in the order of the number of strokes in their surnames):

Wang Ping	Wang Shoudao	Wu Xiuquan
Liu Lantao	Jiang Hua	Li Yimang
Li Desheng	Yang Dezhi	Xiao Ke
Yu Qiuli	Song Renqiong	Song Shilun
Zhang Jingfu	Zhang Aiping	Lu Dingyi
Chen Yun	Chen Pixian	Chen Xilian
Hu Qiaomu	Duan Junyi	Geng Biao
Ji Pengfei	Huang Hua	Bo Yibo
Kang Shi'en	Cheng Zihua	

(Many of these members are former military officers and could be considered members of the Conservative Faction.)

VIII. PROFILES OF CURRENT KEY POLITICAL PLAYERS

With the dismissal of Zhao Ziyang from his post as general secretary in June 1989, the 4th Plenary Session of the 13th Central Committee announced in June 1989 that Jiang Zemin would replace him. In other significant changes in CCP leadership, Jiang Zemin, Song Ping and Li Ruihuan were elected to the Standing Committee of the Politburo of the CCP Central Committee, and Li Ruihuan and Ding Guangen became members of the Secretariat of the CCP Central Committee. Because of his personal ties with Zhao Ziyang, Hu Qili was removed from the Standing Committee of the Politburo of the CCP Central Committee. Rui Xingwen and Yan Mingfu were also removed from the Secretariat of the CCP Central Committee.

A few representative profiles of some of the key political players and Standing Committee members of the CCP's Politburo follow:

Deng Xiaoping, 86, is the doyen of Chinese Communist party leaders, an avowed pragmatist, and a firm advocate of innovative changes in China's political and economic systems. His outlook on political and economic matters is considered moderate or conservative relative to his emphasis on the primacy of an accelerated economic growth, or on the establishment of political institutions insofar as they are supportive of his economic policy objectives. He is a proponent of rejuvenating the leadership by injecting younger party stalwarts into its membership. Although he did not retain any official posts, Deng wields extensive influence and power in the conduct and operation of the Chinese governmental machinery.

General *Yang Shangkun*, 83, has been a Politburo member since 1982 and China's president since 1988. His basis of power is attributable to his position as permanent Vice chairman of the Central Military Commission, and close alliance with the military, including a number of family-related associates occupying senior positions in the military, such as Yang Baibing, head of the army's political department, and Yang Jianhua, commander of the notorious 27th Field Army which dealt a heavy blow among the student demonstrators during the Tiananmen Square unrest.

Li Peng, 63, a protege of Zhou Enlai, is Soviet-educated and considered an expert in electric power and energy resources development. He cultivated close ties with followers of Zhou and veteran Soviet-trained Chinese, as well as with influential party elders. He has been a Politburo member since 1987, a member of the Standing Committee, chairman of the State Planning Commission for Restructuring the Economic System, and premier since 1988. His underlying conservative outlook has been responsible for the rigorous economic retrenchment measures undertaken by China in the last two years. During the rising tide of student unrest unfolding at Tiananmen Square in 1989, it was Li Peng who announced the imposition of martial law on May 20 in Beijing. Li has been trying to consolidate his personal power and improve his image during the past year. Many foreign experts have predicted that Li will be replaced by a more moderate party leader, though his strong ties with the Conservative Faction, make it unlikely that he will be replaced in the near future. No doubt to improve his public image (both at home and abroad) Li has been travelling to many foreign countries during the past few months.

Chin Jiwei, 75, is minister of Defense and a member of the Politburo and the Central Military Commission. He has widespread influence and connections with the military, having served at one time as commander of Chinese army units stationed in Beijing. He is a moderate, and, like Zhao Ziyang, opposed the imposition of martial law in Beijing during the Tiananmen Square student unrest. His view was poorly received by party leaders, and has given rise to much speculation as to his future political role.

Qiao Shi, 66, has been a Politburo member since 1987 and a member of its Standing Committee. He was alleged one of the co-signers of a document critical of Zhao Ziyang's moderate stance and conduct during the pro-democracy demonstration in May 1989. His present main position is that of Chairman of the Central Discipline Inspection Commission, which is responsible for monitoring the nation's intelligence and security interests.

Jiang Zemin, 64, joined the CCP in 1946, and attended Jiaotong University (one of the best engineering colleges in China), graduating from its Electrical Machinery Department in 1947. He went to Moscow in 1955 and worked as a trainee at the Stalin Automobile Factory, returning to China in 1956. Beginning in 1980, he was vice chairman of the State Administration Commission on Import and Export Affairs, the Commission on Foreign Investment, and after 1982 became minister of Electronics Industry. During those years, he concurrently served as secretary of the leading Party members' group of both the Commission and the Ministry. Additionally, he was elected a member of the 12th Party Central Committee in 1982, mayor of Shanghai and secretary of the Shanghai Municipal Party Committee in 1985. He was elected a member of the Politburo of the Party Central Committee in 1987, and a member of the Standing Committee of the Central Committee in 1989, and General Secretary. In addition, he is also the Chairman of the powerful CCP's Central Military Commission since 1989.

Li Ruihuan was born in 1934 in Tianjin. Li is self-educated, and worked as a carpenter in Beijing and Tianjin. He joined the CCP in 1959, and beginning in 1965, served alternately as deputy secretary and secretary of the Party Committees of the Beijing Company of Building Materials, the Beijing Construction Timber Plant (1971), the Beijing Bureau of Building Materials, and successively served as vice chairman of the Beijing Capital Construction Commission, and director of the office in charge of Beijing's capital construction. Additionally, he was vice chairman of the city's trade union federation, permanent member of the All-China Federation of Trade Unions, and was elected during the intervening years a member of the Standing Committee of the Fifth National People's Congress. He was a member of the secretariat of the Central Committee of the Chinese Communist Youth in 1979, as well as a permanent member of the All-China Youth Federation. Li is currently responsible for the party's propaganda and cultural affairs. He is very popular among young workers and artists in China.

Song Ping, 73, studied agriculture at Beijing and Qinghua universities, and after joining the CCP in 1937, he served at the Central Party School in Yan'an, the Yan'an Institute of Marxism-Leninism, the Central Institute of Party Affairs, and the Party's South China Bureau. He joined the Chongqing-based Xinhua Daily and headed Xinhua News Agency's Nanking branch, and served as political secretary to Zhou Enlai. After 1947, he worked in a district Party committee, served as political commissar in Harbin, and held offices in the Harbin and Northeast China Federation of Trade Unions.

After 1952, he was a member of the State Planning Commission, served concurrently as vice minister of Labor and the Commission, and held a position in the Party's Northwest China Bureau as well as being minister of its planning commission. He was a high official in defense construction projects and national defense industry and, after 1972, was active in the revolutionary committee of Gansu Province. He served as political commissar of the Lanzhou Military Command area and of the Gansu Provincial Military Command area.

After 1981, he re-emerged as minister of the State Planning Commission, served as secretary of the Commission's Party group, State councillor, head of the Organization Department of the Party Central Committee, member of the 11th and 12th Party Central Committee, and Politburo member of the 13th PCC.

Yao Yilin, 73, graduated from Qinghua University majoring in chemistry. After joining the CCP in 1935, he served as secretary of the Party section of the Beiping Students' Federation and was one of the organizers of the Beiping students' patriotic movements against Japanese aggression. During the War of Resistance against Japan, he worked underground for the Party in Tianjin and the Shanxi-Chahar-Hebei Bureau, and spearheaded an armed uprising in eastern Hebei Province.

After 1949, he served successively as vice minister of Foreign Trade, vice minister of Commerce, deputy director of finance and trade in the State Council and, beginning in 1960, served as minister of Commerce for seven years. He became a vice premier in 1978, and for a period after 1979, served as deputy secretary-general of the CCP and director of its General Office, and retained the position of vice premier after the restructuring of the State Council in 1982. He was elected an alternate member of the Politburo in 1982, a full member of 1985, and a member of the Standing Committee of the Politburo in 1987. He is a senior economic planner and his main posts today are vice premier of the State Council and minister of the State Planning Commission. He has been instrumental in carrying out many of the new economic policies in China during the past 10 years.

IX. REGIONAL AND PROVINCIAL POLITICAL PLAYERS

Many of these influential regional and local leaders were originally from Beijing and they were transferred or reassigned to their new posts in different regions throughout China.

Among the reform leaders at the provincial level, Ye Xuanping, governor of Guangdong province, and Zhu Rongji, mayor of Shanghai, are considered as important supporters of Zhao Ziyang's reform policies. Ye is responsible for the prosperity of Guangdong where 36 percent of China's foreign trade is conducted, and millions of laborers absorb foreign investment. The province provides a crucial connection to Hong Kong. Ye's father was Marshall Ye Jianying, a powerful political figure who died in 1986. This family background has given Ye Xuanping good connections with the top leadership. As a Central Committee member, Ye held his ground last year against Li Peng's policy of retrenchment. In the recent restimulation of China's economy, Guangdong has quickly revived thousands of small business and increased production output, enhancing its economic ties with Hong Kong and foreign business.

Shanghai and its mayor Zhu Rongji, have recently become more visible in China's press. Shanghai, China's largest industrial city and at one time the country's uncontested financial, trade, and manufacturing center, was overwhelmed by the dynamic Special Economic Zones in Guangdong and Fujian in the 1980s. This year Shanghai has been on the rise. The national stock exchange and other related services are being established there. Once they are complete, the availability of equity finance will improve the environment for domestic and foreign investment. The most ambitious plan is to establish the Pudong district as an industrial, commercial and financial zone designed to push the economic development of provinces along the Yangtze River. In June, 1990 Zhu travelled to Hong Kong and explained to businessmen his preferential policies—the Pudong area would become China's first free-trade zone and the foreign banks will be allowed to operate there.

Zhu is very active both in and out of China to push the reform and takeoff of Shanghai's economy. He is propelling the construction of infrastructural projects, especially transport and construction. Zhu "cut through the swathe of red tape, ... reduced the number of department approvals to 20 from 133" through the Shanghai Foreign Investment Commission to simplify the process for foreign investment.

In contrast to central government denouncement, Zhu used vague terms to talk about the military suppression of the June 1989 demonstrations in Beijing. His image in handling the Shanghai demonstrations seemed conciliatory. On July 7, 1990, he arrived in the United States, heading a delegation of Chinese mayors for a 20-day visit. His mission was to increase Sino-American understanding, telling his American audience about China's open-door policy and its improved environment for U.S. investment.

Both Ye Xuanping and Zhu Rongji have reportedly been candidates for central government posts. Their prominent position in the most important regions of China put them on the list of future top leaders.

X. Prospects and Conclusion

The top leadership has been variously portrayed as contingent upon the source of power deriving from the "first-second lines" of succession men based on age or senility, the first-third echelons of leaders with operational authority in the management of government and party affairs, and members of reform or conservative factions. Out of these layers of political stratification, a strong dictator like Mao might emerge, though this is very unlikely given the trend toward collective leadership during a transition period between conservative and reform factions, and the periodic surfacing of benevolent authoritarian leadership like that of Li Ruihuan and Jiang Zemin.

Another possibility is that China may become divided along regional leadership lines, represented by the influential commanders of the country's seven military districts. Another pattern of leadership succession might be based upon leaders of component provinces favorably endowed with rich industrial-economic resources, such as Guangdong, Fujian, Shanghai, and northeast China.

Against the backdrop of an emergent new leadership, difficult questions still overshadow future prospects. What is the future for China after the first and second echelons have moved on, and the third echelon assumes full power and control of China? Who will pass away first, Deng or Chen and who will be top leader? How will major policies change with the changes in leadership? Providing specific or even tentative answers and speculations about these questions is an impossible task.

APPENDIX A

Selected List of PRC Leaders'

Relatives Holding Important Positions

Bo Yibo (Vice chairman, CCP Central Advisory Commission)

Sons: **Bo Xicheng** (Director, Administrative Bureau of Travel and Tourism of Beijing City)

Bo Xilai (Vice mayor, Dalian City, Liaoning Province)

Bo Quan (General Manager, White Peacock Arts and Crafts Company, Beijing)

Son-in-law: **Jia Chunwang** (Minister, Ministry of State Security)

Chen Yi (Former Minster, Ministry of Foreign Affairs; former mayor of Shanghai)

Son: **Chen Haosu** (Vice minister, Ministry of Radio, Film and Television)

Chen Yun (Chairman, CCP Central Advisory Commission)

Son: **Chen Yuan** (Member, Standing Committee, Beijing Municipal Chinese Communist Party; CCP Beijing Municipal Party Secretary)

Deng Xiaoping (Former Chairman, CCP Central Military Commission)

Sons: **Deng Pufang** (President, The Welfare Fund for Handicapped; former Chairman, Kanghua Trading Company

Deng Zhifang (Ph.D. in physics, University of Rochester; Deputy General Manager, China International Trust and Investment Corporation - CITIC)

Daughters: **Deng Nan** (Bureau Director, State Science and Technology Commission)

Deng Rong or **Xiao Rong** (Director, Foreign Affairs Committee of the National People's Congress; Deputy Director, Personnel Office, General Staff Headquarters, People's Liberation Army - PLA)

Sons-in-law: **He Ping** (President, Poly Technologies, Inc.; former Assistant Military Attache, Embassy of the PRC to the United States; Deng Rong's husband)

Wu Jianchang (General Manager, China's Nonferrous Metals Import and Export Corporation)

Zhao Baojiang (Mayor of Wuhan City and Deputy CCP Party Secretary of Wuhan) Zhao visited the United States with the Mayors Delegation in July, 1990.

He Changgong (High ranking PLA officer; former president, CCP Society on Historical Figures)

Son: **He Qizong** (Deputy Chief of Staff, PLA General Staff Department)

He Long (Marshal; former Vice premier; former Vice chairman, Central Military Commission)

Son: **He Pengfei** (Director, Armament Department, PLA's General Staff Department)

Hu Qili (Former Standing Committee Member of the CCP's Politburo; CCP Central Committee member)

Sister: **Hu Qiheng** (Director, Institute of Automation, Chinese Academy of Sciences; Vice president, Chinese Academy of Sciences)

Hu, Yaobang (Former General Secretary, Chinese Communist Party)

Son: **Hu Liu** (Deputy Department Director, Ministry of Foreign Economic Relations and Trade) Visited the United States with a Chinese Purchasing Delegation in October 1990. He is the Deputy Director of the Technology Import and Export Department.

Li Desheng (Political Commissar, National Defense University; member, CCP's Central Advisory Commission)

    Son: **Li Nanzheng** (Chief, General Staff of Shenyang Military District)

Li Fuchun (Former Vice premier, State Council)

    Son: **Li Changan** (Deputy Secretary-General, State Council)

Li Peng (Premier, State Council)

    Wife: **Zhu Lin** (General Manager of a company in South China)

    Son: **Li Yang** (Vice president, The Industrial Development Company, Hainan Province)

Li Weihan (Former Vice chairman, CCP Central Advisory Commission; former head CCP's United Front Department)

    Son: **Li Tieying** (Member of CCP's Politburo; Chairman, State Education Commission; State Councillor)

Li Xiannian (Chairman, Chinese People's Political Consultative Conference)

    Daughter: **Li Haifeng** (Secretary, CCP's Shijiazhuang Municipal Committee, Hebei Province)

Liao Chengzhi (Former Director of Hong Kong and Macao Office of the State Council)

    Son: **Liao Hui** (Director, Office of Overseas Chinese Affairs, State Council)

Liu Shaoqi (Former President, People's Republic of China)

    Sons: **Liu Yuan** (Deputy Governor of Henan Province; Member, Standing Committee, CCP, Henan Province)

Liu Zhen (Vice mayor, Qingdao City)

Brother-in-law: Wang Guangying (President, Everbright Industrial Corporation, Hong Kong)

Nie Rongzhen (Marshal; former Vice chairman, CCP's Central Military Commission)

Daughter: **Nie Li** (Vice chairman, Science and Technology Committee, Commission of Science, Technology and Industry for National Defense)

Son-in-law: **Ding Henggao** (Minister and chairman, Commission of Science, Technology and Industry for National Defense)

Peng Zhen (Former Chairman, Standing Committee of the National People's Congress; former Mayor of Beijing)

Daughter: **Peng Peiyun** (Director, State Family Planning Commission; Member, CCP Central Commission for Discipline Inspection)

Sons-in-law; **Wang Hanbin** (Member, CCP Central Committee; Vice chairman, National People's Congress; Chairman, Committee on Law, National People's Congress)

Zhang Boxing (Member, CCP Central Committee; Party Secretary, CCP Shanxi Provincial Party Committee)

Qiao Guanhua (Former Minster, Minstry of Foreign Affairs)

Son: **Qiao Zonghui** (Deputy Secretary general, Hong Kong Xinhua News Agency)

Song Renqiong (Vice chairman, Central Advisory Commission)

Son: **Song Ruixiang** (Deputy Secretary of CCP, Qinghai Province and Governor of Qinghai Province)

Tao Zhu (Former Vice premier, State Council)

    Daughter: **Tao Siliang** (Deputy Director, Sixth Bureau, CCP's United Front Department)

Tian Jiyun (Vice premier; Member, CCP Politburo)

    Brother: **Tian Tizhen** (Mayor, Xinxiang City, Henan Province)

Ulanfu (Former Vice-President, People's Republic of China)

    Sons: **Buhe** (Chairman, People's Government of Inner Mongolia Autonomous Region)

            Wujie (Mayor, Huhehote City, Inner Mongolia)

Wang Bingqian (Minister, Ministry of Finance; State Concillor, State Council)

    Son: **Wang Hui** (Mayor, Datong City, Shanxi Province)

Wang Zhen (Vice president, People's Republic of China)

    Sons: **Wang Jun** (Vice chairman, China International Trust and Investment Corporation; Chairman, Planning Commission, Beijing City)

            Wang Zhi (General Manager, Great Wall Computer Corporation, Beijing)

Xi Zhongxun (Vice chairman, National People's Congress)

    Sons: **Xi Zhengning** (Deputy Director, CCP's Organizational Department, Shanxi Province)

            Xi Zhengping (Party secretary, Ningde District, Fujian Province)

    Son-in-law: **Chen Guangyi** (CCP Party Secretary, Fujian Province)

Xiao Jinguang (Former Navy Commander, People's Liberation Army)

> **Son:** **Xiao Congci** (CCP Party Secretary, Datong City, Shanxi Province)

Yang Dezhi (General; Former chief of the PLA General Staff Department)

> **Nephew:** **Yang Xizong** (Member, Central Committee, CCP; CCP Secretary, Henan Province; Chairman, Henan Provincial People's Congress)

Yang Shangkun (President of the PRC; First Vice chairman, CCP Central Military Commission)

> **Brother:** **Yang Baibing** (Secretary general, CCP Central Military Commission; Director of the PLA General Political Department)
>
> **Nephew:** **Yang Shaojun** (Commander, 27th Army)

Ye Jianying (Marshal; former Vice chairman of the Central Military Commission)

> **Son:** **Ye Xuanping** (Governor of Guangdong Province; CCP Deputy Party Secretary of Guangdong Province)
>
> **Daughter:** **Ye Chumei** (former Vice minister, Commission of Science, Technology, and Industry for National Defense)
>
> **Son-in-law:** Zou Jiahua, State Councillor, Minstry of machine Indutry and Electronics
>
> **Daughter-in-law:** Wu Xiaolan (Former Vice mayor, Shenzhen City)

Zhang Aiping (Former Minister of Defense)

> **Son:** **Zhang Haoruo** (Bureau Director, State Council, CCP Party Deputy Secretary, Sichuan Province; Governor, Sichuan Province)
>
> **Son-in-law:** **Yu Zheng-sheng** (Mayor, Yantai City, Shandong Province)

Zhao Ziyang (Former General secretary, Chinese Communist Party)

Son: **Zhao Dajun** (Former Haihua Development Corporation, Hainan Province)

Daughter: **Zhao Liang** (Assistant Manager, Sheraton Great Wall Hotel, Beijing)

Son-in-law: **Wang Zhihua** (Former General Manager, Poly Technologies Incorporated)

EXTERNAL FACTORS AFFECTING THE ECONOMY

By Robert G. Sutter *

CONTENTS

I. OVERVIEW

Events in China leading to the Tiananmen massacre and the political crackdown and economic retrenchment in 1989 and 1990 vividly demonstrated the fault lines that run through the Chinese leadership and society over a range of sensitive domestic and foreign policy questions. Increasingly complex economic problems, rising popular expectations, and widespread disillusionment with the communist system are among the most salient domestic forces expected to test the ability of the Chinese authorities to maintain order and promote policies conducive to the effective economic modernization of the country in the 1990s. Effective administration seems especially difficult over the short term as leadership division and debate are expected to worsen amid the jockeying for power among ambitious officials as the now dominant older generation of leaders headed by 86-year-old Deng Xiaoping approaches its end.[1]

Foreign pressures are part of the equation of forces expected to complicate the development of the Chinese economy through the 1990s. Chinese leaders will have to deal with the western-aligned developed countries that have been appalled by the excesses of communist repression, skeptical of the economic advantages of close association with China in this period of domestic Chinese uncertainty, and attracted to new opportunities presented by the collapse of communism in the Soviet bloc. Some in the West are in-

---

* Senior Specialist in International Politics, Congressional Research Service of the Library of Congress.
[1] For useful background on recent events in China, see *Current History*, September 1990 (entire issue); Report on Economic Sanctions Against China, 101st Congress 2nd Session; House Document 101–192. Washington U.S. GPO 1990; Testimony by Assistant Secretary of State, Richard Solomon before the Senate Foreign Relations Committee, June 6, 1990; U.S. Central Intelligence Agency, The Chinese Economy in 1989 and 1990. EA 90–10023 July 1990.

clined to press hard through economic sanctions, political activities and other measures to force a change in the Chinese system along lines favored by the West. Some authorities in China claim such westerners represent the major foreign "threat" to China in the 1990s.

A strong case can be made in support of the view that holds that such outside pressures could have a decisive impact on the course of Chinese modernization in the 1990s. Available evidence suggests that China's leaders had not anticipated the prolonged alienation from the West that has followed the Tiananmen incident. They also were caught unaware by the radical changes in Eastern Europe, the Soviet Union and in U.S.-Soviet relations. These changes have had the effect of limiting options for developing Chinese relations with the Soviet bloc as a complement to (or substitute for) heavy Chinese reliance on western-aligned developed countries. They have also reduced western interest in sustaining close ties with China.

China's leaders have been so preoccupied with maintaining internal order and control that they have been ineffective in coming up with a strategy to deal with the rapidly changing world order of the early 1990s. Beleaguered and isolated, Beijing leaders have been cut off, at least for the time being, from a large portion of the foreign assistance that used to flow to China from the World Bank, Japan and other western-aligned countries. Tourism receipts in the year after the Tiananmen massacre dropped to less than half of the previous year; foreign investment dropped and technical exchanges were curbed.

Had China been following a more self reliant development strategy, such losses and curbs might not have had a serious effect on the Chinese economy. But the post-Mao reforms saw China's economy become increasingly dependent on foreign trade and exchanges. Thus, total exports (including services) rose to 22.2 percent of China's GNP, up from only six percent in 1980. The level of China's trade relative to its total economy has far surpassed that of other large economies such as Brazil, India or the Soviet Union.

A complicated web of personal, business, academic and other exchanges fostered by the Chinese reformers in the post-Mao period now has come to be seen as threatening to the Beijing authorities. It provides conduits for the safe passage out of China for fugitives from Beijing's repression. Information about the fall of communism in the Soviet bloc, and especially the uprising in Romania and overthrow of China's close ally, Ceasescu, spread throughout cities in China. Outsiders bent on major political change or the overthrow of communism can use these connections to transmit ideas and information deemed to be subversive to the continued authoritarian communist rule. Yet, the imperative of economic modernization and the related need for information and technical support from outside China have checked the tendency shown by some in the Beijing leadership to sharply curb and tightly control this potentially threatening web of outside connections.

An alternate view of the foreign pressures faced by China and their likely effects on the Chinese economy in the 1990s holds that it is easy to exaggerate the effect of outside forces on the course of Chinese leadership and economic policy. This argument adds that the major changes in world affairs in 1989–1990 had positive as well as negative effects on the stability of China's current regime. Thus, it markedly reduced (some would say eliminated) the strategic threat faced by China from the Soviet Union; and it notably increased China's foreign policy leverage and room for maneuver vis-a-vis such important strategic areas as North Korea, Indochina and Southeast Asia. The economic sanctions and curbs on foreign assistance from the western-aligned countries have not been uniform; some countries of East Asia, notably Taiwan, have been rapidly expanding investment and trade with the mainland.[2] Positive international attention to changes in the Soviet bloc could change quickly to disillusionment if the new governing authorities prove unable to come up with effective modernization strategies. Under these circumstances, China might appear as a much better bet for foreign investment and trade.

Meanwhile, it remained unclear how far foreign governments and societies would press for change in China's repressive communist system. And it remained uncertain how people in China would react to such efforts. The fiasco associated with the ship, "Goddess of Democracy," which attempted in vain to broadcast radio programs while stationed off the China coast in June 1990,[3] seemed to demonstrate that established governments remained unwilling to press too forcefully for political change in China.

On balance, therefore, it appeared in mid-1990 that foreign pressures would be likely to serve as an important but secondary set of factors likely to complicate the development of the Chinese economy during the 1990s. Indeed, the Chinese economy had already lost some of the advantages it had derived from close association with western-aligned countries, and international and financial-economic institutions in the 1980s. Those countries and institutions appeared to be unlikely to return to China with the same vigor and enthusiasm, even if China's policies were to return to the pragmatic reform efforts of the 1980s. This "opportunity cost," and other costs to China's modernization associated with the radical changes in world affairs in 1989–1990, were important; but they seemed less important than domestic factors in determining the course of China's modernization and development in the decade ahead. International developments appeared to serve to reinforce domestic pressures affecting the Chinese economy, but, in and of themselves, they seemed to be unlikely to be decisive in determining the course of China's development.[4]

---

[2] See *Financial Times*, June 6, 1990. See also reviews of this issue in August–September 1990 editions of the Far Eastern Economic Review.

[3] See the blow-by-blow coverage of this issue in the *Far Eastern Economic Review*.

[4] Historical comparisons are often inaccurate, because of changing circumstances and other factors. Nevertheless, it is useful to remember that foreign pressure, on its own, only rarely has been decisive in determining Chinese domestic policies, including economic policies. Perhaps the best recent example of foreign pressure causing major changes in domestic policies came in the late 1960s when the Sino-Soviet border clashes escalated to a point where the U.S.S.R. directly threatened to attack China with conventional forces and with nuclear weapons, and China was in no position to defend itself on account of military dislocations and international isolation caused by the Cultural Revolution. This crisis led to major changes in Chinese foreign and domestic policies. It is very hard to imagine Chinese leaders seeing the international pressures they face today as anything like the threat they faced in the late 1960s.

II. Post Mao Foreign Relations and Economic Modernization, 1978–1989

Post-Mao leaders followed general policy lines set at the third plenum of the 11th Central Committee: They viewed effective economic modernization as their primary goal; they understood that their success or failure politically would be determined to considerable measure by their ability to advance the wealth and power of China. As a result, all policies, including foreign policy, were geared to serve this effort.[5]

Chinese foreign policy supported China's quest to achieve economic modernization as effectively as possible in two basic ways. On the one hand, it helped to promote economic contacts with various countries that could benefit China's modernization. On the other hand, it helped to maintain a stable and secure environment in Asian and world affairs that was conducive to Chinese modernization efforts. In this context, Chinese leaders put aside ideological and other constraints to beneficial economic and technical interchange with a wide range of developed countries. They halted or cut back support to Maoist insurgents or political groups that would impede smooth economic exchanges abroad; cut back sharply on Chinese foreign assistance to the Third World; and showed an increased willingness to softpedal past Maoist pretensions to change the world.

Chinese leaders focused their foreign policy concerns on establishing a "peaceful environment" around China's periphery in Asia. China did not control that environment, which remained more heavily influenced by the Soviet Union, the United States, their allies and associates. Since the late 1960s, China saw the main danger of instability and adverse development in Asia coming from the Soviet Union or its allies and associates. And it continued to see reasonably close Chinese relations with the United States, Japan and other non-communist countries as useful to support Chinese security in the face of real or potential pressure.

By the late 1980s, international trends and Beijing's relationships abroad were widely seen to have developed in ways advantageous to Chinese economic modernization:

• Chinese leaders saw the strategic environment around their periphery as more stable and less likely to be disrupted by a major international power than at any time since the 1960s. This development came as a result of changes in Soviet foreign policy, especially those begun by Mikhail Gorbachev in 1985, and continued firm western-backed efforts to check Soviet expansion abroad. Of course, the reduced big power threat did not preclude danger posed by possible conflicts between China and its neighbors over territorial disputes or other issues. Nor did it automatically translate into growing Chinese influence in Asia. Regional economic and military powers (e.g. Japan, Indonesia, India) were becoming more prominent in asserting their influence as East-West and Sino-Soviet tensions subsided.

---

[5] See, *China's Economy Looks to the Year 2000.* U.S. Congress Joint Economic Committee, 1986. Two Volumes.

- Regional security trends were generally compatible with China's primary concern with internal economic modernization and political reform. So long as the regional power balance remained stable and broadly favorable to Chinese interests, Beijing was likely to continue to give the pragmatic development of advantageous economic contacts top priority in its foreign affairs.
- Ideological and leadership disputes had less importance for Chinese foreign policy than in the past. Although Chinese leaders divided between more conservative-minded officials and those who were more reform-minded, the differences within the leadership over foreign affairs had lessened markedly over the past 20 years.
- Reinforcing the more narrow range of foreign policy choices present among Chinese leaders, China had become more economically dependent on other countries, especially the western-aligned, developed countries, than in the past. Particularly as a result of the new openness to foreign economic contacts and the putting aside of Maoist policies of economic self reliance, Beijing had come to see its well-being as more closely tied to continued good relations with important developed countries, notably Japan and the United States, and associated international financial institutions. They provided the assistance, technology, investment and markets China needed to modernize effectively.

Chinese policy planners were on the whole sanguine about China's ability to continue modernization with ample support from the non-communist developed countries and without major disruption to the "peaceful environment" in Asia. Strategically, China was seen as likely to play an increasingly important role as part of an emerging multi-polar world as the contending superpowers, the United States and the U.S.S.R., slowly declined in power relative to other parts of the world. Since Moscow and Washington were expected to remain at odds, they were both thought to be strongly interested in working closely with China and other newly emerging centers of world power (i.e. Western Europe and Japan). Thus, China remained sought after by both superpower adversaries in the U.S.-Soviet-Chinese triangular relationship.

China's location at the center of the most economically dynamic part of the world gave Beijing confidence in China's growing economic as well as continued strategic importance. China's ongoing economic reforms were attracting increasing international attention and support among developed countries and international financial institutions supported by them. China looked forward to even more generous largescale assistance from the World Bank and Japan, as well as growing fruitful economic interaction, technology transfer and training in Chinese relations with the United States, Japan, Western Europe and the non-communist countries of East Asia. Beijing looked forward to the benefits associated with membership in the GATT, and assistance from the Asian Development Bank and other such organizations. Meanwhile, easing Sino-Soviet tensions opened up prospects for broad economic cooperation with the Soviet Union and Eastern Europe.

III. FOREIGN DEVELOPMENTS COMPLICATING CHINA'S SEARCH FOR STABILITY AND MODERNIZATION

Beijing's leaders clearly recognized that much of the non-communist world would react negatively to their decision to crack down on the pro-democracy demonstrations in Beijing and other cities in mid-1989. They almost certainly expected some negative reactions to the intensification of China's concurrent economic retrenchment. Available evidence suggests that party leaders judged that their continued political control required such harsh measures; and at least some felt that sharp negative reactions from the West and elsewhere would pass without longterm consequences for Chinese economic modernization. In particular, Chinese leaders at a conference of returned ambassadors in July 1989 set forth the view that China basically had to wait for a short period in order to allow the storm of international protest over the crackdown to pass. They remained confident that Japan, the United States, the other western-aligned countries and the international financial institutions associated with them would soon restore ties with China because of China's strategic and economic importance.[6]

It is not clear whether or not this Chinese prediction would have come true in late 1989 if other world conditions had not changed. But events in Eastern Europe and the Soviet Union markedly upset the Chinese calculus; they led international factors likely to seriously complicate Chinese modernization efforts into the 1990s.

The rapidly changing political, economic and security policies in the Soviet Union and Eastern Europe in late 1989 and 1990 added to the complications faced by Chinese leaders following their crackdown on pro-democracy demonstrations in Chinese cities in spring 1989. The changes in the Soviet bloc had an obvious "ripple effect" in China, encouraging pro-democracy forces and alarming Chinese leaders who were determined to maintain the monopoly of power held by them as leaders of the Chinese Communist Party. They dampened signs of Chinese interest in pursuing closer ties with the Soviet bloc as a means to balance China's recent strong reliance on economic, technical, and other contacts with the non-communist countries of the West, Japan, and other parts of Asia. (Some in China and abroad had speculated in 1989 that Beijing could offset, to some degree, the sanctions imposed by the western powers and Japan in the wake of the mid-1989 Beijing crackdown by relying somewhat more on growing contacts with the Soviet bloc. At the time, it appeared that economic-technical contacts with the communist-ruled European countries would be accompanied by less of the "spiritual pollution" of pro-democracy ideas challenging the status quo in China. The events of late 1989 and 1990 in the Soviet bloc vividly demonstrated to all in China that the political ideas coming from Eastern Europe were perhaps more directly challenging to the political status quo in China than were the ideas from the West.)

---

[6] See discussion of this view in *Crisis in China: Prospects for U.S. Policy.* Report of the Thirtieth Strategy for Peace, U.S. Foreign Policy Conference. The Stanley Foundation. October 19–21, 1989. 19 pp.

The changes in Eastern Europe and the Soviet Union prompted a strong reaction and attracted positive attention from the developed countries of the West and Japan, and the international financial institutions and businesses associated with them or located there. This had a strong indirect effect on China. Thus, not only did the PRC crackdown and accompanying Chinese economic retrenchment alienate the political, business and foreign assistance decision-makers in the non-communist developed countries and in international financial institutions, but the positive prospects in Eastern Europe served as a magnet to divert their resources away from places like China and toward Eastern Europe and the USSR.

A. SHIFTS IN WORLD POLITICS

On the plane of world politics, the events of 1989–1990 altered the balance of forces in the world that Beijing had been reasonably effective in dealing with, especially over the last 10 years. Heretofore, the Chinese world view had been premised on an international order heavily influenced by the two superpowers, the United States and the U.S.S.R., who would remain in protracted contention or rivalry for the foreseeable future. Because of their rivalry, the superpowers would spend resources on weapons, foreign bases, foreign interventions, and in other ways that would weaken their power relative to newly rising centers of world power such as Japan, the European Community, and China. Given its size, strategic location, large armed forces possessing nuclear weapons, and its demonstrated willingness to use force to pursue its interests in world affairs, China had been seen by many in China and abroad as holding a key position in world politics.[7] It was seen as one corner of the "strategic triangle" in U.S.-Soviet-Chinese relations, or as a critical balancing force between the United States and the U.S.S.R. As such, policymakers in Washington and Moscow paid close attention to Chinese policies for fear of driving China into the arms of their main adversary. Of course, the zero-sum game quality of U.S.-Soviet-Chinese relations varied over time; by the late 1980s, for example, policymakers in Washington appeared confident that the slowly emerging Sino-Soviet detente would not have major deleterious effects on U.S. interests. But the fact remained that U.S. policymakers, and presumably Soviet policymakers, continued to pay close attention to how China's policy affected their respective interests in the U.S.-Soviet competition for world influence.

By mid-1990, the relations between the United States and Soviet Union had changed to such a degree that observers in China and elsewhere could no longer safely assume that U.S.-Soviet rivalry would continue as an overriding international fact into the 1990s. Because of events in Eastern Europe and the U.S.S.R., it was becoming increasingly apparent to western leaders that the U.S.S.R. was unlikely to pose a major threat to the West for some time. Faced with enormous difficulties at home and abroad, the Gorbachev administration was cutting back on overseas commitments, deployment of troops, military spending, and other policy areas

---

[7] Chinese foreign policy expert Huan Xiang and U.S. commentator Henry Kissinger were notable proponents of this view in the latter 1980s.

sensitive to the West. Moscow was actively encouraging political reform in Eastern Europe and in the Soviet Union that seemed likely to make the new governments in Eastern Europe and the administration of the U.S.S.R. more responsive to the desires of the people there to pursue a better material life, with greater freedom of expression and human development. Even though there remained a persisting danger of reversal of policies, should Gorbachev be toppled or under other possible circumstances, it seemed likely that the United States and its allies would find the Soviet bloc more accommodating than confrontational in dealing with heretofore difficult world problems like strategic arms control, force reductions in Europe, and differences over international "hot spots" such as Afghanistan, Cambodia, and others.

Under these circumstances, the United States could increasingly see its interests as better served by encouraging these accommodating Soviet policies. Thus, the dynamic of U.S.-Soviet rivalry, which had been so central to China's world view, was in the process of fundamental change. China had a long record of concern over possible U.S.-Soviet collaboration in world affairs. Chinese officials in the past had portrayed such collaboration as coming at the expense of lesser powers, especially those in the Third World, including China. There were some signs in recent Chinese media coverage that Beijing saw a revival of U.S.-Soviet collaboration at the expense of the Third World.[8] Regardless of how Chinese media wished to portray the recent trends in U.S.-Soviet relations, Beijing leaders almost certainly had to consider possible logical conclusions coming from recent trends in East-West relations. At a time of rapidly improving U.S.-Soviet relations, both powers would likely see their interests as best served by avoiding actions with countries of lesser importance (including China) that could complicate the improvement in East-West relations.

This line of argument appeared to be particularly relevant in explaining Gorbachev's somewhat more cautious approach to China after mid-1989. Since coming to power in 1985, Gorbachev had used various means to pursue improved relations with China as a key element in Soviet efforts to ease tensions around the periphery of the U.S.S.R. and to use the opening to China as a means to break out of Moscow's isolated position in Asia. Events of 1989 and 1990 changed that calculation to some degree, and seemed to lower the priority of improved Sino-Soviet relations in Gorbachev's calculations. (As noted above, Chinese leaders also became more wary of the "spiritual pollution" associated with increased contacts with Soviet bloc countries and the U.S.S.R.) Gorbachev pulled back from China after the Tiananmen massacre for fear of sending the wrong signal to those at home and in the Soviet bloc regarding his intentions concerning political reform. At the same time, Gorbachev almost certainly was aware that an expedient Soviet effort to move closer to China at a time when Beijing hardliners had deeply offended the sensibilities of leaders and public opinion in the West would call into question, in the minds of Westerners, the Soviet leader's ultimate objectives in international affairs. As a result,

---

[8] See for instance, *Liowang Overseas Edition*. Number 2, January 7, 1990, p. 28.

such an expedient effort would have run the risk of causing western officials to be less forthcoming when considering arms reduction, technology transfer, trade and financial assistance policies favorable to the U.S.S.R.

B. POSSIBLE U.S.-SOVIET COLLABORATION IN ASIA

In mid-1990, it remained to be seen how far the nascent trend of increasing collaboration in U.S.-Soviet relations would go. Much would depend on Gorbachev's ability to weather the internal crises and likely political challenges coming from the checkered development of his reform program. Nevertheless, Chinese leaders almost certainly considered that U.S.Soviet relations might continue the pace of improvement seen over the previous year. Under these circumstances, both sides—Moscow and Washington—would likely see their interests as best served by mutual accommodation to deal with international troublespots. In Asia, these troublespots included Afghanistan, Cambodia, and Korea. Both sides showed increasing interest in 1990 in cooperating together or working in parallel in order to ease tensions or settle conflicts in these areas.

The trends in China since mid-1989 also represented a troublespot for policymakers in Moscow and Washington. Both superpowers would have preferred to see a return to a more open, reform-oriented, political, economic, and foreign policy approach in China. Leaders in the United States and the U.S.S.R. were determined to do what they could to encourage such a return to reform in China, without jeopardizing their respective interests vis-a-vis the PRC. Against this background, PRC leaders were forced to deal with a logical outgrowth of these recent trends. That is, both Washington and Moscow might increasingly see it in their interests to exchange information and coordinate their policies toward China, in the interests of fostering an international environment conducive to the resumption of Chinese reform. The United States for many years had carried out coordination of policies with Japan on issues relating to China. If U.S.-Soviet relations continued to improve and China remained a common trouble spot for both powers, one could not exclude the possibility of U.S.-Soviet coordination over China policy in the period ahead.

Of course, any such coordination would have to be carried out very discreetly in order to avoid offending PRC nationalistic sensitivities. Chinese sensitivities would be all the greater because such U.S. collaboration with Moscow would signal a fundamental change in the common strategic orientation that had bound Sino-U.S. relations since the Nixon-Mao rapprochement. Despite differences over a wide range of issues, China and the United States were able to reach common ground in the early 1970s on their fundamental opposition to Soviet expansion in Asia. Historically concerned that a balance of power be maintained in Asia, and no longer able to sustain its longstanding containment system in Asia, the United States under President Nixon looked to a China independent of the U.S.S.R. in order to maintain a favorable balance in Asia as U.S. forces were withdrawn from Asia under terms of the Nixon doctrine. Facing a major security threat from Soviet forces threatening to invade China under terms of the so-called Brezhnev doctrine,

Mao's China saw common ground with the United States, which now seemed more interested in accommodation than confrontation with China.

This common Sino-American understanding continued with varying degrees of activity for two decades. As the Soviet threat to both China and the United States appeared to diminish in the 1980s, both sides adjusted their policies accordingly but still kept in close touch about their respective and often parallel policies vis-a-vis the U.S.S.R. Indeed, the December 9-10, 1989, trip to China of National Security Adviser Brent Scowcroft was initially described as one in a long series of U.S. efforts to keep Chinese leaders fully informed about Soviet policies as seen in U.S.-Soviet arms control and summit negotiations.

Taken together with the downturn in U.S.-PRC relations as a result of the repression in China since mid-1989, the events in Eastern Europe and the U.S.S.R. and resulting changes in Soviet policy held out the distinct possibility of a challenge to this basic anti-Soviet basis of Sino-American policy in Asia. If trends in Soviet accommodation of western interests continued, U.S. policymakers would increasingly see more to be gained from collaborating than contending with the U.S.S.R. over Asian problems. In so far as China followed policies of internal repression, economic retrenchment, and support for such unsavory foreign clients as the Khmer Rouge, U.S. and Soviet policymakers might see their interests as better served by quiet cooperation and coordination of policies designed to foster an atmosphere conducive to a return to economic and political reform in China and to achieve common U.S.-Soviet goals of stability and progress in Asia.

C. DOMESTIC FACTORS AFFECTING FOREIGN INTERACTION WITH CHINA

Policymakers in the United States, Western Europe, Japan and the newly pluralistic and increasing democratic governments of Asia and Eastern Europe do not make foreign policy decisions in a vacuum. They are often heavily influenced by public opinion, the media, interest groups, and the representative members of their respective legislative bodies. In the case of the United States and Western Europe, developments in China and Eastern Europe during 1989–1990 had a profound impact among these groups. The result tended to reinforce the shifts in world politics noted above in ways that appeared to add pressure on China's current leaders and to complicate the prospects of China's economic modernization.

In the United States, for example, the American people, media, interest groups, and, to a considerable degree, U.S. legislators place a strong emphasis on morality or values as well as realpolitik or national interest in American foreign policy. Thus, when the United States moves closer in policy to a heretofore alienated power or powers, these U.S. groups want to see the righteousness of this move, hopefully in terms of common values like freedom, democracy, and free enterprise that are fundamental to the American experience. In the case of the opening to China, American opinion generally accepted the strategic need for the United States to move more closely to China at a time of U.S. withdrawal and strategic realignment in Asia. But China was kept at a distance

and full normalization did not take place until the late 1970s. At
that time, the U.S. move was justified in part by evidence that
post-Mao China was reforming both economically and politically.
Deng Xiaoping was seen moving China in directions that not only
served U.S. security interests in dealing with the expanding power
of the U.S.S.R. and that of its proxies in Asian and world affairs,
but also in directions in domestic Chinese policies that fed the long-
standing U.S. hope to promote a more democratic and prosperous
China.

The Tiananmen massacre and crackdown on unprecedented pro-
democracy demonstrations in China in mid-1989 sharply alienated
American opinion. The leaders in Beijing were now widely seen as
following policies antithetical to American values and therefore as
unworthy of American support. The rapidly changing U.S.-Soviet
relationship, meanwhile, generally meant that there was no longer
evident a realpolitik or national security rationale of sufficient
weight to offset the popularly held revulsion with Beijing's leaders
and their repressive policies.

The other side of the world, meanwhile, saw political, economic
and security changes that attracted wide and generally positive attention on the part of American people, media, interest groups, and
legislators. Eastern Europe and the Soviet Union were increasingly
following policies of reform in their government structures and
economies that seemed to be based on values of individual freedom,
political democracy and economic free enterprise valued in the
United States. As a result, these American groups tended at times
to push U.S. decisionmakers to be more forthcoming in negotiations and interaction with their East European and Soviet counterparts involving arms control, trade, foreign assistance, and other
matters.

The importance of this shift in domestic U.S. opinion regarding
China and the Soviet bloc countries appeared to be greater than it
might have been in the past in determining the course of U.S. foreign policy. Most notably, since the start of the Cold War, the executive branch had been able to argue, on many occasions quite persuasively, that such domestic U.S. concerns with common values
should not be permitted to override or seriously complicate realpolitik U.S. interests in the protracted struggle and rivalry with the
U.S.S.R. Now that it was widely seen that the Cold War was
ending and the threat from the U.S.S.R. was greatly reduced, the
ability of the executive branch to control the course of U.S. foreign
policy appeared somewhat less. Thus, there were instances in 1989
and 1990 where domestic factors seemed to push the Bush administration to be much more generous than it had initially planned in
giving assistance to reforming East European countries. The President's efforts to sustain Sino-U.S. relations at a level higher than
deemed appropriate by Congress and much American opinion resulted in great controversy and a cutback in Administration initiatives. A lesson from these events was that domestic factors were
likely to be even more important in determining U.S. foreign policy
in the period ahead. The ability of the Administration to argue
that the dangers of Cold War contention and confrontation required a tightly controlled foreign policy within the executive
branch would hold less weight and force the Administration to

broaden the circle of actors brought into consultations on foreign policy issues.

Of course, it is unfair to generalize from an U.S. example to make a case for domestic factors influencing behavior of other western-aligned developing countries. Indeed, as is explained below, many U.S. allies and associates in Asia, notably South Korea, Pakistan, Thailand and the Philippines, were careful to keep contacts open with Beijing in the immediate aftermath of the Tiananmen massacre and to avoid association with U.S.-backed sanctions against Beijing. Nevertheless, Japan and the large developed countries of Europe and the international financial institutions associated with them continued to work closely through mid-1990 in limiting economic interchange favorable to China. The reasoning of each government and institution differed according to circumstances. While Japanese people were shocked by Beijing's crackdown, they did not usually press their government to use economic sanctions. But Tokyo chose not to break ranks with Washington in a way that would add friction to an already difficult U.S.-Japanese relationship. The West European people were often quite vocal in pushing their governments to stern actions against China, although the magnet effect of the emerging changes in Eastern Europe and the U.S.S.R. was probably even more important in placing limits on West European interchange advantageous to China.

IV. FOREIGN DEVELOPMENTS SUPPORTING CHINA'S SEARCH FOR STABILITY AND MODERNIZATION

Since mid-1989, analysts of Sino-foreign relations in the United States and elsewhere have generally emphasized how the world changes and international pressures noted above have brought about a series of crises for Beijing's leaders that have challenged the leaders' ability to rule and to carry out the effective modernization of the Chinese economy. What has not received as much attention is an alternate analysis of recent world trends, and China's reaction to those trends. This view tended to play down the likelihood that foreign pressures would lead to major crisis in China. It noted that amid these challenges to Beijing's rule and modernization lie offsetting trends and even important opportunities.[9]

Most important among emerging world trends likely to work to the advantage of China's current rulers were those that relate to the declining military threat to China. Throughout its history, the People's Republic of China had seen itself facing a substantial and often imminent military danger, usually in the form of the United States and/or the Soviet Union. Since the late 1960s, Beijing focused on the U.S.S.R. as its main strategic adversary. Trends in the 1970s and 1980s prompted China to downgrade the immediate threat posed by the U.S.S.R., but Chinese military planners still saw a strong need for active military modernization and vigilance to prepare to meet the threat from the north.

The collapse of the Soviet empire in Eastern Europe and the massive internal challenges to Gorbachev's rule clearly reduced

---

[9] See, for example, weekly coverage of China in *Far Eastern Economic Review* during August-September 1990.

substantially any near term military danger posed to China from the Soviet Union. Chinese military planners remain wary of Moscow, and keep a sharp eye on the growing military power of regional powers like Japan and India. Hardline Chinese leaders also see a "threat" to China's stability posed by U.S. ideology, but they see no sign of U.S. interest to use military means to pressure China.

Thus, trends in the 1990s appeared likely to provide the Chinese leadership with their first significant "breathing space," free from superpower threat, since 1949. Although it was unclear if any significant Chinese "peace dividend" would result in greater Chinese spending on economic modernization, it appeared likely that the Beijing leaders would have an easier time than at any period since the establishing of the PRC to meet the prime demand on Chinese rulers—i.e. to safeguard the integrity and sovereignty of China.

The decline in Soviet power also provides Chinese rulers with opportunities to exert greater influence in areas around China's periphery that have historically been seen as most important to China's security and national pride. Gorbachev's June 1990 meeting with South Korea's President No Tae-Woo was widely interpreted as motivated by the Soviet Union's weak economy and dire need for international economic support. The meeting also capped a rapid decline in Soviet-North Korean relations as Kim Il-song reacted negatively to Gorbachev's support for the radical changes in Eastern Europe and the U.S.S.R. A consequence for China in this new, more fluid situation was to increase China's ability to exert influence in North Korea. It also presumably gave Beijing more leeway to improve economic relations with South Korea, without fear of driving Kim Il-song into the arms of the U.S.S.R.

In Indochina, another area of historically vital importance for China's security and national interests, the decline in Soviet power and changes in Eastern Europe began to result in cutbacks in Soviet bloc support for Vietnam and the Vietnamese-backed government in Phnom Penh. This coincided with widely publicized Vietnamese efforts to reach a compromise in their longstanding disputed relationship with China. Many analysts directly linked the Soviet changes with greater Vietnamese flexibility toward China, although there are many factors which influence the situation in Indochina. It appeared that continued decline in Soviet power and involvement in Indochina were likely to add to Chinese influence in this part of Asia in the 1990s.

Trends in Hong Kong and Macao showed no sign of challenging the attainment of China's longstanding nationalistic goal to recover sovereignty over these two territories in the 1990s. Beijing rulers were often seen as maladroit in managing the acute crisis of confidence in Hong Kong which followed the Chinese June 1989 crackdown. The reported exodus of capital and trained personnel from Hong Kong posed serious problems for the territory's ability to continue to prosper in the highly competitive East Asian economic environment. But the fact remains that Hong Kong is likely to continue to grow in the 1990s. And Hong Kong's investment in the PRC was also likely to continue to grow. Those Chinese leaders associated with the process of assimilation of the valuable territory to

Chinese rule were likely to gain political benefit where it really counts, inside China.

Regarding international economic pressures faced by China, it is important to note that the substantive effects of various sanctions imposed after the Tiananmen incident were mixed. The strength of the sanctions also appeared likely to lessen as more foreign countries and firms tried to restore or develop more normal business interchange with China. Most trade and investment sanctions directed against China were symbolic in nature. The hiatus in World Bank and Japanese foreign aid had a serious effect on Chinese development plans, which had benefitted from the past generous support from both sources. Some World Bank and Japanese aid was transmitted to China in the year after the Tiananmen massacre, and officials at the Bank and in Tokyo were anxious to follow through with gradually expanding aid programs in China, provided conditions in the PRC did not markedly deteriorate.

Decline in foreign investment, tourism and other economic interaction with China began to reverse in 1990. Most notable was the flow of visitors and investment from the nearby newly industrialized Asian economies, especially Taiwan. By the end of 1989 more than 1,000 Taiwanese companies reportedly had invested $1.1 billion in China, and Taiwanese investment exceeded that of the United States and Japan, accounting for more than 60 percent of all foreign investment in the mainland in early 1990.[10] China's leaders were giving special treatment to visiting Taiwan entrepreneurs, with Deng Xiaoping meeting personally with Taiwanese plastic magnate Y.C. Wang to complete arrangements for a major plastics plant in Fujian. Total indirect trade between Taiwan and the mainland amounted to $3.7 billion in 1989 and was heavily in Taiwan's favor. Meanwhile, trade between China and South Korea remained high, at about $4.5 billion in 1989, and the Koreans were continuing to make modest investments in China. Chinese trade with the United States and Japan seemed likely to remain flat or grow modestly in 1990 while the investment picture with these countries was mixed.

Beijing's relatively moderate reaction to the major international challenges and events of 1989 and 1990 added to the arguments of those who saw foreign pressures, in and of themselves, as unlikely to force significant changes in Chinese policy. Although subjected to intense political and economic pressures at home, and facing great uncertainties and rapidly changing events abroad, Chinese leaders in 1989 and 1990 did not fundamentally alter the comparatively moderate course of Chinese foreign policy of the past decade.Thus, much of the basic framework that governed Chinese foreign policy in the post-Mao period remained in tact.

- The top priority of current Chinese leaders remained to promote China's wealth and power. This development still represented a linchpin determining their political success or failure. They did not have the prestige of Mao, who could ignore development needs in pursuit of ideological or political goals. These

---

[10] *Financial Times*, June 6, 1990.10.

officials had to produce concrete results in order to stay in power.
- All policies, including foreign policy, had to serve this goal. Foreign policy still did this in two basic ways.
    a) It helped to maintain a stable security environment around China's periphery. In the past, China worried a lot about the Soviet Union as the main threat to China's periphery. Even though the Soviet danger had declined, China needed to pay close attention to other potential sources of instability—i.e. Korea, Indochina, India, and Japan.
    b) It helped to promote advantageous economic exchanges. Beijing continued this policy while at the same time it tried to pull back from some contacts or regulate them because they were accompanied by potentially dangerous political or social ideas. The continuation of this basic framework suggested a China that was not looking for trouble; rather, it suggested a China that was looking for help.

Beijing's ability to deal with foreign challenges moderately, and to avoid actions that would seriously complicate Sino-foreign relations and exacerbate tensions affecting the Chinese economy in the 1990s, appeared to be based on several factors, including:

- PRC leaders' awareness of their need to focus on economic development and to pursue open interaction with the world to achieve that goal was underlined by their knowledge of the accomplishments of Japan and many other non-communist East Asian states, and their knowledge of the negative development experiences of the rigid communist regimes in North Korea and Vietnam.
- Despite sanctions enacted by the West and Japan, the non-communist world, especially the countries of East Asia, made clear that they had no intention of isolating China. They remained interested in mutually beneficial economic interchange that would grow at a pace determined heavily by China's willingness to remain open to economic interaction with the outside world.
- Soviet bloc changes meant that China could not hope to turn to these countries for support for economic development if Beijing were to decide to cut back economic interchange with the non-communist world.
- The PRC leadership appeared divided and in transition from one generation to another. Making significant changes in foreign policy in most areas remained sensitive politically. It called attention to a leader and made him or her vulnerable to counterattack by opponents in the leadership. Past periods of similar leadership transition (e.g. 1973–1975, 1976–1978) did not see marked changes in foreign policy.
- Leaders who actively promoted reform, interaction with the world and cooperation with the West in the past were not prominent, but they had not been removed from power.
- Even so-called hardliners had proven records of following relatively moderate foreign policies and related defense and domestic policies. Few appeared to favor a return to policies of isolation, autarchy or Stalinist control that were tried but failed in China in the past.

V. Prospects

Christopher Clarke has laid out a series of scenarios that describe how domestic and foreign pressures are likely to affect the course of China's economic modernization in the decade ahead.[11] Most of his predictions rightfully emphasize the difficulties facing Chinese leaders as they deal with largescale internal difficulties and international uncertainties while attempting in the process to construct a stable new "social compact" with the Chinese people following the seeming betrayal of faith and loss of legitimacy in June 1989. The big question for this chapter is to what extent foreign developments and Beijing's reaction to those developments are likely to complicate the difficulties faced by China's leaders and their efforts to promote China's economic modernization.

Carefully weighing international factors likely to complicate or to support China's search for stability and economic modernization suggests that international pressures will have a negative effect on China's future. They will exacerbate the deep economic, social and political problems that will continue to hamper China's drive for economic modernization. Nevertheless, these foreign pressures are unlikely to become of sufficient weight—in and of themselves—to prompt major changes in Chinese policy. Indeed, the international situation in the 1990s promises important opportunities as well as challenges for China's leaders. Even if these leaders become preoccupied with internal conflicts and jockeying for power as the "old guards" die off, Beijing appears reasonably well positioned to weather the challenges posed by a changing world. Despite the turmoil of the past year, Beijing has used international opportunities with reasonably effectiveness, or at least has avoided egregiously counterproductive behavior in the face of foreign challenges. As a result, it appears fair to say that the foreign situation—on its own—will allow Beijing to "muddle through" and meet its basic economic modernization goals regarding the growth of national GNP in the 1990s.

Of course, there are major "opportunity costs" for China in following Beijing's current strategy. The Chinese have already felt some of those costs in the slowdown of foreign investment, aid, trade and other exchanges. The priority that developed countries gave to providing benefits for China will continue, on the whole, to move in directions of less benefit for China. Membership in GATT, the granting of new trade privileges (e.g. U.S. granting GSP treatment to Chinese imports), and aid flows from Japan and international organizations will remain hampered by foreign reaction to Beijing's internal policies and distractions posed by the new regimes in Eastern Europe and the changes in the Soviet Union. A shift toward greater democratization and economic reform in China, foreign disillusionment with failing economies in Eastern Europe and the U.S.S.R., or other possible developments could improve China's ability to attract aid, trade and investment from developed countries. But the fact remains that Beijing's leaders, even if they are successful in muddling through the 1990s, will have lost substantial opportunities that would have enhanced the moderniza-

---

[11] Please see article by Christopher Clarke, on page 1.

tion of China's economy. They will be leading a Chinese government and economy less important and influential internationally than it would have been had Beijing been able to continue reform and avoid the repression of 1989.

COMMENTARIES

CHINA'S BIGGEST PROBLEM: GRIDLOCK, NOT REVOLUTION

By David M. Lampton *

In early 1987 I wrote that China was "driving beyond the head-lights"—that the problems associated with rapid change were mounting so fast that the society and polity were going to hit a wall before its presence was fully visible.[1] While no one could have, nor did, predict the timing or the magnitude of the impact, China hit that wall in the Spring of 1989; the casualties were severe and numerous. In all probability, China will hit more such walls.

However, in recognizing the grave problems China faces, and the human toll its modernization will exact in the future, we should not make the mistake of thinking China is a political and social volcano waiting to erupt in the next few years. It is not in a pre-revolutionary state now or in the mid-term. Although there will be violence and unrest in the future, it will be episodic, localized, and manageable in the short and medium terms, albeit at possibly con-siderable cost. Moreover, there will be abrupt policy changes, with the likelihood that reform impulses will become stronger over time.

Nonetheless, I am uneasy with the cumulative impression left by the chapters in this section. While each author argues that a varie-ty of outcomes are possible, a proposition with which I certainly could not disagree, in the aggregate the preceding chapters portray the People's Republic to be more fragile than I believe it is, at least for the next five or so years.

The chapters in this section have accurately catalogued a stag-gering array of problems facing the People's Republic: rising budg-etary deficits; a money supply that threatens rekindled inflation; diminished legitimacy of the national authorities in the wake of June 4, 1989; unemployment and underemployment of enormous absolute magnitude; rising popular expectations amidst the reality of a real decline in the incomes of about 20 percent of the urban populace and (in the first half of 1990) a 4% income decline among peasants; mounting regional and social inequalities; alienation among intellectuals; little progress in increasing enterprise produc-tivity and the resultant need for huge government subsidies to cover enterprise losses (33 percent of state enterprises lost money in the first half of 1990); a government fearful of engaging in the

* David M. Lampton is president of the National Committee on United States-China Relations in New York. The views expressed in this article are his own, not those of the National Commit-tee, its members, or sponsors.

[1] David M. Lampton, "Driving Beyond the Headlights: The Politics of Reform in China," in David M. Lampton and Catherine H. Keyser, eds., *China's Global Presence* (American Enter-prise Institute: Washington, D.C., 1988), pp. 1–23.

political reform that would provide avenues for the peaceful and constructive expression of popular sentiment; an inability of political leaders to agree on how to manage the transition from a planned to a more market-oriented economy; a succession crisis in which neither the institutions for the peaceful transfer of power exist nor an heir to Deng Xiaoping visible; a less supportive international environment; and, a hemorrhage of power to China's provinces, raising the fearful specter of diminished national integration.

To even list these problems runs the risk of portraying China as a political, social, and economic powderkeg. A principal danger of viewing China's current situation in overly-apocalyptic terms is that American public and private decision makers will be inhibited from building economic, strategic, and cultural relations out of a misplaced expectation that enduring and mutually beneficial links will be unwise because of a looming deluge.

Such a response would damage American interests, hamper realization of the opportunities that do exist, and further retard economic and political development in China. China's future, whatever it may be, will be built upon the human and material foundation of the present. It is better that we be knowledgeable about, and connected to, that foundation rather than relegate ourselves to the sidelines of the future.

Kenneth Lieberthal, Christopher Clarke, and Robert Sutter all observe that there are both stabilizing and destabilizing factors that must be considered in assessing china's prospects for stability. I agree. Nonetheless, the reader needs a broader understanding of the stabilizing factors and a summary judgement about the net result.

Beyond the four factors cited in the Lieberthal contribution, the single most important stabilizing factor is China's peasantry. This mass is not only still comparatively isolated and comparatively uneducated; more importantly, it has benefitted greatly from the last decade of reform. I see almost no evidence that China's peasants currently are motivated to destabilize things, though we must candidly acknowledge that we know little about the thinking and perceptions of China's rural masses. One needs only to go to lively rural markets, see vast new tracts of peasant housing, and observe the last decade's explosion in rural industry to realize that the peasants have done pretty well by any historic standard with which they are familiar. In perhaps the most poignant discussion I have had with a Chinese intellectual since June 4th, we agreed that "the dreams of China's intellectuals seem not to be the dreams of China's peasants and workers."

This brings us to China's workers, notable participants in the later stages of the Tiananmen demonstrations. While careful field research would be needed to validate this assertion, my observations lead me to believe that the bulk of China's urban workers in state enterprises in some ways prefer the security of a planned economy to the uncertainties which are an essential feature of a reformed market economy. The past four decades of an egalitarian work ethic and industrial featherbedding of enormous proportions have taken their toll. Richard Nixon, in his *In the Arena* [2] notes

---

[2] Richard Nixon, *In the Arena* (Simon and Schuster: New York, 1990), p. 320.

that a Soviet economic advisor observed that in the Soviet Union "ideology has become psychology." This appears to be the case among state industrial workers in China as well.

The fears of China's state enterprise workers about a market economy and social instability are quite clear when one considers their opposition to the concept of bankruptcy and their role in helping peacefully clear Shanghai's streets of students and others in June 1989. Further, much of the discontent manifested in Tiananmen Square and elsewhere in China during the spring of 1989 was directed against inflation and corruption—almost unavoidable, short-run results of piecemeal economic reform. It seems to me that China's workers are ambivalent. They support reform (in the abstract), they want less corruption, and they want improved living standards. However, at the same time, they are not excited about the prospects of having to work harder in a much less secure economic environment. Conditions would have to deteriorate sharply for them to overcome these ambivalences.

The material circumstances of urban residents is also an important factor in this assessment. Despite a sluggish market and mounting inventories of many goods (especially durable goods), urban markets are well stocked with produce and consumer items. china's major cities are free from the queues and scarcities that have been a permanent feature in Soviet and Eastern European cities. Life may not be great, but it is literally light years ahead of what has catalyzed the breakdown in the soviet Union and fostered disturbances in Central Europe.

Further, if Mao Zedong's successful revolution had one lesson to teach it was that enduring social change requires a disciplined leadership possessing an ideology capable of mobilizing workers, peasants, and intellectuals alike. An inescapable observation about the present is that no such alternative, either ideological or organizational, exists in China today, as Clarke notes in his contribution. There are no meaningful parties, unions, or religious institutions to provide leadership and an alternative vision. Although the People's Liberation Army is playing a bigger domestic role in the wake of June 4th, and while it may prove decisive in the looming succession, there is very little evidence that the military is anywhere near playing a role analogous to that which the Romanian army played in late 1989.

In short, beyond the largely alienated intellectual class, the conditions favoring massive, widespread, disciplined, potent, and sustained social upheaval appear weak. Instead, the principal danger facing China is interminable policy gridlock resulting from elite conflict and uncertainty, autonomous local authorities who resist needed moves, and a populace that itself is unwilling to make the short-term sacrifices that will lead to a better future. As a result, mounting ecological, demographic, and economic problems will not be addressed effectively.

Given this situation, the question for American policy is how we can respond in ways that take full cognizance of these problems and simultaneously promote our values and interests? I fear that it may be too easy to reach the facile conclusion that China is currently too unpredictable, its relevance to core American interests too limited, and our influence too marginal to justify any American policy beyond "wait-and-see" and "benign neglect." In my view, there are some organizing principles that ought to guide our relations with the People's Republic in this difficult period.

1) If Beijing is ever to build a policy consensus and rebuild social legitimacy, it is going to have to recruit key central players from the localities where, in some cases, economic performance has been comparatively good, recent repression comparatively mild, and where leaders may be comparatively unsullied by the disasters of June 1989. This suggests that American public and private sector leaders should vigorously cultivate ties with local leaders throughout China. It also suggests that while the aggregate performance of the Chinese economy may leave much to be desired, there will be regional pockets of high growth where expanding Sino-American economic relationships may make sense. For instance, the economically growing areas of the Yangtze Delta and the area around Canton (Guangzhou) alone represent huge markets and production potentials. In short, China is a large, diverse country, and should not be treated as an undifferentiated whole.

2) If China is going to achieve improved economic performance and greater social stability, it is only going to do so by systematically righting the balance between "state" and "society", by building the institutions of central "macro" economic control while decentralizing enterprise management (beyond the dead hand of local bureaucrats), by persevering with market-managed price reform, by placing even more emphasis on basic (primary and secondary) education, and by sustained and large investment in agriculture. The United States should be willing to help in these basic development efforts, albeit recognizing that our current economic woes may make any substantial bilateral development assistance infeasible. We need to recognize today, as we did in the 1960s, that involvement in the economic development of others promotes our own long-term economic well being.

3) We need to nurture productive relations with Beijing, based on a policy of speaking truth (as we understand it) and cooperating to solve international and bilateral problems, all the while not deluding ourselves about stability within China's elite. China's cooperation on sanctions against Iraq are of critical importance, as is China's recently more helpful approach to the endless bloodshed in Cambodia. Speaking more broadly, it is unlikely that we will be able to address global environmental, health, and weapons and technology transfer issues if we do not maintain workmanlike relations with China's central rulers.

In short, the chapters in this section speak forcefully, consistently, and largely accurately, to the infirmities of China's governing and economic systems. The key issue is, however, How should Americans respond? Rather than benign neglect, we must pursue a policy of nurturing both central and regional relationships; focusing commercial economic links on areas performing well; concentrating government and exchange relationships on basic institutional, educational, and agricultural development; and maintaining constructive, workmanlike ties with Beijing in the solution of common bilateral and global problems.

This is imperative because the one question these articles did not address, and which should be foremost in the minds of policymakers, is: What are both the practical and human consequences (for China, America, Asia, and the world) of widespread disorder, or poor economic and political performance, in the People's Republic of China?

SOME THOUGHTS ON THE CONTEXT FOR ANALYZING CHINA

by Allen S. Whiting *

As Jonathan Spence has so admirably depicted in his superb history, *In Search of Modern China*, the once renowned Middle Kingdom has experienced prolonged political crises repeatedly during the past 150 years. Yet these crises have seldom been resolved as climatically as with the Chinese Communists ascendancy in 1949. More typically they have been screened by a semblance of rule from the center that concealed the actual or incipient localized freedom from central control. Chinese and foreigners alike continued to treat Peking or Nanjing as a symbolic capital from 1912 to 1937. However, its actual writ in terms of coining currency, collecting taxes, and controlling troops only extended over a portion of the vast area uniformly identified as China on the world map. The same flag flew from one extremity to the other but primary allegiance went to local military commanders.

The warlord domination prevailed in the first decades of the twentieth century because of the virtual independence of various generals enjoyed vis-a-vis the central government. Nor did this entirely end with World War II, by which time the Nationalist regime faced a rival Communist government expanding its own power over entire regions while ostensibly allied against Japan. Only with establishment of the People's Republic of China in 1949 did central rule extend throughout the country, excepting Tibet, which was occupied in 1950, and Taiwan, which remained under American protection after June 1950.

As the accompanying essays suggest, there is cause to question the degree to which the Chinese capital controls the country. What might be called "economic warlordism" threatens Beijing's ability to dictate investment and trade policy throughout China. This applies in particular along the coast and in the south where special enclaves and distance offer the opportunity to pursue fiscal practices for local benefit at the cost of the national economy. What Deng Xiaoping has termed "one country, many systems" with respect to the mainland itself.

The implications of this development are far-reaching. Most immediately, resource allocation will be determined regionally with the exchange of goods, services, and even capital occurring among provinces, counties, and municipalities without Beijing's direction or in some cases its prior knowledge. Foreign entrepreneurs will build on local relationships rather than work through the slow

---

* Allen S. Whiting is the Professor and Director of the Center for East Asian Studies, part of the department of Political Sciences at The University of Arizona.

grinding ministerial machinery in Beijing. Not only will the regime lose control over financial and human resources but its vaunted planning capacity will be seriously eroded except for selected industries and their associated infrastructure.

Over time this erosion of central economic authorities will be exacerbated by two political dilemmas, the recurring problem of leadership succession and the associated but separate ideological crisis. Both issues deserve special attention as threatening the continuation of Communist rule in China. So long as power is personalized rather than institutionalized, the leader's role is critical to exercising authority. This not only places a premium on his ability, it also places a premium on the ability of his cohorts and subordinates who collectively exercise his will as a personal network.

Mao Zedong tolerated, if he did not initiate, the purge of virtually all but a handful of his able associates who had won a civil war and established the first truly national government since the collapse of the Qing dynasty. Mao's chosen successor, Hua Guofeng, could not fill the Chairman's shoes but Deng was able to restore leadership and recruit both new and old associates in a rejuvenated regime. However, Deng failed to keep his chosen successors in place long enough to take over on his death, leaving the likelihood of a power struggle among a host of lesser lights with no visible star in the ascendancy.

The absence of an effective leader becomes particularly serious in an ideological vacuum that leaves no guidelines for behavior with no clear differentiation between right and wrong. The thorough discrediting of Marxism-Leninism-Mao Zedong Thought, especially for the younger generation, was perhaps inevitable, given the incredible human costs of the Cultural Revolution and the necessary rehabilitation of its more prominent victims. But Deng's failure to come up with more than catch-phrases left a society of 1.1 billion people living largely a marginal economic existence with no values or goals other than personal and familial enrichment. The resulting corruption, cynicism, and alienation combined with growing inflation to produce rising resentment against the regime. The Tienanmin Square demonstrations in the Spring of 1989 provided one brief outlet for this resentment. Its forcible suppression restored order but did not establish legitimacy for the regime or assure loyalty among the people, especially in urban areas.

Patriotism or muted xenophobia proved insufficient in the aftermath of June 1989. The leadership's recourse to various well-worn themes failed to mobilize a credible response at home while arousing concern abroad. By mid-1990 the campaign had significantly ebbed in national media, although it had not wholly disappeared in party and military journals. In its place came strong negative themes against pornography and corruption but no positive themes capable of mobilizing energies and evoking sacrifices for the sake of national objectives.

These three factors—economic warlordism, leadership succession crisis, and ideological vacuum—do not necessarily lead to an open collapse of a regime, much less to revolution. China's size and the ability of many sectors to run along on their own power mitigate against the dramatic and sudden changes that racked East Europe in 1989. Furthermore, as the accompanying essays suggest, a population that fears chaos, with good reason, must be pushed to extremes before it will explode. Last, but not least, the People's Liberation Army is unlikely to countenance civil strife, much less break apart in civil war. It remains an effective instrument of national control, perhaps the only one left to the regime.

But if the most probable scenario is a far less dramatic one than that of East Europe or even of the Soviet Union, it is nonetheless challenging to an aspiring post-Deng leadership in Beijing and sobering for all who must deal with the world's largest population. Aside from the various conflicting claims of territorial sovereignty on land and sea that confront most of China's neighbors, non-Han peoples on China's periphery can challenge Beijing's rule with potential spillover effects in India, the Soviet Union, and Mongolia. A different kind of spillover could follow natural disasters, such as several bad years of weather that sharply reduce the food supply so as to trigger mass migration across borders such as that which occurred in 1962. Moreover the problems of pollution, health, environment, and other global issues that require international management cannot be effectively addressed by a rump regime that lacks national authority.

In short, China's dilemma present problems for the world at large. Their resolution, however, depends on the Chinese themselves. Past assumptions of foreign fixes, whether missionary or monetary, do not apply. The crisis is sufficiently deep and longstanding to confront the regime with its own demise unless it manifests dramatic change in political and economic reform while mobilizing the Chinese people in a national ethos that can elicit the response necessary to endure the difficulties and sacrifices that lie ahead. Such an ethos exemplified the first decade of the People's Republic. Whether it can return in the fifth decade remains to be seen.

II. REFORMS

OVERVIEW

By George D. Holliday *

The Chinese leadership's policy of economic retrenchment, initiated in the summer of 1988 and intensified after the Tiananmen Incident a year later, has dealt serious blows to Chinese reformers who had advocated market-oriented economic reforms. The conservative regime has reinstituted some central controls, undermined some of the promising reforms of the 1978–1988 period, and put strict limits on the kinds of reforms that Chinese economists can openly debate.

Does the economic retrenchment of the current regime mark the end of market-oriented economic reforms in China? The authors who contributed to this section do not think so. They emphasize that some of the reforms remain in place and that other reforms are likely to emerge in the coming decade, especially after the aging members of the current regime yield to a new generation of Chinese leaders. Most, however, emphasize that China is unlikely to adopt a market economy "without adjectives," as advocated by the more radical economists in other formerly centrally planned economies in Central and Eastern Europe. Indeed, most of the authors think that China is destined to develop an economic system modified by several adjectives: they variously suggest that China will have a "regulated market economy," a "planned commodity economy," a "more conservative model of a reformed Soviet-economy," an "updated central administrative command system," or a "mixed system." Nevertheless, optimists and pessimists alike foresee a future Chinese economic system that differs significantly from the centrally planned system of China's recent past. Most have a somewhat ambivalent outlook for economic reform in China: they are discouraged by many factors in the current environment that inhibit further reform, but are encouraged by factors that are likely to facilitate reforms in the future.

FACTORS THAT INHIBIT ECONOMIC REFORM

Chinese reformers face formidable economic and political impediments. On the political front, they are opposed by conservative forces in the leadership and by broader segments of the population

---

* George D. Holliday is a specialist in international trade and finance with the Economics Division, Congressional Research Service.

Papers not mentioned in this overview were not available to the reviewer at the time this was drafted.

that stand to lose if economic reforms lead to a redistribution of income. On the economic front, the reformers face a negative appraisal, at least among some elements of Chinese society, of the effects of reforms already in place. They must also overcome uncertainty and disagreement among economists over the best way to proceed with economic reform.

Perhaps the most difficult barrier to overcome in the short run is the political outlook of the leadership. An essential feature of past economic reforms, as Harry Harding points out, was the removal of the Party from microeconomic decisionmaking. Resistance by much of the Party leadership to the loss of control over the economy explains much of the retrenchment since 1988. Harding and others describe a progressive reintroduction of Party controls in domestic enterprises, foreign ventures, and government agencies responsible for economic policy. Thus, one precondition to a resumption of the reform movement appears to be a change in attitude of the current leaders or a change in leadership. Robert Dernberger maintains, however, that the current leaders lack the political will to move toward a true market-socialist economic system. He suggests that they are unlikely to accept even less dramatic reforms to introduce greater efficiencies into the current system.

In the long run, the attitudes of broader segments of Chinese society are likely to determine the direction of Chinese economic policy. Dernberger and others suggest that many Chinese harbor deep suspicions of the market. One reason for their suspicions is that the past reforms redistributed income among various elements of the population. Albert Keidel and Barry Naughton describe, for example, dramatic changes in the structure of relative prices which accompanied the reforms. Since government subsidies and controls distort prices in the centrally planned economy, movement toward market prices creates winners and losers among the population. Increases in food prices relative to other consumer goods, a dominant feature of recent price reforms, threatened the standard of living of urban workers. Keidel concludes that the government's inability to finance the large subsidies needed to maintain urban living standards is a major obstacle to price reform.

Complicating the plight of Chinese economic reformers is the distribution of the benefits and costs of the reforms over time. Harding notes that the economic reforms of late 1970s and early 1980s provided quick economic returns to key economic groups, including peasants and some workers. While such gains generated short-term support, the benefits later began to level off. When the costs of the reforms—inflation, inequality, and corruption—became apparent, many Chinese became disillusioned and rebelled. Even if Chinese leaders were inclined to push further reforms, Harding thinks that they may not have widespread popular support.

Indeed, the Chinese appraisal of the costs and benefits of past economic reforms may differ significantly from that of Westerners accustomed to living in a market economy. Dernberger notes that, while the reform-generated instabilities in real incomes, employment, prices, the balance of payments, and the budget might not seem great to those who have lived in a free market economy, they appear "quite alarming" to those who have lived in a Soviet-type economy. Moreover, Dernberger, Harding, and Naughton note that the retrenchment has succeeded, albeit with significant costs, in moderating the degree of instability experienced in the decade of reform. Most notably, the Chinese government succeeded in ending the hyperinflation of 1988 by reinstituting direct administrative controls and renewing some subsidies. Many Chinese may believe, therefore, that central controls are needed to ensure a stable economic growth.

FACTORS THAT FACILITATE ECONOMIC REFORMS

Despite an imposing array of impediments to reform, the contributors to this section are not totally pessimistic about the prospects for economic reform in China. They point out that elements of the reforms are still in place and appear to enjoy broad support. They also note that some segments of Chinese society have benefitted from past reforms and have a vested interest in maintaining and deepening the reform movement. Moreover, most of the contributors think that further reform is needed to solve China's economic problems: they emphasize the inability of the government to redress such problems with current policies and institutions.

Although the current leadership has clearly pursued a policy of retrenchment since 1988, it has not dismantled all of the reforms of the previous decade. Harding, while acknowledging that the steps taken in the last two years do constitute a "retrogression," points out that China has not resumed rigid central planning, reinstated collective agriculture, or significantly reduced the role of the non-state sectors of the economy. Some of the retrenchment measures, he says, are macroeconomic policies that are consistent with a program of structural reform, and others are purportedly temporary measures. Similarly, Penelope Prime describes a significant reform of China's tax system which, if fully implemented, can raise needed government revenue without subjecting enterprises to direct government control. She sees reason for optimism because the reformed tax system, though partially undermined by retrenchment measures, is still in place. The continuation of some elements of the tax reform program suggests that at least some members of the leadership still support economic reform.

The redistribution of income associated with price liberalization has undoubtedly created economic winners as well as losers. Consequently, some groups in China are likely to support the reform movement. Jan Prybyla maintains that the decade of the 1980s has demonstrated that there is strong sentiment in favor of market reform among Chinese intellectuals. He also notes mounting material frustrations of urban workers and peasants, suggesting that they are potentially strong supporters of economic reform.

David Denny suggests another reason why the reforms may have wide popular support. Acknowledging that the reforms may have widened differences in income among classes of people, he demonstrates that the reform period was accompanied by a narrowing of economic disparities that had previously separated rich and poor provinces. Denny finds that all of the provinces achieved substantial growth, largely due to "the return of more natural economic patterns that offset the extremely irrational and self-defeating patterns that characterized China's regional economic policies in the previous two decades." (According to Denny, central government policies, which reallocated budget resources and influenced the location of foreign investment in China, may also have contributed to more equal growth rates among the provinces.) An implication of Denny's findings is that the reforms may have broad geographical support in China, or, at least, have not exacerbated regional conflicts over economic policy.

Most of the authors suggest that an important rationale for further Chinese economic reforms is the apparent inability of the current system to solve fundamental economic problems. Dwight Perkins and Jan Prybyla, for example, note that the problems of the old centrally planned system—excess demand, inflation, and inefficiency—persist. Solution of such problems, they maintain, requires additional economic reforms.

STRATEGY FOR ECONOMIC REFORM

Harding finds that past reform efforts have suffered from the lack of an effective strategy for reform. While the contributors to this section agree that the Chinese government is unlikely to redress its economic problems under the current system, they differ on the likely or desirable strategy of future Chinese economic reforms.

A key issue is how to avoid inflation during price reforms. Harding believes that China's recent experience with inflation was the predictable result of the government's strategy of microeconomic reform and macroeconomic policies. The government allowed greater financial autonomy to provinces and enterprises, without subjecting them to hard budget constraints. At the same time, the government followed fiscal and monetary policies to increase supply through faster growth rather than to limit demand. Harding suggests that Chinese policymakers have learned the lesson that price reform will be highly inflationary unless it is conducted during a period of relative equilibrium between supply and demand. Keidel, on the other hand, maintains that inflationary periods can facilitate price reform because adjustment of relative prices can take place more easily when all prices are rising.

Perhaps a more fundamental issue is whether to introduce market-oriented reforms quickly and comprehensively or to reform more gradually, maintaining some elements of a socialist system. Prybyla stresses the need for comprehensive "shock" therapy. In the current system, he maintains, the institutional preconditions for applying market remedies do not exist, and the old administrative remedies no longer work. He concludes that the only way to reform the current system is to transform it into a market system. He suggests that the Chinese will reach the same conclusion in the 1990s.

Prime's discussion of the Chinese experience with tax reform also suggests the importance of implementing reforms on a broad front. The tax reform, designed to provide positive incentives for enterprises, is being diluted by failure to implement other reforms. For example, enterprises currently have incentives to reduce the amount of income subject to taxes. They report losses with little threat of bankruptcies and sometimes with expectations of increasing government subsidies. Moreover, because some prices are fixed by the government, enterprise profits may not reflect increases in efficiency and productivity. An implication of Prime's discussion is that useful reforms may be thwarted if they are not complemented by reforms in other parts of the economy.

Perkins and Naughton, on the other hand, maintain that the Chinese government could improve the performance of the economy without a complete transformation of the system. Perkins suggests possible ways of breaking ties between the government and enterprises within a socialist system. An independent banking system which imposes hard budget constraints on enterprises, new forms of public ownership, and retraining of central planners, he says, could help alleviate chronic problems in the economy. Similarly, Naughton believes that there is nothing inherent in the Chinese economic system that would prevent significant reforms, such as creation of an independent central bank, progressive decontrol of prices, and enterprise reform.

Whichever strategy the Chinese adopt, and whichever adjectives are appropriate to describe the future economic system, continued reforms appear likely. The rationales for reform—promoting stable economic growth and improving the efficiency of the economy—remain compelling. The experience of recent years suggests, however, that the reforms may proceed more slowly and take a more circuitous route than many Chinese prefer.

THE PROBLEMATIC FUTURE OF CHINA'S ECONOMIC REFORMS

By Harry Harding *

CONTENTS

I. Introduction

Ever since the Tiananmen Incident of June 1989, Chinese leaders have been attempting to assure foreigners of their continuing commitment to economic reform. As early as five days after the massacre, Deng Xiaoping informed a meeting of military officers that the policies of economic reform and opening to the outside world would continue despite the political turmoil of the preceding months.[1] The Fourth Plenum of the Central Committee, meeting two weeks later on June 23-24, likewise declared that the policies of the 13th Party Congress, including those concerning economic reform, would be sustained.[2] The Fifth Plenum, which met in November 1989, issued similar reassurances.[3] In virtually every meeting with foreign visitors, top Chinese officials, including Jiang Zemin and Li Peng, have reiterated that China remains committed to the transformation of the country's economic system and to extensive interaction with the international economy.

Despite these reassurances, many foreign observers still have doubts about the prospects for economic reform in China. In a cover story in March 1990 on the situation in China, *U.S. News and World Report* asked whether "reform, in the sense of further movement toward a free-market system, had had its day."[4] In the aca-

---

* Harry Harding is Senior Fellow, Foreign Policy Studies Program, The Brookings Institution. This is a slightly modified version of a paper presented to the Workshop on the Chinese Economy, sponsored by the State Planning Commission of the People's Republic of China and the Fletcher School of Law and Diplomacy, Tufts University, held in Peking on May 14-19, 1990.
[1] Radio Beijing, June 27, 1989, in *Foreign Broadcast Information Service Daily Report: China* [hereafter cited as *FBIS*], June 27, 1989, pp. 8-10.
[2] Radio Beijing, June 24, 1989, in *FBIS*, June 26, 1989, pp. 15-16.
[3] Xinhua News Agency [hereafter cited as Xinhua], November 9, 1989, in *FBIS*, November 9, 1989, pp. 19-22.
[4] *U.S. News and World Report*, March 12, 1990, p. 44.

demic community, most scholars of Chinese politics and economics are now more pessimistic about the fate of economic reform than they were in 1987 or 1988. And the most recent annual report on the Chinese economy prepared for the American Congress by the Central Intelligence Agency has also concluded that there is little chance for a "return in the near term to comprehensive, market-oriented reform."[5]

This paper attempts to explain why, despite repeated reassurances by Chinese leaders, the future of China's economic reform now appears so problematic to foreign observers. It is organized around five critical issues facing China's efforts at economic restructuring, each of which raises some important doubts about the fate of economic restructuring in China. These five problems include:

- the uncertain prospects for China's economic retrenchment program
- the damage that the austerity program has inflicted on economic reform
- the wavering commitment of China's leaders to thoroughgoing economic transformation
- the need for a more effective strategy of economic reform in the future
- the flagging support for economic reform among key sectors of Chinese society

Only if subsequent events in China begin to remove their reservations on all five issues will foreign observers begin to view the future of China's economic reform program less pessimistically than is now the case.

II. THE UNCERTAIN PROSPECTS FOR ECONOMIC RETRENCHMENT

In the late summer of 1988, Chinese leaders announced a program of economic retrenchment, aimed at ameliorating the economic and political damage that excessive rates of growth had inflicted on the country's reform effort.[6] Overly rapid economic growth had produced severe bottlenecks, particularly in raw materials, energy, and transportation. It had also contributed to China's international balance of payments deficit, both by stimulating the country's imports and by holding back the nation's exports. And the overheated economy had been one of the major causes of inflation, which in turn was perhaps the most important factor behind the deepening crisis of confidence in economic reform that plagued Chinese politics throughout the late 1980s.

This economic retrenchment effort, which was intensified after the Tiananmen Incident of June 1989, achieved notable results by the end of the year. The rate of inflation, on a monthly basis, dropped to an annual rate of around 7%—well below the government's target of 10%. Industrial growth rates fell, whereas agricultural production remained strong. The excessive growth in the

---

[5] "The Chinese Economy in 1989 and 1990: Trying to Revive Growth While Maintaining Social Stability" (Washington, DC: Directorate of Intelligence, Central Intelligence Agency, June 1990), p. 2.

[6] Xinhua, August 18, 1988, in *FBIS*, August 18, 1988, pp. 16–17.

money supply and in bank credits was halted. China's trade deficit fell from around $7.7 billion in 1988 to $6.6 billion in 1989, and the country scored a small surplus in the first quarter of 1990.

But the costs of retrenchment were also high. Tighter controls on wages and bonuses meant that, for many workers, real incomes continued to fall despite the reduction in inflation. Unemployment rose rapidly in most major cities, to the highest levels since the early 1980s. Many collective and private enterprises went bankrupt, and the losses incurred by state enterprises mounted. Many firms, including foreign ventures, reported their inability to receive payments from customers who owed them money. Provincial authorities complained bitterly about the tight restrictions on credit.

As a result, in late 1989 the central government decided to relax its retrenchment policies so as to avoid a "hard landing." To stimulate the urban economy, wages and bonuses were raised sharply at the end of the year, and both the central and provincial governments channeled more money into capital construction. In the countryside, agricultural credits were increased, so that peasants would be paid for their harvest in cash rather than in the IOU's they had received at the end of 1988. Subsequent reports in early 1990 revealed that more loans were being made available to money-losing establishments, so as to stem the wave of bankruptcies and to ensure that enterprises in the red could still remit taxes to the central government.[7]

Given the lags between adjustments in central government policy and changes in economic performance, and between changes in economic activity and their reflection in published statistics, the net effect of this relaxation remains uncertain. As of the end of March 1990, Chinese leaders appeared to have halted the declines in industrial production, retail sales, and urban employment that had bedeviled the economy at the turn of the year, without restoring high rates of inflation. But there was little confidence among either Chinese planners or Western economists that the nation's economic equilibrium had been fully or permanently restored. Some analysts suggested that the relaxation of credit had not been sufficient to avoid a protracted recession, whereas others foresaw a resurgence of inflation as a result of the growth of wages, credit, and government spending.

These changes in economic policy at the turn of the year are symptomatic of a deeper, long-term issue: whether Chinese leaders can sustain the moderate rates of economic growth and inflation that would be most conducive to further economic reform. The pattern of economic growth in China since 1978 leaves little doubt that the central government can still slow down or speed up the economy, despite the decentralization of economic management over the past decade. What is less clear is whether these central controls, and the leaders employing them, are sophisticated enough to prevent an alternation between severe recession and excessive growth.

Neither of these outcomes is conducive to further economic reform. Recession will complicate the restructuring of urban enter-

[7] *Far Eastern Economic Review*, April 5, 1990, pp. 38–39.

prises by reducing the profitability of industrial and commercial establishments, while simultaneously limiting the prospects of alternative employment for those workers laid off from overstaffed or failing firms. Conversely, an overheated economy complicates price reform by increasing the chances of severe inflation when administrative price controls are relaxed. Only if China can avoid the "boom-bust" cycles of the past can it improve the prospects for further economic restructuring.

III. THE DAMAGE INFLICTED ON ECONOMIC REFORM

To a degree, the economic retrenchment begun in 1988 has been undertaken by macro-economic measures fully in keeping with a program of structural reform. Tightening credit by raising interest rates and reducing the money supply, for example, is a strategy for controlling inflation that does not contradict a long-term commitment to economic restructuring. Cutbacks in government spending for capital construction are also an example of the use of fiscal policy in ways familiar to all market economies.

But in other areas, retrenchment has involved a reversal of course, away from liberalization and back toward government intervention in the economy. One such area has been the reassertion of administrative controls over a wide range of economic activities.[8] Examples include the tightening of price controls over goods in short supply, the reinstitution of mandatory state allocation for critical commodities, the reimposition of government licensing for both imports and exports, the restriction of local autonomy over foreign trade and investment, the use of administrative measures to allocate credit, and the return to government assignment of jobs to college graduates. In some instances, these steps reflect simply the recentralization of decision-making power within the state bureaucracy. But in other cases, the economic retrenchment program has involved renewed government intervention in areas that had previously been decontrolled.

A second area of concern is the renewed involvement of Party committees in the management of both domestic enterprises and foreign ventures, and the reestablishment of Party committees in various government agencies. In China, as in any political system, the ruling party will inevitably be involved in shaping broad macro-economic policy. But one important facet of economic and political reform in China had been to remove from the Party the responsibility for micro-economic decisions. The reintroduction of the Party at the agency and enterprise levels therefore appears to contradict a major premise of both economic and political reform.

Finally, some economic retrenchment measures appear to have been selectively implemented in ways that do greater damage to the private and collective sectors of the economy than to the state sector. Credit controls, for example, have apparently been applied more strictly to township and village enterprises than to state enterprises. Conversely, the recent relaxation of austerity measures seem to be targeted specifically at state-owned factories in high pri-

---

[8] Some of these measures are summarized in the report on economic policy adopted by the Fifth Plenum in November. For the text, see Xinhua, January 16, 1990, in *FBIS*, January 18, 1990, pp. 24–37.

ority sectors of the economy. One measure of the effects of this policy bias is that employment dropped more precipitously in the collective sector than in state enterprises during the economic slowdown of early 1990.

To be sure, the net effect of these three sets of adjustments should not be exaggerated. China has not reinstated rigid central planning, reinstated collective agriculture, or significantly reduced the role of the non-state sectors in industry and commerce. Moreover, Chinese planners insist that some of these measures are only temporary expedients to deal with the severe economic problems of the late 1980s. Still, taken together, these steps do constitute a retrogression in the reform effort. It will therefore be necessary to reintroduce some of these reforms later simply to recreate the structure of the Chinese economy that existed before the Tiananmen Incident.

IV. WAVERING COMMITMENT TO THOROUGHGOING ECONOMIC REFORM

A third obstacle to thoroughgoing economic reform is that the present Chinese leadership does not have the same vision of economic restructuring as it did before the Tiananmen Incident of June 1989. As noted above, Chinese leaders still insist that they are committed to a program of "reform" and "opening." But they now seem to define these two terms quite differently than they did in the late 1980s.

For example, a wave of articles in the Chinese press in the summer of 1989 criticized some of the basic assumptions underlying fundamental economic reform. There was a sustained attack on thoroughgoing marketization of the economy, as well as even sharper denunciations of thoroughgoing privatization. Conversely, the official mass media vigorously defended key institutions and mechanisms associated with the previous economic system, with some articles extolling the role of mandatory plans, others insisting on the primacy of public ownership, and still others proposing a return to collectivized agriculture.[9] Although Chinese leaders have insisted that the program of the 13th Party Congress remains in effect, one of the key passages of the report to that congress—"the state regulates the market, and the market guides the enterprise"—is no longer featured prominently in published discussions of economic reform, presumably because it implied the desirability of a regulated market economy within minimal mandatory planning.

Some of the institutions and individuals which had spearheaded the economic reform effort in the 1980s have also been the victims of the tightening of political controls following the Tiananmen Incident. Both the Party's Rural Development Research Center and the government's Institute for Economic System Reform (tigaisuo) have been disbanded, with their staff transferred to other organizations. The Shanghai *World Economic Herald* (*Shijie jingji daobao*), one of the most reform-minded publications in China, has ceased publica-

---

[9] For typical defenses of mandatory planning during this period, see *Guangming Ribao*, October 7, 1989, p. 3, in *FBIS*, November 1, 1989, pp. 37–39 and 39–41. For characteristic criticisms of privatization, see *Jingji Ribao*, July 4, 1989, p. 4, in *FBIS*, July 21, 1989, pp. 28–31; and *Guangming Ribao*, September 9, 1989, p. 3, in *FBIS*, October 16, 1989, pp. 35–37.

tion. Private "think tanks" pursuing interesting work on the economy, including the Stone Company's Institute for Social Development Research, the Institute of Social and Economic Science, and the CITIC Research Institute, now appear to be inactive. Many reformers are currently living abroad, and others who remain in China do not seem to be publishing actively in the Chinese press. As a result of these developments, the climate for the discussion of China's economic reform program is not as lively and open as it was before June 1989.

To be sure, Chinese leaders have become increasingly specific in their commitment to sustained economic reform. Last summer, Chinese officials spoke in only the vaguest terms about the continuation of a policy of "reform and opening." Beginning in November, however, leaders began to identify a more specific list of "socialist reforms" that would be continued and deepened.[10] These include the various responsibility systems in finance, agriculture, and industry; the foreign trade contract system, the special economic zones, and the coastal development strategy; the reform of the banking, housing, and welfare systems; and the encouragement of a degree of individual and private enterprise. Some administrative price adjustments, involving energy, transportation, and foreign exchange, have also been enacted since June 1989.

Still, the vision of economic reform now held by Chinese leaders is significantly different than it appeared to be in the late 1980s. Then, the ultimate objective seemed to be to create a regulated market economy, with little if any mandatory planning, with producers responsible to the market for their profits and losses, with hard budget constraints on enterprises, and with extensive markets for the factors of production as well as for final production. Now, the goal seems to be more modest. Chinese leaders and economists speak today of a "planned commodity economy," with considerable mandatory planning, with producers responsible to the state for fulfillment of various contracts, with subsidies for enterprises that incur losses, and with markets limited to the allocation of secondary commodities. In short, Chinese leaders now seem to envisage a smaller and more restrictive "bird cage" for their nation's economy than they did in 1987 and 1988.

V. The Need for a More Effective Strategy of Economic Reform

Even if future Chinese leaders should recommit themselves to the goal of a regulated market economy, they will still need to develop an effective and sustainable strategy for creating one. Simply reviving the reform strategies of the 1980s will not be sufficient. Indeed, such a decision could well doom a second round of reform to failure.

By the late 1980s, economic reform in China had begun to experience serious difficulties. Although the country continued to enjoy

---

[10] For lists of reforms to be kept in place, see the Fifth Plenum's decision on economic policy, carried in Xinhua, January 16, 1990, in *FBIS*, January 18, 1990, pp. 24–37; and a statement by Li Peng, in Xinhua, December 12, 1989, in *FBIS*, December 13, 1989, p. 9. A list of the reform experiments to be continued appears in Xinhua, January 8, 1990, in *FBIS*, January 9, 1990, pp. 23–24.

high rates of growth in both domestic production and foreign trade, it was increasingly plagued by such problems as inflation, inequality, and corruption. Moreover, several key indices of the country's macro-economic health were severely out of balance. The government deficit continued to grow, with sluggish revenues unable to keep pace with soaring deficits. The current account deficit also began to burgeon, with an overheated economy drawing in imports and holding back exports. From a sectoral perspective, the economy was out of balance, with vibrant processing, construction, and consumer goods industries increasingly frustrated by bottlenecks in raw materials, energy, and transportation.

In retrospect, it is clear that many of these problems were due to the strategies of reform that Chinese leaders had selected in the decade after the Third Plenum of 1978. Inflation was the predictable result of a decision to grant greater financial autonomy to provinces and enterprises, without simultaneously subjecting them to hard budget constraints. It was then exacerbated by a further decision to address the imbalance between supply and demand by attempting to increase supply through faster economic growth, rather than by decreasing demand. Corruption was the consequence of creating a dual-price system, and then permitting the gap between administered prices and market prices steadily to widen. Allowing individual entrepreneurs and collective enterprises to seek and retain profit, without a rational system of prices and an effective system of taxation, resulted in growing imbalances and inequities among various economic and social sectors. And the failure to impose either stringent financial discipline or adequate tax obligations on industrial enterprises was responsible for imbalance between government revenues and expenditures.

The issue now is whether Chinese reformers have conducted a serious evaluation of the successes and failures of reform over the last decade, and have devised a new strategy for conducting the next round of economic restructuring. The decision on economic policy adopted at the Fifth Plenum last November suggests that two such lessons have been identified: first, that price reform will be highly inflationary (and thus politically intolerable) unless it is conducted during a period of relative equilibrium between supply and demand; and second, that price reform will generate serious corruption unless the gap between administered prices and market prices is steadily narrowed.[11]

But there is less evidence that other, equally important questions, have yet been addressed. One set of issues concerns the *preconditions* for successful economic reform. For example, is it necessary, at an early stage, to impose hard budget constraints on both state enterprises and local governments? Do hard budget constraints, in turn, require a fundamental change in the system of ownership in industry, or at least a transformation of the system of accountability for factory managers? Is it necessary to break down protectionist barriers between provinces, so that provincial enterprises are not given effective monopolies? Can this be done without a great expansion of China's transportation and communications

---

[11] Xinhua, January 16, 1990, in *FBIS*, January 18, 1990, pp. 24–37.

system? Can a system of planning and market exist for the same commodity without severe dislocations?

Another set of critical issues concerns the *strategy* for economic reform. In retrospect, was it wise to attempt to undertake reform in a gradual and incremental manner? Would it be preferable to attempt thoroughgoing reform all at once, by eliminating price controls and enterprise subsidies at one stroke, as has apparently been attempted in both Vietnam and Poland? If an incremental strategy is still deemed to be most effective, what is the most appropriate sequencing of reform measures? Should price reform precede enterprise reform, or *vice versa*? Or should they both be conducted gradually, but in tandem? And, perhaps most generally, how should the costs and benefits of reform be distributed over time? Should the benefits precede the costs, or should the benefits and costs be imposed simultaneously?

Over the next several years, it will be imperative for Chinese leaders to address these questions and to formulate a new and more effective strategy of reform. If they can do so, there is a better chance that, once it resumes, urban economic reform will be more successful in the 1990s than it was in the 1980s. If these issues are not resolved, however, there remains the disturbing possibility that renewed reform will simply encounter the same problems and contradictions in the second round as it did in the first.

FLAGGING POLITICAL SUPPORT FOR FURTHER ECONOMIC REFORM

The misjudgments in reform strategy outlined above had political, as well as economic, consequences. Whether consciously or not, Chinese leaders adopted a strategy of economic reform in the late 1970s and early 1980s that provided quick economic returns to key economic groups, including both peasants (through higher procurement prices and the household responsibility system) and workers (through higher wages and bonuses and the greater availability of consumer goods). This strategy may have garnered support for economic restructuring in the short-run, but it may also have generated expectations that reform would be a smooth and easy process. When, in the late 1980s, the costs of reform started to rise, while the benefits began to level off, the popular reaction was not a readiness to sacrifice, but rather disappointment and disillusionment. The huge protests which swept through Peking and other major cities beginning in mid-April, 1989, were caused in large part by widespread resentment at inflation, inequality, and corruption, and by equally prevalent doubts that the government could address them effectively.

Given the severity of the crisis, it is no longer clear that the Chinese political system can still generate enough support for a renewal of economic reform. We have already noted the pressures to abort the austerity program, and to reinflate the economy. But even if the retrenchment effort is successful, politically painful choices lie ahead. Each of the principal elements in the uncompleted agenda of economic reform—price reform, enterprise reform, and financial reform—will challenge the interests of powerful groups in Chinese society.

As noted above, the inflationary consequences of price reform could be reduced if it were undertaken in a less overheated economic environment, and if enterprises were subjected to competitive pressures that would limit price increases. Even so, given the fact that prices for many key goods and services have been kept artificially low for so long, price reform will inevitably produce some inflationary effects. And the goods and services in question—staple foods, housing, transportation, and utilities—are among the most politically sensitive in any economy. Unless productivity continues to rise, further price reform may yet lead to further decreases in real wages, thus contributing to further popular resentment at the costs of economic reform. Such resentment will be focused, of course, primarily among those sectors of society whose incomes tend to rise more slowly, including officials and intellectuals.

Enterprise reform will also strike hard at vested interests. No matter what form it takes—stockification, privatization, or simply hard budget constraints—the goal of enterprise reform will be the same: to make enterprises responsible for their own profits and losses, so as to reduce state subsidies and increase tax revenues. And yet, as Janos Kornai first pointed out, many powerful sectors of society have a vital interest in resisting hard budget constraints. Workers and managers alike fear the unemployment that would accompany bankruptcy. Workers prefer a loose connection between wages and productivity. And local officials, concerned with maintaining labor peace and maximizing local output, can also be expected to oppose the imposition of tighter financial discipline on local enterprises.

Financial reform—in the sense now of increasing the central government's share of national income—will also be unpopular at the provincial level. Chinese leaders themselves have acknowledged the resistance by provincial officials to a redistribution of state revenues, and have called on them to subordinate their local interests to those of the nation as a whole. Tax reform, to the extent that it means more vigorous collection of taxes from both private, collective, and state enterprises, will be as unwelcome in China as it is in other countries.

In short, now that the benefits of economic reform have largely been distributed, what remains are the costs. Faced with this dilemma, some Chinese intellectuals have proposed the creation of a "neo-authoritarian" political system, so as to impose unpopular but necessary reforms on a reluctant society and a resistant bureaucracy.[12] And yet, it would now appear that large sectors of society want a political system that is more democratic, rather than one that is more authoritarian. For this reason, too, there is reason to wonder whether China today has the political ability to renew and sustain the economic reform program.

This dilemma will be particularly intense if, as is possible, a relatively unreformed economic system can be made to perform reason-

---

[12]Articles by major participants in the debate over neo-authoritarianism can be found in *Shijie jingji daobao*, January 16, 1989, p. 12, in *FBIS*, February 1, 1989, pp. 33–35; *Shijie jingji daobao*, February 6, 1989, p. 14, in *FBIS*, February 24, 1989, pp. 18–19; and *Jingjixue zhoubao*, March 5, 1989, in *FBIS*, March 17, 1989, pp. 16–18. For reviews of the debate, see *Jingji cankao*, March 7, 1990, p. 4, in *FBIS*, March 23, 1989, pp. 26–47; and *Shijie jingji daobao*, March 13, 1989, p. 10, in *FBIS*, March 29, 1989, pp. 39–42.

ably well. If, for example, China can sustain moderate growth rates without significant levels of inflation, corruption, and inequality, there may be a willingness to accept the present economic system as it is. The opportunity cost of this decision—slower growth and less efficiency over the longer term—may appear lower than the price of pushing ahead with necessary but painful reforms. As one Chinese intellectual has pointed out privately, a growth rate of 3% per year could be the greatest threat to renewed reform, in that it would greatly reduce the demands for further economic restructuring. Or, to reverse Voltaire's famous aphorism, the good may in this case be the enemy of the best.

VII. Conclusion

The future of Peking's ambitious economic reform program—what Deng Xiaoping once termed China's "second revolution" under the Chinese Communist Party[13]—is one of the most critical factors influencing the future of China's economy and its role in the world. Over the long run, China's economic productivity, rate of growth, and standards of living will be determined by the fate of its economic reforms. China's ability to produce more sophisticated goods for foreign markets, to attract foreign investment to Chinese shores, and to absorb advanced foreign technology will also be shaped in large measure by the outcomes of economic restructuring.

But this essay has suggested five reasons why the fate of China's economic reform program is in doubt. The most immediate issues are the retreat from economic reform that has occurred since the fall of 1988, and the uncertain prospects for the nation's economic retrenchment program. Even if these setbacks prove temporary, however, reform may face additional barriers that are even more serious. It is not clear whether China's present leaders are still committed to a program of thoroughgoing economic reform, whether economists and planners have developed a more effective strategy of economic restructuring than was implemented in the 1980s, and whether there is a sufficient political base for a resumption of reform. Either separately or in combination, these obstacles could significantly reduce the prospects for a revival of economic reform in the years ahead.

These considerations suggest several possibilities for the future of economic restructuring in China. The most pessimistic is that Chinese leaders do not vigorously pursue further economic reform, either because they no longer accept the desirability of a thoroughgoing reform of the price system and the pattern of ownership, or because they are unable to produce the economic and political preconditions for another round of restructuring. In this first scenario, China would not revert to the kind of central planning characteristic of the 1950s, but would continue to have a high degree of government administrative intervention in the economy, a substantial amount of public ownership, significant levels of government protection and subsidies for state industry, and, as a consequence, relatively low levels of growth and productivity. While facing no imme-

---

[13] Xinhua, March 28, 1985, in *FBIS*, March 28, 1985, pp. D1–2.

diate crisis under this scenario, the Chinese economy could, over the long term, slip into the kind of economic stagnation characteristic of the Soviet Union and much of Eastern Europe in the 1980s.

In a second scenario, the Chinese government does attempt another round of economic reform, whether in the last years of Deng Xiaoping's life or under a new leadership that emerges after his death. But this second effort at reform once again faces serious obstacles, partly because its architects have not developed a more successful strategy of economic restructuring, and partly because the reform program therefore loses much of its political support. The crisis encountered by economic reform under this scenario need not be as dramatic as the one that unfolded in Tiananmen Square in 1989, nor need the retreat from reform proceed any farther than in 1989–90. But under this scenario there would again be retrogression away from a regulated market economy in the direction of more extensive government interference in economic activity, with the same general results for economic performance as in the second scenario.

Finally, the last scenario would envisage a successful renewal of economic reform, presumably after the death of Deng Xiaoping and the other senior leaders of his generation. This most optimistic scenario would assume that all five problems identified in this essay have been overcome, or at least have been rendered manageable. Retrenchment has produced satisfactory preconditions for another round of reform, leaders are determined to push forward, their economic advisers have devised a more effective strategy for transforming China's economic system, and thus the political base for reform remains secure. As a result of renewed reform, China makes a successful breakthrough to create a regulated market economy with substantial levels of private and collective ownership, and therefore achieves significantly higher rates of growth and economic efficiency.

The political uncertainties surrounding the succession in China make it difficult to estimate the probabilities for these three scenarios with any precision or confidence. Perhaps the first scenario, which rules out any new attempt at sustained economic restructuring, has the lowest probability, given the pressure for further reform from important sectors of Chinese society and the contradictions inherent in the present mixture of planning and market. Instead, it is more likely that vigorous economic reform will again be attempted in the next decade, as a new generation of leaders gradually consolidates its power after the death of Deng Xiaoping. If Deng's successors can devise an effective strategy of reform that preserves the domestic political support for restructuring, then their efforts may well succeed. But the difficulties encountered by economic reform in the Soviet Union and Eastern Europe, as well as by China itself in the late 1980s, should caution us that this most optimistic scenario is by no means inevitable. Instead, it is still quite possible that the second round of economic reform in China will meet many of the same problems, and experience much the same fate, as did the first.

CHINA'S MIXED ECONOMIC SYSTEM: PROPERTIES AND CONSEQUENCES

By Robert F. Dernberger *

CONTENTS

SUMMARY

Rather than survey the characteristics of the individual economic reform policies, the problems they have encountered, their impact on economic performance, and their probable fate in the future which is the purpose of many of the other articles in these volumes, this article attempts to critique the results of a new Chinese economic system that is well-defined, dynamically feasible, consistent, and efficient. For this purpose the paper relies on the work that has been done by others in the field of comparative economic systems within the discipline of economics, focusing on three key aspects of any economic system—the degree to which decision-making is decentralized and liberalized from the constraints imposed by political authorities; the role played by markets and market prices in the allocation of resources, goods, and incomes; and how "hard" or "soft" the budget constraints are on the economic decision-making units in the system. It is concluded that the current Chinese economy today, after a decade of economic reform, is not a well-defined, dynamically feasible, consistent, or very efficient economic system.

In the conclusion to the article, the question is raised, what are the more desirable or more probable alternatives open to the Chinese? On the one hand, the objective of the more radical economic reformers, a socialist economy that relied mainly on markets for determining the allocation of resources, goods, and incomes, has been ruled out by the post-Tiananmen, more conservative leadership. On the other hand, contrary to popular reports in the Western press that more conservative leadership has publicly ruled out a return to a traditional Soviet-type economy, a Chinese policy po-

* Robert F. Dernberger is Professor of Economics, University of Michigan. This is a revised version of a paper presented at a workshop in Beijing in May 1990, sponsored by the State Planning Commission and the Fletcher School of Law and Diplomacy, Tufts University.

sition consistent with actual policy implementation in the post-Tiananmen (mid-1989) period. This would leave the Chinese with the choice between muddling through with the existing, incompletely reformed economic system or a better defined and more consistent mixed system, i.e. a rationalization of the existing system to restore a greater role for central planning, administrative controls, and the state-owned sector, while reducing the role of the non-state, local, and market sectors. The current Chinese leadership is experiencing considerable difficulty in its attempt to make the latter succeed before either age or popular discontent creates a new leadership that may well broaden the scope of alternative economic systems being considered.

I. INTRODUCTION

Economists in the field of comparative economic systems develop theoretical models of economic systems not because these models describe reality, i.e., the many different economies that exist in reality, but because the models provide a useful analytical framework for studying those real-world economies. The models greatly simplify reality by concentrating on a few key institutions, managed with a few crucial behavioral assumptions and constraints, to drive the major cause and effect mechanism that determines the allocation of resources, goods, and incomes. Thus, these models allow the more ready identification of the costs and benefits in the observed economic results that are due to the economic system—the system characteristics—and those due to the impact of the exogenous given and stochastic shocks and windfall gains—the environmental effects. After years of blaming poor economic results on environmental effects, poor weather, the Soviet pullout, class enemies, and hostile foreigners, following the death of Mao and the elimination of his most radical followers, the Chinese leadership critically evaluated the economic system and launched the process of economic reform at the Third Plenum at the end of 1978.

Having spent most of my academic career studying and teaching courses on comparative economic systems, when invited to present a background paper for our discussions with representatives of the State Planning Commission on the current problems and prospects of China's economic reform program, I felt my observations on the extent to which a new economic system had been achieved as a result of the economic reform program and my evaluation of that new economic system would be the most useful and informative contribution I could make. That is what I have attempted to do in this article.

I realize, of course, that even after a decade of economic reforms, the reform program remains incomplete and is a long-run process.[1]

---

[1] Several years ago, in an interview with Yao Yilin, then Vice-Premier, I asked him when the Chinese economic reform program would achieve its objective and what the new economic system would look like. His response was most revealing; they had just started the economic reform program and it probably would not be completed until the middle of the twenty-first century, i.e. reform of the economic system, it would be the next generation that would determine where it would end up. About all he could say for sure was that it would be a socialist economy, i.e., have planning and state ownership in a dominant role, but would have special Chinese characteristics, i.e., not be a copy of some theoretical model or of some other country's economy.

The reforms currently (mid-1990) are suffering from indecision and hesitancy on the part of the leaders now in power and there is much to be done before the Chinese economic system can be characterized as a dynamically feasible, internally consistent, and acceptably efficient economic system. Nonetheless, as a result of the economic reforms over the past decade, the Chinese economy—while retaining some characteristics of the previous Soviet-type economic system—can no longer be adequately described by reference to that model. But what model can be used to describe the Chinese economy today?

Three economists, including myself, who have closely followed developments in China's economic reform program over the past decade, independently came to the conclusion that the first decade of reform (1978-1988) has accumulated to produce a "mixed system" and that this system is likely to characterize China's economy for some time into the future.[2] Each of the economists agreed that China's mixed system now lies somewhere well within the boundaries of the Soviet-type economy (state ownership, with highly centralized planned allocation of resources) and a market socialist system (state ownership, with decentralized, market allocation of resources).[3] These economists, however, did not go on to present a detailed institutional and functional description of China's current mixed system, and I do not propose to do so here.

Unfortunately, it is also true economists in the field of comparative economic systems have not developed a commonly agreed upon institutional and functional description or theoretical model for a mixed economic system, and such a system does not exist elsewhere in the world. Thus, I must assume the reader is familiar with the institutional and functional description of China's current, mixed economic system, amply described and analyzed in the other articles included in these volumes. For the purposes of this essay, these other articles readily show why current economic system must be identified as a mixed system rather than as a representation of one of the theoretical models provided in the comparative economics systems literature (Soviet-type economy, market socialism, or free-market capitalism), and it is not

---

[2] The three views can be succinctly stated as follows. "The present unstable state of China's mixed economy ... may well persist over a lengthy period in the future ... (and) there is good evidence for believing that the system of 'socialism with Chinese characteristics,' their stated objective, will retain some elements of the traditional Soviet-type economic system along with the adoption of some elements of market socialism." Robert F. Dernberger, "Reforms in China: Implications for U.S. Policy, " *American Economic Review*, Vol. 79, No. 2, May, 1989, p.21. "Internal bureaucratic politics and the dislike of certain social trends will keep China from achieving full market socialism." Dwight Perkins, "China's Economic Reforms and U.S.-China Relations," in Richard H.; Holton and Wang Xi (eds.), *U.S.-China Economic Relations: Present and Future* (Berkeley, Calif. : Institute of East Asian Studies, University of California, 1989), p. 44. "Short of very drastic and unexpected political changes, this system (China's present economic system) is unlikely to be greatly changed in the next decade." Gregory Chow, "Market Socialism and Economic Development in China," unpublished paper, October, 1988, p. 13.

[3] While the discussant of my paper accepted my designation of China's current economic system as a "mixed economic system," his colleagues from the State Planning Commission were strongly opposed to my use of this term. Apparently, "mixed systems" is frequently used by the Chinese to identify the economies of Western Europe and implies an extensive role for free markets, as well as a more limited role for planning. Thus, our hosts argued for the term "socialism with Chinese characteristics," apparently implying a dominant role for a state-sector and planning and a more restricted role for markets than would be implied by the term "mixed system." They admit the Chinese economy will be a "commodity economy," with commodities produced for exchange values, but that does not necessarily mean exchange on free markets or at values equal to free market prices.

necessary to defend the use of the term "mixed economy" to describe China's current economic system here.

Rather, the objective of this brief article is more limited: to identify several very important properties and consequences of this mixed economic system *as an economic system*. Obviously, considerable modifications are likely to be made as the Chinese try to "consolidate and improve" their economic system, but the system likely will remain a mixed economic system. The following discussion may suggest several areas where serious problems will require further systemic reforms and may even implicitly indicate the nature of the reforms required. Although this paper will not advocate particular cures, it will attempt to identify what I see as systemic problems associated with China's current mixed economic system.[4]

II. DECENTRALIZATION AND LIBERALIZATION

A major institutional and functional characteristic of China's current mixed system, which clearly places it somewhere between the boundaries of a traditional Soviet-type economic system and a market socialist system, is the degree of decentralization and liberalization the reforms have introduced in China's economy. A major theme that has run through the reforms has been the reduction in the state's direct control over allocative decisions in the economy or the removal of controls over and prohibitions on many allocative decisions that can be made by local authorities, groups, and individuals. One of the most obvious consequences of the new mixed economic system, therefore, is a much greater degree of instability in the economy. In the past, the traditional Soviet-type economic system internalized these instabilities within the budget by keeping incomes, employment, prices, the balance of payments, and even the budget itself *relatively* stable, while instability showed up as extreme changes in the level of investment and output. As a result of the economic reforms, however, the former administrative controls and constraints have been greatly relaxed, if not removed, and considerable instability has shown up in real incomes, employment, prices, the balance of payments, and the budget. Crudely summarized, the former instabilities in some real macro variables for the economy have been shifted to the financial variables *and* those variables that affect the daily life of the Chinese.[5]

While the degree of instability being experienced in the Chinese economy during the past few years may be well within the limits of tolerance for the Chinese people who have lived in a free-market, capitalist economy most of their lives, to those who have lived within or managed a Soviet-type economy for three decades, these instabilities can be quite alarming. More important, the Chinese

---

[4] I obviously cannot compare my efforts in this article with those of Marx in his famous three-volume critique of capitalism. It is interesting to note, however, that Sun Yat-sen once argued that Marx was an eminent "social pathologist of capitalism," concentrating on the ills of capitalism. Sun preferred to cite social harmony and conciliation as a driving force of history and a cure for the sick patient. In any event, in the space of the few pages in this article, I hope to emulate Marx's approach and provided a radical diagnosis of China's present, mixed economic system.

[5] For example, while budget deficits, price increases, and balance-of-payments deficits were becoming serious problems compared to the situation in pre-1978 China, the coefficient of variation (standard deviation divided by the mean, expressed as a percent of the annual growth rate of national income) declined from 159.64% in 1952–1978 to 34.75% in 1979–1986.

had rather limited success in their efforts to regain control over their economy and dampen these instabilities in the latter half of the 1980s; that is, until they reinstituted rather stringent and direct administrative controls in late 1988 and in 1989 over credit, the money supply, investment funds, and foreign exchange allocations—controls that many observers found reminiscent of the Soviet-type economic system of the prereform period. Two major characteristics of China's mixed economy, created by the economic reform program, would suggest that the instability associated with this economic system may be even worse than that associated with a Soviet-type economy or capitalist economy.[6]

According to a summary report of the meeting, the error had been the excessive introduction of marketization and privatization which had been due to a misunderstanding of the ground rules for the reforms by the radical reformers. The latter had come to believe that mandatory planning was to be phased out over time; that had never been part of the "official" reform program (the scope of mandatory planning was to be *reduced*, not phased out). The radical reformers also had believed that guidance planning was not mandatory; guidance planning was based on "reference" targets issued by the central planners and lower levels were to work out concrete plans in negotiations with the enterprises using the guidance plans as reference. Nonetheless, those negotiations were to result in targets that were mandatory.

Finally, the radical reformer believed that the desire to introduce market "forces", by "relying on values" to better "balance" supply and demand meant that we must rely on *free* markets to do this. While the Chinese do hope to utilize values that better reflect supply and command conditions in their planning and allocation decisions, this does not mean it was necessary to turn the economy over to private individuals competing on free markets to achieve that objective. For a summary of the statements made at the symposium of Chinese economists and scholars who met "recently" in Beijing to discuss the problems in China's economic reform program, see "Integrating Planned Economy with Market Regulations," in *Beijing Review*, Vol. 33, No. 22, May 28–June 3, 1990, pp. 20–22.

Even before the economic reform program was launched by the Third Plenum at the end of 1978,[7] Hu Qiaomu had called for a transformation from intuitive policies implemented by means of direct administrative controls to a system of indirect economic

---

[6] In this regard, it is interesting to note that in our discussions with representatives of the State Planning Commission they clearly believed a market economy, even a regulated one, was not only unstable, but led to chaos. In fact, they viewed the major problem of the economic reform program in the past as just that, i.e., the too extensive introduction of marketization and privatization, which had led to the loss of control over the economy and chaos. At one point in our discussions, one speaker hinted that China's size and level of development made the danger of market instability even greater. Admitting that a market economic system might have worked well in small island economies (Hong Kong, Singapore, etc.), where prices were largely determined by the world market, the size of China's economy, its level of development, and weak transport and marketing network meant that the introduction of free markets would lead to unacceptable income differences, instabilities, and structural maladjustments (to those Chinese we were meeting with, at least). In fact, at about the same time we were in China, a conference of Chinese economists was being held to determine where and why the reforms had gone wrong and what to do about it.

[7] Hu Qiaomu, "Observe economic laws, speed up realization of the four modernizations," *Renmin Ribao*, October 6, 1978 (translated in *Beijing Review*, Nos. 45–47, November 1978.

levers (incentives). As the reforms unfolded, Chen Yun (the major leader of the conservative reform faction) urged the reformers not to forget to build a bird cage (Hu's indirect economic levers) or the bird would fly away. Nonetheless, the more radical reformers, who had gained control of the reform program by the mid-1980s,[8] showed much greater skill in removing controls and constraints in their pursuit of decentralization and liberalization than they did in developing a system of indirect controls to replace those former constraints. Conversely, the free-market, capitalist systems have adopted extensive networks of indirect economic controls to constrain instability to the extent that economists in the field of comparative economic systems now refer to the latter economies as regulated-market, capitalist systems in parallel fashion, China's mixed system could well be labeled un unregulated, mixed system.

Another institutional feature of China's mixed economic system that reinforces its instabilities is the almost complete absence of well-defined and enforced property rights. Obviously, various regulations have been issued as to who has the right or authority to make specific decisions and carry out specific economic activities, but large areas of economic activity are not covered by these regulations. For those areas that are covered, considerable uncertainty, which facilitates, and even creates, instability, is created by backdoor deals to evade these regulations, arbitrary interference by administrative and party cadre in what are supposedly approved and even encouraged economic activities, outright corruption or criminal activities, and just plain failure of local cadres to implement the new laws and regulations they happen to oppose. The capitalist system is based on well-defined property rights and a legal system to enforce them, while those who live in a Soviet type economy quickly learn who has control over, and the right to allocate, resources and goods. The Chinese, obviously, also must learn who has this power in their mixed economy, but the number of people who *may* be involved in these decisions is very large, may change form one time to the next, and their behavior may be very arbitrary. To function anywhere near its potential, any economic system must have property rights that are much better defined and enforced than is true of China's mixed economic system today.[9]

III. MARKETS AND PRICES

A second major characteristic of China's mixed economic system is the significant increase in the role of markets and market prices

---

[8] In our discussions with the representatives of the State Planning Commission and in our interview with Ma Hong (one of China's leading economists with direct access to the political leaders) made it clear that the reevaluation of the economic reform program made after the summer of 1989 (i.e., after Tiananmen) identifies the early 1980s as the "golden age" of the reforms. Things are now believed to have gone wrong after October of 1984 (i.e., the Plenum that expanded the economic reforms to the urban-industrial and elevated Zhao Ziyang and his more radical reform followers to a more dominant position in control of the reform process).

[9] The Chinese reformers have held considerable debates and published many articles on the different forms of ownership that are to be part of their economic system during the preliminary stage of socialism; state, cooperative, private, and individual. I believe much of these discussions misses the point entirely, being largely concerned with the form 'of ownership and paying little attention to the *property rights* of the owners, whoever they may be. An individual may be given the title of a private owner, but what does it mean if they do not have any property rights in what they "own", i.e., the ability to transfer the property or its services or output to others, and the right to receive and use the income created as a result of that transfer.

compared with their role in the traditional Soviet-type economy. There may be some disagreement about the existing mix or the desired mix of plans and markets, but there can be no denying that the scope of the planner's control over the allocation of resources and economic activities has been significantly reduced over the past decade, while economic activities and decisions subject to market forces have been greatly increased.[10]

Unfortunately, however, the term "market" has been used to indicate many quite different things: free markets, regulated markets, segmented markets, etc. Each type of market, of course, has different properties and consequences. While the Chinese reformers seek the many benefits associated with reliance upon *free* markets, it is doubtful that the type of markets introduced in China by the reformers will produce those results. As defined in comparative economics literature, free markets assume competition on both sides of the market (supply and demand); this competition produces true scarcity prices *that are used* to make choices over alternative uses of resources, goods, and funds. Thus, for example, the competition on the supply side generates reduced costs and technological innovations in attempts to beat the competition; while those suppliers who cannot compete are eliminated. Few of these characteristics of markets and market prices are to be found in China's mixed economic system.

Almost every economy in the world, whatever its economic system, relies upon markets to some extent. In addition, interference in markets in order to redistribute incomes, protect domestic producers, etc., means that markets are no longer free even in the market, capitalistic economies. In China's mixed system, free markets have been introduced for some commodities and activities, especially for selected agricultural products, consumer's goods, and services. In general, however, the terms "market " and "market prices" as they exist in China's mixed economic system identify transactions and price formations that are subject to very severe restrictions and constraints.[11] Competition, to the extent it exists, is largely on the buyer (demand) side, not the supply side. And the introduction of markets for goods has made much more progress than markets for the factors of production. Shortages are preva-

---

[10] None of the readily available statistics can be used to indicate the proportion of economic activities subject to the *influence* of the planners and the proportion subject to market *forces* in China's present mixed economic system. It should be obvious, however, that the share of economic activity carried out by cooperative, private, and individual economic units is not an accurate estimate of economic activities subject to market *forces* and probably is an underestimate of that share. On the other hand, the same share of economic activity carried out *on* "free" markets. See text, below, for a fuller explanation of this important distinction of the determinants of economic activity in China's current mixed economic system.

[11] On the basis of discussions with representatives of the State Planning Commission, it appears that a relatively small share of economic activity in China was being directly determined by assigned planned targets *or* was solely due to market forces. Rather, as a result of the economic reforms, most economic activities were the result of bilateral negotiations at various levels, within the context of various administrative constraints imposed at various levels, even though those activities may appear to have been nonplanned and use what are referred to as market prices. In addition, the data and interview responses from micro-level enterprise surveys being conducted for various collaborative research projects indicate very clearly that most transactions, even those carried out at "market" prices, involve bilaterally negotiated side-payments by the buyer in money or in commodities, which are not reported as part of the transaction. In short, the grey area between plan and market may well dominate China's current economy and that economy may be best identified as a constrained and regulated, barter economy.

lent, with many of the goods in short supply having a fixed official price that is considerably lower than the "market price".

Some observers believe these "market prices" are the effective prices for producers and consumers on the margin or that the share of goods traded at these "market prices" replace the administered prices.[12] On the other hand, the present mix of plans and markets or administered prices and market prices has created an environment that fosters speculation and corruption as much as profit seeking by means of a more rational allocation of goods and resources, cutting costs, and increasing factor productivity.[13] In addition, Chinese leadership that markets repeated decisions to reform prices and remove many of the constraints that the central and local officials impose over market transactions usually cites the need to "consolidate" and "stabilize" the economy before proceeding further with these needed reforms. Thus the present version of China's mixed economic system would appear to be bogged down at a midpoint in the transition form the old economic system to a new one. As a result of the tragic and ominous manner the student-inspired demonstrations of May–June of 1989 were ended by the revitalized conservative-wing of the Chinese Communist Party, attempts to retain and reinforce central controls over the economy dominated the post-Tiananmen leadership's agenda throughout the remainder of 1989. When these attempts resulted in a recession and pessimistic reactions by foreign investors, the Chinese leaders launched an effort to relax their retrenchment and convince the Chinese people, as well as foreigners, of their intentions to pursue domestic economic reform programs and the policy of opening the Chinese economy to foreign trade and investment.[14]

---

[12] For example, in his analysis of the Chinese economic reform program in the 1986 Joint Economic Committee collection of papers on China's economy, it was Barry Naughton who first identified the Chinese economic reform strategy as an attempt to "grow out of the plan".

[13] To analyze and discuss the positive and negative impacts on economic efficiency of China's severely constrained markets and dual price systems is an important topic for research and cannot be dealt with properly here. Most theoretical models that have been developed to represent and analyze China's mixed economic system *assume* enterprises and households are all operating in free markets *on the margin*, i.e., assume the problem being studied away. For example, see William A. Byrd, "Plan and Market in the Chinese Economy: A Simple General Equilibrium Model," in *Journal of Comparative Economics*, Vol. 13, No. 2, June, 1989, pp. 177–204. Using a general equilibrium approach, Terry Sicular is engaged in a project, "Planning and Markets in China's Economic Reforms: Theory and Evidence," with the objective of driving the conditions under which plan and market *can* coexist in a complementary fashion, also believing that present theoretical work and the literature do not provide us with that information. The point being made here in this brief article is that those necessary conditions do not presently exist in China's mixed system; the plan and market exist in a competitive rather than a complementary manner and the markets and market prices that do exist are subject to such constrains that they cannot be expected to achieve the benefits claimed to result from markets and market prices in other economic systems.

[14] Our Chinese hosts at the State Planning Commission presented us with several lengthy and vigorous defenses, illustrated with numerous specific policy changes in the past year, of their dedication to continuing the domestic economic reforms and the policies of opening the Chinese economy to foreign trade and investment. Compared to the many exaggerated and unsupported assertions in the Western press that the Chinese have "abandoned" the economic reform program or are "turning the clock back" to the 1950s, their arguments were very convincing. It is the pace and direction of economic reform that is at the heart of the debate in China, not the question of reform itself. And it is somewhat unfair to accuse the Chinese of "abandoning" a reform they had never adopted, as some observers in the U.S. government claim, i.e., the creation of a free market economy without a state sector and economic plans. To the Chinese, planning and state enterprises define a socialist economy; yet, they do hope to reform that economy to make it work better. In fact, according to many of the Chinese we talked with, it is the period of the early 1980s, not the 1950s (and certainly not the 1960s or 1970s, i.e., the Maoist economic regime) that represents the "golden age" of Chinese economic policy.

Nonetheless, the current efforts at reform and the reforms being considered envisage a limited and cautious pace of reform, with a much greater bias in favor of state-sector enterprises than was true in the past. The foreseeable future, therefore, would not appear to offer any bold new attempts to move forward with privatization, marketization, and price reforms.

"(W)hile it is impossible to see clearly the ultimate destination of China's reform process, it is possible to discern the next stage of the journey: a distinctive Chinese strategy of reform in which market forces are allowed to exert progressively more influence on enterprise decision-making, thus 'squeezing' the administered economy into new patterns. In its most extreme form, this strategy will compel the industrial economy to gradually 'grow out of' the plan, while planners use the transition period to gain experience in the techniques of controlling the economy through indirect means." Barry Naughton, "Finance and Planning Reforms in Industry." [15]

IV. Soft Budget Constraints and Subsidies

Enforcing hard budget constraints on enterprises, cooperatives, and individuals is the way market competition weeds out either the high-cost and inefficient producers, those who produce output for which there is no market demand, or those buyers who have less urgent demands. A soft budget constraint merely means these producers and buyers are provided funds by the banking system or by the state budget so they can continue their activities. Despite much rhetoric about the need to impose a hard budget constraint and their desire to do so, the Chinese have found it very difficult to achieve this objective, not only for broad political and social reasons, but also due to some specific economic interest group pressures. Those who receive the subsidy may profit economically at the expense of those who pay it, while the economy as a whole often suffers an economic and/or welfare loss. Conversely, the advantage of markets and market prices is that they determine who has "earned" the benefits and who should bear the "costs," while the economy as a whole usually gains.

Obviously, there is a significant transition problem in transforming a Soviet-type economy to a mixed economic system. The windfall benefits of this transformation should become a social, not a private gain; while the burden of the costs imposed by the transformation also should be shared by society as a whole. In other words, the Chinese reformers should be devoting their efforts to acquiring the windfall gains of the reforms for society as a whole, rather than allowing them to be captured by individuals and units who in no way earned them. Equally important, the leadership should be steadily phasing out subsidies for producers and buyers who cannot meet the tests of market competition. Yet, to say the least, the Chinese authorities have been rather timid in introducing harder budget constraints.[16] Quite simply, the reformers do not seem to be

---

[15] Joint Economic Committee, U.S. Congress, *China's Economy Looks Toward The Year 2000*, Vol. I., "The Four Modernizations" (Washington, D.C.: U.S. Government Printing Office, 1986), pp. 604–605.

[16] In our discussions with the representatives of the State Planning Commission, compared to earlier meetings with similar groups, the extent to which they relied upon several "excuses" to

Continued

prepared to enforce hard budget constraints. Unfortunately, these transitional problems threaten to become permanent characteristics of China's mixed economic system.[17]

Again, the Chinese reformers have made a normal transitional problem worse than necessary by adopting policies that encourage most people to believe that the costs imposed by any policy or institutional change will offset by the *creation* of a new subsidy to the group that would have to bear the cost. The literature in comparative economic systems suggests that a major distinguishing characteristic of different economic systems is whether or not they impose a "hard" or a "soft" budget constraint on producers and consumers.[18] The Chinese economic reformers have not only had difficulty in trying to "harden" the budget constraint, they have made this already difficult task even harder by awarding new subsidies to those groups that may be hurt by the introduction of a more rational price system and allocation of resources and goods. The resulting inflation, of course, allocates the costs of reforms, but does so in a very inequitable and inefficient manner. In the end, the central government has found it necessary to devote a significant share of budget revenue to subsidies,[19] which has thwarted the achievement of a more efficient allocation of resources and goods.

---

explain why they could not introduce a particular reform policy we were arguing was needed was quite remarkable; "that would lead to unemployment," "that would have a negative impact on the budget," "the workers wouldn't accept that," and so on. In my opinion, such responses indicated that those relying on these arguments either believed they had lost the ability to implement reform policies (or any unpopular policies) at the local level or had lost considerable popular support for the needed economic reform policies, possibly both. If true, this would further support the argument in the text, above, that we should not expect any bold new attempts to move forward with the economic reform program in the near future.

[17] There are those who believe a successful economic reform program must be introduced as a sudden, once-and-for-all complete removal of the old Soviet-type economic system and creation of the institutions of the new economic system, i.e., the approach Poland is pursuing (and, to some extent, Hungary and Yugoslavia have pursued for some time). In fact, it is argued that Hungary and Yugoslavia have not been terribly successful in their reform efforts precisely because they failed to eliminate the dominant role of the Leninist Party in the economy and the very close ties between administrative units of the government and the enterprises, even though they did remove most of the institutions of the traditional Soviet-type economic system. For one of the strongest and somewhat emotional statements of this point of view, see Janos Kornai, *The Road to A Free Economy: Shifting from A Socialist System* (New York: W. W. Norton & Company, 1990). No economy has made this transition successfully yet, but much should be learned over the next decade as to whether sudden and complete political and economic reform of the traditional socialist system or a succession of more gradual and marginal reforms has the better chance of succeeding.

[18] The use of "hard" and "soft" budget constraints as a key variable in analyzing the differences between economic systems, and especially in measuring the degree to which economic reforms work to achieve systemic changes, comes form the writings of Janos Kornai. See, especially, Janos Kornai, *Economics of Shortages* (Amsterdam: North Holland, 1980); idem., "The Soft Budget Constraint," *Kyklos*, 1986, 39 (1), pp. 3–30; and idem., "The Hungarian Reform Process," *Journal of Economic Literature*, 1986, Vol. 24 (4), pp. 1687–1737.

[19] In 1988, despite ten years of economic reform, "subsidies for losses by enterprises amounted to 44.583 billion yuan (and t)his amount was deducted form total receipts." On the expenditure side of the budget, "subsidies to compensate for price rises totalled 31.695 billion yuan." These subsidies, of course, are not the only subsidies included in the budget, i.e., many of the bonuses awarded to workers in state enterprises are little more than direct subsidies, awarded at the expense of the state's revenue. In the draft budget for 1989, these two subsidies were *scheduled* to decline to 20 billion yuan and 5.5 billion yuan, respectively. If these targets had been achieved, it would have represented a major turn around in the authorities efforts to mover towards a "hard" budget. For the quotation and figures cited above, see Wang Bingqian, "Reported on the Implementation of the State Budget for 1988 and on the Draft State Budget for 1989," *Beijing Review*, 1989, 32 (18) pp. xi–xvii (centerfold). Unfortunately, however, in 1989 the actual subsidies paid out for losses of state enterprises and deducted from revenues were 59.976 billion yuan and subsidies paid out to compensate for price rises were 37.034 billion yuan. Thus, instead of declining by two-thirds in 1989, as planned in the draft budget, subsidies increased by 27 percent. Accepting reality, somewhat, the budget for 1990 includes a ten percent increase in

Continued

V. Conclusions

While the Chinese economic reform program has increased the degree of decentralization in decision-making and liberalized the constraints upon those decisions, the leadership has done little to create a system of indirect controls ("economic levers") to replace the direct controls that have been removed, or to create a well-defined set of property rights so that private and cooperative units and managers of public units have the ability to carry out their decisions in the absence of arbitrarily imposed constraints. While markets have been created for large areas of economic activity, continued reliance upon administered prices, the lack of market access, the weak degree of competition on the supply side, the very limited mobility of factors, etc., all mean that market forces fall far short of the objectives for which markets are adopted and relied upon in other economic systems. Finally, while reformers have tried to "tighten-up" budget constraints upon inefficient enterprises and behavior, they have created the expectation and reality of soft budget constraints for individuals, groups, and enterprises to the extent the resulting redistribution of income, goods, and resources needed for their more "efficient" allocation is seriously eroded.

How, then, do we evaluate this new Chinese mixed economic system? To begin, it is interesting to note that the three economists mentioned at the outset of this paper, each came to different conclusions about the merits of that economic system.[20] Dwight Perkins, while agreeing that the present mixed system is preferable to the previous Soviet-type economic system, argued the need for further efforts to push forward to a true "market-socialist economic system (public enterprises, but with profit-maximizing behavior rules for enterprise managers replacing assigned plans determined by planners, and with market-clearing prices being set by the authorities) before the Chinese economy could claim to be efficient. Gregory Chow, on the other hand, argued that the mixed economic system the Chinese were seeking was likely to be more efficient and desirable *than any market socialist system could be expected to function in the real world.* Presumably, Gregory Chow believed that the mixed economic system the Chinese sought would improve the current mixed system of central planning and markets by creating an effective monetary and fiscal policy, adopting and implementing a well-defined set of property rights to complement the mixed system of ownership, removing many of the existing constraints and limitations on market economic activities, and moving toward much harder budget constraints through steady elimination of most subsidies.

---

both subsidies for losses of state enterprises and subsidies to compensate for price rises *as targets.* Recognizing that these subsidies are "equivalent to one-third of the state budget" and that they "have been growing rather rapidly," the Minister of Finance merely states that "[t]his problem calls out for our keenest attention and serious study so that practicable (sic) solutions can be found." Wang Bingqian, "Report on the Implementation of The State Budget for 1989 and on The Draft State Budget for 1990," *Beijing Review*, Vol.33, No. 17, April 23–29, 1990 (centerfold). Cited budget figures are from pp. IX–XII and the quoted phrases are from p. XIII.

[20] For their different conclusions, summarized below the text, see the sources cited in footnote 2, above, in this article.

These modifications in the present mixed economic system undoubtedly would improve the efficiency of the Chinese economy significantly, but the policies of the past year or more represent an attempt to perfect their existing mixed economic system by moving in a direction quite different from either of the options discussed by Perkins or, presumably, by Chow. Rather than try to implement effective monetary and fiscal policy by relying on indirect economic levers, the effective monetary and fiscal policy regimes being pursued rely more on direct administrative controls. Rather than trying to improve the functioning of markets and allowing market forces to play the role they were supposed to achieve, for the sake of stability even grater reliance is being placed on direct interference, prohibitions, controls, etc. Yet, rather than tightening the soft budget constraints on individuals and units throughout the economy, the use of subsidies or grants to prevent discontent and loss of support for the leadership is threatening to change China's economy into yet another type of economic system—a grants economy.

Obviously, as argued by Perkins, the creation of a true market-socialist economy with a large private sector would be much more efficient than the existing mixed economic system in China. Yet, I do not believe the Chinese people, let alone their current leaders, have the political will necessary for pushing reforms further to create a true market-socialist economic system, at least at the present time. In addition, the less dramatic, but vitally important modifications required to make China's present, mixed economic system more efficient than either a market socialist economic system or a traditional Soviet-type economic system also lie well beyond the bounds of political acceptance by China's present leadership. Some observers doubt that their leaders still have the effective political control and administrative capability to implement the needed reforms successfully, even if they desired to do so.

Developments in China's system reforms in the past two years (beginning well before the tragic developments of May–June of 1989), indicate that China's current leaders have been pursuing a mixed economic system best described as (1) a system dominated and controlled by the central authorities, (2) an economic system in which both central plans and markets coexist, but where the planned allocation of key commodities governs the changing structure and growth of the economy and the market sector activities are carried out on very imperfect markets within serious administrative constraints; and (3) a system in which the central authorities rely very heavily on subsidies and grants to achieve the allocation of resources and goods they desire, overriding the results that would hold from decentralized decisions based on true scarcity prices for the sake of maximizing profits. Needless to say, the Chinese authorities encountered considerable difficulty in their attempts to realize this more conservative model of a reformed Soviet-type economy, much to the discredit of the more conservative reform advocates among the current leadership.

To the extent that these observations are correct, the real issue to be addressed by both outside observers and the Chinese themselves is not the merits of a choice between alternative ideal-types of theoretical models of economic systems, inasmuch as both moving forward to a market socialist economic system or returning to a traditional Soviet-type economic system are not among the alternatives actually being considered. Rather, the choice has been narrowed considerably by the existing political environment (i.e. the unreformed political system and the existing political leaders and most likely candidates for replacing them in the near future) to a choice between the mixed system now in place (with all its inconsistencies and inefficiencies) and the reformed Soviet-type economy the current leadership appears intent on creating.

Some may argue this is a false posing of the choices to be made. For example, recent developments in the socialist world indicate to some that there is only one superior choice—a market economy. Others may agree that while a market socialist economic system may not be a feasible choice facing the Chinese at the present time, or even in the near future, the current leadership is bound to die soon and be replaced by those more sympathetic to the radical reformers, who will return to create a market socialist economic system in the not-too-distant future. The political and economic future of Eastern Europe and China is not certain or inevitable and, as a specialist in comparative economic systems, I do not believe in the superiority of a single economic system for achieving the host of objectives, including noneconomic ones, any society may have. Certainly the evidence is not yet in as to the results of the various *different* attempts to reform the Soviet-type economic system throughout the socialist world.

Some socialist economies in Eastern Europe are trying to abandon their previous Soviet-type economic system and adopt a regulated market economy or a market-socialist economic system; still others are trying to rationalize their Soviet-type economies. The Chinese, who have already achieved a mixed economic system, are trying to move that system toward a mix with greater emphasis on central control, planning, and state-ownership. Thus, this generation is most fortunate in having the opportunity to learn a good deal about the feasible and desirable choices in reforming the Soviet-type economic system from one of the few true economic system reform experiments in history, including several different objectives and strategies. It is unfortunate that the Chinese, who have been engaged in the reform of their economic system longer than most other socialist countries now following their lead, have ruled out the attempt to push forward to a socialist system based on markets, which could well be a significantly more efficient economic system than the choices they are now considering.

THE PERFORMANCE OF CHINA'S ECONOMY

By Lee Zinser *

CONTENTS

SUMMARY

In the past three years, China has experienced its sharpest economic swing since Beijing began experimenting with market-oriented reforms in 1979. Inflation reached 30 percent in some Chinese cities in 1988 because economic decentralization during the 1980s created growing investment and consumption demands but reforms did not go far enough to create effective indirect monetary and fiscal instruments that Beijing could use countercyclically. Strict credit and investment controls cut inflation to single-digit rates by late 1989, but they brought economic growth virtually to a halt and caused rising unemployment, slumping industrial efficiency, and a widening government budget deficit. Since early 1990, Beijing has tried to "fine-tune" its retrenchment measures by easing credit while extending central controls. Without efficiency-enhancing market reforms, however, large state enterprises probably will not become engines of growth even with increased government allocations of energy and raw materials; thus Beijing will be reliant on easier credit to spur growth. Strong opposition by pro-

* This paper was written by Lee Zinser, Office of East Asian Analysis, Central Intelligence Agency. The views expressed in this paper are solely those of the author and do not necessarily reflect the views of any US Government agency.

vincial leaders has slowed Beijing's efforts to reclaim financial authority from local governments and enterprises so inflationary pressures could build again as credit controls are eased. Although austerity measures have created favorable economic conditions for proceeding with market reforms, for the near term China's leadership probably will prefer stopgap policies designed to maintain social stability rather than riskier policies for growth and development.

I. ECONOMIC OVERHEATING IN 1988

Chinese leaders confronted an economy in 1988 that was seriously overheated. According to Chinese statistics, real GNP grew by about 11 percent and industrial output—including production by village-level enterprises—surged almost 21 percent. [1] This worsened China's energy and raw materials shortfalls and transportation bottlenecks. As a result of excessive demand pressures, inflation reached post–1949 highs of 18.5 percent overall and almost 30 percent in some urban areas. Moreover, Beijing's budget deficit grew by two-fifths to a record 35 billion yuan ($6.7 billion) and the trade deficit more than doubled to $7.7 billion.

The proximate cause of the economic overheating was excessive monetary growth. After imposing strict credit controls in 1985 to combat overheating then, authorities began implementing easy credit policies in 1986. China's money supply grew at close to a 30-percent annual rate in the first three quarters of 1987 before Beijing slowed credit growth moderately in the fourth quarter. But Beijing relaxed credit controls in early 1988, apparently to spur industrial growth and lay the groundwork for a new round of enterprise reforms. Currency in circulation, one indicator of monetary tightness, grew 47 percent in 1988—the fastest growth since 1984.

The excessive monetary growth, however, was a symptom of a larger problem caused by the incomplete nature of the industrial reforms Beijing had been experimenting with for a decade. Since 1979 Beijing had steadily increased the share of revenues that state enterprises and local governments retained and gave them greater latitude over how funds were spent. Indeed, retained earnings of state enterprises were eight times larger in 1988 than when reforms began, according to the Chinese press. Beijing did not implement meaningful bankruptcy measures, however, and, without that market-oriented control mechanism, factory managers took advantage of increased decisionmaking autonomy to expand investment spending and worker remuneration without regard to efficiency. Local authorities also pushed ahead with ambitious development projects. Consequently, since the early 1980s, investment spending

---

[1] Most figures cited in this paper are official Chinese statistics. They are reported because they provide useful indications of the direction and magnitude of economic performance even though collection techniques are sometimes crude, local officials have been known to deliberately distort data, and some estimation techniques are questionable. For example, annual estimates for retail price inflation probably understated the true rate in 1988 and 1990 and overstated the true rate in 1989 because authorities apparently averaged monthly inflation rates (calculated by comparing the price index in each month with the index in the corresponding month of the previous year) to derive the annual estimates. For a discussion of the reliability of Chinese statistics, see "Allocation of Resources in the Soviet Union and China," Part 14, executive sessions April 14 and July 7, 1989, Subcommittee on National Security Economics, Joint Economic Committee, pages 208–212.

Table 1

Key Chinese Economic Indicators, 1987-90

	1987	1988	1989	1990*
Real GNP growth (percent)	11.0	10.8	3.9	4.4
Real GVAO growth (percent)	5.8	4.0	3.3	5.0
Real GVIO growth (percent)	17.7	20.8	8.3	7.0
State-owned industries	11.0	12.7	3.7	2.9
Collective industries	25.0	28.8	10.7	6.9
Private industries	48.0	46.0	24.1	N/A
GVIO growth of heavy industry (percent)	16.7	19.4	8.2	4.6
GVIO growth of light industry (percent)	18.6	22.1	8.4	7.4
Coal production (million metric tons)	928	980	1,040	1,090
Oil production (million metric tons)	134	137	137	138
Electricity production (billion kwh)	497	545	582	615
Steel production (million metric tons)	56.3	59.4	61.2	66.0
Grain production (million metric tons)	403	394	407	420
Cotton production (million metric tons)	4.25	4.15	3.79	4.25
Labor productivity growth (percent)	7.6	9.3	1.6	-0.8 (through Sept)
Total investment (billion yuan)	364	450	400	N/A
State investment (billion yuan)	230	276	251	N/A
Retail price increase (percent)	7.3	18.5	17.8	2.0
Retail sales (billion yuan)	582	744	810	825
Average per capita urban income (yuan)	1,012	1,192	1,260	N/A
Average per capita rural income (yuan)	463	545	602	N/A
Budget subsidies for enterprise losses (billion yuan)	37.6	44.6	60.0	N/A
Price subsidies (billion yuan)	29.5	31.7	37.0	N/A
Exports (billion US $)	39.44	47.52	52.49	62.07
Imports (billion US $)	43.22	55.27	59.14	53.36
Trade balance (billion US $)	-3.78	-7.75	-6.65	8.71
Foreign exchange reserves (billion US $)	15.2	17.5	17.0	27.0
Exchange rate (yearend, yuan/US $)	3.72	3.72	4.72	5.23

* Preliminary
Source: Official Chinese statistics.

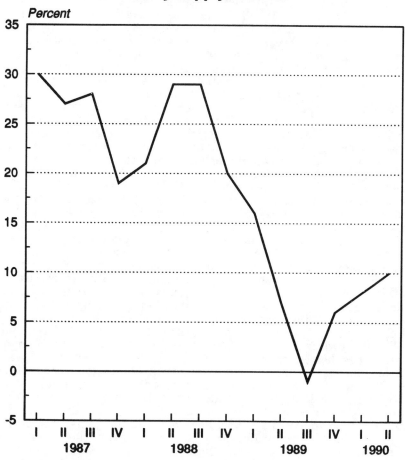

Figure 1

Growth in China's Seasonally Adjusted
Money Supply, 1987-90

Source: IMF International Financial Statistics.

grew at more than a 20-percent average annual rate, and real wages of state industrial workers generally increased faster than labor productivity.

The widespread adoption of an enterprise contract system in 1987 also contributed to inflationary pressures. Under the system, factory managers agreed to remit a specified amount of revenues to the state. Once they fulfilled the contract, additional enterprise profits were to be taxed at a much lower rate, or not at all. Without a meaningful threat of bankruptcy, this provided a strong incentive to factories to boost investment spending and plant output.

Beijing's failure to complete price reform also contributed to the overheating. Although authorities took some significant steps during the 1980s to ease irrationalities in China's pricing structure—including raising state procurement prices for grain, decontrolling prices of nonstaples and many consumer durables, and allowing sales of overquota industrial products at market prices—prices of energy and key raw materials were held artificially low by the state. Because raw materials were relatively cheap, manufacturing industries could generally make profits even if factories used inefficient, outmoded equipment. This encouraged local officials to use their increased revenues to invest in manufacturing industries, which increased the demand on supplies of energy and raw materials.

The inflationary consequences of economic decentralization were somewhat muted in the early 1980s by reform-driven efficiency gains in key sectors. In particular, production of grain and cotton increased about 8 percent and 28 percent annually, respectively, between 1981 and 1984 because Beijing hiked procurement prices and allowed peasants to retain profits from overquota production. This helped Beijing meet rising consumer demands for food and clothing caused by urban wage increases. Hikes in coal prices and policies allowing individuals and local governments to open their own mines helped cause coal output to grow 8 percent a year during the same period, allowing power plants to generate increased amounts of electricity, which contributed to rapid industrial growth, particularly by locally run firms manufacturing consumer items. The production gains from breaking up the communes were exhausted by 1985, however, and the gains from opening individual mines also began to taper off during the latter half of the 1980s.

The surge in prices in 1988, thus, was part of a trend of increased inflation since the mid-1980s, as growing overall demand fed by surging wages and capital construction outstripped supplies of consumer goods and industrial materials. The inflation rate tripled in 1985 to almost 9 percent, pushed along by a rapid increase in the money supply caused by moves the previous year to decentralize the banking system. After remaining near the new plateau for two years, inflation more than doubled in 1988.

The discrepancy between rising consumer demand and lagging agricultural production was particularly notable in 1988. Grain production fell about 2 percent because of adverse weather, relatively low state-set procurement prices, and rising costs of agricultural inputs such as fertilizer, seeds, and plastic sheeting used as mulch. Sluggish production of industrial crops like sugar, ramie,

Figure 2
China's Inflation Rates, 1979-90

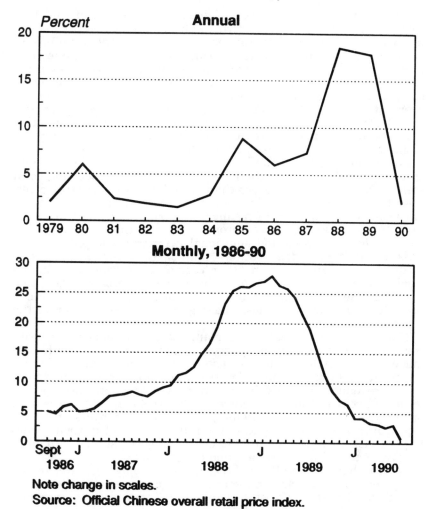

Note change in scales.
Source: Official Chinese overall retail price index.

and cotton caused production costs to rise in food processing and textile industries.

II. LACK OF INDIRECT MACROECONOMIC INSTRUMENTS

The economic consequences of industrial overheating in 1988 were compounded because reforms had not progressed far enough for Beijing to use restrictive monetary and fiscal policies efficiently. When Beijing began decentralizing control over revenues and dismantling the planning apparatus, reformers believed they could use such indirect economic levers as monetary and fiscal policies to compensate for the central government's diminished direct control over enterprises. But because reforms succeeded in delegating administrative authority to local governments, rather than creating markets and financial accountability, Beijing could only carry out monetary and fiscal policies with the help of local officials.

Provincial and municipal officials are more concerned with speeding development of their own economies and boosting local standards of living, however, than complying with central directives to implement restrictive monetary and fiscal policies. Municipal leaders benefit from using increased bank loans and tax revenues to fund new industrial projects because these efforts create jobs for local residents and additional tax receipts for city coffers. This is particularly true because municipalities erect barriers to trade that prevent firms in other regions from competing in the local market. On the other hand, the costs of excessive local spending—increased shortages of raw materials, disruption of planned production by state factories, and higher prices—spill over to the economy as a whole.

Thus the decentralization of planning and financial authority that was instrumental in spurring rapid economic growth also made it difficult for Beijing to use fiscal and monetary policy instruments countercyclically. The system of "tax farming" and multiyear revenue contracts in which provinces guarantee specific levels of tax remittances to central authorities put tight constraints on the use of fiscal policy. Beijing had no market levers to reduce local government spending and was reluctant to cut its own spending for such items as key infrastructure projects, subsidies, administrative expenditures, defense, and education.

Central bank control over the money supply was weakened, moreover, by provincial and municipal leaders who applied pressure to local branches of state banks to accommodate the growing demand for investment spending and wage hikes. Local banks have been responsive to this pressure partly because municipal officials appoint bank personnel and provide housing, offices, and retirement benefits for employees. Branch managers probably also assume that the central bank will ultimately provide the necessary funds if branches become overextended because Beijing does not allow banks to fail. In addition, Beijing's policy of bailing out deficit state enterprises undermines its efforts to reduce overall demand by hiking interest rates.

While decentralization of lending decisions has made it easier for local officials to interfere with monetary policy, reforms shifting the burden of financing investment from the state budget to the banking system have increased the consequences of this interference. This shift not only has reduced Beijing's direct control over the economy but has also meant that excessive growth in bank credit has a much greater impact on demand for investment goods and thus inflation.

III. Imposition of Retrenchment Measures

Faced with rising inflation and widening trade and budget deficits, Chinese leaders announced at a party plenum in September 1988 that they would postpone key market reforms for several years and implement a retrenchment program to cool the economy. In particular, Beijing shelved a price reform proposal that sparked bank runs and panic buying when it was discussed publicly in July and August 1988. In August, retail prices of vegetables and meat soared 40 to 50 percent nationwide and cost of living increases were even higher in many urban areas, according to Chinese statistics.

The retrenchment program Beijing began in September 1988 emphasized the use of administrative controls to reduce inflationary pressure. Beijing announced it would cut state investment spending by 20 percent in 1989, with the burden falling on nonproductive projects such as office buildings and recreational facilities. Although state investment actually fell only 9 percent, Beijing announced it had cancelled or postponed more than 18,000 projects, sharply cutting the value of new projects begun in 1989.

Beijing also tightened credit ceilings for domestic banks, raised reserve ratios by 1 percentage point to 13 percent, and hiked interest rates on bank loans to discourage bank-financed investment outside the state plan. Authorities also called for a halt in loans to private and rural enterprises. China's central bank also raised interest rates on household deposits—indexing those with maturities of three years or longer to the retail price index—and imposed limits on the amounts individuals could withdraw from savings accounts. To gain better control of credit acquired by local authorities through foreign channels, in early 1989 Beijing reduced the number of government entities allowed to borrow funds abroad from 100 to only 10.

Beijing expanded its direct control over raw materials, reimposing price controls for steel, copper, aluminum, and other production materials. It also reestablished its monopoly over the distribution of fertilizer, pesticides, and plastic sheeting to control speculation on farm inputs.

Chinese authorities also extended controls over trade by reducing the number of corporations authorized to import certain products and by tightening controls over foreign exchange and banning imports of some consumer goods and industrial inputs. Beijing also increased the number of exports subject to licenses, quotas, and outright bans.

The administrative measures Beijing outlined in late 1988—and its methods of ensuring local compliance—were similar to retrenchment programs implemented in the early 1980s and again in 1985 to cool the economy. In particular, central authorities tried to create a political environment in which bank managers could resist calls for loans and local officials felt compelled to defer some investment projects. Beijing exerted pressure on local leaders through the press by emphasizing that retrenchment was the party's top economic priority. Central authorities also held numerous meetings of party and government officials to lay down enforcement guidelines and sent inspection teams to localities to report on the extent of compliance with construction and credit targets. In addition, central leaders and government-controlled media touted the role of party committees in factories to make enterprises more responsive to party instructions to cut back spending.

The retrenchment program begun in 1988, however, has taken a much different course than earlier efforts because the student demonstrations in the spring of 1989, which were joined by workers disgruntled with inflation, strengthened the hand of those officials who had been critical of the pace and scope of market-oriented reforms in the 1980s and who had championed retrenchment. The removal of Zhao Ziyang as party general secretary, in particular, silenced an important advocate of balancing retrenchment with market-oriented reforms, and made it difficult for anyone to oppose austerity openly. And a central committee meeting in June 1989 elevated leaders who generally favor reform strategies that emphasize improved central planning rather than experiments with market measures.

By late summer 1989, Beijing's retrenchment program entered a new phase as China's more planning-oriented leadership stepped up calls for recentralization of economic authority to remove the underlying sources of inflationary pressure. The cornerstone of the recentralization program was a desire to reclaim planning and financial authority from local governments and municipally run enterprises. The influence of these orthodox officials was evident at the Central Committee plenum in November 1989, which approved an agenda that called for extending the retrenchment program and strengthening central planning—in part by increasing the share of production that enterprises must turn over to the government and expanding government support to large state enterprises producing energy and raw materials. Moreover, late in 1989 Beijing announced the formation of the Production Commission under the State Planning Commission to strengthen the central government's control over the economy. Fulfilling many of the functions of the State Economic Commission disbanded in late 1987 by then General Secretary Zhao Ziyang, the Production Commission is responsible for allocating capital, raw materials, transportation, and energy to key state-owned industries.

Press accounts indicate that the recentralization agenda also includes increased central control over tax revenues and investment decisions to diminish the ability of municipal officials to use local resources for their own projects. For example, the State Council announced in August 1990 a list of 23 types of investment projects that localities cannot begin without central approval, and press reports indicate Beijing plans to impose a heavy tax on all investment projects not listed in the central plan. Other press reports indicate that some officials want to reduce the scope of decisionmaking authority exercised by local bank branches and restrict the ability of specialized banks, such as the Agricultural Bank of China and the Industrial and Commercial Bank of China, to compete for business. In the fall of 1989, some senior officials called for substantially paring the number of private and rural enterprises, which have been blamed for contributing to inflation by diverting raw materials from state enterprises and using them wastefully with outdated production equipment. Some planning-oriented officials apparently also want to restrict the autonomy of state enterprise managers over personnel, salary, and production decisions.

IV. Economy Reels Under Austerity

Efforts to proceed with the retrenchment program—both its austerity and its recentralization elements—were undermined, however, by worsening economic performance late in 1989. Chinese statistics indicate that by October 1989 austerity measures were creating an economic freefall: compared to the same month a year earlier, inflation slowed to less than double digit rates, but industrial production contracted for the first time in 10 years. For the year, real GNP grew 3.9 percent, about one-third the rate in 1988; industrial output grew at less than a 1-percent rate in the fourth quarter of 1989 and was stagnant in the first quarter of 1990.

Although cutbacks in bank credit reduced inflation to low single digits by early 1990, they also caused massive debt defaults among enterprises and soaring inventories of unsold goods. Some factories, burdened with shortages of cash and excessive inventories, suspended production and laid off workers. A Chinese official admitted that at one point about one-fifth of industrial enterprises had closed; many more had significantly curtailed operations. Urban unemployment consequently reached its highest level since the early 1980s. Rural unemployment also grew because retrenchment policies that curtailed supplies of credit, raw materials, and energy to rural enterprises closed more than one million of these enterprises, and millions of rural workers employed in urban construction projects also were forced to return to the countryside because of the cutback in investment projects.

Some urban factories kept workers at the plant but paid them only 70 percent of their expected wages and no bonuses in late 1989. Real wages fell for the second consecutive year—official statistics indicate that price hikes were responsible for a drop in real income for more than one-third of urban residents. Some workers reportedly complained that the belt-tightening in late 1989 was the worst they had experienced since the early 1960s, when China was recovering from the disastrous Great Leap Forward. According to the Hong Kong press, other workers registered their displeasure by participating in work slowdowns, demonstrations, and strikes.

Not only did rising unemployment and falling living standards threaten to stoke the social discontent that anti-inflationary measures were designed to dampen, but weak industrial growth prevented government revenues from keeping pace with growing subsidies to workers and financially ailing enterprises. Consequently, Beijing's budget deficit widened further by 7 percent to 37 billion yuan ($7.1 billion) in 1989. More than 6,200 enterprises recorded losses, more than double the number in 1988. Lagging labor productivi-

Figure 3
China's Real GNP Growth, 1979-90

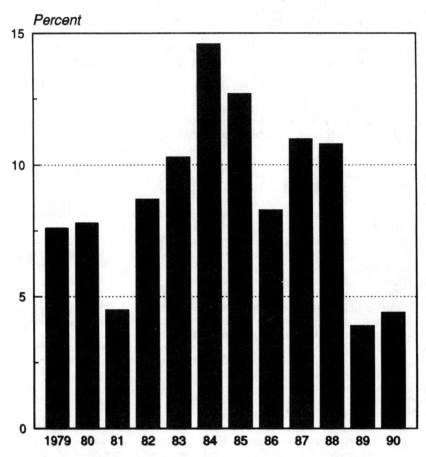

Percent

Source: Official Chinese statistics.

Figure 4

China's Industrial Growth, 1979–90

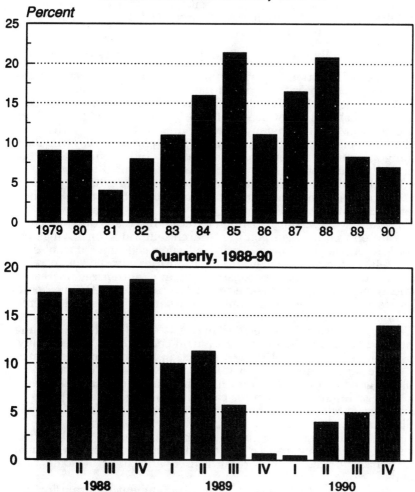

Percent

Quarterly, 1988–90

Note change in scales.
Source: Official Chinese statistics.

ty—per capita productivity grew only 1.6 percent in 1989—and rising inventories contributed to mounting production costs. The inflation-indexed bank rates for consumers made the inventory problem worse by boosting savings deposits by more than one-third to 513 billion yuan ($98.1 billion) by yearend, which accompanied an almost 8-percent real decrease in retail sales.

V. EASING THE BRAKES WHILE STRENGTHENING CENTRAL CONTROLS

To head off additional worker unrest and ease the economic dislocations caused by retrenchment measures, Beijing began to ease up on austerity in late 1989. In the fourth quarter of 1989, the central bank disbursed new loans of 125 billion yuan ($23.9 billion), more than twice the amount released during the rest of the year and 25 billion yuan ($4.8 billion) more than planned. Early in 1990, Beijing announced it would also double to 60 billion yuan ($11.5 billion) the amount of working capital loans it planned to disburse in the first half of the year. By the end of 1990, Beijing had reportedly increased overall new lending by almost 50 percent to 273 billion yuan ($52.2 billion).

To stimulate spending, Beijing reduced interest rates on bank loans by one percentage point in March, cut rates on savings accounts in April, and lowered prices of such consumer durables as color televisions and refrigerators. Authorities also began to relax state controls over capital construction and authorized increased institutional purchases of some products. In addition, Beijing boosted price subsidies and food supplies to urban residents and ordered pay raises for all state employees.

To keep inflation from reemerging as it eased austerity, Beijing continued to emphasize expanded central control over the economy. For example, in early 1990 the Production Commission designated 234 large state enterprises to take part in a "double guarantee" program under which the government guarantees raw materials and energy inputs in return for commitments by the enterprises to turn over specified amounts of revenues and output. Moreover, Beijing targeted increases in bank credit to key state industries. In addition, Beijing tightened control over coal prices in April 1990 to dampen profiteering caused by the discrepancy between in-plan and market prices, and it recentralized allocation of some rare metals.

Beijing's efforts to "fine-tune" the retrenchment program in 1990 yielded mixed results. Industrial growth picked up moderately beginning in May, and by the fourth quarter of 1990 it had returned to double-digit annual rates. This plus a record 420 million metric ton grain harvest pushed real GNP growth up 4.4 percent. China also recorded an $8.7 billion trade surplus in 1990, continuing the turnaround that began in the second half of 1989 as tighter central controls and slower economic growth reduced demand for imports while increased subsidies and allocations of raw materials to export-producing factories helped cause exports to soar.

Although inflation remained in low single digits for much of 1990, it picked up late in the year—prices rose at a 5-percent annual rate in November. China's budget deficit also probably hit a new high. In the first half of 1990, revenues fell short of expenditures, giving Beijing a budget deficit in the first six months of the year for the first time ever. Moreover, industrial efficiency continued to lag, inventories remained high, and retail sales probably fell in real terms for the second consecutive year. By the end of 1990, one-third of all state enterprises were running deficits, according to the Chinese press.

VI. CHINA'S ECONOMIC POLICY DILEMMA

As Chinese leaders face the 1990s, they are confronted with the dilemma of how to stimulate rapid enough gains in living standards to meet the expectations spawned by a decade of rapid, reform-driven growth without reigniting inflation and widespread social unrest. In the past three years, Beijing has demonstrated that strict credit quotas and administrative controls are capable of throttling down the economy, but use of these instruments alone is not likely to provide the basis for rapid, noninflationary long-term development.

Industrial efficiency almost certainly will remain depressed if Beijing continues efforts to expand the scope of central planning because reducing managerial autonomy and forcing factories to sell more goods at relatively low, state-set prices will erode incentives. Guaranteeing large state enterprises increased state allocations of raw materials and energy will further erode incentives to boost productivity. Moreover, policies that favor China's capital-intensive industries will squeeze the dynamic nonstate sector and impede its ability to provide jobs for China's unemployed and underemployed rural workers and to produce labor-intensive goods for export. The unemployment penalty these policies exact may grow over time because Beijing must find jobs for about 100 million workers expected to enter the labor force in the next five years.

Low state-sector productivity will also make it difficult for Beijing to close its budget deficit, and pressures to speed revenue growth and stimulate state industries probably will cause Beijing to ease credit. Indeed, the larger-than-planned expansion of credit in late 1989 was partly designed to help enterprises meet their yearend tax obligations. Easier credit, however, will undermine Beijing's ability to keep inflation in check. Because China is resource rich, credit expansion will spur growth, but without market-oriented reforms, such a policy will not improve the efficiency of investment, and increased aggregate demand will worsen energy and transportation bottlenecks.

Although Beijing will try to reclaim control over tax receipts from local governments as a way of reducing the budget deficit—and its inflationary impact on the economy—it will continue to face stiff opposition from provincial officials. According to a number of Hong Kong press reports, a Central Committee plenum scheduled for the fall of 1990 to discuss a draft of China's 8th Five-Year Plan (1991–95) was delayed by two months because of wrangling over a scheme for revamping the distribution of taxes between central and local governments. When the plenum finally met, it did not publicly address the issue.

Although in the post-Tiananmen atmosphere central authorities have brought enormous political pressure to bear on local govern-

Figure 5
China's Budget Deficits, 1979-89

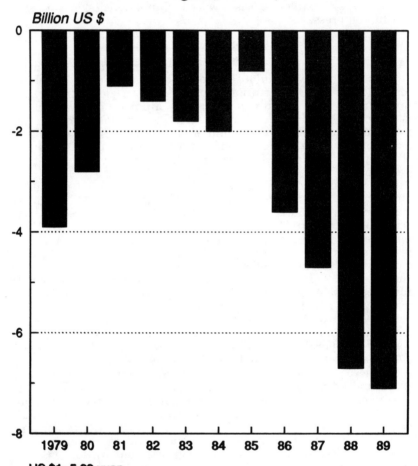

US $1=5.23 yuan
Source: Official Chinese statistics, adjusted according
to Western accounting practices.

ments, municipal and provincial officials also have strong cards to play when they bargain for control of finances. For example, local governments control a significant share of industrial production. By 1988 nonstate enterprises produced more than one-third of China's industrial output—up from one-fifth a decade ago—and localities had gained control of many state enterprises as well. Moreover, they control important sources of raw materials; about 54 percent of coal was produced by locally run mines in 1988, and more than half of China's steel and more than four-fifths of its cement were allocated outside Beijing's central plan.

Provincial and municipal governments also are important sources of foreign exchange. The freer economic rein that Beijing has given provinces along China's southern coast is a key reason that these local governments have rapidly built up export industries and attracted foreign investment. Indeed, over the past 10 years, Guangdong Province has been the recipient of about half of the total foreign investment in China, and in 1989 it accounted for 15 percent of the country's exports. In addition, locally run firms throughout China have become important sources of foreign exchange. For example, rural enterprises in 1990 exported about $13 billion worth of goods, almost 21 percent of China's total, according to the Chinese press.

Beijing also depends on local governments to implement its policies. Almost all tax collectors, for example, are appointed and controlled by local officials. The Chinese press has cited numerous examples of local governments arbitrarily exempting enterprises from taxes or simply refusing to collect particular types of taxes.

VII. Outlook for the 1990s

Because Beijing will have to rely on increased credit allocations to spur growth but will probably not be able to reclaim the financial authority it lost during the 1980s, China's economy is likely to experience boom and bust economic cycles in the 1990s. Beijing is likely to clamp down hard when inflation approaches double-digit levels, so the expansion phase of the cycle may be shorter than in the 1980s. Indeed, some officials are advocating low growth targets, probably because they realize China's macroeconomic instruments are blunt and they do not have a good idea how sensitive overall demand is to changes in credit and state investment spending. Thus they prefer to err on the side of caution. They may also be concerned that the high level of personal savings deposits could accentuate a surge in prices if people withdraw money en masse to purchase consumer durables when inflation picks up.

The economic dislocations caused by retrenchment policies will provide reform advocates opportunities to advance proposals for modest new experiments. The need to fund the growing budget deficit, for example, probably helped win approval recently for the opening of several securities markets and plans to link bond markets in several cities. Hikes in state coal prices in August 1990, an almost 10-percent devaluation of China's currency in November, and discussions of possible hikes in retail grain prices have all been linked to the need to curtail government subsidies. Beijing may have missed its best chance to implement meaningful price reform, however, by not doing it in late 1989 at the trough of the macroeconomic cycle.

The prospects for a return to comprehensive, market-oriented reforms appear dim in the near term, however, despite the inefficiencies and long-term problems inherent in the current planning-oriented, slow-growth approach. Reform momentum began to slow as early as January 1987 when Hu Yaobang was ousted as party general secretary. The sharp inflation in 1988 and massive demonstrations in 1989 underscored the authorities' determination to weigh economic policies according to their potential impact on social stability.

Efforts to fine-tune retrenchment policies further in the next few years are likely to be based on this cautious attitude. Although many in the leadership endorse the primacy of central planning for China's economy, they do not want to return to Maoist-style ideological strictures. For example, they endorse basing economic decisions on objective criteria, including cost-benefit analysis, and requiring that even mandatory planning takes account of supply and demand—thus they support increases in state-set prices of key raw materials. They also favor responsibility systems in industry, agriculture, and foreign trade that hold decisionmakers accountable for profitability, and they endorse the use of economic incentives to guide factories to meet plan targets.

Their agenda also calls for increasing productive capacity through technological transformation of existing facilities, rather than building new factories or importing whole plants. Moreover, they advocate giving priority in investment to agriculture, energy, transportation, communication, and export-oriented projects, and improving the quality of factory decisionmaking by educating managers and allowing scientists and engineers to play a larger role. In addition, they support the importation of technology and capital from Western countries.

There are valuable lessons to be drawn from the experiences of the past three years. Unlike many reforming socialist economies, China demonstrated the will and ability to dampen inflation, at least temporarily. Controls over the trade sector and export promotion policies, moreover, helped push China's foreign exchange reserves up to a healthy $27 billion by the end of 1990. At least for now, this lessens the chance that China's foreign debt will be a burden on development and provides a cushion for any future market experiments. The leadership's commitment to boosting exports during retrenchment will tie China even closer to the global economy; the pressure to keep up with China's market-oriented East Asian neighbors, particularly for foreign investment, may give reformers additional motives for reducing inefficient central planning. The rush by municipal leaders to protect local economies from retrenchment policies by raising internal barriers to trade, moreover, has increased the need for, and the potential gains from, creating national resource and commodity markets. Thus should a less risk-averse leadership gain the reins of government, a return to comprehensive reforms should be possible in the future.

THE CYCLICAL FUTURE OF CHINA'S ECONOMIC REFORMS

By Albert Keidel *

CONTENTS

I. INTRODUCTION

At mid-year 1990, China's reforms and economic future depend on resolving the conflict between price reform and urban subsidies. Initially, price reform creates the need for direct financing of urban subsidies. Ultimately it forces a sharp reduction in subsidies, if not their complete elimination. Such an adverse impact on urban lifestyles inevitably leads to popular resentment—so much so that urban irritation at the inflation and unemployment resulting from price reform was almost certainly a cause of the 1989 Tiananmen uprising.

But there are ways to resolve the price-subsidy conflict. Overall, the best way may be to make good use of the economic cycles of expansion and contraction that have characterized Chinese reforms since their beginning. Periods of inflationary expansion have been best suited for broadening price reform, investing in new jobs, and introducing controversial taxes. Periods of contraction and austerity, on the other hand, can help convince urban workers that layoffs are necessary and push enterprise managers to cut costs, restructure their labor force, economize on urban investments, and reduce subsidies.

China—socialist China—will have economic cycles whether it wants them or not, but it should avoid the extremes of panic infla-

* President, Rock Creek Research, Inc. I am grateful to Mr. Tian Jianghai of the PRC State Planning Commission for his many useful comments and questions on an early draft of this paper. I would also like to thank Ji Feng and Kristen Walker for valuable editing and research assistance. I am especially grateful to the State Planning Commission, The Ford Foundation, and Denis Simon for making it possible for me to attend the SPC Peking conference in May 1990, where a very early draft of this paper was presented.

tion and protracted unemployment. Economic cycles should not be allowed to disrupt reforms by stalling critical stages. It is likely, even without price reform, that China's economy will still grow and prosper in many ways. But its successes will be limited, and its instabilities will be increasingly difficult to manage. If, however, China applies economic cycles themselves to the solution of its urban price reform problems, it could accomplish fundamental reform and at the same time contain cyclical exaggerations.

Economic ups and downs have plagued China since the start of Communist rule, but they were largely political until after 1978, when economic reforms and the introduction of markets induced alternating phases of inflation and financial austerity. These cycles became increasingly intense in the latter 1980s, as financial reforms and the role of market credit eroded central government control over the economy and forced a confrontation between fundamental reform and life-as-usual for state enterprises and for the part of China's urban population that is officially subsidized.

At the time economic reforms began—and by overall Chinese standards—the subsidized portion of China's urban population had grown accustomed to a life with relatively high consumption levels. This standard of living was financed by the Maoist price system. Low prices for rural products and relatively high prices for manufactures generated large urban profits that both financed industrial investment and sustained a privileged urban lifestyle.

Deng Xiaoping's economic reforms, however, introduced higher food prices and two-tiered markets for other rural products such as fuel and construction materials. With the spread of these price reforms in the 1980s, the officially subsidized urban standard of living and large state investment programs became difficult to finance. China's leaders could not rely as much on rural-urban financial transfers through the old price system. Instead, they resorted to government budget deficits and easy bank credit to pay for state-enterprise investments and to sustain urban expectations for a modern life. This monetary accommodation of weak taxes and low urban productivity led to cycles of inflation and fiscal contraction which, in turn, led directly to the Tiananmen uprising of 1989.

By 1990, the two most promising solutions to long-term price reform problems are to raise urban state-sector labor productivity and to introduce direct taxes on the non-state-sector economies. A third route, deficits and inflation, will ultimately fail to accomplish thorough price reform. No monetary, fiscal, or price-system manipulations can avoid the harsh reality that reforms have cut transfers from the rural economy and that real urban consumption levels are higher than justified by the lower productivity of urban workers.

But neither raising productivity nor introducing new taxes is politically attractive. In the rural economy, direct farm and township taxes would be an even more odious transfer of rural wealth to the cities than the old Maoist price system has been. For the cities, raising productivity would mean job changes, layoffs, new jobs from more labor-intensive investments, and management reliance on business cost-effectiveness rather than promoting enthusiasm for selecting technology. Many of these changes would contradict popular urban beliefs that socialism in China means job comfort and security, and that socialist industrialization means heavy investment in an increasingly capital-intensive high-technology productive capacity. The necessities of reform therefore risk arousing the opposition and indignation of urban workers, intellectuals, and communist cadre alike.

The well-timed use of economic cycles can reduce the adverse political impact of urban layoffs, harder work, price reform, and new taxes. This is because economic cycles combine practical policies with matching adjustments in citizen expectations. For example, popular resistance to layoffs and job hunting is weakened if bankruptcy and financial reorganization are enforced during a well-publicized cyclical downturn. Credit restrictions encourage managers to cut out costly and unnecessary equipment and where possible substitute less-expensive labor.

On the other hand, during periods of cyclical economic expansion, new jobs and growing revenues can relieve unemployment and help make higher prices appear more affordable. At the same time, expanding sales can make new or stiffer taxes appear less burdensome than they ultimately will be. Above all, increasing urban productivity requires the new jobs and large investments common during economic booms. Chinese policymakers must therefore learn to manage China's economic cycles so as to avoid the protracted phases of investment stagnation common in the recent past.

Whether or not China solves its basic economic problem of high state-sector consumption and low state-sector productivity, the system reforms in the 1990s appear certain to strengthen the role of most domestic markets and open China even further to the world economic community. Without fundamental price reform, however, the resulting market economy will be twisted and crippled in significant ways, and economic growth will not achieve its potential. Without the painful adjustments to urban expectations and productivity necessary for urban price reform, much of the dynamism in China's economy will remain in rural areas, townships, and smaller cities. Repeated bouts of inflation and state budget crises will generate growing resentment over the government's crude efforts to finance state enterprise subsidies and expensive state investments. If, however, China can make major adjustments in state enterprise productivity through layoffs, new jobs, and more efficient investment design and construction, urban state enterprises could lead the way in developing China's economic growth potential and increasing the industrial sophistication.

In either case, China's economy in the 1990s will grow impressively as an exporter of manufactures and an importer of technology. But if urban labor and management reforms succeed, the economy will be better integrated into a relatively effective national market in most goods and services. Otherwise, China's state-subsidized cities will become barricaded prisons of economic inefficiency, holding the much more competitive non-state economy at bay by means of a hated taxing authority, restrictions on the scope of the non-state economy, and inflationary state finances.

II. China's Cyclical Economic Past

China's economy has been subject to two types of cyclical influence. One kind of cycle is political and has been based on the timing of Communist Party congresses and major national leadership decisions. In the political cycle, new alignments in the Communist Party Central Committee and major leadership shifts have for decades initiated economic instabilities. The other kind of cycle is economic and only became significant in the 1980s under Deng Xiaoping. In the economic cycle, each phase—whether liberalization or renewed financial austerity—has generated economic conditions that by their nature prompt yet another policy shift, leading to the next phase. For example, inflation has generally triggered financial and investment cut-backs, while austerity cash flow problems have triggered spending relaxation. In the 1980s, both political and economic cycles operated, but the economic cycle became increasingly exaggerated and disruptive, especially as financial reforms matured in 1986–88.

Chinese scholars and policymakers have long been aware of political influences on China's economic instability and refer to as many as seven politically induced investment cycles in China's economy since 1953, including the Great Leap Forward of 1958 (the second cycle), the 1966–70 early years of the Cultural Revolution (the fourth cycle), the 1978–80 years of heavy investment following Mao's death (the sixth cycle), and the continuing investment expansion begun in 1982. Most of these cycles are identified either with a particular Party Plenum in which Mao exercised his accumulated power, or with a particular National Congress of the Communist Party, as in 1973 (the Tenth Party Congress), 1977 (the Eleventh), and 1982 (the Twelfth Party Congress, which initiated the long boom of the 1980s).

The economic cycles of the 1980s, however, have been shorter than the political cycles, and they are measured differently. China's political cycles have traditionally been identified from annual data on State investment spending, uncorrected for inflation. But annual data are too aggregate to capture the more frequent economic cycles, especially in the latter 1980s when their periodicity shortened. The economic cycles of the 1980s are instead best measured with monthly statistics on industrial output, corrected for the influence of seasonal variations. Seasonally adjusted data are presented in Tables 1 and 2.

Seasonality in monthly Chinese industrial output means that, even when there is no change in policy or underlying conditions, output from one month to the next can change dramatically because of regular annual shifts in weather and the timing of official output targets. For example, relative to the average output level over many months, June output is on average 9 percent higher than normal every year, while July and August output levels are roughly 5 percent below the average. This is because weather in June is good, and production activity is more intense in order to fulfill mid-year plan targets. In July and August, however, the weather is extremely hot in most of China, and the work pace is more relaxed. Similarly, industrial output in November and December is 3-to-5 percentage points higher than the actual trend in order to meet annual targets. Then in either January or February, output is roughly 12 percent below trend, depending on when Chinese New Year happens to fall. Because of such strong seasonality, measuring month-to-month growth rates from raw data makes it virtually impossible to tell how much of the variation is due to seasonality and how much is due to actual shifts in the underlying growth of industrial output.

While it is essential to correct for seasonality, some corrections are not very satisfactory. The Chinese way of reporting monthly growth rates does correct for seasonality in its own way, but it introduces other inaccuracies, which for China in the 1980s were quite serious. Chinese official monthly growth rates correct for seasonality by comparing a month with the same month in the previous year. Since the month is being compared to itself one year earlier, there is no need to change the data for seasonality; the influence of seasonality is the same for the same month in each year. But this methodology, because it spans a whole year, also includes change during the other eleven months preceding the month under analysis. When these months experience rapid monthly ups and downs, as in China's case, the measure no longer reflects only growth for the month of concern. For example, if there were a sharp downturn in the first half of a 12-month period followed by a strong recovery in the second half, even though industry was growing again at a fast pace, the official Chinese growth rate for the twelfth month could show slow or even negative growth. This is because, given the slump earlier in the year, output for the month under analysis might not be significantly different from what it had been a year earlier.

In other words, the official way of measuring monthly growth really calculates an average of monthly growth rates over the whole preceding year. This helps to understand the second major problem with the official way of calculating monthly growth rates—a shift in the growth trend may not appear in official growth data until as much as three or four months after it has begun. If policymakers rely only on these statistics, they will be unaware of new trends and will be slow in adjusting policy. For example, if after twelve months of rapid growth the industrial economy suddenly turns downward, output for many months will still be much higher than it had been twelve months earlier, and so the official growth rate will show strong industrial growth for many months, when in fact industry is in a decline. Government policymakers would be wrong to think that their austerity program had not yet taken hold.

This problem of timing in official data can be seen in Table I for the period January 1988 to June 1990. The seasonally adjusted data in the second column show what really happened to industrial output during this important period. The country experienced strong expansion and a financial and banking crisis (January–October 1988), an initial austerity program (November 1988–February 1989), a recovery through the Tiananmen uprising (March–May, 1989), a sustained second austerity program (after the June 4 army crackdown), and finally a recovery in industrial output (beginning in March 1990). The first column shows that official data blurred

Table 1
Chinese Monthly* Industrial Output, 1988-90
Comparison of Official and Seasonally Adjusted Growth Rates
(Percent growth*, on an Annual Basis)

		"Official"	Seasonally Adjusted
1988	Jan	15.4**	20.6
	Feb	16.7**	12.7
	Mar	14.6	9.3
	Apr	17.2	27.8
	May	17.9	28.6
	Jun	17.7	36.6
	Jul	15.5	6.3
	Aug	20.1	19.1
	Sep	20.2	30.7
	Oct	20.4	31.8
	Nov	17.9	-1.2
	Dec	18.3	5.5
1989	Jan	8.1	-31.6
	Feb	11.3***	-5.8
	Mar	14.8	23.1
	Apr	13.7	44.2
	May	11.1	14.6
	Jun	8.8	7.8
	Jul	9.5	-2.3
	Aug	6.1	-2.9
	Sep	0.9	-13.7
	Oct	-2.1	-15.7
	Nov	0.9	-5.4
	Dec	3.4	29.7
1990	Jan	1.7**	-27.4
	Feb	-2.7**	-29.0
	Mar	1.1	25.4
	Apr	1.8	60.0
	May	4.6	48.9
	Jun	5.7	29.6
	Jul	2.9	-8.4

*Note: Right-hand column growth rates are based on seasonally adjusted real output levels and are calculated as the average monthly growth for a given month relative to the average output of the three previous months. Hence, the measure is really a two-month average growth rate, converted to an annual basis. This growth rate measure is sensitive to changes in the month in question, but less sensitive to an anomalous change in one of the three preceding months.

**Note: These "official" data for January and February have been corrected for an irregularity in the incidence of the Chinese New Year Festival. Because of the large drop in output associated with the Festival, if it falls in February one year and January the next, or vice versa, comparisons with the previous year are distorted for both January and February. The "official" data for January and February 1988 and 1990 have been corrected for this distortion. As officially published, the data for January and February, respectively, were 25.0% and 11.4% for 1988 and   -6.1% and 5.6% for 1990. "Official" data above for other months are as presented by official government publications, with the exception of February 1989.

***Note: As officially published, this February 1989 growth rate was 7.5%, which is too low, because 1988 was a leap-year, and its February had 29 days rather than 28, causing it to produce more and making 1989's official growth rate appear too low by comparison. The "official" data above are based on average daily output for each month.

Sources: See Table 2.

these trends, and in each case reported the onset of a new period to begin two to four months later than it actually had.

Continuing the analysis of Table 1, official data make it appear that the 1988–89 austerity program never had a very serious impact, when in fact output growth was flat by November 1988. Similarly, official data show negligible growth in the spring of 1990, when in fact output was recovering strongly after February (though most of the output increase was accumulating in inventories). Perhaps most important, these data for winter–spring 1988–89 are consistent with leadership indecision and disagreement about the austerity program. In any event, it should be clear from these examples that in order to study China's economic cycles in the 1980s, one must use seasonally adjusted month-to-month data rather than officially calculated growth rates.

Table 2 presents seasonally adjusted month-to-month industrial growth rates for ten years, from mid-1980 to mid-1990, and describes the many sharp variations in China's industrial economic performance in the 1980s. In general, there have been five obvious major industrial cycles in economic activity, with a number of more minor ups and downs in between. The five major industrial slumps were in the periods September 1980 to February 1981, January to September 1982, June to November 1985, November 1988 to February 1989, and July 1989 to February 1990. The last two slumps are often thought of as one long austerity program, but these data show that there was a significant recovery surge just at the time of the Tiananmen uprising.

Inflation and money growth trends, not shown here, correspond quite closely with these industrial cycles and became increasingly exaggerated in the latter 1980s. While inflation remained low for the first half of the 1980s, there was an inflationary surge in 1984–85 and then an extremely serious inflationary crisis in 1988. Similarly, while money growth fluctuated somewhat before 1984, beginning in that year large increases in loans and circulating cash alternated with strong cutbacks in the money supply. In most cases, the major shifts in industrial output lagged behind money supply changes by about a quarter-year, and the shifts in money supply became increasingly exaggerated, with the most extreme money supply increase coming in the first half of 1988.

Combining all these factors, it is apparent that economic cycles of expansion and contraction became increasingly important in China as reforms matured in the 1980s. Their periodicity, averaging just over two years, was shorter than the political cycles tied to National Communist Party congresses, which tend to meet every five years. What is more, the economic cycles can usually be identified with well-publicized policies to control inflation or inject liquidity into the economy. For example, the slump of 1980 corresponds to Deng Xiaoping's initial readjustment program to control the inflation and budget deficits associated with rural price reform, fighting in Vietnam, and Hua Guofeng's aborted Ten-Year Mini-Leap Forward. The cyclical shifts in 1981–83 were not as well publicized, but the 1984–85 expansion was the direct result of the introduction of China's urban reform program in October 1984 and the preparatory banking reforms earlier that year. The contraction in late 1985 was a highly visible program to control inflation and over-heated investment, although official statistics based on calculations over the previous year generally (and erroneously) show the slowdown to have occurred in early 1986. The rapid recovery in early 1986 was the direct result of the state banking system's response to complaints from state enterprises of serious cash shortages, which financial data show resulted in a direct infusion of new money into enterprise accounts.

Also in 1986 financial reforms moved from an experimental stage to implementation throughout much of the country, enabling a variety of new and less-closely supervised financial institutions to make loans and collect deposits, often in cooperation with provincial and county officials. The subsequent growth surge triggered official attempts to curb overheated investment. The results of these efforts can be seen in the slower growth rates both at the beginning and at the end of 1987.

The mild downturn at the end of 1987 is particularly interesting, because it represented an effort to limit money growth for all of 1987–88, an effort that failed spectacularly as China's 1988 money supply grew at record rates and brought such high inflation that panic buying, hoarding, and runs on state banks created the worst financial crisis in the history of the PRC. This crisis, in turn, prompted the contraction visible in the data for late 1988 and early 1989, a well-publicized austerity program that included the introduction of high interest rates and the cancelation or postponement of most state construction programs. The resulting unemployment among construction workers became so serious by March 1989, however, that growth was resumed in March–May 1989, despite public policy statements that austerity would continue. The June military crackdown suppressing demonstrations also marked a renewed austerity program that extended into 1990; the program finally succeeded in reducing inflation to negligible levels.

The most important lesson in these data is China's inability to avoid economic cycles, in large part because of its ineffective macroeconomic policy tools. China's markets and financial systems are too new and unpredictable to allow fine tuning of investment and price trends. This lesson became clearer when financial reforms in 1986–87 decentralized the economic system even further, forcing the government to accelerate its reactions to unfavorable economic shifts. One of the sources of policy instability was the absence of fundamental price reform. Successful price reforms themselves, however, must be a result and not a cause of successful reforms in other dimensions, especially in the tax system, the structure of urban labor, the productivity of urban state workers, and the pace and productivity of urban state investment.

III. Urban Productivity: Fundamental Price Reform Impediment

In many critical ways, price reform is the essential ingredient in most other economic reforms. Without price reforms, managers and bankers cannot base decisions on profitability and meet social needs at the same time. Without price reform, bankruptcy and labor reallocation may easily do more damage than good; and liberalized exports and imports could generate warped trade patterns

Table 2
Chinese Industry
Seasonally Adjusted Monthly Growth Rates, 1980-1990
(Percent Month-to-Month Growth on an Annual Basis)

1980	Jun	14.7	1983	Oct	19.0	1987	Feb	-3.9
	Jul	18.2		Nov	17.0		Mar	11.3
	Aug	5.0		Dec	-16.3		Apr	17.1
	Sep	-8.7	1984	Jan	6.0		May	17.6
	Oct	-17.7		Feb	21.8		Jun	29.3
	Nov	2.6		Mar	24.8		Jul	19.0
	Dec	-7.1		Apr	10.3		Aug	11.6
1981	Jan	-7.1		May	14.1		Sep	12.1
	Feb	-5.9		Jun	5.3		Oct	17.0
	Mar	12.1		Jul	26.8		Nov	7.5
	Apr	2.3		Aug	24.3		Dec	12.1
	May	12.0		Sep	29.3	1988	Jan	20.6
	Jun	11.2		Oct	23.3		Feb	12.7
	Jul	14.4		Nov	28.1		Mar	9.3
	Aug	19.2		Dec	8.8		Apr	27.8
	Sep	15.9	1985	Jan	50.5		May	28.6
	Oct	22.9		Feb	62.9		Jun	36.6
	Nov	24.2		Mar	14.9		Jul	6.8
	Dec	18.4		Apr	13.7		Aug	19.1
1982	Jan	-5.9		May	5.6		Sep	30.7
	Feb	9.7		Jun	-1.2		Oct	31.8
	Mar	6.3		Jul	10.2		Nov	-1.2
	Apr	-7.4		Aug	-2.6		Dec	5.5
	May	-6.7		Sep	-16.9	1989	Jan	-31.6
	Jun	-5.1		Oct	-14.4		Feb	-5.8
	Jul	7.2		Nov	-6.5		Mar	23.1
	Aug	1.4		Dec	14.4		Apr	44.2
	Sep	3.6	1986	Jan	26.3		May	14.6
	Oct	11.4		Feb	10.9		Jun	7.8
	Nov	21.5		Mar	20.4		Jul	-2.3
	Dec	50.8		Apr	10.7		Aug	-2.9
1983	Jan	13.1		May	12.9		Sep	-13.7
	Feb	-2.3		Jun	15.7		Oct	-15.7
	Mar	-0.5		Jul	12.0		Nov	-5.4
	Apr	8.5		Aug	15.7		Dec	29.7
	May	12.7		Sep	16.1	1990	Jan	-27.4
	Jun	9.5		Oct	25.4		Feb	-29.0
	Jul	9.0		Nov	22.7		Mar	25.4
	Aug	10.5		Dec	23.0		Apr	60.0
	Sep	21.6	1987	Jan	8.6		May	48.9
							Jun	29.6
							Jul	-8.4

Note: Underlying data are monthly flows adjusted for seasonal variation and number of days per month. The growth measure used is calculated as the average monthly increase in one month's output over the average output for the three preceding months. Hence, strictly speaking, the measure is a bi-monthly growth rate. This measure reduces the double variation which occurs with straight month-to-month growth rates, under which one month's sharp variation affects growth rates for both preceding and following months. For a further explanation of seasonal adjustments, see Table 1 and the text.
Sources: Rock Creek Research, Inc. Data Banks. Calculated from data in PRC State Statistical Bureau Monthly Statistical Bulletin, various issues and Economic Information & Agency China Economic News, various issues.

harmful to China's long-term growth. But in China, price reform itself is delayed by the government's inability to finance the large urban subsidies that successful price reforms would require. This is because for decades those urban subsidies have been financed by the gap or "scissors" between low prices for rural goods and high prices for urban manufactures. By correcting this gap, price reforms cut off revenues for urban projects and incomes.

Casual analysis of delays in China's price reform assumes that China's leaders do not understand the importance of price reform and resist it because of an ideological preference for central planning. But there is evidence that this is not the case. On numerous occasions in the 1980s, Chinese policies introduced price reform, in sectors as important and diverse as foods, construction materials, and energy. In virtually every case the reforms were slowed or stopped because the new cost structure made it impossible to finance urban standards of living and urban investment. The subsidies and costs overwhelmed the combined financial capacities of the state budget and state banking system.

Most fundamentally, price reforms threatened the subsidized urban standard of living enjoyed by the 20 percent of China's population legally registered to live in cities as state and collective employees. Put in the simplest terms, if production and consumption are valued at reasonable prices, China's privileged urban population has not earned its own keep. Over the decades, urban state enterprises had added workers but had not made corresponding increases in output and quality of product. Similarly, by the end of the 1970s, the extra output generated by an additional Chinese yuan of investment had fallen to all-time historical lows.

The comparison of rural and urban standards of living is complicated by the various Chinese definitions of who is rural and who is urban. Traditionally, registered urban residents enjoyed special privileges and subsidies. By the end of the 1980s, official statistics reported that 52 percent of China's population lived in cities and towns—a misleading figure implying that the urban population increased by over 350 million in less than 8 years. (See Banister's chapter in this volume). In fact, only 20 percent of the total population was registered by the Public Security Ministry as being "nonagricultural," a designation left over from the early Maoist period, when China's population was formally divided into two groups, those who lived on rural communes and those who lived in cities. Even though, by mid-1990, a large portion of the so-called "agricultural" population is employed in nonfarm rural and urban industries and services, the official "agricultural" and "nonagricultural" distinction still determines which households receive state subsidies for food, fuel, housing, health care, and education, in addition to being guaranteed jobs for life in state enterprises and urban collectives.

Under the Maoist price system, the privileged "nonagricultural" urban standard of living was financed by legislating low prices for rural products and high prices for urban industrial output. Although much of the profit generated in this way was used to finance state investments, a significant portion also went to subsidizing the standard of living of urban residents, including students, so that at least in its cities, China could point to the success of socialism in providing a better life for workers. This "price scissors" rural revenue transfer was thus formalized under Mao. Strict controls on rural-urban migration also ensured that rural-urban income differentials did not result in the growth of shanty towns and urban slums so common in other parts of the world. In this way, although the Maoist price system may not have seemed "rational" or market-determined, it was originally based on a logical scheme to raise funds for investment in rapid industrialization. Its serious drawback was that, over time, the lack of competition and individual incentives in both rural and urban areas allowed productivity in both sectors to stagnate and in some cases decline.

Implementing fundamental price reform under these circumstances leaves China with only three policy alternatives. None of them is politically attractive. Either solution by itself is doomed to ultimate failure, but a combination of the three has a good chance of success. The first solution is to introduce price reform and then implement a direct tax on the rural economy equivalent to the loss in profits and revenues due to price reform. An explicit tax could replace all the financial transfers implicit in the old price system, but such a large tax would not only be extremely unpopular and difficult to collect, it would weaken incentives originally strengthened by the price reform and turn the government into an omnipresent and unpopular landlord. It is true that a direct and more effective national tax system is needed and would help solve the problem, but by itself it could not sufficiently support price reform.

The second policy alternative is to implement price reform but maintain urban subsidies by running state budget deficits and borrowing from an acquiescent banking system willing to postpone repayment obligations indefinitely. This alternative is the default if all else fails, and was in fact used by China in 1985 and 1988, but it leads to inflation, urban unrest, and ultimate erosion of whatever benefits had accrued from the original price reform. Just as for taxation, there is a role for slightly inflationary monetary policy, especially to maximize investment and job creation, but easy money by itself will fail.

The third alternative solution to the subsidy problem is to increase dramatically the productivity of the urban labor force and the productivity of large urban investments, while limiting growth of urban consumption levels. This third alternative attacks the heart of the problem, but is the most difficult politically, because it requires major disruptions to the accustomed urban standard of living. Raising urban productivity requires a restructuring of the urban labor force, job changes, layoffs, and significant investment in new jobs—preferably more labor-intensive jobs. But layoffs and more demanding jobs seem to contradict the promise of Chinese urban socialism, which, if anything, has been understood to mean job security.

The Tiananmen uprising of 1989 revealed the seriousness of the urban population's opposition to the impact of price reform. A quick examination of student demands and worker support for the demonstrations reveals that economic factors stimulated the uprising. The most substantive of the students' "Seven Demands" called for prosecution of corruption, better pay for intellectuals, and punishment of officials responsible for the 1988 inflationary crisis. These demands were complemented by worker efforts to form independent labor unions. In contrast, noneconomic demands for freedom, democracy, recognition of student patriotism, rehabilitation of Hu Yaobang, an end to press censorship, and redress for police brutality were ardent and sincere but were in a sense tactical demands that sought to enhance the political effectiveness of government opponents.

At the time of the 1989 Tiananmen uprising, many students and intellectuals feared—erroneously, it seems—that the austerity program begun in 1988 and reemphasized in early 1989 policy statements was really a cover for the reversal of reforms by conservative leaders. Even though a recovery in industrial output growth had begun by the start of student demonstrations in April, official data had not yet shown the trend (see Table 1). Furthermore, the 1988–89 austerity program had left hundreds of thousands of rural construction workers unemployed. In March and April of 1989 hundreds of thousands of these workers began moving to the cities to look for jobs. Their presence was an implicit threat to the security of jobs in state enterprises and urban collectives.

It is ironic that while students and workers were avowedly pro-reform, their demands for improved conditions ran counter to the inevitable short-term impact of reforms, especially price reforms. Corruption was an important issue because urban residents felt that just when they were being forced to sacrifice in the austerity program, officials were getting rich from selling state-quota goods on the higher-priced second-tier markets. Corruption thus symbolized urban citizen sacrifices during the austerity program. Complaints about inflation and low salaries for intellectuals were complaints about the eroding privileged urban standard of living. And yet, in order for price reform to work, there would have to be inflation; real urban incomes would probably have to fall temporarily; and job security would have to be compromised. The Tiananmen uprising of 1989 illustrates the ground swell of urban resentment brought on by the inevitable consequences of price reform.

The fundamental problem of price reform, then, is intimately related to the political, social, and even psychological dimensions of economic change. If China fails to introduce price reform in the 1990s its economy will shudder and stumble along under the heavy burden of police control over a rebellious nonstate economy. And yet, full implementation of price reform requires a strong and disciplined government hand to the throttle. There are deeply felt urban beliefs which hold that maintenance of a safe and comfortable urban way of life is the true test of China's commitment to socialism. The government's job in forcing unpopular changes can be made easier if their necessity and inevitablity can be made obvious to those most affected. To this end, China's economic cycles, rather than representing policy failure, can become a vehicle for policy success.

IV. USING ECONOMIC CYCLES TO IMPLEMENT ECONOMIC REFORMS

China's economic cycles consist of an expansion phase and a contraction phase—a boom and a bust. Each phase of the cycle can be used to promote parts of China's reform program that are incompatible with reforms more suited for another phase. In many dimensions, the difficulties or exaggerated problems associated with reforms in one phase can be adjusted or corrected in the next phase. But most important, the signs of trouble or difficulty in one phase can help convince the public and policymakers alike that additional reform steps are necessary, which are naturally associated with the succeeding phase of the cycle.

The clearest example of the use of cycles is also the most important for price reform. Price reform is by definition the adjustment of relative prices; it is promoted when some prices change but others do not. Because most prices are more easily raised than lowered, inflationary periods during which some prices go up much more than others is a natural mechanism for price reform. But price reform is also made easier when the labor force is adjusted to meet post-reform needs for higher labor productivity. Major reforms that shift prices closer to their market values leave inefficient state firms with low revenues and high labor costs. In the sense that these labor costs need to be reduced, the layoffs and job changes usually associated with an industrial recession are also an essential part of price reform. But inflation and layoffs are difficult to implement together. Instead, inflationary price adjustments have best occurred in the expansionary phase of China's economic cycle, while layoffs and job changes are more easily enforced during an economic downturn, when workers are aware of economy-wide bankruptcies and revenue shortfalls. Just such cyclical forces have been very effective throughout muct of the 1980s in China's nonstate sectors, especially for village and township industry.

Cyclical implementation can benefit other reforms as well. In the case of financial reforms, new bank and credit facilities can expand and experiment during a cyclical expansion, while in a period of credit discipline, government supervision and macroeconomic control can improve. For foreign trade, periods of credit expansion facilitate experiments in decentralized management of imports and foreign exchange, while during the cycle's contraction phase the government can strengthen indirect controls and correct any damage to its international balance of payments. Finally, cyclical liberalization of the economy also allows for the periodic correction of social consequences to reform which appear to undermine socialist principles and Communist Party authority. Overall, reforms in 1990 have a serious public relations problem, and the judicious use of economic cycles, while avoiding extremes of inflation or unemployment, promise one of the best mechanisms for advancing fundamental system change.

The rhythm of economic cycles also takes advantage of the natural element of forgetfulness on the part of both the urban population and policy-makers. At the height of an inflationary expansion phase, popular opinion is quick to believe that slower economic growth and even significant unemployment are an acceptable burden to bear if only inflation can be controlled. In the depths of the downturn phase, on the other hand, it often seems to many that some resurgence of inflation is not too high a price to pay if only investment and employment growth could pick up. Rational anticipation of such policy swings in a poor economy like China's has insignificant influence on their economic consequences. In fact, just such a dynamic of forgetfulness was common in China in the latter 1980s. In the inflationary periods of 1985 and 1988, the clear priority was to control rapid price rises, even if austerity meant higher employment and cash flow problems. In 1986 and early 1990, however, the seriousness of the asuterity recession encouraged the popular opinion that economic expansion and further price reform would be worth some inflationary risk.

Economic cycles cannot of course solve all the problems of economic reform. The evolution of legal systems, commercial institutions, social security programs, unemployment insurance, management skills, and regulatory sophistication require a slow and gradual process of training, experimentation, and legislative initiative. These take time. But none of them can successfully evolve without the concurrent introduction of price reform, and price reform often comes quickly. Economic cycles not only ease the social impact of price and labor reform, they also draw out the process of price and labor reform, allowing other slower reforms to mature.

Most important, an awareness of economic cycles and of their usefulness for reforms can help avoid the danger of serious instability. If policymakers continue to stimulate the economy when an expansionary phase is already well along, the resulting inflation and overheated investment will provoke hoarding, weaken financial institutions, and encourage conservative opposition to the entire reform program. Conversely, if the austerity program in a cycle's contraction phase is further tightened when inflation is already starting to come down, the resulting unemployment, liquidity crises, and slow wage growth will exaggerate labor dissatisfation, delay new hires, and threaten social unrest. Furthermore, the proper timing of counter-cyclical policy shifts first requires an adequate understanding of what is happening to the economy. Policymakers need seasonally adjusted month-to-month data to track the cycle accurately, followed by early intervention to ensure that cyclical extremes do not reach damaging proportoins. China's economic cycles will not disappear in the 1990s, but how China uses them to complement the needs of price reforms and other economic initiatives will largely determine the nature of China's economy at the end of the century.

V. Alternatives for China's Economic Future

China's economic future faces two realistic economic alternatives: one with successful price reforms and one without. In any event, while there is virtually no possibility that China will return to a system like the centrally planned economy of the Maoist era, large state enterprises and investment programs will remain prominent parts of China's economy well into the next century, even as markets expand and dominate numerous sectors. Markets and market forces will coexist with state enterprises, and state market forces will coexist with state enterprises and state investment projects, but the degree to which they will support one another will depend on price reform. If fundamental price reform is introduced early in the 1990s, then by the year 2000 China's state sector will become successfully integrated into the rest of the national economy. In that case, real GNP growth for most of the decade could average as high as 7–9 percent a year. If, however, price reform continues to stall and the productivity of urban state enterprises stagnates, then the privileged urban population and priority state projects will continue to depend on large state subsidies. The government's efforts to finance those subsidies will lead to large budget deficits, inflation, growth surplus, and increasingly unpopular taxes on farms and nonstate enterprises, with growing corruption throughout the country. Cadres at all levels will come under pressure in their jobs to deliver rural and township revenues to the state and to police nonstate economic activity so it does not compete directly with the state sector. These cadres increasingly will be exposed to temptations for bribery and favoritism. Under these conditions, inflation in the 1990s will be high and seemingly insoluble. Economic growth will be throttled by repetitive austerity campaigns and average no more than 4 to 6 percent.

Whichever course China takes, economic cycles will be important for understanding the overall trend. Both kinds of cycles—political and economic—will be relevant. For example, the next Communist Party congress, probably sometime late in 1992, will be important for setting the pace of reforms and economic growth in 1993–95. What is more, to the degree that reformers in the government try to influence the outcome of the Congress in a pro-reform way, they will do their best to suppress unwanted side effects of reforms in 1991–92.

In the 1991–1992 period before the 1992 Party Congress, China's pro-reform leaders should make every effort to limit inflation, eliminate budget deficits, run a foreign trade surplus, reduce crime, and maximize grain output. These are sensitive economic issues for the swing factions of the Communist Party congress, which will determine the makeup of the new Central Committee. Just such political preparations were observed in 1987. The anti-bourgeois liberalization campaign that year saved economic reforms. Its severity placated worried delegates and reassured them that reforms did not threaten party authority or social stability. To casual observers of conservative steps in 1992, therefore, it might appear that China's economic reforms are suffering a setback, but when seen in the context of the upcoming Party Congress, such conservative policies can be interpreted as part of the preparation for fundamental reforms later in the decade.

Shorter-term econmic cycles will also be important in the 1990s, as policymakers react to economic events that are not completely in their control. Inflationary expansions will prompt austerity programs to cut back on excess demand. Conversely, periods of credit contraction, unemployment, and state enterprise cash flow problems will prompt infusions of new credit and stimulate lower interest rates and revitalization of state investment projects. The important issue is whether these shorter-term economic cycles will be copled with state-sector layoffs and new investments to raise labor productivity. If austerity programs force unemployment in the state sector and are then followed with new investment to absorb the redundant labor, the burden of subsidies will gradually decline and market forces will play an ever larger role in the nationwide economy. But if austerity policies aimed at controlling inflation also continue to guarantee all state jobs, then subsidies will grow, become increasingly difficult to finance, and lead China's econmy into an era of bitter rivalry between a protected state enterprise sector and a relatively independent but constricted nonstate economy based in smaller cities, town and rural areas.

INFLATION IN CHINA: PATTERNS, CAUSES AND CURES

By Barry Naughton [*]

CONTENTS

China underwent an inflationary crisis during 1988–89 that shook the foundations of its political and economic system. Inflation jeopardized the economic reform process and fueled popular discontent, thereby contributing to the political crisis that culminated at Tiananmen Square on June 4, 1989. High inflation occurred in spite of repeated expressions by the Chinese leadership of their determination to hold inflation rates below 10%, and in spite of traumatic historical experience with inflation. China had experienced hyperinflation in the 1940s, and two years of serious inflation in the early 1960s, following the collapse of the Great Leap Forward. The prolonged price stability China then experienced between the mid-1960s and 1978 seemed to demonstrate a profound aversion to inflation on the part of policymakers, reinforced by the fact that most of the urban population lived on fixed incomes diffi-

* Graduate School of International Relations and Pacific Studies, University of California, San Diego.

cult to adjust in the face of inflation. These factors failed to prevent the collapse of macroeconomic discipline during the late 1980s.

This article first reviews the patterns of inflation in China over the past ten years. Stressing that prices have changed at different rates in different sectors, consumer prices and prices of industrial and investment goods are treated separately. Economic consequences of the inflation in different sectors are briefly described. A discussion of the causes of inflation follows. It is stressed that some price increases are needed to accommodate price rationalization; but that the economy has also been plagued with continuing problems of weak and inconsistent monetary policy. A few measures that would lead to modest improvement in China's anti-inflation effort conclude the paper.

I. Patterns of Inflation and Their Measurement

China has many different inflation rates. Chinese markets are segmented, and different kinds and degrees of control are exerted over prices and purchases in different parts of the economy. Moreover, the legacy of forty years of government price controls affects different sectors in markedly different ways. As a result, prices of different kinds of commodities have changed at very different rates over the past ten years. The Chinese environment can be contrasted with the situation in market economies where markets are linked together by the ability of producers and consumers to substitute freely between different goods according to relative prices, and where markets can generally be presumed to be in equilibrium. Even in full market economies, prices of different goods can change at different rates, as the experience with energy prices in the 1970s and 1980s testifies. But it remains meaningful to speak of a basic inflation rate, which is approximately equal to the rate of increase in wages minus the increase in labor productivity.

In China, it is doubtful whether it is possible to speak meaningfully of a single rate of inflation. Price trends for urban and rural consumer goods, industrial products, and building services have all diverged sharply at different periods. As economic reform has progressed, segmentation between different sectors of the economy has decreased, and there may be a tendency for inflation rates in some sectors to converge. Until now, though, different sectors have displayed different inflation rates not simply because of differential changes in productivity and wages, but also because of changing relations between sectors in the national economy. Finally, Chinese price data are of uneven quality; some areas are well served, but information is quite inadequate in others.

However, it is possible to make some meaningful generalizations about inflation in China. There have been two clear periods since 1978. From 1978 through the end of 1984, overall inflation was modest. From 1985 through 1988, inflation was sharply higher, regardless of which sector or indicator we examine. During the first period, in spite of the overall low rate of inflation, prices of nonstaple food, mining products, and construction grew at moderately rapid rates, in the range of 5 to 10% annually. Prices of manufactured consumer goods were stable or declined. Evidence is much weaker for prices of industrial materials and machinery, but they seem to have grown at intermediate rates, around 3–5% annually. There was therefore some realignment of prices, and real incomes grew rapidly given moderate inflation overall. During the second period, inflation accelerated across the board. Driven at first, during 1985, by increasing food prices, by the end of the period, in 1988, the price of everything was increasing rapidly. Changes in relative prices were swamped by the overall rise in the price level. Rapid inflation eroded nominal increases in income, and brought real income gains for the entire 1985–89 period virtually to zero.

II. Consumer Goods

Consumer price inflation was moderate through 1984, notwithstanding a brief spurt of prices during 1979–80. Since 1985, inflation has been consistently high, and it accelerated sharply during 1988. In the final quarter of 1988, government policy shifted to emphasize halting inflation, and inflation has in fact been brought down sharply, marking the end of the second period. Annual rates of increase of several important consumer price indexes are shown in Table 1. The urban consumer price index (CPI) is covered first, and the relationship between this and other measures of inflation is discussed later.

Table 1: Increase in Major Consumer Price Indexes

Annual Percentage Increase

	Urban CPI	Retail	Nonstaple Food	Farmers Market
1978	0.7	0.7	2.2	-6.6
1979	1.9	2.0	3.5	-5.1
1980	7.5	6.0	14.1	2.0
1981	2.5	2.4	3.2	5.8
1982	2.0	1.9	-0.2	3.3
1983	2.0	1.5	4.6	4.2
1984	2.7	2.8	6.0	-0.4
1985	11.9	8.8	23.0	17.2
1986	7.0	6.0	8.3	8.1
1987	8.8	7.3	14.9	16.3
1988	20.7	18.5	31.1	31.9
1989	16.3	17.8	13.8	10.8
Jan–June 90	1.5	3.0	0.2	-5.5

The most important part of consumer price inflation has been the increasing cost of food. Urban food grains are subsidized and supplied by the government at a strictly controlled price, but the cost of other food items has skyrocketed. The most important of these "nonstaple" foods are vegetables, poultry, eggs, and meat. Over the entire 1978–1989 period, the price of nonstaple food items more than tripled, driving a doubling of the overall urban price level. Food prices grew rapidly during both post–1978 periods. Between 1978 and 1984, the urban CPI increased by a cumulative 20%, while urban nonstaple food prices increased by 35%. From 1984 through 1989 inflation accelerated, but the relationship between increases in the overall price level and in food prices stayed roughly constant. The 1989 urban CPI was 83% higher than that in 1984, but urban nonstaple food prices were 128% higher. Only in late 1989-early 1990 did food prices fall below overall inflation due to the drastic deflationary policies that cut into real household income.

Figure 1 shows that there have been three bursts of inflation in the past ten years, and each has been marked by a rapid growth in nonstaple food prices. In 1979–80, 1985, and 1988, large increases in nonstaple food prices paced increases in the overall price level. During the entire period, a steadily increasing proportion of nonstaple foods has been provided through the free market. As a result, increases in nonstaple food prices can be decomposed into two elements: (1) increases in the price charged by state commercial outlets, and (2) an increase in the proportion purchased at higher priced free markets. During each of the bursts of food inflation, the government increased the price of food at state commercial outlets, and simultaneously compensated state employees by increasing their wages. In 1979 and 1985, those wage increases permitted most urban employees to stay ahead of inflation, but in 1988, modest wage adjustments were soon swamped by accelerating inflation.

Table 1 shows the increase in average nonstaple food prices for urban residents (Column 3) and the change in prices in urban farmers' markets (Column 4). The farmers' market price index is usually translated into English as the "market price index," but this is misleading. The index covers only goods sold by farmers, and in urban areas ninety-five percent of these are food products. The index thus covers only one segment, although an important one, of consumption goods. From Table 1, it can be seen that farmers' market prices increased more slowly than overall nonstaple food prices through 1985, actually declining in 1978 and 1979. Thus the increase in state prices gradually decreased the gap between state and market prices. According to official Chinese figures, market prices were 69% above state prices in 1978, but only 28% higher in 1985. Since 1986, state prices have been close to farmers' market prices, particularly when quality differentials are taken into account. Moreover, the farmers' market and overall nonstaple food prices now move closely together, reflecting the fact that urban residents are increasingly dependent on the farmers' market for their nonstaple food purchases.

The increase in the cost of food is particularly important, because Chinese households spend an exceptionally large proportion

FIGURE 1. URBAN CONSUMER PRICES, CPI AND NONSTAPLE FOODS, 1978 TO FIRST HALF OF 1990.

Increase from Previous Year

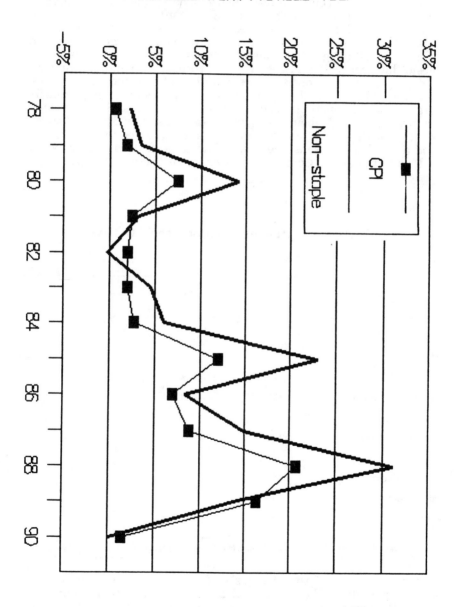

of their income on food. More than half of urban household expenditures are for food, and nonstaple food items account for more than 30% of total outlays (see Table 2). There are two reasons for the large weight of food in total consumption spending. First, because China is a low income country, households spend a larger proportion of income on food than in a rich country (the relationship economists call Engel's law). Second, because the prices of many other items are controlled at a very low level, a larger proportion of money outlays goes to nonstaple foods. The most obvious examples of low, controlled prices are rent, transportation, medical care, and staple grains. Control of rent and public service prices reinforces Engel's law, and gives Chinese consumers an extraordinarily large share of nonstaple food in household budgets. Since consumers are concerned about the prices of things they actually spend money on, this large budget share makes increases in the price of food a particularly sensitive issue. (The same factors were at work in Poland under the Communist government there).

Table 2: Structure of Urban Household Outlays

Unit: Percent

	1982	1988
Food	58.7	51.4
Of Which:		
(Staple Grain)	(12.9)	(6.9)
(Non-Staple Foods)	(32.1)	(31.4)
of which: [Fresh Vegetables]	[6.2]	[6.4]
of which: [Pork]	[8.4]	[7.6]
Clothing	14.4	13.9
Durable Goods	6.4	12.9
Other Goods	8.4	7.4
Rent, Utilities, Fuel & Transport	5.9	4.0

Sources: 1989 TJNJ, pp. 727, 728, 713; Urban Household Survey.

A brief review of the changes in the structure of urban household expenditures between 1982 and 1988 can tell a great deal about the impact of inflation and also clarify the relationship between different consumer price indices. The major changes, displayed in Table 2, were the decline in the share of staple grain, the big increase in the share of consumer durables, and the continuing moderate decline in the share of rent and public utilities. The share of consumer durables is increasing because urban households are buying many more consumer durables, which have had stable or declining prices except during the panic buying of 1988. The share of staple grain and public utilities, on the other hand, is declining because prices of these items (and quantity available) remain tightly controlled by the government, while income is rising.

Nonstaple foods have a stable share, but this stability reflects the offsetting effects of two different factors. Increasing incomes have tended to raise demand for food products, but non-staple foods prices have increased more rapidly that other items, causing consumers to substitute into other goods. While urban consumers spend the same proportion of their rising incomes on vegetables and pork, they are not actually consuming any more of these items. Indeed, the household surveys actually indicate that per capita consumption of vegetables and pork declined slightly between 1982 and 1988. By contrast, consumers are spending the same share of their incomes on clothing and other goods, but the prices of these items have grown relatively slowly, and consumers are consuming more. Overall, urban residents are better off because they have more durable goods, more clothing and miscellaneous goods, and more housing. However, inflation has prevented them from upgrading their diets in the way they would have preferred.

In the urban consumer price index, changes in the price of individual goods are weighted according to the actual importance of those goods in urban household outlays. Those weights are determined from annual household surveys, and the index can be checked for logical consistency: the urban consumer price index is quite reliable. The other main price index, the overall index of retail prices (Column 2 of Table 1), is less useful, because the different components are weighted according to their importance in total retail sales, rather than their importance in household outlays. Rural residents purchase very little nonstaple food—they grow about one-half of the food they consume—so the retail price index gives less importance to food prices, the most rapidly growing component of prices. Indeed, the State Statistical Bureau doesn't even bother to collect prices of vegetables sold in rural areas. In most years the retail price index grows more slowly than the urban consumer price index, and it cannot be used to deflate household income, either for urban or rural households. The urban consumer price index is therefore the best index of the rate of inflation faced by Chinese households. Moreover, its overall rate of increase is quite consistent with the dramatic increase in price of certain of its components, such as fresh vegetables.

The most important consequence of consumer price inflation is the impact on real household income. The rapid inflation in 1988–89 caused a significant reduction in real household income for the first time since the beginning of reform in 1978. Table 3 shows changes in real urban wages and rural per capita incomes. Urban wages increased from 1978 through 1980, and then stagnated until 1983. They then increased by 33% between 1983 and 1986. After

1986, the real urban wage stagnated, then declined by about 5% in 1989. Real rural incomes cannot be calculated with the same degree of precision, because it is unclear how farm-grown food is treated in Chinese statistics. However, we can deflate nominal rural income by the retail price index for consumer goods sold in rural areas through 1987, and the rural consumer price index after 1988, and we derive the real income series in Table 3. Rural incomes grew steadily and rapidly from 1978 through 1985. The calculation may overstate the rate of increase, but the growth of income is so large that more accurate figures would undoubtedly leave substantial real growth. After 1985, however, rapid rural income growth ceased, and in 1989, real incomes declined 9% from the previous year. The acceleration of inflation through 1988–89 clearly halted the growth of real incomes that had marked the reform era generally, and eroded the income gains made by city-dwellers in 1985–86.

TABLE 3. Trends in Real Incomes, 1985 = 100

	Rural per capita income	Average urban wage
1978	41	72
1979	49	77
1980	55	81
1981	62	80
1982	74	81
1983	85	83
1984	96	95
1985	100	100
1986	100	108
1987	103	109
1988	104	108
1989	95	103

If only food prices were increasing, then all of the inflation would be the result of changes in relative prices. Since it is generally recognized that the relative price of food must be raised, this would indicate that the inflation, although painful, was serving a useful economic purpose. Table 4 shows the increase in nonstaple food prices alongside the increase in price of the component of consumer prices with the lowest inflation rate (durables or daily-use items). It can be seen that through 1986, prices were generally stable for the items with the minimum inflation rate. Indeed, through 1984, prices of these items were actually declining slightly. This indicates that through 1986, nearly all the inflation experienced was an inescapable cost of the necessary realignment of relative prices. Indeed, throughout this early period, the Chinese government devoted substantial effort to matching price increases with offsetting price reductions. This effort succeeded in maintaining a low inflation rate, but at the cost of an overall slow pace of economic change. Even the simplest realignment of prices strained Chinese administrative capabilities and required elaborate political compromises before adoption.

From 1987, the relative price stability of non-food items began to change. In 1988–89, even the slowest growing component of the consumer price index increased by 13–14%. This can be taken as a

Table 4: Change in Relative Prices

	Annual Percentage Change	
	Increase in Price of Slowest Growing CPI Component	Increase in Nonstaple Food Prices
1978	0.0	2.2
1979	-0.6	3.5
1980	-4.5	14.1
1981	-2.0	3.2
1982	-2.9	-0.2
1983	-2.2	4.6
1984	-0.1	6.0
1985	1.2	23.0
1986	0.7	8.3
1987	3.2	14.9
1988	12.9	31.1
1989	14.3	13.8

Source: 1989 TJNJ, p. 691, 1990 TJZY, p. 38.

rough measure of the amount of "excess inflation" during those years. This is the amount of inflation that did not contribute anything to realignment of relative prices. The same rationalization of prices could in theory have occurred with an overall inflation rate that was thirteen or fourteen percentage points lower.

The increasing price of food in relation to manufactured goods such as textiles and consumer durables has significantly altered Chinese price relationships, bringing them more in line with world prices, and reducing the degree of discrimination against agriculture. At the same time, however, the overall price level has risen while the prices of staple grains, housing, and social services have remained almost constant. Yet all of these had historically been controlled at extremely low levels, and they needed to be increased relative to other prices. Thus, while there has been some price "reform" in the area of nonstaple foods, the reverse has occurred in relation to these other goods, and price relations that were already distorted have become even more distorted.

The foregoing discussion helps to show how different the inflationary experience of 1988–89 was from the rest of the reform period. The crisis of 1988 was really an unprecedented collapse of macroeconomic stability. (For a detailed account, see Naughton,

1989). The unique characteristics of the 1988 episode emerge even more clearly when we examine monthly inflation rates. In order to do this, Chinese monthly price data must be converted into an internationally comparable form. Chinese publications always compare the price level in a given month with the price level in the same month one year previously. By contrast, in the United States, the price level in a given month is compared with the previous month, and the change is then seasonally adjusted and expressed as an annual rate. The Chinese inflation figure is thus actually the sum of twelve successive month to month increases, and the most recent monthly increase is averaged in with the eleven previous ones to get the annual rate. The U.S. index is extremely sensitive to changes in a given month, while the Chinese index, as published, smooths over individual monthly changes and seems to present a picture of very gradual rise and fall in the consumer price index. Figure Two shows graphically both the official Chinese consumer price index and a recalculation based on those figures that shows monthly changes. (The monthly changes have been slightly smoothed by computing moving averages over three months, in order to minimize the effect of errors in the recalculation procedure.) This conversion allows the characteristics of the 1988–89 experience to stand out clearly.

China experienced a burst of hyperinflation in the summer of 1988. Consumer price inflation was gradually accelerating during the first part of 1988, and prices in the farmers' markets—the least controlled sector of the economy—had been accelerating since 1987. In the spring of 1988, state prices for several nonstaple foods were also increased, and Deng Xiaoping announced that comprehensive price reform would be attempted soon. In the context of growing inflationary pressures, this announcement proved to be exceptionally ill timed. Inflationary expectations among the population were dramatically confirmed, with serious consequences. Individuals began to engage in speculative buying, purchasing whatever they could before prices increased, while enterprises abandoned whatever price restraint they had been exercising in order to position themselves for the coming price reform. As a result, prices exploded during the summer of 1988. For three months, prices were increasing at more than a 50% annual rate, the traditional definition of hyperinflation.

This was an economic crisis that compelled a radical response. In September 1988, policy shifted dramatically to stress fighting inflation. Renewed subsidies and price controls were directed at the most volatile component of consumer prices, vegetables and meat. Controls on investment and enterprise outlays were enacted, and strict quotas on bank lending put in place. These measures quickly ended the hyperinflationary episode, bringing the monthly inflation rate down to approximately its pre-crisis levels. Still, persistent inflation in the 20% range continued until June 1989. After June, contractionary policies were intensified, and the measures begun nine months earlier began to take effect. During the second half of 1989, inflation was brought to a halt, and prices were actually falling for a brief period. As of June 1990, prices were beginning to rise again. Ironically, even though prices were now increasing, the official Chinese inflation index continued to decline and

FIGURE 2. NATIONAL CONSUMER PRICE INDEX, YEAR PREVIOUS AND MONTHLY INCREASE, SEPTEMBER 1986 TO JUNE 1990.

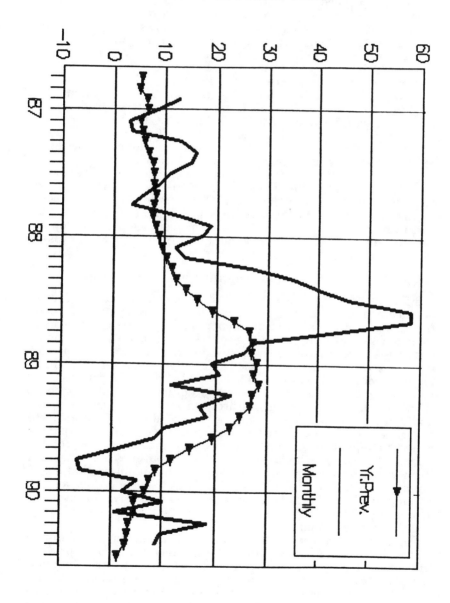

Inflation at Annual Rates

reached its lowest level in years. This was because it was now averaging in the affects of falling prices during late 1989.

One final element of China's consumer price inflation needs to be considered, and that is the regional dimension. Inflationary pressures have rippled out from Guangdong province, where prices have been pushed up by vigorous economic growth and the growing influence of international prices on Guangdong's increasingly open economy. Guangdong's consumer price increase was by far the highest in China with a cumulative increase over the 1978–89 period of 286%. However, the impact was felt beyond provincial borders, and prices increased more than 240% in a ring of provinces around Guangdong, including Hunan, Guangxi, Fujian, and Zhejiang. The impact was also felt Guizhou and Sichuan, where prices increased by 227–230%. These were the only provinces where prices increased at a rate more than five percentage points above the national average (219%). Besides the direct impact of the booming Guangdong economy, higher inflation in these provinces may also be associated with a more progressive attitude toward reform which has resulted in fewer efforts by provincial governments to control prices. The North China plain experienced below average inflation: with the exception of Beijing, inflation in all the north China provinces ran at least five percentage points below the national average. The lowest cumulative inflation, 191%, was recorded in Tianjin.

III. Producers Goods and the Cost of Investment

Inflation has also affected the cost of investment and industrial producers goods. However, while we can be reasonably confident of the accuracy of the urban consumer price index, there is no comparable measure of inflation in the sphere of producers goods. The situation is extremely complex: most industrial producers' goods have two prices, a lower state-set price and a higher market price. Information about the proportion of goods sold at differing prices is fragmentary and difficult to interpret. Additional complexity comes from the fact that many goods are sold at prices in-between plan and market prices, either because of informal controls on ex-factory prices, or because factories exchange lower priced output for access to inputs at similar concessionary prices. In spite of this complexity, it is possible to sketch the main outlines of change. But because methodologies used to compute the numbers that follow are not known, it is difficult to judge the reliability of indexes, and no individual numbers should be taken too seriously. However, the results that follow represent the best efforts of Chinese economists, and the results are plausible.

First, there has been substantial upward adjustment of in-plan prices. Table 5 shows the annual rates of increase in plan prices of the main categories of industrial products over two fairly long periods. The structure of industrial prices bears some similarity to that of consumption goods, in that historically low prices of extractive products, such as coal, petroleum, mineral ores, and lumber, need to be raised relative to manufactured goods. Some realignment of relative prices was carried out, particularly during the period through 1985. After 1985, the rate at which planned prices increased accelerated for all categories of goods, but the differential between rates of increase shrank. Through 1985 prices of extractive materials were increasing annually 4.7% faster than manufactured goods, but this differential shrank to 2.8% in the latter period.

Table 5: Average Annual Increase in Planned Prices

	1978-85	1985-88
Extractive Industry	6.0	9.1
Materials Industry	4.2	7.4
Manufacturing	1.3	6.3

Source: Calculated from Zhang Zhuoyuan et al, p. 23, and Chen Fubao.

After 1985, the most important changes in industrial prices came because of the increasing importance of marketing outside the plan by enterprises. Formal price ceilings on outside-plan sales were removed in February 1985, and some market price data for individual commodities is available from that time. In general, market prices increased during 1985, and then leveled off for a couple of years. Market prices of some products, most notably coal, even declined somewhat between 1985 and 1986. However, wide differentials between plan and market prices remained. Typically, standardized producer goods, such as coal, cement, and ordinary steel products, sold at market prices that were about two to two and a half times plan prices.

The surge of inflationary pressures in 1988 had a severe impact on producer goods prices. Market prices had begun to increase by the beginning of 1988, and the pace of inflation accelerated through the year. General trends are summarized in Table 6. By the third quarter of 1988, a situation close to panic buying had emerged for certain commodities. Market prices of non-ferrous metals and light steel products doubled within a few months. Moreover, by the beginning of 1989, in-plan prices had also increased by 20% as producers increasingly passed on cost increases to their customers, even within the state plan. Inflation truly became a generalized problem in the Chinese economy during 1988.

The most obvious consequence of inflation of producer goods has been a steady increase in the cost of investment. Unfortunately, the Chinese do not calculate an investment goods price deflator. However, two comparisons can provide a general indication of the increase in the price of investment goods. The first is the index of construction costs, which is given in Table 7. The first index covers state-run construction companies, which only perform about one-third of the total construction work. The second index covers all

148

Table 6: Producer Goods Inflation

Unit: Percent Increase from Year Previous

	Within-Plan	Outside-Plan	Average
1987Q2	8.0	15.5	8.8
1988Q1	6.5	12.7	10.4
1988Q2	10.4	18.0	15.5
1988Q3	15.7	28.9	23.0
1988Q4	16.5	34.7	26.7
1989Q1	20.5	36.9	29.4
1989Q2	19.9	39.5	27.5

Sources use different methodologies that may not be completely comparable. 1987Q2 calculated from Li Lei et al; 1988Q1 through 1989Q2 from Xie and Ding.

completed construction, but it only gives the actual cost per square meter of new construction. Because it is not adjusted for quality improvements, it may overstate the degree of inflation. The two indexes are not closely correlated, especially in the early years, but both show construction costs increasing at more than 10% annually after 1985.

Construction prices are relatively difficult to control, particularly in China where much construction is performed by nonstate and rural construction teams. It is possible that prices of industrial machinery, and overall costs for large, state-sponsored projects, have been growing more slowly than overall construction costs. However, a careful study by the State Statistical Bureau of large state investment projects indicates that this is not the case. A comparison of all the large state investment projects completed during 1986–88 with those completed during 1976–80 found sustained cost increases over that period. In five sectors for which detailed comparisons were possible, average investment costs per unit of capacity in the later period were 253% of those in the earlier period, implying an average annual rate of increase of 11%. Undoubtedly this reflects a higher rate of increase during the latter part of the period. One important factor was the devaluation of the renminbi, which resulted in sharp increases in the price of imported machinery.

The rapid increase in the cost of investment implies that the real rate of growth of Chinese investment in the state-run economy has been relatively slow since the beginning of the reform period. State capital construction almost exactly tripled in nominal terms be-

===

Table 7: Increase in Construction Costs

	Annual Percentage Increase	
	State Owned Construction	Overall Cost Per Square Meter
1979	--	8.7
1980	--	8.8
1981	5.1	13.0
1982	2.9	5.8
1983	2.6	12.2
1984	5.8	13.3
1985	9.4	9.6
1986	10.0	12.7
1987	8.4	16.9
1988	13.8	11.5
1989	11.7	--

tween 1978 and 1988. If, however, it is true that average investment costs increased at an 11% annual rate during this period, that would imply that real state capital construction over the entire period grew at an annual rate of less than 1% per year, and total state investment (including decentralized "renovation and replacement") grew by only 4% per year. Overall investment grew faster, because collective and private investment grew at much faster rates, and it is in any case impossible to have confidence in the price deflator used. But this preliminary calculation does indicate that state investment has grown slowly, and may help explain the difficulty the government has had in completing priority investment projects.

IV. Causes of Inflation I: Changes in Relative Prices

Inflation is a monetary phenomenon, and an excessive increase in the money supply is a part of any inflationary episode. Usually, though, the money supply has been allowed to expand in order to accommodate pressures for increased prices created by increased costs in certain areas, or by an unresolved struggle between different social groups for shares of society's output. These factors are particularly important in a socialist economy undergoing economic reforms, for two reasons. First, the structure of relative prices that prevails before reform is typically highly distorted, so that liberalization of the economy creates large changes in prices and corresponding large pressure on costs of certain kinds of products. Second, these changes in relative prices have a big impact on the distribution of income between different social groups.

These two factors can both be easily linked to the characteristic of China's consumer price inflation. As described above, the most characteristic feature has been the more rapid increase in food prices relative to other consumer prices. Low food prices before reform are clearly related to one of the most fundamental characteristics of China's economy: by keeping food and other agricultural prices low, China's leaders kept wage and material costs low for industry. The high profits in industry that resulted from this policy were the primary source of government revenues, and were in turn channelled into the industrialization effort. Rural dwellers paid almost no direct taxes: instead they were taxed indirectly through the low prices paid for their output. Clearly, for China to move to a more market-oriented economy, food prices will have to rise relative to the price of industrial products. Moreover, this change in relative prices will tend to make farmers better off relative to urban dwellers, unless the government enacts other offsetting policies. Difficult political and economic issues are involved in these changes.

When we bring this perspective to bear on the choice of monetary policy, we can see that the government must attempt to resolve a very difficult question: To what extent should the money supply, and therefore the overall price level, be allowed to increase in order to accommodate the higher price of food? It is often accepted in market economies that prices are relatively inflexible downward. That is, although producers are willing to increase prices or maintain them unchanged, they are relatively unwilling to lower them. If this is strictly true, then relative prices can only be changed as part of an inflationary process: some prices will remain unchanged, while the now more costly item will increase in price, resulting in a higher price level overall. This dilemma faced Western policymakers during the 1970s oil crises: if the relative price of energy was to increase, would it be better to keep monetary policy unchanged, thus forcing some prices to decline (at the cost of a recession); or to allow oil prices to increase sharply while increasing demand enough to allow other goods to be sold at their original prices (at the cost of inflation)? Chinese prices are even less flexible downward than prices in a market economy, because government price fixing remains significant in many sectors of the economy. Therefore, presumably Chinese planners should accommodate at least a portion of the increased food prices, allowing the overall price level to rise.

In fact, Chinese policymakers have followed two very different policies on this issue. Until the third quarter of 1984, total credit (and therefore total money supply) grew at modest rates (See Table

8).[1] Extremely conservative about inflation, policy-makers during this period were unwilling to accommodate the gradual increase in agricultural prices. Instead, as shown in Table 4, from 1980 through 1983 they tried to make other prices downwardly flexible by administrative command. Unavoidable price increases in agricultural products were generally matched by price reductions of some industrial product, most obviously when the price of cotton fabrics was increased and the price of synthetic fabrics reduced at the same time. This policy kept the rate of inflation down, but the pace of change was simply too slow. Virtually every individual price change required the approval of the Premier. The magnitude of necessary changes was simply too great, and the political and administrative capabilities of the Chinese government too limited, to permit an adequate adjustment of prices with minimal inflation.

The rate of credit creation accelerated dramatically at the end of 1984 (See Table 8). Between the end of the third quarter in 1984 and the end of the third quarter in 1988, credit grew at well over 20% annually. Rapid growth of credit had the effect of fully accommodating food price increases and stimulating more rapid economic growth. From Table 4, it can be seen that a really dramatic realignment in the relative price of food occurred in 1985 through 1987. Moreover, GNP growth accelerated to over 10% annually. However, these results were purchased at substantial cost. Excess demand conditions were created throughout the economy, and repeated attempts to control them failed, as discussed below. As excess demand conditions spread through the economy, the new inflationary environment described above became established and erupted explosively during 1988. Policy shifted from being too conservative before 1984, to being too expansionary after 1984. A steady middle course would have been preferable.

Up to this point the focus of this paper has been on food prices to examine the tension between the needs of price realignments and the desire for price stability because it is in this area that the past experience in price changes has been most manifest. But note that, even within the sphere of consumer prices, food is not the only such item. Housing and fuel prices are important prices that have been maintained at excessively low levels, and staple grains have always been excluded from food price adjustments. Indeed, it is probable that most of the necessary adjustment of nonstaple food prices has already taken place. While there are still a range of subsidies on nonstaple foods (varying greatly from locality to locality) that need to be removed, these are relatively modest overall. However, there has been virtually no reform of housing, fuel, or grain prices, and we might expect changes here to take center stage in the future.

---

[1] The largest extension of credit comes annually during the fourth quarter, in order to finance agricultural procurement. Since this is the most important component of credit policy, and it has a lag effect throughout the entire economy, monetary policy decisions implemented during the fourth quarter of each year dominate economic conditions through most of the following year. Moreover, dramatic changes in monetary policy typically occur during the fourth quarter, rather than at the beginning of the next calendar year (this was true for the two most dramatic changes, in 1984 and 1988). Finally, year-end figures can be manipulated by varying credit procedures, particularly since the agricultural procurement is still under way at that time. For all these reasons, the most useful figures on monetary policy describe a fiscal year that begins on September 30 annually. Table 8 shows both this figure and the ordinary year-end figures.

Table 8: Growth of Total Credit

==

Percentage Increase over Year Previous

	YEAR-END	END THIRD QUARTER
Dec 1981	14.5	
Sept 1982		11.6
Dec 1982	10.4	
Sept 1983		12.6
Dec 1983	12.4	
Sept 1984		15.0
Dec 1984	28.8	
Sept 1985		31.5
Dec 1985	21.4	
Sept 1986		24.3
Dec 1986	26.8	
Sept 1987		26.3
Dec 1987	19.0	
Sept 1988		21.5
Dec 1988	16.8	
Sept 1989		11.4
Dec 1989	17.6	
Sept 1990		18.0

September 1990 is a preliminary estimate base on
August figures.

Perhaps more important, the process that has been largely completed with regard to nonstaple foods has barely begun in industry. Fuel and raw material product pricing is analogous to past agricultural pricing: the price has been kept low, facilitating collection of revenues in the manufacturing sector. Moreover, besides raw materials, there are a wide range of other cost factors that must gradually make their way into the cost structure of industrial products: these include higher interest rates, depreciation, and social security contributions. A similar policy decision must be made on how much of these increases to accommodate with higher prices, and how much to offset with reductions in prices elsewhere, or in reductions of government revenues. Indeed, a crucial part of price reform will be reform of the tax system, setting new "prices" for the provision of government services. Therefore, we must continue to expect cost pressures to influence the overall level of prices, and a zero inflation policy is not really a viable option.

V. CAUSES OF INFLATION II: WEAK INSTRUMENTS OF MACROECONOMIC CONTROL

The preceding discussion of relative price changes seemed to assume that Chinese policymakers have as much control over the growth of credit and money supply as do policymakers in a developed market economy. However, this is clearly not the case: the Chinese banking system is still relatively weak and underdeveloped, and this makes it more difficult for policymakers to implement a consistent macroeconomic policy. Indeed, there is an extreme point of view that holds that China, in common with other planned economies, is always characterized by shortages, forced saving, and suppressed inflationary pressures. In this view, any liberalization of prices will inevitably result in inflation, because of the pent-up demand for nearly all goods.

Whether this is true for the Soviet Union and the formerly socialist countries of Eastern European is a much debated topic. However, it seems clear that it is not strictly true in China. This argument can be made both from an institutional perspective, and by examining the dynamic characteristics of the Chinese economy. China has been characterized by parallel, free markets for agricultural products for a long time; and similar parallel markets for industrial materials at least since 1984. Whatever excess demand pressures exist can be expected to push prices upward on these parallel markets. Yet we have seen that free market prices for agricultural goods have gradually converged with planned prices. Similarly, prices in industrial markets were relatively stable from the end of 1985 through the end of 1987. Clearly, China is not always characterized by frustrated demand, for if it were, these free market prices would have been constantly bid up.

The dynamics of the economy reveal something about the relationship between the banking system and production enterprises. It may well be the case that enterprises have an "insatiable" demand for investment and production inputs because they are not adequately disciplined by market forces, i.e., because they have "soft budget constraints." But if enterprises do not have access to bank credit to fund their investment projects or input purchases, their insatiable demands will remain wishes, irrelevant to the macroeconomy. In fact, on several occasions, Chinese policymakers have been able to sharply restrict total bank credit, and drastically reshape macroeconomic conditions. This was most apparent at the end of 1989, when tight limitations on bank credit brought the economy to a screeching halt and brought on a brief period of falling consumer prices. This was only the most dramatic example of what the banking system could do, and similar though less intense episodes occurred in 1981 and early 1986. Clearly, under certain circumstances, the banking system can control effective demand. Thus, it is impossible to assert that China is always a shortage economy, not subject to the normal rules of macroeconomics.

But while China is not inevitably characterized by shortage, there are still significant weaknesses to the banking system that make macroeconomic control more difficult (Naughton, 1990). These can be considered in two categories: weaknesses that make control difficult in normal periods, and weaknesses that affect contractionary policies. During normal periods—when the economy is growing and there are no obvious crises—the control exercised by the banking system is continually eroded by the interference of powerful politicians. Government and party officials are deeply involved in economic management at every level, and without checks on political power, these officials are subject to constant temptation to coerce banks to provide funds for their favorite projects. Indeed, generally coercion is not necessary: local government and banking officials are part of a team that works together to foster industrialization, and banks are supposed to follow the priorities laid down by the government. In this context, local bank branches have every incentive to comply with the wishes of local officials (see White and Bowles). When this joint effort breaks down, local officials may then have recourse to coercion. Nor is such behavior limited to local officials: according to one emigre account, fully one-third of the large-scale investment projects approved during the Seventh Five Year Plan (1986–90) were pet projects approved by individual leaders, rather than emerging from the formal planning process (Chen Yizi, p. 51). At the national level, banking officials have more incentives to pay attention to overall macroeconomic relations; but conversely the power of top officials is subject to even fewer effective constraints. Thus, in normal times, there is a built-in tendency for credit policy to be more expansionary than banking officials would like.

Moreover, the banking system itself lacks experience in the control of the economy. As shown in Figure 2 above, policymakers monitor a measure of inflation that is extremely insensitive to short-run changes in prices. As a result, the indicators of inflation do not create clear warning signals that would help to mobilize political support around moderate credit policies. Moreover, the banking system has, since 1983, been making a gradual transition from a system of controlling total credit by means of aggregate quotas to a system of controlling local bank lending by reserve requirements and central bank operations. The new system promises greater efficiency and flexibility in the long run, but in the short run learning costs are significant. Between 1985 and 1988, credit could expand rapidly even without significant new central bank lending because the reserve requirements for local banks were set at low levels (so the money multiplier was large). Central bankers may have underestimated the speed with which local banks could maximize their lending given reserve requirements, and this contributed to the excessive growth of credit during this period.

Thus, there are reasons to believe that there is a kind of built-in bias toward excessively expansionary credit policy during normal times. Pervasive government and party pressure on an inexperienced banking system tends to create overly rapid credit growth. Nevertheless, when inflation accelerates and conditions deteriorate, the central leadership can insist on a strict credit policy. This happened at the end of 1985, the end of 1987, and the end of 1988. However, in the first two cases, strict credit controls were abandoned in the early part of the following year: it was only after the full-scale inflationary crisis of 1988 that contractionary policies could be maintained. Why were the earlier attempts at contraction abandoned before they could be effective?

It seems that the cost of contractionary policies is large in China. In any economy, contractionary policies have a cost. Restriction in the growth of credit and money causes a slowdown in the growth of current price output: typically, this slowdown is composed in part of a deceleration of inflation (the desired outcome), but also in part of a deceleration in the growth of real output. In the long run, the economy adjusts to the slower rate of price increase and returns to its long-run growth path, but the output foregone in the short-run is seldom regained and is the cost of taming inflation. In China, it appears that the short-run impact on real output is especially severe, and the delays before the economy adjusts to a lower rate of inflation especially long.

In China, virtually all credit is extended to enterprises. This contrasts with the situation in market economies where much credit goes to finance housing and the purchase of consumer durables. As a result, in a market economy, increases in interest rates quickly cause consumer to postpone large purchases, and the housing and automobile industries are particularly interest sensitive. Credit contraction, and the associated interest rises, quickly reduce final demand. By contrast, in China credit restrictions have virtually no impact on final demand. Consumer purchases are virtually unaffected, and investment is reduced only when specific bank-financed investment projects are suspended. Instead, the immediate impact comes on enterprises, which experience much greater difficulty in getting the credit they need to purchase inputs and carry on normal production.

This would not matter if enterprises voluntarily cut back their wages and investment spending. But in fact, enterprises respond to the announcement of contractionary policies with strategic behavior. It is here that the existence of soft budget constraints at the enterprise level is particularly important. Enterprises respond to their reduced access to credit by attempting to protect the types of outlays in which they have most interest. Instead of foregoing bonuses and investment projects that have already been approved, enterprises shift the burden of credit restrictions to other areas. They pile up debts to their suppliers, and they may even allow production to decline, due to their inability to purchase supplies, before they allow bonuses and investment spending to decline. This type of behavior would not make sense if enterprises truly believed they were responsible for their own long-run profits and losses. If that were the case, they would do anything to keep up production, sacrificing short-run benefits such as bonuses and investment projects. But enterprises believe that contractionary policies are temporary. If they can protect bonuses and investment in the short run, they have every reason to believe that they will be forgiven for their failure to maintain output and profit taxes to the state. Indeed, they may even realize that by letting production decline, they can put nearly irresistible pressure on policymakers to reverse contractionary policies. In other words, enterprises doubt the credibility of contractionary policies, and try to position themselves well for the economic conditions that will exist after contractionary policies are abandoned.

For example, during 1989, contractionary policies cut sharply into industrial growth. The profit of in-budget state industrial enterprises declined 19%. However, enterprise retained profits declined only 2.6%, while arrears in tax payments and bank loans increased by 72%. (Liu and Lu, 1990). Enterprises were passing the cost of adjustment onto the budget and banking system, delaying the reduction in bonuses and investment that would be required to bring the economy back into balance. Moreover, debt among enterprises exploded, surpassing 100 billion yuan in mid-1989. In this case, the expansion credit among enterprises was simply substituting for the reduction in bank credit, further delaying effective adjustment.

This kind of enterprise behavior only makes sense if enterprises believe that they will be forgiven a substantial portion of these obligations. In fact, this belief has thus far turned out to be extremely well founded. During the previous contractionary episodes of late 1985 and 1987, contraction was speedily abandoned. Faced with the difficulty of maintaining tight credit in the face of declines in real output and increasing complaints from production enterprises, Zhao Ziyang twice abandoned necessary contractionary policies that he had joined in adopting. In 1989, contractionary policies were maintained much longer, and had a real impact on inflation and output. Yet even in this case, it can be said that enterprises never really adjusted. From the final quarter of 1989, credit growth again increased (see Table 8), and during 1990, enterprises were the recipients of all kinds of special financial assistance to help them out of the difficulties created. While the 18% credit growth from the third quarter 1989 through third quarter 1990 may not seem particularly high, recall that this occurred under conditions of price stability and near stagnation of production. Credit grew at least 15% faster than nominal output, and much of the credit was directed to state-run enterprises.

Ironically, because credit was extended to enterprises, it had little effect during the first half of 1990 in increasing final demand. Enterprises in 1990 found they could get access to the credit they needed to produce (and production in fact began to revive gradually from June), but they still could not sell the output created. Just as there is a painful delay before credit cuts down on inflationary pressures, there is an almost equally painful delay before the resumption of credit growth causes a revival of final demand.

For all these reasons, credit policy in China is clumsy and slow. Ultimately, it can be effective, as eventually changes in credit policy must trickle down to final demand. But in the meantime, the costs associated with changing macroeconomic policy regimes is quite large. These problems cannot be fully solved until enterprise budget constraints are hard. But the hardening of budget constraints is a gradual process that cannot come to fruition until the end of the economic reform process. During the transition, the clumsiness of credit policy is a fact of life that must be accepted.

Thus, there are multiple causes of inflation in China during the reform process. The need to accommodate relative price changes means that some inflation is unavoidable and indeed, to be welcomed. However, the intervention of government officials in the economy and the inexperience of the banking system imparts an inflationary bias to the economy. This bias is intensified because contractionary policies are so costly and painful that there is an enormous temptation to postpone them beyond the point when they have become necessary. For all these reasons, inflation is likely to be a persistent problem in the Chinese economy.

VI. REMEDIES

There is no simple cure for Chinese inflationary tendencies. Because of the need to realign prices and the continuing weakness of the banking system, inflation will be significant for the next decade. However, precisely because of the inflationary bias in the economy and the large costs of contraction, it is especially important that credit policy maintain a consistent and tough stance. It appears that at one point in the mid-1980s one group of Chinese policy-makers saw that some inflation was inevitable, and then concluded that it was nothing to worry about. If true, this is unfortunate. Precisely because some inflation is inevitable, it is important that policymakers constantly attempt to restrain it, to "lean against the wind." Only in this way is it possible to restrain the inevitable tendency of inflation to accelerate as inflationary expectations become imbedded.

It is possible to make a few concrete recommendations that would assist in the effort to control inflation.

1. An independent central bank, not subject to intervention by top political authorities, should be established as soon as possible. Of course, given the current political realities in China, there is virtually no possibility of this occurring in the immediate future. However, we should not neglect the central importance of this measure. Even if true independence is unrealistic, policymakers should move in this direction by appointing a strong leader to head the bank and publicly supporting the authoritative character of bank decisions. This would be in the interests of political leaders, since it would enable them to avoid taking specific responsibility for unpopular economic decisions by shifting blame onto the bank, even while they provide general support to the idea of bank independence.

2. The bank should adhere to a policy of moderate, steady growth of total credit. Given the growth potential in the Chinese economy and the need for moderate inflation to accommodate price changes, credit growth need not be exceptionally low. A steady 15% growth of credit would permit both real growth and inflation to be maintained in the 7-8% range.

3. Credit growth should not be completely inflexible, but discretionary changes should be left to the banking system. The independent central bank—or the political authorities controlling the bank—should establish a set of sensitive indicators of monthly price changes, and give these indicators wide publicity. The central bank should have moderate discretion to adjust policy through its control of lending to branch banks. The indicators and bank responses should be given steady publicity so that economic agents can see that policy is consistent, and gradually adapt to a new set of expectations about central government policy. Macroeconomic policy will become much more effective and easy to implement when enterprises come to believe that the bank will regularly tighten credit in response to signs of increasing inflationary pressures.

4. The moderate inflation permitted by this credit growth should be fully utilized to carry out price reform. Progressive decontrol and adjustment of prices, combined with fiscal reform, should be steadily enacted. Adjustment of individual prices would be appropriate only for a few special cases, such as energy or housing prices. In other cases, prices can be "adjusted" by establishing new taxes and accounting rules, while allowing greater price flexibility. Clearly a few important price changes require significant policy decisions by the central government, but it is illusory to think that changes in thousands of prices can be individually managed to control the total inflation rate at some specific level. At the other extreme, keeping prices frozen simply leads to accumulation of inflationary pressures and greater problems in the future.

5. Continued enterprise reform is necessary to produce modest "hardening" of enterprise budget constraints, thereby reducing the costs of adjustment in the economy.

It is unlikely that this set of changes will be quickly implemented. However, there is nothing inherent in the Chinese economic system that would prevent these changes from being made, and it is not utopian to suggest that such changes could sharply reduce the costs of inflation in China. Stable, consistent macroeconomic policies, combined with continued reform, would allow China to gradually escape from its current inflationary dilemma. This would reduce the incidence of boom and bust cycles in the economy, and make crises such as that of 1988–89 substantially less likely.

BIBLIOGRAPHY

Chen Fubao, "A General Account of the Reform of Prices of Means of Production," Gongy Jingji Guanli Congkan [Digest of Industrial Economic Management], 1989: 7, pp. 2–7.

Chen Yizi. Zhongguo: Shinian Gaige yu Bajiu Minyun, [China: Ten Years of Reform and the Popular Movement of 1989], Taipei: Lien-ching, 1990.

Li Lei, Peng Zhaoping and Xue Peng, Gongye Jingji Guanli Congkan [Digest of Industrial Economic Management], 1988:2, p. 22.

Liu Li and Lu Chunheng, "What is the Way Out?" Zhongguo Tongji [China Statistics], 1990: 4, pp. 10–11.

Naughton, Barry, "Inflation and Economic Reform in China," Current History, September 1989.

——, 1990. "Monetary Implications of Balanced Economic Growth and the Current Macroeconomic Disturbances in China," in D. Cassel and G. Heiduk, eds., China's Contemporary Economic Reforms as a Development Strategy, Baden-Baden: Nomos, 1990.

TJNJ. Zhongguo Tongji Nianjian [China Statistical Yearbook]. Beijing: Zhongguo Tongji, various years.

TJZY. Zhongguo Tongji Zhaiyao [China Statistical Abstract]. Beijing: Zhongguo Tongji, various years.

Urban Household Survey Section, State Statistical Bureau, "Liu Wu" Qijian Woguo Chengzhen Jumin Jiating Shouzhi Diaocha Ziliao, [Urban Household Survey Materials, 1981–1985], Beijing: Zhongguo Tongji, 1988.

Xie Minggan and Ding Hongxiang, Zhongguo Gongye Jingji Yanjiu [China Industrial Economic Research], 1990:1, p. 22.

White, Gordon and Paul Bowles, Towards a Capital Market? Reforms in the Chinese Banking System: Transcript of a research trip, Sussex: Institute of Development Studies China Research Report No. 6, 1987.

Zhang Zhuoyuan, Li Xiaoxi, Bian Yongzhuang, and Shi Xiaokang. Zhongguo Jiage Jiegou Yanjiu [Studies in China's Price Structure], Taiyuan: Shanxi Renmin and Zhongguo Shehui Kexue, 1988.

PRICE REFORMS VS. ENTERPRISE AUTONOMY: WHICH SHOULD HAVE PRIORITY?

By Dwight H. Perkins *

CONTENTS

SUMMARY

There is one general theme to this short essay: Can one create some of the elements needed to make a market system work, but retain central commands in other elements and still expect to reap the benefits of greater efficiency? Or must all five of the critical elements for a successful market system be realized? Put differently, if one or more components of an effective market system prove difficult or costly to implement, can one introduce direct controls in selected areas to overcome these difficulties or will selective controls inevitably lead back to a command system?

The five key elements needed to make a market system work are:

1) Goods must be available for purchase (and sale) on the market. Allocation of intermediate and final products by an administrative body is the antithesis of a market system.

2) Prices must reflect the relative scarcities in the economy. "Prices must be right" or the enterprises will get the wrong signals from the market. With the wrong signals, products will end up in the hands of low priority users.

3) Enterprises must behave in accordance with the rules of the market, specifically they must maximize profits by cutting their costs, improving product quality, and increasing sales. Increasing profits by lobbying the state for higher subsidies, lower taxes, or for monopoly control over one's market will lead to behavior inconsistent with what is required by a well-functioning market. If enterprise behavior is inconsistent with what market rules require, then goods will end up in low priority uses, excessive inventories for example, even though prices are properly set at their relative scarcity value.

4) There must be competition between enterprises. Strictly speaking, it is possible to have a market system without competition, but

---

* Harvard Institute for International Development.

many of the benefits of a market system are lost if competition is absent. It is competition that puts pressure on firms to behave efficiently. Monopolists are notoriously slow about improving product quality and cutting costs.

5) Inflation, the rate of increase in prices, must be kept to an acceptable level. What is acceptable or not acceptable is basically determined by politics. In some countries an annual rate of inflation of 20 or 30 percent is evidence of stability, in others it is a rate that may threaten the existence of the government. In Vietnam in 1988, for example, the rate of inflation rose to 700 percent without having any apparent impact on political stability. A 700 percent a year rate, however, does create great uncertainty in the economic sphere, which in turn makes it difficult or impossible to maintain well functioning markets. The uncertainty created by a 20 to 30 percent rate is less damaging unless it triggers a decision by government to institute price controls. Price controls in the presence of continued excess demand lead to queueing, and the inefficiency entailed in long queues leads back to formal rationing through government controlled administrative channels.

There are other elements that contribute to more or less efficient markets, but these are the essentials. The questions in the remainder of this essay all address in one way or another whether it is possible for a market system to live comfortably side by side with elements of a hierarchical or bureaucratic command system. Or are market and command systems fundamentally incompatible with each other such that one or the other must triumph in the end?

I. MUST ALL FIVE COMPONENTS BE IN PLACE?

The first issue is whether all five components of a market system must be in place for a market to function with a reasonable level of efficiency.

Some economists, particularly those familiar mainly with Western market economies, often assume that the main source of inefficiency in an economy is caused by government interventions that distort prices away from relative scarcity values. If one removes these government interventions, prices will find their scarcity values and markets will function efficiently. In the urban industrial sphere of many economies the main distortions in prices are caused by tariffs and other restrictions on foreign trade. Removal of these restrictions and lowering or evening out tariffs brings domestic relative prices in line with world prices. For traded goods world prices reflect relative scarcities in the world at large and hence determine the true cost of these products for any trading nation. With trade restrictions removed, therefore, the prices are right and little more need be done.

But Western economists who analyze the problem in this way take a great deal for granted. Specifically, they assume that the other components of well-functioning markets are already in place. If goods are not available for purchase and sale on the market or if enterprise managers do not behave in accordance with the rules of the market, then getting prices right won't help much. That goods must be available for purchase and sale on the market if prices are to make a difference is obvious. That enterprise managers must behave in accordance with the rules of the market is less obvious and often forgotten, particularly by economists who are unfamiliar with economic systems which have extensive bureaucratic controls over the economy.

Profit maximization by cutting costs or raising sales is not typically the primary objective of enterprise managers in a centrally planned command economy. For decades, both in China and the Soviet Union, the main objective of enterprises was to maximize gross value of output. There were also cost and input targets, but they were often ignored. Firms generally attempted to get and hold onto any raw material or intermediate product that might be of use in meeting the output target. Inventories overflowed with goods that night prove useful at some future point in time. In such a system the only effective constraint on enterprise demand for inputs is in the hands of the government, not the enterprise. Higher prices will not restrain enterprise demand; only the direct controls of planners perform this function.

Chinese enterprises no longer maximize gross value of output, but they do not just seek profits by cutting costs or raising sales either. Enterprise managers do care now about profits, since profits have a direct connection with the level of worker benefits. But profits can be increased by negotiating lower taxes or getting larger amounts of credit at subsidized interest rates. Given the excess demand for a wide range of products and the artificially low price of many inputs, profits can be raised by steadily expanding output even if expanded output raises average cost. Higher input prices will lower the demand for those inputs, but only to a limited degree. Put in more technical language, the price elasticity of demand for industrial inputs is not zero, but it is much lower than it would be in a true market system.

How large is this excess demand in the system? There are no straightforward ways of measuring this demand, but various kinds of indirect evidence give one a general idea of the problem. First there is the size of Chinese inventories. In most market economies the change in inventories from year to year averages about 1 to 3 percent of GNP. In China the average was 7.4 percent before 1979 and still 6.6 percent in the 1980s (circulating capital as a percentage of NMP). The Kornai Index, the ratio of input inventories to output inventories, is also of some relevance. That ratio for a small sample of Chinese industries or was 4.5 to 4.6 in 1983–84 and 3.8 in 1985. The index for most Western market economies hovers around 1.0 and for South Korea, around 2.0. For the Soviet Union and Poland, in contrast, the ratio is over 10.0.

Another way of looking at the problem is through China's exchange rate. China's official exchange rate in 1987 was 3.7: U.S. $1.00 and there is little question that if enterprises were free to import, the demand for imports would have exceeded the supply of foreign exchange by a substantial margin. The black market rate at the time was 5:1 or 6:1, but the black market (or the swap market) was too restricted to be a good measure of the excess demand. What is the exchange rate that would have brought about balance between the supply and demand for imports in the absence of administered quotas? And how does that exchange rate compare with the rate that would achieve this balance in a Chinese economy where all enterprise maximized profits in the face of hard budget constraints?

In the late 1970s China's purchasing power parity exchange rate relative to the U.S. dollar was probably around 1:1 based on the price comparisons attempted by Irving Kravis. Between 1979 and 1987 the inflation rates in both China and the United States were similar, so the purchasing power parity in 1987 was also about 1:1. In developing countries, however, the actual exchange rate always deviates substantially from the purchasing power parity rate, due to the influence of the relative prices of nontraded goods and services. These affect the purchasing power parity exchange rate but not the foreign trade exchange rate. The difference between the two rates is known as the "exchange rate deviation index" and for poor countries this deviation index is typically 2.5 to 3.0. Thus a country such as China, with a purchasing power parity rate of 1:1, could expect to have a foreign trade exchange rate of 2.5:1 or 3.0:1. The latter exchange rate could be expected to create an equilibrium in the supply and demand for imports if enterprise managers were behaving according to the rules of the market. If managers were not behaving in accordance with such rules, the exchange rate needed to achieve equilibrium would rise above 3.0:1. In China, even rates of 5:1 or 6:1 might not achieve equilibrium. The difference between 5.1 or 6:1 or even higher rates relative to the 3:1 rate of a well-functioning market system is another measure of the degree of excess demand of Chinese enterprises caused by the soft budget constraint and other sources of deviations from proper market behavior.

This degree of excess demand relative to what would have existed in a true market system is very large, but it is probably much less than what existed before the reforms of the 1980s. In 1977 and 1978, for example, China encouraged enterprises to import goods from abroad, implying that few restrictions would be placed on such imports. The result, according to the calculations of one Hong Kong company, were contracts or letters of intent to import around U.S. $600 billion worth of goods, a formidable figure considering that China's foreign exchange earnings in those years were well under $10 billion per year. China's enterprises at that time were behaving in accordance with the rules of central planning and bureaucratic commands and it is difficult to imagine how far the exchange rate would have had to rise to keep demand for imports in line with ability of the country to earn foreign exchange to pay for them. One suspects that even a rate of 10:1 might not have been sufficient.

By the standards of 1977–78, therefore, China by the late 1980s had made considerable progress in changing enterprise behavior in the direction needed to make markets work efficiently. But it is also true that China still had a long way to go before Chinese enterprises behaved in accordance with market rules, even to the degree found in places such as South Korea, let alone free enterprise Hong Kong.

III. Choices in the Face of Excess Demand

Given this large and chronic excess demand, what are the choices that face economic policymakers?

One choice would be to free all prices and eliminate all quotas, in effect to create completely free markets even in the presence of substantial excess demand. The initial impact of this decision would be a major across-the-board rise in prices. If interest rates were included in the prices that were freed up, these rates would rise until enterprise demand for credit was brought in line with the value of the goods what could be purchased with that credit, and prices generally would presumably stabilize at that point. Real interest rates, just like the exchange rate, would have to be well above what would be the case in a true market system where enterprises were behaving according to the rules of the market. The real interest rate and exchange rate would then come down to more appropriate levels representing true market equilibrium rates.

The above degree of liberalization, however, is not likely to be realistic in any existing socialist country. More realistic is a decision to free up prices of many industrial inputs and final products, but to hold the interest rate well below an equilibrium level. In that situation the prices of these inputs and final products will rise sharply, and enterprises will go to the banks for increased credit to buy the higher priced goods. Demand for credit will greatly exceed the supply, which will put pressure on the monetary authorities to expand the money supply so that the banks can expand enterprise credits. If the monetary authorities refuse to accommodate this situation, then enterprise will get into a political fight for whatever credit does exist. Depending on their political clout with the banking system, some priority areas will get enough credit while others will not. If the banking system handles credit rationing well, the degree of disruption to the economy may not be excessive. If credit is rationed poorly, the results could be very damaging to the economy.

In the Chinese case, it is probably more realistic to expect that the monetary authorities will lack the political independence needed to hold the line on monetary expansion. In that case credit will expand rapidly, prices will rise, enterprises will raise wages to keep workers from being hurt by inflation, which will increase demand further and lead to more increases in prices. The actual process is more complicated than this, but the likely result is a price spiral caused by a combination of excess demand and cost-push pressures. Something like this is what occurred in China in 1988 and 1989.

If one cannot hold the line on credit but is unwilling to tolerate inflation, the next step is to have the state fix prices directly. Assuming one is not going to fix all prices, the question is, which prices to fix. One option is that practiced in China in the late 1980s of having a two-tier pricing system. Under some circumstances a two-tier pricing system will behave in much the same way as would the complete freeing up of prices. Most decisions of enterprises will be made on the basis of the freed up market prices. Goods distributed by the state at low fixed prices mainly serve the purpose of subsidizing favored enterprises. The overall rate of inflation may be lower than in the completely uncontrolled prices case, mainly because some of the cost-push pressures are absent, but this too is a complex issue and the impact of a two-tier price system on the rate of inflation is not easy to assess.

An alternative to the two-tier price system is to fix prices for some goods but not for others, or to fix prices for some enterprise but not for others. One could fix the prices of certain capital goods and intermediate products deemed to be critical. These products, of course, would have to be distributed through administrative channels in a planned or rationed way since demand would greatly exceed supply.

Fixing prices for some enterprises, the larger ones, for example, but not the smaller ones, probably would not work. The temptation to earn easy profits by selling state allocated goods at low prices to smaller firms which would pay higher prices would be too great.

The only real choice for economic policymakers, therefore, is whether to control the prices of a few products or a great many. The more products there are whose prices are controlled, the more complex the job of the planners, particularly in China where there are so many small-scale enterprises. Inflation caused by excess demand does not disappear; it is channeled on the remaining free markets or shows up as unwanted increases in savings deposits. Controls may reduce the cost push elements in inflation, but it is also possible that they may not. It all depends on how administered prices are managed in practice.

Administered prices and the resulting quotas, of course, eliminate most competition from the system. What competition remains is largely confined to efforts to extract more inputs and subsidies from the central planning authorities. Allocative efficiency will also suffer, but by how much depends on the skills of planning authorities and the complexity of their tasks.

For a nation where enterprises behave not according to the rules of the market, therefore, the choices facing economic policymakers are not very attractive. Either one tolerates a high level of inflation or a high level of inefficiency in the system. One can solve the problem by completely freeing up all prices including interest rates and the exchange rates, but this step is probably too radical to be realistic. One can also return to a more stable and predictable world by reinstituting controls over most prices and quantities, but the Soviet Union is a good object lesson of where that is likely to lead. China is likely to face Soviet style inefficiency much earlier in its growth process if for no other reason than the size of China's population and economy and the large number of enterprises that need to be controlled.

The above analysis, therefore, underlines the importance of changing enterprise behavior so it conforms better with what the market requires. The greater the degree to which this can be accomplished, the easier it becomes to loosen controls over prices without engendering excess inflation, among other things.

But how does one change the rules of enterprise behavior? Early theorists of socialist economies suggested the goal could be accomplished by simply ordering enterprises to maximize profits. No one today thinks the task will be so simple.

The essence of the process involves breaking the ties between the enterprise and the government bureaucracy, but how to do this is the question. An independent banking system that itself faced a hard budget constraint would be a help. Banks that could not pass on their losses to the central bank would have a powerful incentive to ensure that enterprises paid them back and at a profitable rate of interest. Creating new forms of public ownership such as one enterprise owning shares in another might also be a step in the right direction. A board of directors made up such of owners might also be a step in the right direction. A board of directors made up of such owners might be more interested in the enterprise's achieving higher profitability than would the central government's economic policymakers, although on cannot be certain of this. Conceivably it is possible to retrain ministries and central planners so that they reward managers on the basis of those managers' ability to cut costs and raise sales instead of on the basis of a large number of other criteria as is presently the case. As long as the government bureaucracy control appointments and promotions, enterprise managers will attempt to do what they think these government officials want, regardless of what the law might say.

Finally, making a market system work more efficiently in a socialist context requires experimentation. Many of the options discussed above have never really been tried in practice and no one knows precisely how they will turn out. The only way to discover what will work and what will not is to try and make adjustments on the basis of actual experience. For experimentation to be feasible, however, those in charge of reform measures must be able to take risks without fear of reprisals if events do not go precisely as planned. Consistently bad experiments might be a legitimate ground for demotion, but the system cannot be oriented toward rewarding only those who stay closest to whatever the current orthodoxy may be.

TAXATION REFORM IN CHINA'S PUBLIC FINANCE

By Penelope B. Prime *

CONTENTS

SUMMARY

Tax reform is an important component of China's overall economic reform because taxation raises government revenue and influences enterprise decisions, without subjugating enterprises to direct government control. This paper presents an overview of China's tax reform since 1983. The main feature of this tax reform was that state enterprises began paying industrial and commercial taxes instead of remitting profits, referred to as *li gai shui* (changing profit to tax). In principle, this tax reform contained many desirable characteristics, but problems with other aspects of economic

---

* China Branch, Center for International Research, Bureau of Census, Department of Commerce; Department of Economics, Georgia State University.

reform have diluted the positive incentive effects implicit within the new tax system.

I. INTRODUCTION

Taxation is a key determinant of economic behavior and resource allocation. The more decentralized an economy is, the more important the tax structure becomes in enhancing, or hindering, the effectiveness of the public sector. As part of its ambitious economic reform program beginning in 1978, China has paid increasing attention to how taxation affects decentralized decision-making. Although experiments with new taxes have been ongoing, comprehensive changes in the tax system began in 1983. Tax reform is important in China because of its potential effect on government revenue and on the central government's ability to guide enterprises, and local governments, without stifling initiative.

During the period of economic reform, and especially in the second half of the 1980s, China has also experienced persistent budgetary deficits. While these deficits have not been large by international standards, the fiscally conservative Chinese leadership considers deficits a major problem. The deficit problem has caused Chinese policy-makers to be concerned with increasing tax revenue to cover budgetary expenditure.

This paper presents an overview of China's tax reform and recent trends in government revenue collection. The first section discusses the new role China envisions for tax policy. Trends in the state budget, and in growth and sources of government revenue, are presented in the second and third sections. The final two sections look at enterprise reforms and performance, and the potential effect of these on government revenue.

While tax policy would be expected to affect government revenue, a causal relation is difficult to establish in this case because of the many other reforms China has implemented along with tax reform. The purpose here is simply to look at what has been happening on the revenue side of the budget in light of China's new tax policies. The theme that emerges is that while China's tax reform is well intended, the ability of the government to establish a sound but flexible, tax-based public finance system is both essential to, and dependent on, the success of the other economic reforms.

II. A NEW ROLE FOR TAX POLICY

The National Tax Bureau of the Ministry of Finance summarized the purpose of China's tax reform in the following six general goals: [1]

1. Increase the number of tax categories and tax rates.
2. Vary tax rates by product and sector in order to influence the direction of economic development, and to encourage exports while protecting domestic production.

---

[1] Guojia shuiwu ju [National Tax Bureau], *Shuifa daquan* (*SFDQ*) [Complete Guide to Tax Law] (Beijing: Zhongguo caizheng jingji chubanshe, 1989), p.9.

These two goals contrast with policy in the late 1960s and early 1970s when China's goal was to simplify the tax system as much as possible. Within industry and commerce, for example, the number of taxable items fell from 108 to 44. The number of tax rates also fell, with reportedly only 16 in use. Most enterprises paid only one tax.[2] Simplification was consistent with direct government control over enterprises through the planning process, but to encourage enterprise initiative while maintaining some influence over the direction of the economy requires sophistication in tax instruments and adjustable tax rates.

3. Improve management and increase the economic responsibility of state enterprises by changing to a profits tax with retention of after-tax profits, rather than having enterprises remit all of their profits directly to the state budget.

Before economic reforms began in 1978, enterprise remittance of profits made up a larger share of government revenue than did taxes. The goal of replacing enterprise profit remittance with industrial and commercial taxes establishes taxation as an indirect "lever" to influence managers' decisions. This reform separates state enterprises from the government budget. Previously state enterprise accounts were part of China's public finance budget, and were made compatible with plan targets. Enterprises contributed nearly all of their profits to government revenue, but profits themselves were only an accounting phenomenon. Likewise, wage payments and reinvestment decisions had little to do with whether the enterprise was profitable or not, and managers had little control over incentives or production.

Taxation of state enterprise profits would reduce the difference between state and collective enterprises. Unlike state enterprises, collectives have always paid profit taxes and have been responsible for losses if they occurred. The budget has subsidized collectives to some extent, but the operation of collectives has not been part of the budget's function. Therefore one significance of separating state enterprises from the budget would be to put state enterprises in competition with collectives for inputs and customers. Furthermore, profits would become the most important objective for state enterprises, since funds for bonuses and reinvestment would no longer be provided through the budget.

This goal has been implemented via the *li gai shui* tax reform, which is discussed later in this section.

4. Use taxes to adjust enterprise profits that are excessively high or low due solely to the artificial nature of the planned price system.

The purpose of this goal is to reward enterprises by allowing them to keep after-tax profits that are earned as a result of better management rather than as a result of the price system. This goal is necessary because China has gone forward with tax reform before price reform.

This goal has also been implemented as part of the *li gai shui* reform in the form of an "adjustment tax" on enterprise profits.

---

[2] *SFDQ*, p.7.

5. Guarantee that the government will have sufficient revenue while creating incentives for enterprises, localities, and government bureaus to increase their profits by devising ways to share increments in profits.

This goal addresses China's desire to develop a tax policy that will give incentives to enterprises to increase their profits, and to governments to improve their tax collection and supervision functions. It is an extension of goals 3 and 4 in that it addresses increments in profits earned or revenue collected, and would allow higher retention rates for these increments.

To encourage enterprises to increase profits, this goal has been implemented as part of measures designed to make enterprises more "responsible" for their performance. This is discussed in section V of this essay in connection with the enterprise contract system. To encourage local governments to increase revenue collection, the Ministry of Finance has tried various forms of central-local government revenue-sharing. This is discussed in section IV.

6. Divide each tax into central and local (and shared) portions to ensure both levels have taxation authority and sources of revenue.

In the past, local governments have not had the authority to tax for local needs. They have relied on resources that were approved by, and usually shared with, central authorities. At the same time, the majority of government revenue is collected by local governments for the central government. The purpose of this goal, in combination with goal 5, is to establish a less arbitrary division of revenue sources and expenditure responsibility. The division of each tax into local, central, or shared proportions was established in 1985.

In implementing these six general goals, the core program has been the introduction of a new set of industrial and commercial taxes that replaced profit remittance in state enterprises, called *li gai shui*. *Li gai shui* was implemented in two phases. In the first phase, begun in June 1983, enterprises paid a profit tax and remitted a portion of after-tax profits.[3] Various calculation methods of tax and profit payments were used, but total payments for 1983 were set to be approximately the same as in 1982. In the second phase of *li gai shui* all profit remittance was replaced with taxation. This phase began in October 1984, and comprised the following five parts:

1. Divide the industrial-commercial tax into four taxes (product, value-added, turnover, and resource); make the product tax more detailed with adjustable rates.
2. Collect a natural resource tax from mining enterprises. (This tax is in addition to the salt tax, which has existed since 1950).
2. Reintroduce taxes on housing, land utilization, vehicle utilization, and urban maintenance and construction.

---

[3] For details of this phase see Katharine Huang Hsiao, *The Government Budget and Fiscal Policy in Mainland China* (Taipei: Chung-Hua Institution for Economic Research, 1987), pp.162–64.

4. Levy a 55 percent profits tax on large and medium sized state enterprises, and one of eight rates on small state enterprises.
5. Levy an additional adjustment tax on profits (an excess profits tax), using 1983 profits as a base.

Most of these five parts have been implemented. The existing industrial and commercial tax categories as of 1989, and their starting dates are summarized in Figure 1. These changes have substantially increased the complexity and sophistication of China's tax system. If these changes work as intended, this increased sophistication can serve to make China's tax system more flexible and transparent, and therefore a potentially powerful "economic lever" for influencing the direction and performance of the economy.

III. The Government Budget

Several recent trends in China's public finance, however, suggest that the transition from a centrally directed public finance system to one that is tax-based will not be easy. Budget deficits have been one problem that has been particularly sensitive for Chinese leaders. Table 1 reproduces annual official figures since 1978 for China's total (central and local) budgetary revenue and expenditures and the size of the surplus or deficit. These figures show that China's budget deficit problem was consistently worse during the seventh Five-Year Plan (1986–1990) compared with the previous Five-Year Plan period (1981–1985). The seventh Five-Year Plan period began with a deficit of 7.06 billion yuan in 1986. In 1989 the deficit reached 9.54 billion yuan, with a planned deficit in 1990 of 8.90 billion yuan. The average deficit for the five-year period was 8.11 billion yuan compared with an average of 2.42 billion in the previous five-year period.[4]

Furthermore, these official figures include revenue raised from issuing government bonds as budgetary revenue. The practice of counting bonds as revenue is common in socialist planned economies because of the ideological and political importance placed on a balanced budget in a socialist system. This goal has resulted in accounting practices that differ from Western methods, often with the purpose of decreasing or hiding deficits.[5] In Table 2 the official figures are adjusted to exclude foreign and domestic bonds as revenue. With these adjusted figures the deficit situation looks substantially worse, reflecting the fact that reliance on raising revenue by issuing bonds has grown in recent years. The adjusted deficit in 1986 was 20.88 billion yuan. The deficit steadily increased throughout the period to reach 36.97 billion in 1989, with a planned deficit of 42.34 billion in 1990.

---

[4] Part of the deficit increase is explained by a change in accounting practices. Before 1986 both price and enterprise subsidies were recorded as negative revenue. Beginning in 1986 price subsidies have been recorded as an expenditure item. It is unlikely, however, that the three-fold increase in the deficit between the two five-year periods can be explained in this way. See Caizheng bu zonghe jihua si [General Planning Department, Ministry of Finance], *Zhongguo caizheng tongji 1950–1988 (ZGCZTJ)* [China's Finance Statistics 1950–1988] (Beijing: Zhongguo caizheng jingji chubanshe, 1989), pp. 17, 197, and Guojia tongji ju [State Statistical Bureau], (*ZGTJNJ, 1989*).

[5] See P. T. Wanless, *Taxation in Centrally Planned Economies* (New York: St. Martin's Press, 1985), pp. 66–7.

Figure 1. Industrial and Commercial Taxes: 1989

Circulation Taxes	Profit and Income Taxes	Resource Taxes	Special Purpose Taxes	Property & Behavior Taxes
1. Product (1984)	4. State enterprise profit (1984)	13. Salt (1950)	15. Construction (1983)	19. Housing (experimental)
2. Value added (1983)	5. State enterprise adjustment (1984)	14. Natural resource (1984)	16. Oil consumption (1982)	20. Vehicle use (1986)
3. Turnover (1984)	6. Collective enterprise profit (1986)		17. Bonus (1984)	21. Urban maintenance and construction (1984)
	7. Urban-rural individual industrial industrial-commercial profit (1986)		18. Wage adjustment (1985)	22. Slaughter (1950)
	8. Individual income (1980)			23. Animal transaction tax (1953)
	9. Individual adjustment (1987)			24. Market transfer (1962)
	10. Chinese-foreign joint-venture profit (1980)			25. Land use (experimental)
	11. Foreign enterprise profit (1982)			
	12. Private enterprise profit (proposed)			

Sources: Guojia shuiwu ju [National Tax Bureau], Shuifa daquan (SFDQ) [Complete Guide to Tax Law] (Beijing: Zhongguo caizheng jingji bu chubanshe, 1989), pp. 8-13; Caizheng bu zenghe jihua si [General Planning Department, Ministry of Finance], Zhongguo caizheng tongji, 1950-1988 (ZGCZTJ) [China's Finance Statistics, 1950-1988] (Beijing: Zhongguo caizheng jingji chubanshe, 1989), pp. 40-43.

Notes: 1. Dates in parentheses give approximate beginning of implementation.
2. Some of the taxes have been reintroduced. For example, the 1986 vehicle use tax is a new form of the vehicle license tax begun in 1950.

Table 1. Total National Budgetary Revenue, Expenditure,
          and Balance: 1978-1988 (billion yuan)

Year	Revenue	Expenditure	Surplus or deficit
1978	112.11	111.10	1.01
1979	110.33	127.39	-17.06
1980	108.52	121.27	-12.75
1981	108.96	111.50	-2.55
1982	112.40	115.33	-2.93
1983	124.90	129.25	-4.35
1984	150.19	154.64	-4.45
1985	186.64	184.48	2.16
1986	226.03	233.08	-7.06
1987	236.89	244.85	-7.95
1988	262.80	270.66	-7.86
1989	291.92	301.46	-9.54
1990	323.65	332.55	-8.90

Note: The figures for 1986 and later are not compatible with figures of revenue and expenditure from previous years. In 1986, due to the fact that some items previously deducted from revenue were reclassified as expenditure, there were nominal increase in both revenue and expenditure. Figures for 1990 are planned.

Sources: Guojia tongji ju [State Statistical Bureau], Zhongguo tongji nianjian, 1989 (ZGTJNJ, 1989) [China's Statistical Yearbook, 1989] (Beijing: Zhongguo tongji chubanshe, 1989), p. 657, for 1978-1987; ZGCZTJ, p. 12, for 1988; and Foreign Broadcast Information Service (FBIS) 12 April 1990, pp. 16-17, for 1989 and 1990.

IV. TRENDS IN REVENUE COLLECTION

The fact that budget deficits have worsened during the period in which tax reform was implemented raises the question of how government revenue has fared.

UNSTABLE GROWTH IN REVENUE

One salient characteristic, and problem, for China's public finance has been the variability of budgetary revenue. This is shown in Table 3, where bond revenue has been excluded. Revenue actually fell 4.9 percent in 1979, 2.4 percent in 1980, and 2.5 percent in 1981. Revenue increased annually after 1981, but at rates varying from a low of 2.3 percent in 1982 to a high of 22.1 percent in 1985.

Part of this instability was due to inflation, since revenue and expenditure data are reported in current prices. For comparison, Table 3 also gives China's officially reported, annual increases in

Table 2. Total National Budgetary Revenue, Expenditure,
and Balance (Adjusted): 1978-1990 (billion yuan)

Year	Revenue	Expenditure	Surplus or deficit
1978	112.11	111.10	1.02
1979	106.80	127.39	-20.60
1980	104.22	121.27	-17.05
1981	101.64	111.50	-9.86
1982	104.01	115.33	-11.32
1983	116.96	129.25	-12.29
1984	142.45	154.64	-12.19
1985	177.66	184.48	-6.82
1986	212.20	233.08	-20.88
1987	219.94	244.85	-24.91
1988	235.72	270.66	-34.93
1989	264.49	301.46	-36.97
1990	290.21	332.55	-42.34

Note: The official revenue and expenditure data have been adjusted by excluding domestic and foreign bonds. The figures for 1990 are planned.

Sources: ZGCZTJ, pp. 11-12, 16-17, for 1978-1988; FBIS 12 April 1990, pp. 16, 19, for 1989 and 1990.

retail prices. Even considering inflation, however, there was still much variability in revenue growth, and between 1987 and 1989 revenue grew less than the rate of inflation.

Another way to evaluate revenue growth is to account for economic growth using a measure called revenue buoyancy.[6] Revenue buoyancy is calculated in Table 3 as the percentage change in revenue divided by the percentage change in national income (*guomin shouru*). A buoyancy value of one or more would imply that the revenue-generating ability of the public finance system is keeping pace with economic growth. A value less than one would imply that the system is not capturing potential revenue sources as the economy grows. These interpretations are subject to the caveat that this measure does not distinguish between automatic increases in revenue due to growth and increases resulting from changes in the public finance system itself (e.g., new taxes).

Calculations of China's revenue buoyancy are given in the last column of Table 3. With this measure China's revenue collection also appears very unstable. China's revenue buoyancy was just over one between 1983 and 1986, but it was low (and negative)

[6] Luc De Wulf, "International Experience in Budgetary Trends during Economic Development and Its Relevance for China," *World Bank Staff Working Papers*, no. 760 (Washington, D.C.: World Bank, 1986).

Table 3. Annual Percent Change in Revenue, National Income,
          and Retail Prices, and a Measure of Revenue
          Buoyancy: 1978-1989

Year	Revenue	National income	Retail prices	Revenue buoyancy
1978	24.8	13.0	0.7	1.9
1979	-4.9	10.7	2.0	-.5
1980	-2.4	9.6	6.0	-.3
1981	-2.5	6.6	2.4	-.4
1982	2.3	7.7	1.9	0.3
1983	11.7	10.6	1.5	1.1
1984	19.7	17.7	2.8	1.1
1985	22.1	22.0	8.8	1.0
1986	17.8	11.5	6.0	1.5
1987	3.6	17.0	7.3	0.2
1988	6.9	22.9	18.5	0.3
1989	11.5	9.9	17.8	1.2

     Note: The percentage changes in revenue and
national income are based on figures given in current
prices. Official revenue data have been adjusted to
exclude domestic and foreign bonds.

     Sources: Revenue (adjusted data), Table 2;
national income, ZGTJNJ, 1989, p. 29, for 1978-1988, and
Beijing Review 33.15 (9-15 April 1990): centerfold,
p. 1, for 1989; retail prices, ZGCZTJ, p. 180, for
1978-1988, and Beijing Review 33.17 (22-29 April 1990):
documents, p. III., for 1989.

before then, near zero in 1987 and 1988, and then back to more
than one in 1989. There was a jump from 0.3 to 1.1 in the value of
revenue buoyancy between 1982 and 1983, which coincides with the
first phase of *li gai shui*, but this increase was not sustained. So a
problem with variability, and therefore lack of predictability, in
the size of government revenue has continued despite tax reform.

CHANGES IN THE SOURCES OF REVENUE

While tax reform seems to be a minor factor in annual fluctuations of government revenue, it has substantially altered the
sources of budgetary revenue. As a result of *li gai shui*, there has
been an increase in the importance of revenue collected from taxes
and a concurrent decrease in direct transfers of enterprise revenues into the government treasury.

The changes in sources of budgetary revenue are summarized in
Figure 2. The percentage of enterprise revenue in total budgetary
revenue has decreased steadily from 51.0 percent in 1978 to only
1.9 percent in 1988. Concurrently, tax revenue has increased from

46.3 percent to 74.0 percent, respectively, over the same period. Fees generated 7.1 percent of revenue by 1988,[7] and bonds generated 10.3 percent. Neither fees nor bonds were sources of revenue in 1978.

Although revenue from taxes has increased, the makeup of tax revenue itself has not changed, as shown by Figure 3. Industrial and commercial taxes represented 86.9 percent of total taxes in 1978 compared with 88.4 percent in 1988. The rest of tax revenue was comprised of agricultural taxes, customs duties, and a small category of "other taxes." Direct agricultural taxes have always represented a small percentage of total tax revenue in China's public finance.[8] Agricultural tax revenue represented 5.5 percent of total tax revenue in 1978, falling to 3.1 percent in 1988. Customs duties have also been a minor source of revenue. They represented 5.5 percent of tax revenue in 1978, increasing to 6.5 percent in 1988.

Within the category of industrial and commercial taxes, however, major changes have occurred with the introduction of *li gai shui*. These changes are illustrated in Figure 4. The industrial and commercial tax (sometimes referred to as the consolidated industrial and commercial tax), represented 87.5 percent of all industrial and commercial taxes in 1978. With *li gai shui* this tax was replaced with four new taxes: product tax, value added tax, turnover tax, and resource tax. By 1987 the revenue from these four taxes together represented 83.6 percent of all industrial and commercial taxes. The remaining 16.4 percent came from the industrial and commercial profit tax (7.9 percent), taxes on Chinese-foreign joint ventures and foreign firms (0.3 percent),[9] and other, minor taxes (8.2 percent).

CENTRAL-LOCAL GOVERNMENT FISCAL RELATIONS

In connection with tax reform, there has been much discussion in China on the proper division of fiscal responsibility between the central government and the provinces, and between provinces and lower-level governments. A series of experiments in fiscal decentralization have been implemented over the last decade with the intention of finding the best mix of central-local revenue sharing and expenditure responsibility.[10] The goal of these changes has been to introduce incentives for local government to care about the profitability of enterprises in their jurisdictions, and to improve revenue collection. Beginning in March 1985, the revenue collected from each tax has been designated to go to either central or local governments, or to be shared at a predetermined rate.

The division of revenue between the center and localities over the decade, given in Figure 5, shows that the center's share has in-

---

[7] Examples of fees are usage fees paid by enterprises on fixed and working capital.

[8] The actual contribution of agriculture to government revenues has been much higher than direct taxes indicate. Agriculture has also contributed to government revenue through pricing policies and collection of special fees (Hsiao, *The Government Budget*, p.109).

[9] This figure is low because even though foreign business in China has increased rapidly in the last decade, its importance is still small compared with the size of China's economy. Also many foreign companies receive tax "breaks" in the form of low rates or uncollected taxes, although these are often countered with high prices for goods and services bought within China.

[10] For a description of the numerous systems tried, see Hsiao, *The Government Budget*, pp.72–84.

Figure 2. Sources of Budgetary Revenue by
Category: 1978, 1983, and 1988

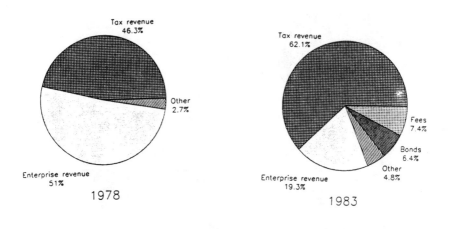

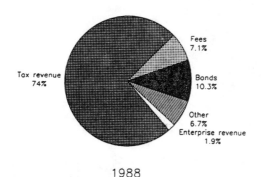

Source: ZGCZTJ, p. 17.

creased, despite the emphasis on decentralizing fiscal responsibility. The center's share in 1979 was 14.3 percent; by 1988 its share
had increased to 36.4 percent.[11] Further, no major changes in the
ratio of central to local revenue appear to have coincided with *li
gai shui* in 1983 or 1984, or with the beginning of determining central and local revenue on the basis of each tax in 1985.

---

[11] These figures are based on domestic revenue only. The center's share would be higher if
foreign revenue was included.

Figure 3. Sources of Tax Revenue by Category
as a Percentage to Total Tax Revenue:
1978, 1983, and 1988

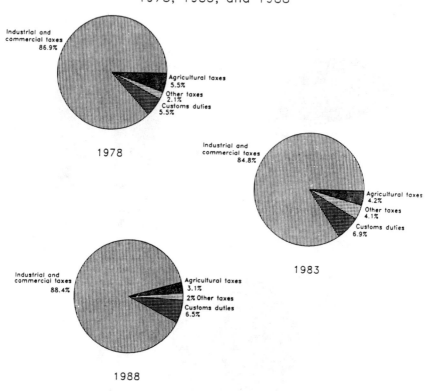

Source: ZGCZTJ. p. 37

Even so, there has been much concern in Beijing that central revenues are inadequate, and that local governments have gained financially at the expense of the center. This apprehension over the size of central funds originates in the distinction between budgetary and extrabudgetary funds. While the center's share in budgetary revenues has increased, budgetary revenue itself has fallen dramatically compared with national income. As Figure 6 illustrates, in 1978 budgetary revenue represented 37.2 percent of national income; in 1988 it represented only 20.0 percent. In contrast,

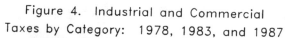

Figure 4.   Industrial and Commercial
Taxes by Category: 1978, 1983, and 1987

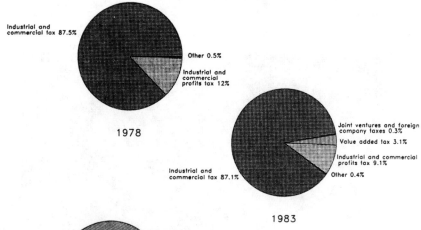

Industrial and
commercial tax 87.5%

Other 0.5%

Industrial and
commercial
profits tax 12%

1978

Joint ventures and foreign
company taxes 0.3%

Value added tax 3.1%

Industrial and commercial
profits tax 9.1%

Other 0.4%

Industrial and
commercial tax 87.1%

1983

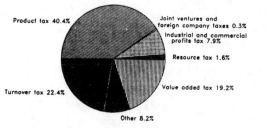

Product tax 40.4%

Joint ventures and
foreign company taxes 0.3%

Industrial and commercial
profits tax 7.9%

Resource tax 1.6%

Value added tax 19.2%

Turnover tax 22.4%

Other 8.2%

1987

Source: ZGCZTJ, p. 40–43.

Note: Data for 1987 are used here, rather than for 1988 as in Figures 2
and 3, because comparable data for 1988 are incomplete.

extrabudgetary revenue increased from 11.5 percent of national
income in 1978 to 19.3 percent in 1988. Since extrabudgetary revenue is controlled primarily at local levels, these trends would explain the central government's concern over its control of revenue.

Figure 6 also suggests that a halt in the rise of extrabudgetary
revenue coincided with tax reform. An inverse relationship between budgetary and extrabudgetary revenue, as a percent of national income, existed until 1982; that is, as budgetary revenue fell,
extrabudgetary revenue rose. Beginning in 1983, their relationship

Figure 5. Central—Local Revenue Sharing:
1979—1988

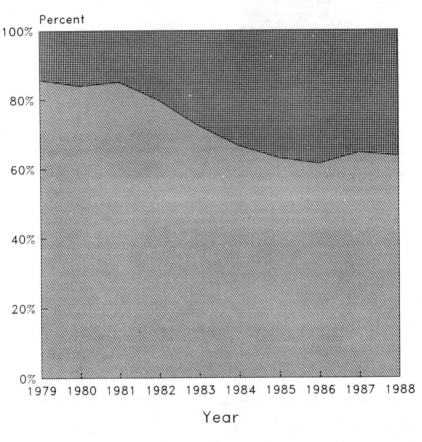

Percent

Year

Local share   Central share

Source: ZGCZTJ, p. 59.

Note: Based on data for domestic revenue including domestic bond revenue.

has stabilized with their proportions in national income generally
moving together (except for a jump in budgetary revenue in 1986).
More research is needed to understand how China's tax system affects extrabudgetary revenue.

V. The "Enterprise Responsibility" Factor

Complicating the tax reform picture are various forms of enterprise reform, or "enterprise management responsibility," begun by the Ministry of Finance in 1987.[12] With these reforms, contracts for fixed periods of time are set up between enterprises and the Ministry. The contracts specify quotas for payment of profit taxes and adjustment taxes. Methods for deciding on the quotas are numerous and complex, but basically the enterprise agrees to pay a set percentage of profits based on previous performance, and then profits earned above this are taxed at lower rates. Since profit tax rates fall as the amount of profits increase, these contracts are supposed to create incentives for enterprises to increase profits.

Under any system that taxes profits there is an incentive to reduce the amount of profit subject to tax. In China this incentive has been strengthened by the tax-contract system, even to the point of reporting losses, because there is little threat of bankruptcy for unprofitable enterprises. In fact, subsidies to unprofitable enterprises may be guaranteed to enterprises within the contract system, although the Ministry of Finance's goal is to build into the contract that subsidies will be phased out over time. As a result, certain practices that reduce accounting profits are very popular, whether an enterprise is profitable or not. For example, wages and nonwage benefits, such as housing, have increased dramatically, as has borrowing for investment, because both worker benefits and repayments on these loans are deducted before the tax liability is assessed.

Another result of the contract system is that taxes on profit are in effect negotiable. According to the tax code, the tax rate on earnings of state firms is 55 percent for medium to large enterprises, and one of eight rates between 10 and 55 percent for small enterprises, plus the adjustment tax.[13] In actuality, because the profit and adjustment taxes are negotiated according to the specific contract, the rates vary for each enterprise. Tax assessors have the authority to consider all sorts of special circumstances when the contracts are made.

Some of these special circumstances are beyond the control of an enterprise. One of these is price. Because some prices are market prices and others are fixed prices, profits may not correspond to the success of management or productivity of workers. Also profitability varies widely across industries. One reason for the new industrial and commercial taxes is to equalize profit rates so enterprises with low profits due to artificially high input prices or low

---

[12] Before 1987 other forms of enterprise responsibility existed, such as the "enterprise fund" and the "profit and loss" responsibility system. The main purpose of these earlier forms was to give enterprises financial resources with which to reward workers. In these forms the amount of funds an enterprise could retain was tied to variables other than profitability per se, such as the size of their wage bill (*Jingji xue wenti* [Problems of Economic Study] no. #1 (1988):15; *Jingji wenti tansuo* [Inquiry into Economic Problems] no. #12 (1988):49–56).

[13] The distinction between "small" enterprises and others varies depending on whether the firm is involved in industry and transport, retail sales, or other services, and whether it is located in Beijing, Tianjin, and Shanghai or elsewhere. The definitions are based on a range of values of fixed assets, size of earnings, and number of people employed. The specifics can be found in Sun Shuming and Zheng Li, "Guoying chiye lirun fenpei de falu guiding" [Legal regulations of state enterprise profit distribution], *Jingji wenti tansuo* [Investigations of Economic Problems] no.12 (1988):51.

Figure 6. Total Budgetary and Extrabudgetary Revenue
as a Percentage of National Income: 1978–1988

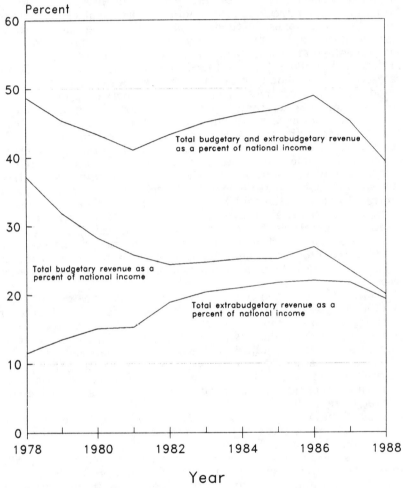

Source: ZGCZTJ, pp. 12, 103, and 173.

Note: Budgetary revenue data exclude bonds.

output prices will not be discouraged from improving efficiency.[14]
In this way economic reform can go forward without having to wait

---

[14] For a discussion of how the product tax can be used to influence price while controlling profitability in Chinese enterprises, see Wang Chuanlun, "Some Notes on Tax Reform in China," *China Quarterly* no. #97 (March 1984):53–67.

for full-scale price reform. Prices will still influence consumption, but their effect on investment and production decisions can be adjusted.

Without price reform, however, the tax-contract system in effect makes all taxes negotiable, and therefore ad hoc. In addition, adjusting taxes for each enterprise is unwieldy, and is hindered by poor accounting, negotiation, and corruption. Therefore the overall, long-run effect of tax and enterprise reform on government revenue is difficult to predict. On the one hand provisions to allow enterprises to keep higher shares of incremental profits should encourage enterprises to increase sales and reduce costs; on the other hand, the combined effects of negotiation, incentives to reduce accounting profits, and administrative costs may overwhelm the increases in revenue due to incentives to increase profits.

VI. Economic Performance and Revenue Growth

The *li gai shui* tax reform has been concerned with making state enterprises efficient and dynamic by subjecting them to the same taxation system as collectives. The achievement of these goals, however, has been undermined by other factors that have adversely affected the performance of state enterprises. For example, inflation in the late 1980s, also a result of economic reform, hurt state enterprises more than others because they are subject to fixed state prices and cannot pass on increased costs. This decreased profits in state enterprises and increased the amount of revenue used for subsidies.[15] Also, attempts to control budgetary expenditure by cutting investment curtailed growth in the state sector, and industry in particular. Investment is a large expenditure, and is easier to cut in major central projects than in smaller, local projects.

Failure to make state enterprises more efficient and dynamic has affected government revenue, especially since industrial and commercial taxes are such a large revenue source. This can be seen in Table 4, which gives the share of revenue collected by ownership category. The figures in this table show that the state sector's share has fallen from 86.8 percent in 1978 to 74.1 percent in 1987. Table 5, which gives the share of revenue collected by economic sector, shows that concurrently industry's contribution to budgetary revenue has also fallen. Industry's share was 75.4 percent in 1978, and only 56.9 percent in 1987. While industry's share was falling, the category of "other" rose from 2.1 percent to 20.9 percent during the same period, as this is where bond revenue is counted. Contributions from the other economic sectors remained about the same. This implies that decreases in revenue from state industry have been largely made up by issuing bonds.

Conclusion

Implementation of the *li gai shui* system is the core of China's efforts to establish a legal, uniform tax system, which gives enterprises autonomy from government and incentives to care about

---

[15] Enterprise subsidies were 44.6 billion yuan in 1988, up from 24.52 billion in 1985 (the first-year figures for these subsidies were made available). Price subsidies increased from 1.1 billion yuan in 1978 to 31.7 billion yuan in 1988 (*ZGCZTJ*, pp.17, 88, 197).

Table 4.   Percentage of Revenue Collected by Ownership Category:
           1978-1987

Year	State	Collective	Individual	Other
1978	86.8	12.7	0.5	0.0
1979	86.5	13.0	0.5	0.0
1980	85.4	14.0	0.6	0.0
1981	84.4	14.7	0.9	0.0
1982	81.6	15.1	3.3	0.0
1983	80.1	16.0	3.0	0.9
1984	78.9	17.2	2.8	1.1
1985	71.6	23.1	4.3	1.0
1986	77.1	16.9	4.1	1.9
1987	74.1	18.4	4.5	2.4

Source: ZGCZTJ, p. 25.

their economic performance. Budget deficits have increased since the introduction of reforms and the share of revenue contributed by state enterprises has fallen, but there is no evidence that tax reform is to blame for these developments. Meanwhile the new system has replaced enterprise remittances with tax revenue, and shares of budgetary and extrabudgetary revenue appear to have stabilized.

One unresolved issue is whether sufficient incentives have been introduced to increase profits and tax revenue. The success or failure of tax reform in this regard cannot be determined yet because the effects of the tax system cannot be separated from the results of other economic reforms being introduced at the same time. However, the intent of establishing a uniform, nonarbitrary tax code has been potentially undermined by the tax-contract system.

Another test of the success of tax reform will come when the new policy instruments are used to resolve problems that arise in the future. If tax policy is not adequate, will central leaders fall back on directives?

So far China's leaders have not passed this critical point. Economic austerity measures in the fall of 1988, and panic directives after economic disruption caused by the student demonstrations in June 1989, are cases in point. Nonetheless, economic reform is still on the agenda, and a new tax system is in place. That Chinese leaders have concerned themselves with these important aspects of the economy is reason for optimism.

Table 5. Percentage of Revenue Collected by Economic Sector: 1978-1987

Year	Industry	Agriculture	Commerce	Transport	Construction	Other
1978	75.4	2.8	12.2	7.3	0.2	2.1
1979	78.8	2.9	4.7	7.7	0.0	5.9
1980	82.7	3.0	1.5	6.5	0.1	6.2
1981	81.9	3.5	0.3	5.8	-0.1	8.6
1982	84.0	4.4	-3.7	4.6	0.1	10.6
1983	86.0	5.4	-7.9	5.7	0.9	9.9
1984	77.8	4.1	-0.8	8.3	0.4	10.2
1985	64.0	4.7	7.7	7.0	0.4	16.2
1986	56.1	3.6	14.7	5.4	1.0	19.2
1987	56.9	5.1	11.5	5.2	0.4	20.9

Source: ZGCZTJ, p. 33.

PROVINCIAL ECONOMIC DIFFERENCES DIMINISHED IN THE
DECADE OF REFORM

By David L. Denny *

CONTENTS

SUMMARY

When China's decade of economic reforms began in 1978, there was widespread concern that the reforms—including increased foreign trade, greater foreign investment and economic assistance, and increased freedom for private economic activities—would increase the disparity in development and income levels between China's "rich" and "poor" provinces.

Despite these expectations, China's decade of economic reform did not produce an ever widening gap between the economic performance of the "have" and the "have not" provinces. As measured

* David L. Denny is Director of Research at the US-China Business Council in Washington, D.C. The author has benefitted from the advice of friends, colleagues and family members too numerous to list. Special thanks to Joel Greene for research assistance and creation of the graphs.

by per capita net material product,[1] the economic disparities that had previously separated rich and poor provinces actually narrowed.

That economic reforms and the open door policies produced greater equality of economic performance in the provinces is, at first, quite a surprising result. After all, in order to increase incentives and economic efficiency, Deng Xiaoping and his pragmatic colleagues are quite rightly credited with introducing a more benign attitude toward increasing income differentials.

'Trickle down' economics, while perhaps effective at promoting savings and effort, is not usually credited with quickly promoting a more equitable structure of economic benefits. Moreover, China's greater emphasis on foreign trade, the aggressive solicitation of private foreign investment, and the activity of multilateral and bilateral lending institutions combined to increase concerns that foreign resources would gravitate to those parts of China already well endowed with sophisticated manpower as well as relatively modern transport and telecommunications systems. Finally, the weakening of central control over key aspects of the economy created doubts about the ability of the central government to redistribute resources from richer to poorer regions. [2]

In practice, however, many of the reasons for believing that provincial economic disparities would widen were exaggerated. The expansion of foreign trade opportunities did not work to the relative advantage of the well developed provinces that effectively monopolized China's foreign trade in the past. Foreign investment was more widely dispersed than is commonly believed but, more importantly, the activity of foreign lending agencies partially offset the tendencies of investors to locate in well developed provinces. And while central planners lost substantial control over fiscal resources, the central government retained its ability to subsidize the budgets of poor provinces from the coffers of the rich.

But the most important reason appears to be that the reforms allowed natural patterns of economic development to re-emerge. At least in the decade of the 1980's, this more natural pattern of regional economic development replaced the extremely irrational—and, in the final analysis, counterproductive—emphasis on egalitarianism that had characterized the Maoist Era.

---

[1] Net material product (the net value of all material producing sectors) is a better measure of ecnonomic performcance than the commonly used gross value output statistics. Nevertheless, NMP statistics systematically undervalue the service intensive economies such as those of Beijing and Shanghai. Unfortunately, at the provincial level the more satisfactory and comprehensive measures of economic activity (GNP/GDP) have only become available in the last few years {For example, Zhongguo Tongji Zhaiyao ,1990 (A Statistical Survey of China), Beijing, May 1990, p.6.}.

[2] A recently published paper provides a useful survey of these ideas and their expected impact on regional economic differences. The author, like most previous researchers, concludes that "in essence, uneven regional development may characterize China's development strategy for quite some time to come despite the government's faith in the diffusion effect of growth". Dali Yang, "Patterns of China's Regional Development Strategy", China Quarterly, No. 122, June 1990, p. 251. Space does not permit a full discussion of the reasons for the differences between Mr. Yang's conclusions and those of the present paper. They are due partly to a different choice of statistics (NMP vs. GVIO), different targets for the comparison (provinces as opposed to large regional groupings) and different time periods. Another significant difference is that this paper focuses on what actually happened to the broadest measure of economic performance during the past decade while much of Mr. Yang's focus is on the regional allocation of new investment (and by implication what may happen in the future.)

While no single theory can completely explain the narrowing of gaps in per capita economic performance during the decade of reforms, this paper describes the course of comparative provincial development over the 1978–88 decade and examines several factors affecting the observed pattern.

I. PROVINCIAL DISPARITIES NARROW

Figure 1 shows that provincial economic growth during this decade bore no simple relationship to the provinces' richness or poorness at the beginning of the period. Indeed, during the 1978–88 decade provinces that were relatively poor at the beginning of the decade tended to grow more rapidly than the richest provinces.

Twenty-eight Chinese provinces (all except Tibet and newly formed Hainan) are arrayed from left to right in Figure 1. Their per-capita products in 1977—the year prior to the beginning of the decade of reform—are depicted by bars which decline from Shanghai's per capita NMP of 1918 Yuan to the 127 Yuan registered in the same year by Guizhou.

If the richer provinces had grown relatively rapidly during the decade, the growth of the provincial economies would have followed the same general trend—and could be represented by a progressively declining line. But the actual result—depicted by the line labled 1978–88 Growth rate—was quite different. The actual growth rates varied substantially around the national average (the horizontal line in Figure 1) but there was certainly no systematic tendency for provincial growth rates to decline as one moves from left to right (i.e. from rich to poorer provinces).

In fact, the five poorest provinces at the beginning of the decade had, on average, higher growth rates than the five richest provinces. But the highest growth rates were achieved neither by provinces that started off "rich" nor "poor" but by those that began the decade in the middle[3]. As a result, as will be demonstrated below, both middle and poorer provinces in China gained on the richest provinces.

While Figure 1 shows substantial differences in the rates of provincial economic growth (from Zhejiang's 14.9 percent per year to Heilongjiang's 7.1 percent), even the slowest growing Chinese province turned in an economic performance that most countries would envy. China as a whole grew extremely rapidly during the decade and the fruits of economic growth, while quite varied across the broad expanse of China, were, nonetheless, widely shared.[4]

Figure 2 "normalizes" the economic status of each province by calculating per capita net material product in relation to the na-

---

[3] These trends were described earlier by the author in "Equalizing Opportunity", *China Business Review*, September–October, 1987, p. 4.

[4] About half of the provinces turned in performances that were consistent throughout the decade. That is to say, their NNP growth consistently lagged behind the national average (five provinces inlcuding three with initially high per capita incomes—Shanghai, Tianjin and Heilongjiang) or were consistently higher than the national average (nine provinces including star performers such as Zhejiang, Jiangsu, Fujian and Guangdong).

However, six provinces (Beijing plus six of the poorer provinces) did well during the first part of the period but fell behind in the second part of the period. Finally, eight provinces turned in a sub par performance during the 1978–83 provinces but then proceeded to accelerate during 1983–88. The eight provinces in the latter category are: Liaoning, Hebei, Shandong, Jiangxi, Shaanxi, Gansu, Qinghai and Ningxia.

Figure 1
Provincial Per Capita NMP in 1977 and
Average Annual Growth Rates 1978-88

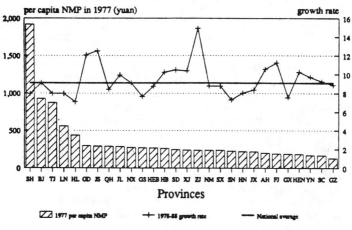

Provinces

Data table

Province and code		Per capita NMP in 1977	Growth rate 1978-88
Shanghai	SH	1,918	7.95
Beijing	BJ	927	9.06
Tianjin	TJ	873	7.96
Liaoning	LN	560	7.96
Heilongjiang	HL	437	7.09
Guangdong	GD	297	12.05
Jiangsu	JS	289	12.51
Qinghai	QH	287	8.40
Jilin	JL	284	9.92
Ningxia	NX	273	9.09
Gansu	GS	271	7.64
Hebei	HEB	267	8.73
Hubei	HB	261	10.23
Shandong	SD	246	10.46
Xinjiang	XJ	239	10.37
Zhejiang	ZJ	237	14.91
Nei Monggol	NM	237	8.76
Shanxi	SX	236	8.74
Shaanxi	SN	226	7.31
Hunan	HN	219	8.02
Jiangxi	JX	217	8.35
Anhui	AH	198	10.56
Fujian	FJ	190	11.23
Guangxi	GX	186	7.55
Henan	HEN	184	10.25
Yunnan	YN	168	9.71
Sichuan	SC	166	9.24
Guizhou	GZ	127	8.87
National average		290	9.09

Source: see appendix

tional average (which is set equal to 100). Thus, Shanghai's per capita net material product of 1918 in 1977 is transformed into 685 after it is divided by the national average of 290 and multiplied by 100. This calculation was made for each province for the year prior to the decade of reform (1977) as well as for the final year (1988).

The result is an unambiguous and consistent shift towards greater provincial economic equality during the period. The fairly steep slope of the curve in 1977 (falling from Shanghai's normalized per capita NMP of 685 yuan, or 6.9 times the national average, and more than 15 times Guizhou's per capita product of 45.4 yuan) is replaced by a substantially flatter curve in 1988. As shown in Figure 2, the five wealthiest provinces at the beginning of the period lost ground relative to the national average, while the five least prosperous provinces all gained ground.

Analysis of the relationship between the average per capita NMP and its standard deviation leads to the same conclusion. As Table 1 shows, the variance of provincial per capita net material product declined throughout the period. It was highest in 1977, declined between 1977 and 1983, and declined again between 1983 and 1988.

This review of the empirical data makes it clear that the per capita net material products of China's provinces did not become increasingly unequal during the decade of reform. In fact, there was a notable tendency for the economic performance of the provinces to become more equal.

But describing *what* happened during this tumultuous decade is much easier than explaining *why* it happened. What are the factors that led to the closing of the gap of per capita net material product? To what extent are they based on fundamental economic factors? To what extent did political power play a role in bringing about this trend towards a more egalitarian regional distribution of economic power? Are these trends susceptible to any consistent explanation or explanations, or do the results merely reflect a myriad of events caused by unpredictable human and natural phenomena?

To answer these questions would require a major research effort. The rest of this brief paper will only proceed a small part of the way towards that goal. Factors such as the power of the central government to redistribute budgetary resources, the impact of the open door policy, and the move away from the previous period's emphasis on regional self-reliance will be reviewed.

II. INTER-PROVINCIAL BUDGETARY TRANSFERS

Much has been made of the erosion of the capacity of China's governmental units at all levels to generate revenues. Between 1978 and 1988, the revenues of governments at all levels grew at an annual average rate of 8.7 percent, failing, however, to keep pace with economic growth. As a proportion of NMP, fiscal revenues declined from 37.3 percent in 1977 to 22 percent in 1988. This decline in revenue-generating capacity has led to concerns that the Chinese government will be unable to continue to fulfill such traditional functions as funding large infrastructure investment projects and transferring budgetary resources from richer to poorer provinces.

Figure 2
Normalized Provincial Per Capita NMP
comparison of 1977 and 1988

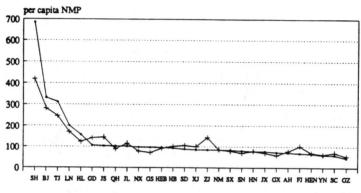

Provinces

— 1977   + 1988

Data table

Province and code		1977	1988
Shanghai	SH	685.0	419.0
Beijing	BJ	331.3	282.1
Tianjin	TJ	311.8	246.7
Liaoning	LN	200.0	169.8
Heilongjiang	HL	156.1	123.1
Guangdong	GD	106.1	141.1
Jiangsu	JS	103.2	144.3
Qinghai	QH	102.5	88.6
Jilin	JL	101.4	115.2
Ningxia	NX	97.5	78.5
Gansu	GS	96.8	71.5
Hebei	HEB	95.4	91.6
Hubei	HB	93.2	101.3
Shandong	SD	87.9	105.8
Xinjiang	XJ	85.4	100.3
Zhejiang	ZJ	84.6	143.2
Nei Monggol	NM	84.6	85.4
Shanxi	SX	83.9	80.0
Shaanxi	SN	80.7	70.2
Hunan	HN	78.2	78.8
Jiangxi	JX	77.5	69.7
Guangxi	GX	72.9	58.7
Anhui	AH	70.7	77.5
Fujian	FJ	67.9	101.3
Henan	HEN	65.7	69.9
Yunnan	YN	60.0	62.5
Sichuan	SC	59.3	70.5
Guizhou	GZ	45.4	53.7

Source: see appendix

TABLE 1. Variation of Provincial Per Capita NMP

	1977	1983	1988
Average of Provincial Per Capita NMP	352.5	595	1180.1
Standard Deviation	364.2	477.5	870.8
Std. Deviation/Average	1.03	0.80	0.74

In addition to the decline in the government's ability to generate fiscal revenues, the expenditures of the central government also declined in relation to expenditures of local governments. The rate of growth of central government expenditures during the decade was 7.1 percent compared to the 10.7% growth of local government expenditures. Since the central government has in the past aggressively used its control over capital construction funds to transfer resources from richer to poorer provinces, one may presume that the decline in the central government's fiscal expenditures probably hit the poorer areas particularly hard. For example, the official estimates of the provincial distribution of fixed asset investment shows a substantial decline in the share of national investment funds going to the poorer provinces in the deep interior regions.[5]

These very significant fiscal changes during the decade of reform raise complex questions of analysis and interpertation. A complete understanding of the fiscal relationships affecting the various provinces would have to assess the regional impact of the central government's own expenditures and analyze which provinces bear the burden of the taxes that are allocated directly to the central government. The growing role of "extra-budgetary" revenues and expenditures would also have to be assessed. Such questions are beyond the scope of this paper.

Fortunately, it is not necessary to assess all aspects of China's fiscal system or how the fiscal system may have changed over time. For the purpose of this paper it is sufficient to show that despite the central government's decline in authority over the period, it still retained sufficient power at the end of the period to affect significant budgetary transfers from rich to poor provinces. The conclusion that the government budget is still an important vehicle for tranferring resources from richer to poorer provinces will, at first, seem inconsistent with the central-local fiscal relationships sketched in Figure 3. As the three graphs show,there has been a substantial change in the division of China's revenues between the central and local governments. Central government revenues have grown much more rapidly than local government revenues.[6] On

---

[5] China State Statistical Publishing House, *Zhongguo Guding Zichan Touzi Tongji Ziliao (Statistical Materials on Fixed Asset Investment in China)*, Beijing, 1989, p. 23.

[6] As will be discussed below, China's fiscal system is based on "unitary" principles. Nearly all tax rates and tax bases are determined by the central government. Similarly, in theory, the central government also determines the appropriate types of expenditures to be made by local and central governments. In such a system, "local" revenues are not determined solely by local authorities nor do they have complete control over their usage. In fact, under China's fiscal system some local governents are required to hand over some of their "local" revenues to the central government. Despite these facts, the classification of some revenue sources as "local revenues" appears to imply some degree of de facto "entitlement" to such revenue sources. For example, all "local" revenues are included in the provincial budgets—even though some portion must be shared with the central government.

the other hand, the expenditures of local governments have grown much more rapidly than the expenditures of the central government.

Figure 3
Central and Local Government Budgets

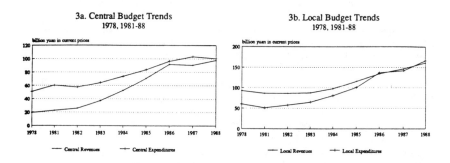

3a. Central Budget Trends
1978, 1981-88

3b. Local Budget Trends
1978, 1981-88

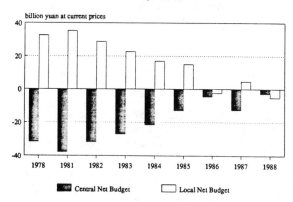

3c. Central, Local Deficits & Surpluses
1978, 1981-88

Source: see appendix

As a result of these trends, central government revenues now provide nearly enough funds to pay for central government expenditures (Fig 3A). The large central government budget deficit (Fig 3C) that existed at the beginning of the decade (which was offset by revenues collected by local governments and transferred to the center) has been all but eliminated.[7] Similarly, the combined

---

[7] This section relies on Chinese official statistics on central and provincial revenues, expenditures and deficits. On a normal "IMF Basis", revenues are overstated (and the deficit is understated) because the Chinese practice is to include governmental revenues from domestic and foreign borrowing as part of budgetary revenue.

budget surplus of all local governments has been systematically el-
minated (3C) as expenditures have been allowed to increase much
more rapidly than local revenues (Fig 3B).

Such a trend has potentially far-reaching implications for the
future. At present, however, local government finance has not been
cut loose and placed on a "pay as you go basis". A recent World
Bank comprehensive study of China's fiscal system emphasizes that
the Chinese fiscal system remains based on "unitary" principles in
which local budgets are subordinated to and included within the
national consolidated budget.[8]

The amalgamation of local budgets into the consolidated national
budget is not simply for accounting convenience. Rather it reflects
the fact that the central government has control or at least strong
influence over revenues and expenditures at all levels of government. The central government determines the tax base and tax
rates that local governments are allowed to use. The center also determines local expenditures in a fair amount of detail. Finally, the
local and central governments bargain over what portions of local
revenues must be turned over to the center.

The result, as will be shown below, is a system in which local expenditures were not tightly linked to local revenues at least for the
1978–88 period. There are, however, good reasons to believe that
the linkage between revenues and expenditures increased during
the decade. In particular, the revenue "contract responsibility systems" introduced at the very end of the period will increase the
ability of local governments to retain revenues when they collect
more than they have contracted for. However, detailed information
on the new systems, such as how many provinces are covered and
how the contracts have worked in practice, is not available. In any
case, the introduction of such reforms so late in the decade was not
a key factor in influencing provincial economic performance during
the period.[9]

In a broad sense, China's fiscal system during the decade of
reform maintained some of the features described by Lardy who
concluded that in the 1950's there was an "absence of a link between local revenues and expenditures".[10] Lardy attributed this to

[8] *China: Revenue Mobilization and Tax Policy,* (A World Bank Country Study), Washington
D.C., 1990). The report contains a wealth of data and insightful analysis about the fiscal relations between the central and local governments. The unitary nature of the Chinese system is
described on page 240: "By comparison with most countries of the world, local governments in
China have little formal independence in matters of structuring their tax system or deciding on
the level and composition of expenditures." Nevertheless, the report goes on to emphasize that
local governments influence taxes and expenditures through negotiations with the central government and through their ability to adjust tax obligations of their subordinate units. As a
result, "provincial governments do indeed have significant room to adjust fiscal decisons to local
needs and preferences (pp. 245–46).
[9] The absence of a tight link between provincial revenues and expenditures during the decade
should be qualified by the fact that throughout the decade fiscal reforms were introduced that
tended to increase the linkage. This was done to give provinces greater incentives to increase
revenues. At the very end of the period, new revenue contract responsibility systems were negotiated between the central and local governments. In some cases, this may have had the effect of
allowing at least some of the provinces to retain all or most of their revenues over their "contracted" responsibilities. The World Bank has expressed concerns over the implications of these
changes: "an important implication of these shifts is that the central government's ability to use
discretionary policy to redistribute among provinces, or to centralize national finances, is much
more limited.", *Revenue Mobilization and Tax Policy,* p. 93.
[10] Nicholas Lardy, *Economic Growth and Distribution in China,* Cambridge University Press,
1978, p. 169.

the fact that "the center imposes a unified tax system and also continues to control the budgetary expenditures of local governments." [11]

As a result of its influence over local government finance, the central government was still able to transfer significant fiscal resources from rich to poor provinces even at the end of the decade of reform. Table 2 indicates that in 1988, only 7 of China's provinces compiled budget surpluses, which totalled 19.5 billion yuan. These budget surpluses offset the combined budget deficits of 24.8 billion yuan in the remaining 23 provinces.

Since the central governments' own revenues were almost evenly balanced with central expenditures, central government revenues were not the source of funds to offset the red ink in the 23 deficit provinces. In addition, local governments are not supposed to run deficits and can borrow only under very restrictive conditions. [12] Finally, in a few cases such as Shanghai, corroborative evidence exists to indicate that the budget surpluses roughly approximate the local revenues that local governments were required to turn over to the center. [13]

Table 2 also indicates that the size of the financial transfers was substantial. Shanghai's surplus, for example, was nearly 60% of its budget revenues—even so Shanghai must have had trouble meeting its obligation to transfer 10.5 billion yuan to the central government.

Moreover, as late in the decade as 1988, many of the poorer provinces continued to run extremely large budget deficits in relation to their own revenues. Six provinces (Tibet, Qinghai, Ningxia, Xinjiang, Hainan and Inner Mongolia) ran deficits larger than their revenues. Another seven provinces ran deficits exceeding one quarter of their own revenue sources. The shortfalls were met by drawing upon budget surpluses amassed by Shanghai, Beijing, Tianjin, Liaoning, Jiangsu and Zhejiang. In other words, the budget surplus provinces were six of the seven richest provinces in China. Budget deficit provinces on the other hand were generally the poorer provinces.

There are some interesting exceptions to the general rule that the richest provinces ran budget surpluses that provided fiscal funds for the poorest provinces. Guangdong is ranked sixth among China's richest provinces but ran budget deficits from 1986 to 1988. Guangdong's 1988 budget deficit reached 7% of its local revenues. This appears to be due to the special consideration the center has granted Guangdong since the beginning of the reform period.

---

[11] Lardy, *Economic Growth and Distribution*, p. 169.

[12] World Bank, *Revenue Mobilization and Tax Policy*, p. 87.

[13] In Zhuang Xiaotian's "Report on Shanghai's 1988 Final Budget Accounts" (*CHINA (?)*,Joint Publicaton Research Service, CAR–89–063, p. 26), he says that "total local revenue was 15,337 million yuan (which overfulfilled) the budgeted revenue and thus accomplished the contracted task of turning 10.5 billion yuan to the central authorities". As reported in Table 2, Shanghai's 1988 budget surplus was 8.9 billion yuan. As emphasized in the text, budget surpluses and deficits only approximate the required revenue transfers to and from the consolidated government budget. Comparison of provincial 1988 budget surpluses and deficits and the World Bank's description of revenue sharing formulas (World Bank, *Revenue Mobilization and Tax Policy*, p. 89) demonstrates that the budget surpluses (deficits) are consistently smaller (larger) than the amount of revenue transfers called for under the sharing formulas. Part of the reason for this divergence appears to be the fact that the central government funds specific line item expenditures included in provincial government budgets.

TABLE 2

Provincial Budget Surpluses (+) and Deficits (-) in 1988

	Surpluses and Deficits	Surplus/Deficit as % of Budget Revenues	Per capita NMP: Provincial Rank
Shanghai	+8.892	57.91%	1
Jiangsu	+3.651	31.61%	7
Zhejiang	+2.242	26.21%	5
Liaoning	+2.070	17.80%	4
Beijing	+1.518	22.28%	2
Tianjin	+0.980	21.91%	3
Hubei	+0.172	2.47%	12
Hebei	-0.273	0.42%	15
Shandong	-0.356	3.95%	10
Anhui	-0.427	10.09%	21
Shanxi	-0.445	11.40%	18
Hainan	-0.518	122.17%	14
Henan	-0.624	8.92%	25
Fujian	-0.692	17.23%	11
Guangdong	-0.763	7.09%	6
Ningxia	-0.875	172.58%	20
Qinghai	-0.921	181.66%	16
Jiangxi	-1.006	31.14%	26
Hunan	-1.010	18.43%	19
Guizhou	-1.018	39.21%	30
Tibet	-1.048	–	27
Shaanxi	-1.071	31.62%	23
Gansu	-1.140	45.64%	22
Heilongjiang	-1.147	18.33%	8
Sichuan	-1.261	14.45%	24
Yunnan	-1.431	28.32%	28
Jilin	-1.794	41.41%	9
Guangxi	-1.939	57.23%	29
Xinjiang	-2.345	151.68%	13
Inner Mongolia	-2.688	111.40%	17

Source: 1989 Zhongguo Jingji Nianjian (1989 Almanac of China's Economy),
Part IV, pp. 1-251, and various 1989 Provincial Yearbooks

Guangdong needs to build its infrastructure rapidly to play its role in attracting foreign investment as well as to present a prosperous face toward Hong Kong. For this reason, Guangdong appears to have been exempt from large budget transfers to the central government budget.

Jilin and Heilongjiang also rank among the top ten in terms of per-capita NMP but still ran substantial deficits. A more careful study of these provinces is needed, but one of the possible conclusions may turn out to be that the poor performances in Jilin and Heilongjiang were due to the increasing losses of state-owned enterprises—which account for a particularly large share of economic activity in the Northeast.

Finally, the provinces that were subsidized most heavily were Tibet, Qinghai, Ningxia, Xinjiang and Inner Mongolia. In addition to being relatively poor, these provinces tend to have large populations of ethnic minorities, they are located on sensitive borders (except for Qinghai), they are sparsely populated and their areas are thought to contain significant underground natural resources. Such factors have forced the central government to place a special emphasis on promoting social stability and economic development in these provinces.

How did these trends affect per capita governmental expenditures in the poorer provinces relative to the richer ones? Were the richer provinces acquiring greater budgetary resources while the poorer provinces were havng a tougher time keeping up?

This question cannot be answered definitively without a detailed study of the regional distribution of central government expenditures, an analysis of extra-budgetary expenditures and the inter-relationship between central and local government expenditures. Nevertheless, Figure 4 takes a step in that direction by providing information on per-capita local government expenditures. The evidence indicates that the poorer provinces ended the decade in a relatively better position to support local expenditures than they were in at the beginning of the period.

Figure 4 and the accompanying data show that nine of the top ten provinces in terms of per capita local expenditures suffered declines in per capita budgetary expenditures relative to the national average. By contrast, six of the ten provinces that began the period with the lowest per capita local government expenditures improved their relative position by 1988.

As a result, despite the general weakening of the fiscal system, the increasing power of local governments, and the new systems that left a portion of incremental tax collections in local hands, budgetary transfers remained an important mechanism whereby the richer rgions of China provided assistance to poorer areas. And poorer provinces ended the period in a relatively better position in terms of their ability to finance per capita expenditures from local budgets.

III. The Impact of the "Open Door" on Regional Economic Inequality

Western and Chinese analysts have both been concerned that China's new policies towards foreign economic relations might exacerbate regional inequalities. These fears appear to have been exaggerated. This is not to say that the fruits of the open door have been distributed evenly throughout China. Indeed, it is quite obvious that in most respects the coastal regions have been much better positioned to seize the opportunities that the open door policies created. Nevertheless, when one takes a comprehensive view of all aspects of the new foreign economic policies, it is clear that the

Figure 4
Normalized Per Capita Expenditures
comparison of 1978 and 1988

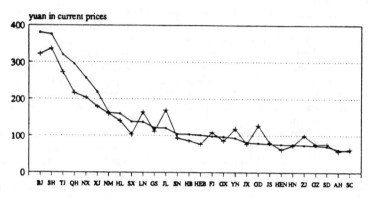

Provinces

— 1978   —+— 1988

Data table

Province and code		1978	1988
Beijing	BJ	380.6	321.9
Shanghai	SH	375.5	336.7
Tianjin	TJ	320.2	272.9
Qinghai	QH	295.4	216.3
Ningxia	NX	257.2	204.2
Xinjiang	XJ	219.1	179.4
Nei Monggol	NM	162.5	160.2
Heilongjiang	HL	159.7	140.5
Shanxi	SX	138.1	103.8
Liaoning	LN	137.3	163.8
Gansu	GS	121.6	112.0
Jilin	JL	120.6	169.7
Shaanxi	SN	104.4	93.5
Hubei	HB	103.9	86.3
Hebei	HEB	101.6	76.6
Fujian	FJ	97.8	108.8
Guangxi	GX	96.8	85.7
Yunnan	YN	93.7	118.6
Jiangxi	JX	81.0	77.2
Guangdong	GD	79.4	127.8
Jiangsu	JS	77.1	80.7
Henan	HEN	75.8	61.9
Hunan	HN	75.1	72.4
Zhejiang	ZJ	73.7	99.5
Guizhou	GZ	72.6	76.0
Shandong	SD	70.6	76.4
Anhui	AH	61.2	57.0
Sichuan	SC	58.3	62.1

Source: see appendix

benefits of the much greater foreign economic relations have been spread quite widely—even to the far interior regions of China.

A. FOREIGN TRADE

The foreign trade system that preceded the open door reforms substantially favored the ports and coastal provinces. Prior to the decade of reforms, the coastal provinces undertook almost all of China's foreign trade. Even though the central government formally monopolized most foreign trade decisions and allowed little foreign exchange to remain in the hands of local officials, the coastal areas derived enormous benefits from shipping and port activities and from establishing export processing ventures. The success of such undertakings was based, in large part, on sourcing low-priced raw materials from inland provinces.

Foreign trade reforms in the late 1970s and in the early 1980s[14] loosened the grip of the central government and the coastal areas on the procurement of foreign trade goods. Provinces were allowed to deal directly with foreigners through their own foreign trade companies. Perhaps more importantly, local branches of the Ministry of Foreign Economic Relations and Trade (MOFERT) foreign trade companies increasingly came under the influence of local officials. One result was that when inland provinces sent products out through the ports, they increasingly did so on a commission basis and retained control over decisionmaking and contracting.

This was not necessarily rational from an economic point of view. In many cases it led to reverse protectionism. Provinces surrounding Shanghai, for example, built their own industries that in many instances turned out to be less efficient. But the net result was a slower growth of Shanghai's export processing industries and a more rapid buildup of the exports of the inland provinces. Indeed, throughout the 1980s, port cities such as Shanghai, Tianjin and Dalian blamed the poor performance of their exports in part on their inability to obtain access to raw materials and exportable products from interior provinces.[15]

These trends are clearly reflected in provincial trade statistics. They show that exports of most of the important exporting provinces (those that exported more than $500 million in 1980) grew much less rapidly than the national average (national exports increased by 2.6 times between 1980 and 1988). For example, Shanghai's exports grew by less than 8.7 percent in 8 years, Tianjin's

---

[14] Chinese sources vary signficantly on when the central government first allowed provinces to have a signficant degree of control over their own foreign trade. Some descriptions allege that certain provinces controlled their foreign trade even prior to the economic reforms of the late 1970's. However, most sources indicate that real self management (ziying) of imports and exports began only in the late 1970's and some provinces did not obtain much control over their foreign trade until the early or mid-1980's. Discussions of provincial foreign trade patterns and strategy are found in the annual economic almanacs (Zhongguo Jingji Nianjian) and the Foreign Trade Almanacs of the Ministry of Foreign Economic Relations and Trade (MOFERT).

[15] A recent article summarized the changes from Shanghai's point of view. "However, when the 1980's arrived, characterized by reform and opening to the outside world, Shanghai not only began to lag far behind Hong Kong and Singapore, ... but its domestic position also began to drop day by day ... The city began to face crises one after another in raw material supply, the sales of its products and its economic performance. Its former economic power and strength was in the process of being overtaken or had already been overtaken by other provinces and cities." Wan Zengwei, "Create a New Situation in Shanghai's Economic Development By Giving Priority to Opening Efforts and Invigorating the Municipal Economy Through Trade", in Foreign Broadcast Information Service, *Daily Report,* August 27, 1990, p. 43.

grew by only 9.1 percent, Liaoning's actually declined by 3 percent and Shandong's were up 69 percent (thanks primarily to the rapid growth of Shengli oil field). The only important traditional exporting provinces that did better than the national average were Guangdong (up 340 percent) and Jiangsu (up 280 percent).

Inland provinces that had been unable to directly conduct their own foreign trade in previous years took advantage of the new system and rapidly expanded their own exports. Shaanxi exports went up 37 fold in eight years, Xinjiang exports were up by 17.5 times, Anhui's were up 13.9 times, Shanxi's up 21.8 times, Inner Mongolia's up 11 times, Sichuan's up 23 times, Zhejiang's up 6.7 times and Heilongjiang's up 8.8 times.

Exports are, of course, a better measure of the cost than the benefit of foreign trade. Unfortunately, the information on provincial imports is much less comprehensive and well defined. In addition, total imports credited to the provinces account for less than 25 percent of all of China's imports. In contrast, exports attributed to particular provinces have tended to account for 80–90 percent of China's total during the 1980's.

Without a much more detailed study of how the inland provinces were compensated for rapidly growing exports (either in terms of a portion of the national import basket or by receiving better terms of trade for domestically produced commodities), it is impossible to determine how much inland provinces benefitted from these high growth rates of "self-managed" exports. Suffice it to say that the rapid growth of "self managed" exports suggests that the inland provinces had meaningful incentives to rapidly expand their exports.

B. FOREIGN DIRECT INVESTMENT

While foreign investors have concentrated on the coastal provinces and the three major metropolitan areas of Beijing, Shanghai and Tianjin, the inland areas have been more successful at acquiring foreign investment than is commonly realized.

As Figure 5 shows, Beijing, Tianjin, Shanghai, Guangdong and Fujian account for 73.6 percent of all foreign investment contracts and 71.1 percent of the dollar value of investment commitments for which China lists the host province. In fact, Guangdong and Fujian province signed nearly two-thirds of all investment contracts and received nearly 50 percent of the investment commitments.[16]

The remaining coastal provinces (Liaoning, Hebei, Shandong, Jiangsu, Zhejiang, Hainan and Guangxi) account for 18.3 percent of the numbers of investment contracts and 16.6 percent of the dollar value of investment commitments. Only 8.1 percent of all foreign investment contracts and 12.2 percent of the investment commitments have gone to China's remaining 18 inland provinces.

---

[16] In Figures 5 and 6, Chinese provinces have been divided into five groups. The three metropolitan areas (Beijing, Shanghai and Tianjin) are grouped as "Metropolitan". Guangdong and Fujian are grouped as "S.China/SEZ" reflecting their special priveleges. The other coastal provinces include Liaoning, Hebei, Shandong, Jiangsu, Zhejiang, Hainan and Guangxi. Inland provinces are divided into "Near Inland" and "Deep Interior". Near inland provinces are: Anhui, Shanxi, Henan, Hubei, Hunan, Jiangxi and Jilin. Deep interior provinces are: Heilongjiang, Inner Mongolia (Nei Menggu), Shaanxi, Gansu, Qinghai, Ningxia and Xinjiang.

Figure 5
Foreign Investment by Region
by commitment value

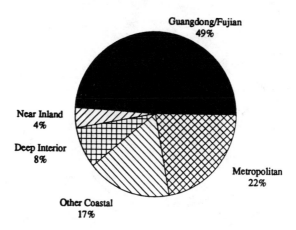

Guangdong/Fujian
49%

Near Inland
4%

Deep Interior
8%

Metropolitan
22%

Other Coastal
17%

1983-1988

Data table

	Number of FIEs	Commitment Value*
Guangdong and Fujian	10,022	9,239
Metropolitan Areas	1,286	4,251
Other Coastal Provinces	2,805	3,153
Deep Interior Provinces	566	1,578
Near Inland Provinces	683	724
Total	15,362	18,945

* million US dollars

Source: see appendix

Figure 6
World Bank Projects by Region
by commitment value

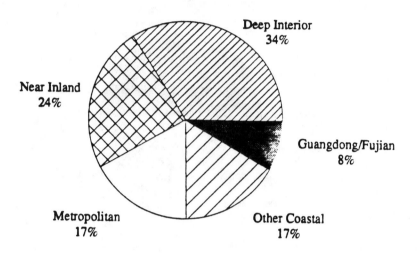

Data table

	Number of Projects or Major Component	Commitment Value*
Deep Interior Provinces	33	1,990
Near Inland Provinces	26	1,398
Metropolitan Areas	15	999
Other Coastal Provinces	21	965
Guangdong and Fujian	9	475
Total	104	5,827

* million US dollars

Source: see appendix

The fact that the inland provinces have lagged behind the coastal and metropolitan areas in acquiring foreign investment will surprise no one. But the degree of success that inland provinces have had in attracting foreign investors should not be minimized. A surprising number of investors have ventured far from the coastal areas to invest in Central China and even in far Northwest and Southwest China. One hundred thirteen investors have gone into Sichuan, one hundred twenty-four are located in Shaanxi, and ninety-two are located in Anhui.

Even the deep interior provinces had attracted a significant number of investors by the end of 1988. Thirty-seven foreign investors were located in Guizhou; thirty-one made commitments to Yunnan; and thirty were established in Xinjiang.

Private foreign investment interest in China is, to an overwhelming degree, simply a natural extension of the Hong Kong economy across the border into South China. The geographical spread of foreign investment does not appear nearly as skewed if the investment commitments made to Guangdong and Fujian are factored out. Three provinces (Beijing, Shanghai and Jiangsu) have more than five hundred investors; Twelve provinces have between one hundred and five hundred, and only four provinces (Ningxia, Qinghai, Gansu and Tibet) have attracted fewer than thirty private foreign investors.

Obviously one cannot argue that foreign investment has been evenly spread throughout the country. However, the usual picture of the domination by a handful of coastal provinces should be balanced by the fact that every province has attracted some private foreign investment and two thirds of the provinces (including many whose population and economies are much smaller) were able to attract at least 100 foreign investment enterprises.

C. FOREIGN ECONOMIC ASSISTANCE PROGRAMS

A third key element of the open door program was China's decision to solicit aggressively the economic assistance of the World Bank, the United Nations Development Program, and a large number of other multinational and bilateral economic assistance donors. In the space of a decade, these lending agencies have implemented very large scale programs. For example, until the suspension of new projects in June 1989, the World Bank had approved 69 projects with a total loan value of over $8 billion, the benefits of which were spread over an exceedingly large portion of China's territory. Twenty-one provinces acquired at least one major World Bank project located entirely within their borders and at least ten provinces had two projects under their sole jurisdiction.

While it is impossible to determine the final destination of all of the World Bank funds, it is possible to determine the provinces that benefitted from the major components of World Bank projects. Assuming that the benefits are equally shared among all provinces that participate in projects crossing provincial boundaries, it is possible to divide the benefits of World Bank funding among the various provinces.[17]

Figure 6 presents data on the number of projects (or major components) and rough estimates for the value of the loans to metroplitan areas, to Guangdong and Fujian, to Coastal Provinces and to the Near and Deep Interior provinces. A comparison of Figures 5 and 6 reveals the striking conclusion that the World Bank has a regional orientation that is almost exactly opposite that of private foreign investors. Guangdong and Fujian account for about half of foreign investment commitments but have acquired less than 10 percent of the World Bank funds. The inland provinces, however, appear to be capturing about half of the World Bank projects as compared to just over 10 percent of private foreign investment.

The regional spread of the World Bank program suggests that there are powerful pressures on both the international organizations and on Chinese officials to distribute the benefits of the programs reasonably widely.

IV. SPREAD EFFECTS: A RETURN TO A MORE NORMAL PATTERN

In previous sections, I have argued that the relatively even distribution of economic performance during the decade was, in part, related to the fact that the Central Government was able to control and utilize strong levers to influence the pattern of economic growth. Budget resources were re-allocated from more prosperous to poorer areas. Moreover, the central government surely played some role in directing foreign investors and foreign lending institutions to many different sections of China to ensure that the reform and open door policies produced benefits for important constituencies.

However, I do not wish to leave the impression that the central government played the key role in preventing the growth of provincial economic differentials. Rather, to the extent that any one single factor may have been responsible for leveling provincial disparities, is best summed up as the return of more natural economic patterns that offset the extremely irrational and self-defeating patterns that characterized China's regional economic policies in the previous two decades.

The work of several observers but most notably Nicholas Lardy and Barry Naughton, have demonstrated the incredible wastefulness and counterproductivity of much of Maoist economic policy during the 1960s and early 1970s.[18] Lardy has shown that the attempt to reach local self reliance forced many poor agricultural areas to abandon crops that they produced efficiently for the market. The policies of near autarky appear to have worked par-

---

[17] These calculations do not include the World Bank's loans to educational institutions and to financial intermediaries. These projects have a myriad of sub-components and tend to have the largest number of beneficiaries. In fact, in several of the educational programs, virtually every province in China was represented by its leading university or research institute. Thus, excluding these projects from the analysis probably leads to an underestimate of the geographical spread of the World Bank program.

[18] Nicholas Lardy, *Agriculture in China's Modern Economic Development*, Cambridge University Press, 1983. Lardy concluded that "to a signficant degree rural poverty in the late 1970s was policy-induced and not merely the consequence of resource endowments or other natural constraints". (p. 176). Barry Naughton, "The Third Front: Defence Industrialization in the Chinese Interior", *China Quarterly*, No. 115, September 1988, pp. 351-386.

ticularly harshly against the poorest areas—perhaps because their only alternative was to retreat to subsistence agriculture. Naughton has reached a similar conclusion about the immense waste of resources involved in the "Third Front" effort to bring industry to the poorest areas. The campaign was usually unsuccessful at its primary objective—building industrial show cases in the rural areas—and it probably also diverted those areas from doing what they could do best.

Largely as a result of these misguided Maoist policies, China's economic map in 1977 revealed a most unusual regional economic development pattern. Guangdong's per capita NMP ranked only slightly above average and Fujian was among the poorest provinces in China. Other apparent anamolies include the fact that Sichuan, China's most productive grain-growing province, ranked second from the bottom in per capita NMP. Shandong and Zhejiang (generally considered relatively advanced because of their long coasts with good ports and other natural conditions) ranked 14th and 16th respectively. On the other hand, Qinghai, Ningxia and Gansu—normally thought of as among the poorest areas of China ranked above all of the provinces just mentioned with the exception of Guangdong.

This pattern of development largely reflected the Chinese Communist Party's pre-occupation with real and imaginary ("sugar coated" in the parlance of the Cultural Revolution) bullets that party stalwarts worried might undermine China's military and idealogical positions. These concerns not only prevented the economic success of Hong Kong from spilling over into neighboring Guangdong province, they also made China's planners unwilling to invest in Fujian (because of fear of possible war in the Taiwan straits) and reduced the possibility of direct contacts between rapidly growing Japan and coastal provinces such as Shandong. Moreover, as argued in the section on foreign trade, China's foreign trade planning systems made it difficult for provinces neighboring the major metropolitan areas to take advantage of their own resources to participate in foreign trade.[19]

While the readjustment of the previous irrational situation often went too far during the decade of reform, the return to a more normal economic pattern is probably the single most important fact that explains why Zhejiang, Jiangsu, Anhui, Shandong, and Henan and Guangdong and Fujian improved their positions so dramatically. They were enjoying the natural spread effects that spilled over from nearby major metropolitan regions and benefitting from the reversal of the previous period's constraints on the exploitation of their own locational advantages and natural resources.

"Economic spread effects", cannot, however, account for every aspect of China's regional economic development pattern during this period. For example, certain provinces such as Xinjiang and

---

[19] One of the enduring ironies of the Maoist era is the fact that despite the best intentions to develop a system to promote a more egalitarian economic development pattern, economic differentials (as measured by provincial per capita net material product) actually increased between 1957 and 1977. Taking the standard deviation over the mean (per capita NMP) as the measure of variation in economic performance there was a 50% rise in the variation of provincial per capita NMP between 1957 and 1977 (.83 in 1957 and 1.24 in 1977).

Yunnan, were too far away from metropolitan areas to expect to benefit from the "spread effects", and yet they grew substantially more rapidly than the national average.

To take another example, Hebei, which surrounds Beijing and Tianjin, grew less rapidly than the national average during the decade (although growth did pick up in the second half of the period—see Footnote 5). If 'spread effects' are the key reason for variations in regional growth one must explain why Hebei did not appear to benefit.

It is always possible that Hebei did ,in fact, benefit from the spread effects so noticeable around Shanghai and Hong Kong. Conceivably other unexplained factors may have offset the spread effects. Suffice it to say that such an anomaly presents an obvious target for more detailed research.

V. CONCLUSION

By most standards all Chinese provinces grew very rapidly during the decade of reform, but the pattern of provincial development tends to contradict the conventional wisdom. The rich did not grow richer (relatively) nor did the poor grow poorer—if anything the opposite happened. And while coastal areas generally had an advantage, some of the most successful performances came from provinces that were far inland.

The results are too diverse to be explained by any single economic or political theory. But one overall perspective that explains a substantial part of the data is that the regional economic pattern during the decade of reform was primarily a reaction to fundamental economic opportunities open to the various provinces. The most rapidly growing provinces took advantage of their nearby location to the relatively developed areas of Hong Kong and Shanghai. These provinces had a comparative abundance of resources, open lands and relatively underutilized utilities. The reforms freed them to use their resources to their own advantage—and often to the disadvantage of more developed areas such as Shanghai and Tianjin.

It is also important to add that the experience of the "decade of reform" may not be repeated in the 1990's. This is partly due to uncertainties about how much of the reform program will be retained in the Post-Tiananmen period. In addition, however, there are other reasons to warn against any simplistic extrapolation of the trends of the 1980's into the 1990's. This is partly due to the fact that the rapid growth of Guangdong, Fujian, Jiangsu, Zhejiang and other provinces had a leveling effect in the 1980's (vis a vis the richest provinces). But continued relatively rapid growth of the same provinces for an extended period of time will obviously bring about the phenomenon of the "rich getting richer". In addition, as discussed above, the new revenue "contract responsibility system" and trends in regional allocation of fixed asset investment could lead to greater variations in provincial economic performance in the coming decade.

Finally, it should be noted that analysis of provincial per capita net material product differences is only one measure of the effect of China's reform policies on the distribution of economic benefits. Provinces are large nation-state type entities and the regional dif-

207

ferences within provinces may be as large as those between provinces. And, most importantly, assessing regional differences does not shed any light on whether there has been a significant widening of differences among classes of people within the same region.

Despite these qualifications, provinces are relatively integrated political and cultural entities. Their populations think of themselves as Cantonese, Fukienese and Sichuanese and intense rivalries separate the provinces. Such inter-provincial tensions underline the importance of the conclusion that the "decade of reform" did not worsen the economic differences among the provinces.

APPENDIX

DATA SOURCES FOR FIGURES 1–7

Per Capita NMP. Provincial and national per capita NMP for 1988 are found in *Zhongguo Tongji Zhaiyao:1990 (Hereafter, TJZY)*, (A Statistical Survey of China: 1990), China State Statistical Bureau Publishing Company, Beijing, 1990, p. 6. Similar statistics for most provinces for 1983 and 1978 are given in *Guomin Shouru Tongji Ziliao Huibian: 1949–1985 (Hereafter GMSRTJZL)*, China State Statistical Bureau publishing Company, Beijing, 1987, pp. 97–421. In a very few cases, it was necessary to use Provincial Yearbooks (Various Editions) and *Zhongguo Jingji Nianjian (Annual Issues-Hereafter, JJNJ)* (Chinese Economic Almanac), Economic Management Publishing Company to fill in holes where data was not available.

Growth of NMP. For 1978–1985, *GMSHRTJZL* gives annual growth rates in comparable prices for most provinces. A few holes in the data were filled by using *JJNJ (Various Years)* and provincial yearbooks. For 1986 and 1987 growth of Provincial NMP in comparable prices is presented in in *Zhongguo Tongji Nianjian (Annual Issues—Hereafter TJNJ)*,China State Statistical Publishing Company, Beijing. The 1988 growth rates of provincial NMP are given in *JJNJ, 1989* (Section VI). The few missing estimates were found in provincial yearbooks.

Provincial and Local Budget Revenues and Expenditures. *TJZY:1990* provides statistics on central government and local government (all governments combined) budget revenues for 1979 through 1988. The same estimates (for a shorter time period) for revenues and additional estimates of budgetary expenditures are available in *TJNJ (Various Issues)*. These estimates were compared to the sum of all provinces reported budgetary revenues and expenditures that can be obtained from provincial yearbooks and from *JJNJ (Various Issues)*. For the same years, the two series are very close. Therefore, for the years when data was not available from *TJZY or TJNJ* the sum of all provincial budgetary expenditures and revenues were used.

Foreign Investment Enterprises by Provinces. Data was obtained from the Ministry of Foreign Economic Relations and Trade Annual Publication *Foreign Trade Almanac*. A Fuller description of this and other data on foreign investment in China can be found in US-China Business Council, *US Investment in China: A Special Report*, Washington, D.C., 1990.

World Bank Loans By Province. The Basic data is found in the World Bank's Appraisal Reports for each project. The reports generally do not give exact figures for how much money will be used in each province. However, for the major components they do identify the provinces that will benefit from the project. The assumption was made that the total loan proceeds for a given major component were divided equally among the benefitting provinces.

A SYSTEMIC ANALYSIS OF PROSPECTS FOR CHINA'S ECONOMY

By Jan Prybyla *

CONTENTS

SUMMARY

The fundamental problem of the Chinese economy is deficient economic performance, which resolves itself into chronic waste, technological retardation, and faulty incentives to labor and management. The suggested contributory causes are some aspects of tradition, "acts of god" (natural population increase, land problems), errors of policy, and—the determining one—the economic system. System-generated problems have to be addressed by systemic reform, that is, change of system, but not by intrasystemic adjustments. This requires the replacement of the institutions and theories of the system responsible for the problems by a minimum critical mass of internally logical, interacting, compatible, integrated institutions and ideas of another system, not by random transplants. If the transition is from central planning to a market system it must satisfy seven operational conditions of a successful market system: free markets, free prices, workable competition, dominant private property rights, macroeconomic instruments of government intervention in the market, rule of law, and dissolu-

---

* Professor of Economics, Fellow, Center for East Asian Studies, The Pennsylvania State University, University Park, PA 16802 USA.

tion of the planning system's *nomenklatura*. In China, where by the late 1970s the fundamental problems of the economy were attributed to the system of central planning, all seven conditions of transition to a market system were violated. Two of them—free prices and private property—are examined. The result was the emergence of a mongrel, half-way nonsystem which did not solve or alleviate the chronic problems, but brought out from hiding some nagging shorter-range troubles (e.g., inflation, unemployment). After September 1989 these shorter-range problems were increasingly combated with old fashioned administrative command weapons. After June 4, 1989 the very idea of marketization and privatization of the system was exorcized on ideological grounds. The current (1990) nonsystemic situation is not viable in the long run. If left structurally uncorrected, it will lead to a collapse of the economy within a few years. Return to (an updated) central administrative command system, presently being implemented, will disguise the short-term problems but not address the fundamental structural problems of waste, technological retardation, and faulty incentives. It will simply postpone the economy's implosion by perhaps as much as ten years. Economic logic dictates that the way out of China's systemic problem of chronic qualitative underperformance is to move all the way to the market system. The logic will probably impose itself before the end of the 1990s, but the exact timing will depend on the pace, sequence, and nature of leadership attrition and change.

I. INTRODUCTION

The predictions made in this essay about the qualitative performance of the Chinese economy in the 1990s are based on my understanding of the trends in China's economic system since 1980. It was during this period that the post-Mao economic changes got in stride under the slogan of the Four Modernizations, of which the ideological-political boundaries were concurrently defined by the Four Cardinal Principles. In other words, the forecasts emerge from my understanding of systemic principles.

As a matter of common-sense prudence, one should point out that the capacity of economics to make reliable predictions is limited by two rather awesome considerations. First, "no scientific law, in the natural scientific sense, has been established in economics, on which economists can base predictions." Second, although the tendency statements (principles) of economics, like those of the natural sciences, presuppose a ceteris paribus clause, in the natural sciences the lesser "disturbing causes" have their own laws specifiable in quantitative terms, whereas the ceteris paribus clauses in economics are either unspecified or specified only in qualitative terms.[1] In its mathematizing drive to become more like the "hard" sciences, economics has tried to put away its moral philosophy origins with all the other things being held equal. However, morality will not conform to the requirements of being equal or fit neatly into its assigned niche of lesser disturbing causes. Yesterday's

---

[1] Stefano Zamagni, "Economic Laws," in John Eatwell, Murray Milgate, Peter Newman (eds.), *The New Palgrave: The Invisible Hand* (New York: W. W. Norton, 1987), pp. 103–104.

"pragmatic" and "liberal" reformers, like Deng Xiaoping, suddenly at three in the morning kill their grandchildren in Tiananmen Square. John Stuart Mill has it right: "It really is of importance not only what men do, but also what manner of men they are that do it." [2]

The following Sections II–IV lay the foundations for the predictions made in Sections V and VI.

II. PROBLEMS

China together with other centrally planned ("Soviet-type") command economies suffers from a chronic deficiency of qualitative performance or inefficiency. This fundamental problem resolves itself into three debilitating, interrelated components that in the past failed to respond to remedial measures of intrasystemic adjustment, such as reorganizations, personnel reassignments, administrative price corrections, and reeducation of those practicing an erroneous work style. The three components of the quality problem are waste, technological retardation, and faulty incentives.

A. WASTE

This resolves itself into chronic shortages of useful goods side by side with chronic surpluses of useless goods, both subsidized by the state budget. Goods are useful when they are wanted and can be used. They are useless when they are not wanted and cannot be used—as when they do not work because of inferior quality or no quality at all (a very common problem in the system), or when they are of the wrong assortment, or are located in the wrong place (e.g., in the north when they are needed in the south and there is no way to get them from north to south), or when they are produced and distributed at the wrong time, or produced at the right time but not distributed, or distributed to the wrong customers, or are damaged or lost in transit, or necessitate scandalously profligate rates of materials and energy utilization, and so on. The waste is not restricted to products. It includes production factors. It has been estimated that at the end of the 1970s one-third to one-half of the rural manpower in China (100 to 150 million people) was unnecessarily employed in agricultural work and could have been used more productively elsewhere. [3]

B. TECHNOLOGICAL RETARDATION

The economy, certainly its civilian segment (but judging by the 1979 expedition against Vietnam, the military as well), has troublesome problems with research, development, innovation, and diffusion of modern technology of both the engineering and social (business know-how) varieties. This has had deleterious effects on the quality of growth. Growth has been based primarily on the addition of production factors (especially labor and capital) of known techno-

---

[2] John Stuart Mill, "Essay on Liberty," Chapter 3, in Marshall Cohen (ed.), *The Philosophy of John Stuart Mill* (New York: The Modern Library, 1961).

[3] Claude Aubert, "Rural Capitalism versus Socialist Economics? Rural-Urban Relationships and Agricultural Reforms in China," Communication for the 8th International Conference on Soviet and East European Agriculture, University of California, Berkeley, August 7–10, 1987, pp. 11–12.

logical content, rather than on factor productivity improvements. Technological sluggishness inhibits China's efforts to work its way out of poverty and to compete on the world market with rising numbers of technologically dynamic newly industrializing market economies.

C. FAULTY INCENTIVES

The way incentives to labor and management are set up contributes to waste and low factor productivity. Merit plays little role. It pays to be inefficient in the system, one of the typical procedures of which has been to use the profits of relatively successful firms to infuse with life the failing ones—the equivalent of $14 billion in 1990, nearly $23 billion (one-third of the planned 1990 budget) if all bailouts are counted.[4] It is not stretching the point to conclude that the system turns out waste as one of its leading products by actively encouraging inefficient worker and managerial behavior.

III. ETIOLOGY

After the death of Mao and until June 3-4, 1989, a great debate took place in China on the causes of deficient qualitative performance and on how to address the combined waste-technology-incentive problem. By 1980 the earlier scapegoat analysis that ascribed every imaginable economic and other disturbance to the Gang of Four had run its course, and with occasional time out to chase ideological ghosts and monsters (bourgeois liberalization), the substance and tenor of the debate became increasingly technical and rational—"pragmatic," was the preferred Western term for it.

Contributing to the quality of economic performance, or the lack of it, are four interrelated and interacting elements. They are: tradition, "acts of god," policy, and system. I suggest that while all are important, the last is determining.

A. TRADITION

Four contributory factors are often brought up in discussion. First, is the Confucian legacy, which is said to have contributed both positively and negatively to the economic performance of various contemporary Chinese communities. The reviewer of Spence's *The Search for Modern China* ascribes to this legacy Deng Xiaoping's distaste for popular participation in politics and his conviction that dissent is synonymous with disloyalty, as well as Liu Binyan's speaking out, despite continuous persecution, against corruption and the abuse of power.[5] Second, there is the spirit of the science and democracy movement going back to the early decades of this century, spreading out from Beida and embracing the ideals and

---

[4] In the absence of rational prices that would indicate the opportunity costs in the system, it is difficult to determine which firms are successful and which are not. The 1990 projected figures are from Adi Ignatius, "Top Official Rules Out Market-Oriented Reforms," *The Asian Wall Street Journal Weekly*, March 26, 1990, p. 3. In 1989 the Chinese government loaned money to unprofitable state enterprises through its banks in order to meet its enterprises' previously negotiated profit-and-tax quota obligations to itself. In this way the government protected its revenues at the risk of rekindling inflation in the economy. Baroque? Robert Delfs, "Creative Accounting," *Far Eastern Economic Review*, April 5, 1990, pp. 38–39.

[5] Vera Schwarcz, review of Jonathan D. Spence, *The Search for Modern China*, (New York: W. W. Norton, 1990), in *The New York Times Book Review*, May 13, 1990, pp. 1, 32–33.

some ideas of Sun Yat-sen. Third, in conversations with Chinese intellectuals, young and old, during my teaching stay in China, what kept coming up was the enormous dead weight of "feudal" peasant ways, glacial in their pace of change, a mind-boggling impediment to modernization, my interlocutors thought, worse even than the socialist system. Fourth, there is the shaping of attitudes by communism, relatively brief, but massively and relentlessly pursued. This includes the inculcation of phobias about private property, profit-making, and individual initiative, historical materialist redefinition of class distinctions, the fanning of class antagonisms, and the raising to historically new heights of bureaucratic elitism, arrogance, nepotism, corruption, and envy.

B. ACTS OF GOD

These are "objective" causes that can have positive or negative effects on the quality of economic performance. In the specific instance of China, two such acts deserve mention: the huge absolute size and rapid incremental increase of the population, and land problems—shrinkage of farmland from an already exiguous base and acute energy shortages. Less than 10 percent of China's land area is suitable for farming. "An average of 200,000–300,000 hectares of the country's cultivated land is lost each year, a loss accompanied by a reduction in irrigated areas, weakened flood control facilities, and lower capacity to drain farmland.... Many places suffer soil erosion and a deteriorated ecological balance." [6] Surveying China's landscape, V. Smil notes that of the millions of trees planted during repeated mass campaigns over the last three decades, only one-third have survived; biomass consumption by peasants is ravaging the countryside while "about half a billion people lack enough fuel just to cook three meals a day for three to six months a year. [7]

A combination of better policies and better system could, one should think, counteract some of the ungodly impacts of these acts or at least limit the damage. Such a combination has eluded China so far. [8]

C. POLICY

Policy errors are the standard communist explanation, in China and elsewhere, for much that goes awry in the system, the perennial low quality of economic performance included. There is some substance to this diagnosis, but it fails to account for the fullness and persistence of static and dynamic inefficiencies. If taken seriously by those who offer it, it can result in intrasystemic policy adjustments that do little to improve the situation, and often make things worse. In China, two monumental policy errors have been the Great Leap Forward—a Maoist variation on the theme of so-

[6] Tian Jiyun (Vice Premier of the State Council), "China's Current Agricultural Situation and Policy," *Beijing Review*, January 8–14, 1990, p. 19.

[7] "Vaclav Smil, *Energy in China's Modernization: Advances and Limitations*, (Armonk, N.Y. and London: M. E. Sharpe, 1988).

[8] On population policy: John Aird, *Slaughter of the Innocents*, (Washington, D.C.: American Enterprise Institute, 1990). In the year 2000 there will be in China 340 million women of childbearing age, up 35 million from 1989. *The Asian Wall Street Journal Weekly*, April 23, 1990, p. 25.

cialist administrative command—and the Third Line (*san xian*) industrial policy pursued for almost two decades beginning in the late 1960s. The *san xian* had as its objective providing China's interior provinces with their own industrial, especially heavy industrial (defense-related), infrastructure through generous infusions of capital and massive assignments of labor. Between 1966 and 1976, out of a total state investment in capital construction of 274 billion yuan, 117 billion yuan went for Third Line projects equipped with "iron pot" incentive systems and 1950s technologies.[9] One result has been that China's industrial structure is probably more distorted than that of other socialist economies that in the past had followed Stalinist sectoral and regional priorities. It is like cleaning up after the dinosaurs.

D. SYSTEM

The implicit assumption behind the policy errors explanation is that the system within which policies are formulated and applied is basically sound and that, therefore, there is no need to dig up the foundations and replace the structure. Although not denying that policy errors are a cause of quality problems, the system-at-fault argument holds that the fundamental cause is structural; that bad policies come not just from fallible or crooked men but from flawed theories and institutions. The policy errors explanation was dominant in China from 1976 through 1978. After that, and until September 1988, the system-at-fault diagnosis gained ground. But effective remedies do not inevitably follow from correct diagnosis. As a rule, accurate diagnosis of the problems of socialist command planning had been followed in the past by the application of partial, unintegrated, insufficient, incomplete, or quack remedies. China, which at one time looked as if it might become an exception to this rule, now exemplifies the rule.

The reason for the failure of central planning is that it is based on an erroneous intellectual premise about the availability and coordination of knowledge in an extended social order known as the economy. The "fatal conceit," as Hayek calls it, is to presume that system-wide planning can be done at all, that it is possible to deliberately construct a rational complex structure, dispensing with the "natural, spontaneous, and self-ordering process of adaptation to a greater number of particular facts than any one mind can perceive or even conceive."[10]

---

[9] Richard Kirby and Terry Cannon, "Introduction," in David S. G. Goodman (ed.), *China's Regional Development*, (London & New York: Routledge, 1989), p. 9; Barry Naughton, "The Third Front: Defense Industrialization in the Chinese Interior," *The China Quarterly*, No. 115, September 1988, pp. 351–376.

[10] F. A. Hayek, *The Fatal Conceit: The Errors of Socialism*, (Chicago: University of Chicago Press, 1988), p. 73. "What Hayek showed was that much modern economics misconstrues the nature of the economic problem facing society by assuming away the problems raised by the fact of dispersed information. To imagine (as earlier critics of Mises and Hayek had proposed) that it would be possible to run a socialist system by simulating the market and promulgating non-market 'prices' for the guidance of socialist managers is to ignore the extent to which market prices—both of consumer goods and of the capital goods that constitute the economy's capital structure—*already* express the outcome of an entrepreneurial discovery procedure that draws upon scattered existing knowledge." Roger W. Garrison and Israel M. Kirzner, "Friedrich August von Hayek," in John Eatwell et al., *The Invisible Hand*, p. 124.

IV. DEALING WITH SYSTEMIC DEFICIENCIES

A. SOME CONCEPTUAL ISSUES

Like other social organisms, an economic system is an internally logical whole of interdependent, interacting, compatible, integrated institutions and ideas, a holistic operation, not a random collection of parts. Economic institutions are socially agreed-on and legally recognized and protected ways of allocating relatively scarce resources among competing alternative uses. The four major functions of economic institutions are discovery, transmission, and processing of information about costs and utilities (supply and demand) in the system; coordination of that information at a point in time and intertemporally; motivation of economic agents (consumers, workers, managers, investors, entrepreneurs); and the designation of socially enforced rights to select uses of economic goods (property). The ideas of an economic system consist of positive theories (economic analysis) and normative rules (economic ethics). The requirement of internal logic, interdependence, interaction, compatibility, and integration applies not only to the system's institutions, but to positive and normative theories, and to the relationship between the institutional framework and its explanatory and justifying ideas. An economic system functions within a broader context of political, legal, cultural, and other systems with which it, too, must interact in compatible, synchronized ways.[11]

When the problem of chronic inefficiency is diagnosed as originating in the system's ideas and its institutions of information, coordination, motivation, and property, and if that inefficiency is seen as keeping people permanently trapped in poverty and making the economy increasingly backward relatively to others, the system has to be removed and replaced by a different system.[12] The term "reform" should be reserved exclusively to describe such systemic transubstantiation.[13] Intrasystemic adjustments will not do, and neither will half-measures sometimes referred to as the "third way." Economic reform must be accompanied by symbiotic reforms of the environmental ecosystems of law, politics, and culture. The Soviet Union's unwillingness and perhaps inability over nearly 40 years to carry out economic and environmental reforms has mired the country in its present frightful condition that threatens to tear it apart.

Systemic reform does not mean the replacement of an operational system (however poorly it operates) by an ideal, pure model of another system; say, inefficient central administrative command planning by a perfectly competitive, allocatively optimal and dynamic market system. What is indispensable, however, is that a certain minimum critical mass of internally logical, interdependent, interacting, compatible, and integrated institutions and ideas be introduced to constitute a working whole (a functioning system); and that each component institution and idea contain within itself

---

[11] Jan S. Prybyla, *Reform in China and Other Socialist Economies*, (Washington, D.C.: American Enterprise Institute, 1990), Chapter 18.

[12] *Idem.*, *Market and Plan under Socialism: The Bird in the Cage*, (Stanford: Hoover Institution Press, 1987).

[13] *Idem.*, "The Chinese Economy: Adjustment of the System or Systemic Reform?" *Asian Survey*, Vol. 25, No. 5, May 1985, pp. 553–586.

a similarly critical minimum mass of internally logical, interdependent, interacting, and integrated elements.

For example, the freeing of prices must be accompanied by privatization of property rights; the abolition of monopolies; the removal of impediments to market entry and exit; the retirement of ethical rules concerning equality of outcomes, guaranteed lifelong employment, and immortality of the firm; and the establishment of the rule of law. Private property rights cannot be truncated, limited, say, to the right of use, without right of transfer or with transfer rights administratively circumscribed by socialist ethical codes concerning the inherently exploitative nature of private property exchanges.

Not all resources in the system have to be or, indeed, can be controlled by private property rights, but where they are, the rights must be comprehensive. Thus, "The owner must have *all* the rights anyone can have over the things in question. The suggestion sometimes encountered in textbooks that ownership can be reduced to a 'right to an income' is inadequate, because it mistakes one element in ownership for the whole... The crucial element in the *ius utendi et abutendi* is the ultimate power of disposal. It is, therefore, not only a question of having all the rights the law allows, but of the law conferring on some person or institution the right of disposal." [14]

While understandable politically, slowness and postponement are not advisable in matters of economic system reform for reasons that have to do with the need to simultaneously introduce a critical minimum mass of structural changes within the economic system and around it. The experience of Eastern Europe, the Soviet Union, and lately China suggests that delay is synonymous with nonreform. Policy steps (e.g., to deflate the monetary demand overhang in a system where money is practically inconvertible into goods) can be taken to reduce the pain of dislocation to politically manageable proportions, but by definition systemic reform *is* dislocation and involves pain. Shock therapy is the only way if one is serious about systemic transformation. An essential precondition is that the people trust their government so they will willingly, if not enthusiastically, put up with the pain of systemic transition. This certainly is not true of the Soviet Union, China, and Romania, among others. The point has been reached where retirement of individual leaders will not restore popular confidence and trust. Only the removal of the Communist party can conceivably do it.

---

[14] Alan Ryan, "Property," in John Eatwell, et al., *The Invisible Hand*, p. 228. In the same volume, Armen Alchian ("Property Rights," p. 233) establishes the inter- and intrainstitutional connections referred to above and their effect on the quality of economic performance: "For the decentralized [market] coordination of productive specialization to work well, according to the well-known principles of comparative advantage, in a society with diffused knowledge, people must have secure, alienable private property rights in productive resources and products tradeable at mutually agreeable prices at low costs of negotiating reliable contractual transactions. That system's ability to coordinate diffused information results in increased availability of more highly valued goods as well as of those becoming less costly to produce. The amount of rights to goods one is willing to trade, and in which private property rights are held, is the measure of value; and that is not equivalent to an equal quantity of goods not held as private property (for example, government property)."

B. MARKET REFORM

When it is determined that the system of central administrative command planning is the primary cause of an economy's inefficiency and that such deficient qualitative performance can no longer be tolerated, the only effective cure is to carry out economic (as distinct from administrative) decentralization, that is, reform the system of the plan into a market system.

Marketization of the plan requires that the following be introduced (almost) simultaneously:

1. Free markets for goods and factors, implying free entry and exit for buyers and sellers, no physical rationing of inputs and outputs, and absence of exogenous compulsion on economic agents to enter into transactions.

2. Free prices for goods and factors. Prices must reflect relative scarcities in the system, i.e., changing relative costs and utilities (opportunity costs). Prices must be the core decision-making device for information, coordination, and incentives, and there must be a tendency toward a single market price for each commodity and service.

3. Workable competition, both domestic and foreign, between and among buyers and sellers, that is, the availability of alternative courses of action. With some strictly circumscribed ("natural") exceptions, monopolies and monopsonies—public and private, central and local—must be removed.

4. Dominant private property rights. These rights, vested in individuals and freely formed associations of individuals, must be comprehensive and cover transfer, use, and income. They must be legally protected and introduced with decent haste on a grand scale.

5. Macroeconomic monetary and fiscal instrumentalities of government intervention in the market process to remedy market breakdowns and failures, and accommodate evolving ethical views on what constitutes social responsibilities within the system. This necessitates the creation of an independent banking system, reform of the tax system, and establishment of national unemployment insurance and pensions systems.

6. Rule of law, that is, a legal order (not just laws) that applies equally to all without exception, government included. "The desirability of the order that emerges as the unintended consequence of human action depends ultimately on the kind of rules and institutions within which human beings act, and the real alternatives they face." [15]

7. Measures to dismantle the vast web of party bureaucratic patronage, the *nomenklatura*, at all levels of society. The system must be promptly and thoroughly detoxified by ditching the apparatchiks.

In the realm of ideas, economic theory based on Marxist categories has to be replaced by market analysis, and the socialist ethical code by market ethic as modified by 5 above. Such modification can go quite far without destroying the essential operational principles of the market system. This was demonstrated by the West German *Soziale Marktwirtschaft*, Sweden's welfare ("soft") capitalism, and

---

[15] Karen E. Vaughn, "Invisible Hand," in John Eatwell et al., *The Invisible hand*, p. 171.

the high degree of government involvement, both formal and informal, in the capitalisms of Japan, Taiwan, Singapore, and South Korea. The market system is flexible and adaptable. It has the "capacity to adapt to different cultural contexts and indeed to survive sometimes remarkable cultural decadence.... This autonomous functioning is precisely one great advantage of capitalism over its rival systems: it is at least relatively 'foolproof,' because the market corrects the actions of fools much more reliably than any planning mechanism." [16] But the market system's flexibility and adaptability have their limits. There is a point beyond which systemic transplants reduce market institutions and ideas below the critical minimum required for the proper functioning of the system. Janos Kornai argues correctly that "the real issue is the relative strength of the components of the mixture." Although there exist no precise measures, "the frequency and intensity of bureaucratic intervention into market processes have certain critical values. Once these critical values are exceeded, the market becomes emasculated and dominated by bureaucratic regulation." [17] China's problem after Mao has been that the critical market minimum was never reached.

C. DEALING WITH SYSTEMIC DEFICIENCIES IN CHINA

The great debate about China's unsatisfactory quality of economic performance produced a consensus among a large majority of economists and many influential officials (although the last were circumspect about it in public) that the villain of the piece was the system of central administrative command planning, that the system had to be changed, and that the change had to be in a market direction (ideologically rightward). Arriving at the consensus was facilitated by bad memories, still fresh, of Mao's attempt to push the system to the left during the Great Leap Forward and the Cultural Revolution. At no time was it said that the socialist economic system would have to be replaced by the market system (capitalism). In China, as in Eastern Europe before November 1989, such a conclusion had been reached by most thoughtful people but could not be openly articulated, although some reform economists came close to it. The exclusion from public discussion of the sensible idea that capitalism is the only viable replacement for socialism—if, that is, socialism's waste-technology-incentive problem is to be addressed effectively—left an intellectual void into which all manner of "third way" pseudo-solutions soon poured in, including the cloudy concept of "socialism with Chinese characteristics."

Although until September 1988 some rather bold structural reforms were carried out (e.g., the dissolution of rural producer collectives), they were incomplete, unfinished, and unintegrated. Put simply, they did not add up to the minimum institutional and theoretical requirements of a market system. The changes made in the

---

[16] Peter L. Berger, "The Market, Morals, and Manners," *The Wall Street Journal*, July 14, 1988, p. 22; *idem.*, *The Capitalist Revolution: Fifty Propositions about Prosperity, Equality, and Liberty*, (New York: Basic Books, 1988); Nathan Rosenberg and L. E. Birdzell, *How the West Grew Rich*, (New York: Basic Books, 1986).

[17] Janos Kornai, "The Hungarian Reform Process: Visions, Hopes, and Reality," in Victor Nee and David Stark (eds.), *Remaking the Economic Institutions of Socialism: China and Eastern Europe*, (Stanford: Stanford University Press, 1989), p. 48.

early to mid-1980s violated every one of the seven basic conditions for the establishment of a successful market system. Only two of the violations can be discussed here: free prices and private property.[18]

1. *Prices.* Some prices, mainly of selected nonstaple farm products, were freed, but most were not—including most factor prices. A multitrack, quite irrational price arrangement emerged in which some prices (including prices of identical goods) were free; others were quasi-free; some were floating, some "negotiated"; others were fixed by the state. There is one set of input prices for domestic firms and another set for foreign joint ventures; one official exchange rate for the renminbi, another for foreign exchange certificates, and another on the black market. Claude Aubert attributes the post-1984 grain production crisis (which threatens the decollectivization reforms) primarily to price distortions flowing from the multitrack price arrangement, accompanied by severe restrictions on the freedom of rural markets and the absolute power of the corrupt state to organize grain marketing and to control essential inputs such as urea, bicarbonate of ammonia, and fuel oil. Although it had been announced in 1985 that above-contract sales to the state marketing network were to be made at free market prices, in fact such sales were made at "negotiated" (i.e., informally state-fixed) prices, which were roughly midway between the contracted and the market price. "Quite often these sales made at 'negotiated prices' were even described as a 'second levy' imposed on the peasants after the 'first levy,' i.e., the contract sales (which were 'contract' only in name)."[19]

By fall 1988 the decision was made to postpone price liberalization for several years. After June 4, 1989, the idea of price freeing was no longer a technical subject to be discussed on the merits of the case. It became part of resurgent socialist economic liturgy and was classified as one of the key Western subversive efforts to bring about China's "peaceful evolution" from socialism to capitalism. In a speech to the National People's Congress (March 20, 1990), premier Li Peng announced that the government would tighten control over market prices in rural and urban areas. Some prices would be readjusted up, some down by the government, but not by market forces. Allocative irrationality (waste) still goes on. It is probably worse now than before.

2. *Property.* As noted, private property rights must be comprehensive and should be introduced quickly on a sufficiently large scale for them to dominate the system. There is bound to be conflict between the need for speed/efficiency and fairness since privatization involves very significant changes in the social structure

---

[18] The violation of the other conditions is discussed in Prybyla, *Reform in China and Other Socialist Economies*, Chapters 11 and 13.

[19] Claude Aubert, "The Agricultural Crisis in China at the End of the 1980s," Paper presented at the European Conference on Agriculture and Rural Development in China, Sanbjerg, Denmark, November 18–20, 1989, pp. 5–10. In 1985 fertilizer cost 630 yuan per ton at the state price, and 930 yuan per ton at the floating price. By 1988 the state price had risen to 800 yuan per ton, while the floating price to 1,437 yuan per ton. Roseanne E. Freese, "The Mixed Blessings of Agricultural Reform," *The China Business Review*, November-December 1988 p. 32. If a farmer wants to get fertilizer from the state at a lower price, he must conform to state directions on what to grow and sell to the state at state-set prices (e.g., grain, the state purchase price of which in May 1989 was barely one-third of the market price and was paid for mostly with IOUs). In any event, he has to bribe the officials. *China Daily*, May 20, 1989, p. 3.

and large redistributions of wealth, and poses difficult questions of how to privatize property in a system lacking rational prices, independent banking, proper accounting, and markets for land and capital (including securities markets), and in which self-recycled members of the privileged party-affiliated class are in the best financial position to buy up state industrial and commercial assets, thus resurrecting the *nomenklautra* in phony privatized form. China's post-Mao privatization effort has failed under each of these headings.

Attention is here focused on agriculture where privatization had been carried the farthest. There has been some privatization of consumer services, but very little in industry where state ownership has remained unchallenged at all times, although state control was administratively decentralized. At no time did private property rights dominate the system. In agriculture the property rights granted to peasant families were restricted to residual rights of use and income. Transfer rights were always extremely narrow. Under the household production responsibility system (*baogan daohu*) what was privatized was the surplus remaining after contractual deliveries to the state and, insofar as the authorities did not interfere with prices on rural markets, to the income derived from sales of the surplus on these markets. At no time were deeds to land granted to the families, and transfer rights were severely restricted and regulated by local governmental authorities. The size of land allotments was determined by the authorities according to the cadres' ideas on distributional fairness (as modified by bribes), and, officially at least, there were restrictions on the hiring of labor and on migration. Essential inputs (chemical fertilizers, machinery, farm plastics) could be obtained only from the state monopolist. The state was the main buyer of farm output at imposed prices. Delivery contracts were not negotiated laterally, as between rough equals, and there was never any question of rule of law or even of half decent and efficient legal framework. "Village cadres reign supreme and the balance of power between the rulers and the ruled has not been altered greatly by decollectivization." [20] In any event, the essential free market-private property ingredient of voluntariness was always missing: no delivery contract (which now includes birth quota obligations), no land.

The inflationary and unemployment surge that began in 1985 led the leadership in 1988 to finally declare that price system liberalization would be postponed. At the time this was viewed as a technical·tactical decision, and was accompanied by a push on the part of some economists (e.g., Li Yining of Beijing University) for more privatization of industry through various stockholding schemes, and the inclusion of the right of transfer in private property rights to agricultural land. After June 4, 1989, all discussion of privatization was relegated to socialist economic demonology. Accused of profiteering, exploitation, bribery, and tax evasion, private business (foreign joint ventures excluded) was increasingly harassed and restricted and, more ominously, put outside the pale of officially proclaimed social morality. The state now defines what is "reasonable" private profit and takes the rest. By law, private firms have to

---

[20] Aubert, "The Agricultural Crisis in China," p. 17.

pay 52 percent of their profits in taxes and put back 30 percent into the business. The remaining 18 percent is subject to various local levies including a tax on "unreasonable" earnings.[21] State banks have been instructed to refrain from lending to private businesses partly to combat inflation, but mostly out of socialist ethics. For reasons of economies of scale, decollectivization is criticized as having produced excessive parceling of land (more than 200 million farms, each of which is about two-thirds of a hectare on average). Land nationalization is being advocated by some establishment economists. The existing system of land tenure is being eroded through reduction in the duration of land leases from the theoretical 15 years to 5 years, 3 years, or even 1 year; increases in extractions from peasants (up to 750 yuan per hectare, or about half the total net revenue of two annual harvests); pressure put on part-time worker-peasants to relinquish their plots and on farm families in general to form of "voluntary" cooperatives to reap the benefits of scale economies. In some places tiny parcels of land are distributed equally to all for private consumption. The remaining land is then auctioned off and subjected to heavy "contract" quotas and collective extractions and extortions.[22]

Since ideas, including half-baked ones, do have consequences, the result in China of applying over the last decade selected, pasteurized, partial, truncated, restricted, and disjointed bits and pieces of market and private property policy—which lacked internal logic and was at odds with partially dismantled but not dead, remnant bureaucratic instrumentalities of the command plan—has been systemic disarray. It is not a mixed system but a mixed-up one, a jumble of two jigsaw puzzles thrown together with many parts missing, a "confused economic order," as Liu Guoguang euphemistically calls it, an institutional and theoretical mess, where things work at odds and official corruption flourishes in the cracks between unfinished markets and discombobulated plans.[23]

The problems that have beset the Chinese economy since 1985 include open and hidden inflation and unemployment, loss of control over the money supply, growing income disparities, too much industrial and too little agricultural investment, massive subsidies, budget deficits, industrial overheating, agricultural underheating, credit crunch, loss-making enterprises, unpaid farm deliveries, neglect of rural infrastructures, excessive parceling of landholdings, mounting foreign debt, growth and strengthening of local monopolies, official corruption, as well as long-standing shortages of useful and surpluses of useless goods, technological sluggishness, and distorted behavior in response to perverse incentives. All of these problems are not the results of too much marketizing and privatizing, but of too little. Chen Yun, no friend of market reform, once said that the relationship between the market and the plan is like that between the bird and the cage. The bird should be allowed to fly, but within the framework of the cage. Otherwise it will fly away. In the Great Leap Forward, Mao crushed the cage and killed

[21] Adi Ignatius, "A Tiny Chinese Venture into Capitalism Feels Icy Chills in Wake of Crackdown," *The Wall Street Journal*, March 8, 1990, p. A11.

[22] Aubert, "The Agricultural Crisis in China," p. 19.

[23] Liu Guoguang, "A Sweet and Sour Decade," *Beijing Review*, January 2-6, 1989, pp. 22-29.

the bird, with resulting systemic nihilism and instant chaos. More slowly ("crossing the river while groping for the stones") Deng Xiaoping enlarged the cage and opened the door a little to the outside world. He also clipped the wings of the bird so it could not fly. The results, although certainly less seismic, are systemically similar to those of the Leap. What has emerged—in consequence of the mistaken idea that a few nuts and bolts from the market system can be used at random to revitalize socialism in a trick of third way social engineering—is yet another nonsystem.

V. PROSPECTS

From late 1987 to early 1988 the Chinese economy reached a juncture at which a critical decision had to be made whether to cross the border to the market system, cope with the recurring crises of the existing half-way arrangement through fire extinguisher-type tactics and minor structural changes, or strategically retreat into central planning. The discussion on what course of action to take was conducted with remarkable professionalism, but not without bitter, albeit muted, ideological and factional-political struggles behind the scenes. A definitive decision was not reached at that time. In September 1987 those counseling (in Aesopian language) that the border be crossed appeared to gain the upper hand, but not for long. The economic situation (especially inflation, unemployment, industrial overheating, and grain output) continued to deteriorate. By September 1988 the centralizers, led by Chen Yun, had regained the initiative in the name of caution, gradualness, and fairness. After the Tiananmen massacre of June 4, 1989, market reform as an idea and a movement was relegated to the lowest level. Once a subject dissected primarily on its technical merits, it was transformed overnight into an antagonistic contradiction, a bourgeois plot. Anxious international lending institutions, foreign bankers, investors, merchants, and governments were reassured that the open-door policy remained in force. After some slight hesitations and misgivings associated with a temporary deterioration in China's Moody ratings, this international element—including "compatriots" from Hong Kong and Taiwan—responded generously with their purse.[24] Internally, the National People's Congress was informed by Li Peng (March 1990) that China "will stand rock firm in the East," (a static version of Mao's "the East Wind prevails over the West wind"), no matter what the bourgeois goings on in other parts of the socialist world.

But to stand rock firm on the quicksand of the present nonsystem is simply not a viable long-term posture. The current neither-plan-nor-market arrangement is a key contributor (in addition to resuscitated Communist traditions, "acts of god," and mistaken policies) to the economy's shorter term problems such as inflation, unemployment, and the agricultural crisis.[25] Nor has China done

---

[24] Jan Prybyla, "Tiananmen: The Economic Cost of the Open Door Massacre," *The American Asian Review*, Vol. 8, No. 1, Spring 1990, pp. 63–87; and *idem*, "The Economic Consequences of Tiananmen Square," Chapter 14 of *Reform in China and Other Socialist Economies*.

[25] For example, the agricultural (cereal) crisis: "According to the farmers themselves, grain prices have been the underlying reason for the growing disinterest in grain production and have resulted in the decrease in both the grain cropped area and the use of fertilizer for grain culti-

Continued

anything constructive about the deeper and longer term problems of waste, technological retardation, and perverse incentives. It has merely brought out into the open problems that for long had been hidden. As under the plan, agriculture continues to finance rudderless industrial development. Other rural problems include increasingly adverse terms of trade for peasants, threats of recollectivization and/or land nationalization, reduction in the duration of land leases, financial restrictions on and bankruptcies of rural industries that once provided farmers with additional income or alternative employment, the resulting return in 1990 alone of an estimated 15–20 million people formerly employed in such industries plus some 5 million from the cities to already overstaffed field work, and obstacles (including physical customs barriers) to interregional trade put up by local authorities. To stand rock firm on unfinished reforms juggling ad hoc expedients is no strategy at all; it may relieve some symptoms for a while, but is ultimately self-destructive. In China's present condition, keeping the door open to foreign loans, investment, technology, and business know-how is useless for China on the long view, and profitless for the foreigners who for reasons of an elusive and illusory future potential keep walking through the door with technophiliac enthusiasm into systemic chaos.

To unfulfilled material expectations and rising worker and peasant discontent, the massacre of Tiananmen Square and the subsequent physical repression and mental obfuscation have added a deep and lasting alienation of the intellectuals, young and old alike, a devastation of the human spirit. Without the participation of the thinking class and the freedom to think, China will never modernize. The alienation of the intellectuals goes beyond disagreement and disappointment with individual leaders. It extends to the Communist party and most of what it stands for.

One false remedy for the present systemless condition in which the Chinese economy is mired is to return to central planning—to rebuild as best one can the partly dismantled cage. This appears to be what the "hardline" post-Tiananmen leadership is doing. Prices will not be freed; on the contrary, more prices are to be set by the planners. The prospect, therefore, is for continued price irrationality. What little decision-making latitude had been granted to firms is to be curbed to assure that planner-sanctioned projects are not starved for funds and materials. Allocation of key industrial inputs (energy, raw materials) is to be increasingly subject to physical rationing ("unified distribution") by the Bureau of Supplies, and allocation of industry-based inputs and infrastructural state investments to agriculture is becoming increasingly contingent on the tenant farmers' adhering to planners' output preferences. Unap-

---

vation. Numerous Chinese economists, too, consider that the price problem is the source of the cereal crisis.... In fact, both the farmers and the economists are right, and prices are the basic factor behind the current crisis: peasants respond well to cereal prices which serve as their point of reference and the basis for their activity. But the reference prices do not necessarily coincide with the average price they get from the state.... Under [the various] constraints, farmers are not interested in the average price at which the state will finally pay them, but far more in the difference between the 'contract' and 'negotiated' prices which are imposed on them, and the market price. Needless to say, the difference is a dissuasive one for the cereal producers who see themselves being obliged to sell their harvests at prices 25–50% below those they could obtain on the free market. Aubert, "The Agricultural Crisis in China," pp. 6–7.

proved extraplan investment is to be penalized by taxes, and investment in general is to be administratively recentralized. The expansion of private businesses is to be more strictly controlled by government departments and spontaneous ("anarchic") growth of the private sector discouraged by levies on "unreasonable" profits. Recentralization will also apply to foreign trade operations. Whether these intentions can be carried out in China's present destructured and corrupt economic condition remains, however, in question.

What is certain is that, should the intent succeed, China's fundamental problem of inefficiency will remain what it has been since the cage was first built. Return to even an updated, mathematized, computerized central planning system decidedly will not solve China's quality problem. In fact, it is this very system that created the problem in the first place. The quality problem will simply be driven underground, hidden from view, and not too well at that. Certainly by reason of its enormous capacity to institutionalize waste, technological lag, and perverse incentives, and because of its origins in an erroneous idea about the nature of extended social orders, China will remain permanently underdeveloped and poor, and the distance separating it from the world's dynamic market democracies lengthens as the years go by.

But there are indications that the intent will not succeed. The decade of the 1980s demonstrated that there is strong sentiment in favor of market reform (and political democracy) in the ranks of China's thinking class, particularly among the young, because only market reform (accompanied by liberalizing changes in the political environment) can put to good use the country's vast unrealized potential ability. Added to this are the mounting material frustrations of urban workers and peasants. Since neither the systemlessness of the present nor return to discredited central planning is capable of addressing China's fundamental problem of the quality of economic performance, and barring a crossing of the border into the market system, the prospect of an economic implosion—a house of cards-like collapse of the economy—is highly probable. Such implosion and its accompanying political disturbances can be averted by change in the present leadership through acts of god, attrition, factional elimination from above, or popular dynamiting from below, and the replacement of those now in charge by people who have the systemic understanding and the political will to take China out of the remnants of the plan into the market system.

VI. Conclusion

The present (1990) nonsystemic situation in which a partially dismantled plan conflicts with an unfinished market is not viable in the long run. Formerly hidden problems, among them inflation and unemployment, coexist with the deeper and unsolved problem of inefficiency made up of waste, technological retardation, and bizarre incentives. In this situation, the institutional preconditions for applying market remedies do not exist and administrative remedies no longer work. Persistence in the nonsystem would mean that the economy lunges from crisis to crisis, going nowhere. Tensions and alienations cumulate in the ranks of peasants, workers, and intellectuals. It is a relatively short act, ending in collapse within a few years.

A return to (an updated) system of central administrative command planning, which appears to have been put on the Chinese leadership's technical agenda in September 1988 and was inscribed in dogma after June 4, 1989, will deal with visible short-term problems by ordering them to be gone, that is, by hiding them (for example, price freezes that translate into suppressed inflation; or replacing open unemployment with overstaffing, that is unemployment on the job). It will do nothing to solve the structural problem of inefficiency of which it is the parent. A return to a fully fledged central planning system may be difficult for several reasons, including deterioration of the plan's institutions, the discredited state of central planning theory, and the intuitive knowledge on the part of most people, supported by several decades of field experience, that the system is a dead end and a recipe for waste, technological lag, and wrong-headed incentives. If actually accomplished, plan recidivism could postpone the economy's collapse by perhaps as much as a decade; but it cannot prevent it.

Economic logic dictates that the way out of China's systemic problem of chronic qualitative underperformance is to reform the plan into a market system. Chances are that this logic will prevail in China and the needed systemic transition will be accomplished. Whether this will be done in the 1990s, as I believe it will, depends to a considerable extent on the order of leadership succession through natural causes, purge, or revolutionary prodding from below: who goes first, and when, and who is left to do it. For "it really is of importance not only what men do, but what manner of men they are that do it."

III. SOCIAL AND HUMAN FACTORS

OVERVIEW

By Leo A. Orleans *

Although it is difficult to generalize or tie together the disparate chapters under "Social and Human Factors," each of the subjects covered has a direct bearing on China's economy. And, in fact, they have as much or more bearing on China's future as any topic covered in these two volumes.

For almost 20 years issues relating to China's population received considerable attention in the U.S. media. Demographers were impressed by the drastic reduction in fertility experienced after 1970 and by the ambitious and audacious one-child program initiated in 1980. Human rights advocates were upset by what they referred to as "draconian" family planning measures initiated by Beijing, and were only partially pacified by the Reagan Administration's termination of support to the International Planned Parenthood Federation and the withholding of some of the grant money to the United Nations Fund for Population Activities—both organizations believed to support China's policies on abortion. As a result, after years of both positive and negative publicity, a large segment of the American public became surprisingly knowledgeable about the magnitude of China's population, her family planning policies, as well as her problems associated with employment, education, urbanization, and other related issues.

In the last few years—aside from the spate of news items that appeared when China's population passed the billion mark—the frequency with which information on China's population appeared in the popular media has greatly diminished. In part because of the foreign outcry against reports of coercion in family planning and in part because following the dissolution of the communes the central government lost much of the clout it had over prescribed family planning measures, Beijing has, somewhat surreptitiously, retreated from the one-child family concept for rural couples. Moreover, aside from the spurt of negative publicity associated with the 1989 Tiananmen tragedy, the world has become much more preoccupied with the dramatic events in the Soviet Union and East Europe. For the most part, China has slipped off the front pages of newspapers around the country.

---

* Leo A. Orleans is China consultant, Congressional Research Service, and publications coordinator for these volumes.

And yet, issues stemming from the size and rate of growth of China's population are just as important now as ever. Although the birth rate in China is once again on the rise, it is fortunate for China (and for the world) that the authorities continue to assign high priority to family planning—albeit minimizing the use of measures that have created such negative publicity around the world. Those who continue to suggest that China should relent in her intense pursuit of reducing the number of births might consider the fact that, were it not for abortion, China would have had at least 100 million more births in the last decade—to say nothing of the births that were prevented because of the many tens of millions of IUD insertions and sterilizations. It is an interesting exercise to contemplate the status of China's economy today if there had not been some 20 years of concerted government efforts to reduce fertility.

As demographers and China scholars, both Judith Banister and Tyrene White are fully aware of the extent to which China's success in achieving her modernization goals depends on a variety of population issues; their conclusions, however, are more scholarly and measured than mine.

*   *   *   *   *

In the short space available, Banister manages to cover all the major issues associated with population, from health issues, to fertility trends, to problems of finding gainful employment for a rapidly growing labor force. On the basis of current trends she predicts that China's mid-1990 population of 1.12 billion will be close to 1.3 billion by the turn of the century. It is easy to get lulled by "the look" of these figures, until one stops to realize that they refer to billions and that over the ten-year period China's population is likely to increase by over 150 million!

In view of the frequent references to China's urban population throughout the two volumes, Banister's brief treatment of the confusion associated with defining and counting urban population becomes especially important. By broadening the definition of "urban" to include large numbers of rural folk living within the wide-ranging urban boundaries, the Chinese have been reporting (for some years now) unrealistically high and therefore confusing urban population figures. As Banister points out, the 1990 census addressed this problem, and by significantly tightening up on the previous definition has come up with a much more realistic urban total of 300 million, or 26.2 percent of the total population.

I would only question the validity of Banister's last sentence suggesting that, were China to shift to a market economy, her "population growth will not appear such a formidable problem." It is, however, a hopeful way to end a chapter.

*   *   *   *   *

In her treatment of China's population dilemma, Tyrene White focuses on the conflict between state-planned child bearing and market reforms and the consequent difficulties of enforcing compliance to the one-child policy in the countryside. Under a command economy cadres were rewarded for accomplishments in reducing fertility and therefore were motivated to enforce birth planning regulations. Now, according to White, local leaders are rewarded for economic achievements first and only get "applause" for low birth rates. Three other factors have been important in causing birth rates to start creeping upward by the second half of the 1980s. First, as the authority of the cadres has greatly diminished, peasants no longer fear them; second, the peasants have become much more mobile and can now have their babies in other localities; and third, funding for birth planning work has been greatly reduced.

It is interesting to note that in family planning, as in many other endeavors in China, there can be a broad gap between a policy and its implementation and that a change in policy is not necessarily preceded by an official announcement. Thus, although the State Family Planning Commission has never admitted an easing of the one-child policy, maintaining that the problem has not been with the policy but with its enforcement, in most areas—after an interval of several years—couples whose first child was a daughter have been permitted to have another child in hopes that it would be a boy. Moreover, many rural families continue to have multiple births and, if necessary, willingly pay the fines.

White concludes that, just as in the case of the economy as a whole, birth planning has been plagued by a "skewed incentive systems that reward 'undesirable' behaviors and decisions, encourage corruption, and waste scarce resources." Finally, it is difficult to disagree with White's prediction that, as China contemplates a population of 1.5 billion by the middle of the next century, her leadership is unlikely to abandon the principle of state-regulated childbearing for a long time to come.

$$* \qquad * \qquad * \qquad * \qquad *$$

The concept of social security is new to China where, whenever possible, the family has always been relied on to provide support in time of need—be it sickness, old age, or unemployment. While for most of China this is still the case, after 1949 Beijing began to experiment with its own version of a social security system that would provide such support for workers and employees within the urban state economic sector—a system that created a gross inequity between the rural and urban populations. However, this inequity and its implications are not the topics of Lillian Liu's chapter; she limits herself to a detailed discussion of the provisions now in effect for the state-sector workers in China.

It is important to understand that whereas in the United States social security is limited to cash benefits for old age, survivors, and disability, for the Chinese urban worker employed in a state enterprise social security constitutes only an extension of a comprehensive package referred to as the "iron rice bowl" by the Chinese. As a member of a *danwei* or work unit, the worker is already entitled not only to life-long employment but also to low-cost housing and extensive food and nonfood allowances. This cradle-to-grave security is obviously attractive to most Chinese workers and the fact that such a system is now considered by many to be a drag on economic efficiency has done little to change it.

Liu points out that a decade of policy changes and experiments with the social security system, originally introduced in the 1950s, has left problems of inadequate funding (despite almost an eight-fold increase in budget between 1978 and 1988), inefficient administration, widespread mismanagement, and large discrepancies between the guidelines set out by the central and local governments and their implementation by individual enterprises, which constantly seek ways of cutting social security costs. Moreover, since workers do not contribute to the funding of social security programs and are still tied to their enterprise for housing, schools, and other benefits, the system discourages the mobility that would be necessary in a market-oriented economy.

Beijing's efforts to overcome many of these problems is made much more difficult by the widespread perception among the workers that social security programs are unreliable. But even if China manages to overcome some of the obstacles currently plaguing the social security system as it is now constituted—and Liu is skeptical that in the near future success will be possible—it is well to remember that the system will still exclude 75 percent of the population living in the countryside and an even larger proportion of the labor force outside the state sector. And finally, the responsible leadership understands very well that only when old age security does not depend on having a male offspring, will China be able to achieve her goals in reducing fertility.

*   *   *   *   *

Baruch Boxer's chapter, "China's Environment: Issues and Economic Implications," might have fit in several other sections of the volume, but it is not at all out of place under "Social and Human Factors."

The retort of developing countries when pressed by advanced countries to show more concern about environment has become quite familiar. They usually insist that measures to control environmental degradation would adversely affect their efforts to industrialize and modernize their country. "Did you worry about pollution when your country was undergoing industrialization?" they ask. In a country with over a billion people, problems stemming from environmental degradation are much easier to understand than elsewhere, but the leadership is plagued by the familiar problem of cost and the ever-growing demands for pieces of the national budget. In China this tug of war between environmental needs and modernization is taking place internally and is therefore especially frustrating.

In his chapter Boxer discusses the early recognition by Beijing of environmental problems and both the successes and failures in the efforts to control them. On the plus side, he mentions the wide-ranging environmental laws and regulations, the numerous educational and propaganda campaigns in support of environmental protection, and the government's support of extensive scientific and technical research and monitoring programs. On the negative side, Boxer deals with the many examples of environmental abuse relating to water, air, and waste management, the confusion over ends and means in environmental protection, and the consequent problems associated with the implementation of environmental regulations when they come up against local attitudes and economic realities.

Although stressing the difficulties of analyzing the economic implications of environmental issues, Boxer raises some interesting questions about steps that might be taken by Beijing, and about what, if any, should be the responsibility of foreign enterprises and the multilateral development agencies as they invest in China's modernization. He concludes that with the exception of a few more advanced areas, it is unlikely that at this time the government has "the expertise or will to implement a national program that can respond satisfactorily to China's special problems of size, physical diversity, resource imbalance, and population concentration."

*   *   *   *   *

Carol Hamrin makes a strong argument that the relationship between the intellectuals and the state has become the central political problem in China. And indeed, it is undeniable that the love-hate relationship between the Beijing leadership and the university-educated segment of the population has been a serious drag on China's cyclical efforts to modernize the country, with the Cultural Revolution representing the height of this antagonism.

Hamrin discusses some of the background in the evolution of this relationship, with an emphasis on the 1980s. She tells of the high hopes for change in the country during the mid-1980s, the increase in political activism, the gradual erosion of confidence in the leadership, culminating with the tragic events in the spring of 1989. She lists the intimidation tactics after Tiananmen and the symbolic measures taken to pacify the intellectuals. She discusses the negative effects China's internal and external brain drain over the past several years, and ends her chapter by concluding that many of the policy errors are due to the isolation of the leadership from the people. Understandably, Hamrin has almost given up hope of any meaningful change in China as long as the current aged or aging leadership is in place, but she does believe the future could be brighter. In her view, the younger leadership is bound to be more forward-looking and will understand that the support of intellectuals will be needed for China to progress into the twenty-first century.

Indeed, the plight of Chinese intellectuals has become well known around the world. They have neither the freedoms, the salaries, or the "creature comforts" we would presume them to have. I do, however, have some important differences with the author and, despite space limitations, I must note at least two of them.

First, Carol Hamrin leaves the impression that the distrust and abuse of intellectuals by the Chinese government started with Mao and the communist regime and that the current repression and alienation of intellectuals is somehow unusual. This, of course, is not the case. Although, as she points out, the traditional practice was for intellectuals to assist and advise the leadership, this reliance was usually limited to revolutionary periods when an emperor or other leader was in the process of assuming leadership. Once the leader came to power, the relationship quickly changed from reliance to distrust and mistreatment of intellectuals. This was even more evident after the social and political turmoil of the twentieth century, when intellectuals, who were so deeply involved in every political upheaval, quickly became suspect as potential trouble-makers. Thus, many intellectuals under Chiang Kai-shek fared little better than the Confucian scholars under the various emperors. The current leaders are as nearsighted as were their predecessors. Tradition!

Second, my view is that the intellectuals' disaffection is not nearly as widespread as Hamrin suggests and that the student-led democracy movement in the spring of 1989 did not have the overwhelming support of intellectuals—especially when using the broad Chinese definition of the word. In fact, China's democracy movement represents the views and aspirations of a small, elitist group of humanists and social scientists who want a greater voice for themselves and frankly disdain the notion that the Party should be more responsive to the Chinese masses. Moreover, with the notable exception of Fang Lizhi, there was an insignificant number of scientists and engineers—by far the largest college-educated group—among Hamrin's "intellectual pace setters and pioneers."

To my mind the best one-sentence analysis of what happened in Tiananmen in the spring of 1989 was by Esherick and Wasserstrom:

> As essentially nonviolent demonstrations that posed no direct economic or physical threat to China's rulers, the power of the protests derived almost exclusively from their potency as performances which could symbolically undermine the regime's legitimacy and move members of larger and economically more vital classes to take sympathetic action. (Joseph W. Esherick and Jeffrey N. Wasserstrom, "Acting Out Democracy: Political Theater in Modern China," *The Journal of Asian Studies*, Nov. 1990, p. 839)

*　　　*　　　*　　　*　　　*

In her chapter on "The Impact of Mao's Legacy on China's Reforms," Marcia Ristaino argues that the Maoist tradition continues to permeate all sectors of the society and body politic and that the current leadership relies on Marxism-Leninism-Mao Zedong Thought to achieve the prescribed goals and solve the country's problems. She believes that despite the destructive Cultural Revolution, Mao continues to have "a deep emotional connection with China's people," and one must agree with Ristaino that Mao, more than any other leader, is associated with China's having "stood up" as a people.

In the first half of her chapter, Ristaino discusses the successes and failures with which Mao has been associated. Maoist tradition was most successful in the rural areas where, through inspiration and indoctrination, he managed to bring basic health care services, education, and other social programs to the peasants. Using his guerrilla heritage as a guide, Mao also successfully utilized the military, not only as a fighting force, but also in civilian affairs, where it participated both in the preservation of social order and played important political and administrative roles. As to economics, culture, and politics, Maoist initiative-stifling ideology and his insistence on centralized control thwarted China's development. Ristaino provides a good summary of Maoist economic policies and contradictions. One of the notable contradictions is that while Mao taught self-reliance and denigrated bureaucracy, his highly centralized system of production fostered dependence and lack of initiative.

The second part of Ristaino's paper is entitled the "Post-Mao Challenges." Here, I agree with much of what she says, but it seems to me that the material she presents contradicts her major thesis: the continuing influence of Mao's legacy. She talks about how increased urbanization has eroded Maoist values and exposed the population to many new ideas; she correctly points to the government's apprehension over the expanded media and communications systems and the freedom of expression which blossomed before to the Tiananmen crackdown; and she touches on the many challenges that the Maoist tradition faces from abroad.

Ristaino believes that, while China's better-educated urban youth does not subscribe chapter and verse to Mao's teachings, some of them now look up to him and the security provided by his authoritarian, centralized model. Perhaps. But I think that there are two more important reasons why Mao's picture is showing up in Chinese homes. First, it is one of the few safe ways to express displeasure with the current leadership; and second, it is a sad commentary on the absence of contemporary leaders for young people to look up to.

I would say that, although there is a considerable overlap between the two, the legacy of tradition is much stronger than the legacy of Mao in today's China. And, as we all know, for over a decade now, the Chinese leadership has been struggling with the impossible task of retaining China's "Chineseness" (traditions), while modernizing and opening to the outside world. They are not anxious to return to Mao.

CHINA'S POPULATION CHANGES AND THE ECONOMY

By Judith Banister *

CONTENTS

SUMMARY

This article briefly describes broad demographic trends in China during the 1980s and 1990s, and how they relate to economic trends. The population continued growing during the 1980s because of low mortality, declining age at marriage, fertility slightly above replacement level in most years, and a young age structure. China has achieved rather advanced mortality conditions for a developing country, with apparent further improvement in the 1980s. The death rate is expected to remain low, which will foster continued population growth. During the early 1980s, age at marriage declined in China, which tended to increase the birth rate. But government pressure to postpone marriage may now have arrested this trend.

China's one-child policy is still in effect and has been very successful in urban areas. But in rural areas it has met with continuing resistance. The national and provincial governments have now backed down to the point of allowing some rural couples to have a

---

* Chief, China Branch, Center for International Research, U.S. Bureau of the Census. The interpretations and opinions expressed in this article are those of the author alone, and do not represent the policy of the United States Government or the U.S. Bureau of the Census.

second child. Couples of the Han Chinese majority ethnic group are forbidden to have more than two children, and the determination of the authorities to stop them has succeeded in continually reducing the proportion of all births that are third and subsequent births. It is expected that fertility levels and population growth rates will remain about the same in the 1990s. If China's Communist government were superseded by a more democratic one, however, compulsory family planning would probably cease, and fertility and the population growth rate would rise.

During the decade of economic reform from 1978 through 1988, China's economic boom facilitated rapid job creation. The employed population increased at 3.0 percent a year while the population of labor force ages grew at 2.5 percent annually. Some of the new jobs were in agriculture, but nonagricultural employment increased at over 6 percent per year. Therefore, the economic reforms helped to further the transformation of China's economy out of agriculture into industrial and service sector employment. This structural change is much needed because there is a huge surplus labor force in agriculture. But the economic retrenchment policies adopted in late 1988, and the political crackdown of 1989, brought on an economic slump and at least temporarily stopped the economic transformation of China's employment structure.

The economic reform period also saw increased geographical mobility of laborers. While some moved to nearby towns, others flooded into the cities or headed for coastal zones where factories now produce for export. Rural-to-urban migration of workers was one component of China's urbanization trend in the 1980s. Though the current economic slowdown is causing some nonagricultural workers to return to their villages and to farming, it is likely that the urban demand for rural workers will remain important in the 1990s, and that rural-to-urban migration will continue.

China's population will probably continue growing at around 1.4 percent a year in the 1990s, and the total population is expected to be close to 1.3 billion by the year 2000. If the economic slump and political stagnation continue, this population growth could exacerbate problems of food supply, employment, and living standards, but if China's rapid economic development resumes, this rate of population growth would be more manageable.

I. INTRODUCTION

China's population size is so huge, and each annual increment to the population so enormous, that we cannot ignore how China's demographic conditions impinge on the country's economic development and quality of life. During the tempestuous years 1957–1977, for example, grain production and population size increased by about the same amount, leaving per capita grain output hardly changed after two decades. Since the beginning of the economic reform period in 1978, the interplay between economic and demographic trends has become much more complex than before. For instance, the sharp increases in agricultural production during 1978–1984 gave China some safety margin in its food supply. Yet the loosening of economic controls over the farmers, which had brought about the surge in agricultural output, also weakened the ability of officials to prevent unauthorized rural births.

The general economic boom of the reform decade 1978–1988 produced a doubling of per capita income accompanied by visible improvement in living standards in both urban and rural areas. Population growth continued, but was so much slower than economic growth that per capita gains in food supply, housing, and consumer goods were impressive, at least for a while. This article briefly traces the interactions between population changes and economic trends in China since 1978, emphasizing the most recent years and prospects for the 1990s. Table 1 includes some available economic and per capita economic indicators for this period.

China, the world's most populous country, counted a total population of about 1.13 billion people in 1990, constituting 21 percent of the world's total population and fully 28 percent of the population in developing countries. Since China's landmark 1982 census, the population has grown 1.47 percent a year on average. This growth rate is very low for a developing country, but in the context of China, it has meant an additional 126 million people in only eight years!

II. MORTALITY AND HEALTH

During the 1980s, the rural people's communes were dismantled, and so were the cooperative medical systems that had been organized and highly subsidized by the production brigades under the communes. Now, in most of China's rural areas, health care has shifted to a fee-for-service system in which the former rudimentary arrangements for health and major medical insurance are gone. Some localities have made ad hoc attempts to guarantee minimal health care to everyone regardless of ability to pay. It is unclear how many people are now experiencing reduced access to medical care as a result of the economic transformation of China's rural areas.

Despite some deterioration in China's famous system of preventive and primary health care for the rural population, the data so far available suggest that during the 1980s, survival chances improved for the rural as well as the urban populations at most ages for both sexes.[1] One exception to this generalization is the mortality trend for infants. According to China's 1988 two-per-thousand-population fertility survey, China's infant mortality rate declined sharply through 1977, then stabilized for a full decade through 1987 at approximately 40 deaths in the first year of life per thousand live births.[2] Until death and age data from the 1990 census become available, it is impossible to document mortality trends in China during the most recent years, nor can we even be certain that mortality above infancy did decline during the 1980s as indicated by presently available statistics.

How is it possible to explain the apparent improvement in survival chances for most age groups except infants, in spite of the dis-

---

[1] Based on analysis of life tables from the 1982 census and the 1987 one-percent sample census. See Banister, 1990.

[2] "China's Infant Mortality Declines in Past Forty Years," *China Population Newsletter*, Vol. 6, No. 2, Apr. 1989, pp. 11, 18; and Banister, 1990, pp. 6–8.

array in the rural medical system during the economic reform decade? The weakening of primary health care may have affected prenatal care and the maternal and child health network the most, which would help explain the lack of further improvement in infant survival. But the doubling of living standards greatly improved food supply, nutrition, and the quality and quantity of housing, all of which may have increased survival chances above infancy. People have chosen to spend some of their higher incomes on medical care and pharmaceuticals, and the numbers of doctors and hospital beds per capita have grown, as shown in Table 1.[3] China worked with the United Nations Children's Fund (UNICEF) and the World Health Organization in the 1980s to immunize over 85 percent of the children in each province against six major diseases, thus greatly reducing child mortality from infectious disease. The government has claimed progress in improving water supply and water quality for most of the rural population in the 1980s decade.[4] Therefore, the economic boom has given people more resources to use for prolonging life and improving health, while the government has continued its emphasis on preventive strategies such as immunization which can significantly reduce mortality.

China's low crude death rate contributes to the continuing population growth. The death rate is low, both because of China's great successes in reduction of mortality, and because the country still has a young age structure due to past high fertility.[5] In a young population, a high proportion of people are in ages with comparatively low mortality.

III. MARRIAGE AND THE TIMING OF BIRTHS

Changes in the ages at which women marry and bear children strongly affect annual fertility and population growth by spreading out births or bunching them together. During the 1970s China's government had successfully promoted and required higher ages at marriage in both urban and rural areas. Rising marriage ages significantly reduced the total fertility rates and crude birth rates of the 1970s.[6] But required postponement of marriage was not popular, and this policy was reversed in the revised Marriage Law adopted in 1980. Thereafter, the mean age at first marriage for Chinese women dropped from 23.1 years old in 1979 to 21.7 in 1985; this trend was seen in cities, towns, and rural areas.[7] In addition, there is some evidence that the average time interval between marriage and first birth (known as the "first birth interval") has been reduced in recent years.

---

[3] China, State Statistical Bureau, Department of Agricultural Statistics, *Woguo nongmin shenghuo de juda bianhua* (Great Changes in the Lives of China's Peasants), Beijing: China Statistics Press, 1984; China, Ministry of Agriculture, Planning Bureau, *Zhongguo nongcun jingji tongji daquan* (A Complete Compilation of China's Rural Economic Statistics), Beijing: Agriculture Press, 1989, p. 563; *Statistical Survey of China 1990*, pp. 46, 109–110.

[4] Zhu Baoxia, "Clean Water Goal Set for Rural Areas," *China Daily*, June 9, 1990, p. 3.

[5] With survival chances the same, a country with a young population like China has a lower crude death rate (annual deaths per thousand total population) than a country with an older age structure.

[6] Coale, 1984, pp. 48–54. The "total fertility rate" is the average number of children who would be born alive to a woman during her lifetime if she lived through all her childbearing years and conformed to all the age-specific fertility rates of a given year.

[7] Wang, Riley, & Lin, 1990, Table 1.

Earlier marriage combined with a shorter first birth interval meant that Chinese women in the 1980s bore their children at younger ages than was the case in the late 1970s. The surge of marriages and the shortening of intervals between marriage and first birth caused a bunching of births, especially first births, in the first half of the 1980s. The government has been trying to reverse this trend, and since 1985 marriage age has stabilized or risen slightly.[8]

China's 1980s marriage boom was encouraged by an expansion of available housing space, and simultaneously increased the need for more housing units. The supply of housing escalated rapidly in the reform decade. Rural residents poured much of their newly increased income into expansion and upgrading of their existing dwellings and the building of new houses for family members. In cities, a boom in housing construction helped alleviate a desperate shortage of living quarters. Table 1 shows that living space per capita expanded in both urban and rural areas. Escalating demand for housing was driven in part by the surge of marriages, and housing construction in turn made it much easier for young couples to set up a new household.

IV. FERTILITY AND FAMILY PLANNING

A. THE ONE CHILD POLICY

Since 1979 China has been in the era of the well-known one-child policy. The rationale for this policy has been that it is unacceptable to allow the population of China to continue growing to 1.4 or 1.5 billion people, which is projected if people bear two children per couple. In 1979, the national government of China boldly presumed that it would be possible under current conditions to educate, cajole, or force urban and rural couples to cease childbearing after the birth of one child. In urban areas, the leadership's confidence was reasonably well-founded. The urban family planning program had been very effective since the early 1960s, and the total fertility rate of the urban nonagricultural population had been reduced to only 1.55 births per woman by 1978.[9] Throughout the 1980s, the urban total fertility rate was around 1.3 births per woman, according to official reports.[10] This is lower fertility than that of almost any country or city in the world, developed or developing, and must be seen as an unqualified success for China's one-child policy.

However, the official goal of one child per couple was severely out of line with rural reality. China's forceful family planning program of the 1970s had already resulted in a steep drop in rural fertility from 6.4 births per woman in 1970 to 3.0 births per woman in 1978, a remarkably rapid shift.[11] But rural couples continued to view it as necessary to have more than one child, including at least one son, to provide farm and household labor for the family. A

[8] Wang, Riley, & Lin, 1990, Table 1.
[9] China Population Information Centre, 1984, pp. 162–164.
[10] Wang Wei, "Guanyu jihua shengyu gongzuo wenti" (Questions about Family Planning Work), *Renkou yu jingji* (Population and Economy), No. 2, Apr. 1986, p. 4; Peng Peiyun, "Why I am Extending the Two-Child Option," *People* (International Planned Parenthood Federation, London), Vol. 16, No. 1, Jan. 1989, p. 12.
[11] China Population Information Centre, 1984, pp. 165–167.

widespread rural attitude is that sons, after reaching adulthood, are needed to carry on the family name, live with or near their parents, and care for their aging parents because a rural social security system is lacking. In addition to these traditional reasons for desiring several children, the shift from communal to family farming in the 1980s made households into economic production units that could potentially benefit from more children to work the fields, carry out sideline activities, transport and sell output, take jobs in rural enterprises and bring home the earnings, or migrate to a town or city and send money home. During the 1980s, occasional surveys asked rural couples about desired family size, and they almost always answered that two, three, or more children were preferred.[12]

From 1979 through 1983, the Chinese government escalated the pressure on rural couples to stop at one child. This policy applied to the majority Han Chinese population; China's 55 minority groups, who constituted 7 percent of China's total population according to the 1982 census, have been encouraged to limit fertility but not required to abide by the one-child rule. What evolved in the early 1980s was a requirement that Han Chinese women with one child accept the insertion of an IUD which would not be removed on request, and that couples who had managed to bear two children in spite of the one-child policy or before it was implemented were required to have one partner sterilized. In many rural as well as urban areas, family planning workers monitored the menstrual periods and pregnancy status of each married woman of childbearing age, so that an abortion could be required for pregnancies outside the local official birth plan. The coercion level reached its peak in 1983, when family planning surgery teams swooped into villages and carried out mandatory sterilizations, IUD insertions, and abortions on those women deemed "eligible." That year, the number of each kind of birth control operation peaked in China at 21 million sterilizations, 18 million IUD insertions, and 14 million abortions (Table 2).

B. EVOLVING FAMILY PLANNING POLICIES

The strength of the rural backlash against the coercion campaign was never directly reported in China's media and must be indirectly inferred from other evidence. Suddenly in early 1984, previously scheduled family planning campaigns were called off, the director of the family planning program was replaced, and "Document Number 7" was promulgated. This national directive was never published, but was referred to for some years. It counseled that, (in contrast to the 1979–1983 period), "family planning policies must be built on a foundation that is fair and reasonable, supported by the masses, and easy for the cadres to carry out."[13] Doc-

---

[12] Karen Hardee-Cleaveland, "Desired Family Size and Sex Preference in Rural China: Evidence from Fujian Province," Ph.D. dissertation, Cornell University, 1988; "The Impact of Rural Family Functions on Fertility Rate," *China Population Research Leads* (Shanghai Population Information Center), No. 2, July 1988, p. 2; *Population and Family Planning*, (Beijing: Foreign Languages Press, 1990), p. 11.

[13] Peng Zhiliang, "Tan jihua shengyu zhengce yao heqing heli" (Family Planning Policy Must Be Fair and Reasonable), *Jiankang bao jihua shengyu ban* (Health Gazette, Family Planning Edition), June 29, 1984, p. 3.

ument Number 7 directed that rural couples with "real difficulties," thought to constitute no more than 5 or 10 percent of rural couples, might be given permission to have a second child.

Meanwhile, through all this turmoil, rural fertility remained above two births per woman on average. Since 1983, rural couples have continued their struggle to have two, three, or more children in spite of official prohibition. In many places in China, this is very difficult and requires getting an illegal IUD removal, hiding the pregnancy, and leaving the village on some pretense for most of the pregnancy until the baby is born. In other localities, however, the family planning system of regulation has broken down along with the commune system, and women are no longer being constantly monitored.[14] For a few years after 1983, the national government backed down a little and expanded the proportion of rural second parity births that were officially approved.[15] In some provinces now, peasants who have a firstborn girl are allowed a second birth (to try for a boy). In other provinces, all peasants are allowed two births per couple. But in the more developed provinces, the one-child limit is still being applied to many categories of rural couples as well as to urban couples; in Heilongjiang, for example, only a minority of villages may permit second births to couples with a firstborn girl. Now the national and many provincial governments are trying to reduce the proportions of rural couples who are authorized to have a second child.[16]

As of 1990, as far as can be ascertained, China's government is still trying to be as strict as it can get away with in enforcing a one-child limit for most urban couples and a one-child or two-child limit for rural couples. National and provincial governments continually exhort local cadres to hold the line on births; indeed, the harshness of the official rhetoric and the penalties to back up official demands have been escalating since 1986.[17] This policy appears to be successful; actual fertility in China is below desired fertility—that is, both urban and rural couples are bearing fewer children than they would without the compulsory family planning program. Today, family planning workers and "volunteers" for the quasi-official local Family Planning Associations continue to monitor the birth control, menstrual, and pregnancy status of the vast majority of urban women and most rural married women in the reproductive ages.[18] They often achieve their goals of preventing unapproved pregnancies through required IUD use or sterilization, and by securing the induced abortion of fetuses whose births are not authorized.

C. FERTILITY AND CONTRACEPTIVE USE

As shown in Table 3, China's birth rate has been steady at the low level of 21 births per thousand population annually for four years, according to State Statistical Bureau surveys. Since 1982, 51 or 52 percent of the births each year have been first parity births.

---

[14] Greenhalgh, 1990, pp. 204, 216, 222–229.
[15] Birth parity means birth order.
[16] Details are compiled in Aird, 1990, pp. 59–89.
[17] This trend is well-documented in Aird, 1990, pp. 59–89 and Appendix B.
[18] Peng Peiyun, "Guanyu 1989-nian de gongzuo" (On the Work in 1989), *Zhongguo renkou bao* (China Population), Feb. 24, 1989, p. 1.

This is extraordinarily high for a developing country and attests to the success of the one-child policy. The main parity trend in the 1980s was a steep drop in the proportion of births that were third or subsequent children, a result of China's continuing official insistence that all births above second parity are resolutely forbidden except to members of minority groups. Meanwhile, the proportion of births that were second births rose to one-third, mirroring the slow growth until about 1986 of official tolerance for rural second births.

Today, China's compulsory family planning program is still functioning and keeping fertility low and more or less steady. Table 2 shows that each year, there are still 10–13 million IUD insertions, 3–6 million sterilizations, and 10–13 million abortions performed. Of married women in the reproductive ages 15–49, 71 percent are practicing family planning. Such a high contraceptive use rate is typical of developed countries but rare in developing countries. Of these couples practicing contraception, 49 percent have one partner sterilized, 41 percent are using an IUD, 5 percent are using the pill, and 5 percent other methods.[19] This means that a very high proportion of couples in China are using modern effective contraceptive methods which prevent pregnancy. Abortions, voluntary or required, are still heavily used to prevent births when pregnancies occur.

Fertility is very low in China, not far above "replacement level fertility," yet the population continues to grow at over 1.4 percent a year. This is partly because of age structure. China had huge cohorts born in the high-fertility period of the 1960s, who reached their twenties during the 1980s. Births are highly concentrated when Chinese women are ages 21–30, so this bulge in the age structure is tending to drive the birth rate up. This trend will be even more pronounced in the 1990s, when the huge numbers of women in their twenties could cause a "birth peak." As shown in Figure 1, the number of women aged 21–30 increased from 81 million in 1983 to about 106 million in 1990. The peak will come in 1993, with approximately 124 million women in their fertile twenties, and the number will decline only slowly to about 109 million in the year 2000 (see Figure 1). Therefore, the birth rate could rise in the 1990s if fertility per woman does not drop. China's government is concerned about the coming "birth peak," and therefore is attempting to reduce fertility further.

V. Labor Force and Employment Trends

A. ECONOMIC REFORM AND EMPLOYMENT GROWTH

Shifts in China's age structure have also meant that the population of labor force ages has been growing faster than the total population in recent years. For example, from the 1982 census to 1990, the population at ages 15–64 grew 2.5 percent a year while the total population increased 1.5 percent annually. During the decade from the adoption of the reform agenda in 1978 until the implementation of economic retrenchment in late 1988 and the political

[19] "The Nationwide Fertility and Birth Control Sampling Survey Ended Successfully," *China Population Research Leads* (Shanghai Population Information Center), No. 4, Apr. 1989, p. 3.

crisis of 1989, China's booming economy was successful at creating jobs for the growing working age population. The tremendous increase in the size of the employed population was due not only to vigorous economic growth but also to the continuing Chinese government attitude that full employment is essential, even if it comes at the cost of low productivity.

Official Chinese statistics on employment show that at the end of 1978 there were about 402 million people working (Table 1). The size of the employed population grew 3.0 percent a year to 543 million at the end of 1988, well ahead of the growth of population in labor force ages. In 1989 under economic retrenchment policies, official data still show employment growth of 1.8 percent.[20]

B. SURPLUS LABOR IN AGRICULTURE

It is characteristic of China that the employment participation rate of adult men is extremely high; this is also true of Chinese women, which is even more unusual in international perspective.[21] This phenomenon is partly a result of the practice in some localities of classifying those adults not working outside agriculture in the residual category of agricultural workers, even if their contribution to agriculture is marginal or sporadic. Workers in agriculture made up 60 percent of total employed workers in 1989.

The number of agricultural workers is high partly because Chinese agriculture is still at a low level of mechanization. On the whole, farmers make intensive use of the available arable land and water resources in order to feed the huge population, and this requires a lot of labor. Even so, Chinese policymakers recognize that the agricultural sector does not need so many workers. Chinese scholars estimate that approximately one-third of the country's farmers are underemployed, meaning that their efforts are needed only at peak planting and harvesting time. The surplus of adult workers stuck on the land holds down per-worker productivity in agriculture well below what it would be if these workers could be usefully employed elsewhere.[22]

C. EMPLOYMENT TRENDS BY ECONOMIC SECTOR

For the last decade, the emphasis in employment policy has been to create jobs for the rising tide of youth entering the work force in urban areas, and in the countryside to absorb some of the excess farm workers into nonagricultural jobs, agricultural sideline occupations, or the production of cash crops. In contrast to the earlier Maoist decades, national policy during the 1980s has allowed self-employment, permitted the reopening of rural and urban markets not run by local governments, encouraged rural enterprises to employ idle agricultural workers, and allowed workers to move in order to find jobs. Until 1989, the results were encouraging. During the period from 1978 through 1988 (based on year-end figures), while employment in agriculture increased at 1.3 percent annually, total nonagricultural jobs grew at a respectable 6.3 percent a year. But the retrenchment policies and upheavals of 1989 stopped the

---

[20] *Statistical Survey of China 1990*, p. 15.
[21] Taylor, 1986, pp. 222–230; Arriaga & Banister, 1985, pp. 170–172.
[22] Taylor & Banister, 1989, pp. 43–46.

growth of nonagricultural employment; the number of jobs outside agriculture stayed at 220 million from year-end 1988 to year-end 1989.[23]

Figure 2 shows that the growth rate of jobs in the industrial sector of the economy dropped from 7.3 percent in 1986 to 3–4 percent annually in 1987 and 1988. Then, however, urban layoffs and the closing of some rural enterprises in 1989 brought a decline in industrial employment from 97 million at the end of 1988 to 96 million one year later. Employment in the service sector, which had been increasing at 5 or 6 percent a year, grew at a modest 0.9 percent in 1989. Those who lost their nonagricultural jobs, as well as the new entrants to the labor force, either became unemployed, shifted to service sector work, or took up agriculture. It is clear from Figure 2 that the growth rate of employment in agriculture increased gradually from 0.4 percent in 1986 to 3.0 percent in 1989.

The return of workers to agriculture represents a (hopefully temporary) reversal of the long-term transformation of China's economy from poor, rural, and agricultural to a more urban, nonagricultural employment structure accompanied by much higher living standards. The setbacks of 1989, however, do illustrate the wisdom of the millions of rural families who, as a precautionary measure, have hedged their bets on China's economic transformation. Since 1978, rural households have acquired rights to the use of small plots of land in the family land contracting system. While utilizing this land to grow food for the family and for profit, household units have encouraged their members to get jobs in nearby rural enterprises, take up transport work, sell goods in markets, migrate for seasonal employment, or move to a city or town for an urban job.

However, even if all or almost all adult workers in the household took nonagricultural jobs, and most family income came from nonagricultural sources, families have strongly resisted giving up any of their land rights. Instead, such households have shifted to farming the land nonintensively or letting it lie fallow.[24] This system is wasteful of quality agricultural land, a phenomenon decried by both Chinese and Western economists, but makes good sense from the perspective of the household. In an economic recession, if household nonagricultural workers lose their jobs, they can temporarily revert to farming the land. Given the lack of a rural social safety net, land rights act as an insurance policy.

Urban workers who are laid off do not have this option, and many former rural residents who had moved to cities and towns resist moving back to the countryside. Therefore urban unemployment has grown since September 1988 when retrenchment policies, including a severe credit squeeze on collective and private enterprises, began to be implemented. China's unemployment statistics

[23] Statistics in this paragraph are from China, State Statistical Bureau, Department of Social Statistics, *Zhongguo laodong gongzi tongji ziliao, 1978–1987* (China's Labor and Wage Statistics, 1978–1987), Beijing: China Statistics Press, 1989, p. 6; *Statistical Yearbook of China 1989*, pp. 106–107; and *Statistical Survey of China 1990*, p. 16.

[24] Sun Zhonghua, "A Glimpse of Grain Production from 1984 to 1988—A Survey of the Grain Output of 13,000 Peasant Households in 155 Villages" [In Chinese], *Zhongguo nongcun jingji* (China's Rural Economy), No. 3, Mar. 20, 1990, pp. 16–24, tr. as "5-Year Grain Production Slump Attributed to Peasant Apathy," *Joint Publications Research Service*, No. JPRS–CAR–90–046, June 26, 1990, pp. 78–79.

are still poor in quality;[25] rural unemployment is not captured in the statistics at all, and urban unemployment is underreported because it includes only those who have formally registered for work and are officially "waiting for employment." Figures on urban unemployment probably exclude unemployed migrants in urban areas who do not qualify for permanent residence there, and thus are not included in urban statistics. The official urban unemployment rate was 2.0 percent of the urban labor force from 1986 through 1988, then rose to 2.6 percent by the end of 1989.[26] By the end of March 1990, it was reported that 3 percent of the urban labor force in China was completely out of work, and another 3 percent was "partly out of work."[27]

VI. LABOR MIGRATION AND URBANIZATION

A. INCREASING MIGRATION OF WORKERS

In the Maoist decades, geographical mobility of Chinese families and workers was severely restricted and curtailed by the location-specific permanent population registration and rationing system. Though the vast majority of people did not move at all, there was a trickle of labor migration. Some laborers were required to move to border provinces, some were allowed to move to newly established industrial cities, and some were sent from their city homes to work in rural areas. Often when laborers moved, they were not allowed to bring their families with them.

This system is still in place, but in the economic reform period, restrictions on worker migration have been relaxed.[28] If surplus rural workers could not find nonagricultural work in the vicinity of their homes, the policy that evolved in the 1980s permitted them to travel elsewhere for work. The official guideline was to promote the development of towns and small cities all over the country so that they could absorb rural out-migrants locally. Especially popular with the authorities was allowing peasants to move to a nearby town to take an industrial job or set up a business, and permitting surplus workers from impoverished rural areas to move to a different rural area or leave for seasonal employment part of each year. Gradually, the Chinese government softened its former rigid opposition to allowing migration of rural residents into established urban areas. Workers were allowed to move to cities and towns under certain conditions, for example, if they were responsible for buying their own grain without rations or subsidy, if they brought capital with them to set up shop, if they came alone to work and did not bring a family, and if their legal registration location remained in the rural areas. Different urban localities set up different criteria.[29]

---

[25] The quality of unemployment data from the 1990 census may be a considerable improvement over currently available figures.

[26] *Statistical Survey of China 1990*, p. 18.

[27] "Unemployment Increases in First Quarter," *Zhongguo tongxun she* (China News Agency in Hong Kong), May 29, 1990, translated in *Summary of World Broadcasts, Weekly Economic Report*, No. FE/W0131, June 6, 1990, pp. A1–A2.

[28] For details on this important policy shift, see Judith Banister, *Urban-Rural Population Projections for China*, Washington, D.C.: U.S. Bureau of the Census, 1986. Center for International Research, Staff Paper No. 15.

[29] For further information on worker migration from the villages, see Taylor & Banister, 1989, pp. 23–38.

In the 1980s, some migrants were formally allowed to move permanently to urban areas, and their legal household registrations were transferred to the city or town. Urban population statistics are so problematic that it is difficult to estimate the numbers of these formal, legal rural-to-urban migrants. After a complex series of calculations, it was possible to estimate that during 1985, net inmigration accounted for only about 1 percent growth in the total legal permanent resident population of China's cities; only approximately 1.9 million people were granted legal residence that year in the cities that had been established before 1985.[30]

More numerous are the rural-to-urban migrants who have not been granted the coveted city or town permanent household registration. People who are away from their rural legal residence are grouped together under the label "floating population," whether they actually moved permanently to the urban place ten years ago, or they left their village two days ago and are just passing through town. Some cities have periodically tried to count their floating populations, and relatively sophisticated cities like Shanghai distinguish among "temporary" residents who have been there for different lengths of time. For example, an August 1984 survey of Shanghai's estimated 590,000 floating population included 338,000 "temporary" residents living in established households, of whom one-third had been residing there for over five years and a total of almost one-half had been living there for over a year.[31] Yet the city had not granted them permanent residence, so they were not included in the reported population of Shanghai. Fortunately, China's 1982 and 1990 censuses both assumed that anyone who had lived in a certain town or city for a year or more was a resident of that place, so the censuses give more realistic counts of the populations of cities and towns than do city registers.

The floating population of Shanghai Municipality increased from 0.7 million by the end of 1984 to 1.11 million in 1985 and further to 1.25 million in October 1988, compared to a legal permanent resident population of 12.62 million at the end of 1988. Other cities and many urban towns have also reported floating populations that are large in relation to their legal permanent resident populations. By the end of 1989, a rough estimate of the floating population nationwide was given as 50 million, of whom 1.83 million were in Shanghai Municipality, 1.35 million in Beijing Municipality, and 1.1 million in Guangzhou (Canton) Municipality.[32] In February 1990, the floating population was estimated to be between 60 and 80 million people.[33] Statistics on the movement of China's workers and resi-

---

[30] In addition, China's city population total grew in 1985 through natural population increase (more city births than deaths) and boundary expansion, and most important, through the establishment of 29 new cities. A similar analysis could be carried out for some more recent years for which the data are now available. Judith Banister, "China: Components of Recent City Growth," presented at the International Conference on Urbanization and Urban Population Problems, Tianjin, Oct. 1987.

[31] Zheng Guizhen et al., "A Preliminary Exploration of the Problem of Shanghai Municipality's Floating Population," [in Chinese], *Renkou yanjiu* (Population Research), No. 3, May 29, 1985, pp. 2–7, translated in *Joint Publications Research Service*, No. JPRS-CPS-85-087, Sept. 4, 1985, pp. 33–43.

[32] Gu Chu, "Floating Population Puts Strain on Urban Areas," *Joint Publications Research Service*, No. JPRS-CAR-90-026, Apr. 9, 1990, p. 65; "Rapid Increase of China's Floating Population," *China Population Newsletter*, Vol. 1, Feb. 1990, p. 16.

[33] "Floating Population Nears 80 Million," *Joint Publications Research Service*, No. JPRS-CAR-90-020, Mar. 14, 1990, p. 58.

dents are unreliable so far, but Chinese statisticians are trying to remedy this situation using migration surveys and the 1990 census as tools.

B. URBANIZATION

The urbanization of China's population is an important aspect of its economic and social development, but unfortunately the annual official urban statistics have become almost unusable without careful and time-consuming decomposition of the components of urban population growth. For example, the mid-year 1982 census counted an urban population of 206 million, which constituted 21 percent of the civilian population.[34] By year-end 1989, only 7 ½ years later, official statistics showed a total urban population of 575 million, 52 percent of the national population.[35] Such figures are usually rejected by Chinese and foreign scholars as unrealistic and misleading. The key problem is that in the 1980s hundreds of new cities and thousands of new urban towns were established, and most of these new urban places are seriously "overbounded." While each new city and town may have a genuine urbanized core deserving of urban status, the new urban boundaries are drawn so wide that they encompass large agricultural areas and populations. This problem is caused by the practices of transforming a former xian (county) into a newly established shi (city) and reclassifying a former xiang (township) into a new zhen (urban town) without adjusting the boundary to include only the urbanized area. The latest available statistics show that over half (53 percent) of the total permanent residents living inside the city proper boundaries of China's cities are designated "agricultural" population. Of the total zhen population, 75 percent is "agricultural." [36]

Because China's annual urban population statistics are so problematic, officials of the State Statistical Bureau (SSB) and other leaders of the 1990 census effort decided to define "urban" more narrowly for this census. The enumeration districts in China's censuses are local neighborhood committees in built-up areas and village committees in agricultural areas. The census leadership instructed that village committees, even those inside city and town boundaries, were to be classified "rural" for census purposes. Therefore, the 1990 census seems to have solved the overbounding problem, and the preliminary hand-tabulated result is that only 26 percent of China's population was classified urban in the 1990 census.[37] Comparing this figure with the 1982 census population recorded as 21 percent urban indicates that there has been only moderate urbanization in China during the 1980s. However, this comparison underestimates the speed of urbanization because 1982 census data need to be adjusted downward using the 1990 census definition in order to measure the trend.

---

[34] China 1982 census volume, 1985, p. 26.

[35] *Statistical Survey of China 1990*, p. 14.

[36] Ministry of Public Security, *Zhonghua renmin gongheguo quanguo fen xian shi renkou tongji ziliao, 1988* (Population Statistics by County and City of the PRC, 1988), Beijing: China Cartographic Press, 1989, pp. 4, 8.

[37] "The 1990 Census," *Beijing Review*, Vol. 33, No. 45, Nov. 12–18, 1990, pp. 17–19.

VII. PROSPECTS FOR THE 1990s

A. THE CITIES

A rapid shift is taking place in the age structure of China's urban areas, especially in the built-up city areas, with major short-term and long-term implications. Because the fertility of China's urban nonagricultural population dropped in half from 1963 to 1966, then declined further in the 1970s and 1980s, school enrollments have declined or stabilized in many cities and towns, thus taking the pressure off the urban educational systems to provide more teachers and schools. The small urban cohorts born in the late 1960s and beyond are now beginning to join the childbearing ages and the labor force. The "birth peak" among urban nonagricultural people will be largely over by the mid-1990s. The need to provide greater numbers of entry-level jobs each year to increasingly large cohorts of urban-born youth will soon be history. In fact, without further in-migration from the countryside, China's urban population aged 15–29 would decline precipitously in size between 1990 and the year 2000.[38]

Population aging has also begun in China's cities. During the 1990s, China's urban areas will experience the aging of their labor force as the huge cohorts born in the 1950s and early 1960s begin entering middle age. The proportion of the urban population at ages 65 and above is expected to increase modestly from about 5 percent in 1990 to 8 percent at the turn of the century. This will not be a serious problem in the short run, but if China maintained its urban one-child policy, in the absence of in-migration the elderly proportion of the urban population would rise from 8 percent in the year 2000 to 17 percent in 2020, 33 percent in 2040, and 36 percent in 2060.[39]

Chinese municipal leaders and Chinese demographers advising the authorities are concerned about avoiding such severe aging of China's urban population in the future. They are already discussing reverting to an urban two-child policy at about the turn of the century, which would result in a greater number of working-age adults in the middle of the coming century to provide for the inevitably large numbers of urban elderly.[40]

A continuation of rural-to-urban migration of young adult workers is likely in the 1990s, especially if there is a resumption of China's economic boom and of the transformation into nonagricultural employment. Even with a long period of political stagnation and economic uncertainty, a distinct possibility, China's cities and towns will probably allow millions more peasants to come in to work each year. In the coming decade, there will be a strong urban demand for workers from the countryside, because of the sharp drop in the number of urban-born youth ages 15–29, because those raised in the city are less willing than peasants to do the least de-

---

[38] Banister, 1989, p. 15.

[39] Judith Banister, "The Aging of China's Urban and Rural Populations," presented at the International Academic Conference on China's Population Aging, Beijing, Dec. 1989, p. 11.

[40] Judith Banister, "The Aging of China's Population," *Problems of Communism*, Vol. 37, No. 6, Nov.–Dec. 1988, pp. 71–73.

sirable jobs, and because there remains a strong unmet demand for all kinds of services in the cities and towns of China.[41]

B. THE COUNTRYSIDE

Age structure shifts in rural areas are a decade behind those in urban areas, and are less pronounced because fertility has not dropped so low in the countryside. School-aged cohorts are no longer increasing rapidly in size, so the provision of basic education is less burdensome now. In the 1990s, couples in their peak child-bearing ages will be much more numerous than in the previous decade, a situation which is causing concern about a "birth peak." Yet rural youth who were born in 1977 and later years, after the steep rural fertility decline of the early and mid-1970s, are half as numerous as some of the 1960s cohorts. As they join the work force in the 1990s, there will be a decrease in the number of rural entry-level jobs required. Unfortunately, this incipient beneficial effect of reduced rural fertility will do little to ameliorate the overwhelming need for hundreds of millions of jobs outside agriculture for the rural surplus labor force.

China's rural areas are burdened with a massive backlog of adults who are really not needed in agriculture but have been unable to find other work. During the 1980s, estimates of the number of surplus laborers engaged in crop production ranged from 60 million to 156 million, depending on the technique of estimation.[42] These farmers still need other work, yet the economic and political reversals of late 1988, 1989, and thereafter are crippling China's ability to create employment opportunities outside agriculture. As long as these reversals continue, we can expect very little progress in transforming China's economy into one dominated by nonagricultural work.

C. NATIONAL TRENDS

China has already achieved relatively advanced mortality levels. The death rate is expected to remain low. Further improvements in mortality and health conditions are likely to be slow, because of the intractability of the leading causes of death and illness today. Chronic diseases like heart disease and cancer are everywhere difficult to prevent or cure. In a poor developing country striving for rapid economic growth, cleaning up the polluted air and water has low priority, yet is important for reducing the prevalence of environmental diseases like parasitic and waterborne viral illnesses and respiratory ailments.

It is possible that age at marriage could rise again under official pressure, as happened in the 1970s in both urban and rural areas. But the Chinese people showed in the 1980s that this policy is unpopular, and that they will marry in their early twenties if feasible. A stalemate is the most plausible outcome. Administrative pressure to stop early marriages may already have arrested the de-

---

[41] This is discussed more fully in Judith Banister and Jeffrey R. Taylor, "China: Surplus Labour and Migration," *Asia-Pacific Population Journal*, Vol. 4, No. 4, Dec. 1989, pp. 17–18; and in Banister, 1989, pp. 12–16.

[42] Taylor & Banister, 1989, p. 3.

cline in marriage age, but popular resistance will probably block full implementation of late marriage policies.

In the 1990s we are most likely to see a continuation of the unstable equilibrium between frequent attempts by couples to have another child and continual pressure from the authorities trying to stop them. Fertility will not drop or rise dramatically under this scenario. With fertility and mortality not much changed, we can expect that China's population growth rate will continue to be around 1.4 percent a year, and that the total population will increase to 1.2 billion by 1995 and reach about 1.3 billion by 2000. This will obviously require further annual increases in food production and availability, which will not be easy given the dearth of arable land and the intensity of agricultural land use already.

If China's democracy movement were to bring about a significant shift in the power structure during the 1990s away from authoritarian Communism, one of the first policies to go would probably be compulsory family planning.[43] This would be followed several months later by a rise in fertility that would be expected to last for many years. Once the policy of required family planning is discredited, subsequent Chinese governments might be hesitant to promote birth control, if the situation in India since the cessation of mandatory sterilization is any guide.

In the 1990s, China's population in the labor force ages (defined as 15–64) will no longer be increasing faster than the total population. Rather, the pool of working-age people will increase at 1.2 percent a year as the population grows about 1.4 percent annually, and the population in the young working ages 15–29 will decline. As long as the economy is in a slump, it will remain very difficult to increase the number of nonagricultural jobs enough to employ the additional numbers of middle-aged workers. If agriculture continues to absorb them, this will exacerbate the already serious problem of the huge agricultural surplus labor force.

For the next couple of decades, China's population structure will be beneficial for economic growth and increased productivity. The population is becoming middle-aged. Because fertility has dropped so low, child dependency has greatly decreased. The population ages 15–29 will peak in 1992, then decline 15 percent in size by the turn of the century only eight years later. The burdens of education and on-the-job training will lighten considerably. Because the process of population aging has only recently begun for the country as a whole, a serious aged dependency burden is several decades away. With a low dependency ratio, and a bulge in the population in their thirties, forties, and fifties, China is entering its "Golden Age." These age groups tend to be those of highest productivity, reasonably robust health, low crime, and high savings rates. China's age structure of the 1990s and first decades of the next century will be beneficial for promoting economic take-off and social stability.

---

[43] It should be noted that in Romania, the fall of Ceauscescu was followed immediately by cessation of the forced childbearing policy, which had utilized the same policies of harassing women and monitoring their birth control and pregnancy status as China uses, but for opposite goals.

VIII. CONCLUSIONS

The period of rapid population growth that China had experienced since the early 1950s had greatly strained the process of economic development and transformation, the limited supply of arable land, the environment, and the political leadership trying to cope with its effects. Finally in 1978, the government decided to loosen its stranglehold on the rural and town economies, and an economic boom followed. Rapid economic growth far outstripped the reduced rate of population growth, and living standards greatly increased.

But the shift away from a command economy to a market economy slowed in the late 1980s. Government control of the city economies and the elaborate system of subsidies given to urban workers were barely touched. The inflation that accompanied partial price reform was so intolerable to China's population and government that economic retrenchment was introduced to stop it. The reform decade had succeeded in part because of the greater autonomy given to individuals and families in their economic, social, and political lives, but this led to further demands for freedom that the government suppressed in 1989. Economic transformation and political liberalization came to a screeching halt, at least temporarily. China's rapid economic development of the 1980s facilitated great increases in real per capita income and the generation of enough jobs to keep ahead of the growth of population in the labor force ages. But the economic slowdown of 1989 stopped most of this progress, and many nonagricultural workers returned to farming.

Continued population growth in the 1990s will necessitate additional production of food, housing, and consumer goods, as well as more jobs. To further improve living standards will require economic growth well ahead of population growth. Short-term prospects are not promising. By the time China resolves its current drawn-out crisis of political succession, which is weakening its capacity to take bold economic initiatives, perhaps one or more Eastern European countries will have discovered how to transform an urban Communist economic structure like that in China's cities into something workable. China could then adapt whatever has worked elsewhere and resume its shift toward a market economy and its economic takeoff. Population growth will not appear such a formidable problem when that happens.

IX. BIBLIOGRAPHY

Aird, John S., *Slaughter of the Innocents; Coercive Birth Control in China*, Washington, D.C.: American Enterprise Institute Press, 1990.

Arriaga, Eduardo E., and Judith Banister, "The Implications of China's Rapid Fertility Decline," in International Union for the Scientific Study of Population, *International Population Conference, Florence 1985, Vol. 2*, Liege, Belgium: IUSSP, pp. 165–180.

Banister, Judith, *China's Changing Population*, Stanford, Cal.: Stanford University Press, 1987.

Banister, Judith, "China: Mortality and Health Under the Economic Reforms," presented at the Seminar on Recent Levels and Trends in Mortality in China, Harvard University, Cambridge, Mass., March 1990.

Banister, Judith, "The Migration of Surplus Laborers in China," presented at the International Academic Conference on China's Internal Migration and Urbanization, Beijing, Dec. 1989.

China 1982 census volume. China, State Council Population Census Office and State Statistical Bureau Department of Population Statistics, *Zhongguo 1982-nian renkou pucha ziliao (dianzi jisuanji huizong)* (Data from China's 1982 Population Census [Results of Computer Tabulation]), Beijing: China Statistical Publishing House, 1985.

China Population Information Center, *Analysis on China's National One-per-thousand-population Fertility Sampling Survey*, Beijing, 1984.

Coale, Ansley J., *Rapid Population Change in China, 1952–1982*, Washington, D.C.: National Academy Press, 1984. Committee on Population and Demography, Report No. 27.

Greenhalgh, Susan, "The Evolution of the One-child Policy in Shaanxi, 1979–88," *China Quarterly*, no. 122, June 1990, pp. 191–229.

Hardee-Cleaveland, Karen, and Judith Banister, 1988a. *Family Planning in China: Recent Trends*, Washington, D.C.: U.S. Bureau of the Census, 1988. Center for International Research, Staff Paper No. 40.

Hardee-Cleaveland, Karen, and Judith Banister, 1988b. "Fertility Policy and Implementation in China, 1986–88," *Population and Development Review*, Vol. 14, No. 2, June 1988, pp. 245–286.

Li Bohua, "Changes in Fertility Rates in China's 28 Provinces, Autonomous Regions, and Municipalities Directly Under the Central Authorities," [In Chinese], *Renkou yu jingji* (Population and Economics), No. 3, 1990, pp. 3–12.

Statistical Survey of China 1990. China, State Statistical Bureau, *Zhongguo tongji zhaiyao 1990* (Statistical Survey of China 1990), Beijing: China Statistics Press, 1990.

Statistical Yearbook of China, annual. China, State Statistical Bureau, *Statistical Yearbook of China*, Hong Kong and Beijing: China Statistical Information and Consultancy Service Centre, annual.

Taylor, Jeffrey R., "Labor Force Developments in the People's Republic of China, 1952–1983," in U.S. Congress, Joint Economic Committee, *China's Economy Looks Toward the Year 2000, Vol. 1, The Four Modernizations*, Washington, D.C.: U.S. Government Printing Office, 1986, pp. 222–262.

Taylor, Jeffrey R., and Judith Banister, *China: The Problem of Employing Surplus Rural Labor*, Washington, D.C.: U.S. Bureau of the Census, 1989. Center for International Research, Staff Paper No. 49.

Wang Feng, Nancy Riley, and Lin Fude, "China's Continuing Demographic Transition in the 1980s," presented at the annual meeting of the Population Association of America, Toronto, May 1990.

Table 1

China: Economic and Social Indicators

	1978	1979	1980	1981	1982	1983	1984	1985	1986	1987	1988	1989
Employed population, millions year-end	401.52	410.24	423.61	437.25	452.95	464.36	481.97	498.73	512.82	527.83	543.34	553.29
Agricultural employment	283.73	286.92	291.81	298.36	309.17	312.09	309.27	311.88	313.11	317.2	323.08	332.84
Industrial and construction employment	70.67	73.40	78.36	81.32	84.79	88.14	97.28	105.24	113.56	118.69	122.95	121.16
Services and other employment	47.12	49.92	53.44	57.57	58.99	64.13	75.42	81.61	86.15	91.94	97.31	99.29
Index of real GNP, 1978=100	100.0	107.6	116.0	121.2	131.8	145.4	166.6	187.8	203.4	225.8	250.2	260.0
Index of real GDP, agricultural sector	100.0	106.1	104.6	111.9	124.8	135.1	152.6	155.4	160.5	168.1	172.3	176.6
Index of real GDP, Industry & construction sector	100.0	108.2	122.9	125.2	132.1	145.8	166.9	197.9	218.2	248.1	284.1	297.2
Index of Real GDP, service sector	100.0	107.8	114.3	122.2	135.2	152.3	178.3	207.9	231.0	260.8	292.4	303.5
Index of real GNP per capita, 1978=100	100.0	106.2	113.1	116.8	125.3	136.6	154.8	172.7	184.7	202.1	220.6	226.1
Urban unemployed population (millions)	5.30	5.68	5.42	4.40	3.79	2.71	2.36	2.39	2.64	2.77	2.96	3.78
Urban unemployment rate as reported (%)	5.3	5.4	4.9	3.8	3.2	2.3	1.9	1.8	2.0	2.0	2.0	2.6

Table 1 (continued)

	1978	1979	1980	1981	1982	1983	1984	1985	1986	1987	1988	1989
Ratio of urban to rural per capita income				2.24	1.98	1.85	1.86	1.88	2.15	2.19	2.19	2.31
Urban per capita income (current yuan)				500.40	535.32	572.88	660.12	748.92	909.96	1,012.20	1,192.12	1,387.81
Rural per capita income (current yuan)	133.57	160.17	191.33	223.44	270.11	309.77	355.33	397.6	423.76	462.55	544.94	601.51
Index of real growth in urban income, 1978=100	100.0		126.9	130.8	136.8	142.7	160.4	177.3	182.5	185.6	187.8	
Index or real growth in rural income, 1978=100	100.0		138.1			198.4	231.3	262.1	267.7	282.3	300.7	
Hospital beds per 1,000 population	1.94	1.99	2.02	2.02	2.03	2.07	2.10	2.14	2.18	2.23	2.30	2.32
Doctors per 1,000 population	1.08	1.12	1.17	1.25	1.29	1.33	1.34	1.36	1.37	1.38	1.49	1.55
Urban living space per capita, square meters*	4.20	4.40	5.00	5.27	5.61	5.90	6.32	5.20	8.04	8.47	6.30	6.60
Rural living space per capita, square meters	8.10	8.40	9.40	10.16	10.73	11.63	13.64	14.70	15.29	16.00	16.58	17.21

*Sudden declines in urban living space per capita were caused by expansion of coverage in urban surveys.

Sources: Data sources are on file at the China Branch, Center for International Research, U.S. Bureau of the Census.

Table 2

Birth Control Operations in China, 1971-1988

Year	Total operations	IUD insertions	IUD removals	Vasectomies	Tubal ligations	Abortions
Total	504,367,707	218,893,842	38,086,687	28,819,630	69,403,310	146,610,067
1971	13,051,123	6,172,889		1,223,480	1,744,644	3,910,110
1972	18,690,446	9,220,297	853,625	1,715,822	2,087,160	4,813,542
1973	25,075,557	13,949,569	1,126,756	1,933,210	2,955,617	5,110,405
1974	22,638,229	12,579,886	1,352,787	1,445,251	2,275,741	4,984,564
1975	29,462,861	16,743,693	1,702,213	2,652,653	3,280,042	5,084,260
1976	22,385,435	11,626,510	1,812,590	1,495,540	2,707,849	4,742,946
1977	25,539,086	12,974,313	1,941,880	2,616,876	2,776,448	5,229,569
1978	21,720,096	10,962,517	2,087,420	767,542	2,511,413	5,391,204
1979	30,581,114	13,472,392	2,288,670	1,673,947	5,289,518	7,856,587
1980	28,628,437	11,491,871	2,403,408	1,363,508	3,842,006	9,527,644
1981	22,760,305	10,334,537	1,513,376	649,476	1,555,971	8,696,945
1982	33,702,389	14,069,161	2,056,671	1,230,967	3,925,927	12,419,663
1983	58,205,572	17,755,736	5,323,354	4,359,261	16,398,378	14,371,843
1984	31,734,864	11,751,146	4,383,129	1,293,286	5,417,163	8,890,140
1985	25,646,972	9,576,980	2,278,892	575,564	2,283,971	10,931,565
1986	28,475,506	10,637,909	2,313,157	1,030,827	2,914,900	11,578,713
1987	34,249,051	13,337,217	2,383,790	1,733,229	3,846,093	10,394,531
1988	31,820,664	12,227,219	2,264,969	1,062,161	3,590,469	12,675,836

Note: These figures are reproduced in full detail because the original source is not widely available.
Source: PRC Ministry of Public Health, *Chinese Health Statistical Digest 1988* Beijing, p. 75.

Table 3

Fertility in China, 1978-1989

Year	Crude birth rate		Total fertility rate	Parity Distribution (percent)		
	SSB surveys	Other sources		First births	Second births	Third and higher order births
1978		20.7	2.73			
1979		21.4	2.75			
1980		17.6	2.26	44	28	27
1981		21.0	2.61	48	26	25
1982	21.1		2.86	51	26	23
1983	18.6		2.42	52	27	21
1984	17.5		2.35	52	28	20
1985	17.8		2.20	52	31	17
1986	20.8		2.42	51	33	17
1987	21.0	23.3	2.59	51	33	16
1988	20.8			52	32	15
1989	20.8					

Notes: Birth rates are annual births per thousand midyear population. The States Statistical Bureau (SSB) has carried out an Annual Survey of Population Change every January starting in 1983, gathering birth and death rates for the previous calendar year. Total fertility rates are based on China's 1988 two-per-thousand-population fertility survey.

Sources: a. Birth rates from the SSB: *Statistical Survey of China 1990*, p. 14. b. Banister, 1987, p. 352. These birth rates are derived from total fertility rates for 1978-1980 measured by the one-per-thousand-population fertility survey of 1982. c. From 1982 census data from 1981. China 1982 census volume, 1985, p. 551. d. "1987 Major Figures from Manual Tabulation of the National Sample Survey on Fertility and Birth Control of China," *China Population Newsletter*, Feb. 1989, p. 5. e. Li Bohua, 1990, p. 4. f. Parity data for 1980-1988 are from "Birth Parity Changes in China (1980-1988)," *China Population Newsletter*, Oct. 1989, pp. 4-5.

Figure 1. **China: Number of Women in Peak Childbearing Ages**

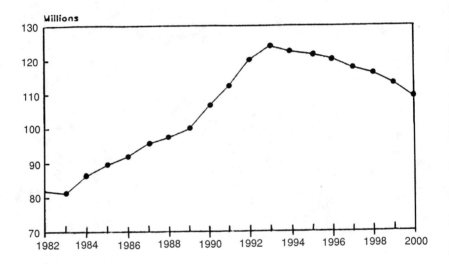

Notes: Peak childbearing ages are 21 through 30. Women in these ages have single-year age specific fertility rates of 0.1 or above (meaning that each year 10% of more of the women bear a child).

Sources: Hardee-Cleaveland and Banister. 1988a p. iv; 1988b, p. 247.

Figure 2. **China: Annual Employment Growth by Broad Sector, 1986-1989**

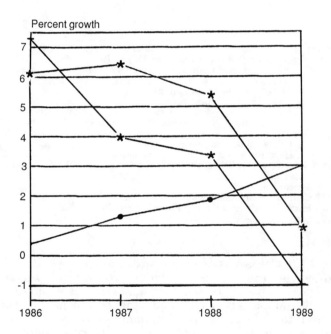

Percent growth

●— Agriculture ╈ Industry ✱— Services & other

Sources: Statistical Yearbook of China 1986, pp. 125-126; 1987, pp. 116-117; 1988, pp. 158-159; 1989, pp. 106-107; and *Statistical Survey of China 1990,* p. 16.

BIRTH PLANNING BETWEEN PLAN AND MARKET: THE IMPACT OF REFORM ON CHINA'S ONE-CHILD POLICY

By Tyrene White [*]

CONTENTS

SUMMARY

Since 1979, China has officially advocated a one-child policy. Motivated by fears that excess population growth would undermine its modernization efforts, this policy was rigorously pursued in the early 1980s. Mobilization techniques honed during the Maoist era were used to enforce rural compliance, but by 1984, campaign methods were in conflict with the goals of rural reform and the changing reality of rural life. That conflict, combined with growing fears of rural instability, led to a progressive relaxation of rural policy between 1984 and 1989. By 1989, a "one-son or two-child" policy was in effect in most areas; in other words, couples whose first child was a daughter gained the right to have a second child after an interval of several years.

Although this relaxation was designed to strike a balance between state birth plans and peasant child-bearing preferences, it contributed to a rise in birth rates above planned levels. By 1988, performance had deteriorated sufficiently to generate open criticism of senior officials who had approved the relaxation, but the policy remained unchanged. The State Family Planning Commis-

* Tyrene White is Assistant Professor of Political Science, Swarthmore College.

sion maintained that the problem was not the policy itself, but poor enforcement. This remained official policy through the summer of 1990, despite a more strident tone in the aftermath of Tiananmen. However, a new campaign was launched to improve rural compliance, and some localities responded with new regulations or directives.

The prospects for improved rural compliance were not good, however. The one-child policy, and China's entire birth planning strategy, was premised on the existence of the structures and processes associated with a centrally planned economy. Although those structures were eroding in rural China in the early 1980s, mobilization campaigns kept birth rates in check. In the second half of the 1980s, mobilization was replaced by routine administrative enforcement, but the conditions which facilitated enforcement during the commune era no longer existed. First, peasants enjoyed a high degree of mobility, making it possible to avoid birth planning by leaving the village permanently or temporarily. Second, cadre-peasant relations had undergone a fundamental change. Cadres no longer monopolized the sources of power and authority in the village, and the peasants no longer feared them as in the past. As a result, they were susceptible to economic retaliation and physical violence from peasants seeking to protect their family's long-term interests. Third, fiscal reforms led to a reduction in funding for birth planning work, and forced the family planning bureaucracy, like other state organs, to seek ways of generating its own revenues. The result was perverse: the bureaucracy whose mission was to prevent excess births relied on fines collected from policy violators to cover its basic operating expenses. In other words, the bureaucracy had more than the usual incentive to turn in a mediocre performance. In addition, fiscal reforms at the township and village levels left village cadres responsible for collecting the fines, but often forced them to turn the monies over to higher levels of government. This reduced incentives for cadre compliance, and made it easier and less risky to falsify reports on local birth trends than to vigorously pursue the policy.

The consequence of these developments has been to relax, but not release, the grip of the state on rural child-bearing. As the conflict between the state-planned child-bearing and market reforms has grown, however, birth planning has encountered the same problems that have plagued the economy as a whole—incentive systems are skewed in such a way as to produce "undesirable" behavior and "irrational" decisions, corruption has flourished, and scarce resources have been wasted. Whereas future leadership or regime changes may lead to more fundamental economic or political reforms, relieving the contradictions between plan and market, even the most liberal population advisors advocate a two-child limit. Although the particulars of policy may change, China is unlikely to abandon the principle of state-regulated child-bearing for a long time to come.

I. INTRODUCTION

In 1979, the leadership of the Chinese Communist Party was poised to embark on an ambitious program of reform and modernization. Although the blueprint for reform remained tentative and incomplete, three elements stood out clearly, even at that early date. First, the climate of political vigilance and mobilization that had been fostered during the previous decade had to be relaxed. Second, the grip of the centralized economic planning apparatus had to be broken; market incentives were needed to supplement and rationalize the bureaucratic allocation process, and to stimulate economic growth. And third, because excessive population growth threatened to stall or negate economic progress, child-bearing had to be subjected to tight planning and control; only one child per couple could be allowed.

Although the relaxation of political and economic controls signalled a change in state policy, the decision to tighten child-bearing controls built on a longstanding policy record. In 1962, the leadership of the Chinese Communist Party asserted the primacy of the state over individual child-bearing decisions and justified intervention on economic grounds.[1] They embraced the principle of "birth planning" (jihua shengyu) as well as birth control (jiezhi shengyu), and shortly thereafter began to draft short- and long-term targets for population growth.[2] Although generally translated as "family planning" or "planned parenthood," the Chinese concept of jihua shengyu is broader than the former terms. Like family planning, birth planning implies conscious household-level decision-making regarding the number and spacing of children, but it also refers to a process of comprehensive state planning and regulation of child-bearing trends. If human reproduction could be regulated in a predictable fashion, it was believed, state plans for economic growth, employment, social services, and food supplies (to cite only a few examples) would be easier to develop and implement.[3]

In practice, the regulation of child-bearing was pursued by subjecting population growth to the same principles of centralized administration that applied to material production. By the early 1970s, annual and five-year targets for population growth were disseminated from the center to the localities along with targets for steel and grain production; party committees and local governments were instructed to make birth planning work a part of their routine, and to create the appropriate mechanisms for bureaucratic oversight. State policy on child-bearing converged on a two-child ideal, and programs that supported pro-natalist tendencies were repealed.[4]

---

[1] An abbreviated text of the 1962 directive, "Zhonggong zhongyang, guowuyuan guanyu renzhen tichang jihua shengyude zhishi" (Central Committee and State Council instructions on enthusiastically promoting planned birth), can be found in Chinese Academy of Social Sciences Population Research Center, Zhongguo renkou nianjian, 1985 (1985 Population yearbook of China) (Beijing: Zhongguo shehui kexue chubanshe, 1986), p. 14.

[2] As early as 1965, for example, Zhou Enlai set a goal of reducing the rate of population growth to one percent or lower before the end of the twentieth century. Zhou Enlai, "Nongcun weisheng gongzuo he jihua shengyu wenti" (Rural health work and family planning), in Zhongguo renkou nianjian, 1985, p. 15.

[3] See, for example, Mao Zedong's discussion of birth planning and economic planning in his speech, "On the Correct Handling of Contradictions Among the People (Speaking Notes)," in Roderick MacFarquhar, Timothy Cheek, and Eugene Wu, eds., The Secret Speeches of Chairman Mao: From the Hundred Flowers to the Great Leap Forward (Cambridge, Ma: Council on East Asian Studies, Harvard University, 1989), pp. 159–161.

[4] Li Honggui, "Zhongguode renkou zhengce," in Zhongguo renkou nianjian, 1985, pp. 217–218.

The one-child policy of the 1980s was the direct outgrowth of this historical approach to fertility reduction—an approach designed specifically for a centrally planned economy. Just as the policy was inaugurated in 1979, however, economic reforms began to chip away at the structures and processes associated with centralized economic planning, and the state relaxed its extreme political grip on private behavior. These changes were most evident in the countryside in the early 1980s, where agricultural decollectivization and decommunization gave the peasantry some measure of economic power and deflated cadre authority. The result was a rapid improvement in rural economic performance, but the enforcement of rural birth limits had never been more difficult.

To enforce a one-child policy during this period of political and economic transition, the state relied on campaign methods that had been a mainstay of the Maoist regime. The campaigns mobilized reluctant cadres to enforce the unpopular regulation, and outside work teams that were sent into villages brought tremendous pressures to bear on rural couples.[5] These pressures reached their peak in 1983, when a massive sterilization campaign targeted all couples under forty with two or more children. The result was a four-fold increase in the number of sterilizations and vasectomies in 1983, as compared with the preceding year, along with a marked increase in the number of IUD insertions and abortions.[6] Within a year, however, the intensity of the campaign had triggered a backlash, and central policy on rural child-bearing limits began to loosen.[7] Despite the search for a satisfactory balance between the competing imperatives of market-oriented reform and birth planning, however, the gap between official goals and rural performance widened steadily in the second half of the 1980s.

II. THE POLITICAL ECONOMY OF BIRTH PLANNING POLICY, 1984–1990

A. THE SIGNIFICANCE OF CENTRAL DOCUMENT 7 (1984)

In the spring of 1984 a new central document on birth planning was issued by the Central Committee and State Council. Consisting of a report by the party group within the State Family Planning

---

[5] Those pressures ranged from economic and political threats to physical coercion. See John S. Aird, "Coercion in Family Planning: Causes, Methods, and Consequences," in U.S. Congress, Joint Economic Committee, *China's Economy Looks Toward the Year 2000, Volume 1: the Four Modernizations* (Washington: U.S. GPO, 1986), pp. 184–221. Campaigns that were effective in the short-run, however, could not prevent young couples from eventually having a second child, or in some cases, a third.

[6] Karen Hardee-Cleaveland and Judith Banister, "Fertility Policy and Implementation in China, 1986–1988," in *Population and Development Review* 14, No. 2 (June 1988), p. 276; Robert Delfs, "The Fertility Factor, " *Far Eastern Economic Review,* July 19, 1990, p. 19.

[7] Apparently, the backlash was experienced at the central level in part through a large volume of letters "inquiring" about the campaign or complaining about implementation methods. In a 1986 document on family planning (discussed below), one passage documents the improvement in cadre work methods by noting that the number of letters from the "masses" had declined by 75 percent between 1983, the peak year, and 1985. For the text of Central Document 13 (1986), entitled "Guanyu 'liuwu' qijian jihua shengyu gongzuo qingkuang he 'qiwu' qijian gongzuo yijiande baogao" (Report on the state of birth planning work during the sixth five-year plan period and opinions on work during the seventh five-year plan period), see Guojia jihua shengyu weiyuanhui xuanzhuan jiaoyu si, Zhonggong zhongyang dangxiao jihua shengyu weiyuanhui, *Shiyizhou sanzhong quanhui yilai jihua shengyu zhongyao wenjian xuanbian* (Propaganda and Education Office of the State Family Planning Commission, Central Party School Family Planning Commission, *Selected Important Documents on Birth Planning since the Third Plenum of the Eleventh Central Committee*), Zhonggong zhongyang dangxiao chubanshe (Central Party School Publishers), 1989, pp. 27–35.

Commission (SFPC) and a statement of concurrence by the Central
Committee, the document made clear that strict birth limits would
continue to be enforced. At the same time, however, the need for
rural political stability was stressed; methods that provoked a serious peasant backlash and endangered their enthusiasm for reform
were to be modified in a way that would make them "acceptable to
the peasants." [8] More specifically, the document signalled a shift in
policy in four important respects.

1. Coercion.

The SFPC report admitted that coercion was a serious problem
in the implementation of birth planning work. In keeping with the
tenor of the central-level party rectification campaign that had
been launched in October 1983, the party group took the blame for
problems with "coercion and commandism," admitting that they
had not paid enough attention to their "work style" or adopted "remedial measures." [9] They also admitted that the demands made on
localities in the implementation of the sterilization campaign in
1983 were too severe, and that the problems began at the top:

> In those places where coercion exists, and no immediate
> solution has been found, the main responsibility is ours.
> We believed that because birth planning work tasks are
> heavy, the appearance of coercion was unavoidable. [10]

With regard to future work, cadres were instructed to avoid rigid
and uniform implementation, or "one cut of the knife" (*yidaoqie*).
Births outside the plan were to be "resolutely checked," but handling the problem "simplistically" was deemed unacceptable. Sterilization was still to be "promoted" on the "principle of volunta-
rism," but lower levels were not to be pressured with unrealistically high targets. In short, cadres were exhorted to continue to take
birth planning and birth targets seriously. At the same time, they
were reminded that birth planning work consisted of more than
the periodic use of administrative pressure and compulsion, and
they were urged to invest in a more comprehensive approach to the
problem.

2. Allowances for second births.

Central Document 7 also marked a turn in policy by increasing
the proportion of households that would be allotted a second child.
In 1982, the quota for second births had been limited to "under five
percent" of all couples; in 1984, the quota was expanded to "about
ten percent." [11] On its own, this small increase was little more
than a cosmetic adjustment to the one-child limit, one much too
small to address peasant grievances. The document went further,
however. It stated that additional concessions would be made as
the rate of forbidden "multiple births" (*duotai*) declined, a policy
that became known as "opening a small hole to close a large hole"

---

[8] Central Document 7 (1984) is entitled "Guanyu jihua shengyu gongzuo qingkuangde huibao"
(Report on the situation in birth planning work). The text may be found in *Jihua shengyu zhongyao wenjian* (Selected important documents on birth planning), pp. 15–25.
[9] Ibid., pp. 18–23.
[10] Ibid., p. 22.
[11] Ibid., p. 20.

(i.e., increasing allotments for a second birth in order to reduce the number of third or higher parity births).[12] This provision opened the door to further relaxations of the one-child limit after 1984, including experiments in some localities with a rural two-child policy.

3. The primacy of rural reform.

In a provision regarding economic penalties for policy violators, the document made clear that family planning was not to take precedence over the requirements for rural reform and development. It explicitly prohibited "infringing upon or destroying the masses' basic means of production or basic means of subsistence" in order to invoke penalties.[13] This new insistence that the implementation of family planning not interfere directly with peasant livelihood or economic production echoed the thrust of another policy document—Central Document 1 (1984). This document, one in a series of crucial agricultural reform documents in the early 1980s, included two elements that had a direct bearing on the implementation of birth planning in the countryside.[14] First, the document called for fifteen year leases on agricultural land; the long-term leases were designed to increase peasant security in their land-holding contracts and encourage investment in agricultural growth. From the perspective of family planning, however, long-term leases made it more difficult to reward one-child couples with extra land allotments. In areas where cadres continued to recognize the land-holding benefit in principle, they were reluctant to enforce it without explicit orders to do so.[15] In other areas, the emphasis on stability and agricultural growth forced changes in birth planning regulations that eliminated the landholding benefit.[16]

Second, to boost peasant enthusiasm and reduce their tax burden, the document called for a reform of township-level finances. Family planning was one of several "government-subsidized projects" specifically targeted for reform; the goal was to reduce excessive expenditures like those incurred in the 1983 sterilization campaign,[17] and to place more of the funding burden on local governments. This reform signalled localities that economic growth took precedence over other central directives. Family planning, however heavily it was stressed in Beijing, could not be allowed to absorb revenues that might otherwise be invested profitably.[18]

4. The relationship between modernization and fertility levels.

The document stressed the "modernization first" theme by inverting the standard argument on the relationship between economic development and birth planning. Over the previous five

---

[12] Ibid., p. 20.

[13] Ibid., p. 21.

[14] For the translated text of the document, see *China Quarterly* 101 (March 1985), pp. 132–142.

[15] Interview with former township-level birth planning official, July 1990.

[16] Susan Greenhalgh, *The Evolution of the One-Child Policy in Shaanxi Province, 1979–1988*, Working Paper No. 5 (New York: The Population Council, 1989), p. 37.

[17] In Wuhan municipality, for example, the 1983 annual budget for birth planning was 600,000 *yuan*, but one million *yuan* was spent on the sterilization campaign alone. Interview with municipal family planning officials, June 1984.

[18] The consequences of this reform are discussed fully in section III, part C, of this paper.

years, propaganda on the one-child policy had stressed that China's modernization effort was dependent on induced fertility control. Without strict birth limits, it was argued, China's development gains would be largely offset by increases in population. In Central Document 7, however, a more complex relationship was implied. The text stated that "high birth rates are a reflection of economic and cultural backwardness," and that "the reasons why the masses demand additional births are many-faceted." [19] This tentative acknowledgement that a decline in fertility levels in the countryside might *result* from the process of development, not *fuel* it, paved the way for a relaxation of rural birth limits during the second half of the 1980s.

B. BIRTH PLANNING POLICY DURING THE SEVENTH FIVE-YEAR PLAN, 1986–1990

1. Policy relaxation and plan goals.

Although the one-child limit was strictly implemented in urban areas throughout the 1980s, after 1984 the policy was progressively relaxed in rural areas. The allowance for a second birth in the countryside was increased from "about ten percent" of all single-child households in 1984 to twenty percent in 1985. In 1986, the first year of the Seventh Five-Year Plan (FYP) period, the quota was raised to fifty percent, and an important new category became eligible for a second child—single-daughter households (*dunu hu*).[20] Over the next few years, provinces were given substantial leeway to determine when and where to implement the provisions for allowing a second birth, including the newly added category. By 1988, fourteen provinces and autonomous regions had declared rural single-daughter households to be eligible for a second child, while six other provinces and municipalities did not.[21] In May 1988, however, the SFPC declared that it was national policy to grant a second child to single-daughter households; localities wishing to implement a more restrictive policy had to apply to the SFPC for approval.[22] By mid-1989, four policy categories had emerged: 1) a two-child policy, operative in six provinces and autonomous regions (Guangdong, Hainan, Yunnan, Ningxia, Qinghai, and Xinjiang); 2) a "one-son or two-child" policy, operative in eighteen provinces, plus less developed areas in Jiangsu and Sichuan; 3) a policy of limited concessions for second births, operative in Beijing, Tianjin, Shanghai, and most rural areas in Jiangsu and Sichuan; 4) a policy

---

[19] "Guanyu jihua shengyu gongzuo," p. 21.

[20] The new provision was a concession to peasant preferences for son, but those couples who gave birth to a second daughter were not allowed a third child. Hu Angang, "Zhongguo renkou shikongde yuanyin ji duice" (Reasons and Countermeasures for China's Runaway Population) *Liaowang Zhoubao haiwaiban* (Outlook overseas edition) 10 (March 6, 1989), pp. 17–18. A second source sets the 1986 quota for second births at sixty percent of rural single-child households. See Wang Yan, Liu Jinghuai, Zhao Derun, Ouyang Huijun, Fang Jinyu, "Renkou wenti yao zhuajin zai zhuajin" (Population problems must be grasped more and more firmly), *Liaowang* 28, July 13, 1987, p. 14.

[21] Hu, "Zhongguo renkou shikongde yuanyin," p. 51.

[22] Peng Peiyun, "Zai quanguo jihua shengyu weiyuanhui zhuren huiyi bimushide jianghua" (Speech at the close of the national meeting of directors of family planning commissions),in *Jihua shengyu zhongyao wenjian*, pp. 108–120; Zeng Yi, "Family Planning Program 'Tightening Up'?" *Population and Development Review* 2 (June 1989), p. 335.

of two or more births per couple, operative among minority nationalities.[23]

The relaxation and decentralization of birth planning policy after 1986 reflected a subtle shift in central priorities. In contrast to the Sixth FYP, emphasis on family planning was distinctly downgraded in the Seventh. In the Sixth FYP, birth planning and population growth were discussed in conjunction with raising incomes and living standards; their importance to the overall modernization process was heavily stressed. In the Seventh FYP and Zhao's explanatory work report, however, they are relegated to the category of "other social programmes," a catch-all category at the end of a list of economic priorities. Similarly, Zhao's speech to the 13th Party Congress in October 1987 grouped birth planning with environmental protection as a serious social issue—one that required political commitment but commanded few resources.[24] In addition, China's official population target for the year 2000 was revised; the original goal of holding population "under 1.2 billion" was changed to "about 1.2 billion," a change soon understood to mean 1.25 billion.[25]

Despite the more moderate tone, the goals set forth in the Seventh FYP remained extremely ambitious. The primary target was set forth in a new directive on family planning; Central Document 13 (1986) called for an average annual rate of population growth of "about 12.5 per thousand."[26] This translated into a total population target of 1.113 billion by 1990, and both targets were registered in the final draft of the Seventh FYP. By 1988, however, it became clear that the population would exceed the target by a substantial margin, and a different kind of backlash began to occur.

2. Hardline offensive and open debate.

As early as 1984, a heated debate over the one-child limit broke out among social scientists and policy advisers in China. Some experts urged a change in rural policy to allow two children per couple.[27] Others, however, voiced their opposition to any relaxation of the one-child limit; they believed that the combination of policy instability and rural concessions would encourage child-bearing

---

[23] Zeng, ibid., p. 335.

[24] For the text of the Seventh Five-Year Plan and Zhao's report, see *Beijing Review* 16 (1986). For the reference to family planning in Zhao's speech at the 13th Party Congress, see Zhao Ziyang, "Advance Along the Road of Socialism with Chinese Characteristics," *Beijing Review* (November 9-15, 1987): X.

[25] The relaxation of the 1.2 billion figure apparently originated in July 1984, when a report was submitted to the Central Committee entitled, "Some Questions On Population Control and Population Policy" (Renkou kongzhi yu renkou zhengce zhong ruogan wenti), in Ma Bin, *Lun Zhongguo renkou wenti* (Discussion of China's Population Problem), Zhongguo guoji guangbo chubanshe (China international broadcast publishers) (Beijing: 1987), p. 2. Subsequently, Wang Wei, then head of the SFPC, used the new formulation of "about 1.2 billion" in a speech at the Central Party School in November 1985. See Wang Wei, "Zai 'Qiwu' qijian ba jihua shengyu gongzuo zhuade geng jin geng hao" (Grasp birth planning work more firmly and better during the seventh five-year plan period), in *Jihua shengyu zhongyao wenjian*, p. 68.

[26] For the text of Central Document 13, see *Jihua shengyu zhongyao wenjian xuanbian*, pp. 27-35.

[27] Peng Peiyun, "Zai quanguo jihua shengyu weiyuanhui," p. 113. Although this alternative has never been accepted by the Chinese government, its popularity among Chinese scholars was fueled by a 1985 article by John Bongaarts and Susan Greenhalgh entitled, "An Alternative to the One-Child Policy in China," *Population and Development Review* 11, No. 4 (December 1985), pp. 585-617. For a discussion of its influence and the diverse views held within the community of Chinese scholars, see Susan Greenhalgh, "Population Studies in China: Privileged Past, Anxious Future," *The Australian Journal of Chinese Affairs* 24 (July 1990), pp. 357-384.

beyond the official limits.[28] When rising birth rates in 1986 and 1987 confirmed their worst fears, these critics were quick to respond. In a series of newspaper articles and other publications, they complained about the "human wave" that was "washing over China," and attributed it directly to the negligence of policy-makers.[29] They argued that it was a serious mistake to loosen rural restrictions on a second birth, and complained that the interference of a few officials had led to the crisis. To stem the flood, at least one author openly advocated the use of coercion to overcome the resistance of the peasantry.[30]

These open criticisms prompted a rebuttal from Peng Peiyun, Wang Wei's successor as head of the SFPC. In 1988, she and other senior officials insisted that the policy relaxation had not been a mistake; instead, they argued that rising birth rates were a function of 1) an increase in the child-bearing age cohort, and 2) poor implementation of policy in some areas.[31] In taking this position, they were backed by the authority of the Standing Committee of the Politburo, which had met the previous March to discuss family planning. The Standing Committee members reaffirmed the existing policy on birth limits, arguing that the policy of allowing single-daughter households to have a second child 1) facilitated rural implementation, 2) prevented female infanticide, 3) generated a positive international reaction, and 4) contributed to the realization of population control targets by reducing the number of third births.[32]

This high-level commitment to the "existing policy" was reiterated in 1989 and 1990. To mark China's arrival at the 1.1 billion population mark in April 1989, a *Renmin Ribao* editorial stressed that the "key" to family planning work was to implement the "existing" policy "100 percent," implicitly rejecting calls for a tightening of policy.[33] Despite a reactionary speech by Jiang Zemin in October 1989, after the Tiananmen crackdown, this remained the basic policy line through the summer of 1990.[34] In February 1990, Jiang Zemin and Li Peng stressed the need to implement "existing policy" in a letter to the national meeting of family planning directors.[35] And in July 1990, Li Ruihuan reiterated the importance of "adhering to the established family planning policies." [36]

[28] Wang Wei, "Zai 'qiwu' qijian," p. 69.

[29] Xie Zhenjiang, "There is No Route of Retreat," *Jingji Ribao*, January 24, 1989, p. 3, in *FBIS*, February 15, 1989, pp. 35–37; Liu Jingzhi, "Experts Concerned Are Not Optimistic About China's Population Situation, and Think That Interference by Officials is an Important Reason Why Birth Rate Has Risen Again," *Guangming Ribao*, March 6, 1988, p. 2, in *FBIS*, March 6, 1988, pp. 14–15.

[30] Xie, "No Route of Retreat," p. 37.

[31] *China Daily*, April 19, 1988, p. 1; see also Peng, "Zai quanguo jihua shengyu weiyuanhui," pp. 108–120.

[32] Peng, ibid., p. 112.

[33] *Renmin Ribao*, April 14, 1989, p. 1. See also, Peng Peiyun, "Controlling Population Enriches the Nation and Makes People Strong," *Liaowang* 1 (January 1, 1990), in *FBIS*, April 24, 1990, p. 53.

[34] According to a report in by Tammy Tan in the *Hongkong Standard*, (October 16, 1989, p. 6), Peng Peiyun read a speech by Jiang at a national symposium in Hangzhou. In it, he reportedly attributed Western criticism of China's birth planning policy to the belief of international businessmen that a larger population would mean higher profits. *FBIS*, October 20, 1989, p. 26–27.

[35] *Zhongguo renkou bao*, February 16, 1990, p. 1.

[36] He was speaking to a forum of advanced family planning workers. *Xinhua*, July 4, 1990, in *FBIS*, July 27, 1990, pp. 14–16.

Nevertheless, anxieties about population growth became more pronounced in 1989 and 1990. They were fueled by the results of a 1988 sample survey that revealed a 1987 population growth rate of 16.16 per thousand, nearly two percentage points higher than the officially reported rate of 14.39 per thousand.[37] This figure raised doubts about China's ability to meet the targets set forth in the Seventh FYP, as well as the long-range target of about 1.25 billion. As a result, in late 1988 the target was revised upward to 1.27 billion. By early 1990, however, even this figure appeared optimistic; China's total population at the end of 1989 exceeded the Seventh FYP target figure for 1990, adding fuel to the hardline argument for tighter child-bearing limits.[38] Rather than change official policy, however, a new campaign was launched to improve performance under the existing policy. Some provinces issued new regulations or special directives, and expert advisors proposed new measures to improve rural performance.[39] The question, however, was whether any set of measures would significantly improve rural enforcement.

II. MARKET REFORM VERSUS BIRTH PLANNING: IMPEDIMENTS TO RURAL IMPLEMENTATION

When the one-child policy was announced by state officials in 1979, it was premised on three assumptions. The first assumption was that governmental regulation of child-bearing decisions was a necessary and valid exercise of state power. Second, it assumed that birth planning would be subsumed within the process of centralized economic planning; population figures and birth targets could be disaggregated and assigned to localities in the same way that economic targets were assigned. Third, it assumed that an effective system of social and political control was in place—one that restricted population movement, facilitated ideological indoctrination, and imposed behavioral norms. A decade later, the state continued to assert the right to set strict child-bearing limits, but the context for implementation had undergone dramatic change, especially in the countryside. The political and economic controls associated with centralized economic planning were significantly weakened, while partial market reforms created irrational reward structures that worked against the state's anti-natal goals. In that context, the gap between state birth plans and grassroots performance began to widen.[40]

---

[37] *Renmin Ribao*, October 28, 1988, p. 3. The survey was conducted jointly by the SFPC, the State Statistical Bureau, the State Planning Commission, the Ministry of Finance, and the Public Security Bureau.

[38] Shih Chun-yu, "NPC Deputies Say the Population Problem is Serious," *Ta Kung Bao*, April 3, 1990, p. 2, in *FBIS*, April 9, 1990, p. 34.

[39] Henan province approved a law on family planning in April 1990. *Henan ribao*, May 10, 1990, p. 9, in *FBIS*, June 1, 1990, pp.36–42. Fujian province issued a party and government directive to shore up implementation of the existing regulations. *Fujian ribao*, March 25, 1990, p. 4, in *FBIS*, May 11, 1990, pp. 42–45. On new measures for enforcement, see *Zhongguo tongxun she*, July 21, 1990, in *FBIS*, July 23, 1990, p. 31.

[40] The declining reliability of the statistical reporting system made it difficult to estimate the precise extent of the problem. The national census that was conducted on July 1, 1990, may help to clarify China's demographic standing as it moves into the last decade of the twentieth century. The census results were not available at the time this article was written, however.

A. PEASANT MOBILITY

During the Maoist era, a tight network of controls over mobility and food supply kept peasant laborers tied closely to the villages. The lack of mobility facilitated close surveillance of child-bearing age couples, and pressures to conform were extremely difficult to resist. To encourage the development and commercialization of the rural economy, restrictions on peasant movement were progressively relaxed during the 1980s. Large numbers began to move into urban areas as private entrepreneurs or temporary workers; others simply moved out of their native villages to nearby towns and small cities. By 1990, it was estimated that this "floating population" numbered more than 20 million.[41]

The increase in peasant mobility vastly complicated the job of enforcing even a two-child limit. Once rural couples moved beyond the jurisdiction of their native village or township, local authorities had neither the ability or the incentive to monitor pregnancy and child-bearing. In towns and cities where migrant laborers congregated, however, local family planning organs were also unable to control their behavior. In some areas, the bureaucracy simply did not have the personnel or economic means to deal with the logistical problems posed by a scattered migrant population; in others their work was thwarted by powerful employers anxious to retain cheap peasant labor. The result was the growth of an "excess birth guerrilla corps" that produced a large "illegal" population.[42]

To counter this problem, the state proposed to substitute indirect regulation for direct administrative control. Beginning in 1987, local branches of the state bureaucracy for commerce and industry were instructed to withhold work permits from individuals who violated the birth limitation policy. Peasants were required to present proof of compliance, and local bureaus were forbidden to issue work papers without this evidence.[43] These procedures were easily skirted, however. Local commerce and industry officials had no interest in becoming adjunct family planning officials, and as the number of migrants increased, fewer and fewer bothered to register locally or acquire the obligatory work permit.[44] By 1990, certain localities had gained a reputation for being safe havens from family planning enforcement.[45]

---

[41] *Xinhua*, June 15, 1990, in *FBIS*, June 18, 1990, p. 37; Zhang Mengyi, "A New Mode of Population Shift and Mobility in China," *Liaowang Overseas Edition* 2 (January 8, 1990), pp. 16–17, in *FBIS*, February 9, 1990, pp. 18–20.

[42] Guo Xiao, "The 'Population Explosion' is Drawing Near," *Jingji ribao* (Economic daily), January 10, 1989, in *FBIS*, February 3, 1989, p. 51; Fan Xiangguo and Huang Yuan, "Zhongguo 'hei renkou'" (China's illegal population), *Xin guancha* (New Observer) 4 (February 25, 1989, pp. 28–32; Report, "Couples with more than One Child Seek Shelter Along Borders of Hunan, Hubei, Sichuan, and Guizhou," *Zhongguo tongxun she* (January 20, 1989), in *JPRS–CAR* 89–014, February 15, 1989, pp. 44–45.

[43] De Ming, "China's Population Situation Remains Grim," *Liaowang Overseas Edition* 17 (April 1988), pp. 9–10, in *FBIS*, May 11, 1988, p. 28.

[44] Those who did were more likely to have used corruption and bribery to acquire the necessary certificates. Pei Gang, "Thoughts on the Present Disarray in Matters of Population Reproduction and Suggested Improvements," *Renkou yu jingji* (Population and economics) 5 (October 25, 1990), pp. 6–10, in *JPRS–CAR* 90–010, February 7, 1990, p. 65.

[45] Report, "Couples with more than One Child Seek Shelter," pp. 44–45.

B. CADRE-PEASANT RELATIONS

A second dilemma for rural enforcement was the changing political climate within the villages. In some localities, powerful village leaders were still able to rule with an iron fist; in others, however, political and economic reforms forced village leaders to be far more circumspect in the exercise of power.

Unlike the commune era, village leaders no longer had a complete monopoly over economic resources or opportunities; neither could they count on an unlimited tenure in office. As a result, policies that provoked peasant opposition (e.g., enforcing birth limits or extracting state and local taxes) were handled with caution, and for good reason. Peasant retaliation or aggressive resistance was a real possibility, and "incidents of revenge" ranged from destruction of cadre property to physical attack.[46] Moreover, village leaders were far more vulnerable to peasant retaliation than were their township superiors; they rarely moved on to higher-level posts outside the village, and they no longer had guaranteed tenure in office. As a result, they and their families had to live with the legacy of their political tenure, in a post-reform social environment where household size and community status were closely linked. Families who saw child-bearing as their best long-term guarantee of strength, respect and stature (and their best defense against weakness, bullying and abuse by powerful families), believed that birth limits represented a profound threat to their existence within the village. Some were prepared to take any steps necessary, including the use of force, to protect that future, and cadres were hesitant to stand in their way.[47]

C. FISCAL REFORM AND FAMILY PLANNING FUNDING

Though rarely discussed in the context of China's family planning efforts, fiscal reforms implemented since 1984 have had a tremendous impact on the program. The fiscal reforms encouraged financial neglect of family planning at the village and township levels, and contributed to a chronic shortage of funding for family planning work.

Until 1984, the costs of contraceptives and all family planning-related medical procedures (IUD insertions, abortions, sterilizations, etc.) were covered within the central state budget. All other expenses (e.g., costs of preparing and disseminating propaganda materials, work subsidies for village cadres and activists involved in mobilization campaigns) were absorbed by local governments or rural villages, whether or not they exceeded budgeted expenditures. In 1984, however, Beijing mandated a reorganization of township-level finances; family planning was one of several categories of local expenses targeted for reduction and rationalization.[48]

---

[46] Su Suining, "There are Many Causes of strained Relations Between Cadres and Masses in Rural Areas," *Nongmin ribao* (Peasant daily), September 26, 1988, p. 1, in *FBIS*, October 7, 1988, p. 13; Fan and Huang, "Zhongguo 'hei' renkou," p. 71.

[47] Yang, "Woguo nongcun jihua shengyu gongzuo zhong xuyao yanjiu jiejuede jige wenti" (Several issues in need of resolution in our country's rural birth planning work), *Renkou yanjiu* (Population research) 6 (1989),pp. 62–64; Pei, "Thoughts on the Present Disarray," p. 65.

[48] See footnote 14.

The impetus for fiscal reform was two-fold. First, central authorities sought to reduce the level of "peasant burdens" (*nongmin fudan*), i.e., the sum of all direct and indirect forms of taxation. Still uncertain in late 1983 how rapidly agricultural performance would improve, they feared that licit and illicit extractions by local cadres could stifle peasant entrepreneurship and impede the reform process.[49] Second, the reform of local government expenditures was part of a larger effort to reduce central-level budgetary commitments and decentralize fiscal authority. By 1984, new revenue-sharing arrangements had been negotiated with individual provinces. As a result, provincial governments gained control over the structure of local spending, and the right to determine their own fiscal arrangements with local governments under their jurisdiction.[50] In turn, counties eventually gained the right to set fiscal arrangements with township governments, placing all levels of government on "harder" budgetary constraints.[51]

This comprehensive reform of the fiscal system had far-reaching implications for the overall pattern of government spending and investment, and for specific budgetary categories like family planning. As governments gained greater control over their budgetary revenues, governmental bureaus and commercial enterprises were pressured to balance their budgets and generate their own sources of revenue for reinvestment or expansion. As more responsibilities were transferred from the central budget to local authorities, therefore, the solvency of local governments came to depend on their entrepreneurial abilities. Government activities that did not generate a profit were often neglected, while profit-making ventures attracted more investment.[52] Agencies that could not compete on the market were starved for funds, and came under increased pressure to find their own sources of revenue simply to maintain their existing operations.[53]

In that climate, the family planning bureaucracy found itself strapped for funds during the Seventh FYP, just as the pressures of an increasing child-bearing age cohort demanded increased investment. In late 1986, SFPC director Wang Wei complained that funding for family planning had dropped off after 1983; he criticized

---

[49] On the problem of "peasant burdens," see Tyrene White, "Below Bureaucracy: The Burden of Being a Village Under the Local State," paper presented at the Annual Meeting of the Association for Asian Studies, Chicago, Illinois, April 6–8, 1990.

[50] James Tong, "Fiscal Reform, Elite Turnover and Central-Provincial Relations in Post-Mao China," *Australian Journal of Chinese Affairs* 22 (July 1989), pp. 13–14.

[51] The arrangements that provincial governments and prefectural governments, between prefectures and counties, and between counties and townships, can and do vary from one locality and the next. This had created an exceedingly complex set of financial arrangements at the local levels. See, for example, "Hebei sheng renmin zhengfu guanyu gaijin caizheng guanli tizhide jixiang guiding" (Some regulations of the Hebei provincial government concerning improving the financial management system), *Hebei jingji tongji nianjian, 1987* (Hebei economic statistical yearbook, 1987), p. 488; Zhonggong hebei shengwei yanjiushi nongcunchu, "Fangshou rang xiang zhengfu dang jiali cai" (Let go and allow township governments to set up their own finances), *Nongcun gongzuo tongxun* (Rural work bulletin) 6 (1986), pp. 32–33. On the distinction between "hard" and "soft" budget constraints, see Janos Kornai, *Contradictions and Dilemmas: Studies on the Socialist Economy and Society* (Cambridge, Ma: MIT Press, 1986).

[52] On the role of township governments in developing profit-making township enterprises, see Jean C. Oi, "Economic Management and Rural Government: Bureaucratic Entrepreneurship in Local Economies," paper presented at the Annual Meeting of the Association for Asian Studies, Chicago, Illinois, April 6–8, 1990.

[53] Christine Wong, "Tax Reform and Central-Local Fiscal Interaction in China," paper presented at the East Asia Colloquia Series, Fairbank Center for East Asian Research, Harvard University, July 1990; White, "Below Bureaucracy."

"some provinces" for drastically reducing their allocation for family planning, and called on them to give priority to family planning in future budgets.[54] By 1988, delegates to the annual meeting of family planning commission directors were pressing central leaders for increased funding and personnel. Premier Li Peng's response, however, was to remind them of the "financial difficulties" with the central budget and request that local governments carry even more of the financial burden for family planning.[55] This left family planning officials to complain publicly about the lack of support at all levels of government. One provincial FPC director was quoted as saying: "During the past few years, we spent half our time lobbying government leaders at all levels. They should take the lead in family planning, but we end up having to push them into action."[56]

The lack of funds to maintain and develop the family planning bureaucracy had serious and paradoxical consequences for rural enforcement. First, family planning work was slowed in some areas due to lack of funding for medical support. In areas where the family planning organization sought to establish medical facilities independent of local hospitals, no funds were available to expand meager facilities.[57] In other areas, local governments did not reimburse hospitals for the cost of sterilization surgeries or other procedures; as a result, the hospitals refused to accept additional family planning patients until the debt was paid.[58] One report claimed that "many" provincial governments owed public health departments "up to 10 million yuan" in tubal ligation surgery fees. To place this sum in relative perspective, one family planning director pointed out that 100 million *yuan* had been spent to renovate the hotel where a family planning meeting had been held. He added, "How come funds just dry up when it comes to family planning?"[59]

Second, the family planning bureaucracy came to rely upon the extraction of fines from policy violators in order to cover ordinary operating costs; *to pursue its bureaucratic mission of preventing excess births, the bureaucracy needed the monies collected as a result of excess births.* In one Sichuan county, for example, the gap between budgeted allocations and actual expenditures during the 1979–1987 period was 606,000 *yuan* annually. To cover the deficit, the county relied on the collection of excess birth fees, making it bureaucratically imperative that couples violate the birth limitation policy.[60] Conversely, counties that were very successful in pre-

---

[54] Wang Wei, "Jihua shengyu gongzuo qingkuang" (Situation in family planning work), *Jihua shengyu zhongyao wenjian*, p. 100.

[55] Li Peng, "Zai tingchu quanguo jihua shengyu weiyuanhui zhuren huiyi huibao shide jianghua" (Talk while listening to the report of the national meeting of directors of family planning commissions), *Jihua shengyu zhongyao wenjian*, p. 62.

[56] Zhu Li, "Family Planning to Emphasize Economic as Well as Administrative Methods," *Jingji Cankao* (Economic Reference), March 10, 1989, p. 4, in *JPRS* 89-047, May 17, 1989, p. 39.

[57] Cheng Linli and Wu Yousheng, "Jiceng jihua shengyu gongzuode fancha xiaoyi yu sikao" (Contrasting effects of basic-level family planning work and reflections), *Renkou yanjiu* 6 (1989), p. 53.

[58] Cheng and Wu, "Jiceng jihua shengyu," p. 53.

[59] Zhu, "Family Planning," p. 39.

[60] Cheng and Wu, "Jiceng jihua shengyu," pp. 53–54.

venting excess births soon recognized the benefit of turning in a more mediocre performance.[61]

Despite the economic incentive to allow excess child-bearing, however, mobilizational pressures to comply with the one-or-two child limit did not cease. Instead, campaigns—presumably the antithesis of routine bureaucratic process—became an essential component of routine bureaucratic process, and targets for fine collections were issued alongside targets for births, sterilizations, and abortions.[62] In one prefecture, campaigns of this type were held three times a year on a regular basis. The collection of fines was one of six key targets issued to each locality.[63] The collection of fines by no means guaranteed that the money would be used to reward one-child couples or provide better family planning services, however. Township and village leaders sometimes took advantage of murky accounting procedures at the grassroots to divert the funds to other projects.[64]

Third, fiscal reforms and fiscal austerity contributed indirectly to the deteriorating quality of China's population statistics. Despite the pressures on grassroots cadres to collect fines, monies raised at the village level were often turned over to higher levels of government. In one Sichuan county, for example, township governments received 70 percent of all monies collected as fines, the district (qu) received 5 percent, the county received 20 percent, and the prefecture received 5 percent.[65] Elsewhere, villages were allowed to retain a portion of the fees, but sometimes as little as 20 percent.[66] This arrangement denied village cadres the fruits of their own labors, and reinforced their distaste for family planning work.[67] Since village leaders were required to undertake the difficult and dangerous job of extracting the levies, but not necessarily allowed to retain them, they had no incentive to accurately report local birth trends.[68]

By the end of the decade, the erosion of the statistical reporting system was one of the most serious issues on the family planning agenda. The statistical "leakage" (shuifen), or exaggeration, begins at the village level, where grassroots reports lay the foundation for nationwide compilations of population trends.[69] Since those reports can only be verified by village cadres who are intimately familiar with village households, the reporting system has always been susceptible to fraud and human error. Since 1985, however, the costs of accurate reporting have grown, while the risks of falsification have declined. As a result, fraud and misreporting have spread to all levels of the system, and political leaders enjoying recognition for their "advanced" family planning work have no incentive to question positive reports from subordinates who are anxious to

[61] Cheng yicai, "Chaosheng zinufei guanli tanwei" (Inquiry into the management of excess birth fines) Renkou yanjiu (Population research) 4 (1990), p. 61.

[62] Elsewhere, I have called this phenomenon "institutionalized mobilization." See "Postrevolutionary Mobilization in China: The One-Child Policy Reconsidered," World Politics (October 1990).

[63] Interview with former township-level family planning cadre, July 1990.

[64] Chen, "Chaosheng zinufei," pp. 61–62.

[65] Cheng and Wu, "Jiceng jihua shengyu," pp. 53–54.

[66] Chen, "Chaosheng zinufei," p. 61.

[67] Ibid., p. 61.

[68] Ibid., p. 61.

[69] Renmin ribao, October 24, 1988, p. 3.

please.[70] Similarly, enthusiastic family planning cadres who uncover statistical errors feel strong pressures to cover them up. As one former cadre put it, an honest report from one township would accomplish nothing but the destruction of one's own career, since higher-level political leaders would be embarrassed and angered by the revelation.[71]

The joint survey conducted in 1988 under the auspices of the SFPC revealed just how serious the statistical problems had become by that time. As shown in Table 1, the survey revealed that the majority of all provinces, municipalities and autonomous regions had birth rates at least 30 percent higher than originally reported for 1987. Despite demands for a more rigorous reporting system, however, in early 1990, SFPC director Peng Peiyun stated that there was a thirty percent gap between household registration figures and actual population size, and that the discrepancy was increasing, not decreasing.[72] This did not bode well for the upcoming national census in July 1990. As preparations got underway in the late spring, therefore, cadres were issued a carrot-and-stick ultimatum: if the census report was accurate, there would be no recriminations, even if the figures implied previous statistical fraud; if the census report was tampered with or poorly prepared, however, the repercussions would be severe.[73] How cadres responded to these warnings in not yet clear, but it is reasonable to assume that they were skeptical of Beijing's amnesty offer.[74]

TABLE 1. Percentage Differences in 1987 Birth
Rates, Statistical Reports versus Survey Results

Number of Provinces *	Percentage Difference
4	under 10%
3	10–20%
6	20–30%
10	30–40%
6	40–50%

* Includes province-level municipalities and autonomous regions.
Source: *Renmin ribao*, October 24, 1988, p. 3.

IV. CONCLUSION

Although Beijing continues to exert formidable pressures on child-bearing age couples, the state's ability to enforce rural child-bearing limits has eroded since 1984. China's birth planning strategy was originally tailored to the political and economic processes associated with a command economy. For birth planning to be effective, fertility and population targets had to be disseminated along with material production targets, and local cadres had to be

[70] Yang, "Woguo nongcun jihua shengyu gongzuo," p. 64.
[71] Interview with former township-level family planning cadre, July 1990.
[72] *Xinhua*, December 13, 1989, in *FBIS*, January 5, 1990, p. 5.
[73] Beijing Domestic Service, March 21, 1990, in *FBIS*, April 17, 1990, pp. 24–25.
[74] Based on one report from Liaoning, that skepticism was probably well-founded. Just after the census was completed, a provincial radio report revealed that significant statistical errors had been uncovered in some localities, and that some "advanced" units did not deserve the title. See Liaoning Provincial Service, July 14, 1990, in *FBIS*, July 17, 1990, p. 45.

held strictly accountable for performance shortfalls. As the process of reform has reduced the number of assigned planning targets, relaxed the pressures to meet others, and generally loosened political constraints on local cadre behavior, the very structure that made it possible to enforce birth quotas has been undermined. That is not to say that local agents of the state are unable to enforce local birth limits when they make a concerted effort to do so, or when they are mobilized from above. Both central and local governments remain capable of bringing formidable powers to bear on individual couples. Nevertheless, market forces set loose since 1985 have fundamentally altered the incentive structures on which rural enforcement depended. Individual provinces and local governments weigh central pressures against local priorities, and discover that the appearance of concern over population growth can substitute for financial investments. Beijing can afford to speak as if all projects are equally important, but local leaders understand that they will be rewarded first and foremost for improved economic indicators; low birth rates will earn them applause, but no political or economic clout.[75] Similarly, grassroots cadres weigh the direct and indirect costs of rigorous enforcement against the risks of neglect; they often conclude that it is more rational and less risky to implement the letter of the law, i.e., collect fines for "illegal" births, and/or falsify statistical reports, than to confront fellow villagers. And finally, many couples have concluded that the rewards for having only one child pale in comparison to the tangible and intangible benefits of having two or more, even if the cost is migration to another locality or boarding one's children with cooperative relatives.

In short, partial market reforms have had the same effect in the realm of birth planning that they have had in the economic realm—creating skewed incentive systems that reward "undesirable" behaviors and decisions, encourage corruption, and waste scarce resources. Unlike the economic realm, however, these problems have generated little attention outside China, since they have helped to undercut the very concept of centrally planned, state-regulated child-bearing, a concept that many find repugnant or immoral. While this outcome may well be applauded and encouraged, it is nevertheless worth noting that it has come at a cost. Millions of children now live with a new kind of class stigma; they are "black" (*hei*, as in black market) or "illegal" children with uncertain status and few prospects. If they are female, they are less likely to be educated, whether legal or illegal. Studies by Chinese scholars show that female education is the single most important predictor of fertility; the failure to educate these children, therefore, increases the likelihood that China's compulsory program will be extended to a new generation. And finally, if declining investment in birth planning allowed some couples to avoid compulsory birth limits, it has also hindered the development of family planning services that many couples want—a ready supply of reliable

[75] Pei, "Thoughts on the Present Disarray," p. 64; Lu Xueyi and Zhang Houyi, "Peasant Diversification, Problems, Remedies," *Nongye jingji wenti* (Problems of Agricultural Economics) 1 (January 1990), pp. 16–21, in *JPRS–CAR* 90–040, May 29, 1990, p. 65. This tendency toward neglect is by no means universal. Certain provinces, like Sichuan and Jiangsu, have been exceptionally attentive to birth planning work. Elsewhere, individual leaders have been motivated by personal conviction, not pressure from their superiors, to focus on birth limitation.

and convenient contraceptives, high-quality medical services, and improved maternal and infant care.

It is true, of course, that China's birth planning program can be blamed for these side-effects. Without it, one might argue, there would be no "illegal" children, and funds invested in the mission of administering birth limits could be deflected to education, health care, and non-compulsory family planning services. Unlike the economic and political sectors, however, where influential constituencies support greater market reform and democratization, even the most tolerant advisors to the SFPC advocate a two-child limit. With the specter of a population in excess of 1.5 billion by the middle of the next century (even if current policies remain in force), reform advocates are cautious about liberalization of birth limits. More far-reaching economic or political reforms are therefore unlikely to result in the abandonment of state-regulated childbearing. At best, they may produce a more moderate, comprehensive and genuinely service-oriented approach to family planning—one that hopes for voluntary compliance but settles for less.

SOCIAL SECURITY FOR STATE-SECTOR WORKERS IN THE PEOPLE'S REPUBLIC OF CHINA: THE REFORM DECADE AND BEYOND

By Lillian Liu *

CONTENTS

I. SUMMARY

This paper deals only with social security for workers in the urban sector. Social security for the state work force, primarily income security programs for state enterprises, faces unprecedented challenges caused by a decade of policy changes and experiments in social security and enterprise and labor force reforms. Serious problems in funding and administering these programs have surfaced. Social security expenditures are rising rapidly. There are also signs of widespread mismanagement and discrepancies be-

* Social Science Research Analyst, Office of International Policy, Social Security Administration (SSA), Department of Health and Human Services. The author is grateful to a number of individuals: Christina Harbaugh of the Office of International Research at the U.S. Census Bureau provided many useful sources; her colleagues at the SSA, Lois Copeland and Leif Haanes-Olsen of the Office of International Policy and John Woods of the Office of Research and Statistics kindly reviewed an earlier draft of the paper; and Teh-wei Hu (University of California at Berkeley), Robert Myers (a consulting actuary), and Anthony Pellechio (World Bank) made helpful comments. Ideas expressed are the author's and not necessarily those of reviewers or of their respective institutions. She is solely responsible for any remaining shortcomings.

tween enterprise implementation and local and central government guidelines, and between local government guidelines and central government regulations. Recent developments suggest that, while the central government is poised to correct some of these problems, some broad policy issues remain: Can China afford the high price of social security for state-sector workers as its population ages? How will Chinese leaders balance their inclination to placate state-sector workers with social security benefits against the need to control these costs?

II. INTRODUCTION

In the 1980s the reformist government in the People's Republic of China (PRC) seems to have pursued a bifurcated social welfare policy for the country's rural and urban populations. Government reforms have apparently taken the social safety net from under the rural population while, at the same time, further enriched statesector workers and retirees in urban areas. By decade's end, critics both in China and in the West have pointed to the gross inequity in social welfare treatment between the rural and urban populations. They have especially noted the large sums provided for the welfare of the comparatively small group of state-sector workers and retirees.[1] The "mini-welfare state" (xiao shehui) in state work units (danwei) seems to be alive and well; state employees therefore are far from being weaned from the "iron rice bowl" that is considered by many reformers as a systemic drag on economic efficiency.[2]

Of the employee welfare expenditures (that is, nonwage compensation), the government-regulated social security programs averaged 72.5 percent during 1978–88.[3] Moreover, in late 1989 and

[1] D. Davis, "Chinese Social Welfare: Policies and Outcomes," China Quarterly (September 1989): 579–97; W. Han, "Woguo zhigongfuli ji qi dui guomin sherufenpei de yingxiang (Welfare for urban workers and its impact on national income distribution, hereafter cited as 'Sherufenpei')," Jinji Kexue (March 1990): 12-9; C. Liu, "Lun zhongguo de eryuan shehui jiegou (On the dualistic structure of the Chinese society)," Shehui (August 1989): 20-5; Ibid (September 1989):22-7; Ibid (October 1989): 13-6; Ibid (November 1989): 4-9. For a contrary view see, M. K. Whyte, "Social Trends in China: The Triumph of Inequality?" in Modernizing China, eds. A. Doak Barnett and R. Clough (Westview: Boulder, CO., 1986), 103-23. For impact of reform on rural social welfare programs, see D. Davis, "The Provision of Essential Services in Rural China," in Rural Public Services: International Comparisons, ed. R. E. Lonsdale and G. Enyedi (Westview: Boulder, CO., 1984), 205-24.

[2] For a brief summary of debates on the culpability of the "iron rice bowl" between reformers and defenders of the system, see G. White, "Labor Contract System," China Quarterly (September 1987): 365–89; comments on "mini-welfare state," ibid, 366-7. For more recent criticism of enterprises as "xiao shehui", see Z. Wang, "Xiao shehui (Mini welfare state)," Shehui (January 1988): 31-2.

[3] Social security for purposes of this paper refers to government-regulated cash and in-kind compensation for lost income and for medical care in old age, sickness, disability (work or non-work related), unemployment, or upon death of the bread winner. This definition is in general agreement with that adopted by the International Labor Organization for comparative studies; it is, however, much broader than the U.S. usage of the term. In the United States, "social security" refers only to cash benefits for old age, survivors and disability.
Social security expenditures in this paper include only old-age and disability pensions and subsidies; costs of free medical care to retirees, employees (whether or not work-related) and their dependents; funeral grants to retirees and employees; and emergency relief grants to employees. Although cash benefits for sick leave, maternity leave, and temporary disability due to work injury are part of social security programs, they are paid out of enterprise budgets for wages and thus are not available for inclusion in social security expenditure. Zhongguo Laodong Gongzi Tongji Nianjian, 1989 (Chinese Statistical Yearbook of Labor Wages, hereafter Laodong Nianjian) (Beijing, 1990), 372-3.
Besides social security, employee nonwage compensation items include, among others, allowances for transportation and personal hygiene; expenses for educational, cultural, and athletic events, and for employee welfare facilities such as canteens and nurseries.

early 1990, as China's economy suffered from the government's austerity program of tightened credits and investment, social security programs for the urban work force have become stabilizing wands the government can wield amidst widespread discontent. Yet all is not well in the freely spending social security programs in the state sector.

III. Pre-1978 Social Security Programs

A. GENERAL DESCRIPTION

In 1978, on the eve of the post-Mao reforms, formal income security programs for the urban labor force were limited primarily to those employed in the state sector. The state-sector workers, almost 75 million strong, constituted 78 percent of urban workers, albeit only 19 percent of the country's total civilian labor force. They represented two groups: about 80 percent of them worked in state-owned enterprises, and the remainder served in the civil service system that included government and party organizations (*jiguan*) and cultural, scientific, and educational institutions (*siye*).[4] These two groups were protected by two formal social security systems providing extensive cash and in-kind benefits, as stipulated by two sets of regulations for nationwide application. First, the 1951 Interim Labor Insurance Regulations (as amended in 1953 and 1958, with subsequent instructions for implementation) detailed provisions for those working in state-owned enterprises. Second, a separate set of regulations provided comparable but somewhat more extensive benefits to those employed in the civil service system.[5]

The income security programs for those in state enterprises or civil service included: retirement pay of at least 60 percent of an individual's last month's standard wage, paid sick leave (up to 6 months per year) and maternity leave at 90 to 100 percent of pay after 6 years' service, and free medical care for employees and pensioners (50 percent of the cost for their dependents). In addition, these programs offered benefits and grants for workers and dependents in case of long-term disability (work or nonwork related), and for dependents upon the death of the worker or pensioner.[6] Employees did not contribute to the funding of the program, and their continuing eligibility was contingent on their employment at the work unit, which was guaranteed regardless of performance so long as they adhered to the "correct" political orientation. Finally, benefit payments were guaranteed by the state budget for all state

---

[4] By 1988, 74 percent of state-sector workers were employed in enterprises, and 26 percent in civil services. See Zhongguo Laodong Gongzi Tongji Ziliao, 1949–1985 (Statistics of labor wages in China, hereafter, *Gongzi Ziliao*, Beijing, 1987), 26–7; and *Zhongguo Tongji Nianjian, 1989* (Chinese statistical yearbook, hereafter, *TJNJ*) (Beijing, 1990), 111. For purposes of this paper, *jiguan* and *siye* are referred to collectively as civil service for lack of a better term. J. P. Burns refers to *jiguan* and *siye* as administrative units and service units, respectively. See his "Chinese Civil Service Reform: The 13th Party Congress Proposals," *China Quarterly* (December 1989): 740.

[5] For a legislative history of state-sector social security provisions, see K. Wang, et al, *Dangdai Zhongguo de Zhigong Gonzi Fuli he Shehui Baoxian (Employee Wages, Welfare Benefits and Social Insurance in Contemporary China)* (Hereafter, *Dangdai*, Beijing, 1987), 302–18; an English summary is in N. Chow's *The Administration and Financing of Social Security in China* (University of Hong Kong: Hong Kong, 1988), 22–7.

[6] For texts of 1951 Provisional Labor Insurance Regulations as amended in 1953, and 1958 together with implementing regulations, see *Laodong Gongzi Wenjian Xuanbian (Selected documents of labor and wages)* (Fujian 1973), pp. 275–306, 407–18, and 447–9.

work units. In the case of state enterprises, benefit expenditures were thus ensured, regardless of an enterprise's financial solvency.

B. INCOMPATIBILITY WITH MARKET-ORIENTED ECONOMY

Social security programs thus constituted part of a large overall package of nonwage compensation items that characterized the "iron rice bowl" for state-sector employees, a package that also included low-cost housing and extensive food and nonfood allowances. However, these very benefits that seemed to have worked well under a centrally planned economy designed to reward its workers in the industrial sector and to complement a wage policy of ensuring job security and equal compensation have been deemed by reformers as antithetical to "market-oriented socialism." Such programs, it is argued, have tended to foster workers' dependence on the enterprise and the state for their well-being without demanding responsibility in return.

Under pre-1978 programs, state-sector employees were tied to their respective work units, which administered all aspects of the social security programs, from determination of eligibility to benefit payments.[7] This highly decentralized administration, in the absence of an established mechanism for portability of eligibility and benefits, discouraged labor mobility across enterprises, industries or sectors—a pre-condition to an open economy. To reformers, pre-1978 social security programs were also seen as inadequate for preparing workers to face the brave new world of a market-oriented economy. There were no formal provisions for adjusting benefit payments to price changes, and no unemployment insurance. The special privilege of benefits awarded to only state employees were regarded as a disincentive for workers to seek employment outside the state sector, thus indirectly hindering the development of collective and private enterprises.[8]

The move toward an open economy would by definition entail a contracting state sector and expanding collective and private sectors. The so-called "big" urban collective enterprises (or *de facto* state enterprises) had adopted provisions equivalent to those for state enterprise workers. In addition, some smaller collectives offered modest retirement plans, their finances permitting. For lack of government backing, collective plans were regarded as unstable sources for income maintenance.[9] There was no income security protection whatsoever for workers in the then negligible private sector.

IV. MAJOR SOCIAL SECURITY POLICY INITIATIVES, 1978–1989

Despite the reformers' concerns, the social security programs established in the early 1950s are still operative today. The reformist

---

[7] For a detailed listing of various subsidies and allowances in English, see Chow, *Administration and Financing*, 92–4. A. Walder has discussed extensively the predominant role of enterprises in all aspects of workers' lives; see his *Communist Neo-Traditionalism: Work and Authority in Chinese Industry* (University of California Press: Berkeley, CA., 1986).

[8] See, for example, "Article Urges Establishment of Comprehensive Labor Insurance System," *JPRS–CAR 89–089*, 33–4.

[9] In 1978, about two-thirds of collective workers were covered by some form of income security programs. See, *Zhongguo Shehui Tongji Ziliao, 1987* (Chinese Social Statistics, hereafter *Shehui ziliao*) (Beijing, 1987), 111–2.

government has kept most of the program regulations intact, making changes in three respects only. First, it improved many of the retirement benefits, including making ad hoc adjustments to pension benefits to offset price changes. Second, in 1986 it set up a special contract workers' retirement pension system for state employees hired under a newly created labor contract system. Finally, it introduced unemployment insurance for state enterprise workers, also in 1986. All three steps reflected the government's efforts to prepare the state-sector labor force for the transition to a market-oriented economy.

A. IMPROVEMENTS TO EXISTING SOCIAL SECURITY PROGRAMS

Most of the improvements to the existing social security programs have related to retirement pensions. They were designed to retire older workers and help make room for unemployed youths. For example, the 1978 amendments to the retirement regulations and subsequent instructions in the early 1980s (1) enforced, for the first time, the statutory mandatory retirement age of 60 for men and 55 for women (age 50 for female blue-collar workers); (2) allowed retirement 10 years sooner if poor health was a factor; (3) relaxed minimum qualifying conditions for retirement (for example, the continuous service requirement was reduced from 20 to 10 years); (4) raised pension benefits; (5) promised the hiring of retired workers' unemployed offspring; and (6) offered, to middle- and upper-ranking Communist party and technical cadres, a special preferred pension benefit (lixiujin)—at full rate of pre-retirement pay plus all the perquisites associated with their position. Since 1985 the government has approved payments by enterprises of periodic ad hoc subsidies to retirement pensions to compensate for inflation. Concurrent with wage increases for state-sector employees in late 1989, benefits for retirees and the disabled were adjusted upward as well.[10]

B. SOCIAL SECURITY FOR CONTRACT WORKERS

The State Council's 1986 Interim Regulations for Implementation of the Labor Contract System by State-Owned Enterprises support labor force reform by putting new state-sector employees on fixed-term employment contracts.[11] Workers thus employed would have their contracts renewed if they performed satisfactorily; they do not have the protection of life-long employment as permanent workers do. It is expected that the life-tenure system will, over time, phase out of practice as enterprises will be populated by a

---

[10] For a full discussion on the liberalization of retirement regulations in the state-sector income security programs for both government institutions and enterprise workers, see D. Davis, "Unequal Chances, Unequal Outcomes: Pension Reform and Urban Inequality," *China Quarterly* (June 1988): 230–7. For texts of 1978 retirement regulations and subsequent amendments to retirement and social security programs, see *Shehui Wenjiao Xingzheng Caiwu Zhidu Zhaibian (Selections on social, educational, administrative and financial systems)* (Beijing, 1979); Zhonghua Renmin Gongheguo Guowuyuan Gongbao (hereafter, Guowuyuan Gongbao) 27 (1989): 973-82; *Xinbian Laodongzhengce Wentijieda* (A new compilation of Q and A to labor policies, hereafter *Xinbian*) (Beijing, 1989), 242–54. Improvements to other programs included extending the paid maternity leave from 56 days to 90 days, for example. Senior professional women may now retire at age 60 rather than age 55. "Nugaozhi tui(li)xiu de singuiding (New regulations regarding the retirement of senior professional women)," *Zhongguo Funu* (September 1990):39.

[11] G. White, "Labor Contract System," 365–89. For text of the Interim Regulations, see *Renmin Ribao*, 10 September 1986, 2.

growing number of contract workers replacing the aging permanent workers.

The 1986 regulations offer workers employed under the contract system a package of retirement pensions, medical care, and other social security benefits comparable to that for permanent workers. There are two major differences in the types of plans offered, however. First, contract workers must help finance their retirement pensions (at 3 percent of their wages, while the enterprise contributes 15 percent toward the buildup of a special retirement fund). Second, instead of individual enterprises, local governments—specifically, newly created social insurance agencies (SIAs) under city or county labor bureaus—are charged with the administration and fund management of these programs. Presumably, as workers under labor contract gradually outnumber permanent workers in the state sector, the predominant retirement pension will be one funded with worker-employer contributions together with state subsidies, and will be administered by local governments.

C. UNEMPLOYMENT INSURANCE FOR REDUNDANT STATE ENTERPRISE EMPLOYEES

As economic reforms continued in the 1980s, the government anticipated the need to provide income security for redundant state enterprise employees. These include workers whose employment contracts expire, employees in bankrupt or near-bankrupt enterprises, and workers who are laid off from state enterprises. The 1986 Interim Regulations for State-Owned Enterprise Workers' Waiting-for-Employment Insurance provide compensation for temporary unemployment to these individuals. Unemployment benefits include medical care as well as 65–70 percent of workers' basic wage for 12 to 24 months, depending on the length of service before unemployment. These programs are financed by the employer, who contributes 1 percent of the standard wage bill, and by local government subsidies. Employees do not contribute.[12]

Having decided to rely on the pre-reform state institutions and enterprises to carry out modernization initiatives, the reformist government seems intent on protecting the privileges of their employees by keeping the pre-1978 social security programs intact and by improving benefits for retirees and workers. On the one hand, the post-1978 social security provisions have thus further enhanced the image of the state work unit as a "mini-welfare state." On the other hand, they represent the government's attempts to remold social security provisions for transition to a new economic order. Provisions have been made to prepare current state employees for contingencies of reforms such as inflation and unemployment. A retirement program requiring contributions from employees under the contract system has been introduced to gradually phase out the noncontributory program for permanent workers.

---

[12] For text of Regulations, see *Renmin Ribao*, 10 September 1986, 2.

V. Program Implementation at the Local Government and Enterprise Levels

More important than central government policies to social security developments in the 1980s were the practices of city and county governments and of enterprises where central policies and programs were implemented and "experiments" carried out. The Ministry of Labor, which has the responsibility for policy development and oversight of social security programs, has no local offices to implement or enforce compliance of its regulations by individual enterprises. Labor bureaus at provincial, city, and county levels are subordinate bodies of their respective governments, and only *indirectly* subordinate to the labor ministry in Beijing.

Throughout the 1980s the central government allowed local governments and individual enterprises to conduct "experiments" in social security as they adjusted to changing conditions induced by enterprise and labor force reforms. In effect, social security programs as stipulated by the central government could best be regarded as the established "national norm" from which local authorities can and still do deviate for their own purposes. The Ministry of Labor appeared far more effective in promoting particular "experiments" deemed constructive to social security developments than in terminating practices that are contrary to its policies.

This decentralized approach may have been necessary in the absence of institutional control from the Ministry of Labor over local government and enterprise labor officials. It was also in keeping with the reformist government's overall policy of loosening central controls. By the decade's end, it has become apparent that certain earlier improvisations at the enterprise and local government levels have evolved into agendas with broad regional and even nationwide implications. Many, however, remained local and isolated practices with or without central government blessings.

A. RETIREMENT PENSIONS AND CITY/COUNTY SOCIAL INSURANCE AGENCIES (SIAS)

1. Permanent Workers

A good example of how enterprise and local government experiments evolved out of pressures from labor force and enterprise reforms and became adopted by the central government as its policy agenda is the resource pooling for retirement pensions for state enterprise permanent workers.

a) Rapid Rise in Retirees Adds to Administrative and Financial Burdens of Enterprises

In addition to improvements in retirement benefits introduced by the central government, three developments in the 1980s contributed to mass retirement by permanent workers who were middle-aged and older. First, many provincial, city, and county governments took advantage of loosened central control and further improved benefits for retirees under their respective jurisdictions. According to one analyst, by 1988 retirement benefits for workers with 20 years' service ranged from 80–95 percent of the pre-retirement basic wage rather than the 75 percent stipulated under the

1978 retirement regulations.[13] Second, since 1978, the increased opportunity for pensioners to earn extra income by working in a "second employment" has made the option of early retirement more attractive. Wage-earning pensioners continue to receive full retirement benefits, complete with free medical care.[14] Third, starting in 1986, a central government initiative to "optimize labor organization" (*yiuhua laodong zhuhe*) by urging enterprises to reduce surplus and unproductive workers has also led to early retirement of middle-aged and older workers.

Some enterprises, taking advantage of their prerogative to administer social security programs, have relaxed the "poor health" or "total disability" requirements so that employees may retire 10 years sooner than the statutory retirement age.[15] All told, the number of pensioned retirees from the state sector increased from 2.8 million in 1978 to 15.4 million in 1988. Expenditures for pensioners—including retirement pensions, health care, and various subsidies—rose from 1.63 billion yuan to 25.7 billion yuan in the interim.[16]

The vast number of retirees has placed unprecedented administrative and financial demands on enterprises. In older industries, where the number of retired workers makes up a large proportion of or even outstrips the number of active workers, the administrative burden of processing claims and paying benefits places extra demands on active employees' time and productive energy. Moreover, the large and escalating retirement expenses have precluded any prospect of profits and bonuses—a disincentive for active employees to work hard, therefore contrary to the overall objective of improving worker productivity.[17]

b) Resource Pooling and the Role of City/County Governments

The intense pressure on enterprises with an inordinately heavy financial burden for retirement pensions has prompted them to propose the pooling of retirement funds. Resource pooling, or unified financing (*tongchou*), began in 1984 as "experiments" in isolated cities and counties when hard-pressed enterprises sought assistance from local labor bureaus to help pay pension benefits to their

---

[13] X. Wei, "Chengshi yanglaojin zhidu gaige chuxin chutan (Preliminary discussions on urban retirement pension system reform)," (unpublished manuscript, Beijing, 1988), 2.

[14] Some 3.6 million out of 22 million state-sector pensioners are earning wages through "second employment." "Laodong bowen (Labor news)," *Zhongguo Laodong Kexue* (hereafter as ZLK) (April 1990): 10.

[15] For examples, see X. Wang, "Henansheng anzhi qiye fuyu renyuan de qingkuang (Making arrangements for surplus workers in Henan province)," *ZLK* (January 1989): 46; "Guanyu funu shixing jieduan jiuye de jizhong yijian (Thoughts on the practice of phased-employment for women)," *ZLK* (January 1989): 38–9; "Gaohao laodong zhidu gaige, tuoshan anzhi fuyu renyuan (Improve labor reform, make proper arrangements for surplus workers)," *ZLK* (December 1988): 33–5.

[16] *TJNJ, 1989*, 152. Separate totals for state enterprise and civil service retirees are not readily available. In 1988 the number of pensioned retirees from *all* urban employment, including those from collective enterprises, was 21.2 million, receiving 32.1 billion yuan in benefits. By the end of 1989, the totals were 22 million urban retirees receiving 37.5 billion yuan in benefits. C. Gu, "Insurance to Benefit All Chinese Employees," *China Daily* 10 August 1990, 1.

1 yuan equaled 61.3 U.S. cents at year-end 1978, and equaled 26.9 U.S. cents at year-end 1988.

[17] S. Pei, "Guanyu gaige tuixiujin zhidu de sikao (Thoughts on the reform of retirement pension system)," *Jingji yu Guanli Yenjiu (Economics and Management Research)* 5 (1986): 36–8; and H. Feng, "Shanghaishi quanmin suoyouzhi qiye shixing tuixiufei tongchoude qingkuang (The implementation of resource pooling in state enterprises in Shanghai municipality)," *ZLK* (June 1987): 12-5.

retirees. By year-end 1988, this practice had expanded to 2,141 cities and counties (out of 2,821, total), and 49 prefectures (out of 334). Local governments have had to overcome the resistance of enterprises with a relatively young work force to take part in the pool, often reimbursing them through tax write-offs. As a result of negotiations involving local labor and finance authorities, and considerable promotion efforts by the Ministry of Labor, these city and county governments have adopted compulsory resource pooling for retirement insurance among enterprises across industry lines.[18]

The local labor bureaus have set up subordinate SIAs (the same agencies administering contract workers' pension programs) to take on all the responsibilities involved in carrying out pension pooling for the retirement program for permanent workers—for example, making certain that enterprises keep accurate accounts of their respective total wage bills (the base for computing enterprise contributions to the pool), lists of retirees, and benefit payments due. These agencies must also verify and transact the amount each enterprise owes to the pooled fund or vice versa.[19]

Having begun as an improvisation to pay benefits for enterprises overburdened with a large number of retirees, pension pooling has led to two potentially significant developments that have gone beyond its original purpose. First, the city and county governments have set uniform contribution rates and benefit levels for all participating enterprises under their respective jurisdictions. Furthermore, for the first time, an enterprise's management of its retirement pension program became subject to local government supervision. One report indicates that the trend is heading toward not only expanding the geographic base of pension pooling, but also transferring a part of retirement program administration to local governments. By the end of 1988 one province (Fujian) had begun region-wide pooling in retirement funds. In addition, SIAs in 235 cities and counties (or 11 percent of those practicing resource pooling) assumed the direct responsibility for paying benefits to pensioners.[20]

Nevertheless, the risk sharing is still limited to individual cities and counties, with the exception of Fujian Province. Cities and

---

[18] *Guoying qiye zhigong tuixiu feiyong shehui tongchou banfa huiji* (Collection of resource pooling arrangements for state enterprise retirement pension funds hereafter *Guoyin*) (Beijing, 1987); G. Zhang, "Guangdong shixian quansheng yi shixian wei danwei tongchou tuixiujijin de tihui (Understanding the city and county-based resource pooling of retirement pension funds in Guangdong Province," in *Guangdongsheng shehuilaodong baoxian ziliao xuanbian (Selected documents on socialized labor insurance in Guangdong Province)*, volume 8 (Guangzhou, 1988), 256–66. "Yijiubabanian quanguo tuixiufeiyun shehui tongchou de jiben qingkuang (Status of resource pooling of retirement expenditures in China in 1988, hereafter, Yijiubabanian tongchou)," *ZLK* (November 1989): 41; and L. Han, "Nuli tuijin shehui baoxian zhidu gaige (Diligently promote the reform of social insurance system, hereafter 'Nuli')," *ZLK* (May 1990): 10–2. Generally speaking, only state enterprises under the jurisdiction of city and county governments must participate in the pool. Provincial-level or national ministry enterprises (such as railway, post, and telecommunications) are exempt.

[19] For descriptions of the duties and responsibilities of these resource pooling agencies, see *Guoying*.

[20] For example, see Jimo County Labor Bureau, "Women shi ruhe dui lituixiu zhigong shixing yanglao baoxian shehuihua guanli de (How we implemented socialized management of old-age insurance for retired workers)," in Qingdao Municipal Labor Bureau's *Qingdaoshi shehui laodong baoxian zhidu gaige cailiao huibian* (Collection of documents regarding socialized labor insurance system reform, hereafter, *Qingdao cailiao huibian* (Qingdao, 1988), 103–15; and H. Li, "Women shi jenyang yunhao tongchou jijin de (How we effectively manage the pooled fund)," *Dandong Diaoyen* (September 1988): 13–5. See also, "Yijiubabanian tongchou," *ZLK* (November 1989): 41; and *TJNJ, 1989*, 3.

counties have made their own arrangements with local enterprises, and they have set their own contribution rates and benefit levels. Also, for most city/county governments the role of SIAs at present is largely limited to monitoring pension pooling; the eventual take-over of the administrative responsibilities involving millions of workers remains in the distant future. With enterprises operating at losses or at reduced capacity, or even lying idle, as a result of the government's austerity program that started in September 1988, these agencies have had difficulty in ensuring that participating enterprises make timely payments to the pool, and that there are adequate funds to pay enterprises which stand to benefit from the pool. Under pay-as-you-go financing, SIAs still have to protect the limited reserves (which amount to only 1.9 months of benefit outgo at year-end 1988, nationwide) from erosion in value and from misappropriation. In cases of shortfalls, city/county governments presumably provide subsidies.[21]

2. Contract Workers

The SIAs monitoring pension pooling for permanent workers are not only responsible for the fund management but also the administration of retirement pensions for contract workers. Because contract workers are comparatively young (typically under age 35) and are years away from retirement, these agencies' primary task at present is the collection of retirement contributions from enterprises, and the registration of contract workers in the retirement program. They have not yet begun to process claims or distribute benefits. At year-end 1988, workers under labor contract exceeded 10 million; only 6.5 million were registered to contribute to the program a year later, however.[22] Protection of these pension funds from erosion in value and from mismanagement is especially important because they are established as a partially funded program. Contributions collected are deposited in special accounts to pay contract workers for benefits due in the future.

B. UNEMPLOYMENT INSURANCE AND CITY/COUNTY LABOR SERVICE COMPANIES

The implementation of unemployment insurance rests with city/county labor service companies (LSCs). These companies were established by city and county labor bureaus as early as 1979. They began by providing job referrals, conducting occupational training, and creating jobs by investing in and setting up collectives for hiring some of the new entrants (averaging about 4.7 million per year during the 1980s) to the urban labor market as a whole. Their responsibilities have expanded since 1986 to encompass the administration of unemployment insurance for dismissed state enterprise

---

[21] M. Fang, "Weishemo zhigong tuixiu yanglaojin shoujiao nan (Why is it difficult to collect contributions to the retirement pension fund)," *ZLK* (April 1990): 32; and "Laodong bumen huyu wanshan yanglaojin shehui tongchou (The labor administration appeals for perfecting resource pooling of retirement pension)," *Jingji Cankao* (Economic Information), 22 June 1990, 1; Z. Shi, "Wei baozheng tingchan qiye lituixiu zhigong shenghuo (To guarantee the livelihood of retired workers of non-operative enterprises)," *ZLK* (April 1990): 47; and unpublished data, Ministry of Labor.

[22] C. Song, "Yijiubajiunian shangbannian quanguo laodong gongzi qingkuang ji quannian zhanwang (Nationwide labor wages during the first half of 1989 and prospects for the entire year)," *ZLK* (December 1989): 12; L. Han, "Nuli," 10–11.

employees, including the collection and management of the unemployment insurance fund and payments to beneficiaries. Benefit levels and implementing procedures are subject to specific provisions determined by provincial, city and county governments based on the national norm stipulated in the 1986 Interim Regulations.[23] In some locales, these companies set up branch and subbranch offices in districts (*qu*) and at the street and resident committee level to help register the unemployed, process claims, and make payments to beneficiaries.

By 1989 there were over 3,000 local government LSCs nationwide. With the majority of their services centering on job training and placement, information is scarce on how well these LSCs have been administering unemployment insurance benefits. National totals are not readily available for the number of state employees who have become unemployed since the 1986 regulations took effect, for those who have since been registered on unemployment rolls, or for those who actually have been receiving benefits. It is believed that, of the average 2.8 million unemployed in the course of 3 years from 1986 to 1988, former state enterprise employees constituted only a small minority. Generally speaking, many enterprises have been reluctant to lay off workers—partly due to lingering commitment to full employment, partly because of the government's belief that keeping workers tied to enterprises can better ease workers' resentment. In late 1989 and early 1990, when, reportedly more than 6,000 enterprises operated at a loss and two-thirds of urban factories were either closed or operating below capacity, many kept their workers on payroll with reduced wages (by 30 to 40 percent), instead of placing them on unemployment rolls.[24]

There are three sources of funding for LSCs: local government appropriations, income generated from affiliated collective enterprises, and contributions to the unemployment insurance fund from enterprises and local governments. Their diverse activities and their major focus on providing jobs for new entrants to the labor force make it difficult to determine whether LSCs have set aside a certain portion of their income for benefit payments to laid-off state enterprise employees. With the central government's rectification campaign in full swing in late 1989, many LSCs have been criticized for laxity in accounting, for widespread misuse and abuse of funds, and for practices such as placing jobs for those with connections rather than ability. Besides, many LSCs and their affili-

---

[23] *TJNJ, 1989*, 123; *Xinbian*, 283-4.

[24] Z. Ren,"Guanyu jiejue qiye fuyu renyuan wenti de sikao (Considerations regarding the resolution of enterprise surplus workers)," *ZLK* (November 1988): 21-3; G. Yao and M. Fang, "Qiyejia de kunao (Entrepreneurs' dilemmas)," *Shehui* (May 1989): 28-31; "Li Boyong fubuzhang zhai quangou laodong fuwu gongshe gongzhohueyi ji zhongguo laodong fuwugongshi yenjiuhui lishihuiyi shang de jianghua (Deputy Minister Li Boyong's speech at the conference of work of All-China Labor Service Companies and the board meeting of the Research Committee of China Labor Service Companies, hereafter, Li Boyong)," *ZLK* (April 1989): 3-5; U.S. Central Intelligence Agency, "The Chinese Economy in 1989 and 1990: Trying to Revive Growth While Maintaining Social Stability," report presented to the Subcommittee on Technology and National Security, Joint Economic Committee, 28 June, 1990; *TJNJ, 1989*, 123. In 1989, the unemployed were reported to total 3.78 million; see *Zhongguo Tongji Zhaiyao, 1990* (A Statistical Survey of China, 1990) (Beijing, 1990), 18.

ated collectives have been established as profit-making enterprises with rather unstable existence.[25]

C. MEDICAL CARE AND OTHER SOCIAL SECURITY PROGRAMS

Besides retirement pensions and unemployment insurance, the central government issued no major policy initiatives in social security throughout the reform decade, except for minor improvements.[26] Whereas retirement pension and unemployment insurance programs have had the benefit of local government agencies (SIAs and LSCs, respectively) in monitoring the funding and, in some cases, in taking over the administration of these programs, this is not the case for remainder of the social security programs—such as medical care, work-injury compensation, and cash benefits for sickness and maternity leave. For enterprises that have adopted the enterprise contract responsibility system and are accountable for their own profits and losses, the funding and administration of these social security programs depends entirely on enterprise management. The status of these programs, therefore, has become far more fluid, or unstable, than retirement and unemployment programs.

Other than retirement pensions, the medical care program (whether or not work-related) has been the most costly and problematic. The total of medical care costs for state-sector employees and retirees has constituted a large, if not always the largest, proportion of social security expenditures overall. Medical care costs rose from 2.73 billion yuan in 1978 to 15.24 billion yuan in 1988, and, respectively, constituted 54.6 percent and 40.0 percent of total social security costs. The 1978 per capita expenditure on medical care for employees and retirees—35.3 yuan, or 66.5 yuan when adjusted to the 1988 price level by the urban consumer price index—almost doubled to 132.3 yuan in 1988.[27]

Attempts to control the rapid increase in health care expenses have met limited success, in part because enterprises have no control over health practitioners and/or hospital administrators who are prone to overcharges, waste and abuses (often in collusion with state employees and retirees requesting free medicines for them-

---

[25] ZLK (March 1990): 36-7; "Guanyu laodong fuwugongsi fazhan he jianshezhong rogan wentide yijian (Thoughts on issues regarding the development of labor service companies)," ZLK (April 1989): 47-8; S. Ni, "Shinian laodong jiuye de huigu yu zhanwang (Review of a decade of labor force employment and its future prospects)," ZLK (March 1989): 3-7; "Zhongda tanwuan beichachu (A serious case of embezzlement under investigation)," Zhongguo Laodong Bao (hereafter, ZLB) 6 December 1989, 1; "Ankang diqu qingli zhengdun laodongfuwu gongsi chengji kexi (Rectification of labor service companies in Ankang prefecture brings good results)," ZLB 24 March 1990, 3; and "Jichen laodongfuwu gongsi ganbuzhigong 'bapan' ('Eight wishes' of the low-level employees at labor service companies)," ZLB 10 January 1990, 3.

It is also difficult to assess the effectiveness of these LSCs because reports about these companies do not distinguish the local government LSCs that have the mandate to administer unemployment insurance from some 50,000 other LSCs created by and affiliated with large state or collective enterprises. Enterprise funded and managed LSCs generally engage in profit-making activities to provide job opportunities for their surplus workers and offspring of enterprise employees. Together, all LSCs have 700,000 employees, more than 4,000 vocational schools, and 230,000 service "points" (dian) extending to districts, and street and resident committee levels in cities and towns and even to rural towns.

[26] In 1988, the paid maternity leave was extended from 56 days to 90 days, for example. Xinbian, 254.

[27] Derived from data in Gongzi ziliao, 1949-1985, 191; Shehui ziliao, 1987, 114; and TJNJ, 1989, 101, 151-2, 688. Separate totals for civil service and enterprises are not available for the years 1978 through 1985.

selves and their families, for example).[28] Some cost-conscious factory managers have introduced various measures (or "experiments") to control health expenditures. The most common approaches adopted, for example, have been to impose co-payments from beneficiaries, or to pay each employee a pre-determined sum per month for medical expenses regardless of actual costs of medical treatments. This latter policy has become especially popular because of its effectiveness in controlling cost and its simplicity in administration. It nevertheless has created hardship for employees and their family members whose treatment for illnesses far exceeds the alloted sum.[29]

The medical care costs cited above represent only the accountable totals of health-related expenditure in social security; paid wages for sick leave, maternity leave, or absence due to work injuries are computed as part of wage totals and not available for inclusion as social security expenditures. Expenses of this type can be substantial, given reports of the widespread practice among workers, who were generally underemployed, taking extended sick leave (available for 6 months per year at full pay after working in the state sector for 8 years) to engage in private businesses or consultative ventures outside the state sector. In some cases, enterprise management has awarded underemployed workers extended leave for as long as 5 years at full or reduced pay as it attempts to "optimize labor organization" or "eliminate" or "digest" (*xiaohua*) surplus and nonproductive workers.[30]

Another problematic aspect in the largely unsupervised enterprise administration of all social security programs is the arbitrary and erratic approach to processing claims. The determination of eligibility and benefit amounts was not always carried out according to central government regulations or local government guidelines, if any. Sometimes there were no observable standards within the same enterprise. Benefit payments were often dependent on the availability of funds, favoritism, or the aggressiveness of the claimant. Such practices have become so prevalent in the administration of compensation for work injuries, for example, that a recent report concluded that government regulations for this program exist only on paper.[31]

---

[28] For examples, see Y. Xie, et al, "Guanyu guoyin qiye laobao yiliao zhidu gaige de jige wenti (Problems in reforming the enterprise labor insurance medical care system)," *ZLK* (November 1988): 10–3; "Minister Urges Better Medical Care, Lower Costs," *FBIS–CHI–90–050* 14 March 1990, 27.

[29] In one city, some 83 percent of sampled enterprises have taken some cost-cutting measures in medical care expenditures. Xie, et al, 10–1; "Woguo gongfei yiliao he laobao yiliaozhidu de gaige (Reform of civil service medical care and labor insurance medical care systems in China)," in *Gaige he wanshan woguo de shehui baozhang zhidu* (Reform and make perfect China's social security system) (Beijing, 1988), 80–8; S. Gui, "Renko laolinghua yu gaige yiliao shoufei (Population aging and reform of co-payment for medical care)," *Shehui* (April, 1987): 18–20.

[30] "Qingdaoshi jiaqiang dui 'changqi binhao' guanli (Qingdao city strengthens its management of 'long-term sick leaves')," *ZLB* 10 January, 1990 1; Xie, et al, 10–3; and "Gaohao," 34. It is estimated that, nationwide, about 15 million urban workers engage in a second employment. See Z. Sun, "Guanyu gongzi shenhua gaige mianlinde wenti he zhence (Problems and policies regarding wage reform)," *ZLK* (May 1990): 3–9.

[31] "Mudanjiangshi laodongju (Mudanjiang city labor bureau)," *ZLB* 8 November 1989, 2; "Dandongshi jiuzheng jiangdi, quxiao zhigong baoxian fuli daiyu de wenti (Dandong city corrects problems in lowering and eliminating workers' welfare insurance benefits)," *ZLB* 8 October 1989, 1; "Chengbao buke diulao ([The adoption of enterprise] contract system should not condone negligence of the aged)," ibid, 2; "Qiye zhigong fuli jijin chaozhi yin yinqi zhongshi (Attention

Continued

Enterprises' disregard for the proper administration of income security programs became evident by the late 1980s. Reports surfaced that the personnel files—including employee information such as position titles, wage records, and service tenure—upon which enterprise officials determine eligibility and benefit amounts, were in disorder and subject to falsification and unauthorized alterations.[32]

Further confounding the breakdown in the administration of social security is the absence of an established appeals system whereby a disgruntled employee can seek redress. The 1987 Interim Regulations for Settlement of Labor Disputes at State Enterprises do not include disputes regarding social security issues. Written complaints have flooded local and central labor offices, reporting nonpayment of benefits and willful reduction in benefits, for example. Many retirees or their offspring visit these offices themselves hoping to get better results. The final resolution of these problems often requires the personal intervention of a local labor bureau chief and other government officials having direct jurisdiction over the enterprise.[33] Certainly, the arbitration of disputes is more difficult if only because of the pervasive discrepancies between enterprise "experiments" and local government guidelines, and between local government "experiments" and central government regulations.

D. SUMMARY COMMENTS

In the 1980s, as the central government clung to social security programs established in the early 1950s, social security developments in the reform decade have been driven primarily by local government initiatives and enterprise "experiments." The most significant development has been the evolution of resource pooling of retirement pensions because it has made social security less dependent on individual enterprises for funding and administration. However, this development has not reached other social security programs. Also important but with limited impact were experiments in social security cost cutting (as in medical care) carried out by some local governments.

Two critical problems have surfaced. First, the 1980s witnessed the unprecedented rise in social security costs at the expense of enterprises and, ultimately, of the state tax revenues because social

should be paid to shortfalls in enterprise employee welfare funds)," *ZLB* 13 January 1990, 1; "Zhigong siwang sangzangfei chaozhi wenti jidai jiejue (Problems of deficits in death and funeral grants for workers urgently await resolutions)," *ZLB* 22 November 1989, 2; X. Zheng and W. Ju, "Xinde gongshang baoxianfagui ying jingkuai chutai (New regulations on workers' compensation should be issued as soon as possible)," *ZLK* (June 1990): 19–21.

[32] H. Cai, "Jiaqiang zhigong dangan guanli, wei gaohuo qiye fuwu (Strengthen the management of employee personnel files, facilitate enterprise services)," *ZLK* (November 1989): 23–4; "Zhigaizhong geren dangan zaojia xianxiang yenzhong (The phenomenon of falsifying individual personnel files in the process of revising position titles is considered serious)," *ZLB* 5 May 1990, 3.

[33] "Wanshan wuoguo laodong zhengyi chuli lifa ruogan wenti (Several issues concerning the improvement of legislation for settling labor disputes in our country)" *ZLK* 3 (1990): 20–1; "Anshanshi Laodong Ju (Anshan city labor bureau)", *ZLB*, 8 November 1989, 2. For additional reports of complaints in recent years against arbitrary practices of the Labor Insurance Regulations, see items for Shanghai municipal labor bureau, Hebei provincial labor bureau, Mudanjiang city labor bureau, and Hubei provincial labor bureau, respectively, ibid. Apparently, civil service retirees were also suffering from administrative problems. In one case, it took a retired cadre 10 years (from June 1979 to May 1989) to finally settle his appeal to correct his service tenure from 28 to 31 years. *ZLB*, 6 December 1989, 3.

security expenditures are operating costs before tax. Total social security expenditures multiplied from 5 billion yuan in 1978 to 38.18 billion yuan ten years later, or 1.4 percent and 2.7 percent of the gross national product (GNP) for the respective years. Annual social security expenditures per covered employee and retiree rose from 77.4 yuan to 331.4 yuan during the same period. The 1988 figure is more than twice the 1978 amount adjusted for inflation (145.8 yuan).[34]

Second, the arbitrary and capricious practices of enterprises in implementing social security programs have made them a less-than-reliable mechanism for income protection. At a time when these programs could have served as effective tools to mollify worker discontent during the 1989–90 economic downturn, the lack of reliability in social security programs may have in itself become a cause of worker frustration. From the perspective of workers, reform-minded experiments such as cutting benefits and imposing co-payments to medical care were regarded as unwelcome violations of central government regulations by enterprises and/or local governments, and as such, they became causes for appeals.

VI. Recent Developments and Remaining Policy Issues

A. Recent Developments, 1989–90

Central and local government measures in 1989–90 have focused on shoring up financing and administration, and revisions of central government regulations of social security programs. In financing retirement pensions, some local governments have merged the pension pools for permanent workers and for contract workers, hitherto set up as separate accounts. As a result, shortfalls in pension pools for permanent workers (which are financed on a pay-as-you-go scheme, and are thus vulnerable to enterprise losses and shutdowns) can be made up, albeit temporarily, by the accumulated retirement reserves for contract workers.[35] These city and county governments, therefore, have moved another step toward transforming an enterprise-managed retirement system into a social insurance system by broadening the base of risk sharing.

Proposals for setting up reserve funds through resource pooling to finance medical care programs and workers' compensation (cash benefits for work-related injuries) have emerged as well. Whether this practice, following the development of retirement pension pools, will take hold and give rise to localized standardization in programs and to city/county government supervision and control over the administration of these programs, remains to be seen. Medical care and workers' compensation programs are more difficult to administer than retirement pensions because of the complicating role of health care providers. The lack of established standards for determining the degree of injury and disability as well as

---

[34] *Gongzi ziliao, 1949–1985*, 191; *Shehui ziliao*, 114; *TJNJ, 1989*, 17, 101, 151–2; 688.

[35] For examples, see J. Mao and Y. Zhang, "Tuixiufeiyong shehuitongchou jitifangshi chutan (Preliminary investigations into methods for computing contributions to resource pooling for retirement expenditures)," *ZLB* 20 January 1990, 3; "Yenchengshi shixing tuixiu yanglao baoxian yitihua tongchou (Yencheng city implements unitary resource pooling for retirement pensions)," *ZLB*, 28 April 1990, 1.

the level of reimbursable care and compensation also causes administrative problems.[36]

Local governments and central government agencies have taken steps to improve the administration of SIAs and their linkages with the Ministry of Labor. Some city and county labor bureaus have announced their plans to acquire computer technology to enhance the SIAs' ability to monitor resource pooling for pension programs. Presumably, automation will also facilitate the SIAs' gradual takeover from enterprises of the administration of the retirement pension programs. Similarly, the Ministry of Labor has announced its support for the general application of computer technology to the management of social security, including the development of a networking capability between local SIAs and a newly established information retrieval center at the Ministry in Beijing. Moreover, the State Bureau of Technological Assessment (*Guojia Jishu Jianduju*) has approved the issuance of social security numbers to workers beginning in April 1990, another step toward facilitating administrative control of social security programs.[37] Mindful of the inadequacy in the existing institutional setup for asserting centralized control over social security administration, the Ministry of Labor has proposed the creation of a separate agency under its auspices at the central government level. It is not clear, though, whether this agency will have its own subordinate branches and subbranches throughout the country.[38]

There are even indications that the central government at last is poised to revise the existing regulations for the retirement pension and work-injury programs. Details are not yet available. The government's intention seems to reassure workers that the established benefit levels will at least continue, if not be improved. Permanent workers in state enterprises, however, may be expected to contribute to the funding of the retirement program. This would represent a major breakthrough for making workers responsible for part of the costs. There is no sign of reforming the medical care program

---

[36] "Sichuansheng zhigong dabin yiliaofei tongchou shidian shouhuanying (Experiments in resource pooling for catastrophic medical care expenditures in Sichuan Province are well received)," *ZLB* 28 March 1990, 2; "Lituixiu zhigong yilaio feiyong shehuitongchou yibi (A look at resource pooling of medical expenditures for retirees)," *ZLB* 14 October 1989, 4; G. Li and Z. Zhang, "Jianli juyou zhongguo tese de gongshang shehui baoxian zhidu (To establish a social insurance system with Chinese characteristics for workers' compensation)," *ZLK* (June 1990): 17-8; X. Zheng, 19-21.

[37] For examples, see "Chengdushi shehuibaoxian jigou shixing jisuanjiwanglou guanli chuju guimo (Chengdu city social insurance agency's implementation of computerized management takes shape)," *ZLK* (June 1990): 47; "Laodongbu jiu jisuanji guanli tuixiu yanglao baoxianjijin tichu juti yaoqiu (Ministry of Labor announces requirements for computerized management of retirement pension funds)," *ZLB* 7 October 1989, 1; Y. Liao, "Woguo shishi shehui baozhang haoma zhidu (China implements social security enumeration system)," *Liaowang* no. 24 (1990): 19-20. The report does not indicate which agency is assigning these numbers or how the adoption of the social security enumeration system is expected to improve the administration of these programs. The author admits that the effective application of the system depends mostly on the pace of automation. At present, individual enterprises keep their own files on employees and retirees manually, and they do not follow any standard procedures or numbering system.

[38] This was proposed by the Director of the Department of Social Insurance and Welfare. See, L. Han, "Nuli," 10-1. In late 1988, a State Taxation Administration was established as an independent agency with direct authority over provincial, municipal and county branches. Former Minister of Labor Luo Gan envisioned the resource pooling of retirement pensions at the national level, with a unified system for budgeting, accounting, and auditing. "Renzhen zhili, zhendun, jiji wentoudi tuijin laodong, gongzi, baoxian zhidu gaige (To seriously manage and rectify reforms in labor, wages and insurance systems and to promote them actively but at a steady pace)," *ZLK* (January 1989): 3-9.

or of revising the much-abused practice of paid sick leave for extended periods, however.[39]

All these developments seem to follow the general trend of spreading risk-sharing among enterprises and shifting administration of the retirement programs to local governments, instead of depending on individual enterprises for funding and administration. Significant as these developments are in the long-term evolution of a social security system suited for a market-oriented economy, short-term necessities have led to expedient practices that might blunt, if not subvert, this general trend—in particular, practices that reinforce employee dependency on enterprises for their social and economic well-being, or make government funding readily available for social security payments.

As layoffs in late 1989 created resentment among those who became unemployed, the government decided to retain workers in factories at reduced pay in order to avert social disorder. In a January 1990 speech, Premier Li Peng specifically lauded the enterprise's function as a "mini-welfare state," responding to workers' social and economic needs.[40] Thus, the practice of the enterprise's functioning as a "mini-welfare state" has regained official sanction. Efforts to lessen workers' dependence on enterprises in order to facilitate labor mobility appear to have taken a back seat to concerns over social stability.

When the general economic downturn in late 1989 and early 1990 caused two-thirds of urban factories to shut down or operate at a reduced capacity, it also exposed the weak financial base of resource pooling in the permanent workers' retirement pension programs that are funded on a pay-as-you-go basis. Dipping into the reserve funds for contract workers has helped to alleviate the shortfall somewhat. But these reserve funds can be easily exhausted given the large number of retirees and the relatively small number of contract workers contributing into the funds. Information is not available regarding the extent to which retirees have been paid during this period of economic hardship nationwide. Some local governments have issued directives that retirees be paid in full regardless of financial status of their former employers (that is, regardless of an enterprise's ability to contribute to pension pools). They have also offered government funding to make up for enterprise shortfalls.[41] It is likely that local and possibly central

---

[39] J. Zhang, "Dui qiye yanglao baoxian zhidu gaige de rogan sikao (Considerations on reforming the enterprise old-age insurance system)," *Jingji Cankao* 14 August 1990, 4 (Mr. Zhang is the director of the Office of Retirement, Department of Social Insurance and Welfare, Ministry of Labor); C. Gu, "Insurance," 1; C. Gu, "Pension System to Undergo Overhaul," *JPRS-CAR-90-040* 29 May 1990, 56; J. Wen, "Reform of worker's insurance under way," *China Daily* 5 September 1989, 1; G. Li and Z. Zhang, 17–8; X. Zheng, 19-21; and "Zhongguo laodong fazhi jianshe ji qushi (The establishment and trends in labor legislation in China)," *ZLK* (March 1990): 3–5. This last reference specifically mentions retirement pension and workers' compensation as among several pieces of legislative proposals already submitted to the State Council for review; labor insurance regulations that stipulate cash benefits for sickness and maternity and medical care are not included.

[40] See P. Li, "Gaige kaifang yao yenzhe jiankangde guidao qianjin (Reform and open policy must march along healthful tracks)," *Guowuyuan Gongbao* no. 4 (1990): 99–106. In the same speech, Premier Li Peng also supported a labor insurance system financed by contributions from employees, employers, and the government, see ibid, 105.

[41] U.S. Central Intelligence Agency, "The Chinese Economy." In Guangzhou city, for example, the government directive instructed the full payment of retirement pensions to beneficiaries of hardship enterprises, and promised making up for shortfalls. Guangzhoushi shehuibaoxian jigou

Continued

government funds have been tapped as a last resort to pay retirement pensions.

It remains to be seen whether this practice of government subsidies to make up enterprise shortfalls is merely a stopgap measure, or whether it will evolve into a routine procedure as during prereform days. The pooling mechanism evolved in the last decade would then become one of channeling local and central government funding to retirement pension payments (or even to medical care and workers' compensation), rather than bona fide pooling of contributions from enterprises.[42]

Recent central and local government measures and proposals have only addressed issues related to developing resources to fund social security (for example, employee contributions to social security, and resource pooling for medical care and work injury programs). No proposals have been put forward to control rapidly rising expenditures. This approach follows the central government's tendency to raise rather than lower benefit levels as evidenced in the 1980s, and probably is also prompted by the current climate of appeasing workers to maintain social stability.[43]

B. IMPLICATIONS FOR TRANSITION TO A MARKET-ORIENTED ECONOMY

During the 1980s, the central government enhanced the social security programs designed in a bygone era and made them the operative programs of today. Only limited progress has been made to adjust social security to a market economy. Both the newly established contract workers' retirement pension program and unemployment insurance program are yet to withstand the test of time. At present, state-sector permanent workers still do not contribute to the funding of social security programs; and they remain tied to their enterprises for receiving social security benefits. As long as resource pooling (for both permanent and contract workers) is limited to retirement pensions at the city/county level, and as long as city and county SIAs operate primarily as clearinghouses for funding rather than administrators of social security programs, the prospect for labor mobility across enterprises even within the jurisdiction of the same city or county will be remote.[44] More important, the central government has yet to set up any government-regulated income security programs for workers in urban collective and private sectors, even though such programs would make these

---

caiqu liudian yingji chuoshi (Guangzhou city social insurance agency adopts six-point emergency measures)," *ZLK* (April 1990): 47.

[42] An alternative route to city and county government funding for enterprise shortfalls and central government subsidies for a specific local pension fund would be expanding the base of pooling to the provincial or even national level. If necessary, the central government would make up the deficit for the national fund, raise contribution rates by enterprises and/or employees, or reduce benefit expenditures. However, it may take years to develop provincial or national pooling because each city or county has negotiated (with local enterprises) its own standards of enterprise contribution rate, retiree benefit level, and various subsidies included in the pension payment. These differences are not easily harmonized.

[43] A related question, given the present economic hardship, is whether the government still considers it appropriate to make workers themselves contribute to social security funding as planned and, if so, whether workers will be compensated with higher wages to cushion the blow.

[44] Employees also depend on their enterprises for housing and many cash and in-kind allowances in addition to social security provisions. Of the reported total nonwage compensation items, the non-social security portion has been about 28 percent of the total during years 1978–88; the social security portion, 72 percent. See note 4 above.

sectors more attractive to new entrants to the urban labor force so not to overload the state sector.[45]

Meanwhile, the skyrocketing cost of providing social security to state-sector employees—a relatively small group of the country's labor force—and its drain on the financial health of enterprises and of the state, is expected to have an adverse impact on the country's national economy. The cost issue will become especially acute as China's population ages and as some 40 percent of its current urban workers retire within the next 20 years. It is estimated that the ratio of employed urban workers to retirees will worsen from 6.4:1 in 1988 to 4:1 by the year 2000. During the same period China's resources will also be needed for investment in economic development and to meet the vast social and economic demands of the rapidly aging rural population who at present must rely on their own resources or family members for support.[46]

C. REMAINING POLICY ISSUES

How the government will resolve this dilemma of allocating China's resources among contending population groups and between social versus economic priorities remains the key social security policy issue. The government might begin with reviewing policy alternatives for state-sector social security programs. A continuation of the current arrangements—that is, reliance on local governments and enterprises to initiate "experiments" conducive to the transition to a market-oriented economy—will probably exacerbate ongoing problems of waste and abuse, and will perpetuate the workers' perception that the social security programs are unreliable.

Should the central government, then, begin to assert leadership in social security policy, as it has begun to recentralize management of state enterprises, prices and investment? If so, it may choose to follow the 1980s policy of adhering to the existing programs, all the while expecting that tightened supervision and control from the center will curb waste and abuse. By taking this approach, the government will be putting an end to a decade of local

---

[45] This is not to overlook that about two-thirds of urban collective workers are reported as having access to some income-security programs which depend mostly on the collective's financial solvency. In addition, the People's Insurance Company of China has begun to offer voluntary retirement plans for collective and private sector employees since mid-1980s. None of these programs can compare with the scope and generosity of state-sector plans. At year-end 1988, 99.8 million workers were employed in the state sector, 35.3 million in urban collectives, and 6.6 million in the private sector. *TJNJ, 1989*, 101.

[46] According to one Chinese analyst, the total cost of the benefit package for state-sector employees and retirees, including the reported total of nonwage compensation items (that is, social security, and cash and in-kind allowances), plus unaccounted subsidies (such as housing, fuel, personal use of government vehicles) amounted to 129.6 billion yuan in 1988, or 9.2 percent of China's gross national product for the same year. W. Han, "Sherufenpei," 14; *TJNJ* , 1989, 17.

S. Zheng and C. Chen, "Zhongguo xianxin shehui baozhang zhidude chulu (A way out for the existing social security system in China)," *Shehui* (February 1990): 6–8; and C. Gu,"Pension System to Undergo Overhaul," *China Daily* 10 August 1990, 1, reprinted in *JPRS–CAR–90–040*, 56. The worker/retiree ratios are based on total urban workers and retirees; the 1988 worker/retiree ratio for the state sector was 6.5:1. *TJNJ, 1989*, 101 and 152.

J. Banister estimates that given the current population policy and restrictions on rural migration to cities, "the proportion of the rural population ages 65 and above would rise from 6 percent in 1990 to 7 percent in the year 2000, 13 percent in 2030, 19 percent in 2040...." In comparison, "the proportion of urban population ages 65 and above would increase from 5 percent in 1990 to 8 percent in the year 2000, 27 percent in 2030, 33 percent in 2040...." See J. Banister, "The Aging of China's Urban and Rural Populations," paper presented at the International Academic Conference on China's Population Aging, Beijing, December 1989, 10-1.

cost-control "experiments," especially in medical care. Besides, given both the lack of an institutional framework for central supervision and control in social security matters, as well as the limited administrative experience of SIAs and LSCs in cities and counties, the savings that can be achieved through regulating administrative procedures, even with the help of computer technology, may be too little and too late to significantly diminish the heavy financial burden in social security over the next two decades.

As an alternative, will the central government decide to reexamine the existing programs and initiate cost-cutting measures as national policy? Will the government overcome its overriding concern for social stability and roll back privileges that state-sector employees and retirees have grown accustomed to expect, especially just after it raised their wages for the purpose of mollifying discontent? Even if that is the direction it takes, to what extent can the central government expect or enforce compliance from enterprise administration?

In sum, at the onset of 1990s, China's leadership faces two policy alternatives. Neither promises easy answers. First, it may continue to use the existing social security system (destabilized as it is) to placate state-sector workers who are disheartened by recent political and economic policies. This will probably drain the country's resources at the expense of meeting the needs of a vast working population outside the state sector, and of further economic development. The second policy alternative is for the central government to decisively control social security costs by modifying existing program provisions and instilling discipline in administration. Meanwhile, it can hold out the hope that an improved economic outlook as the country deepens its economic reforms will help alleviate restlessness among its workers.

CHINA'S ENVIRONMENT; ISSUES AND ECONOMIC IMPLICATIONS [1]

By Baruch Boxer [*]

CONTENTS

SUMMARY

We know a good deal about the extent of China's environmental problems, but little about how to measure their economic impacts. Attempts in recent years to introduce innovative, market-based regulatory programs have resulted from increased foreign investment and the activities of multilateral development agencies. These activities, however, are focused on individual industries, enterprises, municipalities, and provinces. Prospects are reasonably good for development of innovative economic strategies to strengthen existing administrative enforcement measures in a few places, like Beijing and Shanghai, where a great deal of money is being invested, and foreign expertise is available. It is unlikely, however, that the central government in the early 1990s has the expertise or will to implement a national program that can respond satisfactorily to China's unique problems of size, physical diversity, resource imbalance, and population concentration. Despite early recognition of the inevitable environmental cost of pursuing the Stalinist development model, China's leaders made their choice, and still continue to live with the consequences.

I. INTRODUCTION: CATEGORIZATION AND INTERPRETATION

Environmental problems in China seriously threaten 1990s economic modernization plans. Technological remedies and regulatory

---

[*] Baruch Boxer, Professor and Chair, Department of Human Ecology, Cook College, Rutgers University, New Brunswick, N.J.

[1] Research for this paper was supported in part by the Committee on Scholarly Communication with the People's Republic of China, National Academy of Sciences and the National Science Foundation. This chapter draws occasionally on Baruch Boxer, "China's Environmental Prospects," *Asian Survey,* Vol. XXIX, No. 7 (July, 1989), pp. 669–686.

controls at national and provincial levels are generally weak and ineffective despite a constitutional guarantee of environmental protection as a "national principle." Economic productivity suffers from pollution and resource degradation in industry, agriculture, fisheries, animal husbandry, forestry, energy, and other sectors. Problems include rural and urban air and water pollution; arable land encroachment, conversion, and reclamation; soil erosion and fertility loss; deforestation; and health effects of random disposal of municipal garbage and hazardous wastes. In some respects, factors contributing to China's poor environmental condition resemble those in other developing countries. Population pressure overwhelms natural systems' ability to remain productive in the face of pollution insults and physical degradation. Ecosystem processes which support food production, waste assimilation, watershed and aquifer recharge, and other functions essential to human welfare are undermined.

Having recognized this there are major difficulties in moving from description of problems to analysis of their significance. How should economic and other policy aspects of China's environmental situation be assessed? Against what standard? At what scale? Do China's domestic environmental problems have international or global dimensions? Understanding environmental change requires that local events and processes be interpreted in relation to wider economic and social impacts. This facilitates cross-national and regional comparison of problems and remedies.

Analyzing economic implications of environmental issues is made difficult by the tendency in recent years to dwell primarily on the extent and magnitude of China's problems. Many accounts tell of polluted water supplies, foul rivers, degraded natural habitats, choking urban air pollution, and other examples of environmental abuse. [2] Problems frequently are put in the worst light by domestic and foreign observers who draw heavily upon dubious official aggregated data on pollution and resource degradation. This deters attempts to look realistically at economic factors in environmental policymaking. Benefits and costs of environmental protection can be considered at several scales, in various time frames, and in relation to a host of ecological and health considerations. Environmental concerns influence in investment decisions, trade patterns, industrial standards, pricing strategies, and management goals in many ways.

In each case, however, there is much uncertainty regarding economic risks and benefits of environmental regulation and investment, and the costs of neglect to people and the environment. Unresolved issues in the long-term debate over clean air legislation in the United States point up the extent of uncertainties even in countries with strong, long-standing commitment to finding economically equitable solutions to problems like air pollution. [3] Formal analysis in China of economic factors to be considered in managing air pollution or any other environmental problem has barely begun.

---

[2] Vaclav Smil, *The Bad Earth* (Armonk, N.Y.: M.E. Sharpe, Incl, 1984).
[3] Peter Passell, "What Price Cleaner Air," *The New York Times*, August 15, 1990, p. D2.

Economically significant issues with environmental ramifications include toxic waste import and recycling, market factors in pollution control equipment import and export, the effects on industrial development of weakened central environmental and land use regulations in southeast coastal provinces and special economic zones, and factors affecting choice of industrial pollution control standards by line ministries and government agencies. Until now, foreign observers of China's environment have mainly described problems. Comprehensive analysis has focused primarily on the politics of agenda-setting, interpretation of laws and regulations, and problems of policy implementation.[4]

Writers on China's environment, moreover, have only begun to explore the connections between domestic and international policy. Global concerns like climate change, biodiversity, soil loss, and deforestation that currently command the greatest international attention are slow to emerge and are unconstrained by national boundaries. They mainly reflect developed country perspectives. China has actively participated in multilateral negotiations on chlorofluorocarbon reduction to protect stratospheric ozone. Here, as in other multilateral discussions of global environmental issues, however, technical questions of appropriate standards, chemical substitutes, legal precedents, and financial risk-benefit delimit the scope of debate on remedial options.

International demands for domestic policy shifts to address global problems like climate change often are unrealistic in light of national conditions. for example, pressure on China to improve energy efficiency and reduce coal use underestimates difficulties of finding politically and economically acceptable alternatives. Problems include dependency on cheap coal and unwillingness or inability of technical and financial institutions in China to support alternative energy and conservation programs like centralized heating systems for cities. It is assumed by foreigners that information availability, technology and capital transfer, and management assistance are sufficient to bring China into line with international environmental norms.[5] This is questionable. A range of potential climate change phenomena (e.g., sea level rise, temperature migration, spatial shifts in biological productivity, increased ultraviolet radiation) could affect domestic economic performance in unknown ways. There has been little study in China (or elsewhere) of relations between economic and environmental impacts of domestic climate change scenarios.

Another problem facing analysts is that oversimplified environmental quality measures are frequently used to compare China with other regions, countries, and to global norms.[6] These indices are often expressed in per capita units. Per capita data are used in many areas including national resource accounting,[7] pollutant dis-

[4] Lester Ross, *Environmental Policy in China*, (Bloomington: Indiana University Press, 1988).
[5] William A. Nitze, "A Proposed Structure for an International Convention on Climate Change, *Science*, 10 August 1990, pp. 606–608.
[6] Qu Geping, "Shijie huanjing wenti de xin fazhan ji wo gwo de duice" [China's Countermeasures to Newly Developing Global Environmental Problems], *Zhongguo uanjing kexue* [China Environmental Science], 1989, 3, pp. 163–168.
[7] Robert Repetto, "Wasting Assets, The Need For National Resource Accounting," *Technology Review*, January, 1990, 39–44.

charge levels, water resources infrastructure and quality, energy utilization, land management, and resource endowment. Simple comparisons, however, tell us very little about how it to interpret the economic or human significance of China's rapidly deteriorating environment, especially since information overload and self-serving report by competing bureaucracies often confuse the picture.[8]

Problem characterization (e.g., "ecological environment," industrial pollution, hazardous waste, etc.) and reports on enforcement pursue well-trodden paths that are either strewn with superficial observations or prejudices of local and foreign critics, or glowingly hortatory and self-serving in the best tradition of Party obfuscation.[9] Seldom are there attempts to frame problems in analytical terms conducive to estimation of the technical or financial feasibility of regulatory or technical management options.

How will environmental constraints affect China's economic modernization? This paper briefly reviews historical and institutional factors, surveys several key problem areas, and concludes with comments on economic implications of policy choices. My purpose is to point up some difficulties in understanding and applying economic factors in assessment of China's environmental experience.

II. BACKGROUND AND CONTEXT

Several factors influence how environment and resource issues have come to be seen, priorities determined, and technical and policy responses framed. Foremost among these are China's size, population, physical and climatic variability, unevenly distributed resource base, and the contributions of environmental science and administrative work through the 1980s. Since the founding of the PRC in 1949, environment and resource questions have been prominent in theoretical discussions of nature-society relations and in debates over how best to deal with the historical legacy of environmental deterioration. This was best exemplified in the 1950s by the prominence given water conservation. There was great urgency in seeking technical and institutional remedies for controlling physical and human impacts of flooding, soil loss, and drought.[10]

Government and Party have since the late 1960s sought to enhance public awareness of pollution, conservation, and environmental health. This is no small achievement, given economic policy shifts, 1980s decentralization of economic decision-making, changing center-local relations, and the daunting challenge of governing a poor country of China's size and regional diversity. Before the 1960s, environment-related work was tied to public health and sanitation [huanjing weisheng]. These efforts, while an important

---

[8] For example, conceptual and statistical problems of interpreting conflicting data on land and water factors in irrigation management are examined in James E. Nickum, Volatile Waters: Is China's Irrigation in Decline?" In Agricultural Reform and Development in China, T. C. Tso. (ed.), (Beltsville, MD: IDEALS, 1990), pp. 284–296.

[9] Daniel Southerland, "China's Industrial Pollution Posing Severe Health Hazards," The Washington Post, August 12, 1990, p. A18. Song Jian, "Xiang huanjing wuran xuanzhan" [Carry on the War Against Environmental Pollution], Huanjing baohu [Environmental Protection], 1989, 7, pp. 2–7.

[10] Tao Shuzeng, Tao Shuzeng zhishui yanlun ji [Collection of Tao Shuzeng's Speeches on Water Management] (Hubei: Keji, 1983).

early affirmation of government and party concern for public welfare, focused mainly on recycling of household garbage and other nontoxic urban and agricultural wastes, and with sanitary engineering and domestic water supply. Until the 1960s, few institutional or technical measures were taken to deal with burgeoning health and environmental impacts of industry, agriculture, urbanization, and energy development.

In the late 1960s and early 1970s, with the strong encouragement of Zhou Enlai, an institutional base for environmental protection was established, and monitoring and regulatory strategies specific to China's needs were formulated. China embarked on a two-fold environmental initiative. In a national program laid out at an August 1973 conference, problems, goals, and implementing strategies were specified. Initial government efforts were backed by ideological principles which promoted pollution control and resource conservation as economically beneficial. Raw materials were to be conserved, industrial processes improved through materials recycling and residuals recovery, and natural productivity sustained."

Social productive forces," presumably emerging from the synergism of nature and society, were to be maximized to assure the well-being of present and future generations. Theoretically, control over nature leads to more "rational" and efficient use of natural resources, and pollution and waste is reduced. In areas as diverse as desert management and fisheries genetics, impressive scientific efforts were made to probe physical and biological aspects of the interaction between people and nature. The aim was to sustain the productivity of natural systems, thereby minimizing harmful effects of economic development on people and the environment.[11]

From the early 1970s through the 1980s, China promulgated wide-ranging environmental laws, regulations, and standards, supported extensive scientific and technical research and monitoring programs through government agencies, line ministries, and educational institutions, and mounted numerous educational and propaganda campaigns in support of environmental protection. Several principles underlie environmental protection in China: as national policy it should guide social and economic development, provide economic incentives and administrative oversight to prevent and reduce pollution, and combine enforcement of regulations with technology and infrastructure improvement for pollution control.[12] Despite a continuous outpouring of laws and regulations since the late 1970s, however, enforcement is weak and uneven.[13]

There are contradictions between local needs and national directives and standards. On the resource side, localities must feed more people in the face of shrinking land resources. Sichuan's population, for example, is over 100 million. Provincial land use regulations of the 1980s prohibit cultivation on mountain slopes steeper than 20 degrees, but land shortage and population pressure in hilly areas throughout the province make a mockery of these standards. Intensive planting on 40 degree or greater slopes is common, lead-

[11] Baruch Boxer, "Environmental Research in China: Achievements and Challenges," *China Exchange News*, 15, 2 (June 1987), pp. 7-11.
[12] Li Ping, "Environmental Protection in China," *Beijing Review*, 33, 29 (July 16-22, 1990), pp. 18-22.
[13] Lester Ross, *op. cit.*, pp. 172-175.

ing to soil erosion, landslides, and rapid reservoir sedimentation.[14] National industrial pollutant discharge guidelines are similarly undermined in many situations where local production needs take precedence over national environmental goals. Chongqing University officials, for example, have for over a decade unsuccessfully appealed to municipal and national agencies to force several polluting industries located below the University along the Changjiang (Yangtze River) to reduce toxic emissions affecting the health of students and faculty.[15] In rapidly developing coastal cities and provinces, moreover, pollution regulations are increasingly ignored.[16]

The 1970s efforts were distinctive in several respects. They strengthened links between ideology and institution-building both in bureaucratic and scientific and technical realms. In the late 1960s and during the 1970s, pollution control was promoted as broadly supportive of conservation and resource recovery. Health and environmental benefits of point-source control were emphasized along with wider national benefits of resource conservation and nature protection. Mid–1970s appeals for improved "three-waste" (liquid, solid, gaseous) recovery were thus couched in terms of the macroeconomic benefits of integrating environmental protection and development. Much original research was done on regulatory and administrative strategies for maintaining environmental quality while pursuing development goals. A distinctively Chinese approach to environmental protection emerged. Efforts of national research and regulatory agencies were also coordinated with provincial and municipal agencies and activities.[17]

Research and policy development was regionally focused with respect to specific problems. Academy of Sciences institutes and universities took the lead in making research findings available to regulatory agencies that carried out monitoring and enforcement. In Dalian, for example, the Institute of Chemical Physics coordinated industrial pollution monitoring and control studies with provincial and municipal line agencies in the northeast and the Beijing-Tianjin region; the Beijing Institute of Geography took the lead in sophisticated studies of relations between land source and marine pollution in Bo Hai Bay; the desert research institute in Lanzhou coordinated desert control studies and programs with provincial agencies in the northwest; and Academy of Sciences, provincial, and State Oceanic Administration fisheries research institutes in Guangdong and Fujian coordinated their work with researchers in Zhongshan and other universities to control effects of land source pollution on coastal marine fisheries.

China also participated in the 1972 Stockholm U.N. Conference on the Human Environment. She asserted herself as a major participant in emerging international discussions of global environmental issues, especially issues like "pollution export," which served to solidify China's identification with Third World interests

---

[14] Personal communication, Prof. Gu Hengyue, Chongqing University, June, 1988.

[15] Personal communication, University officials, Chongqing University, June 1988.

[16] Daniel Southerland, *op. cit.* See below for further discussion of the situation in the Southeast.

[17] Qu Geping, "Environmental Protection in China: A Brief History," *Chinese Geography and Environment*, Vol. 2, 3 (Fall, 1989), pp. 3–29.

in North-South debates on pollution causes and remedies. Poor countries blamed industrialized countries for causing pollution and resource destruction through their own development and exploitation of resources in developing countries. Poor countries equated pollution with poverty, and maintained that environmental problems could only be solved with technical and economic support from rich countries to assist their development. China was an outspoken advocate of this position throughout the 1970s.

Yet in China it is especially difficult to establish criteria for weighing the costs of doing nothing or something about environmental problems. While problems are interconnected in China as elsewhere, the China case poses special challenges beyond those of size, physical constraints and population pressure on resources. For instance, there is no tradition, as in the West, of neoclassical cost-benefit analysis to test assumptions about how to value natural resources in relation to short or long-term human welfare goals. Nor is there sensitivity to the time value (discount rate) of investment in environmental infrastructure or nature conservation in weighing present versus future environmental and health benefits and costs. Capital investment decisions are the product of a complex system where rivalry among territorial units and bureaucracies and competition among high level agencies for investment funds determines project priority. Most important, cost-benefit concerns seldom enter into the planning process, and capital is not valued as a commodity.[18]

China has for over 20 years forged its own perspectives on what its environmental problems are and how they should be thought about and managed. While it is easy for outsiders to criticize perceived shortcomings in policy development and enforcement, no other poor country has developed a more extensive institutional, research, and educational base for environmental programs. What should be expected of China, given the spotty record of Western countries, including the United States? Why should China be held to a higher standards?

III. MAJOR ENVIRONMENTAL CHALLENGES

Impacts of environmental problems are made worse in China by economic policies that since 1949 give highest priority to industrial and agricultural production. Legal and regulatory directives in recent years to foster environmental sensitivity in the selection of project sites and in their operation have been only partially effective.[19]

Construction of large water, industrial, agricultural, and energy projects like dams and storage reservoirs, irrigation schemes, thermal and nuclear power plants, mines, petrochemical complexes, and steel mills have devastating effects. They severely damage

---

[18] David M. Lampton, "Water Politics and Economic Change in China," *China's Economy Looks Toward the Year 2000*, Vol. I, The Four Modernizations. Selected Papers Submitted to the Joint Economic Committee, Congress of the United States, May 21, 1986 (Washington: U.S. Government Printing Office, 1986).

[19] Li Ping, *op. cit.*; Vanessa Lide, "The Perils of Pollution," *The China Business Review*, July-August, 1990, pp. 32–37; for a somewhat more optimistic view on legal enforcement potential see Lester Ross et al., "Cracking Down on Polluters," *The China Business Review*. July–August, 1990, pp. 38–43.

forest, grassland, mountain, freshwater, marine, and other ecosystems. Growth policies thus contradict and call into question the sincerity of official pronouncements on the need to balance economic growth and environmental conservation. These contradictions reflect the challenges and unique circumstances of various problem areas. Water pollution, energy/environment issues, and waste management are illustrative.

A. WATER

Water pollution is China's most pressing environmental problem because of its widespread, direct impact on human health and natural productivity. Water pollution results from interrelated natural and human causes. These include severe water shortages in the north and in some southern coastal areas. China's annual surface water runoff volume of 264 million m^3 is the world's sixth largest, but uneven distribution of ground and surface water, as well as erratic precipitation patterns, results in regional shortages and difficulties in maintaining timely water availability for agriculture and industry. The Changjiang (Yangtze) Basin, and areas to the south and southwest, for example, have only 33 percent of China's total cultivated land, but nearly 70 percent of the country's water resources. Over the years, there have been many proposed schemes for transferring water from south to north. Ecological and health implications of these schemes have been studied, but debates have mainly centered on costs and engineering feasibility.[20]

Excessive "mining" of groundwater and loss of surface water through poor construction and maintenance of storage facilities contributes to water shortages. Other causes include industrial waste discharge and modification and reclamation of lakes and fresh water and coastal wetlands for urban, industrial, and agricultural development. This leads to species loss, polluted drinking water, aquifer contamination from salt water intrusion, and estuarine siltation. Pressure on rural water supply and deteriorating water quality also results from high agricultural chemical use, poor drainage, and the recent explosive growth of rural industries, especially in southeast coastal areas. In 1987, there were approximately 15 million rural enterprises for building materials, food processing, textile and chemical manufacturing, and other light industry activities. They employ about 80 million people. Few enterprises can treat wastewater, and it is mostly discharged untreated into rural waterways.

Good water supply and management have been crucial to China's economic success since ancient times. Economic activity in China has centered on roughly 5000 river basins with watersheds greater than 100 sq. km. River basins defined China spatially and socially, and focused defense, food supply, marketing, water conservancy, transport, and other key economic activities. These basins still are basic support systems of the national economy because rivers and streams provide surface water, restore groundwater, and collect and disperse wastes. They also serve as the physical base for con-

---

[20] "Diversion of Project Gets a Blueprint," *Beijing Review*, 33, 37 (September 10–16, 1990), p. 11.

struction of flood control, irrigation, storage, and power generating works. A major reason for current widespread water pollution is that natural functions have been undermined through failure to adapt traditional knowledge and practice to modern requirements, as has been done in France, the Netherlands, and other Western European countries.

Recent official views on water supply and pollution emphasize conservation and more effective water reutilization to compensate for inadequate natural supply.[21] Other policy remedies have called for greater attention to demand (economic), rather than supply (engineering) approaches to water management. Price reforms to remove subsidies and foster conservation have not been introduced to any substantial degree, however, although there has been much talk of the need for reforms. Water is priced so low that there are few economic incentives to conserve or reuse water industry and agriculture. Competition for capital investment funds for water projects among political jurisdictions has also hindered attempts to price water more realistically to foster conservation.[22]

Reduction of industrial water pollution, which makes up 70–80 percent of China's total wastewater load, is a top government priority. There has been some success in combining waste reduction, biological treatment, and process modification in smaller installations, and many new factories are required to install pollution control devices. There is little consistency from province to province, however, in use of technical controls or enforcement of discharge standards. Nationally, industrial waste discharge remains the most serious sources of contamination of drinking water crops, and fish and shellfish resources.

Total wastewater discharge in China in 1988 was estimated at roughly 40 billion m[3]. Aggregate supply and demand statistics, however, are not very useful for policy planning except as they can help to clarify specific problems and needs of agriculture, industry, and households. These estimates require confidence in data accuracy, and in assumptions underlying statistical analysis of supply and demand factors affecting water quality, price and the availability of water for various purposes. Date, unfortunately, are notoriously unreliable. There are frequent discrepancies between official sources in reporting wastewater discharge levels.[23] In consistent and excessive data from several agencies with overlapping jurisdictions also reflects poor reporting and interpretation of monitoring results. The National Environmental Protection Agency (NEPA) is unable to coordinate policies and assessments on a national scale. This not surprising, in that NEPA has limited authority and staff (about 300) to implement technical programs. Implementation and enforcement responsibilities mainly rest with bureaus in line min-

[21] Ye Yongyi, "Tigao shuili jianshe jingji xiaoyi de tujing" (Improve Prospects for Economic Efficiency in Water Resources Development), *Kexue yanjiu lunwen ji, Shui ziyuan* (Collection of Scientific Research Papers, Water Resources) (Beijing: Shuili dianli 1983), No. 14, pp. 170–178; Chen Shangkui, "Woguo shuili shiye chengji zhuozhu" (Our Nation's Outstanding Achievements in Water Management), *Dilki Zhishi* (Geographical Knowledge), 4, 1990, 3.

[22] David M. Klampton, *op. cit.*, pp. 387–406.

[23] Final Report of the International Workshop on the Control of Environmental Pollution in China, 12–18 February 1990, Beijing. Prepared for the United Nations Development Program and the State Science and Technology Council (sic) by Richard A. Carpenter, Environment and Policy Institute, East-West Center, p. 12 (henceforth, *Final Report*); Li Ping, *op. cit.*, p. 22.

istries and with thinly-staffed provincial and lower-level environmental units.

Industrial discharge also contributes to the recent sharp decline of fresh water resources in China. Mid–1980s studies indicate that over a quarter of fresh water in lakes, rivers and aquifers is polluted, and water quality is declining rapidly. Already, nearly 25 percent of water flowing in 53,000 km of rivers is unsuitable for irrigation or domestic use, and 86 percent of river water flowing through urban areas is too polluted for irrigation or aquaculture. Surveys of groundwater quality in 47 cities revealed that 43 of them were dependent on groundwater containing toxic contaminants at levels exceeding state water quality standards.

The ubiquity of water pollution challenges national, provincial, and local governments to control individual pollution sources and to coordinate efforts among sectors. Although, on paper, environmental bureaucracies are vertically linked from national to local levels to facilitate research, information exchange, monitoring, and enforcement, for achieving significant reduction of water pollution and improvement control for the nation as a whole are poor.

A major problem is that officials responsible for water pollution in environmental protection, agriculture, urban construction, planning, and water development agencies seldom interact. Environmental agencies are marginalized by politically powerful line ministries, and find it increasingly difficult to enforce laws and regulations through administrative, legal, or economic means. Agency fragmentation and poor coordination hinders policy implementation. For example, a high-level workshop on pollution in China, sponsored by the State Science and Technology Commission and the United Nations Development Program, was held in February, 1990. The workshop report noted that Ministry of Health experts on environmental health were not in attendance. This was seen as seriously weakening prospects for implementing workshop recommendations to improve institutional response to the health effects of water pollution.[24]

B. ENERGY

China is amply endowed with coal (the world's second largest reserves), there is underutilized hydropower potential, and many thermal and nuclear electric generating plants, with associated power grids, are being built throughout the country.[25] In aggregate terms, energy supply from various sources appears adequate for development needs in the 1990s, despite the current financial crisis in the petroleum industry which supplies about 18 percent of China's energy. By comparison, coal provides 76 percent of the country's industrial energy, hydropower 5 percent, and natural gas 2 percent. Problems in the oil industry stem from unrealistic underpricing (now about U.S. $2.00/barrel, compared with a 1980 price U.S. of $9.00), a problem shared with other state-subsidized energy sectors. State oil companies are also reticent to allow foreign oil companies to engage in onshore exploration and production, offshore produc-

---

[24] *Final Report*, p. 8.
[25] ref to Fridley chapter, "China's Energy Outlook."

tion is not at anticipated levels despite heavy investment over the past decade, and there is a continuing need to export about 400,000 barrels of oil a day to earn scarce foreign exchange.[26]

Energy and environmental issues are closely related, but it is difficult to define cost-effective strategies for remedying existing environmental problems and avoiding new ones. The problem is that national energy planning and policy development are not considering energy production impacts on health and the environment. China by necessity will increase its reliance on coal as primary energy source, thereby intensifying already serious air pollution. This will occur even if more flue gas desulphurizing devices ("scrubbers") can be installed in large industries, a doubtful prospect in the presently constrained fiscal climate.

A major reason for mounting energy-related environmental problems is wasteful use of coal to generate electricity that is carried over power grids to grossly inefficient heavy industries. Heavy industry consumes roughly 65 percent of power generated nationally. But China's steel industry uses more than twice as much energy to produce a ton of steel as producers in Western countries or Japan.[27] Energy shortages occur because of both regional imbalance in availability of coal and other energy resources, and poor interregional transportation. The country relies too heavily on centrally distributed power linked to urban and industrial centers, with rural areas undersupplied. More efficient use of existing energy sources, especially hydropower, would better satisfy local needs with reduced environmental costs, and there would be less need for large generating plants.

Although China's coal is generally of good quality, with relatively low sulfur and ash content, high consumption levels and inefficient combustion in industry and households (cooking briquets) results in harmful levels of suspended particulates, sulphur dioxide (SO_2), and carbon monoxide (CO). Pollutant loadings in most urban areas exceed state standards and, especially in northern cities, contribute to high incidence of respiratory disease. Uncontrolled motor vehicle emissions, a growing, but unaddressed problem, aggravates air pollution in urban airsheds. Source breakdown of total suspended particulates and SO_2 from coal combustion is approximately: industry 43 percent; domestic use, 23 percent; thermal power generation, 24 percent; coking plants, 8 percent; and locomotives, 3 percent.[28]

Acid precipitation affects many areas of China including the Chongquing-Yibin area in Sichuan, Guiyang in Guizhou Province, the Liuzhao area of Guangxi Zhuang Autonomous Region, parts of Hunan, Guangzhou.[29] There is superficial evidence of damage to crops, trees, and fresh water bodies, but there has been little careful research on actual sources and sinks and on the dynamics of inter-regional atmospheric transport of pollutants. Secondary

[26] Sheryl WuDunn, "Hopes Fades as Output of Oil Lags in China," *The New York Times*, September 3, 1990, p. 32.
[27] Vaclav Smil, "Missing Energy Perspectives," in *Damming the Three Gorges*, Grainne Ryder e.d., (Toronto: Probe International, 1990), p. 102–103.
[28] *Final Report*, p.6.
[29] Li Ping, *op. cit.*, p. 22.

sources estimate 1 billion yuan in annual damage to farm crops from acid rain.[30]

A basic obstacle to reducing air pollution is the absence of comprehensive and reliable source emission data as well as enforceable control policies. Because mid-1980s emissions survey data have not been made available for national-level impact assessment, it has been impossible to develop effective monitoring and cost assessment procedures to plan and implement national control strategies for industry. These could include using limestone injection in conventional boiler systems, fluidized bed combustion, and other sulfur capture technologies.[31]

Another frequently overlooked energy-related environmental issue is the acute shortage of household fuel in the countryside. Growing demand for household fuel contributes to land loss and deforestation, thereby affecting agricultural productivity. Trees are felled for firewood, and plant stalks (estimated 400 million tons annually) are burned for household fuel rather than plowed under to enhance soil structure and fertility. Risk of erosion and land loss through desert encroachment is also increased, especially in northern arid areas. In the south, biogas generation has partially ameliorated farm household energy shortage (mainly for domestic cooking and preparation of feed for pigs), although biogas generation is feasible only in hot areas with ample supply of organic waste materials. Rural electricity supply could be increased with minimum environmental damage through greater reliance on small-scale hydropower stations. Despite problems with local sedimentation and inappropriate design of facilities for some locations, about 70,000 installations are used in over three-quarters of China's 2,133 counties, with a third of the countries relying on these small facilities for most of their power.[32]

Construction of hydroelectric and thermal power plants, water storage and flood control reservoirs, power lines, and other energy-related structures has wide and immediate social and ecological impact. Especially in the crowded eastern third of the country, construction displaces many people, destroys precious agricultural land and natural habitats, induces erosion from site preparation, pollutes water bodies, and increases deforestation. Offshore oil drilling and production platforms also contribute to marine pollution in biologically productive nearshore areas, although there has been better control in recent years, especially in Bo Hai Bay, an important oil and gas production area.

Environment impacts of energy development are felt at many levels. As with water pollution, however, impacts are difficult to manage comprehensively because of poor program coordination among national and provincial agencies. Separate bureaucracies are responsible for nuclear, hydropower, coal, and petroleum industries. In 1988, the State Council sought to streamline energy bureaucracies by removing the electric power element of the Ministry of Water Resources and Electric Power. The electric power bu-

---

[30] Vanessa Lide, *op. cit.*, p. 34.
[31] *Final Report*, pp. 2–4.
[32] Vaclav Smil, "Missing Energy Perspectives," in *Damming the Three Gorges*, ed. Grainne Ryder (Toronto: Probe International, 1990), p. 105.

reaucracy was merged with other energy groups, although it is not clear if this has improved national policy planning and program implementation.

It is doubtful that administrative measures alone can significantly reduce pollution and ecological impacts of construction and operation of energy production, processing, and distribution facilities. Prospects for improved policy coordination among government agencies became weaker in the 1980s as bureaus, agencies, and research units spawned quasi-governmental corporations to facilitate cooperation with foreign investors and firms. In the early 1990s, in a period of fiscal austerity, it remains to be seen whether this openness will continue. Resistance to foreign contacts on the part of the oil industry has been mentioned, although wider state control in oil and other energy sectors does not necessarily imply that there will be more attention paid to environmental concerns in energy development and distribution. Limited environmentally benign solar, wind, and tidal energy production capability has been achieved, but soft energy contributions to easing environmental impacts remain insignificant.

C. WASTE MANAGEMENT

Despite this foundation, in the 1990s China is faced with overwhelming pollution prevention and cleanup tasks. This is not surprising. Many of today's challenges stem from he leadership's failure in the 1960s to heed those who warned that continued pursuit of Soviet-style development, based on profligate resource use in heavy industry for short-term production gain, would ultimately lead to environmental disaster. Failure to sustain a productive relationship between natural and human systems, the key to China's longevity, is bound to have harmful social and economic, as well as ecological effects.

The traditional system sought maximum efficiency in the exchange and conservation of energy, moisture, labor, and materials. This was expressed physically and culturally in the interplay of soil, water, animals, plants, and people, even in areas like North China with difficult growing conditions. For centuries, engineering and agronomic skills were combined in complex agroecosystems which supplied human needs in face of formidable natural constraints and population pressure. Food crops, aquatic products, and medicinal herbs, along with cash and industrial crops like tung oil, ramine, tea, and pig bristles, were produced interdependently. Forty years of rampant, capital-intensive development, however, has damaged the biological resilience of the productive base. Soil quality, watershed integrity, biodiversity, and clean air and water have suffered.

This decline is well-illustrated in problems of waste management. Traditionally, exchange of organic and nontoxic materials (human and animal waste, vegetables, household garbage, broken glass, etc.) between city and country supported sustained use of densely settled zones near urban centers for food supply. Favorable economies of waste recycling and agricultural production were achieved in spatially-delimited urban-rural exchange zones. The shape and extent of these zones depended upon access to transportation, efficiency of marketing systems, soil fertility, and food price dynamics which governed supply and demand. Labor was never a problem. Nutrients and energy (from food, fertilizer from human waste, and labor) were "cycled" back and forth from city to country, to use the prescient terminology of the American soil scientist, James Thorp, who clearly described the process in the Shanghai area in the late 1930s.[33]

Similar processes were at work as recently as the early 1980s in Shanghai, where complex contractual ties listed between urban districts and municipal recycling and wastewater treatment bureaus to exchange vegetables and other foodstuffs for human waste, organic garbage, and materials like pottery shards and broken bricks. Urban to rural exports were used to fertilizer, compost pile construction, and fowl and animal feed. These arrangements were being rapidly displaced by the mid-1980s, however, as increased market demand for vegetables and desire for quicker harvests and higher profits from private vegetable plots led to greatly increased use of chemical fertilizer, herbicides, and pesticides.[34] Chemical runoff, along with industrial and housing development, has severely polluted soil and waterways in rural Shanghai counties. The sustainable, organic foundation is effectively destroyed.

Evidence of rapid decline in traditional waste recycling capability is clear from recently released statistics. Official sources now report that nationally, only a small portion of solid industrial wastes and urban garbage is being recycled. In 1988, only 26 percent of 560 million tons of solid industrial waste and slag materials from industries and mines were reprocessed, and cities are increasingly surrounded by piles of industrial and mining wastes and garbage for which authorities have not disposal options.[35] Even more disturbing is the seriousness of the hazardous waste disposal problem.

Very few industrialized countries (e.g., Denmark, Sweden, and parts of Germany) have effective hazardous waste management programs. Successful efforts must combine economic incentives, reliable technologies, and administrative authority to assure that waste is either reduced at source or rendered harmless to people and the environment through pyrolysis or other treatment processes. Administrative, economic, and technical components of programs must be coordinated and effectively integrated. This involves source reduction, collection, recycling, and treatment of household, municipal, and industrial wastes. National programs should be supported by public policies that provide tax and other incentives that assure profitable returns at each level of operation and lead to maximum participation of waste generators. China today has no effective hazardous waste management program, and prospects for developing a program are remote.

Failure of the traditional organic recycling system in urban areas is compounded by the overwhelming burden of having to manage nontraditional wastes from industries, mines, and rural en-

---

[33] James Thorp, *Geography in the Soils of China*, (Nanking, 1937).
[34] Personal communications, officials of Changcheng (Great Wall) Commune, Shanghai, June, 1982.
[35] Li Ping, *op. cit.*, p. 22.

terprises. A recent review of the problem identifies chromium wastes, wastes from electroplating, textile dyeing, and leather processing industries, and township and village enterprise wastes, as priority concerns. Suggested remedial measures for chromium wastes include waste minimization, slag pile stabilization, and landfill construction. Chromium wastes have already seriously contaminated drinking water wells in the vicinity of mines and processing works.[36]

Electroplating shops, to take one example, are small, numerous, and scattered throughout large and small cities. There are over 300 in Shanghai and 200 in Beijing alone. This makes it difficult to apply effective controls in individual cases, and to introduce centralized waste collection and treatment operations. It is even more difficult to implement source reduction and recycling policies in the millions of small rural enterprises that have sprung up throughout the countryside in the past decade. The Chinese government has given lip service to controlling this growth as a long-term solution to the waste generation problem, but there is little evidence that this is being done. In fact, devolution of economic decision-making from center to local government levels in recent years mitigates against prospects for effective waste management in these enterprises.[37]

IV. ECONOMIC IMPLICATIONS AND PROSPECTS

Economic policies directly influence environmental protection programs and outcomes. In principle, economic analysis of environmental issues in industrially advanced countries helps inform choice of regulatory options. Mutually satisfactory balance between technical and administrative solutions is seldom achieved, however, because conflicts among government regulators, polluters, and public interest groups often lead to lengthy litigation. As noted above, some disputes remain unsolved for long periods, as with clean air legislation in the United States. Agreement in the U.S. Congress on updating 1977 technical amendments to the Clean Air Act, for example, took over ten years to negotiate.[38]

In China, there is no public participation in environmental law-drafting and management. Public protests over pollution insults to health, or damage to resources (e.g. in agriculture, aquatic products, animal husbandry, or forestry), may lead to improved local controls in isolated cases. Responsibility for policymaking in China, however, still lies with the government. Most important, economic aspects of environmental and resource problems in China still must be initially addressed from the narrow perspective of Party views on acceptable strategies and goals.[39] This differs from many Western countries, the Soviet Union and Eastern Europe, developing nations like Brazil, India, and Mexico. Increasingly, citizen activists influence policymaking through litigation, lobbying of legislative

---

[36] *Final Report*, pp. 15–17.
[37] Dali Yang, "Patterns of China's Regional Development Strategy," *The China Quarterly*, 122 (June, 1990), pp. 256–257.
[38] Peter Passell, *op. cit.*; Keither Schnieder, "Lawmakers Reach an Accord on Reduction in Air Pollution," *The New York Times*, October 23, 1990, p. A1.
[39] Song Jian, *op. cit.*

bodies, government agencies, and professional groups, and by raising public awareness through rallies and protests.

Even in the late 1970s and early 1980s, a time of active (and often productive) searching for theoretical rationales to link environmental protection and economic policy, Chinese analysts were straightjacketed by the need to develop policy in response to vaguely defined theoretical assumptions based on Party dogma. The prevailing wisdom of the time viewed laws of nature and the economy as complementary dialectical poles. Central planners were expected to find ways of "rationally" balancing investment in development and conservation at local and national levels, to avoid pollution excesses while facilitating essential economic growth. The larger aim was to sustain productivity in keeping with "the laws of proportional development," a vague spatial planning concept never meaningfully applied at a national scale. Experiments aimed at adapting theory to local needs, however, were tried in some provinces.[40]

During the 1980s, as China's command economy weakened, consideration of economic dimensions of environmental issues has shifted from broad theoretical approaches to a more specific focus on local and regional concerns. Emphasis has been on finding solutions to specific industrial siting and pollution control problems, nature and habitat protection,[41] and strengthening of urban water supply and wastewater treatment infrastructure to reduce harmful effects of contaminated water.

China's main problem in formulating environmental policy has been inability at the national level to frame regulatory strategies that can be consistently and effectively applied throughout the country. There have been frequent shifts in emphasis among ideological, administrative, planning, legal, and economic approaches. This has made it difficult to set clear environmental goals, and to establish criteria for policies to achieve these goals. There has been much confusion over ends and means in environmental protection. One reason is that the uncertain progress of price and fiscal reforms has slowed emergence of market mechanisms that might improve efficiency in land and resource use and lead to improved resource conservation and materials recycling. Prospects for creative environmental policy development in the present period of economic retrenchment are uncertain.

Progress will depend to a large degree on the rate and level of investment in environmental protection. Several questions arise. Should domestic and foreign investment be directed at technical upgrading of pollution control capability in factories, mines, cities, and provinces, or should investment primarily support institution-building, technical training, education, and public awareness? What are the sources of investment funds? At present, Japan and The World Bank are the main sources of funding to support envi-

[40] See Shi Zhengxin, "Economic Readjustment and Environmental Protection," *Lanzhou Gansu Ribao*, April 23, 1982, JPRS-Worldwide Report, Environmental Quality, September 10, 10982, pp. 19–22 for an account of Gansu's experience in the early 1980s; see also Zhou uxiang, "Solving the Problem of Environmental Protection and Economic Policy," *Hongqi*, 13, July 1, 1982, JPRS-Worldwide Report, Environmental Quality, September 10, 1982, pp. 12–18.

[41] Meng Sha, "Woguo guojiaji ziran baohuqu de jianshe" [Construction of Our Country's national-level nature Protection Preserves], *Dili Zhishi* [Geographical Knowledge], September 1989.

ronmental improvement in China, although loan prospects are still uncertain because of international reaction to the June, 1989 Tianenmen incident. An environmental investment strategy and allocation plan for China are currently under development by that Bank.[42]

Prospects for implementing an effective national environmental investment strategy are also clouded by the growing economic independence of Guangdon and Fujian. In recent years, this independence has weakened central ability to enforce regulatory programs in fast-growing coastal areas.[43] Despite the slowdown in foreign investment in China since 1988, there has been a rapid increase in Taiwanese industrial investment in Fujian, especially around Xiamen. Through early 1990, about 500 Taiwan investors invested $1 billion in consumer goods factories that produce bicycles, appliances, clothing, and shoes.[44] To facilitate investment, local authorities sell "land use rights" for up to 70 years to speculators who have little concern for environmental protection. For example, Wang Yung-ching, the powerful head of Taiwan's Formosa Plastics Group, has been discussing with Chinese authorities for several years the possibility of building a $7 billion petrochemical complex in Fujian. A major attraction of the proposed Fujian site is that it would not be subject to stringent environmental controls. Wang was deterred from building the project in Taiwan by intense pressure from environmentalists.[45]

Finally, there are several ways in which regulators can employ tax and fiscal incentives to further pollution control objectives. These include buying and selling pollution rights to stimulate cost-effective pollution clean-up, introducing least-cost, long-term investment strategies at municipal or provincial levels to foster integrated technical and institutional response to pollution, and recycling effluent fees to factories to improve technical controls. None of these measures, however, are effective on a national scale. The Environmental Protection Law, passed by the Standing Committee of the National People's Congress in December 1989, establishes norms and codifies many existing regulations. It was intended also to improve the efficiency of an effluent fee and rebate system introduce in the 1980s, which has led to reduced pollution in some large industries. However, low fee structures, misleading assumptions in pollutant discharge assessment, and technical flaws in the rebate return system have weakened the effectiveness of this regulatory tool.[46]

Clearly, China's leaders are well aware of the serious environmental problems the country faces. Nevertheless, as is the case in most developing countries, the quest for economic modernization has superceded concern over environmental pollution. Formal analysis of environmental policy issues has barely begun and given

[42] Personal communications, World Bank officials, September–October 1990.
[43] Enforcement problems in the marine environmental area were described by officials of the State Oceanic Administration, Beijing, personal communication, June, 1988.
[44] Adi Ignatius, "China's Old Enemies, Capitalist Taiwanese, Investment in the Mainland," *The Asian Wall Street Journal Weekly*, August 6, 1990, p.1.
[45] James McGregor, "Headstrong Tycoon Defies Pursues Huge China Investment Plan," *The Asian Wall Street Journal Weekly*, August 20, 1990, p. 11.
[46] Lester Ross et al., "Cracking Down on Polluters," *The China Business Review*, July–August 1990, pp. 38–43.

budgetary constraints, institutional inadequacies, and lack of recognition by the population of the seriousness of the pollution problem, China environment is not likely to see much improvement during the decade of the 1990s.

THE ECONOMIC COSTS OF INTELLECTUAL ALIENATION

By Carol Lee Hamrin *

CONTENTS

No one will question the importance to China's future of the loyalty and active contribution of its tiny (16 million) intellectual elite with a tertiary-level education—the faculty and (2 million) students of major educational institutions, professionals working in official research and administrative organs, and specialists in factories, hospitals, and farms.[1] The state's ability to mobilize the creativity of this group may determine whether China becomes a major power or remains a Third World country. Highly educated Chinese must be at the forefront of the immense changes still required to rejuvenate and modernize Chinese culture and society and make China competitive in the high-tech, post-industrial world of the twenty-first century. In a post-industrial era, moreover, the state's relationship with this group will greatly affect the extent of regime legitimacy and the effectiveness of its authority. For an increasing

* Chinese Affairs Specialist at the Department of State and Professorial Lecturer, the Johns Hopkins University School of Advanced International Studies (SAIS). This paper is based on a talk presented at the SAIS "China Forum" in February 1990 and represents the author's personal views, not official views of the U.S. Government.
[1] The 1990 census recorded 16,124,678 persons with a college education, including junior college. See a report in *Beijing Review* (November 12-18, 1990), pp. 21-23. Sun Ling sought to differentiate between the "more than 20 million mainstream intellectuals" and the "very, very small—less than one in 10,000" of them who were the source of bourgeois liberalization and of the Spring 1989 "turmoil." See "Correctly Treating Intellectuals," *Banyuetan* (Bi-monthly Chats) 13 (10 July 1990), p. 14, 15, in Foreign Broadcast Information Service China Daily Report [hereafter FBIS–CHI]–90–159 (16 August 1990), p. 19-20. Guo Lihua and Jiang Zhimin pointed to the serious problem China faces in guaranteeing jobs for its graduates and referred to 500,000 students who graduated in 1989 and 2 million students studying in universities as of 1990. See "An Investigation of Job Assignments for University Graduates and Thoughts Related to it," *Liaowang* [Outlook] 26 (25 June 1990), pp. 29-32, in FBIS–CHI–90–136 (16 July 1990), p. 31.

proportion of state officials is well-educated, and shares the values and interests of intellectuals, as well as personal ties of obligation based on school affiliation.

Yet both the willingness of and opportunity for intellectuals to cooperate with the state toward national goals is now quite uncertain. The leadership's use of violence to resolve state-society conflict at Tiananmen in the spring of 1989, and the ensuing repression and alienation of intellectuals as well as other social groups, has been a personal tragedy for thousands and a national disaster for China. Spring 1989 marked a highly inauspicious entrance into an era of pluralistic politics for the PRC. The polarization between the regime and urban society marked by the confrontation of 1989 was exacerbated by the state's persistence throughout 1990 to reject global trends toward pluralism and prolong recentralizing economic and social policies. This essay will first review the changes in intellectual life in the 1980s that gave birth to opposition politics, and then suggest some of the costs of the open conflict of 1989 and continuing subsurface confrontation in terms of China's modernization program. These significant costs can be sketched in broad brush strokes, although not quantified.

I. THE EVOLUTION TOWARD PLURALISTIC POLITICS IN THE 1980S

The deep roots of the events of 1989 can be found in the previous decade-long transformation of the mental tools and values of the urban, informed Chinese citizenry. Intellectuals were at the vanguard of this "conceptual revolution" and mediated the change for other groups by articulating, debating and dispersing new ideas through the media. A number of the key mediators became involved in the demonstrations and since have been vilified by the leadership as the "scum" of China's intellectuals, e.g. not representative of the mainstream. But in the current environment such slander seems convincing evidence of the strong and continuing influence of their ideas. This tiny but critical subgroup of intellectuals located primarily in Beijing and Shanghai were involved *de facto* in high-level politics by virtue of their national stature as official advisers, researchers, and artists who articulated sensitive issues impinging on regime legitimacy and authority. They were the intellectual pace-setters, cultural pioneers, and opinion-shapers whose thoughts and feelings portended what is to come for the rest of the populace influenced by the mass media—perhaps half of China's total population.[2]

It is impossible to say how many of China's 20 million college graduates share the ideas and commitments of this tiny group of critical intellectuals. There are many distinctions among intellectuals based on class background, generation, profession, and geographic location. Different networks of personal ties and rivalries divide them as well. Presumably, many technically-trained people running factories care more about bread and butter issues than political matters. Moreover, the reputations of some individual dissi-

---

[2] Hong Kong *Ta Kung Pao*, 19 November 1981, estimated that the PRC television audience that year had rapidly reached 36% of the population, or 360 million, compared with an estimated 20–30 million in 1978. Numbers of both television owners and viewers continued to grow at phenomenal rates through the decade.

dents, especially those who left China, have been tarnished in the eyes of their colleagues and the public by actions taken last Spring. Yet the body of ideas generated collectively among the articulate elite still resonate strongly, especially among younger generations. The intellectual revolution will continue, despite the ebbs and flows of economics and politics.

The base line for measuring the 1980s "conceptual revolution" of China's critical intellectuals is their traditional role as assistant and adviser to the leadership in the art of governance, and priest to the people, teaching them proper moral values. In the traditional Chinese view of authority, the exercise of moral and political power was the exclusive right of the state. If there were conflicts, the job of the intellectuals was to voice the inarticulate "murmurings of the people" to the ruler and, through moral suasion, convince the emperor to stem corruption and abuse of power while educating the people to obey.

In the modern era of nationalism, these views of authority resulted in a concept of patriotism that equated loyalty to the nation with loyalty to the state. After 1949, this traditional statism fit well with what may be called the Leninist myth—that the party's interests were the same as those of the society as a whole; that the party was omniscient and infallible; and that absolute and unquestioning loyalty and service was therefore due the party. In practical terms, unlike in traditional and early modern society, there was no independent source of status, employment or income for intellectuals, as the single party-state bureaucracy enforced its right to direct all sectors of society. No competing center of moral, intellectual, or political power was tolerated. Intellectuals seeking a sphere of autonomy were time and again the prime targets of repressive mass campaigns, as the political elite sought to reinforce its monopoly on power with technical and organizational resources much stronger than in traditional society. Even in less coercive times, regime determination of permissible language and thought, and control over information, created a climate of self-censorship that minimized critical thought. This combination of ideology and organization produced a modern version of the traditional scholar-officials—what might be called "establishment intellectuals," highly dependent on the state psychologically, organizationally, and financially.[3]

Current state policy is to reinforce this traditional role for the intellectuals, and most Chinese intellectuals believe that this is their ideal role. Certainly, in the current atmosphere the only means of political security is to adopt this stance outwardly. But in a number of fundamental ways, intellectuals have been breaking with tradition and exploring multiple new roles in society. The Spring 1989 crisis was only the latest step in a long process of intellectual emancipation that was speeded up and made irreversible once the leadership decided in the late 1970s to open up China to external ideas and intellectual exchange.

---

[3] For a more detailed discussion of the role of establishment intellectuals in China, both traditional and modern, see Carol Lee Hamrin and Timothy Cheek, *China's Establishment Intellectuals* (White Plains, N.Y.: M.E. Sharpe, Inc., 1986), and the introduction to Merle Goldman, Timothy Cheek and Carol Lee Hamrin, *Chinese Intellectuals and the State: Search for a New Relationship* (Cambridge, Mass.: Harvard University Contemporary China series no. 3, 1987).

A. SPIRITUAL BREAKTHROUGH

The terrifying and degrading experiences of intellectuals during the Cultural Revolution produced a spiritual rejection of the statist mindset and a commitment to personal fulfillment; this is fundamental to what is happening today. By the time Mao died, if not long before, most thinking people—and especially the Red Guard generation—had lost the blind faith in the party so dominant in the 1950s. Cynicism and aversion to political activism replaced the worship of Mao and willing service to the communist cause. The reforms of the post-Mao leadership have been driven by the imperative to redress this "crisis of confidence."

B. IDEOLOGICAL BREAKTHROUGH

In the early 1980s, the political and cultural elite forged a new cooperative relationship as they worked to undermine the political base for remnant Maoists and create a new constituency for reform within the one-party system. Nevertheless, there emerged an ideological departure from the total dependency of the Mao era to a new relationship of mutual dependence, which had been attempted only sporadically and unsuccessfully in previous decades. As the goal of modernization replaced that of class struggle, the state needed intellectuals to rejuvenate the economy and culture, and also, one might say, to "modernize" Marxism-Leninism—the fundamental ideas legitimating the regime. In the process of critiquing the Stalinist model and legitimating alternative definitions of socialism, intellectuals began to investigate and absorb all Western systems of thought as well as to revive and rethink China's own pre-Marxist intellectual heritage. And they reclaimed their traditional right to participate in state affairs.[4]

Outside observers spoke of an ideological vacuum and pragmatic decision-making in China. In fact, it seems that an alternative ideology was developing based on the slogans of the May Fourth era that were reborn on the banners at Tiananmen—science and democracy. As the elite explored new ideas, politicians asked whether these ideas socialist and Marxist-Leninist, while thinkers asked if they were scientific and democratic.

The high tide of this cooperative relationship came in 1986, following periodic setbacks like the campaign against "spiritual pollution". An atmosphere of near-euphoria developed as intellectuals prepared for symposia celebrating the thirtieth anniversary of the Hundred Flowers Movement (part of the mid-1950s post-Stalin thaw throughout the socialist world). They intended to mark the demise of leftism and the triumph of the campaign to "emancipate the mind." There was a strong hope and desire that policies promising intellectuals improved status, expanded influence, better living and working conditions, and greater material reward, would

---

[4] The following summary of intellectual trends in the 1980s is based on my interviews and research for Carol Lee Hamrin, *China and the Challenge of the Future* (Boulder, Co.: Westview Press, 1990), especially pp. 30–40, 64–79, and 177–191. My focus on a series of "breakthroughs" was inspired by the excellent analysis of the transitions made in intellectual thought prior to Tiananmen in David Kelly, "Chinese Intellectuals in the 1989 Democracy Movement," in George Hicks, ed., *The Broken Mirror: China after Tiananmen* (Chicago: St. James Press, 1990), pp. 26–50.

finally bear fruit, and they could find personal fulfillment in helping the state become rich and strong.

C. FINANCIAL AND ORGANIZATIONAL AUTONOMY

Even though intellectuals' good will toward the state still prevailed, by the late 1980s they were beginning to break away from
their economic dependency on the state. To improve both the economy and the material livelihood of intellectuals, the leadership allowed them to moonlight or leave government jobs to develop new
enterprises such as venture capital corporations and consulting
companies, even private schools and medical clinics. Semi-autonomous think tanks, newspapers, and journals were spun off from
government institutes. Foreign as well as private or collective funding provided financial resources for this activity. Some younger intellectuals of the Red Guard generation had been working toward
this goal of organizational independence since the late 1970s. They
eagerly began to set up polling organizations and cultural foundations. Older intellectuals were more hesitant, but still involved, as
evident in the popularity of semi-autonomous media such as the
World Economic Herald.

These experiments in organization also helped foster a modern
role for intellectuals as specialists rather than priests. Traditional
and Marxist concepts of scholars as a morally superior elite gave
way as technical skills were put to work for other social groups in
a commercial exchange of service for cash. Examples included
young lawyers helping newly-rich peasants go to court to protect
their profits from greedy local cadres; journalists working for specialized journals and newspapers; and the Si Tong (Stone) Research
Institute, an affiliate of the Stone Computer Company, drafting
and publicizing legislation to protect private enterprise.

As they played new roles, intellectuals developed personal and
organizational linkages with other social groups. An example
would be young researchers at the Economic System Reform Institute, who implemented factory and municipal reform experiments
and conducted public opinion polls at all levels of society on behalf
of the State Economic System Reform Commission. As an infant
civil society began to emerge under decentralizing reforms, intellectuals became potential advocates for themselves and other social
groups against the demands of the state as well as tools of the state
and bridges between state and society. In these sprouts of autonomy springing up in the cracks of the monolithic party-state the
party leadership saw the specter of political opposition groups.

II. SYSTEMIC CRISIS

By the late 1980s, China was experiencing flagging economic performance, inadequate political responsiveness to new social demands, and an unsettled leadership succession.[5] The populace was
dissatisfied with spiraling inflation and political-economic corruption. Unhappiness was exacerbated by the heightened expectations

---

[5] See Hamrin, *China and the Challenge of the Future,* chapter 6, and Harry Harding, "China
in the 1990s: Prospects for Internal Change," *National Bureau of Asian and Soviet Research,* no.
1 (September 1990).

created by inflated promises of the reform wing of the leadership. The ouster of General Secretary Hu Yaobang in early 1987, by political means widely perceived in the elite as illegitimate, promoted an erosion of popular confidence in the government and growing hostility between and among politicians and intellectuals. Events outside China fueled this loss of legitimacy. As political reform sped up in the Soviet Union and Eastern Europe, and Taiwan made a peaceful transition to pluralistic politics—all of which was widely reported in China—the mainland leadership appeared to be in slow motion by comparison. Erratic decision-making over economic policy in 1988 reflected insecurity and heightened tensions within the leadership.

The reemergence of leadership struggle in late 1988 galvanized intellectuals into unprecedented political activism in a desperate attempt to stave off the retrogression or even demise of reforms that began to seem inevitable after the death of Hu Yaobang. Through the spring of 1989, intellectuals marshalled all their moral and organizational resources on behalf of the reform program. Increasingly convinced that the party was incapable of addressing China's urgent problems and deserved to lose its monopoly on the shaping of the national agenda, some leading intellectuals took upon themselves the responsibility to shape a "new enlightenment" agenda, seizing back the legacy of the May Fourth Movement long usurped by the party.

Even delegates to the National People's Congress chastised the Premier for allowing the annual economic plan they had endorsed to be thrown aside for ill-timed and poorly-conceived *ad hoc* policies. Unanswered petitions to Deng Xiaoping to release political prisoners to celebrate the PRC's fiftieth anniversary—initiated by astrophysicist Fang Lizhi and eventually involving a spectrum of natural scientists, science administrators, artists, educators and social scientists—led to the largely unplanned, *de facto* emergence of the PRC's first civil rights movement. This marked an important turn from reliance on moral solutions to demands for legal-procedural checks on the power of the state.

The events of April and May 1989 brought all these trends together in a single historic moment. The exhilarating experience of marching together and helping the students peacefully govern Tiananmen and its environs throughout weeks of demonstration boosted intellectuals and many other citizens across a psychological divide in their attitudes toward the state and each other. Those from formerly quite separate social groups, institutions, professions, factions and generations discovered for the first time solidarity among themselves, as well as massive overseas support. And this experience was shared to a lesser extent nation-wide, directly in local demonstrations or vicariously through the mass media and the grapevine.

III. Trying to Turn Back the Clock

A divided leadership hesitated in responding to the burgeoning crisis until it was too late for any peaceful solution not involving major departures from the Leninist system of governance. The alternative of violent repression was chosen by the party elders over much opposition, albeit largely passive, from within the political elite, thus crippling the authority of the party, government, and even the military. The repressive response to the Spring 1989 crisis at home was prolonged into 1990 by the collapse of East European communism. Events abroad—wherein dissident intellectuals inside and outside the party played a key role in bringing down communist regimes—appeared to justify the interpretation of the Tiananmen demonstrations as a foreign-backed political conspiracy requiring a crackdown and encouraged further repression to prevent its reemergence. The impact of 1989 on the elders seemed quite similar to the effect of the outburst of anti-regime sentiment at home in the 1956 Hundred Flowers Movement in conjunction with the post-Stalin thaw in Europe. In both situations, ensuing suspicion and fear in the leadership brought about a number of repressive changes in behavior toward intellectuals.

Beginning in the summer of 1989, Chinese leaders adopted traditional intimidation tactics aimed at squelching the emergence of any opposition into the next century. These included:

- A prolonged purge process involving security investigations, study and criticism sessions, quotas for purge targets in each work unit, and arrests or demotions for supporters of the demonstrations throughout the bureaucracy [6];
- The withholding of degrees and jobs from uncooperative 1989 graduates; mandatory military training for reduced numbers of incoming students at Beijing and Fudan Universities; a further reduction of 30,000 in the numbers of students entering key universities for 1990–91 [7]; and sending recent graduates in government work to do "grass-roots" work, under threat of loss of urban residency permits for noncooperation;
- An aggressive media censorship, budget cuts or forced closures for hundreds of cultural organs, restrictions on foreign contacts, and a propaganda campaign against proponents of "bourgeois liberalism" involving the slandering of democracy activists as national traitors, to reinforce self-censorship and unquestioning loyalty among intellectuals [8];
- Discriminatory treatment favoring "loyal" (e.g., less political) natural scientists and engineers over social scientists and writers;
- A resurgence of praise for the military as an instrument of socialization and a model for social discipline, most notably in the campaign to emulate Lei Feng, the 1960s soldier paragon of blind obedience and self-sacrifice in the interests of the communist party;

---

[6] See David Kelly and Anthony Reid, "Weathering the Political Winter—The Chinese Academy of Social Sciences, 1990," for a report on the purge at CASS based on a mission to China on behalf of the joint committee of academic exchanges with China of the Australian Academies of Social Science and Humanities, February 10, 1990.

[7] *Hong Kong Standard*, August 28, 1990, p. 10, citing Chinese sources on the plans to cut enrollments in most key schools for the 1990–91 academic year.

[8] See Linda Jaivins, "Cultural Purge Sweeps Clean," *Far Eastern Economic Review*, (August 23, 1990), pp. 47–48. A *Guangming ribao* [Enlightenment Daily] commentator article (June 27, 1990), p. 1, put forth the rationale for a continuing purge of bourgeois liberal ideas in the realm of art and literature.

- Tests of political loyalty affecting promotions and demotions during the reorganization of leading groups and the reregistration of party members; and
- A return to anti-intellectual themes, as exemplified in a *Wenyibao* article that asked rhetorically, "Who are patriots and who are traitors? Laboring people or the handful of intellectual scum?" and in General Secretary Jiang Zemin's lament that "Intellectuals have failed to integrate themselves with the working class." [9]

For intellectuals, the Tiananmen crackdown brought disillusionment, loss of hope, and a strong sense of betrayal, especially when contrasted with liberalizing trends in the Soviet Union and Eastern Europe. Both personally and as a group, intellectuals came to view their life options as severely limited in China. Alienation from the regime was evident in the rash of defections, an upsurge of visa applications for overseas study, direct and indirect refusal to carry on research work or to participate in political activity, and early retirements. For some, the sense of despair led to depression and even suicide. Others in search of meaning and community for the first time explored religious values, as witnessed by the growth of attendance in both official and unofficial churches and an upsurge of interest in the mystical practices of ancient Taoism.

By mid-1990, there was a moderation of regime policy and a resigned acceptance of the status quo on the part of intellectuals. This appears to be a temporary truce, however, founded on the lack of effectiveness of either harsh state repression or active intellectual resistance. Regime gestures to buy compliance and to weaken international moral and political sanctions included:

- the lifting of martial law in Beijing amidst continued tight security;
- the release of Fang Lizhi and groups of nearly 1000 Tiananmen detainees [10];
- allowing some family members of political exiles to leave China;
- the pro forma involvement of economic specialists in a months-long discussion of options for the 8th Five Year Plan (1991–95) and the ten year (1991–2000) program, sponsored by the State Council [11];
- periodic reiteration of pro-intellectual rhetoric [12];

---

[9] Such informal remarks by Jiang Zemin while touring in the provinces were never included in more formal remarks addressing policy toward intellectuals.

[10] *South China Morning Post*, 11 September 1990, p. 10, in FBIS–CHI–90-176 (11 September 1990), p. 31, stated that 881 people had been released in three batches in January, May and June. More were released without publicity in October–November.

[11] *Renmin ribao* [People's Daily], September 24, 1990, p. 5, in FBIS–CHI–90-193 (4 October 1990), p. 16–17, reported on Li Peng's views upon reading the results of a forum sponsored by *Jingji ribao* [Economic Daily]. See also a summary of a seminar on theoretical questions in economic rectification and reform, *Jingji yanjiu* [Economic Research] 8 (20 August 1990), pp. 25–31, in FBIS–CHI–90-211 (31 October 1990), pp. 27–52.

[12] Jiang Zemin first spoke of maintaining pro-intellectual reform policies in his speech to young people to commemorate May 4th, *Xinhua* (3 May 1990), in FBIS–CHI–90-087 (4 May 1990). But his tone was strident and almost hectoring as he emphasized the duties of intellectuals to be patriotic, become one with the working class, and contribute to modernization. Few pro-intellectual themes were heard again until late July when a *Renmin ribao* editorial, 23 July 1990, recalled Jiang's speech. Again, the tone was one of warning, however. While the party

Continued

- invitations to activist students and scholars abroad to return to China without punishment in exchange for confession of guilt and cessation of political activity[13];
- forums for CCP "discussions" with the noncommunist political parties, and the promotion of a few noncommunists to the State Council, in an effort to publicize the alleged superiority of the "multiparty consultation system" compared with the competitive multiparty pluralism being adopted in the Soviet Union and elsewhere in the socialist world.[14]

Yet, these developments for the most part were hollow policies—form without content—representing short-term coping strategies on each side, with intellectuals waiting for the succession struggle to resolve itself, and the leadership buying time until the next turn of events. How long it will take and by what means this tenuous relationship can be reshaped is impossible to tell, since it will depend on contingencies at home and abroad that no one can predict. In the meantime, severe damage has already been inflicted on China's modernization prospects in several aspects.

IV. ANOTHER LOST GENERATION?

Some observers have compared the non-return or delay in return of many of the more than 100,000 PRC students and scholars overseas, along with disciplinary measures against college students and graduates in Beijing, to the effects of the Cultural Revolution. From one perspective this would seem an exaggeration, since the earlier ten-year hiatus in all educational activity nationwide created a generation gap in China's educated elite that more limited recent developments have not. As Leo Orleans argues elsewhere in this volume, China may have sufficient numbers—for its current needs—of educated professionals involved in high-level education and basic research. China-educated rather than returned students are adequate to fill the mid-level production-oriented jobs in the sciences and technologies of immediate concern, especially given current slow-growth policies. Eventually, however, with expanded growth, if students currently overseas fail to return at all, and cuts in new student enrollments in China continue, another serious gap in researchers, educators, as well as technicians could emerge as current personnel retire.[15]

---

should "give more play to the role of intellectuals," it must also "set strict demands on them and guide them correctly." The focus continued to be on regaining central control over the affairs of intellectuals. See FBIS–CHI–90–142 (24 July 1990), pp. 12–31.

[13] *Xinhua*, 28 September 1990, in FBIS–CHI–90–190 (1 October 1990), p. 34, cited remarks by State Councilor and Education Commissioner Li Tieying in which he specified that those students who had joined organizations opposed to the PRC government would not be harmed "if they quit those organizations and admit their mistakes." Implicitly, those who had said or done something against the government in 1989 but who had not joined an organization could return without conditions.

[14] *Xinhua* (29 September 1990), in FBIS–CHI–90–191 (2 October 1990), p. 27, echoed these themes and gave background information on the five nonparty members newly appointed to leading posts (making 18 total).

[15] A report in *Liaowang* [Outlook] 26 (25 June 1990), pp. 3–5, in FBIS–CHI–90–136 (16 July 1990), pp. 23–28, quoted S & T professionals telling senior party and government leaders that over the next eight years, China would begin to experience the lack of Cultural Revolution generation specialists, as those now in their fifties retired. One scientist also pointed out the results of a survey showing that at least one-third of current S & T professionals were "not able to bring their roles into play" (presumably due to mismatch of skills to jobs, poor equipment, etc).

From another, less quantitative, perspective, China's current student body may well represent another "lost generation" like the former Red Guards now in their forties. Both groups have experienced a strong disillusionment with politics that breeds deep cynicism and both carry a political stigma that will diminish career prospects. In fact, many of the older activists of 1989 both at home and abroad were former Red Guards, a fact that fueled regime suspicion at the time. Now, this suspicion will poison attitudes between the regime and the younger siblings and protegees of 1989 as well. Unhealed wounds will enhance the prospects of future bouts of rebellion and repression as China proceeds through new transitional stages in socio-economic development.

V. COMPOUNDING THE INTERNAL BRAIN DRAIN

Given the escalating pace of global technological change that places a premium on intellectual activity in all types of employment and the sharp competition China faces from other rapidly-developing economies, any detour for advanced education and for intellectual policy in China now will have much greater proportional consequences than earlier crises. There is a large, albeit immeasurable, cost in terms of lost potential with the reversal of or delays in reform policies regarding education and job placement. These policies exposed an expanding number of professionals to international trends in all fields through travel, exchanges and education; gave greater job mobility to intellectuals to better match training with tasks; introduced more competition among students to obtain financial assistance and desirable employment; and replaced highly politicized and mind-numbing educational approaches with more modern curricula and teaching methods as well as more professional management. These reforms held out hopes of stemming China's hidden but enormous internal brain drain—the lack of development or misuse of human creative potential [16]. This may in the end prove to be the critical drag on China's economic modernization and cultural revitalization.

VI. FURTHER SETBACK FOR MASS EDUCATION AND CULTURAL ADVANCE

The negative impact for modernization of neglecting or repressing intellectual development and reinforcing a culture of falsehood and mistrust spreads far beyond the elite. Current policies exacerbate already serious problems in education caused by economic and social trends, including low levels of local funding for education and high drop-out rates due to the attraction of alternatives under the reform program. Prolonging the economic retrenchment program, apparently planned to last at least through 1991, will inevitably cause further loss of revenue, increasing the current gap of technically-educated workers in a population with 25 percent illiteracy and an unknown percentage of functional illiteracy.[17] The

---

[16] For a discussion of China's human "stunted development," see *Ta Kung Pao*, July 24, 1990, p. 26.

[17] *Liaowang* 41 (8 October 1990), pp. 16, 17, in FBIS–CHI–90–201 (17 October 1990), pp. 29–31, cited scholars at the State Council's Development Research Center on these figures and the problems they pose for China's development.

economic cost in terms of industrial accidents, production malfunctions, and loss of competitive edge with foreign investors who turn to countries with better-educated workers must be considered. The social cost in terms of stunted individual development, lack of civic virtues, and the "desertification" of Chinese culture is incalculable.[18]

VII. LEADERSHIP INFLEXIBILITY AND POLICY ERROR

If Chinese history is any guide, a major nonquantifiable, yet critically important cost of intellectual repression and alienation will become manifest in the policy arena. In any political system there is always a problem of leadership becoming isolated from peoples lives, particularly in China even in the best of times. Beginning with the events of early 1989, however, it appears that China's leaders even less welcoming than usual to all facts and options regardless of the sources. Earlier attempts in 1986–88 to enhance information feedback, "transparency" of exchanges of ideas within an expanding group that included specialists, and "scientific" decision-making procedures have given way to secrecy and even deception within a small, closed decision circle on most issues. This is bound to lead to more policy errors, large and small.

A number of semi-autonomous central policy research institutions set up during the 1980s under then-Premier Zhao Ziyang's patronage to provide some competition to recommendations coming from within the state bureaucracy have come under intense political scrutiny, with many being reorganized or even disbanded. Meanwhile, similar research organs attached to state bureaucratic units, which tend to reflect their narrow institutional interests, have regained a monopoly on policy research.[19]

Although this kind of reshuffle always accompanies a turnover of leadership, and was underway to a lesser degree under the new Premier Li Peng in late 1988–early 1989, the current repressive atmosphere and tighter controls on information and discussion have severely constricted policy debate and input from specialists. In many noneconomic areas of social research, specialists are finding it quite difficult to pursue their work and expect to have little influence on government decisions. There are much larger "forbidden zones" for policy research on international affairs, for example. The Hong Kong press has reported that while more reformist economic projections for the 8th Five Year Plan were permitted, they had little impact on the official draft plan from the State Council's research office and planning commission that proposed continued pursuit of the stabilization program.[20]

---

[18] *Ta Kung Pao*, above.

[19] On economic policy, the State Council Research Office and the Planning Commission's Research Office dominated the drafting of the eighth Five-Year Plan, making the process much more closed than the seventh Five-Year Plan process, which involved considerable input from other think tanks as well as The World Bank. See Hamrin, *China and the Challenge of the Future.*

[20] For published versions of the contribution by the Development Research Center, see *Jingji yanjiu* [Economic Research] 7 (20 July 1990), pp. 20–37, in FBIS–CHI–900–197 (11 October 1990), pp. 28–44; for contributions by the Economic Research Institute of the Chinese Academy of Social Sciences, see *Jingji yanjiu* 7 (20 July 1990), pp. 3–19, in FBIS–CHI–90–075 (10 October 1990), pp. 9–28.

VIII. CRISIS OF LEGITIMACY AND AUTHORITY

It seems apparent that the most important net result of the Beijing massacre was the fundamental loss of legitimacy of the CCP among the educated elite and the informed urban populace as a whole, whose sentiments and views intellectuals articulate. While some people are just angry at Deng Xiaoping and other elders and their protegees, many have lost confidence that the basic Leninist system of central party monopoly on power can either provide personal meaning for their lives or fulfill the national mandate to make China rich, strong, and respected in the family of nations. The collapse of communism in Eastern Europe and the shift toward pluralism even in the Soviet Union has encouraged this change of mind. There is now a widespread assumption that there is an historical "inevitability" of the shift to a post-communist era.

This does not mean, of course, that anti-regime political activism will follow. The traditional Chinese preference for moderation and fear of chaos has also been buttressed by the current situation in Eastern Europe and the Soviet Union. The CCP can effectively argue—at least temporarily—that there is no desirable alternative to its rule. Nevertheless, the social result is a far cry from the civic enthusiasm, creativity, and active support for government policy that would be a strong asset for rapid modernization. Rather, a stance of collective passive resistance to central authority—unprecedented in China—has spread widely among urban intellectuals and officials as well as workers. This echoes, of course, a long Chinese tradition whereby intellectuals out of favor with the court keep silent and try to preserve personal integrity, but the current situation has gone far beyond the intelligentsia and is much more a silent collective social act than individual moral protest. The resulting nonimplementation of unpopular central policies and the spreading maverick behavior by local officials, social groups and individuals both reflects and speeds up the weakening of central authority already well underway in the 1970s and 1980s. This is a strong liability for development.

IX. THE IMPORTANCE OF THE STATE-INTELLECTUAL RELATIONSHIP

The dramatic and traumatic events of 1989 revealed in the starkest terms that the relationship between intellectuals and the state had become a central political problem for China. By the end of 1990, Chinese leaders reportedly were becoming quite concerned about the demoralization of intellectuals and the impact this had on the general mood of society.[21]

The leadership's approach to relations with intellectuals in coming months and years will be important not because intellectuals by themselves are the most powerful asset or threat to the leadership, or because changes in thinking alone will produce solutions to China's daunting problems. Rather, this relationship will be critical in determining the relative harmony or turbulence involved in China's accommodation to an irreversible shift in the locus and

---

[21] Chang Mu, Hong Kong *Ching Pao* 160 (10 November 1990), pp. 30–33, in FBIS–CHI–90–220 (14 November 1990), pp. 24, citing Jiang Zemin's remarks to noncommunist personages in late October.

mechanisms of exercising authority as it modernizes. How this political process takes place will be fundamental to the speed and success of China's modernization.

It seems inevitable that younger central leaders—or more likely, newly emerging leaders from the provinces—will soon begin exploring new options rather than relying on outmoded political tools and policies of the past. And they will turn to intellectuals as a key constituency for the legitimation of a new program.

THE IMPACT OF MAO'S LEGACY ON CHINA'S REFORMS

By Marcia R. Ristaino *

CONTENTS

SUMMARY

A central part of Mao's legacy is what is referred to in this essay as the Maoist tradition. It contains the values and concepts inherent in Mao's approach to China's society, culture, economy, military, and politics. The Maoist tradition comprises a body of thought, policies, and programs that together represent a repertoire from which China's leaders still reference and project their policy choices. In addition, Marxism-Leninism-Mao Zedong Thought constitutes the state philosophical framework from which solutions and goals relevant to China's future continue to be expressed.

Historically, Mao remains closely identified with China's revolutionary success in establishing the People's Republic of China in 1949. He is credited with originating the winning strategies that defeated foreign and domestic enemies, unified the country, and brought it recognition from the modern world. This historical part of the legacy provides Mao with a deep emotional connection with China's people, even though his reputation later became tarnished by the calamitous Cultural Revolution which he originated and led.

Beyond Mao's historical role, the Maoist tradition has found concrete expression in social programs, laudable for their heavy emphasis on staying attuned with public interests, for community solidarity, and for a commitment to egalitarian social goals, especially concerning China's huge impoverished rural population. The expansive delivery of basic health care services and mass educational

---

* Technical Information Specialist, Order Division, Library of Congress.

programs are important examples. These efforts made extensive use of the unique Maoist mass line concept that sought to arouse and consolidate popular support around Party goals through intensive ideological indoctrination. According to the Maoist tradition, the military, inspired by its guerrilla heritage, plays a key role in civilian affairs to the extent that when issues of social stability are addressed, the military's role becomes a natural and integral part of planning and choices.

The Maoist tradition has been less successful in the realms of economics, culture, and politics, especially as China has attempted to approach the outside world for expertise, ideas, and techniques for modern development. Maoist economic policy has been criticized for being overly centralized, utopian, unresponsive to local conditions, and stifling of human initiative. The topics and boundaries of cultural affairs have been determined by the agendas of Maoist ideology, thus arresting spontaneous and creative expression.

In the political realm, the Maoist tradition has distorted the basic concept of democratic centralism as it was originally understood and practiced in China's early revolutionary period. Mao, through his assumption of complete power and through the systematization of his writings into a unitary body of thought, eliminated any possibilities for other fruitful avenues of thought and action. The representational framework of a people's congress system, balancing Mao's political power, was essentially discarded except on paper. Even the Communist Party structure became undermined by Mao's cult of personality. The regular interjection of class struggle to motivate change and instill political awareness has mainly substituted abstract and utopian goals for well-planned and rational approaches to China's growth and development.

China's post-Mao reform program has set in motion ideas and processes that seriously erode the Maoist tradition, especially the political and cultural aspects always so closely interrelated in China's experience. The urbanization of China's peasant society has inspired and accelerated diversity, the transfer of job skills, and the implantation of new values such as self-assertiveness and even acquisitiveness. Accompanying urbanization has been an increase in exposure to new sources of information. Expanded media channels have offered greater opportunities for variety, cultural diversity, and the formation of independent opinion. The recent condemned television production, *He Shang*, clearly displayed a new creativity and a challenging of China's traditions.

China is confronted with the tension between two different approaches to realizing its twentieth century goal of achieving prosperity and power. Especially in times of stress, the Maoist approach, with its clear-cut and familiar authoritarian essence, still holds attraction even for the post-Mao generation. For those now holding office, who were heavily indoctrinated and actively participated in Maoist politics, the Maoist tradition still remains as one very important source of policy options and solutions to China's difficult problems.

I. INTRODUCTION

Mao Zedong's legacy provides the theoretical underpinnings for the People's Republic of China through the body of writings known as Marxism-Leninism-Mao Zedong Thought. This state philosophy represents the legitimizing framework for socialist governance within which all official policies and actions must be expressed and referenced.

But Mao's legacy has another dimension that allows it to act upon China's state and society in ways which both foster and inhibit China's struggle to developand become part of the increasingly interrelated world community. This active dimension is derived in part from Mao's colossal historical role in leading the revolutionary movement in 1949. Mao is credited with having developed the winning strategic concepts of the countryside surrounding the cities, the mass line, and guerrilla warfare strategies and concepts. Mao also was a leading participant in the legendary Long March and later published his famous integrative political theses on the New Democracy.

Most key aspects of what has become Mao's legacy actually were nurtured and developed by others in the course of the revolutionary movement. But with Mao's gradual accumulation of predominant state, party, and military power within the movement, and the systematization of his writings into a singular body of thought, the many creative aspects of the Chinese revolution became associated with him. In retrospect, a strong argument can be made that within the historical context of wartime conditions, extreme poverty, and social deprivation, the times demanded an imposing leader to provide focus to the otherwise dispersed and mainly rural revolutionary movement.

Mao's historical standing certainly was diminished by his identification with the disastrous Great Leap Forward and the Great Proletarian Cultural Revolution. Nevertheless, these policy disasters still do not appear to have diminished Mao's close association-and emotional connection with the national triumph of 1949.

Mao's legacy, or "tradition" is not limited to political, economic, social or cultural matters. By contrast, one can identify other leaders, such as Chen Yun, specifically with complex models of economic development. Rather, the Maoist tradition is comprisedof a broad spectrum of ideas and concepts that can still be evoked in ways that sometimes are unifying and ameliorative and other times, disruptive and retrogressive.

This paper first examines residual aspects of the Maoist tradition, providing examples of its renewed influence especially in Post-Tiananmen China. Secondly, this paper identifies key developments in post-Mao China arising with reforms, which challenge his legacy and operate in tension with the Maoist tradition.

II. THE MAOIST TRADITION

This discussion of Mao's legacy considers how elements of the Maoist tradition support or inhibit China's twentieth century goals of achieving wealth and power within the socialist framework requiring an egalitarian distribution of resources. Although many of the social outreach and collectivist aims are protected under the

Maoist tradition, flexibility and diversity in thought and action are undermined.

A. BASIC HEALTH CARE SERVICES

The only program initiated by Mao himself and still functioning in China, concerns the provision of basic health care services to China's rural masses. Launched during the Cultural Revolution, this program trained young "barefoot doctors" in practical skills essential to basic public health work. Oriented toward preventative rather than curative medicine, these medical personnel provided services such as inoculations, immunization against prevalent diseases, instruction concerning the proper preparation of foods, water purification methods, public sanitation, and personal hygiene. The program's aim was to elevate the health standards of China's largest population segment without taxing human and material resources that were often in short supply or nonexistent. Delivering health care and preventive treatment to the countryside has relied heavily on the large numbers of neighborhood health workers driven by a Maoist ideological commitment to serve the rural masses. This Maoist program constituted an innovative approach to a widespread problem by a system with limited resources.[1]

The present health-care program continues to display certain predispositions and basic values characteristic of the Maoist tradition. First is a fundamental mistrust of the "elitist" urban medical establishment, buttressed by a continued allegiance to traditional Chinese medicine which is often still preferred by the rural population. Second, the program stresses the importance of local autonomy and initiative in the planning and delivery of health care services. Third, it emphasizes the equal status between patients and health-care providers.

Because the Maoist program has been criticized for subjecting people to poor and unskilled medical treatment, the government has been attempting to professionalize the barefoot doctors by implementing selection criteria for candidates, by training those selected in modern medical techniques and practices, and by offering certification as a "country or village doctor" for the best candidates. Nevertheless, peasants who can afford to do so often by-pass the village clinic for more professional services available at the county-level tier of the medical system. Nevertheless, characteristic of Maoist values, the government's health care program aims to evoke a substantial measure of voluntaristic support directed at providing equitable services to the greatest number of primarily poor rural inhabitants without creating a new class of medical elite.

B. CULTURE AND EDUCATION

Mao's "Talk at the Yan'an Forum on Literature and Art" written in May 1942 in the context of the War of Resistance against Japan, remains the basic text concerning artistic and literary endeavors in China. The influence of wartime conditions on this docu-

---

[1] Marilyn M. Rosenthal and Jay Greiner, "The Barefoot Doctors of China: From Political Creation to Professionalization," in *Health Care in the People's Republic of China: Moving Towards Modernization*, M. M. Rosenthal, ed. (Bolder, CO: Westview Press), 1987, p. 5.

ment is conveyed in one of its key lines: "fight the enemy with one heart and one mind.[2] According to Mao, the main function of artistic expression is to serve the people. This is to be accomplished by writers and artists going to work among the workers and peasants and learning about their daily lives. Artists are to use their creative talents to "concentrate" what is discovered during this exposure for expression through the medium of their artistic work.[3] These works have the primary purpose of inspiring the masses and elevating their cultural level by giving it a coherent but focused expression, asdetermined by politics.

Mao's writings clearly indicate the subordinate status of art to politics. To serve the masses well, artistic works must have revolutionary content as well as artistic form. They must unite and educate the population around themes enunciated in the Party's political programs, and be able to evoke in the masses a new level of political and social consciousness and enthusiasm that can be harnessed to achieve the Party's goals. The cadres working in the fields of art and literature acquire the vision and means of expression to carry out their work through their own emersion and study and application of the teachings of Marxism-Leninism-Mao Zedong-thought.

Mao regarded works of art and literature as particularly powerful in shaping the thinking and consciousness of the masses, or in creating "one heart and one mind." He noted that works lacking artistic quality carry no force, regardless of how progressive politically they might be. On the other hand, those with artistic quality but bad political content he described as extremely dangerous. And because of their potential power and influence, Mao regarded intellectual groups which create these works with suspicion and subjected them to regular Party supervision and discipline. Also, Mao warned artists and intellectuals against the pitfalls of copying wholesale Western traditions or styles or of falling into a stagnant traditionalism in the artists' prescribed mission to establish a modern national cultural identity. Mao's famous writings on the subjects of literature and art are again being emphasized as the basic reference works for guiding and evaluating current literary and artistic activities.

Political and ideological concerns also are central to Mao's approach to education. Emphasis on correct ideology has required students to undertake lengthy periods of study in Marxism-Leninism-Mao Zedong Thought. This study is meant to instill in them a commitment to serving the community and strengthening the state, and to mold young thinking along orthodox lines. Educational programs are to have the broadest reach within the population, to stress moral training and enhancement, and to inspire unity of thought and social stability.

Anti-intellectual and anti-expert biases are pervasive in the Maoist approach to education. This was clearly evident during the Cultural Revolution when the system of higher education was shut down as tens of thousands of college students responded to Mao's

---

[2] Mao Zedong, *Selected Works of Mao Tse-tung*, vol. 3 (Beijing: Foreign Language Press, 1967), p. 82.
[3] Ibid., p. 82.

call to join Red Guard organizations. China in effect lost a rising generation of trained talent required to build a viable future.

In place of rigorous academic programs, Maoist training programs included periods of work "among the masses" in order to inhibit or dispel elitist tendencies that segregate mental and manual labor. Basic education was stressed over the highly developed specialized skills of the "expert" as having the primary role in education. Students underwent military and physical training and were indoctrinated in the model behavior of heroes such as Lei Feng, the super patriot who spent his short life "serving the people." They were exhorted to emulate the social and political discipline of the Chinese Communist Party and to participate in its mobilization campaigns to raise popular standards of literacy and education. In short, the Maoist emphasis in education was upon serving broad community needs first, instilling ideological understanding and commitment among China's young, and building a basis for solidarity with the Party's current and future political goals and programs.

Concern with these conservative values has reappeared, especially following the "political turmoil" of 1989. In his authoritative government Work Report, Premier Li Peng called on the educational system to stress moral education and give "top priority to a firm and correct political orientation." Further, Li emphasized the importance in the curricula of teaching Marxism-Leninism and Mao Zedong Thought, learning from the masses, and serving the people.[4]

C. ECONOMICS AND SOCIETY

Maoist economics emphasize collective gains and social welfare as opposed to the privatization of the collective economy.[5] In Mao's system, social goals constitute an essential part of the process of economic development. It is a socioeconomic system that purports to treat each member at least similarly. At the basic level of the system's performance, peasant households were incorporated into collective and ultimately into communal units which subsequently guaranteed the livelihood and community of the members. The Communist Party, through the State Plan, sets the economic program to be strictly followed within the vast communal system and exercised complete control over all available human and natural resources. Industrial projects, massive in scope and in scale, were also part of the planned structure.

The system was energized by the concepts of class struggle and a campaign style of operation. "Class enemies," such as former landlords, were targeted time and again for the purpose of arousing the masses to participate in common endeavors. Participation in these campaigns was fueled by mass emotion, which "advanced elements" or party cadre were charged with transforming into a level of political consciousness effective in bringing about desirable eco-

---

[4] Li Peng, "Work Report to the Third Session of the Seventh National People's Congress," March 20, 1990, in Foreign Broadcast Information Service (FBIS) Daily Report: China, (April 6, 1990), p. 20.

[5] For a comparative discussion of China's economic models, including the Maoist approach, see Dorothy J. Solinger, ed., *Three Visions of Chinese Socialism* (Boulder, CO: Westview Press, 1984).

nomic and social change. Thus, change was expected to occur not through broad participation in institutions or representative bodies, but by the orchestrated mobilization of the masses directed at realizing Party goals and programs. The power of this approach and its capacity sometimes to exceed rational bounds are illustrated by the social and economic disasters of the Great Leap Forward and the Cultural Revolution. Both were essentially utopian campaigns aimed at achieving a modern transformation of the Chinese economy, society, and even the Chinese people, within a short timespan.

There are important contradictions which were inherent in the Maoist economic approach. Maoist policies taught self-reliance and denigrated bureaucracy and its procedures. And yet, because of the highly vertical nature of the Maoist organizational style, the system fostered dependence and lack of initiative at lower levels. Also, the projected Maoist developmental models exacerbated this failing by taking a "one size fits all" approach, applying a singular model to the entire country without careful consideration of existing and inevitable variations in local conditions.

China's present leaders continue to display basic concern over inequalities in distribution and income, and to emphasize solidarity and the priority of serving common needs rather than profit. There has been some movement back towards a limited degree of collectivization and curtailment of family enterprises in the recent course of economic "readjustment." The heavily endorsed "Spark Plan" and "Torch Plan" are Maoist in flavor because they rely upon the mobilization of cadres trained in technical fields and dispersed to serve in rural and urban areas in order to raise general skill levels. Programs such as these perpetuate the Maoist concern with broad reach and social mobilization to achieve developmental goals. These recent mobilization programs, however, have the added dimension of supporting integration of modern knowledge into the general population.

D. POLICE, THE MILITARY, AND STATE POWER

The Maoist tradition has always inculcated a substantial measure of fear, threat, and intimidation in the course of its existence. To some extent, this feature arose from the agrarian wartime conditions under which the revolutionary movement developed and from its political evolution under Mao into a totalitarian state. The well-known Maoist teaching "political power comes from the barrel of a gun" has had applications in China's internal affairs, as was shown again in the decisions made about the Tiananmen demonstrations in June 1989.

According to the Maoist teachings, the People's Liberation Army (PLA) was regarded as the "pillar of the people's democratic dictatorship."[6] It is the guardian of the revolutionary Yan'an Era (1937–45) spirit of solidarity, patriotism, public service, self-sacrifice, and plain living. Also characteristic, the military was closely interrelated with police and civilian powers, a condition that arose out of the guerrilla heritage developed during the early base areas

---

[6] Li Peng, "Work Report," (March 20,1990), p.6.

and rural soviets period.[7] Guerrilla cadres served as soldiers, Party leaders, and government administrators. This Maoist ideal, of the omnicompetent cadres, insured that political, military, and administrative roles overlapped and eventually became fused. It also meant that in the course of maintaining social order and discipline, the military performed a natural and necessary role.

The guerrilla heritage has given the PLA a strong voice in China's civilian affairs. PLA cadres have held concurrent positions in both Party and government posts. Frequently, police recruits are drawn from former PLA personnel. Thus, when issues of social stability and order are addressed, the military's role becomes an integral part of the planning and the resulting choices and programs.

Traditionally, the PLA has played a key role in fostering ideological development and instilling social discipline. These roles are currently apparent in China's renewed emphasis on the popular emulation of the military hero Lei Feng, and also by the PLA's providing military training to university students in Beijing and Fudan universities. Further, the Party, operating under the perceived threat of social instability, has delayed planned political reforms directed at separating Party and government functions. Such separation would likely promote and develop specialized functions and probably have the added important effect of reducing the military's role in civilian affairs. Apparently, this latter outcome is one which the Party still cannot support.

E. POLITICS

The Maoist political tradition constitutes an important revision of the basic organizational principle of China's political system known as democratic centralism. This principle has two cardinal requirements. One is that discussion and debate of major local issues take place among organizational members at the various levels of the hierarchical system and that the results of those discussions be transmitted and become integrated into formal Party policy decisions. The second is that once policy decisions are made, obedience of lower to higher levels of the structure in following Party policy must be complete. Mao upset this system's balance by shifting political power away from democratic, representational forms and toward his own authoritative person and approach. The result was creation of the cult of personality and an imposed unity of thought that together curtailed the development of diversity and representative institutions.

A multi-level people's congress system within which local ideas and initiatives could be presented and debated before being forwarded for consideration at higher policymaking levels in the political system never was given the opportunity to develop. Yet the concepts and the system had firm indigenous roots in China's own historic revolutionary base areas.[8] Social, economic, and political

---

[7] David S. G. Goodman, "State Reforms in the People's Republic of China," in Stephen White and David Nelson, eds., *Communist Politics: A Reader* (New York: New York University Press, 1986), pp. 128–31.

[8] The vital predecessor organizations to the people's congress system were China's multi-level soviets. See Marcia R. Ristaino, *China's Art of Revolution: The Mobilization of Discontent, 1927 and 1928* (Durham, N.C.:Duke University Press, 1987), pp. 126–39.

pressures that might have found constructive release through such a system instead found often violent expression in Mao's campaign approach aimed at achieving what were more frequently utopian ends.

China's wartime conditions no doubt promoted and perhaps required a revision of the principle of democratic centralism. But after 1949, when politics concerned governing the country and establishing its institutions and economy, the political system required more balance. Greater balance between centralization and representational/democratic forces does not in itself constitute a serious challenge to the utility or efficacy of the mass-line campaign approach aimed at accomplishing equality and social justice. Omitting a functioning representative system, however, does remove popular participation in identifying the issues and setting priorities to be realized by these campaigns.

In this vein, the Maoist tradition injected into the political system the concept of class struggle against internal and external enemies. This was done in order to trigger change and instill political awareness, yet it seemed only to substitute abstract and largely meaningless targets for real economic goals and political issues. As the Cultural Revolution showed, the outcome of this political approach was to produce a momentum for destruction that ultimately overwhelmed any constructive activity and growth. In its present context, class struggle is again being discussed and defined not as the principal contradiction in China's society but as one that still exists. Its current target is bourgeois democracy or the Western multi-party system which, if initiated, would undermine the predominant role and status of the Party.

III. POST-MAO CHALLENGES

Two years after Mao Zedong died in September 1976, China embarked on a comprehensive reform program that posed basic challenges to the Maoist tradition. The new reformist thinking has posited the goals of making China prosperous, culturally progressive, and a functioning part of the world community. The following discussion considers some of the key aspects of the reformist challenge which, viewed against the Maoist tradition described above, illustrates how China is indeed confronted with having to integrate two very different approaches to national growth and development.

A. URBANIZATION

An important influence on China's current condition is the rapid growth of urban population. Between 1982 and 1986 the country's urban population increased from 20.6 percent to 37 percent. Part of the reason for this considerable increase was the 1984 decision to broaden the criteria for classifying an area as a city or town. Nevertheless, some demographers estimate that by the year 2,000 nearly half of China's population will live in cities and towns.[9] (For a more detailed discussion of urbanization, see Banister's chapter in this volume.) When that occurs, tho popular conceptions of

---

[9] Robert L. Worden, Andrea M. Savada, and Ronald E. Dolan, eds., *China: A Country Study* (Washington, D.C.: Federal Research Division, Library of Congress, 1987), pp. 81–82.

330

China as either an enigmatic peasant society or one that is comprised of a rural Communist society in which the roles of peasant, soldier, and cadre are necessarily entwined no longer will suffice.[10] As this urbanization process develops an ever larger segment of the population is exposed to the diversity of urban living, the specialization of livelihood, the increased availability of information, and the relative abundance of urban goods and services.

Township enterprises, emerging under the reform program, have become a major contributor to the national economy. They also serve as an important bridge between urban and rural areas by absorbing the otherwise unemployed rural labor. Perhaps just as important, job functions and skills previously limited to large urban areas begin to be disseminated and understood on a broader basis within society. Thus, job responsibilities become more similar and transferable, helping to bridge the previously enormous gap between city, town, and countryside. With increasing urbanization also comes increased exposure to the variety of information, institutions, trades, professions, and skills that make up a more urban environment. The diversity and complexity inherent in this urban milieu contrast with the relative homogeneity of rural China and certainly with the "unity of thought" that existed under Mao.

It is most unlikely that the leadership will be able to control urban growth, as it did in earlier years. In addition, the reforms have opened up large areas of the country, especially coastal China, to extensive development projects that have required a large work force and, by drawing upon pools of unemployed agricultural workers, have promoted further integration of urban and rural populations.

The urbanization process by its very nature and unfolding erodes key Maoist values such as ideological purity, a unified formula approach to problems, committed self-sacrifice, and emulation of national model heroes. In their place, new values such as self-assertiveness, acceptance of diversity, and the nonideological formulation of problems are gaining support and meaning. Adherence to these different values seems to include a rising level of expectation by urban residents that the social and political systems will indeed serve the people honestly and effectively.

B. THE MEDIA

Accompanying the reform program and urbanization process are the development and proliferation of print and broadcast media. While Mao made sure that the media were limited and carefully controlled, in the post-Mao era the publishing industry has expanded beyond its two major centers in Beijing and Shanghai. Newspapers have increased in number and circulation and exhibited more leeway for diverse and even critical opinion. Before the Tiananmen crackdown, China's journalists showed at times remarkable determination in reporting accurate and reliable information. Their contributions and the enhanced flow of information have helped broaden the forum of ideas and have promoted more awareness among the population of contemporary issues both within China

---

[10] John Fincher, "Zhao's Fall, China's Loss," *Foreign Policy*, No. 76 (Fall 1989), pp. 20–21.

and in the world. Since Tiananmen, the number of newspapers and periodicals have decreased and they are again being censored.[11]

Foreign information sources and facilities now based in China contributed to the reformist trend before June 1989. Also, China now has telecommunications and broadcast satellite capabilities that facilitate television and radio transmission internally and link China to communication centers around the world. Radio broadcasts serve remote areas of the country. Official estimates claim that two-thirds of the population have access to television broadcasts. China's development of facsimile, data transmission, and computer-controlled telecommunications services permit the retrieval of international news as well as scientific, technical, economic, and cultural information.[12] It is well known that these avenues of information came into play during the Tiananmen events.

Thus, although the government continues to exercise close supervision over the contents of broadcast programming and still uses these channels as a powerful tool for molding and controlling public opinion, the population has become the direct recipient of information to an extent never before realized in China. An important by-product of the information explosion is the expected narrowing of the gap between urban and rural communities. Further, it is not inconsequential that more than one-hundred million of China's rural and urban inhabitants now live within broadcast distance of Hong Kong and Taiwan.

In short, the expanded capabilities of print and broadcast media have provided direct information to the population that can be discussed, debated, and digested, especially since most television viewing in China takes place in groups. The opportunities were, and to a more limited extent, still are present for expanding the mind-set and horizons of a people previously constrained by limited information and the narrow perimeters of the Maoist tradition.

C. SELECTING A CULTURE—THE *HE SHANG* EXAMPLE

China's expanded mass media channels acquired new significance in mid-June 1988 when a group of prominent intellectuals produced a six-part television documentary, with the title *He Shang* (River Elegy), exploring the past and future of China's culture. The production was a remarkable success, was rebroadcast by local television stations, and became the subject of letters and critical commentary in the print media. *He Shang* locates the sources of China's contemporary weaknesses and problems in the traditional continental culture, which is symbolized by both the nurturing and destructive roles played by the Yellow River throughout China's history: "There would be no internal dynamism and no one-hundred flowers blooming without extensively assimilating the essence of a foreign culture."[13] The negative argument presented is that the Yellow River tradition stifles individual thought and action, focuses attention inward, and prohibits the growth of entre-

---

[11] "Let the Publication of Newspapers and Periodicals Develop in a Healthy Way,"*Ban Yue Tan*, No. 16 (August 25, 1990), in FBIS *Daily Report: China* (October 3, 1990),pp. 20–21.

[12] Worden, Savada, and Dolan, *China: A Country Study*, pp. 366–369.

[13] *He Shang* (River Elegy), JPRS Report (JPRS–CAR–88–002), Washington, D.C., December 6, 1988, p. 17.

preneurial activity, all factors that promoted development in the West, and factors inherent in the Maoist tradition.

The series calls for nothing short of a revolutionization of China's culture in the direction of the sea—towards opening to outside influences in order to create a modern culture. It argues that China must integrate or incorporate cultural changes into its plans for economic growth. Thus, parallel to cultural developments are recommendations that China follow a coastal economic strategy designed to expand the development of capitalism contained mainly in China's coastal cities in the course of introducing the ideas and concepts of Western industrial civilization.

This kind of cultural-historical programming initially can appear rather benign except for the important fact that in China, culture, politics, and history are closely interwoven. Traditionally, intellectuals have placed a high value on moral leadership and service to society, in addition to developing their specific disciplines. When this approach is taken today, it brings intellectuals into conflict with Party cadres, who see themselves as the sole developers and disseminators of any theoretical information. Further, the series completely sets aside any attempt to describe China's history by using Marxist categories. Produced outside the Party's vertically-defined propaganda channels, *He Shang* made direct and effective contact with the population by providing interesting and provocative issues for discussion and debate. While the government was able to suspend broadcast of the series, it is unlikely that the experience of viewing and responding to the material, especially for China's post-Mao generation, will soon be forgotten.

He Shang displays no sense of awe for Mao Zedong. In one segment, Mao is described as "China's greatest contemporary leader" and "a man of great talent and bold vision," but when confronted with the symbolic Yellow River issue, Mao reportedly had little to offer other than his "dissatisfaction." [14] Further, Mao's disappointing reticence on this key problem was exacerbated by his disastrous utopian policies culminating in the Cultural Revolution. Couched in historical allusion, Mao probably was the historical figure described in He Shang who continues to be worshipped by visitors while Liu Shaoqi (identified by name), the former Chairman of the Republic, is ignored. Liu's ill fate during the Cultural Revolution is ascribed to the backward nature not only of China's culture but also its politics, economy, and social structure.

A western reader/viewer of *He Shang* can easily be struck by the totality of the condemnation of China's traditional culture. The work has the heavily dramatic and merciless tone of a national cultural self-criticism session. The West is constantly extolled for having undertaken foreign conquest and trade expeditions while China slept in agrarian torpor. The great Chinese maritime expeditions carried out in the fifteenth century are condemned for lacking conquest or trade motivations when, in fact, they might be viewed in a more favorable light in the context of today's world. Also, one scholarly participant in the production, *He Shang*, recommends that only a thorough "self-questioning" of history will pro-

---

[14] Ibid., p. 29.

mote a genuine understanding of history and lead China to "historical wisdom." [15] Such reasoning raises the issue of whether such a long and rich tradition can be understood in some whole or complete way. Perhaps it is a pattern of thinking characteristic of a society that has had only repeated indoctrination and for whom only "total" answers or solutions to problems are adequate.

D. THE CHALLENGE FROM ABROAD

The Maoist tradition, as it continues to operate in China, has many external challenges. The foreign media and incoming publications have already been noted. Likewise, commercial contacts, especially through Hong Kong and Taiwan, expose the population to knowledge about a "better life" and to different systems and ideas. The events in the Soviet Union and Eastern Europe have posed a severe challenge to the validity of Marxism-Leninism, and by extension and association, Mao Zedong and his thought.

Thus a conflict has developed between China's nationalistic concern with guarding its cultural and political autonomy and foreign values such as human rights requirements and economic sanctions. These outside pressures on the still-present aspects of the Maoist tradition, complicate and frustrate a forceful or effective policy response.

IV. PROSPECTS

The long-standing concern among China's leaders is the phenomenon described as the "heap of loose sand" in which society lacks all cohesion, is unstable, and easily degenerates into chaos. Within this context, the Maoist tradition continues to win allegiance and gain supporters and its policies and values provide a full repertoire from which leaders can enforce orthodoxy, break or reverse movement toward change and reform, and limit the country's full integration into the world community.

A significant portion of the population, particularly the younger and better educated urbanites, no longer subscribes chapter and verse to Maoist teachings. Yet during difficult times even they probably respond to the familiar security provided by the authoritarian, centralized model created under Mao's tutelage. The generation now in office was heavily exposed to the Maoist era political campaigns and indoctrination, and no doubt these influences remain.

There are press reports that the study of Mao's works again is being emphasized and undertaken in some of the educational institutions. A university symposium organized around the theme "the quest for Mao Zedong" was convened in February 1989.[16] Photographs and songs about Mao's famous exploits are for sale in shops. New works and films are being produced showing Mao's all-encompassing role in the revolution. An author writing in *Renmin ribao*

---

[15] Ibid., p. 31

[16] "From 'Sartre Craze' to 'Mao Zedong Craze,'" *Renmin ribao* (overseas edition), March 1, 1990, translated in FBIS *Daily Report: China* (March 25, 1990), pp. 1–2.

in July described Mao Zedong Thought as no less than "the spiritual pillar maintaining the unification of our nation state." [17]

The increased urbanization of the population and the exposure to media that promote diversity in thought and experience probably will continue to erode the power of the Maoist tradition, but this is a gradual process. It is generally recognized that China needs to act swiftly and with flexibility to develop the economy and improve the lives of the people. Another challenge to China's leaders is the confrontation with Western values and concepts that accompany modern scientific and technical knowledge and introduce flexibility and innovation. These challenges severely tax the integrative capacity of China's current political system and leaders. China's land mass and population are burden enough to slow growth and cultural integration without having also to cope with retrograde political traditions.

The debilitating and regressive effects of Mao's political legacy will continue to operate and impair China's development until the political system is rid of the residual influences of Mao's personality cult. This feature of the Maoist tradition centers power in charismatic individuals, sometimes regarded as "saviors", and undercuts the legitimate powers of others serving in office. Countering the cult requires that those in office be awarded the powers of their office, but that fixed terms of office holding be established. This is to prevent any leader, over time, from acquiring unusual personal powers that can distort the functioning of leadership that is working collectively and practicing a balanced version of democratic centralism in guiding China's future. Without these changes, the Maoist political tradition, or the practice of people following a personality cult, will continue to inhibit and disrupt China's plans for stability and development.

---

[17] Jin Huiming, "The Precious Wealth of the Party and People ..." *Renmin ribao*, (July 20, 1990), translated in FBIS *Daily Report: China* (July 30, 1990), p. 27.

IV. MODERNIZATION

A. Agriculture

OVERVIEW

By William H. Cooper [*]

Accounting for about one-third of GNP and two-thirds of the labor force, agriculture is a critical sector in the Chinese economy.[1] One could assert that as agriculture goes, so goes the rest of the Chinese economy. Indeed, when Chinese policymakers launched economic reforms in the 1970s with the "four modernizations," they focused on agriculture to give the economy a jump start.

During the last several years, reform of China's agriculture has lagged and, in some cases, has gone in reverse. China's economic decisionmakers appear to have reached a critical juncture with implications for the future of Chinese agriculture in particular and the economy as whole. They must decide whether to continue with the retrenchment of the late 1980s, that is, reverting to the old ways of conducting agriculture policy, or to once again bring market forces into play, and with them, a degree of economic rationality.

The five papers that are presented in this section address the issues of agricultural reform in China and the prospects for Chinese agriculture in the 1990s. Two of the papers—one by Terry Sicular and one by Shwu-Eng Webb and Francis Tuan—provide analyses of problems and prospects for Chinese agriculture as a whole. The other three papers examine specific aspects of Chinese agriculture. Frederick Crook's paper analyzes China's grain economy, Leo Orleans's contribution focuses on land use policy in China, and David Zweig's paper analyzes Chinese rural industries.

Both the Sicular and Webb-Tuan papers cite vast improvements in the agricultural sector in the early 1980s and attribute these improvements to the rather bold reform measures Chinese policymakers undertook in the late 1970s to early 1980s. These measures were designed to reduce the role of administrative controls and to increase the role of market forces in determining the allocation of resources in the agricultural sector. The reforms consisted of breaking up huge collective farms into smaller plots and establishing a household contract system under which individual households

---

[*] William H. Cooper is a Specialist in International Trade and Finance, Economics Division, Congressional Research Service.
[1] Figure derived from data found in The Economist Intelligence Unit—1988–89. *Country Profile: China, North Korea.* p. 17, 24.

would have more control over production and output distribution for their farms. Thus, the farmers would determine what they would produce and how they would dispose of the output after meeting tax and quota sale obligations to the state. At the same time, the state diminished its reliance on mandatory production targets in agriculture and allowed farmers to make decisions based on profitability and other economic criteria. Webb and Tuan point out that agricultural productivity surged in the early 1980s. So did the diversification of agricultural production as farmers were given more leeway in what they produced. In their paper, Webb and Tuan attribute overall improvements in Chinese economic growth and living standards in the early 1980s to improvements in agriculture.

But after 1984, the fortunes of Chinese agriculture declined. For example, the gross value of agriculture output, which had been growing at average annual rates of in the early 1980s of 8–9 percent, grew only 3–4 percent after 1984 (Sicular). Why the decline occurred is a point of difference between the Sicular and Webb-Tuan treatments of Chinese agricultural reforms. Webb-Tuan blame the downturn in agriculture on the limited scope of the reforms and on how the reforms were implemented. Sicular, on the other hand, blames policies that Chinese decisionmakers imposed subsequent to the reforms.

Webb and Tuan argue that the Chinese have not reformed their legal system to allow the agricultural reforms to operate fully. For example, Chinese law and the legal system could not deal with contract disputes and property rights—legal concepts that are fundamental to the operation of the household contract system. As a result, according to the authors, households have not felt secure in investing in their farms but have spent profits on current consumption that has inhibited the development of agriculture. In addition, when the government established the household contract system, it divided the collective farms into small plots that Webb and Tuan claim were inefficient. The land tenure rights of the farmers have been ambiguous, reducing incentives to invest. Furthermore, a policy of double track pricing (charging different prices for urban dwellers and rural dwellers) and the continued practice of subsidizing food supplies in the urban areas prevented a mature market system for agricultural products from developing and discouraged agricultural production.

Sicular, on the other hand, while recognizing some of the weaknesses of the implementation of the economic reforms, argues that they were not the cause of the abrupt downturn in agricultural production after 1985. Rather she points to policies in three areas as contributing to the downturn: agricultural pricing, investment in agriculture, and the promotion of rural industries. In the area of pricing, Sicular blames the adoption of a proportionate system of state procurement prices for agricultural products. The system was designed to lower the average price the state would have to pay for each unit in order to reduce severe budget deficits and to curtail production that had reached oversupply levels. Proportionate pricing was a shift from an early reform pricing policy using a two-tier pricing system to stimulate production—one set of prices for sales made within quotas and a second set of higher prices for above-quota sales.

Sicular argues that the reversion to a proportionate pricing system—half way between the two sets of prices—lowered marginal revenue and led to farmers decreasing production to levels below what the government expected. The result was the overall downturn in agricultural output.

In the area of investment, Sicular asserts that private and local government investment failed to replace the decline in central government investment in agriculture. Private investors, for example, put their money in rural enterprises and housing rather than in farms as Chinese policymakers had expected which affected agricultural productivity. Sicular also blames agricultural problems on Chinese government programs to promote the development of rural industries, that is, nonagricultural production in the rural areas. Lending policies were revised to give agricultural financial institutions more latitude in lending decisions. Because of the surging profitability of rural enterprises, the financial institutions diverted investments from farms to the rural enterprises, depriving the farms of needed capital. In addition, workers became attracted to rural enterprises, diverting human resources away from the farms as well.

The Chinese government responded to the problems in agriculture by reverting to old methods of agricultural management and abandoning some of the reforms. The government has increased its use of mandatory deliveries, thus reducing the discretion of the farmers to dispose of their output and returning some control back to the hands of the central authorities. And the government has instituted policies to encourage the growth of grain crops and waged a campaign against privately owned rural industries. The government succeeded in establishing some degree of economic stability. But, the long-term prognosis for Chinese agriculture remains an open question, the answer to which depends in large part on whether the Chinese return to a path of economic reforms or return to the inefficient policies of old.

The rural industries have become an important element of Chinese economy and a subject worth special attention when considering the future of Chinese agriculture. According to David Zweig, rural industries consist of enterprises, firms, hotels, and shops that are cooperatives, private establishments, and enterprises run by the local governments. They encompass a broad range of goods and services, such as household appliances, textiles, farm machinery, food, and energy, among others. Dating from the mid-1950s and Mao Tse-tung's "Great Leap Forward" program, the rural industries have long been a staple in Chinese agriculture. They were once considered ancillary to urban production and a means of employing surplus labor without placing more demands on the overburdened urban sector. But rural industries now account for over 25 percent of Chinese industrial production. Zweig implies that the success of the rural industries results from their relative independence from central authorities.

However, as with the rest of the economy, rural industries have been subjected to the vagaries of policymaking at the center—at times encouraged, other times constrained. To reduce the competition with state-run enterprises in urban areas, the government's present retrenchment program has included a campaign to reign in rural industrial activity by curtailing central government credits and restricting access to raw materials supplies. As a result, the rural industries have contracted.

Zweig concludes that rural industries will remain a staple in the Chinese economy and a barometer of official thinking on reform in agriculture and in the economy as a whole. Chinese leaders are once again acknowledging the importance of rural industries as stimuli to manufacturing and as earner of hard currency. However, the rural industries will likely present problems in the future for Chinese policymakers. Among these problems, Zweig indicates the tendency of rural industries to exacerbate regional inequalities in economic development and the competition they exert for raw materials and other resources with state-run industries.

Along with the rural industries, another significant element of Chinese agriculture is grain production. As Frederick Crook explains in his paper, China is the world's largest grain producer. The future of grain production has implications for the Chinese economy and for international grain markets. Crook outlines two general scenarios for Chinese policy in the grain economy for the foreseeable future. The first is one in which the government makes no changes in policy, that is, the government largely determines the size and composition of grain production and distribution. The second is one in which the government reforms the agricultural sector to allow market forces—namely market-determined prices— to make those determinations. The author analyzes the implications of the two scenarios for various aspects of the grain economy—land availability, yield and production, marketing, grain reserves, consumption patterns, and foreign trade.

In some cases the implications of the two scenarios differ very little. For example, technical and natural resource limitations will constrain grain yield and production no matter which road the Chinese take, according to the author. However, prices for grain and, consequently, consumption of grain would differ under the two scenarios.

From the U.S. perspective, perhaps one of the most important implications would be for trade, since China is an important market for U.S. wheat. Under the "no change" scenario, Crook forecasts a decline in grain exports as domestic demand for cereals and feedgrains would grow. At the same time, such a scenario would lead to an expansion of grain imports as the government would maintain low, fixed prices for food in the urban areas that would require a replenishment of urban stocks from foreign sources. Under the "reform" scenario, lifting of government controls would permit regional diversities to emerge in grain production.

Perhaps central to the prospects for Chinese agriculture will be how the Chinese policymakers address the problem of diminishing availability of cultivated land. While China has made impressive gains despite the loss of cultivated land, the land crisis, as Leo Orleans describes it in his work on the issue, constrains agricultural productivity and the Chinese will have to develop policies that limit losses and make better use of the land that is available.

In underscoring the significance of the land crisis, Orleans notes that between the early 1950s and mid-1980s, cultivated land per capita declined 50 percent in China. While the rapid growth in the Chinese population contributed to this trend, the absolute loss in cultivated land was also a major factor. Orleans attributes the loss to a number of factors: the growth in urban population and industrial development that has encroached on rural areas; an expansion in rural housing and enterprises that have encumbered land that could be used to grow food; hoarding of land by urban and rural occupants, preventing precious land from being efficiently used; and an underdeveloped legal system that does not adequately define property rights and tenure.

The author attributes the loss of cultivated land to other policy failures as well, such as environmental problems, some of natural causes, but most of them man-made. Orleans considers deforestation as the primary environmental problem that results in severe soil erosion destroying the fertility of the land. Furthermore, China's land reclamation process, opening virgin lands or returning land to agricultural production, has been of marginal value and unable to compensate for the loss to agriculture of the most fertile lands in the densely populated regions of China.

Because of the constraints imposed by the declining availability of land, Orleans concludes, China must try to protect the existing arable lands and make those lands more productive. The first objective requires stricter control of land-use. The second requires a combination of initiatives both systemic and technological. In the first case, the author believes that household farms should be larger so that they can achieve economies of scale. In terms of technology, the author holds out hope for China to be able to take advantage of existing techniques and technology practiced by advanced developed countries and to develop its own technology, including biotechnology, to improve land productivity.

Clearly, Chinese policymakers face critical decisions on the future of agriculture. From their analyses, the authors of the five papers conclude that China would be best served if it returns to the path towards market-oriented reforms. Whether it heeds that advice appears to be an open question at this time.

CHINA'S AGRICULTURAL POLICY DURING THE REFORM PERIOD [1]

By Terry Sicular *

CONTENTS

SUMMARY

After unprecedented growth in the early 1980s, China's agricultural performance weakened abruptly in 1985 and has stagnated thereafter. Several explanations have been proposed for this slowdown: the exhaustion of one-time gains from decollectivization; the limited amount and uneconomic distribution of arable land under small-scale household farming; and insufficient agricultural investment. This paper argues that such factors were not the primary causes of the slowdown. Rather, government policies enacted in 1983–85 brought about a sudden change in agriculture's fortunes, and the absence of comprehensive countermeasures in ensuing years hindered agriculture's recovery.

In the early 1980s decollectivization and reforms in production planning enhanced incentives and reduced administrative controls over farming. After agriculture's performance began to weaken, increasing attention was given to potential drawbacks of these reform measures. Some have proposed that steps be taken to consolidate farms and reassert control over agricultural production. Administrative intervention by local cadres in farm decision making apparently persists and has probably grown in recent years.

The temptation to rely on administrative interventions remains strong because private economic incentives conflict with government objectives for agriculture. Private incentives were greatly af-

* Associate Professor, Department of Economics, Harvard University, Cambridge, MA 02138.
[1] The author would like to thank Ti Zhongwang and Ye Qiaolun for their assistance in preparing this paper. Financial support from the Rockefeller Brothers Fund; the Committee on Scholarly Communications with the People's Republic of China with funds from the U.S. Information Agency; the American Council of Learned Societies/Social Science Research Council with funds from the Andrew W. Mellon Foundation; and the National Science Foundation under grant no. SES-8908438 is gratefully acknowledged.

fected by policy changes in 1984/85 that substantially reduced the relative profitability of agriculture. Farm prices and material incentive awards, which had been raised in the late 1970s and early 1980s, were reduced. Commercial reforms permitted extra-plan sale of farm inputs at high and rising market prices. The government condoned the growth of private rural business and liberalized rural credit policies. These actions diverted rural financial, material, and human resources from agriculture to rapidly developing nonagricultural activities.

Insufficient investment in agriculture was part of the picture, but in large part as an effect rather than as the underlying cause. In the early 1980s the government reduced direct state investment in agriculture with the expectation that this reduction would be offset by growth in local and private investment. Local and private investment in agriculture, however, has not increased as hoped: instead, funds have flowed to more lucrative nonagricultural businesses. Government policies lowering agriculture's relative profitability have contributed to the outflow of resources.

Since 1985 the government has taken steps to bolster agricultural performance, but with limited success. The government raised farm prices and incentives, but the new prices and incentives were not implemented fully at the local level. Moreover, the price increases were too small and outpaced by inflation. The government also increased controls over cultivation and imposed restrictions on market trade of farm products. These steps, however, only enhanced the relative attractiveness of the many nonagricultural activities not subject to such restrictions.

Government policies in the mid- and late 1980s thus placed agriculture at a disadvantage. Agriculture's relative standing only began to improve in 1989/90 when the austerity program began to slow the growth of rural industry and services. These developments highlight the close connection between the agricultural and nonagricultural sectors of the economy. Ultimately, China's economic development requires growth of both sectors, which will require that agriculture be given equal footing.

I. INTRODUCTION

During the past decade the Chinese government has undertaken substantial reforms in agricultural policy. These reforms have reduced administrative interventions in the the rural economy, increased reliance on economic 'levers', decentralized economic decision-making, and expanded the role of markets. Mandatory planning of production and procurement have been reduced or eliminated, and direct government investment in agriculture has declined. Increasingly the government has relied on pricing and incentives to guide agricultural production, marketing, and investment.

These measures have been undeniably successful in promoting agricultural growth. Between 1978 and 1989 the gross value of agricultural output (in constant prices) nearly doubled, agricultural productivity and farm incomes rose, and the quality and quantity of food available to consumers improved vastly. Success was most apparent, however, prior to 1985. Since 1984 agricultural performance has weakened: growth in the gross value of agricultural output has fallen from average rates of 8 or 9 percent to average rates of 3 to 4 percent. The slowdown was most abrupt for crop production, output of which dropped in absolute terms in 1985 and stagnated thereafter. (See table 1.)

Table 1. Growth in Gross Value of Agricultural Output[*]
(percent growth over previous year, comparable prices)

Year	Growth in Value of Agricultural Output	Of which: Crops
1979	7.6	7.2
1980	1.4	-0.6
1981	6.5	5.9
1982	11.3	10.3
1983	7.7	7.9
1984	12.3	9.9
1985	3.5	-2.0
1986	3.4	0.9
1987	5.8	5.3
1988	3.2	-0.5
1989	3.1	1.8

[*] Includes crops, forestry, animal husbandry, aquaculture, and sidelines.

Source: ZGTJZY, 1990, p. 53.

China's agricultural policy in the 1990s will almost certainly aim at bolstering agricultural, and especially crop production. Effective policies, however, require a clear understanding of the reasons for the slowdown in the late 1980s. Several explanations have been proposed. Some observers argue that the slowdown was unavoidable because agricultural growth had to decelerate as the one-time gains from decollectivization were played out. Some have attributed the slowdown to the declining amount and uneconomic distribution of land. Small family farms with numerous, fragmented plots could not capture economies of scale, and China's limited shrinking arable land area constrained further growth. Others have blamed the slowdown on reduced investment in farming. Certain of these factors undoubtedly weakened agriculture's performance in the late 1980s; however, none of them explain why growth slowed so abruptly in 1985.

This paper presents a different explanation for the slowdown: policies enacted in 1983–85 caused the abrupt change in agriculture's performance. Beginning in 1983 but especially in 1984/85 the Chinese government implemented a set of measures that individually and as a group affected agriculture negatively. These measures included policies directly aimed at agriculture, for example, reductions in the prices and incentives farmers received for deliveries of crops to the state. Equally important, and too often overlooked, were changes in industrial, commercial, and financial policies that had repercussions for agriculture. One such policy change was the 1984 decision to officially sanction the development of private rural enterprise. Concurrently the government allowed rural credit cooperatives to lend more freely to rural industry and services. Together with certain other nonagricultural measures discussed below, these actions caused a flood of resources to flow out of agriculture.

In the wake of such agricultural and nonagricultural policies, agricultural growth declined abruptly and, in the absence of comprehensive countermeasures, remained weak in the years that followed. Inflation hindered agriculture's recovery. Only with the retrenchment in 1989–90, when the environment for nonagricultural activities worsened, did agriculture begin to recover.

The discussion below examines economic policies that contributed significantly to the initial acceleration and consequent slowdown in agricultural growth during the 1980s. The first section discusses decollectivization and production planning. The second section examines procurement and pricing of farm products, and the third section analyzes policies affecting agricultural investment. The fourth section discusses nonagricultural policies that contributed to agricultural trends. The conclusion raises some lessons for policy in the 1990s.

II. DECOLLECTIVIZATION AND PRODUCTION PLANNING

Decollectivization and reforms in production planning are closely related, in that both have affected who makes economic decisions in agriculture. Decollectivization has shifted the basic decision-making unit from the collective farm to the household. Reforms in production planning have changed the degree and nature of administrative control over the basic decision-making unit. These reforms have been given credit for the burst of agricultural growth in the early 1980s; some claim that they also underlie the agricultural slowdown in the late 1980s.

Decollectivization has been treated extensively elsewhere, and so is discussed only briefly here.[2] During the early 1980s the house-

---

[2] See, for example Reeitsu Kojima, "Agricultural organization: New forms, new contradictions," *China Quarterly*, No. 116, Dec. 1988, pp. 706–735.

hold contracting system, under which land was contracted to individual households who could then make their own input decisions and dispose as they wished of their output after meeting their tax and quota sales obligations to the state, became widespread (see table 2). By linking rewards directly to effort, the contracting system enhanced incentives and promoted efficient production based on economic considerations. One study estimates that the incentive effects of decollectivization may have explained over 70 percent of agriculture's growth between 1978 and 1984.[3]

Reforms in production planning accompanied decollectivization. Prior to 1980 collective farms faced mandatory targets governing sown areas, yields, levels of input applications, planting techniques, and so on. Of these targets, those governing sown area were most important, in part because they were relatively easy to monitor and enforce. During the early and mid-1970s sown area targets governed the planting of all major and many minor crops, and they covered a substantial proportion of cultivated area.

During the reform decade the government moved away from mandatory production planning. The number of production planning targets in agriculture was reduced substantially in the early 1980s.[4] Production planning was now to pay greater attention to local soil and weather conditions, economic considerations, and the desires of producers. As surpluses of grain and other crops emerged in 1983 and 1984, mandatory planning of production no longer seemed necessary, and in 1985 the government announced that mandatory production planning in agriculture was no longer permitted. Thereafter planning targets were to serve only for guidance or reference.[5] Local implementation of the production planning reforms varied, but the overall effect was to reduce the degree of intervention in agricultural economic decisions. These reforms contributed to agriculture's rapid growth in the early 1980s by permitting the diversification of agricultural production, greater regional specialization, and a decline in the previously over-intensive cultivation of grain.

The slowdown in the late 1980s has raised questions about decollectivization and the relaxation of controls over farming. Chinese publications have given increasing attention to the potential drawbacks of the household contracting system.[6] One drawback is that decollectivization may have reduced agricultural investment. Despite ongoing proclamations that decollectivization was correct and announcements extending the length of land contracts, rights to land under the contracting system remain vague. Until farmers feel that they have a permanent, secure claim to the land, they will be reluctant to make long-term investments. Decollectivization

[3] John McMillan, John Whalley, and Lijiang Zhu, "The impact of China's economic reforms on agricultural productivity growth," *Journal of Political Economy* 97(4), August, 1989, pp. 781–807.

[4] Changes in production planning are discussed in Wu Xiang, "Lianchan chengbao zeren zhi yu nongye guanli," *Zhongguo renmin daxue fuyin ziliao* (hereafter ZGRMDX) 3 (1983), pp. 97,98; "Guowuyuan pizhuan guojia jiwei 'Guanyu gaijin jihua tizhide ruogan zhanxing guiding'," *Renmin ribao* (hereafter RMRB), 10 October 1984; and "Zhonggong zhongyang, guowuyuan guanyu jin yibu huoyue nongcun jingjide shixian zhengce," RMRB, 25 March 1985, section 1.

[5] "Zhonggong zhongyang, guowuyuan guanyu jin yibu huoyue nongcun jingjide shixian zhengce," RMRB, 25 March 1985, section 1.

[6] Kojima, *op. cit.*, pp. 729–730.

also has contributed to a decline in large-scale water conservancy and irrigation projects. With the weakening of collective organizations, water control and irrigation works have deteriorated.

Another alleged drawback to the household contracting system is that small, fragmented farms are less productive than large, consolidated farms. This view underlies recent proposals to promote farm reconsolidation as a solution to the current agricultural malaise. Although household labor could undoubtedly be saved if each household's plots were consolidated, it is questionable whether combining small farms into large farms would bring about additional gains. Studies of other countries, and some preliminary evidence from China, have shown that small farms are not significantly less productive than large farms.[7]

Although the government has not reversed decollectivization or rehabilitated mandatory production planning, it has encouraged increased collective leadership by local governments and through the formation of cooperative organizations (*lianheti*). In many places household land contracts now specify the land area that households are required to plant in grain.[8] In some localities village cadres directly manage certain aspects of agricultural production. For example, a county in Shandong has promoted a program called the "five unifieds" (*wuge tongyi*), i.e., unified ploughing, sowing, irrigation, harvesting, and threshing by villages.[9] Implementation of the "five unifieds" requires planning and coordination of agricultural production at the village level.

Measuring the extent of collective management of farm production is difficult. Western field researchers have observed the continued importance of village-level management in some localities.[10] A recent survey carried out by the Ministry of Agriculture's Policy Research Center (table 2) provides more systematic evidence. Although the surveyed villages report that by 1987 over 95% of their land was contracted out to households, the role of collective organizations was apparently still quite large. As late as 1987 40% of the land in these villages was ploughed, 45% of irrigated area irrigated, and roughly one-third of fertilizer, insecticide, and diesel oil inputs supplied in a unified fashion by villages (or groups).[11] The proportion of villages planning crop layout and rotations also remained high: in 1987 63% of the villages set plans for crop layout

---

[7]See Sicular, "Distribution in rural China: Observations from a recent survey in Hubei," unpublished manuscript, Harvard, 1989, and also R. Albert Berry and William R. Cline, *Agrarian Structure and Productivity in Developing Countries*, Baltimore: Johns Hopkins University Press, 1979.

[8]For an example of a household contract in 1989, see Frederick W. Crook, "China's current household contract system (part I)," in USDA, *CPE Agriculture Report* 2(3), May/June 1989, pp. 26–30, and Frederick W. Crook, "China's current household contract system (part II)," in USDA, *CPE Agriculture Report* 2(4), July/August 1989, pp. 27–33.

[9]Author interviews, Zouping County, Shandong Province.

[10] See discussions in Jean C. Oi, "The fate of the collective after the commune," in Deborah Davis and Ezra Vogel, *The Social Consequences of Chinese Economic Reforms*, Cambridge: Harvard University Press, forthcoming; in Jean C. Oi, *State and Peasant in Contemporary China: The Political Economy of Village Government*, Berkeley: University of California Press, 1989; and in Jean C. Oi, "Peasant grain marketing and state procurement: China's grain contracting system," *China Quarterly* 106 (1986), 272–290. Author interviews and observations in Shandong and Hubei also revealed this.

[11] Ministry of Agriculture Economic Policy Research Center Rural Cooperative Organizations Task Force, "Zhongguo nongcun diyu xing hezuo zuzhide shizheng miaosu—quanguo 100 ge xian 1200 ge cun diyu hezuo zuzhi xitong diaocha," *Zhongguo nongcun jingji* 1 (1989), p. 13.

and rotations, and 58% set plans for farmland basic construction.[12] The importance of collectives in farm management is highest in the eastern regions, where over three-quarters of the land is under unified ploughing and 80% of villages set plans for crop layout and rotations. These statistics suggest that the role of collectives in farm management has declined less than previously thought.

Table 2.   Survey Statistics on Collective (Unified) Production and Planning Activities

	1978	1984	1987 All	East	Central	West
I. Percent of cultivated area						
A. Under unified management	99.4	5.0	2.4	--	--	--
B. Contracted to households	0.2	93.2	95.7	--	--	--
C. Other	0.4	1.8	1.9	--	--	--
II. Percent of land under unified ploughing	--	49	40	76	34	20
III. Percent of irrigated land under unified irrigation	--	47	45	85	36	16
IV. Percent of inputs subject to unified supply						
A. Chemical fertilizer	--	56	32	50	30	21
B. Pesticides	--	54	28	51	26	23
C. Diesel oil	--	48	33	65	29	20
V. Percent of villages (groups) setting plans for						
A. Crop layout and rotations	73	64	63	80	52	58
B. Farmland basic construction	73	58	58	38	57	36

"--" indicates no data provided by source.

Notes: 1. These survey data are from 1200 randomly selected villages in 100 counties that are designated "rural economic information" counties. All provinces, municipalities and autonomous regions are covered except Tibet and Hainan.

2. The term "collective" refers to the Chinese term jiti, and "unified" to tongyi. Collective and unified activities are carried out by villages and groups, which this source lumps together using the expression cun(zu).

Source: Ministry of Agriculture Economic Policy Research Center Rural Cooperative Organizations Task Force, pp. 5,12,14.

Involvement of local leaders in the management of farm production is qualitatively different than central planning through vertical channels. Local leaders are more likely to be aware of local conditions and the desires of the farmers. Moreover, certain aspects of agricultural production such as irrigation and basic construction are probably better handled collectively than by households. Nevertheless, village and other local cadres belong to formal governmental bodies, their decisions are likely to be influenced by administrative or political considerations, and they have a tradition of infringing on the decision-making rights of households. The persistence,

---

[12] It is possible that villages draw up plans but do not seriously enforce them. Even before the reform period, however, village cadres were known not to carry out the official plans.

and in some regions resurgence, of local government involvement in agriculture thus reflects administrative intervention under a new guise.

Increased use of administrative interventions has arisen because of difficulties guiding production using indirect policies. Efforts to influence farm household decisions using prices and incentives have not had the desired effects. Economic incentives continue to conflict with, rather than complement, the government's objectives for agriculture. So long as farm-level incentives and government objectives conflict, farm behaviour will diverge from that desired by higher levels, and the temptation to directly intervene in production decisions will remain strong.

III. PROCUREMENT POLICIES: PRICES, QUOTAS, AND INCENTIVES

In the 1980s China's policy makers relied heavily on pricing, procurement, and related measures to influence agriculture. Such policies can raise farm profits and enhance agriculture's ability to attract resources, and so spur production. The allocation of resources depends, however, not on agriculture's absolute profitability, but on the relative profitability of farming in comparison to alternative pursuits. Nonagricultural developments therefore can, and have, counteracted efforts to encourage agriculture using prices and incentives. Incentive measures have also been hindered by the continued link between pricing and the state budget. Increasing farm prices raises, while reducing prices lowers, government budgetary outlays. In a period of persistent budget deficits, the government has shown greater willingness to lower than raise farm prices.

Major adjustments in procurement policy began in 1978. Initially the basic structure of the procurement system remained unchanged: farm products were subject to mandatory delivery quotas at planned prices, in some cases with a price bonus or other incentive award for beyond-quota deliveries. Adjustments were made, however, in prices and incentives. The government implemented substantial, across-the-board increases in quota procurement prices in 1979 (table 3). In the early 1980s further adjustments in quota prices took place, and seasonal and quality price differentials were widened.[13] By 1983 quota prices for grains exceeded their 1977 levels by 15 to 20 percent, oils and oilcrops by 27 percent, sugar crops by 26 percent, cotton by over 30 percent, and hogs by 27 percent. These price adjustments followed more than a decade of constant quota prices.

The government concurrently expanded bonuses for above-quota deliveries. Prior to 1979 grain and oilcrops had received a price bonus of 30 percent for deliveries beyond the quota level. In 1979 this bonus was increased to 50 percent. Cotton, which had earlier received no above-quota bonus, now began to receive a nationwide 30 percent price bonus for sales to the state exceeding the average quantity delivered over the three year period 1976–78.[14] Price bo-

---

[13] Table 3 and Ministry of Commerce Institute of Commercial Economic Research, *Xin zhongguo shangye shigao*, Beijing: Zhongguo Caizheng Jingji Chubanshe, 1984, p. 386.

[14] Price Theory and Practice Editorial Department, *Wujia dashi ji*, Beijing: Zhongguo Caizheng Jingji Chubanshe, 1986, p 386.

348

Table 3: State Quota Procurement Prices (yuan per ton, standard grade)

A. Grains and Oil Crops

	Indica Paddy	Japonica Paddy	Wheat	Corn	Soyabean	Shelled Peanuts	Rapeseed
1971	196.2		268.6	181.8	326.0	760.0	560.0
1977	196.2		268.6	181.8		760.0	560.0
1978	196.2		272.2	176.0	401.2	760.0	560.6
1979	231.4	297.2	329.6	214.4	461.4	965.8	714.6
1980	231.4	297.2	314.4	214.4	461.4	965.8	714.6
1981	231.4	297.2	314.4	214.4	692.1	965.8	714.6
1982	231.4	297.2	314.4	214.4	692.1	965.8	714.6
1983	231.4	297.2	314.4	214.4	692.1		
1984	231.4	297.2	314.4	214.4	600.0		

B. Economic Crops and Hogs

	Cotton, North	Cotton, South	Sugar Cane	Sugar Beet	Tobacco	Live Hogs (per 100 kg.)
1971	1,869.4	1,869.4	34.6	54.6	1,355.0	95.72
1977	2,116.0	2,116.0	34.6	60.0		98.86
1978	2,304.8	2,304.8	34.6	60.0	1,369.6	98.92
1979	2,765.0	2,655.2	43.7	76.0	1,369.6	125.38
1980	3,031.4	2,921.6	43.7	76.0	1,369.6	125.38
1981	3,065.8	2,956.0	43.7	76.0	1,680.0	125.38
1982	3,065.8	2,956.0	43.7	76.0	1,680.0	125.38
1983	3,065.8	2,956.0	43.7	76.0	1,680.0	125.38
1984			43.7	76.0	1,680.0	125.38

Source: Sicular, "Ten years of reform...," table 3.

nuses for other farm products were also implemented, in some cases by provincial governments.[15] The increased above-quota bonuses were multiplied by the now higher quota prices, so that between 1977 and 1983 above-quota prices rose 36 percent for grains,

[15] Ministry of Commerce Institute of Commercial Economic Research, *op. cit.*, pp. 391–393.

47 percent for oils and oilcrops, and over 80 percent for cotton (table 4).

In addition to the above price measures, the government expanded a variety of material incentive programs under which farmers were awarded the right to purchase low-priced or scarce commodities in return for delivering farm products to the state. For example, in 1978 the central government raised the nationwide award of chemical fertilizers per 100 kilograms cotton delivered to the state from 35 to 40 kilograms, and starting in 1979 also gave farmers in cotton-growing areas 100 to 200 kilograms grain at the low, urban retail price. Similar incentive programs applied to grain, oilcrops, sugarbeet, sugarcane, hemps, and tobacco. By the early eighties the overall number of material incentive programs and the quantities of items awarded had grown quite large. According to incomplete statistics, products eligible for encouragement grain awards numbered 206 at the end of 1981, as compared to only 68 in 1971.[16] The quantity of grain supplied under encouragement sales programs rose to an historical high of 24 percent of total state grain procurements in the early 1980s.[17]

The price and incentive measures described above were accompanied by a gradual reduction in quota levels and in the overall scope of procurement planning. Quota levels for some products, most importantly grain, were lowered. Between 1978 and 1982 the national grain quota and tax was reduced by 20 percent (table 5).[18] Efforts were also made to adjust the geographical distribution of quotas to permit greater regional specialization. Finally, the number of farm products subject to centrally planned procurement and distribution was reduced, while the number of products handled by lower level governments or traded on free markets was increased. As early as 1978 the government began to encourage the revival of rural markets. By 1980 all products except cotton were allowed on the market after state delivery quotas were fulfilled.[19] By 1982 restrictions on private long-distance trade had been lifted for all farm products allowed on markets except grain, and private individuals were permitted to specialize in transport and trade.[20] The expansion of free markets provided an alternative channel for the sale of farm products, often at prices exceeding those offered by the state.

The government participated in market trade through "negotiated price" procurement (yijia shougou). The state commercial system bought and sold beyond-quota farm products at the negotiated prices, which, according to central directives, were to be agreed upon jointly by both sides, to apply to voluntary above-quota deliveries, and to be decided on the basis of regional, yearly, seasonal, varietal, and quality considerations. These prices were to follow trends in demand and supply, but were in general not to

---

[16] Ministry of Commerce Institute of Commercial Economic Research, op. cit., p. 394.

[17] Ibid, and An Xiji, "Lun woguo nongchanpin jiage tizhi gaige yu jiage zhengce tiaozheng," Nongye jingji wenti (hereafter NYJJWT), Number 10 (1985), pp. 23–24, 26.

[18] Producers also faced obligatory above-quota deliveries, but information is not available on the level of or changes in these obligations.

[19] An Xiji, op. cit., p. 24. Substandard cotton was permitted on the market in the early 1980s, but prohibitions on graded cotton remained.

[20] Price Theory and Practice Editorial Department, op. cit., pp. 137–38; "CPC document no. 1 on rural economic policies," Foreign Broadcast Information Service, Daily Report 1(072), K6–8.

Table 4: State Above-quota and Contract Procurement Prices[*] (yuan per ton)

A. Grains and Oil Crops

	Indica Paddy	Japonica Paddy	Wheat	Corn	Soyabeans	Shelled Peanuts	Rapeseed
1971	255.1		349.2	236.3	423.8	988.0	728.0
1977	255.1		349.2	236.3		988.0	728.0
1978	255.1		353.9	228.8	521.6	988.0	728.8
1979	347.1	445.8	494.4	321.6	692.1	1,448.7	1,071.9
1980	347.1	445.8	471.6	321.6	692.1	1,448.7	1,071.9
1981	347.1	445.8	471.6	321.6	692.1	1,448.7	1,071.9
1982	347.1	445.8	471.6	321.6	692.1	1,448.7	1,071.9
1983	347.1	445.8	471.6	321.6	692.1	1,255.5	929.0
1984	347.1	445.8	471.6	321.6	600.0	1,255.5	929.0
1985	312.0	401.0	424.4	289.4	600.0	1,255.5	929.0
1986	312.0	401.0	424.4	289.4/316.4	692.1	1,255.5	929.0
1987	312/342	401/436	424.4	289.4-336.4		1.448.7	929.0
1988	312/352	401/446	454.4/464.4	289.4-336.4		1,448.7	1000.4

B. Economic Crops

	Cotton, North	Cotton, South	Tobacco
1971	1,869.4	1,869.4	1,355.0
1977	2,116.0	2,116.0	
1978	2,304.8	2,304.8	1,369.6
1979	3,594.5	3,451.8	1,369.6
1980	3,940.8	3,798.1	1,369.6
1981	3,985.5	3,842.8	1,680.0
1982	3,985.5	3,842.8	1,680.0
1983	3,985.5	3,842.8	1,344/2,016
1984	3,665.4	3,310.7	1,344/2,016
1985	3,576.8	3,310.7	1,392/2,088
1986	3,488.1	3,310.7	1,392/2,088
1987	3,576.8	3,399.4	1,497/2,246
1988	3,576.8	3,576.8	

[*] 1971-1984 prices are above-quota prices; 1985-88 prices are the new contract prices.

Source: Sicular, "Ten years of reform...," table 4.

exceed local market prices.[21] The revival of negotiated price trade gave the state commercial system more flexibility in responding to market conditions and provided a lever for influencing the market.

Table 5: Marketing and State Procurement of Grain (million tons trade grain)

	(1)			(2)	(3)	(4)	(5)
	Marketed Grain:[a]			State Procurement[b]	Planned Quota or Contract[c]	(3)÷(2)[d]	Share of Procurement at Quota/Contract Prices[a] (%)
	Total	% to State	% to Market				
1977	47.67	100.0	0.0	47.67	37.75	.79	
1978	50.73	100.0	0.0	50.73	37.75	.74	
1979	60.10	95.8	4.2	57.57	35.00	.61	63
1980	61.29	93.1	6.9	57.07	34.33	.60	58
1981	68.46	92.4	7.6	63.24	30.38	.48	50
1982	78.06	92.4	7.6	72.09	30.32	.42	50
1983	102.49	94.4	5.6	96.74			35
1984	117.25	91.7	8.3	107.48			29
1985	107.63	84.2	15.8	90.62	75		
1986	115.16	83.5	16.5	96.15	60.75	.63	67
1987	120.92	82.0	18.0	99.20	50.0	.50	57
1988	119.95				50.0		
1989	121.38				50.0		

Notes:

a. Data are for the calendar year. Percentage sold to the state is calculated using data in column (2); the remainder is assumed to be sold on the market.

b. Includes purchases by state commercial departments and supply and marketing cooperatives. Data are probably for the calendar year.

c. Data prior to 1985 are for the state procurement quota and tax, and from 1985 on are for the planned level of contract procurement. These data are for the production year (April of the current year through March of the following year).

d. These numbers are approximate, as the data in column (2) are for the calendar year, and in column (3) for the production year.

e. 1979-84 shares are given by Dangdai Zhongguo Liangshi Gongzuo Editorial Committee. 1986-87 shares are estimated by the author. Contract procurement for these years is estimated as state procurement minus negotiated-price procurement (ZGSYNJ, p. 55), and the share is calculated accordingly.

Sources:

Sicular, "Ten years of reform...," table 5.
Dangdai Zhongguo Liangshi Gongzuo Editorial Committee, Dangdai zhongguo liangshi gongzuo, Beijing: Zhongguo Shehui Kexue Chubanshe, 1988, p. 179.
ZGSYNJ, pp. 55, 659.
ZGTJZY 1990, p. 95.

The commercial reforms in the late 1970s and early 1980s successfully promoted agricultural growth, but they also led to expanding budgetary outlays on trade in farm products. As production expanded the government found itself buying ever-increasing quantities of farm products at the higher, above-quota prices. The share of procurement at quota prices declined dramatically, in the case of grain, from 63 percent in 1979 to only 29 percent in 1984 (table 5).[22] Meanwhile, the government continued to sell farm products at low ration prices. State retail prices of grain had not changed since the 1960s and had already been lower than quota

---

[21] Wang Dahuai, "Nongchanpin jiage zhishi jiangzuo: Liangshi he youliao jiage (shang)," *Jiage lilun yu shijian* (hereafter JGLLYSJ) 2 (1985), pp. 50–53.

[22] Above-quota procurement, conversely, rose from 37 percent in 1979 to 71 percent in 1984.

prices before the 1979 price increases. The combination of rising procurement costs and low, unchanged retail prices generated growing price subsidies on state commerce in farm products. Attempts were made to stem these subsidies by raising retail prices for nonstaple foods like meat and vegetables; however, increases in retail prices were invariably accompanied by income supplements or wage increases for urban residents, the costs of which offset subsidy reductions.[23]

By the mid-1980s budgetary losses from price subsidies on farm products grew to a critical level. In 1984 price subsidies on grain, oilcrops, and cotton had reached 20 billion yuan, equal to 14 percent of total government revenues.[24] Similar subsidies also existed for other farm products and on foreign trade in farm products.

Growing budgetary costs prompted an overhaul of procurement policy. First, the government abandoned the two-tiered quota/above-quota pricing system and instituted a single, "proportionate" procurement price for each crop. The new proportionate prices were weighted averages of the old quota and above-quota prices, with the weights varying somewhat by region and crop. Proportionate pricing was implemented for oilcrops in 1983, for cotton in 1984, and for grain in 1985. The new grain price was set equal to 30 percent of the quota price plus 70 percent of the above-quota price (dao san qi).[25] Proportionate pricing stopped the upward drift in the costs of procurement as above-quota deliveries expanded. It also eliminated the incentive to evade quotas in order to receive higher above-quota prices.

Second, on January 1, 1985, the Chinese government announced that, except for a few products, it would do away with the old procurement system and no longer send down mandatory delivery quotas to farmers. For grain and cotton, mandatory quotas were to be eliminated and replaced by a combination of voluntary contract and market purchases. State commercial departments were to negotiate purchase contracts with farmers before the sowing season: the contract prices would be set at the new proportionate prices, and farmers could choose freely whether or not they wished to sign contracts with the state or dispose of their products on the market. The state no longer promised to purchase grain and cotton beyond the contract amount. Only if market prices fell below the old quota price would the state guarantee to buy additional grain, and then it would only pay the old quota price.

Planned procurement of other farm products was to be gradually eliminated and replaced by market allocation. State commercial departments thus would increasingly buy and sell at market or near market prices. Through market participation the state would meet its needs for continued planned supply to urban areas, to industry,

---

[23] Terry Sicular, "China: Food pricing under socialism," in Terry Sicular, ed., *Food Price Policy in Asia: A Comparative Study*, Ithaca: Cornell University Press, 1989; Price Theory and Practice Editorial Department, *op. cit.*, pp. 30–31, 34–35.

[24] State Statistical Bureau, *Zhongguo tongji nianjian* 1990 (hereafter ZGTJNJ), Beijing: Zhongguo Tongji Chubanshe, 1990, p. 244, and ZGTJNJ 1989, pp. 748–749. Official statistics for government revenue include government borrowing. Since government borrowing is not considered a form of revenue in Western definitions of budgetary revenues, I have subtracted borrowing from the official revenue data before calculating these percentages.

[25] JGLLYS 4 (1985), p. 51.

and for export. Through market participation the state would also exert influence on market trends.[26]

If fully implemented, the 1985 reform would have eliminated mandatory state quotas, drastically reduced the scope of commercial planning, and greatly expanded the role of markets in allocation and price determination. Together with concurrent reforms on the retail side, they would also have reduced budgetary outlays on state commerce. This budgetary objective would be accomplished both by establishing a maximum level of state outlays on the procurement of farm products, and by reducing the scope of low-priced state sales. For all farm products except grain, oils, and cotton, both state purchases and sales were eventually to take place at market prices.[27] For grain and oils, planned supplies to urban residents were to continue at unchanged, low prices, but starting in 1985 sales of grain in the countryside were to take place at the higher, proportionate procurement prices.[28] Since in the early 1980s government resales of grain in rural areas had exceeded 40 percent of state grain procurements, the budgetary savings from raising rural sales prices were potentially substantial.[29]

Although the 1985 reforms were meant to slow growth in agricultural output and reduce government procurement of farm products, subsequent declines in crop production and deliveries exceeded expectations. Cotton deliveries fell from 6 million tons in 1984 to only 3.5 million tons in 1985, and grain deliveries from 107 to 91 million tons. These delivery levels were well below the expected amounts: contract-price deliveries of cotton were only 70 percent, and of grain only 72 percent of the totals promised under contracts signed.[30] (See table 5.)

Price and incentive reforms undoubtedly contributed to these trends. The shift to proportionate pricing, although designed to maintain the average prices paid for deliveries to the state, effectively lowered marginal prices. Marginal prices—the prices received for additional output or sales—determine the profitability of increasing or decreasing production levels. Previously farmers received above-quota prices for additional deliveries; now they received proportionate prices. The proportionate prices were lower than the old above-quota prices by about 13 percent for oilcrops, 10 percent for grains, and 12 to 14 percent for cotton (table 4). The switch to proportionate pricing therefore discouraged farm production, and, together with low market prices in 1983 and 1984 due to

---

[26] Ibid.

[27] When subsidiary food prices were raised in 1979, some of the budgetary savings were offset by wage increases to protect urban living standards. With the release of hog and pork prices in 1985, the state announced that it would give urban residents a subsidy or income supplement (Price Theory and Practice Editorial Department op. cit., p. 252).

[28] Ibid. pp. 252–53.

[29] "Taolun nongye ruhe guanqie yi jihua wei zhu, shichang tiaojie we bu," ZGRMDX 15 (1982), p. 75. Some portion of these sales were probably at negotiated prices.

[30] Terry Sicular, "Ten years of reform: Progress and setbacks in agricultural planning and pricing," Harvard Institute of Economic Research Discussion Paper No. 1474, March, 1990, pp. 20–21, and footnotes 55 and 56. Note that these percentages overstate the degree of contract fulfillment, as some beyond-contract procurement occurred at contract prices. For example, in 1987 total grain procurement at the contract price exceeded by 7 percent procurement in fulfillment of the contract responsibility. See Almanac of China's Commerce Editorial Committee, Zhongguo shangye nianjian 1988 (hereafter ZGSYNJ), Beijing: Zhongguo Shangye Chubanshe, 1988, pp. 55, 659.

oversupplies of farm products, adversely affected expectations about the potential for profits from farming.

Concurrent reductions in material incentive awards reinforced the negative effects of price measures. In 1985 grain incentive awards for cotton deliveries were eliminated, and chemical fertilizer awards were to apply only to within-contract, and no longer to beyond-contract, cotton deliveries.[31] Furthermore, in 1985 the price of grain supplied under material incentive programs was raised from the old quota price to the higher proportionate price.

Declines in production and deliveries led the government to back away from some of its 1985 initiatives. Voluntary contracts for grain soon became mandatory. Numerous local reports confirm that delivery contracts were indeed obligatory quotas under a new name.[32] Problems with grain procurement also prompted greater administrative intervention in free markets. To ensure contract fulfillment, local governments closed markets during the procurement seasons and blocked trade of farm products across administrative boundaries.[33]

In 1987 and 1988 the central government imposed further restrictions on markets as part of the effort to slow inflation. Measures taken included allowing local governments to set ceilings and floors on free market prices of grain, oils, animal products, vegetables, and other farm products. In some regions the central government established responsibility systems with local governments for control of the retail price index.[34] In 1988 the State Council issued a decision that starting in the Fall, 1988, procurement season, procurement of rice would be subject to monopoly by the Ministry of Grain. Other departments, units, and individuals were not permitted to supply rice.[35]

The government also began to improve incentives for crop production. Over the two years 1986 and 1987, the central government reduced nationwide planned delivery contracts for grain by one-third (table 5). Although in part a practical step in response to the unrealistically high 1985 contract target, the contract quota reductions were also meant to allow farmers to sell more grain at negotiated and market prices. Furthermore, in 1987 the central government reinstituted material incentives for contract deliveries of grain and cotton. For grain, the "three link" (*san guagou*) policy awarded cash advances and tied sales of high-grade chemical fertilizer and diesel oil at low state list prices for contract deliveries. Similar "link" awards were instituted for cotton and certain other

[31] Price Theory and Practice Editorial Department, *op. cit.*, p. 186.

[32] Lu Wen, "Dangqian nongcun gaige zhongde sange zhongyao maodun," ZGRMDX 23 (1985), pp. 33–35; Jean C. Oi, "Peasant grain marketing and state procurement..."; Liu Wenbao and Zheng Xinwu, "Wanshan liangshi hetong dinggou zhidude tujing," NYJJWT 11 (1986), pp. 60–61; Institute of Development General Topics Group, "Nongmin, shichang, he zhidu chuangxin: Baochan daohu banian hou nongcun," *Jingji yanjiu* (hereafter JJYJ) 1 (1987), pp. 3–16; "State urged to improve purchasing of grain," *China Daily*, 26 November 1988, p. 1; author interviews in Shandong, Hubei, Guangdong.

[33] Reports of restrictions on marketing can be found in Institute of Development General Topics Group, *op cit.*, pp. 1–16; Liu Wenbao and Zheng Xinwu, *op.cit.*; and Zhan Zhongde and Zhao Huazhou, RMRB, 3 July 1989, p. 5.

[34] "1987 nian wujia shangzhang qingkuang fenxi ji jiage gaigede zhuyao cuoshi," JGLLYSJ 3 (1988), p. 59, and "Guojia Wujia Ju tongzhi jiaqiang liangshi shichang jiage guanli," JG JGLLYSJ 3 (1988), pp. 52, 54.

[35] "Guanyu wending liangshi shichangde jueding," JGLLYSJ 12 (1988), p. 55.

crops.[36] The amounts of these material awards were increased further in 1988 and 1989.[37]

The government began to raise contract procurement prices in 1986 (table 4). In contrast to the dramatic, across-the-board procurement price increases of the early 1980s, the price adjustments of the late 1980s were modest, occurred gradually, and applied only to particular products in particular regions. Overall, the price adjustments in 1986–88 raised grain and oilseeds contract prices by between 8 and 16 percent over their 1985 levels in the regions where they applied. For cotton, as of 1988 the contract price in the North had recovered to its 1985 level, and in the South was 8 percent higher than in 1985. The state implemented additional price increases in 1989, including an 18 percent rise in grain contract prices.[38]

The intent of these quota, incentive, and price measures was to revitalize farm production and encourage deliveries to the state. Crop production and deliveries, however, did not respond (tables 1, 5). One reason is that local implementation of these measures was uneven. Local meddling with the "three link" incentive program has received considerable attention in the Chinese press.[39] Local governments did not supply, and farmers did not receive, the promised inputs. A nationwide survey of over 10,000 farm households revealed that in 1987 tied sales of fertilizer and diesel fuel for grain contracts were 20 percent below levels promised in central directives. Cash advances were only 86 percent of the stipulated amounts.[40] Local governments also did not pay farmers the prescribed prices in a timely way. In 1987 and 1988 local governments issued IOUs (da bai tiaozi) to farmers instead of paying them cash. One article estimates that in 1988 the nationwide average debt owed farmers for each 100 yuan deliveries of farm products was 20 to 40 yuan.[41] These debts often remained outstanding for several months or longer, in some cases for up to a year.[42] Such practices seriously eroded farmer confidence in government policies.[43]

---

[36] The national "three link" program for grain awarded 6 kg. good quality fertilizer, 3 kg. diesel oil, and a 20 percent interest-free cash advance for each 100 kilograms contracted grain (ZGSYNJ, p. 54–55).

[37] In 1989 fertilizer awards were reportedly raised to 15 kg. per 100 kg. for contract deliveries of paddy and soybeans, and to 10 kg. for wheat and corn (USDA, *China Agriculture and Trade Report*, 1989, p. 8). In 1988 cotton began to receive 5 kg. diesel oil per 100 kg. deliveries (author interview).

[38] Adi Ignatius, "China unveils raft of austerity moves to cool the economy," *Asian Wall Street Journal Weekly*, 27 March 1989, pp. 1, 11.

[39] "Jianjue luoshi liangshi hetong dinggou 'san guagou' zhengce—guojia jingwei fuzhuren Ye Qing jiu guowuyuan jingji tongzhi da benbao jizhe wen," RMRB, 2 July 1987, 2; Wang Shiqiang, "Jiangshou huafei weihe duixian buliao"; and Yao Guang, Jie Guozhi, *et al*, "Mian jiang huafei buneng kong dui kong," *Jingji cankao*, 13 May 1987. 1986 Document No. 1 also refers to this problem.

[40] Central Rural Policy Research Office Rural Survey Office, "Nongcun gaige yu nongmin," NYJJWT 8 (1988), p. 49.

[41] The estimates of debt owed farmers are from " 'Pay up' call on IOUs to farmers," China Daily, 10 January 1989, p. 3, which quotes an article in *Nongmin ribao*.

[42] Hou Shoulong, Han Ku, and Lu Huaifu, "Lingren youside baitiaozi," RMRB, 8 Aug. 1989, p. 6; Hao Wenkai and Tang Kunran, "Shou zhu da baitiao, nongmin shoubuliao," RMRB, 5 August 1989, p. 6; Zhan Zhongde and Zhao Huazhou, "Tougou fengshou kan 'shengwen',"RMRB, 30 July 1989, p. 5.

[43] The actions of local governments often reflected real obstacles faced at the local level. In the case of "link" incentive sales, for example, the central government had apparently not given local governments supplies of inputs sufficient to meet their tied sales obligations. In 1987 the central government only gave Henan province half the amount of fertilizers it needed to fulfill

Continued

In addition, the increases in contract prices were inadequate. At best the 1988 price adjustments only raised contract prices back to the level of above-quota prices before 1985. For many crops in many regions, contract prices in 1988 remained lower than the old above-quota prices. Only in 1989 did contract prices begin to exceed the old above-quota prices, and then only for some crops in some regions. While contract prices were just regaining their previous levels, market prices were rapidly rising. Inflation far outpaced contract price increases: between 1984 and 1988 the price level rose 47 percent.[44] Inflation caused the gap between contract and market prices to widen considerably. Chinese publications report that by 1988, market prices for grain were three to four times higher, and for oilseeds 18 to 63 percent higher, than contract prices.[45] Under these circumstances, the contract price increases had little effect.

IV. POLICIES ON AGRICULTURAL INVESTMENT

One explanation given for the slowdown in agriculture is insufficient investment. Available evidence indeed suggests that the level of agricultural investment grew slowly, and that, since farm output rose substantially, the rate of investment in agriculture declined. The reasons behind lagging investment are twofold: first, during the early and mid-1980s the government reduced direct state investment in agriculture, and second, local and private investment did not expand as hoped. Initially private resources were used for housing construction rather than productive investment. Even after the housing boom began to slow, however, agricultural investment still did not increase sufficiently. Reductions in crop prices and incentives and policies increasing off-farm opportunities drove local investment funds, along with other financial, human, and material resources, towards more profitable nonagricultural activities.

Table 6 presents available data on government investment in agriculture. State budgetary outlays on basic agricultural construction declined from levels of 5 to 6 billion yuan a year in the late 1970s to between 3 and 4 billion yuan in the mid-1980s. Agriculture's share of government outlays on capital construction fell from over 11 percent to less than 7 percent.[46] As costs of construction rose during these years, the reduction in real investment was even greater.

The government reduced direct investment with the expectation that pricing and incentive policies would elicit substantial local and private investment. Higher prices would increase the returns

---

tied sales obligations for its 1987 cotton contract responsibility. Henan's provincial and local governments made efforts to make up the difference by purchasing higher-priced fertilizer on the market and subsidizing the price differential; this raised supplies to 70 percent of tied sales obligations. Similarly, the central government's drastic reduction in credit allocations during 1988 and 1989 contributed to the use of IOUs. Banks did not lend local procurement departments funds adequate to carry out procurement, and so they resorted to IOUs. See Sicular, "Ten years of reform. . .," pp. 30–32.

[44] This is calculated using the national retail price index. ZGSYNJ, p. 837, and *Zhongguo tongji zhaiyao 1989* (ZGTJZY), p. 89.

[45] Sicular, "Ten years of reform. . .," table 6; Liu Dizhong, "Snow gift encourages big harvest," *China Daily*, 12 January 1989, p. 1; and China Daily, 1 April 1988, p. 3.

[46] These data do not include extra-budgetary outlays on agricultural basic construction, which data are unavailable. Note that these data are different than those cited by some other authors. See table 6 for an explanation of the data definitions.

Table 6. Government Budgetary Appropriations for Investment in Agricultural Basic
Construction[*] (million yuan)

Year	Current Prices	Constant 1981 Prices[**]	Share of total government appropriations on basic construction (%)
1978	5114	5513	11.3
1979	6241	6570	12.1
1980	4859	5005	11.6
1981	2415	2415	7.3
1982	2881	2800	9.3
1983	3425	3184	8.9
1984	3363	2955	6.9
1985	3773	3042	6.5
1986	4387	3276	6.5
1987	4681	3224	7.5

[*] These data include grants and, after the 1985 reform converting direct grants to loans, funds issued to the Construction Bank as credit to be used for budgeted agricultural construction projects. They do not include extra-budgetary outlays on agricultural investment (for which data are not available). Note that these numbers differ from those cited by some other authors. Both Chinese and Western authors commonly cite data that measures the value of work completed calculated using budgeted (yusuan) prices, i.e., the prices used to draw up contruction plans. If actual prices diverge from budgeted prices, or if appropriated money is not spent in the year it was appropriated, then these two series will differ. From 1980-84, the data on appropriations are lower, and after 1984 higher, than the data for work completed at budgeted prices. The series on actual appropriations is, in my opinion, a better indicator of the government's willingness to devote money to agricultural investment.

[**] The constant price series is deflated using a construction price index as a deflator. This construction price index is derived from the nominal series on gross value of construction and the comparable price index of gross value of construction given in ZGTJZY 1990, p. 82. It is an index of budgeted, not actual, construction prices. An index of actual construction prices would be preferred, but no such index is available.

Sources:
  Statistical Bureau Department of Fixed Asset Investment Statistics, Zhongguo guding zichan touzi tongji ziliao. 1950-1985, Beijing: Zhongguo Tongji Chubanshe, 1987, pp. 74-75.
  ZGTJNJ 1989, pp. 665, 669.
  ZGTJNJ 1990, p. 239.
  ZGTJZY 1990, p. 82.

to agricultural investment, and, by raising farm incomes, also enlarge household savings which could be used for that investment. In addition, the government modified credit policies. Rural credit cooperatives, the major source of formal credit to farm households, were allowed to lend out a larger proportion of their deposits, and were in general granted more independence in their lending decisions. Informal cooperative and even private credit institutions were allowed to emerge so as to help match the supply and demand for funds.[47] Such measures were meant to increase the supply of investible funds.

Another approach to promoting agricultural investment was reflected in the policy of "using industry to support agriculture" (*yigong bunong*). Under this policy the central government urged local governments and rural enterprises to devote a share of their profits to agricultural subsidies and investment. These monies could be contributed directly by the enterprises, or could come out of local government tax revenues from industry.[48]

Although data on rural investment are incomplete, available statistics show that local and private investment in agriculture did not increase as anticipated (table 7). Profits of rural township and village enterprises used to aid agriculture declined in the early 1980s and then rose but did not recover fully. Nominal investment in agricultural fixed assets by rural collectives similarly declined in the early 1980s, and then recovered in 1987/88. These data suggest that, despite the campaign to "use industry to subsidize agriculture," the contribution of collective enterprises to agricultural investment in the late 1980s was not substantially greater than it had been in the early 1980s. Moreover, any nominal gains largely reflected higher prices rather than real growth. In constant price terms such investment appears to have declined.

Available data on private investment unfortunately are not broken down between agricultural and nonagricultural components.[49] Farm household purchases of fixed agricultural and nonagricultural productive assets rose substantially through 1983, levelled off at about 17 yuan per capita in 1983–85, and then rose rapidly again in 1987 and 1988. For reasons discussed below, it is likely that much of the growth in later years reflects purchases of nonagricultural assets. Once again, real growth was considerably lower: holding prices constant, household purchases of fixed assets show no real improvement after 1983.[50] Thus neither collective nor private investment in agriculture displays significant real growth, and neither kept pace with agricultural output.

In the late 1980s policy makers responded to slowing agricultural growth by raising direct state investment. In Autumn, 1988, the government called for an expansion in large-scale agricultural capital construction and water conservancy.[51] By 1989 the real level of government investment in agriculture had begun to rise, as had the share of agriculture in the total government budget for capital construction.[52] The 1990 national economic plan calls for an addi-

---

[47] For a detailed discussion of credit policies and related developments, see On-Kit Tam, "Rural finance in China," *China Quarterly*, No. 113, pp. 60–76; Andrew Watson, "Investment issues in the Chinese countryside," *Australian Journal of Chinese Affairs* 22(1989), pp. 85–126; and Loraine West, "Rural credit markets and the cost of capital," mimeo, Stanford University, 1990.

[48] Sicular, "Ten years of reform. . .," pp. 6, 23.

[49] These numbers also exclude in-kind investment such as investment with unremunerated labor.

[50] Nominal purchases of productive assets is deflated using the price index for agricultural inputs.

[51] He Kang, "Seizing the opportunity for rich harvests," *Beijing Review* 33(3), January 15–21, 1990, p. 26.

[52] Data on budgetary appropriations are not available for 1989, but data on state investment in agricultural basic construction (completed work, valued at budgeted prices), show a 50 percent rise in 1989 over 1988 (it rose from less than 5 billion yuan in each of the years 1986, 1987,

Continued

Table 7. Statistics on Investment by Rural Collectives and Farm Households

Year	Profits of Township and Village Enterprises Used to Aid Agriculture (million yuan)[a]	Investment in Agricultural Fixed Assets by Rural Collectives (million yuan)[b]		Per capita purchases of productive fixed assets by farm households (yuan)[c]	
		Current Prices	Constant 1981 Prices	Current Prices	Constant 1981 Prices
1981	2270	3380	3380	2.61	2.61
1982		5205	5059	11.69	11.47
1983		3337	3102	18.44	17.56
1984		2899	2547	16.89	14.78
1985	880	2073	1672	18.70	15.61
1986				16.66	13.76
1987	850	4252	2929	20.52	15.83
1988	1160	4290	2597	25.14	16.69

a. Includes all aid to agriculture by these enterprises, both for investment and other purposes. From State Statistical Bureau Department of Rural Socioeconomic Statistics, Zhongguo nongcun tongji nianjian. 1989, Beijing: Zhongguo Tongji Chubanshe, p. 210.

b. Includes investment in both productive and nonproductive fixed assets. Statistical Bureau Department of Fixed Asset Investment Statistics, op. cit., pp. 348-49, 351; ZGTJNJ 1988, p. 641; and ZGTJNJ 1989, p. 559. Deflated using the construction price index discussed in table 6 (see table 6 footnotes).

c. Investment in productive agricultural and nonagricultural fixed assets. Zhongguo nongcun tongji nianjian. 1989, pp. 296. Deflated using the price index for agricultural inputs from ZGTJNJ 1989, p. 693-94.

tional 30 percent increase in central government investment in agriculture, and for similar increases in local government invest-

and 1988 to over 7 billion yuan in 1989). In real terms—deflated by the construction price index—the increase in 1989 was 36 percent. As a share of total government investment in basic construction, agriculture's share rose from 3 percent to 4.6 percent. See ZGTJNJ 1989, pp. 482, 487-488, 490; ZGTJZY 1990, p. 23; and table 6.

ment.[53] Statements by the central leadership indicate that this upward trend is likely to continue.[54]

V. Nonagricultural Policies That Influenced Agriculture

The agricultural slowdown in 1985 was not solely the result of reduced prices and incentives for farm products. A spate of concurrent changes in industrial, financial, and commercial policies expanded profitable opportunities outside of agriculture and lowered the relative attractiveness of farming. These policies continued to detract from agriculture through 1988. Only with the economic retrenchment in 1989–90 did agriculture begin to recover.

From agriculture's standpoint, one of the most important nonagricultural policies was the decision to relax restrictions on private rural business. Restrictions on private business had been eased gradually in the late seventies and early eighties, but in 1984 private business was for the first time officially condoned and encouraged. The rationale for this change of policy is explained in the 1984 No. 1 Document, which states that in the process of rural development more and more people must necessarily leave the land to enter into small industry and services. The new attitude was echoed in a speech by Wan Li in December, 1984:[55]

[Some people's] conceptual understanding of rural enterprise (*xiangzen qiye*) is incomplete. They only consider the mass-run, collectively-owned enterprises of the original townships, villages, and teams to be rural enterprise, and they do not count the more recently established businesses that farmers run themselves or using pooled funds. Some people go so far as to look down on such businesses. This is incorrect... People should treat them equally and without discrimination, give them encouragement and support.

A variety of measures reflected this new attitude. In February, 1984, a State Council decision permitted individual businesses in rural areas to engage in urban-rural transport, set up stalls or stores in towns, and hire a few employees or apprentices.[56] In 1984/85 rural credit cooperatives, the primary credit institutions at the village level and a major source of agricultural credit for farm households, were explicitly allowed and, furthermore, mandated to provide credit for rural industrial and commercial businesses. Available statistics show the resulting diversion of credit from agricultural to nonagricultural borrowers. By 1985, of total loans by rural credit cooperatives, 45 percent went to township enterprises and household-run industry and services and only 36 percent went to agriculture. In 1986 the share of nonagricultural loans had risen further to 51 percent of the total, while the share going to agriculture had fallen to only 33 percent.[57] The diversion of funds from

---

[53] Zou Jiahua, "Report on implementation of the 1989 Plan for National Economic and Social Development and the draft 1990 Plan (excerpts)," *Beijing Review* 33(17), April 23–29, 1990, p. V.
[54] See, for example, "Decision on further improving the economic environment, straightening out the economic order, and deepening the reforms (excerpts)," (Adopted at the fifth plenary session of the 13th Central Committee of the CCP on November 9, 1989), *Beijing Review 33(7), February 12–18, 1990, p. VI.
[55] Xinhua Tongxunshe Guonei Ziliao Shi, *Shinian gaige dashiji, 1978–1987* Beijing: Xinhua Chubanshe, 1988, pp. 270–71.
[56] See Xinhua Tongxunshe Guonei Ziliao Shi, *op. cit.*, pp. 267–68.
[57] Chinese Finance and Banking Studies Association, *Zhongguo jinrong nianjian, 1987*, Beijing: Zhongguo Jinrong Chubanshe, 1988, p. III-130. Unfortunately, statistics are not available for 1983 and 1984.

agriculture was further facilitated by policies on fund raising (*jizi*) outside of bank channels. At this time rural businesses were granted permission to raise funds by selling bonds and shares. Thus rural residents who did not themselves set up businesses were given a means of investing in industry rather than agriculture.[58]

Christine Wong describes how such measures, combined with a general wave of credit expansion in 1984–85, benefited both private and collective rural enterprises. In 1984 bank credit to township and village enterprises more than doubled to 47.5 billion yuan; in 1985 net borrowings by these enterprises increased by an additional 27.8 billion yuan.[59] Growth of private rural business was phenomenal, especially in 1985: their number rose from 4.2 million in 1983 to 4.4 million in 1984, and then more than doubled to 10.7 million in 1985. By 1985 employment in rural private businesses surpassed 28 million.[60] Total employment in rural enterprises, both private and collective, increased from about 30 million in 1983 to 70 million in 1985, and then to 95 million in 1988. Official statistics show that by 1988 rural enterprises employed almost one-quarter of the rural labor force.[61] These statistics reveal the rapid movement of both financial and human resources from agriculture into industry and services.

During these years other reforms in industrial and commercial policies also detracted from agriculture. In 1983 the central government began to permit the sale of manufactured products at market prices. Extra-plan marketing of important farm inputs began in 1983 when the State Council allowed the sale of imported fertilizers at higher prices. In mid-1984 supply and marketing coops and other local suppliers were permitted to purchase farm inputs independently and to sell the inputs at prices that reflected their purchase and handling costs. Fertilizers, pesticides, and fuel were now increasingly sold at market prices. Since market prices were higher than state list prices, the liberalization of commercial policies raised the cost to farmers of additional farm inputs.[62] One author writes that by 1985 chemical fertilizer prices were 43 percent, pesticide prices 83 percent, and farm machinery prices 92 percent higher than in 1983, and that the prices of diesel fuel, electricity and water had all doubled.[63]

Although it began later, inflation further contributed to the deterioration in agriculture's status. Fiscal and monetary actions caused large budgetary deficits, rapid growth in the money supply, and unprecedented inflation in 1987–88. The inflation had several disadvantages for agriculture. First, as mentioned above, inflation outpaced increases in state contract procurement prices. As the differential between market and state prices for farm products grew, farmers became increasingly unwilling to sign or fulfill delivery contracts to the state.[64] Local governments, which were responsi-

---

[58] See Christine Wong, "Interpreting rural industrial growth in the post-Mao period," *Modern China* 14(1), January 1988, pp. 11–12.

[59] Wong, *op. cit.*, p. 11.

[60] Wong, *op. cit.*, p. 12.

[61] Wong, *op. cit.*, p. 4, and ZGTJZY 1990, p. 65.

[62] Terry Sicular, "Ten years of reform...," pp. 19–20.

[63] Duan Yingbi, "Liangshi liutong tizhi bixu da gaige," NYJJWT 11(1986), p. 37.

[64] Institute of Development General Topics Group, *op. cit.*, pp. 8–9; Liu Wenbao and Zheng Xinwu, *op. cit.*, NYJJWT 11 (1986), p. 60.

ble for ensuring contract fulfillment, responded by restricting free market trade of major farm products. Not surprisingly, such behavior only increased the relative attractiveness of the many off-farm activities not subject to price and market interventions. Second, inflation exacerbated increases in the costs of farm inputs. By 1986/87 market prices for urea were 20 percent to 50 percent higher, and by 1988/89 more than double, state list prices.[65] Thus inflation prolonged the outflow of resources from agriculture.

The austerity program that began in late 1988 reversed some of the policies discussed above. In order to stem inflation, the government severely restricted credit. Inflation slowed, and market prices began to level off. This permitted increases in contract prices to reduce, although not eliminate, the gap between planned and market prices.

One aim of the economic retrenchment was to slow growth in rural industry. Rural enterprises were denied new credit and expected to raise funds internally. Supplies of raw materials and energy were tightened. The government hoped that a large number of township enterprises would either go bankrupt, become accessories to state-run urban firms, or shift to production based on local resources. Private business was a particular target: the government announced in August, 1989, a nationwide campaign to inspect private firms for tax evasion and illegal activities and called for the closing of a large number of private businesses. The effects of these measures was perceptible. In 1989 more than 3 million rural companies (collective and private) were either shut down or shifted to other lines of business, and 8 million employees had to return to farming.[66] These measures improved agriculture's relative standing: rural industry's loss was agriculture's gain.

VI. CONCLUSION

During the 1980s China's leaders demonstrated an unprecedented willingness to relinquish direct control over agriculture. Central policies abolished mandatory production planning and reduced the scope of mandatory procurement quotas. Price and incentive measures became important policy tools. Restrictions on private trade were relaxed, and markets were permitted to play a larger role in resourceand allocation. These initiatives contributed to a period of dynamic growth in the early 1980s.

Agriculture's fortunes reversed in the mid-1980s. Planned prices and incentives for farm products were reduced, and market prices began to fall. Commercial reforms permitted extra-plan sale of farm inputs at high, and rising prices. The government condoned the establishment of private rural businesses, and adopted credit policies that diverted funds from farming to nonagricultural activities. Together, these measures caused resources to flow out from agriculture. Growth in farm, and especially crop, production slowed dramatically.

---

[65] See table 7 in Sicular, "Ten years of reform..."

[66] "Rural firms to face period of austerity," *Beijing Review* 33(4), January 22–28, 1990, pp. 39–40; "Beijing launches probe of private firms' taxes," *Asian Wall Street Journal Weekly*, 7 August 1989, p. 3; David E. Sanger, "Crackdown on China businesses," *New York Times*, 29 August 1989, p. D1.

Steps taken in the ensuing years did little to bolster agricultural performance. Both the central and local governments increased controls over cultivation and restricted market trade in major farm products. Policies raising planned prices and material incentives were not implemented fully. Inflation increased the relative attractiveness of activities subject to fewer restrictions and of products that could be sold at market prices. Only with the austerity program in 1989 and 1990 did agriculture's relative standing begin to improve.

Thus agriculture's slowdown in 1985 and stagnation in ensuing years can be explained largely as the result of policy measures enacted during those years. Other explanations for the slowdown have also been proposed—that the slowdown was inevitable as the one-time gains from decollectivization were exhausted, that arable land area was declining and uneconomically distributed, that uncertain land rights discouraged necessary farm investment, and so on. Such factors may have contributed to the slowdown, but several considerations suggest that they were only secondary causes. First, none of these factors explains why agricultural performance declined so abruptly in 1985. Second, evidence from studies of other countries does not support the conclusion that small farms are inefficient. Third, rural residents were apparently willing to invest heavily in private nonagricultural businesses despite the fact that such activities had equally uncertain prospects and little legal protection.

If the slowdown was largely the result of changes in policy, what implications can be drawn for farm policy in the 1990s? Some might conclude that the way to promote agriculture is to discourage or restrict the development of competing nonagricultural activities in rural areas. This conclusion is incorrect. Economists have long recognized that the development of nonagricultural sectors, and the flow of resources from agriculture to those sectors, is a key part of the development process. Yet resources must be allowed to flow in both directions: the expanding nonagricultural demand for labor and raw materials should bring about rising farm prices and incomes. Higher prices for agricultural products and the growth in rural demand resulting from rising incomes then draws resources back to agriculture.

Unfortunately, in China government policies, especially the planned procurement and distribution of farm products, place agriculture at a disadvantage. In order to maintain planned procurement, the government prevents farmers from switching to the production of the most profitable crops and from selling their products to the highest bidder. When market prices for farm products begin to rise, a necessary precondition for the reversal of the resource outflow, price ceilings are imposed and market trade blocked. Such actions discourage farm production and cause imbalance in the development process.

Macroeconomic policy has contributed to agriculture's unequal standing. During the 1980s the Chinese government has experienced persistent budgetary deficits, and price subsidies on farm products have contributed to those deficits. Due to the link between pricing and the state budget, budgetary concerns have greatly influenced agricultural price and incentive policies. Growth in price subsidies could be stemmed if the government were willing to raise planned sales prices in step with procurement prices. A combination of budgetary pressures and urban bias thus place agriculture at a disadvantage. Budgetary considerations have also contributed to local government interference with central measures. Local governments bear part of the financial burden of price and incentive programs, and this reduces their willingness to carry out such programs. So long as prices and incentives are closely linked with government finances, budgetary considerations rather than the aim of promoting efficient agricultural growth will continue to interfere with the making of farm policy.

The effects of nonagricultural concerns on agriculture highlights the close connection between agriculture and other sectors of the economy. Nonagricultural development both competes with and complements agricultural growth. Nonagricultural policies can reinforce or detract from agricultural programmes. Effective agricultural policy in the 1990s will thus require a broad view, attention to policy coordination, and a true willingness to give agriculture equal footing.

CHINA'S AGRICULTURAL REFORMS: EVALUATION AND OUTLOOK

By Shwu-Eng H. Webb and Francis C. Tuan *

CONTENTS

I. INTRODUCTION

China's 1979 rural reforms brought rapid growth of agricultural production and trade, particularly for the first half of the 1980s. Reforms included policy changes in farming institutions, prices, procurement, marketing, and the trade system. However, agricultural growth slowed after 1985 and grain production, a key component of China's agricultural sector, stagnated. Rural reforms stumbled during the second half of the 1980s, because the state hesitated to make reforms in urban food policy necessary to complete the move towards an open market for agricultural commodities. The state also hesitated to place hard budget constraints on state-owned enterprises. The mounting financial burdens contributed to spiraling inflation in late 1980s, and stagnation of grain production caused the state to adopt austerity measures, and reimpose central control on grain production and trade. Economic reforms were placed on the hold.

The outlook for the 1990s depends on how China's policy makers view the results of their latest retrenchment policies. In the short-term, the recent policy changes have generated some of the desired results including higher grain production and lower inflation. But over the longer run, the disincentives and inefficiency created by these measures will weigh heavily on the economy. Now that grain production has increased and inflation has been brought under control, Chinese leaders may perceive a new opportunity for further economic reform. If so, further production of various agricultural commodities will be increasingly driven on economic forces and trade will increase. However, there is possibility that leaders will view the success of re-centralization policies as a vindication of cen-

* Agricultural Economists, Economic Research Service, U.S. Department of Agriculture. Views expressed in this paper are those of the authors' and not necessarily those of the U.S. Department of Agriculture.

tral planning and continue to emphasize grain, oilseeds, and cotton self-sufficiency while minimizing grain imports. To project China's economic outlook in the 1990s, one must ask the crucial question: Where does the reform movement stand now?

II. 1980s: THE REFORM DECADE

Rural economic reforms since 1979 can be divided into three periods. The first period, from 1979 to 1984, focused on the restructuring of the rural economy through institutional changes to increase agricultural production. These changes, introduced in the early part of the 1980s, had a profoundly positive impact on economic growth. China's total agricultural production, excluding village enterprises, grew by about 7.5 percent per year between 1978 and 1984. The second period, from 1985 to late 1988, concentrated on extending the restructuring reforms by increasing the role of markets and prices. This period was generally characterized by slower growth. Total agricultural production grew at slightly less than 4 percent annually. The last period, from late 1988 to the present, marks the beginning of a retrenchment period, in which austerity measures were adopted to combat spiraling inflation and central control was reimposed over the economy. These measures included a decision by the government in 1989 to reemphasize administrative mechanisms for increasing grain production.

REFORM POLICIES

Four sets of major policy changes were responsible for the successes of the economic reforms in rural areas. First, the introduction of the Household Production Responsibility System (HPRS, which later developed into the household contract system) in the early 1980s gave peasants incentives to improve agricultural productivity, thus contributing to rapid economic growth in rural areas. Second, there was a substantial rise in procurement prices, which significantly increased rural incomes. Third, the opening up of labor and commodity markets facilitated the transfer of resources within and out of the agricultural sector and accelerated agricultural specialization and rural industrialization. Finally, an increase in local autonomy allowed township and village enterprises to develop rapidly, using local capital and labor resources released from increasing productivity in the agricultural sector.

OVERALL ACHIEVEMENT

These policy changes introduced in the early part of the 1980s had a significant impact on economic growth in China. Growth, by any measure, was much higher during the 1979 to 1988 period than the period from 1952 to 1978 (table 1). National income, per capita income, and gross value of output (in current value) took only 10 years in the 1979–88 period to triple the growth achieved in the 26 years from 1952 to 1978. If the retail price index is used as a deflator, per capita income in real terms in 1988 was about 5 times that of 1952, and about twice that of 1978.

Liberalization of agricultural production systems brought a faster increase in agricultural productivity than in industrial productivity. Gross value of output per worker in the agricultural

Table 1. Trends in the major economic indicators in China,
1952-78 VS. 1978-88

Item	Unit	1952	1978	1988	Annual growth 1952-78	1978-88
					Percent	
Population	Million	574.8	962.6	1096.1	2.0	1.3
Labor force	Million	207.3	401.5	543.3	2.6	3.1
National income	Billion yuan	58.9	301.0	1177.0	6.5	14.6
Gross Value Output	Billion yuan	101.5	684.6	2984.7	7.6	15.9
industrial GVO	Billion yuan	34.9	423.7	1822.4	10.1	15.7
agricultural GVO	Billion yuan	46.1	139.7	586.5	4.4	15.4
Per capita income	Yuan/year	102.5	312.7	1073.8	4.4	13.1
Agricultural output						
food grain	Million tons	163.9	304.8	394.1	2.4	2.6
oilseeds	Million tons	4.2	5.2	13.2	0.8	9.7
meat	Million tons	3.4	8.6	21.9	3.6	9.9
aquatic	Million tons	1.7	4.7	10.6	4.0	8.6
Per capita production						
food grain	Kilogram	285.2	316.6	359.5	0.4	1.3
oilseeds	Kilogram	7.3	5.4	12.0	-1.1	8.3
meat	Kilogram	5.9	8.9	20.0	1.6	8.4
aquatic	Kilogram	2.9	4.8	9.7	2.0	7.2
Price indices						
Procurement price	Percent	100.0	178.8	437.4	2.3	9.4
Resale price	Percent	100.0	121.6	210.0	0.8	5.6
Living expenditure	Percent	100.0	125.3	236.3	0.9	6.5

Source: (7,1989, pp.17-19)

sector increased from 475 yuan per year in 1978 to 1,815 yuan in 1988, an annual growth rate of 14.4 percent. Gross output value per worker in the industrial sector increased from 8,459 yuan in 1979 to 18,864 yuan in 1988, or an annual increase of 8.35 percent.

Prior to the 1979 rural economic reforms, the growth rates for the production of major agricultural commodities were either less than or barely exceeded population growth between 1952 and 1978. Per capita production of oilseeds fell at a rate of 1.1 percent per year. Per capita food grain production expanded at a rate of only 0.4 percent and meat products 2 percent. Since the 1979 reforms, per capita grain production increased from 317 kilograms (kg) in 1978 to 360 kg in 1988, reaching a peak of 395 kg in 1984, a growth rate of 1.3 percent per year. This growth was achieved despite an annual population growth rate of 1.3 percent, a decrease of grain sown area by 3.4 percent, and a decline in labor force devoted to crop production. The per capita production of oilseed and meat products, which earned higher relative returns than grain crops, increased at a rate of over 7 percent a year (table 1).

With increasing autonomy under the HPRS, peasants have been guided by economic returns in their decisions as to what and how much of a commodity to produce, subject to meeting the state contract requirements and other institutional constraints. With agricultural production becoming more efficient, economic reforms encouraging the development of household and township enterprises, economic structures in rural areas became more diversified (table 2). For example, in 1978, 90 percent of the rural labor force was engaged in primary industry such as farming and mining, and accounted for about 70 percent of the value of products produced in rural society. The proportion of rural laborers employed in the non-primary industrial sector doubled from 1978 to 1988 and accounted for 47 percent of gross value product in rural society.

Tables 2. Changes in economic structure in China between 1978 and 1988

	1978		1988		Annual growth (1978-88)
	GVO billion yuan	Percent of the total	GVO billion yuan	Percent of the total	Percent
Gross value output	684.6	100.0	2984.7	100.0	15.86
industry	423.7	61.9	1822.4	61.1	15.71
argiculture	139.7	20.4	586.5	19.7	15.43
others	121.2	17.7	575.8	19.2	16.86
	Total number million	Percent of the total	Total number million	Percent of the total	
Labor force	405.81	100.0	543.336	100.0	2.96
industry	50.09	12.3	96.608	17.8	6.79
argiculture	294.26	72.5	323.083	59.5	0.94
others	61.46	15.2	123.645	22.8	7.24
	GVO per capita yuan	Percent of the average	GVO per labor force yuan	Percent of the average	
GVO per labor force	1687.0	100.0	5493.3	100.0	12.53
industry	8458.8	501.4	18863.9	343.4	8.35
argiculture	474.8	28.1	1815.2	33.0	14.35
others	1972.0	116.9	4656.8	84.8	8.97

Source:(7, 1989, p.44 & p.102)

Peasants were given more freedom to select types of production activities. The state also began to permit land use rights to be transferrable and extended land leases to 3-5 years. In some areas, land lease contracts are granted for 15 or even 50 years. With the reestablishment of labor and commodity markets in rural areas, peasants can specialize in crop production and purchase grain from the open markets to fulfil obligatory state procurement. As a result, more households have specialized in crops and livestock production and increased their scale of operations to specialize in single crop production instead of a mix of grain crops for self-sufficiency.

AGRICULTURAL DEVELOPMENTS

The changes in incentive structure stimulated agricultural productivity. Gross value of agricultural output (GVAO) [1] in current price increased from 170 billion yuan in 1979 to 587 billion yuan in 1988, growing at an annual rate of 15 percent. In China, the agricultural sector includes five subsectors —crop, animal husbandry, sideline products (handicraft etc.), forestry, and fisheries. Aquatic production has been the fastest growing subsector with an annual growth rate of 32 percent (table 3). Because growth in fisheries, sideline products, and animal husbandry was so much faster than in the traditionally dominant crop subsector, the composition of the agricultural sectors has changed dramatically in the past decade. The share of the crop sector fell from about 75 percent of GVAO in 1979 to 56 percent in 1988. The share of animal husbandry increased from 17 percent in 1979 to 27 percent in 1988. Sideline products increased from 3.4 percent in 1979 to 6.7 percent in 1988. Fisheries grew from only 1.5 percent of GVAO in 1979 to 5.5 percent in 1988, overtaking the forestry sector. Forestry fell from the third largest subsector (3.6 percent) in 1979 to the smallest sector in 1988 (4.7 percent).

Table 3. Trends in agricultural output value in China, by branch, 1979 - 1988

Year	Agriculture	Crop	Forestry	Animal husbandry	Sideline products	Fishing
	Agricultural product value based on current value (billion yuan)					
1979:	169.76	126.73	6.07	28.56	5.80	2.60
1988:	586.53	327.69	27.53	159.76	39.31	32.25
Annual growth between 1979 - 1988 (percent):	14.8	11.1	18.3	21.1	23.7	32.3
	Percent of the total					
1979:	100.0	74.7	3.6	16.8	3.4	1.5
1988:	100.0	55.9	4.7	27.2	6.7	5.5
Changes between 1979 and 1988:	345.51	-18.78	1.12	10.41	3.28	3.97

Source:(7, p.166)

As the agricultural sector became more diversified, resources were shifted out of the crop sector. Total crop sown area declined

[1] The GVAO comparison between 1979 and 1988 is based on current prices. The accuracy of the price data used to calculate GVAO vary from one subsector to the other. There are national reporting system of physical outputs and official prices in the crop subsector. Price data for crop subsector are the most accurate among all subsectors. For subsidiary subsectors with high proportions of products traded in the open markets, data are least accurate. Many other problems in using GVAO data are pointed out in Robert Field's article, *Trends in the Value of Agricultural Output.* (2)

from 148.5 million hectares in 1979 to 144.9 million hectares in 1988, a 2.4 percent decline (table 4). Although grain procurement prices have increased substantially over the last 10 years, the returns on grain crops still fall far behind cash crops. For example, using 1987 domestic procurement prices to calculate net returns, the profit per hectare on cotton was about twice that of grain crops.

Table 4. Trends in crop sown area in China, 1979 - 1988

Year	Food grain	Economic crops	Other crop	Multiple cropping index	Total sown area	Cultivated area
			Percent			
1979:					(1,000 hectares)	
	80.3	9.9	9.7	149.0	148477.0	99649.0
1988:						
	76.0	14.8	9.1	153.3	144868.9	95749.5
Changes between 1979 and 1988:						
	-7.7	45.6	-8.3	1.5	-2.4	-3.9

Source:(7, p.192)

As a result, in 1988, area sown to grain crops fell by 7.7 percent from 1979. The proportion of sown area devoted to grain production decreased from 80.3 percent of total crops in 1979 to 76.0 percent in 1988. Other crops, including green manures, forage, and vegetables, also suffered a decline of about 8 percent. The sown area devoted to economic crops, such as oilseeds, increased substantially, from 14.7 million hectares in 1979 to 21.4 in 1988, an increase of 45.6 percent. The proportion of sown area devoted to economic crops increased from 9.9 percent to 14.8 percent during the same period.

The area sown to rice and corn declined at an annual rate of 0.6 percent and 0.2 percent, respectively, over the period of 1979 to 1988 (table 5). Soybean (considered a grain crop in China) is the only grain crop that expanded sown area in the last 10 years, from 7.3 million hectares in 1979 to 8.1 in 1988, an annual increase of 1.3 percent. Peanut and cotton sown area also increased at annual rates of 4.1 and 2.3 percent respectively over the last decade.

The rural economic reforms had a significant effect on commodity productivity. Despite decreases in grain sown area, output of rice, wheat, and corn expanded at annual rates of 2, 4, and 3 percent respectively (table 5). The production of soybeans, cotton, and peanuts grew at an annual rate of 5, 7, and 8 percent, respectively. In the last decade, the annual growth rate in productivity tended to correspond with the changes in the sown area. Crops such as cotton, peanuts, and soybeans, which had higher growth rates in sown areas, also had higher productivity growth.

Table 5. Trends in sown area, production and productivity in China, by crop, 1979 - 1988

Year	Rice	Wheat	Corn	Soybeans	Cotton	Peanuts

Sown area: 1,000 hectares

Year	Rice	Wheat	Corn	Soybeans	Cotton	Peanuts
1979:	33873	29357	21033	7247	4512	2075.0
1988:	31987	28785	19692	8120	5535	2977
Annual growth rate between 1979 and 1988 (Percent):	-0.6	-0.2	-0.2	1.3	2.3	4.1

Production: 1,000 tons

Year	Rice	Wheat	Corn	Soybeans	Cotton	Peanuts
1979:	143750	62730	60035	7460	2207	2822
1988:	169107	85432	77351	11645	4149	5693
Annual growth rate between 1979 and 1988 (Percent):	1.8	3.5	2.9	5.1	7.3	8.1

Productivity: tons/hectare

Year	Rice	Wheat	Corn	Soybeans	Cotton	Peanuts
1979:	4.244	2.137	2.982	1.029	0.489	1.360
1988:	5.287	2.968	3.928	1.434	0.750	1.913
Annual growth rate between 1979 and 1988 (Percent):	2.5	3.7	3.1	3.8	4.9	3.9

Source:(4)

AGRICULTURAL TRADE EXPANDED

China's overall exports and imports expanded rapidly, an almost 13-percent annual growth between 1981 and 1988, except for 1982. In general, China's agricultural trade also grew, but at a slower rate of 11.7 percent per year since 1983. Agricultural trade has contributed only about 14 to 15 percent of China's total trade value in recent years, compared with over 20 percent in the early 1980s (table 6). However, with the exception of 1982, agricultural trade was in surplus, in contrast to deficits for overall trade since 1984. The agricultural trade surplus decreased towards the end of 1980s but remained around $3 billion in 1989.

The agricultural trade surplus grew sharply in the mid-1980s as China decided to export more and import fewer agricultural commodities when commodity production peaked in 1984 and infrastructure was not adequate to handle interregional transfers and storage. The country started shipping corn, oilseeds, including soybeans, and cotton to many Pacific Rim countries, such as Japan, South Korea, and Hong Kong. The expansion of commodity exports has slowed in the last couple of years as crop production stagnated

Table 6 -- China's agricultural trade

Year	Total trade	Annual growth	Agricultural trade						
			Total	Annual growth	Ag trade over total	Exports	Ag Exports over total	Imports	Ag Imports over total
	Bil US$	Percent	Bil US$	Percent	Percent	Bil US$	Percent	Bil US$	Percent
1981	44.02	NA	NA	NA	NA	NA	NA	NA	NA
1982	41.61	-5.5	8.84	NA	21.3	4.00	17.9	4.84	25.1
1983	43.62	4.8	8.46	-4.3	19.4	4.55	20.5	3.90	18.3
1984	53.55	22.8	7.99	-5.6	14.9	5.23	20.0	2.75	10.0
1985	69.60	30.0	8.73	9.3	12.5	6.28	23.0	2.44	5.8
1986	73.85	6.1	9.85	12.9	13.3	7.12	23.0	2.74	6.4
1987	82.65	11.9	11.92	20.9	14.4	8.03	20.4	3.89	9.0
1988	102.79	24.4	15.28	28.3	14.9	9.46	19.9	5.83	10.5
1989	111.63	8.6	16.41	7.3	14.7	9.70	18.5	6.71	11.3

Source:(14, p.45)

and domestic demand for feedgrain, soybean meals, and cotton grew.

On the import side, China sharply reduced all imports of agricultural commodities after 1984. For example, corn and cotton imports were largely eliminated for a number of years, and wheat purchases were reduced to only about 6 million tons in 1985 and 1986, from a previous high of almost 14 million tons. China also began to sell cotton in 1985 and became a major cotton exporter after being a major importer at the beginning of the 1980s. The situation of imports, similar to the exporting side, also changed in the last 2 or 3 years because of stagnating agricultural production. In general, imports of corn, oilseeds, and cotton have resumed, with cotton imports picking up significantly in 1989. Because of severe shortages, China also sharply increased raw sugar and agricultural chemical imports, including fertilizer, in the last two or three years.

IMPROVEMENT IN LIVING STANDARDS

The economic reforms have been successful in improving the living standards of China's people. Per capita income increased from 316 yuan in 1978 to 1,182 yuan in 1988 in urban areas (a nominal rate of 14 percent per year), and from 134 yuan to 545 yuan in rural areas (an annual rate of 15 percent). Consumption expenditure increased from 311 yuan in 1978 to 1,104 in 1988 for urban residents, while in rural areas it increased from 116 yuan to 477 over the same period of time. Consumers are spending a declining share of their budget on food: for urban areas it decreased from 58 percent to 51 percent from 1978 to 1988, and declined for rural areas from 68 percent to 53 percent. Living standards improved substantially as real income increases and a larger proportion of income is available to spend on non-staple food items.

Nonetheless, China's per capita consumption of agricultural commodities has increased markedly in the 1980s. For instance, per capita grain for human consumption was 198 kilograms in 1958 and 196 kilograms in 1979, but rose to 254 in 1985 and remained at around 250 in the last two or three years, although grain supplies have been much tighter in that period. Grains consumed by the livestock sector have also increased continuously in the last decade. Per capita meat and vegetable oil consumption increased from 8.1 and 1.6 kilograms in 1978 to 16.7 and 5.9 kilograms in 1988, respectively.

Per capita consumption of livestock products is still low compared with world averages, despite impressive increases in the 1980s. This is also true for vegetable oil, cotton, and sugar consumption. The per capita consumption of agricultural commodities, especially meat, will continue to grow, and therefore domestic demand for feed grains should expand despite slower growth of per capita income in the 1990s. Consequently, long-term exports of feed grain, particularly corn, will gradually shrink during the next 10 years.

III. Emerging Problems in the later 1980s

Rapid economic growth and increases in agricultural productivity slowed down after 1984 and many problems started to emerge. Failure to move reforms beyond agricultural production became a major stumbling block for sustained economic growth. The unwillingness of current leaders to reform the political system contributed to the slow development of designing legal supports, including an acceptable legalized property rights structure. Heavy subsidies for urban residents resulted from the irrational pricing system, and inefficient state-owned enterprises in the urban areas continue to be a major drag on the economy.

LACK OF LEGAL, INSTITUTIONAL, AND ADMINISTRATIVE EXPERIENCE

One of the most important problems in implementing the household contract system has been the lack of a legal system which guarantees contract fulfillment. The court system has not been well developed. There are few judges trained to hear contract dispute cases and fewer lawyers to represent farmers. Local tradition encourages negotiated settlements and courts are used only as the last resort. The rule of a village leader rather than law continues to be the modus operandi in rural areas.

Legal system reforms are key to allowing individual profit-maximizing goals can be orderly pursued within contractual arrangements. Only when personal profits earned from hard work can be guaranteed through legal systems will individuals have the incentive to continue to work hard. Proper tax laws could be designed to channel a portion of these profits to state coffers for supporting investment in infrastructure instead of lining corrupt officials' pockets.

Lack of a legal system to protect property rights creates very little incentive to increase investment or to improve productivity in the long-run. Because of the uncertain future, farmers often use their profits to purchase consumer goods, such as TV sets, or to build houses to improve living standards. Since peasants cannot own their land and land-use rights are uncertain, they farm contracted farmland only to maximize short-run profits and make very little investment to improve land productivity for the future.

LAND TENURE SYSTEM

Under the household responsibility system, the collective land in general was contracted out to each of the households in proportion to their labor size for one to three years.[2] The short-term lease provides very little incentive to invest in improving land productivity in the long-term. Reform policies were introduced to correct these problems: households were allowed to exchange or hire limited laborer services and extend the lease to 15 years in some areas. However, the lack of a legal system prevents the effective implementation of these policies. In many areas, the contract land is still subject to each year negotiation as well as local cadre approval.

In addition, farmland has been divided into many small parcels since the introduction of the household production responsibility system. When the system was established in the early 1980s, all big tracts were divided into several different grades, and households were then allocated a parcel from each grade. On the average, each household's holding of 1.2 acres were fragmented into nine tracts. This type of land tenure system undoubtedly inhibits efficient use of farmland.

LACK OF MARKET DEVELOPMENT

In China, the government interferes in agricultural commodity marketing through the enormous state commercial network of collective supply and marketing cooperatives under its direct control. Peasants in China are unable to predict how the government will interfere in agricultural production in relation to input supplies and procurement decisions. The state often uses input delivery policies to manipulate agricultural commodity production and procurement, supplies of chemical inputs, for example, are still tightly controlled. Peasants take great risks in deciding what to produce and a wrong decision can result in a large loss of potential income.

Many economists thought that China missed a golden opportunity for a full-scale introduction of a market-oriented economy in 1984. The production of most agricultural commodities were plentiful in that year and rural marketing systems would likely have been able to perform as well as the state system in distributing agricultural products. Instead, the government adopted a double-track pricing system for most agricultural goods, raw materials, and almost all major industrial outputs. Urban residents and state-owned enterprises often paid for raw materials with low state-fixed prices. The markets that could have raised prices to reflect actual demand and production costs were therefore very limited.

The double-track pricing system does not allocate resources efficiently. Producers often try to secure low fixed prices regardless of whether higher market prices exist. Farmers have little incentive to produce those commodities. Because the government heavily subsidizes consumption of most agricultural commodities, and because of limited transportation facilities, the state maintains a

---

[2] In some places with both higher population pressure and land productivity, Village land is divided into food plots and duty plots. Food plots are free, distributed on a per capita basis, and intended to provide for a family's own consumption. The remaining land is then divided into duty plots, allocated contractually to laborers and subject to tax in the form of quota delivery.

quasi-monopsony over the purchase of most agricultural commodities. Agricultural commodity prices are distorted by government policies and the prices do not signal consumer demand and producer supply behavior.

While the government's failure to reform the legal systems encourages corruption and erodes individual incentive to work hard, the price differentials created under the double-track pricing system provide incentive for enterprises to be intermediate links between corrupt officials and the next buyers. Commodities change hands several times and prices rise each time without any value being added. Profits earned by an enterprise very often depend on its capability to buy at a lower price and then sell at a higher price, and not on the adoption of improved technology or enhanced labor productivity.

Even many individuals and state-run enterprises guaranteed to receive low-priced inputs must bribe officials. The costs of operating enterprises have increased. Shrinking profits have reduced the enthusiasm of private enterprises and the government budget is stretched as state-run enterprises pass on these increasing costs.

The lack of infrastructure development prevents markets from developing and causes rural consumption of agricultural commodities to be very distorted. Rice in the south and wheat in the north are used to feed livestock because corn can not be transferred to where it is needed. Market prices of major agricultural commodities in many rich urban areas are often three or four times the market prices peasants receive. In some regions, surpluses of agricultural products have piled up while other regions have suffered shortages because of inefficient marketing.

URBAN SUBSIDIES

China has a policy of low wages for government employees including industrial workers in large cities, to support heavy industry development. Heavy industry development had been the top priority for the period from the 1950s through the 1970s. In return, the government provides cheap food, housing, utilities and public services to urban residents. The Communist Party has evolved as essentially an urban-based proletarian party. It was difficult for the Party to reform marketing structures when those reforms meant that urban food prices would rise, lowering the standard of living for its urban constituents.

Rather than broaden the reform process to urban areas, China implemented a double-track pricing system which gave the appearance of reform in the distribution system. It did allow for state-fixed prices and market negotiated prices to coexist for major agricultural products and intermediate materials. But it avoided dismantling the urban food subsidy system and created tremendous opportunities for corruption. The subsidized consumption of some major agricultural commodities in urban areas is perhaps the largest policy distortion of China's food and agricultural sector. The amount guaranteed by ration coupons was set in 1955 when grain and edible oils accounted for a large portion of the consumer diet. Economic reforms brought substantial increases in per capita incomes. Consumers were willing and able to diversify their diets.

With prices of food grains and edible oils at artificially low levels, there was no incentive for users to conserve. As grain and edible oils are sold at both fixed and negotiated prices, coupons for these products have actually become a currency which can be traded in open markets for almost everything despite prohibitions against coupon transfers or sales. The government is committed to sell the rationed amount. Over the last decade, the government raised procurement prices many times without raising the retail prices for ration coupon sales. Government subsidies for urban consumption have thus increased dramatically. Subsidies for grain and edible oils alone have increased from around 6 billion yuan in 1979 to over 30 billion yuan in 1989.

IV. Estimates of Government Intervention

Although the 1979 economic reforms have brought increasing liberalization to the agricultural sector, the government still intervenes heavily. For example, by 1986, the government had increased six-fold the portion of food grain procurement at negotiated prices, but this accounted for only about one third of total procurement.

PSE/CSE ESTIMATION

The producer subsidy equivalent (PSE) and consumer subsidy equivalent (CSE) measures are used in this study to evaluate the degree of policy intervention among major agricultural commodities in China. The PSE/CSE measures are estimates of the amount of the cash subsidy or tax needed to compensate farmers/consumers for removing government intervention. Estimates of PSE/CSE for 1986 presented here do not account for government investments in infrastructure such as irrigation, transportation, or any services that contributed value-added to commodities. However, in this report it is assumed that government services were proportionately applied across all agricultural commodities. The PSEs/CSEs, when compared across agricultural commodities, show the degree of intervention among different agricultural commodities.

GOVERNMENT INTERVENTION IN AGRICULTURAL PRODUCTION

The government procured about one-third of grain output and three-quarters of peanut and pork output. Almost all cotton is procured by the state. Therefore, it is extremely difficult to estimate a domestic market price. No attempt is made in this article to estimate PSE due to procurement for cotton. Because of the difficulty of getting market information on pork, this study also did not estimate PSE due to procurement for pork.

The world reference price for a specific commodity was based on the total value of the imported commodity divided by the total quantity imported into Hong Kong. If Hong Kong prices were not available, then, prices based on imports to Asia were used. In this article, official exchange rates were used to convert world reference prices into domestic-valued prices. The shadow exchange rates were often much greater than the official rates, suggesting the yuan was overvalued. For example, during the period 1986–88, the official exchange rate was $1/ 3.72 RMB, but in the open market the rate was $1 for about 7 RMB. The yuan has been devalued continuously since reforms began, except in 1980, and the current rate is 4.72 (since December 1989) (table 7).

Table 7. Official exchange rate of US$ to renminbi (RMB): 1978-88

1978	1979	1980	1981	1982	1983	1984	1985	1986	1987	1988	1989
				Unit: RMB per US$							
1.67	1.55	1.50	1.70	1.89	1.98	2.32	2.94	3.45	3.72	3.72	4.72

Source:(18)

Two components of PSEs are estimated in this report: 1) the effects due to domestic procurement policy measures calculated as the sum of the input subsidies and the difference between the procurement and market prices, and 2) effects due to border measures, calculated as the difference between prices domestic producers are getting and alternative prices that they could have received if there were no government measures to restrain trade.

A negative (positive) PSE indicates a tax (support) on the producers of that commodity. Negative PSEs due to procurement policy indicate that procurement prices are less than market prices and the price difference more than offsets the estimated input subsidies. For each unit of grain procured, taxes from procurement policy ranged from 5 percent of market prices for soybeans to 12 percent for rice (table 8). For peanuts, the main source of edible oil in China, but also is a major export, the government tax through procurement policy is about 14 percent. The effect of the procurement policy is negative for all major agricultural commodities except cotton. China's cotton is of better quality than that traded in the international markets. The calculation of PSE for cotton in this study does not account for this quality difference.

The border measure component of PSEs varies widely across commodities. The government tends to use border measures to maintain the price competitiveness of major exports such as peanuts and rice (table 8). Among the grain products rice has the biggest difference between the domestic market price and world price. Domestic prices for wheat, corn and soybeans are about the same as their respective world prices. That food security is still a top priority is reflected in the price ratio of wheat and rice—the reverse of the world price ratio. To encourage wheat production, the government set the price of wheat higher than the price of rice. China's rice farmers are taxed much more heavily than wheat producers.

GOVERNMENT INTERVENTION IN CONSUMPTION OF AGRICULTURAL COMMODITIES

Estimates for CSEs also contain two parts: 1) budget expenditures as urban rationing policy in making up the price difference between government procurement prices and subsidized resale prices, and 2) border measures reflecting the difference between what domestic consumers are paying and what they would likely pay if there were no measures to restrain trade.

Table 8. Estimates of China's Producer Subsidy Equivalent, 1986

Crop	Production	Quantity Procured	Domestic Market Price	Reference Price	Value of Subsidies	Policy transfers Border	PSE Percent
Units	Mil. metric tons	Mil.metric tons	Yuan/Ton	Yuan/Ton	Mil. Yuans	Mil. Yuans	%
Rice	129.2	40.7	562.3	680.2	-2712.8	-15230.8	-24.7
Wheat	90.0	34.6	496.6	522.7	-1173.3	-2352.5	-7.9
Corn	70.9	22.4	389.6	392.1	-672.1	-176.8	-3.1
Soybean	11.6	3.7	889.5	916.8	-174.7	-317.7	-4.8
Peanuts	5.9	4.3	1228.5	1833.4	-740.7	-3558.3	-59.5
Pork	18.0	12.1	3034.2	4706.7	0.0	-30037.5	-55.1
Cotton	3.5	3.8	3216.0	2655.1	0.0	1985.4	17.4

Source: (17,18, and 19)

Government data on subsidies are very limited. In fact, the only available information regarding budget expenditures on agricultural subsidies is the aggregate expenditures making up the difference between procurement prices and government resale prices to urban residents. A weighting scheme was developed based on the procurement amount and the ratio of market prices to government resale prices to allocate the total subsidies to each individual commodity. CSEs due to the rationing policy for major agricultural commodities are all positive (table 9), reflecting government support for urban consumers. The size of the urban subsidy varies and depends on the individual commodity. Staple foods are subsidized more heavily than non-staple foods. In 1986, prices of farm to non-farm sales for food grains, oilseed crops and meat were about 83, 57 and 4 percent higher than the corresponding urban subsidized prices (p.138). CSEs due to border measures, in general, are the same magnitude as the PSE but of the opposite sign.

V. RETRENCHMENT

In 1987 and 1988, the reluctance of China's leaders to initiate political reforms led them to make continued economic concessions to urban constituents and continue to support poorly managed state-run enterprises. The government financial burden continued to build and the inflation rates continued to rise. The inflation rate was 18.5 percent in 1988, and prices increased by more than 25 percent in the first quarter of 1989. China's enthusiasm for economic reforms in the past ten years has been dampened by four consecutive years (1985–88) of stagnation in grain production, high inflation rates, and political instability. As a result, the Communist Party Central Committee decided to increase central control and adopt austerity measures to slow down consumer spending in late March, 1989.

Since grain production had fallen short of targeted production and stayed below the record 1984 production level for four years since 1985, the government decided to make grain production a top priority in early 1989. The government raised procurement prices of food grains and cotton by 18 and 10 percent respectively, increased taxes on peasants who produce crops other than grains and cotton, and reimplemented many of the old centralized policies. For instance, the government again restricted the use of land for crops other than grain and cut off the flow of rural laborers to urban areas.

The economic retrenchment was successful in reducing inflation, which fell to around 6 percent in the first half-year of 1990. Recentralization of grain production did boost grain production to a record level of 407.5 million metric tons (mmt) in 1989, barely exceeding the 1984 level of 407.3 million. It is predicted that in 1990 grain production might even reach 435 mmt. However, overemphasis on grain production may have affected overall economic efficiency in rural China. A major problem in China's grain economy is the lack of price-guided markets to direct the supply and demand for grains. Increasing centralized control and emphasis only on grain production might have severe adverse effects on rural economic efficiency.

Table 9. Estimates of China's Consumer Subsidy Equivalent, 1986

Crop	Consumption	Consumer Price	Reference Price	Value of Subsidies	Policy transfers Border	CSE Percent
Units	Mil. metric tons	Yuan/Ton	Yuan/Ton	Mil. Yuans	Mil. Yuans	%
Rice	128.5	562.3	680.2	7434.7	15146.8	31.3
Wheat	95.4	496.6	522.7	4549.7	2491.2	14.9
Corn	65.5	389.6	392.1	3190.4	163.6	13.1
Soybean	10.4	889.5	916.8	582.6	285.1	9.4
Peanuts	5.6	1228.5	1833.4	1747.6	3399.5	74.6
Pork	17.6	3034.2	4706.7	2943.6	29502.0	60.6
Cotton	3.0	3216.0	2655.1	1363.3	-1669.7	-3.2

Source: (17, 18, and 19)

VI. OUTLOOK

How China will affect international agricultural markets in the future hinges on the direction of its policy—whether it continues to employ government intervention in the agricultural sector or becomes more reliance on market-oriented systems.

GOVERNMENT INTERVENTION VS. ECONOMIC EFFICIENCY

In this section, the PSE/CSE estimates are compared with the corresponding economic efficiency index across major agricultural commodities to evaluate the possible effects of further reforms on grain production and trade.

Domestic production and prices of major agricultural commodities are distorted in comparison to their open market values. The calculated returns for these commodities show large price distortions if domestic producer prices are used. Since all of the major agricultural commodities are tradable internationally, the world prices are used to calculate the relative returns across major agricultural commodities. The quality in the input markets of fertilizer, labor, and other variable inputs do not vary significantly from producing one crop to another. Hence, the domestic prices of these inputs are used to calculate variable costs of production.

The net returns to variable inputs per ton of output produced are calculated as the ratio of value of a ton of output priced at its corresponding world price to the total variable costs of material and labor (valued in domestic prices) in producing the ton of output. This ratio shows the rate of return per yuan spent on variable inputs to produce this unit of output. Among the major grain crops produced in China, rice has the highest efficiency ratio of 2.75 (each yuan spent on variable inputs yields an output value of 2.75 yuan), as compared to 1.83 for wheat. When this set of economic efficiency indices is compared with PSE measures, it demonstrates that, in China, the heaviest government taxes fall on the crops that are produced most efficiently. Returns (relative to wheat) to fixed inputs, such as land, for major agricultural commodities are shown in Figure 1. The order of the return ratios for these commodities follows the order of magnitude of government taxes per unit of output for these crops.

PROSPECTS FOR TRADE

China has a population of more than 1.1 billion but only 96.7 million hectares (1 hectare = 2.47 acre) of cultivated land. Per capita income is still very low and capital for development is not readily available. Land and capital are relatively scarce resources and labor, in contrast, is an abundant resource. In theory, China should have a comparative advantage in engaging in labor-intensive enterprises such as textile or other light industries. Returns from manufacturing light industrial goods are much higher than from producing agricultural commodities.[3] Among agricultural commodities,

---

[3] This study used the per capita income earned in urban area (916 yuan) and rural area (463 yuan) in 1986 as a proxy for relative returns on light industries and farming activities. To more accurately assess comparative advantages of different activities, an economic efficiency index such as the one discussed in the previous section would need to be developed.

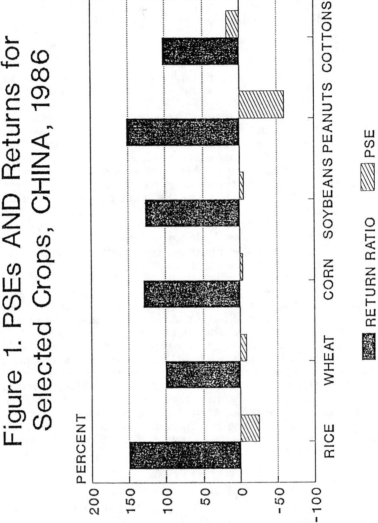

Figure 1. PSEs AND Returns for Selected Crops, CHINA, 1986

RETURN RATIO: WHEAT=100

the returns for meat, aquatic products and other cash crops (e.g. fruits and vegetables) production are much higher than for grain crops and cotton. Hence, if economic reforms are to be continued—if the agricultural sector continues to decentralize, and economic efficiency is stressed—we can expect that grain production will decline in importance in China.

As mentioned previously, two of the most efficient crops, rice and peanuts, are the two most heavily taxed crops in China. Their domestic producer prices are about 70 and 50 percent below world market prices. Increasing liberalization in the agricultural sector will therefore encourage farmers to increase the production of these two crops and other cash crops which yield much higher profit margins.

If there were no border measures or procurement quota requirements, Chinese farmers could produce and export more rice and peanuts, but more wheat, soybeans and even corn would be imported. Wheat is more land-intensive than rice. In China, the labor requirement for rice is about 131 work days per acre sown as compared to 83 work days for wheat. Because land is a relatively scarce resource and labor a relatively abundant resource, China should have a comparative advantage in growing rice vis-a-vis wheat.

China's continued reforms would likely mean increased decentralization and, consequently, a more diversified economic structure in which more types and levels of economic activities will help maximize net economic returns to the society. However, current austerity measures adopted by the state to deal with inflation problems and stagnation in grain production appear to have put economic reforms on hold and the continuing austerity program certainly will have an adverse effect on China's longterm prospects as a promising market for foreign grain and cotton exporters.

If, however, China's economic reforms continue and government controls are further relaxed, the country would become a very promising market for major grain and cotton exporters, because returns to grain crops (with the possible exception of rice) are lower than cash crops and other economic activities. Currently, grain crop production is kept relatively high mainly because of government intervention. Since the peasants' objective is to maximize net returns, the production of these crops should decrease as government intervention is gradually removed.

In the next 10 years, per capita income would grow with continuous and successful economic reforms. Increases in household income would certainly see an increase in consumption of wheat, meat, dairy products, etc. as consumers improve their diets. The increasing demand for wheat for food consumption and feed demand for corn and soybeans would accompany increases in income, leading to a potential increase in grain imports.

If, however, China continues current austerity measures emphasizing grain production and maintaining grain self-sufficiency, the outlook for the agriculture sector will likely be just an extension of the situation in 1989 and 1990. Under this policy regime, despite higher grain output, the 1990s are expected to be characterized by slow overall economic growth. Total grain production may at best reach 500 mmt and China will maintain low levels of wheat imports, probably only 15–20 million metric tons. However this import level might further restrained by the lack of foreign exchange. China's ability to import wheat in the 1990s would be curtailed sharply if Uruguay Round of the agricultural trade negotiations reach a consensus and wheat prices increase in the international markets.

REFERENCES

1. An, Xi-Ji, "The Development and Improvement of Agricultural Marketing in China," in *China's Rural Development Miracle: With International Comparisons*, edited by J. Longworth, 1989, University of Queensland Press, Australia.
2. Ash, Robert F., "The Evolution of Agricultural policy," in *The China Quarterly*, No.116, School of Oriental and African Studies, December, 1988.
3. Carter, Colin A., and Fu-Ning Zhong, *China's Grain Production and Trade: An Economic Analysis*, Westview Press, Boulder, Colorado, 1988.
4. China's State Statistical Bureau, *China Agriculture Yearbook*, various issues (*Zhongguo Nongye Nianjian*, various issues in Chinese), Beijing, China.
5. China's State Statistical Bureau, *China Price Statistics*, 1988 (*Zhonggu Wujia Tongji Nianjian, 1988*), Beijing, China.
6. China's State Statistical Bureau, *China Rural Statistical Handbook*, 1988 (*Zhonggu Nongcun Tongji Nianjian,1988*), Beijing, China.
7. China's State Statistical Bureau, *China Statistical Yearbook, 1988* (*Zhonggu Tongji Nianjian, 1988*), Beijing, China.
8. Committee for Economic Structural Reform, *Ten Years for Economic System Reform of China*, Beijing, China, 1988.
9. Crook, Frederick, "Primary Issues in China's Grain Economy in the 1990 Decade," in *China's Dilemmas in the 1990s*, U.S. Congress, Joint Economic Committee, 1991, Washington D.C.
10. Economic Research Service, *China: Agriculture and Trade*, U.S. Department of Agriculture, July, 1990.
11. Lin, Justin F., Brucroff, R., and Feder, G., "Reforming the Agricultural Sector in a Socialist Economy: The Experience of China," in the conference on *Agricultural Reform in Eastern Europe and the USSR: Dilemmas & Strategies*, Fall 1990, Budapest, Hungary.
12. Longworth, John W. (editor), *China's Rural Development Miracle: With International Comparisons*, 1989, University of Queensland Press, Australia.
13. Field, Robert, "Trends in the Value of Agricultural Output, 1978-86," in *The China Quarterly*, No.116, School of Oriental and African Studies, December, 1988.
14. Tuan, Francis, "China's Agriculture and Trade: Development and Prospective," in *World Agriculture: Forces for Change in the 1990s*," WAS-59, June 1990, Economic Research Service, U.S. Department of Agriculture, Washington D.C.
15. Webb, Alan J., Lopez, M., and Penn, R., *Estimates of Producer and Consumer Subsidy Equivalents: Government Intervention in Agriculture*, Statistical Bulletin No. 803, April 1990, Economic Research Service, U.S. Department of Agriculture, Washington D.C.
16. Webb, Shwu-Eng H., *The Role of China in the International Grain Markets*, Invited paper presented at the session on "Trade Horizons with the Socialist Economies in the 1990's" at the 1989 Western Agricultural Economics Association annual meetings, Coeur d'Alene, Idaho, July 9-12, 1989.
17. ———, "China's Grain Policy at a Crossroads," WAS-56, September, 1989, Economic Research Service, U.S. Department of Agriculture, Washington D.C.
18. ———, "Agricultural Commodity Policies in China: Estimates of PSE's and CSE's, 1982-87," in *China: Agriculture and Trade*, Economic Research Service, U.S. Department of Agriculture, November, 1989.
19. ———, "Estimating China's Grain Procurement by Individual Crop: Contracted vs. Negotiated, 1979-88," in *CPE Agriculture Report*, Vol.III, No.2, March/April 1990, Centrally Planned Economies Branch, Economic Research Service, U.S. Department of Agriculture.
20. ———, "Estimating China's Grain Procurement and Market Prices, 1979-88," in *CPE Agriculture Report*, Vol.III, No.2, March/April 1990, Centrally Planned Economies Branch, Economic Research Service, U.S. Department of Agriculture.
21. ———, and Crook F., "China's Experience With Economic Reforms: Successes and Failures," presented in the organized symposium, *China, Eastern Europe, and the USSR: Alternative Approaches to Political and Economic Reforms and the Implications for Agriculture*, 1990 American Agricultural Economics Association annual meetings, Vancouver, British Columbia, Canada, August 2-7, 1990.
22. Wen, Guanzhong J., "China's Rural Institutions and Their Impact on Sources of Growth," in *China Report*, Vol. 1, No. 2, April 1990, Washington Center for China Studies & Theoretical Research Committee of IFCSS, Washington D.C.

PRIMARY ISSUES IN CHINA'S GRAIN ECONOMY IN THE 1990s

By Frederick W. Crook *

CONTENTS

I. INTRODUCTION

A. SUMMARY

China has the world's largest grain economy. Authorities in Beijing define grain to include wheat, rice, corn, sorghum, millet, barley, oats, soybeans, potatoes, and other grains (buckwheat, field peas, and beans). China is the world's foremost producer of rice and is a major producer of many of the crops listed above. China is probably the world's largest holder of grain stocks. It is a major exporter of rice, corn, and sorghum, but is also, at various times, one of the world's largest importers of wheat. This grain economy supports the world's largest population, but the 1.1 billion population also means that China does not have large per capita grain surpluses. It produces large quantities of feed grains which supports the world's largest hog industry and one of the world's largest brewing industries. The functioning of this grain economy affects important aspects of China's overall economic development, and through international grain markets, it affects American farmers and the U.S. economy.

In the next ten years important changes are likely to occur in China which will affect the grain economy. Rather than describe all the possible scenarios, this paper examines the two most likely to occur: one in which there is no major change in policies and institutions, and a second, in which "reforms" are initiated which increasingly use markets to solve basic economic problems.

Land for Grain to Decline in 1990s

In the coming decade, economic growth will foster new residential housing, factories, roads, and airfields which will reduce avail-

---

* Economic Research Service, U.S. Department of Agriculture.

able cultivated land. Area sown to grain crops in both the "no change" and "reform" scenarios will probably decrease as a result, and also because profit margins for raising grain are likely to be less than that for raising other crops.

Slower Growth for Grain Yields

From 1979 to 1984 yields increased at an annual average rate of 5.3 percent, but the rate of growth slowed to only 1 percent in the 1985–89 period. In the "no change" scenario, yields are forecast at 1.5 percent, similar to the rate in the past four years. In the "reform" scenario, incentives will encourage farmers to boost yields to 1.9 percent a year—still well below the rate of the early 1980s.

Grain Production to Grow at a Slower Pace in the 1990s

By the year 2000, grain production likely will not reach the target of 500 million tons set by China's authorities. With falling grain area and slowly rising yields, grain output is forecast to range from 459 to 466 million tons.

Reforms Could Substantially Affect Grain Marketing

The termination of the grain purchase and supply system would raise grain prices for urban consumers, which could exacerbate tensions in the cities. But over the decade, greater reliance on market forces will discipline producers to supply the proper kinds of grain to users and encourage consumers to use scarce grain resources more efficiently. Alternatively, the use of the present grain purchase and supply system will continue to drastically distort incentives for producers, insure enormous government budget deficits to finance the gap between purchase and retail prices, and encourage black markets in the cities.

Reforms Alter Grain Stocks

The break-up of the commune system encouraged farm families to store grain, and farmers are now holding large quantities of grain stocks. The "no change" scenario predicts grain stocks will rise to 86 million tons by 2000, about 20 percent of consumption. In the "Reform" scenario, Government authorities will continue to set aside grain for strategic purposes and to maintain market stability, but the actual quantity of stocks could fall as grain holding companies (or entities) use grain prices and interest rates to calculate benefits and costs for storing grain.

Cereals vs. Feed

The "no change" scenario predicts that per capita cereal consumption will be reduced by several kilograms by 2000 as output is shifted to feed grains. To close the gap between supply and demand for feed grains, government authorities likely will switch some grain from the food to the feed category; try to implement grain saving programs by improving feeding efficiencies and switching from pork to poultry production; and try to restrain the growth of the livestock sector.

Grain Exports

In the "no change" scenario, China's grain exports are forecast to decrease because of increasing domestic demand for cereals and feed. In the "reform" scenario, exports of rice, corn, potatoes and sorghum likely will increase.

Grain Imports

The "no change" scenario predicts that grain imports will rise to nearly 23 million tons. Most of the imported grain will be wheat, but small quantities of feed grain also will be imported to support livestock feeding operations in suburban areas. In the "reform" scenario, large quantities of wheat likely will be imported, but if China's consumer demand for meat parallels that of compatriots in Taiwan and Hong Kong and if government authorities allow foreign exchange to be used, then large quantities of feed grains could be imported also.

B. PURPOSE AND SOURCES

The purpose of this paper is to highlight primary issues in China's grain economy in the 1990s. Issues explored include limitations on cultivated land, yield prospects, marketing arrangements, stocks, adequacy of grain for cereal and feed consumption, and grain exports and imports. The analysis of each issue includes a short review of institutions and trends to place the issue in proper historical perspective. Projected features of the grain economy in the coming decade are then sketched by examining how problems would be solved if "reforms" are initiated or alternatively, if there is "no change" in existing policies and institutions.

In the "no change" scenario it is assumed that structures and policies in place in 1990 persist throughout the decade. China's leaders are expected to make few major changes in the economic and political system in the 1990s. They will probably make minor adjustments in the system in response to changing conditions and priorities but could experiment with some reform measures such as the Zhengzhou (Honan Province) wholesale grain market. In the "reform" scenario it is assumed that China's leaders will initiate reforms similar to those begun in the 1979–84 period. Markets will be frequently used to solve economic problems. Firms will increase the use of comparative advantage and regions will specialize. Factors of production will enjoy greater mobility. The government will continue to play a major role in the economy, but will use more indirect means such as taxes and subsidies rather than direct management of the economy as in past decades. The central government will continue to manage foreign trade and will follow patterns similar to those in Japan, South Korea, and Taiwan. The government will modify its self-sufficiency policy and will adjust the grain purchase and supply system accordingly.

This paper is based on historical data for area, yield, production, consumption, and trade which came from statistical yearbooks published by China's State Statistical Bureau, the Ministry of Agriculture, the Ministry of Commerce, and U.S. Department of Agriculture's "World Agricultural Supply and Demand Estimates."[1] The bulk of the report is based on previous work completed by USDA's Economic Research Service's China Section.[2] Studies of China's grain economy by China's government authorities and scholars, U.S., and foreign scholars were used in preparing this report.[3]

II. WHAT ARE LAND AND POPULATION LIMITS FOR GRAIN PRODUCTION?

China's cultivated land base decreased from 107.9 million hectares in 1952 to an estimated 95.6 million in 1990. Cultivated land is defined as the area farmers plow up each year to plant crops. Over the past four decades, new factories, roads, airfields, dams, ports, and houses used up more cultivated land than was replaced by reclamation projects.

China's population rose from 574 million in 1952 to an estimated 1.11 billion in 1990. The combination of more people and less land prompted farmers to use available area more intensively, availing themselves of such techniques as intercropping and planting more crops on the same piece of land during one cropping year. Actual sown area is therefore about 1.5 times as much as cultivated land. Sown area increased from 141.3 million hectares in 1952 to an estimated 147 million in 1990.

Rising population and decreasing cultivated land reduced per capita cultivated area by more than half from 0.188 hectares in 1952 to 0.086 by 1990. On the average, each citizen is supported by 853 square meters (there are 10,000 square meters in a hectare) of cultivated land which is roughly equivalent in area to two basketball courts. By comparison, each citizen in the United States is supported by 7,350 square meters of cropland.

Analysts in both China's Ministry of Agriculture and the USDA forecast that continued economic growth and the building of infrastructure projects in the 1990s will reduce cultivated land area.[4] If reforms are implemented, USDA analysts forecast cultivated land will decrease from 95.3 million hectares in 1990 to 93 million in 2000. This means that with an expected population of 1.28 billion by 2000 each citizen will be supported by only 728 square meters of cultivated land (Figure 1).

A review of past trends provides perspective on how farmers dealt with this issue in past decades. China's rural statistical system reports three categories of sown area data: grain crops (defined above); economic crops (cotton, oilseeds, and sugar crops); and

[1] Agricultural Yearbook Editing Committee, Minister He Kang, Chairman, Zhongguo Nongye Nianjian, 1988 (China Agricultural Yearbook, 1988), Beijing, Nongye Chubanshe, 1989.

[2] Frederick W. Crook, "China's Grain Production to the Year 2000," China, Agriculture and Trade Report: Situation and Outlook Series, U.S. Department of Agriculture, Economic Research Service, June 1988, pp. 30–38.

[3] Joseph R. Goldberg, "Grain Options for China—1990–2000," in T.C. Tso, Editor, Agricultural Reform and Development in China, published by Ideals Incorporated, Beltsville, MD, 1990, pp. 113–122. Also see Colin A. Carter and Zhong Fu Ning, China's Grain Production and Trade: An Economic Analysis, Westview Press, Boulder, CO, 1988.

[4] See Frederick W. Crook, "Allocation of Crop Sown Area: Analysis of Trends and Outlook for the Future," China, Agriculture and Trade Report, Situation and Outlook Series, U.S. Department of Agriculture, Economic Research Service, July 1990, pp. 37–44; and State Council, Research Center for Rural Development, and Institute of Agricultural Economics, Chinese Academy of Agricultural Sciences, Zhongguo Nongcun Fazhan Zhanlue Wenti (Problems in China's Rural Development Strategy), Beijing, Zhongguo nongye keji Chubanshe, Nov. 1985.

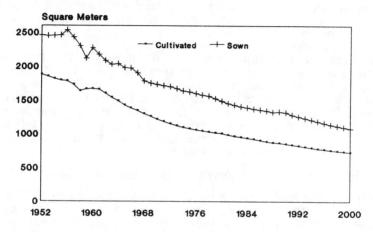

Figure 1
Per Capita Cultivated
and Sown Area, 1952-2000

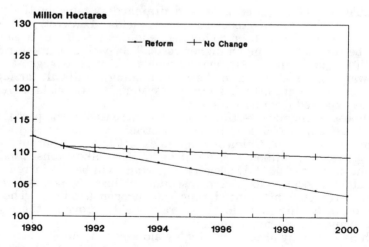

Figure 2
Grain Area Estimates, 1990-2000

other crops (fruits, vegetables, and forage). Grain crops fell from 124 million hectares in 1952 (87.8 percent of total sown area) to roughly 112 million in 1990 (76.2 percent), an annual average decrease of 2.1 percent. Area sown to economic and other crops expanded accordingly.

If China holds to a "no change" strategy, USDA analysts forecast that cultivated area will decrease from 95.3 million hectares in 1990 to 94 million in 2000. The area sown to grain will fall from 112.4 million hectares (76.2 percent of total sown area) to 109.4 million in 2000 (75.3 percent). Grain area will fall because of the decrease in cultivated area and because land will be shifted to raising economic crops. Government policy stressing the importance of grain in the economy will be a countervailing force limiting the decrease (Figure 2).

If China's leaders initiate additional reforms in the 1990s, economic growth will expand and infrastructure projects will increase, reducing the cultivated land base from 95.3 million hectares in 1990 to 93 million in 2000. With less stress on grain production, farmers likely will allocate marginal grain growing land to more profitable uses. Area sown to grain crops are forecast to fall from 112.4 million hectares (76.2 percent of total sown area) in 1990 to 103.3 million in 2000 (74.8 percent).

III. What Are the Prospects for Yield and Production?

Grain yields rose from 1.3 metric tons per hectare in 1952 to 3.6 in 1989, an annual average growth rate of 2.8 percent. China's farmers probably will not be able to sustain this growth rate in the 1990s in either the "reform" or "no change" scenario. Yield increases in the coming decade will depend on both technical and economic factors.

WHAT ARE THE TECHNICAL PROSPECTS FOR GROWTH IN GRAIN YIELDS?

Expansion of irrigated area and drainage systems in the past three decades greatly boosted grain yields. Low-cost, efficient projects have already been completed; additional irrigated area can only be completed at much higher costs. Tube-well irrigation in the North China Plain greatly boosted yields, but reports suggest that the water table is falling in the area, making it difficult for farmers even to maintain their irrigation system.[5] Little yield increase can be expected from irrigation.

The use of chemical fertilizers greatly increased in the past three decades, from 78,000 tons in 1954 (nutrient weight basis) to 23.7 million tons in 1989. China's planners expect fertilizer output to increase from 90 million tons in 1990 to 150 million tons (product weight basis) by 2000.[6] Especially important will be the increase in output of phosphorous and potassium fertilizers which will help balance the current preponderance of nitrogen fertilizers. The expansion of fertilizers could boost grain yields, provided there is a proper mix of economic incentives.

China's farmers already use high-yield seeds. About 42 percent of total grain area is sown with hybrid rice and corn seed and improved varieties of wheat.[7] Plant breeders have been most active in

[5] Jiang Zaizhong, "State Councilor Chen Junsheng Urges Water Saving Agriculture," Beijing, Xinhua Domestic, Mar. 7, 1990; translated in U.S. FBIS, CHI-90, No. 48, Mar. 12, 1990, p. 33. Also see Wen Jia, "Crops Gain in Plan That Save Water," *China Daily*, Mar. 22, 1990, p. 3.

[6] "More Fertilizers for More Grain," *China Daily*, May 5, 1990, p.2.

[7] "Jinnian Tuiguang Sanda Liangshi Tsowu Liangzhong Bozhong Zhongmianji Yuji Da 7.1 Yimu" ("This Year Improved Seeds for the Big Three Grain Crops Are Estimated to Reach 7.1 Hundred Million Mu"), *Renmin Ribao*, Mar. 1, 1990.

raising wheat, rice, and corn yields, but some improvements probably can yet made for these grain crops. Plant breeders could well expand yields for barley, sorghum, oats, soybeans, and potatoes.

The agricultural extension system supported yield growth in the past three decades and can be expected to maintain that support in the coming decade. Continued reforms would encourage individual farmers to use cultivation practices which would raise yields, reduce costs, and boost profits.

Table 1 lists wheat, rice (milled), and corn yields for China and selected countries. The comparison of China's grain yields with those from other countries clearly shows that China's farmers already are producing world class grain yields. For example, in 1989 only three countries had higher rice yields than China: Japan, Australia, and the United States. Clearly, if U.S. farmers can obtain 4.4 tons per hectare there are no technical reasons why China's farmers cannot replicate those yields. Some yield growth will occur in the 1990s, although China's yields are already very high.[8]

WHAT ARE THE ECONOMIC PROSPECTS FOR GROWTH IN GRAIN YIELDS?

There are not strong economic incentives to boost grain yields in the "no change" scenario. Government policy and prices in the period from 1985–89 provided an economic environment in which farmers could earn more money raising economic crops and working in rural industries. For example, farmers in this period earned 498 yuan per hectare raising wheat compared with 711 for peanuts, 1,180 for cotton, and 1,882 for sugarcane.[9] The Government's grain purchase and supply system embodies considerable coercive elements which greatly reduce incentives to produce grain.

From 1984 to 1989, grain yields rose from 3.608 tons per hectare to 3.632, an annual average growth rate of only 0.13 percent. If this same policy and price package is projected to the year 2000, then the combined effect of technological and economic factors is projected to produce a yield growth of 1.456 percent a year (Figure 3).

Economic incentives for grain production in the "reform" scenario are complex. As market forces increase in the economy, grain producers and consumers will make adjustments. Before reforms are implemented, it is difficult to predict how grain farmers will respond. As the government grain purchase and supply system is altered, urban grain prices likely will rise. Urban residents and in-

[8] One possible explanation for high grain yields is that China's statistical authorities may underestimate grain area and production. From travel in rural areas and discussions with many rural authorities our general impression is that there is more grain in rural areas than is reported. While constructing grain supply and use balance sheets and working with livestock production and feed requirements we have noted a discrepancy—using official PRC data there is a gap between grain use for cereals and feed and meat output. Given official data there is not enough grain in China to sustain such a large population and still have enough grain to produce the kind of meat that they report. One possible explanation for this discrepancy is that farmers underreport grain area and production. The unreported grain is fed to livestock which boosts farm income. In this case perhaps grain yields are not as high as reported which means that further yield growth is possible if the proper technical and economic environment is created. See Frederick W. Crook, "Notes on China's Grain Supply and Use: A Trip Report," U.S. Department of Agriculture, Economic Research Service, International Economics Division, September 1986, p. 7.

[9] In 1987 3.72 yuan equalled 1 U.S. dollar. U.S. Department of Agriculture, Economic Research Service, Agriculture and Trade Analysis Division, China Section, "China Agricultural Statistics Data Base," January 1990; and Agricultural Yearbook Editing Committee, Minister He Kang, Chairman, *Zhongguo Nongye Nianjian, 1987 (China Agricultural Yearbook, 1987)*, Beijing, Nongye Chubanshe, 1988, pp. 393–394.

TABLE 1. China's wheat, rice and corn yields compared with selected countries.

tons per hectare

Country	Production conditions for wheat	Wheat 1989	Rice 1989	Corn 1989
China	mostly irrigated	3.04	3.90	3.88
Pakistan	mostly irrigated	1.87	1.53	1.44
India	mostly irrigated	2.24	1.69	1.33
Mexico	mostly irrigated	4.12	2.62	1.72
Japan	mostly irrigated	3.47	4.49	2.00
Australia	mostly dry fields	1.56	5.86	3.61
Argentina	mostly dry fields	1.86	2.15	3.09
USSR	mostly dry fields	1.94	2.56	3.71
Poland	mostly dry fields	3.87	n.a.	5.00
France	mostly dry fields	6.35	3.53	6.76
Canada	mostly dry fields	2.06	n.a.	6.25
United States	mostly dry fields	2.51	4.40	7.39

Source: USDA Data, August 1990.

Figure 3
Forecasts For Grain Yields
For "No Change" and "Reform" Scenarios

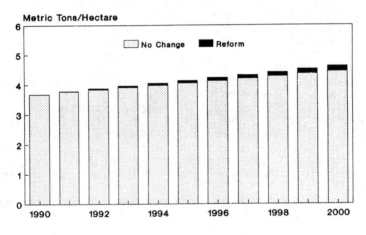

dustrial users of grain will initiate grain substitution and conservation strategies. Government pressure (primarily using coercive elements) to continually increase grain production will subside and farmers will begin to respond more to market pressures. In this case there will probably be less demand for rice and coarse grains for human consumption, but the demand for grain in the form of livestock products, meat, eggs, fish, and milk may well increase. Individual farmers will have an interest in raising grain yields and cutting costs of production.

From 1979 to 1984 grain yields increased at an annual average rate of 5.3 percent. In the "reform" scenario, the combined effects of technological and economic factors will boost yields only slightly to 1.851 percent a year. In sum, rapid yield increases are not expected for either the "no change" or the "reform" scenario.

GRAIN PRODUCTION BY THE YEAR 2000

These area and yield estimates for the "no change" and "reform" scenarios suggest that the annual average growth rate for grain production in the 1990s will be considerably lower than the rates for the previous two decades, and production by 2000 will range from 459-466 million tons compared with China's goal of 500 million tons.[10]

Grain production rose from 160 million tons in 1952 to 407 million in 1989, an annual average growth rate of 2.55 percent. During the turbulent "Great Leap Forward" period (1958-63) grain production fell by minus 2.36 percent a year. In the 15-year period from the end of the "Great Leap Forward" to the beginning of reforms in 1978, grain output increased at an annual rate of 4.39 percent. During the initial phase of the reform decade (1978-84), the growth rate jumped to 5.24 percent a year. But in the five-year period from 1984 to 1989, there was no growth in grain output because price and incentive policies introduced in 1985 discouraged further growth. In the "no change" scenario the growth rate is only 1.22 percent, well below the rapid growth rates of the past. The growth rate for the "reform" scenario is even slower at 1.09 percent (Figure 4).

Figure 4
Grain Production, 1980-2000

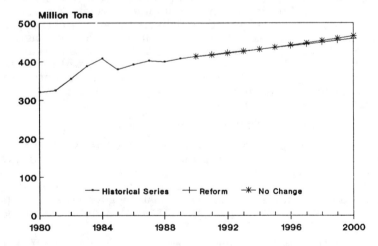

[10] Chinese Academy of Agricultural Sciences, "Analyses on Long-Term Development of Grain Production in China," *Zhongguo Nongye Kexue (Scientia Agricultura Sinica)*, No. 5, 1987, pp. 1-5; translated in U.S. JPRS, CAR-88, No. 11, Mar. 8, 1988, pp.29-33. See also "More Fertilizers for More Grain," *China Daily*, Beijing, May 5, 1990, p. 2.

IV. How Will Grain Be Marketed?

For hundreds of years China's grain flowed through marketing channels shaped by three elements. First, China's farmers produced grain primarily for their own use and only secondarily for the market. Second, local and regional grain markets were the primary means of linking supply with urban demand. Third, the central government often intervened in the marketing of grain to supply the requirements of military border garrisons and civil servants in the capital, to generate revenue to sustain government functions, and to stabilize market prices.

In 1953–55 China's leaders chose to disrupt this ancient grain marketing system by eliminating the use of grain markets. The government established a grain purchase and supply system which forced farmers to sell their excess grain to purchase stations at government-fixed prices.[11] The Grain Bureau stored, transported, milled, and sold grain to urban residents and government workers at relatively low fixed prices. These citizens were issued grain ration coupons based on their age, sex, and occupation related to caloric requirements. Only citizens with coupons could purchase grain at government- owned retail shops. Since 1955, government leaders have used monopsonist pricing practices to capture gains from agriculture to support national development projects. To increase farm marketings in the early 1960s, the government increased grain purchase prices while holding retail prices firm. The government subsidized the difference between farm gate and retail prices from government revenues. In 1978, the price subsidy for all agricultural products was only 5.6 billion yuan, but by 1987 it had grown to 50 billion yuan—a large chunk of the government's budget.[12]

In the early 1980s, the government allowed local free markets to function again. But it also has prohibited farmers from selling grain in those markets until they delivered grain purchase quotas to government-owned grain stations. Currently, farmers agree to sell part of the grain to the government based on local open market prices.[13] Given this historical context, how will the government relate to grain marketing in the 1990s? Will it continue the current system, or will it return to more traditional practices that rely more heavily on markets?

NO CHANGE IN GRAIN MARKETING SCHEME

In the "no change" scenario, the government is expected to purchase large quantities of grain and keep the retail price of grain low—and to have difficulty financing the subsidy. In the 1980–87 period the government purchased about 30 percent of production. If this ratio is maintained, by the year 2000 the government will purchase over 140 million tons of grain a year. Assuming that the gov-

[11] Audrey Donnithorne, *China's Economic System*, Praeger Publishers, New York, 1967, pp.337–364.

[12] Hao Si, "Price Subsidies—A Heavy Burden for the Chinese Government," Zhongguo Tongxun She, Hong Kong, Jul. 1, 1988; translated in U.S. FBIS, CHI-88, No. 128, July 5, 1988, p. 48.

[13] Nickolas R. Lardy, *China's Interprovincial Grain Marketing and Import Demand*, U.S. Department of Agriculture, Economic Research Service, Agriculture and Trade Analysis Division, Staff Report No. AGES 9059, Sep. 1990.

ernment will not be able to face urban unrest stemming from increasing retail prices for staple grains, then purchasing this quantity of grain will be very expensive. Either the government will have to raise the purchase price to encourage more production from farmers—which will make the subsidy problem even more severe—or it will have to increase the use of coercive elements, making rural residents even more unhappy than they already are. As the economy becomes more complex, government bureaucrats will have an increasingly difficult time trying to equilibrate supplies with demand for grain for use as cereals, in industry (starch and alcohol) and as feed.

REFORM OF THE GRAIN MARKETING SYSTEM

In the "reform" scenario, open market activity likely will increase so that resources will be allocated more efficiently. In the past few years, grain stations have paid a special price for above-contract grain. These prices were based on open market prices and grain purchased at this higher price was passed to users such as restaurants, factories, and feed mills that in turn passed the costs to end users. As an increasing quantity of grain is sold at higher retail prices, urban consumers will adjust their consumption patterns and will begin to conserve grain. These adjustments may alter the specific kinds of grain grown, i.e., more corn embodied in livestock products and less rice production.

The government will have difficulty weaning the urban population away from low-priced grain. For almost 40 years city dwellers have had cheap grain, which has become an income subsidy because they receive more grain than they require and sold their excess coupons in the black market for cash or trade them for other commodities.[14]

The government will continue to be a player in grain markets to facilitate grain transactions, grading, storing, strategic stocks, stocks to dampen fluctuations in the market, and will have some kind of control of international grain transactions. Internal transportation problems will continue to hinder grain marketing in the coming decade. But increasingly, markets will allocate grains to users, which in turn will prompt producers to grow the kinds of grain consumers want.

V. What Quantity of Grain Stocks Will Be Maintained?

In the 1949–84 period, the government took primary responsibility for maintaining grain stocks. There is little information about grain stocks because the government considers such data a state secret. Grain stock information in Figure 5 came from the construction of grain supply and use tables which used available production, import, export, and consumption data to estimate stock numbers.[15] In 1961 stocks reached an estimated low of about 10

---

[14] James P. Houck, "Parallel Markets, Price Theory, and China's Grain Policy," Department of Agricultural and Applied Economics, University of Minnesota, St. Paul, Minnesota, Staff Paper No. P89-21, June 1989.

[15] Frederick W. Crook, "China's Grain Supply and Use Balance Sheets," *China, Agriculture and Trade Report: Situation and Outlook Series*, U.S. Department of Agriculture, Economic Research Service, June 1988, pp. 22-29.

million tons, only 7.3 percent of grain consumption, but in 1985 they peaked at 111 million tons, 32 percent of consumption. Note that stocks are estimated to have fallen sharply since 1985 (Figure 5).

Figure 5
China's Grain Stocks

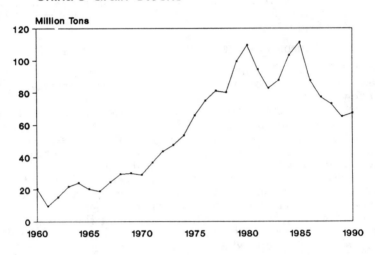

STOCKS IN THE "NO CHANGE" SCENARIO

Grain stocks fell sharply from 1985–89 because production increases stalled, grain exports increased, domestic demand for grain surged, and imports slowed for a time. By the end of 1990, stocks were assumed to be 71 million tons, or 19 percent of consumption. Throughout the 1990s, the government likely will slowly build stocks to about 86 million tons, about 20 percent of consumption.

In 1984 the commune system was reorganized into the township-household contract system.[16] Under this system, farm households made contracts with economic cooperatives to farm parcels of land and sell specified quantities of goods to the state, and were permitted to sell surpluses in local markets or consume the goods themselves. In this economic environment, households have begun to store grain. There is little quantitative data on the aggregate size of on-farm grain stocks. The author visited numerous farm families in various parts of China during the 1987–90 period and found that farmers routinely stored grain as an insurance policy against ill health, crop failures, and fluctuations in purchase prices.[17]

---

[16] See U.S. Congress, Joint Economic Committee, *China's Economy Looks Toward the Year 2000, Vol. 1, The Four Modernizations*, May 1986, pp. 354–375 for a brief description of the new household contract system.

[17] Frederick W. Crook, "Reports on Rural People's Communes (Townships)," unpublished data set, Great Falls, VA.

STOCKS IN THE "REFORM" SCENARIO

In the "reform" scenario three institutions will hold grain stocks. First, the government will hold some grain for strategic reasons and as a buffer to maintain orderly markets. Second, farm families will continue to hold grain stocks. This will be especially true in areas where the probability for crop failures is high and transportation networks are not well developed to bring food and feed grains into areas suffering from disasters. Third, grain companies may begin to hold grain stocks.

It is difficult to forecast the quantity of grain stocks held under the "reform" scenario. As markets become more important, prices and interest rates are expected to become increasingly important in determining stock levels. Currently the costs for grain stocks are hidden from consumers. In the reform scenario these costs will become more transparent and grain stocks could be reduced.

VI. How WILL GRAIN BE CONSUMED?

For hundreds of years China's consumers have subsisted primarily on a diet of grains supplemented with beans, vegetable oil, vegetables, fruits, sugar, and a little meat. In the early 1930s, for example, 93 percent of the calories in rural diets came from grains, while animal products accounted for a little over 2 percent.[18] Per capita food grain consumption rose from an estimated 170 kilograms in 1950 to a peak of 226 kilos in 1956. Consumption fell to 169 kilos in 1961 during the "Great Leap Forward", but rose steadily to 246 kilos in 1984. Note that after 1961 per capita consumption did not exceed the 1956 peak until 1979 (Figure 6).

Since 1949 China's consumers have eaten an increasing quantity of meat. Per capita annual red meat consumption rose from 5.9 kilograms in 1952 to 21.1 kilograms in 1989. Pork accounts for over 90 percent of the meat production. Since 1962, when meat consumption hit a low of 2.9 kilos, consumption rose at an average rate of 8.3 percent per year. An increasing number of citizens are choosing to consume grain both as a cereal and as livestock products which have come from grain-fed livestock. This rapid rise in meat output implies feed grain consumption rose from an estimated 8.5 million tons (5.9 percent of total grain production) in 1952 to 92 million (22.6 percent) in 1989 (Figure 7).[19]

Also since 1949 increasing quantities of grain have been used to manufacture alcoholic beverages. Beer (barley) and distilled liquor such as maotai (sorghum) output have risen especially fast in the 1980s, so that by 1988 12.5 million tons of grain were allocated to the beverage industry.[20]

Each season a percentage of China's grain harvest is lost during harvesting, transporting, storing, and processing. Authorities in China estimated in the mid 1980s that about 15 percent of the crop

---

[18] John L. Buck, *Land Utilization in China*, The University of Chicago Press, Chicago, Illinois, 1937, p. 411.

[19] Francis C. Tuan, *China's Livestock Sector*, U.S. Department of Agriculture, Economic Research Service, International Economics Division, FAER, No. 226, April 1987, p. 39.

[20] "Booze Boom Against the Grain," *China Daily*, Nov. 23, 1988.

Figure 6
Per Capita Grain Consumption, 1960-89

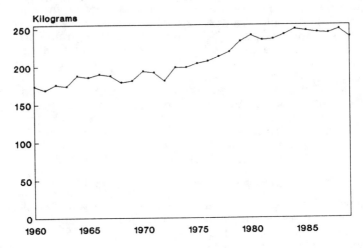

Figure 7
Per Capita Meat Consumption, 1952-89

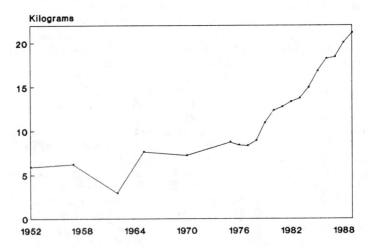

dropped out of their grain system into the waste category (about 57 million tons in 1985).[21]

GRAIN VS. MEAT CONSUMPTION IN THE "NO CHANGE" SCENARIO

The "no change" scenario assumes that current policies and institutions will remain in place to the year 2000. Government authorities will allocate scarce grain resources to competing users. Grain allocated for cereal consumption is forecast to decrease slightly from 240 kilograms per capita in 1990 to 238 kilos by 2000. In the next ten years, government-led efforts will be made to build better storage facilities to reduce the waste grain ratio. But these efforts will be partly blunted by the cheap grain policy which leads to misuse of this resource. As incomes rise, citizens will also want to consume greater quantities of grain in the form of alcoholic beverages, which will reduce the quantities available for cereal use.

The primary problem for government authorities will be to find feed grains to support the growing livestock population. Given falling cultivated land area, decreasing area sown to grain crops, slowly rising grain yields, and government policy preference to maintain basic food cereal rations, then forecasted feed grain output does not match meat production goals. Differences in demand and supply conditions for feed grains can be resolved by either 1) augmenting feed grain production by reducing grain for cereals and industrial use; 2) increasing feeding efficiency; 3) adjusting growth rates of livestock products; or 4) allocating foreign exchange to purchase feed grains in the international market.

First, allocation of grain for cereal and industrial uses are already fairly close to the margin. Given China's natural resources, little can be done in the short term to expand grain production. China's authorities have little room to maneuver with regard to shifting grain production from cereals to feed grain. When push comes to shove, the allocation question will turn on whether to consume grains directly as cereals or as meat. Given this choice, central planners likely will choose cereals.

Second, more adjustments probably will be made in livestock production targets. In the mid-1980s, government authorities, flushed with full grain bins, announced plans to expand total meat output by 2000 to 27.8 to 30 million tons. A "food basket" project was initiated to increase the supply of meat to urban residents. Resources were allocated to improve storage and transportation facilities and to build animal breeding stations, feed mills, and modern livestock feeding operations near large urban areas. But as increases in grain production levelled off from 1985 to 1989, government leaders began to initiate grain-saving strategies. Poultry production was encouraged because chickens are better converters of grain to meat than hogs. Authorities also promoted the production of ruminant animals like goats and sheep because they can convert grass to meat and thus conserve on grain consumption.[22]

---

[21] Tang Qingzhong, "Woguo liangshi shouhou jiagong sunshi yenzhong" ("There Are Serious Post Harvest Grain Losses in My Country"), *Renmin Ribao (People's Daily)*, Beijing, Jan. 8, 1989, p. 1.

[22] "State Council Circular on Nonstaple Food," Xinhua Domestic Service, Beijing, Sep. 6, 1990,; translated in U.S. FBIS, CHI-90, No. 175, Sep. 10, 1990, pp. 44–46.

Third, central planners could decide to import large quantities of feed grains. A review of China's grain imports reveals that corn and barley have been imported. Barley has been imported primarily to meet the demand for brewing. Corn in past decades has been imported primarily to meet cereal, not feed, requirements. In the past five years (1984–89), corn imports averaged 560,000 tons and a good portion of this corn probably was used for feed (about 1 percent of the estimated quantity of corn fed to livestock in those years). Given the constraints on foreign exchange and the government's desire to accelerate industrial production through imports of key industrial equipment and technology, it is unlikely that authorities will allow large quantities of foreign exchange to be used to purchase corn. Corn in this context can be considered a luxury item like tobacco, alcohol, and color TV sets—items consumers want but which authorities deem unaffordable at this stage in China's development.

GRAINS VS. MEAT IN THE "REFORM" SCENARIO

The "reform" scenario assumes increased use of markets, specialization, and comparative advantage. But government authorities will continue to play a major role in the economy, especially in managing foreign trade.

For institutions handling grain in the next decade, "price" will be a more severe taskmaster than government cadres. Grain handlers will be disciplined by price and profit margins to initiate waste reducing measures. These measures could make several million tons of grain available each year.

Price will also discipline cereal consumers to save grain. Per capita cereal consumption is expected to decrease in the coming decade both because of grain-saving strategies and because consumers will get more of their calories from processed foods, vegetables, fruits, beans and meat.

Industrial use of grain likely will increase. As the economy expands, an increasing portion of the grain crop will be used for industrial purposes. For example, starch and sugar production using grain likely will increase. Grain used to manufacture alcoholic beverages probably will increase, but the expansion will be disciplined by price, rises in income, and limited by foreign exchange in the case of barley to brew beer.

How much grain will the market allocate to meet the demand for livestock products? Population growth, expansion of incomes, and reduced government constraints will encourage meat consumption. On the other hand, given falling cultivated land area, decreasing area sown to grain crops, slowly rising grain yields, and government policy preference to maintain basic food cereal rations, feed grain output might not match the demand for meat.

How consumers will respond in markets to purchase cereals and meats cannot be foreseen clearly. The published target of 27.8 to 30 million tons of meat by 2000 implies feed grain requirements of 182 million tons compared with 132 million tons for feed in the "no change" scenario, a gap of 50 million tons. Our best guess is that this gap will be adjusted in three ways. First, a rise in price for feed grains certainly would induce more feed grain production.

Second, some feed grains will be imported. For reasons already given, the government likely will limit the foreign exchange allocated to purchase feed grains on the international market. More feed grains will be imported than under the "no change" scenario, but, on the whole massive quantities of feed grain probably will not be imported. For example, the governments of Japan and South Korea have managed meat production, and meat and feed grain imports, so that per capita consumption in 1989 was 34.7 kilos and 27.4 respectively. Third, higher meat prices will prompt consumers to purchase less meat until there is a balance between supply and demand.

VII. How Much Grain for Export and Import?

China's exports expanded from $1 billion in 1953 to 7.6 billion in 1977, an average annual rate of increase of 8.7 percent. After 1978, a liberal open door trade policy encouraged exports, which reached $59.1 billion in 1989—an average rate of increase of 18.7 percent. China's imports followed a similar pattern with growth rates slightly smaller than exports. China has been both an exporter and an importer of grain in the past four decades, but for most years has been a net importer (Figure 8).

Figure 8
China's Grain Trade, 1960-90

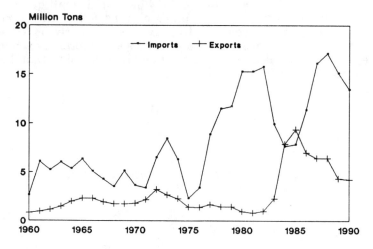

INTERNATIONAL GRAIN TRADE IN THE "NO CHANGE" SCENARIO

In the "no change" scenario, China's exports are assumed to expand from a three-year (1987–89) average of $48.7 billion to over $92.4 billion by 2000, an average growth rate of 6 percent a year. Government authorities likely will attempt to constrain import growth, which is expected to grow from a three-year average (1987–89) of $50.3 billion to 77.4 billion in 2000, an average growth rate of

4 percent a year. Considerable foreign exchange reserves will be generated in the 1990s.

In the coming decade, China's grain exports should decline because of increasing domestic demand for cereals and feed. Small quantities of rice, corn, and sorghum will be exported. Grain imports are forecast to expand from 15.1 million tons in 1989 to 22.9 by 2000. Government authorities in the 1980s allocated 3 to 5 percent of their import bill to purchase grains. Growth in exports should provide sufficient foreign exchange to finance these purchases. Government authorities will continue to emphasize grain self-sufficiency and will import grain to maintain the urban grain ration system. Government authorities probably will import sizeable quantities of wheat and small quantities of feed grains to support livestock feeding operations in suburban areas.

INTERNATIONAL GRAIN TRADE IN THE "REFORM" SCENARIO

In the "reform" scenario, China's exports are assumed to expand from a three year (1987–89) average of $48.7 billion to over $102 billion by 2000 at an average growth rate of 7 percent a year. Government authorities likely will have less control over imports than in the "no change" scenario and import growth is expected to expand from a three year average (1987–89) of $50.3 billion to $105 billion in 2000, also an average growth rate of 7 percent a year.

Under reform conditions, China's grain exports will rise, with certain regions exporting rice, sorghum, potatoes, and corn. Other regions will import large quantities of wheat, and small quantities of rice, soybeans and corn. If China's citizens follow the path of Taiwan, whose citizens consumed an average of nearly 58 kilos of meat in 1989, and if government authorities allow foreign exchange to be used to purchase feed grains, then it is possible that large quantities of corn will also be imported.

LOSS AND MISUSE OF CHINA'S CULTIVATED LAND

By Leo A. Orleans *

CONTENTS

SUMMARY

When, earlier in this century, parents admonished children to finish everything on their dinner plates because Chinese people were starving, the cliche simply reflected the prevalent and well-founded truism, overstated rather emotionally in 1948 by ecologist William Vogt: "China quite literally cannot feed more people.... The greatest tragedy that China could suffer, at the present time, would be a reduction in her death rate.... Millions are going to die.... There is no way out. These men and women, boys and girls, must starve as tragic sacrifices on the twin altars of uncontrolled human reproduction and uncontrolled abuse of the land's resources." [1]

Now, of course, few people consider China to be on the verge of a Malthusian disaster. Aside from the major famine which followed the Great Leap Forward and scattered regional food shortages, China has managed not only to feed a population which doubled in the past 40 years, but actually to increase per capita grain production.[2] Even more impressive, she is feeding over 20 percent of the world's population on probably less than 5 percent of the world's arable land.[3] The fact that China's per capita grain production has

---

* Leo A. Orleans is a China consultant, Congressional Research Service, and publications coordinator for these volumes.

[1] William Vogt, *Road to Survival* (New York: William Sloane Associates, Inc., 1948) pp. 224–5. Brought to my attention in Frances Moore Lappe and Joseph Collins, *Food First* (Boston: Houghton Mifflin, 1975) p. 97.

[2] In 1952 every person received 570 jin (2 jin = 1 kg) of grain; in 1981 the person share rose to 652 jin. (*China Daily* (hereafter CD), Feb. 1, 1983, p. 1).

[3] Chinese sources cite various figures for China's proportion of the world's arable land. Perhaps two extreme examples are 2 percent (*Jingji Ribao*, Jan. 10, 1989; FBIS–CHI–89–022, Feb. 3, 1989, p. 51) and 6.8 percent (Taiyuan Shanxi Provincial Service, Oct. 8, 1988; FBIS–CHI–88–197,Oct. 12, 1988,p. 42.) Some of the differences may be the result of confusion between arable or

Continued

increased despite the rapid population growth can be attributed to
two factors. First, advances in science and technology have made it
possible for China to increase the sown area by intercropping and
planting two or more crops on the same piece of land during one
cropping year. As a result, while cultivated land has been decreasing, the sown area has increased from 141.3 million hectares in
1952 to 144 million in 1990.[4] And second, the credit must also go to
the resourceful and hard-working Chinese peasants, who, in the
course of these decades, managed to overcome fluctuating and
often irrational goals and policies. Or, as someone else put it,
"Rather than geographic determination of human fate, China illustrates human determination of geographic fate.... The Chinese
were, and are, adept at making the land serve their ends rather
than allowing it to constrain them...." [5]

China's agricultural performance, however, is covered elsewhere
in this volume. (See chapter by Webb and Tuan and other chapters
in this section) Here the discussion will center on China's loss of
cultivated land, which is having a serious effect on agricultural
production and is becoming more acute each year. As we shall see,
the land crisis relates to the growth of urban areas, the expansion
of rural industries, the explosion in new rural housing, inadequate
and poorly implemented laws, the general mismanagement of land,
as well as a variety of environmental factors.

I. AMOUNT OF CULTIVATED LAND AND ITS RATE OF LOSS

China has some of the oldest statistics on cultivated land of any
country, but they suffer from a variety of problems: the use of
measuring units which changed not only over time but also regionally; the often-difficult mathematical problem of measuring irregu-
lar pieces of land; and serious underreporting because land was
generally used to determine the local tax base.

Over the past decade China has made great improvements in the
quality of her statistics, but even now they should not be taken at
face value or used without caveats and explanations.[6] Although numerical precision is not necessary to appreciate the magnitude of
the farmland disappearance problem, a few words on the nature of
the pertinent statistics are still in order.

Given the variety of land figures reported in contemporary Chinese sources, it is clear that many of the difficulties of measuring,
aggregating, and reporting these statistics are legitimate. As with
other statistics, however, there continues to be a traditional "cha-
buduo" ("more or less") attitude toward them. To make matters
worse, casual users of land statistics (both Chinese and foreign)
often use figures for cultivated land and sown land (includes land
which is double and triple cropped) interchangeably, creating con-

tillable land, cultivated land (land plowed up each year), and sown area, which may include two
or more crops on the same piece of land during one cropping year (discussed below).
[4] Frederick W. Crook, "Allocation of Crop Sown Area: Analysis of Trends and Outlook for the
Future," China Agriculture and Trade Report, U.S. Department of Agriculture, July 1990, p. 37.
[5] E. N. Anderson, The Food of China (New Haven, Conn.: Yale University Press, 1988) as cited
in Jerome B. Brieder, "Millions of Mouths to Feed," Natural History, Oct. 1988, p.36.
[6] See Michael Field's chapter in this volume. Also, see L. A. Orleans, "China's Statistics: The
Impossible Dream," American Statistician, May 1974. Many of the problems and attitudes I discuss in this early article are still valid today.

siderable confusion. Translations are notorious in reporting what is obviously "sown land" as "cultivated land" or "arable land." Conversion of units between mou, hectares, acres, and, on occasion, square kilometer, adds to the difficulty of finding matching figures. But the conclusion is not as bleak as this confusion might suggest. More recent figures reported by the Ministry of Agriculture and the State Land Administration Bureau have become quite consistent—albeit still often distorted in secondary sources.

Table 1 presents rounded, order-of-magnitude figures on cultivated land for selected years and shows the growth in the number of people each hectare of farmland must support. (Perkins' hardgained but illusive figures for the early years, when China was expanding her borders, are included mostly as a curiosity.) It is important to understand that since 1949 the annual changes are net figures: the difference between land lost due to natural factors (deforestation, erosion, salinization, etc.) plus the expansion of urban and rural settlements, less the land gained as a result of China's land reclamation program. The new lands programs were especially successful in the 1950s when millions of people were conscripted to reclaim wasteland, level and terrace mountain sides, transform deserts through the construction of irrigation and drainage systems, and, in every way possible, increase land that could be cultivated, including lands that were neglected during the war period. In this way, China's cultivated land acreage managed to keep pace with population growth throughout most of the 1950s.

Table 1 shows that the land loss problem became more serious in the 1960s; in the 1970s the number of persons per hectare increased primarily because of population growth rather than loss of land, although the 100 million hectares of cultivated land reported between 1973 and 1982 are more likely to reflect an absence of statistics, rather than stability; in the 1980s, with the introduction of the responsibility system and other economic reforms (discussed below), the land problem reached crisis proportions.

Indeed, by 1986 there were twice as many persons in China per hectare of cultivated land as there were in the early 1950s. Or, to put it another way, "In 35 years, per capita cultivated land decreased by about 50 percent; between 1957 and 1977 the decrease in cultivated land amounted to the total cultivated land of 11 provinces, including Guangdong, Gwanxi, Yunnan, and Szechwan." [7] On the whole, despite some of the usual inconsistencies, statistics on cultivated land and its loss have become plentiful and are probably reasonably accurate.

II. CAUSES OF LAND LOSS

The many factors which are responsible for misuse, abuse, and consequent loss of arable land in China can be divided into three broad categories: the first relates to development and modernization, the second to rural reforms and changing attitudes toward land, and the third to the environment. And, as will be seen, perhaps the basic stumbling block to coping with the loss of land are the ubiquitous and self-serving work units (both urban and rural),

---

[7] *Liaowang*, No. 29, July 20, 1987; JPRS–CAR–87–046, Sept. 10, 1987.

TABLE 1. Approximate Figures of Cultivated Land and Population, Selected Years

(Land and population figures rounded to nearest million)

Year	Cultivated Land (million hectares)	Midyear Population (millions)	Persons/hectare
1400	25	61	2.4
1600	33		
1685	49		
1766	63	215	3.4
1873	81	349	4.3
1893	83	387	4.7
1913	91	430	4.7
1933	98	503	5.1
1949	98	560	5.7
1950	100	563	5.6
1951	104	568	5.5
1952	108	575	5.8
1953	109	584	5.4
1954	109	595	5.5
1955	110	607	5.5
1956	112	619	5.5
1957	112	633	5.7
1958	108	647	6.5
1965	104	716	6.9
1970	101	820	8.1
1973	100	883	8.8
1975	100	918	9.2
1979	100	972	9.7
1981	100	995	10.0
1982	100	1,008	10.1
1984	98	1,032	10.5
1985	97	1,043	10.8
1986	96	1,056	11.0
1988	93	1,087	11.7

Sources: Cultivated land—1949–79: As provided by the Ministry of Agriculture to the World Bank and reported in a document entitled *China: Socialist Economic Development*, Annex C: Agricultural Development, June 1, 1981, p. 61. 1984 and 1985, as derived from information in China Daily, Feb. 21, 1987, p. 3; 1986: *Renmin Ribao*, May 18, 1987; JPRS–CAR–87–013, July 1, 1987, p. 85. 1988: *China Daily*, Oct. 21, 1988, p. 1. Population—1949–1981: Judith Banister, *China's Changing Population* (Stanford University Press: Stanford, CA, 1987), p. 352. Post 1982: Mid-year estimates of the U.S. Bureau of the Census, provided by Banister.
Note: The pre-1949 approximations are included primarily as a curiosity. They are taken from Appendix A ("Chinese Population Data," pp. 207 and 212) and Appendix B ("Cultivated Acreage Data," p. 240) in Dwight H. Perkins, *Agricultural Development in China 1368–1968* (Chicago: Aldine Publishing, 1969).

and especially their leaders, who have had long experience in circumventing state policies for personal gain.

A. DEVELOPMENT AND MODERNIZATION

Urban Growth. National development and urban sprawl have always gone hand in hand. China's 1953 census reported an urban population of only 77.2 million or 13.2 percent of the total population; the 1982 census reported an urban population of 206.6 million or 20.6 percent; and in the next seven years (to the end of 1989) it was reported to be 315.7 million, or 28.6 percent of the total.[8] The fourfold increase in urban population resulted in an even greater increase in the urban area, from 2 percent (at some unspecified

---

[8] *Xinhua*, May 5, 1990; FBIS–CHI–90–088, May 7, 1990, p. 37. For a more detailed discussion of urban population, other estimates, and definitional problems, see chapter by Judith Banister in this volume.

date, most likely 1949) to 9.1 percent of China's area in 1986.[9] Despite the inclusion of large rural tracts within the urban boundaries, this figure seems grossly exaggerated. Nevertheless, to accommodate the millions of new urban immigrants each year, there is no doubt that large areas of arable land have been lost to agriculture through the construction of factories, housing, roads, parks, communication, and other facilities.

In terms of arable land loss, perhaps even worse than the expansion of large municipalities has been the rapid growth in the number and size of small and medium-sized towns scattered throughout the country. While trying to control the growth of large municipalities, the government has pushed the development of smaller urban areas, which could use local resources and absorb some of the excess rural labor. As a rule, these settlements start out as agriculture-based market towns on some of China's most fertile soils.

Millions of peasants have indeed been leaving the back-breaking activities of agriculture and going to work in nearby urban areas. In fact, nonfarm activities became a lucrative novelty even while communes were still intact and there were reports that, even then, under the rubric of "developing integrated operations by combining agriculture, industry, and commerce," local cadres would take fertile land out of agriculture and rent or sell it to operators of small factories.[10]

In a land-short society there is also a tendency to hoard land. Urban enterprises and institutions frequently manage to acquire more land than they can use and, because land was allocated by the state and is free, they consider it to be "their own property and let it lie idle for possible future use, thus aggravating the urban land shortage." [11]

Even in 1987 the statement by the director of the Rural Development and Research Center that "China plans to shift 100 million people from agricultural work to local industries in the next few years," [12] seemed grossly exaggerated. Now that China has initiated an austerity program to cut down on excessive capital construction and fixed assets, reduce inflation, and improve the economic environment, there has been a reverse movement and millions of peasants have been forced to return to the farms. It is safe to say, however, that the slowdown in urban growth is temporary and that the loss of cultivated land due to urban expansion is bound to continue for a long time.

Rural Development. Nothing reflects more clearly rural China's prosperity in the 1980s than the boom in the construction of rural housing, a phenomenon frequently commented on by visitors to China. According to *Guangming Daily*, between 1979 and 1988, 6.2 billion square meters of housing were built in rural China; 86 million rural families moved into new houses; the average per capita living space in rural areas was expanded from 10 to 19.4 square meters—at least triple the average in urban areas; and 672 million

[9] CD July 8, 1987, p. 1.
[10] *Red Flag*, No 20, Oct. 16, 1981; JPRS No. 79, 712, Dec. 22, 1981.
[11] *Red Flag*, No. 16, Aug. 16, 1986.
[12] CD, Sept. 4, 1987, p. 1.

square meters of rural public facilities were constructed.[13] This is, of course, great for the peasants, 80 percent of whom are said to live in attractive new brick homes, but what effect has this had on land loss? The director-general of the State Land Administration complained that between 1985 and 1988 more than 227,000 hectares of farmland were used by farmers for private housing sites.[14] This is a tremendous amount of land, but considering the fact that many farmers are accused of building "villa-style apartment buildings," (at least from the exterior) it may not be an exaggeration.

As did the cities, the Chinese countryside saw the proliferation of small-scale industries and other nonagricultural enterprises, often making it difficult to draw lines between city and countryside. The problem, however, is the same. Whether through the expansion of towns or villages, land that was previously used for agriculture is now being used for other purposes. Large tracts of valuable farmland around the country have been occupied by rural enterprises— of which the most land-hungry, apparently, are brick and tile kilns with their yards. One good indication of the extent of nonagricultural activities in the Chinese countryside is that by 1988, 95 million Chinese farmers, or one-quarter of the nation's rural labor force, were involved in township enterprises, whose total output value (regardless of quality) topped 640 billion yuan, surpassing that of agriculture.[15] Such a boom in township enterprises must inevitably consume large chunks of farmland, but the process may be halted at least temporarily. It was reported that as part of the current retrenchment process, China has closed or transferred 3 million rural enterprises, eliminating 3 million jobs[16]—which tells us something about the size of the country, the nature of rural enterprises, and some interesting aspects of Chinese statistics!

As in the cities, there is also hoarding of land in the countryside. Some farmers become involved in sideline production and other nonagricultural work and as a result many either neglect their land or do not cultivate it regularly, but refuse to give it up for others to cultivate. The official explanation for this "hoarding" mentions "the legacy of feudalism," insecurity of income from industrial jobs and sideline production and, most important, that there is no penalty for taking fertile land out of production.[17] From the peasants' perspective, holding on to their small strip of contract land makes great sense. Because of the insecurity of urban and township employment, the main function of "this stretch of land which the peasants neither cultivate well nor wish to abandon" becomes an "indispensable safety net for social stability."[18] To put it simply, if the peasants lose their jobs in towns or in townships, as many do, they can always return to their land.

Finally, there is considerable concern over the loss of arable land that remains in agriculture (produces food) but is no longer cultivated. The introduction of a market economy into the countryside has caused many farmers to convert their land from grain produc-

[13] *Xinhua*, Sept. 22, 1989; FBIS–CHI–89–192, Oct. 5, 1989.
[14] CD, Jan. 18, 1990, p. 1.
[15] *Beijing Review* (hereafter BR), April 30–May 6, 1990, p. 21.
[16] *Xinhua*, April 9, 1990; FBIS–CHI–90–072–S, April 13, 1990, p. 43.
[17] CD, Oct. 19, 1988, p. 4.
[18] *Jingji Ribao*, April 14, 1990; FBIS–CHI–90–091, May 10, 1990, p. 30.

tion into more lucrative uses, such as fishing ponds, poultry farms, and orchards.

B. REFORMS, AMBIGUOUS OWNERSHIP AND CHANGING ATTITUDES TOWARD LAND

In addition to the "normal" losses of cultivated land due to urbanization and the expansion of nonagricultural rural activities, it is important to note the changing attitude of Chinese farmers toward land—a change caused, to a large extent, by introduction of the responsibility system and which has resulted in some new and unanticipated problems. The controversial Chinese television series, "River Elegy," ascribes much of China's backwardness and resulting ills to the narrowness and conservatism of the Chinese people and to their stubborn worship of land. If this were in fact true, Deng's reforms seem to have altered this "fixation on the land." Because of the emergence of changing conditions and new incentives, all too many Chinese peasants are willing to abandon their land.

In this connection, the most glaring problem spawned by the demise of communes and introduction of the responsibility system is the fuzziness of land ownership and use rights. There is a great deal of uncertainty about the demarcation between collective ownership and land use rights of farming households and about the length of time a family will be able to farm a specific piece of land. While in theory land is assigned for 15 years, in many localities it is reassigned every few years. Conflict over land allocation has become common. In one county 90 percent of civil disputes had to do with lack of distinction of land ownership.[19] One scholar from the Agricultural Development Research Institute adds: "Since communes have died out no one actually owns the land," so that "people in rural areas with power, influence and money find it easy to use land to obtain gains."[20]

It is easy to see how this land allocation system not only increases the chance that land will be misused but limits optimum investment by individual families and thereby adversely affects the yield. At the household level, ambiguous property rights have, at best, caused peasants to operate their land for short-term gains and, at worst, to lose their enthusiasm for farming and, in many cases, to leave farming altogether. Many farmers are spending their increased income on food, clothing, and houses, ignoring investment in the land. At the institutional level, since enterprises and units occupy land at no cost, there is no incentive to use land efficiently, resulting in "rampant construction projects and cheap uncontrolled land allocation" and the shrinkage of farmland.[21]

Concern over loose ownership standards have given rise to frequent scholarly meetings and seminars to discuss various types of land ownership schemes.[22]   But although, at least so far, there

[19] *Liaowang* Overseas Edition, Dec. 19, 1988; FBIS–251, Dec. 30, 1988, p. 43.
[20] *Xhongguo Nongcun Jingji (Chinese Rural Economy)*, No. 5, May 31, 1989; JPRS–CAR–89–095, Sept. 13, 1989, p. 37.
[21] CD, Jan. 30, 1989, p. 2.
[22] See, for example, *Qiushi (Seeking Truth)*, No. 12, Dec. 16, 1988; JPRS–CAR–89–031.

have been no practical solutions to this problem, a few localities are experimenting with land registration certificates for both units and individuals, which specify definite land boundaries and proof of compensation for the transfer of land use rights.[23]

C. ENVIRONMENTAL FACTORS IN LAND LOSS

The history of Chinese civilization is intimately tied with land and with an unending battle against environmental factors. Here I will limit the discussion to a brief review as it relates to the loss of cultivated land.

Although China is spending more of her limited funds on programs designed to protect farmlands from "natural" causes, the magnitude of the problem is increasing. According to the *People's Daily* every year 133,000 hectares of land is washed away by flood, turned into desert, or destroyed by other natural disasters.[24] Deforestation is probably the primary reason that millions of tons of soil are washed into the sea every year. Along with quarrying and mining, the cutting of forests causes silting, which, in turn, raises the level of river beds, making floods more frequent, transportation more erratic, and seriously damaging existing farmland. At the same time, and despite efforts at control, China's deserts are growing at a rate of 1,560 square kilometers a year, according to the director of a desert control institute.[25]

To manage these problems China has been carrying on a seemingly endless program of afforestation, reporting both significant achievements and major failures. The Green Great Wall shelterbelt extending across North China—which includes the planting of grasses and bushes, as well as trees—is a good example of this. On the one hand it is reported that this 10-year effort freed 10 million hectares of farmland from sand storms and, in the process, helped water conservation and controlled soil erosion; on the other hand, mismanagement of this expensive project and a lack of funding to compensate the peasants who provide seedlings for trees and do the planting, have caused serious difficulties and almost half of the new forest suffers from insect damage.[26] Similar problems are reported from around the country and all result in extremely low survival rates for newly planted trees. Planting goes on, however, and the Minister of Forestry provides us with figures that seem incredible even for China: in a 1989 nationwide afforestation drive, 300 million people planted a record 1.7 billion trees (fewer than 6 trees per person) on 5.4 million hectares of land.[27]

Other causes for the deteriorating ecological environment and consequent loss of farmland are an increase in salinization; an increase in sandy soils due to denudation, improper reclamation, and excessive grazing of animals; soil erosion, especially in South China's hilly areas; and pollution of fields, especially by foul water.[28] According to the latest figures, 6.7 million hectares of

[23] Xinhua, Jan. 6, 1988.
[24] CD, Aug. 10, 1989, p. 4.
[25] BR, Mar. 14–20, 1988, p. 12.
[26] CD, Oct. 4, 1988, p. 1.
[27] Xinhua, March 5, 1990; FBIS–CHI–90–044, March 6, 1990.
[28] See, for example, Hefei, *Anhui Ribao*, June 22, 1985; JPRS–CAG–85–027, Sept. 12, 1985, p. 4.

farmland are contaminated by waste water, petroleum products, and cinder, reducing the annual grain harvest by 10 billion kilograms.[29] Additional pollution was caused by the introduction of pesticides and chemical fertilizers into Chinese agriculture so that, according to the *Farmers Daily*, 13 million hectares of the country's farmland are polluted by these chemicals.[30]

As farmland is lost and degraded, China is in the constant process of adding land through the reclamation of wastelands. In 1986 alone some 250,000 hectares of land were "reclaimed and newly created."[31] Current land reclamation plans appear not only too ambitious, but perhaps not altogether realistic. For example, the National Committee on Agricultural Zone Planning estimates that more than 6.6 million hectares of wasteland in "remote and seashore areas" will be reclaimed before the turn of the century. It also projects that nearly 10 million hectares of seashore or beach areas can be turned into farmland capable of feeding more than 100 million people![32] Past experience proves that unfettered land reclamation for agriculture can seriously damage the land without adding any significant production. Most frequently this happens during periodic drives to grow more grain, when the performance of the cadres is judged by the acreage added to cultivated land rather than its productivity. Frequently grain was planted on marginal reclaimed land—often valuable grassland—only to be abandoned after a few years to experience even more severe erosion.[33] In the 1990s the Chinese authorities have become much more aware of the need to protect the regressing grasslands,[34] but there is certainly no guarantee that the next drive to expand grain acreage (which is sure to come) will not commandeer the most readily accessible grasslands.

Whatever China's success in opening up new lands, three points must be kept in mind. First, despite land reclamation, the amount of arable land has decreased every year since 1957.[35] Second, most of the lost farmland is in the most fertile, densely populated areas of China, while the reclaimed land is of much lower fertility and tends to be located in remote areas where transport facilities are poor. It is not an equal exchange. And third, a significant proportion of cultivated land lost to environmental factors results from massive efforts to add land through reclamation. As already discussed, the liberal felling of forests and destruction of grassland in order to create farmland in some areas ("blind reclamation of

---

[29] Xinhua, March 30, 1990; JPRS–CAR–90–030, April 24, 1990, p. 57. "Waste water is responsible for almost half of all farmland pollution." (*Anhui Ribao*, June 22, 1985; JPRS–CAG–85–027, Sept. 12, 1985, p. 7.)

[30] CD, Nov. 5, 1988, p. 4.

[31] *Renmin Ribao (People's Daily)* (hereafter RMRB), July 24, 1989; FBIS–CHI–89–151, Aug. 8, 1989, p. 46.

[32] CD, March 23, 1988, p. 1.

[33] See, for example, "Status of Grasslands in China," an unpublished paper by Yang Li and Hsin-i Wu presented at a CSCPRC Grasslands Meeting in Washington, D.C., May 30, 1990.

[34] In this connection, it is interesting that a 1989 circular demanding that local governments open up new farmland was jointly issued by the State Land Administration Bureau, the State Science and Technology Commission, the Ministry of Finance, and the Ministry of Agriculture. (*Jiefangjun Bao*, Oct. 25, 1989; FBIS–CHI–89–215, Nov. 8, 1989.)

[35] For example, "Looking at conditions over the past 20 years (approximately 1960 to 1980), each year an average of 16 million *mu* of wasteland was reclaimed whereas 25 million *mu* of land was occupied for other uses." (*Jingji Guanli*, No. 7, July 15, 1980; JPRS No. 76, 462, Sept. 22, 1980, p. 8. Also see Table 1.)

land") has cost China millions of hectares of farmland through soil erosion, floods, and shifting sands in other areas.[36]

III. LEGAL RESPONSES AND PROBLEMS OF IMPLEMENTATION

Between 1949 and 1979, almost all the concern over the loss of arable land was limited to the negative effects of pollution on land. Not unlike other third world countries, economic progress was deemed much too important to be sidetracked by concern about how land was used. For over 30 years it was almost inconceivable for anyone to object to the use of farmland to construct a factory, with adjacent workers' housing and other amenities. There were, of course, complaints even in the late 1970s and early 1980s about "anarchy" in land use, pointing, for example, at commune cooperatives, tractor stations, and brick workshops occupying much more land than they needed,[37] but public outcry was muted because under the commune system land was collectively owned. There was always opportunity to misuse the land, but the possibility of personal gain through some form of land manipulation was, for all practical purposes, impossible until decollectivization and the greatly increased opportunities for profit by individuals.

With the introduction of the responsibility system and the subsequent confusion about the control and management of land, the people in the countryside found new and previously nonexistent opportunities to make money from land. The peasants profited from the new market economy in agriculture and by developing sideline enterprises, but the primary profiteers and culprits in the misuse of land were the local officials who, with every passing year, seemed to exhibit more and more disregard for rules and regulations on land use. In 1987 an investigation by the State Land Administration showed that 40 percent of the land was seized unlawfully and that in some localities the illegal use of arable land reached 60 percent.[38] The custom of taking land first and seeking approval later—whether by individuals or enterprises—was widespread, as was the practice of taking much more land than was approved by the authorities.[39]

Despite widespread corruption, it was not until June 1986 that the Standing Committee of the National People's Congress passed what the Chinese refer to as the first land management law.[40] It was to become effective in January 1987 and was designed to prevent the confiscation of land for industrial use and construction and to protect it from a variety of other abuses by using administrative, economic, and legal means to strengthen land management.[41] This law was supplemented by the "Regulations on Land

---

[36] See, for example, RMRB, July 24, 1989; FBIS–CHI–89–151; Aug. 8, 1989.

[37] RMRB, June 22, 1980; JPRS 76,574, Oct. 9, 1980, p. 20.

[38] *Liaowang*, July 20, 1987; JPRS–CAR–87–046; Sept.10, 1987, p. 35.

[39] See, for example, *Jingji Wenti (Problems in Economics)* No. 6, June 25, 1985; JPRS–CEA–86–050, April 29, 1986, p. 38.

[40] A copy of the 57 articles of the law was released by *Xinhua* on June 25, 1986 and translated in JPRS–CAG–86–029, Aug. 1, 1986, p. 1.

[41] Only joint ventures, cooperative enterprises, and enterprises with exclusive foreign investment could get preferential treatment in the use of land. (Hong Kong, *Zhongguo Xinwen She*, Dec. 9, 1986; FBIS, Dec. 15, 1986, p. K15). For more information on the foreign land-use policy, see Perry Keller, "Liberating the Land," *The China Business Review*, March–April 1988, pp. 40–44.

Rehabilitation" which were announced by Premier Li Peng in November 1988 and which were to go into effect on January 1, 1989.
The lengthy regulations can be boiled down to this: whoever
(whether enterprises or individuals) is responsible for damaging
land in any way will be responsible for rehabilitating it.[42] The
whole concept of restoring land damaged by mining, timber cutting, or solid-waste pollution is brand new to the Chinese and in
order to encourage units to use "re-improved" land for agriculture,
animal husbandry, fish breeding, or tree planting, they were
exempt from the agricultural tax.[43]

Statistics on the "wanton occupation" of arable land are both
plentiful and contradictory, but they make clear that the immediate effect of the law on land-related corruption was negligible.[44] As
already alluded to, the most obvious obstacle to the law's implementation was that the implementers themselves were not only
the ones most likely to profit from ignoring it, but, as pointed out
by one Chinese commentator, they were "not even able to accept
the fact that the violation of the Land Law was a crime." Local
party and government officials who are in control of the land—i.e.,
in a position to sell, lease, or approve its use—were responsible for
more than half the illegal land transactions. The *People's Daily* put
it more vividly by saying that the difficulty of checking the abuse
of farmland stems from the fact that "the pen which determines
the fate of the land has not been really brought under control." [45]

Just three of the endless examples of how cadres profit from
land—which theoretically has no value and cannot be traded under
Marxism—should adequately illustrate the problem.

An article in the *People's Daily* tells a story of a government department in Jinan City which, in order to build cemeteries, took
over 13 hectares of farmland on which 400 villagers made a living.
Officials then auctioned off the cemetery plots, "pocketing with
smiles" the 1,500 to 2,400 yuan each plot brought. The article goes
on to say that since only 27 percent of the country's 6 million
deaths last year were cremated, it is clear that "the dead are competing and will continue to compete with the living for the country's limited land." [46]

Another interesting tale comes from Hebei Province. After getting approval from the village committee, a party secretary had a
brick kiln built which, with its field, occupied 3.2 hectares of farmland. He neglected, however, to get the necessary approval of
higher authorities. The farmers complained; the county investigated; the party secretary admitted his fault, but the kiln continued to

---

[42] *Xinhua*, Nov. 13, 1988; JPRS–CAR–89–003, Jan. 3, 1989.

[43] CD, Nov. 16, 1988, p. 3.

[44] For example, one report states that even though in 1987 the illegal occupancy of farmland
showed a decrease over the previous year, the country still lost about 800,000 hectares of farmland in this way (CD, March 3, 1989, p. 3). Incomplete statistics for 1988 (from just 24 provinces)
showed 387,000 cases of illegal building on cultivated land, implying a decrease (*Xinhua*, Oct. 26,
1989; FBIS–CHI–89–206, Oct. 26, 1989, p. 52), while another *Xinhua* report states that the
number of violations of the land law increased in 1988 (*Xinhua*, Nov. 5,1988; FBIS–CHI–88–219,
Nov. 14, 1988).

[45] RMRB, Feb. 5, 1990; FBIS–CHI–90–037–S, Feb. 23, 1990.

[46] CD, 12–29–88, p. 4. Another article in the *China Daily*, entitled "Burials Gnaw Away
Arable Land," included detailed figures on the area occupied by burial mounds, the amount of
timber used in each coffin, and savings in arable land and timber that accrue when bodies are
cremated. (CD, Dec. 1,1988, p. 4).

operate. Now the farmers have taken the case to provincial authorities and vow, if necessary, to take it to the central government.[47] But while more and more peasants apparently sought justice from the courts, local authorities gained reassurance from the fact that noncompliance with the law did not result in severe criminal sanctions for the offenders, but only fines or possible dismissal from the job—a relatively small price to pay when 1 hectare of land could bring from 28,000 to 72,000 yuan.[48]

There are also apparently instances when the cadres are willing to share their booty with the peasants. Some villages on the outskirts of cities sell off their (common use?) land "to government agencies or enterprises," invest or deposit the proceeds in banks, and distribute the interest to all the peasants, "who are thus living very well." And they well might if, as reported for the outskirts of Chengdu in Sichuan province, land is going at 750,000 yuan per hectare![49] By the end of 1989, Beijing realized that something more drastic had to be done to strengthen the 1986 land law. Wang Xianjin, Director-General of the State Land Administration, listed the measures intended to reinforce its implementation. He pledged not only to reduce the construction targets and tighten up on land-use approvals given by authorities, but even to take back land-use rights from projects that were halted or cancelled by the current austerity drive. Because of the newly established quotas on the amount of land that can be taken out of agriculture each year, large land users such as coal and nonferrous metals producers, airports, railways, highways, irrigation networks, and oil fields will have to apply to the State Land Administration for special permission to build new projects.[50] The building of private houses in rural areas is also to be restricted and there is to be a 20-year freeze on the expansion of existing private housing sites. Cadres desiring to build private homes will have to get two types of approval, first from local officials and then from the State Land Administration. And most important, those who do not abide by the regulations set down in the land law and acquire land either for themselves or for their relatives will be severely punished "no matter who they are."[51] As part of these regulations, Wang also set a goal for the amount of land that will be reclaimed in 1990, showing a net increase in farmland of 1 million *mu* or about 67,000 hectares for the year.[52] So much for theory. Significantly, what he did not mention is the need to prolong land-contract tenure in order to give peasants an incentive to stay on the land and invest in it.

To have better control over producing farmland, the State Land Administration intends to bring most of it under State protection, especially the high-yield farming areas of east, central, and southeast China and in the coastal areas. Since 70 percent of the land is said to be managed by township-level governments, it is not quite

[47] CD, March 3, 1989, p. 3.
[48] CD, Mar. 23, 1989, p. 1. For a more detailed account of the land- and housing-generated tensions between peasants and cadres, see David Zweig, "Struggling Over Land in China: Peasant Resistance after Collectivization, 1966–86," in Forrest D. Colburn, ed., *Everyday Forms of Peasant Resistance* (Armonk, N.Y.: M.E. Sharpe, 1989), pp. 162–8.
[49] *Jingji Cankao (Economic Information)*, Feb. 13, 1989; JPRS–CAR–89–029, Apr. 4, p. 54.
[50] CD, Oct. 21, 1988, p. 1.
[51] CD, Aug. 19, 1989, p. 1.
[52] CD, Jan. 18, 1990, p. 1.

clear how this consolidation will be accomplished. One important step, however, will be to reinforce the inadequate ranks of local land officials, 60 percent of whom perform their duties on a part-time basis. Another innovation, at least in some "experimental areas," is for farmers to sign agreements "not to build houses, make bricks, grow fruit trees, or dig fish ponds on protected farm-lands" and in return the government promises not to allow the confiscation of their land for use by developers.[53]

It is difficult to say how effective these new laws and regulations are likely to be in protecting arable land. Perhaps Li Peng's call for more efficient management of existing farmland in his report to the National People's Congress on March 20, 1990,[54] will show a degree of concern by China's top leaders which will assure better implementation. For the time being, however, the conclusion of heads of land bureaus at a March 1990 conference that "the tend-ency of sharp losses of arable land has been checked in recent years"[55] seems premature.

Finally, it is useful to place the land law into perspective and point out that the noncompliance with and nonenforcement of laws are not limited to land and are said to be "almost universal." A survey of law enforcement conducted in 1988 in Zhejiang Province showed that only 30 percent of the laws were enforced "fairly well," while 50 percent were "generally enforced" and 20 percent were "fairly poorly" enforced. And just as in the case of land laws, the primary culprits are the "leading cadres who hold power."[56]

IV. The Hereafter

Political leaders can be replaced and the economy can be struc-turally corrected or "fine tuned," but China's population of over 1.1 billion will keep growing, and as long as China pursues a policy of modernization and development—and no one is predicting other-wise—farmland will continue to be taken for nonagricultural uses. Without raising the spectre of the moth-eaten Malthusian devil, it is easy to imagine an impending crisis and to understand Beijing's concerns. While the complex subject of China's food/population bal-ance is beyond the scope of this paper, a few comments—superficial though they may be—are nevertheless most relevant to the subject at hand.

If population growth is taken as a given, then the answer seems all too simple: China must try to protect the existing arable lands and, at the same time, make them more productive. In other words, China must continue doing what she has been doing, but must do it more efficiently.

Observers from societies with a strong legal tradition find it diffi-cult to understand why law enforcement is so capricious in China. In fact, traditional concepts are so deep-rooted in China that it will obviously take time to overcome what seems to be a perpetual tug-of-war between the rule by man and the rule by law. In the case of

---

[53] CD, Dec. 12, 1989, p. 1. Quoting from RMRB.
[54] BR, Apr. 16–22, 1990, p. XIX.
[55] *Jingji Cankao*, Jan. 6, 1990; JPRS–CAR–90–018, Mar. 5, 1990, p. 54.
[56] Hong Kong, *Liaowang Overseas Edition*, No. 27, July 3, 1989; JPRS–CAR–89–103, Oct. 17, 1989, p. 51.

land, as in other cases, individuals, and especially cadres, will continue to seek and find ways to circumvent the existing rules and regulations. Consequently, although land laws are becoming more stringent and the rate at which arable land is taken for nonagricultural purposes is declining, the problems brought about by the loss and misuse of arable land will not disappear for many years.

As to increasing the productivity of the cultivated acreage, here too China must approach the problem on two fronts: one systemic, the other scientific.

In the first instance, it is extremely important for China to create stability and confidence in the countryside by putting an end to the post-commune debate over whether land should be owned collectively, be privatized, or whether some middle ground should be sought. The decision is not an easy one and the best answer may have regional variations. The economic stimulation brought about through the introduction of the responsibility system into agriculture was impressive indeed, but in the future productivity may stagnate in many parts of China simply because household ownership of land has created serious problems of scale, which only increase as land acreage diminishes. Small plots in China may be manicured, but in many parts of the country they are also among the most fragmented in the world. Tillers of such postage stamp plots with ambiguous land rights may understand the advantages of technical improvements, but find it either impractical or impossible to invest in fixed assets, thereby continuing to rely on brawn to plow the land and to turn the soil. In the meantime, irrigation canals, rural roads, and other responsibilities previously taken care of at the commune level have suffered through neglect and lack of investment of both capital and manpower. The impracticalities of carrying out modernization and mechanization on small, scattered plots is well known, so that in areas where small-scale agricultural operations predominate, some type of community cooperatives, or dual management of land, is already under experimentation. On the other hand, the potential problems associated with the simultaneous existence of privately owned and cooperatively owned land are readily apparent.

In the second instance, China must obviously continue to increase the productivity of lands now under cultivation. It is, after all, through the introduction of new means and methods to improve traditional agricultural practices that she has managed to feed a population which has doubled since 1949. Granted that per acre productivity will likely increase much more slowly in the future, the agricultural know-how now practiced by advanced countries could still significantly raise current yields, especially if irrigated and double-cropped acreage is expanded. The availability of food could be further increased by decreasing the huge losses now experienced between field and market—a serious condition in all third world countries. For the short-term, then, and assuming political and economic stability in the country, increased mechanization and electrification, improved seeds, fertilizers and pesticides, and improved management at all stages, should make it possible for food production to keep pace with China's population.

Looking into the more distant future, indications are that scientific and technological potential in food production is almost beyond the imaginations of most lay persons. Although some critics contend that, if unrestricted, new developments in the biological sciences will bring about ecological disaster, there is little doubt that many of the promises held out by biotechnology (one of China's priority sciences), which may now read like science fiction, will come to fruition and thereby change farming around the world.

In China, nature and man have colluded to make the loss of cultivated land a serious problem. To overcome the potential crisis, Beijing will have to control nature, reorient man's values, and invest in science.

RURAL INDUSTRY: CONSTRAINING THE LEADING GROWTH SECTOR IN CHINA'S ECONOMY

By David Zweig *

CONTENTS

I. SUMMARY AND INTRODUCTION [1]

China's rural industry has been the most vibrant sector of the national economy since the mid-1980s. For several decades after they first emerged from the 1958 Great Leap Forward as a product of "self-reliant" development, rural factories were seen both in and outside of China as an anciliary part of China's economic development. They offered a means by which rural surplus labor could effectively use local resources. By the late 1960s, rural industry became a conduit for introducing urban technology to the rural areas. Yet it remained part of Mao's cellular approach to development and his goal of protecting the urban sector from the economic demands of the countryside. Rural, not urban, industry would supply finances and material for agricultural modernization, leaving urban, state-owned industry free to fulfill urban demands.

Since the mid-1980s, the increased interdependence of the urban and rural sectors has transformed the role and status of rural industry. Following the reintroduction of "household farming," and the freeing up of tens of millions of surplus rural laborers,[2] promoting rural industry and developing a rural service sector became

* David Zweig is Associate Professor of International Politics at The Fletcher School of Law and Diplomacy, Tufts University.

[1] Research for this paper was supported by a grant from the Social Sciences and Humanities Research Council of Canada, Ottawa, two travel grants from the Sackler Foundation, Washington, DC, the Kearny Foundation, Hong Kong, the China Executive Development Program, at The Fletcher School of Law and Diplomacy, Tufts University, and the Luce Foundation's, "U.S.-China Collaborative Research Grant." Research assistance was provided by Sonny Lo at the University of Waterloo, and Xu Ziwang, Mulatu Wirtu, and Alexis Feringa Thurman at The Fletcher School, Tufts University.

[2] According to China's leading analyst of rural development, Du Rensheng, at least 200 million rural inhabitants would have to find work in the rural nonagricultural sector. Du Rensheng, "Second-stage Rural Structural Reform," *Beijing Review*, No. 25 (24 June 1985): 15–17, 22.

vital national policy to stem the tide of rural-to-urban migration. According to *Peasant Daily* of 24 February 1988, by 1987 the output value of rural enterprises, including industry and the service sector, surpassed the total output value of agricultural production. The rapid increase in rural living standards following decollectivization created a huge market for home appliances and construction materials, as peasants demanded amenities previously reserved for urban residents. Rural industry now produces many light industrial goods for everyday living, such as electric fans, cooking utensils, and clothing, undermining the state sector's monopoly on light industrial production. As these consumer goods were removed from the state plan, rural industry, with its more flexible production lines, responded rapidly to increased nationwide demand. By 1988, rural industry, excluding services, accounted for over 26 percent of total nationwide industrial production.

As the quality of these light industrial products improved, rural industry in the coastal regions moved swiftly into the export sector; in 1989, rural industry directly earned almost 20 percent of China's foreign exchange. Local governments have also used flaws in the banking system to siphon enormous amounts of scarce funding from central coffers for developing local industry, which has become the local governments' "cash cow." Although the central government has tried on numerous occasions to limit the growth of the rural industrial sector, local resilience has always succeeded in weathering the storms, progressing rapidly once the environment improved. Today, rural industry remains a major challenger to the state sector in light industry and export earnings and has shifted from a supplementary economic role to what Bo Yibo now refers to as "a major pillar of the national economy." [3] This change calls for more attention to be paid to this booming and critical sector of China's political economy.

II. HISTORICAL DEVELOPMENT

Even before rural industry rose to such prominence in China's economic development, its history shows a remarkable resiliency and a penchant for irrepressible autonomous development. Today, as leaders who favor more planned development with greater emphasis on the state sector try to inhibit rural industry, they confront a sector that has weathered numerous assaults from the central government, emerging from each confrontation better equipped for continued economic growth.

During the Great Leap Forward (1958-60), peasants were mobilized to produce steel in backyard furnaces and to set up small workshops as part of the People's Communes. Soviet-built plants, coming on line in 1957-59, did not improve life in the countryside, so the state promoted rural industry to address the rural-urban gap. But central plans for guiding and promoting small-scale rural industries, drawn up in 1957-58, were ignored as local initiatives to set up factories took over. At least 7.5 million new factories and workshops, with the majority processing agricultural produce, were

---

[3] See Bo Yibo, "To Develop Township and Town Enterprises is a Task of Strategic Significance," Speech to the Delegates to the Inauguration of the Chinese Township and Town Enterprise Association, 11 January 1990, in *FBIS*, No. 9-S (9 February 1990): 41–43.

set up in the first nine months of 1958.[4] But the economic catastrophe of 1960–62 dried up material resources, so state policy which called for the closing of all loss incurring industries also stipulated that 90 percent of China's rural labor force remain in agriculture. In response, local officials shut down many rural factories.

From the mid-1960s through the early 1970s, rural industry grew for two reasons. Responding to the US escalation of the Vietnam War in fall 1964, China moved one-third of its industrial base to the hinterlands, creating a "Third Front." [5] With almost one-third of its national budget going to establish this new industrial heartland, rural areas were left to develop on their own. Second, China's burgeoning "green revolution" called for increased production of chemical fertilizer and cement for both water conservation projects and power plants for pumping water. When the 1970 Northern Districts Agricultural Conference promoted agricultural mechanization,[6] and the "five basic industries—cement, agricultural machinery, power generation, fertilizer, steel—local enthusiasm led to excessive factory construction, which the Chinese called "blind development." [7] The August 1971 National Conference on Rural Mechanization, which decided that rural industry should promote agricultural mechanization, made rural industries eligible for bank loans and fiscal support.[8]

These policies led to rapid growth in county-owned rural industry. Between 1965 and 1969 the production capacity of small, nitrogenous fertilizer plants grew five times, and their share of national fertilizer output increased from 12 percent in 1965 to 60 percent in 1971. The number of cement plants increased tenfold between 1965 and 1973, and came to produce almost half of China's cement. Similar growth occurred in pig iron production, small-scale power generators and farm equipment.[9]

After 1972, commune and brigade enterprises grew rapidly. Urban youths sent to the rural areas in the Cultural Revolution persuaded urban factories to set up workshops in their villages as a way of getting themselves out of fieldwork and into factories. A 1974 policy, implemented in parts of rural Jiangsu Province, called on all communes to promote brigade-level factories, while another policy carried out in suburban Nanjing allowed local officials to demand that state enterprises, which took village land, build workshops in these villages and employ displaced rural laborers.[10] Finally, the 1976 founding of the National Rural Industry Administration formally legalized the position of rural firms.[11]

---

[4] Carl Riskin, *China's Political Economy: The Quest for Development Since 1949* (Oxford: Oxford University Press, 1987): 125–126.

[5] Barry Naughton, "The Third Front: Defense Industrialization in the Chinese Interior," *The China Quarterly*, No. 115 (September 1988): 351–386.

[6] *Zhonghua renmin gongheguo jingji dashiji, 1949–1980* (Major Events in the PRC, 1949–1980; Beijing: Zhongguo shehui kexue chubanshe, 1984), p. 463.

[7] *Major Events in the PRC, 1949–1980*, op.cit, p. 472.

[8] Luo Xiaopeng, "Ownership and Status Stratification," in William Byrd and Lin Qinsong, eds., *China's Rural Industry: Structure, Development and Reform* (New York: Oxford University Press, 1990).

[9] Riskin, *China's Political Economy*, op.cit., pp. 214–15.

[10] Information collected by the author during his various research trips to rural Jiangsu Province.

[11] Luo, "Ownership and Status Stratification," op. cit.

In the late 1970s and early 1980s, decollectivization, which shifted resources from collectives into private hands, decreased funding for rural industry. Twenty thousand commune and 85,000 brigade enterprises closed in 1981, with the loss of 500,000 jobs.[12] However, local capital accumulation in the 1970s through "extra budgetary funds;" a 1979 financial reform allowing local government to retain and invest larger shares of its revenues; [13] a doubling of Agricultural Bank of China (ABC) loans to rural industries in 1979–80; and three-year tax-free development for new enterprises in the late 1970s and early 1980s all gave local governments the funds and incentives to promote rural industry. Reforms in agricultural procurement created new opportunities for food processing plants, while the legitimization of private enterprises in the mid-1980s boosted rural industry.[14]

Since the 1984 issuance of State Council Document No. 4, which renamed "commune and brigade enterprises" as "township and village enterprises," rural industry has become a major factor in all aspects of the national economy. Loans to rural industry in 1984 were 2.3 times those of 1983.[15] Local data collected by the author in counties around Nanjing reflect major industrial expansion in 1984–85. In one township, output increased from 4.6 million yuan in 1983 to 7.3 million in 1984, and 9.97 million in 1985. In Jiangpu County, outside Nanjing, from 1983 to 1984 industrial output increased 24 percent; by 1985 it was up another 26 percent. Weakened central government control over allocation of producer goods, along with increased local control over investment funds, fueled further growth, particularly in areas with strong industrial bases. In Jiangsu and Zhejiang provinces, rural industrial growth far surpassed overall industrial growth, as much of the industrial expansion in these provinces was due to growth in rural industry.[16]

A new period of growth followed then General Secretary Zhao Ziyang's November 1987 call for China's coastal areas to implement an export-led growth strategy.[17] Dissatisfied with the results of his 1984 urban industrial reforms, Zhao argued that rural enterprises, not state-run ones, would be the "new impact force" for establishing an export-oriented economy and for earning foreign exchange.[18] Since then the role of rural industry in China's foreign trade has expanded rapidly (Table 1). In spite of the current retrenchment, 1990 estimates from officials in the Ministry of Agriculture are that rural industrial exports will climb by another 25 percent to over US$12.5 billion.[19]

---

[12] Christine P.W. Wong, "Interpreting Rural Industrial Growth in the Post-Mao Period," *Modern China,* Vol. 14, No. 1 (January 1988): 8–9.

[13] Wang Bingqian, "Report on Financial Work," *Beijing Review,* 29 September 1980.

[14] Wong "Interpreting Rural Industrial Growth," op. cit., pp. 7–9.

[15] *Zhongguo jingji nianjian, 1985* (Chinese Economic Yearbook), p. v–228.

[16] Robert Delfs, "The Rural Uprising," *Far Eastern Economic Review,* 11 July 1985. According to Delfs, between 1978 and 1984, annual growth in rural enterprises of nearly 25 percent in Jiangsu Province increased the privince's industrial output vaue by 19 percent/year.

[17] David Zweig, "Internationalizing Rural China: The Domestic Politics of Rural Exports," *Proceedings of the 19th Annual Sino-American Conference on Mainland China* (Taipei, forthcoming).

[18] "Zhao on Coastal Area's Development Strategy," *Beijing Review,* 8–14 February 1988, pp. 18–23.

[19] Interviews by author in Nanjing and Beijing, summer 1990.

The latest retrenchment began in fall 1988, following the October 1988 Third Plenum's decision to deflate China's overheated economy. With rural industry a major target of that effort, the number of enterprises, and the total number of employees in rural enterprises, decreased for the first time since 1981. However, after June 4, 1989, the newly dominant planning faction, whose base of support lies in the state-owned, heavy industrial sector, resurrected the centrality of state enterprises and squeezed rural industry mercilessly by closing off most forms of credit. The "39 Points," put forward at the 5th Plenum in November 1989, called on all rural enterprises that waste energy, produce shoddy goods, pollute, or compete with state enterprises for materials, to close down, suspend production, merge with other firms, or shift product lines. Rural enterprises were to process only local materials "instead of scrambling with large enterprises for raw materials and energy." [20] As a result of these measures, almost two million firms closed or were taken over by other firms, and almost three million workers lost their jobs (Tables 2 and 4). According to estimates by the Ministry of Agriculture's Township and Village Enterprise Bureau, as of early 1990, only 30 percent of firms were making a profit; 50 percent lacked inputs or could not sell their products; 10 percent are ready to go bankrupt, while another 10 percent had gone bankrupt. An extremely hostile environment compelled many private entrepreneurs to close shop, while those who had contracted collective enterprises returned firms to the collective, causing the firms to stop production. Unofficial estimates suggest that the contraction in rural industry has forced 15 million farmers back to the land.

By spring 1990, policy towards rural enterprises was forced to respond to popular anxiety and economic reality.[21] China's looming foreign debt crisis made it unwise to restrict a major foreign exchange generating sector. China's state budget faces an increasing deficit, and rural industries have supplied over 50 percent of new state taxes since 1980. With almost 100 million rural inhabitants employed in rural enterprises, nationwide plant closings and massive unemployment would lead to further rural-to-urban migration and both urban and rural unrest. Party leaders, including an important member of the old guard who reemerged during the events of spring 1989, lobbied on behalf of rural industry.[22] Further speeches, national conferences, exhibitions, and press reports supporting rural industry forced Li Peng to visit Jiangsu Province in February, where he admitted that "insufficient stress has been laid" on rural industry, and that its significance must be again recognized.[23]

---

[20] See "Decision on Further Improving the Economic Environment, Straightening Out the Economic Order, and Deepening the Reforms (Excerpts), adopted at the Fifth Plenary Session of the 13th Central Committee of the Chinese Communist Party on November 9, 1989, in *Beijing Review*, Vol. 33, No. 7 (Feb. 12–19, 1990).

[21] The most important article was a commentary in *Peasant Daily* on 15 March, entitled "Correctly Appraise the Role of Township and Town Enterprises." See *FBIS-CHI-90-078*, 23 April 1990, pp. 51–53.

[22] In January 1990, Bo Yibo called on his old comrades to deepen their understanding of rural industrialization, reminding them that it was party policy (i.e., not just the reform faction's policy) and the creation of the peasants. Rural industrialization was the "inevitable trend in Chinese economic development," and a "strategic task" for invigorating the rural economy. See Bo, "To Develop Township and Town Enterprises," op. cit.

[23] Li's comments were quoted in *Peasant Daily*, "Correctly Appraise the Role of Township and Town Enterprises," op. cit.

Yet despite this crisis, rural industrial growth has persisted at a stable rate of 15–16 percent (as compared to earlier rates of 45 percent in provinces such as Jiangsu). Funding has come from rural credit cooperatives not controlled by the Agricultural Bank (Table 8), those linked to state firms or that earn foreign exchange, and from bank loans to nonpolluting rural industries that use local resources, as well as various local strategies including forcing workers to invest in factories, setting up local savings and loan companies outside the banking system, and local government surcharges.[24] Some local officials feel that this retrenchment has allowed them to close inefficient firms, preparing them again for a rapid development once funds become more accessible.

III. THE ADMINISTRATIVE STRUCTURE SUPERVISING RURAL INDUSTRY

When dealing with China's economy, precise definitions are often problematic. For example, the Chinese have applied the term— "township and village industry" (TVE) (*xiangcun qiye*)—to a wider category of firms than those simply run by these two levels of local government. Also, since the mid-1980s they increasingly referred to "township and town industry," (*xiangzhen qiye*), which includes former townships now incorporated as towns. In this paper, the definition of rural industry includes any factory, enterprise, firm, hotel or shop situated in the rural areas or rural towns and owned cooperatively, privately or by local governments (village, township or town), below the county level (Table 9).

Unlike most industrial sectors in China, which are defined by product types, rural industry is defined by the level of ownership— township, village, cooperative or private—and its geographic location—in the rural areas. At the top of the bureaucratic structure guiding rural industries is the Township Enterprise Administrative Bureau (*xiangzhen qiye ju*), established in 1979 under the Ministry of Agriculture (MOA). According to the recently published *A List of Chinese Government Organizations*, the Bureau's major tasks include researching and directing rural industry's planned development, management, laws, economic structure, technological development, and liason with other ministries to improve the quality of rural industrial products.[25]

Other ministries and commissions have their own offices for rural industry. According to one official in the MOA, every ministry has a particular interest in TVEs (which may suggest that several of them have specific offices for dealing with TVEs), and the MOA's responsibility is to work out all the relationships among the different ministries.[26] For example, the State Planning Commission has a Division of Township Enterprises (*xiangzhen qiye chu*), whose task is to organize the work of different units to support rural industry. Given the fact that rural industrial production crosses so many product lines and therefore challenges the prod-

---

[24] Jean Oi, lecture at Fairbank Center, Harvard University, 10 August 1990.

[25] The *Name List of Chinese Government Organizations, Vol. 1, 1989* (Zhongguo zhengfu jigou minglu; Beijing: Xinhua chubanshe, 1989), pp. 191–92.

[26] One would assume that the TVE Bureau in the MOA calls together all the different offices relating to TVEs in the central bureaucracy to coordinate work. On the issue of exports from rural areas, national conferences are always run by both the MOA and the Ministry of Foreign Economic Relations and Trade.

ucts of so many ministries, most ministries need to coordinate with rural industries in some manner.

At the provincial level, the Township Enterprise Department (*xiangzhen qiye ju*) is separate from and reportedly has equal bureaucratic status to the provincial Department of Agriculture (*nongye ting*). Within this department are several bureaux, one of which is now an office for promoting external economic relations. The provincial Planning Commission also has an office for coordinating the relationships among the different industrial bureaucracies related to rural enterprises. Similar structures exist at the municipal level, with the MOA replaced by a Rural Work Department within the city government. The city's Industrial and Commercial Bureau (*gongshang guanli ju*), and its Individual Household Department (*getihu chu*) are responsible for collective and private commercial endeavors in the suburban counties. While the scale of bureaucratic supervision is vast, these overlapping bureaucracies mean that direct control often lies with the level of government which owns or directly supervises the enterprise.

Thus real control over rural enterprises lies at the county level and below; in suburban areas, the city's district government (*qu*) plays this same role. Here the most important organization for fostering the expansion of rural enterprises is the County (or District) Planning Commission which is responsible for determining economic priorities and apportioning local funds. It allocates foreign exchange to different factories in the county and townships. Other important organizations responsible for rural enterprises include the Bureau of Township and Village Enterprises (*xiangzhen qiye ju*), which helps foster township, town and village enterprises, and the county Industrial and Commercial Bureau (ICB), which is responsible for licensing, training, and overseeing all commercial enterprises in the county. The ICB's Individual Household Department (*getihu ke*) supervises all private industrial and commercial activities within the county.

While these bureaucracies monitor or promote development, many county-level organizations own rural factories directly. While these enterprises would not be included in the statistics on rural industry, because they are owned by administrative units at the county level, they form part of the ever-increasing landscape of rural industrialization. For example, county Supply and Marketing Cooperatives, which until the mid-1980s had a monopoly on the purchase and sale of most agricultural inputs and production, control a large number of rural enterprises. In Wujiang County of Suzhou Municipality, the Supply and Marketing Coop owns 42 factories and employs over 8,000 workers. According to its vice-director, there are about five cooperatives like this in China. In Zuoping Country, Shandong Province, Walder found that of 26 collective enterprises under county control, 11 were owned by the Supply and Marketing Coop, six were run by the Light Industrial Collective, three by the Construction Commission, two by the Grain Bureau, two by the Bureau of Public Affairs and one each by the Commerce

Bureau and the Agriculture Bureau.[27] At the township level, the most direct control belongs to the Industrial Company (*gongye gongsi*).[28] Before these companies were established in the mid-1980s, all rural enterprises were controlled by the Commune Party Committee and the Commune Management Committee. In the 1983 reform of the commune structure, the commune administration was split into a township government, a township party committee and an Economic Association Committee (*jingji lianhe weiyuanhui*) responsible for supervising all economic activities.[29] Underneath it were four offices responsible for agriculture, industry, sidelines, and an office for economic management. When this Economic Association Committee was disbanded in February 1986, the industrial, sideline, and agricultural companies remained under the supervision of an Office of Economic Management (*jingying guanli bangongshi*). According to interviews in 1986, however, the industrial company was actually under the direct supervision of the district planning commission, and the Office of Economic Management was under the district party committee's Agricultural Work Department.[30] While the sideline company ran a tree farm and a small cattle business, all commercial and sideline endeavors owned by the township where really under the management of the industrial company, and would be considered part of rural industry. Interviews with the township party secretary showed, however, that he retained great influence over economic decisionmaking.

Finally the administrative villages (*cun*) work within the same broad framework, with the village management committee supervising all industrial enterprises owned by the village, and the village party committee often interfering in local economic management. However, in regions where the administrative villages are highly industrialized, townships may wield little control.

IV. ESTABLISHING THE RURAL-URBAN LINKAGE

Since 1984, a major reason for rural industrial growth has been the increasing connection between urban and rural factories. After the State Council raised the status of rural enterprises, city governments and rural officials were called upon to establish economic linkages between these two industrial sectors. In some provinces, the new policy of "cities leading the counties" (*shi lingdao xian*) increased the authority of urban administrators over the rural areas. In 1986, all factories in Nanjing with outputs of over 3 million yuan had to help rural industry. One official in the Wuhan city planning commission was given the task of establishing economic linkages with rural factories, sending retired workers and technicians to them and opening training courses for their new manag-

---

[27] Andrew G. Walder, "A Profile of Zouping County Industry and Finance," Shandong Field Research Project, 1988 Field Report, presented at the conference at Wingspread Center, Racine, Wisconsin, Nov. 4-6, 1988.

[28] In some locations, such as Nanhai County, Guangdong Province, the industrial company at the township level is called the Township Industrial and Trading Company. Luo, "Ownership and Status Stratification," op. cit.

[29] This describes the process in Zijingshan Township, in the suburbs of Nanjing.

[30] At the county level, this would mean that township industrial companies are not under the direct leadership of the county TVE Bureau; rather they would also be under the county planning commission, which we always assume to be the most powerful economic organization in the county.

ers. Much of southern Jiangsu Province's rural industrial boom was due to the migration of many technicians from Shanghai factories into rural areas around Wuxi, Suzhou and Changzhou municipalities.[31]

These linkages benefit urban factories. As the growth of the market economy undermines many urban factories' planned markets, linkage with rural factories enlarges the scope of their sales. Urban factories lack land for expansion; rural governments can expropriate land for new factories. Piece goods or certain parts of the product cycle can be efficiently subcontracted to lower-paid, rural industrial workers who do not receive state-mandated welfare benefits.

V. Sectoral Breakdown

Rural industries cover numerous economic sectors. While rural governments cherish these contacts because they allow people to enter the nonfarm sector without migrating to the cities, they also make localities more vulnerable to fluctuations in the planned economy. "The five basic industries" promoted in the 1960s and 1970s, and aimed at making the rural areas self-reliant, linked rural industry with the urban enterprises in the chemical, cement, agricultural machinery, iron and steel, and energy sectors. Since the 1970s, the sectoral breakdown of rural enterprises has changed significantly. While we do not possess detailed comparative data for pre-1980 on output by products, Tables 2 through 7 show the breakdown by broad sectors. In both total output and employment (Tables 5 and 7), agriculturally oriented firms declined, as did industrial firms, with the major exodus from agricultural labor moving into transportation, construction, and commerce (including small restaurants and food stands).[32] According to *People's Daily*, in 1980–81, rural industries shifted from low-profit enterprises, such as those making small farm tools, to high-profit ones producing consumer goods.[33] Table 10 presents sectoral breakdowns for 1980, 1985, and 1988. Significant changes since 1980 have occurred in textile production, paper making, mining and chemical production. While construction boomed between 1978 and 1980, it has developed significantly in terms of total output, and its role in rural industry has steadily declined.

When these different rural factories are linked with state-owned factories, they fall into different bureaucratic systems *(xitong)*. Textile factories fall under the light industry system; chemical plants fall under the chemical industry system. But overall, linkages between central ministries and rural enterprises are quite weak. While the State Planning Commission might include output from TVEs in its projected growth data, it does not include transfers of output or inputs to rural industry even in the guidance aspects of the plan. These firms have access to planned goods only if the

---

[31] For an analysis of urban-rural relations in the 1980s, see David Zweig, "From Village to City: Reforming Urban-Rural Relations in China," *International Regional Science Review*, Vol. 11, No. 1, pp. 43–58.

[32] By 1986, many urban construction projects were contracted to rural governments who sent labor teams all over the country. For example, in 1986, Qidong County, in Jiangsu, was carrying out projects as far away as Guizhou Province.

[33] *People's Daily*, 1 April 1981.

larger firms with which they deal allocate planned commodities to them.

VI. State Controls

While the central government has few direct controls over rural industry, Beijing has carried out frequent retrenchments of rural industries. In the 1960s, the state closed 20,000 commune enterprises and laid off 500,000 workers. In October 1985, *People's Daily* called for another such retrenchment, and in 1988–89, especially after the June 4 crackdown, the state forced over one million inefficient enterprises to close.

The major source of central control is the supply of loans to rural industry. While wealthy counties may have sufficient capital to generate industrial growth, most counties and townships need loans. Through its control of the Agricultural Bank, the Ministry of Finance and the People's Bank of China control the flow of funds to rural industry. Constraints imposed on new capital construction can cut the flow of funds to new factories. The central administration can stop rural factories from withdrawing their own funds from the bank [34] or force them into bankruptcy by simply insisting that banks call in all outstanding loans.

The effort to promote more technologically advanced products from rural enterprises also increases central government influence. In 1985, to improve the quality of rural enterprises and agricultural production, the State Council approved the "Sparks Plan," put forward by the State Science and Technology Commission. Under this plan the SSTC is able to allocate funds, scientific information, management skills, new crops, and technological innovations to rural industry, and to promote linkages between scientific research institutes and rural industry. Rural firms that became part of the "spark" program could receive more loans, but at the cost of being included in the state plan. [35]

The new emphasis on promoting exports from rural areas has increased central governmental control over TVEs. The Ministry of Foreign Economic Relations and Trade (MOFERT) now assigns export quotas and foreign exchange quotas to counties which divide them among county-run firms and township governments, which further divide them among township-run firms. Negotiations over these quotas allow for only minor adjustments at the margin. [36] More recently, 190 township enterprises whose products will be promoted overseas will be brought more directly under state control by becoming part of the export-oriented manufacturing system. [37]

Finally, in the recently published "Regulations Governing Rural Collective-Owned Enterprises," the current leadership declares township, town, and village-owned enterprises—as distinct from cooperatively and privately owned firms—as component parts of China's socialist "public ownership economy." [38] Throughout, the

---

[34] *China Daily–Business Weekly*, 1 May 1989, p. 3.
[35] *China Daily–Business Weekly*, 16 January 1989, p. 4.
[36] Interview in Beijing in April 1989.
[37] *China Daily–Business Weekly*, 14 May 1990, p. 1.
[38] *FBIS*, 15 June 1990, pp. 31–35.

document stresses the state's role in encouraging, promoting rural
enterprises while still guiding them. Firms are warned that they
must produce goods that accord with the state's industrial policy;
those that continue to produce low quality products will be shut
down.

VII. LOCAL GOVERNMENT CONTROLS

Although rural enterprises are either leased to individuals by
contract with the local government or privately owned, they
remain tightly controlled by different local officials. While collectively owned rural enterprises are nominally independent of local
political controls, work by Western scholars such as Oi and Walder,
and Chinese scholars such as Wang, Zhao, and Luo show that
county, township and village governments wield significant power
and in many cases completely determine the decisions of factory
managers. Even private firms have shown a propensity to become
closely entwined with local governments in many parts of China,
although in some cases local entrepreneurs may wield important
political influence. Thus the formal management structure may obscure the locus of real decision-making authority.

The most important reason for government interference is that
rural industry has become the local government's main source of
revenue. Under the "financial responsibility system" introduced in
the mid-1980s, whereby each level of government contracts with its
immediate superior to turn over a fixed sum of funds—with the
surplus remaining with the local government—a predatory system
of tax farming has been established. As a result, local governments
use every method possible, including many which straddle the
boundaries of legality, to promote rural industry, at the same time
milking it to supplement their government budgets.

In some prosperous locations, townships and villages have sufficient funds to generate their own rural enterprises. Red Flag
Township, near Wuxi, invested 12 million yuan in 1978–84, of
which 80 percent came from retained profits from other enterprises
in the county.[39] According to one press report, there are 13 different ways for local governments to raise funds for rural enterprises.[40]

Local banks and local governments have close relations. While
the state calls for cutbacks on capital investment, the county and
township governments get new funds through the efforts of local
branches of the ABC, in particular the Rural Credit Cooperatives.
The credit coops rely primarily on peasant deposits for their investment funds; as a result the central government cannot prevent
them from loaning deposits to rural industries, particularly when
local governments apply strong pressure. As mentioned above,
rural credit coops expanded the scale of their loans even during the
peak period of the government's recent prohibition against loans to
rural industry.

---

[39] Delfs, "The Rural Uprising," op. cit., p. 94.
[40] These include: selling stock or dividends; making new workers contribute funds as they join
factories; cooperating with state, other collective, or specialized households; private credit loans;
cooperating with educational or research institutes; loans from other enterprises; cut backs on
other new projects; efficiently using capital, etc. See *Peasant Daily*, 16 August 1985, p. 2.

Because township industries pay a high rate of tax to the county, county governments have become their active protectors. According to Luo, since TVEs are "the political and economic foundation for Wuxi County as a whole," local banks have consistently come to their rescue.[41] When funds were short in Wuxi in 1986, banks borrowed 100 million yuan from other areas which they loaned to rural industries at cost. They also reduced interest rates for loans to the lowest legal level, even though lending rates are subject to central government regulations. Walder's findings show that rather than compel the banks to make loans, the county assumes the financial risks that the banks would face by promising that they will give enterprises continued tax breaks until the enterprises repay the loans. In this way, expanding rural industry in the short-run costs the county, and probably township governments, short-term tax revenues.[42]

County and township governments aggressively defend their own economic interests, particularly from challenges by private firms. In 1985, when burgeoning private firms and village enterprises drew labor and business away from county- and township-owned firms, Wuxi County's government imposed restrictions on these firms. It thoroughly investigated village-owned firms, and if they were defacto private and only nominally collective, they were closed down. Relatives of skilled workers who left collective enterprises to work for private ones were permanently barred from jobs in TVEs. By these methods, the county drove out the competition, allowing private enterprises to survive only in commerce, transport and services.[43] Since June 4, 1989 and the reemergence of a political climate critical of excessive private profits, taxes on private enterprises, as well as new restrictions on how they use their profits, have increased.[44] Also, if managers who leased collective enterprises earn salaries that are several times higher than those of their workers, the local government can force them to reinvest more in the collective.[45] When local enterprises, including factories, orchards, and other collective enterprises, were first leased in the early and mid-1980s, local officials grossly underestimated the size of profits that leases could earn. As profits soared, peasants and cadres often demanded renegotiation, triggering a rash of contract disputes. As a result, China has found it necessary to uphold the legality of rural contracts.[46]

To maximize political and economic security, private firms take on various ties to collective firms or local governments. Researchers in Jieshou County, Anhui Province, found one case in which an individual peasant opened a firm that was nominally called a town-

[41] Luo, "Ownership and Status Stratification," op. cit.

[42] This fact explains why some wealthy counties with expanding industrial bases pay peasants with IOUs for the grain it procures; all government and bank-funds are tied up in promoting rural industry.

[43] Luo, "Ownership and Status Stratification," op. cit.

[44] Adi Ignatius, "Beijing Reins in Wenzhou Experiment," *Asian Wall Street Journal*, 13 February 1990.

[45] Jean C. Oi, "The Fate of the Collective After the Commune," in Ezra Vogel and Deborah Davis, eds., *Social Consequences of Chinese Economic Reforms* (Cambridge, MA: Harvard Contemporary China Series, forthcoming).

[46] David Zweig, Kathleen Hartford, James Feinerman and Deng Jianxu, "Law, Contracts and Economic Development: The Case of Rural China Under the Reforms," *Stanford Journal of International Law* (Summer 1987).

ship enterprise, but which was under the direct control of the county. This peasant got easy loans, tax exemptions, a bank account, and the opportunity to purchase land in the county seat.[47] In the reverse situation, another case featured four individuals who opened a food processing plant that nominally belonged to the district, yet the district never interfered in their business decisions. In Nanhai County, Guangdong Province, local governments established joint private-collective ownership, where successful private firms or factories were financially reinforced by local governments who needed their products. A contractural division of profits was worked out. Similarly, in Wenzhou District, Zhejiang Province, because private businessmen cannot do business with the socialist sector, they establish formal affiliations with collective or state enterprises, to which they pay a fee for the privilege. Local cadres help businessmen form such collective or "partnership firms" to protect them; in return they get voluntary donations and assistance for local government projects.[48]

Unclear rural property rights allow governments to expropriate firms owned by other levels.[49] In Jiangpu County, Jiangsu Province, the author discovered that a successful export-oriented factory owned by the county-seat government was taken over by the higher-level county government in 1986, while in Jieshou County, Anhui Province, researcher Luo Xiaoping found that some private firms were also taken over by the county. Factory workers hoped that by turning these private firms into county-owned collectives they would be eligible for benefits similar to those received by state workers. The private owners could also become state cadres and their families could get access to urban household permits.

VIII. Conclusion: Problems and Prospects for Rural Industry in the 1990s

Because rural industries have grown at a rather remarkable rate, they constantly generate and confront new problems. Many of these problems will continue to affect state and local policy towards rural industry.

As rural industry becomes more capital intensive, it no longer serves as a major repository for excess labor. Yet by the year 2000, it must absorb at least another 50 million workers. Already estimates suggest that surplus rural labor runs anywhere from 70 to 156 million.[50] To avoid massive rural to urban migration, rural industries, including the service sector, must continue to expand if they are to play a major role in resolving future rural employment problems.

[47] Report by Zhao Yang at the Fairbank Center-Development Institute Seminar, Nanjing, China, January 1989.
[48] Liu Ya-ling, "The Reforms from Below—the Private Economy and Local Politics in Rural Industrialization—the Case of Wenzhou in the Post-Mao China," Department of Sociology, The University of Chicago, July 1988.
[49] Unclear property rights, or what one scholar called "soft" property rights, are part of China's traditional heritage. Under the communists, such expropriations become commonplace during "leftist" or radical periods. See David Zweig, *Agrarian Radicalism in China, 1968–1981* (Cambridge, MA: Harvard University Press, 1989), pp. 145–168.
[50] Jeffrey R. Taylor, "Rural Employment Trends and the Legacy of Surplus Labour," *China Quarterly*, No. 116 (December 1988): 136–166.

As rural industries become more complex, they challenge state industries more directly. Their unquenchable need for resources has increased the price of raw materials. Resultant bidding wars prompt localities to keep resources in their own region, decrease profitability in the all-important state sector, and foster inflation. Yet if rural industries are prevented from seeking resources outside their localities, they will not be able to attain economies of scale or develop the necessary scientific and technical knowledge that will allow them to produce high quality products efficiently.

Rural industry exacerbates interregional inequalities.[51] With expanding ties to urban industries, suburban industries and those in developed areas near state firms should develop much faster. Coastal rural industry's increased access to foreign exchange offers workers, managers, and local governments benefits unavailable to inland rural areas. Data already shows clearly that some provinces earn greater amounts of foreign exchange and have higher retention rates than others.[52] Moreover, by selling foreign exchange at the higher market rate, coastal areas like Guangdong, Fujian, and Jiangsu provinces can pay a higher price for raw materials from the hinterland. These areas then process these goods for export, generating a cyclical process of "internal colonialism" whereby the inland areas supply raw materials to the coastal areas, who earn the "value added."

In advanced areas of the countryside, rural industry has moved beyond the stage of autonomous development. For various reasons—its role in exports, the need for technology, better management and quality control, rural industry became more embedded in the state bureaucracy, and with less autonomy—it may develop more slowly. On the other hand, because local governments used funds pried from local banks to keep many inefficient rural factories afloat, market mechanisms could not play the necessary role in rationalizing production. So long as these inefficient rural firms kept up their level of employment and paid their taxes to the local government, scarce capital continued to be wasted, even as the central government needed these funds for high priority projects in the energy and transportation sectors. Finding a proper balance among regional interests and between national and local interests, all the while ensuring steady development within the various regions and levels of the system, remains the major dilemma facing rural industry's future development.

---

[51] For a more detailed analysis of this issue, see the chapter in this volume by David Denny, "Regional Economic Patterns During the Decade of Reform."

[52] See *Xiangzhen qiye nianjian, 1987* (Township and Villages Enterprises Yearbook, 1987; Beijing, Agricultural Publishing House, 1988), p. 616.

TABLE 1. Foreign Exchange Earnings From Township & Village Enterprises (TVEs)

(billions US dollars)

Year	Total Earnings	China's Total Export Earnings[6]	Percent of Total Export
1989	10.01	52.5	19.3
1988	[2] 8.02	47.66	16.8
1987	[3] 5.1	39.46	12.9
1986	[4] 4.5	31.37	14.3
1984–85	[5] 2.38	53.74	4.5

[1] *Foreign Broadcast Information Service*, 23 April 1990.
[2] *China Daily*, 25 September 1989, p. 1.
[3] Interview REBDHZ–4/89.
[4] *China Daily*, 15 December 1987, p. 1.
[5] Based on *FBIS*, 13 April 1990, which reported that 1984–1989 TVE exports totalled US$30 billion.
[6] IMF, *Direction of Trade Statistics Yearbook*, 1989.

TABLE 2. Number of Town Enterprises (TTEs) by Sector

(in 1000s)

Year	No. of Enterprises	Agriculture	Industry	Construction	Comm'n & Transport	Commerce & Catering Industry
1978	1,524.2	494.6	794.0	46.7	65.2	123.8
1979	1,480.4	743.9	767.1	49.7	82.1	137.6
1980	1,424.6	378.3	757.8	50.8	89.4	148.3
1981	1,337.5	319.0	725.4	48.3	88.9	155.9
1982	1,361.7	292.8	744.0	57.0	95.8	170.5
1983	1,346.4	269.8	744.0	57.0	91.6	184.0
1984	6,065.2	248.4	4,812.2	80.4	129.6	794.6
1985	12,224.5	224.2	4,930.3	82.6	106.1	6,881.3
1986	15,153.1	239.7	6,355.0	892.5	2,619.8	5,046.0
1987	17,446.4	231.2	7,082.5	901.3	3,237.8	5,993.6
1988	18,881.6	232.8	7,735.2	955.8	3,725.5	6,282.3
1989	18,686.0					

SOURCE: *Statistical Yearbook of China: 1989*, p. 245. 1989 figure from *A Statistical Survey of China*, 1990, p. 65.

TABLE 3. Number of TTEs by Sector

(percentage)

Year	No. of Enterprises	Agriculture	Industry	Construction	Comm'n & Transport	Commerce & Catering Industry
1978	100	32.5	52.1	3.0	4.3	8.1
1979	100	30.0	51.8	3.3	5.6	9.3
1980	100	26.6	53.2	3.6	6.3	10.4
1981	100	23.9	54.2	5.6	6.6	11.7
1982	100	21.5	55.0	4.0	7.0	12.5
1983	100	20.0	55.3	4.2	6.8	13.7
1984	100	4.1	79.3	1.3	2.4	13.1
1985	100	1.8	40.3	0.7	0.9	56.8
1986	100	1.6	41.9	5.9	17.3	33.3
1987	100	1.3	40.6	5.2	18.6	34.3
1988	100	1.2	41.0	5.1	19.7	33.0

SOURCE: *Statistical Yearbook of China: 1989*, p. 245.

TABLE 4. Total Employment in TTEs by Sector

(in 1000s)

Year	No. of Enterprises	Agriculture	Industry	Construction	Comm'n & Transport	Commerce & Catering Industry
1978	28,265.6	6,084.2	17,343.6	2,356.2	1,038.3	1,443.3
1979	29,093.4	5,330.0	18,143.8	2,984.5	1,169.0	1,466.1
1980	29,996.7	4,560.7	19,423.0	3,346.7	1,135.6	1,530.7
1981	29,695.6	3,799.4	19,808.0	3,488.3	1,073.8	1,526.1
1982	31,129.1	3,440.0	20,728.1	4,212.9	1,129.4	1,618.7
1983	32,346.4	3,092.2	21,681.4	4,827.2	1,097.1	1,648.5
1984	52,081.1	2,839.3	36,560.7	6,834.9	1,293.0	4,553.2
1985	69,790.3	2,523.8	41,367.0	7,899.5	1,141.8	16,858.2
1986	79,371.4	2,408.0	47,619.6	12,703.7	5,412.6	11,227.5
1987	87,764.0	2,441.1	52,653.7	13,740.0	6,153.5	12,875.7
1988	95,455.0	2,499.9	57,033.9	14,848.1	6,841.6	14,231.0
1989	93,662.0					

SOURCE: *Statistical Yearbook of China: 1989*, p. 246. 1989 data from *A Statistical Survey of China*, 1990, p. 65.

TABLE 5. Total Employment in TTEs by Sector

(percentage)

Year	No. of Enterprises	Agriculture	Industry	Construction	Comm'n & Transport	Commerce & Catering Industry
1978	100	21.5	81.4	8.3	3.7	5.1
1979	100	18.3	62.4	10.3	4.0	5.0
1980	100	15.2	64.8	11.1	3.8	5.1
1981	100	12.8	66.7	11.8	3.6	5.1
1982	100	11.1	66.6	13.5	3.5	5.2
1983	100	9.6	67.0	14.9	3.4	5.2
1984	100	5.5	70.2	13.1	2.5	8.7
1985	100	3.6	59.3	11.3	1.6	24.2
1986	100	3.0	60.0	16.0	6.8	14.2
1987	100	2.8	60.0	15.5	7.0	14.7
1988	100	2.6	59.7	15.6	7.2	14.9

SOURCE: *Statistical Yearbook of China: 1989*, p. 246.

{}

TABLE 6. Total Output Value TTEs by Sector

(100 million *yuan*)

Year	No. of Enterprises	Agriculture	Industry	Construction	Comm'n & Transport	Commerce & Catering Industry
1978	493.07	36.19	385.26	34.80	18.77	18.05
1979	548.41	38.46	423.52	46.77	23.06	16.60
1980	656.90	39.38	509.41	60.05	24.52	23.44
1981	745.30	38.97	579.34	70.28	25.06	31.66
1982	853.08	40.06	646.02	100.38	29.27	37.35
1983	1,016.83	43.22	757.09	136.20	32.73	47.09
1984	1,709.89	52.91	1,245.35	216.54	42.31	147.78
1985	2,728.39	58.70	1,827.19	316.60	49.99	482.51
1986	3,540.87	68.87	2,413.40	522.73	255.93	279.44
1987	4,743.10	88.70	3,243.49	641.88	257.89	411.14
1988	64,956.6	115.27	4,529.38	827.70	473.46	694.95
1989	84,028.0					

SOURCE: *Statistical Yearbook of China: 1989*, p. 247. 1989 data from *A Statistical Survey of China*, 1990, p.65.
NOTE: The *Survey*'s data or total output value for other years differs somewhat from data in *Yearbook*, so except for 1989 *Yearbook data are used*. While final numbers may vary, the trends are similar.

TABLE 7. Total Output Value of TTEs by Sector

(percentage)

Year	No. of Enterprises	Agriculture	Industry	Construction	Comm'n & Transport	Commerce & Catering Industry
1978	100	7.3	78.1	7.1	3.8	3.7
1979	100	7.0	77.2	8.5	4.2	3.1
1980	100	6.0	77.6	9.1	3.7	3.6
1981	100	5.7	77.7	9.4	3.4	4.3
1982	100	4.7	75.5	11.8	3.4	4.4
1983	100	4.3	74.5	13.4	3.2	4.6
1984	100	3.1	72.8	12.7	2.8	8.6
1985	100	2.2	67.0	11.4	1.8	17.6
1986	100	1.9	68.2	14.8	7.2	7.9
1987	100	1.9	68.4	13.5	7.5	8.7
1988	100	1.8	69.7	12.7	7.3	10.7

SOURCE: *Statistical Yearbook of China: 1989*, p. 247.

TABLE 8. Rural Credit Cooperative Loans to TVEs, Dec. 1987–Sept. 1989

(billion *yuan*)

	Dec./87	June/88	Dec./88	June/89	Sept./89
RCC Loans to TVEs	32.9	46.3	45.6	51.2	53.7

SOURCE: People's Bank of China, cited in World Bank, *China: Country Economic Memorandum Between Plan and Market*, Report No. 8410–CHA, May 8, 1990, p. 16.

TABLE 9. Rural Industry By Level of Ownership, 1984, 1985, 1988.

	No. of Enterprises	No. of Employees	Output Value (billion *yuan*)
1984(a)			
COLLECTIVE			
Township	401,513	18,791,661	143.3
	** (6.6)	(36.1)	(86)
Village	1,248,128	19,689,332	
	(20.6)	(37.8)	
PRIVATE			
Cooperative *	1,119,583	6,559,453	15.9
	(18.4)	(12.6)	(9)
Private	13,295,900	7,020,462	11.7
	(54.3)	(13.5)	(7)
TOTAL	16,065,124	52,060,908	170.9
1985(b)			
COLLECTIVE			
Township	419,476	21,113,565	198.78
	(3.44)	(30.3)	(72.9)
Village	1,149,595	20,407,813	
	(9.4)	(29.2)	
PRIVATE			
Cooperative	1,402,012	9,463,290	74.06
	(11.5)	(13.5)	(27.1)
Private	9,253,509	18,805,660	
	(75.6)	(27)	
TOTAL	12,224,592	69,790,328	272.84
1988(c)			
COLLECTIVE			
Township	420,000	24,900,000	243.9
	(2.2)	(26.1)	(37.5)
Village	1,170,000	24,040,000	192.4
	(6.2)	(25.2)	(29.6)
PRIVATE			
Cooperative	1,200,000	9,770,000	56.1
	(6.4)	(10.2)	(8.6)
Private	16,090,000	36,750,000	157.2
	(85.2)	(38.5)	(24.1)
TOTAL	18,880,000	95,450,000	649.6

SOURCE: (a) Wong, "Interpreting Rural Industrial Growth," op. cit. p. 13; (b) *Zhongguo nongye nianjian, 1986* (China's Agricultural Yearbook; Beijing: Nongye Chubanshe, 1986), pp. 158, 160; (c) Ministry of Agriculture, P.R.C., *A Survey of China Township Enterprises* (August, 1989).
* While the data for 1984 and 1985 divides cooperatives into "peasant joint cooperatives" and "other types of cooperatives," I put them together for simplicity. The ratio between these two types of cooperatives in terms of number of firms, employees or total output value, based on 1984 and 1985 was approximately 4:1 or 5:1 favoring peasant joint cooperatives.
** Numbers in parenthesis give a percentage distribution of the totals.

TABLE 10. Industrial Output Value in Township and Village Industries, 1980–88

(in 100 million RMB/percent of total production)

	1980 Output/Percent		1985 Output/Percent		1988 Output/Percent	
Mining/Metallurgy	10	2.0	49	3.3	150	4.3
Electric power	2	0.4	5	0.3	8	0.2
Coal	21	4.1	56	3.8	75	2.2
Petroleum	1	0.2	2	0.1	7	0.2
Chemical, Plastic	42	8.3	122	8.4	361	10.5
Machinery	132	25.9	372	25.5	847	24.6
Building	104	20.4	275	18.8	546	15.9
Forestry	15	2.9	43	2.9	89	2.5
Food	41	8.1	114	7.8	271	7.9
Textile	34	6.7	182	12.5	476	13.8
Sewing	19	3.7	53	3.6	130	3.8
Leather	8	1.6	23	1.6	59	1.7
Papermaking/Stationery	20	3.9	78	5.3	221	6.4
Other	55	10.8	79	5.4	199	5.8
Total	509	99.08	1459	99.21	3438	99.8

SOURCE: 1980 and 1985 data came from *A Survey of China Township Enterprises*, (Ministry of Agriculture, PRC, June, 1988). 1988 data came from *A Survey of Township Enterprises in China*, (Ministry of Agriculture, Township Enterprise Bureau, August 1989).

B. Industry

OVERVIEW

By Phillip Kaiser *

Over the past decade, significant advances have occurred in many of China's industrial sectors, including communications, transport, energy, and aviation, which are especially critical to economic development. However, the growth experienced by these sectors has been unable to keep pace with the demands engendered by China's rapid development so that communications, energy, and transportation have become serious bottlenecks to future growth. To make matters worse, the response of the current leadership to the economic and political problems which arose during the second half of the 1980s, is to revert to greater centralized control and planning. The authors agree that the unwillingness of the government to continue with market-oriented reforms will delay modernization and inhibit efficiency. Moreover, as new opportunities have opened up in Eastern Europe and the Soviet Union, China faces greater competition in attracting foreign investment and joint ventures, without which economic modernization will be hampered.

The energy sector provides an example of both the progress made and the difficult prospects ahead. As David Fridley points out, in the 1980s energy production increased substantially. By 1989 output of hydropower was up 100%, coal up 68%, and oil up 30% over 1980. However, as new coal-fired power plants have come on line and the iron and steel industries have expanded, demand has increased even more. Power shortages and temporary blackouts have been experienced in some areas. In the oil industry profits have evaporated because while the policy of providing industry with low-cost energy persisted, the costs of producing oil continued to rise. Without an injection of funds the exploration and development of oil reserves will be crippled. According to Fridley, the growing imbalance between energy supply and demand will cause China to experience "a prolonged and chronic energy shortage."

In the area of telecommunications the situation is also troublesome, with vast disparities between urban and rural areas, and generally poor service. In fact, Ken Zita points out that "basic telephone service is among the poorest in the world, and the lack of computer-to-computer data communications is a major bottleneck in China's economic reforms..." In spite of an increase in phone

---

* Philip Kaiser, Consultant, Congressional Research Service.

lines and improvements in service since 1979, the number of telephones is "well below even the developing world's average."

Development of telecommunications is hampered by regional and ministerial turf battles, and a lack of sufficient financing. Some of the problems could be overcome if administrative responsibility for research and development and manufacturing were not split between two competing ministries, which wastes resources according to Zita. Private networks are increasing and their further development may help the modernization process. The army, railways ministry, and national bank have or are developing such systems.

Zita also points to the "double edged sword" aspect in introducing advanced technology into the country. On the one hand, technology which improves public communication is likely to enhance the prospects of democratization; on the other hand, it would allow Beijing to monitor thousands of calls simultaneously.

The past decade "has been the most fruitful in the history of Chinese aviation," according to Charles Barton. Both passenger and freight traffic have increased dramatically (although from a very low base). Increased domestic demand as well as foreign business and tourist needs are likely to outpace the ability of China to provide services. This growing sector, with ten new airports planned and increasing numbers of aircraft, will find current support services such as air traffic control and navigation services to be insufficient.

In the production of aircraft and aircraft components, China has done well. Serving essentially as subcontractors, Chinese factories have supplied components to companies such as GE, Pratt & Whitney, Boeing, and McDonnell-Douglas. China has also found an export market for the aircraft it produces in developing countries such as Laos and Sri Lanka. The government sees commercial production of aircraft as an important opportunity for industrial growth.

Transportation bottlenecks are a serious constraint to economic development. While this sector has also experienced considerable growth, it has not kept up with the demands of either freight or passenger traffic. Ralph Huenemann points out that although there is severe overcrowding in all modes of people transport, it is especially bad in passenger rail traffic, which is also an excellent illustration of the interconnected nature of the various industrial sectors. Increases in passenger rail traffic exacerbate the bottlenecks in freight traffic which, in turn, cause delays in trains carrying coal (the bulk of which is carried by rail), which then exacerbate the country's energy problems.

While many needed improvements were made in the rail system in the 1980s, much more needs to be done to modernize it. China is already in the process of changing from steam to new diesel and electric engines, and by now almost half of the locomotives are non-steam. In the future, China hopes to improve her railroads by introducing a variety of new technologies, including the highly desirable but expensive computerized signalling system.

In highway construction the focus in the 1980s has been on upgrading existing routes rather than building new roads. The number of unsurfaced roads has decreased and the quality of highways is improved. Roadway traffic has increased dramatically and this has reduced some of the burden on the railroads, as well as providing more efficient handling of short-haul shipments.

The transport of freight on waterways has increased significantly in the past decade, but inadequate port and dredging capabilities restrict water transport growth.

Perhaps the biggest disappointment, from the perspective of reform of industrial capacity, is the unchanged nature of large state factories, discussed by James Stepanek. For the most part they remain the inefficient core of China's planned economy. Protected from most competition, and increasingly requiring subsidies, they typically use excessive amounts of labor and capital. Moreover, intense regionalism and rivalries between the central and local governments for control cause duplication of efforts and inefficient allocation of resources.

In China individual enterprises are not simply production units, but must also provide their workers and staff with schools, housing, health care, and other services. Such a system is an obvious distraction to the main production goals of the enterprise, and an administrative nightmare to its managers. As they are now constituted, state factories also inhibit worker mobility and therefore represent a serious disincentive to private enterprise. A worker contemplating leaving such a position would be giving up his "iron rice bowl:" a permanent job, health care, housing, education for the children, and retirement benefits. Since the government finds it difficult to "close" what is essentially a small city, and thereby face the wrath of the workers, inefficient plants continue to operate throughout China.

As the decade of the 1980s came to a close the Chinese leaders could look at major accomplishments in the industrial sector, as well as increasingly apparent and interconnected bottlenecks. At the same time, they showed a persistent willingness to recentralize control. As China enters the 1990s, it remains to be seen whether the leadership will be willing to take the steps necessary to provide incentives for domestic production and to attract foreign investment in an increasingly competitive global market. Great hurdles will have to be overcome for further development of China's industrial sector.

CHINA'S ENDURING STATE FACTORIES: WHY TEN YEARS OF REFORM HAVE LEFT CHINA'S BIG STATE FACTORIES UNCHANGED

By James B. Stepanek *

CONTENTS

SUMMARY

China's "reform decade" of 1979–89 failed to achieve management reforms in state factories because of the government's reluctance to terminate subsidies to state factories. Planners refused to cut off subsidies principally for two reasons. First, to penalize a factory—the main vehicle of social services—for poor management would have serious social consequences in the absence of a nationwide net for the unemployed, sick, and uninsured. Secondly, the profits and taxes paid by state factories provided the central government with the largest share of its revenues.

I. THE EARLY YEARS OF REFORM

When Deng Xiaoping was in the United States in 1979 he toured the Ford auto plant in Atlanta. Remarkably, he allowed that visit to be shown on Chinese TV. That was an unprecedented event. China had suppressed news about the U.S. moon landing and other world events, and told its people that Chinese factories had substantially caught up with ones in the West. The brief glimpse of an automated car factory on TV showed just how far behind China was, and it sent a message to Chinese industry that the government would tolerate complacency no longer.

---

* James B. Stepanek is a Visiting Lecturer, Yale University School of Organization and Management.

Back in China, Deng energetically pursued his reform program. The results were spectacular. By the mid-1980s agricultural output was soaring. Industrial production by township and collective factories grew impressively. Private markets flourished. Trade with the outside world doubled during the years 1978 and 1979, which ushered in a period of closer ties with the West. Contacts with foreigners grew. In one minor incident, the government allowed the Gezhouba Construction Bureau to talk directly with Caterpillar Corp. of the USA for the first time in March 1980. Caterpillar's D9 bulldozers had arrived in China a few years before, and vanished. The Chinese refused to reveal who the end-user was. Everything was a state secret. Though seemingly a minor reform, the simple step of allowing people to communicate directly with each other sent information from the outside world surging throughout the entire economy.

A stunning admission in 1980 by the Chinese Vice-Premier at the time, Bo Yibo, was that Soviet-style central planning did not work. Henceforth, the government would experiment with "interest rates, taxes, and prices" to control China's economy.[1] A total of 6,600 factories were singled out for accelerated reform, which began the slow process of bringing back many "capitalist" management practices condemned in the Cultural Revolution, such as increasing the importance of profit as a planning tool, allowing factories to sell "above plan" products on their own, and giving local government more control over a factory's retained earnings.[2]

New slogans reflected the sense of excitement. At factory gates, the big red Chinese characters, four on the left and four on the right, were repainted. The new slogans said "Customers First, Quality Tops!" and things like "Small Margins, Big Sales!" The old Cultural Revolution couplet, "Heighten Vigilance, Defend the Motherland!" was taken down everywhere except at places like the Beijing Ordnance Factory and Norinco battle-tank testing range west of the Marco Polo Bridge.

II. PENETRATING STATE FACTORIES

That amazing period of rapid change has come and gone, leaving many things intact. The reforms, for all their impact on collectives, hardly penetrated China's state-owned factories. These are the grey buildings on the horizon that stand well behind the colorful street markets and China's gleaming international hotels. These factories are the core of China's planned economy. Because they seldom see them, most foreigners imagine these big factories operate much like China's small factories, the dynamic export collectives that are filling America's store shelves with appliances, apparel, and toys.

But the big state factories are operationally unique. They are laid out on a grand scale. They consume the nation's best resources in prodigious quantities. A few make enormous sums of money for the state, including the many plants that exploit China's vast re-

---

[1] "Vice-Premier Bo Yibo on China's Current Priorities," *The China Business Review*, November–December, 1980, p. 10–11; and "China's Planning System in Transition," *The China Business Review*, November–December, 1980, p. 15–19.

[2] Thomas H. Pyle, "Reforming Chinese Management," *The China Business Review*, May–June 1981, p. 7–19.

serves of minerals and produce rationed consumer goods. However, a growing proportion of state factories depend on subsidies—the government openly acknowledges—equal to about one-half billion dollars a month in the first half of 1990.[3]

These losses are a major concern of the central government, since the profits and taxes from state enterprises are the linchpin of Beijing's budget.[4] Moreover, declining revenues have caused the central government to lose influence over China's provinces and major cities, which were in a stronger financial position than the central government in the late 1980s and now control more than half of total revenues.

III. BEHIND THE GATES

A few steps inside the front gate of a state factory reveals how little has changed. Many plant managers I first met in 1980 were still doing essentially the same jobs in 1989. The cavernous buildings, unhurried pace of work, and fatuous briefings probably have changed little since the Polish, Czech, and Russian technicians helped build these plants in the 1950s. As an American businessman in China I had to know who really controlled the large state factories and who were my customers. Western press reports about China's reforms completely missed what I was seeing. For those of us working inside the gates of state factories, the only useful published guides were the Old Testament writers on China's economy, like Barry Richman, Ta-Chung Liu, Audrey Donnithorne, and Franz Schurmann.[5] They warned about the system's rigidity. So prophetic were their warnings, that the much-heralded changes that swept across China in the 1980s never touched the large state factories, and the few reforms that did penetrate their front gates were merely dusted off experiments from an earlier era.

One example is free markets. Beginning in the late 1970s, free markets were reintroduced, first in agriculture and then in urban retailing. Most of China's leaders, except for those who denounce "petty capitalism" in all its forms, have always advocated that a centrally planned economy needs free markets around its edges. Private barbers and vegetable hawkers can do no harm, if kept to their side of the street. To the horror of conservative leaders these petty capitalists not only flourished in the 1980s, but brazenly crossed the street. They set up private stores that threatened state stores, and private trucking companies that offered factory-to-factory service that undermined the state supply system.

Most alarming of all, the entrepreneurial spirit infected local officials, who enthusiastically expanded these profitable businesses, which in turn reduced their financial dependence on Beijing. This sharpened the conflict between China's two power blocks: China's

[3] Nicholas D. Kristof, "At the Businesses Owned by Beijing the Ink is Red," *The New York Times*, November 18, 1990, p. 2E.

[4] James McGregor, "Beijing Faces Tough Choice between Reform and Political Ideology in Charting Economic Course," *The Asian Wall Street Journal Weekly*, October 29, 1990, p. 17.

[5] See, for example, Barry M. Richman, *Industrial Society in Communist China*, New York: Vintage Books, 1969; Ta-Chung Liu and Kung-Chia Yeh, *The Economy of the Chinese Mainland: National Income and Economic Development, 1933–1959*, Princeton: Princeton University Press, 1965; Audrey Donnithorne, *China's Economic System*, New York: Praeger Publishers, 1967; and Franz Schurmann, *Ideology and Organization in Communist China*, Berkeley: University of California Press, 1966.

governors and mayors, on the one hand, and the central government leaders, on the other. They are engaged in a historic competition, despite the fact that they are all Party members and believe in socialism, as far as anyone can tell. In the absence of open debates or a free press, all that can be seen of the political differences at the top are vague shadows cast upon the factory floors of China. The provinces and cities back collective and private enterprises and give first priority to foreign investment that earns money for the local government regardless of how low-tech it may be. In contrast, the central government has spent nearly $23 billion on Western technology and equipment and put nearly all of it in state enterprises, where much of it is being wasted.[6] For example, I got a call from an end-user complaining that our high-density recorder did not start. Our technician discovered that the $100,000 recorder had been sitting untouched in its box for four years.

IV. DECENTRALIZATION, ROUND THREE

Another old reform that reappeared in the late 1970s is decentralization. An example of decentralization is a factory under central government control that is turned over to a lower administrative level like a city, and hence "decentralized." Advocates of decentralization believe that a factory runs better if it is taken out of the hands of bureaucrats in faraway Beijing and put in the hands of local bureaucrats in Tianjin or Huhehaote, or wherever the factory is located. Decentralization was twice carried out in earlier decades, and twice abandoned. The government of Premier Li Peng is now attempting to re-centralize the economy for a third time.

But decentralization will be hard to reverse. It would require changing the policies that promote decentralization, the main one being the policy known colloquially as "who establishes, who controls, and who utilizes," or *shuijian, shuikong, shuiyong.* "Who establishes" refers to the level of government making the initial investment. Thus, if a township government invests in a factory, it basically controls it. As the words "who utilizes" imply, the township government would also get to keep the after-tax revenues from that factory.

This principle allows local governments to enjoy the fruits of their investments. The principle also provides the mechanism that is driving decentralization forward, for as local governments expand their investments faster than the central government, more enterprises come under local control and are "decentralized." For example, Factory 4 at the Sichuan Instrument Plant was financed by Beijing and pays profits to Beijing. But Factory 20 at the same plant is being financed by the Chongqing municipal government, which hopes to make a big profit for the city. Factory 20 is an example of a "decentralized" unit within a larger "centralized" state factory. Confusing cases like this make it hard to pin down the number of decentralized plants in China, though managers have told me that most state factories are decentralized and virtually all have some component of local control—workers in even the

---

largest state factories are normally hired through local labor bureaus, for instance.

Thus, it is Beijing's poor financial health and inability to make new investments that are frustrating Li Peng's efforts to recentralize industry. The drop in foreign loans to China after Tiananmen added to Li Peng's frustrations. The large investments needed by the state sector—to shift resources away from provinces and cities and back into the planner's grip—can only come from Western financial institutions.

To those of us conducting business in the state sector, September 1988 was a turning point as important as, if less publicized than, the Tiananmen massacre that occurred ten months later. That was when the conservative leaders in the central government finally shouted, "Enough!" and seized control. They consolidated control at the third plenum of the thirteenth Chinese Communist Party Central Committee—exactly ten years after Deng launched his reforms at the now-historic third plenum of the eleventh CCP Central Committee in late 1978.

The government immediately stopped conducting minor renovations of state factories, and rushed to fortify the Soviet-style planning system that had been condemned as being too rigid ten years earlier. The number of state plan items was increased from 19 to 29. This helped the government expand its control of top priority commodities in order to ensure the survival of central planning. By gaining control of ten additional key commodities, the government also took over the many factories producing these commodities.

Every single state factory threatened by closure or bankruptcy by the economic downturn in late 1989 was quickly subsidized. A group of 234 "large and medium-sized" state factories received emergency injections of cash.[7] When conditions failed to improve in 1990, subsidies continued, despite the fact that the share of state enterprises losing money exceeded one-third,[8] or was as high as two-thirds, according to one unofficial report.[9] These moves make it clear that state factories are too important to reform. As we will see below, the central government cannot discipline factories that lose money, and it lacks any incentive to change those that do make money.

V. A Look Inside a Model State Factory

The Zhengzhou Coated Abrasives Works makes sandpaper and other abrasive materials, and also boasts its own high-rise hotel and dairy farm that produces real ice cream. Before a plant tour begins, visitors are served large quantities of hot tea and statistics. The statistics trumpet the size of the factory's floor space and its large inventory of imported equipment. The plant is clearly a big success. Awards cover the walls of the conference room. A plaque from Henan Provincial authorities calls Zhengzhou a technological "pace setter." Another from the State Economic Commission in Beijing praises its contribution to the sixth Five-Year Plan. Amidst

---

[7] *The Herald Tribune,* March 6, 1990, p. 15.
[8] *The Economist,* October 20, 1990, p. 38
[9] James McGregor, "Beijing Faces Tough Choice between Reform, Political Ideology in Charting Economic Course," *The Asian Wall Street Journal Weekly,* October 29, 1990, p. 17.

the awards is a photo of the factory grounds taken from an airplane. China's big state factories love to print these "bird's eye view" or *niaokantu* photographs in their literature, because only from an airplane can one see all the buildings and surrounding walls and gates.

Inside the Zhengzhou facility, the factory buildings are spacious and poorly utilized. Heaps of materials in-process testify to the factory's ability to hoard raw materials. The air is foul. Nobody fixes the dryers leaking hot air. Imported machinery is in disrepair. The only people who cannot read the "Safety First!" slogans in Chinese are the foreign visitors, who also happen to be the only people wearing helmets.

After one tour, my business colleagues and I returned to the conference room for a wrap-up meeting. Because we hoped to make another sale, we did not mention our main finding: that with the same equipment but with only one-fortieth of the work force in a far smaller space, Zhengzhou could produce more. A lecture was not in order. They knew the facts as well as we. Instead we congratulated Zhengzhou for getting more foreign currency from the government, and turned to the matter of contract terms. We lowered our price again and made the sale, giving Zhengzhou even more equipment it could not use.

The Zhengzhou Works is one of roughly 10,000 *zhongdian*, or "key" state factories that report to Beijing. They are the pillar of Chinese industry. They account for less than a tenth of all state enterprises in China, but produced in 1989 most of the state sector's industrial output.[10] Despite the subsidies many receive, these enterprises as a group still provide the government most of its tax and profit revenues. In return, the government lavishes everything on these factories—the best engineers, preferred access to resources like coal, steel, and foreign exchange, and cheap water and electric power. Even in the dry north, water and power are heavily subsidized. For example, the city of Qingdao suffers shortages of both power and water, but its key state factories were charged less than 2.5 U.S. cents for each kilowatt of electricity consumed in 1989 and less than 5.0 U.S. cents for each cubic meter of water. This is roughly 4 and 12 times cheaper, respectively, than the rates charged American factories in the water-rich and highly electrified New England states.

Meanwhile, the government does little to encourage private and collective plants, which have nevertheless flourished. Since 1980, virtually all of the net increase in industrial employment has occurred in private and collective firms.[11] In the southern provinces of Guangdong, Fujian, Jiangsu, and Zhejiang, these plants produce more than the state sector by a wide margin. Today Guangdong challenges Shanghai for first place in industrial output—up from only half of Shanghai's output in 1984—due to the growth of private and collective industries in just six years.[12] Altogether there

---

[10] Robert Delfs, "Coming of Age," *Far Eastern Economic Review*, October 25, 1990, p. 17; and *China Market*, No. 12, 1989, p. 12–15; and James McGregor, "Beijing Faces Tough Choice between Reform, Political Ideology in Charting Economic Course," *The Asian Wall Street Journal Weekly*, October 29, 1990, p. 17.

[11] Carl Riskin, *China's Political Economy: The Quest For Development Since 1949*, New York: Oxford University Press, 1987, p. 354.

[12] *Far Eastern Economic Review*, March 15, 1990, p. 38.

are roughly 1.8 million collectives of all types in China, and more than 5 million private establishments. They have continued to top the production statistics in 1990 despite Beijing's threat to shut their doors if they compete against state factories.

These statistics really mean something: collectives differ radically from state factories. For example, I once spent the night in a guest house next to a collective factory in Sichuan. Its machine tools made so much noise I went to see what was going on. At 8 p.m. it was still turning out tractor parts. Everybody was busy. At the state factory I was visiting the workers regularly quit at 4:00 P.M. In the morning I asked my hosts about the collective. I said I was impressed. It reminded me of Taiwan factories years ago. My hosts thought this sounded funny. They assured me, "it's only a township factory." Its technical level is low, they said. It uses anything. Even scrap. The only people who support it are the customers.

That was my last visit. The state factory didn't have anything to export. We had been trying for years to find something to export so that they could pay in dollars for equipment I hoped to sell them. Looking back, why they failed to export is best summed up perhaps in that five minute chitchat about the humble tractor parts factory that satisfied "only" customers.

VI. The Inherited System

Interestingly, state factories trace their origins to the Soviet Union, and before that to the capitalist giants that appeared nearly a century ago. Henry Ford's mammoth automotive complex on the Rouge River was an example of the totally integrated plant that later stirred the imagination of Soviet and Chinese planners. As the wall of ignorance about the outside world rose higher, the Russians and Chinese nevertheless held to their vision—to build immense factories with forests of chimneys and thousands of workers, and to build them in the shortest possible time. China threw itself into its first Five Year Plan beginning in 1953–57 in an effort to dot the country with industrial behemoths. An entire generation passed before the Chinese realized that the integrated capitalist giants had long since given way to more specialized forms of industrial organization.

Following the received Soviet wisdom, the Chinese also erected a planning bureaucracy. People trained in Marxist economics began to run everything by decree, without a free marketplace in either prices or ideas. And like their Russian advisors, they purged from their minds the concept of money or profit and learned to think in physical terms alone. As a result, building a factory was thought of as putting quantities of steel, cement, and other physical inputs together at the correct time and place, and running a factory was even easier, in theory, because the steel, parts, and so forth were combined according to fixed ratios handed down by ministries and these ratios changed only when a new factory was built.

Finance and law, two essential policy instruments in most of the world, play a minor role in this management scheme of things. Banks release money only when they see the *gaizhang* or seal of the competent planning authority. A factory can have a million dollars in the bank, but cannot touch it without the *gaizhang*.

The laws promulgated by China in the past ten years fill entire walls in Hong Kong law firms, and these laws play a role in China's foreign trade. However, inside the state sector, ministry regulations remain as good as law, the state plan is law, and what the bureau director says is better than law because it overrules the utterances of all officials below the director level. For example, in March 1985 a factory ordered that high-pressure agricultural pumps made in Beijing for export to St. Paul, Minnesota, be stamped "Made in the Philippines." This policy violates China's own customs regulations, not to mention U.S. law, but a foreign trade bureau chief nevertheless approved the order. He said many parts were being stamped "Made in Hong Kong" so it surely didn't matter.

VII. FACTORIES AS SELF-CONTAINED ISLANDS

A small Chinese town is erected each time a state factory is built. For example, what had been a desolate patch of gravel along a shoulder of the ancient Silk Road is, 20 years later, the Baoji Nonferrous Metal Works—the nation's leading producer of titanium sheet and tubing for the nuclear industry. More than 50 structures were built including dwellings for 10,000 people. Likewise, the Northeast General Pharmaceutical Factory is located inside Shenyang, yet separate. It occupies more than a million square meters of urban space. Within its high walls a town has been built, with 236 school teachers and vocational education instructors, and its own construction company to build the factory's roads, stores, and apartments. One gets the impression that making vitamins and hormones is one of the community's least important activities.

These supporting facilities consume a big share of factory revenues and confront managers with a confusing array of community problems that have nothing to do with production. For example, the Capital Iron and Steel Corporation in western Beijing employs approximately 135,000 staff just to grow vegetables and rice, run the schools, parks, buses, theaters, and bakeries that support the less than 15,000 workers who actually make steel. The same situation exists at the 650,000 kilowatt Liaoning Power Plant, which has 3,000 workers. But only 20 technicians and roughly 100 maintenance engineers are needed to run the plant. At least a quarter of all state factory employees are "surplus," according to the China Enterprise Management Association.[13] Because state factories give preference to worker's children, the redundant staff are often the worker's own family members.

Today every state factory is essentially a small municipality with roads, theaters, schools, and hosts of other services that in other countries would be provided by local governments. Under the circumstances it is perhaps easy to forget that these factories were originally built to make things—to produce—and not to provide social services to thousands.

---

[13] *The International Herald Tribune*, October 30, 1989, p. 13.

VIII. Danwei Socialism

Factory directors often hear the flattering words, "you are really a mayor." Their responsibility for both production and social services makes it hard for foreign visitors to think of any parallel position in the West, unless the mayor of Corning, New York, were also the president of Corning, Inc., the giant multinational corporation. But visitors are also forced to ask, "how does the government discipline a factory that is really a town?" The traditional solution was to maintain a strong Communist Party cell in every *danwei*, or work unit, in Chinese society. Each cell was responsible for carrying out government policies.

In 1985, the World Bank advocated instead that work units divest themselves of responsibility for social services. As a first step, the World Bank advocated that units sell off apartments to their tenants.[14] This was done on a very limited scale, for example, in the Number One Deshengli District in northwest Beijing. The Chinese press floated the idea that stores and restaurants should also be sold off, or at least turned over to their managers under long-term lease agreements, or *chengbao* contracts. *Chengbao* contracts are widely used only in the south. The idea of universal unemployment insurance was also broached in 1985, but not seriously pursued.

In the end, no consensus emerged on what to do about factory-run social services, and for a very good reason. These services are not provided by the state, but by an individual's *danwei*. The quality of services depends on a unit's resources. A *danwei* with many trucks, for example, can forage for luxury foods, consumer goods, and raw materials. The highways of China are jammed with factory trucks carrying Tianjin shrimp, television sets, and cement back to their units. The Chinese-American joint-venture boilermaker in Beijing, the Babcock & Wilcox Beijing Co. Ltd., sends its trucks all over China to secure steel plate. It is a "mad rush to get there first," an official explained to me on December 14, 1988. "Our drivers even had to sleep next to our steel plate at the Panzhihua Steel Mill to keep other drivers from stealing it."

In addition to trucks, a wealthy *danwei* might have its own buses, theaters, fish ponds, orchards, and even fishermen. For example, the Fiber Glass Factory near Badaling fails to turn out quality panels for passenger trains, but the workers eat fresh fish because the plant director allows them to spend a lot of time fishing at the Guanting Reservoir. Just as the availability of higher-quality food may depend on how many trucks a worker's *danwei* has, so too will the quality of housing depend on how many cement mixers and cranes a factory owns. None of these benefits are transferable. A 50-year old worker nearing retirement cannot transfer his pension to a new employer, even in the unlikely event that he changes jobs.[15] Therefore one's *danwei* matters far more than pay, at roughly $30–$50 per month, which is the same for everyone.

---

[14] Edwin Lim, Chief of Mission, *China: Long-Term Development Issues and Options*, Baltimore: The Johns Hopkins University Press, 1985, p. 11.
[15] *Far Eastern Economic Review*, October 25, 1990, p. 18.

Next in importance to the *danwei* is the *xitong*, which literally means "system," but refers to all the work units under a single ministry or equivalent body at the State Council level. The *xitong* to which a person belongs can be a matter of life and death, because ministries generally run the big hospitals that are only open to staff within that *xitong*. For example, the Ministry of Energy Resources has excellent facilities for treating blood clots, as I learned when visiting a friend in its hospital. But if a worker in a factory under the Ministry of Railways were dying of a thrombosis, it would be impossible to receive treatment at the Energy Resources hospital, unless his spouse worked in the Energy Resources *xitong*.

Because these many services are not provided by the central government, but by units, in the final analysis China is not a socialist state but remains a collection of socialist units. Thus, it is hard to talk about socialism in China without asking the question, "Ni nar?"—which literally means "where are you?"—but really is a way of asking "what unit are you from?" It is the first question asked on the phone, since the response depends on the rank of the caller's *danwei*. It is also the first question asked at the front door of many hospitals. After a bicycle accident at Tiananmen Square on April 29, 1987, a man with a broken collar bone was rushed to the Union Medical College. He was turned away because he did not belong to any unit and was carrying no cash, and went home untreated. He was one of the growing legions of workers who have no *danwei* at all. Poor people enter hospitals in China clutching wads of cash. Street vendors and private entrepreneurs, too, are completely on their own. Even people in state factories have few benefits if they are contract workers. Since 1986 contract workers have no guarantee of lifetime employment.[16]

Clearly Chinese socialism would come tumbling down if factories concentrated only on production. Until a nation-wide net exists to catch the unemployed, sick, hungry, and uninsured, the state is reluctant to permit managers to fire workers. This makes it possible for managers to blame their unsatisfactory economic performance on poor labor discipline that results from guaranteed lifetime employment—the so-called "iron rice bowl."

IX. RIGID WORK RULES

When asked, "who is to blame for the mess in state factories?" Chinese officials do not hesitate a second. The managers and workers have absolutely no *zerengan*, or sense of responsibility, they say, and that is why tools are stolen and raw materials are wasted. Deng Xiaoping's original "20 Points" that outlined China's reform policies placed great emphasis on stricter work rules.

Work rules make it easier to assess blame, the thinking goes. Hence the clearer the rules, the easier it is to point the finger and administer the fine. Other countries have work rules too, but normally in combination with higher pay for good work. Western managers generally prefer the carrot, but keep the stick handy. But in a Chinese state factory bonuses are normally the same for every-

---

[16] *Far Eastern Economic Review*, October 25, 1990, p. 17.

one regardless of performance. The iron rice bowl makes the stick more like a noodle. Out of frustration, the government has encouraged state factories to write up in detail each person's tasks, and levy fines accordingly. Behind the gatekeeper as one enters a Chinese factory there is usually a large poster saying who can enter the plant and under what conditions. The gatekeeper must enforce the rules, and likewise the machinery operator and the accountant must observe the regulations on the wall behind the machinery and on the wall of the office. Sometimes the regulations are painted in large red characters or chiselled in cement for everybody to see. The real message is "We mean it this time!" but in the absence of an enforcement mechanism, managers cannot do much.

Most work rules are based on fixed ratios, which reflects the idea that production relationships are fixed for all time. For example, when Chinese go on buying trips to Western factories they tend to ask strange questions about ratios: What is the ratio of supervisors to workers? Or quality control inspectors per plant? Or the ratio of inventory and production floor space? The Chinese are gathering information about the ratios in order to translate everything they see into precise work rules that can be followed by the most indolent worker. Otherwise they cannot be sure the equipment will work in China.

This nurtures technological rigidity, which is reflected on the shocked faces of foreign executives when they see their own equipment operating in China. Instead of the usual changes and improvements one expects to see five or ten years later, they see their equipment operating just as it did on the occasion when the Chinese visited and asked all those questions about ratios.

Nearly 50 years ago, the Ford Motor Co., for example, sold its jeep designs to the Russians during World War II, who later sold the designs to the Chinese. Years later, American Motors established a joint venture in China that happened to be at the same factory that made the old Ford. American's joint venture, later taken over by Chrysler, assembled the Cherokee Jeep. But the joint venture partners also agreed to keep producing the old Ford—now called the "212 Jeep." The Chinese resisted Chrysler's efforts to change the jeep's Russian-style production. After years of trying, Chrysler's chief engineer admitted to me on October 15, 1988, that only a few improvements in the old Ford had been made, including bucket seats in front, thicker canvas on the roof, doors for winter use, and a cigarette lighter in the dashboard. The Chinese fought even these changes. Why change manufacturing procedures, they wondered, and upset the work rules?

Such rigidity makes it hard for China to manufacture advanced products, except in the laboratory environment where innovation is possible. For example, the display cabinets in the reception rooms of state research institutes often contain copies of advanced Western products, like TID's high-speed 101 tape recorder. This proves that Chinese scientists and engineers are first rate, and can produce almost anything in their well-equipped laboratories. But when the brilliant engineering prototypes are turned over to state factories to be mass produced, quality plummets. For example, the Suzhou Aircraft Instruments Factory makes China's most advanced prototypes of cockpit instruments for jet fighters, but has

failed to mass produce anything except simple parts for home refrigerators.

X. THE ROLE OF FOREIGN JOINT VENTURES

Foreign joint ventures in China, some officials hoped, would succeed where rigid work rules and everything else had failed by turning factories over to ruthless capitalists to administer shock treatment. Many state factories were indeed shocked when foreign companies finished their feasibility studies and said, "Yes, a joint venture is possible—in that little corner building, and 25 workers is
plenty." The Yokogawa joint venture in Xian, for example, utilized
a tiny slice of its partner's vast operations, and still produces a
large volume of industrial control equipment.

In the end, foreign joint ventures probably received more shocks
than they administered. Many were crippled by supply problems.
The biggest headache for Mr. Yang Tong, the general manager of
the Shanghai-Foxboro Co. Ltd., was supplies made in China. Supplies were delivered by the state, he noted on May 4, 1988, but the
poor quality and delivery forced him to continue importing supplies. That raised costs and made it harder to win orders.

To the disappointment of the Chinese government, there were
few joint ventures in the manufacturing sector and any remedial
impact they may have had on management was correspondingly
small. Most joint ventures were in hotels and export processing,
and in other areas not dependent on the state supply system. In
fact, total foreign investment in all of China in recent years has
been less than total investment in Bangkok. Most investment is
concentrated on the coast, where private and collective firms predominate. Two-thirds of China's entire foreign direct investment in
1988 was in Guangdong Province. It is only a slight exaggeration to
say that foreign investors still prefer to locate their factories by a
pier facing Hong Kong, which is very telling indeed in a country of
China's vast land mass and diverse industrial base that has supposedly experienced ten years of reform.

XI. FACTORY AUTONOMY

A possible path to factory autonomy was outlined for me on July
9, 1988, by a State Planning Commission official, Xing Youqing. He
said that beginning "soon" all enterprises outside the state plan
would be turned over to private managers, who would sign long-
term leases and pay rent to the government. After this system
"had invigorated the economy making it safe to move ahead," state
factories could adopt the same system, he said. Then, planners
would step back and only engage in *choujian*, the colloquial word
for macro planning. Finally, all enterprises would be allowed to
freely issue, buy, and sell stocks. Complete privatization would take
place as ministries sold off their stocks in what had once been state
enterprises.

Factory autonomy was the most talked-about reform of all. Yet
factory people will tell anyone who cares to listen that the reform
never made it past the front gates. "We are called corporations, but
we are not like your corporations," said an engineer from the Jilin
Chemical Industry Corporation. The Director General of the For-

eign Investment Administration, Liu Yimin, admitted on June 27, 1988, that "state enterprises will have to make money one day, or they will be abolished. But right now they are not legal persons and basically have little responsibility."

Zhao Ziyang himself, the former Party General Secretary now under house arrest, said that factory autonomy "had not really been carried out." In his January 23, 1988 interview in the *Guangming Daily*, he warned that "efforts to improve large and medium state enterprises will be wasted unless we adopt a system that works." This was a significant admission, since Zhao played a major role in formulating both the October 20, 1984 "Decision of the Central Committee on Reform of the Economic Structure" that launched urban industrial reforms, as well as the State Enterprise Reform Law that passed the last session of the National People's Congress on April 13, 1988.

Factory autonomy was thwarted mainly by the power of city governments and their subordinate bureaus and corporations. For example, the man who once ran the Wuhan Instrumentation Industrial Co. from his office in the Bureau of Instrumentation Industry in Beijing complained on February 25, 1988, that the factory no longer even sends him reports. Now the factory gets money from the Wuhan bureau of industry, and takes orders from the Wuhan government, not Beijing.

Not surprisingly, cities and provinces squeeze factories for as much cash as possible. In the late 1980s, I was frequently approached by decentralized state factories that were desperate for money. The city of Qingdao, one factory complained, had cut off loans and told it to find a foreign investor willing to refurbish its plant and equipment. The Qingdao Pressure Gauge Factory sent this appeal for help: "Dear Sir: Our factory was established in 1966, and covers 7,914 square meters of which 7,084 is factory space. We have 380 workers, of which 28 are technicians. Our annual output is 300,000 pressure gauges. Using the form of joint venture management, with our side providing plant, equipment, and labor, and your side providing the equipment, know-how and cash, we propose selling abroad using your company's access to foreign markets." [17] Nothing came of their letter.

But cities and provinces fight tenaciously when it comes to protecting the markets of their factories. For example, Liaoning Province nearly stopped the No. 47 Research Institute in Beijing (under the Ministry of Aeronautics and Astronautics) from selling its control software to the Liaoning Power Plant (under the Ministry of Energy Resources). Making the sale was like "crossing the Great Wall," I was told on August 1, 1988, because the customer was under a different ministry, and even worse, in a different province. Foreign companies are terribly disillusioned when they set up a factory to serve all of China, then discover that their market is limited to regions where they enjoy political support. For example, during one joint venture negotiation, the foreign side asked about a marketing plan. The Chinese side said, "the provincial bureau chief once worked in this factory, so don't worry." Later the bureau

---

[17] June 2, 1989, letter from the Deputy Director of the Qingdao Pressure Gauge Factory, 25 Yichang Road, Qingdao, Shandong Province.

chief showed his face at a banquet. That was proof enough, the Chinese believed, that the joint venture's market would be protected in that province, and a marketing plan was unnecessary.

Such intense regionalism compels factories to be very self-reliant, and they are. When the Sichuan Instrument Plant needs mechanical or electrical parts, for example, it assigns the task to factories 1, 3, 6, or 13, which employ hundreds of workers making parts used in the plant's other 16 factories. The Sichuan Plant never thinks of giving the job to an outside factory. The reasons are interesting: outside factories are considered unreliable and sloppy, and when it is time to deliver the goods, outside factories will demand that the buyer's trucks come and pick up the goods and bear the risk of damage during shipment.

Curiously, factories in other regions have exactly the same complaints about the Sichuan Instrument Plant. For example, the Wuhan Iron and Steel Corporation gets such bad service from the Sichuan Instrument Plant, and other domestic suppliers, that it has built its own instruments factory, called the Iron and Steel Instrument and Meter Plant. Its vice director, Yu Chuanwen, admitted on January 27, 1989, that it was a waste to make instruments themselves, "but we have no choice." Likewise, the Fushun No. 2 Refinery told me that the Sichuan Instrument Plant's products are "always late." So are their other suppliers, hence they still make instruments themselves. "We were told to stop being self-sufficient by 1988," a plant official said in mid-1988, "but we couldn't change because the system hasn't changed."

XII. CONCLUSION

Following a decade of reforms, China enters the 1990s with its key industries surviving virtually unchanged under the equally unchanged leadership of men like Chen Yun, the 85-year-old patriarch of central planning.

The central government's dependence on the income from state enterprises creates a crippling fear of innovation. Rather than encourage private and collective enterprises, whose revenues go to cities and provinces, the central government reserves its best engineers, scarce foreign currency, and key materials for state factories. These factories cling to the obsolete ideal of the self-sufficient factory that produces everything it needs while providing its workers with education, health care, entertainment, and even fresh fish. In the absence of an alternative safety net, these services cannot be divorced from the state factories: what could China do with the unemployed millions who would be dismissed from their jobs as bakers, teachers, and drivers at state factories?

A major obstacle to reform of state factories is the planning system itself. In 1985, the World Bank suggested that planners guide the economy by indirect means, using monetary policies, for example.[18] But it became obvious in 1989 that China neglected this advice. Inflation hit the double-digit zone, and Beijing panicked.

---

[18] World Bank, *Long-Term Development Issues*, p. 14; and United Nations Development Program (UNDP) contract with the China International Center for Economic and Technological Exchange, signed in 1989, p. 28.

Planners grabbed the brakes and cut off credit to everybody. Banks were ordered to approve nothing.

The rate of inflation did decline, but the economy was almost paralyzed. State factories could not pay their bills, and many private and collective industries reportedly went out of business. Instead of tightening credit, Beijing eliminated credit. Had the planners followed the World Bank's advice and employed indirect policies, the banking system could have continued to extend loans to strong enterprises that were capable of paying higher interest rates. This would have helped the planners distinguish between profitable and unprofitable enterprises, something they have professed to want for the past ten years.

Instead Beijing cut off the money supply, waited a few weeks to see who screamed the loudest, and then slowly relaxed its grip, giving first priority to factories with the greatest political clout— not those that were necessarily profitable. When credit was eased, the government's first rescue package for the equivalent of U.S. $1.7 billion was given to a preferred list of large-scale state enterprises.[19] Is it any wonder that China's state enterprises don't change?

---

[19] *The New York Times*, March 8, 1990, p. 1.

MODERNIZING CHINA'S TRANSPORT SYSTEM

By Ralph W. Huenemann *

CONTENTS

I. SUMMARY INTRODUCTION: THE TRANSPORT BOTTLENECK

In the 1972 volume in this series, P. Vetterling and J. Wagy surveyed China's transport system over the period from 1950 to 1971 and characterized it as "generally adequate to meet the demands of the economy, with only infrequent instances of congestion of a local or seasonal nature." [1] Unfortunately, this optimistic assessment was soon out of date. When it was announced at the famous Third Plenum in December 1978 that the growth targets proclaimed just a few months earlier were being abandoned as overly ambitious, energy shortages were cited as a key reason for the policy change. [2] In the Chinese economy, where coal is the prime source of energy, energy shortages are closely linked to transport bottlenecks. Thus, a transport system that was "generally adequate" in the early 1970s had become a major problem area by the end of the decade. Inadequate transport capacity has remained a serious constraint ever since, often being identified (along with energy) as a "key bottleneck" or a "prominent weak link" in the economy. [3]

These qualitative impressions are reflected in the quantitative record, as shown in Table 1. During the rapid economic growth period of 1952–59, when the gross value of industrial and agricul-

---

* Ralph W. Huenemann is a Professor in the School of Public Administration and Director of the Centre for Asia-Pacific Initiatives, University of Victoria, Canada.

[1] Philip W. Vetterling and James J. Wagy, "China: The Transportation Sector, 1950–71" in Joint Economic Committee, 92nd Congress, 2nd Session, *People's Republic of China: An Economic Assessment*, Washington, D.C.: Government Printing Office, 1972, p. 150.

[2] Hua Guofeng, "Report on the Work of the Government," *Beijing Review*, July 6, 1979, pp. 5–31.

[3] See "Go All Out to Improve Railway Transport," *Beijing Review*, February 25, 1977, p. 3; Zhao Ziyang, "The Current Economic Situation and the Reform of the Economic Structure," *Beijing Review*, April 22, 1985, p. iv; Wang Yuanzhi, "Tantan jiaotong yunshu touzi qingxie de ruogan wenti (A discussion of several questions concerning the emphasis in communications and transport investment), *Touzi Yanjiu* (Investment Research), June 1989, p. 30; and "Decision on Further Improving the Economic Environment, Straightening Out the Economic Order, and Deepening the Reforms (Excerpts)," *Beijing Review*, February 12, 1990, p. vii.

tural output (GVIAO) grew about 15% a year on average, freight traffic and passenger traffic (on mechanized modes) grew by 23% and 16% respectively, suggesting that the income elasticity of demand for modern transport is greater than 1.0. The experience of 1959–65, when China's economy suffered great distress, is shown in Table 1 for completeness but tells us little about more normal circumstances. During the period of 1965–78, when GVIAO grew by 8.5% a year despite the adverse effects of the Cultural Revolution, freight traffic grew at 8.4% and passenger traffic grew at 7.3%—both somewhat slower than would have been predicted from the income elasticities observed in the 1950s. Not surprisingly, this was a period when complaints about transport bottlenecks became more frequent. Finally, in the period of the economic reforms since the Third Plenum, GVIAO has grown at about 11% a year, while freight and passenger traffic have grown at about 9% and 12% respectively. Despite this rapid growth of passenger traffic, which was achieved only by severe overcrowding on trains and buses, many would-be travellers could not buy tickets. At the same time, however, the expansion of passenger traffic that did occur made the freight bottleneck just so much worse, especially on trunk routes. In this context, the continuing complaints about transport as a weak link in the economy are not surprising, but it is important to remember that the complaints arise, not because transport has been stagnant, but because the transport sector has been scrambling—with only partial success—to keep up with the demands of a rapidly growing economy.

TABLE 1. Growth Rates of Economy and of Modern Transport

[average * per annum]

Time Period	Real GVIAO [2]	Modern Ton-Km	Modern Passenger-Km
1952–59	14.9	23.1	16.3
1959–65	0.2	1.0	−0.4
1965–78	8.5	8.4	7.3
1978–89	10.9	9.1	12.0

[1] Traditional transport remains important in the Chinese economy, but mainly for short trips, so these traditional modes contribute relatively little to total ton-km and passenger-km.
[2] Real GVIAO is the gross value of industrial and agricultural output, measured in constant prices.

II. The 1980s: A Decade of Expansion and Upgrading

A. RAILWAYS

Network: In 1949, China had a railway network of only about 21,800 kilometers, and large areas of the country had no rail lines at all. For the next three decades, the government worked vigorously to extend the network, with new routes being opened at the average rate of 1,000 km a year between 1952 and 1979 (see Table 2). Substantial investment went to the upgrading of existing routes (such as the double tracking of the Tianjin-Pukou line), but the main focus was on new routes, especially in the frontier regions of the northwest and southwest, where population is sparse and the terrain extremely inhospitable to railways.

In the arid northwest, where the Baotou-Lanzhou and Lanzhou-Urumqi lines were completed in the late 1950s and early 1960s, the key engineering problem was to stabilize shifting sand dunes. In the mountainous southwest, the problems were even more daunting. For example, the Chengdu-Kunming line, completed in 1970, contains over 400 km of bridges and tunnels in its 1,085 km length. Vetterling and Wagy call it "one of the great engineering feats of the modern world." [4] Other lines in the region—such as the Baoji-Chengdu (1958), Chongqing-Guiyang (1965), Guiyang-Kunming (1966), Yangpingguan-Ankang (1972), and Zhuzhou-Guiyang (1972)—also traverse difficult terrain. In a 1979 interview, the Minister of Railways suggested that the most difficult new route of all was perhaps the Xiangfan-Chongqing (1978), which runs over bridges or through tunnels for 45% of its 901 km.[5] And it might be argued that an even more difficult engineering challenge is the Xining-Lhasa line, which was carried as far as Golmud by 1980 and then—sensibly—postponed indefinitely.

Toward the end of the 1970s, a major shift in railway policy occurred. One indication of the shift came at a national railway conference in April 1978, when the Minister stressed the need to upgrade existing routes.[6] Other authoritative statements of the period reinforced the message that, while China would continue to build some new lines, priority would be given to modernizing the existing lines in heavy-traffic corridors.[7] As can be seen from the data on route length in Table 2, this shift in priorities persisted right through the 1980s, with only about 350 km of new routes being opened per year on average. Furthermore, the new routes of the 1980s were mostly prosaic heavy-haul coal lines radiating from Shanxi province toward the industrial areas on the east coast, not heroic nation-building links to the frontier regions. One of the few exceptions to this pattern in the 1980s was the 460-km line from Urumqi to Alataw on the Soviet border, which was officially opened on September 1, 1990.[8] Of course, by the late 1970s, many of the earlier gaps in the network had been filled in, so it was natural to de-emphasize new construction to some extent. But this tendency was probably reinforced by the economic reforms after the Third Plenum, which encouraged greater attention to the rate of return on investment.[9]

To increase carrying capacity on existing single-track routes, 50 kg/m rail has largely replaced the earlier 43 kg/m standard, and some corridors are being provided with 60 kg/m rail. Also, the

[4] Vetterling and Wagy, p. 153.

[5] "Building Up China's Rail Transport," *China Reconstructs,* October 1979, p. 76.

[6] "China's Railway Minister on Modernizing Faster," *Economic Reporter,* April–June 1978, p. 29.

[7] Wang Peixian, "Railway Development: Moving on a Faster Track," *China Business Review,* January–February 1982, p. 32.

[8] "New Railway Spans Asia, Europe," *Beijing Review,* September 17, 1990, p. 10.

[9] See for example Cao Yaolin and Wang Yongyin, "Tigao woguo tielu jianshe de jingji xiaoyi" (Increasing the economic effectiveness of China's railway construction), *Jingji Yanjiu* (Economic Research), December 1982, p. 49, where it is argued that on eight long-established heavy-traffic lines each 10,000 RMB spent on upgrading enabled an extra 307,000 ton-km of traffic to be carried per year on average, while for fourteen recently-constructed new lines each 10,000 RMB of investment generated only 76,000 tonkm of traffic per year on average.

TABLE 2. Growth of the Railway Subsector, 1952–89 [11]

Year	Route [2] Length (000 km)	Freight Traffic (million tons)	Freight Turnover (billion ton-km)	Passenger Traffic (million)	Passenger Turnover (billion pass-km)
1952	22.9	132.2	60.2	163.5	20.1
1957	26.6	274.2	134.6	312.6	36.1
1965	36.4	491.0	269.9	412.5	47.9
1978	48.6	1101.2	534.5	814.9	109.3
1979	49.8	1118.9	559.9	863.9	121.6
1980	49.9	1112.8	571.7	921.2	138.3
1981	50.2	1076.7	571.2	952.2	147.3
1982	50.5	1135.0	612.0	999.2	157.5
1983	51.6	1187.8	664.7	1060.4	177.7
1984	51.7	1240.7	724.8	1133.5	204.6
1985	52.1	1307.1	812.6	1121.1	241.6
1986	52.5	1356.4	876.5	1085.8	258.7
1987	52.6	1406.5	947.1	1124.8	284.3
1988	52.8	1449.5	987.8	1226.5	326.0
1989	53.2	1514.9	1039.4	1138.1	303.7

[1] Data for 1952–88 from *Zhongguo Tongji Nianjian 1989* (1989 Statistical Yearbook of China); data for 1989 from *Zhongguo Tongji Zhaiyao 1990* (A Statistical Survey of China 1990).
[2] Includes central and local standard gauge lines (and the metric lines near Vietnam) but not the light railways used in forestry and mining.

standard siding length on many routes is being increased from 850 m to 1050 m. These measures permit longer, heavier trains, but by themselves are inadequate in major corridors. On the latter routes, electrification (25 kV) or double tracking, or both, are being extended. By 1989, about 25% of the rail network had been double tracked and over 10% had been electrified.

Recently announced projects for the Eighth Five-Year Plan (1991–1995) suggest that extending the railway network over new routes will receive more attention in the 1990s than in the 1980s. Some of the routes proposed are in mountainous frontier regions (such as the Chengdu-Daxian, Xi'an-Ankang, and Nanning-Kunming lines), but the primary expenditure seems destined for two new north-south routes (Beijing-Jiujiang and Beijing-Kowloon) as well as for expanded capacity on the vital Datong-Qinhuangdao and Shenyang-Qinhuangdao corridors.[10]

Fleet: As every railway romantic in the world surely knows, China still operates several thousand steam locomotives. However, the days of steam are numbered, and already nearly half of the locomotive fleet (46% in 1989) is non-steam. The last of the Qianjin 2-10-2's was built at Datong in December 1988; all future additions to the fleet will be diesel or electric. In 1980, China produced about 130 diesels (some diesel-electric and some diesel-hydraulic) and about 40 pure electrics.[11] Domestic production of locomotives has expanded through the 1980s as key factories have been modernized, and Chinese sources indicate that output will be about 630 diesels and 200 electrics in 1990, rising further to 700 diesels and 350 electrics in 1995.[12] Substantial numbers of locomotives have also been

[10] "More Railways for the 1991–95 Period," *Beijing Review,* September 24, 1990, pp. 10–11.
[11] Wang Peixian, p. 33.
[12] Gong Wei, "China's Railway Rolling Stock Industry Development Strategy," *China Market,* July 1989, p. 11.

imported, including 50 French diesel-electrics, 34 West German diesel-hydraulics, and a significant number of Romanian diesel-electrics in the 1970s, followed by 420 American diesel-electrics in the 1980s. Pure electrics have been imported from France, East Germany, and Czechoslovakia.[13] Even including the imports, however, China's locomotive fleet has been growing by only about 3% a year over the past decade (reaching 13,524 units in 1988).[14]

Where freight cars and passenger coaches are concerned, the situation is similar to that for locomotives. The quantity and quality of domestic production is improving, as factories are modernized and expanded, and this domestic output has been supplemented by some imports of specialized equipment. In 1980, China produced about 1,000 passenger coaches and 10,500 freight cars.[15] By 1990, production has risen to about 2,800 passenger coaches and 26,000 freight cars.[16] Some of this output merely replaces older cars being retired; the net addition to the fleet is correspondingly less. In net terms, the freight car fleet has grown only about 3% per annum over the past decade (reaching 340,299 units in 1988), and the passenger coach fleet only about 6% (24,917 units in 1988).

Traffic and Operations: Historically, the modernization of transport in China has been synonymous with the building of railways. In recent years, however, the modal split has gradually become more diversified, as highways, shipping, airlines and pipelines have been developed. Also, non-mechanized transport continues to play an important role, though only for short-haul traffic. Since the Third Plenum, the rail share of measured freight turnover in the modern sector (excluding ocean shipping) has fallen from 73% in 1978 to 59% by 1988. For passenger turnover, the rail share has fallen from 63% to 53%.[17] These trends will undoubtedly continue. Despite these declining shares, however, the absolute level of traffic on the railways rose dramatically over the same period and put severe pressure on the system's capacity. Since 1978, the ton-km carried by rail have increased by 6% a year—twice the growth rate of the freight car fleet. Similarly, the passenger-km carried by rail have increased by nearly 10% a year—as against the 6% annual increase of coaches in service.

This performance was achieved by the intensified utilization of equipment and track that were already heavily utilized. Inevitably, there have been some adverse consequences. The most pervasive is poor service. On the passenger side, severe overcrowding has become the norm, even though many would-be passengers are turned away for lack of space. The standard hard-seat carriage, designed to hold 108 people, is often packed with as many as 236 pas-

---

[13] This account of imports may not be complete. See Peter Clark, *Locomotives in China*, Waterloo, N.S.W.: Roundhouse Press, 1983; Joachim Petersen, *Die Eisenbahn in China*, Stuttgart: Motorbuch Verlag, 1983; Huang Zhihe, "Tantan woguo tielu qianyin dongli de xianzhuang he fazhan" (A discussion of China's railway tractive power, present and future), *Tiedao Zhishi* (Railway Knowledge), May 1987, pp. 2–3; Wang Yanping, "Locomotives Running Out of Steam," *China Daily Business Weekly*, June 28, 1987, p. 2; and Thawat Watanatada, Clell Harral and Pam Baldinger, "Railways," *China Business Review*, March–April 1989, pp. 14–19.

[14] Basic data on railway fleet size can be found in the various issues of *Zhongguo Tongji Nianjian* (Statistical Yearbook of China).

[15] Wang Peixian, p. 33.

[16] Gong Wei, p. 11.

[17] The actual rail share is almost certainly less than these measured amounts, because data on rail traffic are reasonably accurate, while substantial highway traffic goes unrecorded.

sengers, and the Ministry of Railways has even resorted to using converted boxcars to carry passengers at peak periods.[18]

The discomfort and inconvenience of this situation have been exacerbated by a rising crime wave. Commercial travellers who go to the coastal regions to obtain consumer goods for inland markets often carry large sums of cash, and theft on trains has become a serious problem. The illegal resale of tickets by scalpers is another element in the crime wave. On the freight side of the picture, volume and axle-load limitations constrain the temptation to overload, but the resulting severe rationing of capacity means that shippers often find their requests for cars delayed or denied. The temptation to offer—and accept—bribes is obvious. In 1989, 224 major embezzlement and bribery cases involving the railway system were handled by the courts. The bribery problem came to a head in early 1990, when a Vice Minister named Luo Yunguang was fired for taking bribes and for failing to discipline subordinates who also took bribes.[19]

Another adverse consequence of intensive utilization is that safety margins are compressed. On March 24, 1988, two passenger trains collided near Shanghai, killing 28 people (most of whom were Japanese visitors). This was the fourth serious railway crash in the space of four months, and it forced the resignation of the Minister of Railways, Ding Guanglen.[20]

Fundamentally, there are only two solutions to the congestion problem: to add capacity, or to deflect demand. Both are being pursued. The efforts to increase capacity by increasing the length and frequency of trains (longer sidings, greater tractive power, double tracking, etc.) have already been mentioned. On relatively light traffic routes, the further diffusion of existing technology would be quite adequate, so the problem is essentially one of financing the necessary investment. Given the limitations of the central government's budget, an alternative that has received increasing attention recently is the building of local railways by provincial authorities. These should not be confused with the narrow-gauge railways that have long been used in mining and forestry work in various parts of China.[21] The new local railways are built to standard gauge and will share rolling stock with the national pool. Of the 10,000 km of new rail lines planned for construction in the 1990s, about half are expected to be local railways.[22]

On heavy-traffic routes, however, current Chinese railway technology is being pressed to its limits; further expansion of traffic will require a new generation of high-tech equipment, utilizing modern electronics for signalling, marshalling, and other tasks.

[18] "Passenger Trains Overloaded," *Beijing Review*, July 25, 1988, pp. 11–12.
[19] "Police Fight Crimes on Trains," *Beijing Review*, October 17, 1988, pp. 12–13; Yi Hong, "China's Railways: Getting on Track," *China Reconstructs*, October 1988, pp. 13–15; "Vice-Minister Sacked in Scandal," *Beijing Review*, March 26, 1990, p. 13; Ben Chi, "Gains and Losses of China's Railway Construction," *China Market*, May 1990, pp. 13–15.
[20] Yi Hong, p. 13.
[21] Rudi Volti, *Technology, Politics and Society in China*, Boulder, Colorado: Westview Press, 1982, pp. 184–85; "New Advances in Transport," *Beijing Review*, February 15, 1974, p. 22.
[22] Watanatada, Harral and Baldinger, p. 15; Yang Yuying and Lu Baogui, "Ji-Tong tielu" (The Jining-Tongliao railway), *Tiedao Zhishi* (Railway Knowledge), January 1990, pp. 8–9; Cui Jinlai, Bai Jianhong, and Wang Minxuan, "Henan sheng difang tielu" (Local railways in Henan province), *Tiedao Zhishi*, February 1990, pp. 1011; Wang Mingkui, "Kun-Yu tielu" (The Kunming-Yuxi railway), *Tiedao Zhishi*, March 1990, pp. 10–11.

Here the problem is not merely a capital budget constraint (though the necessary investments in computers and telecommunications will certainly be expensive) but some fundamental and rather intractable issues in systems design and technology transfer. To date, the Chinese have carried out extensive investigations of computerized railway operations in other countries but appear not to have made any final decisions about the configuration of their own system.

The other solution to overcrowding is to shed demand. In a centrally planned economy, the traditional answer to excess demand is to ration supply—either by applying a "first come, first served" rule (more common on the passenger side) or by allocating scarce space to favored shippers (more common on the freight side). Both methods cause frustration and resentment. An obvious alternative is to curtail demand by raising fares, but China's leaders have been extremely cautious about doing this, since inflation is also unpopular.

Over a period of three decades, railway freight rates were changed only once (in 1967)—at which time they were reduced, not increased. Finally, rail charges were increased in steps in 1983, 1985, 1989 and 1990. As can be seen from Table 2, these price increases appear to have caused some decline in passenger traffic in 1989, but overcrowding continues to be a serious problem.[23]

B. HIGHWAYS

Network: In many respects, the phases of development of China's highway network have paralleled the pattern for railways. In 1949, large areas of the country had no highways at all, so the first phase—quite naturally—was one of rapid expansion of the network. As can be seen from the data in Table 3, the highway system expanded from 127,000 km in 1952 to 515,000 km in 1965, for an average growth rate of nearly 11% a year. Most of these new roads were of low quality, however, since funding was being stretched to the limit. This first phase witnessed the construction of many frontier highways, with nation-building and strategic purposes receiving greater attention than economic calculations. Examples include the Chengdu-Lhasa, Xining-Lhasa, and Yecheng Burang roads into Tibet (built in the 1950s), and the roads built with Laos, Nepal, and Pakistan in the 1960s. Like the railways built in this same southwestern quadrant of China, these highways often posed daunting engineering challenges. The 1,455-km Yecheng-Burang road, for example, has an average elevation of 4,200 meters—making it the highest road in the world.[24]

In 1965-1978, the expansion of the highway network decreased dramatically, to about 4% a year. In part, this slowdown reflected the policies of the Cultural Revolution, which aimed to reduce economic transactions between regions. The emphasis on local

[23] Tomoyuki Uchida, "Problems in Transportation in Development of Pingsu Coal Mines in Shanxi," *JETRO China Newsletter,* No. 70, September–October 1987, p. 9; Watanatada, Harral, and Baldinger, P. 15; "China Will Execute Unified Price of Coal Transport in 1989,11 *China Market,* April 1989, p. 52; Xiao Zhu, "China to Raise Railway Freight," *China Market,* July 1989, pp. 16–17.

[24] "China Facts and Figures: Communications and Transport," Beijing: Foreign Languages Press, 1982, p. 2; Vetterling and Wagy, pp. 161–63.

TABLE 3. Growth of the Highway Subsector, 1952–89

Year	Route Length (000 km)	Freight [2] Traffic (million tons)	Freight Turnover (billion ton-km)	Passenger Traffic (million)	Passenger Turnover (billion pass-km)
1952	126.7	131.6	1.4	45.6	2.3
1957	254.6	375.1	4.8	237.7	8.8
1965	514.5	489.9	9.5	436.9	16.8
1978	890.2	851.8	27.4	1492.3	52.1
1979	875.8	3710.4	74.5	1786.2	60.3
1980	888.3	3820.5	76.4	2228.0	72.9
1981	897.5	3636.6	78.0	2615.6	83.9
1982	907.0	3792.1	94.9	3006.1	96.4
1983	915.1	4014.1	108.4	3369.7	110.6
1984	926.7	5333.8	153.6	3903.4	133.7
1985	942.4	5380.6	169.3	4764.9	172.5
1986	962.8	6201.1	211.8	5442.6	198.2
1987	982.2	7114.2	266.0	5936.8	219.0
1988	995.6	7323.2	322.0	6504.7	252.8
1989	1014.3	7258.3	333.0	6424.1	264.0

[1] Data for 1952–88 from *Zhongguo Tongji Nianjian 1989* (1989 Statistical Yearbook of China); data for 1989 from *Zhongguo Tongji Zhaiyao 1990* (A Statistical Survey of China 1990).
[1] Freight data through 1978 are only for state-owned vehicles.

self-reliance in this period was epitomized by the exhortation to curtail the "irrational" exchange of grain from south to north and coal from north to south.

In the period since 1978, the expansion of the highway network has slowed even further, to a mere 1% a year. This does not reflect an intensification of the policy of local self-reliance, however. Rather, the highway investments of recent years—which have been substantial—have been concentrated on the upgrading of existing routes in heavy-traffic regions. While unsurfaced dirt roads constituted 39% of the network in 1979, this fraction had been reduced to 17% by 1988.[25] Much of this surfacing is still done with inadequate materials (mixed bitumen, sand, and gravel), requiring high maintenance, but the average quality—and hence traffic capacity— of China's highways has definitely been improving in recent years. In a few locations, highways that can accurately be called expressways are being built, including the Shenzhen-Guangzhou-Zhuhai, Beijing-Tianjin-Tanggu, and Shenyang-Dalian projects.[26] However, superhighways of this sort, while undoubtedly very useful on heavy-traffic routes, carry a price tag of between 6 and 12 million RMB per kilometer and therefore have only limited applicability in China.

Fleet: Production of motor vehicles in China began in 1956, when the No. 1 Vehicle Factory in Changchun turned out the first "Liberation" 4½-ton trucks, modeled on the Soviet ZIL-150 that was in turn a copy of a pre-war Ford.[27] Other major production facilities that have come on-stream over the years include those in Beijing

[25] Volti, p. 191; Chen Yuanhua, "Highways," *China Business Review*, March–April 1989, p. 28.
[26] Chen Yuanhua, p. 30; *Beijing Review*, September 3, 1990, p. 9.
[27] Volti, p. 194; Vetterling and Wagy, p. 163; Albert S. Peterson, "China: Transportation Developments, 1971–1980, " Joint Economic Committee, 97th Congress, 2nd Session, *China under the Four Modernizations, Part* 1, Washington, D.C.: Government Printing Office, 1982, p. 152.

(jeeps), Shanghai (sedans), Jinan (8-ton trucks), and Nanjing ("Leap Forward" trucks). Particularly important is the No. 2 Vehicle Factory, which—as a model of Maoist regional self-reliance—was deliberately located in the remote village of Shiyan in Hubei province.[28] The No. 2 Factory began serial production in 1975. Although China now has more than 100 vehicle production or assembly plants, located in all provinces (except perhaps Tibet), and although these factories produce a wide variety of vehicle types and sizes, the No. 1 and No. 2 factories dominate the industry. For example, in 1986 the No. 1 produced about 85,000 vehicles and the No. 2 about 95,000, which together amounted to 49% of that year's national output of 370,000 cars, trucks, and buses.[29] Because the "Liberation" truck produced in Changchun and the "East Wind" truck produced in Shiyan are very similar in size and function, China's truck fleet has suffered from a lack of diversity—in particular, a shortage of smaller vehicles to serve the needs of rural modernization. The result has been that agricultural tractors, especially the small two-wheel type, are widely used for transport purposes, which causes congestion and wastes fuel.[30] Over the years, China has imported a significant number of vehicles to supplement the domestic fleet, especially specialized vehicles like off-road dump trucks for the mining industry and deluxe sedans for the tourism industry and for high-level cadres. With some fluctuation from year to year, imports averaged about 10,000 vehicles per year in the 1950s, fell to about 5,000 per year in the 1960s, and then began a steady climb in the 1970s, from about 10,000 in 1970 to at least 25,000 in 1979.[31] Because of the economic retrenchment of the early 1980s, vehicle demand was temporarily flat, but then the success of the economic reforms brought about an explosion of demand. In 1984, although domestic vehicle production rose to 316,000 units from the previous year's 240,000, local supply could not begin to meet demand, and imports shot up to 149,000 from the 1983 figure of 25,000. Then, in 1985, despite domestic production of 437,000 units, imports ballooned to 354,000 units. Many of these imports came into China through Hainan Island, where a major corruption scandal was brewing.[32] Despite the ensuing crackdown, vehicle imports in 1986 numbered about 150,000, and have averaged about 90,000 units per year since then.

Predictably, this surge of imports has been greeted by a protectionist reaction from China's vehicle producers.[33] One policy response has been to increase tariffs and other taxes on imported vehicles to very high levels, so that a Volkswagen Santana that

---

[28] Masaharu Hishida, "A Visit to China's 'Second' Automobile Factory," *JETRO China Newsletter*, No. 71, November–December 1987, pp. 2–8.

[29] *Beijing Review*, February 9, 1987, p. 10; Hishida, p. 5.

[30] It is estimated that a two-wheel tractor uses three-fourths as much fuel as a 4-ton truck, while pulling a maximum cargo of perhaps one ton. See Jacques Yenny, "Modernizing China's Transport System," *China Business Review*, July–August 1986, p. 21. Of course, the larger vehicles ensnared in the congestion also use extra fuel.

[31] The vehicle import data, taken from the *Statistical Yearbooks* are for trucks only. For early years, virtually all imports were trucks, but by the late 1970s other vehicle types were becoming important as well.

[32] Martin Weil, "Overhauling the Automotive Industry," *China Business Review*, July–August 1986, p. 28; Jim Mann, *Beijing Jeep*, New York: Simon and Schuster, 1989, p. 152.

[33] See, for example, "Auto Makers Urge Import Curb," *Beijing Review*, October 17, 1988, p. 10.

would sell for about $10,000 in the U.S. has a retail price of $43,000 or more in China.[34] Another policy response has been to encourage the transfer of technology to domestic factories by permitting them to form joint ventures with foreign partners, in the hope that this will accelerate import substitution. The best known of these agreements is certainly the one between American Motors Corporation and the Beijing Auto Works to form the Beijing Jeep Company (signed in 1983), but other important examples include the Volkswagen ventures in Shanghai (Santana) and Changchun (Audi 100) , Peugeot in Guangzhou, Citroen in Wuhan, Iveco (Fiat) in Nanjing, and Steyr with a consortium of heavy-duty truck factories led by the Jinan truck plant.[35]

TABLE 4. Production and Imports of Motor Vehicles

Year	Domestic Production (000)	Imports [2] (000)
1952	—	1.8
1957	7.9	1.6
1965	40.5	6.2
1978	149.1	21.9
1979	185.7	24.8
1980	222.3	22.0
1981	175.6	9.9
1982	196.3	16.1
1983	239.8	25.2
1984	316.4	148.7
1985	437.2	354.0
1986	369.8	150.1
1987	471.8	90.2
1988	664.7	94.7
1989	573.7	85.8

[1] Data for 1952–88 from various issues of *Zhonggguo Tongji Nianjian* (Statistical Yearbook of China); data for 1989 from *Zhongguo Tongji Zhaiyao 1990* (A Statistical Survey of China 1990). Includes cars, trucks, buses and some specialized vehicles, but not tractors or motorcycles.
[2] Import data through 1981 are for trucks only.

These automotive joint ventures have had serious problems. In most cases, the basic business plan has been to begin by assembling imported CKD ("complete knock-down") kits and then gradually to substitute local items for the components of the kits, until production becomes largely domesticized. An important additional element in the business plan, though apparently only tacit in many of the agreements, has been the hope that the joint venture would not be a drain on China's foreign exchange earnings, either because it would save hard currency by displacing imports or—preferably— would earn hard currency by exporting. In the event, these plans have proven to be unduly optimistic, because local suppliers of components have had difficulty meeting the quality and price requirements of the world market. As imports of components run at higher than projected levels, while exports of vehicles fall short of

---

[34] Kim Woodard, "The Automotive Sector," *China Business Review*, March–April 1989, p. 39.
[35] The literature on these joint ventures is extensive. Mann's book on Beijing Jeep, already cited, is particularly detailed, but see also "How Volkswagen Performs in China," *Beijing Review*, July 21, 1986, pp. 24–25; Weil, pp. 28–35; Woodard, pp. 38–43; and a series of articles on the heavy-duty vehicle industry in the August 1989 issue of *China Market*.

projections, the joint ventures are caught in a nasty foreign exchange scissors. For Beijing Jeep, this problem was solved by a secret agreement, signed in the spring of 1986, under which the Chinese authorities in effect made the RMB convertible for this one company (up to a limit of $120 million). This led to what Jim Mann has characterized as the "ultimate irony:" Beijing Jeep earned hard currency by selling an existing Chinese product (the old BJ212 jeep) to Chinese customers for RMB.[36]

Traffic and Operations: The official data on highway traffic, as given in Table 3, must be treated with caution. The data through 1978 measure only the traffic on "public" vehicles (those operated by the Ministry of Communications through its local bureaus). In principle, the data from 1979 onward include the traffic of own-account vehicles operated by factories, collectives, and individuals (which the Chinese refer to collectively as "social" vehicles), but this information is almost certainly incomplete.

Despite the imperfections of the data, certain characteristics of highway traffic in China are indisputable. The congestion of mixed traffic is a constant headache throughout the country, but it has not prevented an explosive growth of freight and passenger turnover. Since the Third Plenum, both ton-km and passenger-km on the highways have increased at about 16% a year on average (according to the official data), as compared to the 6% annual freight growth and 10% passenger growth on the railways. Quite likely, the true growth rates of highway traffic were even faster.

In some instances, the traffic moving on the highways would have been better served by rail, if rail capacity were available. This is undoubtedly true of the coal trucks from Shanxi province that one sees on the streets of Beijing, for example. For the most part, however, the shift of modal shares from rail to road that has been so evident over the 1980s represents a predictable and appropriate adjustment to the changing sectoral structure of the economy. The railways are simply not so well suited as trucks to handling the diverse, short-haul, breakbulk shipments that are essential to agriculture and light industry.

C. WATER TRANSPORT

Network: Broadly speaking, China's large navigable rivers are grouped in three basins: the Heilongjiang (Amur River) system in the northeast, the Changjiang (Yangtze River) system in central China, and the Zhujiang (Pearl River) system in the south. The Huanghe (Yellow River), which drains the north China plain, is plagued by heavy silting; its navigational use is quite limited. The generally west-to-east flow of these rivers is complemented by the north-south Grand Canal (completed 700 years ago), which still provides an important transport corridor between Hangzhou and Beijing. China's 18,000-km coastline provides a second north-south channel for waterborne transport.

At the end of 1988, China had about 109,400 km of navigable inland waterways.[37] However, "navigable" in this context means a

---

[36] Mann, pp. 216 and 228.
[37] *Zhongguo Tongji Nianjian 1989*, p. 396.

depth of 0.3 m—a mere foot of water. Of China's waterways, only about 20,000 km are regularly maintained to a depth of 1.0 m or more year-round, and fewer than 5,000 km can accommodate vessels of 1,000 tons or more. Thus, China's waterways are really two separate systems: four major corridors (coastal, Changjiang, Pearl River, and Grand Canal) on the one hand, and a spiderweb of shallow rivers and canals on the other.

For transportation purposes, both inland waterways and coastal routes have faced serious difficulties. On the coastal routes, fear of sending ships through the Taiwan Strait hampered the development of cabotage for many years. In the 1980s, however, with the easing of military tension in the Strait and the increasingly overt trade between Taiwan and Fujian, coastal shipping has belatedly developed, though it is still hampered by the legacy of inadequate investment in port facilities. On inland waterways, the scarcity of funding for port facilities (and dredging) has also been a problem, which has been compounded by conflicts over jurisdictions and uses. Decisions on flood control, power generation, etc. were made with little regard for the needs of water transport. Thus, by 1979, more than 2,000 obstructive dams and flood gates had been built on navigable waterways.[38] No doubt many of these obstructions were on minor waterways with modest traffic levels, but some were not. A particularly egregious example is the bridge across the Changjiang at Nanjing, opened in 1968, which prevents vessels larger than 5,000 DWT from traveling upstream, even though the channel of the Changjiang will accommodate vessels of 10,000 DWT as far inland as Wuhan.

Fleet: On the minor waterways, vessels are small in size and traditional in configuration, though motorization is now common and hulls are often constructed of ferro-cement, not wood. On the large rivers, pusher tugs are just beginning to displace the more traditional (and less fuel efficient) tow boats.[39]

Traffic and Operations: As can be seen from Table 5, freight turnover on the waterways has grown by about 9% per year on average since 1978—which significantly exceeds freight growth on the railways but falls well short of the growth on highways. On the passenger side, water traffic grew by about 7% a year in the same period, which was significantly slower than traffic growth on either railways or highways but by no means negligible.

D. PIPELINES

In the early days of the petroleum industry in China, most products were shipped by tanker car on rail. However, the construction of pipelines for oil and natural gas got underway in the 1960s. One particularly important landmark was the completion of the 1152-km line from the Daqing oil field to Qinhuangdao in 1973, and its extension to Beijing (an additional 355 km) in 1975.[40] The current

[38] Zhou Mingjing, "China's Inland River Transport, " *Dili Zhishi* (Geographic Knowledge), September 1984, pp. 2–4; David M. Lampton, "Water Politics and Economic Change in China," in Joint Economic Committee, 99th Congress, 2nd Session, *China's Economy Looks Toward the Year 2000*, vol. 1, Washington, D.C.: Government Printing Office, 1986, p. 393.
[39] Robert Delfs, "Changjiang Shipping," *China Business Review*, September–October 1981, pp. 17–20; Paul Jensen, "Ports," *China Business Review* , March–April 1989, pp. 20–26.
[40] "Taching Oil Pipeline Reaches Peking," *China Reconstructs*, October 1975, pp. 15–16.

TABLE 5. Growth of the Waterway Subsector, 1952–89 [1]

Year	Freight Traffic (million tons)	Freight Turnover (billion ton-km)	Passenger Traffic (million)	Passenger Turnover (billion pass-km)
1952	51.3	11.8	36.1	2.5
1957	153.8	33.9	87.8	4.6
1965	227.5	43.3	113.7	4.7
1978	396.3	129.2	230.4	10.1
1979	389.8	139.3	243.6	11.4
1980	383.8	152.1	264.4	12.9
1981	369.6	150.7	275.8	13.8
1982	397.2	170.8	279.9	14.5
1983	403.0	181.1	272.1	15.4
1984	413.5	196.1	259.7	15.4
1985	567.0	237.1	308.6	17.9
1986	757.3	270.0	343.8	18.2
1987	730.0	288.9	389.5	19.6
1988	807.5	310.4	350.3	20.4
1989	n.a.	n.a.	319.0	18.7

[1] Data for 1952–88 from *Zhongguo Tongji Nianjian 1989* (1989 Statistical Yearbook of China); data for 1989 from *Zhongguo Tongji Zhaiyao 1990* (A Statistical Survey of China 1990). Includes inland and coastal traffic, but not overseas shipping. Data through 1984 cover Ministry of Communications vessels only.

system extends for 15,100 km and makes an important contribution to easing congestion on the railways. (In 1989, the freight turnover by pipeline was about 6% of railway turnover.)

As can be seen from Table 6, pipeline traffic has grown quite slowly since 1978 (less than 4% per year on average), even though the network was being expanded by about 5.2% a year. This pattern reflects the production constraints that were occurring in the petroleum industry, rather than problems with the pipelines themselves.

TABLE 6. Growth of the Pipeline Subsector, 1952–89 [1]

Year	Route Length (km)	Freight Traffic (million tons)	Freight Turnover (billion ton-km)
1952			
1957	—		
1965	400	n.a.	n.a.
1978	8300	103.5	43.0
1979	9100	113.4	47.6
1980	8700	105.3	49.1
1981	9700	109.3	49.9
1982	10400	111.7	50.1
1983	10900	116.2	53.4
1984	11100	125.4	57.2
1985	11800	136.5	60.3
1986	13000	148.3	61.2
1987	13800	151.4	62.5
1988	14300	156.2	65.0
1989	15100	156.4	62.9

[1] Data for 1952–88 from *Zhongguo Tongji Nianjian 1989* (Statistical Yearbook of China 1989); data for 1989 from *Zhongguo Tongji Zhaiyao 1990* (A Statistical Survey of China 1990).

In the early 1980s, some Chinese agencies expressed great enthusiasm for the possibility of using pipelines to move coal (in slurry).

Outside observers have generally been critical of these proposals, both because of their high construction cost and because of the scarcity of water in China, and little has been heard of these plans in recent years.[41]

E. CIVIL AVIATION

Recent developments in civil aviation are discussed in detail in the accompanying article by Charles Barton, and therefore I will make only a few brief comments on traffic levels. As can be seen from Table 7, the growth of freight traffic by air has averaged nearly 20% a year since 1978, and passenger traffic has grown almost as fast (about 19% a year). This is even more explosive than the growth of traffic on the highways in the same period. However, this growth occurred from a very small base, so the share of traffic carried by air in 1989 was still extremely modest accounting for only about 3% of total passenger-km on all modes, and for less than 1/10 of 1% of total ton-km.

TABLE 7. Growth of Civil Aviation, 1952-89[1]

Year	Freight Traffic (thousand tons)	Freight Turnover (million ton-km)	Passenger Traffic (thousands)	Passenger Turnover (million pass-km)
1952	2	2	22	24
1957	8	8	69	80
1965	27	25	272	248
1978	64	97	2309	2791
1979	80	123	2980	3499
1980	89	141	3431	3956
1981	94	170	4013	5016
1982	102	198	4452	5951
1983	116	229	3915	5896
1984	150	311	5542	8350
1985	195	415	7468	11695
1986	224	481	9964	14631
1987	299	650	13100	18700
1988	328	730	14420	21448
1989	310	690	12830	18700

[1] Data for 1952-88 from *Zhongguo Tongji Nianjian 1989* (1989 Statistical Yearbook of China); data for 1989 from *Zhongguo Tongji Zhaiyao 1990* (A Statistical Survey of China 1990).

[41] Martin Weil, "Coal Slurry in China," *China Business* Review, July-August 1983, pp. 21-24.

CHINA'S GROWING AIRLINES AND AVIATION INDUSTRY

By Charles Barton [*]

CONTENTS

INTRODUCTION

Tang Xiaoping, executive vice president of the China National Aero-Technology Import Export Corporation (CATIC), said in Beijing on June 26, 1990 that a major goal of China's aviation industry in the coming decade is to shift from military to commercial production. He sees the tremendous world-wide demand for commercial aircraft as a major opportunity for China.

American aerospace leaders and policy makers need to know more of China's growing aviation industry, its importance to China's modernization, and its potential in the international aviation marketplace. This paper reviews the capabilities, problems, current developments, and future goals of both the air transportation and manufacturing sectors of China's aviation establishment.

I. AIRLINES

The last ten years have been a time of change and growth for China's airlines, representing the fastest upgrading of a national civil air transport system in history. The improvements have not come without problems, however.

During the 1950s period of Sino-Soviet cooperation, the Soviet Union assisted China in building up an internal air transport system. Soviet influence survives to this day in the air navigation system, air traffic control, instrument approach procedures, and in airport architecture. Soviet-built aircraft still exist in the Chinese inventory.

---

[*] Aviation Writer/China Specialist. Most of the material in this paper was collected through on-site visits, discussions with Chinese officials and Western repreresentatives of corporations, and various meetings. Most of the historical background is based on information in *China Today: Aviation Industry*, The China Aviation Industry Press, Ministry of Aero-Space Industry, Beijing, 1989.

In 1972, the Boeing 707 that carried President Nixon to China so impressed the Chinese that they bought seven and started on the fleet modernization of CAAC, an acronym which stands both for the Civil Aviation Administration of China and for the airline it operates. The second major catalyst of China's aviation modernization program was the new economic policies of 1978 that opened China to foreign investment and tourist travel.

Demand skyrocketed for air transportation of both passengers and goods. CAAC, with its structure, procedures, and equipment based on 30-year old Soviet models, and a staff of former air force personnel influenced by military rather than commercial attitudes, could not cope. Frequent delays, poor service, and a poor safety record aroused a storm of complaint. The Hong Kong media called CAAC "the airline the world loves to hate." But unchallenged by domestic competition, the object of this scorn continued as before— grossly inefficient, bureaucratic, and indifferent to travelers' needs.

Government circles outside of CAAC pressed for change. A 1985 reshuffle of the State Council, the highest administrative level of the government, made then Vice Premier Li Peng, the Soviet-trained former chief engineer for China's largest hydro-electric complex, responsible for aviation. Li, now China's premier, is comparatively young, energetic, and technically proficient. Also in 1985, the government sent abroad a high-level delegation from the State Council, the Ministry of National Defense, the Air Force, CAAC, and the Ministry of Aviation Industry to study the interaction of government, industry and military in the aviation systems of the leading countries of the world.

In a further action, Beijing named another relatively young technocrat, aviation engineer Hu Yizhou, as director general of CAAC. He replaced Shen Tu, who had failed to take necessary action to reform the old system. Hu's task was to restructure the CAAC empire, separating the governmental and operational functions and forming a modern aviation system.

To do this, Hu wrestled with problems of decentralizing and modernizing a 57,000-employee monopoly during a time of unprecedented growth in numbers of aircraft and routes flown—a Chinese puzzle of immense proportions. New regional airlines were split off from the old monolithic parent and authorized (conditionally, and not immediately) to negotiate and sign contracts with foreign airlines, tourist agencies, cargo agents and other organizations. They could also make suggestions for purchasing and leasing airplanes, selecting air routes, and arranging flights, but CAAC to this day retains final say in these matters. Eventually, however, CAAC is intended to resemble the U.S. Federal Aviation Administration (FAA) in function and responsibility.

The government also allowed the formation of local airlines other than those spun off from the state-run monopoly. Some of these local aviation enterprises are jointly run by local authorities and CAAC, such as Xiamen Airlines, or by provincial or municipal authorities, such as Shanghai Airlines. One of the more successful independent airlines to grow out of this move is United China Airlines, which uses air force aircraft, crews, and facilities. This operation has spawned an air-cargo affiliate, the Baoji Corporation. The new terminal and cargo facilities built at Nan Yuan Air Force

Base near Beijing to support these civil operations have given that military base the look of a civilian airfield.

As part of these ongoing reforms, China's civil airports are becoming independent units. China has about 100 airports for civil use. According to state plans, a total of 10 new airports are to be put into service, and another eight new airport projects started during 1990, but airports will still be far too few for a nation of one billion people—even for its urban population of some 300 million. The United States, a country of about equal size but with less than one-fourth of the population, has 430 airports served by scheduled airlines. Another plan calls for a separate service organization that will handle aeronautical information, telecommunications, navigation and weather reports.

Today, the needs of China's growing air transport fleet (over 100 new aircraft purchased since 1985) exceed the capabilities of the nation's ground support, air traffic control, navigation, and approach control systems. Chinese pilots, air traffic controllers, dispatchers, electronic engineers, and ground support personnel all recognize the need for immediate improvement—a very expensive undertaking. Furthermore, the great variety of aircraft types complicates parts support, maintenance, and the training of flight crews to support the increased level of flight operations.

CAAC's customer relations are still far from smooth, but progress is being made, especially on international flights. One particularly sore point is ticketing. It has heretofore been impossible to buy round-trip tickets for domestic flights, to buy tickets to destinations beyond the first stop, or to arrange confirmed space for each leg of a journey at the time of purchasing a ticket. In a nation where the demand for air transportation exceeds the supply and where poor internal communications have precluded the development of a nationwide computerized reservations system, it is perhaps inevitable that abuses in ticketing and reservations occur.

This situation is being improved by a new computerized reservation system being implemented with the help of UNISYS. However, ticketing and reservations are not just a problem of infrastructure, communications, and computers, says one American businessman in Beijing. There's also an attitude problem—the Chinese way of doing things, a resistance to changing old ways, and the persistence of political connections as the primary means of accessing "luxury" items such as airplane tickets. The problem is complicated by China's cash economy, which make local regions especially reluctant to relinquish their own ticketing and reservations authority.

To develop the aviation infrastructure, China needs technical and financial aid from joint venture partners in industrialized nations and innovative financing to overcome China's chronic shortage of hard currency.

One of Hu Yizhou's first acts as director general was to sign a memorandum of understanding in June 1985 with Lufthansa Chairman Heinz Ruhnau, under which the German airline provided management consulting services in all technical areas, advised on improving the efficiency of CAAC's engineering workshops, and developed a long-term plan for the expansion of CAAC's technical facilities.

This initial memorandum has led to the formation of the Ameco Beijing Aircraft Maintenance and Engineering Corporation, a joint venture of Lufthansa and Beijing-based Air China Airlines, that offers aircraft maintenance and engine overhaul services to both Chinese and foreign airlines. Lufthansa has also joined in a joint venture technical training center to be located at the Bejing Airport maintenance base.

What will Lufthansa gain from these joint ventures? Like other foreign companies operating in China, Lufthansa views its joint venture as a potentially valuable toehold not just in China, but in the entire Far East. By helping to modernize China's aviation industy, Lufthansa hopes to enhance its visibility and reputation abroad, particularly with other potential client governments in Asia.

Maintenance is being provided to China's airlines not only by Lufthansa, but also by Boeing, McDonnel Douglas, Airbus Industrie, British Aerospace, and others who have sold modern aircraft to China. In addition, Lockheed Aircraft Service-International of Ontario, California, and Hutchison Whampoa China Trade Holding Ltd. of Hong Kong have joined with CAAC GRA (Guangzhou Regional Administration) to establish and operate the Guangzhou Aircraft Maintenance and Engineering Company (GAMECO), Ltd., at Baiyun Airport in Guangzhou with an initial investment of $30 million.

The China National Machinery Import and Export Corporation, a commercial operating entity of the Ministry of Foreign Economic Relations and Trade, was at one time the sole organization authorized to negotiate and purchase civilian aircraft. It is still responsible for commerical negotiations for aircraft under the trade agreement with the U.S.S.R.

The Ministry of Aerospace Industry, a combination of the former Ministry of Aviation Industry and Ministry of Astronautics Industry, now oversees and administers China's domestic aerospace industry. Its commercial arm is the China National Aero-Technology Import and Export Corporation (CATIC). CATIC is responsible for the import of foreign technology and equipment to improve China's domestic aerospace production. CATIC often requires that no major aircraft purchase be approved unless the foreign vendor agrees to offset a portion of the aircraft price with purchases of components made in China.

The procurement arm of CAAC is the China Aviation Supply Corporation (CASC). CASC handles the purchase of aircraft, aircraft parts and equipment for CAAC and the regional airlines as well. However, the new joint venture maintenance companies are being empowered to deal directly with foreign vendors of aircraft parts, equipment and components.

A 1980 World Bank report on "Aviation and Development" points out that air transportation is more important to developing countries than to developed countries. Developing countries can build airlines with less capital and in less time than they can build road and rail nets. Furthermore, the benefit to the overall economy is almost immediate.

Chinese leaders agree. Despite problems, much has been accomplished in a short time. Much remains to be done. But China's airlines are on the way.

II. AVIATION INDUSTRY

The accomplishments of China's aircraft factories surprise those who think of China as a labor-intensive agricultural country with little modern industry. China is a land of contrasts. Rockets that place satellites in precise orbits thunder up from launch pads next to peasants tilling the soil with caribou-drawn wooden plows. And in a country that is still poor and underdeveloped in many ways, there are factories that build sophisticated modern aircraft.

1950S: EARLY GROWTH

Since the early 1950s, China has placed heavy emphasis on developing an aviation industry. In May 1953, China and the Soviet Union signed an agreement under which the Soviet Union assisted China in 143 major projects (later increased to 156) of which 13 were for the development of China's aviation industry. These projects included an aircraft factory, an aero-engine factory, and an airborne equipment factory.

In 1953, the Nanchang Aircraft Factory in central China's Jiangxi Province was built to produce piston engine trainers. This was followed by the Zhuzhou Aero Engine Factory near Changsha in Hunan Province producing piston engines, the Shenyang Aircraft Factory in Liaoning Province producing jet fighters, and the Shenyang Aero Engine Factory for jet engines.

Starting in 1956, the focus shifted to the construction of factories such as the Xian Aircraft and Engine Accessory Factory, the Xinping Aviation Electronics and Wheel Brake Accessory factories, and the Baoji Aviation Instrument Factory in Shaanxi Province. These plants were furnished with complete sets of equipment bought from the Soviet Union.

By the end of 1957, China's aviation industry had grown from a small business capable of aircraft repair to an emerging industry with a growing capability to mass-produce piston trainers and jet fighters based on Soviet designs. However, China's own research, development, and independent design capability lagged behind developing production capability.

In 1956, a 12-year development program for science and technology was launched that included mastering and developing jet technology. In 1958, the JJ-1 jet fighter trainer, the first aircraft to be designed and manufactured in China by Chinese—the airframe in the Shenyang Aircraft Factory, the PF-1A jet engine in the Shenyang Aero Engine Factory—was successfully test-flown.

Although the JJ-1 flew successfully, it was not mass-produced because of changed air force training requirements. However, the JJ-1 provided vital design experience basic to subsequent successful designs by the Shenyang design team: the CJ-6 primary trainer (PT-6 in Western nomenclature), the Q-5 series attack aircraft (A-5 outside China), and the J-8 (or F-8) series jet fighters.

By 1960, China's aviation industry had delivered 1,086 aircraft to the air force, including 767 fighters, 278 trainers, and 41 trans-

474

ports, and delivered 216 transports and 17 trainers to China's civil aviation sector. The trouble, however, came with the turmoil casued by the "Great Leap Forward" near the end of the 1950s, followed by the July 1960 cancellation of Soviet technical assistance, the attendant withdrawal of Soviet experts, and three years of natural disasters. In combination, these events greatly retarded the development of aviation.

1960S: READJUSTMENT AND RESURGENCE

The early 1960s was a time of adjustment and reorganization. In September 1963, the government created the Ministry of Aviation Industry (the Third Ministry of Machine Building) under Minister Sun Zhiyuan to organize and direct a resurgence in aviation development.

By 1965, as a result of government and industry efforts, the total industrial output of China's aviation industry was 1.6 times that of 1960. During 1963–65, 1,055 aircraft and 3,081 engines were produced and delivered.

An essential part of this progress was the development of indigenous sources for aeronautical materials and equipment, such as superalloys for jet engines, precision bearings, acrylic plastic sheeting for canopies, aluminum alloys, large castings and forgings, rubber products, special textile materials for high-speed parachutes, and aviation fuels and oils. The mass-produced J–6 jet fighter and the Z–5 helicopter needed 12,319 items and 9,019 items of such materials respectively, of which only 20 percent could be supplied domestically in 1960. By 1965, these items could be fully supplied within China.

Scientific research was key to much of this development. In the early 1960s, in order to organize and administer research, the government set up the Chinese Aeronautical Establishment (the Ministry of Defense's Sixth Research Institute) and a number of subordinate science and product design institutes. In 1964, the Chinese Aeronautical Establishment was merged with the Ministry of Aviation Industry.

Initially, copy manufacturing and reverse-engineering was practiced to train technical personnel, improve design skill, and accelerate the design of new aircraft. Later in the 1960s, there was a shift from copy manufacture to design, and the attendant construction of scientific research and test facilities.

In the late 1960s, the Cultural Revolution again caused great setbacks in aviation education, quality inspection, and rational planning. According to *China Today: Aviation Industry*, published by the China Aviation Industry Press, "capital construction was carried out blindly without planning and feasibility study," plants were dispersed in mountain areas and inside tunnels, and "the investment was not only wasted, but it also left over many outstanding problems which could not be solved for a long time."

During the 1960s and 1970s, the United States, the United Kingdom, France, and the Soviet Union had invested heavily in aeronautical research and development while China's aviation industry stagnated and fell further behind. However, with the downfall of the "Gang of Four" in 1976, the adoption of socialist modernization as the nation's goal, the beginning of new economic policies, and the opening to the outside world, aviation industry began a new period of development.

To counteract the "wrong thinking" of the Cultural Revolution that "production was more important than scientific research," Deng Xiaoping stressed that science and technology were productive forces vital to economic construction. In July 1978, the Ministry of Aviation Industry held a working meeting on aviation science and technology in Tianjin, stressing the vital role of advanced research as a technical base for project development. As one speaker put it: "There is no way of cooking without rice."

OPENING CHINA'S DOORS

The period from 1979 to the present has been the most fruitful in the history of the Chinese aviation industry. A big factor in this development has been the opening of China doors to international investment and cooperative endeavors.

In China, "offset" and "countertrade" agreements must be part of nearly every sale by foreign aviation manufacturers. The resulting technology transfer and the manufacture of parts and subassemblies in China are helping China toward a bigger role in the international aviation market. "We have to start with these small steps," said Mr. Hua Runxi, director of CATIC's Number Two Production Department with responsibilities for engine components, parts export, and engine offsets. "We understand that in the world's aviation industry there is a pyramid. At the top are Boeing, McDonnell Douglas, and Airbus Industrie—these three. On the engine side there are General Electric, Pratt & Whitney, Rolls-Royce, and SNECMA in France. But they have many subsontractors, main component suppliers. We think China should be some place in that pyramid today, but close to the top."

To that end, since 1981 CATIC has established cooperative relationships with nearly all the major aircraft engine manufacturers in the United States: Pratt & Whitney, General Electric, Pratt & Whitney Canada, General Motor Allison of Indianapolis, Textron Lycoming, and Garrett. More recently, Revmaster of the United States, and SNECMA, Turbomeca, Aerospatiale and Messier-Hispano-Bugatti of France have joined the list of customers. Most subcontracted items are related to compensation trade (see appendix A for details of China's aviation factories and their arrangements with foreign manufacturers).

As to products other than engines, one of the first Sino-foreign cooperation projects, the joint manufacture of French Dauphin helicopters in 1980, started with final assembly in China, according to He Wenzhi, Deputy Minister of Aero-Space Industry. Now most of the airborne equipment and airframe components are Chinese-made, he says.

Since 1979, CATIC has manufactured aircraft parts, components and subassemblies under subcontracts from 14 world-famous aircraft manufacturers such as Canadair, Boeing, McDonnell Douglas, British Aerospace (BAE), Aerospatiale, and Messerschmitt-Bolkow-Blohm (MBB). These products include vertical fins for the Boeing 737, the outboard wingbox for the ATR-42, the center wing of the

UK's Shorts Brothers SD360, and doors and control surfaces for a variety of aircraft. A 1988 contract between McDonnell Douglas and CATIC calls for producing complete MD–82 nose sections by the Chengdu Aircraft Corporation, and building horizontal stabilizers by the Shanghai Aviation Industrial Corporation (SAIC). CATIC's Tang Xiaoping said in Beijing in June 1990 that by the first part of 1991 the Chinese will have built the fourth nose secton for the McDonnell Douglas MD–82, and that they are talking with Boeing about increasing the contract for building vertical fins. This relationship between McDonnel Douglas and SAIC, which includes the co-production of 25 MD–82 twin-jet transports, is giving McDonnell Douglas unique access to the Chinese market and helps China prepare for a major role in the international aviation marketplace.

China has a long way to go to approach the top of the international aero-space market pyramid, but progress since 1980 shows that Chinese factories are definitely on the way. In July 1988, Gareth C. C. Chang, then-president of McDonnel Douglas China, noted that there is no longer any question in his mind that since the start of China's cooperation with foreign aircraft companies, the Chinese have proved that they can manufacture, assemble, and fabricate parts "as well if not better" than anyone else. "China is fully capable of building a 50-passanger airplane all by herself," he said, "and can compete with anybody else in the world."

In advising the Minister of Aviation Industry, Chang insisted that "the argument that you are going to build an airplane only for China because you can use lower grade materials, more backward design, that's pure bullshit. Either you're in the aviation business or your're not. If you're in the aviation business, you build an airplane for world consumption."

Perhaps reflecting this attitude, a contract for 20 more McDonnel Douglas MD–80 series aircraft to be built in Shanghai was signed last year. West Germany's MBB is cooperating in developing a 75-seat feeder airliner, the MPC-75, scheduled to fly in 1994. In addition, China has asked for final proposals from Boeing, and McDonnell Douglas for the manufacture in China with Chinese participation about 150 mid-size "trunk airliners" for China's airlines.

China's new emphasis on building commercial aircraft for export is already bearing fruit. In December 1988, the Civil Aviation Administation of Laos signed a contract for two Chinese-built Y–12 aircraft, a 17-passenger high-wing, twin-prop jet airplane that can take off and land on rough, short runways. The Y–12, built by the Harbin Aircraft Manufacturing Corporation in Heilongjiang Province, has a maximum take-off weight of 11,680 pounds and a maximum ceiling of 23,000 feet, cruises at 204 mph, and can carry 3,748 pounds of passengers and cargo a maximum distance of 2,190 miles.

On June 20, 1990, the British Civil Aviation Authority gave the Y–12 an air worthiness certificate which boosted sales. A week later, Tang Xiaoping reported that 10 Y–12 aircraft had been sold abroad so far, six to Sri Lanka and four to Laos, and that other countries were interested in the aircraft.

Sun Zhaoqing, CATIC president, said on June 20 that Sri Lanka had previously purchased two Y–8s in addition to their six Y–12s. The Y–8, build by the Shaanxi Aircraft Factory, is a four-engine turbo-prop transport similar in size and function to the Lockheed Hercules C–130, but non-pressurized and at only half the price.

Tang listed two problems in the development of China's aviation industry in the 1990s: lack of money, and lack of certification from the U.S. FAA, the CAA (the British Civil Aviation Authority), or European countries. Without such certification, Tang noted, China would not be able to enter the world aircraft market. Certification by Western countries involves many new concepts for the Chinese and costs a lot of money. China has received CAA certification for the Y–12 aircraft, but, Tang observed, "the bigger aircraft are another story." China has learned a lot about the FAA certification process from the co-production of the MD–82 in Shanghai.

Developing China's human resources is another priority for China's aircraft industry, and essential if China hopes to compete in the high tech market. In his 1986 book, *China Takes Off*, E. E. Bauer of Boeing described situations where Chinese mechanics had a simplistic view of complex equipment. Furthermore, as a result of a legacy of national poverty, they were reluctant to discard any parts or equipment which they considered to be remotely reusable. For example, the Boeing technical representatives found that Chinese mechanics would clean non-reusable high pressure hydraulic system filter cartridges with gasoline and then re-install them even though "non-reusable" was steel-stamped on both ends of the filter element. In additional efforts to save money, the Chinese also substituted Chinese-manufactured oils, greases, gaskets, and O-rings that did not meet required specifications. In general, there was a tendency (not unique to the aircraft industry) to neglect preventive maintenance. As Bauer discovered, the Chinese preferred to solve problems after they developed and not to do anything extra unless there was a direct threat to safety or unless operational experience convinced them it would cost more if the work was not done.

On the other hand, the Chinese skill at "making do" can have its benefits. One McDonnell Douglas quality assurance advisor (QA) was pleasantly surprised by the fine quality of the Chinese workmanship considering what they have to work with. "If they don't have it, they make it," he said. "A couple of Chinese QA people I know will be of great benefit to the company after we leave." Other McDonnell Douglas advisors expressed their admiration for the technical ability and motivation exhibited by Chinese workers, commenting that "American workers are going to have to look out." This does not mean, however, that Chinese workers on the MD–82 project are all highly motivated paragons. An hour before quitting time there is a noticable slackening of effort among those not involved in the priority actions of the moment and the Chinese traditional mid-day "xiu xi," or rest period, results in long lunch periods. This led one American to observe that "to the Chinese, work is a place to which you go for lunch."

Another workforce problem, according to Werner Hupe, Lufthansa's senior technical advisor and general manager of their Technical Joint Venture Project, is that the Chinese are somewhat inexperienced in the paperwork processes used to ensure that jobs are done completely, correctly, and on time, and that the record is signed by the responsible people. The Lufthansa advisors, with German thoroughness and attention to detail, responded by standarizing all the aircraft log books and other maintenance forms to make the process easier for the Chinese.

Despite the problems, most American manufacturers seem to feel that overall, Chinese aviation mechanics, factory workers, and technicians are doing very well, and their efforts are paying off. In November 1987, the FAA granted a production certificate extension for the co-production of MD–82 aircraft in Shanghai, and in June 1988 granted a fabrication assembly certificate to the Shanghai Aviation Industrial Corporation for manufacturing parts for this aircraft. At the Beijing Maintenance Base, FAA granted a repair station license to the wheel shop. Other licenses are pending as technology and up-to-date equipment are transferred to the Chinese. Slowly but steadily, the Chinese are meeting their 1990s goals.

Unlike some of the other industries, China's civil aviation sector appears to have suffered little in the aftermath of the Tiananmen Square events and subsequent austerity measures imposed by Beijing. Gareth Chang, President, McDonnell Douglas Pacific & Asia, summed up the impact by saying, "As far as the industry is concerned, it's a non-event. Our relationship has not deteriorated or improved as a result."

Underlying China's drive for modernization is the desire to restore China to greatness, to restore pride and place after two centuries of humiliation. But it is also in the interest of other nations to have a developed, prosperous China as a trading partner. The development of Chinese air transportation and aviation industry contributes to these goals.

III. Appendix: Aviation Factories in China [1]

AIRCRAFT AND COMPONENTS

BADDING PROPELLER FACTORY, P.O. Box 818, Branch 608, Baoding, Hebei Province. The only propeller manufacturer in China. About 4,000 employees. Aero-products include: propellers, governors, speed limiters, feathering pumps, helicopter rotor hubs, tail rotors, etc.

CHANGHE AIRCRAFT FACTORY, P.O. Box 109, Jingdezhen, Jiangxi Province. Telex 95027 CHAF CN. Employs 6,000 staff and workers. Aero-products include the Z–8 helicopters with 13 tons takeoff weight. (Many civil automotive products)

CHANGZHOU AIRCRAFT FACTORY, P.O. Box 16, Changzhou, Jiangsu Province. Telex 361019 BOOTH CN. Employs 1,200 staff and workers. Aero-products include light and small helicopters, pilotless aircraft, and high pressure gas bottles.

CHENGDU AIRCRAFT CORPORATION, P.O. Box 800, Chengdu, Sichuan Province. Telex 60132 CCDAC CN. The J–7 (F–7) high altitude high speed fighter has been produced here since 1967. It produces MD–82 nose sections for McDonnell Douglas. Has about

---

[1] Source: *Survey of Chinese Aviation Industry*, 1989/1990, Aviation Industry Press, Beijing, People's Republic of China, 1989.

20,000 workers and staff of which more than 2,700 are technical staff. Main-aero products: four types of fighter, one trainer.

GUIZHOU AVIATION INDUSTRY CORPORATION, P.O. Box 38, Anshun, Guizhou Province. Telex 66018 AIMGA CN. A grouping of many different enterprises, factories and institutes engaged in R&D, advanced computer applications for quality control and CAD/CAM, manufacturing technology, etc. Employes 18,000 technical and professional people. Main products: a high altitude high speed fighter and its trainer version, two series of turbojet engines, air-to-air missiles, fuel pumps, rocket launchers, hydraulic pumps, various airborne DC and AC generators, electrical converters, relays switches, connectors, electro-operated mechanisms, electro-magnetic valves, hydraulic valves, etc. Especially strong in design and production of small to medium size aircraft with wing span less than 20m (65 ft).

HARBIN AIRCRAFT MANUFACTURING COMPANY, P.O. Box 201, Harbin, Heilongjiang Province. Telex 87082 HAF CN, Fax 0451-227491. Has more than 15,000 staff and workers of which over 2,000 are engineering and technical people. Owns three design and research institutes. Aero-products include the Y-12 (a 17 passenger, high wing, twin prop-jet airplane that was granted a UK CAA airworthiness certificate in June 1990), and Z-9A helicopters. Subcontracts central wing panels and cabin doors for Short Bros., eight kinds of mainlanding gear and other doors for BAe, machined products and composite material components for Skorsky, cabin doors for Dauphin helicopters, etc.

NANCHANG AIRCRAFT MANUFACTURING COMPANY, P.O. Box 5001, Nanchang, Jiangxi Province. Telex 95068 NHMC CN, Fax 41112 ext 2272. Over 20,000 staff and workers, 22% of which are technical people. An integrated complex of factories and design institutes—4 R&D institutes, 9 subsidiaries and factories, several dozen workshops. (Has an advanced level production line for motor-cycles.) Aero-products include: Q-5 (A-5), Q-5III, Q-5M attack, and L-8 aircraft, as well as FL-1, FL-2, and FL-3A missiles.

SHAANXI AIRCRAFT COMPANY, P.O. Box 35, Chenggu, Shaanxi Province. Telex 70141 STAF CN. Employs 10,000 staff and workers, 15% engineering and technical people. Company combines R&D and production. Has 11 divisions, 2 design and research institutes, 2 workshops, and the largest final assembly building in China. Aero-products include the Y-8 four prop-jet transport, comparable to Lockheed C-130 Hercules. Two have been sold to Sri Lanka.

SHAANXI AERO-HYDRAULIC COMPONENT FACTORY, P.O. Box 43, Yang County, Shaanxi Province. Telex 71207 SAITC CN. A specialized factory for the production of landing gears, hydraulic accessories, rubber and plastic products, and arc welding rods. Employs more than 2,600 staff and workers. Aero-products include landing gear and all hydraulic components and rubber parts for the Y-8 transport.

ENGINE AND COMPONENT MANUFACTURERS

CHANG KONG MACHINERY FACTORY, P.O. Box 924, Beijing. Telex 222819 CKMF CN. More than 2,000 employees, 20% are technical staff. Aero-products include engine fuel pumps, fuel governors, and other engine accessories.

CHANGZHOU LAN XIANG MACHINERY WORKS, P.O. Box 37, Changzhou, Jiangsu Province. Cable 5046. Has 11 specialized factories, 8 shops, 2 product development departments, 1 tooling department, 3 meteorological inspection and test centers, and equipment service center. Employs over 5,000 of which more than 1,000 are technical staff. Main aero-product is the WZ–6 helicopter engine. (Much non-aero, industrial production)

CHENGDU ENGINE COMPANY, P.O. Box 613, Chengdu, Sichuan Province. Telex 60142 CET CN. Fax 442470. More than 20,000 employees in 9 specialized factories, 2 subsidiary companies, and 2 research institutes. Of over 5,000 technical staff there are nearly 2,000 engineers and 500 senior engineers. Has a 25-year contract with United Technology Corporation for producing FT–8 industrial gas turbines. Aero-products include WP–6 and WP–13 turbojet engines as well as the flame tube, gas collector section, ring and pipe of the Pratt & Whitney JT–8D turbofan engine. Much non-aero production.

CHINA NATIONAL AEROENGINE CORPORATION, No. 67, Jiao Nan Dane, Beijing. Cable 9696. Engaged in scientific R&D production and operation of aero-engines and other products, and is authorized to independently handle foreign trade. Has 16 factories and research institutes located in Beijing, Harbin, Shenyang, Xi'an, Chengdu, Changzhou, Zhuzhou, Jiangyou, and Wuxi with a total of 130,000 employees. Much non-aero production and marketing.

CHINA NATIONAL LIGHT-WEIGHT GAS TURBINE DEVELOPMENT CENTER, No. 67 Jiaonan Dajie, Beijing. Telex 22318 AEROT CN, Fax 4015381. A division of the China National Aeroengine Corporation founded in 1985. Main product is the FT–8 gas turbine engines , jointly designed, manufactured and sold by the Center and Pratt & Whitney and Turbo Power & Marine Systems, soon to be available on world market.

DONGAN ENGINE MANUFACTURING COMPANY, P.O. Box 51, Harbin, Heilongjiang Province. Telex 87082 HEF CN. Since 1948, the company has moved from repairing to manufacturing, from piston engines to turboprop engines, and from military production to both military and civil products. Has two design departments (for aero- and non-aero- products) and six specialized factories. Employs 10,000 of which 12% are technical people. Aero-products include the WJ5A–1 engine for the Y–7 aircraft, reduction gear box for the Dauphine helicopter, repaired Mi–8 helicopter engines for Pakistan, Sudan, and other countries.

LIMING ENGINE MANUFACTURING CORPORATION, P.O. Box 424, Shenyang, Liaoning Province. Telex 80025 CMMCS CN, Fax (024)732221. China's first turbojet engine factory, founded iin 1954. Employs more than 20,000 of which over 3,000 are technical staff and engineers. Products: aeroengines WP6–B and WP7–C and their parts; co-generating gas turbine sets rating at 4,500 kw; and civil products.

LIYANG MACHINERY CORPORATION, P.O. Box 5, Pingba, Guizhou Province. Telex 66044 LYMCG CN. Began manufacture of aero turbojet engines in 1970. It employs over 10,000 of which 15% are technical staff including about 1,500 engineers. It combines

R&D with production, has 3 specialized factories and one research and design institute. Aero-products include WP7 and WP13 turbojet engine series in 11 versions. It has begun to export these to 6 countries and since 1985 has built up a development and production capability for dozens of non-aero-products.

SHANGHAI AEROENGINE MANUFACTURING PLANT, No. 600 Guangzhong Road, Shanghai. Telex 33136 SHAIR CN. Fax 651482. Employs about 2,000 including over 500 technical staff. In the 1970s the plant successfully developed China's first turbofan engine, repaired JT3D-7 engines for CAAC and manufactured more than 20,000 military engine spare parts. Main aero-products include WS8 turbofan engines, 3K42 light duty gas turbines, and a variety of jet engine parts.

SHANGHAI AERONAUTIC MACHINERY PLANT, P.O. Box 254, Shanghai, Cable 8215. Employs more than 1,300 including 139 engineers. Except for aero-hydraulic products is now mostly engaged in civil production of hydraulic and refrigeration machinery, etc.

SOUTH MOTIVE POWER AND MACHINERY COMPLEX, P.O. Box 211, Zhuzhou, Hunan Province. Telex 995002 CHENF CN. Fax (086) (0733) 24220. China's first aero-engine was built here. Has over 10,000 employees including 3,000 technical personnel. Main aero-products include WJ6 turboprop engine for medium transport planes, WZ8A turboshaft engine for light helicopters, HS6A to HS6K series engines for small transports and agricultural planes, and WJ6Gl through WJ6G4 engines for industrial and marine applications.

XI'AN AERO-ENGINE CORPORATION, P.O. Box 13, Xi'an, Shaanxi Province. Telex 70102 XIARO CN. Employs more than 10,000 with more than 4,000 technical staff. Main products include turbojet and turbofan engines, 6,000 and 13,000 hp gas turbines, and many civilian products.

ZHONGNAN TRANSMISSION MACHINERY FACTORY, formerly in Yuanling, now has new plant in Wangcheng, a suburb of Changsha, Hunan Province. Cable 2830 Wangcheng. Has 3,000 staff, 15% engineering. Aero products include gears for HS-5, HS-6, WJ-6, WJ-9, and Z-9 engines; main and tail reducing gears, accessories such as oil pump, and middle and tail speed reducer for Z-8 helicopters. Many commercial products.

CHINA'S TELECOMMUNICATIONS AND AMERICAN STRATEGIC INTERESTS

By Ken Zita *

CONTENTS

SUMMARY

China's antiquated telecommunications infrastructure is a serious impediment to broad scale modernization of the Chinese culture and economy. Part I examines the overall state of telecommunications development in China and the formation and implementation of industrial policy. The roles of various organizations are assessed in the context of telecommunications services, private networks, organization and political control, and research and development. Part II is an assessment of American strategic interests in the telecommunications sector in China, both from the security and the commercial perspectives. "Soft loan" financing is also assessed, along with other questions relevant to U.S. policy.

INTRODUCTION

China is preparing for its next revolution: the Information Age. Telecommunications has been a state strategic priority since 1985, when the government of Zhao Ziyang first began to recognize how the power of information networks could support the broad-based effort to modernize and reform the national economy. For China to step successfully into the modern era, the entire archaic public telecommunications infrastructure needs to be replaced. Basic telephone service is among the poorest in the world, and the lack of

---

* Ken Zita is an independent consultant.

computer-to-computer data communications is a major bottleneck in China's economic reforms—regardless of the ideology of the nation's leaders. China needs to surmount considerable barriers in the telecommunications modernization effort, including organizational restructuring, financing, and improved supervision over network operations.

This paper is divided into two sections. Part I, Modernization Goals, is a review of current organizational challenges facing China's national planners. Part II, Considerations for American Policy, is an analysis of the American strategic interests relevant to telecommunications development in the PRC.

PART I: MODERNIZATION GOALS

The shortcomings of China's telecommunications are well known.[1] Despite an increase in switching lines from 6.2 million in 1979 to 14.9 million in 1988 and steady improvements in calling service, nationwide telephone density is only 0.75 telephones per 100 population, or one phone for every 133 citizens. In China's vast countryside, density falls to an astonishing .17, or one phone for every 500 residents.[2] Both figures are well below even the developing world's average density of three telephones for every 100 people. Most of China's 7.8 million telephone stations, moreover, are in offices with limited public access. Only officials with deputy director status (or who have special political connections—and a lot of money) are entitled to private telephone service.[3]

The telecommunications industry in China is crippled by three strategic weaknesses. First, there is little vertical integration of local and toll services, which skews economies of scale in capital investment and revenue collection, and leads to technical inconsistencies among regional networks. Second, R&D and telecommunications manufacturing are split helter-skelter between two rival entities, the Ministries of Posts and Telecommunications (MPT) and Machine Building and Electronics Industry (MMEI), and the competition between them strains already scant resources. Third, state funds—especially foreign exchange for imports and joint ventures—are extremely limited, and impending financial reforms in telecommunications will sharpen the crisis.[4]

China hopes to raise the number of telephones to 33.6 million by the year 2000, adding some 10–15 million virtual circuits or line equivalents. Analog service is expected to be extended to the smallest towns, and digital switching and transmission corridors are slated to link provincial capitals and big cities. Fiber and sophisticated switching systems will upgrade urban centers.

Success of China's long-range development plan is contingent on a number of factors, including:

---

[1] See Ken Zita, *Modernising China Telecommunications* (*MCT*) (London: The Economist Publications, 1987) and Pyramid Research, *China's Telecom Strategy*, (Cambridge, MA: Pyramid Research, 1989).

[2] Ken Zita, "Telecommunications in China," International Telecommunications Society (Cambridge, MA), June, 1988.

[3] Ken Zita, "China's Great Leap Forward," *International Herald Tribune*, October 20, 1987.

[4] Ken Zita, "Telecommunications: China's Uphill Battle to Modernize," *China Business Review* (*CBR*), November–December, 1989.

- The MPT assuming a more balanced leadership role. MPT needs to hand over responsibility for policy planning and operations in local areas to provincial authorities, and simultaneously consolidate and strengthen its primary role as the national long distance carrier. MPT allows provinces latitude in local daily management decisions but continues to manage foreign exchange quotas for local import purchases, often overriding local planning sentiments.
- The adoption of a coherent policy for managing domestic manufacturing. Currently, China's industrial base for telecommunications is fragmented by regionalism, inter-ministry rivalries, inefficient factory management, and a lack of reliable financing.
- Local bureaus of the MPT boosting internal generation of funds through local tariffs by encouraging municipal governments (and indeed the central government) to allow placement of long term bonds. China's shortage of domestic capital and foreign exchange is a serious obstacle to growth, and reappraisal of both the telecommunications cost/pricing and external financial systems are essential.[5]

SERVICES

Local telephone services throughout China are controlled by state-run monopolies, usually at the provincial or municipal level. Affluent and relatively sophisticated cities are building modern networks based on the latest foreign technology, while poorer regions are making do with basic technology. The government hopes to spearhead advances in selected regions to raise the overall capabilities of the network, thereby catalyzing cultural and commercial development—technology and economic "trickle-down," with Chinese characteristics. Suburbs of cities with big construction budgets will benefit, though most areas will have to wait. Even with Li Peng's stated attempt to rationalize the economic disparities between the coastal provinces and the interior, network growth will occur fastest along the seaboard. The result is the formation of a two-tier network. Until recently, telephone service in China was everywhere the same: that is, poor. Now, the cities of the east coast are installing advanced imported systems while the nation's interior—the agricultural belt with increasing riches but limited urbanization—lags behind.

Network stratification poses an important social and economic question: Who will benefit from new information technology? In a macroeconomic sense, any municipality that can afford imported equipment can proceed immediately with network modernization. Other regions must compete for an ever-shrinking share of direct government spending, attempt a "middle-road" course of network development based on domestic analog technology (if available), or simply postpone development of the local telephone infrastructure—resulting in relative economic and cultural isolation. Even

---

[5] Financial issues are a complex area and beyond the scope of this paper. For further details, see: Ken Zita, "Steps Toward Political and Financial Reform in China's Telecommunications Sector," in *Telecommunications in the Pacific Rim*, Eli Noam, Ed., (New York: Columbia University Press, 1990).

though 80 percent of the Chinese population lives in rural areas, rural network development has none of the fanfare and little of the potential surrounding the bustling digital expansion in the cities. Before 1949, telephone service in the hinterlands was nonexistent. Today, rural areas are still considered poor country cousins: at year-end 1987, only about 3.09 million lines served a rural population exceeding 800 million.[6] The cumulative waiting list for local service in China is estimated at 850,000, with 100,000 or more in Beijing alone, and the numbers would be higher if the public realistically believed it possible to obtain service.[7] Further, distinction can be made among different classes of services available, related to the various grades of equipment being installed. Priority calling status on quality equipment is assigned; as a result, some users get instantaneous local dial tone and international long distance dialing over digital circuits, while others wait for lines on crackling and decrepit systems. Who gets what, when and on which terms?

Information technology presents special difficulties to China's concept of distribution of public resources. Though the state has been relatively effective in providing health care, housing, and transportation, China simply cannot afford to provide everyone with a telephone, with a resultant disparity of opportunity. With access to effective telecommunications comes access to prosperity, social mobility, and virtually limitless horizontal communication within society. Consider the discrepancies between China's new information "haves" and "have nots": a small packaged goods enterprise in Nanjing is granted three clean local trunk lines via which it can source price information for raw materials all over Jiangsu Province. A competing enterprise, without equal political access or financial clout can scarcely holler across town over a single faltering or perennially blocked line. One firm can meet the dynamic demands of the emerging market economy in China; the other is held back by antiquated infrastructure. So far, however, telecommunications expansion in China today is a business phenomenon: most new systems are installed in government agencies, institutions or cooperatives. The goal of universal service—that every citizen is entitled to telephone service—is not a stated goal of the PRC, and given development constraints will not likely be a viable priority before the turn of the century.

PRIVATE NETWORKS

The second dimension of Chinese telecommunications is the development of private national networks. Beginning in 1976, the central government granted permission to four ministries—those of coal, petroleum, railways and water and power—to build their own systems to handle internal communications. At the time, the Ministry of Railways and the People's Liberation Army (PLA) already had systems in place, and it was widely recognized that the public

---

[6] Liang Xiong-Jian and Zhu You-nong, "The Development of Telecommunications in China," in *Telecommunications in the Pacific Rim*, Eli Noam, Ed., (New York: Columbia University Press, 1990).

[7] Chen Weihua, "Growth Requires Better Communications," China Daily Business Weekly, June 27, 1988.

network was a liability to effective communications—a critical consideration in the wake of the cultural revolution.

Today, private networks are proliferating. The People's Bank of China is investing an estimated $1 billion on a private network, and with China speeding toward reunification with Hong Kong in 1997, greater access to international networks will be required by all major enterprises.

The private network development strategy within China is vital to full-scale modernization of the national economy. Each of the ministries can be viewed as separate lines of businesses in a state-run conglomerate, each with headquarters in Beijing, each contributing to the government's centrally planned bottom line. With economic decentralization racing to divest operational control from Beijing, the state needs a national management information system (MIS) to keep track of geographically disperse activities and resources. Without an MIS structure to keep planning policies in line, Beijing could lose yet more control over profit and loss centers (provincial or outlying offices, factories, independent enterprises and cooperatives) than intended by economic restructuring. Private networks are insurance that all roads will continue to lead to Beijing.

As with private telephone companies in the United States, the MPT is threatened by large users "bypassing" the public network with private systems. In response, MPT is planning an "overlay" data network based on satellite technology to be developed in conjunction with AT&T and Japan's KDD to meet the special communications needs of large organizations.

ORGANIZATION AND POLITICAL CONTROL

Telecommunications equipment manufacturing in China is a fragmented, and sometimes bitter, competition between MPT, the national long distance carrier and manufacturer of selected products; and MMEI, the State Council's "favorite son" and a highly subsidized research center for components and software. The principal result of the competition is that despite formidable resources, China can report few economies of scale and only poor synergy among R&D, product definition, and manufacturing of telecommunications.

The current strategic framework for industrial development in the information sector was formulated by the Group for the Revitalization of the Electronics Industry (ELG), a council of high-level technocrats within the State Council, during the group's short-lived tenure from 1985–1988. Under the tutelage of Li Peng, the ELG set the strategic path and development priorities for five electronic industry subsectors: computers, telecommunications, software, integrated circuits, and sensors. Though functionally disbanded, the ELG has left an indelible mark on the industry's future by establishing structural rules and guidelines for many of the most important development decisions facing the information industry in China.

The ELG's conceptual recommendations, such as limiting the number of foreign electronics suppliers and targeting specific technologies for exploration and growth, are given tangible form by the

State Planning Commission (SPC) and the State Science and Technology Commission (SSTC). The SSTC recommends how R&D funding should be spent, while the SPC actually controls the budgets. In late 1984, the SPC sought to ease the rivalry between the MPT and MMEI by parceling specific R&D tasks to each organization. The compromise made the MPT primary user of telecommunications equipment, while MMEI was viewed as the primary manufacturer. See Figure 1.

This demarcation is deceptively neat. The MPT manufactures a great deal of telecommunications equipment and will continue to do so in the future. It currently commands the central office and PBX manufacturing sector and is a stakeholder in optical electronics and line multiplexer equipment. MPT manages China's only digital switching facility, the Shanghai Bell Telephone Company joint venture with Alcatel. MMEI, on the other hand, makes approximately 90 percent of all telecommunications components, from mechanical relays and printed circuit boards to capacitors, transistors and integrated circuits, and is slated to boost central office production at two new facilities, with Germany's Siemens and Japan's NEC. A further distinction between the two ministries is that MPT's systems are installed almost exclusively in the public network, while MMEI's equipment is sold chiefly to the military and private networks. (Figure 2).

Under SPC/ELG guidance, a program has evolved to support "leading" research institutes that pursue key development projects. The MPT's Research Institute No. 1 in Shanghai, for instance, is slated to become China's foremost (domestic) PBX design center; MMEI's Factory No. 738 in Beijing is destined to be the center for new research in large switches. Similar assignments—in some instances more than one—have been made for all strategic technologies: lightwave fiber (MPT in Wuhan and Shanghai); satellite earthstations (MMEI in Nanjing); PCM (MPT in Chongqing); integrated circuits (MMEI in Beijing and Nanjing), and so on. Leading research and manufacturing sites are all reported to have ample budgets, access to foreign exchange, highly qualified staff, preferential taxes and, frequently, permission to licence technology from abroad.

The assignment of government-sponsored leading enterprises and factories contrasts sharply with the dominant industrial structure in China. Ministries and municipalities have historically encouraged local self-reliance, a strategy that surrendered manufacturing efficiency to community rule. For example, one can still find crossbar switch factories that also build assembly line machine tools, test equipment, postal delivery bags, sewing machine motors, household lamps—whatever was needed (or was independently profitable) in the past.

Leading research and production centers will encourage R&D and factory floor specialization, coordinate talented personnel, and do away with ancillary activities. If pursued with conviction, the "leading site" strategy may establish better linkage between research, competent factory management, and production by investing in organizations most likely to meet with technological and commercial success.

488

FIGURE 1.

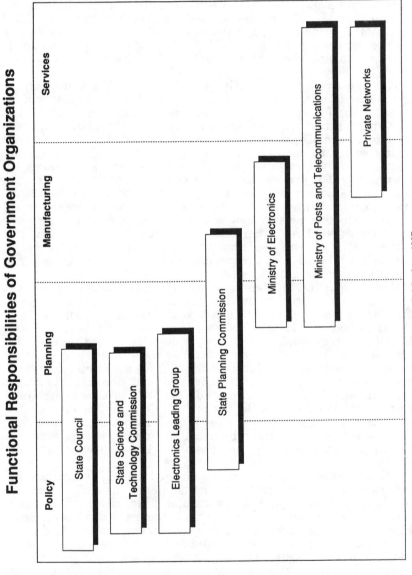

Functional Responsibilities of Government Organizations

Source: Modernizing China's Telecommunications, The Economist Publications, 1987.

FIGURE 2.

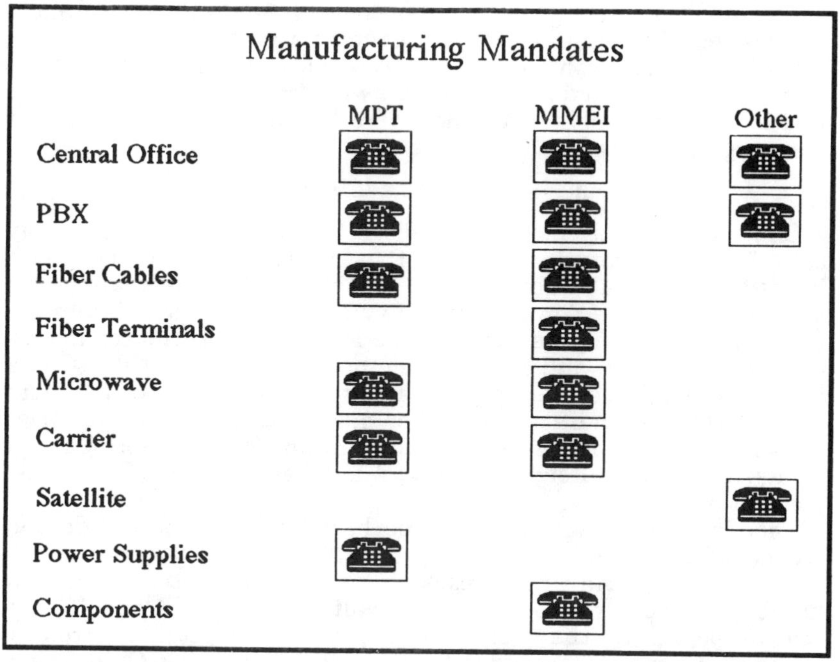

Manufacturing Mandates

	MPT	MMEI	Other
Central Office	☎	☎	☎
PBX	☎	☎	☎
Fiber Cables	☎	☎	
Fiber Terminals		☎	
Microwave	☎	☎	
Carrier	☎	☎	
Satellite			☎
Power Supplies	☎		
Components		☎	

Responsibility for actually implementing ELG/SPC policy rests largely with MMEI. MMEI has no clear bureaucratic mechanism to coordinate planners, R&D facilities, and factories in large-scale projects, however. The ministry can encourage limited association among affiliated factories (which are managed as independent enterprises), but lacks the managerial infrastructure to marshal major development efforts. No single point of strategic control exists within MMEI to harness scattered resources, and planning decisions are often made according to strict financial considerations—that is, who has foreign exchange—and not in line with SPC "leading site" recommendations, developed according to carefully considered research and manufacturing efficiencies.

A case in point is a joint R&D and planned manufacturing venture for a small central office exchange between Italtel, the Italian national suppliers, and MMEI Research Institute No. 54 in Shijiazhuang. Following the ELG's advice, the State Council limited the number of urban central office ventures to three. Feeling left out of the market, Italtel appealed by proposing a project to design and eventually manufacture a small rural central office exchange, while the Italian government made available a soft loan to underwrite the project. In this way, Italtel effectively maneuvered through restrictions established by the central government bureaucracy, and a fourth switching venture was consummated in principle without violating established rules.

The MPT's manufacturing is managed by the Posts and Telecommunications Corporation (PTC), currently a wholly owned subsidiary which tightly controls 27 factories and 100 affiliates. MMEI's more than 1,000 factories, by contrast, were fully divested in the mid-1980s, with only R&D and overall strategic and production planning guided by Beijing.

RESEARCH AND DEVELOPMENT

China's emerging industrial policy for information technology calls for the commercialization of basic research combined with limited strategic alliances with foreigners.[8] The state realizes the shortcomings of its domestic industry and understands the importance of both moving its R&D talents into the marketplace, and acquiring technology and research methods from abroad. But China is keen to avoid the branch plant syndrome—assembly rather than true R&D—that characterizes other newly industrialized countries in Asia, notably Hong Kong and Taiwan. Furthermore, China wants to acquire foreign technology but keep its own R&D independent and evolving.

Though well more than a decade has passed, the scientific and technological community is still reeling from the impact of the cultural revolution. Advanced research (with the exception of certain military projects) was brought to a halt between 1966 and 1976, a critical period in the global development of digital electronics. China's progress in integrated circuit technology, by Chinese accounts then virtually on par with the West, essentially ceased. The result is that Chinese information technology is two to three technological generations behind the West. The engineers and technical workers who suffered most effectively lost 10 years of research and practical experience; they are now the industry leaders holding senior and middle management positions.

Recovery from the "decade of chaos" is complicated by deep currents in Chinese science and technology. Basic science has high status in China; applied science does not. One reason for the dichotomy is the distinction the Chinese make between a quest for knowledge and a search for practical application. Technology is the business of packaging the fruits of scientific endeavor, not of seeking truth. Like traditional Chinese military science, Chinese technological modernization attempts to absorb Western technology without absorbing too much of its culture. Deng Xiaoping has said: "We study advanced technology, science and management to serve socialism, but these things do not by themselves have a class character." This is not entirely true. Technology is a highly political activity and the social context in which it is employed, as well as the managerial system which gives rise to it, reflect highly particular organizational philosophies. To make the step into the information age, a technology management infrastructure has to be created—and it will have to be borrowed from abroad.

---

[8] This section is excerpted in its entirety from *Modernising China's Telecommunications*, Chapter 4, "Research and Development."

Some of the effects of Chinese attitudes toward technology, as they affect telecommunications, are as follows:

> The result of a shortage of applied science, or conversely, an overemphasis (from the industrial point of view) on basic research is that China has impressive theoretical potential but little seasoned managerial know how.
>
> Similarly, the advances of basic research do not effectively lead to product innovation. There does not exist an adequate product development cycle (from conception to approval, prototype, testing and production) for important developments. With no technology management, good ideas often never leave the labs.
>
> There are no formal mechanisms for the diffusion of innovations. Chinese technical advances and transferred foreign processes and products often stay within the group which first adopted them, leading to reduplication of research efforts, wasted capital, and limited market penetration.
>
> There is poor allocation of trained personnel due to vertical segmentation of industries and longstanding government policies regulating worker assignments. The R&D environment is not conducive to the cross-fertilization of expertise. The problem is compounded by increased competition and protectionism among newly privatized independent research institutes.

PART II: CONSIDERATIONS FOR AMERICAN POLICY

American strategic policy toward China for more than a decade has been to encourage a stable and prosperous China, and to promote democracy and market-oriented economic activity. Telecommunications, as the salient technology making possible the free flow of information and ideas, is intrinsic to China's progress toward democratic reform. However, the same technologies that make possible the free flow of information are also extraordinarily powerful at restricting it.

In a society like China's—where the need for technological modernization and the potential for political repression are equally great—the power of information networking and processing technology represents a double-edged sword: networking technologies can help decentralize political and economic power, but can also be applied to tighten restrictions on civil liberties. International facsimile transmissions to and from China, for instance, are largely credited with preserving contact with the West during the Tiananmen crisis in June, 1989. At the same time, however, closed circuit CATV cameras in Beijing's streets have been used to identify protestors in the Tiananmen movement, and new call management capabilities are being deployed which enable authorities to potentially intercept and monitor thousands of telephone conversations and fax messages simultaneously from a central source. Similarly, the same satellite and microwave facilities that allowed American audiences to view the movement live were used to restrict coverage to the Chinese public.

Generally speaking, advanced telecommunications networking technology—from telephones and fax to elaborate computer communications architectures—stimulates and distributes economic activity. Networks allow information to flow horizontally within society according to the needs of markets, unimpeded by interference or intervention from bureaucratic control. Modern networks also help reduce computing transaction costs, making data transfers faster and more efficient. These aspects of modern networking directly support American interests to create a strong, market-oriented Chinese economy. Endorsing such progress, however, comes at a cost.

With the introduction of digital switching and optical transmission systems, China's networks will be better able to dodge two important elements of American security interests: network "survivability" and electronic eavesdropping. With latest generation digital central office switches (running the Common Channel Signalling System #7 (SS7) protocol, at present restricted by CoCom), call processing management and intelligence is distributed, and the network can automatically re-route traffic when congestion and outages are encountered. This capability is extremely desirable from a systems administration perspective, and U.S. carriers are rapidly deploying the technology in domestic networks. While SS7 dramatically improves network efficiency, strategic doctrine suggests that an SS7 network could continue operation even after sustaining damage from "surgical strikes" in the event of war. Traditional switching systems, based on a hierarchy, are more vulnerable to disruption. A similar case is made regarding high-speed optical fiber transmission systems. Fiber optics do not radiate electromagnetic signal information (as do conventional copper cables), and so are relatively impervious to existing electronic interception and deciphering techniques. CoCom restricts export of high speed fiber technology to China, paralleling the posture maintained with the Soviet Union; in June, 1990, proposals for a high speed fiber backbone across Siberia were rejected. China currently has indigenous fiber technology and is aggressively investing in optical R&D and manufacturing, and will have widespread optical facilities installed by the turn of the century.

These considerations pose a particularly knotty, and at present unresolved policy question: at what point do the macroeconomic and political advantages gained from improvements in the public network outweigh the liabilities posed to national security concerns? Conflicting positions within the government have led to the current paralysis on the matter, and a clear, unambiguous breakthrough is required for American interests—strategic or commercial—to be fully met in China.

SOFT LOANS

The American competitive position in China is extremely weak compared with Japan, France and Sweden. AT&T, the largest domestic manufacturer of central office network systems, has less than 1 percent share of public network contracts in China, and less than 2 percent share when private networks (such as the military) are included. This inferior market position can be attributed in part to an absence of competitive "soft loan" financing. With the cost of telecommunications infrastructure so great and Chinese buyers so poor, soft loans and concessional "trade aid" have become a sine qua non for most network sales. For many regional telephone bureaus, the use of foreign subsidies is irresistible; as much as 20 percent of Guangdong's capital in the early 1990s may come from abroad.

A U.S.-led embargo on soft loans following the 1989 Tiananmen crackdown was tacitly lifted by mid-1990. The Japanese government has reinstated its commitment to pledge over $5 billion in trade financing to Beijing, a package which includes $300 million in loans slated specifically for telecommunications.

Sweden has underwritten telecommunications contracts in China from 1980–89 worth a total of $183 million, and France contributed an estimated $169 million over the same period. The total value of telecommunications contracts supported by soft loans during the same period for all countries combined amounts to some $727.5 million. This level represents the fourth highest area of infrastructure soft loan spending after electric power, chemical plants, and railroads.[9] Payback terms for government-sponsored concessional loans and mixed-credit packages average 2 to 5 percent with payback over 6–30 years, and may offer a 10–15 year grace period. American firms, armed only with EximBank's token and uncompetitive credits and no concessional funds, continue to be left out of most major development projects.

The issue of potential American soft loan financing for telecommunications projects in China also raises several difficult questions. Specifically, American policymakers need to determine if it is in the nation's strategic interest to ensure American presence in the telecommunications sector in China. With American presence, the U.S. government may be in a better position to assess the relative strengths and weakness of the Chinese information infrastructure. Similarly, the U.S. bargaining position in multilateral export control bodies, notably CoCom, would be more credible if American companies were more viable market actors. Further, American corporations operating in the PRC could extend domestic enterprise network architectures more efficiently on American technology installed abroad.

While these arguments are persuasive, the rationale for spending American tax dollars on more tangible and more immediate opportunities, particularly in a period of budget austerity, are equally compelling. American policy planners must necessarily ask which sector of the population in China would benefit from American trade aid in telecommunications, and how American policy and strategic and industrial interests would gain. The most successful American telecommunications projects in China to date—AT&T's sales to the military, and Motorola's contracts for cellular radio—benefit the established political regime and the nation's elite. Are broader American policy goals of promoting political stability and democratization best met by empowering such groups?

[9] U.S.-China Business Council, "Foreign Soft Loans to China Telecom Projects 1984–89," *China Business Review*, November–December 1989, pp.26–27.

Proponents of trade financing argue that without export credits, only the elite can afford high-cost, high-performance American technology—and that without convincing support from Washington, American firms will be left out of perhaps the largest growth market in the world. Policymakers could best serve U.S. interests by examining carefully the exact network application for credits proposed for the future. Carte blanche spending for telecommunications export projects would be careless; contracts intended to improve the public communications infrastructure, however, could well prove to be a worthwhile investment in China's development program.

CHINA'S ENERGY OUTLOOK

By David Fridley *

CONTENTS

SUMMARY

Economic reform in China has given a major boost to the development of China's energy industries. Demand for energy has risen steadily in response to the rapid expansion of the economy over the past ten years, while economic liberalization and deregulation have stimulated energy output as the energy industries found new sources of capital, labor, and investment opportunities. In the first half of 1980s, the coal, oil, and electric power industries all experienced accelerating rates of growth. After mid-decade, however, an overheating economy, rising inflation, and lower international oil prices had a serious impact on the vitality of the energy industries. At a time when energy demand was soaring, the state-owned energy industries faced a decline in the real value of their output, excessive debt, falling productivity, and sharply higher costs of production. These trends have continued into 1990 despite the economic slowdown engineered in late 1988 and, if left unmanaged, will constrain the ability of the domestic energy industries to meet the energy needs of China's modernization program. This in turn could lead to progressively higher imports of energy, particularly oil, and could limit the speed and scope of economic expansion in the 1990s and beyond.

---

* Research Associate, East-West Center, Honolulu, Hawaii.

I. Overview of the 1980s

The past decade of development in China has wrought enormous changes to the country's economic, political, social, and demographic foundations. The radical shift from strict Maoist central planning to limited market reforms left virtually no one untouched. The economy boomed, sometimes overheating, and the standard of living for nearly all Chinese rose. The energy industries also experienced economic and structural reform in the 1980s, but their strategic importance kept them more closely under central control. Prevented from exercising autonomy over most production and pricing decisions, the energy industries failed to enjoy the boom that deregulation produced in so many other sectors of the economy. Fearing the inflationary consequences of a much-needed rise in domestic coal, oil, gas, and electricity prices, the government stabilized most energy prices, which began to fall rapidly in real terms after mid-decade. As a result, even the immensely profitable refining sector began to see red ink.

Energy output initially fell or stagnated in 1980 and 1981 as the industry closed down many inefficient producers, reduced investment, and reorganized its administrative structure. By 1982, output began to rebound, boosted by the adoption of a second, higher tier of prices applied to marginal (above-quota) production. Except for the natural gas sector, which remained in a prolonged slump, all energy sectors experienced healthy rates of output growth in the first half of the decade, lulling planners into a false optimism about an easing energy crunch. With stockpiles of coal growing and electricity output rising rapidly, investment was scaled back, especially in large state-run energy projects, and price reform was repeatedly put off.

After 1985, a number of factors contributed to a slowdown in energy output. High inflation robbed the industry of part of its purchasing power, and delays in commissioning of new capacity and underutilization of existing plants plagued the coal and power sector. Shocked by the electricity shortages of 1984–85, planners redirected investment capital to the power industry without full coordination in the production and transport of sufficient coal supplies to the new plants. Nevertheless, by 1989, output of hydropower and coal managed to expand by 100% and 68% respectively over 1980, while crude oil output rose by 30%. The laggard has been natural gas; suffering from decades of underinvestment, high costs, and low prices, the industry barely managed to exceed the output level reached a decade earlier (Table 1).[1]

While growth in energy output slowed in the latter part of the 1980s, demand shot up (Table 2). Double-digit growth in virtually every sector of the economy (with the notable exception of agricul-

---

[1] Conversion standards used here are those adopted by the State Statistical Bureau, based on a coal equivalent (ce) value of 7,000 kcal/kg (29,307 kJ). Raw coal output (5,000 kcal/kg) is converted at 0.7143 kg/kgce; crude oil (10,000 kcal/kg) at 1.4286 kg/kgce; natural gas 9,310 kcal/m³) at 1.33 kg/m³, and electricity, including hydropower and thermal power, at the average rate of coal-equivalent consumption per kWh generated each year. In the 1980s, this ranged from 413g/kWh to 397g/kWh. Conversion of crude and aggregate product volumes to barrels per day (b/d) is based on a standard 7.3 barrels per ton, while individual products are converted based on their specific gravities. Tce figures are first calculated in oil equivalent (oe) volumes before conversion to barrels per day.

Table 1
Primary Energy Production, 1980-89

	Coal ('000 tons)	Oil ('000 b/d)	Electricity (GWh)	Natural Gas (million m³)	Total ('000 bdoe)
1980	620,150	2,119	58,200	14,270	8,923
1981	621,640	2,024	65,500	12,740	8,852
1982	666,330	2,042	74,400	11,930	9,349
1983	714,530	2,121	86,400	12,210	9,978
1984	789,230	2,292	86,800	12,430	10,898
1985	872,280	2,498	92,400	12,930	11,976
1986	894,040	2,614	94,500	13,760	12,337
1987	927,960	2,683	100,000	13,890	12,777
1988	979,880	2,741	109,100	13,910	13,412
1989	1,040,000	2,752	116,400	14,900	14,076
Average Annual Growth (%)					
1980-85	7.1	3.3	9.7	(2.0)	6.1
1985-89	4.5	2.5	5.9	3.6	4.1

Source: State Statistical Bureau, *China Energy Statistical Yearbook 1989* (Beijing: Statistical Bureau Press), Feb. 1990, p. 81. Hereafter cited as *CESY 1989*.

Table 2
Final Energy Consumption, 1980-88

	Coal ('000 tons)	Oil* ('000 b/d)	Electricty (GWh)	Natural Gas** (million m³)	Total ('000 bdoe)
1980	388,042	1,262	276,340	13,660	6,995
1981	391,890	1,188	284,070	11,970	6,949
1982	416,831	1,198	301,780	11,440	7,286
1983	448,736	1,240	324,410	11,650	7,760
1984	487,805	1,309	348,400	12,120	8,354
1985	527,044	1,370	381,330	12,370	8,995
1986	516,779	1,479	417,490	12,850	9,213
1987	544,870	1,595	462,400	12,820	9,852
1988	577,052	1,706	508,730	13,510	10,557
Average Annual Growth (%)					
1980-85	6.3	1.7	6.7	(2.0)	5.2
1985-88	3.1	7.6	10.1	3.0	5.5

Source: *CESY 1989*, various pages.
*Including non-power direct crude burning.
**Including oil/gas field use.

ture) created immense strains on the infrastructure for energy production, conversion, transportation, and distribution. Growing shortages of petroleum products induced the government to relax import restrictions on both products and crude oil. A worsening shortfall in electricity production led a number of coastal provinces to import diesel fuel for use in small and inefficient power generators, and a growing volume of above-quota fuel oil began to find its way back to mothballed oil-fired plants. Faced with these fuel and power shortages, many localities adopted the much-publicized policy of *ting san, kai si*—closing plants for three days of the week—and a growing number of urban residents suffered from regular rolling blackouts. Although the three-year economic "readjustment" policy adopted in September 1988 brought economic growth to a virtual standstill by early 1990, energy demand continued its sustained rise, fueled by a high level of suppressed demand that heretofore had remained unsatisfied. In 1989 and 1990, a number of top officials admitted that China is facing a prolonged and chronic energy shortage. [2]

COAL

The coal industry forms the backbone of China's energy economy. Accounting for 73% of total primary energy production and an even higher 76% of consumption (on a calorific basis), coal has found widespread use in industry, transport, household consumption, and as a chemical feedstock. Few other major economies in the world—Eastern Germany, Poland, and Czechoslovakia aside— have such a high dependence on coal in their energy mix.

The 1980s was a period of rapid development of the coal industry, characterized by large-scale investment in central mines, promotion of local mines, and expansion of collective and individual-run mines. Production fell in 1980 from the 1979 high of 635 million tons but resumed its upward trend in 1981. Although the coal industry ended the decade with production two-thirds higher than in 1980, much of the growth came from local mines, which accounted for 75% of the increase between 1980 and 1988; village mines in turn accounted for 70% of the increase in local mine output (Table 3). [3] Village mines currently number about 79,000, of which more than half are unlicensed. In general, they are under-capitalized, under-mechanized, and unsafe, with a mortality rate 4.5 times higher than in central mines.

Production capacity expanded significantly during the 1980s. State investment of over Y45 billion added 165 million tons of new central-mine production capacity between 1980 and 1988, including large collieries of 4 million-ton capacity at Kailuan and Datong. [4] China's largest foreign investment to date, the 15 million-ton Antaibao open-cast mine at Pingshuo, Shanxi, constructed as a joint venture with Occidental of the United States, also began production.

With foreign trade playing only a minor balancing role, coal consumption rose in parallel to production (Table 4). The most rapid increase occurred in the power sector; with the commissioning of numerous new coal-fired plants after 1985, demand growth accelerated to around 12% per year. Rapid growth in the iron and steel industry led to a revival of demand for coking coal, while industrial use grew steadily throughout the decade at an average 6.6%. A decision to move away from steam engines to more efficient diesel- and electric-power-driven locomotives caused transport demand for coal to fall slightly after 1985. A slowdown was also evident in the

[2] See, for example, the report by Ye Qing, Deputy Director of the State Planning Commission at the Working Meeting on the Conservation and Comprehensive Utilization of National Resources, January 1990, as reprinted in *Zhongguo Nengyuan* (Energy in China), no. 1, 1990, pp. 13–17.

[3] Following Chinese usage, "central" mines refer to those mines under central jurisdiction of the China National Coal Corporation and its related companies in the Northeast and Inner Mongolia. Output from these mines is allocated centrally (*tongpei*), and prices are fixed by he state. "Local" mines refer to state-owned mines under control of the province, county, or district, while "village" mines (*xiangzhen eikuang*) are collectively and individually run enterprises.

[4] *CESY 1989*, p. 22. This figure excludes new capacity from "renovation and transformation" investment, which totalled more than Y18 billion between 1980 and 1988.

Table 3
Coal Production, 1980-89
(million tons)

| | Total | State-Run Mines | | Local Mines | |
		Subtotal	%	Subtotal	"Village" Mines
1980	620	344	55.5	276	105
1981	622	335	53.9	287	117
1982	666	350	52.6	316	137
1983	715	363	50.8	352	159
1984	789	395	50.1	394	195
1985	872	406	46.6	466	238
1986	894	414	46.3	480	243
1987	928	420	45.3	508	261
1988	980	434	44.3	546	295
1989	1,040	480	46.1	560	na
Average Annual Growth (%)					
1980-85	7.1	3.3		11.0	17.8
1985-89	4.5	4.3		4.7	7.4*

*1985-1988.
Source: CESY 1989, p. 83. 1989 figures are preliminary.

Table 4
Coal Consumption, 1980-88
(million tons)

	Total	Power Generation	Coking	Industry	Transport	Household Use	Stock Change*
1980	626.0	126.5	66.8	216.4	19.3	115.7	10.2
1981	624.3	127.0	59.1	214.5	20.9	120.9	7.3
1982	658.7	134.3	60.8	231.6	21.7	124.6	(3.3)
1983	697.6	143.2	63.9	253.8	21.9	130.6	(12.5)
1984	767.7	159.4	69.6	278.4	22.8	139.8	(17.1)
1985	827.8	164.4	73.0	297.1	23.1	156.2	(39.1)
1986	875.9	180.1	80.6	311.3	23.0	158.2	(13.5)
1987	935.3	202.9	87.7	338.5	22.4	164.9	16.2
1988	999.1	228.3	88.8	360.9	22.6	175.3	30.8
Average Annual Increase (%)							
1980-85	5.7	5.4	1.8	6.5	3.6	6.2	
1985-88	6.5	11.6	6.7	6.7	(0.8)	3.9	

*positive figures are stock withdrawals.
Source: CESY 1989, p. 228-244.

household sector, where a concerted program of fuel substitution reduced incremental demand for coal (see Natural Gas, below).The rapid increase in production from local mines in the early 1980s allowed the accumulation of large stockpiles of coal; nearly 100 million tons of coal accumulated at minemouths by 1986. Although transport constraints were in part responsible for the stockpiling, planners mistakenly regarded this "surplus" as a sign that the squeeze on coal supplies was easing. By 1989, however, it became evident that demand was outstripping supply, and shortages were being avoided only by drawing down on stocks, which were largely depleted by the end of 1988. The current shortage of electric power, most severe in the coastal regions, is exacerbated by a growing shortage of coal. [5]

The geographical mismatch between coal production and consumption centers has necessitated the transport of hundreds of millions of tons of coal each year. Coal is the single largest commodity carried by China's railroads, accounting for an average 40% of the total volume of shipments throughout the 1980s (Table 5). Nearly 15% of all domestic coal shipments originate in Shanxi province, which in 1988 dispatched more than 122 million tons from central mines alone, and this figure is expected to top 300 million tons by the end of the century. Destinations are less concentrated; eight provinces, all located on China's eastern coast, received more than 10 million tons of centrally allocated coal in 1988, with Liaoning alone taking delivery of 24 million tons. [6] A small, but growing, volume of coal reaches international markets. Major expansions at the northern China ports of Qinhuangdao and Shijiusuo have allowed coal exports to reach 15 million tons in 1989, but numerous officials in the National Coal Corporation question the wisdom of coal exports given the tightness of supply in the domestic market. Coal imports, stable at around 2 million tons a year, are largely the result of barter trade with North Korea, though some specialty coals are imported for industry.

Table 5
Domestic Coal Transport and International Trade
(million tons)

	Domestic Transport				Export	Import
	Total	Rail	Road	Water		
1981	..	424.95	..	..	6.57	1.93
1982	..	450.62	..	..	6.44	2.19
1983	..	473.21	..	..	6.56	2.14
1984	751.64	500.92	159.35	91.37	6.96	2.49
1985	791.23	534.31	159.47	97.45	7.77	2.31
1986	820.89	547.86	167.61	105.42	6.83	1.94
1987	839.67	562.60	164.59	112.48	9.95	1.72
1988	872.37	585.62	162.46	124.29	12.41	1.69
1989	..	..	..	..	15.34	2.29

Note: ..—not available.
Source: CESY 1989, p. 370; China Customs Statistics.

UPSTREAM OIL

As one of the first sectors of the Chinese economy to open to the outside world, the petroleum industry benefited quickly from access to foreign markets. After falling from a peak of 2.12 million b/d in 1979 to 2.02 million b/d in 1981, onshore production began to rise as new technologies were imported and introduced into the domestic oil fields. At Daqing, the granddaddy of China's oil fields and the source of the bulk of China's crude exports, infill drilling and the widespread use of submersible pumps brought production

---

[5] The 1989 shortfall was estimated at 30 million tons. See Jiang Xianrong, Ministry of Energy, "Review of and Outlook for Conservation Work in China," Zhongguo Nengyuan, no. 5, 1989, p. 41.

[6] CESY 1989, p. 369.

up to 1.1 million b/d in 1985, peaking at 1.11 million b/d in 1988. Shengli oil field was the big hope of the 1980s, as expanded exploration and improved drilling techniques boosted output by nearly 12% a year from 1980 to 1985. Total output reached nearly 2.5 million b/d in 1985, with growth averaging 5.4% a year since 1981.

Since 1985, the increases have slowed sharply, and in 1989 total crude output grew a mere 0.4% over 1988. Part of the slowdown was due to the faster-than-expected decline in the Huabei oil field south of Beijing. This so-called "buried hill structure" is not well understood geologically, and its decline by nearly 50% from 1985 to 1989 exceeded even the most pessimistic forecasts. Unfortunately, this oil field is the source of a significant proportion of Beijing's natural gas supply, which may indicate that the plans for expanding gas use in Beijing to displace coal may be set back. Smaller fields, such as Zhongyuan in Henan and Karamay in Xinjiang, have been the main source of expansion outside the main fields, but together with a dozen other small fields contribute only about 20% of total output.

The other big hope for increasing oil production in the 1980s was the offshore areas. In the 10 years since the first Western companies began seismic surveys, the results have been disappointing. In general, the geology has been unfavorable—highly fractured small structures—meaning high costs and low yields. Furthermore, after international oil prices crashed in 1986, Western companies reduced expenditures, and some withdrew altogether. Nevertheless, in 1985, the first joint Sino-Japanese field came onstream in the Bohai, followed by two smaller fields brought on in 1987 and 1989, but total production has reached only 10,000 b/d. The total (France) find in the Beibu Gulf off southern China was first expected to produce up to 20,000 b/d itself, but again geology and technical problems have kept production below 8,000 b/d. In 1990, the Huizhou field, discovered and developed by the ACT (Agip-Chevron-Texaco) consortium, began production, bringing total offshore production to over 20,000 b/d for the first time. This will be followed in 1991 by production from the JHN Lufeng 13-1 field in the Pearl River Basin, which is expected to add 10-15,000 b/d to the total.

DOWNSTREAM OIL

The refining industry as well has undergone a significant transformation in the 1980s. [7] After shutting down a number of small refineries in the early 1980s and consolidating most of the rest under Sinopec—the China National Petrochemical Corporation—in 1983, China embarked on a program of refinery upgrading to reduce the output of fuel oil and increase the output of more valuable products such as gasoline, kerosene, diesel, and petrochemical feedstocks. After some US$10 billion in expenditures, primary distillation capacity has reached 2.4 million b/d—fifth largest in the world—and China now has the highest ratio of upgrading capacity to distillation after the United States (Table 6).

---

[7] For further details on the Chinese refining sector, see David Fridley, *From Toppers to Bottoms: a Survey of the Chinese Refining System* (Washington, DC: US Department of Energy), Jan. 1988.

Table 6
Upgrading to Distillation Ratios: International Comparisons, 1989
('000 b/d)

	China*		US		Japan		Indonesia	
	Capacity	% Dist.	Capacity	% Dist.	Capacity	% Dist.	Capacity	% Dist.
Distillation	2,213	100	15,418	100	4,199	100	714	100
FCC/RCC	685	31	4,749	31	617	15	13	2
Hydrocracking	100	5	1,078	7	153	4	100	14
Thermal#	295	13	1,730	11	86	2	82	11
Reforming	112	5	3,528	23	532	13	62	9
Total Upgrading	1,192	54	11,085	72	1,388	33	256	36

*Sinopec only.
#includes coking, visbreaking, and thermal cracking.
Source: Oil and Gas Journal, 26 December 1989; personal communication.

After declining for a few years in the early 1980s, throughput rose only slowly as the export market received preference over the domestic refiners. This policy was changed in 1986, as low international prices, combined with a rising volume of suppressed demand in China, led the government to reallocate more crude to the domestic system. Since 1986, throughput (including non-Sinopec refineries under the China National Oil and Gas Corporation [CNOGC], the former Ministry of Petroleum) has risen an average of more than 100,000 b/d each year; in 1990, total runs are expected to rise a further 90,000–100,000 b/d (Table 7).

Table 7
China's Petroleum Product Output, 1980-89

	1980	1985	1989	1980	1985	1989	Growth, 80-89
	Million tons			Thousand b/d			%
Gasoline	10.8	14.4	20.6	252	335	480	90.5
Kerosene	4.0	4.0	4.0	85	85	85	0.0
Diesel	18.3	19.9	25.7	363	394	509	40.2
Fuel Oil	28.7	28.4	30.2	521	515	548	5.2
Throughput	78.7	84.5	107.2	1,574	1,690	2,144	36.2

Source: Sinopec.

Gasoline output has increased the most rapidly, primarily owing to the overwhelming reliance on catalytic cracking in secondary processing and the high profits from gasoline production. Kerosene production has remained flat in the 1980s, but output of lamp kerosene—which is consumed largely in rural areas and accounts for about one-third of the total—has actually fallen, while jet fuel production has jumped in response to the expansion of the domestic and international airline network. Output of diesel fuel, the mainstay of China's product mix, has risen less dramatically than gasoline, despite burgeoning demand from the agricultural, industrial, and power sectors, and has only slightly outpaced growth in throughput over this period. Since 1988, with diesel imports soaring, there has been a steady reorientation toward maximizing diesel production, and output promises to jump to 600,000 b/d in 1990. Fuel oil output (including the volume used as refinery fuel) has remained nearly flat at about 530,000 b/d, but its yield as a proportion of throughput has fallen from 40% in 1980 to 28% in 1989. [8]

Production of nonenergy-use products has increased significantly as well. Other products—including chemical feedstock, lubricants, asphalt, coke, paraffin, and solvents—now yield over 14% on throughput, with growth in chemical feedstock production paralleling the expansion of ethylene and other petrochemical facilities. Lubricants production has been stagnant in the 1980s; 1990 production of 37,000 b/d is virtually the same as in 1980. Despite good feedstocks from Daqing vacuum gas oil, lube production facilities are relatively simple, and China is still reliant on imported lubricants for many of its modern automobiles and much of its imported machine stock.

Since 1986, consumption of petroleum products has outpaced the rise in refinery throughput. By loosening regulations on imports, China allowed many once-deficit regions to import products for local use. With diesel being in greatest shortage, especially in the developed coastal regions, imports rose dramatically, from near zero in 1985 to over 80,000 b/d in 1989. Guangdong and other coal-short regions in the south have imported fuel oil, while gasoline imports remain for the most part limited to retail outlets in the Special Economic Zones, largely owing to high (85%) custom duties levied on imports for inland delivery. [9] Domestic consumption has also been boosted from a reduction in product exports. Since peaking in 1985, total product exports have fallen by nearly 30,000 b/d, although this decline has been stemmed by surging refinery throughput; exports in 1990 are expected to rise from their 1989 levels. Higher throughput, however, has required the expansion of crude oil imports, despite a 22% drop in crude exports since 1985. The majority of crude imports come from Indonesia—whose heavy waxy crude is very similar to most Chinese grades—and from Oman, which produces a low-sulfur (0.8%) crude suitable for Chinese refineries and yielding larger volumes of much-needed middle distillates. Since 1985, the total shift in China's oil trade has reached 330,000 b/d, equivalent to the total consumption in Thailand in 1989 (Table 8).

Trade with Japan and Singapore dominated in the 1980s. Since establishment of a government-to-government deal for crude exports in the late 1970s, Japan has remained China's largest export market. Although the long-term contract is set at 180,000 b/d until 1991, Japan regularly imports 80,000–100,000 b/d in addition from the spot market, primarily of Daqing. The bulk of Daqing imports, however, are not refined; its low sulfur content makes it a favored crude for direct burning in power plants.

China's exports to Singapore commenced in 1980, but volumes remained below 10,000 b/d until a long-term processing deal for 60,000 b/d was agreed upon in 1984. Within one year, exports for processing in Singapore shct up to over 160,000 b/d, leading to severe downward pressure on the regional price of low-sulfur waxy

---

[8] In weight-percent terms.
[9] China National Chemical Import and Export Corporation (Sinochem), personal communication.

Table 8
China's Crude and Product Trade, 1980-89
('000 b/d)

	Exports				Imports			
	Crude	%	Products	%	Crude	%	Products	%
1980	266		84		7		neg.	
1981	275	3.4	92	9.5	1	(85.7)	neg.	
1982	304	10.6	105	14.1	13	1,200.0	neg.	
1983	304	0.0	102	(2.9)	7	(46.2)	neg.	
1984	446	46.7	116	13.7	5	(28.6)	neg.	
1985	623	39.7	124	6.9	0	(100.0)	1	
1986	570	(8.5)	109	(12.1)	9		39	3,800.0
1987	545	(4.4)	99	(9.2)	0	(100.0)	40	2.6
1988	521	(4.4)	96	(3.0)	17		61	52.5
1989	487	(6.5)	95	(1.0)	65	282.4	107	75.4

Note: neg.—negligible.

Source: CESY 1989, China's Customs Statistics. Before 1985, import and export figures were collected by the Ministry of Foreign Economic Relations and Trade (MOFERT), which recorded trade only within its system. Inconsistencies with Customs figures arise from the MOFERT practice of recording trade based on the date of contract signing, and, in the case of crude, recording as imports crude oil which was actually resold in Singapore. Since 1985, Customs figures have been recognized officially.

resid (LSWR). By increasing the proportion of higher sulfur Shengli crude in the export mix, China reduced the output imbalance, but Singapore was already beginning to lose its significance in China's export strategy. With booming regional oil demand after 1986, Singapore refiners found it more profitable to increase runs of Middle Eastern crudes, and to increase runs on their own accounts. Processing fees, which were once as low as $0.55 per barrel, rose to over $1.30 by late 1989 and early 1990, sharply reducing China's incentive for Singapore processing. Total crude exports to Singapore fell to 70,000 b/d in 1989.

NATURAL GAS

Natural gas production in China began growing in importance with the discovery and exploitation of the vast natural gas fields in Sichuan province. From a mere 290 million m^3 in 1959 (the year the Daqing oilfield was discovered), production jumped to over 1 billion m^3 in 1960—98% of which was nonassociated gas—and nearly tripled again by the beginning of the 1970s. With development of the extensive associated gas reserves in the major oilfields, total production rose to a peak of 14.5 billion m^3 in 1979, after which the industry entered a prolonged period of stagnation. By 1982, production had fallen 18%.

China's natural gas production is small in relation to its potential reserve base and crude oil production. Table 9 compares the major non-OPEC oil and gas producers; China is ranked fourth in oil production but twelfth in natural gas. On an oil-equivalence basis, the ratio of oil and gas production in the United States and the Soviet Union is roughly one-to-one, but in China, gas production totals less than one-tenth of crude output. Natural gas constitutes less than 3% of the national primary energy supply, whereas oil supplies 20%. Nearly all gasfields suffered from the cutback in production in the early 1980s, with the notable exception of the

Zhongyuan field, located in the Yellow River valley in Henan province. Discovered in the late 1970s, Zhongyuan has also become China's fourth largest oil field, surpassing Huabei, which is now in a period of rapid decline. A concerted program of exploration in the Dongpu depression, in which Zhongyuan is located, has increased natural gas reserves at a rate of more than 10 billion m^3 per year, and, on average, every ton of crude oil produced from this area contains 100 m^3 of dissolved gas. [10] In 1988, despite rapid growth, the 1.29 billion m^3 of output from Zhongyuan ranked it fourth in associated gas production after Daqing (2.23 billion m^3), Liaohe (1.64 billion m^3), Shengli (1.42 billion m^3), though it is far larger than the Xinjiang (460 million m^3), Dagang (391 million m^3) and Huabei (209 million m^3) fields. [11]

Table 9
Oil and Gas Production by Major Non-OPEC Countries, 1989

		Oil				Natural Gas (Oil Equiv.)	
		mill. tonnes	'000 b/d			mill. tonnes	'000 b/d
1	USSR	607.5	12,150	1	USSR	644.5	12,890
2	USA	433.8	8,676	2	USA	438.4	8,768
3	Mexico	141.2	2,824	3	Canada	88.2	1,764
4	China	138.3	2,766	4	Netherlands	52.9	1,058
5	United Kingdom	91.9	1838.0	5	Algeria	40.2	804
6	Canada	80.2	1,604	6	United Kingdom	37.9	758
7	Norway	74.9	1,498	7	Norway	28.8	576
8	Libya	54.8	1,096	8	Mexico	23.9	478
9	Algeria	50.4	1,008	9	Argentina	21.6	432
10	Egypt	44.5	890	10	Italy	15.3	306
11	India	34.2	684	11	West Germany	13.6	272
12	Brazil	30.9	618	12	China	12.9	258

Source: *BP Statistical Review of World Energy*, (London: British Petroleum), June 1990.

Sichuan province, location of China's major nonassociated gas fields, is currently the largest natural gas producer and accounts for more than 40% of China's total. Its importance is heightened by the fact that, at 90%, Sichuan has the highest ratio of commercial sales to production and accounts for more than 60% of national sales. Other gas producers such as Daqing, Liaohe, and Shengli consume a significant proportion of their production in oilfield uses. In 1987, for example, total commercial natural gas sales from all oil/gas fields amounted to 8.4 billion m^3, or only 61% of total production of 13.76 billion m^3. [12] At the Daqing field in far northeastern China, where ambient temperatures are often far below the 60 F pour-point of Daqing crude, less that one-third of natural gas production is sold commercially. Much of the gas is used to heat crude for pipeline transportation, while some is reserved for reinjection and for household use by oilfield workers. Nationally, an average 20–30 m^3 of gas is burned per ton of oil transported. Low heater efficiency (about 60% compared to 85% in developed

---

[10] *Almanac of China's Economy 1987* (Beijing: Economic Management Press), 1987, p. VI-41.
[11] *CESY 1989*, p. 127.
[12] *Almanac of China's Economy 1988*, (Beijing: Economic Management Press), 1988, p. V-21.

countries) and a lack of natural gas transport facilities lead to high use and waste by fields. [13]

Consumption of natural gas is dominated by industry. In 1988, industrial consumption (including oil/gas field use) reached 11.9 billion m³, or 83% of the total. The balance was consumed by the construction industry (760 million m³, 5%), household/residential use (1.53 billion m³, 11%), and transport and other uses (170 million m³, 1%). Within industry, two-thirds of the commercial volume of natural gas is consumed by fertilizer plants, both as feedstock and fuel. Other major industrial users include the metallurgical and synthetic fiber industries; a declining share of the gas—290 million m³ in 1988—is used for power generation. Fastest growth has been recorded in residential consumption, which increased from 0.2 billion m³ in 1980 to 1.53 billion m³ in 1988. Currently, over 5.3 million people are served by natural gas in the cities of Beijing, Tianjin, Shenyang, Dalian, Zhengzhou, Chengdu, and Chongqing. [14]

ELECTRIC POWER

Electric power has recorded the fastest growth of all energy forms in the 1980s yet remains most seriously in short supply. Development of the industry since 1980 has been characterized by an initial concentration on hydropower development, followed by a sustained effort to expand thermal generation capacity and to replace oil with coal. In 1980, thermal generation accounted for 80% of total output of 300 TWh, falling to 75% in 1983, then rebounding to 81% in the first half of 1990 (Table 10).

Table 10
Power Generation Capacity and Output, 1980-89

	Capacity (MW)			Output (TWh)		
	Thermal	Hydro	Total	Thermal	Hydro	Total
1980	45,549	20,320	65,869	242.4	58.2	300.6
1981	47,203	21,930	69,133	243.8	65.5	309.3
1982	49,400	22,960	72,360	253.3	74.4	327.7
1983	52,280	24,165	76,445	265.0	86.4	351.4
1984	54,517	25,600	80,117	290.2	86.8	377.0
1985	60,638	26,415	87,053	318.3	92.4	410.7
1986	66,277	27,542	93,819	355.1	94.5	449.6
1987	72,710	30,190	102,900	397.3	100.0	497.3
1988	82,800	32,700	115,500	436.0	109.2	545.2
1989	na	na	124,500	462.7	117.1	579.8
Average Annual Growth (%)						
1980-85	5.9	5.4	5.7	5.6	9.7	6.4
1985-89	10.9*	7.4*	9.4	7.4	8.1	7.6

*to 1988.
Note: na—not available.
Source: *CESY 1989*, p. 137.

---

[13] Qu Shiyuan and Dong Luying, "Study of the Rational Utilization of China's Natural Gas," *Zhongguo Nengyuan*, No. 3, 1986, p.4.
[14] *CESY 1989*, p. 376. Nearly 10 million people are served by low-BTU town gas from coking plants and gasification plants. In 1988, total own gas consumption reached 1.72 billion m³, up from 1.37 billion m³ in 1980. Over 14 million people have access to LPG, consumption of which totalled 1.32 million tons in 1988, equivalent to 1.9 billion m³ of natural gas.

Thermal power generation has become increasingly reliant on coal. In 1980, coal constituted 82% of total fuel use (coal, oil, and gas), but with the displacement of oil by coal, oil consumption in power generation has fallen from 400,000 b/d in 1980 to 300,000 b/d in 1988, with coal now providing 95% of total fuel supply. [15] This heavy reliance on coal has created logistical and transport problems, as the major thermal power plants are concentrated in the eastern and northeast coastal provinces, while supplies are sourced from the major coal mining regions of interior Shanxi, Inner Mongolia and Shaanxi provinces. Even distant Guangdong province, which has few indigenous energy resources, is heavily reliant on Shanxi coal to fuel its coal-fired plants.

As the industry grew in the 1980s, new and larger generation and transmission facilities were developed. In 1980, the majority of generating units were rated 200 MW or less, but at the end of 1988, China had brought on line two (imported) 600 MW units, and 32 units of 300–350 MW capacity out of a total of 296 units of 100 MW or larger. Units were imported from Japan, France, Italy, the Soviet Union, and Eastern Europe, and these imported plants now account for nearly 20% of total generation capacity. [16] Transmission lines have increased both in length and capacity. From zero in 1980, China now has nearly 6,000 km of 500-kV transmission lines, while the length of 330-kV lines has risen nearly 500% and 220-kV lines have tripled in length to over 65,000 km. Major grids have developed in North China, East China, Central China, and the Northeast.

Nevertheless, electric power shortages have worsened in virtually all parts of the country as growth in power output has averaged only half that of GNP growth. In 1988, China was short an estimated 78 TWh of electricity, or 14% of actual generation, but this number is widely regarded as understated since the estimate was based on minimal needs for industry, agriculture, and transport without consideration of urban and household demand. [17] In certain provinces such as Guangdong, estimates of power shortages range from 25% to 35%. These shortages have resulted in billions of yuan of lost output and have caused considerable inconvenience to urban dwellers, who often find themselves in the dark at least once a day. One indication of the magnitude of the shortage is the ratio of power generation capacity to power consumption capacity as measured in megawatts; in 1982, this ratio stood at 1:2.1 but had grown to 1:2.8 by 1988, compared to a preferred ratio of 1:1.7. [18] Contrary to recent official statements, the much publicized trend of expanded home use of consumer electronics and appliances such as washing machines and refrigerators has had little impact on the worsening power crisis; household consumption capacity remains at less than 10% of the national total and actual consumption at less

[15] *CESY 1989*, p. 154. Oil use includes direct burning of crude (47,000 b/d in 1988), fuel oil (214,000 b/d) and diesel (39,000 b/d).

[16] Chen Wangxiang, Xie Aidi, China Electric Power Industry Association, "Review the Past, Look to the Future," *Zhongguo Nengyuan*, no. 5, 1989, p. 46.

[17] Xia Meixiu, Ministry of Energy, "Analysis of the Crisis in Quota-Price Electricity," *Zhongguo Nengyuan*, no. 1, 1989, p. 27.

[18] Zheng Gongchang, "The Energy Industry Must Grasp Both the Present and the Long-Term," *Zhongguo Nengyuan*, no. 1, 1989, p. 8.

than 7% of the total. In contrast, industry accounted for over 78% of final consumption in 1988.

NUCLEAR

China's nuclear plans have been scaled back considerably from the initial target of 20,000 MW of capacity on line by the year 2000. Current plans include three major goals: first, to have 6,000 MW of capacity completed by 2000; second, to have an additional 6,000 MW under construction by 2000; and third, to bring on line 1,200 MW of capacity each year after 2000. Though of more modest scale than earlier plans, this target as well may be compromised by a lack of financial and technical resources (Table 11).

Table 11
China's Nuclear Power Program

Location	Capacity (MWe)	Type	Vendor	Status
Qinshan 1	300	PWR	Domestic	UC, end 1990
Daya Bay	2x900	PWR	Framatome (reactor); GEC (turbine)	UC, 1992 (1), 1993 (2)
Qinshan 2	2x600	PWR	Domestic; cooperation with Germany	Approved, under negotiation
Liaoning	2x1000	PWR	USSR	Planned, under negotiation
Guangdong	2x900-1000	PWR	na	Planned
Local	300	PWR	Domestic	Under negotiation

Note: UC—under construction.
Source: Lu Yingzhong, Director, Institute of Techno-economics and Energy System Analysis, Beijing, "The Challenges and the Hope: Nuclear Energy in Asia, Status and Prospects," paper presented at the American Nuclear Society Annual Meeting, Nashville, TN, June 10-14, 1990, p. 9.

China's first domestically designed commercial plant—the 300 MW pressurized water reactor (PWR) at Qinshan in Zhejiang province near Shanghai—is scheduled to be synchronized with the East China grid in late 1990 or early 1991, while the first 900 MW unit of the Daya Bay nuclear plant in Guangdong province, is expected to begin generation in 1992, followed by the second 900 MW unit in 1993. Currently, China is considering the construction of a second plant in Guangdong of 1,800–2,000 MW capacity and plans to follow the commissioning of the Qinshan plant with a second employing domestically designed 600 MW units now under development. After the visit of Prime Minister Li Peng to Moscow in 1990, China announced that it would import nuclear technology from the Soviet Union for installation in Liaoning province, which is home to China's highest concentration of industry. This plant would also be of the PWR design and have a total capacity of 2,000 MW. Aimed at solving the serious shortage of electricity in the major coastal industrial areas, nuclear power "bases" are being developed for Guangdong, Liaoning, and the Yangzi River Delta region.

II. CHALLENGES IN THE ENERGY SECTOR

The partial nature of the economic reforms in the 1980s have put China's energy industries in a classic "squeeze." Controls on many elements of cost to the industries—such as material prices, interest rates, and wages—were loosened considerably, while output prices remained fixed by the government. This squeeze is a major cause of the deterioration of the industries' performance in the latter part of the 1980s, but it has coincided with a number of other developments which present immense challenges to industry revitalization.

PRICING, COSTS, AND FINANCIAL PERFORMANCE

Energy pricing policy in China has been based primarily on the provision of low-cost energy to the industrial sector. With the broadening of economic reforms in the 1980s, pricing became a central issue in the reform of the energy industries. The major development during this period was the adoption of "double-track" pricing, which involved the establishment of a higher price—usually 2 to 3 times higher—for oil, coal, natural gas, and electric power produced above planned or contracted levels or produced from collective or private mines and plants. The intent of this reform was to promote marginal production, since producers were able to sell the above-quota amounts directly to end users without guidance from state plans. The effects of this policy were quite pronounced in the early and mid-1980s, but rising production costs and falling profits have wiped out many of the early gains (Table 12).

Table 12
Costs Increases and Losses in the Energy Sector*, 1980-88

	Change in Costs (%)				Total Reported Losses (million yuan)			
	Oil/Gas	Refining	Coal	Power	Oil/Gas	Refining	Coal	Power
1981	5.93	na	(5.68)	2.40				
1982	7.87	na	(2.08)	6.87				
1983	2.95	na	(1.03)	5.38	na			
1984	2.05	na	4.67	5.95				
1985	10.12	na	22.25	6.47	1	1	1,571	123
1986	9.90	1.88	8.03	8.69	18	9	2,218	213
1987	4.21	2.27	4.67	7.73	199	1	2,624	270
1988	21.86	13.84	14.16	13.20	1,142	2	3,011	709

*state-owned independent accounting units only.
Source: State Statistical Bureau, *China Statistical Yearbook*, various years.

The oil industry was among the first to adopt the two-tiered pricing system. The price of the oil produced within the state plan (quota oil) remained at the Y100 per ton level set in the 1970s, while above-quota production was set at the *yuan* equivalent of international prices prevailing in 1982. Daqing crude, for example, was priced at Y650 per ton ($45/bbl). [19] Petroleum products also received new above-quota prices, although essential fuels such as diesel and fuel oil remained heavily subsidized.

The new pricing system played an important role in the rapid expansion of onshore oil production in the early 1980s, and it created a favorable environment for the development of offshore deposits. Price reform in other sectors of the economy, however, has created unexpected pressures on the industry. Deregulation in other sectors such as steel, cement, machinery, and other basic construction materials led to a surge in their prices, forcing oil production costs up at an unprecedented rate. At the same time, the industry faced an average 20% per year increase in the price of imported equip-

---

[19] Yuan-to-US dollar conversions are based on the period average exchange rate of the year in question.

ment, compounded by frequent devaluations of the yuan before 1986. In 1980, crude production costs averaged Y44 per ton but by 1988 had reached nearly Y100, or the price received for each ton of quota crude production. [20]

Changes in the international market also had an unfavorable impact. With the collapse in international prices in 1986, the domestic above-quota price (for Daqing crude) was lowered to Y545 per ton ($21/bbl), resulting in a sharp drop in income from above-quota production. Even with a slight increase to Y555 per ton in 1989, currency devaluation has brought the dollar-equivalent value down to only $16.15 per barrel.

To fund its operations in the 1980s, the petroleum industry amassed huge amounts of debt, which by the end of 1989 totaled nearly Y20 billion ($5.4 billion), half of which was in the form of foreign loans mostly denominated in Japanese yen. Amortized over production, debt has reached over Y145 per ton, or over $4.00 a barrel. With crude priced at Y100 per ton, rising debt raised the specter of insolvency for the industry, and the government faced a ballooning subsidy burden. In January 1988, the official price was finally raised to Y110 per ton ($4.07/bbl), and further to Y137 ($5.07/bbl) in January 1989. In January 1990, it was hiked to Y167 per ton ($4.85/bbl), but this did not even make up for the devaluation in December 1989, much less account for the more than 20% inflation in 1989 (Figure 1).

Figure 1
Domestic Price of Chinese Crude Oil, 1980-90

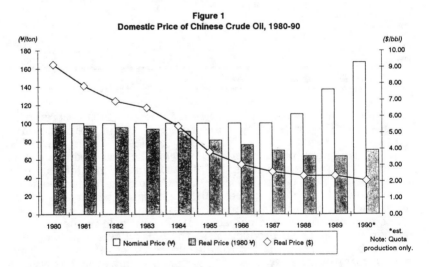

Profits in the industry have disappeared. In 1980, the upstream oil industry reported profits of nearly Y11 billion ($7.3 billion), but in 1989, total losses in the industry (before offsetting subsidies) reached Y3.9 billion ($1.05 billion). The petroleum industry has found itself increasingly short of money to fund further exploration

---

[20] *Zhongguo Nengyuan*, no. 5, 1989, p. 63.

and development work, potentially crippling future output increases from the mature Eastern fields. This is particularly relevant in the 1990s as the government hopes to begin full development of the potentially massive reserves in the Tarim basin, which would involve billions of dollars of expense in building a pipeline to bring the oil east.

In the downstream sector, prices have affected both the type and degree of upgrading in Chinese refineries. The price differential between light and heavy products—which determines in part a refiner's incentive to upgrade fuel oil—reached as high as $23/bbl in the early 1980s, but has since fallen to around $15/bbl; in Singapore, this differential has averaged $5/bbl over this same period. Combined with a large differential between gasoline and diesel (now $6.30/bbl compared to an average $2.00/bbl in Singapore), these pricing signals have shaped the refining system into a strongly gasoline-oriented system. Price distortions also exist among various grades of the same product and have reduced incentives to upgrade quality. Current policy is to raise the average octane of gasoline from a low 83 RON to 92 RON, but with only $1.50/bbl differential between these grades, compared to some $2.50 in Singapore, refiners have generally forgone the added costs of higher quality. Similarly, shortages of low-pour (± 20 C) diesel fuel affect northern China every winter, but since the ± 20 grade is priced the same as ± 10 grade, and is only $1.30/bbl higher than the 0 grade, refiners are reluctant to absorb the extra cost, despite the economic losses caused by the shortages.

Sinopec has also suffered the effects of rising input costs and controlled output prices. After jumping rapidly in the years after its formation, profit growth has slowed sharply. In 1985, profits were up 48% over the previous year, but the rise slowed to about 14% in 1986 and 1987, and was reduced to only 2% in 1988. With sagging domestic demand yet continued higher prices in 1989, Sinopec suffered an 11% fall in profits; already, virtually every simple refinery and many complex refineries have reported losses. [21] In Chinese parlance, these are "policy losses," the result of unfavorable state policies on pricing and other financial matters, though there are many indications that many Chinese refineries would not be competitive at international price levels.

Foreign loans have been as critical in the expansion of the refining industry as in upstream development. A wide range of modern refining equipment was imported in the 1980s, including hydrocrackers, visbreakers, alkylation units, resid cat crackers, and reformers, even though China has a domestically produced version of nearly all of these technologies. Petrochemical expansion also added to Sinopec's total debt burden. Four major ethylene-centered petrochemical complexes—at Daqing, Qilu, Yangzi, and Shanghai--opened during the decade, raising total ethylene capacity from 500,000 to 1.8 million tons. Seven years of foreign borrowing has brought Sinopec's total foreign debt to $6 billion (out of China's total of some $45 billion), repayment of which begins in 1990 and peaks in 1994. This repayment burden is additional to Sinopec's re-

---

[21] *Sinopec Annual Report 1989.*

quirement of about $1 billion per year for upgrading current units and expanding existing refineries.

One of the most serious obstacles to the revitalization of China's natural gas industry is the long-term impact of low prices. For most of the past decade, costs in the gasfields have been higher than the sales price, which is set by the state on a field-to-field basis. Between 1985 to 1987 alone, the national average sales price of natural gas per 1000 m³ rose from Y59.07 to Y68.47, while the average sales cost per 1000 m³ increased from Y74.30 to Y99.28, resulting in soaring losses. [22] The seriousness of the situation moved the State Council to raise prices in April 1987, when the Ministry of Petroleum Industry (now CNOGC) and the State Council signed a contract raising the price of the first 6.5 billion m³ of natural gas to Y130 per thousand m³ ($0.99 per thousand ft ³), up from the previous price range of Y50-Y80 per thousand m³ ($0.38-$0.61 per thousand ft ³). In parallel with the two-tiered pricing system in effect in the oil industry, the above-quota volume of natural gas was to be sold at double the new price. This price rise allowed some producers to make a marginal profit, though high-cost gas fields such as Huabei were already incurring sales costs in excess of Y200 per 1000 m³ in 1987.

Costs of natural gas production rose sharply as production conditions deteriorated. Large increases in field maintenance and major repairs have become necessary at fields in the middle or late stages of their production lifespan, but often these costs have been concealed to keep accounting costs low. At some fields, expenditures on such items as field maintenance, exploration in current producing areas, depreciation, bonuses and welfare allowances, and other nonoperational expenditures have either been omitted or only partially recorded in accounts (Table 13). Producers have responded to the state policy on subsidization which stipulates no additional subsidy for excessive losses over the "loss quota" (set by the state), and retention of surplus subsidies by the fields for losses below quota. As a result, fields have tried to make their costs look as small as possible to have more subsidized money at their disposal.

As a perennial loss-maker, the coal industry has also eroded its productive capacity as losses have become unmanageable. In 1980, production costs averaged Y20.05 per ton—lower than the mine-mouth price of Y21.33. After eight years of rapidly rising prices, production costs nearly doubled to Y39.97 per ton, while the average sales price reached only Y27.94; in 1988 alone, 93% of central mines reported losses totaling Y3.011 billion. From 1984 to 1988 alone, central mines spent a total of Y6.063 billion to make up for financial shortfalls, including Y3.779 billion originally targeted for production development and technical renovation, Y2.063 billion of repair and maintenance funds, and Y206 million of salary funds, seriously affecting technical preparedness and workers' incomes. [23]

In contrast to central mines, local and village mines are able to sell their output either at market prices or within a price ceiling

---

[22] "Low Prices Are a Serious Obstacle to Development of the Natural Gas Industry," *Tianranqi Gongye (Natural Gas Industry)*, no. 5, 1989, p.3.
[23] Chi Chu, China National Coal Corp., "A Review of Ten Years of Reform and Development in the Coal Industry," *Zhongguo Nengyuan*, no. 5, p. 19.

Table 13
Reported and Unreported Costs in the Natural Gas Industry, 1985-87
(million ¥)

		1985	1986	1987
	a. Actual costs	280	220	250
I. Depreciation/major repair	b. Listed costs	120	140	130
	c. Difference	160	80	120
	a. Actual costs	620	670	780
II. Field maintenance	b. Listed costs	200	210	220
	c. Difference	420	460	560
III. Unreported exploration in producing areas		660	530	560
Subtotal (Ic+IIc+III)		1,240	1,070	1,300
Adjusted complete costs		1,860	1,870	2,050
Percentage of unreported costs		66	57	63

Source: *Tianranqi Gongye (Natural Gas Industry)*, No. 5, 1989, p. 7.

set by the provincial price bureau. Facing lower production costs as well, many mines are able to make a profit, but these profits have been falling as local governments have adopted a series of special "land-use" and other fund-raising taxes. Dependent on these local and collective mines to boost national output, the government has been reluctant to force the implementation of numerous regulations on mine safety and modernization, as they would raise the low start-up and operating costs of these mines; currently, large central mines require an average Y300–500 of investment per ton of new capacity, while local mines average Y150–160 and village mines only Y75–80. [24]

The electric power sector has suffered a gradual erosion of profits during the 1980s. Recognizing the inadequacy of central funding for this capital-intensive industry, the government in July 1984 tacked on a Y0.02/kWh consumer surcharge for a dedicated Electric Power Construction Fund, but at the same time raised the tax on the production and sale of electric power from 15% to 25%, including a Y10/MWh charge on producers and a 10% revenue tax on distributors. [25] These measures, combined with a steady rise in costs of construction materials and fuel, had a strongly negative impact on the profits of thermal-power plants, especially oil-fired ones (Tables 14, 15).

The July 1984 regulations also permitted construction of new plants by enterprises, localities, collectives, and individuals. Following the principle of "whoever invests has ownership and receives the benefits," the government allowed the price of electric power from these plants to be set at a higher, negotiated price (*yi jia*), but it also meant that the owners themselves as consumers faced higher electricity prices. This has resulted in an unintended disincentive for enterprises to invest in power plant construction, since they are otherwise able to petition for the provision of quota-priced

[24] Di Fangsi, Ministry of Energy, "My Views on Accelerating the Development of the Local Coal Mining Industry," *Zhongguo Nengyuan*, no. 1, 1989, p. 31.
[25] Xia Meixiu, Ministry of Energy, "Analysis of the Crisis in Quota-Priced Electricity," *Zhongguo Nengyuan*, no. 1, 1989, p. 26.

Table 14
Fuel Costs in Power Generation, 1980-87
(¥/ton of coal equivalent)

	Coal	Oil	Average
1980	36.68	69.74	46.14
1981	40.39	71.82	47.71
1982	43.25	99.20	55.40
1983	47.89	115.40	61.32
1984	53.15	116.46	64.10
1985	59.77	112.33	69.21
1986	67.04	130.68	75.21
1987	72.42	134.90	79.46
Avg. Ann'l Increase (%)	10.2	9.9	8.1

Source: Xia Meixiu, *Zhongguo Nengyuan*, no. 1, 1989, p. 25.

Table 15
Electricity Prices, Costs, Taxes, and Profits, 1980-87
(¥/MWh)

	Sale Price	Sales Cost			Taxes	Profits
		Total	Fuel	Depreciation		
1980	64.79	32.38	17.06	5.46	9.69	22.72
1981	65.05	33.49	17.31	5.89	9.72	22.35
1982	66.13	35.59	19.19	6.03	9.69	20.85
1983	67.16	37.47	20.31	6.04	9.64	20.05
1984	68.96	39.75	21.50	6.14	11.04	18.17
1985	70.85	42.95	22.88	6.24	15.59	12.21
1986	75.26	47.66	25.03	6.67	16.09	11.43
1987	78.66	52.82	na	na	16.16	9.48
Avg. Ann'l Increase (%)	2.8	7.2			7.6	(11.7)

Source: Xia Meixiu, *ibid.*, p. 27.

electricity at less than half the cost of their own power. [26] The severe shortage of electricity, especially after 1984, has led a number of regions to seek additional electricity at virtually any cost. Since 1985, hundreds of sets of diesel-power generators have been imported, primarily in the south and eastern coastal regions. Powered by diesel fuel (most of which is imported), these generators have provided guaranteed supplies of electricity to hotels, office buildings, and factories, but at a cost of up to Y0.50/kWh, compared to the basic tariff of Y0.0745/kWh for large industrial users and Y0.0912/kWh for other industrial and commercial establishments.

Although the power industry as a whole remains profitable, the return on capital has fallen from 12% in 1980 to less than 4% in 1988. With normal bank loans charging 7.2% interest, new power plants are almost all running at a financial loss and banks have become increasingly unwilling to fund new ventures. Until 1989, most of the debate on energy price reform concerned the need to raise prices, increase the role of market-based floating pricing, and move eventually to international price levels. The severe inflation of 1988 and 1989, combined with a partial return to central plan-

[26] Xia Meixiu, *ibid.*, p. 28.

ning, has caused much of this earlier debate to be replaced by an emphasis on the controlled pricing system, quotas on losses, and cumbersome formulas to be used for price adjustment.[27] Discarding many tenets of market pricing theory, planners have called for a continuation of the dual-price system and a rise in quota-priced energy to a level guaranteeing each sector an average return on capital no less than the national industrial average. For virtually every sector, this would involve a doubling or tripling of prices, but would still leave most energy prices substantially below international levels. The natural gas industry, for example, has proposed a price rise to around Y175 per thousand m^3 ($1.35 per thousand ft ^{3}), providing the industry with an overall profit, but still leaving a number of major gasfields in the red.

INVESTMENT

A major development in energy investment in the 1980s has been the move away from state allocation of investment capital at no interest to a combination of financing channels including bank loans; retained profits; special conversion funds; local financing; floating of enterprise, city, and provincial energy bonds; and foreign loans and foreign joint ventures (Figure 2). In 1981, central-budget investment accounted for 66% of total investment in the energy sectors, dropping to only 27% in 1988.[28] Other major sources of funding, including domestic bank loans, foreign borrowing, and self-financing, have grown at over 25% per year during this period, but each sector has developed a different degree of reliance on each financing source. The coal industry, for example, still relies heavily on state investment, but has accounted for only 15% of domestic bank loans to the energy sector. In contrast, bank loans to the oil industry—including offshore development—have accounted for only 4% of total bank loans, whereas the sector accounts for nearly 50% of all foreign exchange loans. The power industry dominates the use of domestic bank loans and self-financed investments, and has managed to raise over Y7 billion in other sources, including local, enterprise, and private investment. It has also led the industry in the variety of foreign financing sources; since 1981, the power sector has received loans from the World Bank, Japan External Cooperation Fund, Kuwait, and credits from a number of national export-import banks (Table 16). Investment in the energy industries is widely regarded as inadequate. Averaging only 14%–15% of total investment in the 1980s, funding to the sector has been vastly exceeded by investment in energy-consuming ventures. The Ministry of Energy has called for a rise in the investment ratio to 20%–23% of the total, with the proportion dedicated to the electric power industry increased to 9%–10%, as is typical in many industrialized countries.[29]

The shift from central funding to a reliance on loans and retained profits has generally worsened the financial position of the

---

[27] See the annex to Document 1071 (1989) of the Ministry of Energy on "Several Policy Suggestions Concerning Support for Development of the Energy Industry," reprinted in *Zhongguo Nengyuan*, no. 1, 1990, pp. 18–23.

[28] *CESY 1989*, p. 29.

[29] Ministry of Energy, Document 1071 (1989), *op. cit.*, p. 19.

Figure 2
Investment In Energy Industries* by Source, 1981-88

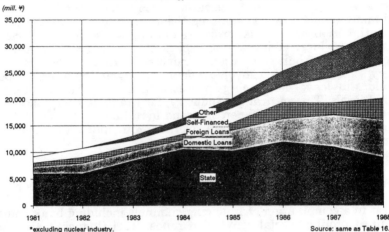

*excluding nuclear industry.

Source: same as Table 16.

Table 16
Fixed Asset Investment*
(billion ¥)

	Total Investment	Energy	Energy as % Total	Coal	Oil/Gas	Electric Power	Refining	Coking & Town Gas
1981	96.10	14.20	14.8	3.63	4.69	4.78	0.74	0.36
1982	123.04	17.41	14.2	4.87	6.20	5.53	0.70	0.11
1983	143.01	21.34	14.9	6.21	7.42	6.91	0.65	0.15
1984	183.29	27.91	15.2	8.19	9.46	8.90	0.99	0.37
1985	254.32	36.84	14.5	8.80	13.03	12.73	1.21	1.07
1986	301.96	44.77	14.8	9.31	13.78	18.42	1.63	1.63
1987	364.09	55.00	15.1	9.94	16.62	24.08	2.64	1.72
1988	449.65	65.29	14.5	10.80	19.70	28.58	4.21	2.00

*including public, collective, and private investment.
Source: *CESY 1989*, p. 21.

energy industries. The coal, natural gas, and upstream oil industries have had to resort to using other funds earmarked for repair, maintenance, and exploration to fund shortfalls in construction and operating expenses. The increase in bank loans has added to total industry debt, but there has been little tax relief from the central government, and in many cases tax rates have risen. In 1984, for example, the electric power industry changed from profit remittance to a taxation system. Under this system, profits remaining after debt repayment on investment loans (converted from earlier state allocations) are subject to a 55% income tax; the balance is then subject to a 28.5% "adjustment" tax, leaving the enterprise with less than 10% of its original earned profits. These profits are then divided according to a state-set formula among development, preparedness, social security, and employee bonus funds. Between 1985 and 1988, the power industry paid Y1.83 billion more in taxes to the government than it received in public investment. [30]

As a primarily military-oriented sector, the nuclear industry has remained outside direct state investment channels. At present, much of the investment capital for the industry depends on an annual contribution of 3.5 million tons of "dedicated oil" (gongxian you) from CNOGC, worth about Y800 million, although financing of the Daya Bay nuclear plant in Guangdong has involved domestic and foreign bank loans, including state-guaranteed foreign exchange loans. As a way to stimulate the development of the industry, the State Council has issued a circular calling for the incorporation of the nuclear industry into the Ministry of Energy, subject to its overall planning, financing, and management, and to list the nuclear budget for the Eighth Five-Year Plan as "nonoperational" expenses, relieving the first few domestic nuclear plants from debt repayment burdens. [31] Nevertheless, the needed investment for conversion of military plants to civilian production, treatment of nuclear waste, environmental protection, and repair and maintenance is expected to exceed central government capabilities; as a result, the industry has also promoted the involvement of provincial and local governments and enterprises in nuclear-related development.

PRODUCTIVITY AND EFFICIENCY

The need for higher production in the face of limited capital has highlighted the importance of productivity in increasing unit energy output. As with many sectors of the Chinese economy, the energy industries suffer from high rates of waste, low utilization, and numerous inefficiencies in production, transport, conversion, and consumption. Although productivity in the energy industries was enhanced by a number of reform policies in the 1980s, reversals began to appear after 1985 as investment slowed, costs rose, and limits to current production techniques were reached. Geological factors as well exacerbated the turnaround.

In the oil industry, the high rate of oilfield use and loss declined steadily in the early 1980s. At a number of fields, crude was used as fuel to heat crude for pipeline transportation and to generate power but has since been largely replaced by natural gas or coal. Between 1980 and 1984, oilfield use of crude fell by 11% but rose 16% between 1984 and 1988 as more crude was consumed in fueling enhanced recovery processes. The program of enhanced recovery has also increased oilfield losses. In 1988, production losses and oil field self-use together reached 3.6% of total output, or nearly 100,000 b/d. With further development of marginal fields, this percentage is expected to continue to rise.

The oil industry has also suffered from a sharp drop in well productivity. Although the number of oil wells in production has more than doubled since 1981, average output has dropped from nearly 100 b/d to just over 60 b/d. Part of this is due to the increased use

---

[30] Chen Wangxiang et al., *op. cit.*, p. 47.
[31] Jiang Xinxiong, China Nuclear Industry Corporation, "Accelerate the Development of China's Nuclear Industry," *Zhongguo Nengyuan*, no. 6, 1989, p. 12.

of infill drilling to maximize total output from field complexes such as Daqing, but it is mainly due to the declining proportion of flowing wells, which now account for only 10% of the total. [32] With artificial lift—meaning water flooding, steam flooding, and pumping—incremental yields are smaller and costs higher than with wells flowing under natural pressure. This decline in productivity is also reflected in rising unit costs of capital investment in the oil industry. By 1985, average costs for development of one barrel per day of production capacity had fallen to 6,520Y (in 1980Y); in the three years to 1988, this figure doubled in real terms to Y13,065 per b/d, or Y24,100 per b/d in current money. With a 40% fall in the average output per well from 1980 to 1988, higher investment was needed simply to maintain output.

The electric power industry has seen a number of its efficiency and productivity measures rise over the past decade, although the rate of improvement has slowed significantly. The industry is generally plagued by high unit fuel consumption and low conversion efficiencies. In China, fuel costs account for an average 50–55% of power industry operating costs. In 1980, an average 413 grams of coal-equivalent fuel was consumed for each kWh of power generated; renovation measures and the installation of newer equipment quickly brought the rate down to 398 grams by 1984, but it had fallen only 1 gram further by 1988. Unit fuel consumption varies widely around the country depending on the configuration of the installed capacity, ranging from a high of 485 gce/kWh in Hunan to only 338 gce/kWh in Beijing, compared to an average 328 gce/kWh in the Soviet Union. [33] Each gram decline in China's consumption rate equates to a savings of over 400,000 tons of coal, but further improvements are hampered by the proliferation of small (25 MW or less) locally built power plants, built in an attempt to find a quick solution to worsening power shortages. Energy consumption in these plants ranges up to 1,000 gce/kWh, pollution measures are minimal, and operating costs more than double that of an average 200 MW plant, but they can be designed and built in only one-half to one-third the time; for many counties, these plants are the only way to increase the local supply of electricity. Between 1985 and 1988, total capacity of these plants grew from 15,000 MW to 22,000 MW, accounting for about one-quarter of total thermal generation capacity. [34]

Low utilization and overstaffing depress productivity measures. Most 1,000 MW plants in China have 2,000 to 3,000 workers, compared to only 500 in a 700 MW plant built by Huaneng International in Dalian. Many plants suffer derating as a result of the high ash content of the coal burned; these problems in turn reduce the number of operating hours per year, in some cases to as few as 3,000 hours. In contrast, newly built plants average some 6,000 hours of operation annually. [35]

---

[32] *World Oil*, January 1990, p. 28.

[33] Jiang Xianrong, Ministry of Energy, "Review and Outlook of Energy Conservation Work in China," *Zhongguo Nengyuan*, no. 5, 1989, p. 40.

[34] Ye Qing, State Planning Commission, "Report to the State Council on the Fifth Energy Conservation Working Group Meeting," *Zhongguo engyuan*, no. 5, 1989, p. 6.

[35] Huang Yicheng, Minister of Energy, "Thoroughly Undertake Adjustment in the Energy Industries, Increase Labor Productivity and Economic Returns," speech to National Energy Working Meeting of 5 January 1990, reprinted in *Zhongguo Nengyuan*, no. 1, 1990, p. 5.

Nearly 16% of power generated in China is lost before reaching the consumer. Thermal power station use has risen slowly to nearly 8% of total generation, but line losses, though declining slightly, were still a hefty 8.2% in 1988. Although low transmission voltage contributes to the high rate of line loss, in some areas such as Guangdong, theft from line-tapping adds significantly to the overall total.

The coal industry has struggled to improve its performance over the past decade. Overall productivity (i.e. of total employees, including non-miners) rose to 1.092 tons of coal per worker-shift in 1988, only 0.2 tons higher than in 1968; 30% of the coal bureaus under central control average less than 1 ton per worker-shift. The mechanization rate of central-run mines has increased to a nominal 58%, accounting for about 25% of national output, but over half of the 400-plus sets of integrated mining equipment now in use are past their useful lives. [36] Low mechanization and overstaffing at mines contribute to the high percentage of output consumed by the mines themselves. In 1988, mine use accounted for 4% of total output, but at a number of major mines the rate is as high as 10%–15%; at Yantai, it has reached 55%. In contrast, British mines consume an average 0.45% of their output. [37]

Besides the mines, the coal industry is handicapped by a lack of washing plants. In 1988, 175 million tons of coal—only 18% of total production—was washed, but cleaned coal averaged 10% ash, compared to only 2%–3% ash in coal from U.S. or Australian plants. Most of the washed coal is directed to the coking industry, leaving power plant and other industrial consumers with raw coal containing an average 18% ash. With over 585 million tons of coal transported by rail in 1988, this percentage translates into roughly 100 million tons of dirt and other nonvolatile matter carried by the overloaded rail transport system.

Declining real prices, rising taxes and production costs, spiraling losses, high debt burden, insufficient investment, low productivity and low efficiency are among the major problems facing China's energy industries. Problems in management structure, environmental pollution, technology development, and ownership have also been examined by the leadership, but few solutions have been forthcoming. Without a major overhaul of the way the energy industries are financed, operated, and managed, these problems will present an almost insurmountable hurdle which will increasingly frustrate the government's plans for economic modernization.

III. Outlook

Over the next decade, China's energy industries will face immense challenges in meeting the energy requirements of an expanding economy. In 1979, a long-term energy strategy was formulated to support the quadrupling of gross industrial and agricultural output by the year 2000. By assuming a primary energy elasticity of demand of no less than 0.5 and no less than 1 for electric power, the quadrupling of economic activity could be supported by

[36] Huang Yicheng, *ibid.*, p. 3.
[37] Jiang Xianrong, *op. cit.*, p. 40.

a doubling of primary energy production and a quadrupling of electric power output. Moreover, an implicit assumption was that China could remain energy self-sufficient; domestic production targets were thus set to achieve this long-range goal. Output targets for 2000 were set at 200 million tons (4 million b/d) of crude oil, 1.43 billion tons of coal, 30 billion m³ of natural gas, and 1,200 TWh of electricity, including 240 TWh of hydropower and 20 TWh of nuclear power. Based on 1989 output, these targets imply an annual average rate of growth for the remainder of the century of 3.5% for crude oil, 2.9% for coal, 6.8% for hydropower, and 6.6% for natural gas, or 3.3% for total energy production.

The progress over the last decade has brought achievement of these production targets within reach, but only if the government can reverse the unfavorable trends in investment, productivity, and finances that have worsened considerably since 1985. Major commitments to sustain investment flows, increase efficiency, rationalize prices, promote exploration, stress conservation, and improve the financial situation of each sector are now of vital importance. Measures in these areas could arrest or reverse the slowdown in output growth experienced in the latter half of the 1980s.

Major projects currently under way in the "energy base" of Inner Mongolia, Shanxi, Shaanxi, western Hebei, and Ningxia—including a number of large-scale opencast mines—are expected to boost coal output in this region to 700–800 million tons by 2000, relieving the pressure on local and village mines to sustain as rapid growth as in the past decade. Crucial for success of this plan is the expansion of transport facilities, since 400–500 million tons of coal will need to be transported out of the region by the end of the decade. Since nearly half of this volume constitutes coal for power plant use, pressure has been growing for the government to undertake a program of mine-mouth power plant construction and transmit power to consumption centers. In response, the government in mid-1990 ordered a speed-up in construction of 8,700 MW of coal-fired capacity at the Huolinhe, Yiminhe, Yuanbaoshan, Zhungeer, and Dongsheng mines in Inner Mongolia. [38] Throughout the entire northern "energy base" region, current plans call for a total of 120,000 MW of coal-based thermal capacity to be built over the next 20 years, though environmental degradation, lack of water resources, and insufficient funding remain major obstacles to its realization. [39]

Nationally, over 45,000 MW of new power generation capacity is currently being planned or under construction. Major additions of more than 3,000 MW are slated for the developed eastern provinces of Anhui, Jiangsu, Shanghai (including Shidongkou, China's largest thermal plant of 3,600 MW total capacity), and Zhejiang; the heavily industrialized province of Liaoning and neighboring Jilin; and the rapidly growing province of Guangdong in the south. A similar amount of capacity will be needed in the latter part of the 1990s to reach the target capacity of 175,000 MW in 2000.

---

[38] "Acceleration of Construction of Five Large Coal-Power Bases in Inner Mongolia," *Renmin Ribao*, 23 May 1990, p. 1.

[39] Peng Fangchun, State Planning Commission, "Important Measures to Ameliorate the Current Power Shortage," *Zhongguo Nengyuan*, no. 6, 1989, p. 33.

Hydropower production will be boosted by the addition of more than 30,000 MW of capacity, including major additions in Sichuan, Yunnan, Guangxi, Gansu, and Qinghai, and output is likely to achieve the target of 240 TWh in 2000 assuming investment funds remain adequate. With the squeeze in central funding, provincial governments have become more directly involved in construction projects: recently, Yunnan, Guangxi, and Guangdong set up a joint investment organization to accelerate construction of a series of dams on the Hong Shui (Red River), which, when completed some time after 2000, will provide an additional 11,000 MW of capacity. Prospects for the production of nuclear power will depend as well on the ability to channel additional resources into this sector, but assuming at least 5,000 MW of capacity by 2000 (i.e. Daya Bay, Qinshan I and II, and Liaoning), total output could reach 27 to 30 TWh.

Both the oil and natural gas industry, however, are unlikely to meet their production targets. With over half of China's gas production in the form of associated gas, declines in the major eastern fields will result in declines in gas production as well. Without a concerted effort in exploration, onshore gas production is unlikely to exceed 20 billion m^3 by the end of the century, 10 billion m^3 less than the target. A major variable is offshore natural gas; already, CNOOC considers natural gas to have a more promising future than oil in its offshore fields, and it hopes to exploit the estimated 3 trillion m^3 of reserves in the South China Sea, Beibu Gulf, and Pearl River basins. Given the independent financial status of CNOOC, large-scale exploitation of offshore gas resources is unlikely without state backing and funding; indeed, CNOOC has proposed incorporating its gas exploration and production plans into the central budget for the Eighth Five-Year Plan period. Without centrally backed funding, however, only the ARCO find off Hainan island is likely to be brought into production in the next decade, but the bulk of its output may be exported to Japan in the form of LNG to provide foreign exchange.

A shortfall in oil production poses a major challenge. With few substitutes for its use as a transport fuel and petrochemical feedstock—and little leeway for further substitution of fuel oil by coal—oil provides a critical and valuable source of energy to the Chinese economy. Diesel fuel is the primary commercial energy used in agriculture, and—unlike most other countries—gasoline fuels over 80% of China's trucking fleet. Oil is also a major earner of foreign exchange, providing over $3.6 billion in export revenues in 1989, down from a peak of $6.7 billion in 1985. Most of these earnings have come from the export of crude oil, production of which has consistently exceeded the capacity of the refining system. Since 1986, however, refining capacity has expanded rapidly, and throughput has risen at an average of over 100,000 b/d each year, compared to an average 63,000 b/d annual increase in crude production—and a mere 11,000 b/d increase in 1989. Although Sinopec targets 4 million b/d of refining capacity in 2000, equal to projected crude production, neither is likely to exceed 3.4 to 3.5 million b/d (see Table 18, below). Declining or stagnating production at eastern fields such as Daqing, Huabei, Dagang, and Zhongyuan may offset expected increases at Shengli and Liaohe, while exploitation of the estimated large reserves in the Tarim Basin of western China faces severe financial and logistical constraints, not the least of which is the construction of a multibillion-dollar pipeline to bring the crude east to the refining and consuming centers.

Implicit in many of the discussions on production prospects is the assumption that China will remain largely self-sufficient in energy, with "demand" in 2000 equaling production. For certain energy forms, such as electricity and natural gas, this identity is likely to hold, since neither is easily imported. Recent demand forecasts, however, have attempted to separate the concept of demand from consumption and provide estimates of demand based on energy requirements of projected economic activity (Table 17). Concerned with primary energy demand, these forecasts do not provide estimates of total final electricity demand, but given current shortages and the expectation that power demand growth will exceed growth in primary energy production, it is highly probable that total electricity supply will continue to lag demand. Indeed, China's economy is likely to continue to suffer from chronic shortages of virtually every energy type. This prospect has underlaid the recent stress on energy conservation, increased productivity, and "comprehensive utilization" of resources, all policies designed to take advantage of the immense latent energy potential in China's largely energy-inefficient economy. [40]

Table 17
Energy Demand Forecasts*, 2000

	Total (million tce)	Coal (million tons)	Oil (million b/d)	Natural Gas (billion m³)	Hydro (TWh)	Nuclear (TWh)
Range	1,416-1,540	1,329-1,531	2.8-4.8	9.8-50	239-286	0-44.8
Average	1,478	1,465	3.94	33	260	20

*Summary of five forecasts: Energy Research Institute (1987, 1989), Qinghua University (1987, 1990), and the World Bank (1985).
Source: *Zhongguo Nengyuan*, no. 3, 1987; no. 6, 1989; Lu Yingzhong, *Comparison of Energy Consumption, Supply, and Policy of the People's Republic of China and Some Other Developing Countries* (Washington, DC: Washington Institute for Values in Public Policy), 1990.

Shortfalls in coal production in 2000 could take two forms: shortages of coal for power generation, thus exacerbating power shortages, and shortages of coal for industrial uses. Assuming coal demand of 1.4 to 1.5 billion tons, the supply gap may reach some 70 to 170 million tons (or 50 to 130 million tons on an import-equivalent basis). Although China is not prepared to undertake large-scale imports of coal—and indeed still promotes coal exports to compensate for declining oil exports—coal shortages in the resource-poor southern provinces may well be solved through imports from Vietnam, Indonesia, or Australia. Other regions may need to adopt other measures, such as rationing fuel, freeing up household coal consumption through substitution by gas or electricity, strict conservation measures, or limits on industrial expansion.

[40] Although these policies were first promoted at the Eleventh Party Congress in 1980, they were heard with decreasing frequency over the ensuing decade. Since 1981, there has been an annual meeting of the Energy Conservation Working Group of the State Council, but no meeting was held in 1988. With Prime Minister Li Peng's stress on energy conservation at the Seventh National People's Congress, the group was reconvened in June 1989, and the reports reemphasized the need to give priority to energy conservation in the near term.

China is presently a net oil exporter, but the slowdown in domestic production and rapidly rising demand will transform it into a net oil importer, perhaps as soon as mid-decade. Based on a number of assumptions on output, refinery expansion, and demand, Table 18 presents an alternative forecast for China's supply and demand balance to 2000, with the attendant implications for trade. On the crude production side, financial difficulties, declining production at onshore fields, and marginal output from offshore fields will likely limit output growth to some 3.2 to 3.5 million b/d—the narrower range here reflecting the geological fundamentals involved—while demand, though subject to manipulation by the government through ration and import controls, may reach 3.5 to 4.5 million b/d. Though the high production/low demand scenario for 2000 appears to be in basic balance, the critical variable in relating production to demand is refining. In even the most optimistic projection—requiring that China build a 100,000 b/d grassroots refinery every year between now and 2000—a shortfall in refinery capacity will limit product output to a band centered around 3 million b/d. As a result, total import demand for products could soar from the current 100,000 b/d to over 500,000 b/d, or even to nearly 1.7 million b/d with lower production and higher demand. Similarly, rapid expansion of China's refining capacity, combined with lower growth in crude output, could also place China in the market for over 500,000 b/d of crude.

Table 18
Outlook for Petroleum Supply and Demand
('000 b/d)

	1980	1988	1989	1990 Low	1990 High	1995 Low	1995 High	2000 Low	2000 High
CRUDE SUPPLY									
Onshore:									
Daqing	1,030	1,114	1,110	1,090 —	1,100	900 —	1,000		
Shengli	352	666	667	680 —	700	800 —	900		
Others	737	946	956	990 —	969	1,161 —	1,099		
Offshore:	0	15	19	20 —	24	60 —	100	75 —	140
Total:	2,119	2,741	2,752	2,780 —	2,793	2,920 —	3,100	3,150 —	3,510
DEMAND	1,472	1,937	2,053	2,156		2,860 —	3,140	3,540 —	4,480
REFINERY OUTPUT	1,556	1,975	2,041	2,148		2,450 —	2,590	2,800 —	3,320
IMPORTS									
Crude	0	17	64	100 —	120	0 —	200	0 —	510
Products	0	61	107	90 —	100	270 —	740	220 —	1,690
EXPORTS									
Crude	266	545	488	440 —	490	50 —	370	0 —	390
Products	84	99	95	90 —	110	0 —	50	0 —	0

Source: East-West Center.

These volumes, though massively larger than those at present, are not particularly high for a country the size of China, nor are imports historically unprecedented. In the "worst-case" scenario of China importing 1.7 million b/d of products, imports would constitute some 40% of total demand, a level last seen in 1960. Nevertheless, the absolute volume involved is unprecedented, and imports of this magnitude may pose a problem for China's balance of payments. Assuming China's total exports double by 2000 to around \$100 billion, lower levels of imports of some 500,000 b/d would account for only 6–7% of total export revenues, up from the current 2.5%, but in the high case of 1.7 million b/d, imports would require around 20% of total export income. The latter figure is most likely unsustainable, since China also faces a higher import bill for foodstuffs, minerals, other raw materials as well as equipment to modernize its aging industrial base.

Nor does China have much leeway to limit oil demand as it did in the 1970s and early 1980s. With fewer than 300,000 private automobiles out of a motor vehicle fleet of over 4.5 million, there is little discretionary driving, and petrochemical feedstocks, demand for which is expected to exceed 320,000 b/d by 2000, form the basis of the rapidly expanding synthetic fibers, plastics, and rubber industries. Currently, textile exports (including synthetics) constitute China's largest source of foreign exchange earnings. In addition, the decentralization of procurement has allowed cities and provinces with foreign exchange surpluses to import oil directly, largely bypassing the limitations imposed by the national plan.

Demand growth will not stop in 2000. By 2020, total energy demand is expected to top 2.4 billion tce (33 million bdoe), including 1.6 billion tons of coal, while the long-range forecast for 2050 posits a demand of 5.2 billion tce (73 million bdoe), including over 3.1 billion tons of coal—equivalent to twice current U.S. energy consumption and about 40% of current world energy consumption. Although little credence should be paid to such forecasts, they do illustrate that China cannot afford to slacken its efforts in expanding energy output, increasing the efficiency of energy use, promoting conservation, and developing alternative energy sources. Moreover, the worldwide concern over the environmental impact of fossil fuel burning poses an even greater dilemma: though blessed with abundant coal reserves, China may face the need to restrict its use in order to limit CO_2 emissions. None of the forecasts to date, however, have factored in this issue, but China appears to have little flexibility in the short term in moving away from its heavy dependence on coal.

Conservation is likely to provide fewer returns than in the past. The record of conservation in the 1980s has been impressive, but estimates of total energy conserved since 1980 range from 250 million tce (based on changing energy intensities in GNP) to 1.1 billion tce (based on changing energy intensities in U.S. dollar terms and the import of energy intensive products such as fertilizers and rolled steel). As with many other indicators, the rate of savings has declined since 1985, averaging 4.7% per year from 1981 to 1985, and only 3.1% per year since then. [41] This decline is in part due to a decline in conservation investment, which fell to Y1.3 billion in 1989 from over Y2 billion in the mid-1980s. Moreover, the cost of conservation has risen significantly, from an average Y300 per ton saved during 1981–1985 to over Y500 per ton in 1986–1989. [42]

Largely ignored in most discussions of China's energy future is the role of noncommercial energy in rural areas. Estimated at

[41] *CESY 1989*, p. 11.
[42] Ye Qing, *op. cit.*, p. 6.

about 28% of the volume of commercial energy, noncommericial sources provide over 80% of energy use in the countryside. [43] Split 38% to 61% between wood and agricultural wastes, noncommercial fuels provide energy for heating, lighting, and cooking, but the lack of alternatives has led to serious ecological damage in certain regions from overcutting, diversion of wastes from composting and soil enhancement, and overuse of fertilizers and pesticides. Current policy promotes the development of small-scale hydroplants, provides long-term low-interest loans for energy projects, stresses the use of local resources, and allows greater flexibility in pricing, but solutions are often cast in terms of a long-term 100-year strategy, effectively admitting that in the near-term, little can be done to substantially change the situation in rural areas.

IV. CONCLUSION

After a decade of remarkable expansion and modernization, China's energy industries are entering a new decade that promises to pose even greater challenges than those met in the 1980s. Financial, economic, and political instability all have a direct effect on the health and vitality of the industry through their impact on budgeting, price reform, industrial restructuring, demand, and trade. The record of economic reform in the 1980s has demonstrated that the Chinese respond rapidly to new opportunities, reflected in the take-off of a number of sectors such as agriculture that had previously been moribund. The economy has also responded well to changes in the international environment—witness the rapid adjustment of foreign trade to lower oil export revenues after 1986. Nevertheless, the current return to reliance on central planning to solve the problems generated by the partial reforms of the last few years does not bode well for the energy industries.

As is the case in all centrally planned economies, central planners do not have access to nor can they process the amount of information needed to run an entire national economy efficiently. Politicization of the process also interferes with optimum allocation of resources and can actually create long-term damage to certain sectors, as seen in the underdeveloped and problem-plagued state of the natural gas industry. Moreover, the information that planners do receive is not always of best quality, since the system often contains incentives to distort production and financial figures, which in turn give the central planners a distorted picture of investment productivity.

Without true markets to provide and process the information needed by the energy-producing and consuming sectors, little sustained improvement in the current situation can be expected. Although raising prices alone would significantly alleviate the industry's financial crisis, problems of compartmentalism and isolation, centralization of planning, bureaucratic and political dominance, and insufficient capital are serious obstacles to revitalization of all energy sectors. Moreover, a conceptual obstacle to price reform is the traditional assertion by central planners that China needs to

---

[43] Lu Yingzhong, *Comparison of Energy Consumption, Supply and Policy of the People's Republic of China and Some Other Developing Countries*, p. 31.

keep its raw material prices low in order to maintain export competitiveness. Unfortunately, the leading role of productivity in export competitiveness is often lost in this debate, despite the glaringly obvious examples from raw-material-short Japan, Korea, and Taiwan.

Reforms are needed. The multiple salutary effects of price reform are widely recognized, but this should be accompanied by decentralization of planning and enhancement of local flexibility; adoption of standard accounting and costing methods; rationalization of the tax regime; liberalization of trade, including the broadening of import rights; and further deregulation at the retail level, among other policies which would help ultimately to reverse many of the unfavorable trends that have emerged over the last decade of stop-and-go partial reform. As the world's third largest producer and consumer of energy, it is in more than China's own interest that its domestic industry remain healthy and capable of providing for the needs of its economy and population.

China also faces serious challenges internationally. Rising imports of crude oil and petroleum products raise the question of how and where to access the required volumes. China now depends primarily on Singapore for its product imports, but even with complete dedication to the China market, Singapore would be unable to supply a sufficient amount of products if import demand rises at its current rate over the next decade. A large product deficit may provide an opening to greater foreign participation in the downstream sector, which to date has been limited to technology sales, engineering contracts, product sales, and retailing in the Special Economic Zones. Foreign-backed joint ventures in refining would bring to China the marketing and technical expertise of the international oil companies along with a lessened reliance on product imports.

The reforms needed in the energy sector would compel a host of related legal and economic reforms. Without them—or even with some of them—China is likely to be left with an increasingly limited number of options in the 1990s as the imbalance between energy supply and demand grows. The experience of the 1980s has shown that the current situation is counter-productive and most likely unsustainable, but it has also demonstrated that industry can and will respond to new incentives and policies. It is critical, however, that these incentives provide the proper signals to producers and consumers. With such a fundamental commodity as energy, China must ensure that it enters the twenty-first century with a healthy and vital industry.

C. Science and Technology

OVERVIEW

By Genevieve Knezo *

Multiple contradictions consistently hamper China's science and technology modernization. China's early technological preeminence—for instance, in printing, gunpowder and armaments, the use of wind and water power to drive machines, porcelain, and cast iron—predated European discoveries by four to ten centuries. But European technology eventually dwarfed these achievements because of the inertia of Chinese cultural orthodoxy, which sapped creativity; population pressures, which reduced China's need to use technology to increase industrial productivity; corruption; and bureaucratic mismanagement. Similar constraints curb China's science and technology today.

Of the "four modernizations" announced by China in 1978, clearly the most important was the goal, later down-scaled, of reaching technological parity with the West by the year 2000. The current belief is that the development of science and technology will not only augment the productivity of China's abundant manpower, but will enable China to develop the industrial and agricultural capabilities and defense base needed to help forge a modern economy.

China has achieved some success. Richard Suttmeier reports that it has the largest scientific and technological infrastructure (including personnel) of any developing country and that it has geographically dispersed its scientific and technical resources. Leo Orleans describes the world class scientific caliber of Chinese students and scholars now in the United States, who are overqualified to work in China's science and technology infrastructure and whose return to China might adversely affect the work of U.S. laboratories.

The 1985 decision of the Communist Party Central Committee to emphasize applied science and technology in order to drive economic growth deemphasized basic research and forced more cooperation between researchers, industrial firms, and entrepreneurs. Institutes involved in R&D under the Chinese Academy of Sciences are now required to supplement the funding they receive from the State by contracting work with individual enterprises.

Suttmeier cites as effective the Chinese Government-directed "863" National High Technology Development Program, which

* Genevieve Knezo is a Specialist in Science and Technology at the Congressional Research Service, Library of Congress.

Papers not mentioned in this overview were not available to the reviewer at the time this was drafted.

gives priority to biotechnology, space technology, information technology, laser technology, automation technology, energy, and advanced materials. This program also aims to divert some military technology research resources to the civilian sector.

China's space program began in the 1960s with military support, and continued at modest levels during the Cultural Revolution because of Zhou Enlai's personal endorsement. Civilian activities seem to be paramount now. Marcia Smith concludes that despite China's economic problems, the U.S. restrictions on technology transfer, and the lack of a cooperative U.S.-Chinese space agreement, China is now considered a world class space power with 27 successful launches of its own or foreign-owned satellites (telecommunications, weather, resources, reconnaissance).

Suttmeier and Eric Baark discuss the decentralized, but government-managed, technology promotion programs. The Spark Program was formulated in 1985 by the State Science and Technology Commission (SSTC) to develop more middle- and high-technology enterprises and to train technical workers in the rural areas. This was followed in 1988 by the Torch Program, to accelerate the commercialization of research results generated in national institutes. The government encouraged the creation of "start-up" firms and "technology incubators" in existing special economic zones and in new high-technology development zones that give firms preferential tax treatment and access to foreign exchange. Under the Torch Program, the government finances priority projects in electronics, information, and new materials. The *minban* program consists of non-State run science parks and some private industrial firms that entrepreneurs have "spun off" from State-funded research institutes whose government-guaranteed funds were cut. They generally have some form of collective ownership and a relationship with the district government. One often-cited success story is the Haidian district in Beijing, an area known as "electronics street." Suttmeier estimates there are 894 such firms located in at least 30 cities.

Notwithstanding these successes, most of the authors cite major obstacles to China's science and technology reform. Baark assesses the various "policy cultures" in Chinese society—bureaucratic, entrepreneurial and academic—that generate inertia which constrains innovation and reform. Pressures to maintain centralized party and bureaucratic control over the political and social order, or at least over the speed and direction of reform, need to be reconciled with the growing independence and dispersion of power that accompany scientific and technological modernization. This dilemma is seen in the attenuation of the technological goals set out originally by leaders Deng Xiaoping, Hu Yaobang, and Zhao Ziyang and opposed by conservative party elements because they implied unacceptable levels of social and political freedom and the introduction of "contaminating" Western ideas. The government's attitude was manifested in its violent suppression of student demonstrations for democracy in June 1989.

Conservatives continue to try to maintain a command economy over the decentralized initiatives, and Soviet-trained science and technology bureaucrats continue to oppose policy reforms that link the innovative capacities of economy to the "mainstream of productive activity." The party's role in the industrial economy has been reinforced by China's need to curb inflation stemming from recent relaxations of some of the austerity measures imposed on the economy in the late 1980s and the shortage of local financing for industrial activity. Centralized party control continues to limit the development of the non-State economy and China's access to high-technology joint ventures and foreign capital. Baark and Suttmeier believe that the current political uncertainty and uneasy climate for business following the Tiananmen demonstrations will further depress technological reforms.

The momentum of scientific and technological modernization often clashes with the "traditional Chinese" way of doing things. This involves such practical issues as determining the balance between foreign and domestic sources of technology and the degree of freedom to give to intellectuals. In this regard, Suttmeier describes the need to placate the children of the old guard, the elite families who now control technological firms, and to induce them to invest in nonmilitary commercial ventures. Uncertainty about the ownership of intellectual property rights also undermines China's high-technology future and foreign high-technology trade. Baark contends that fraud permeates the growth of direct contacts between researchers and the nascent businesses that came with decentralization. He says the SSTC's regulatory reforms—the Patent Law of 1985, the Technology Contract Law of 1987, and the organizations created to manage markets—have increased centralized bureaucratic control. Suttmeier contends that China's commitment to maintaining its socialist system will deter innovation, risk taking, and creativity.

Historically, China opposed the import of Western knowledge, but now an external orientation is condoned, especially since 1978, when a decision was made to send foreign students abroad to supplement the deficient knowledge base of the "old scientific elite," who had been trained in the West prior to the Communist revolution or in the Soviet Union. Orleans focuses on "brain drain" issues and on the approximately 50,000 Chinese students and scholars who are currently in the United States. Over the years China has accepted some loss of young professionals as an acceptable cost of training students abroad, but brain drain has been getting larger because China cannot absorb all its trained personnel. Orleans and Mary Bullock conclude that it is in the best interests of both China and the West to solve the problem of student defection.

The flow of students abroad did not abate following the Tiananmen disaster despite the Chinese government's imposition of requirements for students to undergo political education and to reimburse the government for their preparatory education. Numerous exceptions are made for those who have private funding from relatives abroad or who can bribe or buy their way out. Also foreigners have continued to be receptive to Chinese students.

Bullock notes that following the Tiananmen incident and the imposition of martial law, the foreign intellectual community has been torn between sustaining or canceling programs with China. Those advocating continuity argued that the Chinese intellectual community would become more vulnerable and isolated if outside ties further diminished. Those advocating suspension hoped to influence, by protest and sanctions, more ameliorative government policies."

For the most part, however, most of the papers in this section conclude that there is a continuity of relationships. China wants to maintain its open door to the West and to seek international markets for its products. The West seeks to promote China's development for both commercial and strategic reasons. According to Bullock, the harshest reaction to the crackdown was from American scientists. The U.S. Government sent mixed signals, with some agencies continuing to maintain contacts and renew cooperative agreements despite bans on high-level negotiations and travel advisories. The United States has even once again temporarily extended the umbrella Science and Technology accord, which expired in January 1987. The major obstacle to renewal is disagreement over intellectual property rights, not Presidential human rights policies regarding Tiananmen.

There is, however, some evidence of weaker ties with the West. Chinese government action to suppress democracy damaged West European ties with China, and, according to Bullock, Europe is now more interested in ties to Eastern Europe. Overall, "As West Europe, Japan and the United States begin to renew or extend their scientific and technical agreements with China, it is apparent that they are seeking less technologically advanced fields for cooperation because they link international relationships to political reform in China. Environmental science rather than robotics, for example, will be given priority."

Bullock also foresees a significantly enhanced role for Japan in China—a factor that may realign power relationships in the Pacific. Initially there was some slowdown in student exchanges and Japanese financial assistance, but "Japanese political leaders and academics alike also maintained that Japan had a special (more realistic) understanding of China and that China should not become internationally isolated." Bullock reports that since June 1989, Sino-Japanese science and technology cooperative activities have more than doubled and Japanese funding has been expanded to include more technical assistance, educational relations, and economic assistance.

Whether China will achieve its technological reform by the year 2000 is debatable. What is clear is that China's present leaders do not want to sacrifice party ideology, Chinese traditions, and existing power alignments to modernization. Apparently, Western leaders have little choice but to respect this orientation.

FRAGMENTED INNOVATION: CHINA'S SCIENCE AND TECHNOLOGY POLICY REFORMS IN RETROSPECT [1]

By Erik Baark *

CONTENTS

SUMMARY

The aim of reforms [1] in China's science and technology (S&T) policy and management during the 1980s was to provide a new impetus for a substantially different pace and performance level for technological innovation. The analysis proposed in this paper suggests that this objective has not been fully achieved. The fate of the reforms has been shaped by what I refer to as the tensions between policy cultures on the one hand and the inertial forces of Chinese society on the other, both of which act to constrain innovation.

I identify three S&T policy cultures: bureaucratic, entrepreneurial, and academic. Each of these cultures has been associated with particular development priorities, a set of preferred policy instruments, and represents a particular "network" of political and institutional interests. Reformers of a fundamentally entrepreneurial outlook struggled in the early 1980s to integrate innovation and production by means of new, market-oriented organizations. Failing to overcome the resistance of a middle-aged, Soviet-trained network of administrators and the rehabilitated academic elite, how-

* Erik Baark is Associate Professor, Technical University of Denmark.
[1] Research for this paper has been conducted with financial support from the Swedish Agency for Research Cooperation with Developing Countries. In addition, I am greatly indebted to Andrew Jamison for criticism and suggestions, and to many Chinese friends for assistance in the collection of relevant material. The responsibility for views presented in the paper is, however, completely my own.

ever, these reformers had to accept compromises in the late 1980s which deprived them of a good deal of their influence over the basic resources for technological innovation in the Chinese society. As a result, the innovative capabilities of China's economic system remain fragmented, i.e. separated from the mainstream of productive activity. The difficulties in establishing the new technology markets promoting technological entrepreneurship illustrate the continuing problem of fragmentation. The concluding section of the paper discusses the forces of fragmentation in the context of the new imperatives of technological modernization in the 1990s.

I. HISTORICAL FRAMEWORK

The reforms in China in the 1980s must be seen in the perspective of that nation's modernization endeavor. Three important goals have been to find a balance between foreign and domestic sources of technology, create adequate technological capabilities to meet perceived defense needs, and satisfy the nationalist urge to "catch up" with the advanced industrialized countries.

These concerns were superimposed on a science and technology system that had, since the founding of the People's Republic of China, sought to integrate science into "socialist reconstruction." This process had generated its own particular set of issues with the establishment of a range of indigenous organizations for research and development. The core questions concerned the role of science and technology—and, by extension, the practitioners: scientists, engineers, and technicians—in China's modernization.

It is useful to distinguish between two fundamental issues. One issue pertains to the question of intellectual autonomy of scientists—or freedom of expression. The leadership wished to ensure the "correct" ideological consciousness and allegiance to the political priorities of the Chinese Communist Party, while scientists have often upheld traditions of intellectual and academic freedom. Another issue has been concerned with the manage ment of science and technology and thus centered around the professional or institutional autonomy of scientists. Here the key question has been whether and to what extent scientific research and technological development should be directed by central planning and resource allocation. In addition, the issue of professional autonomy has become increasingly concerned with questions of research funding and debates over management approaches.[2]

The first three decades of policy debate were dominated by the conflict over intellectual autonomy in which there were two fundamental rival policy viewpoints, the "ideologist" and the "neutralist." The ideologist view emphasized the class interests of the proletariat, endorsed and articulated by the Party, as a guideline for research and development. It was felt that the propagation of communist political consciousness among scientists would enable them to conduct science relevant to the people and to the nation. Those who were ideologically biased in "capitalist" directions would not be motivated to produce such results. The first serious attempt to

---

[2] For an illuminating discussion of the struggle for autonomy by Chinese scientists, see Richard P. Suttmeier, "Reform, Modernization, and the Changing Constitution of Science in China" *Asian Survey*, Vol. 29, No. 10 (October 1989), pp. 999–1015.

implement this view came during the Anti-Rightist Campaign and the "Hundred Flowers" campaign in the late 1950s. The Cultural Revolution in the late 1960s and its aftermath represented another radical effort to exercise intellectual control as a means of directing S&T. This effort also failed to achieve much more than a disruptive effect on the development of science and technology.

The neutralist viewpoint, in contrast, argued that ideology was largely irrelevant to the production of scientific and technological results. In a socialist system of centralized planning the influence of the Party should be limited to establishing the priorities for the system as a whole; only the main guidelines of development needed to be selected at the top political echelons with due reference to the political goals of the Party. Deng Xiaoping's aphorism that it does not matter whether the cat is black or white as long as it catches mice, which was so strongly attacked by the Cultural Revolution radicals in the early 1970s, epitomized the pragmatism espoused by the neutralist view. The neutralist view dominated the S&T policy debate in the early 1960s and has been the official principle underlying reforms since 1978. The turning point came when Deng Xiaoping made the crucial announcement that scientists belonged to the working people and thus needed no extra ideological schooling. In reality, however, the ideological castigation of intellectuals recurred at regular intervals during the 1980s. The rhetoric concerning criticism of "bourgeois liberalization" and the necessity of Party leadership forced upon the scientific community after the crackdown in June 1989 indicates that the influence of an ideologist policy view is dormant, but far from dead.

China entered the 1980s under the domination of a neutralist policy perspective to meet the twin challenges of revitalizing an alienated and weak scientific and technological infrastructure and "catching up" with the industrialized countries. The legacy of the past—regardless of the conflicts between the neutralist and ideologist viewpoints—was a strongly regimented pattern of S&T management. This pattern had evolved from copying the Soviet, Stalinist model during the "golden years" of S&T planning in the 1950s. Key components of this system were the central research organizations such as the Academy of Sciences, the comprehensive system of military and sectoral research and development institutes, and the concentration of research and development resources to specific, defense-oriented projects.

The system failed to provide a significantly higher technological level in the majority of industrial enterprises. Apparently less than 10 percent of the results of research and development activities was put into production in the 1970s, and the designs of the vast majority of equipment dated from the 1950s. Chinese and foreign observers agreed that it would require an enormous effort to raise the level of technology to those current in the industrialized countries. The new reform measures of the 1980s were seen as a solution to this problem; in Figure 1 some of the most important are briefly described.[3]

---

[3] A detailed description of the whole range of S&T reforms and their implementation is beyond the limits of this paper. A fairly recent overview is provided in Denis F. Simon and

Continued

FIGURE 1. SCIENCE AND TECHNOLOGY POLICY MEASURES OF THE 1980s.

Technology markets	It became possible to sell the results of research and development, which had previously been transferred without any compensation. Most commercial transactions since 1981 have taken place at local or national technology fairs
Technological transformation	Upgrading the technological level of equipment in state-owned enterprises. This program was initiated in 1982. It was implemented by the State Economic Commission and has involved both import of technology and domestic innovation activities
Key breakthrough S&T projects	Since 1982 the State Planning Commision (SPC) has formulated key breakthrough projects under the five-year plans. The projects are inceasingly open to tenders from competing research institutions
Patent system	Patent Law promulgated 1985. Introduced as a complement to S&T awards in order to provide incentives for the discovery and dissemination of new technology
Open Laboratories	Key laboratories equipped with advanced instruments have been established in various fields by the SPC since 1985. The laboratories should receive both domestic and foreign guest researchers
S&T Firms	Promotion of new research, development and production ventures. These may be established jointly by research and production units or may be independently operated by entrepreneurial units
Spark Program	In order to diffuse new technology in the countryside, the SSTC initiated this plan in 1985. It involves demonstration projects and major training programs. Funding is envisaged to come from both government and local sources
Funding reform	Since 1986 government allocation of funds for operating expenses were reduced for research units engaged in applied research and development, since these units were expected to raise financial resources on the technology market
Appointment system	New regulations for professional appointments issued in 1986 in order to create opportunities for mobility of scientific and technical personnel
National Science Foundation	Established in 1986 to support basic science research according to criteria of academic exellence
High Technology Plan	A large number of research projects announced in March 1986 to support new industries in microelectronics, biotechnology, new materials, space, etc.
Torch Program	A series of projects initiated since 1988 to ensure the development and diffusion of results from the High Technology Plan. Projects are approved by the SPC but funding is to be raised locally
Science Parks	Experimental zones set up since 1988 to provide special incentives to high technology industries

Merle Goldman (eds.), *Science and Technology in Post-Mao China* (Harvard University Press, Cambridge, Mass., 1989). Another useful source of information is the series of White Papers on S&T that the Chinese have published in recent years. They are entitled *Zhongguo kexue jishu zhengce zhinan (Guide to China's Science and Technology Policy)* and have been published by the State Science and Technology Commission (SSTC) annually for 1986 to 1989.

II. Policy Culture Tensions

In the course of the 1980s, three different "policy cultures" have emerged within the neutralist framework to provide guidelines for reform. They may be classified as bureaucratic, entrepreneurial, and academic (see Figure 2). While in practice they often become intertwined in the process of policymaking, for analytical purposes it is useful to separate them as "ideal types." They exist primarily as interest lobbies, or institutional networks, and as such exercise significant influence over practical policymaking.

The process of reform during the 1980s can be said to have started at the level of development priorities and then moved gradually "down" to the more pragmatic issues of choosing the means by which to implement these priorities. At a later stage, these issues were further transformed into the conflicts and compromises of institutional power struggle.

FIGURE 2. Science and Technology Policy Cultures: A Matrix.

Policy Culture

	Bureaucratic	Entrepreneurial	Academic
Development priorities	National needs	Market demand	Knowledge frontiers
Policy instruments	Planning guidelines	Commercial transactions	Peer review
Institutional networks	Planning and Economic Commission/ Defense S&T and Industry Commission	Science and Technology Commission	Chinese Academy of Science/ Universities

The initial challenge to the previously hegemonic bureaucratic policy culture came with the acceptance of market-oriented reforms at the Third Plenum in December 1978. The focus of development priorities shifted away from "national needs" defined primarily by the military-industrial complex. A report prepared by the State Science and Technology Commission (SSTC) in 1981 proposed to coordinate S&T priorities more closely with economic development, although it still operated largely within the framework of administrative plans. The document did, however, provide preliminary designs for new policy instruments; experiments with technology markets, opportunities for technical consultancy, and eventually the establish ment of new firms thus proliferated in the first half of the decade. Interestingly, research institutes in the defense sector had pioneered some of the new approaches, but they were quickly superseded by a large number of civilian research institutions.

The endorsement of the reforms by the CCP Central Committee came in March 1985 in its "Decision on the Reform of the Science and Technology Management System." Ironically, this took place as the bureaucratic policy culture reasserted its influence after a few years of alleged economic "overheating." The market-oriented policy instruments formulated by the entrepreneurial reformers also mobilized academic resistance to the reforms, since they forced the large majority of research institutes to look for new sources of financial support.

In practical terms, the tensions among policy cultures seriously limited the effectiveness of the range of policy initiatives taken. These initiatives formed a spectrum ranging from an emphasis on planning and centralized decision-making to the free search for scientific results, illustrated by some examples in Figure 3. The identification of particular initiatives with the different policy cultures is only approximate since many compromises were made in the process of policy-making.

FIGURE 3. EXAMPLES OF POLICY INSTRUMENTS FOR EACH POLICY CULTURE.

Bureaucratic	Entrepreneurial	Academic
* Technological transformation program	* Technology markets	* Open laboratories
* Key S&T projects (Five-year plan)	* Patent system/ S&T laws	* National Science Foundation
* High technology plan	* S&T Firms, Science Parks	* Appointment system
	* Spark and Torch Programs	

For example, both the Spark Program and the Torch Program have been seen as a means of decentralizing decision-making by the transfer of funding responsibilities to local authorities. Nevertheless, the shortage of local funds has made it very difficult to implement these programs without the assistance of the bureaucracy. The setting of priorities for the Spark Program has largely been the responsibility of the SSTC, and thus the program tends to combine the planning approach with the promotion of entrepreneurial initiatives.

Other compromises emerged between the bureaucratic and the academic policy cultures. The establishment of open laboratories and the High-Technology Program was based on criteria of academic excellence, and has provided an important means to strengthen advanced fundamental research in China.[4] In the process of actual implementation of these schemes, however, the influence of the State Planning Commission has tended to shift priorities in the direction of applied research. In the case of technology markets and entrepreneurship, as we shall see below, the pervasive influence of the bureaucratic culture has also forced the entrepreneurial reformers into compromises regarding the regulation of innovative activities.

The bureaucratic and the entrepreneurial cultures have shared an interest in the promotion of technological development and diffusion. In the 1980s there has thus been a significant shift in policy concern along the innovation cycle, from measures designed to promote invention to measures intended to enhance the diffusion of technologies. Earlier the academic and bureaucratic policy cultures had been preoccupied with the earliest phases of the innovation process. The entrepreneurial reformers have tried to direct more attention to—and generate more funds for—the later phases of the process, as delineated in Figure 4.

FIGURE 4. POLICY INSTRUMENTS IN THE INNOVATION PROCESS.

Discovery	Development	Diffusion
Science Foundation	Key S&T Projects	Spark Program
S&T Awards	High Technology Programme	Torch Program
	Patent System	Technological Transformation Programme

This shift has reflected the demand-side orientation of the entrepreneurial policy culture, and has been viewed as an important step in making the S&T system more responsive to the needs of the economy. The new approach also created a greater need for ensuring that the new measures had internal consistency and that support was provided throughout the innovation process. The conflicting priorities of each policy culture have reduced the actual possibilities for integration. The bureaucratic and academic cultures, in particular, entail a legacy of concepts that perceives of innovation as a supply-oriented, one-way flow from research units to production enterprises. Such concepts inhibit the potential of the majority of Chinese policymakers to see and, to an even greater extent, support and exploit the crucial forward and backward linkages that characterize modern innovation processes. Even the integration of the High-Technology Program and the Torch Program has tended to ignore the potential contribution of feedback linkages with production enterprises.

---

[4] For a recent overview, see Marc Abramson, "Open Labs in China," *China Exchange News* Vol. 18, No. 1, pp.8–13.

In addition, there has been a tendency for institutional interest lobbies to develop separate networks struggling for ultimate power over financial resources. The entrepreneurial reformers attempted to create a network around progressive political personalities in the CCP Central Committee, the State Council, and the recently abolished Science and Technology Leading Group. The entrepreneurial network was thus based on an unusual alliance between high-level politicians such as Hu Yaobang and Zhao Ziyang, who had become opposed to the rigid Soviet model through their largely domestic experience, and an expanding group of young technocrats inspired by Western economic and managerial philosophies. A stronghold of this network was the SSTC, but the influential research organizations known as "think tanks" established by Zhao Ziyang have also played a major role.

In the early 1980s these people were on the offensive supported by the crucial, but ambivalent, personal charisma of Deng Xiaoping. Since the mid-1980s, however, they have been finding it more difficult to maintain the pace of reform, against the reaction from bureaucratic and academic networks. The austerity measures and difficult political climate following the crackdown in June 1989 marked a further weakening of entrepreneurial reforms.

The resistance came from a new generation of bureaucrats trained in the Soviet Union or by Soviet experts in the 1950s. Premier Li Peng is archetypical of this generation. The formidable personal network created by these people provides the core political and administrative support for the military-industrial complex in China including, of course, the National Defense S&T and Industry Commission. The network has also maintained a strong position in the State Planning Commision and the State Economic Commsission. Finally, it is extremely influential in the industrial ministries and in the well-funded aeronautic and space technology establishment headed by prestigious scientists such as Qian Xuesen, a rocket expert who returned to China from the United States in the 1950s. The reluctance of this group of people to relinquish control, despite reformist rhetoric, has repeatedly provided a barrier to the implementation of S&T policy reforms.

The academic policy culture was, at least in the initial phases of reforms, not so much at odds with the entrepreneurial approach. Through the rehabilitation of intellectuals and the position granted to "scientific" advice in policymaking, the protagonists of the interests of universities and the research community were able to lobby for important new initiatives. The reform measures included the establishment of open laboratories for advanced research, science foundations, and expensive equipment for high-energy physics research. At the same time, however, reforms of the system of research and development funding presented new challenges for scientists. Antagonism to cuts in central state funding and other measures undermining basic research became particularly important in 1986–87, and for many institutions a new spate of key breakthrough S&T projects and a high-technology research plan provided a welcome chance to seek alliances with the bureaucracy.

This latest compromise between the bureaucratic and academic policy cultures was confirmed by Premier Li Peng in August 1989, when the theme of reform was being toned down considerably.[5] In his view, the reforms have "basically been successful"—i.e., terminated. Two remaining issues regarding bureaucratic and academic interests include the choice between serving the immediate needs of national economic construction or the long-term developmental needs on the one hand, and determining the relationship between basic and applied research on the other. The leadership adheres to a fundamental belief in dictating applied research priorities according to the needs of national economic construction so characteristic of the bureaucratic policy culture, but in order not to alienate the academic network there is a token support for basic research in official statements.

III. COMMERCIALIZATION AND ENTREPRENEURSHIP

It is instructive to look at two areas where the tensions between different S&T policy cultures have limited the success of the reforms. The successful growth of commercial transactions in knowhow and the remarkable performance of new S&T firms during the 1980s led to an exposure of the contradictions existing between various groups and indicate the difficult environment for innovation in China.

A. COMMERCIALIZATION: THE TECHNOLOGY MARKETS

In the efforts to shift the attention of the Chinese research and development organizations toward market demand, the entrepreneurial reformers have emphasized commercial transactions to integrate research with production. The concept behind the new approach was borrowed from the theory of a socialist commodity economy that had gained so much popularity in the early 1980s. The key assumption was that the results of research and development—designs, prototypes, or simply know-how—constitute a commodity. Mechanisms for exchange of these "commodities" were then quickly established, initially in major industrial cities such as Shenyang but rapidly spreading to other cities. The primary vehicle for exchange of technology was the trade fair in which research institutes could exhibit the results of their work. In addition, during 1985–86, an increasing number of intermediary organizations emerged which served as brokers linking suppliers and customers.[6]

The growth of technology trade has continued to expand throughout the 1980s, as indicated by the estimates provided in Figure 5. Many transactions took place during the national or local technology trade fairs, but a new practice of direct contacts between research institutions and their customers was also gaining popularity. At the same time, however, instances of fraud and other questionable activities began to occur. The reaction was to increase control.

The entrepreneurial reformers at the SSTC reacted by strengthening indirect regulation: a more extensive legal frame-

---

[5] "Woguo keji tizhi gaige jiben shi chenggong de (The Reform of China's S&T System Reforms Have Basically Been Completed)" *Keji Ribao (Science and Technology Daily)* 8 August 1989, p. 1.
[6] See E. Baark, "Commercialised Technology Transfer in China 1981–86: The Impact of Science and Technology Policy Reforms" *The China Quarterly* (September 1987), pp. 390–406.

FIGURE 5. THE VALUE OF TECHNOLOGY TRADE, 1985–87.

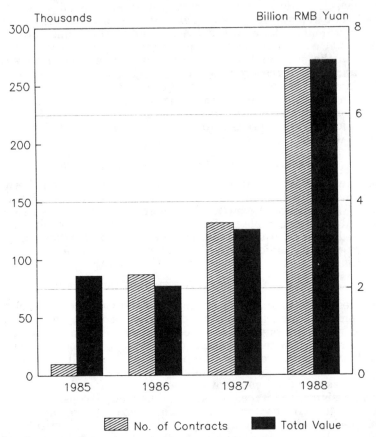

work for transactions in technology-related services was introduced with the Patent Law of 1985 and the Technology Contract Law promulgated in 1987. A Basic Science and Technology Law has also been discussed, but the process of formulating such a law appears to have slowed down significantly.[7] The bureaucratic reaction, in contrast, emphasized direct management of technology markets by specialized organizations. In October 1986 a China Technology Market Joint Development Group was established at the national level, and similar organizations were created at lower levels of regional administration. In theory, these organizations were intended to accelerate commercial transfer; in practice, they simply brought the market under the purview of the bureaucracy and created an

[7] The plans for legislation is discussed are S&T White Paper No. 2 issued in 1987. All the White Papers have contained useful collections of important laws and regulations in the sector.

intermediate level of management that levied new charges on the transactions.

The expansion of the number and value of transactions in the technology market, which subsequently took place in 1988, was thus, to a considerable degree, the result of "regularization" of the market and better statistics. Moreover, a substantial number of transactions derived from plan projects. These included the increasing number of research and development projects for which government organizations issued contracts after a tender. To assure broader diffusion, during the last few years there has also been a tendency of licensing technology which was originally developed under state plans, for use in the market. According to recent statistics, such projects constituted 30 percent of the total value of contracts in 1988.[8]

Many Chinese observers have, however, felt that the growth of the technology market was constrained by the economic system. In particular, the value of technology is generally considered very low, i.e., the remuneration for technical services, commissioned technological development, etc. undertaken by scientific institutions is rather meager. In 1987 the average value of technology license contracts was 29,200 RMB yuan, which was raised to 53,700 RMB yuan in 1988. Contracts for technology development averaged 66,500 RMB yuan, while technical services involved transactions that reached an average sum of only 17,500 RMB yuan.[9] These sums do not appear to indicate a lucrative market for the technology suppliers, particularly considering the rate of inflation and the devaluation of the Chinese currency.

Another constraint has been the low demand for new technology, particularly from the major state-operated enterprises. This characteristic is reflected in the prices, as indicated above, but is also found in the composition of buyers. The reformers had been particularly worried that the largest proportion of technology purchases during 1985–86 was made by small-scale and rural enterprises. The lack of demand from the large, state-owned sector confirmed a fear that the S&T institutions were still marginalized in relation to the core industrial sectors. They have been encouraged by statistics from 1987–88 indicating that an increasing proportion of buyers in the market belong to the category of large- and medium-scale enterprises.[10] The problem is, however, that most of the growth of this category may be derived from a larger demand from medium-scale enterprises. The possibility exists that the introduction of plan projects under the formal procedures of a technology market has led to a token increase in the demand for technologies from large state-owned enterprises. If this is the case, the technology market may be as marginal as ever in providing crucial inputs in the process of technological innovation in China.

---

[8] Interviews, summer 1990.

[9] Figures provided in interviews during summer 1990. Prices are simply left to be determined by supply and demand, and a lot of theorizing concerning ways to fix prices has proven largely futile. See Erik Baark, "The Value of Technology: A Survey of the Chinese Theoretical Debate and Its Policy Implications" *Research Policy* No. 17 (1988), pp. 269–282.

[10] Interviews during summer 1990 indicated that this category occupied 58 percent of technology sales to industrial enterprises in 1987, and 68 percent in 1988.

542

B. ENTREPRENEURSHIP: SCIENCE AND TECHNOLOGY FIRMS

The commitment of reformers to entrepreneurship in the mid-1980s provided opportunities for the formation of new technology-based enterprises.[11] For research institutes and universities this meant the creation of a practical way of profiting from existing know-how. The main breeding ground for new S&T firms was the so-called "Electronics Street" in the Zhongguancun area of the northwestern suburbs of Beijing, which is also the site of many advanced research institutes in China.

The fate of Electronics Street and its entrepreneurial spirit is symptomatic of the tensions generated by entrepreneurial reforms in China. The history of the S&T firms in Electronics Street dates back to a "Service Department for the Development of Advanced Technology," which had been created in 1980 by a group at the Chinese Academy of Sciences, led by Chen Chunxian from the Institute of Physics.[12] Inspired by visits to Silicon Valley and Route 128 in the United States, this bureau was an attempt to combine R&D with production. Chen Chunxian's initiative was discussed by Hu Yaobang and other members of the CCP Central Committee in January 1983; their conclusion was approval of the "new road taken." In April 1983 an independent unit was formed under the name "Huaxia New Technology Development Institute."

The "overheating" of the Chinese economy in 1984–85 subsequently provided a fertile base for new technology firms. This was particularly the case in electronics, where a demand was generated by the somewhat naïve reactions to the "New Technological Revolution."[13] Electronics subsequently flourished, with annual growth rates of more than 100 percent, and pioneers such as Chen Chunxian's "Huaxia" firm became overshadowed by a core group of very prosperous companies. By 1987 eight companies led by a newcomer, Stone Computer Company, had captured a large part of the rapidly growing market for microcomputers in China. Figure 6 shows that the turnover of electronics firms rose from 18 million RMB yuan in 1984 to over 900 million RMB yuan in 1987.

The majority of new entrepreneurial units were collectively owned with participation by state-owned units or local authorities. There are virtually no genuinely "private" entrepreneurs, and even an unusually independent figure such as Wan Runnan from the Stone Computer Corporation had allegedly relied on intervention from higher authorities in the central government.

People associated with the academic policy culture have reacted to these new forms of interaction with society in an ambivalent fashion. On the one hand, many scientists respond with disdain. In their view, the entrepreneurs were not really engaged in technolog-

---

[11] The reforms initially encouraged "Research-Production Alliances" (*Keyan shengchan lianheti*), but as firms gradually became independent from their original units, the term "Science and Technology Firm" (*Keji qiye*) was coined. In the remainder of this paper the generic term "S&T firms" is used.

[12] For details see Yu Weilian (ed.), *Xiwang de huoguang (The Blaze of Hope)* (Beijing: Zhongguo renmin daxue chubanshe, 1988). Some results from this study have also been published in White Paper No. 3 on S&T (1988). Another valuable source of information has been Miao Qihao "Science Parks for Development: the Chinese Case," Paper presented to the Research Forum of the conference on R&D, Entrepreneur and Innovation, Manchester, U.K., July 1990.

[13] The demand was apparently also fueled by the introduction of new formal criteria: in order to be classified as "advanced," for example, the enterprises needed to install a computer!

FIGURE 6. Electronics Street: Number of Firms and Turnover.

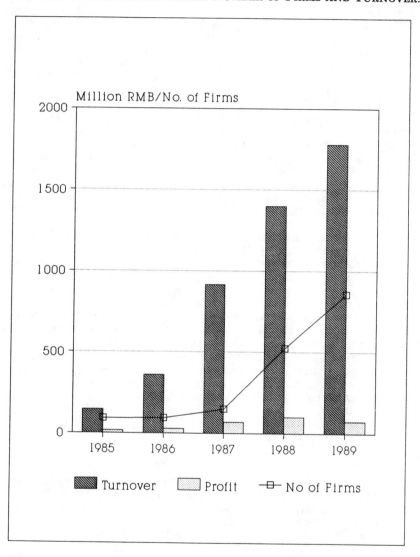

ical development, but only in the marketing of imported computer hardware. On the other hand, the scientists are under considerable pressure to earn money through entrepreneurship themselves, and the need to solve this problem has made it necessary to accept a much broader definition of their work.

In 1987 it became clear that the spin-off entrepreneurial firms were more effective than most state-operated units—in both generating profits and developing new technology rapidly. An investigation carried out in early 1988 confirmed that the firms on Electronics Street were capable of conducting product innovation and exploiting domestic and international markets at an unprecedented rate. More than 75 percent of the research and development projects carried out by the entrepreneurial firms were finished within a year; the majority of the results were marketed in China and many were marketed abroad.[14] These were precisely the qualities that were desired by the reformers; but in addition to the academic contempt toward such commercial flair, which is a distinctive feature of both traditional Chinese Confucian values and more recent communist dogmatism, there was a fear of the political consequences of "private" enterprise. The *enfant terrible* buried in most of the entrepreneurs of Electronics Street represented a challenge to the political system. Wan Runnan thus engaged the Stone Corporation in the student demonstrations in spring 1989, and had to escape to the United States and France after the crackdown.

The apparent success of the entrepreneurs on Electronics Street led to another interesting development: the proliferation of "Science Parks"[15] in China. The first park was established by the Chinese Academy of Sciences in Shenzhen. After a feasibility study commissioned by the SSTC, the State Council in 1988 approved the establishment of a new zone in Beijing, comprising many of the enterprises set up in the Electronics Street. The preliminary experience gained in the zones established in Beijing and Shanghai indicates, however, that the Chinese science parks are seldom a spontaneous phenomenon, but a kind of program sponsored by local or central government. The future of these programs depends to a large extent on the macroeconomic situation, and although many of the enterprises in the existing zones have continued to grow during 1989, they have also been affected by the austerity measures of the government.

IV. CONCLUSIONS

The paradox of fragmented innovation in China derives from two interacting forces: the schisms of policy compromises and the inertia of the economic system. Arguably, China's many enterprising and talented scientists, technicians, and managers are caught in "scissors" that limit their innovative capability and marginalize their efforts contribute effectively to economic growth.

My own view is that the political reaction to reform in the last half of the 1980s, which culminated in the dramatic confrontations of May–June 1989, will continue to constrain the innovative policy instruments introduced by entrepreneurial reformers. Compromises between major institutional networks will continue to characterize the reform process, rendering it partly ineffective. The problem is also the existing structure of the economy, with its

---

[14] See table 2 on page 48 in White Paper on S&T No. 3 (1988).
[15] Officially known as "*Xin jishu chanye kaifa shiyanqu* (New Technology Industrial Development Experimental Zone)." Enterprises in such zones are provided with a package of incentives such as lower tax rate, longer tax holiday, promotional activities, etc.

biased price system, the lack of venture capital outside official channels, and the pervasive interpersonal relations in economic transactions. This structure constitutes a gravitational force that, in a sense, "pulls" the activities of innovative units and persons down toward earlier modes of conduct. The conservatism and inertia of S&T management in China can thus be expected to continue to influence innovation in the 1990s.

CHINA'S HIGH TECHNOLOGY: PROGRAMS, PROBLEMS, AND PROSPECTS

By Richard P. Suttmeier *

CONTENTS

SUMMARY

Since the suppression of the demonstrations in Tiananmen Square on June 3 and 4, 1989, international interest in China's economic technological and scientific development has declined. Programs of exchange and cooperation with China were suspended by many countries. With the dramatic changes in Eastern Europe and the Soviet Union, the spotlight which China enjoyed for the better part of a decade shifted elsewhere. While these changes in the international environment have clearly had important consequences for Chinese development programs, we should not lose sight of the fact that these programs go on.

Before June 4th, China's high-technology aspirations had just been redefined and were beginning to attract international attention. China, after all, with its large technical community, represented an intriguing possibility for a Western Pacific region which increasingly saw its economic future in terms of high-technology development. Where China was going with its high-technology pro-

* Richard P. Suttmeier is Director of the Center for Asian and Pacific Studies, University of Oregon.

grams, and the chances for their success, had implications not only for China's future, but also for the future of the region. These kinds of issues are no less important today, after June 4th, than they were before.

Unlike the Asian newly industrializing economies (NIEs)—South Korea, Taiwan, Hong Kong, and Singapore—whose interest in high-technology industry stems from the successful exhaustion of their labor-intensive industrialization strategies, China has only begun to exploit its comparative advantage in low-cost labor. The NIEs, on the other hand, in the face of rising labor costs, have concluded that their continued prosperity will require industrial restructuring to achieve higher value-added manufacturing through high technology.

The Chinese rationale for its high-technology initiatives is somewhat different.[1] First, many Chinese leaders are ambivalent about overreliance on labor-intensive industrialization. According to Li Xu'e, the Vice Minister of the State Science and Technology Commission (SSTC) responsible for the "Torch" Plan (discussed below),

> "... although in labor-intensive industries China has the advantage of cheap labor, we lack clear advantages in such other factors critical to product competitiveness as product quality, modern management, and after sales service ... the added value produced by these industries is small, and the competition among undeveloped countries is fierce."[2]

These leaders reason that, although China remains an underdeveloped country by many measures, in one respect—its larger number of scientists and engineers—it is more like a developed country. Furthermore, China has had considerable experience with high-technology research and production as a result of its strategic weapons programs, and already has a high-technology industry which produced goods and services worth 70 billion yuan in 1987. Finally, the leaders of China's technical establishment fear that unless China at least "pays its dues" to high-technology development, it will fall further behind other nations in a world where, in their view, a nation's wealth and power will increasingly be based on science and technology.

The main components of China's evolving strategy for high technology include (1) the support of research, development, and applications through the mechanisms of annual and five-year plans; (2) the initiation, in 1987, of a high-priority national high-technology program, the so-called "863" Program; (3) the initiation of the "Torch" Plan in 1988 to encourage the industrial application of research results; (4) the encouragement of high-technology entrepreneurship, the start-up of new firms, and the support of special high-technology industrial zones; and (5) the conversion of military research and production facilities to civilian use. Before discussing each of these in greater detail, I will explore further some of the conditions affecting high-technology development.

---

[1] See Li Xu'e. "Some Problems in the Development of China's High Technology Industry." *Zhongguo Keji Luntan, (Forum on Science and Technology in China)*. No. 6, November 18, 1990. In JPRS–CST–90–008. March 15, 1990. This discussion also draws on the author's interview with Zhang Binfu of the "Torch" Plan office, August 1989.

[2] Li Xu'e. "Some Problems."

I. China's Technical Resources

There is little doubt that China's investments in the development of science and technology over the last 40 years have had extremely disappointing economic consequences. Yet, there is also little doubt that those investments have produced a very large technical establishment, second to none in size in the developing world. The number of scientists and engineers in major centers, like Shanghai or Beijing, alone, exceed the number for most countries—including such development exemplars as South Korea and Taiwan. That this establishment has been inefficiently run, and has failed to maintain reasonably uniform quality standards, cannot be denied. But it still represents a large pool of human and material resources waiting to be exploited. Let us consider its dimensions.

By the end of 1988, China had 5,275 state-run research institutes, including some 120 in the Chinese Academy of Sciences (CAS). These employed approximately 384,000 scientists and engineers (50,000 in CAS), of whom 345,000 (30,000 in CAS) were in research and development. In addition to another 2,498 institutes at the country level, which employed 64,000 personnel, 12% of whom were scientists, the 1980s also saw the growth of some 4,870 collective and privately owned research establishments. These employed 61,000 scientists and engineers in 1988.

Finally, China's 1,063 institutions of higher education employed 541,000 science and technology personnel in 1988, with 161,000 full time equivalent scientists and engineers engaged in R&D. While it is still difficult to arrive at internationally comparable indices of levels of effort, the data above suggest that as many as 450,000 scientists and engineers are engaged in R&D.[3] Total expenditures for R&D in 1988 were probably on the order of RMB 15 billion.[4]

One of the more interesting features about Chinese technical capabilities is their spatial distribution. While we often correctly assume that Beijing and Shanghai are major centers of Chinese science and technology (S&T), they are not alone. Past policies and historical accidents have in fact distributed China's technical resources well beyond those two cities, as Table 1 illustrates.

Table 1 indicates that each major region of China is represented by at least one province as a technical nucleus. It is clear from Table 2, however, that when the regions are taken as a whole, not surprisingly, there are considerable differences in resources among them. Nevertheless, these data do show that there is a much wider distribution of capabilities in the country than visits to the more internationally visible centers along the coast would lead one to suspect.

---

[3] Based on Richard P. Suttmeier. "Science and Technology Resources in China," unpublished report to the National Science Foundation, and on the author's discussions with Zhao Yuhai and Dong Liya of the State Science and Technology Commission (SSTC), August 1989.

[4] This figure is based on published figures of state expenditures and amounts spent by industry which are estimated to be 50% of the former.

TABLE 1. Leading Provinces in S&T Resources

Number of Institutes		Number of S&Es		Expenditures	
Beijing	393	Beijing	79,540	Beijing	2,627,553
Liaoning	332	Shanghai	30,624	Shanghai	1,088,324
Jiangsu	301	Sichuan	23,122	Sichuan	882,675
Sichuan	277	Shaanxi	18,324	Liaoning	634,002
Shandong	267	Jiangsu	17,742	Shaanxi	619,488
Guangdong	258	Liaoning	17,548	Jiangsu	560,126
Hubei	248	Hubei	11,648	Guangdong	380,530
Shanghai	242	Tianjin	10,810	Tianjin	369,959
Heilongjiang	231	Guangdong	10,101	Henan	360,822
Hunan	201	Henan	9,613	Hubei	324,188

Source: Richard P. Suttmeier. "Science and Technology Resources in China," unpublished report to the National Science Foundation, and on the author's discussions with Zhao Yubai and Dong Liya of SSTC, August 1989.

TABLE 2. Concentration of S&T Resources by Region

Number of Institutes		Number of S&Es		Expenditures (Yuan)	
East	1,392	East	108,739	East	3,525,106
South Central	1,038	North	76,120	Northeast	2,499,097
Northern	1,023	Northeast	43,125	South Central	1,499,834
Northeast	712	South	34,449	Southwest	1,164,546
Southwest	557	Southwest	31,779	North	1,096,870
Northwest	549	Northwest	30,548	Northwest	1,034,120

Source: Richard P. Suttmeier. "Science and Technology Resources in China," unpublished report to the National Science Foundation, and on the author's discussions with Zhao Yuhai and Dong Liya of the SSTC, August 1989.

As is shown below, the growth of high-technology initiatives is also not limited to a few centers. The data in Tables 1 and 2 illustrate why this is so.

II. THE "MAIN BATTLEFIELD"—THE REGULAR PLANS

Chinese commitment to high technology through the planning process goes back to the 1950s with the adoption of a 12-year plan (1956–67) for S&T developments. This plan led to the introduction into China of capabilities in such fields as computers, semi-conductors, automation, radio electronics, nuclear and jet propulsion technologies.[5] During the course of this plan period (the actual plan objectives had been met by the early 1960s, and a new plan was introduced in 1962), Chinese science became both more militarized (and thus increasingly, in high-technology areas, cut off from the civilian economy), and more subject to radical politics. The planning process was seriously disrupted by the Cultural Revolution, but highly focused high-technology work continued in support of military missions. The goal of the mid-1950s to develop a broad base of generic, science-based technologies—fell victim (to the great detriment of the economy and of scientific research) to the development

---

[5] State Science and Technology Commission. *Guide to China's Science and Technology Policy, 1986. (White Paper on Science and Technology, No. 1, hereafter, "White Paper")* Beijing, 1987, p. 16.

of more specialized (and highly classified) competence in the military sphere.

The first major effort at broad-based science planning in the post-Mao period, the National Science and Technology Development Plan for the 1978–85 period, was strongly oriented toward high technology. It identified 108 key projects in 8 priority areas: agriculture, energy, materials, microelectronics, lasers, space, high-energy physics, and genetic engineering. Within a year of its announcement, however, this plan was being reconsidered. By the early 1980s its emphasis on basic research and high technology had been toned down considerably. These priorities were too far removed form China's immediate economic needs, it was thought, and shortages of both money and high-quality manpower argued against a major push into high technology at the time. Policy and planning attention for S&T, therefore, turned to the more pragmatic concerns of the sixth Five-Year Plan (FYP) (1980–85) for the economy.

High-technology development was not entirely excluded, however. Though not on the list of priorities for the sixth FYP, work on large-scale integrated circuits, computers, computer software, communications (including optical fibers, microwaves, satellites, digital exchanges, and networks), biotechnology, new materials, space technology and remote sensing, lasers, and isotopes and radiation technology was mentioned.[6] Many of these areas of research received a boost when they were included in the "Scientific and Technological Key Projects Program" of the seventh FYP when it was adopted in 1986.[7]

Since the five-year plan continues to be an important mechanism for relocating the nation's resources ("the main battlefield"), one of the more important modes of support for high technology is through the conventional planning process. In the sixth FYP, some RMB 1.5 billion was set aside for science projects organized around 38 major "programs," but most of them were not in high technology. The commitment to science in the seventh FYP was substantially greater, RMB 5 billion in support of 76 programs.[8]

Support of research relevant to high technology through the regular planning process continues to be evident in the recently announced basic research priorities for the eighth FYP. These include high-temperature super-conductivity, the structure and properties of optoelectronic materials, semi-conductor super-lattice physics, as well as projects pertaining to biotechnology, geophysics, and the environment.[9]

A. THE "863" PROGRAM

By the mid-1980s, with more funds becoming available for S&T, the expansion of the technical manpower pool,[10] (including the

---

[6] *White Paper, 1986*, 189–215.
[7] *White Paper.* p. 153.
[8] *Keji Ribao*, (Science and Technology Daily), 8 April, 1989. In JRPS–CST–89–015, August 18, 1989, p. 1
[9] *Keji Ribao (Science and Technology Daily)*, December 23, 1989, On JPRS–CST–90–007, March 6, 1990, p. 3.
[10] The number of individuals working in S&T in state organizations increased by 38.6% between 1982 and 1987. In this same period, there were 1,863 million college and university gradu-

Continued

return of technical personnel from advanced study of abroad), and a deepened appreciation of the world high-technology revolution, a consensus was developing that China could not afford not to get into high technology more ambitiously. In March of 1986, laser specialist Wang Dahang and three other senior scientists wrote to Deng Xiaoping urging the initiation of a new national high-technology program. The Party Central Committee approved the idea in October, and the program began in early 1987 as the National High Technology Development Program (referred to in China as *baliusan* literally, 86/3, or March 1986). The Program reportedly, "... aims to pool together the best technological resources in China over the next 15 years to keep up with international high technology development, bridge the gap between China and other countries in several most important areas, and wherever possible, strive for breakthroughs. The programme also aims to provide technological backup for economic development and train large numbers of talent for the future." [11]

The national high technology program has the following priorities: [12]

1. *Biotechnology* (High-yield, high-quality, adversity-resistant plants and animals; New medicines, vaccines and genic therapy; protein engineering)

2. *Space Technology*

3. *Information Technology* (Intelligent computer systems; Optoelectronic devices and microelectronic optoelectronic systems integration technology; information acquisition and processing technology)

4. *Laser Technology*

5. *Automation Technology* (Computer-integrated manufacturing systems; intelligent robots)

6. *Energy* (Coal-fired magnetohydrodynamic power generation; advanced nuclear reactors)

7. *Advanced Materials*

The overall management of the Program is divided between the Basic Research and High Technology Department of the State Science and Technology Commission and the National Defense Science, Technology and Industry Commission, but its actual administration employs an innovative (for China) peer-review system. Each of the seven areas above has a senior expert advisory committee (the average age of the members is 72). Below these are 15 "expert task groups" (involving a total of 106 scientists and engineers with an average age of 48) who designate projects warranting support, and who review the progress of grants on an annual basis. In project selection, the Program uses a "bottom up" approach, with project ideas originating from potential investigators (inspired by U.S. practice), and the "top down," more targeted approach favored by the Japanese. [13]

---

ates, and some 69,000 recipients of graduate education in China (in all fields). (11 April, 1988). In JPRS–CAR–88–023, p. 17.
[11] "An Outline of the Hi-Tech Development Programme in China." Beijing. The Science and Technology Leading Group of the State Council, 1987.
[12] *Ibid.*
[13] Based on author's interview with Ma Junru, Head of the Fundamental Research and New Technology Department of SSTC, August 1989.

Approximately RMB 500 million has been spent on the Program since it began.[14] The number of projects supported, some 1,000 thus far, is expected to ebb and flow from year to year, depending on quality and size of project (one of the larger projects, in semi-conductor lasers, has consumed RMB 30 million, but others have been less costly). The Program has involved some 10,000 scientists and engineers in 500 organizations from the three main sectors of the R&D establishment—CAS, institutions of higher education, and ministerial research institutes. In 1988, the distribution of funding by sectoral performer was as follows:[15]

FIGURE 1. "863" PROJECTS, BY PERFORMER.

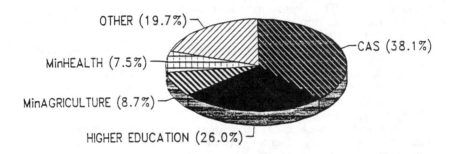

OTHER (19.7%)

CAS (38.1%)

MinHEALTH (7.5%)

MinAGRICULTURE (8.7%)

HIGHER EDUCATION (26.0%)

A small fraction (2%, or RMB 7.5 million in 1988) of the Program's budget has been transferred to the National Science Foundation of China to be administered by that agency in support of exploratory research.[16] About 2,000 technical personnel have been involved in some 200 exploratory basic research projects.

Figure 2 summarizes the distribution of funding in 1988 by major subject area.[17]

Successes to date have been reported in projects dealing with optoelectronics, lasers, rice germination, hepatitis-b vaccine, and new materials. In the belief that it would be more cost-effective to concentrate resources, new national centers have been established in three areas of technology—optoelectronics, computer-integrated manufacturing systems, and robotics. More generally, with big projects that require cooperation from different institutes, there is often fierce competition for the right to host the project, and thus reap the long-term benefits of keeping the new equipment involved. While an administrative problem, this competition is also a measure of the keen interest taken in the Program by the research community.

---

[14] Approximately RMB 200 million was expended in 1988, with some RMB 300 million to be spent in 1989 (Ma Junru interview). These figures would suggest that the 863 Program is budgeted at about twice that of the National Science Foundation of China.

[15] Shang Mu. "Progress in China's High-Technology Research and Development Plan." *Keji Ribao* (*Science and Technology Daily*). November 17, 1990. In JPRS-CST-90-005, February 8, 1990, p.4.

[16] China's total expenditure on basic research in 1987 has been estimated to be RMB 800 million, or 7% of the total R&D expenditures. *Jiefang Ribao*, February 14, 1989, p. 3.

[17] Shang Mu. "Progress in . . . ."

FIGURE 2. "863" PROJECTS, BY FIELD.

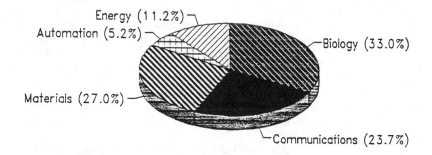

Energy (11.2%)
Automation (5.2%)
Biology (33.0%)
Materials (27.0%)
Communications (23.7%)

The primary purpose of the Program—is to prepare China for the high-technology challenges of the turn of the century—through research and international technology monitoring. Nevertheless, some of the results of the 863 program are finding their way into applications, and research results during the 1990s are expected to have commercial potential. Questions of property rights are among the more important issues surrounding commercialization. One response has been the promotion, under the SSTC, of a new technology brokerage firm called "Xe Zhao." Should patentable discoveries result from 863 projects, Ke Zhao would acquire licenses to these patents which it would then relicense to enterprises.[18] As discussed further below, ownership questions have been further clouded by political developments since June 4, 1989.

B. THE TORCH PLAN

Concerns for the commercialization of research, including but not limited to the 863 Program, prompted the initiation of the "Torch" Plan in August 1988. Torch, which is administered by the Torch High Technology Industry Development Center (established in 1989) under the Industrial Science and Technology Department of the SSTC, is in many ways a product of the reform decade. Its approach to problems of moving research to production shows the influence of 10 years of exposure to foreign innovation systems, and its foci of attention are the new organizational forms (e.g., start-up firms), and institutional possibilities (e.g., high-technology development zones) which emerged in the 1980s.

The Plan's main objectives include the following:[19]

1. *Policy Guidance.* Provide policy guidelines conducive to the growth of high-technology industry and the transfer of knowledge from laboratory to enterprise. The main focus of this work is to coordinate policy for, and oversee, existing (or planned) special eco-

---

[18] Ma Junru interview.
[19] Based on interview with Zhnag Binfu of the Torch program Office, SSTC, August 1989. See also three important articles translated from *Zhongguo Keji Luntan* (*Forum on Science and Technology*) No. 16 November 18, 1989, pp. 2–14, in JPRS–CST–90–008, March 15, 1990, pp. 1–13.

nomic zones for high technology and new technology, some 30 of which now exist (see below).

2. *Establishment of Technology Enterprise Service Centers.* Some 30 of these are to be established during the first few years of the Program (25 had been set up by April, 1990). Borrowing from the Western concept of "technology incubators," the centers are to provide comprehensive services and information pertaining to finance, equipment procurement, marketing, taxes, foreign travel, etc. to those (especially scientists and engineers) seeking to establish new companies. The Donghu New Science and Technology Startup Services Center in Wuhan served as the prototype.

3. *Training.* During its first few years, the Program aims to provide management training for up to 20,000 individuals in various aspects of operating high-technology firms for both the domestic and international markets.

4. *Finance.* The Torch Program has a limited budget, and thus approaches the financing of high-technology start-ups more as a broker than a banker. The Program uses its influence to facilitate loans and investments from banks and local governments with promises of payback periods of 3–4 years. The Industrial and Commercial Bank of China has been especially active in supporting the Program, providing RMB 200 million and 10 million in U.S. dollars in 1988 and 1989.[20]

5. *Organize Specific Projects Valued by the State.* Some 272 such projects (out of 1500 project proposals received) have been supported during 1988 and 1989 in five major areas designated as priorities—new materials, microelectronics and information, energy (high-efficiency and conservation technologies), biotechnology and electromechanical devices ("megatronics"). Approximately RMB 1.5 billion has been invested in support of these projects. This investment is expected to produce returns of RMB 5.6 billion annually and earn some 580 million U.S. dollars in annual exports.[21]

Torch originally was not intended to focus on large state enterprises which have their own research to production strategies. After two years experience, and the realization that economic benefits may in some cases be a function of scale economies, this may now be changing.[22]

Table 3 shows the distribution of Torch projects for 1988 and 1989 according to province and priority technology.

The large number of projects in the electronics and information and new materials categories is consistent with Chinese interests and strengths in these technologies. It is somewhat surprising that there are not more projects in biotechnology, and that there are as many as there are in megatronics. (See Figure 3).

The geographical distribution of projects is suggestive. The Plan has reached all of China's provinces except four (Xinjiang, Qinghai, Yunnan, and Tibet), but as Figure 4 indicates, the greatest concentration of activities is in three regions: North China, East China,

[20] *Xinhua*, April 19, 1990, FBIS–CHI–90–077, April 20, 1990, p. 34.
[21] *Ibid.*
[22] *Renmin Ribao*, (*People's Daily*), February 3, 1990, FBIS–CHI–90–039, February 27, 1990, p. 21.

TABLE 3. Torch Projects by Region and Technology, 1988 and 1989

City	Materials	Biotech.	Electronics and Information	Megatron.	Energy	Other	Totals
Beijing	16	8	24	8	4	2	59
Guangdong	5	8	10	0	4	1	28
Hubei	9	3	3	3	1	2	21
Liaoning	10	0	0	6	1	1	18
Jiangsu	4	1	5	5	0	1	16
Zhejiang	3	1	2	6	1	2	15
Shandong	4	6	2	0	2	1	15
Henan	4	1	3	1	2	0	11
Shanghai	4	1	3	3	0	0	11
Anhui	1	2	7	1	0	0	11
Guangxi	2	0	3	2	0	0	7
Fujian	1	0	5	1	0	0	7
Hebei	1	0	5	0	0	0	6
Hunan	3	0	0	1	0	2	6
Sichuan	2	0	2	2	0	0	6
Tianjin	2	2	2	0	0	0	6
Heilongjiang	1	0	2	0	1	1	5
Shaanxi	1	0	4	0	0	0	5
Hainan	0	1	3	0	0	0	4
Gansu	1	1	1	0	1	0	4
Jilin	1	0	2	0	0	1	4
Nei Mongu	1	0	0	1	0	0	2
Jiangxi	2	0	0	0	0	0	2
Ningxia	1	0	0	0	0	0	1
Shanxi	0	0	0	1	0	0	1
Guizhou	0	0	0	1	0	0	1
TOTALS	79	35	85	42	17	14	272

Source: *Keji Ribao.* (*Science and Technology Daily*). August 6, 1990. In JPRS–CST–89–024. November 1,1989. pp. 1–9. This report also provides the topics for each of the 271 projects.

FIGURE 3. TORCH PROJECTS, BY FIELD, 1988–1989.

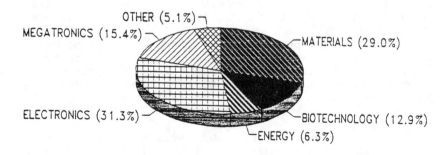

OTHER (5.1%)
MEGATRONICS (15.4%)
MATERIALS (29.0%)
ELECTRONICS (31.3%)
BIOTECHNOLOGY (12.9%)
ENERGY (6.3%)

and the South Central region (which includes Guangdon and Hubei).

Eighty percent of projects in the north are in Beijing, presumably a reflection of the large concentrations of S&T talent in the capital, *and* the fact that Beijing has been a leader in high-technology entrepreneurship (discussed further below).

FIGURE 4. TORCH PROJECTS, BY REGION.

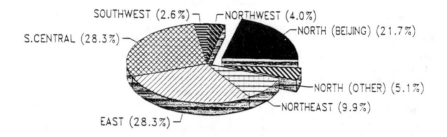

SOUTHWEST (2.6%) ⌐NORTHWEST (4.0%)
S.CENTRAL (28.3%) ⌐NORTH (BEIJING) (21.7%)
NORTH (OTHER) (5.1%)
NORTHEAST (9.9%)
EAST (28.3%)

On the other hand, the extensive activities in East China are not a reflection of a concentration in Shanghai; projects are distributed rather evenly among most of the provinces (Shandong, Jiangsu, Zhejiang, Henan, Anhui) which make up the region. The low number of projects in Shanghai, especially in comparison with Beijing, is interesting. It is less a measure of Shanghai's importance as a center of high technology, than of the fact that the Torch plan is not attempting to compete with high-technology activities which are part of other national programs, of which Shanghai is a major participant. On the other hand, East China (minus Shanghai) has been a center of collective and township enterprise during the past decade, and also has a large number of collective and private research organizations.

The same can be said of the South Central region, especially its two main centers, Guangzhou and Wuhan. Guangdong province has perhaps been the greatest beneficiary of the decade of reform; both institutionally and attitudinally, this province is likely to feel quite comfortable with a program such as Torch. Wuhan, like Beijing, is both a major center of technical resources *and* has been active in high-technology entrepreneurship. It should be noted, however, that Torch projects in Guangdong and Hubei provinces are not exclusively located in these two major cities.[23] The spatial distribution of Torch projects seemingly reflects the influence of the coastal development strategy and, as we shall see below, it is closely related with the establishment of high-technology enterprise zones (the distribution of which also seems biased toward the coastal regions).

When it began, the Torch Plan assumed an active level of international cooperation as part of its activities. The plan is open to foreign investment, and contracts have been made with foreign venture capital firms. As noted above, the Chinese market for high-technology is still relatively small; the international market is thus very important for the program. China, of course, also hoped to enter into joint ventures which would combine Chinese expertise

[23] This is true for the plan in other provinces as well, where projects are located in a number of smaller cities. Of Shandong's 15 projects, for instance, 6 are in the provincial capital of Jinan, 3 are in Quingdao, 3 are in Zibo, and 1 each in Qufu, Weihai and Rongcheng.

and the "critical elements"—finance, special materials, management, and marketing expertise—from abroad which are not available in abundance in China. While progress toward the internationalization of Torch has been slowed by the events of June, 1989, the perceived importance of international cooperation, apparently, has increased.

At a national Torch conference held in May 1990, the questions of internationalization received prominent attention. Emphasis was placed on the establishment of "bridge" and "showcase" firms in the United States, Japan, Germany, Hong Kong, and Macao, and on more foreign participation in the training of management personnel for high-technology enterprises.[24] In June 1990, Torch officials signed an agreement with a U.S. firm, Omega Orient Industrial Company, to establish a company in Houston to serve as a "window" on the international market for the Program.[25]

While the Chinese press during the past year has been filled with enthusiastic reports about progress of the Torch Plan and its prospects for the future, it is difficult at this stage to render any serious evaluation of it. Torch is best assessed in the context of the high-technology strategy more generally, a subject discussed further below.

III. New Enterprises and New Enterprise Zones

Since its initiation in August 1988, the Torch Plan has been given a special responsibility to foster new high-technology firms and to oversee and promote the development of special high-technology enterprise zones. But activities in these two areas predate Torch and illustrate another side to China's high-technology development story.

As early as 1984, in its talent-rich Haidian district, Beijing began to see the appearance of new firms growing out of the many research institutes located there. Most were being spun off from CAS and still had formal ties with the Academy. Some, however, were started by individuals who broke with "the system" and began pushing the limits of what the reform environment would allow. These became known as the *min ban* (nonstate) enterprises, most of which employed some form of collective ownership, with many also had some sort of relationship with the Haidian district government.[26] The Stone Corporation, which became deeply involved with the political demonstrations of early 1989, was one (but not the only one) such firm.

Under the reform conditions of the 1980s, the numbers of both kinds of enterprises continued to grow. Reform policies of two sorts were at work. One, as noted, encouraged the growth of collective enterprises and technical entrepreneurship, and more generally made the possibilities for technical careers outside of the state sector real for the first time since the 1950s. The other policy

[24] *Xinhua*, June 6, 1990, In FBIS–CHI–90–112, June 11, 1990, p. 7.
[25] *Xinhua*, June 6, 1990, in FBIS–CHI–90–112, June 11, 1990, p. 7.
[26] Cf. Marc Abramson. "Minban Science Firms in China." *China Exchange News*. Vol. 17, No. 4. December 1989, pp. 12–17. See also Richard P. Suttmeier. "Listening to China." *Issues in Science and Technology*. Fall 1988; and Richard P. Suttmeier. "Laying the Corporate Foundations for China's High Tech Future." *The China Business Review*, July–August 1988.

thrust pertained to the research establishment and attempted to force research institutes to better serve the economy by cutting their guaranteed annual appropriations. Along with other reforms internal to CAS, shrinking budgets pushed research institutes to seek new ways of generating revenues. Starting their own firms became one of the means chosen.

The number of firms in the Zhongguancun area of Haidian district grew rapidly after 1987, and its main thoroughfare, Haidian Road, became known as "electronics street." While many of these firms can be legitimately described as high-technology companies (selling products, technology, or both which they themselves developed), many others have been (and still are) better described as technology traders (often offering hard-to-obtain foreign hardware) and technical service firms.[27]

In May 1988, after a thorough investigation by the Party Central Committee, the State Council approved the designation of the area as the Beijing New Technology Development Zone, entitling its firms to preferential tax treatment and foreign exchange regulations.[28] While Beijing is legitimately seen as the leader in the new entrepreneurship, start–up companies and special zones were also appearing elsewhere after the mid-1980s, including the special "science park" sponsored by the CAS in Shenzhen (begun in 1985), Shanghai's Caohejing (which, with its 15 foreign-invested enterprises now leads other zones in attracting foreign investment), and Guangzhou's Wushan. According to one report, the number of high-technology enterprises had reached some 15,000 nationwide by the end of 1989, with a work force of 80,000 people.[29]

The Beijing experience seemingly has been quite successful. Some 790 companies (including 139 established by CAS) had been approved as of June 1989, employing 26,000 people. In 1988, the firms in the zones had total earnings of RMB 1.4 billion (470 million yuan of which were from sales of technology), and had also earned $US 13 million through exports.[30] By May 1990, the total number of firms had risen to 894, the 50 largest of which had business networks around the country and annual incomes exceeding 5 million yuan.[31] The Stone Company alone generated about one-sixth of the total revenue of Haidian district.[32]

Since the formal State Council approval of the Beijing zone, there has been a rush to start high-technology zones elsewhere (or to provide formal designation, and thus policy preferences, to already existing zones). Most of these new designations have come as a result of local, rather than of central government action (though they are subject to central guidelines), and as a result, there is no

---

[27] During the past year, revenues from trading dropped from 60% of the total for firms in the area to 32%, while technical service revenues increased from 20% to 40%. *Xinhua*, April 14, 1990. In FBIS-CHI-90-074. April 17, 1990, p. 49.

[28] This includes a three-year tax holiday, followed by another three years of reduced tax rates.

[29] Radio Beijing interview with Zhang Binfu of SSTC. February 7, 1990. In FBIS-CHI-90-043. March 5, 1990, p. 29.

[30] Zhang Binfu and Tang Juan. "An Excellent Start in Implementing the Torch Plan." *Zhongguo Keji Luntan Forum on Science and Technology*. No. 6. November 18, 1989. In JPRS-CST-90-008. March 15, 1990, p. 11.

[31] *Xinhua*. May 17, 1990. In FBIS-CHI-90-097. May 18, 1990, p. 23.

[32] *Beijing Review*. No. 1. January 1-7, 1990. In FBIS-CHI-90-004-S. January 5, 1990, p. 39.

one model for the zones. Special high-technology zones, of one sort or another, are now found in the following 30 cities.[33]

IV. The Defense Sector

A large concentration of technical resources exists in China's defense R&D and defense industries. S&T personnel in defense industries constitute 13% of the work force, in comparison with an average of 3% in civilian industry.[34] China's programs in nuclear weapons and space have spurred development in a whole range of attendant technologies—materials, electronics, new processing techniques, etc.—of potential commercial value.[35] Institutions such as the National Defense Science and Technology University in Changsha, which developed the Galaxy supercomputer, are also active in such fields such as artificial intelligence, precision guidance, stealth and counterstealth technologies, simulator technologies, and flexible manufacturing.[36]

Since the early 1980s the defense sector has been given the charge to assist the civilian economy by technology transfers and through the conversion of its plants to civilian production. According to one report, some 3,000 long-standing civilian production problems during the 1980s were solved with technologies from the defense sector, netting the latter more than 2 billion yuan for the know-how supplied; by 1989 the value of production for the civilian economy from defense plants had risen to 66% of total output value, up from 10% in 1979.[37]

While the exploitation of the technical talents of the defense establishment is not without problems,[38] the Chinese believe it holds great potential. The latest moves to accelerate the use of assets from the defense sector include a late 1989 decision to declassify some 2,300 defense R&D achievements,[39] to spur foreign sales of defense sector technology, and to issue the "Provisional Regulations for the Examination and Approval of the Export of State Secret Technology," on December 6, 1989.[40]

V. Discussion and Assessment

The Chinese experience with high-technology is perhaps poignantly illustrated by the following example. On April 16, 1990, the *Xinhua* news agency carried a brief note to the effect that the 27th Research Institute of the Ministry of Machine Building and Electronics Industry, in conjunction with the Zhengzhou Municipal Telecommunications Bureau, had successfully developed a new device,

---

[33] Based on Zhang Binfu and Tang Juan. "An Excellent Start."

[34] Xiao Qinfu. "The Shortest Route To Two Way Development of S&T and the Economy." *Keji Ribao. (Science and Technology Daily).* December 25, 1990. In JPRS–CST–90–007. March 6, 1990.

[35] See, for instance, Di Naiyong. "Research and Development of Long March Family of Launch Vehicles." *Shijie Daodan Yu Hangtian. (Missiles and Spacecraft).* No. 137. September 1989. In JPRS–CST–90–007. March 6, 1990, p. 19.

[36] *Keji Ribao. (Science and Technology Daily).* February 4, 1989, p. 1.

[37] Xiao Qinfu. "The Shortest Route."

[38] See, *Ibid.*

[39] *China Daily.* January 24, 1990. In FBIS–CHI–90–018–S. January 26, 1990, p. 42.

[40] The text of the Regulations can be found in *Keji Ribao. (Science and Technology Daily).* December 30, 1990. In JPRS–CST–90–005. February 8, 1990, pp. 1–2.

"for detecting unregistered or unauthorized fax users ... This instrument can detect and record the telephone numbers of any unauthorized fax user transmitting fax messages through the public telephone network." [41]

This report calls attention to two very important features of Chinese high-technology development. The first is that most foreigners, indeed most Chinese as well, may never have heard of the 27th Institute, nor of many of the other, literally thousands, of government research centers which have developed outside the international purviews of cosmopolitan science and commercial technology. While their qualitative levels still remain uncertain, we are now better able, at least, to gauge the size of this reservoir of human talent. It is clear, that China has a very large technical community, with technical resources distributed widely across space, disciplines, and technologies. What actually goes on in this establishment, and how well it is done, remains only incompletely understood.

The achievements in Zhengzhou, however, also call attention to a more fundamental issue about Chinese technological development. During the mass demonstrations in China in the spring of 1989, we saw technological ingenuity being used by both demonstrators and government to advance their political agendas. The fax was a favorite tool of the demonstrators, while sophisticated imaging and intercept devices were employed by the government. When the achievement of the 27th Institute is seen in this context, the question of whose ends are to be served by new technologies is inescapable.

For the better part of 40 years, the best scientific and technological talent in China was harnessed to the service of the state. This produced a tradition of research and production capable of achieving successes in certain areas of strategic technology. But it also led to the bottling up of research results in laboratories, thus denying the civilian economy—*and* the military—of a regular source of innovation. While the defects of this system are now widely understood, both inside and outside of China, the events of the last year have more graphically called attention to how the fate of high technology in China is closely linked to the nation's political future.

International experience continues to accumulate in support of the view that national high-technology strategies cannot be based on a philosophy which puts technical assets, in the first instance, at the service of the state. The experience of poor, socialist China supports this proposition, as does the growing consensus that large commitments of technical talent to national defense projects places even the rich, capitalist, and democratic United States at a competitive disadvantage in high technology. The underlying lesson seems to be that a high-technology strategy which is cut off from competition in a mass market is ultimately unsustainable without enormous government subsidies.

A competitive mass market is not solely a matter of large numbers of consumers having increasing amounts of disposable incomes. It is also a matter of consumers and producers having genuine autonomy to use their resources as they see fit. That is, it is a

---

[41] In FBIS–CHI–90–078–S. April 23, 1990, p. 28.

matter of rights and liberties that are recognized and respected by the State.

China's reform policies of the 1980s clearly set in motion a process of economic and political liberalization. But as many observers have now noted, the extent to which economic change would call attention to the needs for political change was grossly underestimated, as we saw so tragically in Tiananmen. Less dramatic, but of direct relevance to the question of China's high-technology future, is how reform comes to affect the often subtle questions of rights and liberties pertaining to property.

The question of the ownership of productive assets had become increasingly pressing during the 1980s. Liberalization had made possible the proliferation of industrial activities outside the state sector. Many of these activities came to compete with state-owned enterprises, but for markets and (especially) for inputs. Absent a coherent property rights regime and protected economic liberties, this competition contributed as much to the growth of corruption as to economic discipline. For many reform theorists and strategists, changing the ownership principles for state enterprises had come to be seen as inescapable if the benefits of marketization were ever to be realized. In this context, the role of high-technology enterprises—as innovative means to the amelioration of long-standing problems of considerable national importance—occupied a special place. In continuing to force property rights questions to the center of thinking about reform, their special quality is likely to continue.

The need to confront the meaning and implications of property rights issues becomes unavoidable with the encouragement of high-technology enterprises, and the implementation of such programs as 863 and Torch. When an institute of the CAS spins off a new company, for instance, who owns its assets and who bears responsibility for their use? More import, who has the rights of appropriation over the profits it makes from new discoveries and products?[42] How will these rights be handled in a plan like Torch, which seeks to facilitate the transfer of research results to production? Are property rights sufficiently clear and assured to permit the kinds of risk-taking behavior which seems necessary for successful high-technology development?

China clearly has given thought to these issues. With the introduction of a patent system, and with commitments to strengthen trademark protection, relative to the pre-reform era, China has taken major steps toward modifying its property rights regime. As noted above, the government has begun to think about who will own the results of the 863 Program. The existence of the Technical Contracts Law, which deals mainly with unit-to-unit relations, provides some guidance for the Torch Program.[43] Recently issued "Interim Regulations on Strengthening the Registration and Administration of Science and Technology Development Enterprises" also try to clarify the rights and obligations of firms with different pat-

---

[42] The economic success of the Stone Company and the controversy surrounding it are closely related to ownership questions. Stone started with an investment of RMB 20,000 from the local government, but its fixed assets had grown to RMB 80 million, and it had RMB 1 billion in sales last year. To whom does all this belong?

[43] Zhang Binfu interview.

terns of ownership. Equally important, China continues to recognize the existence of collectively and privately owned firms.[44]

As further support for the idea of diversified ownership, the Haidian district in Beijing has initiated a new program for the provision of retirement and health insurance for personnel working in nonstate organizations, thus tackling one of the major problems of personnel management associated with the growth of the nonstate sector.[45] The Chinese Academy of Sciences, inspired by the example of the defense industry in Singapore and public corporations in Europe, has begun to experiment with the establishment of a holding company to manage shares issued by the many start-up companies being spun off by its institutes.[46]

Despite these developments and changes in attitudes toward property rights, China at present is committed to maintaining its socialist system. This will inevitably limit experimentation with ownership schemes to those within an acceptable ideological range, and keep in doubt the long-term viability of guarantees of nonstate ownership. China thus seems still quite some way from respecting those rights and liberties normally thought to be essential for the operation of a competitive mass market.

Unable to rely on demand from the domestic economy, the leaders of China's technological community have increasingly been focusing on international markets. Foreign relations, thus, become the other main area where the prospects for high technology are contingent on political direction.

China's "open policy" of the last decade, and the engagement with international S&T which it has made possible, have been of enormous importance for the revitalization of its R&D and for its high-technology development strategy. This is recognized by the leaders of the technological community. Although China is loathe to admit it, the international sanctions imposed following June 4, 1989 have upset planning assumptions for high-technology development. Joint venturing, technology transfer, and venture capital investments as important components for programs such as Torch, have become considerably more uncertain in the face of strained foreign relations *and* the inevitable cooling of business interest in the face of political uncertainty.

In the period since the Tiananmen events, Chinese orientation toward international S&T seems to show a curious combination of attitudes. On one hand, there has been a resurgence of technological nationalism, a proud reaffirmation of China's own technical capabilities won through self-reliance. On the other hand, there is also a sharpened sense of the importance of gaining access to international markets and to international cooperative research. These two orientations are nicely illustrated in domestic reactions to China's successful launch of AsiaSat, and they are also evident in an important, recently completed, two-year study of high technology conducted by SSTC, CAS, the Chinese Academy of Social Sci-

---

[44] See *Xinhua*. March 29, 1990. In FBIS–CHI–90–072–S. April 13, 1990, p. 21.

[45] *Xinhua*. January 10, 1990. In FBIS–CHI–90–018–S. January 26, 1990, p. 9. In the absence of insurance and housing opportunities on the open market, technical personnel were reluctant to make complete breaks with their state employers which had a monopoly on the provision of these welfare benefits.

[46] Interview with Hou Ziqiang, CAS, August, 1989.

ences, and the Commission for Science, Technology and Industry for National Defense. The study finds that China must,

* develop an economy oriented to the world market ..." which aims at the world market's high standards and high efficiency..."
* ... take high tech industry ... as the leading forces, to the international stage...";
* ... join the world network of high tech economy...";
* ... give full play to China's advantages. China's research institutes have accumulated in recent decades a certain number of world-level scientific achievements which have potential commercial prospects. In addition, China has tens of thousands of scientists, businessmen and overseas students who are relatively familiar with contemporary frontier science and technology and economic management." [47]

The theme of high-technology internationalization was also sounded recently by SSTC Vice Minister Zhu Lilan, whose responsibilities include the 863 Program, in stating that the Program would seek expanded international cooperation. Zhu also called attention to the role of 863 in attracting China's overseas students back to China as a result of its contributions to improving the research atmosphere.[48]

There is, of course, another side to the relationship between China's high-technology development and foreign relations. China has been an exporter of strategic goods and technologies to nations of the world engaged in regional conflicts or those who aspire to regional power status. Its capacity as a supplier of strategic technologies will only increase as a result of its high-technology development commitments. China's high-technology development thus poses interesting challenges and opportunities for foreigners. It is of great international importance to continue to induce China to join in international regimes dedicated to the responsible use of strategic technologies in international commerce and foreign relations. But how this is done depends on the nature of domestic politics in China, and again, is related to the question of whose interests are served by technological development.

For some, Chinese behavior as a strategic supplier is more understandable if seen as the actions of a "wheeler-dealer" rogue military-industrial complex, rather than as the coherent and intentional foreign policy of a government. Control over the military industrial complex, while by no means unified, is thought to lie in the hands of those having family ties to China's senior leaders. The military industry is thus the source of considerable political influence as well as scientific and technological prowess. In this line of thought, inducing these relatives of the elite—members of the Chinese high-technology business community—with economic opportunities that are more attractive than destabilizing strategic exports may be a promising approach in the short run (short of a change in government) to securing China's international responsibility. More generally, the sooner a workable and acceptable formula can be

---

[47] *Xinhua.* June,1990. In FBIS–CHI–90–117. June 18, 1990, p. 39.
[48] *China Daily.* June 13, 1990. In FBIS–CHI–90–116. June 15, 1990, p. 29.

found for harnessing China's technological resources to economic development and high-quality scientific research, the better for China and for the international community.

Finding that formula is increasingly linked to China's domestic political evolution, a process which has a complex relationship with high technology. For reasons discussed above, significant political liberalization seemingly is needed if China's high-technology aspirations are to be met. Interestingly, given their involvement with high technology, the children of the old guard may have more of an interest in liberalization than is commonly assumed.

At the same time, if it is the case, as suggested above, that high-technology development carries an imperative to expand international contacts, induce institutional innovation, and keep property rights issues at the center of reform thinking, high-technology strategies can be a force for liberalization. Foreign governments and businesses can ultimately do little to determine Chinese political developments, but their continued engagement with China's high-technology programs can help orient these programs more toward economic growth than toward strategic exports. For foreign governments and for foreign companies who have found their dealings with China this past decade disappointing and exasperating, China's expanding commitment to high technology offers opportunities for a revised "China strategy."

CHINA'S ACQUISITION AND ASSIMILATION OF FOREIGN TECHNOLOGY: BEIJING'S SEARCH FOR EXCELLENCE

By Denis Fred Simon *

CONTENTS

I. Introduction

In August 1987 in Dalian, a major national conference on foreign technology import was held as part of an effort by Chinese leaders to review past policies and to identify whether or not China had indeed taken full advantage of its increased exposure to foreign technical know-how and equipment. The meeting was important because it provided a forum for a rather sharp critique of both the State Science and Technology Commission and the former State Economic Commission respectively for their ongoing policies and practices. Out of the meeting emerged a general agreement that new efforts would have to be made to ensure more effective and efficient assimilation of imported technology, and that perhaps it was time to consider creation of a special State Council-level organization to monitor and coordinate foreign technology acquisition. Even

* Denis Fred Simon is Associate Professor of International Business and Technology at the Fletcher School of Law & Diplomacy of Tufts University. He is also the Director of the Center for Technology and International Affairs at the Fletcher School.

more significant, however, despite recognition that the open door policies of the previous several years had yielded substantial benefits, there was an apparent consensus that China had not made the best of its opportunities with respect to the importation of foreign technology and equipment.

The ideas and opinions that emerged from the Dalian meeting led to the issuance of a series of new policy guidelines in the latter part of 1987 covering technology import activities. These new guidelines have taken on added significance since the turmoil that occurred on June 4, 1989 in Tiananmen Square. In spite of the dramatic events associated with the political demonstrations in the square, the subsequent removal from power of Party Secretary Zhao Ziyang, and the imposition of economic sanctions as a protest against China's human rights policies by most of the industrialized nations, Chinese leaders have remained steadfast in their commitment to continue the country's "open policy" and to acquire foreign technology and equipment when and where appropriate. While many questions continue to surface within the highest echelons of the PRC leadership regarding the inflow of undesirable social and political influences—many of which are associated, directly and indirectly, with the borrowing of foreign technology—there does not appear to have been a fundamental retreat from the policies that have been in place over the last decade or so.

Yet, what is increasingly clear with respect to China's experience with managing and utilizing foreign technology over the last several years is that many of the same issues that were on the economic and political agenda during the initial period of the "great leap outward" have continued to plague the leadership. In essence, the contribution of foreign technology has been uneven at best. Technology acquisition has gotten caught up in the various problems associated with the overall program of economic reform, with the consequence being that a variety of distortions have occurred that have affected, in a rather negative fashion, the degree to which the PRC economy has been able to take advantage of the presence of modern equipment and advanced know-how. As a result, while articles extolling the contributions of foreign technology continue to appear in the Chinese press, an overall assessment of the place of foreign technology leaves one with a rather indeterminate set of findings. In some cases, the contributions of foreign technology have been appreciable and substantial progress has been made, e.g. the expanded application of advanced, automated machinery into the textiles industry and the introduction of quality control systems for the production of consumer electronics and automobiles. Yet, even acknowledging these gains, the reality is that progress has not been fast enough given the monies and level of effort expended, raising a number of critical questions about how to improve the existing system and how to better target enterprises that will have a higher probability of success with respect to foreign technology absorption and digestion.

II. CHINESE VIEWS OF THE TECHNOLOGY TRANSFER PROCESS

China's post-Tiananmen leadership continues to place a great deal of emphasis on the maintenance of the open door policy and the current policy of importing foreign technology and equipment. Underlying the PRC's continued willingness to rely on the import of foreign technology to support its modernization program are several factors. First, and perhaps most important, Chinese leaders continued to be concerned about the rapid development of high technology abroad and the growing linkages between economic, military and diplomatic influence, on the one hand, and advanced technological development, on the other hand.[1] Simply put, Chinese leaders remain fearful about falling too far behind the West in both qualitative and quantitative terms. It is estimated, for example, that over the next ten years, China will invest U.S. \$2.1 billion in high technology development, which while being a substantial amount for China seems almost insignificant when compared to the current investments being made in the U.S., Japan, and Western Europe.[2] Second, Chinese leaders realize that their country lacks the domestic resources, financial and technological, to catch-up in a reasonably short period of time. Even taking into account current efforts such as the high technology-oriented "863" or TORCH plan, the only way to overcome the present shortage of ample resources is to utilize foreign technology.

This is not to suggest that Chinese leaders are particularly enamored by their need to depend on the global technology market for meeting internal technological needs. Self-reliance continues to be a high priority in China among the leadership. According to one commentary, ". . . the import of technology has not turned out to be a major tool for improving China's self-development capacity in science and technology."[3] From the perspective of the current PRC leadership, one of the most disconcerting and even distasteful aspects of the sanctions imposed by the U.S. in the aftermath of China's alleged missile sales to Saudi Arabia and Iran *and* the regime's actions in Tiananmen Square, was the ability of a foreign power to leverage its control over technology to get the Chinese to alter their behavior.[4] Still, China has little choice but to keep these channels open to overcome current production shortfalls and technological inadequacies.

And third, Chinese leaders remain committed to foreign technological borrowing because of the increasing entanglement of technology and national security issues. Even as the Cold War has wound down and the tensions on the Sino-Soviet border as well as on the Korean peninsula have moderated, China remains vitally concerned about maintaining its military strength. Foreign technology is needed to boost programs in microelectronics, computer-integrated manufacturing, advanced materials, etc.—all of which have applications and relevance for the country's defense-industrial base.

---

[1] Feng Zhaokui, "High-Technology Competition in the 1990s," *Shijie Zhishi* [World Affairs], Number 10, May 16, 1990, pp.2–3.

[2] "New Emphasis on High Technology," *China Daily*, October 1, 1990, p.3.

[3] Yang Lincun and Qiu Chengli, "Major S&T Policy Issues to be Faced in the 1990s," *Liaowang Zhoukan* (Outlook Weekly), Number 19, May 7, 1990, p.41.

[4] There are rumors to the effect that spending for both civilian and military S&T science and technology increased appreciably in the aftermath of the Tiananmen crisis and the foreign sanctions against the PRC, as many Chinese leaders remained steadfast in their refusal to accept as a *fait accompli* the ability of outside powers to use China's need for foreign technology as a source of political leverage.

China's current concerns regarding technology transfer are reflected in the vocabulary that has emerged to describe the various facets of the process. The term "technology introduction" or "*jishu yinjin*" is used to describe the importation of foreign technology. On occasion, the term "*jishu zhuanrang*" is also employed, but in most instances, this refers to domestic technology transfer. A related term, "technical transformation" (*jishu gaizao*) refers to the upgrading of industrial enterprises through the introduction of both domestic and foreign technology and equipment. In formal discourse about the subject of technology transfer, the acquisition side is clearly distinguished from the assimilation side of the equation. The two key terms in this regard are "absorption" (*xishou*) and "digestion" (*xiaohua*). Both of these refer to the ability to make effective use of the imported technology once it is received by the recipient. Clearly, there is a sense, particularly in the aftermath of the Dalian meeting, that simple "importation of technology" is not enough to make a difference in terms of the projected contribution to economic development and national technological self-reliance.[5] Accordingly, sharp criticisms have appeared in various newspapers and journals regarding the country's poor performance with respect to absorption and digestion.

What is urgently required at the very least, according to current Chinese thinking, is an ability to utilize the technology fully and adapt it (*jishu shiying*) to local circumstances. Even more desirable is to have the foreign technology serve to catalyze some form of indigenous innovation (*jishu gexin*). According to official Chinese statements regarding the import of foreign technology, it is simply not enough to acquire and use the technology in one location; two things must occur for technology transfer to be considered successful. There first must be diffusion of technology (*jishu kuosan*) beyond the immediate recipient and secondly there must be increasing degrees of localization of production (*guochanhua*) of critical components or raw materials.

One of the major debates that has surrounded Chinese technology import policy has been the designation of just what constitutes the importation of technology.[6] Even though in 1981 when the "Interim Regulations on the Administration of Technology Introduction and Equipment Import" were adopted by the State Council and a formal distinction was made between import of "technology" versus import of equipment, the reality is that confusion continues to persist regarding just what is considered to be "*jishu yinjin*." According to the 1981 regulations, "the import of general machinery, electric machinery, electrical appliances, and instruments" are not classified as forms of technology import. The orientation of the regulations is clearly in the direction of distinguishing "software" (*ruanjian*) from hardware and equipment (*shebei*).

---

[5] According to Chinese thinking, assimilation of imported technology and equipment includes the following: a) putting the imported technology into operation and reaching the planned output of the project; b) localization of the components and raw materials; c) research on and manufacture of the imported equipment through trial and/or batch production; and d) development and innovation regarding the imported technology and equipment. Interviews in Beijing and Shanghai, August 1987.

[6] Sun Quichang, *Jishu Yinjin Yu Xiandaihua* (Technology Import and Modernization), (Chongqing: Chongqing Publishing House, 1989). [in Chinese]

Yet, a debate has prevailed throughout the decade over whether or not imports of production lines, for example, are acceptable as a form of technology transfer. At the Dalian meeting in 1987, just to cite one example, officials from the State Planning Commission and the former State Economic Commission argued about the validity of pursuing "hardware" imports as a means to acquire technology since items such as a production line contain *embodied* engineering technology, manufacturing technology, etc." This position was quickly attacked by persons from China's State Science and Technology Commission, many of whom acknowledged the immediate benefits of "direct imports of productive capacity," but also stressed the limited potential for actual transfer of technology into Chinese enterprises. The debate has not ebbed whatsoever insofar as there continue to be those in China who believe that given China's mediocre S&T system, the best strategy, in the short term, is to concentrate on the import of production lines and assembly lines in order to manufacture higher quality, competitive products for both China's home market and for export.

The situation with respect to software versus hardware imports can be best appreciated by examining the statistics from the pre-1978 period and comparing them with the evolving situation since the open policy of the 1980s. From 1952 to 1978, approximately 97.7% of the contracts for technology import were for hardware, mainly focused on the import of complete plants and equipment. Perhaps the best examples of this policy orientation are the 156 industrial plants imported from the USSR in the late 1950s and early 1960s as well as the 20-plus petrochemical and fertilizer plants imported from Japan, Western Europe and the U.S. in the mid-1970s. By 1984, however, the value of software as a percentage of the overall value of contracts jumped up to almost 50%. Between 1981 and 1984, the contract value for software acquisition ranged around 30–50%. Since 1985, these figures have declined, falling to about 14% in 1989. This suggests that despite an initial surge in the mid-1980s, the current orientation seems to be more in the direction of hardware and equipment purchases.[7] (See Table 1).

One of the consequences of this still unresolved debate is that the statistical system for keeping track of technology imports is seriously flawed in a number of important respects. To begin with, different accounting systems are ostensibly used by the Ministry of Foreign Economic Relations and Trade (MOFERT), the State Planning Commission (SPC), the Chinese Customs Bureau, the Ministry of Finance, and the State Science and Technology System (SSTC). MOFERT only counts in its statistics formal contracts reviewed and approved by itself or its subordinate import/export corporations, such as the China National Technology Import/Export Corporation. The Customs Bureau does not have any systematic way to classify "technology" or "know-how" imports, and thus its calculations tend to be based on "hardware" imports and explicit fees paid for technology licensing only. In many instances, it can only account for expenditures that appear explicitly as "equipment" imports. In reality, many of the contracts for the purchase of machin-

---

[7] Zhou Hongqi, "Pros and Cons of Technology Imports," *China Daily*, March 31, 1990, p.4.

TABLE 1

SOFTWARE AS A PERCENTAGE OF OVERALL

TECHNOLOGY IMPORTS, 1987-89

Unit: U.S. $ Millions

	LICENSE	TECHN SERVICE	CONSULT SERVICE	CO PRODUC-TION	COMPUTER EQUIP	TOTAL
1987						
TECH IMP VALUE	350.87	15.59	10.19	509.95	2097.89	2984.89
SOFTWARE VALUE	166.98	5.76	10.01	14.56	261.39	458.70
% OF TOTAL	47.6%	36.9%	98.3%	2.9%	12.4%	15.4%
1988						
TECH IMP VALUE	476.58	14.24	27.51	10.04	3019.87	3548.26
SOFTWARE VALUE	294.48	14.04	18.20	4.53	345.11	676.79
% OF TOTAL	61.9%	98.6%	66.2%	45.1%	11.4%	19.1%
1989						
TECH IMP VALUE	148.45	38.45	6.18	6.58	2723.35	2923.00
SOFTWARE VALUE	69.81	11.52	5.90	2.01	328.49	417.74
% OF TOTAL VALUE	47.0%	30.0%	95.5%	30.5%	11.8%	14.3%

SOURCE: MINISTRY OF FOREIGN ECONOMIC RELATIONS & TRADE, BEIJING, 1990.

ery and related equipment, for example, contain provisions and fees for training programs and other related forms of "technology transfer." These amounts may never be calculated into the final statistics, or on the other hand, the entire "package" may be classified as a "technology import." In the MOFERT statistics, a distinction is now made to identify the exact proportion of the total contract value that can be considered "software."

Nonetheless, it still is unclear just what is or is not being included in the final calculations. When one takes into account the fact that most of the statistics being provided are for "central government" agencies and do not include the activities of local organizations, as well as the reality that many projects are divided into smaller components with their true intent obscured in order to avoid certain regulatory and administrative provisions, all of this suggests that the numbers being produced by the various agencies in the PRC government probably do not reflect an accurate picture of just what has transpired in terms of "actual" technology import.

Another dimension of technology import work that further causes problems derives from the absence of a formal system for approving, managing and coordinating the various tasks associated with the acquisition of foreign technology. MOFERT's responsibilities extend simply to the review and examination of the contracts associated with the import of foreign technology; it is not principally concerned with the choice of the technology or the selection of the supplier, though it may offer advice to the Chinese buyer in both instances. MOFERT merely ensures that the terms of each contract do not violate Chinese law and regulations. The State Planning Commission's role is somewhat more substantial insofar as it is concerned with defining the priority industries and technologies contained in the respective five year and annual economic plans. The SPC also is intimately involved in technology import activities by virtue of its responsibilities for overseeing the program for technical transformation, which frequently involves the acquisition of key equipment and technology. The State Science and Technology Commission's role in technology import work is actually very limited, especially since a great deal of its prerogative was surrendered to the SPC after the departure of former Minister-in-Charge Fang Yi in the early 1980s. The SSTC is primarily concerned with the long-term technological development of the country, and therefore, does not get involved in the nitty-gritty aspects of technology import work, except in an advisory capacity. It is here where one of the fundamental points of contention can be found between the SPC and the SSTC as the former is concerned with increasing the production capabilities and output of Chinese industry and agriculture while the latter focuses primarily on research. As a result, says one official, "the goal of technology import continues to be more linked to expanding production capacity and less concerned with the general advance of in Chinese technological development."

The essence of China's problems on the organizational side regarding technology import is that no one organization seems to possess an overall integrated perspective on technology import work. The situation has been greatly aggravated by the past decentralization of authority to local areas that has been part of the reform of the foreign trade system. According to an article in *Guoji Maoyi Wenti*, "the most serious problem with China's current policy of delegating authority for importing technology to lower levels is the lack of coordination between departmental and local levels." [8]

> The most urgently needed [measure] is the creation of a 'State Commission for Coordinating Technology Imports' to provide consolidated leadership, uniform legislation, and

[8] Wang Suzhi, "Perfecting an Improved Technology Import Strategy," *Guoji Maoyi Wenti* (International Trade Journal), Number 4, 1987, translated in JPRS-CAR-88-004, February 12, 1988, p.53.

strong macro-economic control over all technology importing activities. The current system of importing has failed
since too many departmental-level bureaus, all lacking
unified direction and acting independently, have been created to deal with different aspects of the problem. This
loss of control at the departmental level is to blame for the
tensions that have arisen both inter-departmentally and
between the departments and local levels. [9]

In spite of the efforts by the central government to set up a multi-
tiered review system to ensure that projects requiring major expenditures of scarce foreign exchange received adequate assessment, numerous mechanisms were devised to escape from these
regulatory safety valves. This has meant that a great deal of duplication, and therefore waste of foreign exchange, has occurred because of inadequate controls on the behavior of local level organizations. In effect, many enterprises without sufficient engineering,
management or technical skills were able to import production
lines and technology. In many cases, the results have been deleterious as far as both the economic and technological interests of the
country have been concerned, leading to much waste and under-uti-
lized capacity.

According to recent criticism of the previous policies, unlike
countries such as Japan and South Korea, China has lacked a
master plan for technology import. As one source has suggested,
"although the PRC has many special and specific technology
import laws and regulations, [there] still [is] no authoritative and
comprehensive basic law and our various special regulations are
neither coordinated nor systematic ..." [10] There is no explicit link
between economic priorities and some type of blueprint for foreign
technology acquisition. In fact, aside from the recent list of licensed
commodities and products for export and imports, Chinese authorities have yet to produce a list of restricted, controlled, or prohibited
technologies. As a result, this same source suggests, "the lack of
provisions in our current legislation on the sphere of imported
technology has caused us to import less technology for production
than for services, less advanced than ordinary technology, and less
technology for developing power and transportation than for concentrating on output value and efficiency." [11]

III. A STOCKTAKING OF TECHNOLOGY IMPORT

Between 1979 and 1989, Chinese entities signed over 4,700 contracts for the import of foreign technology, with a value of U.S.
$36.4 billion.[12] As recorded by MOFERT, the quantity and value of
technology import agreements peaked in 1986 when the total
number of agreements reached 744 and the total contract value
surpassed U.S. $4.45 billion. These increases reflect the expanded
openness of the trading system, including the decentralization of

---

[9] Ibid.
[10] Guo Junxiu, "Perfecting Technology Import Legislation," *Guoji Shangbao* (International
Commerce), March 17, 1990, p.3.
[11] Ibid.
[12] MOFERT, *Almanac of China's Foreign Economic Relations and Trade, 1990*, (Beijing, 1990),
p.48.

decision authority to lower levels. Licensing and import of "complete sets of equipment (*chengtao shebei*) remain the predominant forms of technology acquisition. The number of licenses and complete sets of equipment imports both peaked in 1986, reaching 305 and 328 cases, respectively. While licensing is recognized as the preferred form of acquiring "technological know-how," however, foreign exchange limitations have led China to focus increasingly on foreign investment as its major mechanism for technology transfer. Heretofore, this has not proven to be the most appropriate strategy for China as many foreign partners in these ventures are investing in the PRC for access to the potentially large domestic market; most Chinese organizations seem primarily focused on technology transfer in these ventures, thus leaving both partners somehow dissatisfied with the outcome of their business collaboration. The category known as "complete sets of equipment" may constitute a whole plant, a single production line, or an integrated system of machinery and know-how to manufacture a particular type of product. In pursuing the import of technology, there continues to be a general tendency to shy away from excessive expenditures on both consulting and advisory services *and* technical services. In many instances, Chinese buyers of technology remain locked into the notion that "hardware" represents the only tangible proof that the recipient has actually received something for his money. While at various times, a consulting or technical service agreement may accompany a licensing agreement, the reality is also that few Chinese entities seem willing to pay for these kinds of "extras"; with a scarcity of foreign exchange, it is usually the "services" part of the contract that gets dropped if and when a financial crunch occurs, frequently leaving the recipient ill-equipped to handle the complex tasks of operationalizing and maintaining the various pieces of equipment. This tendency is compounded by the fact that intended Chinese purchasers of foreign technology tend to make their "buy decisions" on the basis of price rather than quality, which leads to purchases of "stripped down" or second-hand equipment without much in the way of technical support.

Over the last three years, the primary suppliers of technology to China in terms of value have been Italy (U.S. $1.71 billion), France (U.S. $1.25 billion), and Japan (U.S. $1.19 billion).[13] In 1989, China's purchase of foreign technology declined from U.S. $3.54 billion in 1988 to U.S. $2.92 billion (See Table 2). The decline was due to a combination of the sanctions imposed on China, including the fact that there was a 51% decrease in new foreign loan agreements, and the economic retrenchment program, which resulted in tighter policies regarding credit.[14] The largest single supplier was Italy, which provided China with technology and equipment with a value of U.S. $687 million, accounting for 23.5% of the total value of foreign technology acquired by the PRC. One interesting development has been the growth in technology imports from the USSR,

[13] Data used in the following paragraph come from the Ministry of Foreign Economic Relations and Trade (*Almanac of China's Foreign Economic Relations and Trade*) 1988, 1989 and 1990 editions (in Chinese).
[14] *China Economic Weekly*, January 29, 1990, p.4.

which provided the PRC with technology and equipment worth U.S. $468 million, making the Soviet Union the second largest technology supplier to the PRC (in terms of value) in 1989.

Another interesting development has been the fact that 74.3% of the monies used to engage in technology import came from foreign bank loans, which while representing a 16.6% drop from the previous year, still represents a substantial dependence on foreign capital.[15] In terms of the number of contracts, however, the picture is somewhat different. Between 1987–89, the U.S. accounted for the largest number of cases (279), while Japan was second (271 cases) and the Federal Republic of Germany was third (221 cases). In 1989, the PRC entered into a total of 328 contracts for technology import, a sharp drop from 581 contracts in 1987 and 437 contracts in 1988. Both Japan and Canada were responsible for the largest number of contracts, each having 52 (15.9% of the total number respectively).

Although neither the data issued by MOFERT nor the Customs Bureau contain statistics regarding formal technology transfers from Taiwan and South Korea, it should be noted that a substantial contribution is being made to the PRC by firms from these two economies. In the case of Taiwan, as many firms on the island gradually move many of their factory operations offshore—in industries ranging from textiles to consumer electronics—to Fujian and Guangdong to utilize cheap labor on the China mainland, they are providing considerable know-how to PRC enterprises in terms of quality control techniques, production scheduling, inventory management, product design, etc. Taiwan's links with the world market and its need to meet both the cost and quality requirements of its distributors and customers in the U.S. and Western Europe, have made it essential for its companies to assist many PRC enterprises upgrade their operations and master the basics of low cost, high quality manufacturing. The same can be said about firms from South Korea, which in their growing number of operations in both Shandong and southern China, are bringing their valuable experience to Chinese factories in way that may ultimately facilitate greater absorption on the part of the PRC. Obviously, the same also can be said about the activities of firms from Hong Kong as well, which through their assembly operations in Shenzhen and the other special economic zones, are helping to create an appreciable export-oriented, manufacturing base in the PRC.

From an industry perspective, it is clear that since 1978 the major beneficiaries of foreign technology have been the energy sector, the petrochemicals sector, the metallurgy sector and the telecommunications sector. According to MOFERT statistics, in 1988, the contract value for key technology import projects in three industries—energy, telecommunications, and raw materials—accounted for 56.3% of the total technology import contract value. In 1989, a similar picture emerges. Energy (27.4%), petrochemicals (16.4%) and chemicals (11.8%), and telecommunications (5.0%) ac-

---

[15] It also reflects China's tight situation with respect to foreign exchange reserves. The central government in Beijing supplied only 2.7% of the foreign exchange needed to support technology import work in 1989. See "Work Regarding the Import and Export of Technology," *Economic Yearbook of China, 1990* (Beijing, 1990), p.III–209.

TABLE 2

CHINA'S IMPORTS OF FOREIGN TECHNOLOGY, 1981-89

Unit: U.S. $ Millions

YEAR(a)	LICENSES	CONSULT SERVICES	TECH SERVICES	CO-PRO-DUCTION	COMP SET EQUIP	TOTAL
1981-1984	294	28	59	36	209	726
	368.49	16.20	391.46	70.85	1,145.70	1,992.70
1985	291	21	30	34	295	671
	219.80	8.93	12.92	385.43	2,234.31	2,961.39
1986	305	31	46	34	328	744
	419.36	12.11	235.84	136.40	3,651.82	4,455.53
1987	235	24	30	25	267	581
	350.87	10.19	15.99	509.95	2,097.89	2,984.89
1988	169	19	27	10	212	437
	476.58	27.51	14.24	10.05	3,019.88	3,548.26
1989	96	14	13	11	194	328
	14,844	618	3,845	658	272,335	2,923.00

SOURCE: Ministry of Foreign Economic Relations & Trade, Beijing, 1990.

a. For each year or period, the first line (reading across) shows the number of cases of import subsidies; the second line shows the dollar value ($ U.S. Millions).

counted for the bulk of foreign technology and equipment acquisition. The situation regarding imported technology to support the technical transformation of enterprises program, however, reflected somewhat different priorities. The largest recipients by sector of foreign technology in terms of the number and value of contracts were the textile industry (16.9%), the electronics industry (6.2%), and the chemical industry (4.5%).[16]

As indicated previously, the data concerning foreign technology import into China does not contain statistics regarding the import of advanced machinery and related equipment. This data falls in the category of "trade statistics." Nonetheless, because China has spent considerable funds for the import of advanced machinery and equipment covered under the SITC Categories 7 and 8, it is important to consider this data and to somehow tie it into the overall technology imports (See Table 3).

The data indicate that China has added substantially to its industrial base over the last three years in terms of new productive capacity. The large increase in imports of both specialized and general machinery indicate that efforts are underway to replace, when

---

[16] This allocation was consistent with the overall distribution of domestic funds as well. See *Almanac of China's Foreign Trade & Economic Relations, 1990* (Beijing, 1990), pp.50–51 (in Chinese).

TABLE 3
CHINA'S IMPORTS OF MACHINERY, COMPUTERS AND RELATED ITEMS,
1987-1989   **Unit: U.S. $ Millions**

MACHINERY			
EQUIPMENT IMPORTS	1987	1988	1989
POWER EQUIPMENT	56.7	104.1	136.5
SPECIALIZED MACHINERY	497.7	459.9	567.3
METALWORKING EQUIP	97.9	139.8	98.5
GENERAL MACHINERY	173.9	213.5	238.7
OFFICE MACHINES	72.2	69.0	64.9
TELECOMM/SOUND EQUIP	146.0	182.4	179.3
ELECTRICAL MACHINERY	159.3	230.4	239.6
ROAD VEHICLES	129.9	149.1	143.6
OTHER TRANSPORT	127.0	118.4	152.5
TOTAL MACHINERY	**1,460.6**	**1,666.6**	**1,820.9**
SPECIFIC EQUIPMENT AND INSTRUMENTS			
INSTRUMENTATION	86.3	81.8	81.6
PHOTO/OPTICAL EQUIP	43.2	36.5	39.8
TEXTILE MACHINERY	88.7	105.8	150.6
NC MACHINE TOOLS	9.2	9.5	9.5
TOTAL SPEC. EQUIP. AND INSTRUMENTS	**227.4**	**233.6**	**281.5**
COMPUTER			
DATA PROCESSING >16 BIT	5.4	2.7	3.5
DATA PROCESSING <16 BIT	18.7	18.9	16.3
COMPLETE CENTRAL PROCESSING UNIT	1.7	1.3	2.0
COMPUTER PERIPHS	NA	NA	14.8
TOTAL COMPUTERS	(25.8)	(22.9)	36.6

SOURCE: *China's Customs Statistics, 1988-1990* (Beijing, 1990).

possible, a good deal of the obsolete equipment that sits in many Chinese factories today. Of course, within the country's 400,000+ enterprises, that is no small task, especially given the huge strains on both the foreign exchange and domestic budgets. Still, it is clear that industries such as textiles have received a big stimulus by virtue of the new equipment entering into production. The data also reflect the strong and continued concern with modernization of the infrastructure, especially the energy and telecommunications sectors.

It also should be remembered that the statistics contained in this chart do not reflect any equipment, e.g. computers or machine tools, that might have been included as part of the importation of an entire production line. Taken together, these equipment purchases have not only added significantly to Chinese industrial production capacity, but they have also been responsible for improvements in productivity, quality, and product sophistication within selected industrial sectors. While it is true that there may not be much in the way of so-called *disembodied* technology and know-how that has been made available by the presence of this machinery in China's numerous industrial enterprises, the reality is that through reverse-engineering and other forms of technical learning, Chinese end-users as well as equipment manufacturers in the domestic machine-tool industry have benefitted from their intimate access to the various pieces of equipment.

China has also continued to engage in a broad-based program of scientific and technical cooperation with various countries in the developed and developing world. According to Song Jian, Minister-in-Charge of the State Science and Technology Commission, China has signed agreements with 57 countries and has cooperative relations with 108 countries and regions.[17] It has joined 187 international non-governmental science and technology organizations and has also become a member of more than 30 scientific and technological organizations under the United Nations.[18] In addition, China's S&T organizations have participated in more than 280 international academic organizations. The Chinese Academy of Sciences, for example, has signed cooperation agreements with counterparts in more than 50 countries and regions. Of the PRC's 340 sister-city relationships, approximately one-third are oriented toward science and technology collaboration. Taken together, these relationships not only give a boost to "science" and education in China, but also have broad implications for the modernization of the country's industrial technology base. A good example is the agreement signed in early 1989 between China and the FRG to set up three automation training centers in Beijing.[19] Under the agreement, AEG of West Germany will provide China's Ministry of Metallurgical Industry, Ministry of Coal Industry, and the China National Non-Ferrous Metals Industry Corporation with about U.S. $1.2 million in the latest automation equipment in coal mining and metallurgy as part of an effort to familiarize Chinese technical per-

---

[17] "Song on Foreign Science Exchange," *Xinhua*, September 3, 1990, translated in FBIS–CHI–90–171, September 4, 1990, p.29.

[18] "International Science and Technology Exchanges," *China Economic Weekly*, June 7, 1990, p.10.

[19] "Beijing and Bonn Sign Automation Accords," *China Daily*, February 2, 1989, p.2.

sonnel with the latest developments in high-technology electric drive and process control equipment. Similar types of industry-oriented programs of cooperation have been developed with Japan, France, and Sweden.

IV. TECHNICAL TRANSFORMATION OF ENTERPRISES

In an effort to improve economic performance and rectify overall productivity problems in the industrial sector, Chinese leaders in Beijing have placed special emphasis on the technical renovation and upgrading of plant and facilities. In fact, one of the most salient aspects of the entire modernization program is the attention and resources that are being devoted to the "technical transformation of enterprises (*jishu gaizao*)" program (See Table 4). While many of the renovation efforts underway in China's provinces and municipalities do not seem to stand out from the perspective of size or scope, there remains little doubt that collectively they constitute one of the most important features of the modernization program. According to current statistics, about 1/3 of the investment in fixed assets during the past decade (1978–88) has been made for updating equipment and technological transformation.[20]

Four main activities have been associated with the ongoing program of technical transformation begun in 1981 under the 6th Five Year Plan.[21] First, there has been the "550 renovation projects" in the machine-building and electronics industry. A list of 550 key factories and research institutes was prepared as part of an attempt to identify the most critical entities requiring assistance in restructuring and upgrading. Second, there has been the program known as the "three transformations" within the textiles and light industries.

This program has been aimed at improving quality, variety and reliability of products with an eye toward increasing exports. Third, there has been the shift to civilian products in the defense industry. This has involved former military factories utilizing their specialized equipment and personnel to manufacture products for both the domestic market and export. According to one source, the proportion of civilian products manufactured by the defense industry jumped from 8.1% in 1979 to 66% of the value of total output in 1989.[22] And fourth, there has been the "12 dragons" project, which has been mainly aimed at localization of components and raw materials as well as improving the digestion and absorption of foreign equipment and know-how.[23] In industries such as electrical appliances and consumer electronics, e.g. televisions, where a large number of complete production lines had been imported, Chinese leaders have wanted to ensure that strong reliance on imported components and spare parts would not make China excessively dependent on foreign countries. In each of these four areas of activi-

---

[20] Li Jingwen, "Promoting S&T Progress and Deepening Economic Structural Reform," *Renmin Ribao*, April 4, 1988, p.5.

[21] "Concentrate Strength on Doing Several Big Things," *Renmin Ribao*, November 25, 1990, p.2.

[22] Wang Jin, "Remarkable Achievements Made in Making Defense Technology Serve the National Economy," *Renmin Ribao* (Overseas Edition), September 6, 1990, p.1.

[23] "The Idea and Practice of Establishing China's Own Industrial System—The Dragon System," *Science and Technology Daily*, March 17, 1988.

TABLE 4
Investment in Technical Transformation of Enterprises
by Sector, 1981-89
Unit: 100 Million Yuan

SECTOR	1981	1985	1986	1987	1988	1989*
INDUSTRY						
ELECTRONIC	6.70	20.01	21.99	17.48	24.21	22.87
SHIP BUILDING	NA	1.78	1.44	2.43	2.63	1.01
NONFERROUS METALS	16.54	41.17	60.14	79.23	99.28	92.52
COAL	13.01	25.31	29.69	31.94	34.67	43.10
PETROLEUM	26.69	11.84	13.62	15.54	29.69	25.95
PETRO-CHEMICALS	NA	9.49	12.40	19.32	22.03	26.32
CHEMICALS	13.31	28.81	38.62	52.60	85.32	74.73
POWER	7.38	13.51	17.75	21.87	27.84	27.87
MACHINERY	6.41	31.76	43.43	59.84	65.62	60.54
AUTOS	NA	5.56	5.88	7.92	15.73	16.19
BUILDING-MATTER	4.19	17.56	25.19	27.13	28.90	30.35
TEXTILES	17.77	38.40	53.77	65.25	92.91	59.75
LGT INDUST	22.84	55.97	74.86	88.14	108.32	110.72
OTHER IND	7.20	26.20	36.71	43.78	61.25	31.27
INDUSTRY	142.04	337.64	452.39	552.55	721.65	623.19
AGRIC	5.73	10.28	13.96	18.12	19.75	11.51
TRANSPORT/ TELECOMM	23.32	42.13	58.55	71.52	76.10	64.37
COMMERCE	9.27	22.40	32.23	45.76	52.23	23.37
URBAN CONS	7.70	21.81	40.39	43.57	51.33	36.44
OTHER	7.24	14.88	21.69	27.07	33.45	22.01
GRAND TOTAL	195.30	449.14	619.21	758.59	954.51	788.78

Source: *China Statistical Abstracts, 1989*, p.67; *Statistical Yearbook of China, 1990*, p.189.

*NOTE: Data for 1989 are compiled slightly differently from that for 1981-88, which may explain why, even taking into account the overall decrease in spending for 1989, the data available for the "other industries" category are relatively lower.

ty, a series of "special projects" was designated to receive targeted loans and related funds, including foreign exchange allocations, though by the latter part of the 7th Five-Year Plan, support for the program came out of a more general budget allocation that was somewhat less targeted (and therefore more susceptible to local distortion).

The issue of technical transformation takes on special importance from the perspective of technology import insofar as the Chinese hope to accomplish much of their technical upgrading and plant modernization through expanded contacts with foreign firms and industrial specialists. In fact, one of the primary reasons for adopting the open door policies now in place has been to attract foreign involvement in the Chinese economy. By relying on a variety of forms of foreign involvement, the Chinese have hoped that foreign participants would contribute their know-how, their production technology, and their managerial expertise to assist local manufacturing in becoming more efficient and effective producers.

There is little doubt that the task of updating production equipment, product designs, processing technologies, and testing and measurement capabilities constitutes a major undertaking. Surveys taken in the mid-1980s revealed that 10–20% of the equipment in industrial enterprises was from before the 1950s, 60% was from the 1950s and 1960s, and only 20–25% was from the 1970s and 1980s. Estimates suggest that 25% of the state-owned enterprises in the industrial sector require *complete* renovation; another estimate contends that 60% of the government-owned industrial equipment in state-owned enterprises needs to be replaced or renovated.[24] For example, while China possesses more lathes than any other country in the world, only 10% of them can be considered "state of the art." Moreover, due to the combined impact of Western export controls and China's own trade policies, much of the equipment has been sourced from different countries, leaving many factories with problems of equipment compatibility.

In essence, China's strategy for modernizing its domestic industrial technological capabilities is a multi-faceted one, reflecting a combination of top-down, market-oriented, and horizontal policy initiatives. The effort is under the direction of the State Planning Commission, which took over responsibility for the program when it merged with the former State Economic Commission. The current drive is largely characterized by the strong emphasis being given to both organizational reform and structural change—though it must be acknowledged that the Chinese have not entirely backed away from the "big push" approach to technological advance. At a March 1990 conference on the tasks for science and technology (S&T) development in the 1990s, Li Xu'e, Deputy Director of the Standing Committee of the SSTC, advocated the establishment of the chief-engineer responsibility system under the leadership of the enterprise director as a means to enhance technological development in industry.[25] In spite of the retrenchment efforts over the last year or so, the degree to which the leadership is prepared to initiate fundamental change in the technology area is still fairly significant. This commitment was first reflected in the March 1985 Central Committee Decision on "Reform of the Science and Technology Management System" and has been carried forward in the various other innovations that have been introduced, such as the technology market, the establishment of various "high technology zones throughout the country, and programs such as the Torch

[24] "Industry Needs Big Technological Lift," *China Daily*, August 27, 1990, p.4.
[25] *Keji Ribao* (Science and Technology Daily), March 10, 1990, p.1.

Plan." [26] While the S&T reforms come at the technology problem from the R&D side, they are significant for industrial performance (and thus the State Planning Commission) because they spell out a broad array of modifications regarding the funding of science and technology activities, including the use of contracts to encourage R&D institutes and production units to develop more intimate working relations. Even more important, the reforms in S&T since 1985 serve to complement a number of other initiatives introduced over the past few years in the area of economic reform, e.g. the production responsibility system, and overall industrial policy,[27] many of which are aimed at encouraging enterprises to rely more on China's technical work force for helping with such tasks such as the assimilation of foreign technology.[28]

Propelled by a desire to gain expanded access to foreign technology, China has set in motion a series of acquisition programs to support the technical transformation program. During the period 1981–1989, China signed over 18,000 agreements and over 30,000 contracts for the introduction of technology and equipment to support the upgrading of Chinese enterprises for a total of over 415,000 projects. In total, the State pumped in 463.2 billion yuan (U.S. $ 98.5 billion). More than 17,000 projects involved the use of foreign exchange funds for the import of technology and equipment to support technical transformation. Estimates are that close to U.S. $27 billion was expended. In the 7th Five-Year Plan (FYP) itself, the State allocated a total investment of 276 billion yuan for technical transformation, but initial estimates are that the actual amount of investment for the first four years (1986–89) was over 314 billion yuan with one year still left to calculate. A report in the *Renmin Ribao* in mid-November 1990 indicated that the total figure will likely exceed 400 billion yuan.[29] During 1989, however, the total investment in technical transformation declined some 20% from 95.5 billion yuan in 1988 to 78.9 billion yuan (See Table 5). This was the first significant drop in investment level in this area since the program began, reflecting the severity of the economic crisis confronting the leadership and its need to introduce controls on spending due to two budget shortfalls and excessive subsidies to problem-plagued enterprises.[30] Approximately 1,300 of the projects required foreign purchases, and therefore an expenditure of foreign exchange, which apparently totalled U.S. $1.3 billion.

---

[26] In spite of various problems, China's technology market continues to expand. In 1989, for example, the value of national transactions totalled 8.14 billion yuan, up from 72 million yuan in 1984. See *Xinhua*, September 3, 1990, translated in FBIS–CHI-90-171, September 4, 1990, p.28.

[27] Gao Shangquan, "Deepening Enterprise Reform Should be Carried Out in a Comprehensive Fashion," *Liaowang* (Outlook), Number 32, August 6, 1990, pp.5–6.

[28] One of the eight tasks proposed at the National Work Conference on Science and Technology in March 1990 was to encourage research institutes to play a more active role in importing technology and absorbing new technology. See *Keji Ribao* (Science and Technology Daily), March 10, 1990, p.1.

[29] "Important Strategic Thinking—On Strengthening Technical Transformation Among Enterprises," *Renmin Ribao*, November 13, 1990, p.1.

[30] Subsidies to unprofitable enterprises amounted to nearly 60 billion yuan (US$12.6 billion) in 1989 or nearly 20 percent of the government's annual expenditure. Early indications are that funds for technical transformation in the first half of 1990 continued to decline by 3.4%. "Industry Needs Big Technological Lift," *China Daily*, August 27, 1990, p.4.

TABLE 5
Technical Transformation of Key Items:
Purpose, Use of Funds and Type of Construction, 1981-89
Unit: 100 Million Yuan

	1981	1985	1986	1987	1988	1989
PURPOSE OF PRODUCTION						
SAVE ENERGY	7.79	17.37	22.75	25.90	30.77	25.25
EXPAND PROD	NA	160.35	211.20	273.26	375.30	303.08
INCREASE VARIETY	93.20	61.30	97.88	108.61	134.74	119.00
IMPROVE QUALITY	7.08	26.58	39.16	42.82	49.15	39.38
WASTE TREATMENT	2.98	9.08	11.78	14.33	17.67	14.99
OTHER	49.67	106.02	131.73	157.63	188.82	156.19
TOTAL	**195.30**	**449.14**	**619.21**	**758.89**	**954.51**	**788.78**
LESS NON-PRODUCT	34.58	68.44	104.71	136.04	158.06	128.57
TOTAL	**160.72**	**380.70**	**514.50**	**622.55**	**796.45**	**660.21**
USE OF FUNDS						
CONSTRUCTION	113.77	196.23	267.79	339.51	461.49	377.25
BUY EQUIPMENT	76.15	224.94	308.58	353.29	412.23	355.89
UPDATE EQUIPMENT	NA	58.36	88.85	119.99	89.33	55.64
CONSTRUCTION						
NEW CONSTRUCTION	19.75	23.06	36.26	41.22	69.72	38.87
EXPANSION	75.01	194.45	274.59	350.33	423.51	345.54
RE-BUILDING	89.02	191.16	261.84	313.18	386.43	363.49

Source: *China Statistical Abstracts, 1989,* p.71; *China Statistical Yearbook,* 1990, p.191.

As in the past, the basic framework of the program for the initial portion of the 7th FYP was laid out in a list of 3,000 key items (actually the number ended up totalling 3,900 items) designated by the SPC (by components of the former State Economic Commission) for purchase during the 1986–88 time period. As noted, these items placed the import of technologies to support the technical transformation of enterprises in the forefront—with the State Planning Commission and its local counterpart organizations—still being the lead unit in this effort. Most of the focus is on the import of *know-how*, with emphasis on technologies in the electronics and machinery area. While technology imports are not confined to this 3000 item list, the list does appear to contain the priority items.

The salience of the so-called "3,000 projects" list can be seen in a recent Chinese assessment of the impact of those technologies imported under this program during the last three years of the 6th FYP. According to the evaluation, which was made in late 1986, "the 3,000 projects have enabled some Chinese industries and products to leap-frog technically, significantly narrowing the gap with the advanced nations. Ten percent of the products of the machinery industry today reach international standards of the late 1970s and early 1980s. In electronics, the manufacturing of color TV sets, video cassette recorders, tape recorders and copiers has grown and matured. More than 30 percent of [our] electronic products are now on par with the best of the world in the late 1970s and early 1980s, up from 15% in 1982." [31] While perhaps somewhat over-optimistic in its tone, the assessment reveals the critical value that such a program could have if properly supported and managed, especially since, as the source suggests, "these projects require limited outlays, have a short construction period, pay off quickly, and yield good economic results." [32]

Improved use of foreign technology has been made possible, in many cases, by the fact that acquisition mechanisms have been created at the enterprise level with the establishment of so-called "technology introduction or import departments." In many cases, these departments were created on an ad hoc basis to handle the process of technology import. Subsequently, they have been formally institutionalized and are now a permanent part of the Chinese enterprise. Their primary value is that they constitute a critical mass of individuals responsible for all facets of an import-related project. In some instances, in addition to having a small core staff, there is a rotating staff of technical and financial specialists that move in and out of the office as needed during the inception, negotiation, agreement, and implementation phases of particular projects. Enterprises are now responsible for preparing in-depth feasibility studies to justify not only the need for the purchase, but also to indicate their capabilities and resources for effectively implementing the new technology. The increasing reliance on loans to finance technical transformation projects has also helped to ensure greater success in the various projects, especially since enterprises are now responsible for paying back the monies they use for upgrading their facilities, buying new equipment, etc. In 1989, for example, only 1.8% of the total funds allocated for technical transformation came from government grants, 57.3% was from self-investment, and 40.9% was derived from domestic and foreign bank loans

---

[31] Jiang Shaogao, "3,000 Pieces of Technology Imported in 3 Years," *Renmin Ribao* Overseas Edition, December 4, 1986, p.3.
[32] Ibid.

(See Figure 1).[33] Total funding for technical transformation increased from 18.7 billion yuan in 1980 to 78.9 billion yuan in 1989.

Accordingly, it is clear that China's enterprises covered under the technical transformation program have begun to benefit substantially from the growing presence of foreign technology in the local economy. First, it is estimated that large amounts of both domestic funds and foreign exchange have been saved. According to one estimate, approximately U.S. $11 billion in foreign exchange will have been saved by import substitution associated with the technical transformation program. Chinese analysts claim that 45% of the increase in China's exports of light industrial goods, textiles and machinery over the last several years has been achieved through the upgrading of old workshops with imported technology and equipment.[34] In the city of Shanghai, where approximately 25 billion yuan (U.S. $4.9 billion) had been invested in technical transformation, of the 725 projects completed between 1986–88, more than 14 billion yuan in production value has been generated and close to 900 million yuan in foreign exchange earned.[35] Second, in the electrical appliance area, for example, product quality and designs have been greatly improved. A good example is the Yingkou Washing Machine Factory in Liaoning Province, which after extensive cooperation with a Japanese firm—including the completion of two large scale technical upgradings and the set up of 22 computerized production lines, now produces seven models of washing machines. In the chemical industry, the Luzhou Natural Gas Chemical Company in Sichuan used a World Bank loan, in conjunction with assistance from the UK-based firm H&G Engineering, to update its production techniques and increase its output capacity.[36] After its three-year program of technical renovation, the Luzhou company's daily 300 metric ton output of synthetic ammonia was increased to 450 metric tons. Moreover, energy consumption was sharply reduced. And third, according to one study of imported technology and equipment which have been put into operation in Beijing, Shanghai, and Tianjin, each yuan of investment in imported technology for technical renovation has increased output value by 2.5–2.8 yuan.[37]

This is not to suggest that the technical transformation of enterprises program has been without its problems. The most significant problem continues to be the general reluctance of many enterprise managers to give a high priority to technical transformation as well as overall technological progress. According to one article, Chinese managers are said to lack the three main ingredients necessary for promoting technological advance: 1) a strategic vision and strong enterprising spirit; 2) the courage to take risks and be a pioneer; and 3) a high level of scientific culture and strong aptitude for management. "Currently, many factories and enterprises are

[33] "The Situation Regarding China's Investment in Fixed Assets," *Economic Yearbook of China, 1990* (Beijing, 1990), p.II-35.
[34] "Foreign Technology Purchases Pay Dividends," *China Daily*, August 29, 1989, p.1.
[35] "Renovation Projects to Bring Industry Up-to-Date By 1995," *China Daily*, (Shanghai Focus), December 10, 1990, p.1.
[36] "Renovation Completed at Chemical Complex," *China Daily*, November 27, 1990, p.2.
[37] Wang Xiaodong, "Results and Prospects for China's Technology Imports," *Liaowang Overseas Edition*, No.1, January 5, 1987, pp.13–14 translated in JPRS–CEA–87–014, February 26, 1987, pp.53–54.

Figure 1

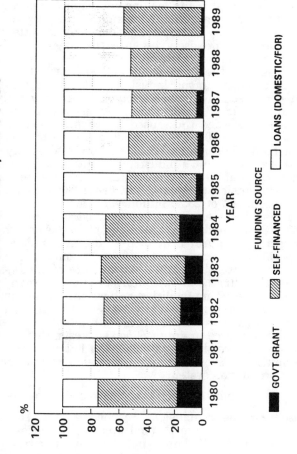

FUNDING SOURCES FOR TECHNICAL
TRANSFORMATION, 1980-89

FUNDING SOURCE

■ GOVT GRANT   ▨ SELF-FINANCED   ☐ LOANS (DOMESTIC/FOR)

UNIT: % OF TOTAL

lukewarm in the pursuit of technological progress, ... an important reason is that many leading cadres and departments in charge do not take the evaluation of technological progress in enterprises seriously.... Many enterprise leaders pay no attention to technological progress precisely because the higher levels' demand for such progress is a soft criterion." [38]

As a result of the above-mentioned situation, there has continued to be a tendency among industrial enterprises to use funds designated for "technical transformation" for primarily capital construction. While after 1985, the funds used to purchase and update equipment exceeded those used for construction, the fact remains that between 40-50% of the funds are used for some form of construction. While some new construction is to be expected given the dismal state of China's industrial facilities, this problem is part of the general inability of the central authorities to control spending effectively outside the plan. Between 1986-88, for example, out of total investment of 23.25 billion yuan for technical transformation in the machinery and electronics industries, only 7.85 billion yuan (about 1/3) was budgeted within the plan. [39] And, while the austerity program inaugurated in 1988-89 did help reduce the severity of this problem, it promises to reemerge once the controls are removed. And last, the largest expenditure of funds continues to be used for the purpose of expanding production, many times through expansion of existing facilities rather than actual upgrading. Funds for the purpose of increasing variety and improving quality do not generally equal or surpass those allocated for production expansion. As one source in *Jingji Ribao* suggests, this leads to the enactment of what are simply extensions of low-standard projects rather than new initiatives based on a thorough restructuring of the prevailing production system. [40]

CHINA'S TECHNOLOGY IMPORT PRIORITIES

Based on the conclusions reached at the Dalian meeting in August 1987, the State Council approved a series of recommendations concerned with improving the results of technology importation. [41] During the last three years of the 7th Five Year Plan, these recommendations became the foundation of China's revised technology import policy. Enacted with the help of the former State Economic Commission, a five-point preferential policy package was introduced and was applied specifically to 300 key projects ("300 dragons") identified by the commission as central to China's economic modernization. [42] The five points included the following provisions: 1) the product or value-added tax will be reduced or exempted on items produced with foreign technology that have replaced imports; 2) buyers of items produced with foreign technology may be asked (with approval by the State Administration of Ex-

[38] Gu Jiekang, et.al., "How to Make Enterprises More Desirous of Modern Technology," *Zhongguo Keji Luntan*, Number 2, 1988, pp.36-38.

[39] He Guangyuan, "More Regulation and Control of Machine-Building and Electronic Industries Urged," *Jingji Ribao*, September 22, 1989, p.2.

[40] Ibid.

[41] "State Council Policy on Imported Technology," *Xinhua*, November 20, 1987, translated in FBIS-CHI-87-226, November 24, 1987, p.29.

[42] Zhang Yuan, "Preferential Policy Begun for Imported Items," *China Daily*, February 4, 1988, p.2.

change Control) to pay some foreign exchange when purchasing such products on the domestic market; 3) import duties and product tax may be reduced or exempted for import of items that are difficult to manufacture in China, but are critical to economic modernization; 4) central government departments and local governments are responsible to give the 300 projects advantages in foreign exchange, bank loans, supply of materials, etc.; and 5) enterprises that complete the absorption and digestion of the imported technology and increase localization will be eligible for special rewards or bonuses. Taken as a whole package, these new provisions are designed to stimulate interest in foreign technology acquisition, while at the same time providing incentives for successful absorption. The emphasis in the revised policies is clearly and unequivocally on improving "digestion and absorption" of imported technology.

Even though China will continue to adhere to its policy of economic consolidation and rectification for the next 1-2 years, the emphasis on technology import will not subside. In keeping with the above principles, during the 8th Five Year Plan, China will place emphasis on the following areas: 1) high technology—as a means to help facilitate the formation of a batch of research centers in such fields as high-energy physics, microelectronics, computers, biotechnology, ocean engineering, and new materials; 2) key technology for enhancement of the economic infrastructure, including energy, communications, raw materials, and agriculture; and 3) new techniques, materials and equipment that can boost the quality of export products.[43] According to Xie Yangan, deputy director of the Foreign Economic Relations and Trade Office of the State Planning Commission, the emphasis will be on the acquisition of design and manufacturing technologies that will help promote the development of new equipment and products as well as enhance the overall competitiveness of Chinese exports.

These priorities will also be reflected in the guidelines for technical transformation for the 8th Five Year Plan. Approximately 300 large and medium key enterprises will form the focal point for the program.[44] Three main tasks have been delineated for the technical transformation program a) reduction of energy use and consumption of raw materials; b) improvement in the quality of products and development of new products; and c) expansion of exports and an increase in foreign exchange earnings.[45] In all likelihood, funding will increase overall, though during the initial period, there may be a slight decline due to prevailing economic conditions. According to officials at the People's Construction Bank of China, hard currency loans will mainly go for technical renovation projects in key industries, including energy, transportation, raw materials, light industry, and textiles.[46]

---

[43] "More Foreign Technology Needed," *Beijing Review,* March 12-18, 1990, p.39.
[44] Qin Hanshan, "China's High-Tech Development," *China Market,* Number 4, 1990, p.17.
[45] "Important Strategic Thinking—On Strengthening Technical Transformation Among Enterprises," *Renmin Ribao,* November 13, 1990, p.1.
[46] "China To Go Ahead with Tight Credit Policy," *China Daily,* October 30, 1990, p.2.

V. China's Assimilation of Foreign Technology

The central focus of attention regarding technology import in China has shifted away from primary concern with issues such as U.S. export controls and COCOM and is now aimed at the question of assimilation. This is not to suggest that Chinese officials remain fully satisfied with the degree to which China still falls under American export control restrictions. For example, the PRC leadership was obviously not pleased with the decision of the Bush Administration to force China's National Aero-Tech Import and Export Corporation (CATIC) to sell its interests in MAMCO Manufacturing, a Seattle-based producer of aircraft parts, due to "national security" concerns.[47] Nonetheless, after spending several billions of U.S. dollars for imported equipment and know-how, Chinese officials are seeking ways to ensure that previous deficiencies are eradicated. As noted, there remain a range of opinions regarding the effectiveness of previous efforts at absorption of foreign technology. Some official statements suggest that as much as 90% of the cases involving technology import have yielded "desired results." Other more pessimistic analyses, for example, indicate that the number of so-called "success" cases may be less than 50% and even as low as 20%.[48] For example, in a review conducted in 1987, out of 996 cases of technology import in the machine-building industry carried out between 1975–86, only 210 cases (21%) can be considered under full operation.[49]

Clearly, some progress has been made. According to an official from the State Planning Commission, as a result of technology imports over the last decade, China has been able to expand steel production annually by 15 million tons, copper by 90,000 tons, aluminum by 1.5 million tons, ethylene by 900,000 tons, synthetic fiber by 1.1 million tons, and cement by 4.8 million tons.[50] Improvements in management, manufacturing technology, and personnel utilization have all helped to eradicate some of the previous problems of the late 1970s and early 1980s. The successful startup of the 300,000 ton ethylene project in the Shanghai Petrochemical Complex is one such example.[51] With equipment and know-how imported from Toyo Engineering of Japan, this project will provide China with the capacity to produce 1.3 million tons of petrochemical products per year. This project is the last of four such installations China imported from Japan in 1978. The other three projects are in Daqing (Heilongjiang), Qilu (Shandong), and Nanjing (Jiangsu).[52] Originally, this installation had been placed in Nanj-

---

[47] "Bush Orders Chinese Firm to Sell Stake in US Aircraft-Parts Maker," *Asian Wall Street Journal Weekly*, February 12, 1990, p.19. Some have suggested, however, that the Bush Administration's decision, which was authorized by the 1988 Omnibus Trade Bill, had very little to do with actual national security concerns, but rather was a reflection of the tense bilateral political climate induced by the events in Tiananmen Square. See Keith Eastin, "China Case Highlights a Flawed US Law," *Asian Wall Street Journal Weekly*, April 2, 1990, p.14.

[48] Song Zhuci and Hong Lujian, "Strengthening the Macro-Mechanisms for Machinery Technology Import," in *Industrial Policy Research on China's Machine-Building Industry* (Beijing: Machine-Building Industry Press, 1989), pp.259–271.

[49] Ibid.

[50] "Foreign Technology Purchases Pay Dividends," *China Daily*, August 29, 1989, p.1.

[51] "New Plant Sets Record," *China Daily*, December 18, 1989, p.1.

[52] "Petrochemical Trade Prospers," *China Daily*, October 16, 1989, p.4.

ing, but in 1983 it was transported to Shanghai. Unfortunately, while sitting idle in Nanjing, many problems arose, such as corrosion of the pipes and meters. Repair of these problems cost a considerable sum of money. Nonetheless, with the help of experts from the three other facilities, the plant was finally able to complete a successful test run in December 1989.

Similar gains have been made in the turbogenerator industry, which has been a high priority sector since the 1950s.[53] Between 1953–58, China established two large manufacturing bases for turbo-generator production; one is in Harbin which imported Soviet technology and the other in Shanghai which relied on technology obtained from Czechoslovakia. The principal means of acquiring technology was through imitation. Between 1958–80, the PRC entered a period characterized by the emphasis on self-reliance. Through indigenous efforts, Chinese engineers were able to master some of the key water and hydrogen cooling technologies, circulation techniques, rotor balance and speed calculations, and stator and rotor coil water systems.[54] Between 1980 and 1985, China entered its current open door phase and signed 13 agreements for acquisition of generating equipment manufacturing know-how. Included in these 13 agreements signed by the PRC was a February 1981 15-year agreement for importing technology from Westinghouse to upgrade the quality of Chinese turbogenerators in terms of parts and components as well as overall performance.[55] Through these imports, which included a substantial element of joint design and production work between Westinghouse and the relevant Chinese entities, Shanghai and Harbin have been able to perfect near state-of-the-art techniques to procure the 300MW completely hydrogen inner cooled generator and the 600MW hydrogen and water cooled generator, respectively. The availability of this technology within China has saved substantial foreign exchange, and has also contributed in a big way to helping China improve its hydropower generating capacity.[56]

Still, assimilation problems abound. One of the more revealing cases involves the Yunnan Tobacco industry, which over the past several years has invested 750 million yuan and expended U.S. $140 million in foreign exchange to import one tobacco leaf composite flue-curing production line (600,000 boxes annual capacity), seven cut tobacco-making production lines with an annual capacity of 2.4 million boxes, 187 cigarette rolling units with an annual production capacity of 1.96 million boxes, and 123 packaging units with an annual production capacity of 800,000 boxes.[57]

[53] Shen Liangwei, "The Status of and Prospects for Turbogenerator Manufacture in China," *Dadianji Jishu* (Large Electric Machines and Hydraulic Turbines), Number 6, November 1986, pp.1–9.

[54] Ibid.

[55] For a discussion of China's ability to produce the materials and metals needed to manufacture turbine rotors and blades see Sun Huilian, "Material Technology Progress in the Power Equipment Industry," *Dongli Gongcheng* (Power Engineering), Volume 9, Number 2, April 1989, pp.14–24.

[56] This is not necessarily to suggest that China's turbogenerators are without their problems. Nor is it to suggest that China's power problems have been resolved. For an overview of the current situation see Zhu Chengzhang, "Achievements, Problems and Countermeasures in China's Electric Power Industry," *Keji Daobao* (Science and Technology Review), Number 30, March 1990, pp.3–6.

[57] Zhang Kaihan, "Digesting Imported Technologies and Raising the Equipment Utilization Coefficient," *Yunnan Ribao*, April 15, 1990, p.2.

On the surface, the project appears to have been a success, especially if we measure the performance of the technology in terms of increases in economic output. Compared with 1981, for example, Yunnan's cigarette output reached 3.5 billion boxes (3.4 times that of 1981); the imported equipment accounted for about 50% of the increase. The value of the output was 3.7 times that of 1981, taxable profits were 4.29 billion yuan or 7.6 times that of 1981, and the output of filter-tip cigarettes was 1.42 million boxes or 20.8 times that of 1981—95% of which was produced on imported equipment.[58]

Based on Chinese assessments of the project, however, certain shortcomings were revealed. First, despite the rapid increases in output, the fact is that the efficiency of imported equipment is much lower than that of equipment made in China. The average production efficiency of the main tobacco machines and equipment in Yunnan is 75%; equipment made in China has an 89.41% rating, while imported equipment has a rating of 51.04%. Overall, compared with the efficiency levels in the U.S. and Europe, Yunnan's imported equipment has not yet reached the 40% level. Since the technology imported from abroad (West Germany) is more complex than the domestically-made machinery and has different maintenance and material requirements, Chinese workers feel much less comfortable with using it. "... because the technical level of operation is low, the daily maintenance and care of equipment is not good, the quality of raw and supplementary materials does not meet requirements, and the work environment for the equipment is bad—all of which has accelerated the wear and tear on and the aging of the equipment. The supply of spare parts is not timely enough, the equipment's maintenance technical standards and data are not complete, there is lack of high-quality technicians who have been systematically trained and can correctly adjust and maintain the imported equipment, there is pressure from heavy production tasks, and so forth."[59]

The situation with respect to Yunnan's import of tobacco processing equipment and technology appears to derive from the number of rather generic problems. First, there has been an excessive focus on technology importation and not enough attention given to digestion and absorption. The tasks of complete digestion and absorption have not been made a high enough priority by the plant managers. If Yunnan's tobacco industry can increase the effective utilization rate of the imported cigarette-making and packaging equipment by 10% over the next year or two, it could reduce future outlays of foreign exchange by U.S. $12.6 million and add 64.33 million yuan in taxable profits to the state. Second, not enough time and attention was given the problem of training. Third, the industry lacks much of the support structure to keep it alive and operating efficiently. There are an inadequate number of repair plants and parts supply centers to sustain the industry. Fourth, the operating environment for the equipment needs to be improved to avoid constant equipment breakdowns. Relatedly, there frequently does not exist some form of "equipment management responsibility system" to

[58] Ibid.
[59] Ibid.

ensure that the imported items are not just operating effectively, but are fully incorporated into the mainstream operations of the entire production endeavor.

The types of problems found in Yunnan's tobacco industry are indicative of those found elsewhere in the PRC. As noted, requirements exist for the preparation of comprehensive feasibility studies by intended foreign technology recipients. These feasibility studies, which are reviewed by the local economic and/or planning commissions as well as the relevant banks if a loan is involved, oblige the enterprise to specify the nature of the technology being sought, the appropriateness of the supplier, and the competence of the enterprise in terms of management, equipment and personnel, to make effective use of the imported items. However, while funds are made available for the acquisition of foreign know-how and equipment, there rarely is a budget set aside for covering the costs of assimilation. One of the major failures heretofore has been the lack of direct participation by China's scientific and technical R&D institutions in the digestion and absorption process.[60] As one source has indicated, "... institutions of higher education and scientific research units, China's main forces in scientific research, are cut off from digesting absorbing and innovating work."[61] Lacking appropriate incentives, neither the technology recipients, nor the R&D institutes seek out one another on a regular sustained basis. A sample survey of 620 items imported by China between 1973–86 showed that scientific research units were called upon to help with the assimilation of foreign technology in fewer than 2.0% of the cases![62] Ironically, however, when such organizations do come together, the results are not necessarily optimal, as those who are responsible for R&D frequently tend to push up the level of know-how and equipment being demanded from the foreign supplier beyond the capacity of the recipient to utilize the technology.

Assimilation problems are also manifested in the serious situation regarding duplication of technology imports. While some in China claim that the country's problems with redundant technology imports stem primarily from the poor macro-economic management and oversight system, others argue, quite persuasively, that the main cause is related to the lack of adequate absorption and digestion. Since the demands of the domestic market cannot be satisfied by importing merely one set of equipment (because of poor performance with technology absorption), other potential suppliers quickly jump in to secure their share of the market. The validity of this argument is supported by several studies conducted by the National Research Center for Science and Technology for Development under the SSTC. According to one study conducted within the machinery and electronics industry, market competition was stated as the driving force behind the desire of various enterprises to advance their technical levels.[63] This may sound ironic in an econo-

---

[60] Theodor Leuenberger, ed., *From Technology Transfer to Technology Management in China* (Berlin: Springer-Verlag, 1990).

[61] Hu Jiexun, "On the Role of Institutions of Higher Education and Scientific Research Units in Digesting, Absorbing, and Innovating Imported Technologies," *Keyan Guanli* (Research Management), Number 2, March 1989, p.14–18.

[62] Ibid.

[63] Bao Ke and Zhou Weimin, "The Assimilation of Imported Technology in the Machinery and Electronics Industries," *Jingji Cankao*, January 21, 1988.

my that supposedly relies on the planning mechanism for formulating and implementing economic policy. Still, whether perceived or real, enterprise managers do have a sense of their participation in China's so-called "big market." Moreover, despite the admonition to focus on exports, the primary motivation for technology imports among Chinese enterprises has continued to be access and share in the domestic market in China.[64]

Perhaps the sector where redundant imports have been the most distressing has been in the television industry, where estimates suggest that at least 113 production lines for color TV assembly and production were imported.[65] The total capacity of these lines is over 15 million sets. Approximately 51.0% of China's urban residents have a color television set; the percentage among families in the rural areas is about 4.0%.[66] Total TV production reached 27.7 million sets in 1989, 34% (9.4 million) of which were color televisions (See Figure 2 and Tables 6 and 7). Aside from the obvious problems of duplication and perhaps under-utilization resulting from excessive production capacity, the main problem associated with these 113 production lines is that the depend primarily on imports for key parts and components. For example, a television plant in Jiangsu Province with a capacity to produce 175,000 color TVs a year can only manufacture 5,000 sets because of its limited foreign exchange.[67] In 1988, one study estimated that 85–87% of the tubes needed to be imported for the 10.28 million color TV sets produced.[68] Similar foreign exchange issues have emerged with respect to semiconductors, integrated circuits, and printed circuit boards used in the manufacture of color TVs. From an overall perspective, despite concerted efforts to revitalize the domestic semiconductor industry and build up production capabilities in places such as the Caohejing High-Technology Zone in Shanghai, estimates are that anywhere from 50%–70% of the internal market demand for ICs is still met through imports.[69]

To remedy the situation, Chinese leaders have given a high priority to the localization of key components. Official estimates are that China can now produce 90% of the supplementary components for TV sets, reducing the cost of imported components from U.S. $60 to U.S. $20. The two most important primary components, i.e. color picture tubes and integrated circuits, are currently the target of major investment activities. In the case of the latter, the major project initiated to overcome the domestic shortfall of TV set integrated circuits (ICs) was the import from Toshiba of a complete IC production line by the Jiangnan #742 Radio Equipment Factory in Wuxi in the mid-1980s.

In addition, with improvements in domestic production techniques, China can provide many of the less-complex linear ICs used in television manufacturing. The government has also chosen to

---

[64] Denis Fred Simon and William A. Fischer, *China's Experience with Foreign Technology* (New York: Ballinger/Harper and Row, forthcoming).
[65] "China's Television Receiver Industry Developing in a Beneficial Direction," *Zhongguo Dianzi Bao* (China Electronics News), March 31, 1987, p.2.
[66] "Sluggish TV Sales Expected to Boom," *China Daily* (Business Weekly), June 4, 1990, p.2.
[67] "Exchange Woes Put TV Producers in Bind," *China Daily*, February 15, 1989, p.4.
[68] "Home Target for Tube Makers," *China Daily* (Business Weekly), April 24, 1989, p.2.
[69] "Current Problems and Demand Forecast of China's Semiconductor Market," *Dianzi Shichang* (Electronics Market), June 22, 1989, p.2.

Figure 2

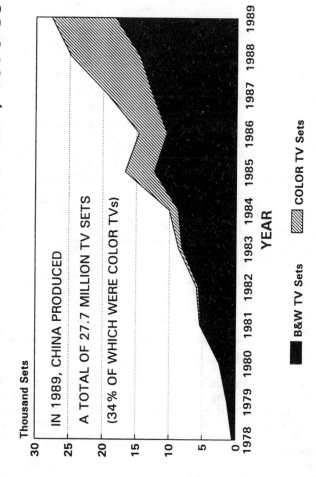

TV SET PRODUCTION IN CHINA, 1978-89

Thousand Sets

IN 1989, CHINA PRODUCED

A TOTAL OF 27.7 MILLION TV SETS

(34% OF WHICH WERE COLOR TVs)

YEAR

■ B&W TV Sets   ▨ COLOR TV Sets

UNIT: 1,000 SETS

TABLE 6

China's Leading Television Manufacturers, 1989

Unit: 1000s of sets

FACTORY	OUTPUT	COLOR TV	TOTAL SALES	SALES % /OUTPUT
WUXI TV FACTORY	1,187	235	1,117	94.2%
SHANGHAI #18	1,150	142	1,101	95.7%
SHANGHAI #4	1,148	101	1,121	97.7%
NANJING RADIO	1,071	237	944	88.1%
SUZHOU TV	1,018	204	1,005	98.7%
SHANGHAI #1	886	38	868	98.0%
HANGZHOU TV	788	131	628	79.7%
TIANJIN BROADCAST EQUIP	658	381	535	81.3%
CHANGHONG	651	448	412	63.4%
DALIAN TV	601	126	463	77.1%
TIANJIN TV	545	192	394	72.2%

Source: *Zhongguo Dianzi Bao*, April 1990.

regulate the chip circuits that can be employed in the production of color TV sets; starting in early 1990, for example, certain chip sets used by Hitachi and Sony declared ineligible as far as the State production of optimized chip circuits.[70] In the case of the former, a strategy was put in place to significantly expand domestic production capacity.

Starting in 1981 with the opening of the Shaanxi Color TV Tube Factory in Xianyang, the central government has encouraged the development of four (including the Xianyang facility) color TV tube bases, with Beijing, Nanjing, and Shanghai being the other three sites. The Beijing project involves a U.S. $152 million joint venture with a capacity of 1.8 million tubes between Japan's Matsushita, the Beijing Electronic Tube Factory, and the Beijing branch of the China Electronics Import and Export Corporation.[71] The Shanghai project is a U.S. $109 million joint venture with a production capacity of 1.0 million tubes between the Hong Kong Novel Technology

---

[70] According to officials in the ministry, the TDA double-chip circuit has been determined to be the best optimized circuit for use in China. Those manufacturers who do not use the approved chips will not receive preferential treatment in pricing and sourcing from the central authorities. See *China Informatics*, April 30, 1990, p.121.

[71] "Kinescope Firm Highlights China's Investment Climate," *Beijing Review*, January 15-21, 1990, pp.27-29.

TABLE 7

SELECTED EXAMPLES OF PRC COLOR

TV PRODUCTION LINE IMPORTS[a]

Unit: Single Lines

COUNTRY	TOTAL # LINES	COMPANY	# OF LINES
JAPAN	50		
		MATSUSHITA	8
		HITACHI	7
		JVC	13
		TOSHIBA	6
		SANYO	4
		NEC	3
		SHARP	5
		OTHER	4
WESTERN EUROPE	2		
		PHILIPS	1
		GRUNDIG	1
HONG KONG	18		
		LU-DI	6
		KANG-LI	5
		OTHER	7

Source: Ministry of Machine-Building and Electronics Industry, Beijing, 1989.

[a] The number of production lines noted in this table does not account for the total of 113 lines imported in 1981-88. Several lines apparently came from non-designated sources, including knocked-down lines from Taiwan and South Korea as well as several discontinued lines from Hong Kong.

Development Company and the Shanghai Vacuum Electronic Parts Company; the picture tube technology comes from the Toshiba Corporation of Japan. The third project in Nanjing is a joint venture with a capacity of 1.6 million tubes named the Huafei Color TV Tube Factory involving technology from Philips of Holland and the Huadong Electron Tube Factory.[72] The Xianyang Factory in Shaanxi has a capacity of 960,000 color tubes, though last year it

---

[72] "Philips Signs More Electronics Agreements," *China Daily*, November 11, 1987, p.2.

produced 1.06 million tubes. It relies on technology from Hitachi, Toshiba and the U.S. A fifth project appears underway in Shenzhen involving technology from the Hitachi Corporation of Japan. Four related projects to produce the glass bulbs for color TV tubes have also been inaugurated: one in Shijiazhuang, one in Anyang in Henan with Corning Technology, one in Shenzhen with Corning Technology as well, and the last one in Chengdu involving technology transfer from Asahi Glass of Japan.

The major question confronting China, however, as it moves ahead with a projected plan to manufacture approximately 10–13 million color TV tubes a year is whether or not it is economically feasible to become basically self-reliant in this area.[73] Because of China's continued need to import the raw materials to make the bulbs and tubes, preliminary estimates are that it would cost China U.S. $150 million in foreign exchange to sustain 10 million tubes of output.[74] China is also still dependent on foreign companies for advanced designs used in state-of-the-art color televisions.

Moreover, there are major questions about the ability of the Chinese market to absorb color TV sets at the pace required to keep the industry financially viable. Many of the sets being produced are not state-of-the-art; in early 1990, for example, there were indications that over U.S. $40 million worth of "ordinary" color TV sets were being stockpiled.[75] The Chinese government ordered production of color TV sets reduced by 30% in 1990 in response to a sluggish domestic. This is a major step in view of the fact that the production value of color TVs was U.S. $3.3 billion in 1989, accounting for 24.4% of the total value of electronics production.[76]

Finally, there is the question of high-definition television. Ultimately, China, which already is the largest producer of black and white television sets in the world, may also become the largest manufacturer of color TVs, especially if labor and material costs in Taiwan, South Korea, and Hong Kong continue to climb. In 1989, total TV exports reached 3.9 million sets (1.8 million were color TVs), an increase of 49% over 1988. If HDTV takes off, however, China could be stuck with an expensive infrastructure designed to manufacture TVs primarily for the Third World and perhaps the former socialist countries in Eastern Europe.

VI. PROSPECTS AND CONCLUSIONS

The expanded use of new technology in Chinese industry and agriculture is essential if the PRC is to achieve its long term goal of closing the gap with the Western industrialized nations. In some cases, Chinese leaders realize that the most practical answer is to make better use of existing equipment through improvements in plant layout and more efficient use of energy and raw materials. In other cases, there is no choice but replacement—whether through imports or from domestic suppliers. Nonetheless, the central questions remain the same. How does China choose which enterprises

---

[73] "TV Industry Approaches Self-Sufficiency," *China Daily*, October 1, 1990, p.3.
[74] "Make Less Color TV Tubes—Think Tank," *China Daily*, July 31, 1989, p.2.
[75] "Color TV Sales Rise in April," *China Daily*, May 2, 1990, p.3.
[76] See *China Electronics Industry Yearbook*, 1990 (Beijing, 1990). See also "TV Exports Rose to 1.89m by May," *China Daily*, June 29, 1990, p.2.

should be targeted for access to scarce funds? At what level should decisions be made for implementing technological upgrading? What criteria should be used in the selection of appropriate technologies, equipment, suppliers? Unless these questions are answered satisfactorily and systematically, and in a manner consistent with the central thrust of overall economic policy, the result will be a series of unfulfilled expectations as far as the investment in technology import is concerned.

Any assessment of China's performance with respect to foreign technology acquisition and assimilation must remain preliminary in view of the fact that many projects have yet to be completed, and it is hard to measure just to what extent the Chinese scientific and engineering community has truly advanced its indigenous technological capabilities over the last several years. Of course, there have been a number of very positive developments, including the substantial improvements in manufacturing techniques and processes, expanded training of individuals, and a more sophisticated understanding of the challenges associated with effective use of foreign technology. Legislation covering the transfer of technology has also been enacted, including a patent law and a copyright law. Major gains have also occurred in the science and technology system, with some fairly dramatic improvements taking place in research dealing with automation, new materials, microelectronics, and biotechnology. These gains promise to have positive spillovers into the economy as a whole, and for technology import activities in particular, as a result of the concerted effort being made by both the SSTC, the Chinese Academy of Sciences, and the SPC to ensure that S&T and the economy do not remain as disjointed as in the past. Given the degree to which production of various critical raw materials, components, etc. has increased, the overall contribution of foreign technology must be acknowledged. In other words, collaboration with foreign technology suppliers has proven to be of pivotal value to China.

Yet, the fact remains that there are significant problems in the Chinese system that detract from the country's ability to fully realize the potential benefits in both economic and technological terms. In many respects, China is facing a two-fold problem. On the one hand, the Chinese are coming up against the constraints within their own system. Problems of uncertainty associated with the economic reforms, e.g. incomplete price reform, and the tensions between the central and local governments for control and decision-making autonomy, combined with a host of factors associated with low labor productivity, poor quality control, and ineffective management, make it difficult to create a workable system for coordinating and monitoring technology import work. The Chinese continue to use the term "wujihuaxing" meaning "no planning" to describe the fact that a great deal of technology import activity occurs in a blind fashion, causing serious waste of time and resources. In this regard, the effort by Beijing to assert greater control over the foreign trade sector in the aftermath of the 1988–89 economic crisis may not have been such an irrational thing to do, particularly given the fact that local spending had gotten nearly out of control. Some appreciable tightening up by the central government in the field of technology import work may not only yield benefits to the domestic economy by providing more gudiance and direction, but also may prove attractive to foreign firms that have been bewildered by the pulling and tugging from various quarters within the Chinese bureaucracy. Greater central government involvement in the form of high level project sponsorship could also mean better guarantees as far as the availability of production inputs are concerned, power availability, etc.

Still, the various efforts by the Chinese to attract foreign know-how and expertise that could help overcome many of the country's prevailing problems have been slow to materialize because of continuing questions about China's investment climate, its actual commitment to protect proprietary information, and a series of related issues. In reality, there are many other attractive investment alternatives to China where the local skill levels, managerial capabilities, and investment environment are all less problematic. In a world in which themes such as globalization and regionalization are occupying the attention of corporate executives and economic policymakers, Chinese leaders must begin to find ways to project an image that reflects a more systematic approach to working with foreign companies. Otherwise, China's ability to gain access to desired foreign technology and leverage its technological capabilities in the international marketplace may be extremely limited. This may be a rather disconcerting thought to current Chinese leaders as they seek to identify what role China should play—in both political and economic terms—in the world of high technology in the next decade and beyond.

CHINA'S SPACE PROGRAM

By Marcia S. Smith *

CONTENTS

SUMMARY

China launched its first satellite in 1970, and by the end of August, 1990, had successfully completed 26 launches [1], placing 29 satellites into orbit (see Appendix 1). China is currently focussing its attention on the practical applications of space technologies, such as communications and weather satellites, and on the potential of commercial space activities.

China's entry into the international commercial launch services market has prompted considerable debate in the United States over whether U.S.-made satellites should be launched on Chinese vehicles. Asiasat-1, built by Hughes Aircraft Co., was launched by a Chinese Long March 3 vehicle in April 1990, and export licenses have been granted for two more Hughes-built communications satellites (AUSSAT 1 and 2) for launch in 1991 and 1992. The issue continues to be very controversial, focussing on whether the Chinese are charging unfairly low prices for their services, and therefore undermining U.S. (and European) companies offering similar services. Technology transfer and the political situation in China are also concerns. Another commercial activity is launching experi-

---

* Marcia S. Smith is a Specialist in Aerospace Policy, Science Policy Research Division, Congressional Research Service.

[1] The Chinese have acknowledged an additional three launch failures, although there may have been other, unacknowledged failures during the 1970s and early 1980s when the Chinese were less open about their space program.

ments for foreign companies on Chinese satellites. In 1987 and 1988, China launched experiments for France's Matra, and West Germany's Intospace consortium.

China has expressed interest in a broad range of future space activities, including building space shuttles and space stations. Such programs probably will be prohibitively expensive for many years to come, however.

I. LAUNCH VEHICLES AND LAUNCH SITES

China has developed a family of launch vehicles called Long March, and several versions of it are in use today. The Long March 2C is used for satellites destined for low Earth orbits, and is launched from the original Chinese launch site at Shuang Chengtzu (41.2 ° N, 100.1° E), near Jiuquan in the Gobi desert. The Long March 3 and Long March 2E vehicles are used to place satellites in geostationary orbit [2] from China's second launch site, inaugurated in 1984, at Xichang (28° N, 103° E) in southeastern China. The Long March 4 is launched from the newest Chinese launch site, Taiyuan (38° N, 112° E), south of Beijing, for launches into polar orbits.[3] Taiyuan and the Long March 4 have been used only once so far (in 1988) for China's first weather satellite; another weather satellite launch is scheduled for 1990. (The launch vehicles and their capabilities are listed in Appendix 2.)

All of the Long March vehicles are available for commercial launches, although the most interest is in the Long March 2E and Long March 3 since most commercial satellites are for communications and need to be placed in geostationary orbit.

II. CHINESE SATELLITES

As detailed in Appendix 1, several of the satellites launched by the Chinese have been recovered back on Earth. The recovery of a satellite usually means that its payload is either a scientific experiment that requires analysis by researchers on the ground, or, more often, film for recording images of the Earth for military reconnaissance or civilian remote sensing of the land and oceans. As discussed below, two of the recovered satellites (in 1987 and 1988) carried materials processing experiments for French and German firms. The Chinese have stated that another (in 1987) was for scientific purposes. The remaining recovered satellites also could have been for scientific purposes, but are thought by Western analysts more likely to have been related to developing a military photographic reconnaissance capability. The Chinese have never admitted to developing such a capability, referring only to "reconnaissance surveys of natural resources" and "photographic surveys" using this type of satellite.[4] Additional Chinese satellites that were

---

[2] Geostationary orbit exists 35,800 kilometers over the equator. Satellites placed there maintain a fixed position relative to a point on Earth, and therefore the orbit is very useful for communications satellites. Some weather satellites and certain types of reconnaissance satellites are also placed in this orbit.

[3] A polar orbit circles the Earth's poles and a satellite placed there will pass over every point on the globe. Polar orbits are used primarily for weather, science, and reconnaissance satellites.

[4] *Zhongguo Xinwen She*, 1335 GMT, 31 Jul 90. In Foreign Broadcasting Information Service (FBIS) China Daily Report, 8 Aug 90, p. 31.

not recovered but whose missions have never been announced are thought to be related to the development of other types of reconnaissance (electronic intelligence, for example).

One other Chinese launch, in 1981, was definitely for scientific purposes: three satellites were placed into orbit simultaneously for space physics experiments. China has launched one weather satellite (which failed shortly after launch), and another is planned for launch in 1990. In recent years, an increasing number of Chinese satellites are for domestic communications, and as discussed below, the Asiasat-1 spacecraft (partially owned by China) is for regional communications. China also has launched an experimental satellite for Pakistan (Badr-1).

III. COMMERCIAL SPACE ACTIVITIES

The main areas of commercial interest in the Chinese space program are selling launch vehicle services to place satellites in orbit for commercial customers, or carrying experiments for foreign companies on Chinese satellites.

A. MATERIALS PROCESSING FLIGHT OPPORTUNITIES

Only China and the Soviet Union currently offer flights of materials processing in space (MPS) experiments on free-flying satellites.[5] These commercial activities involve purchasing space aboard a Chinese satellite, rather than buying a launch vehicle service.

In 1987, the French company Matra paid for the launch of a MPS experiment on a Chinese satellite launched by a Long March 2. The West German consortium Intospace flew experiments on a Long March 2 in 1988. The Chinese reportedly charge about $20 million for use of the entire Long March 2 spacecraft, and between $30,000 and $50,000 per kilogram for a partial payload.[6] This is consistent with the fee Intospace was charged: about $1 million for a 20-kg experiment, or $50,000/kg.[7]

B. LAUNCH VEHICLE SERVICES

China offers launch vehicle services through the China Great Wall Industry Corp., and launch insurance through the Peoples Insurance Co. The Chinese have made a concerted effort since 1985 to market launch vehicle services internationally; the main competitors are three U.S. companies (McDonnell Douglas, General Dynamics, and Martin Marietta) and Europe's Arianespace.

---

[5] MPS experiments include a number of fields of research into producing substances in the low gravity environment of space that may be superior to similar substances produced on Earth. The research includes growing crystals (like gallium arsenide, that could be used in computer chips, or protein crystals for use in pharmaceuticals), or electrophoresis in which an electrical current is passed through a liquid to produce pure vaccines. MPS experiments can be conducted using airplanes or sounding rockets (which can provide seconds or minutes of microgravity), and the U.S. space shuttle or the Soviet space station Mir. Flights on free-flying satellites are often preferable, however, because the experiments are exposed to microgravity conditions for a longer time versus sounding rockets or airplanes, and do not have astronauts nearby who may accidentally interfere with their operation by creating vibrations. Flights on free-flying spacecraft also are probably less expensive than using the space shuttle or Mir.

[6] "Chinese Bid for Reentry Business", *Aerospace America*, Mar. 1988, p. 19.

[7] See: Covault, Craig. "Chinese Prepare Long March Booster for Launch with German Payload." *Aviation Week and Space Technology*, July 25, 1988, p. 26.

To date, the Chinese have signed four contracts for launches: Asiasat–1, two AUSSATs, and Arabsat 1–C (these agreements are discussed in more detail below). A commercial agreement to launch a Swedish satellite apparently has fallen through, since it has been announced that the satellite will now be launched on a U.S. vehicle.[8] The Chinese launched a Pakistani test satellite in 1990, but there is no indication that this was a commercial arrangement (this was the first launch of the Long March 2E, and its primary purpose was launching a simulated AUSSAT satellite to demonstrate the rocket's capability).

1. Asiasat and AUSSAT: the U.S.-China Agreement on Launch Services.

China's first launch contract was signed with AsiaSat Co., which is owned by three entities, each having a one-third share: Cable and Wireless PLC of London, Hutchinson Telecommunications Ltd. of Hong Kong, and CITIC Technology Inc., a subsidiary of the China International Trust and Investment Corp.(CITIC). Cable and Wireless has overall management responsibility for Asiasat; the company is based in Hong Kong. The Asiasat–1 satellite (which is the refurbished Westar 6 satellite that was recovered by a space shuttle crew in 1984 after it failed to achieve the proper orbit) was purchased by AsiaSat Co. At about the same time that China and AsiaSat signed their launch agreement, China completed a contract with the Australian government for the launch of AUSSAT 1 and AUSSAT 2 in 1991 and 1992.

Virtually all communications satellites in the free world are either built by U.S. companies, or U.S. companies serve as major subcontractors to European or Canadian firms. Thus, export licenses are required from the United States, and approval must be sought from the Coordinating Committee on Multilateral Export Controls (CoCom).[9] All three of these satellites—Asiasat 1, AUSSAT 1, and AUSSAT 2—are built by Hughes Aircraft Inc., an American company.

Export license requests were made to the U.S. State Department in July 1988 to send the three U.S.-built satellites to China for launch. Two major issues arose at that time which continue to generate controversy today. The first is technology transfer—whether China might obtain U.S. technology by having access to U.S. communications satellites. The second is whether the Chinese will abide by fair trade practices in pricing their launch services. In early September 1988, during a visit to China, then-Secretary of Defense Carlucci expressed no reservations about technology transfer from launching U.S.-built satellites on Chinese launchers.[10] In fact, he reportedly felt that there would be expanded technology transfer with China in the future. However, the following specific procedures to protect against technology transfer were agreed upon: 1) all customs inspections of the satellites would be waived; 2) no Chinese technician would touch or have access to the satellites;

[8] "OSC Signs Launch Agreement with Swedish Firm." *Defense Daily*, Dec. 20, 1989, p. 431.
[9] CoCom members are all the NATO countries except Iceland, plus Japan.
[10] *Defense Daily*, Sept. 8, 1988, p. 1.

and 3) in the case of an accident, all satellite debris would be returned to the United States.

For the Asiasat and AUSSAT contracts, the Chinese offered an "introductory" price of about $30 million each, far below rates for comparable launch services by Western companies.[11] The Chinese contend that the price was "promotional," intended to build a customer base. The term "promotional" was never clearly defined.

Consultations between the two nations continued, and on December 17, 1988, the U.S. State Department announced that China had agreed to the following conditions:

- That it would sell no more than a total of nine commercial satellite launches to anyone through 1994;
- That it would offer its launch services, including insurance and reflight guarantees, on prices, terms, and conditions on a par with those offered by companies in market economies.

The phrase "on a par" was never explicitly defined in the negotiations or the agreements.[12]

All these conditions were met by January 1989. Approval for the export of the AUSSAT and Asiasat satellites was granted by CoCom in March 1989. Following the Tiananmen Square demonstrations in June, however, the Bush Administration suspended all export licenses for items on the Munitions Control List, including the three satellites.

Congress subsequently passed legislation (P.L. 101-192, section 610) prohibiting the export of the satellites unless conditions improved in China, or unless the President certified to Congress that it was in the national interest of the United States to reinstate the licenses. In December 1989, the President made that certification to Congress. Asiasat-1 was exported to China and launched in April 1990.

The AUSSAT satellites are still under construction in California. On June 10, 1990, the House passed a bill (H.R. 4643, the Export Facilitation Act) that includes a provision prohibiting export of U.S.-made satellites to China for launch. Since the AUSSAT satellites have not left the country, the language, if enacted, apparently would apply to them, although the sponsor of the language, Representative Solomon, stated that he did not intend to affect the existing export licenses.[13]

2. Controversy Over the Arabsat Contract

In March 1990, the European launch services company Arianespace, which launches the Ariane rocket, charged that China was violating its agreement with the United States by selling launch services to the Arabsat Consortium for below fair market prices. The issue developed in connection with the planned launch of

---

[11] These launch cost figures were provided by AsiaSat Co. and AUSSAT officials during congressional testimony on the Reagan Administration's decision to license the export of satellites for launch on the Chinese Long March launch vehicle. One U.S. ELV industry official testified that a fair price for a equivalent launch on a Delta rocket would be $50 million. See: U.S. Congress. House Committee on Science, Space and Technology. "The Administration's Decision to License the Chinese Long March Launch Vehicle." Hearings. 100th Cong., 2d Sess. Sept. 23 and 27, 1988. Washington, U.S. Govt. Print. Off., 1989. pp. 91, 110, 288.

[12] Telephone conversation with State Department official, June 1, 1989.

[13] *Congressional Record*, June 6, 1990, p. H 3302.

Arabsat 1–C on a Long March vehicle for a reported price of $25 million, approximately half of what would be charged by Arianespace or a U.S. company.[14] Although the satellite was built by Aerospatiale (a French company), Ford Aerospace was a major subcontractor and approximately 60 percent of the components are American-made.[15] Thus, Arianespace appealed to the French and U.S. governments to deny an export license for the satellite.

This issue reportedly was raised during already scheduled trade talks between the U.S. and China in July 1990, but the outcome is unclear. The head of the U.S. delegation, Donald Phillips, from the Office of the U.S. Trade Representative, said that the Chinese "presented information and their own rationale" for their actions, and that the issue is "still under review."[16]

Chinese space officials assert that they are abiding by the agreement, and that this is primarily a matter of China being able to offer lower prices because it has lower costs. Chen Shouchun, vice president of China Great Wall Industry Corp., points out that it took only 18 months to develop the Long March 2E booster (the newest version), compared to the 3–4 years it would have taken in the West.[17] He also noted that there have been more failures in the Ariane launch vehicle program than with the Long March, and Arianespace's customers must bear those costs. The opinion that China may be able to charge lower prices even if it fairly takes into account all its costs may have some following in the United States. During the debate over the Asiasat and AUSSAT export licenses, an unnamed U.S. industry official estimated that even without promotional pricing, the cost of a launch by the Chinese would be 30 to 50 percent cheaper than a similar launch on a U.S. or European vehicle.[18]

Another Chinese official, Lin Huabao, deputy chief of engineering at the Chinese Academy of Space Technology, feels that the entire U.S.-China agreement itself is unfair. "China is a sovereign country. There should not be any limits imposed by outside governments like this. For a sovereign nation, this is not a good thing."[19]

China's ultimate success in commercial space depends on several factors. For free-flying materials processing experiments, the Chinese have only one competitor (the Soviet Union), but it is not clear how large the market is for these types of experiments. For communications satellites, China can offer launches in the near term, a significant advantage since European and U.S. launch services companies are often booked up years in advance. Although low prices also might attract business, if the United States or other governments conclude that the prices do not follow fair market standards, they could respond by denying export licenses for the satellites, which would significantly undermine China's prospects.

[14] Lawler, Andrew. "U.S. to Confront China on Launch Sales." *Space News*, July 9–15, 1990, p. 1, 29.
[15] Lawler, Andrew. "U.S. Urged to Protest Arabsat Launch." *Space News*, Mar. 26–Apr. 1, 1990, p. 29.
[16] Quoted in: "Group Seeks Launch Satisfaction." *Space News*, July 30–Aug. 5, 1990, p. 2.
[17] Chen Shouchun, vice president of Great Wall Industry Corp., quoted in: Chen Gengtao. "Defending Chinese Launch Pricing." *Space News*, Aug. 20–26, 1990, p. 15.
[18] See *Defense Week*, Aug. 8, 1988. p. 3.
[19] Quoted in: de Selding, Peter. "Chinese: Launch Accord Unfair." *Space News*, Apr. 30–May 6 1990, p. 20.

A potential disadvantage is that the Long March vehicles do not have a long track record, making their reliability difficult to estimate. The perceived political stability or instability of the Chinese government may also influence potential customers.

IV. REMOTE SENSING AND COMMUNICATIONS SATELLITES

The Chinese are also involved in the areas of satellite remote sensing (including weather) and communication satellites.

The Chinese operate a remote sensing receiving station that acquires data from the U.S. Landsat remote sensing satellites.[20] The Chinese pay an annual lease fee of $600,000 to EOSAT, the private U.S. operator of the Landsat system, and in return are free to sell the data to anyone. In addition to their own sales, the Chinese have an agreement with EOSAT to market data for them in China.

In late 1988, China launched its first weather satellite, which apparently failed soon after launch. Another weather satellite is planned for launch in the fall of 1990. Both of these are polar orbit satellites; the Chinese state that they will also build geostationary weather satellites in the near future.[21]

To date, the communications satellites built and launched by China have been relatively small and are used for domestic Chinese telecommunications. The Asiasat-1 satellite, however, is larger and provides communications not only for China, but for neighboring countries on a commercial basis. Since China is a one-third partner in AsiaSat Co., this will generate revenues for China. The Chinese are planning to develop a larger and more sophisticated communications satellite for its domestic use as well, and reportedly hope to enter into the market of selling satellites someday (in addition to launch services).[22]

V. INTERNATIONAL COOPERATION

In addition to its commercial space activities, China has signed several agreements for international cooperation in space (which usually does not involve an exchange of funds). In 1984, China signed three agreements for cooperation in space technology with the Federal Republic of Germany, Italy, and France. More recently, China has formed a joint venture with Brazil, called the International Satellite Communication Ltd. (INSCOM), to sell communications satellite launching, tracking and networking services on the world market.[23] In 1988, the two countries announced plans to jointly build a remote sensing satellite for launch by China in 1992 (and perhaps a second in 1994), but the current status of that project is unclear.

Also in 1988, the Chinese signed an agreement with Australia for joint technical and commercial ventures (including the AUSSAT launches, cooperation in remote sensing and satellite ground sup-

[20] Landsat data are used for many purposes including crop forecasting, land use planning, mineral exploration, and pollution monitoring.

[21] The United States is the only other country that has weather satellites in both geostationary and polar orbits.

[22] Barton, Charles. "Chinese Plan Trio of Satellites to Broaden Marketing Prowess." *Space News*, Aug. 6–12, 1990, p. 4, 39.

[23] Kolcum, Edward. "Brazil, China Form Space Launch Venture." *Aviation Week and Space Technology*, May 29, 1989, p. 35.

port). The agreement provides for creation of a joint space commerce and technology working group to coordinate activities. The launch of a Pakistani satellite on a Chinese launch vehicle in 1990 heralded cooperation between those two countries; there seems to have been no prior announcement of this joint space activity and it is unclear whether there will be additional cooperative projects between China and Pakistan.

There is no U.S./China agreement for space cooperation, although discussions have been held between the two countries for several years. The Chinese have selected two student experiments to fly on the U.S. space shuttle, but they are being flown as part of the Get Away Special (GAS) program where anyone can purchase a small container (called a GAS-Can) for experiments that require no interaction with the crew or use of shuttle systems (like electricity). An individual working at the Jet Propulsion Laboratory [24] purchased the GAS-Can for the Chinese, so the flight involves no cooperation on a government-to-government or agency-to-agency level. The Chinese experiments are scheduled for the STS–42 mission (currently scheduled for launch on April 1991). A second Chinese GAS-Can flight is being planned, which will involve one experiment from China and one from Hong Kong.

VI. FUTURE

The Chinese talk boldly about future space plans such as building space stations, but also have nearer term objectives of building larger and more sophisticated communications and weather satellites. Any assertions by the Chinese about future space plans must be viewed with caution, however, since they have changed quite abruptly in the past. During 1979 and 1980, the Chinese proclaimed great expectations for utilizing space, and reportedly even had astronauts in training.[25] In late 1980 and early 1981, however, the Chinese retreated from their expansive plans because of a reassessment of the Chinese economic situation, and announced that their human spaceflight program had been postponed for at least the remainder of the decade.

In the mid-1980s, prospects for building a Chinese space station and space shuttle were raised by Chinese space program officials, who then quickly pointed out that approval for such projects was far from certain.[26] A 1988 Chinese report did assert that astronauts were being trained, but there were no specifics about what missions would be flown.[27] While some reports suggest that the Chinese might fly astronauts on a Chinese spacecraft launched by a Long March rocket,[28] it may be that these astronauts are being

---

[24] JPL is a government-owned contractor-operated facility in California that is responsible for most NASA planetary missions. It is operated for NASA by the California Institute of Technology.

[25] Early Chinese interest in placing humans in space was indicated by the 1967 suborbital flight of a puppy, Xiao Bao (Little Leopard), who was successfully recovered (in both the United States and the Soviet Union, human flights were preceded by animals). Also, in 1968 the Chinese established a Space Flight Medical Program Research Center which included simulators for human spaceflight.

[26] *South China Morning Post*, 6 Feb 87, p. 5. In FBIS China Daily Report, 11 Feb 88, p. 2.

[27] *Zhongguo Tongxun She*, 1158 GMT, 15 Dec 88. In FBIS China Daily Report, 28 Dec 88, p. 31.

[28] *South China Morning Post*, op. cit. See also: Covault, Craig. "China Developing Technology for Future Manned Space Flight." *Aviation Week & Space Technology*, June 29, 1987, p. 22.

trained for prospective flights with either the United States or Soviet Union. The Chinese have shown interest for years in flying an astronaut on the U.S. space shuttle, and in June 1990, the possibility of a Chinese astronaut visiting a Soviet space station [29] was raised during a visit to the Soviet Union by Lt. Gen. Liu Huaqing, vice chairman of China's Central Military Commission. The discussions do not appear to have been very specific, however.[30]

For the present, the Chinese are focussing on practical applications of space such as communications and weather satellites, and on commercial space opportunities. With or without commercial customers, China seems committed to its space program. The investment in three launch sites and a range of launch vehicle capabilities would not be easily forsaken whatever the country's economic or political future. The only real question is how vigorously they will pursue space activities in the years ahead.

---

[29] The Soviets have launched representatives of many nations to their space stations since 1978. Today, these flights are made on a commercial (rather than cooperative) basis, and cost approximately $10 million. Austrian, Japanese and British astronauts are now in training in the Soviet Union.

[30] Moscow International Service in Mandarin, 0200 GMT, 6 Jun 90. In FBIS Soviet Union Daily Report, 12 June 90, p. 14.

APPENDIX 1

CHINESE SPACE LAUNCHES
THROUGH AUGUST 31, 1990[1]

Name	Launch Date	Launch Site[2]	Comments
China 1	04/24/70	S	Engineering test. "East is Red" song played until 05/20/70.
China 2	03/03/71	S	Housekeeping test and possible science.
China 3	07/26/75	S	Science? Reconnaissance? Not recovered.
China 4	11/26/75	S	Possible reconnaissance test. Recovered.
China 5	12/16/75	S	Like China 3.
China 6	08/30/76	S	Possible electronics intelligence gathering test and/or science. Not recovered.
China 7	12/07/76	S	Possible reconnaissance test. Recovered.
China 8	01/26/78	S	Possible reconnaissance test. Recovered.
China 9-11	09/19/81	S	Triple scientific payload for space physics experiments.
China 12	09/09/82	S	Possible reconnaissance test. Recovered.
China 13	08/19/83	S	Possible reconnaissance test. Recovered.
China 14	01/29/84	X	First Long March 3 launch; upper stage failed.
China 15	04/08/84	X	First Chinese geostationary communications satellite.
China 16	09/12/84	S	Possible reconnaissance. Recovered.
China 17	10/20/85	S	Possible reconnaissance. Recovered.
China 18	02/01/86	X	Communications.

Name	Launch Date	Launch Site[2]	Comments
China 19	10/06/86	S	Possible reconnaissance. Recovered.
China 20	08/05/87	S	Materials processing experiment for a French company.
China 21	09/09/87	S	Science. Recovered.
China 22	03/07/88	X	Communications.
China 23	08/05/88	S	Materials processing for German company. Recovered.
China 24	09/06/88	T	Weather.
China 25	12/22/88	X	Communications.
China 26	02/04/90	X	Communications.
ASIASAT 1	04/07/90	X	Communications (commercial launch).
BADR 1	07/16/90	X	Pakistani test satellite plus engineering test satellite.

1.Prepared by CRS based on data from Chinese news bulletins; *World-Wide Space Activities* (House Science and Technology Committee, 1977); and Clark, P. S. The Chinese Space Programme. *Journal of the British Interplanetary Society*, v. 37, 1984. p. 195-206.

2.S = Shuang Cheng-tzu. X = Xichang. T = Taiyuan. Launch dates are in Greenwich Mean Time.

APPENDIX 2 CHINESE LAUNCH VEHICLES				
Launch Vehicle	Launch Site	Kilograms to Low Earth Orbit	Kilograms to Geostationary Transfer Orbit[1]	Price ($ millions)
Long March 2C	Shuang Cheng-tzu	2,500	-------	20
Long March 2E	Xichang	8,800	2,500-4,000	25-30
Long March 3	Xichang	-------	1,400	25-30
Long March 4	Taiyuan	2,500 (polar)	-------	?

1. Geostationary transfer orbit (GTO) is an elliptical intermediate orbit into which a satellite is placed enroute to geostationary orbit (GEO). A satellite in GEO will maintain a fixed position relative to a point on Earth, and therefore is very useful for communications satellites. Some weather and reconnaissance satellites are also placed in GEO.

THE EFFECTS OF TIANANMEN ON CHINA'S INTERNATIONAL SCIENTIFIC AND EDUCATIONAL COOPERATION

By Mary Brown Bullock *

CONTENTS

SUMMARY

The Tiananmen massacre, China's ideological repression, and subsequent Western sanctions have shaken, but not destroyed, the foundation of China's international scientific and educational cooperation. China's extensive network of formal agreements and personal *guanxi* have weathered a sea-change in international policies and public opinion. Notwithstanding a marked reduction in foreign participation, the institutional structure of China's intellectual cooperation remains in place and is beginning to return to normal. China's educational door remains open, and the numbers of scholars and students studying abroad have not yet diminished. Brain drain has, however, become a more divisive reality.

Intellectual partners in the United States, Japan, Germany, the United Kingdom, and France reacted differently to Tiananmen, revealing the complexity of national and individual motives for engagement with China. Sino-Japanese relations have gained new salience, whereas European and American ties, more acutely influenced both by Tiananmen and the reforming Soviet Union and Eastern Europe, have lost momentum. The net result is not the collapse of intellectual cooperation, but a restrained resumption more overtly linked to encouraging future political reforms in China.

* Mary Brown Bullock is Director of the Asia Program at the Woodrow Wilson International Center for Scholars. Research for this paper was partially supported by a travel grant from the National Science Foundation. Interviews were primarily conducted in the summer of 1990. Nobuko Kamimura and Chris Davies provided research assistance.

I. Pre-Tiananmen: The Scope of China's Scientific and Educational Cooperation

In March 1978 Deng Xiaoping startled China and the world by ending China's self-imposed intellectual autarky:

> Independence does not mean shutting the door on the world nor does self-reliance mean blind opposition to everything foreign. Science and technology are a kind of wealth created in common by all mankind. Any nation or country must learn from the strong points of other nations and countries, from their advanced science and technology.[1]

He then went on to proscribe: "We must actively develop international academic exchanges and step up our friendly contacts with scientific circles of other countries." Making up for lost decades, China unleashed an unprecedented level of scientific and educational diplomacy. By the mid-1980s, it had established a truly impressive international scientific and educational presence.

Western scientists and educators responded enthusiastically. A French scientific administrator recalled: "The French felt emotionally close to China; we wanted to help."[2] A German diplomat, citing historical antecedents of the 1920s and 1930s, attributed his countrymen's enthusiasm to the "exotica of China: it was everything we were not."[3] Many Japanese referred to a post-World War II "guilt syndrome"—the hope for expiation. And Americans found deep satisfaction in the discovery that China was not "lost." To be sure, political and economic interests established the initial parameters of Sino-Western relations. But intellectual and cultural relations, driven by public enthusiasm, quickly became the cutting edge.

The nature and scope of intellectual cooperation between socialist China and the democratic West, including Japan, was surprising. The U.S.-China Scientific and Technical Agreement became the largest formal American scientific partnership with any country.[4] The China Program of the United Kingdom's Royal Society exceeded its other international commitments, and China ranked close to India in the commitments of the British Council.[5] Formal partnerships between German and Chinese universities dwarfed previous educational relationships, and China became the largest educational client of the German technical assistance agency, the Deutsche Gessellschaft Fur Technische Zusammenarbeit (GTZ).[6] In

---

[1] Deng Xiaoping, "Speech at Opening Ceremony of National Science Conference," March 18, 1978, p. 4.

[2] Interview with Francoise Aubujeault, Centre National de la Recherche Scientifique, Paris, July 9, 1990.

[3] Interview with Albrecht von der Heyden, German Foreign Ministry, Bonn, July 16, 1990.

[4] The best summary of U.S.-China relations at the time of Tiananmen is in Kerry Dumbaugh and Larry Z. Nowels, "China-U.S. Cooperation: Military Sales, Government Programs, Multilateral Aid, and Private-Sector Activities." Congressional Research Service Report for Congress, June 9, 1989. For an overview of China's educational relations with the West see Ruth Hayhoe, *China's Universities and the Open Door* (M.E. Sharpe: Armonk, New York, 1989).

[5] Interviews with Peter Warren, The Royal Society, and Tim Callan, British Council, London, November 13, 1989.

[6] Interviews with von der Heyden, July 16, 1990; Munchend Imohl and Manfred Lindau, Deutsche Gessellschaft Fur Technische Zusammenarbeit, Eichborn, Germany, July 12, 1990.

less than a decade, Chinese students and scholars in the United States increased to more than 40,000—the largest component of America's large international student population.[7] Likewise, by 1989, the total number of Chinese students and scholars in Japan had also grown to perhaps 40,000.[8]

For the Chinese government, this extensive international exposure has had ambiguous results. Frequent Chinese statistical litanies testify to satisfaction with the quantitative dimensions of intellectual diplomacy: scientific agreements with 108 countries, membership in 280 international organizations, and the initiation of 14,300 cooperative scientific projects in 1988 alone.[9] Yet, successive campaigns against spiritual pollution and bourgeois liberalism revealed persistent deep-seated hostility toward Western culture. Growing concern about "brain drain" began to cloud the educational "open door." Even science was not immune from suspicion, as far-reaching scientific reforms, patterned after Western institutional models, enhanced professional independence and reduced the influence of the Communist Party.[10]

Nonetheless, the political prestige and economic benefit which accrued to China were incalculable. "Scientific tourism" gave way to substantive, in-depth collaboration, which included high technology and applied technology, space science and railway engineering, solar energy and cancer epidemiology, engineering education and arid land development, laboratories and M.A. and Ph.D. degrees sponsored jointly by China and the West. It is difficult to name a discipline, a level of training, or a research field that did not experience Western expertise and collaboration during the 1980s. China's most sophisticated research and educational community, if not its infrastructure, was transformed and revitalized as a result of its incorporation into the world academic community.

What is historically unique about the 1980s is that the most advanced nations were drawn into close, and frequently reciprocal, collaboration with a poor, developing country. Intense interest in China's climate, environment, geology, flora, fauna, economy, and human diversity coupled with the growing sophistication of China's own intellectuals yielded a complex and highly professional network of Sino-Western collaboration. This was greatly augmented in the mid-1980s when most Western countries adopted technical assistance programs for China. It was this rich international network of human and material resources that was jeopardized by China's Tiananmen tragedy.

[7] Leo Orleans, *Chinese Students in America* (National Academy Press: Washington, D.C., 1988).

[8] This includes more than 30,000 language students. *Statistics on Foreigners and Japanese Arriving and Leaving Japan in 1988* (Japan Immigration Association, Tokyo, 1989), p. 20. Student Outflows between China and Japan, May 21, 1987, Ministry of Science and Education, Tokyo, Japan.

[9] Wu Yikang, "Country Report or Workshop on Science and Technology Cooperation in Asia-Pacific Region," February 1990.

[10] Pierre Perrolle, "After Tiananmen: Science Relations with China," *Issues* (Winter 1989/90). Denis Simon and Merle Goldman, ed., *Science and Technology in Post-Mao China* (Harvard University Press: Cambridge, Mass., 1989).

II. Post-Tiananmen Intellectual Relations

The May Tiananmen student demonstrations symbolized the reforming China that the West applauded. The June violence and subsequent strident return to repressive ideological campaigns galvanized world opprobrium, at first nationally and then in concert. At the July Economic Summit, the Group of Seven curtailed economic assistance, commercial credits, and defense-related technology transfer. But Western governments did not abrogate education relations, and official sanctions generally excluded science. The European Economic Community's policy of "maintaining working level relations" in science and education, while postponing or cancelling new ventures, was in theory widely accepted.[11]

International sentiment was transferred from the student demonstrators in Beijing to the Chinese students abroad, many of whom demonstrated openly against Beijing. Public opinion came to equate these students with the Beijing martyrs. Protection of Chinese student visa status became a worldwide priority. Legislatures, the political entities most responsive to public opinion, in Canada, the United Kingdom, the Federal Republic of Germany, and the United States mandated protection. Canada was most generous: under a "humanitarian and compassionate review process" all Chinese students and scholars in Canada were offered permanent resident status. Concern for stranded students also led to emergency fiscal measures. France and Germany diverted previously allocated funds for programs in China to student relief. In addition, Germany also appropriated an extra 5 million DM for emergency student support. The United Kingdom created a special privately funded trust fund.[12] No federal fiscal action was taken in the United States, but the National Science Foundation dispensed $1.8 million in discretionary institution-wide funds to Chinese students, nearly twice its annual China program budget.[13] American universities and foundations also provided emergency support.

There was more initial consensus on sanctuary for Chinese students than for the nature of post-Tiananmen intellectual relations with China itself. In the year since Tiananmen, the international community has been torn between sustaining or cancelling programs with China. Those advocating continuity argued that the Chinese intellectual community would become more vulnerable and isolated if outside ties further diminished. Those advocating suspension hoped to influence, by protest and sanctions, more ameliorative Chinese government policies. Both positions have been embraced, sometimes simultaneously, within most Western countries. Brief examples from the United States, Japan, Germany, the United Kingdom, and France will be followed by a discussion of the

[11] Dru Findlay, "The Impact of Recent Events in China on International Professional and Academic Exchanges and Related Development Activities," Ford Foundation report, August 31, 1989.

[12] Ibid. Carol Strevy, "Financial Status of Students/Scholars from the People's Republic of China on U.S. Campuses," Institute of International Education, February 1990. Interview with von der Heyden; interview with Patrick Bonneville, Ministry of Foreign Affairs, Paris, July 11, 1990.

[13] Interview with Pierre Perolle and Patricia Tsuchitani, National Science Foundation, May 1990.

longer-term consequences of Tiananmen upon China's international cooperation.

THE UNITED STATES

Tiananmen intensified the politicization of cultural relations between the United States and China. A national debate over President George Bush's management of the China relationship was symbolized by the debacle over the Pelosi Bill (H.R. 2712), which provided five-year visa extensions for Chinese students. The differences between congressional and executive views of the Pelosi Bill highlighted continuing American uncertainty over the appropriate role of human rights in the overall bilateral relationship.[14] This debate was not limited to the political arena: the American scientific and educational community was deeply divided over the question of post-Tiananmen relations with China.[15] Of all nations, the American response to Tiananmen appeared most schizophrenic.

The harshest scientific reaction to Tiananmen came from American scientists, and yet the U.S. government continued, almost without interruption, some of its more important bilateral scientific programs. During the fall of 1989, a number of previously scheduled government scientific missions to China continued.[16] After only a short hiatus, negotiations on renewing the umbrella U.S.-China Scientific and Technical Agreement resumed with some progress toward resolving the longstanding intellectual property rights dispute. In early 1990, both the U.S. Department of Agriculture and the U.S. Geological Survey signed new, expanded cooperative agreements in agriculture and the earth sciences. Several months later, in May, 1990, the United States quietly once again extended (but did not reach final agreement on renewing) the umbrella S&T accord. This was publicly announced in China, but not the United States.[17]

The strongest reaction against China from the two national scientific organizations most closely linked to the American university community—the National Science Foundation (a government agency), and the National Academy of Sciences (a nongovernmental organization). In protest of Tiananmen and the violation of human rights, both the National Academy of Sciences (NAS) and the National Science Foundation (NSF), the two most prestigious scientific organizations in the United States, suspended cooperation with China immediately after Tiananmen.[18] In contrast with other U.S. government agencies, NSF cancelled working group meetings, travel, and grants related to China except U.S.-based research projects. The NAS maintained communication with China, but can-

[14] New York Times (December 15, 1989), p. A43.
[15] For the debate in the United States see Science, June 9, 1989, p.131–1132; August 4,1989, p. 461–462; Chronicle of Higher Education (August 16, 1989), B3–B4; China Update: An Occasional Bulletin of the China Scholars Coordinating Committee, No. 1 (August 1989).
[16] U.S. Department of State, "Status of US/PRC Science and Technology Activities," Document 256784, Telegram, August 11, 1989.
[17] Interview with Wu Yikang, State Science and Technology Commission, Beijing, March 2–3, 1990; Interview with Jin Xiaoming, Chinese Embassy, Washington, D.C., May 11, 1990; Xinhua, May 18, 1990, in FBIS, May 21, p. 5.
[18] "NAS Suspends Collaboration with Chinese Institutions," NAS Media Advisory, June 7, 1989. Interview with Pierre Perrolle and Patricia Tsuchitani, National Science Foundation, May 10, 1990; interview with Erich Bloch, National Science Foundation, November 2, 1990.

celled the research visits of American scientists to China as well as bilateral group projects. These positions mirrored the sentiments of many, but not all, American scientists. Employing punitive sanctions as a means of protesting human rights violations has been a growing tenet of the American scientific community. NSF had limited contacts with the Soviet Union for many years due to human rights violations, and the NAS had followed suit when Andrei Sakharov was banished. Many drew analogies between Sakharov and Fang Lizhi's enforced protective custody in the American Embassy in Beijing. Yet, perhaps reflecting very sudden disillusionment with China, NAS China sanctions greatly exceeded those earlier leveled against the USSR during Sakharov's exile.

In the social sciences, an almost reverse scenario took place. The official Fulbright Program was cancelled by the Chinese government in late summer 1989, the only such action taken by the Chinese side. On the other hand, nongovernmental relations were less affected, at least on the American side. Chinese social science institutions, especially the Chinese Academy of Social Sciences, remained under tight political scrutiny. But most individuals and institutes welcomed foreign contact if not formal programs. Key American nongovernmental organizations maintained ties with China. The Ford Foundation continued grants in the social sciences, staying open even during the summer of 1989. The Social Science Research Council and the American Council of Learned Societies sponsored American research in China during the fall of 1989. Other social science programs were sustained, including the United Board for Christian Higher Education in China, Yale-China, and the Lingnan Foundation. Somewhat surprisingly, several new ventures were initiated, including an American international relations program at Beijing University.

The views of American academia began to moderate during the winter and spring of 1990. This "softening" occurred worldwide, and can be attributed to four factors. The first was the continuing flow of bona-fide Chinese scholars abroad. Their participation at international conferences and in response to very specific invitations gave some assurance of continued professional freedom. Second was the successful informal diplomacy of a number of senior Chinese intellectuals. For example, Chinese Academy of Sciences President and Central Committee Member Zhou Guangzhao made an informal visit to the United States in January 1990, meeting with NAS President Frank Press and other influential American scientists. Third, although the Chinese government announced new worrisome restrictions on Chinese study abroad, the numbers remained high in 1989–1990, with many educational programs continuing on schedule.[19] Finally, American scientists and social scientists also began to revisit China during the first half of 1990. They returned with reports of politically discouraged Chinese intellectuals and renewed anti-intellectualism, but also of a scientifically engaged community more anxious than ever for international cooperation. These pleas for continued foreign contact from Chinese

[19] For Chinese students coming to the U.S. see Strevy, *op. cit.* Also, Ken Yates, U.S. Embassy, Beijing to Mary Bullock, December 8, 1989.

intellectuals were perhaps the most persuasive element in the resumption of foreign scholarly contacts with China.

Believing that a protest had been made and acknowledging that further isolation would probably hurt intellectuals more than it would speed political reform, the NAS and NSF began to resume programs in the spring and summer of 1990. Other institutions, which had reduced or postponed activities, also stepped up contacts, including convening bilateral conferences in Beijing. September 1990 brought the return of American Fulbright scholars to China and the reopening of the NAS/Committee on Scholarly Communication with the People's Republic of China Beijing office, both symbolizing the resumption of American intellectual ties to China.

Even as exchanges have resumed, the continuing presence of large numbers of Chinese students and scholars in American institutions of higher learning remains an important, and somewhat unpredictable, force.[20] In addition to the five-year visa extension, proposed changes in U.S.immigration laws, designed to attract foreigners in needed skills, will further ease permanent residency for many Chinese.[21] Employment opportunities (at least in the sciences and engineering), combined with a welcoming Chinese-American community, facilitates future U.S.-based careers. Concern and political sympathy for this new wave of potential immigrants remains strong, but this empathy does not now preclude resuming ties with individuals and institutions in the People's Republic of China.

This survival of American governmental and non-governmental institutional structures for scientific and educational relations with China does not necessarily mean the survival of American resources and enthusiasm for China. There are currently mixed signs. One recently conducted institutional survey reports that 57% of Chinese respondents experienced a slowdown in projects with the United States, while 60% of the North American institutions reported a similar slowdown.[22] On the other hand, a forthcoming survey from the Institute of International Education is expected to reveal that most reporting American universities (over 200) have resumed cooperation at nearly pre-Tiananmen levels.[23] NSF likewise reports that a year after Tiananmen, American scientists are requesting funds for China cooperation at fairly normal levels, with little concern for the political climate. In fact, despite the earlier NSF ban, FY90 grants for China research are nearly equal to those of FY88 and FY89, with most of the FY90 grants awarded in the summer of 1990.[24]

For Americans, the identification with China as a liberalizing country had been central to the expanding relationship. Intellectual relationships were not closely tied to economic interests, as in Europe, nor to developmental assistance programs as in both Europe and Japan. They were far more closely linked, implicitly if

[20] Kerry Dumbaugh, "Chinese Student and Scholar Organizations in the United States," Congressional Research Service Report 90–558 F, Oct. 15, 1990.
[21] New York Times, August 27, 1990, p. A16.
[22] Hanmin Liu, "Issues in American-Chinese Scholarly Exchange Activities: A Survey." Paper prepared for International Health Forum: Building a common Ground, October 16–19, 1990.
[23] Information provided by Carol Strevy, IIE, September 1990.
[24] Interview, Patricia Tsuchitani, NSF, July 30, 1990.

not explicitly, to the American historical mission of "changing China." In justifying a return to post-Tiananmen China, most reaffirm that mission.

THE UNITED KINGDOM

The United Kingdom's post-Tiananmen policies toward China have been the least volatile, emphasizing continuity. Mindful of ongoing negotiations over Hong Kong, the British have been anxious to preserve as many channels of Sino-British cooperation as possible. This is in keeping with the tenor of British policies since a concerted effort was made to strengthen Sino-British scientific and education cooperation in the mid-1980s.[25] Continuity has also been linked to hope for ongoing political reform and Sino-British trade:

> The Government's attitude however had been not to isolate China but to maintain people-to-people contact (both as a way of maintaining access for Western ideas in China and to encourage those who are working for reform) and to maintain commercial business links. [26]

The position of the Royal Society, which has led the way in defining the nature of the British scientific relationship with China, is illustrative. Normal relations were to be combined with protest and selective cancellation. Shortly after Tiananmen the Royal Society sent a cable to the Chinese Academy of Sciences expressing hope that relations would not be affected by Tiananmen, that exchanges would be continued. This was in keeping with long-standing Royal Society philosophy that: "The flow of ideas should continue as long as there are appropriate institutional links." In protest of Tiananmen atrocities, the Royal Society simultaneously elected to let lapse agreements with Chinese "government" organizations—the Ministry of Geology and the National Science Foundation of China—and dropped support for international conferences in China that it feared would become a propaganda front. The Chinese Academy of Sciences expressed appreciation for British empathy, noting that ties had been "very regular," but British scientists did not rush to take advantage of continuing institutional channels. During the post-Tiananmen year, there was nearly a 50% drop in British scientific travel to China under Royal Society auspices.[27]

Educational and social science relations have been fairly stable. The British Academy, representing the social sciences and humanities, was one of the few international organizations to maintain programs with China during the summer of 1989, albeit at a very reduced level. And the British Council, with its broad array of education and scientific programs, has maintained a consistent level of cooperation with China. This is not surprising given the heavy emphasis on applied science and engineering, fields of Chinese priori-

[25] For an overview of Sino-British cultural relations at the time of Tiananmen see British Council, "Narrative Review of the Year: China 1988/89," and The Royal Society, "Royal Society Relations with China, 1987," and the British Council, "Programme of Cultural, Educational and Scientific Exchanges between Britain and China, 1988–1990."

[26] The British Council, "Notes of the Seminar on British Academic Relations with China Held at the Royal Society, 25 September 1989," p. 1.

[27] Interview with Peter Warren, Royal Society, November 13, 1989; Phone interview with May Ling Thompson, Royal Society, September 20, 1990; Interview with Cheng Erjin, Chinese Academy of Sciences, March 6, 1990; Royal Society Press Releases, August 7,1989; July 2, 1990.

ty, and British commercial interests. Agreement is expected in the early fall on the renewal of the overall Sino-British Cultural Agreement, little changed from previous years. Although Britain has experienced few Chinese "brain drain" problems, in part because of the dearth of appropriate jobs, fewer Chinese Ph.D. candidates are expected in the future.[28]

This continuity of core Sino-British scientific and cultural relations may partially explain Fang Lizhi's release to the United Kingdom. The Royal Society issued a scientific invitation in December 1989; it was formally accepted by Fang in January, and he was permitted to leave the American Embassy in July 1990. Fang's initial outspoken criticism of the Chinese government while in the United Kingdom (he has since left for the United States), is unlikely to affect the future course of Sino-British cooperation. On the other hand, declining British interest, muted criticism, concern about the future of Hong Kong, and shift of resources to Eastern Europe, are expected to dampen Sino-British relations.

FRANCE

Of all Western countries, Sino-French intellectual relations appear most damaged by the Tiananmen crisis. This is, however, only partially due to French reactions to Tiananmen. During the 1980s Sino-French economic and cultural relations failed to meet expectations on either side.[29] Tiananmen provided further provocation for a reassessment, which is likely to bring significant change in bilateral relations.[30]

Tiananmen occurred just before France's bicentennial celebration of human rights, the French Revolution. President Francois Mitterand immediately condemned China's leaders as "unfit to govern," the harshest criticism by any Western leader. Chinese student demonstrators wearing black mourning arm bands were given the place of honor leading the July 14 Champs d'Elysse parade extravaganza, replacing Chinese acrobats. A succession of leading Chinese dissidents, smuggled out through Hong Kong, were steered toward political asylum in France. Since Charles DeGaulle's 1964 opening to China, symbolic affinity has been at the heart of the Sino-French relationship: "France is the China of Europe; China is the France of Asia." After Tiananmen, the affinity collapsed, the symbolism reversed, and a hard-headed realism has now

---

[28] Interview with Nicola MacBean, Great Britain China Centre; Allison Cooper, British Academy; Tim Callan, Marilyn Goodwin, Thelma Howard, British Council, November 14–15, 1989; David Marer, British Council, Beijing, March 8, 1990; Wu Lingmei, Chinese Academy of Social Sciences, March 9, 1990. See also David Shambaugh, "The British Council/Economic and Social Research Council China Exchange Scheme; A Programme Review, 1980–1989," February 28, 1990.

[29] Jean-Luc Domenach, "Sino-French Relations: A French View," in Chun-tu Hsueh, *China's Foreign Relations: New Perspectives* (New York: Praeger, 1982). Jean-Pierre Cabestan, "Western Europe in China's New World Strategy," Paper presented at China Symposium, Oiso, Japan, June 1989.

[30] This assessment and the information that follows is based primarily on the following interviews. Annette Alfsen, CNRS; Claude Cadart, CNRS; Jean-Claude Rossignol, CNRS; Claude Aubert, Institut National de la Recherche Agronomique Economie et Sociologie Rurales; Pascal Meunier, Ministry of Foreign Affairs; Michel Culas, Ministry of Foreign Affairs; Paul Jean-Ortiz, Ministry of Foreign Affairs; Jean-Pierre Baudry, Ministry of Foreign Affairs; Yves Chevnier, Ecole des Hautes Études en Sciences Sociale. All interviews conducted the week of July 9, 1990, Paris. Also Bernard Commere and Maurice Oberreiner, French Embassy, Beijing, March 7, 1990.

emerged.[31] The subsequent "freeze" in Sino-French relations may have been deeper than with any other country. The highly centralized nature of educational and scientific ties with China, funneled through the French Foreign Ministry, held them hostage to the declining political relationship. Yet, a surprising number of programs continued. During 1989–90 France maintained its flagship Wuhan University program, reduced but continued its French language program, and selectively continued scientific programs. The Centre National de la Recherche Scientifique (CNRS), comprising institutes throughout France, postponed all programs with China save the most important—the Kunlun Geotraverse. Geological exploration of China is one of France's highest scientific priorities, and the large six-month expeditions had long been planned for the summer of 1989. After debate at the highest level of French government, the expedition went ahead as scheduled, but only after the Chinese pledged to avoid all publicity.

The hiatus in social science and humanities programs was more complete, and, with individual exceptions, continued through the summer of 1990. Social science exchanges are largely negotiated through the French Foreign Ministry, compounding their political sensitivity. With a number of Chinese social science leaders taking initial refuge in France, including Zhao Fusan, Vice-President of the Chinese Academy of Social Sciences, and Yan Jiaqi, Director of the Academy's Political Science Institute, neither the Chinese nor the French have been prepared to resume official bilateral relations.

Since January, and especially during the summer of 1990, there have been some efforts to improve Sino-French relations. The French decision not to sell frigates to Taiwan in February reversed the downward political spiral, and may have been linked to Chinese responsiveness to French bids for the Guangdong metro contract. (Among the French economic disappointments were the loss of the Shanghai subway contract to Germany, and the Beijing contract to the United Kingdom.) French scientists in fields ranging from agriculture to oceanography to geophysicists revisited China, exploring the potential for resuming normal scientific ties. A number of Sino-French scientific conferences were convened in France. An office of the Alliance-Francaise opened in Shanghai, as if to give some hope to France's long-standing interest in reestablishing its historical cultural presence.

In July 1990 an official French delegation was dispatched to China to begin negotiations toward the formal resumption of scientific and education relations. Amid these signs of normalcy, however, it is also clear that Tiananmen dealt a major blow to Sino-French cultural and scientific relations. Although the quasi-independent CNRS reported level funding for scientific programs with China for 1990–91, the French Foreign Ministry, which funds most other Sino-French scientific and educational programs, almost halved the 1990–91 China budget (from 50 million francs to approximately 30 million francs). During the same period French support for similar programs with Vietnam suddenly rose to 50 million

---

[31] See, for example, Francis Deron, "La Chine de M. Peyrefitte," *Le Monde*, July 11, 1990, p. 1, 4.

francs. Long-standing frustrations with China, new opportunities in Vietnam (where residual French culture is much stronger), and most important, in East Europe, are widely cited by both Chinese and French as reducing and ultimately reshaping the future of French involvement with China.

THE FEDERAL REPUBLIC OF GERMANY

Tiananmen evoked a German public outpouring of anti-Chinese government sentiment nearly equal to that in France, but its complex bilateral network has been less severely disrupted. Two June Bundestag denunciations officially curtailed new commercial credits or economic assistance, the backbone of German scientific and educational cooperation with China. Many individual German states, or *Landers*, which had been leaders in Sino-German cooperation, took even more punitive measures. In some states, university professors were discouraged from China travel: they had to take an official leave of absence to do so. Yet, this decentralization, which characterizes Sino-German cooperation, also provided the flexibility which France lacked. Within Federal agencies and private organizations alike, the operational policy that emerged was: "the continuation of cultural, scientific, and educational relations without contributing to the prestige of the regime." [32] As one German official explained it, "within these guidelines, we have been as flexible as possible." [33]

German scientific and educational cooperation with China is second in scope and size only to the United States, and is characterized by a network of cooperative projects in China.[34] By fall, many of these projects and institutes had resumed their China operations.[35] This included German advisors in Tibet, scientists in the Sino-German Cell Development Institute in Shanghai, instructors in vocational education institutes, language teachers in the Göethe Institute, and professional staff in the Beijing, Chengdu, and Shanghai offices of the Frederich Ebert Foundation.

At home, key German academic bureaucracies and institutions endeavored to preserve China relations. The Max Planck Gesellschaft Institute, like the French CNRS, decided not to cancel a large-scale geological expedition. Following internal debate, the Max Planck Gesellschaft Institute (encompassing more than 30 institutes) also decided to renew its 2 million DM agreement with the Chinese Academy of Sciences, six months early. Many German institute heads opposed the extension, citing loss of enthusiasm for cooperation with China. But, a March 1990 visit from CAS Presi-

---

[32] Interview with von der Heyden.

[33] Interview with Hans-Deiter Scheel, Ministry of Foreign Affairs, Bonn, Germany, July 16, 1990.

[34] For a comprehensive survey of German relations with China see Erhard Louven and Monka Schader, *Wissenshaftliche Zusammenarbeit Zwischen der Volksrepublic China und der Bundesrepublik Deutschland* (Hamburg: Institute of Asian Studies, 1986).

[35] The summary that follows is based on the interviews cited above and the following additional interviews. Frank Mann and Christine Althauser, German Embassy, Beijing, March 8, 1990; Werner Menden and Peter Gottstein, Federal Ministry for Research and Technology, Bonn, July 16, 1990; Dietrich Papenfuss and Heinrich Pfeiffer, Humboldt Foundation; The-Quyen Vu, Friedrich Ebert Foundtion; Joachim Wiercimok, German Research Council; Bonn, July 17, 1990. Barbara Spielmann and Dietmar Nickel, Max Planck Institute, Munich, July 23-24, 1990; Rudolph Wagner, University of Heidelberg, Heidelberg, July 13, 1990; Manfred Lindau and Munchend Imohl, German Institute for Technical Assistance, Eichborn, July 12, 1990.

dent Zhou Guangzhao personally convinced Max Planck President Staamb of the urgency of reaffirming external support for Chinese science. Likewise, Dr. Heinrich Pfeiffer, Secretary-General of the prestigious Humboldt Foundation, was personally involved in negotiating the continuation of Humboldt programs for Chinese scholars with the Beijing government. Even more important to China, the Federal Ministry of Industry and Technology and the Ministry of Economic Cooperation continued many of their ongoing scientific programs with China's State Scientific and Technical Commission and numerous related agencies.

Germany's technical assistance to China has included more than 60 million DM annually for science and education, linked in many instances to economic development in fields of commercial interest to Germany. Although G7 sanctions curtailed new grants, Germany joined Japan in Summer 1990 in signaling the resumption of these programs. In July, Dr. S. Lengl, Minister of Economic Development, travelled to China and signed new agreements opening two national research centers for vocational education. Vocational education has been the single most important German program, absorbing more than 50% of the technical assistance budget. Lengl's visit, the highest-level German political visit since Tiananmen, clearly signaled that Germany would continue its involvement in China's scientific, educational and economic development.[36] Nonetheless, strains in educational activities and funding persist. As elsewhere there is new difficulty in recruiting German scientists for participation in China-based activities. More Chinese students and scholars are remaining in Germany. Several years ago, the Chinese Ministry of Education complained that Chinese students failed to return from Germany. This is now a reality as individual states are continuing to extend visas. There are perhaps as many as 4,000 Chinese students and scholars in Germany with significant concentrations at selected universities: at the University of Heidelberg there are more than 500 Chinese students and scholars. Although the numbers of new Chinese students and scholars arriving in Germany remain stable, there are changes in the patterns of study. The Volkswagen Foundation was recently informed that China cancelled several German-funded Ph.D. programs for Chinese students. German funding for cooperation with China, heretofore on the increase, is beginning to decline. The opening of East Europe, German responsibilities toward a newly reunified country, and apathy toward China will certainly reduce future support.

The pre-Tiananmen strength of Sino-German relations, the close personal relationships that many senior German institutional leaders had developed with Chinese academic leaders, and the decentralized independent role of key national institutions have, however, protected the basic framework of Sino-German cooperation. In a year which began with East Germany avoiding "the China solution," and ended with national reunification, this was no small accomplishment.

---

[36] *Xinhua*, July 10, 1990, in FBIS, July 11, 1990, p. 10. "Concept & Implementation of Institutes for Vocational & Technical Education & Training," State Education Commission, Ministry of Labor, Gesellschaft Fur Technische Zusammenarbeit (May 22, 1990).

JAPAN

Sino-Japanese relations have gained new salience in the post-Tiananmen period.[37] While acquiescing in international economic sanctions, Japan is leading the way toward overall renormalization. Scientific and educational relations, long relatively underdeveloped, have become an important arena for sustaining and even expanding the relationship.

Given geographical proximity and cultural affinity, post-Mao Sino-Japanese educational and scientific relations had been relatively slow to develop. At the beginning of the century more than 300,000 Chinese students may have studied in Japan, but in 1985 only 2,730 were enrolled in Japanese colleges and universities, close to the numbers of Chinese studying in the Federal Republic of Germany.[38] Science officials in both countries repeatedly complained about the modest level of scientific collaboration. For example, Japan in 1988 still ranked fifth among the Chinese Academy of Sciences foreign partners, behind not just the United States and Germany, but also France and the United Kingdom. Intellectual relations were eclipsed by the rapid development of Japanese technical assistance projects that provided all-important grants, but did not necessarily nurture higher level professional collaboration, more extensively developed in China's scientific relations with West Europe and the United States.

As economic, political, and cultural problems between the two countries intensified in the mid-1980s,[39] both governments sought to strengthen educational relations as a long-term buffer. China increasingly benefited from Japan's "internationalization" of higher education: by 1988 nearly 8,000 Chinese were enrolled in Japanese institutions of higher learning. The exchange of prime ministerial visits in 1988 and 1989 also promised increased cooperation in science and education, primarily to be funded by Japan. At the time of Tiananmen, plans were under way for numerous new initiatives—an expanded scientific agreement, secondary school programs, a Ph.D. program in Japanese studies at Beijing University, a bilateral environmental research institute, and a huge cultural center for Sino-Japanese student exchanges and cultural events in Beijing.[40] The only nagging new issue in cultural relations also resulted from Japanese relaxation of student visas: a sudden influx of more than 40,000 Chinese language students in 1987 and 1988. Attracted by frequently fraudulent language programs and the lure of jobs, most Chinese in Japan at that time quickly disappeared into Japan's growing underclass of foreign workers—waiters, prostitutes, and hospital workers. China accused Japan of exploiting

[37] Kim Hong-nack, "Perspectives on Recent Sino-Japanese Relations," *The Journal of East Asian Affairs* (Summer/Fall 1990), pp. 403–435.

[38] *Student Outflows between Japan & China, May 21, 1987*, Ministry of Science and Education, Tokyo, Japan.

[39] Allen S. Whiting, *China Eyes Japan* (University of California Press, Berkeley, 1989); Laura Newby, "The Linkage between China's Domestic Politics & Foreign Policy as Reflected in Sino-Japanese Relations," Paper Presented at China Symposium, Oiso, Japan, June 1989.

[40] Interviews with Kanema Ikeda, Science and Technology Agency, Tokyo, June 26, 1989; Masayoshi Enomoto, Japan International Cooperation Agency, Tokyo, June 27, 1989.

Chinese youth, and the problem of Chinese student workers became hotly debated in the Japanese press.[41]

The Tiananmen events, broadcast live in Japan as elsewhere, brought an immediate, but fairly short-lived, suspension of most Sino-Japanese intellectual activities. Chinese students resident in Japan, critical of the Chinese regime, became temporary media figures, although not to the same extent as counterparts in the United States and Europe. Japanese faculty in the Japanese Studies Program at Beijing Normal University returned home, and the Japan Foundation temporarily cancelled most of its programs. Likewise, scientists under the auspices of the Japan Society for the Promotion of Science returned from China. The Japanese Chinese Studies Association voted to discontinue travel to China.[42]

Many Japanese intellectuals urged that the Japanese government take a more condemnatory attitude toward the Deng regime. Formal statements by Japanese political leaders did become more critical as Chinese executions continued, and Western leaders urged Japan to join in censuring China. Japan eventually postponed large-scale credits and technical assistance grants. But Japanese political leaders and academics alike also maintained that Japan had a special (more realistic) understanding of China and that China should not become internationally isolated.[43]

It is within this context that Japanese intellectual relations with China have evolved during the post-Tiananmen year. The suspension of Japanese credits and grants, particularly the 810 billion yen economic assistance grant, had more impact on the Chinese economy than all other bilateral international sanctions. Faced with escalating Chinese pressure to resume loans and grants, Japan has endeavored to be flexible in other areas. The Japanese government initially quietly managed two emotional issues—requests for visa extensions by Chinese students and the ongoing visa, social, and economic problems of Chinese student workers. Selected Chinese students, legitimately concerned about their political vulnerability, were quickly given visa extensions, and public and private organizations provided emergency financial assistance. Restrictions on Japanese language schools and tighter Japanese visa restrictions, efforts which had begun just before Tiananmen, continued. The flood of Chinese language students slowed.

Japanese and Chinese organizations reported that almost all Chinese visiting scholars returned to China after Tiananmen, and that most official educational exchange programs continued unimpeded during 1989–90. For the first time, however, Chinese Ph.D. students began to remain in Japan. China's State Education Commission reported that 90% of the Chinese Ph.D. candidates scheduled to return from Japan in 1989 failed to do so, in contrast to a 90% return rate the previous year. Long-term employment possibilities

---

[41] Interview with Hajime Wakabayashi, Ministry of Education, Tokyo, June 27,1989; Interview with Peng Jiasheng, Education Counsellor, Chinese Embassy, Tokyo, June 28, 1989.

[42] Interview with Masaharu Yamada and Akira Oguma, Japan Foundation, Tokyo, June 23, 1989; Interview with Nakahide Onozawa and Shigeru Torigai, Japan Society for the Promotion of Science, Tokyo, Japan, June 26, 1989.

[43] *Mainichi Daily News*, June 23, 1989, B12; June 25, 1989; *New York Times*, June 20, 1989, A2; "China is China and the West Best Not Forget," *The Japan Economic Journal*, July 29, 1989, p. 11.

are limited, but Japanese companies are providing extended contracts for well-trained Chinese scientists and engineers.[44]

The flow of individuals between China and Japan remained well below previous levels during the fall and spring of 1989–90. Both Chinese and Japanese officials, however, made numerous efforts to reinvigorate cultural, scientific, and educational ties.

Tiananmen initially postponed plans to expand the Sino-Japanese bilateral scientific program. But in January 1990 the two sides met in Beijing and signed a new Science and Technology Agreement. The new agreement, which focused on agriculture, the environment, and oceanography, more than doubled the previous level of cooperative efforts. While still behind levels of European and American scientific cooperation with China, this accord marked a new stage in Sino-Japanese scientific cooperation, and both sides expressed satisfaction with the results. Zhou Guangzhao travelled to Japan in the spring, negotiating agreements for closer cooperation between CAS and the Ministry of International Trade and Industry (MITI). Negotiations resumed on plans for the Japan-funded modern environmental research center to be built in Beijing. And the scientific exchanges sponsored by the Japan Society for the Promotion of Science continued more or less as before.[45]

In the summer of 1990, Sino-Japanese relations accelerated, with the Japanese government signalling that both economic and cultural relations should resume pre-Tiananmen patterns. This renormalization was spurred on by the Houston Economic Summit's tacit approval for Japan's resumption of economic assistance grants and loans to China. In a broader sense, Prime Minister Kaifu met repeatedly with visiting Chinese commercial, educational, and cultural delegations, publicly calling for increasing contacts. To avoid criticism from China, but amid growing controversy within Japan, the Japanese government began to take a stricter position concerning Chinese dissidents, delaying visa extensions and threatening forcible repatriation. In this context, Li Tieying, State Councilor, Minister of Education, and spokesman for China's more restrictive study abroad policy, visited Japan in July.[46] His official visit, including symbolic meetings with Prime Minister Kaifu and Chinese students, could not have been duplicated in the United States or Europe in the summer of 1990.

As controversy over the political role of Chinese students in Japan demonstrates, these overall trends do not mean an end to the many cultural and economic tensions between China and Japan. It is clear, however, that scientific and educational relations between China and Japan were less hurt by Tiananmen than those with Europe and the United States. Indeed, they appeared to continue a trend toward overall improvement which pre-dated June 4. During the 1990s, they are likely to be a more important component of the overall Sino-Japanese relationship.

[44] Interview with Yu Fuzeng, State Education Commission, Beijing, March 7, 1990.
[45] Interviews with Wu Yikang, Li Shubao, State Science and Technology Commission, Beijing, March 2, 1990; Cheng Erjin, Chinese Academy of Science, Beijing, March 5, 1990; Yasuo Nazaka and Tsuyoshi Yamaguchi, Japanese Embassy, Beijing, March 8, 1990.
[46] Asia Watch, "Japan: Harassment of Chinese Dissidents," October 4, 1990. *Xinhua*, June 30, 1990 in *FBIS* July 2, 1990, p. 4; *Xinhua*, July 2, 1990 in *FBIS*, July 3, 1990, p. 3; *Xinhua*, July 4, 1990 in *FBIS* July 5, 1990, p. 9; *Renmin Ribao*, July 24, 1990, in FBIS, July 26, 1990, p. 6.

III. Renormalization? The Consequences of Tiananmen

Fifteen months after Tiananmen there is increasing talk of re-normalization, not just in Japan but in Europe and the United States as well. In the mid-1970s, normalization meant the establishment of diplomatic relations and governmental cooperation ranging from medical to military. For the Chinese government today it means the resumption of higher-level political ties and the removal of economic sanctions. This has already begun. More senior officials have resumed their trek to Beijing, and Japan's resumption of economic assistance and loans is likely to be followed elsewhere. But outside Beijing, renormalization still carries an additional connotation: continued progress toward human rights and political reform *in* China. By their very resumption, cultural and intellectual relations with China are again at the cutting edge of that agenda. Beyond normalized political discourse and economic cooperation with China, the deeper cultural and societal contours of post-Tiananmen Sino-Western relations are taking shape. There is more continuity than change.

First, the continuity. The tenacity of cultural, scientific, and educational institutional connections with China is rather remarkable. For all their initial and particular differences, the post-Tiananmen responses to China in Europe, Japan and the United States have many similarities. It is as if once relations were reestablished in the post-Mao era, no one (on either side) wants to let go. Even in France and the United States, where the reaction to Tiananmen was most negative, a gradual resumption of intellectual relations is taking place. Overall, this is in part the result of vested bureaucracies, public and private, national and international, with well-defined interests in the China relationship. Beyond bureaucratic self-interests, however, friendships, working relationships, and the desire to continue ongoing projects have provided much of the renewed momentum. In a deeper sense, despite far greater political and economic uncertainty, Tiananmen has not dissipated the historic Western desire to be involved in China's modernization.

In China there has also been continuity. "Open-door" policy proclamations have proved valid. Thousands of students and scholars continue to go abroad for short visits and long-term training. Internal Chinese assessments of international scientific relations reaffirmed the necessity of foreign collaboration.[47] Accordingly, China has embarked on a new stage of scientific and educational diplomacy designed to reassure the outside world. Continuity in most academic leadership positions has contributed to this effort.

Two old issues have become more acute: brain drain reality, and constraints on the international flow of science and technology. These are essentially North-South issues, pre-dating Tiananmen.

Brain drain reality, exacerbated by Tiananmen, has dictated significant changes in Chinese educational policies and has created grave problems for Chinese scientific and educational institutions. During the first post-Tiananmen year, 1989–90, there was little appreciable change in the outward flow of students and scholars. For

---

[47] Interviews with Wang Dan and Kong Deyong, State Science and Technology Commission, Beijing, March 2, 1990.

the most part, foreign visa and immigration limitations, not Chinese restrictions, determined the numbers and categories who left China. Since January 1990, however, new restrictions on study abroad for immediate post-B.A. and post-Ph.D. students have been announced. France, Germany, the United Kingdom, and selected programs in the United States report a decrease in Ph.D. candidates and some enforcement of the requirement that they all be at least 35 years old. Visa statistics for the United States also illustrate the change in general categories studying abroad, if not the age of the applicants or the degree being sought. The numbers of new students and scholars leaving for the United States has increased slightly since 1988. There has, however, been nearly a 100% increase in visas (self-sponsored), and a corresponding decrease in J1 visas (officially sponsored).[48]

There is every indication that the numbers leaving China will remain high, and visa applications are overwhelming foreign embassies. Once again China's remaining intellectual community, faced with yet another "lost generation," is confronted with the need to revitalize its own institutions. The loss of morale and momentum is palpable. Those who have stayed are politically sympathetic with those who leave or do not return, but are also increasingly supportive of government restrictions designed to prevent further "brain drain." Even a rapid return to political reforms will not fully solve these problems. Sino-Western educational relations during the 1990s will confront an increasingly complex agenda that requires mediation between the growing numbers of disaffected Chinese students and scholars remaining abroad, the continuing outward flow of intellectuals, and pressing domestic needs.

Prior to Tiananmen, the emerging issue in China's international scientific relations was a more intense clash on issues such as intellectual property rights and high technology cooperation. Deng Xiaoping's "science is a part of the wealth of all mankind" sounds idealistic today. His science minister's recent "self-reliance" statements evoke more contemporary reality. While others warned of the dangers of foreign ideas, Song Jian has consistently reaffirmed the critical role that foreign scientists and scientific ideas have played in China, beginning with Mateo Ricci. Nonetheless, he also repeatedly warned that in an era of increasing techno-nationalism, China is ready to go it alone:

> Cooperation in any field of science and technology, especially in high technology, must be based on our own strength. We must put emphasis primarily on self-reliance instead of cherishing any unrealistic illusion.... A nation that is incapable of gaining superiority with the aid of science and technology in the international arena will only find itself in a position of being neglected, discriminated, and exploited.... High technology has become a weapon in the hands of certain Western countries to bully and op-

[48] Glenn Shive, "New Rules on PRC Students Studying Abroad: Who Can Leave, Who Cannot, and Why," IIE Report, March 23, 1990; "China Reforms Its Policies on Officially Sponsored Students Going Abroad," IIE Report, October 1990; "New Restrictions Stimulate the Flow of Self-Sponsored Students from China to American Universities," IIE Report, October 1990. Interview with Yu Fuzeng, March 7, 1990.

press ... it has also become an important means for them to exploit and plunder the resources of developing countries. ...[49]

As international scientific relations are restored, this rhetoric may recede. But these statements, and others like them, reflect Song Jian's understanding of growing constraints on the flow of science and technology across national boundaries.[50] Tiananmen, and the temporary hiatus in scientific and technological relations, has only toughened the position of Western negotiators. As West Europe, Japan and the United States begin to renew or extend their scientific and technical agreements with China, one may expect less flexibility in areas of advanced technology. Continuing debate over the nature of international scientific and technological cooperation between China and the West, including Japan, should be expected.

This relative continuity does not mean that 1989 will not be a watershed in Sino-Western cooperation. Two changes are directly linked to Tiananmen and the collapse of China as a reform model. First, as is evident in the preceding discussion of European and American relations with China, East Europe and the Soviet Union have become the new models of reform. This has resulted in the shift of some resources and enthusiasm away from China. European technical assistance programs have made major contributions to China's scientific and educational infrastructure. Although these programs are now resuming, it is not likely that they will continue to expand; more likely they will be reduced in the immediate future. It is most unlikely that the United States will consider technical assistance for China, leaving multilateral organizations, private foundations, and universities to define the parameters of assistance. The net result will be an enhanced role for Japan, which is already expanding rather than reducing funding for science and education in China.

Second, there is now overt linkage between resuming intellectual cooperation with China and China's political reform process. Perhaps the most powerful result of Tiananmen was the politicization of international scientific and educational exchanges. The rationale for the resumption of ties has become more explicitly political and ideological: a distinction between cooperation with the government and cooperation with the people, the expressed hope that continued exposure to Western ideas and intellectuals will nurture the now-repressed seeds of political reform.

The combination of these various pre-and post-Tiananmen trends and expectations suggest that the future course of China's intellectual relations with the West will be difficult. China's post-Cultural Revolution structure of international relationships has emerged remarkably intact from Tiananmen, but inherent contradictions persist in its ongoing encounter with the West.

---

[49] *Xinhua*, May 24, 1990, in FBIS June 8, 1990, p. 25. See also Song Jian, "Science and Technology to the People," State Science and Technology Commission, December 1989; *Qiushi*, No. 19, October 1, 1989 in *JPRS*, December 14, 1989, pp. 5–11.

[50] Kenneth Keller, "Science and Technology," *Foreign Affairs* (Fall 1990), pp. 123–139; Robert Reich, "The Rise of Techno-nationalism," *Atlantic Monthly* (May 1987), pp. 63–69.

PERSPECTIVES ON CHINA'S BRAIN DRAIN

By Leo A. Orleans *

CONTENTS

I. INTRODUCTION

Since the end of World War II, many thousands of young people from less-developed countries have come to the West, especially to the United States, to pursue higher education. While many return home after completing their training, others manage to change their student status and remain abroad. This flight of intellectual capital from developing countries—which has come to be known as "brain drain"—is usually of concern only to governments losing potential professionals and to scholars of labor and migration trends. The situation of Chinese students and scholars now in the United States, however, has caught the attention not only of bureaucrats and scholars, but of a large segment of the American population. There are several reasons for this. First, the 50,000 Chinese students and scholars now in the United States—more than from any other single country—are scattered throughout the country, and thus have contact with many Americans. Second, the Chinese students' reputation for being bright, hard-working, and personable has spread well beyond the academic community. Third, many of the students have found ways either to remain in this country or to postpone their return, providing them with additional opportunities to meet and interact with large numbers of Americans.

But most important in capturing the sympathy of the American people for the Chinese students studying here were the Tiananmen Square demonstrations in April–May 1989 and their tragic culmination on June 4. Every night for weeks, televisions in American homes featured images of Chinese students in Beijing marching, making speeches, and crying in an emotional plea for understanding. Interviews with Chinese students in this country also served to

* Leo A. Orleans is China consultant, Congressional Research Service, and publications coordinator for these volumes.

highlight the link between the students' aspirations and the American ideals they professed. Millions of Americans began to feel as if they knew these students personally, to sympathize with their cause, and eventually to support their efforts to remain in the United States. And indeed, the tragedy of Tiananmen provided many Chinese students with at least a temporary reprieve in their duel with the U.S. Immigration and Naturalization Service (INS).

II. THE CHINESE PERSPECTIVE

Over the past ten years Beijing's policy regarding sending students and scholars abroad for advanced study has evolved but never wavered. Surprisingly, even after Tiananmen, when many students in the United States publicly declared their intentions not to return to China until the current regime has passed from the scene, the composition of individuals permitted to leave China was somewhat changed, but their flow did not abate.

A. THE FIRST 10 YEARS (1979–89)—A REVIEW.

Chinese students have been going abroad for knowledge and know-how for a century now. Until 1949 most went to the United States, Europe, and Japan; in the 1950s, the flow shifted to the Soviet Union. Except for language training, few Chinese students studied abroad during the 1960s and most of the 1970s while China isolated herself from both East and West. The overseas flow finally resumed after Mao's death.

In 1979, with the normalization of relations between China and the United Sates and after China's shift in priorities from security considerations to national modernization, access to foreign—especially American—scientific and educational institutions became an important short-cut in acquiring the knowledge and experience of the previous two decades. The first wave of Chinese who came to the United States were, for the most part, older scholars from the institutes of the Academy of Sciences and universitites under the then-Ministry of Education, with previous training in the West or Japan. They went abroad to catch up with advances in their disciplines and renew contacts. Gradually, however, as Chinese educational institutions began to overcome the setbacks of the Cultural Revolution, the pool of younger individuals qualifying for admission to foreign universities increased, and as a result, so did the number of degree-seeking students coming to the United States.

During the 1980s the issue of sending students abroad was discussed at various official levels, as well as in educational and scientific institutions, and several national conferences were held to discuss policy.[1] While rules and regulations were made and changed and implementation varied between provinces and between institutions, the basic aim was to get as many students and scholars into foreign universities and research institutions as Chinese funding and foreign scholarships would allow. Soon, "study-abroad fever" swept China's urban youth and gathered so much momentum that it was almost impossible for the authorities to control. Between

---

[1] Much of the information in this section was adapted from my *Chinese Students in America: Policies, Numbers and Issues* (Washington, D.C.: National Academy Press, 1988)

1979 and mid-1989, the U.S. Immigration and Naturalization Service issued some 80,000 visas to Chinese students and scholars, of whom about two-thirds came on J-1 visas, issued to government-sponsored individuals, and one-third on F-1 visas, issued to students sponsored and supported by family or friends.

Beijing was aware of the considerable risk involved in sending so many of the brightest scholars abroad but concluded that the non-return of some would not negate the value of the exchange programs. Throughout most of the 1980s this was a relatively easy conclusion to sustain, since most of the students were still in the midst of completing their studies abroad in the United States and the question of return was not yet at issue. Moreover, at least through 1986, almost all of China's government-sponsored and perhaps a fifth of the self-supporting students and scholars returned home upon the completion of their studies. Thus, it was not until 1987—when two developments brought the issue to the fore—that the likely non-return of a large proportion of students created a minor crisis in government circles.

In December 1986 and January 1987, what started as relatively mundane student demonstrations protesting campus conditions and job assignments took on political overtones when a handful of participants (supported by some off-campus intellecuals) added democracy and human rights to the list of demands. Beijing's efforts to minimize the significance of the demonstrations faltered when conservative elements in the leadership forced the expulsion of some highly placed intellectuals from their posts and dismissed Hu Yao-bang as general secretary of the Communist Party. Immediately, students both in China and on American campuses assumed that fewer Chinese would be permitted to come to the United States—the cradle of "bourgeois democracy." By late 1987, however, it became clear that China was not reversing economic reforms, closing the door to the outside world, or, for that matter, altering the policy of sending students and scholars to the United States.

Unfortunately for the Chinese, the student demonstrations in January 1987 also occurred at a time when much larger numbers of students were completing degree programs in the United States. Doubts about China's ability to utilize their new skills and a nagging unease about political prospects at home were reinforced by the government's reaction to the demonstrations and widespread uncertainty about China's policies regarding foreign education. As a result of the perceived political instability and uncertain future, many more students in the United States began to seek ways to remain in this country or postpone their return.

For its part, the government was trying to mitigate the situation by proposing measures to influence students to return, and by changing the student and scholar selection process to reduce the future likelihood of defection.

Measures intended to persuade students to return have had little success. During the past decade of impressive economic progress, the government has failed to make good on promises to increase salaries and improve living conditions for intellectuals, many of whom lag behind workers in these respects. Directives instructing work units to give special considerations to returning scholars were resented by colleagues who did not have an opportunity to go abroad, and were therefore ignored or unevenly implemented.[2] A more creative and, if more scholars were returning, a more practical step was the establishment of "open research laboratories." These independently funded entities are affiliated with institutes of the Chinese Academy of Sciences and some of the major universities. In addition to providing a supportive research environment for some of China's top scientists, these laboratories also serve as temporary workplaces for returning Chinese PhDs in science and engineering, until it can be decided where best to apply their skills.

While attempting to smooth the way for returning students, Beijing also approached the problem from the other end by changing selection policies to decrease the likelihood of non-returns. First, visits to American universities by officially sponsored individuals were limited almost entirely to older scholars, who would remain abroad for a shorter period of time. Second, the number of scholars sent by the State Education Commission and the universities under its control would decrease, while more individuals would be sent by their *danweis* or work units. Study programs for these individuals, also older, would be attuned to the needs of the work unit, to which they would return. From Beijing's perspective these are indeed reasonable steps which are likely to achieve their goals.

Broadly speaking this was the situation when all hell broke loose in Tiananmen.

B. AFTER TIANANMEN

Following the violent suppression of students and their supporters in Tiananmen Square, there was great confusion regarding the future of foreign study, especially in the United States.

Since Chinese leaders had no doubt that the "very small number" of students who "fabricated lies about the government" were under the influence of Western political and capitalist forces, students were convinced that Beijing would take drastic steps to stop or sharply curtail study opportunities in the United States. Numerous statements by high Chinese officials that the open door policy would not change and that students and scholars would continue to be able to study abroad seemed to be contradicted by some depressing new regulations. It was reported, for example, that freshmen entering Beijing and Fudan Universities would first have to undergo a year of military training. On the other end of the educational system, after graduating and before starting their work assignment to a permanent work unit, all university graduates were to spend at least a year in practical work or manual labor at the "grass roots level." This was to serve two purposes: first, to provide—even on a temporary basis—college-educated individuals to work in units which sorely lack them; second, to give college graduates "an opportunity" to "get in touch with workers and farmers and cultivate the habit of bearing hardships"—a disturbing throwback to Maoist years.[3]

---

[2] See, for example, Leo A. Orleans, "China's Changing Attitude Toward the Brain Drain and Policy Toward Returning Students," *China Exchange News*, June 1989, p.2.

[3] This practice, as it is practiced by the Capital Steel and Iron Company in Beijing, is described in *Beijing Review*, Oct. 29–Nov. 4, 1990, p. 29.

Regardless of how strictly enforced or how widely implemented, the return to the glorification of practical work and manual labor—intended to "combat Western democratic influence"—was upsetting to all college students and did not seem to bode well for any young person wishing to pursue advanced education abroad. Throughout this period, then, many contradictory signals came out of Beijing that left students and foreigners alike confused as to whether, which, and how many students would be allowed to study in the United States. It was an atmosphere ripe for rumors.

The most authoritative early policy statement on sending students abroad was made by He Dongchang, vice-minister in charge of the State Education Commission, in an August 1989 interview with the weekly *Liaowang*.[4] The reporters asked He to respond to author Han Suyin's charge that the tragedy in Beijing was directly linked to the policy of letting students study abroad. The vice-minister reiterated that the sending of students and scholars abroad was a fundamental national policy and would not change, but then acknowledged that the "turmoil-turned-riot" in Beijing made it necessary to place a "screen" over the open door to prevent "flies and worms" from passing through it.

He Dongchang went on to explain that in the last 10 years China's higher education system, including the graduate level, had been greatly improved, so that in the future most students seeking graduate degrees would be able to obtain them in China. But while the number of state-sponsored students sent abroad for advanced degrees would be sharply reduced, the number of visiting scholars would be "considerably increased." Furthermore, by stating that "we cannot confine openness to just a few developed Western countries" he implied that in the future more students and scholars would go to other countries besides the United States. Finally, He stressed once again the need to improve the planning process so that foreign education would mesh with national needs. To illustrate the disparity between individual study programs and national needs, He claimed that 1,000 Chinese students in the United States are getting doctorates in optical physics—an obvious exaggeration.

Many of He's points were not new, but simply affirmed the changes that had already been announced prior to Tiananmen. But although his interview received much attention in the Western media, confusion and rumor persisted because some of his points were misinterpreted and some of the measures he described have not been implemented.

After months of deliberation came additional clarification of the new policies. In January 1990, the State Education Commission issued lengthy provisions, effective Feburary 10, for students going abroad at their own expense.[5] The stated intent of the document was to strengthen the "guidance and control" over these students by requiring them to work a specified number of years before going

---

[4] Hong Kong, *Liaowang Overseas Edition*, Aug. 21, 1989; FBIS–CHI–89–166, Aug 29, 1989, pp. 16–17.

[5] "Announcement Concerning Promulgation of 'Supplemental Provisions for Personages with University Graduate and Postgraduate Qualifications Studying Abroad at own Expense,'" State Education Commission, January 25, 1990. A good discussion of this policy and its ramifications was published in *Kuang Chiao Ching* (Wide Angle), Hong Kong, April 16, 1990; JPRS–CAR–90–049, July 11, 1990, pp. 7–10.

abroad in order to repay the state for their education. The length of service varied from two to five years and was determined by a confusing formula that takes into account level of education, type of school, full-time or part-time status of students, and then factors in the number of years of work experience an individual may have already had. The document did provide for an important exemption. Students with relatives overseas (and the word is that their number skyrocketed after the release of this document) could essentially buy their way out of China by paying fees ranging from 1,500 to 6,000 yuan.

Not surprisingly, the release of this document caused yet another media sensation, for it did indeed appear that "China Acts to Restrict Study Abroad," as the headlines proclaimed. In fact, the document's provisions are being implemented loosely if at all. The most dramatic proof of this is that while there had been some internal shifts in the composition of the new arrivals to the United States since June 1989, at least so far, there has been no reduction in overall numbers. On the contrary, their numbers have increased, as the following figures, released by the Chinese, show: [6]

Year	Privately Supported	Government Supported	Total
1988	4,771	1,159	5,930
1989	7,386	1,446	8,832
Jan. thru May	1,684	537	2,221
June thru Dec.	5,702	909	6,611

Similarly, U.S. data on the number of visas issued in China during FY90 (Oct. 1989–Mar. 1990) show a slight decrease in J–1 visas but a significant increase in the number of F–1 visas over the previous fiscal year. However, the final test of China's policies with regard to sending students and scholars to the United States may come in the fall of 1990—more than a year after Tiananmen.

Be that as it may, it is still appropriate to ask why is it that contrary to so many predictions, the Chinese government continues to permit students and scholars to come to the United States where, presumably, they pick up so many dangerous notions? A few reasons can be suggested.

First, science and technology are still seen as the answer to many of China's problems and the United States is still considered to be the most advanced country in these fields. Second, a sharp reduction in scientific and educational exchanges would send the wrong message not only to Washington but to American scientists and engineers in academic institutions and industrial enterprises, with whom Chinese colleagues have valuable contacts. Third, the Chinese continue to have a high regard for American higher education, with which so many Chinese scholars have had first-hand experience. Fourth, because of its image, reputation, and the large Chinese communities in many American cities, the United States

---

[6] *Newsletter*, The Embassy of the People's Republic of China, Washington, D.C., May 12, 1990.

continues to be the country of choice for the overwhelming majority of Chinese students and scholars. Putting a tight lid on the desire to study in the United States may have seemed too dangerous. And finally, since Beijing still hopes for the eventual return of the students now in the United States, restrictive policies toward study abroad would send the wrong message and any intimidation would have an opposite effect on the new generation of Westernized scholars. Instead, Beijing continues to promise better living and working conditions for the returnees and much publicity is given to those few who do return and receive "a warm welcome" and "preferential treatment." [7]

China's real hope, however, is that the special attachment the Chinese people have for their homeland will eventually draw them home. To show that ties with the motherland are not easily broken, they point to the large numbers of scientists and other professionals who returned to China in the early 1950s, to the support so many Chinese-American scientists provided after normalization, and to the eventual return to Taiwan of thousands of U.S.-educated scholars. Moreover, the thinking is that if and when they do return the scholars will have gained much more experience and they will be much better equipped to make important contributions to China's development. In the meantime, Chinese scholars in the United States will continue to maintain relations with many of their colleagues at home, and thereby serve as yet another channel through which knowledge and know-how can be transferred to China.

An official of the Ministry of Personnel summarized China's attitude toward students remaining abroad in a very straightworward way: "We should not have a prejudice against those who linger a bit. . . . What we should do is create a more attractive environment for them." [8]

III. THE U.S. PERSPECTIVE

The apolitical scientific and academic links between Chinese and American scholars and institutions were pursued with enthusiasm by both sides and have played a vital role in forging friendly ties between the two countries since the normalization of relations in 1979.[9] The most tangible sign that three decades of tension and suspicion were over was the ever-growing number of Chinese students on American campuses. Some Americans welcomed the new relationship because of sentimental attachments stemming from missionary and educational contacts through the first half of the 20th century, others saw China as an intellectual and scientific frontier without which our knowledge of the world would be sorely lacking, and yet others were simply thrilled with the novelty of having Chinese in our midst and showing them our country. Thus, through most of the 1980s a kind of love affair seemed to develop between the two countries. And at least until 1987, the question of

---

[7] See, for example, *Renmin Ribao*, June 5, 1990; FBIS–CHI–90–114, June 13, 1990, p. 19.
[8] *China Daily*, Dec. 15, 1988, p. 1.
[9] For a detailed discussion of exchange programs and sponsors, see David M. Lampton, *A Relationship Restored*, (National Academy Press, Washington, D.C.,1986), Ch. IV.

"brain drain" and the potential problem of the non-return of Chinese students was of marginal concern to the U.S. government.

The cordial relations between China and the United States came close to the breaking point following Beijing's crackdown against the students in Tiananmen, and created a rupture between the Bush Administration and Congress. While President Bush was convinced that "this is not the time for an emotional response" which might jeopardize the entire relationship with China, the students' calls for democracy (and the vision of the Goddess of Freedom in Tiananmen Square) elicited a very different response on Capitol Hill, where a resolution supporting the democracy movement was quickly passed by voice vote. Members of Congress vied with each other to see who could come up with the most stirring rhetoric about the brave students who risked their lives to bring democracy to China and criticized the President for not taking more forceful actions to punish the Chinese government. To members of Congress already critical of China's policies regarding family planning and Tibet, the Tiananmen incident was further proof of China's disregard for human rights—a position that was greatly reinforced by what appeared to be an endless stream of Chinese students testifying about Beijing's atrocities.

President Bush did, of course, take immediate steps to show U.S. displeasure over Tiananmen, and an executive order was issued to assure a sympathetic review of requests by Chinese students in the United States to extend their stay when their visas expired. The order applied to all students in the United States on June 6, 1989 and, upon application, provided for an extension of all expiring visas for one year, until June 5, 1990.

Since students who came to the United States on F-class visas can apply for immigrant status as aliens seeking permanent residence, the order applied primarily to government-selected scholars with J-class visas who, according to the immigration law, could work in the United States for 18 months after finishing their studies, but had to leave the country for at least two years before changing to another nonimmigrant category or to permanent resident status.

Chinese students were not overjoyed by the executive order. Unsure what their status might be after one year and concerned that they would have to return to China or become stateless, many students felt that by accepting a deferred departure they would be making a public statement against their country and would be branded as counter-revolutionaries. Consequently, few applied for the extension while many slowed down their academic progress in order to hold on to their visas.

Convinced that if students returned to China they would be immediately arrested, many members of Congress felt that Bush's actions did not provide adequate protection. Several bills were introduced to allow students to remain here under the INS "hardship" provision, or to apply immediately for permanent-residency status. Most notable was the Pelosi bill, which would have allowed students to remain in the United States after their visas expired. The bill passed both houses of Congress by large majorities but ran into stiff and expected opposition by the White House. Bush, upset by what he considered to be Congressional intrusion on presidential authority, vetoed the bill, pointing out that existing administrative directives assure the Chinese students essentially the same protection. The attempt to override the veto succeeded in the House but failed by four votes in the Senate. Congressional pressure on the President did not stop, however, and on April 11, 1990 Bush issued an executive order formalizing all the administrative steps already taken and deferring until January 1, 1994 any deportation proceedings against Chinese who arrived in the United States before April 11, 1990.

Actions by Congress and statements by Bush elicited predictable complaints from the Chinese government for "interference in Chinese internal affairs and fomenting discord between the Chinese students and Chinese government." [10] Beijing voiced "great indignation and strong protest" to Bush, maintaining that his statements on changes in the status of Chinese students not only "undermined the educational exchanges," but did not take into account the long-term interests of the two countries. In fact, even those Chinese leaders who may have believed that there was American involvement in the anti-government demonstrations in June, knew very well that whatever Bush did or did not do with regard to Chinese scholars and students, would not cause them to run for plane reservations for the return trip. Characteristically, many of these protests and allegations were related to "face"—a show of displeasure that a situation which needed defusing through silence would be formalized through executive orders.

China's post-Tiananmen complaints about U.S. "interference" in the fate of Chinese students and scholars were more serious, but not new in themselves. For several years Beijing had expressed concern that not enough was being done by the INS and the U.S. Information Agency, which administers many of the national programs, to force Chinese nationals to comply with existing regulations and return home as scheduled. Moreover, they suspected collusion between the U.S. government and American professors—especially those working in mathematics, physics and chemistry—to appropriate China's most talented young scholars. Although no such plot exists (and the Chinese, most likely, know this), many American professors have indeed become dependent on the intelligent and hard working Chinese students as teaching and research assistants. And some of them lobbied hard (before and after Tiananmen) to find ways to keep the Chinese in this country.

Official U.S. sanctions against China seriously affected most of the scientific and educational exchanges between the two countries: scientific and technical protocols signed by the two governments became inactive; federal funding for programs involving travel to China was stopped; the National Science Foundation drastically cut back its scientific exchange program with China; the National Academy of Sciences suspended its exchange programs; and many academic associations and universities put their programs with China on hold. As an aside, it should be noted that many scholars disagreed with the wisdom of cutting off scientific and academic contacts with China. This position was cogently expressed by Pierre

---

[10] See, for example, *Xinhua*, July 26, 1989; FBIS–CHI–89–143, July 27, 1989, p. 24.

Perrolle: ". . . the type of broad-based progress reflected in the pro-democracy demonstrations in Tiananmen Square is not the result of U.S. pronouncements on democracy and human rights but the outgrowth of extensive direct contacts between Americans and Chinese." [11]

By the spring and early summer of 1990 tension between China and the United States had started to subside. China moderated her rhetoric, resumed the suspended Fulbright and Peace Corps programs, released several hundred imprisoned dissidents, and permitted Fang Lizhi and his wife to leave the country. And with the ending of the heated and divisive Congressional debate over the most-favored nation status for China—in which the Chinese student issue was frequently raised—the tension between Congress and the Administration regarding U.S-China policy has also been muted as of this writing.

IV. The Students' Perspective

It is not facetious to say that for a large number of Chinese students today, the primary concern about the "brain drain" is how to become part of it. This was not true earlier in the decade, when the desire to go abroad to study did not imply a desire to remain there. The gradual change in attitudes came as a result of professional considerations, the example of others (and safety in numbers), a desire for a better life style, and the lack of political reform to match the economic progress of the past decade.

It is not difficult to sympathize with the "study-abroad fever" which gripped the student population in the mid 1980s. By then, China's universities were graduating large numbers of bright youths who wished to do graduate work and, at the same time, "see the world." Students were aware that many of China's top academic and research positions were filled by individuals who received their education in the West prior to 1950, in the Soviet Union during the 1950s, or who were members of the somewhat younger crop of PhDs trained abroad after 1980. Since success seemed to be tied to foreign education, a "blind desire" to study abroad developed among students in Chinese universities, causing some educators to profess that the study a foreign language (usually English) was taking precedence over all other courses and that some of China's best universities were becoming "study-abroad prep schools." The complaints of the authorities seemed to have little effect on students intent on getting into an American institution of higher education. And once accepted, their primary anxiety was not a passport from China's security people, as one might expect, but a visa from the American Embassy or from one of the consulates. There is a widespread belief that every year U.S. visas are getting more difficult to obtain. There are, in fact, more rejections, but only because the number of applicants for visas has been growing. The total number of visas issued has not decreased. [12]

---

[11] Pierre Perrolle, "After Tiananmen: Science Relations with China," *Issues in Science and Technology*, Winter, 1989–90, p. 54.

[12] The process of obtaining a U.S. visa is considered to be a nerve-racking experience and is dreaded by all. In a biting and somewhat exaggerated description of this "humiliating" process,

Continued

In 10 short years, students and scholars from China became the largest contingent of foreigners on American campuses. As with their predecessors who came to the United States in the first half of this century, the new generation of Chinese students quickly impressed the academic community with their seriousness of purpose, dedication, and appealing manners. Appreciation of these qualities and the novelty of having students from the PRC in American universities bolstered the recognition of the importance of academic exchanges in opening relations with China, and created what many consider an unprecedented amount of goodwill in and beyond the academic community.

Inevitably, after living in the United States for several years, students went through a major transformation collectively and as individuals—as much because of what they learned about this country as by their new-found ability to look at their own country more objectively. It is not really surprising that many of them got spoiled by the special attention shown them and soon learned to take shortcuts and to seek special considerations from the academic institutions and favors from their friends and acquaintances.[13] Neither is it suprising that these bright and affable youths quickly learned how our system works, how to push the right buttons and how to use the "back door." This change was clearly visible in their activites following the Tiananmen incident.

We can only imagine what went on in the minds and hearts of the Chinese students and scholars watching the events in Tiananmen Square from across the ocean. All of them, no doubt, felt grief, concern for their families and friends, and frustration over their own helplessness; for many, the military crackdown affirmed the resolve to remain in this country. Beijing's never-ending assurances that there will be no reprisals for participating in demonstrations fell on deaf ears and, so far, probably no more than 100 students and scholars have returned to China since June 1989. Most are convinced (without any real evidence) that the government has compiled lists of demonstrators and speech-makers in the United States and that to return is to end up in jail.

Thus, the primary concern of the overwhelming proportion of students and scholars now in the United Satates is to complete their education and, at least for the time being, find a way to remain in this country. Funding was not a problem and according to a survey taken by the Institute of International Education and coordinated by Carol Strevy, there was little change in the circumstances of Chinese students who resumed their studies in the fall of

a Shanghai reporter wrote of the long lines, the "indescribably melancholy" atmosphere inside the Shanghai consulate, the questions that are asked and often not understood, and the need to prove to the "unsympathetic visa-issuing officer" sitting behind "iron bars" that the desire for a student visa is to study and not to use it as a means of getting into and staying in the United States.(Zhou Jiajun,"Shanghai Residents Under the Stars and Stripes Banner," *Jiefang Ribao*, Nov. 17, 1988; FBIS–CHI–88–226, p. 8.

[13] The following example expresses one of the many frustrations experienced by foreign student advisors: "My staff is exhausted, frustrated, angry, resentful, etc. when it comes to Chinese. We spend an inordinate amount of time in dealing with Chinese students and scholars (both in the admission process and once they arrive) and I feel we do things for (with?) the Chinese that we would never do for other nationalities. . . . " (From an informal survey of foreign student advisors conducted in 1988 by Becky Roach, then a foreign student advisor herself, at Iowa State University. I am indebted to Bernard La Berge for providing me with a copy of the survey.

1989.[14] As in earlier years, U.S. academic institutions continued to provide most of the financial support for Chinese students and scholars—most of it secured prior to June 1989—so that students rarely experienced any serious financial problems. Assistance from national donor organizations also continued with few interruptions and some emergency support to students was made available at the local level. But while students were as well off financially after Tiananmen as they were before, the worry about their visas has become a continuing obsession: whether and how to extend it, how to change status, how to make sure none of the available options are overlooked.

Once their studies are completed, work opportunities for Chinese graduates vary greatly. For the most part, those majoring in fields of science and engineering are in great demand in the United States and should have a relatively easy time of finding employment within the academic community or in the economy at large. Moreover, English language competence is not as vital a factor as it is likely to be in other fields. Conversely, opportunities in the social sciences are limited by demand and usually require a standard of language proficiency which many foreign students, whatever their country of origin, find it difficult to attain.

While most Chinese students and scholars resumed their academic work in the fall of 1989, others found an alternative commitment in student protest activities which mushroomed after June 4. Dissident organizations grew, multiplied, and, for a time, seemed to speak for the vast majority of the students. Their goals were imprecise, but what tied them together was a desire to get rid of the current leadership and bring some undefined form of "democracy" to China. To achieve their aims these organizations focused on disseminating information through a sophisticated communications network, providing speakers to address public gatherings, and attempting to lobby Congress on a variety of subjects, ranging from censure of Chinese treatment of imprisoned Tiananmen demonstrators to the issue of renewing the U.S. most favored nation trade status for China in 1990.

Initially, the dissidents experienced no serious problems in raising funds for their activities and publications. Donations were received from the American public, particularly Chinese Americans, and from overseas Chinese communities, especially Taiwan—a sensitive topic for many of the organizations. By 1990 the influence of dissident organizations began to wane and fund-raising became much more difficult. In part, the slowing of activities was due simply to the passage of time and the students' preoccupation with studies and research. Some students, moreover, got fed up with the movement's harshly antagonistic stance toward Beijing that demonstrated little concern for or influence on the developments in China. The most important reason, however, for the dwindling support of the dissident organizations were stories in U.S. newspapers, both in English and Chinese, about "fiscal mismanagement, crippling factionalism and lavish lifestyles in the dissident communi-

---

[14] *Financial Status of Students/Scholars from the People's Republic of China in U.S.*, (Institute of International Education: New York, February 1990).

ty." [15] The most dramatic case in point was the rise and fall of Wu'er Kaixi, the brash young "revolutionary" who became familiar to TV viewers during the demonstrations in Beijing, came to the United States to lecture to the American people about the importance of introducing democracy into China, and eventually stumbled from the pinnacle of public approval on the familiar rocks of wine, women and song. Talk of merging some of the organizations for greater effectiveness was grounded on yet another familiar obstacle: the unwillingness of individuals to give up or share their leadership positions.

V. A Personal Perspective

As someone who has followed Chinese student issues for many years, I would like to stray from the more academic format and end this paper not with a summary/conclusion, but with some personal observations which, because they are at variance with majority opinion, can only be expressed in the unbecoming first-person-singular mode. I would also like to express the hope that more than a year after Tiananmen, passions have cooled and my views will no longer be regarded as "genuinely nauseating," to use the words of one respondent to an article I published in July 1989.[16]

Most Chinese students, whether here or in China, are members of the "me generation" that matured under Deng Xiaoping's reforms. This generation views patriotic dedication and sacrifice as "corny" notions, and with the tacit approval of the leadership, has come to appreciate the power of the all-mighty dollar (or yuan, as the case may be). Spoiled by their parents, who vowed that their children would not have to suffer as they did during the Cultural Revolution, these young people could not and did not appreciate the great economic and political progress that China has made in the last decade. Their dreams have much more to do with their own future than with the future of China. This is not a criticism but simply a recognition that Chinese students may be different from the preceding generations, but are no different from many other students around the world. In the meantime, in the minds of many Americans, the image of Chinese students as self-sacrificing martyrs fighting to liberate the Chinese people from the communist dragon in order to bring democracy to the country is fading, but not entirely gone.

Most of the privately funded students who originally came to the United States on F–1 visas, and therefore had an opportunity to change their status in order to remain here, never intended to return to China, and few did. Most of the government-supported students and scholars who came here on the J–1 visa knew they had to return to China, but some, no doubt, secretly wondered if they might eventually find a way to remain in the United States. It seems safe to presume that their proportion kept increasing with the number of years they spent on an American campus. What happened in Tiananmen was a tragedy for all of them, but it also presented an unusual opportunity for those seeking ways to stay.

---

[15] See, for example, *U.S. News and World Report*, April 30, 1990, p. 34.

[16] "Students Bear Much of the Responsibility for the Tragedy in China," *Chronicle of Higher Education*, July 19, 1989, p. A36. The unfortunate title was provided by the editors.

They knew that the United States would not force them to go back and President Bush and the Congress quickly confirmed their convictions.

As a group, students and scholars who might return at this time would be no better and no worse off than the rest of the intellectuals in China—not an incentive, to say the least. Except for a few highly visible and vocal leaders, there is no reason to believe that they will be in any way abused. To assume otherwise is to assume that Beijing has lost all hope of getting them back—which is not the case. Conversely, to insist that the life of a student would be in danger if he or she returned to China provides excellent insurance against being forced to return.[17] Chinese students have also learned that the words "human rights" can work magic in the United States. No matter that the Western concept of human rights may not yet be applicable to China's very different social, cultural, and religious traditions and environment. No matter that if asked about human rights and free elections for Chinese peasants or, God forbid, the people of Tibet, most students would likely respond with a blank stare of incredulity.

As discussed earlier, even prior to Tiananmen, students' reluctance to return to China after completing their advanced degree programs was due as much to professional concerns as to political or economic considerations. Most Chinese students in science and engineering, especially those who have earned their PhDs, are over-qualified for China's current needs. With best intentions, China could not provide them with the type of facilities, equipment, and challenges that they have here.

The key question, then, is: How vital are the scholars who are now in the United States to China's economy? Both here and in China one frequently hears that China "desperately" needs the scholars who have been trained abroad. I belong to a small minority of observers who don't believe that at this time the loss of U.S.-trained PhDs creates a "desperate" situation for China—although, it *is* a painful loss of face. Briefly stated, all the institutes of the Chinese academies of sciences, agriculture, and medicine, which are located in major cities, as well as the teaching positions in key comprehensive universities are already fully staffed with highly competent individuals, most of whom were either trained abroad or have had some research experience abroad. This may not be the case in some of the academy branches in the more distant provinces, but because they would be less likely to have up-to-date facilities and equipment for research, sending returning scholars there would be both coercive and a waste of their talents. Using them at a different level or in other capacities would also mean sacrificing years of education and experience gained in the United States. Even if China were able and willing to make additional investments in basic research in order to provide the type of facilities that would attract foreign-trained PhDs, the question would remain whether, given the level of economic development and more immediate priorities, such expenditures could be justified. There is undoubtedly a need for top-notch scientists and engineers

---

[17] See, for example, Li Lu, "In China, I'd Be Dead," *New York Times*, Dec. 24, 1989.

in many less prominent institutions of higher education and in industry, transportation, communications, and a host of other fields, but again, allowing for some individual exceptions and special situations, Chinese scholars with foreign experience would not find these positions attractive. This was exactly the complaint leveled at highly-trained scientists by Mao: the country needs them on the production line, so to speak, while they want to do basic research and, to use Mao's words, work in an "ivory tower."

Recognizing that China's higher education is extremely uneven and that it is built on, what one observer referred to as, "an illiterate and barren wasteland," it must still be admitted that in the past ten years Chinese universities have expanded and greatly improved their capacity to train middle and high level personnel. There has also been a rapid expansion of graduate education which, since 1983, trained well over 3,000 PhDs, most of them in the physical sciences and engineering. Although the politically suspect social sciences and humanities continue to suffer from Beijing's insecurities, recent visitors report that in many fields the climate is, once again, improving. Thus, I believe that the two million or so people enrolled in various types of institutions of higher education should, for the most part, meet the diverse needs of China's economy. Of course there are still shortages in some fields—no doubt an aspect of fluctuating educational policies and the impossible task of planning enrollment—but scholars currently abroad are not likely to fill these gaps.

Over the past few years Chinese students and their organizations have played a significant role in influencing U.S. relations with the People's Republic of China. But while their input is entirely legitimate and, in some cases, useful, it is well to keep in mind that their goals are not necessarily those of the United States. Another point to remember is that although Chinese scholars have been filling important slots in our universities, in industrial research, and in other capacities, it is in the interest of both the United States and China for them to eventually return home. Tiananmen delayed this process, but I am sure that as conditions improve in China many of them will do just that. And when they do return, they will make a vital contribution not only to China's development but to a better understanding between our two countries.

D. Military

OVERVIEW

By Richard F Kaufman *

Through most of the 1980s, China's military program was given the lowest priority, in terms of resource allocations, of the major sectors scheduled for modernization: Agriculture, Industry, Science and Technology, and the Military. Defense budgets were cut; the size of the army was reduced; and the replacement and upgrading of weapons lagged. Now that is changing. Military strategy has been altered; policies concerning roles, missions, and force structure are being modified; and defense budgets are being increased.

As Paul H.B. Godwin shows, Chinese military policy will be much different in the 1990s. Military strategy underwent a fundamental shift in the mid 1980s from a focus on a general war with the Soviet Union to concerns about small-scale or local wars around China's periphery. In large part, this was the result of Beijing's assessment of a change in the global balance of power away from the bipolar dominance of the two superpowers, toward greater multipolarity. The decline of the Soviet military threat under Gorbachev confirmed this assessment. In the future rising economic strength in Japan, Europe, and some less developed countries, Chinese analysts believe, will be accompanied by growing military strength in those quarters. Military threats could come from a number of sources.

The change in strategy caused the military to be more aware of its shortcomings. Limited war contingencies require a credible capacity for quick response, with a high degree of mobility and command and control. China is weak in these areas and in military hardware and technology generally: "Chinese equipment is not on a par with advanced Western systems—it may not even be close." In addition, the possibility of a major war cannot be ruled out. But the task of modernizing the military establishment to achieve competence at all levels of warfare will be time consuming and expensive.

The paper by Robert Skebo, Gregory Man, and George Stevens discusses China's military capabilities and the obstacles to modernization. Combat capabilities have steadily declined relative to the Soviet Union and even some of its smaller neighbors. Nevertheless, China still retains considerable military power. Its nuclear forces are roughly equivalent to those of France, with long-range missiles

---

* Richard F Kaufman, General Counsel, Joint Economic Committee, United States Congress.

that can launch space satellites and probably strike targets throughout the United States. Its bomber and undersea forces are mostly medium- or short-range and outmoded. China's large ground forces are capable of defense but have only limited ability to project power. There is a lack of logistical support, transport, air defense, communications, armor, and air support.

The navy is slowly expanding its coastal defense force to develop regional power projection capabilities. But its surface fleet and submarines are obsolescent. It has a relatively large number of destroyers and frigates, modest amphibious capabilities, and diesel submarines designed in the 1950s. Naval aviation is severely limited. The Air Force faces similar problems of aging and obsolescence.

Modernization is constrained by three types of factors: economic, technological, and political-social. Rapid replacement is not possible because of costs. The leadership is aware that defense is an economic burden, and limited budgets and the need to support the large number of forces are likely to hold back new weapons development and production. Limited access to advanced Western technology continues to hamper efforts to improve manufacturing techniques and management in the Soviet designed defense industrial base. Added to these problems are a controversy over the proper amount of political indoctrination to be included along with professional training, the negative effects on morals and efficiency of a variety of corrupt practices, and the failure of the military to attract high calibre recruits.

The trends in defense spending, examined by James Harris and other analysts of the Central Intelligence Agency, reflect the changes in strategy and policy as well as more recent events. The decline in defense spending was reversed in 1990 when it was announced that the defense budget had been increased. Depending upon estimates for inflation, the real increase could be about 10 percent. The share of GNP spend for defense is estimated at 3.5 percent.

While there are growing pressures for weapons modernization, most of the increased allocations will be used to address problems related to domestic security and military morale. On the assumption that there are no immediate external threats, and in the wake of the Tiananmen crisis of 1989, resources are being channelled to the stationing of troops in the Beijing area, increasing internal security throughout the country, maintaining equipment, constructing barracks and other facilities, increasing food supplies, and ensuring adequate military pay and retirement.

The military leadership anticipates intensified arms races in the Asian-Pacific region, a resurgent Japan, and potential challenges from Taiwan and India, among other regional powers. Such concerns form the basis of current efforts and military demands for increased resources to replace and modernize the inventory of nuclear and conventional weapons, and to accelerate long-term research and development. Military spending is likely to continue rising over the next several years.

The complicated role played by the military establishment in China's political economy is discussed by Ronald N. Montaperto. Historically, the distinction between civilian and military leaders has been blurred, and a symbiotic relationship between the two developed. The senior military leaders have enjoyed a high degree of access to and influence over their civilian counterparts which has allowed them to be deeply involved in the political succession and many broad policy issues.

This interaction is changing as the old leadership passes from the scene and as personal relationships are replaced by institutional structures and arrangements. A new military professionalism has given rise to leaders and constituencies whose career advancement is based on specialized knowledge and expertise and who define their political interests in ways that elicit from the system the resources necessary to modernize the military. The technocrats, for example, are a group of officers educated as scientists and engineers rather than as professional soldiers. They are interested in acquiring advanced foreign technologies and in coordinating the research and acquisition plans of the military services. They also appear to advocate foreign military arms sales, much of which are conducted by military run enterprises.

Shirley Kan provides an account of China's emergence as a major arms supplier in international markets, and the consequences for China and the world. Chinese weapons have been sold exclusively to developing countries and deliveries soared in the latter part of the 1980s. In the Iran-Iraq war sales totaling $7.5 billion were made to both sides. China became the fifth largest arms merchant selling weapons to developing countries during this period, behind the Soviet Union, the United States, France, and the United Kingdom.

Arms exports play an important role in military modernization by promoting technical progress, through contacts with foreign experts, and through the infusion of foreign exchange earnings. The profits from arms sales are an important source of revenue for the military. This activity also furthers some of the objectives of industrial reform by encouraging industrial decentralization and the spread of profit-oriented commercial sectors.

China has been accused of reckless conduct in arms transfers, but its decision to discontinue sales to Iraq following that country's invasion of Kuwait placated many Western critics. In the 1990s, Kan concludes, China can be expected to continue a vigorous program of arms sales to advance its position as a world power and to earn hard currency.

CHINESE DEFENSE POLICY AND MILITARY STRATEGY IN THE 1990s

By Paul H.B. Godwin *

CONTENTS

SUMMARY

China's interpretation of the changes in the international security environment from a condition where the United States and the Soviet Union dominated a bipolar world to one where the trend is increased multipolarity has been reflected in its defense policy and military strategy. In 1985, the Chinese People's Liberation Army (PLA), as all three services are collectively known, was required to redirect its development of military strategy from a myopic focus on general war with the U.S.S.R. to the more probable source of military conflict: small-scale and potentially intense wars around China's periphery. New enemies did not emerge; rather, the kinds of conflicts that could arise required a fresh look at defense policy and military strategy.

Over the past five years, even as the military threat from the U.S.S.R. diminished, the Chinese armed forces developed new defense strategies and concepts of operations to support these strategies. The eleven military regions (MR) within which all Chinese forces are deployed were reduced to seven, with each MR seen as a potential theater of operations. The ground forces were reorganized into Group Armies and their training focused on the development of quick-reaction capabilities in combined arms packages utilizing all branches of the armed forces. The MR commander became, in

---

* Professor of National Security Policy, The National War College, Fort L.J. McNair, Washington D.C. 20319–6000. The views expressed in this essay are those of the author and are not to be construed as those of the Department of Defense, The National Defense University, The National War College, or any other agency of the U.S. Government.

essence, the commander of a unified theater of command responsible for a theater of war or "war zone."

These changes, although important in themselves, left the PLA even more conscious of its technological obsolescence. Developing concepts of military operations in which speed and lethality were to be the principal characteristics of combat, rather than defensive operations based upon attrition warfare and a society mobilized for war, served only to highlight one of the PLA's primary weaknesses. As in all the years since the beginning of Chinese defense modernization in the late 1970s, these technological weaknesses led the armed forces to demand swifter modernization of their arms and equipment.

Even with these limitations, however, the new paradigm of war reflected in the PLA's military exercises will do little to alleviate the apprehensions of China's smaller neighbors. Beijing states that its defense policy *is* defensive. Nonetheless, the military strategy and operations developed in support of this policy contain concepts and capabilities with offensive elements. These offensive elements are currently severely limited by the inability to provide the logistic support for force projection much beyond China's border. The decade of the 1990s could see this change.

I. MILITARY STRATEGY AND SECURITY

In the spring of 1985, the Military Commission of the Central Committee of the Communist Party of China (*Zhongyang Junshi Weiyuanhui*—CMC) ordered a critical change in the strategic guidance directing the Chinese People's Liberation Army (PLA) military strategy and training. The new guidance directed the armed forces to refocus their strategy formulation and operational training from preparation for an "early, major, and nuclear war" to what the CMC declared the most likely form of conflict in the foreseeable future—local limited war (*jubu zhanzheng*) around China's borders.[1] This CMC decision remains the authoritative guidance for Chinese defense policy and military strategy five years later.

The Central Military Commission, until recently chaired by Deng Xiaoping, is the highest level of authority in the Chinese defense establishment. The Ministry of National Defense functions primarily as the CMC's administrative arm. Although the precise manner in which the CMC contributes to security and defense policy decisions is not known, its membership indicates the weight it carries in policymaking. The 14 members in 1985 included the defense minister, the PLA chief of staff, and the directors of the PLA General Logistics and Political Departments. They were accompanied by China's three surviving marshals serving Deng Xiaoping as his vice chairmen. With Deng as chairman of the commission, it is reasonable to assume that the views of China's leading soldiers were

---

[1] See Generals Zhang Zhen and Li Desheng's discussion of the May–June 1985 Military Commission's guidance at a meeting with the editorial board of *Jiefangjun Bao* (Liberation army daily) reported in *Ta Kung Bao* (Hong Kong), 16 February 1986, in *Foreign Broadcast Information Service: People's Republic of China* (hereafter FBIS–CHI), No. 032 (18 February 1986), pp. W11–12.

heard and carried great weight in decisions influencing security and defense policy.[2]

CHINA'S PERCEIVED SECURITY ENVIRONMENT

The threat perceptions of China's leadership changed dramatically over the years 1978-1985. The Third Plenum of the Eleventh Central Committee, meeting in December 1978 under Deng Xiaoping's predominant influence, concluded that the Soviet Union was not an *immediate* military threat to China's security. Although not an immediate threat, the U.S.S.R.'s aggressive foreign policy was seen as threatening China over the long-term, and Soviet military forces deployed along the Sino-Soviet border were seen as the most direct military threat to China's security. Defending against a massive Soviet assault deep into the political and industrial heart of China was the principal objective of the military strategy and concepts of operations developed by the PLA over the years 1978-1985.[3]

The "strategic shift" directed by the 1985 CMC meeting came shortly after Gorbachev became the general secretary of the Communist party of the Soviet Union (CPSU), but more than a year prior to his July 1986 speech in Vladivostok. Thus there is no connection between Gorbachev's implementation of a more conciliatory policy toward China and the change in China's threat perceptions. Far more relevant was Beijing's assessment that there had been a shift in the global balance of power over the years 1978-1985. By the early 1980s, Chinese journals specializing in international security affairs were concluding that the Reagan Administration's policies had not only created a shift in the military balance of power, but that there was a new American resolve to oppose Soviet expansionism. They further concluded that a military balance had been created in which the United States had an edge, but that the two superpowers essentially stalemated each other. The superpower stalemate would continue into the 1990s, and perhaps into the twenty-first century, thereby making a world war very unlikely.[4] This same shift in the global balance of power and the superpower stand-off would prevent the Soviet Union from attacking China.

Even as the Reagan Administration was strengthening U.S. military power and was viewed by Beijing as systematically opposing the predatory foreign policy objectives of the U.SS.R., Chinese analysts also saw the international system as undergoing a major change. The long-term dynamics of the international system were perceived as creating a condition in which both the U.S.S.R. and the United States would have decreased influence in the world. Both were viewed as being impoverished by their mutual competition. Their economic decline would reduce the political influence of

---

[2] The best analysis of this problem is found in A. Doak Barnett, *The Making of Foreign Policy in China: Structure and Process* (Boulder: Westview Press, 1985), especially pp. 96-102.

[3] See Paul H. B. Godwin, "Changing Concepts of Doctrine, Strategy and Operations in the Chinese People's Liberation Army 1978-1987," *The China Quarterly*, No. 112 (December 1987), pp. 578-581; and Ngok Lee, *China's Defense Modernisation and Military Leadership* (Sydney: Australian National University Press, 1989), pp. 146-174.

[4] Banning Garrett and Bonnie Glaser, "From Nixon to Reagan: China's Changing Role in American Strategy," in Kenneth A. Oye, Robert J. Lieber, and Donald Rothchild (eds.), *Eagle Resurgent? The Reagan Era in American Foreign Policy* (Boston: Little, Brown, 1986), p. 283.

both superpowers, while the rapidly growing economic strength of Europe, Japan, and a number of Third World economies would grant them greater independence from both Moscow and Washington. Growing military strength would accompany rising economic strength, thereby contributing to what Chinese analysts as early as 1983 saw as an emerging multipolar world.[5]

Multipolarity was not viewed as necessarily favorable to a tranquil international environment. Rather, whereas the balance of power between the United States and the Soviet Union would not permit either to launch a war against the other, thereby making a global war unlikely, the chances of local wars flaring up was increased by the growing military strength of local and regional powers. The most threatening aspect of the emerging global environment perceived by Chinese analysts was the increased probability of small-scale wars around China's periphery.[6]

The 1985 decision of the CCP Central Military Commission to shift the PLA's war preparation and training toward a primary focus on potential small-scale wars fits the pattern of global power evaluations and threat assessments presented by China's leading journals of international affairs for some years. Because independent research centers do not exist in China, it is reasonable to assume that these journals reflect basic strategic questions postulated at the highest levels of China's decision-making process. Further, when a consensus emerges in these journals, it can be assumed that such agreement reflects the general pattern of strategic analysis held by China's security policy elite.

The "normalization" of Sino-Soviet relations in May 1989, went far toward reducing Chinese perceptions of the Soviet threat even further. The progress made in Soviet force reductions in the Mongolian People's Republic was complemented by direct discussion with Moscow of confidence and security-building measures along the Sino-Soviet border.[7] Although not openly stated by Chinese analysts, the economic problems faced by the USSR and the reductions in Soviet defense spending would also reinforce their sense of confidence that the Soviet military threat was quickly dissipating.

Nonetheless, analyses of Soviet military strategy in January and March of 1990, while noting force reductions in Europe and Asia and the shift toward a defensive military doctrine announced by Gorbachev, adopted very cautious and conservative positions. They stressed that Soviet forces were in *transition* to a more defensive military doctrine and force structure and that, in the words of the official newspaper of the PLA, *Jiefangjun Bao* (Liberation army daily), "At the same time it must be made clear that the Soviet Army presently remains an offensive force; even if the change to a "defensive structure" is realized in the future, the Soviet Army will still carry tremendous potential of launching in-depth at-

---

[5] Xing Shugang, Li Yunhua, and Liu Yingna, "Soviet-American Balance of Power and Its Impact on the World Situation in the 1980s," *Guoji Wenti Yanjiu*, No. 1 (January 1983), in FBIS–CHI, No. 028 (21 April 1983), pp. A1–12.

[6] Zong He, "Changes and Developmental Trends in the International Situation," *Shijie Zhishi*, No. 11 (1 June 1983), in FBIS–CHI, No. 141 (21 July 1983), pp. A1–5.

[7] See the Agence France Presse (AFP) Hong Kong report, 27 January 1990, in FBIS-CHI, No. 124 (27 June 1990), p. 3; and Foreign Minister Shevardnadze's interview with A. Bovin on Moscow Television Service reported in FBIS-SOV, No. 180 (17 September 1990), pp. 13–14.

tacks." [8] Nor was such a cautious interpretation limited to military journals. *Shijie Zhishi* (World knowledge), a journal focused on issues of international politics and security studies, was similarly cautious about any near-term change in Soviet military strategy. While recognizing that Soviet forces were going to be cut by some 500,000 and that a reduction in strategic nuclear forces would occur, a January 1990 essay stressed that these reductions were balanced by the technological upgrading of Soviet weapons and equipment, including space systems. The author concluded that "the forward-deployed offensive posture of the Soviet Union has not been fundamentally changed." [9]

This cautious interpretation of changes in Soviet military capabilities and strategy brings into focus an important aspect of Chinese evaluations of their security environment. Whereas multipolarity is the predominant *trend* in the dynamics of the international system, the military strengths of the U.S.S.R. and the United States will continue to give them an important role in international politics for some time to come.[10] Furthermore, the security policies of the U.S.S.R. and the United States remain the most significant forces for change in the immediate future. Their current policies of dètente and dialogue with each other, although driven by their own internal weaknesses, are seen by Chinese analysts as the major contributor to the present international environment.

The security environment perceived by Chinese analysts for the 1990s is therefore one in which the trend toward multipolarity will continue as the influence of the U.S.S.R. and the United States continues to lessen. There is no world conflict threatening the international system, but in the words of the Chinese foreign minister, "the 1990s will witness fierce turbulence and recurring struggles in the general course of dètente and dialogue." [11] It is this turbulence and unpredictability that, for Chinese analysts, creates the possibility of conflict around China's periphery. The multipolar world perceived by China's analysts is created by the decreasing influence of the superpowers and the growing political, economic and military strength of regional powers. Thus there is within Chinese analyses, especially their military appraisals, growing sense of China's vulnerability within an increasingly unpredictable global security system.

II. DEFENSE POLICY AND MILITARY STRATEGY

With the CMC's new strategic guidance in 1985, Chinese military strategists were tasked with preparing the PLA primarily for small-scale limited conflict. While the U.S.S.R. remained the only state capable of launching a major war with China, the chances of such a conflict were minimal at best. The U.S.S.R.'s primary protaganist remained the United States, and the principal focus of this

---

[8] Wang Haiyun and Zhou Yi, "New Trends in Soviet Army's Theoretical Study of Combat," *Jiefangjun Bao*, 23 March 1990, in FBIS–CHI, No. 075 (18 April 1990), p. 9.
[9] Zhou Aiqun, "The Soviet Union Adjusts Its Military Strategy," *Shijie Zhishi*, No. 2 (16 January 1990), in JPRS–China Report, No. 037 (14 May 1990), p. 6.
[10] Wang Lin, "Looking Towards the 1990s," *Beijing Review*, No. 1 (1–7 January 1990), p.12.
[11] "Foreign Minister Qian Qichen Answers Questions Raised by *Shijie Zhishi* on Current International Situation on 20 December 1989," *Shijie Zhishi*, No. 1 (1 January 1990), in FBIS–CHI, No. 022 (1 February 1990), p. 2.

confrontation remained in Europe. With the superpowers militarily stalemating each other, and with the United States sustaining a military edge in Europe and the Pacific, the possibility of a major military confrontation with the Soviet Union was small. What China now faced as it looked to the future was the possibility of small wars erupting along its borders—including the remote possibility of a limited war with the Soviet Union. These wars required a distinctly different preparation from the principles of protraction and attrition that had dominated the armed forces' preparations for war with the U.S.S.R.

Chinese analysts view "local wars and limited wars" as a category of conflict circumscribed both in geographical scope and political objectives, but as a type of war that can vary widely in intensity and duration. They state that the purpose of military force when used in these wars is not to totally eliminate the adversary's capability and will to resist, but to "assert one's own standpoint and will through limited military action, . . This being the case, the further progression of modern limited warfare is mainly not decided through military action as such, but rather determined by the needs in the political and diplomatic struggle." [12] While recognizing that these kinds of wars can be quite lengthy in duration, such as the Korean war, the American war with Vietnam, and the Iran-Iraq war, the primary focus of Chinese military analyses has been on the operational requirements for localized wars of short duration.

Chinese military journals have designated five types of limited war to be of special importance:

1) Small-scale conflicts restricted to contested border territory.

2) Conflict over territorial seas and islands.

3) Surprise air attacks.

4) Defense against deliberately limited attacks into Chinese territory.

5. "Punitive counterattacks" launched by China into enemy territory to "oppose invasion, protect sovereignty, or to uphold justice and dispel threats." [13] The characteristics common to all of these scenarios are the limited political objective behind the use of military coercion and the requirement that the forces used be able to respond quickly to either defeat the presumed political purpose of the attack, or gain the political objective sought by the limited use of force.

Nonetheless, the new focus of the PLA's military training, both in the field and within China's centers of professional military education, did not exclude the Soviet Union. What changed was the nature of a potential conflict with the U.S.S.R., for the Soviet Union was included in the PLA's new concentration on local and limited wars that potentially endangered China's periphery. The

---

[12] Jiao Wu and Xiao Hui, "Modern Limited War Calls for Reform of Traditional Military Principles," *Guofang Daxue Xuebao*, No. 11 (1 November 1987), in JPRS–China, No. 037 (12 July 1988), p. 49.

[13] Jia Wenxian, Zheng Shouqi, Guo Weimin, and Long Zhuoqun," "Tentative Discussion of the Special Principles of a Future Chinese Limited War," *Guofang Daxue Xuebao*, No. 11 (11 November 1987), in JPRS–China, No. 37 (12 July 1988), p. 48, contains this particular categorization, but over the past three years a number of essays in a variety of journals have tended to focus on these types of potential conflicts.

kinds of conflicts most likely to be fought required a new look at defense policy and military strategy. As one essayist noted in 1986, preparation for a world war while neglecting local war "will lead to dangerous strategic planning and erroneous macro-policymaking." [14]

There is a strange ahistorical cast to Chinese analyses of limited, local war appearing in military journals over the years following the CMC's decision. Although most of the essays recognized the importance of the Korean war and China's 1979 incursion into Vietnam within their analyses of the different kinds of limited war and local conflicts that had occurred since the conclusion of World War II, they did not note that all of the conflicts fought by the Chinese armed forces since 1949 fall into this category. From the Korean war in 1950 to the March 1988 seizure of atolls in the Nansha (Spratly) Islands, Chinese armed forces have been used in precisely the kinds of confrontations the CMC concluded would be the most likely form of military conflict for the foreseeable future.

Since the summer of 1985, there has been a continuing series of exploratory essays analyzing the operational requirements of small-scale wars. Local wars and unanticipated military crises involving only limited political objectives require the swift and effective application of military force. This characteristic demanded a major reorientation of the armed forces' approach to military strategy and operations. As a *Liberation Army Daily* article defined the situation at the end of 1989, "the main task of our Army is to deal with sudden incidents or limited wars." [15]

Within this framework, the issue of a three-stage approach to campaigns, where the war is divided into defensive, stalemate, and counteroffensive stages or phases, has been questioned for local war in much the same manner as it was when Chinese military strategists were preparing for a major war with the Soviet Union. In essence, Chinese analysts now state that modern military technology grants an aggressor the capability to seize the initiative in the opening battles of the war—that the first battle will be of crucial importance in local wars. This means that mobilizing the entire country and people for war is no longer an appropriate policy.[16] The nature of contemporary and future warfare requires standing forces capable of quick and lethal response to crises involving the threat or application of military force. This operational need resulted in considerable discussion both of the weaknesses in China's military technology and the preparation of its armed forces for war.

LOCAL WAR AND THE MILITARY REGION

Preparation for local wars required the PLA to review its defense posture around the periphery of China and make an assessment of the most likely conflicts to be fought in each sector. Given the diversity of terrain, weather, and potential adversaries, different

[14] Zhang Qinsheng, Liang Hunan and Yan Xiaonin, " A Study of Local War Theory," *Liaowang* (Outlook—Overseas edition, Hong Kong), No. 37 (15 September 1986), in FBIS-CHI, No. 183 (23 September 1986), p.K5.

[15] Chen Yutian, "Pay Attention to Forecasts of 'Small Wars,' " *Jiefangjun Bao*, 29 December 1989, in JPRS–China, No.011 (12 February 1990), p. 65.

[16] Ibid.

border regions were faced with distinctly different operational requirements. This led to the conclusion that each of China's seven military regions (MR) should conduct independent training and field exercises for local war.[17] The concept of "war zone" was introduced, with the observation that "war zone independent campaign operations will probably be the most frequently seen mode of action in the Army's campaign operations for some time to come."[18]

1988 saw four major regional exercises conducted under the direction of their MR commanders. These exercises were designed to test the extent to which the previous three years of preparation had developed new capabilities within the armed forces to respond to the changing nature of warfare. Three of the exercises focused on the U.S.S.R. as the potential adversary: West–88, conducted by the Lanzhou Military Region in northwestern China; Yanhang–88, conducted by the Beijing MR in northern China; and Qianjin–88, conducted by the Shenyang MR in the northeast. Guangzi–15, conducted by the Guangzhou Military Region in the South China Sea, where the postulated enemy had to be Vietnam, rounded out exercises.[19] The only potential adversaries not faced in these campaign-level maneuvers were India and Taiwan, and there has been no reporting of exercises on the Sino-Indian border or near Taiwan equivalent to those directed at the U.S.S.R. and Vietnam.

The capabilities tested were primarily rapid deployment and combined arms operations responding to "border clashes, accidents, and local warfare."[20] Equally important, however, was the principle that the exercises should test theater operations fought by individual military region commanders as independent campaigns. In each of these exercises, the MR commander was clearly defined as being responsible for the campaign and, presumably, the concept of operations behind the campaign.[21] The three exercises directed against a Soviet attack focused on the ability of the Chinese armed forces to respond quickly to a "blitzkrieg" assault. There was no reference to a massive mobilization of the society at large. They were not exercises designed to test the PLA's ability to conduct a prolonged defensive war, but rather campaigns built around combined arms warfare to disrupt and eject Soviet forces as early in the confrontation as possible. The exercises reflected Beijing's concern that a Soviet attack on China could be conducted for immediate political objectives rather than a war to subdue and conquer China itself. For example, when China attacked Vietnam in 1979, the U.S.S.R. could have considered a limited assault on the PRC to force Beijing to back down from the invasion and withdraw its forces from Vietnam.

The importance of these exercises was demonstrated by the presence of the Chief of the General Staff, General Chi Haotian, and the President of the PLA National Defense University (PLA/NDU),

[17] Zhao Tianxiang, "Militia Reform and the Strategy of Theater Development," *Jiefangjun Bao*, 10 June 1988, in JPRS–China Report, No. 069 (4 November 1988), pp.29–30.
[18] Xu Jingyao, "1988: A Year of Reform for the Chinese Army," *Liaowang* (Overseas edition, Hong Kong)No. 3 (16 January 1989), in FBIS-CHI, No. 014 (24 January 1989), p.36.
[19] Ibid., p. 37.
[20] Ibid., p.36.
[21] Beijing Domestic Service, 14 October 1988, in FBIS–CHI, No.202 (19 October 1988), p.29.

General Zhang Zhen, as observers in the West–88 exercise.[22] The PLA/NDU is deeply involved in preparing analytic studies of the requirements for small wars, and its students at the Group Army and military region command-levels have undertaken courses and analytic studies of local war requirements. These ideas are tested in field and command post exercises undertaken when the officers return to their MR commands.

Guangzi–15, conducted by the Guangzhou MR in the South China Sea, was designed to test the PLA's ability in both coastal defense and the protection of China's territory in the South China Sea. It was a combined arms campaign like those in the north, but was rendered more complex by the need to coordinate land, air, and naval forces, including the naval air arm, in a force projection exercise. It should be noted that the PLA's brigade-sized Marine Corps is deployed in the Guangzhou MR on the island of Hainan, where it is trained specifically for force projection into the South China sea. Once again, the importance of this exercise can be seen in the presence of Lieutenant General Han Huaizhi, a deputy chief of the General Staff Department (GSD), together with representatives of the GSD Training Department and observers from the PLA/NDU and the PLA's Academy of Military Science (AMS).[23]

The exercises all referred to the use of "special forces" as an integral part of the campaigns. Such forces are quite new and have played a prominent role in Chinese analyses of local war requirements. The size of these units is not known, but they are probably small, well-trained combat forces. They are trained to fulfill four major functions in a campaign: as "door openers" striking at critical targets and widening a breach in the enemy's position; as a "scalpel" to strike at targets that, when destroyed, will paralyze the adversary's combat potential; as "steel hammers" to seize crucial enemy positions; and as "boosters" to speed up the tempo of a campaign by opening up new battle areas within the invaded area.[24]

Forces with these roles are often referred to as "fist" (quantou) units and have been the focus of considerable discussion in Chinese military journals over the past five years. Air-mobile forces are one focus of Chinese interest, and units of the airborne forces of the PLA have been selected for training as "fist" units and "rapid response units" capable of being deployed anywhere in China within 12 hours.[25] Each military region has been reporting the development of "fist units" and rapid deployment forces designed to fit its own local situation and potential adversary. The PLA Marine Corps has received considerable publicity in these reports. Originally founded in 1953 but disbanded in 1957, the Marine Corps was reestablished on 5 May 1980 as the "fifth arm of the Navy." Headquartered at Zhanjiang, Guangdong—the fleet headquarters of the

---

[22] Ibid.

[23] Zhu Dacheng and He Delai, "Guangzhou Military Region Organizes Land, Naval, and Air Force Commanders and Organs to Stage a Joint Exercise," *Jiefangjun Bao*, 8 November 1988; in FBIS–CHI, No. 227 (25 November 1988), p.37.

[24] Li Qianyuan, "A Cursory Analysis of the Characteristics of Limited War of the Future," *Jiefangjun Bao*, 19 December 1986, in JPRS–China, No. 048 (23 September 1987), p.91.

[25] Tan Jun and Hong Heping, "A 'Fist Battalion' of a Certain PLA Airborne Unit," *Jiefangjun Bao*, 14 June 1988, in JPRS–China, No. 045 (9 August 1988), pp.59–60.

South Sea Fleet—the Marines have received special attention as China's amphibious force capable of "sudden landings." [26] Their deployment with the South Sea Fleet and Chinese analyses of the Marines' role in local war clearly identifies them as the "fist" unit for operations in the South China Sea.

COMMAND AND CONTROL IN SMALL-SCALE WARS

Force projection in small-scale wars raised questions about the distinction that Chinese military thought makes between strategy, campaign, and tactics and their implication for command and control during small-scale wars. Normally, these three levels of the military art are viewed as having distinct borderlines. Small wars, some Chinese analysts suggest, blur this traditional distinction as the significance of tactical actions increases. Whereas in major wars tactical actions will have little influence on the "overall war situation," in small wars, tactical actions may achieve strategic objectives. Furthermore, the objective, location, and timing of an action or strike can be so significant that even tactical actions will require a decision by the highest level of command, including the head of state. Thus, those in charge of the strategy for a local war campaign may well have to pass over all intermediate levels of command and communicate directly with the tactical units. [27]

These analysts see three potential command patterns for localized conflicts. In the first, the campaign commander recognizes that on occasion he will be bypassed and therefore accepts the combat order given directly to a subordinate commander and does not interfere with the action itself. In the second, the strategic-level command authority is also in operational command and communicates directly with tactical units. In the third, an independent command is created with specific restrictions placed on the commander's freedom of action.

Within this third pattern of command, the commander can act independently of higher authority. The military objective, forces to be used, geographical constraints, and time of the attack would be strictly delineated, but, within these restrictions, the field commander could act independently without the need to report or request instructions through the chain of command. Chinese analysts note that this type of authority was given to Rear Admiral Woodward as commander of the British task force in the Malvinas (Falklands) campaign. They also note that similar restrictions had been placed on General MacArthur, but when he demonstrated intent to overstep the constraints placed upon his authority, President Truman relieved General MacArthur of his command. [28]

This analysis raised an important issue, for the emphasis in the 1988 exercises was on campaigns fought within a military region under the direction of the MR commander. Yet the logic of small wars, where political objectives are as limited as the conflicts' geographic scope, could result in reducing the campaign commander's freedom of action. The central authorities controlling the political

---

[26] Deng Huaxu and Li Daoming, "A visit to the PLA Marine Corps," *Renmin Ribao* (People's Daily), Overseas Edition, 2 August 1988, in FBIS-CHI, No. 149 (3 August 1988), pp.30–31.
[27] Jiao Wu and Xiao Hui, "Modern Limited War" pp.50–51.
[28] Ibid.

strategy directing the campaign may also be required by the logic of the situation to assume command, or at least direction, of tactical actions because they can have a profound effect on the outcome of the war.[29] By raising the examples of General MacArthur and Rear Admiral Woodward, the analysts were looking at one of the most significant questions raised by small wars—what limits need be placed on a field commander's freedom of action in order to ensure that the combat operations of a campaign do not undermine the political objectives of the war itself?

Ultimately, of course, this question and most others dealing with command and control in small wars is dependent on the specific setting and objectives of the conflict. Although Chinese analysts agree on the principal characteristics of small wars, they are still investigating the diversity of issues raised by these confrontations.

Chief of Staff Chi Haotian stated the underlying principle of the PLA's approach to local war in a commentary on the 1988 exercises: "Our country has a vast territory and the conditions vary in different parts of the country. Instead of indiscriminate imitation, all Army units should conduct their studies in the light of their different conditions.This should be the basic starting point in our study of local war." [30]The occasion of this speech was a meeting with officers who had participated in the West–88 exercises in northwest China. Each of China's military regions faces different conditions under which it has to conduct operations, even if, as in the case of three MRs facing the U.S.S.R., the potential adversary is the same. Thus the character and operational demands of the campaigns will vary, the force structures employed in combat will differ, "fist" units and other special forces will range in their size and composition, and the intensity of the combat also will vary. This being the case, there can be no common mold directing each MR commander's preparations. Each MR, seen as a potential theater of operations, will develop its own campaign plans in view of its own unique conditions.

Despite this diversity, however, one problem was common among all campaigns. The operational demands of local wars raised once again the difficulties created by the armed forces' backward military technology.

III. MILITARY TECHNOLOGY AND SMALL-SCALE WARS: THE PLA'S CONTINUING DILEMMA

Chinese analyses of the requirements for small-scale wars and unanticipated military crises have paid close attention to the need for a quick, lethal response by China's armed forces. Even if military force is not applied, a credible capacity to quickly respond to a crisis must be available if China is to maintain an effective deterrent posture at this level of warfare. Current levels of Chinese military technology severely limit both the mobility and lethality of the PLA.

---

[29] Liu Zhiwei, "A General Forecast of the War Patterns in the 1990s," *Jiefangjun Bao*, 9 February 1990, in FBIS–CHI, No. 041 (1 March 1990), p.34.
[30] Chi Haotian, "Meet the Needs of Military Struggle in the New Period, Constantly Increase the Defense and Combat Capacity of Our Army," *Jiefangjun Bao*, 16 October 1988, in FBIS–CHI, No. 211 (1 November 1988), p. 26.

An example of the quick response tactic, Chinese analysts believe, was the Israeli invasion of Lebanon which was deliberately launched when the eyes of the world were focussed on the war in the Falkland islands. Beirut was under siege in three days, and the operation was completed in five days. In the minds of these analysts, the effect was a *fait accompli* before world opinion had been formed.[31]

The operational requirements for small-scale wars identified by the PLA place great emphasis on the need for mobility and lethality, and for command, control, communications, and intelligence (C3I) capabilities to direct swiftly moving combined arms combat integrating air, land, and naval forces. The PLA's weaknesses in these areas are readily recognized by Chinese analysts, who state that "divorced from advanced military science and technology, we cannot possibly build an army capable of stopping and winning a modern war."[32]

Nonetheless, and despite continual reporting in the Chinese press and journals of the extent to which the PLA is modernizing its combat aircraft, naval combat vessels, armored fighting vehicles, antitank/antiair/antiship missiles, and developing computer-based command and control systems, Chinese equipment is not on a par with advanced Western systems—it may not even be close. Even with the force reduction by 1 million undertaken since 1985, the Chinese armed forces themselves remain very large—perhaps some 3.2 million, with the ground forces accounting for 2.3 million.[33] Added to this are 9,000 main battle tanks (MBT), 2,800 armored personnel carriers (APC), some 7000 fixed-wing combat aircraft (including naval aircraft), 115 submarines (including 1 SSBN and 3 SSNs), and 53 destroyers and frigates as the major naval surface combatants, this is a very large force to bring up to advanced Western standards. Indeed, the task is too large and too expensive to be completed in a short period of time. Once again, this is something the Chinese readily admit and discuss quite openly.

The approach taken by China in recent years has been to modernize selectively. The leadership has chosen to upgrade key units. It appears that the "fist" units, which come in various types and sizes according to the military regions' operational requirements, are those where the most modern equipment is introduced and tested in field exercises.[34] This, the Chinese note, is the practice followed by advanced military forces in the West.[35] While undoubtedly the most sensible way to introduce new weapons and equipment into the armed forces, it will not result in a "modernized"

[31] Zhang Taiheng, "Local Conflicts and Special Forces," *Jiefangjun Bao*, 14 March 1986, in JPRS–China, No. 055 (3 November 1987), p. 37.

[32] Wang Chenghan, "On Coordinated Development of National Defense and the Economy," *Hong Qi* (Red Flag), No. 17 (1 September 1987), in JPRS–China, No. 11 (7 December 1987), p. 18. This essay in what was until 1989 the Communist party's theoretical journal is but one of many over the past decade stressing that the need to modernize the PLA's military equipment in coordination with its modernization of strategy and operations requires greater defense outlays than Beijing is willing to provide.

[33] These figures and the others used in this section are taken from *The Military Balancen 1988–1989* (London: The International Institute for Strategic Studies, fall 1989).

[34] He Chong, "Let Some Units Modernize First," *Jiefangjun Bao*, 6 November 1987, in JPRS–China, No. 006 (19 February 1988), pp. 85–86.

[35] Dongfang Tie, "What Can We Learn From Other Countries' Practice of Strengthening Key Troops," *Jiefangjun Bao*, 19 March 1988, in FBIS–CHI, No. 66 (6 April 1988), p. 39.

PLA except over a very long period of time. But, as Chinese analysts observe, with the sole exception of the U.S.S.R., the most likely sources of local war around the Chinese periphery do not involve countries whose forces have the capability to fight high-technology warfare in same capacity as the major Western powers.[36] Needless to say, this condition does not satisfy the Chinese military leadership, who continue to press for larger military budgets and the acquisition of advanced military technology. The operational requirements of local wars provide yet another arrow in their quiver of defense budget demands.[37]

IV. LOCAL WAR AND TOTAL WAR: LINKAGES ACROSS THE SPECTRUM OF CONFLICT

Chinese analysts insist that if China wishes to contain a local war within the parameters set by its limited political objectives, the PLA must also have the capability to deter and fight a major war. In presenting this argument, these analysts note that major foreign military powers prepare for major war, small-scale wars, and unexpected crises ("random eventualities") as part of their preparation for all levels of warfare.

Preparation for "total" war is seen as performing two functions: it serves as a deterrent and prepares the armed forces for such a war should it occur. Preparation for a major conflict also complements readiness for small-scale wars. The conclusion drawn by Chinese military authorities is that while their forces must now prepare for the entire range of possible military conflict, the current international situation requires them to place greatest importance on preparing for small-scale wars and unanticipated crises. The PLA must therefore follow the principle of "walking on two legs" in its operational training.[38] Thus, even though the CMC's strategic guidance for the PLA's operational and tactical training over the past five years placed preeminent emphasis on preparation for local war, the armed forces have also sustained a focus on general and nuclear war.

NUCLEAR WEAPONS AND LOCAL WAR

A 1987 *Liberation Army Daily* essay stated that China's strategy for national defense in the twenty-first century "should be based on fighting major wars and fighting nuclear wars." [39] China's focus on major war prior to 1985 was deemed of critical importance because these preparations had prevented a major war and minimized the potential scale of such a war had it broken out. The author concludes that if China had focused only on preparations for limited and small-scale wars, then a major war could well have occurred. To be confident that future wars can be limited, preparation for large-scale and nuclear wars must continue.[40]

---

[36] Jia Wenxian et. al., "Tentative Discussion of the Special Principles," p. 48.

[37] Zhang Taiheng, "Local War, and Development of Weapons and Equipment," *Jiefangjun Bao*, 1 June 1990, in FBIS–CHI, No. 116 (15 June 1990), pp. 26–227.

[38] Wang Chengbin, "Changes in Strategy and Deepening the Reform in Training," *Jiefangjun Bao*, 6 February 1987, in FBIS–CHI, No. 40 (2 March 1987), pp. K32–35.

[39] Zhang Jian, "It Is Still Necessary to Base Our Plans On Fighting a Major War," *Jiefangjun Bao*, 24 April 1987, in FBIS–CHI, No. 085 (4 May 1987), p. A2.

[40] Ibid.

This and other essays sought to establish linkages across the spectrum of conflict, with close attention to the role of nuclear weapons deployed by "medium" nuclear powers, such as Britain and France. It was asserted that at the root of any strategy pursued by a medium nuclear power is the understanding that their nuclear weapons free them from manipulation by the superpowers, thereby permitting them to play their role preferred in world affairs.[41] In particular, and in what may have been a reference to Vietnam, the argument was that in border conflicts or small wars where lesser nations act as agents for great powers, the nuclear retaliatory capability of medium-sized powers can perhaps prevent the interference of great powers.[42]

This approach to nuclear weapons and deterrence as they affect small wars is not new; observing that nuclear weapons make the world safe for small wars is a common, and seemingly accurate, position. To return to the four major exercises of 1988, the 2nd Artillery Corps—China's "Strategic Rocket Forces"—was a participant,[43] but no specific discussion of its roles and missions was provided. On the other hand, the Chinese armed forces have conducted exercises involving simulated battlefield nuclear weapons, and the East Sea Fleet conducted widely reported exercises in which they were required to operate in a nuclear environment.[44] Essays in *Liberation Army Daily* over the past five years have raised the issue of limited nuclear war and the role of nuclear weapons in offsetting weaknesses in conventional capabilities. Moreover, one author suggested that improvements in accuracy and the reduced explosive power of nuclear warheads has increased the possibility of their use in theater warfare.[45]

Citing a Brookings Institution study, *Liberation Army Daily* took note of the study's conclusion that in the 215 incidents involving American forces since World War II, the use of nuclear weapons was considered in at least 33 cases. Although nuclear weapons were not used, the author contends that China is surrounded by a "complicated environment, with more and more nations and regions possessing nuclear weapons in particular." As China prepares for conventional local wars, it must also develop measures for dealing with limited nuclear wars.[46]

Perhaps reflecting these concerns, China's missile forces have conducted exercises in which they prepared for "nuclear counterattack operations" during maneuvers designed primarily to test conventional war capabilities. Presumably, the responsibility of the 2nd Artillery Corps in the 1988 exercises was to be operationally prepared to launch a quick response to any use of nuclear weapons by the adversary—the PRC's stated doctrine and policy for the use

---

[41] Zhang Jianzhi, "Views On Medium-Sized Nuclear Powers' Nuclear Strategy," *Jiefangjun Bao*, 20 March 1987, in FBIS–CHI, No.062 (1 April 1987), p.K29.

[42] Ibid., p. K31.

[43] Xu Jingyao, "A Year of Reform," p. 36.

[44] (n.a.), "PLA Navy Carries Out Multi-Arms Defensive Exercise Under Conditions of Nuclear Warfare," *Jiefangjun Bao*, 19 July 1988, in FBIS–CHI, No. 144 (27 July 1988), pp.1819; and Wu Xuelin and Cao Guoqiang, "Naval Base Conducts Defensive Exercise Under Conditions of Nuclear War," *Renmin Ribao*, 2 July 1988, in FBIS–CHI, No. 128 (5 July 1988), p.47.

[45] Zhai Zhigang and Guo Yuqian, "We Should Not Overlook the Threat of Limited Nuclear War," *Jiefangjun Bao*, 11 September 1987, in FBIS–CHI, No. 186 (25 September 1987), p. 22.

[46] Ibid.

of nuclear forces. Beyond the stated policy, such exercises would also fit Chinese military analysts' evaluation of the PRC's nuclear strategy. These analysts view China's nuclear forces as preventing a major power from threatening the People's Republic with nuclear war in order to deter Beijing from the course of action it had chosen. In this manner, nuclear weapons doctrine, strategy, and operations are brought together by theater-based campaign exercises in which conventional war fought for limited political objectives is the central focus.

V. Conclusions: Chinese Defense Policy in the 1990 s

Chinese military analysts believe that a successful defense policy and military strategy for China requires competence at all levels of warfare. In their view, success in small wars requires the ability to prevail in major conflicts, including those involving nuclear arms for deterrence and nuclear combat. With the normalization of Sino-Soviet relations in May, 1989, and the discussions of confidence and security building measures between Moscow and Beijing over the past year, China's defense problems are significantly reduced from what they were only five years ago. The military threat from the USSR is now minimal even though Chinese military analysts remain cautious in their interpretation of Soviet military capabilities. Thus emphasis on a defense policy placing primary importance on small-scale ware was prescient.

Nonetheless, a defense policy that places greatest importance on a military strategy focussed on China's periphery will do little to ease the apprehension of China's neighbors as they evaluate Beijing's growing military capabilities. This apprehension may be reduced for the near-term by the recognition that currently internal security requirements divide both the PLA's attention and funding. They will have noticed that elite "fist" units from several of China's military regions were among the forces used to bring order to the streets of Beijing. Over the longer term, however, if the present orientation toward defense policy and military strategy continues, including the role of nuclear weapons, the PLA's demands for more advanced technology to support the military operations required to implement China's military strategy will only serve to exacerbate the foreboding felt within the PRC's neighboring states. Although China insists that its military doctrine and strategy are defensive, the concepts of operations formed around the new paradigm of war are equally applicable to offensive force employment. Given the PLA's currently limited force projection capabilities, extended operations outside China are simply not plausible. For the longer term, however, the uneasiness of China's smaller neighbors will likely remain.

CHINESE MILITARY CAPABILITIES: PROBLEMS AND PROSPECTS

By Robert J. Skebo, Gregory K.S. Man, and George H. Stevens *

CONTENTS

BACKGROUND

During the last ten years, the combat capability of the People's Liberation Army (PLA), despite a broad-ranging modernization plan, has steadily declined. The Chinese military is falling behind rather than closing the gap on its principal threat, the Soviets. Indeed, even smaller regional neighbors are surpassing China's military technology base and deploying more sophisticated weaponry such as F–16s in Indonesia, Pakistan, Thailand and Singapore and K–1 tanks in South Korea.

The PLA began to modernize in the mid-1970s. Later, the lesson taught by the Vietnamese in 1979 provided impetus for expanded efforts. Eventually, in the mid-1980s, the leadership launched a systematic modernization program it hoped would produce a modern force capable of combined arms operations, with enhanced ground, naval and air strengths. However, because there was not enough money for large-scale deployment of modern weapons, Beijing adopted a two-track, interim approach involving reducing the size of the force, streamlining PLA organization, and improving training while simultaneously upgrading and fielding certain critical systems such as tanks, artillery, aircraft avionics, and command and control systems.

---

* This paper, originally presented at the First Annual Staunton Hall China Conference, September 14–16, 1990, was prepared by Major Robert J. Skebo (U.S. Air Force), Major Gregory K.S. Man (U.S. Army), and Major George H. Stevens (U.S. Army Reserve). The comments and analysis do not necessarily reflect the views of the Defense Intelligence Agency or the Department of Defense.

After eleven years, and a world-wide search for weapons, technology, training, and assistance, there has been some progress. The size of the PLA has been reduced by over 1 million troops, its organization has become more efficient, and development of new weapons continues. However, the PLA is not well equipped, either to deal with the Soviet threat or to implement its new doctrine for prosecuting so called local wars of limited duration.

This evolving doctrine of "local wars" will only supplement the flexible, older, Maoist principle of "People's War Under Modern Conditions." People's War doctrine envisioned swift and mobile guerrilla harassment of an aggressor's over-extended supply line (and which therefore has severe limitations against an enemy with limited territorial objectives). This active and total defense strategy is based on the PRC's strengths of geography, manpower, organization, and size. It is a total war concept in which the entire population plays a role.

Local Wars doctrine, on the other hand, emphasizes rapid reaction, limited conflict, flexible response, preemptive action, and limited power projection to China's "strategic boundaries." The idea of power projection is a critical point in the doctrine of "local wars" since it implies that China wishes to operate beyond the nation's geographic borders. The Navy, in particular, will focus on the capability to defend territory within expanded operational areas that may reach to the limits of China's coastal seas.

II. OBSTACLES IN THE WAY OF MODERNIZATION

While Chinese military doctrine is changing, a number of obstacles stand in the way of achieving the capabilities to implement it. These problems fall into three basic, interrelated categories: economics, technological capabilities and political-social.

China's interim objective seems to be to upgrade its current generation of weapons, based mostly on Soviet designs, and to improve them with newer, primarily western subsystems. This is a difficult task, on which progress so far has been uneven (although impressive by lesser developed countries' standards). Much of China's effort appears directed at the export market rather than immediate domestic application so that Beijing can earn the foreign currency necessary to support its own research and development programs. Although the PLA has deployed limited quantities of newly developed equipment to demonstrate its effectiveness to potential buyers (like the A–5M FANTAN aircraft), there is no evidence suggesting plans for comprehensive replacement of any major category of equipment. This will not occur until well after the turn of the century because of China's overall domestic economic problems, its technological backwardness, and the tentativeness of the political climate.

A. ECONOMIC CONSTRAINTS

Beijing realizes that economic constraints rule out any attempt to rapidly replace all of the PLA's largely obsolete equipment. Given the size of the force the cost even of maintaining present capability constitutes a severe economic burden. An article in *JingJi YanJiu* (*Economic Research*), Sep. 1990, states that the recent, total published defense spending has remained at about 6-8 percent of GNP and that the upper ceiling for defense economic spending for the period 1985–2000 for China will be limited to roughly 5-8 percent of GNP. The defense budget appropriation increased by 5.22 billion yuan or about 30 percent during the 10 year period 1980–1989. However, during this period the official inflation rate rose 98.9 percent meaning that by 1989, the PLA actually had 50 percent less negotiable funds to operate with. In addition, official inflation rates are thought to reflect about half the real inflation in China. For example, actual inflation in China during 1989 was estimated to be about 33 percent, although the government's announced inflation was 17.8 percent.

Budgetary constraints have obvious impact on PLA operations and acquisitions. For example, the army is forced to devote a greater share of its total funds to the daily support of its deployed forces. As Major General Wan Qikan, President of the Academy of Military Economics in Wuhan, stated (in an interview published in *Renmin Ribao* of 29 June 1990) "as the rate of increase in military spending has been lower than that of price increases in recent years, to maintain the stability of the army, we had to increase the proportion of living costs in national defense spending and relevantly cut the proportion of purchases and maintenance of weapons. The decrease in spending and increase in prices means a drop in purchase power by a wide margin."

Also, the shortage of funds has forced the PLA to concentrate on building a foundation for weapons development rather than weapons production, and indeed Chinese research and development facilities can design and build some state of the art prototypes. However, defense industries cannot afford to make the facilities improvements that will make it possible to produce the prototypes in adequate quantities. China's progress in this regard was probably set back by the restrictions Western nations and Japan placed on military and financial transactions with Beijing in June 1989.

In order to help compensate for these shortfalls, the PLA itself is forced to generate about one-third of its funds. Under the policy of "self-subsidy and self-development," some PLA units sell civilian services and food staples and approximately one-half of PLA controlled factories produce consumer goods. The army also is a major player in the international arms market. However, it is not likely that these activities will solve the problem.

B. TECHNOLOGICAL CAPABILITIES

A *Jiefangjun Bao* (*PLA Daily*) 1 June 1990 article warns of the danger of war in China's remote border regions and that the PLA's weaponry "... cannot meet the needs of fighting in cold, hot, or jungle areas. When they reach 4,000 meters (13,125 ft) then weak points emerge." Later the article states that ..."to deal with local war the PLA needs to introduce technology and purchase patent rights from abroad and put more resources into China's own weapons programs." Finally it states, "we should fully realize that developing efficient military equipment is an important link in improving our army's combat effectiveness."

PLA leaders acknowledge that equipment obsolescence is probably the most serious long-term constraint on capabilities. Most of China's large conventional defense industry was established with Soviet help and along Soviet lines in the 1950s, and has developed little since the break with the Soviet Union in the 1960s. Dated Soviet designs, management methods, and production techniques are still in use. Workers lack state of the art skills, production is poorly integrated with research and development, and Beijing does not yet have broad access to advanced Western engineering and design methods. In short, China's defense industrial complex is simply not capable of the precision work necessary to produce new, modern weapon systems.

Chinese leaders acknowledge that these problems can only be overcome gradually. They further recognize their best chance lies in a policy that seeks limited and selective improvements in areas of greatest weakness, emphasizing self-reliance and economy. This less costly 'substitution value' road to modernization has as its basis getting better use out of what the PLA currently has in its inventory and in its technology base. The difficulties with this approach are illustrated by Beijing's experience with upgrading its F–8 fighter aircraft.

The F–8 was deployed in the early 1980s after a development program that lasted from 1964–1979. However, even after deployment the Air Force was not satisfied and sought to upgrade its capabilities in a new version to be called the F–8-II. The two basic areas for upgrade were the avionics and the engine. The F-8-II completed flight testing in 1987, but since the Air Force specifications were still not met, the Ministry of Aviation Industry and the Air Force decided to approach the U.S. government to upgrade the aircraft's fire control system at a cost of $500 million USD. Despite a promising beginning, and the expenditure of more than $200 million the program came to an end in May 1990 because of cost overruns, unforeseen technical problems, and schedule interruptions. The F-8-II program remains stalled in the development phase. After 26 years of work there are only a limited number of aircraft in the inventory, and none meets the operational requirements of the Air Force.

C. POLITICAL AND SOCIAL IMPEDIMENTS TO MILITARY MODERNIZATION

Since the founding of the PLA there has been an ongoing debate over the proper mix of political vs professional training. To date, there is no sign that a resolution of the tension is in sight.

Before the Tiananmen demonstrations, political training had virtually become the handmaiden of military training. However, since June 1989, up to 50 percent of all PLA training time is now focused on politics and ideology. A 17 June 1990 *JFJB* editorial on the three revised PLA regulations (Internal Management, Discipline, and Formation Drill) which were promoted and signed by the Chairman of the Central Military Commission (CMC), Jiang Zemin, on 16 June 1990, states that "the new regulations stress the party's absolute leadership over the army and the principle of strengthening the army politically." A 28 June 1990 *SCMP* article states that this call for military unity came directly from Deng Xiaoping during a late May informal meeting with the CMC. Deng is quoted as saying that "... the unity of the army is the lifeline of the republic. If the army is unified, it signals that the entire country is stable."

A 6 March 1990 *Ming Pao* report based on a Xinhua Wenzai article titled "General Trends," gives a different point of view and highlights some of the serious problems in today's PLA. Twenty PLA generals at group army (GA), military district (MD) political commissar (PC), and military region (MR) deputy commander levels strongly criticized unspecified leaders who were obstructing military reforms. In addition, these generals were worried about the decrease in PLA combat effectiveness.

Major General Chen Xianhua, former GA Commander and now Chief of Staff (COS) for Guangzhou MR, in a comparison of Chinese and Pakistani military training, said the PLA's training "is like middle school students attending a sports class." In an effort to solve the training problems, the leadership unveiled a new training regulation in July 1990. Initial impressions are that it is the most comprehensive and specific to date. It outlines specific individual, combined arms, and operational training. The regulation is designed to promote military-wide standardization, which has been lacking in the past. Furthermore, the regulation establishes strict standards for evaluating unit progress in training and prescribes detailed methods for higher headquarters to test subordinate units. Only time will tell if this new training program bears fruit. However, the competition imposed by required political indoctrination is certain to subvert its effectiveness.

Corruption is also a problem. In the same article Major General Ma Chunma, Political Commissar of Heilongjiang MD, points out that he can "punish corrupt officials (officers) but cannot change the practice of seeking personal gain by abusing power or officials harboring them." With increased contacts with non-Chinese manufacturers and agents and as the guarantor of party supremacy, the PLA has become fertile ground for corruption, influence peddling, and nepotism. Accordingly professional standards and orientations are degraded, military resources are diverted to other quarters, and overall capabilities decline.

A final point concerns the quality of PLA recruits. In the same March 6th report, Major General Li Guangxiang (no position given) states that the PLA is "backward in terms of professionalism, psychology, and social quality." He asks, "where is the first grade combat capability? The combat capability will not come from the annual recruiting effort." Even before Tiananmen the prestige and opportunities for advancement gained by joining the military were evaporating. A 29 April 1989 China Daily summary of a *China Youth News* article highlights the unsatisfactory physical and educational levels of PLA recruits. Quotas are not being met, urban recruits bring increased disciplinary problems. Because they lack educational background, rural recruits require additional basic education to prepare them for basic military instruction. The PLA is not attracting the high-calibre recruits necessary to use modern weapons and equipment.

III. CURRENT AND FUTURE CAPABILITIES

Having discussed some of the pitfalls facing today's PLA let us now consider China's military capabilities. A review of the PLA's numbers, developments, capabilities, and future prospects for each service is given below.

A. NUCLEAR FORCES:

Since its initial nuclear explosion in 1964, China has gradually deployed modest but survivable nuclear forces in order to deter both nuclear attack and coercive threat from external nuclear or conventional forces. Beijing takes great pride in having broken the U.S. - Soviet nuclear monopoly and it has developed autonomous nuclear forces that allow it to pursue an independent foreign policy in its own national interest. Chinese nuclear forces are roughly on a par with those of France; Beijing has neither the resources nor the desire to become a nuclear superpower and is content to maintain relatively small but credible deterrent forces. China has pledged never to initiate the use of nuclear weapons; its strategy is to ride out an initial strike and then retaliate with surviving nuclear assets. The credibility of China's nuclear deterrent is based on:

—survivability, which derives from the transportability of intermediate-range launchers,
—hardening and concealment of intercontinental silos and deployment within rugged terrain—thus complicating preemptive targeting,
—a periodic rotation of mobile launch units between hardened underground facilities and austere launch pads,
—varied modes of air, land and sea-based deployment,
—and from camouflage, deception and uncertainty.

China's initial land-based ballistic missile systems were of limited range and used non-storable propellants. The DF-1/SS-2 (*Dongfeng* or East Wind) and CSS-1 short and medium range ballistic missiles (SRBM/MRBMs) had ranges of 600 and 1200 km, used non-storable propellants, and carried small fission warheads with a yield of about 15 kilotons. By about 1969 Beijing developed the more reliable CSS-2 intermediate-range ballistic missile (IRBM), which used storable, more stable propellants and could deliver a 1-3 Megaton thermonuclear warhead over a distance of some 3,000 km. By adding a second stage to the CSS-2, Beijing achieved the CSS-3, an intercontinental ballistic missile (ICBM) with a limited range of some 7,000 km which was used to launch China's first two satellites in 1970-71. Still heavier satellites were launched by a new booster after 1975; known as the CSS-4, this ICBM was launched over a distance of approximately 10,000 km into the Pacific in 1980; it can probably strike targets throughout the U.S.

The SS-2 SRBM and CSS-1 MRBM are now retired to parks and museums in Beijing. The mobile CSS-2 IRBM is still widely deployed and is the backbone of China's survivable deterrent. Beijing probably has over 100 CSS-2 IRBMs for four to five dozen CSS-2 launchers, although recent sales of the system to Saudi Arabia may have slightly reduced this force. China probably has less than 30 ICBMs. Chinese publications indicate that the CSS-3 is transportable and is launched from both silos and launch pads. The much larger CSS-4 is probably confined to silos. Although the CSS-4 originally carried a 4-5 Megaton warhead, Beijing now has the technology to multiply the effectiveness of its limited number of ICBMs by reequipping the CSS-4 with 3-4 multiple independently-targetable reentry vehicles (MIRVs). Refire missiles probably are available for CSS-3 launchers, but not for hot-launch CSS-4 ICBM silos.

In addition to its land-based ballistic missile forces, China also has a small stock of nuclear weapons for air and sea delivery. During the 1960s, to overcome the range limitations of the SS-2 and CSS-1, Beijing developed a thermonuclear bomb with a yield of 1-3 Megatons that could be carried to a distance of some 3000 km by its fleet of at least 100 B-6/BADGER (Tu-16) intermediate bombers. China also has over 150 B-5/BEAGLE (Il-28) medium range bombers and some 500 A-5/FANTAN ground attack fighter which can carry small fission bombs to distances of about 1000 and 800 km, respectively. Beijing's combined stockpile of nuclear bombs probably totals less than 100, and the older fission bombs likely will be replaced by newer, small-yield thermonuclear warheads, such as the neutron bomb Beijing is now developing. Today, however, this aerial component is the weakest link in Beijing's nuclear triad. For example, China's Il-28 BEAGLEs are almost ready for retirement, and replacement bombers are unlikely. An H-Bomb laden Tu-16 BADGER, formidable in the late 1960s, probably would not survive contemporary Soviet air defenses. The A-5 FANTAN is more likely to be used in a tactical role rather than as a strategic system.

China has one older GOLF Class diesel powered ballistic missile submarine (SSB) with tubes for 2 JL-1 (*Julang* or Great Wave) submarine launched ballistic missiles (SLBMs) and one XIA Class nuclear powered ballistic missile submarine (SSBN) with tubes for 12 JL-1 SLBMs. The JL-1 has a range of about 2,000 km, and was successfully launched from the GOLF in 1982 and from the XIA in 1988. The JL-1 is also the first of an entirely new generation of solid propellant missiles that eventually will displace China's older and more cumbersome liquid propellant systems. Several new SRBMs are being developed for the international arms market; two of these, the M-9 and M-11, are good candidates for deployment in a tactical nuclear mode. Solid propellant MRBM, IRBM and ICBM classes probably are already in design and could be deployed within the decade.

In the 1990s Chinese nuclear forces will continue to modernize at a slow, yet deliberate pace to improve the accuracy, reliability and survivability of future systems. Deterrence will remain as the primary strategic use of the force due to its limited size and the uncertain accuracy of its warheads. China will probably need to try to develop:

—a new generation of more stable solid propellant missile systems,
—a tactical nuclear weapon to support ground forces,
—the effectiveness of its ICBMs with the use of Multiple Independently-targetable Reentry Vehicles (MIRVs), and

—the ability to deploy Submarine Launched Ballistic Missiles (SLBMs) to augment the present land-based force.

Advances in these areas will be slowed by the technological, economic and political constraints discussed earlier.

B. GROUND FORCES

The PLA remains basically an infantry force. Despite some small improvements in truck mobility and mechanization since 1979, the ground forces do not have the mobility required of a modern army.

China's ground forces have the firepower to deter and, if necessary, mount an effective defense against any conventional attack. However, even after eleven years of modernization efforts the PLA has very limited ability to project its power. Away from rail lines and airfields, the lack of adequate logistical, transport, air defense, communications, armor, and air support severely limits its capabilities. Development of rapid reaction units in each group army, many of which were employed against the demonstrators in June 1989, will eventually result in enhanced ground force projection capabilities, but this probably will not happen until well into the future.

The Type 59 (Soviet T–54) continues to be the PLA's primary tank. Of late 1950s vintage, the Type 59 has been followed by incrementally improved models known as the Type 69, 79 and 80 tanks. Although these improved versions mount western cannon, optics, and range finders, they have been produced principally for foreign sales and only about 200–300 have been deployed to PLA units. Prototype tanks to replace the Type 59s have been under development for over 10 years with the help of various nations. However, Beijing seems unable to decide which prototype will best meet the needs of the next century

Currently, China's self propelled (SP) artillery, towed artillery and multiple rocket launchers have strength in numbers and have achieved significant systems and ammunition enhancements. However, SP systems continue to have difficulties. For example, the Type 83 152mm SP was put together for the 1 October 1984 National Day Parade, then returned to the factory to solve integration problems. The system did not work and is still not deployed in significant numbers. PLA artillery capabilities have been helped in some areas by the acquisition of counter battery radars, which are used in the destruction or neutralization of indirect fire weapons systems. These radars will increase capabilities somewhat, but the problems of integration still remain.

With respect to surface to surface missiles (SSM), the M9 and M11 solid propellent systems are still under development and testing, but the overall status of the program is not known. Prototype missiles were first shown at arms shows in Beijing in 1986 and 1988. The M9 was said to have a maximum range of 600 kilometers and the M11 290 kilometers. The incentive to export these systems is high and, as with tanks and military aircraft, China may well continue to assert its role as a supplier of these types of low cost military equipment.

Gun systems still form the backbone of PLA Air Defense Artillery (ADA) units. China only has two operationally deployed air defense weapons, the HN5 and the HQ–61, both of which use older technology. The HN5 infra-red (IIR) surface-to-air missile (SAM) is based on 1960s Soviet SA–7 Grail technology and the HQ–61 is based on 1970s technology similar to that found in the U.S. Sparrow. ADA requires significant coordination between air defense brigades and SAM units and China still encounters problems in command and control of these systems.

The PLA Aviation Corps comprises a polyglot mix of Soviet and Western systems running the gamut from Soviet HIP to French GAZELLE helicopters. Testing and experimentation continues on lift, antiarmor capabilities and tactics. Apart from acquisitions and standardization, a major problem facing army aviation is the apparent difficulty of maintaining and keeping modern equipment operational. This diversity of equipment may well reflect PLA inability to determine the scope, roles and missions of its Aviation Corps. The Chinese apply maintenance to their army aviation assets only when a weapon system is broken. Preventative maintenance is not accomplished on a regular basis and a significant number of DAUPHIN and S–70C/BLACKHAWK crashes have occurred.

Ground force units demonstrated excellent use of civil and military rail and air assets to move over 200,000 main force troops to the capital in 1989. This was the largest movement of troops, given the short time span, since the Korean conflict. However, operations in the capital revealed many problems. The PLA was not a trained internal security force, there was little or no riot control training or equipment, and the leadership was confused. This led to tragic results.

Improvements in logistics, organization, personnel management, and training will continue to lay the foundation for later integration of more sophisticated weaponry. This is the least costly solution since it avoids buying weapons from outside sources and at the same time builds indigenous weapons development programs. By placing more emphasis on military training, China will improve the capabilities of both the officers and individual soldiers at a lesser cost and thereby increase overall the PLA's capability.

Budget constraints will force the Chinese to concentrate on building a defensive army capable of limited regional offensive operations. To that end, the future will bring an increase in the formation and deployment of rapid reaction units to fight in local war situations. Together the group armies will deploy about 10,000 tanks which will be improved to achieve a slight increase in capabilities. The ground forces will also increase the number of APCs—from the present 3,000 to improve mobility. The number of field artillery weapons—currently at about 13,000—will remain about the same, but mobility and survivability will be enhanced. Finally, the ground forces will attempt to improve light armed helicopter assets to better support the local war doctrine.

C. NAVY

Traditionally a coastal defense force, the PLA Navy is slowly developing a limited regional power projection capability. Currently the major surface combatants are its destroyers and frigates. The submarine force, although large, is limited to engaging surface ships with older torpedoes using WW-II tactics. China's submarines are no match for a modern anti-submarine warfare force. The Navy does have significant value in asserting China's claims to disputed islands in the South China Sea.

China has one operational XIA class SSBN equipped with CSS-N-3 SLBMs. It is doubtful that any more of these expensive systems are under construction. Four HAN class SSNs are operational but do not venture far from their home ports. The principal tactical submarine is the ROMEO class diesel submarine, which is a 1950s vintage, Soviet designed system. Both the HANs and ROMEOs are fitted with dated, 1970s-type sensors and weapons.

The PLA Navy's 56 principal combatants make it the third largest navy in the world. The LUDA destroyers and JIANGHU frigates have significant problems with on board weapons, equipment, and powerplants. The Navy is trying to upgrade these platforms with both indigenous and foreign systems and engines. Key deficiencies and areas targeted for development are air defense, surface-to-surface missiles, electronic warfare, command control and communications (C3), and integrating these systems for effective operations.

The majority of China's three naval fleets are made up of patrol and coastal combatants. These are organized geographically into the North Sea, South Sea and East Sea Fleets. Because of their age, most of the vessels are ineffective on the open seas but useful for coastal defense. Navy minelaying capabilities have been strengthened with the deployment of the WOLEI minelayer which represents China's largest class of domestically produced minelaying vessels, able to carry over 300 mines.

The amphibious fleet grew during the 1970s but, little has been added since that time. Currently, the Navy has the basic sealift for one infantry division with tanks for a 30 day deployment. This could provide enough force for a South China Seas Spratly Islands operation but nothing larger. Also hundreds of civilian merchant and fishing vessels could be employed to transport troops in a non tactical operation.

PLA Naval Aviation units can cover Chinese ports and installations but the lack of aerial refueling capability prohibits coverage of fleet operations beyond the range of coastal airfields. Also, open ocean training with naval units is rare. The Navy's primary attack aircraft is the A-5/FANTAN which has a particularly limited combat radius of about 150 to 400 nautical miles—with an auxiliary fuel drop tank. This severely limits its over water strike capability. In addition, most aircraft operations are limited to clear weather, daytime operations, due to a lack of sophisticated avionics and pilot training.

Naval modernization will constitute an increased threat to Taiwan. The threat could manifest itself through an increased emphasis on antishipping roles or a blockade of the island. It would be difficult for Taiwan to counter either of these operations effectively.

In the 1990s the naval forces will continue to build an organization able to defend territorial claims out to the limits of China's coastal seas. The production rates for ships will slow, but quality will continue to be stressed over quantity. Weapons and electronic upgrades will continue on existing ships and concentrate on improving ASW and air defense capabilities to support limited power projection to the limits of China's coastal seas.

D. AIR FORCES

The evolution of aircraft in the PLA has taken many twists and turns. Western acquisitions have improved the A-5/FANTAN with a relatively up to date navigational/attack system. Avionics are being acquired for the F-8-II. However, as noted earlier the direction of this program is not clear at this time. The F-7 AIRGUARD (an upgraded MiG-21) has been improved with foreign radar, head-up display, a new computer, radios, and identification friend or foe (IFF) systems. Joint development has begun on a new jet trainer with Pakistan. Chinese aerial missile systems are being significantly improved with access to foreign missiles. However, PLA Air Force capabilities are seriously hindered by obsolete airframes and powerplants.

Many aircraft are reaching the end of their operational life. In the West most fighter airframes are considered reliable only through 25–30 years of service. At that time, regardless of the number of hours flown, point stress fractures, corrosion, and fatigue make the airframe less stable and reliable. Most Chinese aircraft are reaching this stage. China's tradition of poor periodic maintenance compounds the difficulties.

China's 2,700 F-6 fighters are based on the Soviet MiG-19 FARMER, which began production in the late 1950s. This aircraft is the backbone of the Air Force and a possible replacement aircraft is under development. According to Chinese reporting this aircraft, called the *Xin Jian* (new fighter), will approximate mid-to late-1970s design technology.

China also deploys the F-7/FISHBED, the Soviet MiG-21, which was first delivered to China before 1960. Although the FISHBED is a proven fighter, only about 500 have been deployed. Improved versions such as the AIRGUARD and F-7-3 have been flown. However, these aircraft will not be produced in sufficient numbers to replace the F-6 FARMERs, since the Chinese realize the inherent limitations of the 1960s designed airframe.

The F-8 interceptor began development in the late 1960s, and the PLA currently has about 80 in the inventory. Under the U.S. Peace Pearl program, the F-8 was to have been a stepping stone to a next generation fighter. However, as noted, the program is unlikely to be revived due to financial and technical problems.

The A-5 ground attack aircraft began in 1958 as a design to transform the MiG 19 into a close air support aircraft of which there are about 550 in the inventory. A prototype flew in 1965 and a number were deployed to the flying units. Some were sold to North Korea and Pakistan in the 1970s and 1980s. Under a 1986 contract, the A-5 was upgraded with Italian avionics based on the Italian AMX fighter and an improved Chinese engine. The aircraft is being produced mainly for foreign sales but some Air Force and Navy A-5s can be refitted in the future.

In 1988, the FB-7 fighter-bomber was unveiled and is being developed as a maritime attack aircraft for the Navy and an all weather interdictor/strike aircraft for the Air Force. The Chinese state that it will be in the same class as the Soviet SU-24/FENCER. If it enters production it may have a terrain following radar and avionics of Chinese design and manufacture. However, at this time it appears that little progress has been achieved.

China's bomber force is dependent on the 1960s vintage B-6 BADGER, with about 130 in the inventory. Its slow speed and poor electronic counter measure capability give it a low probability of survival in the modern aerial warfare arena. The C601 antishipping missile will help the B-6's standoff capabilities but lack of aerial refueling limits any fighter protection for China's bomber force.

Of China's 250 transports, 200 are short range, 45 are medium range, and 5 are long range transports. Most short range aircraft are Y-5 COLT biplanes. Some Tridents are available for VIP and special cargo flights and there are limited numbers of Y-7 and Y-8 aircraft based on the Soviet AN-12 and AN-24 transports. The Y-8 is being developed in a number of variants for refueling, AEW, and surveillance missions. The cutoff of Western contracts and military assistance has hindered these programs. As in 1989, China's civil aviation corporations stand ready to support PLA operations.

In the coming decade, capabilities will continue to fall behind Western nations due to the PRC's dependence on western technology, political instability, and inability to indigenously produce and field modern aircraft. As interceptors, ground attack, bomber and transport aircraft age, they will not be replaced by any new airframes, because there are no airframes ready to go into production. Existing aircraft will continue to have incremental upgrades to avionics and weapons systems, but the government will find it difficult to maintain a modernization momentum into the next decade. To this end Beijing may be forced to cut back or completely drop some of its new systems envisioned for the 1990s and beyond. If it is forced to drop one of its programs the New Fighter—a follow on to the F-8-II—will be the first to go.

IV. Conclusion

For the past 15 years the PLA has been a force in transition trying desperately to reform itself and join the ranks of the world's modern military forces. To date actual improvements have been slow and incremental. Manning has been reduced, the reorganization has established a solid foundation to build upon, and some excellent research and development and think tanks have been established. However, professionalism continues to be hampered by the requirements of correctness, weapons upgrades cannot be adequately funded, and a real question remains about China's defense industry's capability to produce functional modern weapons and equipment.

As in the rest of China, much emphasis is placed on symbolism rather than substance. For example, the Navy's XIAs and HANs rarely get underway. If China should acquire an aircraft or helicopter carrier it too would be a symbol. What aircraft or helicopter can or will China obtain or develop to put onboard? How would it fight off enemy air, surface combatants, and submarines? Although the PLA's capabilities to defend the homeland are high, there is little fear of successful Chinese military operations beyond the Spratlys.

There is some optimism for the future. There are outstanding, highly-professional military leaders who want to bring the PLA into the modern world. They support the economic reforms necessary to provide technologically advanced production facilities and the funds to operate them. But until these military leaders can be sure of the political and ideological winds and of a new leadership that will support their efforts, these professionals will be forced to make do with the equipment, men, and opportunities they presently possess.

INTERPRETING TRENDS IN CHINESE DEFENSE SPENDING

By James Harris et al. *

CONTENTS

SUMMARY

Beijing raised the official state defense budget for 1990 to 29 billion yuan ($6.1 billion)—the first real growth in formal defense spending in eight years and a reversal of a decade-long decline in the military's share of the state budget. Beijing is probably responding to operational and morale problems in the People's Liberation Army (PLA) that are increasing its concerns about the ability of the Chinese military to meet future domestic crises. Some of the increase is undoubtedly intended to defray the costs of deploying troops during the Tiananmen crisis in June 1989 as well as the continued costs of garrisoning large numbers of paramilitary police and soldiers in Beijing. In addition, a portion of the new funds is likely to be used to improve the living conditions of the average soldier as well as to help pay for the retirement and demobilization of over a million Chinese soldiers since the mid-1980s.

The true increase in resources devoted to the Chinese military is clouded by the fact that the PLA receives an equivalent level of funds from such extrabudgetary sources of revenue as arms sales and Army-run business as well as from defense-related allocations in the budgets of other Chinese Government organizations. These funds may actually push China's defense budget for 1990 past 57 billion yuan ($12 billion). Thus, while Beijing claims it spends less than 1.8 percent of gross national product (GNP) on defense, the actual number may be closer to 3.5 percent.

---

* This paper was prepared by James Harris and other analysts from the Office of East Asian Analysis, Central Intelligence Agency. Information available as of November 20, 1990, used in this report.

There are indications, moreover, that China's military spending may be ratcheted up further in years to come. Beijing is likely to come under continuing pressure from its various military services for greater outlays for weapons modernization. They seek more funds for priority weapon development programs that Chinese press accounts indicate have lagged as a result of the PLA's shrinking budget. Military demands for increased research and development funding are also likely to grow significantly over the next decade if China is to bring new military technologies on line by the twenty-first century. Chinese press reports suggest that an increasing proportion of these funds may go to achieve breakthroughs in such high-technology areas as space, composite and new materials, advanced manufacturing processes, and information systems.

In arguing for additional funds, China's military leaders will probably play successfully on Beijing's sense of vulnerability over the loyalty of the army as well as the Chinese leadership's fears of such potential regional adversaries as India and Japan. The remaining question will be how much of China's defense spending comes from the official budget and how much is financed from other sources. In either case, the key issue facing Beijing today is probably not whether defense spending will grow, but by how much.

I. China Reverses Trend Line on Defense Spending

Chinese Finance Minister Wang Bingqian on 21 March 1990 announced a 15.2 percent hike in official state funding for the People's Liberation Army (PLA) in 1990,[1] the first real growth in the official defense budget since 1983 and the second consecutive year that Beijing has increased monies allocated to defense.[2] If annual inflation remains below Chinese predictions of 5 percent for 1990—the inflation rate rose only 2.3 percent in the first nine months of this year, according to recent Chinese statistics—this year's budget of 29 billion yuan ($6.1 billion) will represent a real increase of at least 10 percent for the PLA.

The true increase in resources devoted to the military is clouded by the fact that it receives an equivalent level of funds from such extrabudgetary sources of income as arms sales and Army-run businesses as well as from defense-related allocations in the budgets of other Chinese Government organizations. These funds may actually push China's defense spending past 57 billion yuan ($12 billion). Thus, while Beijing claims it spends less than 1.8 percent of gross national product (GNP) on defense, the actual number may be closer to 3.5 percent. This is still very small compared to the 6 percent of GNP that the United States spends on defense each year and the 15 to 17 percent spent by the Soviet Union.

---

[1] "Wang Bingqian's Budget Report," Xinhua News Agency, 7 April 1990.

[2] Beijing announced a similar 15-percent increase in the military budget for 1989, but an unexpectedly high inflation rate of 17.8 percent eroded the benefits of that raise. Moreover, in previous years the military budget fared even worse, declining at an average annual rate of 5.8 percent in real economic terms during the 1980s, according to Chinese Government reports. The last real growth in the military budget occurred in 1983, when real spending power increased by only 4 percent.

There are several sources of revenues and subsidies available to the PLA that do not appear to be included in the official Chinese defense budget (see figure 1):

- **Arms sales.** Despite Chinese arms' low prices and the high variability of profits on each sale, arms sales are an important source of hard foreign currency that can be used to import Western military technology and equipment. One Western research organization estimates that between 1985 and 1989 China exported $6.9 billion worth of military hardware.[3]
- **Entrepreneurship.** PLA-run commercial enterprises also generate significant revenues, and profits have been increasing 15 to 20 percent annually during the past several years, according to Chinese press reports.[4] The PLA's business activities are likely to continue to increase, even with government austerity measures in place.
- **Agricultural production.** Extensive agricultural cultivation by PLA units also contributes to the military budget by reducing the amount of money Beijing has to allocate for subsistence. For example, PLA farms in 1989 grew more than 2 billion kilograms of grain, meat, and dairy products, according to the Chinese press.[5] If purchased at market prices, these foodstuffs would have cost the military over $1 billion. Moreover, PLA agricultural production is likely to increase this year to offset inflated retail food prices, to better meet soldiers' nutritional needs, and to sell more produce at higher, free market prices. Recent Chinese press reports indicate that PLA farms reaped a bumper summer harvest this year as agricultural output increased 10 percent over 1989.[6]
- **Other budgetary funds.** There may be allocations in the state budget that are intended for national defense projects. For example, money earmarked for the National Defense Science, Technology, and Industry Commission (NDSTIC), the State Science and Technology Commission (SSTC), and defense-related ministries may be used to fund military research and development.
- **Military pensions.** According to Chinese press reports, there are now more than 5 million former military personnel and dependents receiving assistance from the Ministry of Civil Affairs.[7]
- **People's Armed Police and military reservists.** The People's Armed Police (PAP) annual budget is not accounted for in published defense figures because it was removed from PLA control in the mid-1980s. In addition, the costs of China's reserve forces—more than 50 divisions are cited in the Chinese press—are probably being paid out of provincial budgets.

[3] Stockholm International Peace Research Institute, us SIPRI Yearbook 1990, Oxford University Press, London, 1990, p. 221.
[4] Liberation Army Daily, 29 December, 1989.
[5] Xinhua News Agency, 13 April 1990.
[6] Xinhua News Agency, 13 July 1990.
[7] Xinhua News Agency, 27 March 1990.

II. Paying for Domestic Security

The bulk of the increased defense allocations will probably not be used to buy weapons to meet an external threat but primarily to meet pressing problems that are increasing Beijing's concerns about the ability of the Chinese military to quell any future domestic crisis. Senior Chinese leaders have repeatedly referred to a window of opportunity that may last for the next 15 years in which Beijing will face no immediate external threats.[8] Thus, the money will probably be targeted primarily on three areas: to pay for the added operational expenses associated with deploying troops to Beijing since last year's crackdown and increasing the internal security apparatus throughout China, to improve the readiness level and morale of units by increasing spending on equipment maintenance and salaries for the soldiers, and to ease the lot of retired PLA soldiers.

Although Beijing has provided no specific information, part of the budget increase will almost certainly defray the costs of deploying troops to Beijing during the Tiananmen crisis in June 1989 as well as the continued costs of garrisoning nearly 100,000 paramilitary police and soldiers in Beijing.[9] Although no major unrest has occurred since mid-1989, the leadership's fears of the population will no doubt compel it to maintain a large garrison in and around the city for the foreseeable future.

FIGURE 1. PLA Budget: The Decision Making Process.

The General Logistics Department (GLD) in Beijing holds the overall responsibility for creating the annual PLA budget, but final authority rests with the Communist Party's Central Military Commission (CMC) and the State Council. Rather than mandate the budget from above, the GLD assembles the budget through consultation with the General Staff Department, the service arms, and the military regions. The decision-making process may be as follows:

- In the first part of the year units down to the division level appraise their current strength and assess their fiscal requirements.
- Staff departments and military regions submit their budgetary requests to the GLD in the fall. The GLD reviews these submissions and makes adjustments it believes appropriate.
- The Ministry of National Defense probably submits the proposed budget to the State Council, which returns the budget to the GLD by the end of the year for implementation.

The CMC probably focuses on weapons procurement and development—deciding what funds are to be allocated on key weapon systems and determining what proportions of this funding will come from the military budget, the State Council, and separate budgetary accounts. Finally, the National People's Congress rubber-stamps the military budget each spring.

---

[8] "Chen Yun Presents New Political, Economic Strategy," Asahi Shimbun, 18 September 1989.
[9] "Security Forces 'Boosted' in Beijing for Asian Games," South China Morning Post, 5 September 1990.

The Chinese military also appears to be enhancing the operational readiness of its military and paramilitary forces in the Beijing area by replacing equipment lost during the Tiananmen incident with new, more advanced gear. The Chinese leadership, for example, is equipping its paramilitary forces in Beijing with riot-control equipment as demonstrated in the September issue of *People's Liberation Army* Pectoral. Most of it is such nonlethal equipment as helmets, face shields, water cannons, rubber bullets, and tear gas, but the Chinese have also fielded armored, antiriot vehicles with their security forces.

Additional funds will probably also go to maintaining security outside Beijing. China is significantly increasing the size and operational capabilities of the PAP by creating new riot-control units in major cities throughout China and by staging public displays of their skill, according to Hong Kong press reports.[10] The new PAP unit formed in Guangzhou, for example, demonstrated its riot-control tactics and equipment to city officials this summer. The Chinese media also announced this summer an unusual winter recruitment drive possibly to flesh out some of these newly formed units.[11]

Beijing is also evidently revamping largely moribund party militia units—composed of ideologically reliable workers—under the control of provincial party officials. Shanghai officials mobilized over 20,000 militia during the 1989 crisis to assist local security forces in removing student roadblocks, monitoring worker attitudes, and controlling traffic. Since then, Beijing has been encouraging local authorities to establish "emergency militia detachments" and step up training to ensure that local militias could respond quickly to new unrest.[12]

Finally, the Chinese military is maintaining a substantial—and costly—presence along its remote frontiers. Beijing has long garrisoned a substantial security force in Tibet and it is still in place, even after martial law was lifted from the Tibetan capital of Lhasa in May 1990, according to Western travellers who have recently visited Tibet. Over the past two years, China has been building and maintaining a presence on islands it occupies in the South China Sea, as demonstrated in various Chinese publications, such as *Jianchuan Zhishi (Ship Knowledge)*.

III. OTHER AREAS REQUIRING FUNDS

The Chinese military will probably also spend a large portion of this year's additional money on projects to improve the living standards of the average soldier, in order to make the troops—which the regime is counting on for support—happier. Soldiers' poor living standards no doubt are a major contributor to the low morale and discontent that Hong Kong press accounts indicate have plagued the PLA since the Tiananmen incident.[13]

---

[10] Kuan Chiao Qing, No. 212, 16 May 1990, pp. 6–9.
[11] Liberation Army Daily, 7 July, 1990.
[12] "Grasp Key Points, Do a Good Job in Reorganization," Liberation Army Daily, 20 January 1990.
[13] Willy Wo-Lap Lam, "Analysis," South China Morning Post, 3 October 1990.

Some of the new funding will probably be used to augment existing programs designed to bolster morale:

- **New construction.** According to reports in the PLA's *Liberation Army Daily,* Beijing is constructing numerous new facilities for the troops including multistory barracks, improved roads, and training and logistic bases. Many of the old barracks had cracked walls, broken doors and windows, and tiles falling from roofs.
- **Increased food supplies.** Liberation *Army Daily* reports also indicate General Logistics Department (GLD) Director Zhao Nanqi told an all-Army forum on grassroots production in April that the PLA would step up its agricultural production to increase food supplies.

Finally, Beijing's decision to drastically reduce the size of its standing army from some 7 million men in the late 1970s to less than 4 million men today has imposed **retirement costs** that the PLA must currently bear.[14] The costs associated with demobilizing more than 600,000 men each year, including providing generous retirement benefits for the 32,000 ranking PLA and PAP officers discharged this year, are also likely to be a heavy drain on PLA finances.[15]

IV. THE COMPETITION FOR FUTURE RESOURCES

Although the Chinese leadership appears to be using increased defense spending for needs other than hardware, the PLA's various service arms will no doubt press for a greater share of state funds to support individual weapons modernization programs. Senior service arm commanders are likely to support their arguments for increased funding by citing articles in the official Chinese military press predicting that regional arms races, particularly in the Asian-Pacific region, will intensify in the 1990s and raise the danger of local wars breaking out on China's periphery. These PLA officers are also likely to play on Beijing's fear of a militarily resurgent Japan to buttress their calls for increased spending on new weapon technologies for the 21st century.[16]

Nuclear Missiles. On the basis of the wide variety of new missile and rocket technologies displayed at international arms fairs over the last several years, China is probably engaged in a major—and costly—modernization program to replace most of its 1960s-vintage nuclear missile systems with new technology.[17] Because maintaining a credible deterrent will continue to be a top priority of Chinese leaders, Beijing will almost certainly provide the nuclear forces with sufficient funds for major projects even if it means re-

---

[14] Central Intelligence Agency, "The Chinese Economy in 1988 and 1989: Reforms on Hold, Economic Problems Mount," p. 17.

[15] China Daily, 19 October 1990.

[16] A recent analysis of the present world military situation published in the *Liberation Army Daily* on 7 September 1990 exemplifies the current strategic thinking of many Chinese military officers. The author predicts that the diminution of US-Soviet military rivalry will cause some large countries in the Third World to "step up the pace of military buildup and to carry out military intervention in other countries." The analysis singles out Japan for criticism, noting that Tokyo's military expenditures rank third in the world and concluding that Japan "possesses the conditions to become a military power."

[17] Jane's Information Group, "China in Crisis: The Role of the Military," Surrey, United Kingdom, 1989, pp. 109–116.

FIGURE 2. THE PLA BUDGET: SHORT SHRIFT FOR THE COMMON SOLDIER.

For the past several years, top PLA leaders, including Chief of General Staff Chi Haotian, have publicly argued that the military budget was inadequate. As late as this June, PLA officials continued to make calls in academic journals for increased defense spending to ensure the livelihood of their soldiers as well as to modernize the military.

Soldiers' pay lost much of its real purchasing power during the second half of the 1980s, according to the analysis in *Junren Gongzi (Military Wages)*, published last year by the PLA-run Liberation Army Press. By 1989, for example, first-year enlisted men had no disposable income as compared with a modest 12–13 yuan each month in 1985. Many, if not most, junior enlistees rely on friends, family, sideline work, or illegal activities to augment their pay. In contrast, while the average urban worker's disposable income has fallen over the past few years because of inflation, It remains over 25 percent of his basic wages or about 25 yuan each month, according to Chinese Government figures. Rural workers also retained a sizable portion of their annual earnings as disposable income, ranging from 22 to 32 yuan each month.

Not surprisingly, officers receive much better treatment from the PLA than enlisted men. According to the same PLA publication, they receive enough money to support themselves and half the expenses of an additional person. This may not meet many officer's needs, however, because Chinese Government statistics indicate that, on average, each employed person must care for three other people—including children and aging parents.

ducing the amount of money allocated to other service arms for procurement.

Naval Programs. The Chinese Navy also appears to be pressing for more funds for modernization in the wake of its clash in March 1988 with Vietnamese naval forces in the disputed Spratly Islands. Senior Navy officers are also concerned about the potential threat posed by other regional navies; India's acquisition of powerful surface warships and Japan's goal of developing its naval forces to defend its sea lanes out to 1,000 nautical miles are particularly worrisome. Various reports in the Western media suggest that the Navy's priorities include surface-to-air missiles to provide protection from an attack and allow Chinese warships to operate at greater ranges from the mainland, in-flight refueling to extend the combat ranges of the Navy's fighter and ground attack aircraft, and an airborne early warning capability to better monitor air and sea traffic in the ocean areas bordering China.[18]

---

[18] Ngok Lee, "Chinese Maritime Power: Towards Modernisation," *Naval Forces*, Vol. 11, No. 2, 1990, pp. 89–95.

Air Force Programs. Beijing continues to stress air force modernization to offset the challenge posed by the increasingly advanced aircraft that India and Taiwan have already deployed or will soon field. The acquisition of foreign technology has been a costly, but crucial part of the Air Force's modernization drive over the past decade; Beijing will probably continue to plan major spending for a new-generation fighter aircraft, advanced radar-guided missiles, and upgrades to existing combat aircraft.[19] China, for example, has initiated competing programs with Italian and French firms to improve the weapons delivery capability of its ground attack aircraft, the A–5. The Chinese Air Force's need for modern weapon systems is apparently urgent enough that Beijing is considering acquiring jet fighters from the Soviet Union.[20]

Ground Force Programs. China's ordnance industry appears to be pursuing an aggressive—and costly—research and development strategy designed to "leapfrog" the technology gap between China's obsolescent ground force weapon systems and those of the West and the Soviet Union. Chinese weapon manufacturers, for instance, have unveiled numerous prototypes of new ground force equipment at international arms exhibitions. According to Western journalists attending the shows, it is comparable to modern equipment in Western and Soviet inventories.[21] Given the absence of any pressing external threat to its security, Beijing is likely to field limited numbers of new weapon systems to a few elite units for evaluation and training. Nonetheless, China has the military production infrastructure to quickly begin producing an array of high-quality weapons—including main battle tanks, armored fighting vehicles, artillery, and air defense weapon systems.

V. RESEARCH FOR LONGER-RUN REQUIREMENTS

In addition to outlays for ongoing weapons programs, increased funding for research and development will almost certainly be needed if Beijing is to field more advanced weapons in the twenty-first century. The goal of such long-term development programs would probably be to provide the military with sophisticated weapon systems that might include more capable strategic missiles, stealth and counterstealth technologies, new ships and submarines for the Navy—possibly including an aircraft carrier—and rapid mobility for the Army.[22]

Besides these programs, the Chinese military probably will require more money to research and develop even more advanced, defense-related technologies in the mid-to-late 1990s. Although most of the funding for such long-term research probably does not come directly out of the military budget, the PLA nonetheless will have to pay a portion of these costs. Consequently, the Chinese military and its subordinate research and development units are likely to be heavily involved in a 13-year modernization plan—the 863 pro-

---

[19] James C. Wilson, "The Chinese Air Force: Roadblocks to Modernization," *United States Air War College*, May 1990, pp. 5–6.

[20] Far Eastern Economic Review, 6 September 1990, p. 20.

[21] Jane's Defense Weekly, 19 November 1988, pp. 1285–1286.

[22] "Radar ECCM's New Area: Anti-Stealth and Anti-ARM", Dianzi Xuebao, March, 1987; "China Considers Carrier Plans", Jane's Defense Weekly, 16 June 1990, p.1186.

gram—that Beijing has publicly revealed as designed to close the gap between China and the West in such key technologies as space, composite and new materials, advanced manufacturing processes, and information systems.

VI. Prospects

Senior military leaders are likely to continue to press Beijing to increase budgetary support to the PLA throughout the 1990s, arguing that such funds are long overdue and essential to improving morale and maintaining loyalty, meeting operational expenses, and financing weapons modernization. An analysis in China's prestigious journal *Economic Research* on 20 June 1990 is probably a reflection of this pressure. Its author argues that the state must increase its defense allocation at a rate comparable to national economic growth for several years to offset a decade of declining military spending. Otherwise, the author warns that defense modernization will be held up and the livelihood of China's officers and men will become more difficult, resulting in lax discipline and a decrease in the PLA's combat effectiveness.

In arguing for morale-boosting programs, China's military leaders are likely to play on Beijing's current sense of vulnerability over the loyalty of the PLA. They will probably succeed in obtaining higher levels of funding for items designed to improve living standards, such as housing and food subsidies. Meanwhile, Beijing will probably face mounting operational expenses over the next few years to meet the costs of expanding the police and security presence in Beijing and other key cities. Maintaining or expanding a presence in remote border regions, including Tibet and the Spratly Islands, is also likely to pose an increasing drain on military resources for the foreseeable future.

Although the military is in a strong position to press for more funding because the leadership depends on it for continued rule, some interest groups within the leadership may argue that a greater emphasis on defense is unwise given the faltering state of the Chinese economy and the diminished Soviet threat. They can, for example, point to Gorbachev's announced force reduction of over 200,000 men from the Soviet Far East by next January and the withdrawal of Soviet divisions from Mongolia as well as the reduced border tensions with Vietnam and India. Much may depend, therefore, on the relative influence of the PLA within China's leadership.

In summary, the increase in defense spending in 1990 reflects both real needs caused by the neglect of the military during the economic growth of the 1980s and the increased reliance of the leadership on the military. It is likely that the leadership will feel compelled to try to assuage the military by increasing defense spending over the next few years to ensure military readiness to quell potential domestic unrest. The remaining question will be how much of China's defense spending comes from the official budget and how much is financed from other sources. In either case, the key issue will probably be not if defense spending will grow in the next few budgets, but how much.

CHINA IN TRANSITION: MILITARY CONCERNS AND ABILITY TO INFLUENCE EVENTS

By Ronald N. Montaperto *

CONTENTS

I. INTRODUCTION

China has entered the twilight of the Deng Xiaoping era of reform and openness. In 1991, age, infirmity, and the passing of its members will undoubtedly lead to the deterioration of the uneasy leadership coalition that has ruled China since the events at Tiananmen Square in June 1989.

The Chinese People's Liberation Army (PLA) will be deeply involved in the effort to achieve a smooth succession and shape the course of future policies. Some national military leaders—both retired and on active duty—will be direct participants in the process while nearly all will closely monitor the full range of Beijing's policies and attempt to influence those that bear upon military interests.

Their ability to achieve success will be affected by the reality that the PLA too is experiencing a period of institutional transition that influences most aspects of its activities. For example, the basis of PLA political power is beginning to change and the focus of military political concern is becoming more narrowly focused. Also, the means by which the army strives to achieve its political goals is beginning to reflect a new and increasing reliance on formal institutions and regularized procedures. Networks of personal relations—

---

* Defense Intelligence Agency.

guanxi networks—are being supplemented by formal institutional relations. This essay analyzes and describes changes in the patterns of PLA political influence and speculates on the ways in which that influence is likely to be used in the immediate succession period and beyond.

II. THE CHINESE PEOPLE'S LIBERATION ARMY: SOURCES OF POLITICAL INFLUENCE

A. JUNE 4, 1989: THE IMPACT OF TIANANMEN

The suppression of the Democracy Movement illustrates vividly the loyalty of the PLA to Deng Xiaoping and the senior Party leadership. Despite some misgivings, and probably mindful of the cost to be paid in terms of morale, the army as an institution responded to Deng's call, routed the Beijing demonstrators, and upheld China's leaders in the face of the challenge to their authority.

The PLA's role in suppressing the Tiananmen demonstrators does not appear to have produced an increase in the army's formal institutional power. Since June 1989, the PLA role in supervising the media may have become more active and the continuing campaign to learn from Lei Feng has certainly raised the visibility of the military. Overall, however, the proportion of military personnel serving on various Party and government organs remains basically as it was before the events at Tiananmen.

On the other hand, it is reasonable to assert that the informal political influence of individual senior military leaders has probably grown since the summer of 1989, if only because the challenge of the democracy demonstrations increased the need for military support. In the mind of the civilian leadership collective, maintaining social stability, and, especially, preventing new outbreaks of demonstrations, requires that the populace view the PLA and the People's Armed Police (PAP) as reliable, dedicated supporters of the Party and government. The need to maintain the loyalty of the leaders who control the military and police apparatus therefore remains intense and their opinions are likely to loom large in certain types of policy deliberations throughout the succession period. This is one source of military influence in the current political environment.

B. EXPERIENCE AND PERSONAL RELATIONS

Apart from their control of military force, senior PLA leaders are also guaranteed authoritative participation in the larger political process by virtue of the symbiosis that exists between them and China's senior civilian leaders. To illustrate this, a brief excursion into Chinese Communist history is necessary.

As the concept of "People's War" evolved between 1935 and 1949, CCP emphasis on the political functions of conflict, the corollary doctrine of strict military subordination to the Party, and the shared difficulties of an arduous wartime environment caused a blurring of the distinction between civilian and military leaders. As a result, there grew up a class of revolutionary leaders, such as Deng Xiaoping, Li Xiannian, Nie Rongzhen, and many others whose abilities, achievements, and reputations transcended the boundary between the civilian and military sectors. After 1949, some, like Deng, returned to their essentially civilian roots while others, like Nie, remained in uniform.

However, in subsequent years, the relationships continued and, in many cases became stronger. Throughout China's post–1949 history, what is now the older generation of military leaders has derived added lustre from its close association with China's present senior civilian leaders. The civilians too, both individually and as a group, have gained additional strength from their relations with senior military leaders.

Even though age, declining physical capabilities, and actuarial attrition are gradually eroding the ties, the symbiotic relationship in which the members of each group use the members of the other as political resources continues to exist. As a result, even though the PLA is institutionally subordinated to the Party, its senior leaders possess a degree of political access and influence exceeding that mandated by their formal positions. Their status as old-line revolutionary heroes legitimizes their claim to speak on issues of broad policy.

Few of these senior military leaders remain on active duty, although Defense Minister and Politburo member Qin Jiwei and Central Military Commission Vice Chairman Liu Huaqing continue to hold official office. Most, such as former PLA General Staff Department Director Yang Dezhi and General Political Department Director Yu Qiuli retired from the service. Insofar as the retired PLA leaders have a common institutional locus, it appears to be in the Central Advisory Commission (CAC). More than two thirds of the members of the CAC are either active or retired military personnel.

The objections of senior military leaders may well have been one of the factors that prevented Hu Yaobang's accession to the Chairmanship of the Central Military Commission and also an important cause of his dismissal from the post of Party General Secretary. If so, it shows that senior military leaders are able to utilize the influence that accrues from their status to achieve favorable action on a variety of issues related to PLA interests or to problems of national policy. Indeed, the influence derived from the considerable status of its retired and active senior leaders probably remains as the most important link between the PLA and the larger political system.

However, with the decline and gradual passing of the older military generation, the sources of status within the PLA and therefore the nature of the military leadership in China is changing. So too are the linkages between the PLA and the larger political structure and the basic manner in which the army articulates the full range of its political concerns. To illustrate how this is so, it is necessary to turn to a consideration of the impact of rising military professionalism.

III. CHANGING PATTERNS OF POLITICAL INFLUENCE: THE IMPACT OF PROFESSIONALISM

In 1985, the reduction in the size of the force, the implementation of a significantly improved education and training system for officers, and a force-wide reorganization into group armies signaled that the PLA quest to build a modern, professional army had reached a new stage. However, it is important to note that the vision of the professionalism that was to be achieved appeared to be solidly grounded in the Chinese notions of democratic centralism. Like "socialism," "military professionalism" in China was to have uniquely Chinese characteristics.

In the context of Chinese Communist history and values, military professionalism does not require that the PLA withdraw from active participation in either the political or social systems. As the PLA becomes more "professional" the nature of the political issues on which the army is engaged is shifting and becoming more narrowly focused on military matters. As noted above, professionalism is also producing a new type of leader. Advancement and status is coming to be based upon command of specialized knowledge and expertise rather than on historical experience and revolutionary associations. Finally, professionalism is producing a style of engagement that is more intense than was generally so in the past.

The shift in orientation became evident after the Cultural Revolution when the army began its move "back to the barracks." By 1987, PLA representation was reduced from 57 percent to 11.1 percent in the Politburo, from 31 percent to 18.6 percent in the Central Committee, and from 29.5 percent to zero of Provincial First Party Secretaries. Eight military officers who served as heads of machine industrial industries had been replaced by 1980. For the PLA, the "back to the barracks" movement signaled a shift from performing government and Party-centered administrative and supervisory functions to building a modern fighting force.

In addition to shifting the focus of political concern and encouraging the emergence of a different kind of leader, professionalism is also posing a new challenge to the coherence of the PLA as an institution. Modernization necessitates acquiring sophisticated weapons technologies, developing the new fighting doctrines and the training patterns to use them effectively, and managing relations with foreign military establishments. This in turn requires leaders who have mastered the new skills and gained the expertise required to perform these functions.

It seems apparent that such a group of technocrats and commanders is emerging and that the new leaders are beginning to define PLA political interests in ways that increasingly focus on coaxing from the political and economic systems the resources and supports required to modernize the military. The new leaders have also begun to articulate their professional concerns at the highest levels of the military and civilian bureaucracies.

In the context of scarce resources, the demands of the leaders responsible for nurturing different aspects of professionalism and modernization are often conflicting, and the process of brokerage by which competing claims are reconciled assumes the aspect of a zero-sum game. Officers with similar orientations and priorities draw together and use connections with officers at higher levels to promote their common interests.

As a result, the rise of military professionalism in China is also producing new constituencies within the PLA as well as the new-style leaders to represent them. Competition for resources within and between the different PLA groupings will continue to grow and, overall, the process by which the military engages the larger political system will become more difficult to define. Most important, the basis for rising to the higher levels of the PLA leadership is beginning to change as the specialized expertise of the generation concerned with building professionalism combines with and begins to replace the more general revolutionary experience of the Long March generation. As with China's civilian institutions and leaders, the PLA too is in the midst of a succession process.

For heuristic purposes, it can be asserted that four main constituencies seem to be emerging. The categories are neither logically exhaustive nor mutually exclusive. Moreover, because all share similar historical roots, the boundaries between them are not firmly fixed and indeed transcend the more traditional divisions between the ground, naval, and air components of the force. Additional groupings almost certainly exist, but those discussed below are the most useful for a preliminary analysis of the changing political role of the PLA.

A. COMMANDERS AND OPERATORS

Potentially the most politically powerful of these constituencies is a group of men who serve or who recently have served as commanders of different group armies or as leaders within the military science and technology establishment. Their political influence derives from several sources.

First, although they have yet to achieve the highest rank, these officers are able to use connections with their superiors at the military region and national levels to articulate their professional concerns which, by definition, center on the capabilities of the group armies to perform their basic military missions. Second, because they compel attention to these basic needs and requirements, the inputs of the group army commanders are central to defining PLA demands for resource allocation, and the social supports that facilitate maintaining training programs and morale. These inputs also justify the flexibility necessary to implement new doctrinal formulations. Third, the group army commanders are able to supplement their essentially indirect sources of influence by direct participation in certain aspects of the formal political process at the national level; they and the younger commanders within the various military regions comprise roughly one half of the total military representation on the Chinese Communist Party Central Committee. Finally, the members of this group will replace the old guard as that generation passes from the scene. One such individual is Li Jijun, who formerly commanded the 38 Group Army and who now works in the General Office of the Party Central Military Commission. Li is also a member of the Party Central Committee.

B. TECHNOCRATS

A second group is located squarely within the science and technology establishment and its members often are connected with the network of companies controlled by the Commission on Science, Technology, and Industry for National Defense (COSTIND) or with those associated with the General Staff, General Political, and General Logistics Departments at the PLA national level. Technocrats, scientists, and engineers rather than professional soldiers, these colonels and generals have an interest in acquiring both whole systems and the technologies required for indigenous programs of weapons development. They also form an important part of the interface between the PLA and foreign armies.

The highly-educated technocrats are important, not only because of the obvious significance of their concerns for the future of the PLA, but also because, in many cases, its members are either related to or have very close personal relations with China's highest civilian leaders. These connections mean that they are extraordinarily well-positioned to ensure a hearing for their interests and plans in national political councils. In terms of function, the technocrats recommend priorities for acquiring advanced foreign technologies, coordinate the research and acquisition plans of the army, navy, and air force, and manage the military dimension of China's opening to the outside. It is probable that the members of this group strongly advocate a broad and active PLA engagement with foreign military establishments and the aggressive pursuit of foreign military sales. Lieutenant General Ding Henggao and Major General He Pengfei are examples of the members of this constituency.

C. STRATEGISTS

Although it was truncated by ten years of Cultural Revolution emphasis on Maoist conceptions of People's War, the PLA actually possesses a rich tradition of critical writing on strategy and doctrine. The recent revival of this tradition appears to have produced a third constituency that is concerned with formulating the strategic concepts intended to guide the PLA into the 21st Century.

This group is located within a network formed by the National Defense University, the Academy of Military Sciences, and such think tanks as the Chinese Academy of Social Sciences. The strategists appear to be a more fluid group than the two mentioned previously and probably also have less coherence than the others. Its members appear to arise from the division command level and below and probably cycle through the various schools and institutes as part of the new pattern of career development that has emerged in the 1980s. However, a small number remain to become permanent members of the defense intelligentsia.

Although the strategists appear to have little direct influence in the larger political process, they are important in two respects. First, they articulate the concepts that help to define China's strategic assessment and thus influence the ordering of national priorities. Second, and following from the first, they appear to have influence in establishing priorities for developing future military capabilities. For example, China's recent emphasis on building the capabilities necessary to prosecute so-called local wars of limited duration is probably based upon the work of this group. Finally, the strategists define and execute the terms of reference for the enhanced system of military education that has become so important for the PLA. They help to form the mindset of future PLA leaders.

D. THE POLITICAL COMMISSARIAT

Ten years of military reform do not appear to have produced a synthesis of the longstanding dialectic between "red" and "expert." The tension between the two concepts will probably continue for as long as "the People's Army" exists. For that reason, the PLA's political commissars will continue to function as a critically important constituency.

The most immediate effect of rising military professionalism after the changes of 1985 was to sharply reduce the proportion of time devoted to political study and training. However, the 1987 appointments of Chi Haotian, Yang Baibing, and Zhao Nanqi, all of whom had long experience as political officers, to head the PLA General Staff, General Political, and General Logistics departments illustrated the continuing importance and vital role of the political commissariat, both within the PLA and as a voice to be heard as the PLA formulates its position on important national political issues.

Under their leadership, the role of the political officer appeared to focus on easing the stresses and strains engendered by the reorganization and force reduction. Political officers explained the rationale for the new policies, performed liaison functions with local government organs and enterprises to help the transition of the retirees to civilian life, and saw to maintaining the morale and quality of life of the troops who remained on active duty. The overall message appeared to be that participation in the military modernization process was in itself a political value of major importance.

However, since Tiananmen, apprehension about the political reliability of the force has brought a dramatic increase in the influence of Yang Baibing's General Political Department and in its influence at all levels of command. Political study now occupies more than half of total training time. At the same time, having adopted a "correct" stand on the PLA role in suppressing the Tiananmen demonstrations appears to be a major consideration as the General Political Department and political commissars at all levels vet candidates for promotion. As a result of Tiananmen, the pendulum within the military appears, as was the case after 1959 and during the Cultural Revolution, to have swung towards the political commissariat.

At the national level the locus of influence for the political commissariat certainly resides with Yang Baibing who, in addition to his role as Director of the General Political Department, is also General Secretary of the Party's Military Commission and a member of the Party Secretariat. Through his half-brother, President Yang Shangkun, and also by virtue of his wide-ranging dominance of the PLA's political commissar system, Yang is able to press the case for ideological correctness, maintaining the primacy of the Party over the army, and for maintaining political stability. It is probable that Yang's primacy, and with it the ascendancy of the political commissariat, will obtain at least until the larger issues of the succession are resolved. Moreover, traditional military conservatism on social and political issues will be reenforced for a time.

IV. Professionalism and PLA Unity

In the short run, the emergence of new PLA constituencies will pose some challenge to military unity. For example, the dominance of the political commissars will eventually spark the resistance of other constituencies that are deeply concerned with readiness, equipment acquisition, and training.

However, over the longer term, it is not likely that the competition of the new constituencies will seriously degrade overall PLA unity. Longstanding PLA values emphasize loyalty to the civilian Party leadership and the concept of the PLA as the guardian of China's national security. These values provide a strong incentive to achieve compromise.

Also, as mentioned earlier, the military elders derive a large measure of their political power and influence from their ability to mobilize military support for civilian leaders and because they can ensure a hearing for military concerns. To do this effectively requires that the PLA speak with one voice. Accordingly, the prestige of the military old guard is used—sometimes even by younger officers—to forge consensus before potential conflict becomes disruptive. PLA advocates are under some pressure to compromise their positions in accordance with the preferences of their senior patrons.

As the military elders pass from the scene, a new mechanism for consensus building will have to be found. However, for some time to come, the PLA will on the whole continue to speak with one voice on the larger issues of national policy.

V. Issues of Concern

Overall, the PLA's political priorities for the future will probably be determined by two overarching considerations. First, and ultimately more important, the PLA will desire to restore, and, if possible, to increase the momentum of its equipment modernization program. Second, and of more importance in the immediate future, will be the desire of the military to maintain a stable social and political environment.

These concerns will frame and influence the PLA's approach to political engagement on other issues that hold a different level of importance. Because the world view of China's highest military leaders seems to mirror the ideological conservatism and nationalistic bias of their civilian counterparts, the army will probably continue to support the present civilian leaders. However, the constancy of military support will obviously be conditioned by the perception of how well the civilian leaders manage China's pressing economic and social problems and, of course the extent to which the civilian leaders support the military modernization effort.

A. THE SUCCESSION

In keeping with established practice and convention, it is most likely that PLA succession concerns will be articulated mainly by the military elders in combination with the members of the Party Military Commission and the officers who serve on the Party Central Committee and its Politburo. These men will represent the views and preferences of the lower command levels who will not become directly involved.

At this time, the senior PLA leadership appears to support the combined leadership of Party General Secretary Jiang Zemin and Premier Li Peng. However, judging by the pattern of military response to the events at Tiananmen, their support is probably rooted in the personal loyalty that senior leaders hold for Deng Xiaoping. If Deng should suddenly pass from the scene, or if he were to become incapacitated, continued military support for Jiang and Li is by no means assured.

When the attrition of the senior leadership begins, the PLA will probably use all of its considerable resources to reduce the tensions the transition is bound to produce. As noted above, senior military leaders will work through established, although informal and highly personalized, channels to assure a smooth transition.

President and Military Commission First Vice Chairman Yang Shangkun will perforce be a key player in this process, assuming he remains in good physical and political health. With his more than sixty years of Party and military experience, Yang seems well-positioned to play the leading role. However, he also faces a number of difficulties. For example, despite his revolutionary credentials and military associations, he simply lacks Deng's stature. Also, having made his mark as a bureaucratic administrator, he is not a soldier in the same sense as China's other senior military leaders.

Given what appears to be an almost universal acknowledgement within the high military and civilian leadership of the need to maintain an atmosphere of continuity, direct military intervention involving either the threat or actual use of force does not appear to be very likely. However, if succession politics produces a prolonged stalemate, and if new outbreaks of demonstrations occur, military concerns about stability will rise.

Even then, it is most likely that the People's Armed Police will be responsible for dealing with popular demonstrations. However, PLA leaders at all levels will monitor events quite closely. If stalemate and or unrest continues, PLA leaders will become more assertive and eventually align themselves with the group they feel will bring stability and a program that supports PLA modernization interests. This is the point at which support for Jiang or Li, or both, could be withdrawn.

B. THE BUDGET AND ACQUISITIONS

Given its strong commitment to restoring the momentum of the modernization program, and irrespective of the additional funds that might be available from other, "off-budget" sources, the PLA will undoubtedly continue to press for increases in the overall defense budget. The recent 15.2 percent increase in defense expenditure to 28.97 billion yuan, while highly welcome, cannot but be regarded by PLA modernizers as anything other than partial compensation for nearly a decade of gradually shrinking support. Overall, the increase has probably accomplished little more than to whet the appetite for additional funding.

The desire to overcome the deficiencies resulting from these shortfalls is the major impetus driving PLA efforts to develop a modern, professional force. Senior military leaders will attempt to use their influence, which has been bolstered by the PLA defense of the Party in June, 1989, to support demands for increased funding. However, China's overall economic situation appears to be such that the economy will not be able to sustain military budgets at the level demanded until well into the future. The resulting tension will test the ability of the system to produce a satisfactory compromise. It will also be a continuing problem for any successor regime.

C. FOREIGN RELATIONS

In foreign relations, most senior PLA leaders appear to share the essentially conservative, nationalistic world view of their counterparts. The views of leaders at the military region and below are less clear, but they probably agree with their senior colleagues and patrons. Consequently, it is likely that PLA leaders will continue to support China's "opening to the outside" and press for expanded military and defense relations with the west and Japan, but simultaneously uphold the policies designed to counter the spread of "bourgeois liberalism."

The intense nationalism of military leaders appears to produce an ambivalent view of the proper course for China's foreign relations. PLA leaders apparently recognize that broadly defined diplomatic and economic ties with the external world are essential to the economic, scientific, and technological development required to provide a firm foundation for China's national security. They particularly value foreign military contacts as a source of modern weapons and for the stimulation they provide in developing and adapting their own military doctrines.

However, these reasons for expanding external relations tend to be offset by an innate suspicion of foreign ideas and concepts. The end result is that, while PLA leaders will continue to support expanding bilateral relations—especially with the west and Japan—they will also insist the relationships not become what they consider to be too close.

D. SOCIAL POLICY

Through the succession period and into the future, it is likely that the PLA leadership will continue to try to exert a conservative influence on all aspects of Chinese social policy. Since the early 1980s, military leaders have frequently voiced dissatisfaction with various aspects of reform and openness because, in their view, the policies subvert socialist values. Such allegations reportedly formed and important dimension of PLA opposition to both Hu Yaobang and Zhao Ziyang.

Moreover, the PLA appears to be playing an active role in the present effort to inculcate orthodox political values. Since June, 1989, PLA personnel are reported to be active in managing the policies of *People's Daily* and the party theoretical journal *Qiu Shi*. Sensitive as they are to currents in Beijing, provincial media officials have been quick to fall into line between the PLA-inspired exponents of orthodoxy.

Although they will probably support reform and openness for the professional benefits they bring, PLA leaders are also likely to maintain a fairly narrow view of ideological acceptability. If the succession produces a leadership that is more reform-minded than the present coalition, the PLA voice on social matters is likely to become increasingly strident.

VI. Conclusions

The leadership succession and economic problems facing China in the 1990s will frame PLA concerns and the capacity to influence events and national policies. The PLA will be less able to express its professional concerns and promote its professional efforts effectively until overriding issues of national leadership and policy direction are resolved.

Also, the PLA's strongly felt desire for modernization and higher levels of professionalism will compel the military to use its political strength to achieve the political stability and economic progress that will eventually make modernization possible. Yet the demands of building professionalism will continue to conflict with some of the PLA's more traditional political and social roles. For all of these reasons, it is likely that the overall modernization effort will progress only slowly and that accommodating PLA interests will continue to be a nettlesome problem for any successor regime.

Third, there is little prospect of complete withdrawal of PLA support for whatever political combination emerges in Beijing. Debates on leadership, budget allocations, foreign policy, and the proper role of ideology will all intensify through the succession period and probably continue through the decade. PLA positions on these issues are likely to be less flexible and more conservative than those of some civilian leaders. However, because PLA and civilian leaders are motivated by generally similar values, and because these values actually require military access to the larger political process, it is likely that future political leaders will remain sensitive to military concerns across the board, but not be dictated to by a unified military voice.

Finally, the PLA will undergo significant change. The emerging constituencies within the PLA and the parochialism it will inevitably entail will at times cause the army to appear divided. But, to the contrary, the long range effect of building more specialization into the PLA system will increase unity by making each constituency aware of the others' needs and positions. This heightened awareness will probably encourage coherence and cooperation on key issues that address overall PLA requirements.

CHINA'S ARMS SALES: OVERVIEW AND OUTLOOK FOR THE 1990S

By Shirley Kan *

CONTENTS

I. INTRODUCTION

In the last decade, China emerged as a major supplier in the international arms market, especially in the strategic Mideast region. The transfers of low cost and low technology Chinese weapons have been exclusively to the developing world. For the 1982–1989 period, China ranked fifth in terms of arms deliveries to developing countries—behind the Soviet Union, United States, France, and the United Kingdom. Moreover, Chinese arms deliveries increased 37 percent from the 1982–1985 period to 1986–1989.[1]

The Chinese have reaped economic, political, and other benefits from their arms sales. By marketing primarily to the Mideast, China's state-run arms trading corporations have collected enormous profits from Egypt, Iraq, Iran, and Saudi Arabia. Geopolitical

---

* Shirley Kan is an Analyst in Foreign Affairs with the Congressional Research Service (CRS).
[1] Grimmett, Richard F. *Trends in Conventional Arms Transfers to the Third World by Major Supplier, 1982–1989.* CRS Report 90–298F, June 19, 1990. Table 2F.

motivations have continued to play the most important role in decisions on weapons shipments to countries outside of the Mideast region. China has provided weapons to Pakistan, Cambodian guerrilla factions, Thailand, and Myanmar's regime. Beijing has used this policy to increase China's political leverage in Asia and to help check feared Soviet, Vietnamese, and Indian expansion. China has earned influence through its contribution to the arms buyer's efforts in addressing regional balance of power situations or internal political struggles.

Technological, intelligence, and diplomatic benefits have also motivated China's enthusiastic pursuit of arms sales. Two arms buyers, Egypt and Iraq, reportedly provided Chinese defense researchers with Soviet equipment, allowing them to extract technology more advanced than China possessed. These Middle Eastern buyers also probably furnished intelligence about Soviet weaponry and military doctrines.[2] Furthermore, China's arms sales to Saudi Arabia helped pave the way for Riyadh's recognition of the People's Republic on July 21, 1990—a major diplomatic victory for Beijing at the expense of the Nationalists on Taiwan.

China's increased arms sales have important ramifications for world stability. Attempts at global conflict management or weapons non-proliferation now requires cooperation from Beijing. In other words, Chinese behavior conditions to an unprecedented degree the ability of the superpowers to manage world events, such as a Cambodian peace settlement and the Iraq-Kuwait crisis. In addition, economic and technological benefits from arms sales have contributed to Chinese military modernization—an important ingredient in China's status in world affairs.

Arms sales also have important implications for China's efforts at reforms, modernization, and interdependence. Within the defense industrial establishment and the People's Liberation Army (PLA), an entrepreneurial sector with a significant stake in China's reforms and foreign contacts has developed. The arms trade has contributed to both the short-term aim of incremental upgrading of military hardware, as well as the long-term objective of strengthening the defense research and development base. On the other hand, the aggressive commercial marketing of arms has called into question China's commitment to global weapons non-proliferation and stability. U.S. charges of irresponsible behavior in arms transfers have hampered Beijing's efforts to promote foreign technology transfers.

In the 1990s, China can be expected to continue arms sales with vigor, in order to further advance its position as a world power and pursue foreign currency earnings, but these efforts will probably be tempered by external factors. The internal factors influencing Chinese arms sales will be leadership goals, political requirements, bureaucratic compromises, industrial capability, as well as military requirements. External variables include changes in the international arms market, regional instability, the nature of superpower relations, China's security situation, and economic and technological leverage on the part of countries or world organizations in re-

---

[2] Shichor, Yitzhak. "The Middle East," in Gerald Segal and William Tow (eds.). *Chinese Defence Policy*. London, Macmillan Press, 1984. p. 271-2.

stricting weapons transfers. At times, policy-makers in Beijing must choose between benefits of Western linkages and gains from arms sales, and between military and civilian production needs. Overall, Beijing's pursuit of sustained or increased arms sales will be circumscribed by the continuing decline in demand for arms, greater emphasis on nuclear and conventional weapons non-proliferation in wake of the Cold War, and the resolution of tensions along China's borders with the Soviet Union, Vietnam, and India.

The next section will review the significance of Chinese arms sales and the major weapons deals. Then, the ramifications for world politics, and the implications for China's reforms, modernization, and interdependence will be summarized. Finally, the last section will cover the internal and external factors which will influence the prospects for Chinese arms sales in the 1990s.

II. HISTORICAL SUMMARY OF CHINESE ARMS SALES

In the decades prior to 1980, due to both Maoist outlooks and market conditions, China's goals in weapons transfers did not include commercial profits. Military aid was provided on a grant basis, and the modest levels amounted to less than $5 billion between 1963 and 1980. For strategic interests, the Chinese furnished military supplies to North Korea, North Vietnam, Pakistan, Tanzania, and different insurgent groups.[3]

In the 1980s, several internal and external factors encouraged China's eager pursuit of arms deals for foreign exchange earnings. China's new pragmatic leadership under Deng Xiaoping perceived a reduced security threat and emphasized an economic development role for the military. The Chinese policy-makers established foreign trading corporations in the various defense industrial ministries and the PLA. Opportunities surfaced when oil-rich, high-demand markets emerged in the Middle East, especially with the start of the Iran-Iraq War.

ROLE OF ARMS SALES IN CHINA'S EXPORTS

Chinese arms sales have become an important foreign exchange earner. Although the Chinese Ministry of Foreign Economic Relations and Trade does not report statistics on military sales,[4] the ratio of arms exports to total Chinese exports can be estimated, as provided in Table 1 below. The contributions of China's arms exports to total exports during the 1980s were significant relative to the ratios in other countries.

PAKISTAN

Neighboring South Asia was one of the first arenas where Beijing employed arms transfers to further Chinese interests, and Pakistan has been key to China's geopolitical strategy regarding India and the superpowers since the 1960s. Following serious deterioration in relations between Beijing and Moscow, the Sino-Indian

---

[3] Joffe, Ellis. *The Chinese Army After Mao.* Cambridge, MA, Harvard University Press, 1987. p. 114.
[4] Fletcher, Noel. "China Talks More Openly About Plans for Arms Sales," *Journal of Commerce*, Oct. 4, 1988.

TABLE 1. Ratio of Estimated Arms Exports to Total Chinese Exports

Year	Arms Deliveries (millions of US$)	Total Exports (millions of US$)	Arms Deliveries as a Percentage of Exports (%)
1983	1,560	26,542	5.9
1984	2,060	30,784	6.7
1985	670	30,311	2.2
1986	1,250	31,933	3.9
1987	1,800	41,947	4.3
1988	2,580	49,961	5.2
1989	1,950	51,667	3.8

Sources: Value of Arms Deliveries from Richard Grimmett, *Trends in Conventional Arms Transfers to the Third World by Major Supplier, 1982–1989*, Congressional Research Service, June 19, 1990. Table 2.

Figures for Total Exports based on merchandise exports plus other goods, services, and income credits in *International Financial Statistics* (IMF, September 1990); and adding the value of arms deliveries for each year to IMF total, because the Chinese Ministry of Foreign Economic Relations and Trade does not include arms sales in its statistics.

border war of 1962, and India's subsequent military build-up with Soviet assistance, Beijing committed support to Islamabad's conventional and nuclear defense.[5]

In pursuit of mainly strategic goals, China has continued its contribution to Pakistan's efforts to build its defense in face of India's military acquisitions. Over 1978–1982, the value of Chinese arms deliveries to Islamabad was $230 million (in constant 1984 dollars), and during 1983–1987, that value was $270 million (in constant 1988 dollars). In the more recent period, Beijing became Islamabad's most important arms supplier after Washington.[6] Willingness to ally with Pakistan in maintaining the local balance of power has earned Chinese leaders their cherished influence in this region for decades. China's role may grow in relative importance as there have appeared signs of weaker American commitment to providing aid for Pakistani defense over concerns about its nuclear capability.

Pakistan is not exempt from the general desire on the part of developing countries to acquire sophisticated Western equipment. The attractiveness of the outdated Chinese models is chiefly their low cost. Pakistan must make up for the technological disadvantage of these items by installing Western avionics systems. Still, in 1989, Islamabad's air force accepted 50 F7P fighters from Beijing, adding to the existing inventory of 300 Chinese jets. Moreover, the Pakistani navy is negotiating the purchase of a Chinese Han class nuclear-powered attack submarine for $63 million to match India's acquisition of a Soviet Charlie class submarine in 1989.[7]

EGYPT

While the Chinese arms transfer policy in South Asia has been marked by continuity, China's relations with the Middle East experienced astonishing transformation in the 1980s, catapulting Beijing into a position of significant influence in that strategic region.

[5] Vertzberger, Yaacov. "South Asia," in Gerald Segal and William Tow (eds.) *Chinese Defence Policy*. London, Macmillan, 1984. p. 248–50.

[6] United States Arms Control and Disarmament Agency. *World Military Expenditures and Arms Transfers (WMEAT)*, 1984, 1988.

[7] Cheung, Tai Ming. "Air Arms Race Builds Tensions," *Far Eastern Economic Review (FEER)*, Feb. 15, 1990. p. 54–55; and "Nuclear Deal on Han," *FEER*, Sept. 6, 1990. p. 20–21.

The initiation of Sino-Egyptian military ties was announced by then President Sadat in March 1976, just ten days after he had broken relations with Moscow. The circumstances allowed China to play a valuable role in providing supplies of MiG engines, spare parts, ammunition, maintenance for Soviet-made equipment, and Chinese versions of Soviet MiG aircraft. However, the value of military transactions was low and the deals were part gift, part sales. Chinese arms transfers to the Middle East during the 1975–1979 period were limited to about $70 million, or 0.2 percent of the total military supply to the region.[8]

In 1980, pragmatic Chinese leaders began to provide more significant levels of arms to Egypt on commercial terms. From 1980 to 1983, Beijing concluded deals with the Egyptians valued at the time as something between $500–700 million by one scholar. The writer also notes that China had become Cairo's third largest weapons supplier—after the United States and France.[9] During 1983–1987, Beijing exported $550 million in arms to the Egyptians.[10]

Apart from the economic and political benefits of the relationship with Cairo, Beijing also gained access to more sophisticated Soviet—and perhaps even Western—military technology and intelligence. The more advanced samples of fighters, engines, bombers, missiles, and tanks were not the most up-to-date and may have already been familiar in China. However, the close relationship with the Egyptians was advantageous, because it allowed the Chinese to take back to China working and diversified models with manuals for reverse-engineering and experimentation.[11]

IRAQ AND IRAN

The experience with Egypt gave Beijing confidence in dealing with the next sales opportunity in the Middle East. During 1982–1989, the Chinese made $7.46 billion in arms deliveries to Iraq and Iran.[12] In that period, with 57 percent of its arms shipments destined for the two belligerents, China ranked fifth among all arms merchants to the developing world—behind the Soviet Union, United States, France, and the United Kingdom. As one specialist notes, "the Iran-Iraq War proved to be a bonanza for the PRC, enabling it to sell in the first three years of the conflict more arms than it had exported in the preceding quarter-century." [13]

In spite of its announced neutrality, China had begun to supply weaponry to Iraq in 1981, soon after the start of the Iraq-Iran conflict in 1980. Like Egypt, Iraq lacked Soviet replacement parts and ammunition, and had to turn to China for a quarter of its military acquisitions, including tanks, fighters, light arms, and artillery. Chinese equipment was available without political strings, relatively cheap, simple to use, and could be supplied at an extensive scale. In return, Iraq, like Egypt, probably provided more updated military technological information for China.[14]

---

[8] Shichor, p. 264-7.
[9] Ibid., p. 268.
[10] WMEAT, 1988. p. 113.
[11] Shichor, p. 271-2.
[12] Grimmett, Tables 2G and 2H.
[13] Miller, Morton S. "Conventional Arms Trade in the Developing World, 1976–86: Reflections on a Decade," WMEAT, 1987. p. 21.
[14] Shichor, p. 268, 272.

In addition, China had exported combat aircraft and other weaponry to Iran—apparently through North Korea—since the beginning of the Iran-Iraq War. By the mid-1980s, China had begun direct shipments to Iran and became its most important supplier of arms.[15] While Chinese arms deliveries to Iraq were valued at $3.11 billion (in 1990 dollars) during 1982–1985, deliveries to Iran were a modest $570 million over the same period. In the 1986–1989 period, the pattern was reversed. China's arms deliveries to Iraq dropped to $1.05 billion, while deliveries to Iran climbed to $2.73 billion.[16]

Reports that Chinese shipments to Iran included Silkworm surface-to-surface missiles which threatened shipping in the Persian Gulf prompted the United States in October 1987 to ban further liberalization of technology sales to China. In response, Beijing announced its intent to "prevent Silkworm missiles from flowing into the international market" while denying direct sales to Iran. In early March 1988, then Chinese Foreign Minister Wu Xueqian visited Washington where he reiterated the vague assurance, without committing support for a U.N. Security Council resolution to impose an arms embargo on Iran. After Wu's statements, the State Department announced on March 9 the resumption of export-control liberalization for China. However, U.S. intelligence found that Beijing had also exported C–801 anti-shipping missiles and CSA–1 anti-aircraft missiles—items not mentioned in the official Chinese assurance.[17]

SAUDI ARABIA

Ironically coinciding with Foreign Minister Wu's visit, the United States, on March 6, 1988, obtained confirmation of American intelligence reports about Chinese deliveries of CSS–2 (East Wind) intermediate range ballistic missiles to Saudi Arabia. Reports indicated that the Sino-Saudi deal was initiated in 1985. The shipments, which first reached Saudi Arabia in late 1987, were reportedly disguised as weapons bound for Iraq.[18] The actual number of missiles sold has not been made public, but the transfer was believed to be sizeable, with the cost to the Saudis estimated at $3–3.5 billion.[19] Indeed, the monetary value of total Chinese arms deliveries peaked in 1988, amounting to $2.58 billion.[20] The sale had serious implications for dangerous missile proliferation in the Middle East.

In addition to significant economic profits, Beijing also scored diplomatic points in its rivalry with Taipei, as Saudi Arabia had been one of the few remaining countries to maintain formal recognition of the Republic of China on Taiwan. The CSS–2 missile sale signaled the development of increasingly friendly Sino-Saudi ties,

[15] Van Vranken Hickey, Dennis. "New Directions in China's Arms for Export Policy: An Analysis of China's Military Ties with Iran," *Asian Affairs*, Spring 1990. p. 18; Michael Weisskopf. "China Sells Arms to Iran Via North Korea," *Washington Post*, April 3, 1984.

[16] Grimmett, Tables 2G and 2H.

[17] Van Vranken Hickey, p. 18–19; Chanda, Nayan. "Much to Do About Nothing," *FEER*, March 24, 1988. p. 19.

[18] Ottaway, David B. "Saudis Hid Acquisition of Missiles," *Washington Post*, March 29, 1988. p. A1.

[19] Seib, Gerald F. "Saudi Purchase of Long-Range Missiles Rekindles Debate on U.S. Arms to Arabs," *Wall Street Journal*, April 4, 1988. p. 13.

[20] Grimmett, Table 2.

which culminated in the establishment of diplomatic relations between Beijing and Riyadh on July 21, 1990.[21]

CAMBODIAN RESISTANCE

While the Chinese have exported arms to the Middle East primarily for monetary gains, in Indochina, Beijing used military instruments as part of a geopolitical strategy toward Vietnam and the Soviet Union. China became a major supplier of weapons to the three Cambodian resistance groups in 1979, after Vietnam's invasion. Most supplies have been channeled to the communist Khmer Rouge, the strongest faction with 30,000–40,000 guerrillas. In addition to the 1979 PLA attack on the Sino-Vietnamese border [22] and continued naval activities in the South China Sea, arms transfers have been one of three military tools employed for Beijing's objectives of a Vietnamese withdrawal from Cambodia and an end to their alliance with the Soviets.[23] U.S officials estimated the Khmer Rouge to have received $100 million a year in military and other support from their Chinese patrons.[24]

During Hanoi's troop withdrawal from Cambodia in 1988–1990, reports said that the Chinese continued to supply large new shipments of arms to the Khmer Rouge.[25] In July 1990, China agreed to halt arms transfers to the guerrilla faction, perhaps to be a more constructive international actor. Beijing's commitment was necessary for U.S. foreign policy objectives. The agreement came a day before Secretary of State James Baker announced that the United States was dropping diplomatic recognition for the resistance coalition and opening talks with Vietnam, in efforts to prevent the Khmer Rouge's return to power.[26] However, in spite of the Chinese pledge, reports in the fall of 1990 have claimed the Chinese may be supplying tanks to the Khmer Rouge in their last grab for strategic territory before the conclusion of peace talks.[27]

THAILAND

As part of its strategy to isolate Vietnam, Beijing has also placed priority on improving ties with the Association for Southeast Asian Nations (ASEAN).[28] China's rise in prominence as the second largest military supplier to Thailand since 1986 was one result of this emphasis. The Thais made the most purchases in 1987 and 1988 from the Chinese, all based on low "friendship" prices, perhaps below cost. The special Sino-Thai military relationship developed as

---

[21] Beijing International Service. "Commentary Discusses Ties." in *FBIS-CHI*, July 24, 1990. p. 6.

[22] After Vietnam's invasion of Cambodia in 1978, Beijing sought "to teach Vietnam a lesson" about aggression. The PLA, with its outdated equipment and procedures, failed to achieve a decisive victory in this limited incursion and lost an estimated 20,000 soldiers.

[23] Niksch, Larry A. "Southeast Asia," in Gerald Segal and William T. Tow (eds.). *Chinese Defence Policy*. London, Macmillan, 1984. p. 236–37.

[24] Sterngold, James. "China Faults U.S. Shift on Cambodia," *New York Times*, July 20, 1990. p. A2.

[25] Pear, Robert. "China is Said to Send Arms to Khmer Rouge," *New York Times*, May 1, 1990.

[26] Krauss, Clifford. "U.S. Says China Backs Halt in Weapons to Khmer Rouge," *New York Times*, July 21, 1990.

[27] *The Nation* (Bangkok). "Officer on PRC Logistic Support to Khmer Rouge," in *FBIS-EAS*, October 12, 1990. p. 68; Pringle, James. "Thieves in the Temple," *Washington Times*, November 1, 1990. p. A8.

[28] Niksch, p. 241.

a result of common goals regarding Vietnam's invasion of Cambodia, a Thai military modernization program with limited funds, and a dramatic drop in arms sales assistance from the United States—Thailand's most important arms supplier.[29] According to the latest available figures, Beijing delivered $90 million worth of weapons to Bangkok in the 1983–1987 period.[30]

BURMA (MYANMAR)

In Southeast Asia, China has most recently extended its political influence through arms sales to Burma (formerly Myanmar), where a repressive military regime has ruled since September 18, 1988. After violently suppressing pro-democracy demonstrations, the State Law and Order Restoration Council (SLORC)—as the regime is called—came to power isolated from the world democratic community which imposed an embargo and cut off Western supplies of arms. In addition, India expressed its support in September 1988 for the "undaunted resolve of the Burmese people to achieve democracy." India was also the only neighbor to adopt an explicit refugee policy when thousands of dissidents fled SLORC's takeover a week later.[31] The regime seems determined to retain power in spite of the opposition's overwhelming victory in the May 1990 elections and to bolster its military force. For the above reasons, the SLORC may have decided to abandon its former neutrality in the Sino-Indian rivalry and turn to China for arms.

Reports indicate that a shipment of Chinese munitions arrived in Yangon (formerly Rangoon) in August 1990. That delivery appears to be only the beginning of a significant arms deal whereby China would supply Burma with a package amounting to $1.2 billion worth of assistance. Twelve F–6 jet fighters (modified MiG–19) are reportedly scheduled to arrive in December 1990. Other items in the agreement include 60 medium-size tanks, 25 anti-aircraft guns, a number of 120-mm and 105-mm howitzers, six 30-knot patrol boats, twelve F–7 jet fighters (modified MiG–21), a number of shoulder-fired HTM 5–A missiles, and nine armored personnel carriers.[32] China quickly dismissed the reports as "sheer rumor."[33]

III. IMPLICATIONS

GEOPOLITICAL EFFECTS

The pattern of Chinese weapon transfers has important ramifications for international politics. Beijing delivered 91 percent of its arms exports to the Middle East and South Asia in the 1982–1985 period, and 94 percent in 1986–1989. In 1989, China was the most important source of arms for Iran, with deliveries valued at $1.29 billion.[34]

---

[29] Stier, Kenneth J. "Chinese Edge Out Americans in Arms Sales to Thailand," *Journal of Commerce*, April 20, 1990.

[30] *WMEAT, 1988.*

[31] *FEER. Asia 1990 Yearbook.* p. 97, 99. India built camps for Burmese dissidents, and its Minister for External Affairs stated that no genuine Burmese refugees seeking shelter in India would be turned back.

[32] A reliable diplomatic source told *The Nation* (Bangkok), reported on Nov. 27, 1990, p. 1; in FBIS–EAS, Nov. 27, 1990. Also see, Lintner, Bertil. "Chinese Arms Supply Suggests SLORC Digging In," *FEER*, Sept. 13, 1990. p. 28.

[33] Hong Kong AFP, Nov. 29, 1990; in *FBIS–CHI*, Nov. 29, 1990.

[34] Grimmett. Tables 2D, 2K.

As a result, Chinese cooperation has become crucial for U.S. interests in the strategic and unstable Mideast region. In the recent Iraq-Kuwait situation, Beijing's actions regarding the trade embargo against Iraq have been one of the most closely monitored aspects of that round of crisis-management. The United States sought reassurances that China would enforce the ban on weapons to Iraq after a British paper, *The Independent*, reported on September 30 that Norinco, a Chinese defense corporation, agreed to supply Iraq with seven tons of lithium hydride, a chemical used for ballistic missiles.[35] Other critical observers have noted the foreign ministry's assurances on halting Chinese arms sales to Iraq, but not arms deliveries.[36]

Arms sales have also provided significant influence for Beijing in Indochina and South Asia. Chinese cooperation in halting arms transfers to the Khmer Rouge is necessary for American efforts to bring about a peaceful settlement in Cambodia and preclude the communist faction's return to power. Chinese military transactions to Pakistan also have particular impact for the arms race in South Asia, especially on the issue of nuclear non-proliferation. Arms sales have gained Beijing valuable leverage in foreign relations.

On the one hand, the important position that China attained in the 1980s produced a more confident and satisfied power on the world stage. On the other hand, Beijing's objective willingness and proven capacity to supply in quality and quantity the developing world's demands for arms, including missiles, has caused considerable concern for weapons proliferation.

RELATIONSHIP TO INTERNAL REFORMS

China's elevated status as a world power has also been closely linked to the contributions of its arms sales to efforts at reforming and modernizing the military and economy in general. While Deng Xiaoping's reform of the defense structure after 1978 made possible the extensive Chinese arms sales of the 1980s, that trade in turn has had ramifications for continuing efforts at military and economic reforms. The Chinese military industrial complex developed features of decentralization of control with a proliferation of arms trading corporations in a dual PLA and ministerial structure (see Table 2 below).

Starting in 1979, with one exception, the pragmatic Beijing leadership established foreign trading corporations under the various defense industrial ministries, such as machine-building and electronics.[37] The expansion of military-related sales abroad prompted the PLA to also set up its own front companies to sell off excess stocks of equipment and secure a share of the foreign exchange earnings from the lucrative arms sales. These export and procurement arms of the military have also directly imported advanced military technology and equipment for the PLA's modernization.

---

[35] Sun, Lena. "Chinese Said to Sell Chemical to Iraq," *Washington Post*, October 1, 1990. As usual, the Chinese foreign ministry denied China had violated the trade embargo against Iraq and called the report "totally groundless," adding that "China is a responsible country."

[36] Delfs, Robert. "The Gulf Card," *FEER*, September 20, 1990. p. 19.

[37] U.S.-China Business Council. "China's Military Procurement Organizations," *The China Business Review*, Sept.–Oct. 1989. p. 31.; U.S.-China Business Council files. The North Industries Corporation (Norinco) had been secretly set up in 1973.

Table 2 below shows the Chinese arms trading corporations which were formed under reorganized defense industrial ministries subordinate to the State Council and also under General Departments and service arms supervised by the Communist Party's Military Commission.

Table 2: China's Arms Trading Corporations

CCP Military Commission
(PLA Corporations)

State Council
(Defense Ministerial Corporations)

COSTIND:
    Xinshidai Corporation
    Xiaofeng Technology and Equipment
    Corporation

GSD Equipment Department:
  Polytechnologies, Inc.
  Pinghe Electronics Co. Ltd.

MMBEI:
  China North Industries Corp.
  China National Machinery and
    Equipment Import-Export Corp.
  China Shipbuilding Trading Co.
  China National Electronics
    Import-Export Corp.

GSD Communications Department:
  China Electronics Systems
    Engineering Company
  China Zhihua Corporation, Ltd.

MAS:
  China National Aero-Technology
    Import-Export Corp.
  China Precision Machinery Import-
    Export Corp.
  China Great Wall Industry Corp.
  Beijing Wan Yuan Industry Corp.
  Beijing Chang Feng Industry Corp.
  Chinese Academy of Space Tech.

Air Force:
  Lantian Corporation

Navy:
  Xinghai Corporation

GPD:
  Kaili Corporation

GLD:
  Xinxing Corporation

MER:
  China Nuclear Instrumentation
    and Equipment Corp.
  China Nuclear Energy Industry
    Corp.
  Rainbow Development Corp.

PAP:
  Jingan Equipment Import-Export
    Corporation

Abbreviations:
CCP — Chinese Communist Party
COSTIND — Commission of Science, Technology, and Industry for National Defense
PLA — People's Liberation Army
GSD — General Staff Department
GPD — General Political Department
GLD — General Logistics Department
PAP — People's Armed Police
MMBEI — Ministry of Machine Building and Electronics Industry
MAS — Ministry of Aerospace Industry
MER — Ministry of Energy Resources

Source: Corbett, John F. Jr. and Clinton B. Mullen. *China's Defense Industrial Trading Companies*, Defense Intelligence Agency Reference Aid, VP-1920-271-90, unclassified, September 1990.

Three implications for reforms can be identified. First, the defense sector has also been subject to policies of decentralization.

The growth of civilian and military import/export companies has further decentralized authority over commercial production and sales decisions within the state. In the dual defense industrial structure, PLA corporations have been separate from defense ministerial corporations. These "subordinate but highly autonomous" defense ministerial corporations have also set up their own subsidiaries.[38]

Corporations in the PLA have been formed under all three General Departments: Logistics, Staff, and Political, in addition to those in the People's Armed Police, PLA Navy, and PLA Air Force. However, the absence of evidence pointing to Chinese arms shipments to Iraq in the first few months after the invasion of Kuwait may have indicated that the top leadership in Beijing, at a minimum, retains the reins on politically sensitive arms sales.

The Commission of Science, Technology and Industry for National Defense (COSTIND) was formed in 1982 to ensure the PLA's needs are met. COSTIND coordinates budget allocations, research and development (R&D), and production. However, most defense corporations have not been subordinate to it. Responsible to both the State Council and the Party's Military Commission, COSTIND is supposed to link the military and civilian hierarchies. It has played a coordinating role, as when one company needs the supplies of a factory not under its jurisdiction.

Second, arms sales have generated an increasingly large constituency for reforms and foreign trade within the profit-oriented sectors of both the military and civilian defense hierarchies. High-level cadres have opportunities to obtain top management positions in the lucrative corporations situated in attractive coastal cities. The PLA now includes within its ranks soldiers and political officers who have become professional entrepreneurs. As a result, support has been enhanced for continued economic reforms to obtain funds and advanced technology.

Third, the transfer of some PLA officers to import/export corporations and the sale of excess military supplies have facilitated efforts to streamline the military. The PLA's export of its outdated, surplus stocks of military equipment and spare parts was to complement paramount leader Deng Xiaoping's one million man demobilization to restructure the PLA into a leaner war machine. In sum, export of military supplies has played a role in Chinese reforms to adopt more efficient utilization of military facilities and resources, promoting modernization of the forces.

MODERNIZATION OF THE MILITARY

Chinese military modernization involves two dimensions: the short-term goal of improving the combat effectiveness of forces and the long-term aim of building a scientific and defense industrial base capable of developing the country's own weapons with advanced technology.[39] On the positive side, arms sales have promot-

---

[38] Latham, Richard J. "China's Defense Industrial Policy: Looking Toward the Year 2000," in Richard Yang (ed.) *SCPS Yearbook on PLA Affairs 1988/89.* p. 85.

[39] Godwin, Paul H.B. "Overview: China's Defense Modernization," in *China's Economy Looks Toward the Year 2000.* Joint Economic Committee, May 21, 1986. p. 133.

ed the incremental and ongoing progress in both areas through the infusion of economic profits and advanced technology.

The significant levels of foreign exchange earned from arms sales have been a very important source of extra-budgetary revenue for the PLA in funding R&D and procurement of advanced equipment and technology. With only 70 percent of operating expenses in maintaining troops covered by the state budget,[40] the PLA must make up for the rest and still find supplemental funds for modernization. For example, the General Logistics Department's Xinxing Corporation, which has an annual business volume of several hundred million U.S. dollars, has been allowed to keep 100 percent of its foreign currency earnings.[41]

The increased financial autonomy of the PLA provided by arms sales has made ongoing modernization possible in spite of reductions in defense allocations, which dropped from 17.5 percent of national spending in 1979 to 7.4 percent in 1989.[42] Arms sales also apparently gave access to more advanced technology through China's arms buyers in the Middle East. These contributions have allowed the modernization of the PLA through extensive research and development, and less so by large-scale import of more sophisticated equipment.[43] Finally, with reforms aimed at reducing the isolation of the defense research and production sector, technology transfers have stimulated the upgrading of civilian facilities and products as well.

There is an opposing viewpoint that the Chinese arms marketing structure has obstructed the development of a cohesive modernization program for the PLA.[44] According to this argument, jurisdictional conflict has arisen among several key groups placed in the dual defense industrial structure. Rival armed services perceive different operational requirements. Defense industries aim to upgrade manufacturing facilities to maximize economic gain, while military officers prefer more timely improvements in combat capabilities. Moreover, the lines of authority have been blurred by the impotence of the defense ministry and the dual foci of responsibility. The defense industries, political leaders, and COSTIND all have exhibited a bias toward exports and commercial gain. As the result, no comprehensive force development program for the armed services has been implemented. "Too often, procurement decisions within the PLA itself represent a compromise rather than a clear set of priorities. . . . Economic and commercial issues distort the decisions on upgrading military doctrine, force structure, and equipment."[45]

INTERDEPENDENCE IN THE WORLD ECONOMY

Finally, arms sales present implications for China's efforts at greater integration with the world economy. As seen in the Silk-

---

[40] *Ming Pao* (Hong Kong), April 24, 1988, p. 9. Interview with PLA General Logistics Department Director, Zhao Nanqi; cited by Latham, p. 87.

[41] U.S.-China Business Council files.

[42] Gillespie, Richard E. "The Military's New Muscle," *The China Business Review*, Sept.–Oct. 1989. p. 27.

[43] Shichor, p. 271.

[44] Richard Gillespie and Richard Latham argue this view.

[45] Gillespie, p. 29–30.

worm sales to Iran, arms sales have conflicted with another modernization goal of acquiring Western technology. Especially in the view of the United States, China's deliveries of arms and missiles, plus repeated denials of such, in regions of instability have harmed its pronounced standing as a responsible actor. The Chinese arms transfer record on missiles raises concern for nuclear proliferation and escalated arms races, particularly in South Asia. Western charges of reckless arms transfers complicate the work of diplomats in the foreign ministry as they lobby for foreign investments, trade, World Bank aid, favorable tariff treatment, or entrance to the GATT. Thus, consideration of trade-offs by China's policy-makers will partly affect Chinese arms sales in the next decade.

IV. OUTLOOK FOR THE 990s

In the 1990s, China can be expected to continue its aggressive marketing of weapons for both political and commercial reasons. Indeed, U.S. intelligence reported in early 1990 that China appeared to be preparing for a new round of missiles sales to Iran and Syria.[46] However, China's pursuit of sustained or increased arms sales will likely be circumscribed by increased economic interdependence, continuing global decline in demand for arms, greater American efforts to emphasize nuclear non-proliferation in a new era of superpower cooperation, and the resolution of tensions along China's borders with the Soviet Union, Vietnam, and India.

INTERNAL FACTORS

One domestic factor that may encourage arms sales is that political leaders in Beijing realize the imperative of raising morale within the PLA after having assigned to the military lower priority in the modernization efforts of the last decade and after using troops to suppress pro-democracy demonstrations in June 1989. This need to placate the PLA has been reflected in the military's 11.5 percent share in the 1990 budget, the first increase after ten years.[47] With political realities and budgetary constraints, the PLA could argue its case for the continued pursuit of arms sales earnings to meet its needs.

Another positive factor is the improved capacity of the Chinese defense industry that will allow it to take advantage of market opportunities. Chinese military suppliers have proven capable of providing huge quantities of low-technology weapons at competitive prices to the developing world. At the same time, ongoing Chinese efforts to upgrade older Soviet models and develop an "interim generation" of more advanced Chinese weaponry will allow China to remain on the scene as a major arms supplier.[48]

There may be domestic issues that would mitigate the enthusiastic production and marketing of arms for export. First, one scholar points out the increased relevance of the "guns and butter" trade-off for Chinese policy-makers. The question of resource allocation between military and civilian purposes will be more salient in the

---

[46] Gordon, Michael. "Beijing Avoids New Missile Sales Assurances," *New York Times*, March 30, 1990. p. A7.

[47] Cheung, Tai Ming. "Political Payoff," *FEER*, April 5, 1990. p. 28–9.

[48] Miller, p. 21.

1990s because of efforts over the last decade to integrate the military and civilian research and production sectors.[49] For example, 50 percent of production by the giant defense corporation, Norinco, are now civilian goods,[50] reflecting efforts to divert the excess capacity of the military complex for the civilian sector of the Chinese economy. Second, state management of the greatly expanded defense industrial bureaucracy may involve efforts to control redundancy and corruption. Finally, there will continue to be conflict between the business of arms dealers and the tasks of diplomats.

EXTERNAL VARIABLES

It appears that several external circumstances in the 1990s will constrain China's continued marketing of arms for profits and influence. Increased economic interdependence has brought a trade-off for China between arms sales profits and potential economic and technological gains from cooperating with the West on strategic issues. After Iraq's invasion of Kuwait in early August 1990, China promised to withhold arms sales to Iraq in hopes of increasing Western trade and investments. China's constructive role against Iraq in part led to the easing of sanctions by the European Community[51] and the continuation of most-favored-nation status on tariffs for Chinese goods, despite the passed U.S. House of Representatives resolution to disapprove it.[52] Beijing appears to have calculated that gradual progress towards the resumption of trade, investment, and loans to levels prior to the violent crackdown in June 1989, as well as continued friendship with Saudi Arabia, represent potentially greater gains than any arms sales profits from or leverage over Baghdad.[53]

The ending of the Cold War has given Washington greater maneuverability to stress weapons non-proliferation in the developing world. One consequence was the Bush Administration's October 1990 suspension of $240 million in annual military aid to Pakistan due to suspicions about its nuclear capability.[54] The change in superpower relations may translate into heightened American sensitivity and willingness to use economic and technological leverage to prevent the spread of arms, and missiles in particular, by Beijing.

Chinese arms sales will also be affected by changes in the international arms market. The value of arms sales agreements with Third World buyers has generally declined during 1982–1989.[55] This trend can be mainly attributed to the completion of many force improvement programs in the developing countries.[56] High

---

[49] Latham, p. 80.

[50] U.S.-China Business Council files.

[51] Sun, Lena. "EC to Ease Sanctions on China," *Washington Post*, October 24, 1990. The sanctions were imposed in response to the Tiananmen crackdown in June 1989.

[52] Farnsworth, Clyde. "Assailing Beijing, House Votes a Rise in China's Tariffs," *New York Times*, October 19, 1990. p. 1. House Joint Resolution 647 passed 247–174 on October 18, 1990, and was received in the Senate.

[53] Sun, Lena. "China Hopes Its Cooperation Will Yield Benefits," *Washington Post*, September 15, 1990. p. A13.

[54] The suspension was required by Sec. 620E of the Foreign Assistance Act, which makes U.S. assistance conditional upon presidential certification that Pakistan does not possess a nuclear explosive device. Also see, Coll, Steve. "Rifts Appear in U.S.-Pakistani Alliance," *Washington Post*, October 22, 1990. p. A13.

[55] Grimmett, Table 1.

[56] Miller, p. 19.

growth rates and continued arms races, especially in air power, continue to make Asia a favorable market for arms. However, Asian militaries tend to prefer advanced Western equipment over Chinese supplies. This view is held prominently by Thailand's Air Chief Marshal who put a purchase of Chinese F7M fighters on hold after he took office in October 1989.[57] Moreover, the pattern of ASEAN countries matching each other's acquisitions of Western hardware is likely to continue.[58] The late 1980s have seen the scaling back of Third World conflicts, including the end of the Iran-Iraq War, the Soviet pullout from Afghanistan, and Vietnam's withdrawal from Cambodia. In the future, China may no longer be able to count on arms sales opportunities of the same lucrative and urgent nature.

On the supply side, China's arms sales prospects will be affected by its existing (e.g., Soviet, American, French, British) and potential (e.g., Brazilian) competitors in the arms market. After Iraq's invasion of Kuwait, the Bush Administration's decision to sell multibillion dollar packages of weaponry to Saudi Arabia may have cut China off from that market. The Soviet Union appears to be in possession of a large stock of surplus arms after a number of East European countries terminated contracts.[59] Further, one specialist notes that "Brazil has long been building the kind of industrial infrastructure which can support an arms industry at the upper edge of the middle technological level." [60] Finally, although the effects are not yet fully apparent, changes in former Soviet bloc countries, which have been important arms exporters, will affect the market—either through the countries' dumping of Soviet supplies on the market or creation of a vacuum for further Chinese expansion.

Lastly, China's improved external security situation in the 1990s may also affect its decisions on arms sales. At the time, China appears ready to enjoy the lowest level of tensions along its borders since the 1950s. The recent gradual normalization of relations between China and India was highlighted by then Prime Minister Rajiv Gandhi's end of 1988 visit to Beijing. After Vietnam's military retreat from Cambodia, China has agreed to halt arms shipments to the Khmer Rouge and invited top Vietnamese leaders for a secret summit in the southwestern Chinese city of Chengdu in early September 1990.[61] Beijing's new friendship with Moscow has expanded to military transactions.[62] In sum, reduced fears of Soviet-Vietnamese encirclement will lessen the urgency of Chinese arms sales to neighboring countries for political goals.

---

[57] Cheung, Tai Ming. "Air Arms Race Builds Tensions," *FEER*, Feb. 15, 1990. p. 55; Tasker, Rodney. "Political High-flier," *FEER*, Dec. 7, 1989. p. 21.

[58] Tasker, Rodney. "Reaching for the Sky," *FEER*, Feb. 22, 1990. p. 22.

[59] Cheung, Tai Ming. "A Sale is in the Air," *FEER*, Sept. 6, 1990. p. 20.

[60] Miller, p. 22.

[61] Delfs, Robert, "Carrots and Sticks," *FEER*, October 4, 1990. p. 11; Also see, Chanda, Nayan. "Vietnam's Vice Premier Sees Progress Toward Normalizing Relations with U.S." *Asian Wall Street Journal*, October 15, 1990. p. 24.

[62] In the first sale of military items since rapprochement, Moscow agreed to sell China two dozen troop-carrier helicopters (*FEER*, October 11, 1990, p. 8). Also, the Chinese have been negotiating the purchase of 12 Soviet Su27 ground attack fighters for the PLA Air Force (Cheung, Tai Ming. "A Sale is in the Air," *FEER*, September. 6, 1990. p. 20).

V. Conclusion

The leaders of China face complex domestic and international dilemmas in making arms sales decisions. Yet, the political and military leaders in Beijing, with general consensus about the objectives of exporting arms, are not likely to relinquish the contributions of arms sales to modernization and foreign policy. Chinese decision-makers will continue to choose between arms sales and further Western linkages on a case by case basis depending on the perceived net gains for the Chinese national goals of both power and wealth. Thus, the United States will continue to face issues stemming from the effect of Chinese arms sales on American interests globally.

V. INTERDEPENDENCE

OVERVIEW

By Arlene Wilson *

China's economic isolation from the Western world changed dramatically after the Third Plenum of the Eleventh Communist Party Congress in late 1978. Spurred by a desire to modernize, acquire new technology, and stimulate economic growth, the Chinese leadership, headed by Deng Xiaoping, initiated a policy of "reform and opening up." Although the policy included both domestic and international initiatives, the papers in this section focus on the "open door policy" aimed at encouraging foreign trade and investment.

NATURE AND EFFECTIVENESS OF THE OPEN DOOR POLICY

In general, China's integration into the world economy included institutional and legal changes to decentralize the foreign trade bureaucracy, protect the interests of foreign investors, and facilitate borrowing from abroad. More specifically, China enacted joint venture laws, established local foreign trade entities, set up special economic zones (SEZs), joined multilateral institutions, and liberalized import, export and foreign exchange restrictions. But progress in opening up was sporadic. Three times during the 1980s, retrenchment followed a period of rapid economic changes, creating much uncertainty for foreign businesses. Typically the reform periods in 1979–80, 1984 and 1987–88 were characterized by expansionary monetary policy, increased investment spending, liberalizing measures for exports, imports and foreign investment, decentralization of foreign trade decisions, and the establishment of special economic zones and coastal areas. But, sometime after new measures were initiated, imports swelled, creating foreign exchange problems, and inflation, fueled by easy credit and shortages of supplies, became severe. With few economic levers to control the economy and Beijing's fear of social unrest, the leadership retracted some of the reforms in 1980, 1985 and late 1988. For example, investment spending was strictly curtailed, foreign trade decisions were recentralized by abolishing some local trade entities, and the SEZs' autonomy was reduced. During the retrenchment phases, Western exports to China declined, as did foreign investment in China.

---

* Specialist in International Trade and Finance, Economics Division, Congressional Research Service.

Papers not mentioned in this overview were not available to the reviewer at the time this was drafted.

The basic framework of laws and regulations on foreign investment in China were enacted in the years 1979 through 1982. These legal changes protecting the rights of foreign investors made possible the unprecedented increase in foreign direct investment contracts in China from $1.7 billion in 1980 to $5.6 billion in 1989. In his paper on Chinese law, James Feinerman explains why foreign investors, despite the reforms, continued to express many legal concerns. For example, the many different Chinese tax regimes complicated foreign investment in China. Getting approval to market products in China was difficult, and approval of potential investment projects could be slow. Foreign exchange problems remained, despite Chinese efforts to resolve them. The Chinese sometimes interpreted legal contracts as nonbinding, and did not always permit foreign investors to make personnel decisions. Recent legal reforms in April 1990 attempted to address these issues. The author concludes that China, after making some mistakes, now seems to have a clearer system of law and regulation. The goals of SEZs are to attract foreign investment, facilitate export industries, and serve as a link between the foreign and domestic market. To that end, investors in SEZs receive tax and tariff preferences, flexible labor and wage policies, more modern infrastructure, and more freedom from bureaucratic control. SEZs were successful in stimulating foreign trade and investment, but have been criticized for their high infrastructure cost, their use of domestic funds (diverting funds from domestic projects) and possible corruption. Economic criticism, as well as political discord, led to several periods of retrenchment. But, George Crane, in his paper, notes that periods of retrenchment were usually short because foreign investment, needed for modernization, declined. He concludes that SEZs are inherently unstable because they are subject to ideological and economic criticism, but, at the same time, cannot be ended by opponents who are interested in modernizing because foreign investment would then decline.

As China opened up, those provinces most actively engaged in foreign trade and investment grew more rapidly, had a higher standard of living, and enjoyed more autonomy from Beijing's policies than did other provinces. For example, coastal provinces avoided to some extent Beijing's 1988–89 austerity program by selling in foreign markets and borrowing from foreign investors. Erin Endean, in her paper on China's foreign commercial relations, maintains that the gulf between the coastal provinces and others will widen in the future. But, at the same time, the coastal provinces will be more vulnerable to a downturn in global economic conditions than the other provinces.

According to Martin Weil, foreign businesses did not have an easy time operating in China in the 1980s, despite the increasing openness. In particular, the cycles of reform and retrenchment, as well as interference by the Chinese bureaucracy in business decisions, increased the uncertainty and the cost of doing business in China. He concludes that those foreign companies which had large sales volumes or which produced for export in the coastal provinces, usually profited. But for others, perhaps the majority, optimism for the future was China's main attraction.

Membership in multilateral economic institutions began when China joined the International Monetary Fund and the World Bank (and its affiliated agencies) in 1980. After acquiring observer status in the GATT in 1983, China applied for GATT membership in 1986. China also joined the Asian Development Bank in 1986. According to William F. Feeney, the grants, loans and credits China received from its participation in international economic institutions have been "indispensable in accelerating China's modernization." For example, from 1981–90, China's cumulative borrowings from the World Bank and its affiliate, the International Development Association, were $9.2 billion. Moreover, China also benefitted significantly from the research analysis, advice and consultation provided by the institutions' highly qualified staff. China's external debt from all sources, estimated at $40 billion to $50 billion, is considered well within China's ability to pay.

The acquisition of foreign technology is a major goal of China's opening up. According to Roy Grow, although the national government and local authorities are involved in the decision to acquire new technology, the enterprise is the most crucial. Successful enterprise managers define the need for foreign technology, discuss the options with end users within the enterprise and initiate the process of acquiring new technology. Since the enterprise is so important in the process, national policies affecting enterprise managers will have a large effect on the success or failure of future technology projects.

During the 1980s, China benefitted from the policy of export-led growth, as standardized products (especially textiles and apparel) mass produced by low-wage workers were sold in large developed-country markets. But, as William Fischer discusses, this strategy may be less successful in China in the future. Problems in Chinese infrastructure, recentralization of authority during the retrenchment periods, the possibility that automation will replace workers in some industries, and growing trade barriers in industrial markets may limit future growth of mass-produced items. The author concludes that China needs more intimate relationships with foreign countries to overcome export barriers abroad and infrastructure difficulties in China. In order to attract foreign technology and managerial skills, China must rely on its comparative advantage of a potentially large market, not low-wage labor.

CHINA'S CHANGING TRADE PATTERNS

From 1979 to 1989, China's foreign trade grew from $29 billion to $110 billion. Over the same period, China's exports increased from 5 percent to 22 percent of GNP, an indication of the tremendous importance of international trade to China's modernization program.

More than half of China's trade is with Asia, and such trade is growing at a rapid rate. Not surprisingly, Hong Kong, through which many of China's exports and imports are transshipped, is China's largest Asian trading partner. Other evidence of the close economic linkage with Hong Kong is the large amount (70 percent) of foreign direct investment that comes from Hong Kong, much of it going to Guangdong province in southern China. Japan, China's second most important Asian trading partner, is a source of crucial technology and foreign loans. In recent years, China's trade and investment with Taiwan and South Korea, although still relatively small, have grown rapidly and are particularly important in some areas. For example, the recent growth of the Xiamen SEZ in Fujian province reflects significant investment from Taiwan. John Frankenstein concludes that Asia's importance in China's trade will probably increase in the future, but, at the same time, China's future trade depends crucially on the way in which China deals with the absorption of Hong Kong in 1997.

China's bilateral trade with the United States grew from $2.3 billion in 1979 to $17.8 billion in 1989. Growth of U.S. imports from China was strong and steady, while U.S. exports fluctuated considerably from year to year, partly as a result of periodic retrenchment in the Chinese open-door policy. The steady upward trend in U.S. imports from China resulted in a widening of the U.S. bilateral trade deficit to $6.2 billion in 1989. As Nai-Ruenn Chen notes in his paper, the U.S.-China trade deficit may widen further as other countries, especially Taiwan, shift production of exports to China.

U.S.-China bilateral trade issues reflect divergent philosophies and interests. U.S. export control policy, for example, frustrates the Chinese desire to import high-technology products. U.S. firms invest abroad to make profits or to gain market access for the future, while China views foreign investment as a means of acquiring new technology, management skills and funds to stimulate modernization. Other often contentious bilateral trade issues are the protection of U.S. intellectual property rights in China, textile trade, the application of U.S. import control laws to products from China, and the U.S. granting of most-favored-nation status to China. China's bilateral trade of $3.9 billion with the Soviet Union in 1989, although growing rapidly since trade ties were renewed in 1983, is small compared with its importance to China in the 1950s. The bulk of Sino-Soviet trade, still centrally planned, is low because both countries are focusing on selling to hard-currency countries to acquire technology. Nevertheless, Sino-Soviet border trade, usually outside official trade channels (although permitted by both governments) appears to be growing rapidly. Sharon Ruwart concludes, in her paper, that, although China fears the recent political changes in the Soviet Union, "pragmatism will prevail and trade will be encouraged."

THE TIANANMEN INCIDENT AND THE FUTURE OF THE OPEN DOOR POLICY

Foreigners were already scaling back new investment in response to the austerity program of 1988–89 when the Tiananmen incident occurred in June 1989. After the shock of Tiananmen, however, international institutions, banks and individual countries strongly curtailed lending to China. For example, World Bank lending to China, which had been projected at $1.5 billion–$2 billion before June 1989, fell to $500 million in the 12 months beginning June 1989. Tourism from the United States and Japan declined dramatically, but an increase in tourism from Taiwan mitigated the total decline. The reduction in lending and decline in tourism fueled a foreign exchange crisis in China, and administrative controls were reimposed.

Although the Chinese leadership continues to publicly support the open door policy, the Tiananmen incident dramatically changed the perception of Western business regarding China. Perhaps most important, the close link between politics and economics in China is now very evident. Most authors of papers in this section agreed that the Tiananmen incident seriously reduced confidence in China, at least for the near future. Foreign investors (other than those from Taiwan, who continued to invest in China) will likely wait until the aging Chinese leadership is replaced and the political situation is clarified before committing large amounts of funds in China.

Nevertheless, by 1990, some of the foreign economic links were improving. Western governments lifted some of the economic sanctions they imposed right after the shock of Tiananmen and multilateral institutions resumed some lending. For example, in 1990 the World Bank authorized loans for basic human needs and some Western governments resumed export credits for China.

Many authors suggested that the changing world environment does not bode well for China's economic links to the West in the near future. Recent political and economic changes in the Soviet Union and Eastern Europe may make them more attractive to foreign investment and also weaken China's negotiating position as a strategic buffer between the United States and the Soviet Union. Markets in the West may not be as open to Chinese exports as they were for Japan and the newly industrializing countries in the past. A world recession, if it occurs, would likely inhibit China's exports.

COSTS AND BENEFITS OF INTERDEPENDENCE: A NET ASSESSMENT

By Wendy Frieman * and Thomas W. Robinson **

CONTENTS

SUMMARY

Interdependence—whether economic, political, scientific, security, or cultural—is a fact of modern life and therefore a normal component of China's development strategy. The questions for Beijing concern the degree and direction of interdependence, connections between economic and other aspects of interdependence, how China evaluates the costs and benefits of interdependence, and what Beijing's actual policy is regarding its several facets. One approximation is to consider which of the several approaches to interdependence China favors—traditional international trade theory, dependencia, developmentalism, export-led growth, the "Who is Us" approach, and the "They Own Us" school. The answer appears to be a mixture of dependencia and developmentalism. In terms of the facts, China's economic interdependence has grown rapidly in the last decade to the extent that its "trade dependence" is more than 25 percent of gross national product, while its interdependence with the advanced industrial nations (but not the Third World) is strong in terms of commodity composition. China has also

---

* Director of the Asia Technology Program at Science Applications International Corporation.
** Director of the China Studies Program at the American Enterprise Institute. He would like to thank Will Eisenbeis, Mehlika Hoodbhoy, M. Walsh McGuire, Craig Peterson, Tonya Thesing, and Kathleen Walsh for research assistance and Lin Zhiling for helpful commentary and research on Chinese language sources.

become highly interdependent in scientific, security, political, and cultural spheres, and interdependence in these areas in many instances is mutually transmutable. The Beijing leadership has generally not worried about this, except in the cultural sphere.

Chinese analysts strongly favor interdependence as highly beneficial to the country's developmental strategy and, generally, are willing to accept costs—in terms of limits on China's foreign policy freedom and the domestic influence of foreign ideas—in order to avail themselves of the benefits. A complex analysis of those costs and benefits can be made, from which it can be concluded that China will continue to move further toward interdependence, although probably not as rapidly as in the past. The dilemma for current and future Chinese rulers remains the same as that facing every Chinese leading group for the past 200 years: how to gain the benefits of economic interdependence, and hence of modernization, without suffering the concomitant costs of political and cultural transformation away from nativist exclusivism and toward genuine global partnership. The "bottom line" is that the leadership will continue to try to have things both ways but if the costs of interdependence appear to rise even modestly beyond present levels, the door will once more swing shut—if never again entirely closed—and overall modernization will suffer accordingly.

I. GENERAL IDEAS CONCERNING INTERDEPENDENCE

Interdependence has been a fact of human activity since the dawn of civilization. People and social institutions always have had to depend on each other to survive or to achieve their goals; in that sense, interdependence can hardly be controversial. Differences do arise, however. Is interdependence sometimes inequitable, so that the "balance of dependence" tilts too heavily in favor of one partner? Does economic interdependence spill over to other spheres, particularly into politico-military affairs, thus greatly complicating equity balance calculations and postulating the danger of overall dependence for small or developing countries? If interdependence is multifaceted, how can it be calculated, especially if the "units" of calculation differ from field to field and if some fields have no quantitative capability of measurement? How, in the face of such problems, can a nation's leaders make policy decisions on important questions of economic life, trade, and other domestic and foreign matters?

There are at least six types of answers to these questions drawn, respectively, from traditional international trade theory, the dependencia approach, development economics, export-led growth, the "Who is Us" school that interdependence is innately good, and its opposite, that it is by nature bad.

- Traditional international trade theory does not generally use the term "interdependence" but rather looks to the idea of mutual advantage. Nations trade with each other only when each gains in the exchange, and attention is devoted largely to questions of comparative advantage, the advantages derived from mutual specialization of production, the setting of the terms of trade through exchange rates, the consequent linking for mutual betterment of the internal economies of the coun-

tries in question, and the distortions from the ideal that gov-
ernment-imposed tariffs, quotas, and other restrictions on
trade bring. The assumption is that nations are rational actors
and that they therefore engage in trade (and become interdependent) only when it is in their interests to do so and end
such a relationship of they find this not to be the case. Moreover, it is believed that governments should refrain from interfering in the trade arena and leave such matters to private entrepreneurs. The terms of trade, set by the marketplace, are by
definition mutually advantageous to both parties, even if internal markets are severely affected and even if mutual specialization leads some countries to be permanently consigned to an
"underdeveloped" status.

- Dependencia argues that the terms of trade between more and
  less developed nations is by nature unequal by retarding the
  growth and industrialization rates of the latter. Nations consigned over the long run to be raw materials suppliers to the
  industrially more advanced nations and receiving in return the
  manufactures of the latter are kept in a relatively underdeveloped, and hence dependent, state. The means to this end are
  unequal terms of trade by the actions of transnational corporations, grossly distorted distribution of wealth between a small
  group of rich and a very large number of poor nations, perpet-
  uation of authoritarian forms of government, and through superior power and knowledge, undue interference by rich nations in the affairs of poorer nations. Unless severely modified
  by agreed-on international action, this system is self-perpetuat-
  ing. The way to meliorate the relationship is for more developed nations to make trade concessions to the lesser developed,
  thus equalizing the terms of trade, and for less developed nations to take government action to raise the price of raw materials, expand capital transfers, reduce foreign control of capital, and nationalize the assets of transnational corporations.
  Dependency theory takes equity and development as principal
  values, to which trade must be subordinated. Essentially it is a
  political theory of trade which assumes an alliance between
  imperialist (e.g., strong, developed, Western) nations and local
  authoritarian governments and bureaucracies for purposes of
  keeping the vast majority of the people of lesser developed nations in economic and political servitude. This theory also pre-
  sumes that only in a post-colonial era of anti-foreign nationalist governments will development have a chance, and even
  then the former imperialists will attempt to extend their hold
  by dominating international economic institutions and proclaiming the benefits of "interdependence." In the dependency
  approach, genuine interdependence is impossible.
- Developmentalism begins where dependencia leaves off but
  takes a more optimistic view. So long as economic and political
  barriers to growth and industrialization are removed, "natural" (generally market-driven) processes within a lesser developed nation will impel it forward. The critical impediment is
  not external, as in dependencia, but internal: the drag imposed
  by traditional socio-cultural attitudes, customs, and institutions. These must be removed for progress, which will then

easily move the economy in the direction already taken by Western countries. Indeed, lesser developed countries should deliberately copy Western practices, especially capitalism. On the other hand, democracy is not a necessary condition for development, at least in the initial stages. Rather, the prerequisite is political and social stability, which can be supplied perhaps better by an authoritarian government. Lesser developed nations should Westernize themselves rapidly, hold themselves open to free trade, and encourage foreign investment, aid, and technology transfers. Therefore, tariff barriers, quotas, and other deliberately-raised obstacles to free trade should be avoided, which means that export-led growth strategies should be eschewed despite their obvious success. Proponents of developmentalism believe that interdependence is a good that is the natural product of a nation's gradual entrance into the "modern" world, which is to say that interdependence and internationalization are nearly synonymous. The best example of this approach is Japan between 1868 and 1931, which deliberately opened itself to Western influence, modernized all of its domestic institutions, joined the developed world on equal terms within a comparatively short time, and still preserved the essential features of its own civilization.

- Export-led growth strategies stand between dependencia and an emphasis on development through Westernization. Former colonies did not wish to exchange their previous political servitude for economic dependence but greatly desired to develop as rapidly as possible. A middle way was, fortuitously, discovered. It combined, in a resource-poor land: state-led capitalism; administratively-imposed very low wages; authoritarian government; high tariff and other barriers against Western manufacturers; high risk-taking in the international market through massive state-led investment in a few modern industries (shipping and steel, for example) not justified on the basis of the internal market; massive acceptance of international loans (but not much foreign investment); artificially low (and highly controlled) exchange rates; and aggressive marketing of products in the wide-open markets of the West, particularly the United States. A high balance of payments deficit is deliberately run for many years (and financed through additional loans and constant downward adjustment of exchange rates) on the assumption that later it will not only be balanced by successful sales in developed countries but that substantial surpluses will be achieved. Only in the long run would barriers be lowered, authoritarian political controls be relaxed, foreign capital allowed relatively free reign within national borders, and mutual interdependence achieved. By then, the nation would be fully industrialized, strong enough to compete internationally on an equal basis, and able to participate in the construction of an interdependent regional and global economy. The "four dragons"—South Korea, Taiwan, Hong Kong, and Singapore—are the obvious examples of this model, which has been tried but with much less success elsewhere.
- Interdependence as an approach is based upon certain shared notions. The degree of interdependence is defined by the per-

centage of a nation's gross national product taken up by foreign trade, i.e., imports plus exports of goods and services. It is
noted that for smaller and lesser developed nations, this percentage is higher than for larger and more industrialized countries, but it is also realized that, in the second half of the twentieth century, this ratio is rising for the developing countries
as well. Interdependence is not limited to economic matters
and is also present in politics, culture, security, etc. And none
of these spheres are autonomous: nations can, and do, (or are
constrained to) exchange degrees of interdependence in various
arenas. Finally, there is a basic division between an emphasis
on interdependence as a set of linkages or connections between
societies, with little or no judgment attached, and an emphasis
on interdependence as a set of mutual dependencies between
two or more nations that may be both differential in their
manifestations and corrosive in their effects. All agree, however, that the closely connected nature of the global economy
makes it inevitable that economic activity or economic policy
within a given country will, often rapidly, necessitate a response and consequent changes in the military, political, cultural and other spheres.

Thus, American monetary or fiscal expansion, undertaken for
purely domestic economic purposes, will spill over to the international economic sphere through balance of payments changes, linkages between interest rates in American and other nations, exchange rate adjustments, changes in demand for imports, and inflation. Differences in opinion arise only when judgments are attached as to whether such activity, and the responses that decision-
makers in other nations feel necessary to take, are "good" or
"bad." Most agree, however, that the policy concerns of interdependence among developed, industrialized nations are different in
kind and quantity from problems of interdependence between
lesser and more modernized nations. Nonetheless, the issues that
have arisen among the more developed interdependent nations are
also reflected, although to a lesser degree, between the less and the
more developed countries and are likely to gain prominence as the
former move up the value-added chain of development. Because a
rapidly developing China is already facing many of these policy
choices, it is useful to examine the two schools of thought that
have developed among analysts in the more advanced industrial
countries especially as they relate to the effects of interdependence
between the United States and Japan.

Two schools of thought on interdependence dominate the American policy community. Essentially, the "Who is Us" school, so labeled in a title of an article by Robert Reich that appeared recently
in the Harvard Business Review, argues that interdependence is by
and large a good thing. Foreign companies that open plants in the
United States, Reich argues, are not only employing U.S. workers
who might not otherwise have jobs, they are also transferring technology to the United States and thereby increasing the value of US
exports. The United States maintains a high degree of control over
these investments, and the risks of repatriation, minimal at most,
are more than offset by their benefits. Ultimately, Reich main-

tains, American competitiveness should be measured not by the market share or profitability of American corporations, but by the degree to which U.S. workers can add value to the world economy and attain a higher standard of living without going into debt. To the degree that foreign investment helps the United States achieve those objectives, the policy community should look on it not with alarm, but with favor. American economic and investment policies should reward any company, American or foreign, that invests in upgrading the quality of the domestic work force, since manpower skills are critical to long-term competitiveness. Growing levels of international trade and investment result in a larger pie for everyone.

The opposing point of view centers on foreign control of American assets and foreign influence over the US policy process. It argues that, although the pie might be getting larger, the United States is getting a smaller and smaller slice. US companies are increasingly threatened by competition from countries that use government subsidies and incentives to incubate fledgling American corporations. In order to circumvent American charges of unfair trade practices, these countries, notably Japan, have begun buying manufacturing plants in the United States. They have simultaneously begun investing in the treasury bond market (which helps finance the American budget deficit) and in American real estate. These events have contributed to a general sense in the United States that there *is* a "they" and an "us," and that "they own us." The "They Own Us" school contends that foreign investment in real American assets gives foreigners (especially the Japanese) the power to control the future of our domestic economy. The policy prescriptions emanating from this perspective range from protection of domestic industry through tariffs and other entry barriers, to formulation of an industrial policy that "picks winners" and targets key sectors for government subsidies.

II. FACETS OF CHINESE INTERDEPENDENCE

What does interdependence look like in the Chinese case? With what nations is China interdependent and to what degree? Can interdependence be specified within China, that is, are some regions or industries more interdependent than others? Aside from economic interdependence what other types of interdependence exist in China? What measures are available to Beijing to control interdependence? And does, or can, China exchange interdependence in one sphere, say national security, for interdependence in another, say economic?

In the current international environment, all nations are interdependent to some degree. And for China, neither isolation nor complete dependence are workable or desirable policies. What Beijing wishes is to walk a middle ground between these extremes, maximizing the benefits of interdependence while minimizing the risks. Moreover, its entire modernization program rests on its ability to tap the international environment for resources: monetary, technological, and human. Some useful distinctions are nonetheless apparent. First, engagement is not the same as interdependence. China can be part of an international organization, or reach out to

the international community in some way, without necessarily becoming inextricably intertwined with it. Second, economic and
technological interdependence is not generally symmetrical between the parties involved. Hence, states need not behave in
mirror image fashion toward each other, since the calculus of costs
and benefits are different for each. Third, the ultimate test of Chinese interdependence with the rest of the world is what happens
when China or one of its partners loosens ties. A premise of American policy toward China, for instance, is that if China is enmeshed
in a network of international ties, it will fear losing them and will
avoid angering major trading partners. It will therefore have a
stake in behaving responsibly by international standards. Chinese
behavior at Tiananmen in June 1989, when coupled with American
policy changes thereafter, demonstrated that whereas the degree of
"enmeshment" was less than had been supposed, China was still
susceptible to the notion of an international behavior standard and
has accordingly modified its foreign economic and diplomatic policies—if not its domestic orientation—accordingly.

There are a number of measures of Chinese economic interdependence. One is the very large growth, in percentage and absolute
terms, of Chinese foreign trade since the early 1980s. From 1980 to
1989, exports grew from less than 27 to 195 billion yuan, while exports grew from 30 to 220 billion yuan. Another is the degree to
which China permits foreign investment, including foreign equity
participation and foreign management of Chinese plants. China has
encouraged the establishment of joint ventures in virtually every
industry, some quite large and many foreign managed. By late
1989, direct foreign investment in China totaled $32.1 billion over
20,000 projects. A third is China's willingness to borrow from foreign commercial and multilateral institutions. Loans give foreigners a say in how the economy is managed and exposes China to the
vagaries of international financial markets. China has minimized
the risk by borrowing less than "safe" limits for developing countries and has adeptly managed its external debt. The Chinese debt-
to-gross national product ration (a high of 11.9% in 1987) and debt
service as a percentage of exports (which reached a high of 10.7%
in 1986) are well below the norm for developing countries.

But China is not highly interdependent economically if by that
term one means exports or imports as a percentage of gross national product. Generally speaking, neither figure in recent years has
been much above one-eighth of the total. On the other hand, if the
degree of economic interdependence is defined as the sum of imports and exports as a percentage of gross national product,
China's degree of "trade dependence" has risen greatly in the last
decade, from less than 10 to more than 25 percent. This is illustrated in Table 1. These figures can be compared with similar numbers
for other relevant economies. Thus, the United States in 1989 was
about 20 percent trade dependent (i.e., imports plus exports as a
percentage of gross national produce), Japan 27 percent, Hong
Kong near 100 percent, Taiwan 78 percent, West Germany 63 percent, and South Korea 66 percent. So by this definition of the term
"trade dependence," China was near the low end of the spectrum.

Nonetheless, China's imports supplied a critical portion of the
wherewithal for its industrialization and overall modernization,

while that is not always the case for these other countries. Those at a high level of industrialization produce a larger portion of their modern equipment at home. Those that are hard currency economies have less difficulty purchasing needed goods abroad. Therefore, "trade dependence" figures must be modified according to the level of industrial development of the country in question. While there are many measures of economic modernization, for trade dependence comparison purposes perhaps the percent of the population engaged in non-agricultural pursuits is an acceptable measure. In the case of the United States, about 98 percent of the population is engaged in non-agricultural pursuits, while in China the figure is 29 percent, or nearly a 3:1 ratio. If such reasoning be accepted, China is much more trade dependent than the United States, even though both nations are relatively low in terms of the percentage of gross national product devoted to trade. Probably China's trade dependence, if that term now be refined to mean the degree to which the country depends on trade for powering economic modernization, is much higher than that of the United States and probably is closer to that of South Korea. In other words, some multiplier needs to be attached to the trade dependence figure to take into account the difference in modernization between and the advanced economies. But such a multiplier is undoubtedly not as high as 3:1 (which would place China's trade dependence as high as 80 percent).

If one looks at the composition of imports and compares it with the kinds of commodities—mostly industrial equipment and high technology items—necessary for successful economic modernization, it becomes clear that China has a much higher degree of interdependence with the more developed industrial nations than with the Third World. This is illustrated in Table 2.

Further, if one considers the regions of the world with which China trades, it is again clear that China is economically linked with the developed countries of Asia, Europe, and North American so far as imports and exports are concerned, as shown in Table 3, but not the Third World nations of Asia, Africa, and Latin America.

Finally, the different regions of China are differentially interdependent with other nations. The coastal provinces, especially Guangdong, Zhejiang, Jiangsu, and Shangtong, and some of the coastal or Yangtze Valley cities, such as Shanghai, Guangdong, Anhui, Beijing, and Tianjin, have since 1978 been oriented increasingly toward the international market, while the inland provinces have concentrated on the internal Chinese market. Figures indicating the degree of such interdependence for the coastal provinces are not available. However, the Chinese press is filled with stories and debates as to the efficacy and consequences for China's modernization of the increasing bifurcation of the economy into a modern, foreign trade-oriented, and interdependent coastal sector and a traditional, internally-oriented, and independent inland sector.

China's interdependence is to be found not only in the economic realm. There is also interdependence in the spheres of science, security, politics, and culture. In science, China has clearly become an active participant in the international research community, tap-

TABLE 1

China's Relative Foreign Trade Dependence since 1978
(in Billions Yuan)

Year	GNP	Exports	Imports	Exports & Imports	Exports and Imports as % of GNP
1978	358.8	16.76	18.74	35.50	9.89
1979	399.8	21.17	24.29	45.46	11.37
1980	447.0	27.12	29.88	57.00	12.75
1981	477.3	36.76	36.77	73.53	15.41
1982	519.3	41.38	35.75	77.13	14.85
1983	580.9	43.83	42.18	86.01	14.81
1984	696.2	58.05	62.05	120.10	17.25
1985	856.8	80.89	125.78	206.67	24.12
1986	972.6	108.21	149.83	258.04	26.53
1987	1,135.1	147.00	161.42	308.42	27.17
1988	1,401.5	176.76	205.44	382.20	27.27
1989	1,578.9	195.60	219.99	415.59	26.32

Source: China Statistical Yearbook 1989

ping into the wealth of international scientific literature, attending and participating at international conferences, participating in scholarly communications, establishing personal relations with non-Chinese colleagues, and setting up exchange programs in many fields. Both government-to-government and privately funded projects have proliferated to the point where no once can keep track of all that is taking place. During the 1980s, more than 70,000 Chinese students enrolled in American colleges and universities. Much of China's scientific progress since 1978 has been the product of international scientific cooperation.

In the national security realm, China has also become highly interdependent with the Asian and global security systems. Its own security depends not only on its own efforts but on the structure of Asian and global security and on the foreign and national security policies of other nations, especially the United States and the Soviet Union. During the Cold War, centered around the competi-

TABLE 2

Commodity Composition of China's Exports/Imports

In Percentages

Year	Agriculture	Minerals	Chemicals	Light Industry/ Textiles	Heavy Industry	Misc.
1982	21.19/ 38.61	23.78/ .95	5.35/ 15.22	19.25/ 20.25	5.65/ 16.61	24.78/ 8.36
1983	22.29/ 26.63	20.99/ .52	5.63/ 14.88	19.64/ 29.41	5.49/ 18.64	25.96/ 9.92
1984	22.60/ 18.49	23.06/ .51	5.22/ 15.46	19.33/ 26.70	5.71/ 26.43	24.08/ 12.41
1985	24.48/ 12.11	26.08/ .41	4.96/ 10.58	16.43/ 28.16	2.82/ 34.83	25.23/ 10.31
1986	24.53/ 12.00	11.90/ 1.17	5.60/ 8.79	19.02/ 26.09	3.54/ 39.11	35.41/ 12.84
1987	22.03/ 14.75	11.52/ 1.25	5.67/ 11.59	21.73/ 22.51	4.41/ 33.08	34.63/ 16.10
1988	22.00/ 16.80	8.36/ 1.42	6.09/ 16.54	22.07/ 18.84	5.82/ 30.18	35.66/ 16.22

Source: China Statistical Yearbook 1989

tive alliance-alignment systems of the two superpowers, China's security depended on its agility within the American-Chinese-Soviet strategic triangle. Sometimes China played that game well, sometimes not; but its security was not determined by its own efforts. With the end of the Cold War in 1989-1990, the Soviet threat declined greatly, as did China's need to depend for security on the United States. But China remained security interdependent, not only on the policies of the remaining superpower, the United States, but also on the rapidly changing structure of power and organization in Asia and elsewhere. Thus, when the Gulf crisis emerged in the late summer of 1990 and China found its national security even mildly subverted by a distant Middle East strongman, it looked to interdependence and the principles of the United Nations and the procedural rules of the Security Council.

TABLE 3

Direction of China's Foreign Trade
Value of Exports/ Imports in Millions of U.S. Dollars

Year	Industrial Countries	Africa	Asia*	Europe	Middle East	Western Hemisphere	U.S.S.R. and Other Countries
1978	6,094/ 8,056	533/ 192	727/ 450	564/ 544	661/ 183	108/ 458	1,185/ 1,060
1979	8,708/ 11,788	603/ 261	1,044/ 508	625/ 747	808/ 165	229/ 782	1,353/ 1,576
1980	12,719/ 16,561	685/ 360	1,514/ 855	773/ 825	985/ 357	410/ 719	1,283/ 1,484
1981	15,378/ 16,473	676/ 375	1,528/ 796	743/ 739	1,059/ 346	506/ 639	820/ 923
1982	15,200/ 14,446	760/ 261	1,393/ 1,123	548/ 661	2,725/ 272	528/ 597	707/ 1,186
1983	15,686/ 16,330	525/ 311	1,291/ 886	539/ 646	2,742/ 294	432/ 1,290	869/ 1,261
1984	18,202/ 20,883	543/ 310	1,552/ 1,169	507/ 799	2,435/ 280	449/ 888	1,129/ 1,393
1985	20,617/ 34,823	421/ 285	1,493/ 2,093	754/ 1,290	1,764/ 194	501/ 1,825	1,764/ 1,901
1986	23,567/ 35,004	574/ 254	1,695/ 2,071	1,034/ 1,624	2,109/ 150	363/ 1,550	2,101/ 2,530
1987	29,623/ 35,507	1,230/ 154	2,121/ 1,860	1,190/ 1,393	2,642/ 279	410/ 1,161	2,223/ 2,319
1988	37,127/ 43,528	1,642/ 245	2,626/ 2,677	1,090/ 1,546	2,089/ 577	231/ 1,925	2,748/ 3,302

SOURCE: U.N. Trade Statistics

* Hong Kong and Singapore are grouped with the Industrial Countries.

China is also politically interdependent with foreign nations. Whether Beijing is able to obtain developmental loans from Europe, Japan, and the United States, or from the World Bank, depends on the political attitudes toward China of those nations and of the multilateral economic institutions. After Tiananmen, those attitudes soured, resulting in a cutoff or a major slowdown of loans, as well as a severe dropoff of investment, trade, technology transfers, and tourism. It was in the hope of re-establishing the flow of such external economic assistance that China in mid-1990 changed its foreign policy orientation to one of cooperation with other countries on such important international political issues as Cambodia, Korea, Kashmir, and Iraq. China's economic development is thus strongly linked with the political relations Beijing maintains with relevant foreign countries and with the foreign policies of the latter.

China is, finally, culturally interdependent with other countries and this too affects Beijing's success in economic development.

With an attractive traditional culture, China continues to appeal to many peoples, in Asia and beyond, and there is, in effect, an "outflow" of Chinese cultural influence to the rest of the world. That is why, in normal times, large number of tourists come to the country and why certain nations, such as the United States, take a special interest in the lives of the Chinese people and adopt generally favorable policies toward China. But China also receives a great deal of cultural influence from abroad, particularly in the post–1978 reformist, open door period. Returned students, the international media, exchange scholars, tourists, foreign businesspeople, entertainment personalities, translators of books, are all conveyors of foreign cultural influence to China. And it has long been established that it is impossible to "cleanse" foreign technology, capital, and trade from their cultural content. Thus, China's cultural interdependence is an important factor in its economic development and, in particular, in its foreign trade.

Once the notion of different arenas of interdependence is introduced, the question arises as to how they interrelate among themselves and how each affects China's economic interdependence. The problem is complicated, and perhaps insoluble, for two reasons. First, there is no clear way to measure the interdependence created by these influences. No quantitative measure exists in most of the four spheres just described. Even if a measure existed, there would still be the problem of how to relate one quantitative measure to another. Currency equivalents are a rough measure in the trade arena, and perhaps destructive power in the national security realm could also be measured, if very roughly, by military budgets established in national currencies. But political and cultural influences are, by their nature, not measurable although their influence is real and often pervasive. Second, the above illustrations demonstrate that the various sectors of China's interdependence are themselves interdependent. Economic and security interdependence, for instance, clearly and directly influence each other and each, in turn, depend on China's political interdependence. And the nature and degree of these mutual interdependences vary from period to period.

Nonetheless, some preliminary conclusions may be in order. First, Chinese interdependence in one sphere, say science, encourages and supports interdependence in other spheres, say the economy. Once the "door" of interdependence is open in one arena, therefore, it is easier to open the door in other arenas and to keep them open. Second, interdependence in one arena can be converted into or substituted for interdependence in other arenas. It has long been established, for instance, that security and economic interdependence can substitute for each other over a broad spectrum of variables; and this has been so in China's case since the 1950s. In particular, much of China's foreign trade between 1978 and 1989 has been with the United States and its allies rather than with the Soviet Union. This is true not only for reason of economic development but also because of Beijing's need to assure its security, through American ties, against the Soviet military threat. Third, given this, the way is open for China to stress interdependence in areas that seem least harmful to state or party interests. Interestingly, and contrary to what might be supposed by outsiders, the

Beijing leadership has usually taken cultural interdependence (i.e., in their eyes to allow foreign cultural influence to penetrate Chinese society) to be much more threatening than security or economic interdependence, which by comparison is generally viewed as less harmful and more tolerable—and probably more necessary. In recent years, there have been several campaigns against Western "spiritual pollution" but not against the dangers of the "parallel tracks" Chinese-American anti-Soviet national security policy nor, needless to say, against conducting an increasing volume of foreign trade with China's Western security partners.

III. CHINESE PERCEPTIONS OF INTERDEPENDENCE

China's attitude toward interdependence has evolved over the post–1978 period to such a degree of prominence that by the end of the 1980s it had become the subject for careful study and, not infrequently, debate by the leadership. Before 1978, Beijing did not, generally speaking, have a separate policy toward the issue or, if it did mention the subject, placed it in the context of more general foreign policy orientations.

Contemporary Chinese policy toward interdependence must first and foremost be related to the historic attitude toward the outside world. During the many centuries of dynastic rule, Chinese emperors and their courts looked upon foreigners, their countries, and their products as perhaps interesting but always inferior in culture and material attainment to that of Chinese civilization. The well-known tributary relationship was the product of this attitude, which by its very nature prohibited even the thought of interdependence. With the coming of the West to China's doorsteps during the 18th and 19th centuries and its use of pressure and force, this attitude gradually began to change to one which begrudgingly accepted equality in international relations.

By contrast, during the late Ching, the warlord period, and the Republic, from 1842 to 1949, China found itself in a position of inferiority abroad: the country fell far behind the West in terms of power and development as dynastic decline, imperialist attempts at colonization, civil war, and foreign invasion all ate into the fabric of Chinese society and its sense of self-respect and well-being. A positive orientation toward the mutual benefits of trade, the presence of large numbers of foreigners in the country, cooperative scientific and technical exchanges, and other nations' investment in and technology transfer to China could hardly be expected under such circumstances. Chinese rulers and many of the intelligentsia saw these as the baleful and inevitable by-product of China's weakness and disunity. They concluded that the way to overcome the country's relative backwardness, while concomitantly preserving the greatness of the culture, was to take only what was necessary from the West, strip it of its cultural connections, and build a new China of restored power and pre-eminence largely through internal efforts.

The post-1949 communist regime also adopted this stance, while stressing the dangers of "neo-colonialism" and Western cultural dominance. Self-reliance and Third World unity against the developed nations (even including developed socialist nations) was therefore the leitmotif of Chinese foreign and trade policies during the Maoist period ending in 1976. With such an attitude, interdependence could have no basis of support in most Chinese eyes, even though in the 1970s and 1980s the immense benefits to be obtained from it in many spheres were becoming increasingly obvious to any Chinese decision-maker who glanced abroad.

With the Deng Xiaoping-led reform era beginning in late 1978, however, interdependence took on a different connotation in line with the new emphasis on the positive aspects of investment, trade, technology transfer, and scientific exchange. That is not to say that the term always received a favorable press, or that the Party was in fact willing to drop its more basic policy of wariness toward foreign cultural influence. Indeed, during several campaigns in the 1980s against "spiritual pollution" and "bourgeois influence," and in favor of self-reliance, interdependence was highly criticized. Moreover, a strain of opposition to the benefits of interdependence continued to be included in generally favorable articles and pronouncements. If there is a consensus among Chinese writers and political leaders on the topic, perhaps it is that interdependence is seen more as a one-way street, with the onus primarily on the Western nations to provide benefits to China. Consequently, to many Chinese interdependence is not the inevitable political, social, and cultural result of economic development and the complex international economic relations that accompany it. If anything, there is a tendency to stick to the neo-colonialist/dependencia approach outlined in Part I.

As the reform impetus peaked in the middle to late 1980s, however, there was a pronounced tilt in favor of interdependence and its benefits to China. China recognized the absolute necessity of opening the door wide and keeping it that way. The close connection between internal economic reform and interdependence, the necessity for China to join all the major global and regional economic organizations (and thus submit itself to their rules), and the realization that the collectivist economic model of autarky and excessive self-reliance all were spelled out in policy pronouncements and scholarly analyses. This was particularly true during the late 1988–early 1989 peak reform period, when it was stated that other nations' "development and well-being are an indispensable condition for one's own progress" and that trans-Pacific economic competition is desirable so long as all remained within the framework of higher common interests and interdependence.

Shortly after the 1989 Tiananmen incident, and as a cover for Western "pressure" on Chinese Party culture, the regime reverted for a time to extreme emphasis on self-reliance and was highly critical of interdependence. Such pressure would merely cause China to struggle more arduously in the spirit of self-reliance to develop the economy. Even then, however, there was a back-handed recognition that China could no longer isolate itself from the international community. The opinion was set forth that Western-led (i.e., American) attempts to punish and isolate China for Tiananmen through imposing sanctions or denying most favored nation treatment could only fail. China had become too important for the world economy for that, both as a supplier of raw materials, a locus for Western investment, and as a major trading nation in its own

right. Much of the post-Tiananmen literature and policy statements was set forth in terms of the responsibility of developed nations to recognize the special needs of developing countries, including China. That placed the Chinese approach within the context of
so-called North-South relations: the Third World debt crisis, the
question of special treatment for developing countries, reversing
the flow of financial resources out of developing nations, stabilizing
global commodity prices, lowering global interest rates, eliminating
developed countries' trade barriers, and generally raising economic
growth rates. In early 1990 much of the Chinese literature on
interdependence has therefore been couched in these terms.

A year after Tiananmen, however, the analytic Chinese approach
had evolved to a further stage, becoming both variegated and sophisticated in outlook. A review of the Chinese language press
during the latter portions of 1990, as well as interviews in China by
the authors during the period, support this conclusion. Several
themes emerge.

- Interdependence is not only a fact of contemporary international life, but both a favorable condition and an indispensable
  factor in China's own economic development. Interdependence
  was sometimes defined as including international economic cooperation, including capitalist investment in factories and
  other facilities in China, increasing scientific and technical
  interchange, complementarity of natural resources, cooperation in production of material goods and services, and the establishment by Chinese cities and provinces of ties with like
  foreign entities.
- Chinese writers recognized that interdependence involves
  international division of labor, i.e., the internationalization of
  production, economic regionalism, linked growth rates, and
  international interest rates set by the advanced capitalist
  countries.
- It was clearly recognized that economic interdependence promoted international peace and security, that there was inter-
  penetration between the two spheres, and the substitutability
  of economic and security factors for each other, was great; and
  that economic interdependence tended to promote diplomatic
  cooperation and recognition.
- China recognized a need to promote a new international economic order stressing equality, mutual benefit, and cooperative
  prosperity alongside the desired international political order
  consisting of Chinese-led anti-hegomonism and the five principles of peaceful co-existence.
- China saw its trade with Hong Kong and Taiwan as a particularly instructive example of the benefits of interdependence:
  China needs the capital, technology, and expertise the others
  can provide, while they in turn need China's resources and
  markets.
- North-South (developed-developing countries) relations should
  be viewed within the context of interdependence. The mutual
  benefits are obvious: the South (i.e., China) needs the capital
  and expertise of the North, while the North needs the markets,
  investment sites, raw materials, and the inexpensive labor of

the South. On the other hand, there is an obvious need to narrow the North-South gap by solving the debtor crisis, stopping the outflow of funds from the South, by stabilizing commodity prices, by combating protectionism, by raising up grow rates in the North as a means of also raising them in the South, by opening markets in Northern countries and also lowering interest rates, and increasing Northern foreign aid to the South.

- Finally, Chinese writers and editorialists inveigh against post-Tiananmen sanctions as being against interdependence. If most-favored-nation treatment promotes mutual benefits (one of the components of interdependence), then taking it away leads to one-sided benefits and exploitation.

Comparing these notion with the six general approaches to interdependence set forth above, it appears that Chinese writers—and therefore the Chinese Communist Party and its government—understand but do not support traditional international theory. They are still taken by the dependencia argument (that is the basis of the North-South emphasis) and either ignore or oppose developmentalism as too capitalist-oriented and too dependent on external political and social influences. They also apparently reject export-led growth strategies although the latter-day coastal-inland division of China into export-dependent and domestically self-sufficient parts would seem to support such an orientation, and come down strongly in support of interdependence as innately "good." One thing is clear: if one were to judge China's approach to economic interdependence, the weighted average of the notions conveyed in the written literature seems amazingly liberal. There is little that most analysts of the costs and benefits of interdependence could criticize. The important question, however, is how much these opinions are reflected in China's trade practices.

And here a problem arises. Even before Tiananmen charges have been made that China is engaging in a mercantilist, one-sided emphasis on exports, and on the amassing of a large hard foreign currency surplus (in 1990 about $26 billion). What is worse, it is accused of dumping, circumventing American trade quotas, and engaging in other unfair trade practices to build up export earnings. The problem is particularly prominent in textiles and toys. At the same time, the centrally-directed Beijing economy restricts American imports, through trade quotas, targeted production, and central directives to enterprises to restrict imports. This issue could become of central concern to overall American-Chinese relations, since the linkage with the most favored nation issue—and hence the human rights question—is direct. Before drawing hasty conclusions as to Beijing's "real" intentions toward the interdependence issue, however, it is possible to supply some reasonable economic explanations for such a policy. First, the major decrease in the rate of gross national product growth after Tiananmen affected the country's ability to purchase foreign goods as well. Imports therefore declined swiftly—but probably temporarily—while exports remained at higher levels as foreign demand did not decline. Second, Beijing changed its exchange after Tiananmen to reflect the lowered global value for the *renminbi*. This also had the effect of pro-

moting exports and retarding imports. Third, China found it necessary to begin massive repayment of loans made in the late 1970s
and early 1980s, and was constrained to save up foreign currency
to cover these costs. Merchantilism fails as an explanation for this
policy. As in the case of previous surpluses, the $26 billion can, and
probably will, be spent rapidly, since the purpose of storing up foreign currency is precisely to purchase foreign technology and capital imports necessary to further industrialization. A major buying
spree was in fact begun in the fall of 1990, thus attesting to the
validity of this proposition.

IV. BENEFITS AND COSTS TO CHINA OF INTERDEPENDENCE

This section analyses the gains China anticipates and the risks it
faces by pursuing policies that increase its interdependence. As
argued earlier, autarky is not a real option for China, so the relevant debate is not over interdependence versus autarky but over
what degree of interdependence is suitable for and acceptable to
Chinese leaders. As noted previously, no easy terms are available
to characterize degrees of interdependence, nor do numerical scales
exist for measuring how intertwined China is with the rest of the
world. Indirect indicators—such as international debt and import
and export activity—measure particular activities and not China's
total economic or other behavior. So what follows will simply use
the terms "more interdependence" and "less interdependence" to
describe arbitrary points on the continuum.

A. BENEFITS OF A HIGHER DEGREE OF ECONOMIC INTERDEPENDENCE
AND COSTS OF A LOWER DEGREE OF ECONOMIC INTERDEPENDENCE

Benefits are obvious. The spectacular growth in the Chinese
economy between 1980 and 1990 was possible largely because of the
opening to the West and the ability of foreigners to gain access to
the Chinese market—albeit not the supposedly lucrative consumer
market. Interdependence makes it possible for China to import the
equipment and human resources desperately needed for modernization. So the more open China became, the greater the benefits. In
examining the costs of less interdependence, the time-frame distinction is critical. The costs to China of pursuing a less interdependent policy in 1979 or even 1982 would have been the risk that
the economic gains would be relatively insignificant. Only in hind-
sight can anyone see exactly what would have been sacrificed. But
that cost is very different from the economic cost associated with
China's decision to pursue a less interdependent path in 1990. The
spectacular growth of the early 1980s was from a comparatively
low base, and probably would have leveled off in time. If in the
1990s China chooses to be less interdependent, the rate of economic
growth (likely to be much smaller than in the 1980s) might not
suffer unduly as a result. In fact, the economy prior to June 1989
was overheated to the point where a severe retrenchment and reassertion of central control were the only possible remedies within
the confines of a socialist system. Thus, simply because during one
ten-year period more interdependence meant more growth does not
mean that the same will apply in the next ten-year period.

The central question in assessing costs of a less interdependent policy is the reaction of the outside world. Chinese policies during the Deng decade of reform inspired confidence in industrialized countries about China's economic future. This led to the participation of foreign firms in developing Chinese industry and to a lesser extent agriculture. Would a less interdependent, less forthcoming, less involved China discourage foreigners who have the capital and the skills China needs? Has China become involved enough in the world economy to avoid the consequences of a lower degree of involvement?

The answers to these questions will be debated for many years. By 1990, China had not yet moved very far away from a higher degree of interdependence compared to where it was in 1980. But the events of June 1989 did test the interdependence proposition and it is possible to draw some tentative conclusions. Despite the outrage over the Chinese government's military response to the student demonstrations, the worst-case economic consequences never materialized. First, foreign investors did not pull out across the board and no existing joint ventures closed or even ceased to operate for more than a few days. On the contrary, foreign firms involved in joint ventures seem determined to persevere. Second, China was adroit at managing its external debt. There was no widespread panic. And whereas China's credit rating fell and many loans were temporarily suspended, the country's balance sheet remained in surprisingly good condition—$11 billion in 1990 and perhaps $15 billion in surplus in 1991. There were no immediate financial problems related to international debt. Third, import and export figures are not dramatically lower than they might have been without sanctions and reprisals from trading partners. The events of June 1989 certainly shook the confidence of foreign buyers in China's reliability as a vendor, as well as the confidence of Hong Kong and Southeast Asian entrepreneurs whose investments have been critical to the growth of China's export industries. Also contributing to a drop in both imports and exports were tight credit policies. However, the reassertion of central control over the economy and the careful scrutiny over import decisions would have probably been imposed independently of sanctions by trading partners.

The more important costs of the Tiananmen incident are probably in the scientific and technical areas. Many in the West were anxious to have contact with a more open, outward looking China, to which Chinese students enrolled in overseas universities would have some incentive to return. Many Western scientists, whose contacts with their Chinese counterparts have done much to advance the state of science in China, are now cynical and disillusioned, and therefore much less interested in bilateral exchanges. And many Chinese students in the United States are either uninterested in or afraid of returning to China. While China is enduring these effects with what appears to be a minimal degree of pain, the costs are nonetheless high.

B. COSTS OF A HIGHER DEGREE OF ECONOMIC INTERDEPENDENCE AND BENEFITS OF A LOWER DEGREE OF ECONOMIC INTERDEPENDENCE

A higher degree of economic interdependence has entailed substantial costs. Costs can be grouped into two general categories: effects on the domestic economy and less tangible political and social effects. For China to be an effective player in the international economic arena and to reap the benefits of interdependence, the Beijing leadership had to undertake far-reaching reforms of the domestic economic and financial systems. Reforms in turn resulted in a tremendous loss of central control over provincial activities, a buying spree that wasted millions (if not billions) of hard-currency dollars badly needed for critical projects, and inflation that by early 1989 was close to thirty percent. China also ran the risk that foreign partners, for political or fiscal reasons, might withdraw and force autarky on the country.

Political and social costs have been equally troublesome to the Chinese leadership and at the same time are much more difficult to quantify. Mainly, they involve Chinese exposure to Western political and intellectual values. These have already had a profound influence on a critical, if small, segment of Chinese society: urban, educated professionals and students on whom the modernization program is vitally dependent. The ultimate nightmare for the current leadership is that foreign values will begin to take hold of the population, as was evident by the Tiananmen Incident in Beijing, and similar demonstrations in many other Chinese cities.

Some potential benefits accrue for China from policies that entail less economic interdependence. Critical is the opportunity to regain control over the economy. It is again important to distinguish, however, between choosing less economic interdependence in 1980 and less interdependence in 1990. If China had chosen a less interdependent path in 1980, it is possible that the population could have remained relatively isolated from foreign values. However, because of the genie-in-the-bottle phenomenon, choosing a less interdependent path in the 1990s does not mean that foreign influence can be held to a minimum.

This discussion can be summarized in four propositions. First, benefits of a high degree of economic interdependence are real, but will probably not be as dramatic as in the past. Second, costs of pursuing a less interdependent path exist but are less significant than they would have been in the early 1980s. Both of these judgments argue for more autarky and less interdependence. Third, costs of a high degree of economic interdependence are high and will probably remain so even if the potential benefits are not likely to be as great in the immediate future as they have been in the immediate past. But fourth, moving to a less interdependent strategy would not necessarily eliminate or reduce the most significant of those costs, due to the genie-in-bottle phenomenon.

C. BENEFITS AND COSTS TO CHINA OF NON-ECONOMIC INTERDEPENDENCE

In Section II, we discussed some types of non-economic interdependence and their relationship to China's economic interdependence. Here we consider three particular benefits and two costs. The first benefit is enhanced military security. Between 1972 and 1989, China was militarily interdependent with the United States, as both took the Soviet Union as their common designated foe, partially integrated their respective security strategies, and integrated this aspect of their foreign policies toward each other with other components, including transfer of some American and other nations' military technology to China. Indeed, the opening of most of the COCOM list of proscribed items was crucial to the very great rise in China's foreign trade and to the entire post-1978 modernization effort. The point of security interdependence, however, is that by placing its security partially in the hands of the Americans, a much greater "amount" of security was made available to China. It was a highly cost-effective operation for Beijing, especially during the critical years 1972–1984 when perception of the Soviet invasion threat was at its peak. And by lessening the need to devote such high percentages of gross national product to arms production and to maintain a very large military force, huge resources were freed to devote to rapid economic development. Such security interdependence was, of course, vital to the United States and its allies in Asia and elsewhere. Thereby Washington, Tokyo, Seoul, Bangkok, and the NATO countries benefitted immeasurably by the effective addition of at least a portion of the Chinese military to the general program of deterring Soviet aggression. There is no way to measure the gains derived from such mutual security interdependence, since war did not occur. But if such gains were somehow monetized, they would have to be somewhere near the level of a large percent of the total assets of the Chinese economy, since China would have inevitably lost a nuclear war with the Soviet Union and found itself dismembered and surely in a chaotic state after such a war.

The second specific benefit to China of non-economic interdependence is that it has helped enable China to become an important player in the "big league" of international relations. For many years, even at the beginning of the Deng-led reforms, China was not taken seriously in international relations. For all its geographic size, large population, and economic and military potential, it was largely discounted in the cabinets of the major post-World War II powers. China in fact was more a international relations dependency, in the sense that its security and development stemmed from its protection or assistance by the Soviet Union or the United States, than it was an independent or at least an important interdependent player. It was also an international outsider by choice, after 1960 belonging neither to the Soviet-led nor the American-led alliance systems nor to the Third World Group of 77.

With Deng's policy of relative openness, however, China began to count in international relations and the various elements comprising its national power began gradually to add together. Trade, security, cultural, and diplomatic components of Chinese foreign policy more and more integrated with, and became in turn penetrated by (i.e., became interdependent with) these same components of the foreign policies of the other major powers. For instance, China became a security protector of South Korea against North Korea, along with the United States, from which followed the development of South Korean-Chinese trade, technology transfer, and the establishment of quasi-diplomatic trade offices in the two capitals. China strongly aligned itself with the United States against the Soviet Union during the latter's occupation of Afghanistan, and this orientation was of considerable assistance in convincing the American government to relax export restrictions and to encourage transfer of much high technology to Beijing. And during the 1990 Gulf Crisis, China's support of American-Russian initiatives helped bring Beijing out of the semi-isolated diplomatic state in which it was placed following the Tiananmen Incident. It also assisted in constructing a somewhat less negative image of the country as a whole (the reality was different, of course—suppression of human rights in the country continued unabated), which in turn was one factor in the American Administration's decision to relax some economic sanctions and the Congress' inability to force reversion of China's most favored nation status.

This last example points up a third benefit of interdependence to China. It is a means to help avoid international isolation in various fields, as well as a safeguard—to the extent the Beijing leadership so desires—against over-emphasis on China-centeredness. By deliberately making itself interdependent in security, diplomatic, and cultural terms as well as through economic interchange, China changes the very term of its international intercourse. And since the country has already proceeded reasonably far down the path of interdependence in these various spheres, it is becoming increasingly difficult, if not impossible, to revert to a policy of self-imposed isolation. Thus, so long as the Beijing leadership desires to be integrated with the international community, interdependence assists China in achieving that end. Avoiding isolation and avoiding China-centeredness are therefore different expressions of the idea of a more positive emphasis on participation in regional and global developments. It also assures that China is accepted not merely as a relatively equal partner in various arenas but, perhaps more importantly, that by being so heavily involved in international affairs it will become a leader that other nations will look to. Interdependence, then, becomes a means for restoring China's centrality that it lost in the early 18th century.

These benefits to China come with at least two concomitant costs. The first is partial control by foreigners of China's foreign relations, especially its military security. Decisions vitally affecting the defense capabilities of the country, its diplomatic position, and its cultural and ideational reputation are now made in foreign capitals as well as in Beijing. Washington and Moscow heavily influence Beijing's military defense posture, its defense budget, and its capability to project military power abroad. The United States and its allies and associates in Asia, Europe, and elsewhere at least partially determine China's diplomatic alignment, regionally, globally, and in international institutions. And China's general reputation is not only a function of what the rulers inside the Chung Nan Hai decide is best for the country—as in the Tiananmen Incident and its long aftermath—but of how other peoples perceive China and its cultural-intellectual acceptance abroad. For a country that, perhaps above all others, has prided itself on its ability to determine its own fate on the basis of its own values and actions, that cost is high, and is perceived so by the leadership. In fact, the line between benefit and cost derived from the various types of interdependence is often judged to be very fine. That helps explain why China switches so frequently between favoring interdependence and the benefits it brings and opposing it for reason of the costs it imposes. It also helps explain why continuous internal party-led political-ideological campaigns ("Anti-Spiritual Pollution," "Resist Bourgeois Influence," etc.) are imposed on the Chinese people and why, in all probability, they should be expected to persist.

The other cost follows from this. Interdependence obviously carries the risk of perceived excessive foreign cultural penetration. As noted previously, every Chinese regime stretching back for several thousand years has been hypersensitive to this possibility. The communist ruling group is hardly an exception. Until the institution of the post-1978 open door policy, the only time foreign cultural influence was allowed into the country in any but token degree was when China was too weak to resist. This was clearly the case during the Warlord and Republican periods, i.e., much of the 20th century. The Mao Zidong-led party came to power in 1949 at least partly on a platform of getting rid of foreign penetration and that policy, implemented strongly thereafter, was generally popular. While modernization has modified this resistance to some extent, anti-foreign feelings still run high among large segments of the populace and the party, if not always the intelligentsia. The question for China, as it has always been, is whether the perceived high cost of foreign cultural penetration can be justified by the benefits stemming from modernization of the country as a whole. The Tiananmen Incident and the repressive policies that followed demonstrate once again that the tolerance of outside cultural influence is still very low.

It follows that, even though the benefits of interdependence are known and admitted, the regime, if forced to choose, will almost always come down on the side of closing the door to the outside and thereby limit the degree to which they perceive China as becoming interdependent. Therein lies the dilemma for the Chinese rulers, of course, for they also know that the road to full modernization runs through a large city called interdependence. So far, no Chinese leadership has found a way to have it both ways, i.e., to modernize, to obtain therewith the benefits of interdependence, and still minimize the perceived costs of foreign cultural penetration. The trouble is that even a relatively small degree of foreign influence appears to produce a highly disproportionate response among the Chinese people in terms of their attitudes toward the communist regime and hence in terms of the ruling group's ability to govern. Tiananmen was, in that regard, a very strong lesson to the leadership and it will not be forgotten soon.

V. Options for China's Future

The "bottom line" is rather easy to describe, if trends extant at the beginning of the 1990s continue. First, China will probably continue a modest degree of interdependence in most spheres, high when compared with the beginning of the 1980s but relatively low in relation to the more highly industrialized nations. Second, the Beijing party leadership will attempt to control the degree of its

interdependence in all spheres, lest the combination of domestic opposition and the continual waves of external influence threaten its
very capacity to rule, indeed to survive. Much, of course, will
depend on the character of various successor leadership groups exercising power after Deng Xiaoping's demise. But barring a breakdown of party rule, a la East Europe, or the re-emergence of liberal
reform groups within the party (both relatively unlikely in the
judgment of both authors), little change can be expected from
China with regard to its attitude and policy toward interdependence, throughout the 1990s. Third, it follows that the Beijing leadership will continue to try to have it both ways: reap the benefits
from interdependence and avoid excessive costs. That will not be
easy, obviously, since secular trends throughout the globe all point
to greater degrees of, and benefits from, interdependence in all
spheres, especially the economic. A fourth conclusion therefore is
apparent: the disjunction between global trends and Chinese pro-
pensities implies that China will not modernize as fast as it could
were it to allow interdependence to exert its full influence over the
country.

China will not therefore cease to move ahead. But it will fall progressively behind, not only as compared with where it could be but
also in relation to the degree of modernity of the other nations of
relevance to Beijing. In the long run, the costs of avoiding full-scale
interdependence will mount and become increasingly obvious.
China will surely be able to live with such costs, as it has always
done. But the toll, in terms of lost opportunities and actual burdens
imposed upon the Chinese people, will be high. In the medium
term, i.e., the decade of the 1990s, that will merely be one more
tragedy for China. But beyond the turn of the century, it could, in
combination with other, mostly domestic trends, weigh increasingly
heavily in favor of a broad popular push to replace the Chinese
Communist Party with a non-communist, possibly democratizing
successor regime. Such a group could well take interdependence as
one of the planks in its program to modernize the country as rapidly as possible.

CHINA'S FOREIGN COMMERCIAL RELATIONS

By Erin McGuire Endean *

CONTENTS

SUMMARY

The coming decade holds many uncertainties for China and, consequently, for Beijing's foreign trade, investment, and financial relations with the rest of the world. Chief among these is the transition to a post-Deng Xiaoping leadership, and the direction economic policies will take under a new regime. Policy liberalization would encourage broader foreign contacts, but Beijing's failure to return to the reform path would probably deter some potential investors and bankers from committing large sums to China projects. Chinese exports will probably continue to grow fairly rapidly whether

---

* This paper was written by Erin McGuire Endean, Office of East Asian Analysis, Central Intelligence Agency. The views expressed in this article are those of the author and do not necessarily reflect the views of the U.S. Government.

Beijing resumes market-oriented reforms or not, but exports would probably grow more rapidly if Beijing adopts comprehensive reforms that encourage factories to streamline production and to respond quickly to world market forces—and that permit China to improve its access to foreign markets by securing membership in the General Agreement on Tariffs and Trade (GATT). Other important unknowns that will shape China's foreign commercial relations include Western openness to Chinese exports and the willingness of foreign governments, bankers, and businessmen to invest in China, particularly as new markets and investment sites in Eastern Europe are clamoring for funds.

Despite these uncertainties, foreign trade, technology, and financing are certain to become even more important determinants of China's economic growth and modernization in the coming decade than they were in the 1980s. Export markets will become increasingly vital to Chinese factories and workers, and foreign-invested projects will generate a growing share of China's industrial output. Foreign borrowing may grow more slowly if exports continue to perform well and if Beijing retains tight controls on overseas borrowing to keep its nearly $50 billion foreign debt from swelling and to minimize its reliance on foreign funds—a reaction to Western sanctions imposed after the Tiananmen incident. Nonetheless, Beijing will continue to draw on concessional foreign financing for major infrastructural improvements.

One consequence of China's increasingly outward orientation will be the reduction of Beijing's influence over the regions most closely integrated into the global economy. Foreign economic links, for example, have already blunted the impact on coastal provinces of the economic austerity program Beijing has been implementing over the past two years. In Guangdong, China's most outward-oriented province, tighter domestic credit and sluggish domestic demand resulting from austerity policies have encouraged factories to rely increasingly on global markets for their products and on foreign partners for needed investment funds. Accordingly, austerity policies may have actually intensified Guangdong's movement away from central control—the opposite effect Beijing intended.

Beijing's growing trade prowess will make urban coastal areas increasingly vulnerable to a downturn in global economic conditions, however. For example, a slump in Western import demand or a revocation of China's most-favored-nation trading status with the United States could cause Chinese unemployment to balloon and factory losses to mount in export-producing regions. A deteriorating operating environment for foreign investment, or more attractive opportunities elsewhere, might also cause Chinese exports to slow; foreign investment has been one of the most important factors contributing to Chinese export growth in the 1980s. Finally, restrictions on Chinese access to low-interest foreign funds could delay needed port, railway, and energy-sector modernization efforts, and sharply higher interest rates on commercial loans could slow development in the cities and regions that rely on borrowed funds to accelerate industrial growth.

I. Foreign Trade, Investment, and Finance in the 1980s

One of the most striking successes of China's economic reform program has been its transformation from an autarkic economy to one that is increasingly open to international economic forces. After nearly two decades of adhering to an import-substitution strategy that focused on creating domestic industries capable of minimizing China's reliance on outside sources of machinery and equipment, Beijing began, in the late 1970s, to permit imports of equipment and commodities needed to accelerate economic growth. Chinese leaders acknowledged that the transformation of the domestic economy Deng Xiaoping envisioned at the watershed Third Plenum of the 11th Party Congress in December 1978 would require foreign technology, expertise, and funds. A law on joint ventures and the creation of four special economic zones followed in 1979, and a year later Beijing resumed its seats in the International Monetary Fund and World Bank and began to borrow from them as well as to take on commercial debt.

These moves, plus the dismantling of China's cumbersome central trade bureaucracy and the introduction of financial incentives that encouraged traders to export, caused trade to burgeon. Total trade more than tripled from 1980 to 1990 to over $110 billion, equivalent to 41 percent of China's GDP—up from just 12 percent in 1980.[1] Exports averaged 13-percent annual growth from 1980 through 1990, a rate matched during the period only by South Korea, Hong Kong, and Taiwan among major exporters; China became the world's 14th-largest exporter in 1990, up from 23rd place at the beginning of the decade. Legislation and regulations designed to encourage foreigners to invest in high-priority sectors and regions induced foreign partners to sign more than 29,000 investment contracts worth nearly $40 billion, $19 billion of which had been transferred by the end of 1990. China's access to international credit markets dramatically improved, and, accordingly, its foreign borrowing mounted steadily, raising external debt from less than $1 billion in 1978 to roughly $50 billion at the close of the decade.

Open-door policies over the past decade have transformed the Chinese economy and fundamentally altered Beijing's economic relations with the rest of the world. For example, export incentives have encouraged China to specialize in the labor-intensive light industrial goods in which it has a comparative advantage, fueling an expansion of rural industries that specialize in consumer goods production. Imported goods, meanwhile, have improved standards of living and boosted factory productivity and product quality, a process aided by the influx of technical and managerial expertise that has accompanied foreign investment. The impact of China's open door has been particularly pronounced in coastal areas, where 90

---

[1] Because China's national accounts are calculated in domestic prices not strictly comparable to the world prices in which its foreign trade statistics are denominated, these ratios cannot, strictly speaking, be compared to the export-to-GDP ratios of more market-oriented economies, such as Taiwan, Japan, or the United States. Nonetheless, the ratios accurately reflect the trend over the last decade of China's economy becoming increasingly exposed to outside influences as a result of growth in the trade sphere having outpaced growth in the domestic economy.

percent of the foreign investment and two-thirds of China's trade activities are centered.

China's appetite for foreign capital and drive for new export markets have influenced Beijing's economic relationships with Asian neighbors as well as with the United States. China and Hong Kong have developed a symbiotic relationship beneficial to both sides; Hong Kong investment—which accounts for two-thirds of the foreign investment in China—has transformed southern China into a series of dynamic export-processing zones, while low-wage Chinese labor has enabled entrepreneurs from the territory to remain competitive in world markets despite soaring wages and shortages of skilled workers. Japan has emerged as China's largest source of loans, supplying nearly three-fourths of borrowed funds. China's economic contacts with South Korea and Taiwan—virtually non-existent in the first half of the decade—have blossomed. This has propelled closer dialogue between Beijing and Seoul as officials have sought to mediate trade and investment disputes and to provide a new framework for contacts between the countries in the absence of diplomatic relations. Investment by Taiwan firms in China—albeit indirectly—has linked the two economies despite Taipei's continuing proscriptions on direct contacts; investment and travel by Taiwan businessmen helped offset the downturn in investment and tourism from the West following the Tiananmen crackdown on prodemocracy demonstrators. The United States, crucial to China in the first half of the decade primarily as a source of technology and training, has emerged as China's foremost export market, a trend that is likely to dominate the bilateral economic relationship in the coming decade. China's barter trade ties to the Soviet Union and Eastern Europe have grown steadily, particularly at times when hard currency shortages encouraged Beijing to trade with countries that would accept Chinese products, rather than scarce foreign exchange, as payment for imports.

II. A Decade of Trade Reforms and Reversals

Beijing has attempted three times since 1978 to implement reforms in the trade sector that would expose traders—and factories—to global economic forces and wean them away from state subsidies. Exports have grown fairly steadily over the past decade, but the relaxation in central oversight of imports has led to several spending sprees that caused trade deficits to balloon and foreign exchange reserves to drop precipitously. On each occasion, when the trade deficit grew at an alarming rate or corruption and mismanagement became rife, Beijing has stepped in to regain some of the trade authority it had relinquished.

The first wave of reforms began in 1978, when Beijing began dismantling the unwieldy, Soviet-style trade bureaucracy that for nearly 30 years had given 10 national import and export corporations under China's trade ministry sole authority to sign import and export contracts with foreign firms. Beijing began to permit individual provinces, municipalities, and industrial ministries to set up their own trade entities, undermining the trade ministry's monopoly. At the same time, Beijing undertook a $10 billion import program that centered on purchases of complete plants and equipment from Japan, the United States, and Western Europe. Beijing also opened four special economic zones (SEZs) in southern China to serve as windows on the West by attracting foreign investment and technology and generating exports. Imports ballooned 44 percent in 1979 before cutbacks in domestic investment spending in 1980 reduced demand for capital imports and sparked the cancellation of many of these contracts and the beginning of a three-year readjustment phase.

A second wave of trade reforms began in 1984, when Beijing announced plans to open 14 port cities and Hainan Island to foreign investment. Beijing also permitted local authorities to sign trade contracts and approve foreign investment projects up to a ceiling amount, which varied from region to region. Thousands of independent trading companies sprang up in these cities and in the SEZs. Again, trade burgeoned, producing some unforeseen problems. Many of the independent traders engaged in lucrative—but unproductive—transactions; some, for example, made money by exporting and then reimporting Chinese goods and collecting state subsidies on both transactions. Strong demand for consumer goods such as televisions, tape recorders, and microcomputers caused imports to soar 60 percent in 1985. Another problem surfaced when local officials in the SEZs approved hundreds of hotels and office buildings but failed to attract manufacturing investment. The SEZs became known as centers of real estate and currency speculation, rather than the industrial hubs planned when Beijing funded billions of dollars worth of infrastructural improvements. Beijing curbed the SEZs' autonomy, scaled back foreign investment in "nonproductive" sectors, and reasserted control over the trade sector by closing down more than a thousand independent trading companies after the trade deficit soared to nearly $15 billion in 1985 and a billion-dollar car import scandal on Hainan Island touched off charges of widespread corruption and mismanagement. In addition, Beijing sharply devalued its currency against the U.S. dollar in July 1986, following several years of gradual depreciation.[2]

Beijing began its third round of trade reforms in January 1988, after import growth had successfully been reined in to less than two percent annually for two consecutive years. This round of reforms was centered on developing export-processing enterprises along the coast that would capitalize on China's cheap labor and make use of factories and infrastructure already in place. This plan, dubbed the "export-led coastal development strategy" by its primary proponent, Zhao Ziyang—who was Communist party General Secretary at the time—was timed to take advantage of China's improved export competitiveness resulting from currency appreciation and labor shortages in Japan, South Korea, and Taiwan.

---

[2] Beijing saw currency devaluation as a means of reducing its need to subsidize exports of manufactured goods; the currency adjustments had the effect of narrowing the gap between high state-set Chinese prices and the relatively lower prices prevailing internationally for many of these goods. Devaluation was also another means to curb Chinese imports, since it raised the dollar prices on these items. For imported commodities that China could not substantially reduce, Beijing's subsidy burden grew; the central government had to cover the difference between high world prices for grain, steel, and other primary products and the low state-set prices in China.

Two key characteristics differentiated this round of reforms from those in 1978 and 1984. First, unlike the earlier reforms, this round featured the introduction of financial changes, rather than simply decentralized command planning. Beijing granted local branches of central trade corporations greater autonomy over what they exported and imported, replacing volume quotas with contractual targets for earnings and profits. Beijing permitted successful export corporations to retain a higher share of their above-quota hard currency earnings.[3] Second, this round sought to make individual factories more responsive to market forces; the earlier reforms had focused on the next level up—foreign trade corporations. Beijing began billing factories directly for their imports; China implemented an "agency system" under which Chinese customers paid trade corporations a commission for purchases made on their behalf. On the export side, Beijing gave export-producing factories a share of earnings from foreign sales of their products. Beijing also began to permit several hundred export-producing factories to sign sales contracts with foreign buyers directly, bypassing the trade bureaucracy altogether.[4]

A. BEIJING REVERTS TO ADMINISTRATIVE CONTROLS IN 1988

True to form, this latest round of reforms enabled both imports and exports to balloon. The trade balance took a turn for the worse, however, when the domestic economy began to overheat as a result of massive infusions of credit that were intended to spur industrial production. Overly rapid industrial growth and serious shortages of energy and other raw materials drove inflation in urban areas to 30 percent. Beijing turned to foreign suppliers for many of the industrial and agricultural products it could not supply domestically. Imports rose 19 percent in the first half of the year, with purchases of foreign fertilizer, sugar, and cotton rising dramatically.

At the same time, a sharp increase in exports of primary goods— a result of the incentives to trading companies introduced during the third round of trade reforms—was a mixed blessing. Rapid export growth worsened domestic shortages of energy and raw materials and bid up domestic prices.[5] Inflation, in turn, eroded the competitiveness of Chinese products in foreign markets, slowing export growth in the second half of 1988. Chinese Customs statistics indicate that, after growing at a nearly 30 percent rate in the first half of 1988, exports slipped to just over half that pace from July through December 1988. Even China's premier foreign exchange earner, the textile sector, was squeezed; Chinese prices for

---

[3] By 1988, Beijing was permitting exporters of light industrial goods, arts and crafts, and garments to keep 70 percent of their earned foreign exchange and the machine-building and electronics industries to retain 50 percent—in contrast to the roughly 30 percent permitted most other sectors.

[4] Beijing also granted China's special economic zones additional trade and investment privileges, including the right to retain 100 percent of the foreign exchange they earned from exports. Hainan Island received provincial status and became China's fifth SEZ in early 1988.

[5] Because China's domestic price structure severely underprices raw materials and energy, trading companies rushed to export these commodities when Beijing eased control over the foreign trade sector. Exports of pig iron, steel, coal, nonferrous metals, raw silk, and cotton all jumped even though domestic factories were reporting shortages of the same goods. Trade corporations reaped large profits by buying these goods at low prices set by the central government and exporting them at higher international prices.

textile fibers increased about 30 percent in 1988 while international prices for fabrics dropped by 15 percent on average, according to Chinese press reports. Pinched by these price adjustments—and freed from centrally mandated export quotas by the 1988 trade reforms—many factories found it more profitable to sell to the domestic market.

Beijing included the trade sector in the comprehensive austerity program it began implementing in late 1988 to cool the overheated economy. As with other austerity measures, Beijing's policies essentially invoked administrative measures to regain central control over economic decision making, reversing many of the market-oriented reforms implemented over the previous decade. For example, Beijing recentralized trading authority, slashing by one-third the number of authorized foreign trade corporations and requiring a larger share of imports to be subject to import licenses, import substitution regulations, and bans. Beijing also tightened controls over foreign exchange allocation for imports and imposed new restrictions on the discretionary use of exporters' retained foreign exchange earnings. At the same time, Beijing expanded the number of primary products subject to export licenses, quotas, and bans, and boosted subsidies to exporters of manufactured goods. Beijing also set up chambers of commerce to coordinate sales volumes and prices for similar products exported by more than one trader. To slow the flow of foreign credit to Chinese enterprises that found their access to domestic funds reduced when Beijing cut state investment and curbed bank lending, Beijing tightened its supervision over foreign borrowing, reducing the number of government entities authorized to borrow funds abroad from 100 to only 10.

B. CONSEQUENCES OF THE JUNE 1989 CRACKDOWN

Inflation, shortages of key raw materials, and tight domestic credit had begun to take their toll on exports and had caused foreign investors to scale back expansion plans even before the spring 1989 pro-democracy demonstrations in Tiananmen Square. The country's deteriorating current account balance and mounting debt-service obligations had also led commercial bankers to begin reassessing their lending plans for China. The crackdown accelerated the decline: in the year following Beijing's decision to use force to suppress the demonstrations, China probably lost an additional several billion dollars in tourist revenue, foreign loans and aid, and foreign investment.

One of the areas that suffered most immediately was the tourism industry. China earned $1.8 billion from tourism in 1989—$800 million below the total that had been projected prior to the unrest and 20 percent below the level in 1988. Decreases of 40 percent and 30 percent, respectively, in the number of visitors from Japan and the United States were only partially offset by a 24-percent increase in visitors from Taiwan. The shortfall in tourism earnings forced China to reschedule several foreign loans used to build tourist hotels, moves that may have added to foreign bankers' worries about China's creditworthiness.

International financial institutions and countries with low-interest loan packages pending froze billions of dollars worth of credits, the largest of which were a yen credit from Japan worth $6 billion to support energy, telecommunications, and transportation projects; $780 million from the World Bank; and several hundred million dollars from the Asian Development Bank. Most Western nations also froze government-backed export credits to China.

Although the freeze on long-term official lending had little immediate effect on capital inflows—most of the delayed projects would not have transferred funds to China for several more years—it made commercial bankers more cautious, which had a serious near-term impact. After reevaluating both China's political stability and its creditworthiness, many bankers reduced medium- and long-term commercial loans from earlier projections, scaled back short-term trade credit lines, and raised the interest rates assessed on loans. The international bond market also downgraded China's credit rating. In all, the sanctions renewed caution among commercial bankers, recentralized borrowing authority, and reduced demand for funds under the austerity program caused China to sign less than $5 billion in loan agreements in 1989, half the level of a year earlier. Foreign commercial borrowing dropped by nearly 70 percent.

Beijing drew down its foreign exchange reserves sharply in the weeks immediately after the Tiananmen crackdown. Much of the drawdown can be traced to withdrawals by overseas depositors in Bank of China branches in Hong Kong, Macao, and Singapore. The drop in commercial lending also caused Beijing to use its reserves to pay for imports and make payments on outstanding loan obligations. China's foreign exchange holdings dropped by $3 billion in June and July, to $13.6 billion—barely sufficient to cover three months' imports, a level Beijing generally regards as a minimum.

Foreign investors postponed many of the projects that were under discussion at the time of the crackdown and began to reassess the risks and rewards of operating in China during a period of economic austerity as well as political and social instability. By year-end, foreign investment commitments—which, at $5.6 billion, slightly exceeded the level reached a year earlier—were $2 billion–$3 billion below the level that might have been reached had the pace set in the first half of the year continued.

More broadly, the crackdown also derailed China's efforts to secure membership in the General Agreement on Tariffs and Trade (GATT) before the December 1990 close of the Uruguay Round.[6] Although GATT contracting parties resumed consideration of China's membership request in December 1989 after a six-month delay, many of them had, in the interim, grown increasingly concerned that China was not making progress toward making its economy

---

[6] China applied for GATT membership in July 1986 and submitted a memorandum describing its foreign trade regime in February 1987. Since then, members of the working party formed to consider China's application have been reviewing the memorandum and questioning Chinese officials about the compatibility of China's state-dominated economy with the GATT's free trade principles. A key impediment to China's accession is Beijing's insistence that it be admitted to the GATT as a less developed country (LDC), rather than as a nonmarket economy (NME). LDC status would permit Beijing to use high tariffs and quantitative import restrictions to protect infant domestic industries or to reverse balance-of-payments difficulties. GATT membership as a nonmarket economy, however, would have far fewer advantages for China because it would enable other GATT members to retain quotas and other nontariff barriers on imports from China to protect them from a flood of exports at state-set—often subsidized—prices.

more compatible with the GATT's free-trade principles and was unlikely to do so anytime soon given the three-year hold on major economic reforms announced by China's leaders. At the same time, China's damaged international image in the wake of the crackdown probably influenced Taipei's decision to apply for GATT membership as an independent customs territory on 1 January 1990, a move that will complicate China's accession negotiations.[7]

C. BEIJING TIGHTENS ITS GRIP

Chinese leaders' concern that foreign exchange reserves might drop quickly as a result of sharp declines in tourism, foreign loans, and foreign investment—as well as the deteriorating trade balance—prompted those in charge of economic policy to further tighten the center's grip on the foreign trade sector after the crackdown. The removal of many of China's most vocal proponents of market-oriented economic reforms from positions of influence after Zhao Ziyang was ousted as General Secretary of the Communist party in June 1989 cleared the way for greater use of administrative measures by advocates of stronger central control.

On the import side, Beijing began to require central approval for purchases of grains, sugar, steel, fertilizers, petroleum, timber, cotton, pesticides, and several other key commodities in July 1989. Chinese leaders subsequently banned imports of 20 electronic and machinery products and some associated assembly lines, boosted tariffs on dozens of other products—in some cases by as much as 100 percent—and subjected hundreds of import goods to stringent new inspection requirements.

Beijing's financial difficulties in the wake of the crackdown also renewed its interest in stimulating exports. Beijing began to provide export-producing factories with priority access to electricity, raw materials, and transportation, as well as increased allocations of credit. In December 1989, Beijing devalued its currency 21 percent against the U.S. dollar, the first change in the state-set exchange rate in more than three years. A second devaluation of nearly 10 percent followed in November 1990, and there are numerous reports that Beijing plans another 10- to 15-percent devaluation for 1991.[8]

---

[7] At a minimum, Beijing probably fears that it will have to expend considerable effort persuading GATT members to postpone consideration of Taiwan's membership bid until after Beijing becomes a GATT member—time and effort that could have been spent lobbying for China's membership. Beijing may also be worried that the simultaneous consideration of the two applications could make GATT members even more critical of China's economic system; on economic merits alone, Taipei presents a strong case for membership because it has significantly liberalized its financial and trade system over the past few years. Finally, Beijing probably fears that if Taiwan accedes to the GATT first, Taipei could influence the terms under which Beijing becomes a member.

[8] As with other nonmarket economies where export prices are set by state-owned trading corporations, the link between exchange rates and export competitiveness is indirect. Devaluation is a way for Beijing to limit state subsidies that must otherwise be paid to trade corporations that lose money on government-mandated exports of items—such as manufactured goods—with domestic production costs greater than prevailing international prices when converted to domestic currency at the official exchange rate. Orthodox officials are believed to have endorsed the currency devaluation—postponed in 1988 because of concerns that higher import prices would fuel inflation–because they recognized the need to stimulate exports as well as to reduce government expenditures on export subsidies, which grew sharply in 1989 as inflation boosted domestic production costs. Objections to the move had diminished by late 1989 because Beijing had succeeded in bringing the inflation rate down to 6 percent, compared to 27 percent at the beginning of the year.

Immediately after Tiananmen, Chinese officials launched a propaganda campaign to assure businessmen that the country remained open to foreign investment, and at the same time warned foreign investors that Beijing would retaliate if they used the crackdown as an excuse to cancel or suspend already concluded deals. In late 1989, to prop up investor confidence, Beijing began promising foreign investors special allocations of credit and raw materials. China adopted an amendment to its joint-venture regulations in April 1990 that permitted foreigners to function as chairmen of joint ventures in China and allowed firms to operate in perpetuity if so specified in contracts. The amendment also included a pledge from Beijing not to nationalize or expropriate joint ventures.

III. FOREIGN ECONOMIC LINKS RECOVERING

Beijing's reassertion of control over the trade sector brought about remarkable results. Rapid export growth and tough import controls gave China a record $9 billion trade surplus in 1990, compared with a $6.6 billion deficit a year earlier. The slump in the domestic economy was partially responsible for the turnaround because it slashed demand for imports and freed up goods for export. Foreign sales were 18 percent above the level posted in the first eight months of 1989. Imports, meanwhile, dropped 10 percent, with sharp cuts in purchases of synthetic fibers, timber, nonferrous metals, steel, motor vehicles, and consumer goods. China's year-end current account surplus is estimated to have approached $9 billion in 1990.

Hard currency inflows from foreign investment and tourism remain below what they would likely have been without the Tiananmen crackdown, but signs in the second quarter of 1990 pointed to a partial recovery in these areas. Although foreign investors signed only $870 million worth of new contracts in the first quarter of 1990, 42 percent below the level achieved a year earlier, they pledged nearly $1.5 billion worth of new investment in the second quarter—just 2 percent below the level of the second quarter of 1989. The third quarter showed continued improvement, with more than $1.6 billion in new investment contracts. In the final quarter of 1990, China signed an unprecedented $2.6 billion worth of investment contracts with foreign firms, bringing the year-end total— $6.6 billion—to record levels. Investors from the United States and Japan remained cautious about China projects—in many cases testing the waters by signing investment contracts valued at a fraction of their original amount—but investment by Taiwan businessmen made up for much of the slack. Several large European-funded projects, including a $920 million Sino-German automobile joint venture, further bolstered investment levels. Record travel by tourists and businessmen from Taiwan in the first half of 1990—arrivals from Taiwan were up 64 percent as of October—caused a thirteen-percent gain in the total number of tourists traveling to China. Despite China's currency devaluations in 1989 and 1990, which reduced the dollar value of tourism inflows, earnings nonetheless surpassed the 1990 target of $2 billion.

Economic sanctions against China were gradually dismantled in 1990, further contributing to the balance of payments turnaround.

The World Bank began to authorize loans for "basic human needs" in February 1990 and five months later key donor countries agreed to begin considering new Bank loans for projects that would encourage market-oriented reforms. In July 1990, Tokyo lifted its freeze on the massive $6 billion yen-denominated credit program. Many Western governments have resumed export credits for China. The European Community formally lifted its economic sanctions on 22 October. The gradual resumption of lending from multilateral development banks and official creditors, in turn, encouraged commercial lenders to boost lines of credit to China, although Beijing apparently did not take on significant levels of new commercial debt. Altogether, these factors enabled China's foreign exchange reserves to burgeon, reaching $27 billion by year end, nearly double the level posted immediately after the Tiananmen crisis.

IV. THE COMING DECADE

Although China's foreign commercial links are recovering from the post-Tiananmen chill, Chinese leaders do not have a comprehensive strategy for maintaining and enhancing these ties in the 1990s. For one thing, China's leaders, preoccupied since Tiananmen with ensuring social stability and maintaining party control, have focused on near-term solutions to economic problems such as inflation and unemployment that threaten to re-ignite anti-government demonstrations. Externally, their major concerns have been chipping away at economic sanctions and assuring foreign businessmen that China remains open to foreign investment.

Second, they have apparently not yet achieved a consensus on long-range economic strategies. On the domestic side, orthodox officials can claim some successes—sharply reducing inflation and improving China's external accounts—but critics can also point to negative side effects resulting from austerity policies, such as increased unemployment, higher government subsidies, spiraling losses in state enterprises, and reduced tax revenues. Regarding trade policy, although the traditionalists that dominate economic policy making continue to fear that a reduction in central oversight would cause imports to balloon, some Chinese officials are questioning the need for retrenchment policies now that Western sanctions are easing and foreign investment and tourism are recovering. Proponents of looser controls also are concerned that tight import controls are hampering economic growth in industries that use foreign inputs and will harm China's long-term export prospects. They contend that it is unreasonable for a country with factories as outmoded as China's to shut out needed capital equipment imports and that developing countries ought to accept trade deficits incurred to build infrastructure and modernize industries.

Third, these debates are taking place against a backdrop of shifting political alliances among China's aging leaders that could alter the balance of power in Beijing. Deng Xiaoping may be maneuvering to resuscitate his stalled economic reform program. It is unclear whether he will succeed in splitting his more orthodox rivals or exploiting their handling of the economy to regain the initiative. But the trade sector might be a promising target for renewed reform efforts given its strong performance over the past year and Deng's desire to eliminate Western sanctions and attract foreign investment by demonstrating that China's economic reforms are continuing.

Finally, Beijing appears uncertain what its role will be in the post-Cold War world, in particular how changes in the Soviet Union and Eastern Europe will affect China's foreign economic links. Chinese leaders probably wonder if Washington might devalue Beijing's importance as an anchor of the strategic triangle and focus instead on nettlesome bilateral economic friction points. They recognize, moreover, that other reforming economies will place new demands on the investment and low-interest funds available from Western Europe, Japan, and multilateral institutions. China's trade relations with the Soviet Union and East European countries are also undergoing a significant transformation—from barter to hard currency trade—and it is unclear how this will affect exchanges. Beijing is also concerned that the European Community's EC-92 program of market integration will make it tougher for Chinese exports to make inroads in EC markets.

A. ERRATIC IMPORT TRENDS

Without arriving at a grand strategy for external economic relations, boom-and-bust import cycles almost certainly will continue over the coming decade. In the near term Beijing intends to allow imports to rise modestly. Beijing apparently will retain its tight grip over imports, however, and in late 1990 began boosting foreign purchases by instructing its trade corporations what to purchase, and from whom, rather than by dismantling its administrative controls over the trade sector or implementing the systemic price and enterprise reforms needed to encourage factories to make responsible import decisions; China's current leaders are more likely to approve additional requests by factories for foreign exchange allotments and import licenses than to do away with licensing requirements or foreign exchange restrictions altogether. This approach will probably enable Beijing to raise imports at a controlled pace in the near term. Depressed industrial and consumer demand resulting from China's austerity program will also tend to keep imports from rising dramatically until the domestic economy begins to grow more rapidly; the economy grew by only 4.4 percent in 1990, half the average annual rate posted over the previous decade.

If Beijing eases controls over imports as a means of absorbing excess liquidity in the economy, as it did in 1985, or if China's industrial sector picks up, imports could again balloon rapidly because the problems characteristic of China's half-planned, half-reformed economy that caused erratic surges and slumps in imports during the 1980s remain unresolved.[9] It is unclear when—or if—

---

[9] Without administrative controls, Chinese traders would rush to import goods rather than seek suitable domestic substitutes because China's overvalued currency makes foreign goods relatively cheaper. Imports of machinery and consumer goods would grow most rapidly; these items can be sold domestically for a substantial windfall because China's skewed domestic price structure assigns excessively high prices for manufactured goods. Factories make purchasing decisions with little regard for long-term considerations such as expected earnings because they do not face hard budget constraints; Beijing is loathe to institute bankruptcy proceedings against unprofitable factories.

China will have leaders that are committed to, and capable of, implementing the vast array of reforms needed to prevent sudden import surges from following a reduction in central oversight of trade decision making.

B. PROMISING EXPORT PROSPECTS

It appears that China will be able to sustain double-digit annual export growth throughout most of the 1990s, although growth in some years may slow to less than 10 percent and in others accelerate to more than 20 percent.

China's potential as a high-volume producer of labor-intensive products sold at prices well below those offered by its competitors is immense, and still largely untapped. China's labor force of some 160 million in the relatively well-developed urban coastal areas that produce more than two-thirds of China's exports is larger than the labor forces of Japan and the Asian Newly Industrializing Economies combined. Wages remain low relative to those prevailing in China's competitors, averaging less than $2 per day in urban state-owned factories.

Moreover, the dynamic non-state sector is becoming an increasingly important source of China's exports. Rural industries have proven themselves adept at making inroads in foreign markets; according to the Chinese press, China now has more than 300,000 export-oriented rural enterprises, up from just 1,500 in 1980. Last year, these enterprises exported $12.5 billion worth of goods, one-fifth of China's total exports. Moreover, these factories have demonstrated their ability to maintain rapid export growth even under adverse conditions; in 1990, despite Beijing's deliberate discrimination against these factories in allocating credit and raw materials, exports by rural collective industries grew by nearly a third.

Further, reform-minded officials and traditionalists agree that exports are vital to the country's long-term modernization strategy, and have been able to set aside differences to unite in efforts to promote exports. Most recently, Beijing instituted new trade reforms designed to spur exports and reduce export subsidies in January 1991, despite continuing differences over domestic economic policy.

Beijing will probably achieve export growth regardless of whether it maintains closer central controls over the economy or reinstitutes more market-oriented policies. Productivity-enhancing reforms contributed to China's export boom in the 1980s. But Beijing's reassertion of controls over the economy in 1989 also boosted exports by slowing domestic demand, freeing excess consumer products, industrial equipment, and construction materials for export. Beijing's greater supervision over raw materials allocation—and export—boosted supplies to factories and thus enabled China to increase exports of value-added industrial goods. Tighter central supervision also helped Beijing boost export prices and curb the cutthroat competition that under trade reforms had trimmed export earnings. Exports could grow more rapidly if a new reformist leadership emerges and successfully implements trade reforms in tandem with comprehensive domestic economic reforms that include price decontrol and bankruptcy measures. These measures could prod factories to improve efficiency as well as encourage them to respond quickly to changes in world demand. Comprehensive reforms would over time enable Beijing to avoid a recurrence of the boom/bust cycle that occurred in 1988 and early 1989 when Beijing gave traders more autonomy over their exports without adopting enterprise and price reforms that would hold them accountable for profits and losses.

In part, China's promising long-term export prospects result from the massive investment and technological improvements—both domestic and foreign—that were made in export-producing factories in the latter half of the 1980s. China has more than 12,000 foreign-invested enterprises that produce for export. In 1990, they generated foreign sales of $8 billion, up nearly 60 percent from a year earlier. Apart from equity investments, some 50,000 Chinese enterprises are now assembling export goods using foreign-supplied materials; in 1990 they generated $12 billion in export earnings—one-fifth of China's total exports. Furthermore, export growth in the 1990s will be sustained by the thousands of export-oriented co-production agreements initialed between Chinese and foreign firms in recent years, many of which are only beginning to produce for export. Even if foreign investment in large, technology-intensive operations slumps for the next few years in the wake of the Tiananmen crackdown, small labor-intensive operations will doubtless remain attractive to many new investors because of China's low wage rates.

Domestic investment in export-generating factories over the past few years will also probably sustain export growth into the mid-1990s, when many of the new facilities begin exporting. Capital construction expenditures in the textiles, consumer electronics, plastics, chemicals, food processing, and metalworking industries ballooned in 1987 and 1988, and the same sectors installed $10 billion–$15 billion worth of foreign equipment during the same timeframe. Export growth later in the coming decade could slow, however, if Beijing maintains its current restrictions on capital goods imports for several more years.

C. SLOWER GROWTH IN FOREIGN INVESTMENT

Foreign investment will continue to grow. Some investors from Japan, Western Europe, and the United States may delay major commitments for large, technology-intensive ventures, although many will doubtless try to keep their options open by signing investment contracts for small ventures that can be used to test the waters. Larger, more risky ventures may have to await a verdict on Beijing's handling of the volatile transition to a post-Deng Xiaoping leadership. China's attractiveness as an investment site will be influenced by the direction economic policy takes at that time as as well as by the degree of unrest among workers and students. Prolonged periods of political and social instability almost certainly would disrupt factory production and exacerbate transportation bottlenecks, dimming China's chances of attracting foreign investment. China's ability to attract overseas Chinese investment nevertheless will buoy export performance over the next few years. Asian investors, particularly from Taiwan, will remain keen on small, labor-intensive manufacturing operations that produce for third-country markets.

D. MANAGING A GROWING FOREIGN DEBT

China's experience following the Tiananmen crackdown, when many governments suspended new loans to China and commercial bankers slashed lines of credit, will probably lead Beijing to reinvoke the rhetoric of self-reliance to justify scaled back foreign borrowing over the next few years. In reality, China's strong external accounts have reduced Beijing's need for new foreign loans over the next few years, particularly from commercial banks, which—despite the improvements in China's balance of payments—will probably keep interest rates above their pre-Tiananmen levels while political stability remains tenuous. Yet, China will probably continue to borrow judiciously from multilateral lending institutions and from foreign governments that offer concessional interest rates and extended timetables for repayment.

Without major new demands for short-term foreign loans, Beijing is unlikely to have difficulty making payments on its roughly $50 billion foreign debt over the next few years.[10] China's debt-service ratio is about 10 percent, according to International Monetary Fund estimates, well within manageable levels. Even in 1992, the year that debt repayments peak, China should have no difficulties meeting its obligations, provided its exports continue to post strong growth and China does not experience another foreign credit crunch like the one that occurred following the Tiananmen crackdown. China's healthy level of foreign exchange reserves provides Beijing added protection even if exports falter or additional social unrest reduces China's access to foreign funds.[11]

V. OTHER UNCERTAINTIES AHEAD

A variety of external factors will influence how China's foreign economic relations unfold. The pace of the dismantling of Western sanctions imposed after the Tiananmen crisis will affect China's access to Western credits and export markets. The restrictions on World Bank lending to China limiting loans to those that promote market-oriented reforms leave much leeway for interpretation, and could make the difference between whether China receives several hundred million or more than $1 billion a year in low-interest loans. Failure to receive MFN status from the United States when

[10] Estimates of China's foreign debt as of the end of 1989 vary considerably, ranging from the official Chinese figure of $43 billion to International Monetary Fund estimates of $51 billion. The Chinese statistics are likely understated because they fail to tally all loans taken on by local-level entities—some of which doubtless have occurred without either Beijing's knowledge or approval—and because they do not include suppliers credits of less than 90 days. The IMF numbers and comparable OECD data estimated on the basis of creditor information may overstate China's debt, however, because they sometimes include the value of short-term lines of credit instead of amounts actually drawn. Moreover, they may include some borrowing by foreign joint-venture partners.

[11] China is not expected to use its hefty foreign exchange reserves to prepay a portion of its outstanding foreign debt. Foreign debt held by the central government, which constitutes about one-third of outstanding debt, is primarily on concessional terms; it makes no sense to prepay loans that carry below-market interest rates. Another third of the debt is commercial; repayment of these obligations is not the central government's responsibility—it is the responsibility of the enterprises and localities that incurred, or guaranteed, the debts. The trade finance and commercial loans that comprise the remaining third also are not generally the responsibility of the central government.

it comes up for annual review would hurt China's trade balance because China's exports to the United States—its primary export market—would drop. A steep drop could, in turn, cast doubts on China's ability to repay its foreign debts.[12]

The pace of China's anticipated export growth will also be influenced by whether or not—and on what terms—China secures membership in the GATT. In the near term, provisional GATT membership would probably not increase China's access to foreign markets much because it would permit other GATT members to continue imposing quantitative restrictions and other nontariff barriers on Chinese products as long as Beijing's economy remains state-dominated. If Beijing becomes a GATT contracting party—and is able to persuade other GATT members that market reforms in China have evolved to the point that safeguards are no longer necessary—Beijing's exports could grow by as much as 15 to 20 percent annually.

Exports and foreign investment would also receive a boost if China becomes eligible for U.S. trade privileges under the Generalized System of Preferences (GSP), as it wishes. GSP status would encourage other economies that want to make inroads in the U.S. market to boost their investments in export-producing factories in China. Businessmen in Taiwan, South Korea, Singapore, and Hong Kong—economies "graduated" from their GSP eligibility in 1987—would be especially responsive to a change in China's status.

Other uncertainties are the health of the world economy—particularly given higher oil prices resulting from the Gulf crisis—and global demand for, and openness to, the types of manufactured goods China will export. China's ability to draw foreign investment and loans, moreover, will be influenced by the relative attractiveness of the new markets and investment sites opening up in Eastern Europe and the Soviet Union. Finally, Taipei's willingness to permit investment and trade ties to the mainland will be increasingly important to Beijing; in 1990, investment contracts signed by Taiwan businessmen were second only to those from Hong Kong. If Taipei permits investment in China—even indirectly—by large, technology-intensive ventures moving offshore to escape the island's environmental protection regulations and high operating costs, China could become a more efficient producer and more competitive exporter of products such as chemicals, plastics, and steel.

VI. IMPLICATIONS FOR CHINA

If foreign demand for Chinese products remains strong, foreign investors remain active in China, and foreign governments and bankers restore lending activity at least to pre-Tiananmen levels, standards of living in the coastal regions that are most open to outside economic influences will rise, and the gap between these provinces and the more closed inland regions will widen. This trend could probably occur regardless of whether Beijing maintains re-

---

[12] The conditions Congress may attach to renewal of China's MFN status would make future eligibility less predictable. This uncertainty, in turn, is probably already reducing China's attractiveness as a site for foreigners to invest in factories producing goods exported to the United States; investors are doubtless concerned that if Beijing failed to receive MFN status, goods produced in China would be uncompetitive in the United States because tariffs would increase as much as tenfold.

trenchment policies or accelerates economic reforms; even under austerity policies, the economies of China's coastal provinces have grown more rapidly than those in the interior. Moreover, even China's more orthodox leaders have found it difficult to argue against special treatment for coastal regions. Premier Li Peng, for example, reversed his original position and began trumpeting the importance of China's special economic zones in his March 1990 work report to the National People's Congress, a move probably designed to align himself with policies that enjoy broad popular support.

Another consequence of China's increasingly outward orientation will be the reduction of Beijing's influence over the regions most closely integrated into the global economy. Foreign economic links, for example, have already blunted the impact on coastal provinces of the economic austerity program Beijing has been implementing over the past two years. In Guangdong, China's most outward-oriented province, tighter domestic credit and sluggish domestic demand resulting from austerity policies have encouraged factories to rely increasingly on global markets for their products and on foreign partners for needed investment funds. Firms found they needed to export to grow and they needed foreign partners to help upgrade export quality and penetrate foreign markets. According to the Guangdong statistical bureau, the province's industrial output grew nearly 17 percent in 1990, largely as a result of the stellar performance of foreign-invested firms, whose output nearly doubled. According to Chinese press reports, foreign-funded enterprises now produce nearly one-third of Guangdong's industrial output and generate more than 40 percent of the province's export revenues. Accordingly, austerity policies may have actually intensified Guangdong's movement away from central control—the opposite effect Beijing intended.

Beijing's growing trade prowess will make urban coastal areas increasingly vulnerable to a downturn in global economic conditions, however. For example, a slump in Western import demand or a revocation of China's MFN trading status with the United States could cause Chinese unemployment to balloon and factory losses to mount in export-producing regions. Exports could also slow if foreign investors do not transfer the technologies China needs over the next few years to remain competitive with other Asian exporters of more sophisticated manufactured goods. Restricted access to low-interest foreign funds could delay needed port, railway, and energy-sector modernization efforts, and sharply higher interest rates on commercial loans could slow development in the cities and regions that rely on borrowed funds to accelerate industrial growth.

TABLE 1.

China: Key Imports, 1990

	Value[a] (Billion US $)	Percent of Total[b]	Percent Change from 1989[b]
Total	53.4	100	-10
Specialized machinery	4.6	9	-19
Iron and steel	2.8	5	-52
Textile yarn and fabrics	2.6	5	-9
Grain	2.5	5	-18
Telecommunications equipment	1.8	3	0
Electrical machinery	1.8	3	-25
General industrial machinery	1.7	3	-28
Transport equipment	1.7	3	12
Power generating equipment	1.6	3	19
Textile fibers	1.5	3	-35
Petroleum	1.4	3	-4
Resins and plastics	1.3	2	-43
Road vehicles	1.2	2	-18
Manufactured fertilizers	1.1	2	9
Organic chemicals	1.0	2	-28
Metal ores and scrap	1.0	2	28

a Yearend projections based on official Chinese Customs statistics available for January through September 1990. Imports are c.i.f.

b January through September 1990.

TABLE 2.

China's Major Export Commodities, 1985-90

Million US $

	1985	1986	1987	1988	1989	1990	Average Annual Growth Rate, 1985-90
Textile yarn and fabrics	3,277	4,282	5,790	6,458	6,994	6,742	16
Clothing	2,079	2,969	3,749	4,872	6,130	6,706	26
Petroleum and petroleum products	6,766	3,207	4,003	3,372	3,581	3,792	-11
Miscellaneous articles	874	1,266	1,326	1,675	2,283	2,641	25
Telecommunications equipment	93	252	503	789	1,140	1,758	80
Vegetables and fruit	839	1,113	1,290	1,617	1,623	1,659	15
Footwear	260	335	485	727	1,096	1,619	44
Manufactures of metals	430	563	797	1,006	1,210	1,451	28
Fish and shellfish	288	500	721	969	1,039	1,419	38
Nonmetallic mineral manufactures	229	322	439	579	793	1,285	41
Electrical machinery and parts	120	191	336	571	819	1,267	60
Iron and steel	118	167	422	1,010	709	1,091	43
Textile fibers	1,156	1,165	1,508	1,672	1,546	1,005	-3

Note: Data are f.o.b. Commodities listed represent products for which China's 1990 exports exceeded $1 billion.

Source: Official Chinese Customs statistics. Data for 1990 are projected using data available through September.

TABLE 3.

China: Foreign Investment Contracts,[a] 1980-90

	Number of Contracts	Value (Million US $)
1980	344	1,675
1981	981	1,328
1982	465	1,125
1983	470	1,732
1984	1,856	2,651
1985	3,073	5,932
1986	1,498	2,834
1987	2,233	3,709
1988	5,945	5,297
1989	5,779	5,600
1990	7,236	6,570

Source: State Statistical Bureau of the People's Republic of China, as published in annual statistical yearbooks and in the Chinese press.

[a] Includes joint oil development contracts.

TABLE 4.

Sources of Foreign Investment* in China, 1979 to 1989
(Contracted Value)

Million US$

	1979-84	1985	1986	1987	1988	1989	Cumulative total	Share of total
National total	10,327.5	6,333.2	3,330.4	4,319.1	6,190.7	6,294.1	36,795.0	100.0
Hong Kong, Macau	6,494.6	4,134.3	1,773.4	2,364.7	4,161.2	3,734.0	22,662.2	61.6
United States	1,025.0	1,152.0	541.5	361.5	384.3	654.9	4,110.2	11.2
Japan	1,158.0	470.7	282.8	386.3	370.6	515.4	3,183.7	8.7
Singapore	117.0	75.5	140.8	79.8	136.9	147.7	697.7	1.9
Germany	141.8	20.3	55.6	139.6	69.2	159.6	586.1	1.6
United Kingdom	334.0	44.3	51.7	28.6	56.4	33.3	548.2	1.5
France	212.6	49.9	11.9	73.8	32.9	17.6	398.6	1.1
Italy	113.0	24.5	91.6	19.4	22.9	63.3	334.7	0.9
Canada	65.6	8.7	91.0	34.3	39.5	49.1	288.3	0.8
Australia	91.2	14.1	31.6	47.4	17.4	83.7	285.3	0.8
Netherlands	2.0	2.7	0.3	0.1	153.3	17.7	176.1	0.5
Thailand	25.8	14.6	13.2	4.5	41.7	56.8	156.6	0.4
Switzerland	22.2	0.7	25.0	57.1	38.7	11.8	155.6	0.4
Austria	0.0	0.0	90.1	0.9	3.4	9.4	103.8	0.3
Philippines	6.4	40.6	3.8	30.5	15.5	4.7	101.5	0.3
Belgium	50.1	2.7	0.3	1.7	0.6	21.2	76.5	0.3
Sweden	32.9	5.0	0.0	5.3	0.8	27.6	71.6	0.2
Denmark	3.0	3.6	42.6	0.6	0.5	0.0	50.2	0.1

Note: Includes equity and cooperative joint ventures, wholly foreign-owned enterprises, joint offshore oil exploration, leasing, compensation deals, and processing and assembly.

Source: Business China, 25 June 1990.

TABLE 5.

China's Balance of Payments, 1985-1990

Billion US $

	1985	1986	1987	1988	1989	1990
Current account	**-11.4**	**-7.0**	**0.3**	**-3.8**	**-4.3**	**8.5**
Trade balance	-13.1	-9.1	1.7	-5.3	-5.6	7.0
Exports	25.1	25.8	34.7	41.0	43.2	51.0
Imports	38.2	34.9	36.4	46.4	48.8	44.0
Nontrade income (net)	1.5	1.7	1.7	1.1	0.9	1.1
Unrequited transfers (net)	0.2	0.4	0.2	0.4	0.4	0.4
Capital account	**9.0**	**5.9**	**6.0**	**7.1**	**3.7**	**1.5**
Long-term capital (net)	6.7	8.2	5.8	7.1	5.4	5.5
Short-term capital (net)	2.3	-2.3	0.2	0.1	-1.5	-4.0
Change in reserve assets	**-2.4**	**-1.3**	**6.3**	**3.3**	**-0.5**	**10.0**
Memo items:						
Total external debt	16.7	22.8	31.0	40.9	41.3	45.4
Tourism receipts	1.3	1.5	1.9	2.2	1.8	2.0
Foreign direct investment inflows	2.0	2.2	2.3	3.2	3.3	3.4
Foreign direct investment outflows	0.3	0.3	0.6	0.9	1.0	1.3
Yearend foreign exchange reserves	11.9	10.5	15.2	17.5	17.0	27.0

1. Merchandise trade data are based on Customs statistics, adjusted in accordance with balance-of-payments specifications.

2. Nontrade income includes shipment fees, tourist revenues, investment income, labor contracts, and other nontrade services.

3. Official unrequited transfers include grants and donations to and from international organizations and foreign governments; private transfers include remittances and payments from abroad by residents.

4. Long-term capital carries a maturity of one year or longer. It includes foreign direct investment; portfolio investment; international organization and foreign government loans; loans to Chinese banks, government agencies, and localities, deferred payments and collection; processing, compensatory trade and leasing payments; Chinese loans abroad; and other long-term capital.

5. Short-term capital includes loans to Chinese banks, government agencies, and localities; deferred payments and collections; and other capital to be repaid within one year.

6. Change in reserve assets: in this table, contrary to standard practice, a negative number denotes a drawdown in foreign exchange reserves; a positive number indicates an addition to foreign exchange reserves.

Source: China's State Administration of Exchange Control (1985-89) and CIA estimates (1990).

FIGURE 1.

Chinese Trade Trends, 1980-90

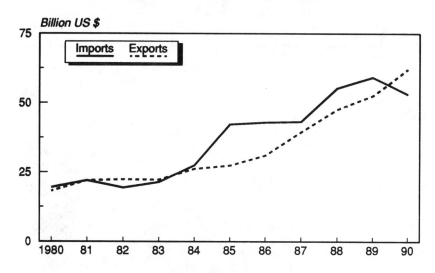

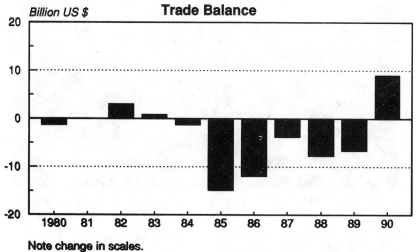

Note change in scales.

FIGURE 2.

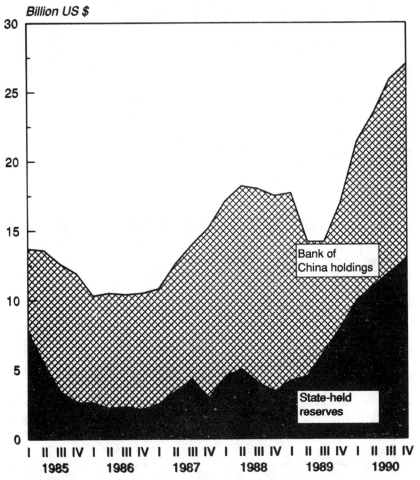

China: Quarterly Foreign Exchange Reserves, 1985-90

Note: State-held reserves and Bank of China holdings for the last four quarters are estimated. All other data are from official Chinese statistics.

FIGURE 3.

China: Export Earnings by Foreign-funded Firms

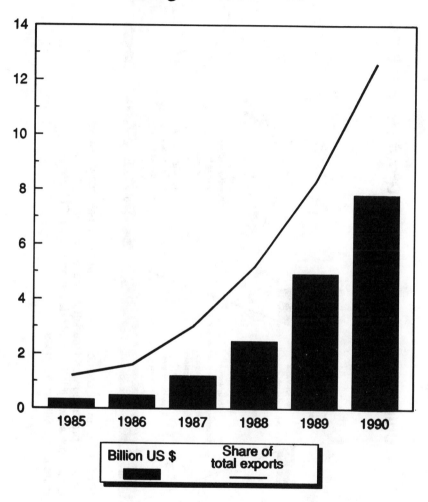

FIGURE 4.

China: Prospects for Export Growth in the 1990s

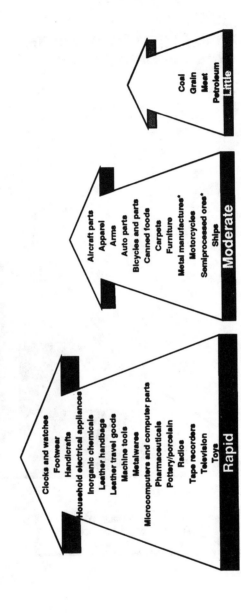

Rapid

Clocks and watches
Footwear
Handicrafts
Household electrical appliances
Inorganic chemicals
Leather handbags
Leather travel goods
Machine tools
Metalwares
Microcomputers and computer parts
Pharmaceuticals
Pottery/porcelain
Radios
Tape recorders
Television
Toys

Moderate

Aircraft parts
Apparel
Arms
Auto parts
Bicycles and parts
Canned foods
Carpets
Furniture
Metal manufactures*
Motorcycles
Semiprocessed ores*
Ships

Little

Coal
Grain
Meat
Petroleum

*Export growth will be more rapid if China's domestic prices remain far below prevailing world market prices; exports will, conversely, grow more slowly if inflation or price reforms bring Chinese prices more in line with world prices.

FIGURE 5.

Growth in Chinese Exports Relative to Growth in World Markets, 1980-90

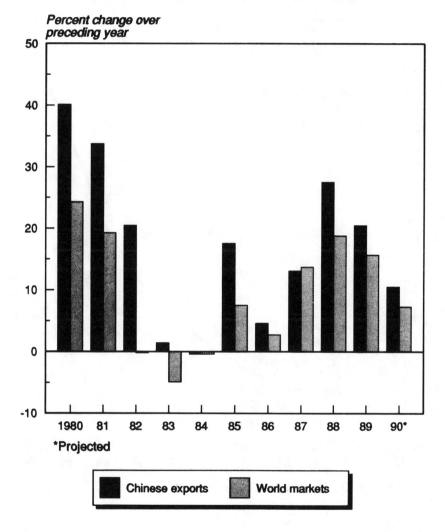

Percent change over preceding year

*Projected

Chinese exports   World markets

FIGURE 6.

China-US Trade, 1980-90

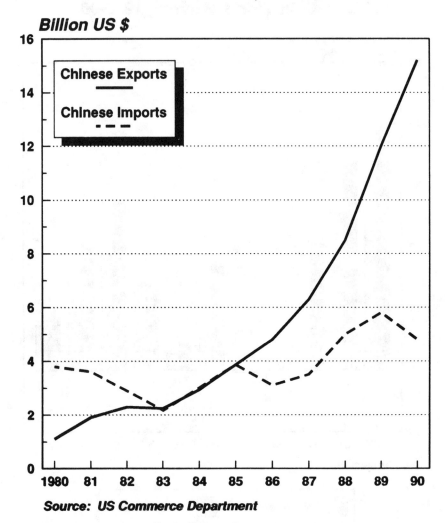

Source: US Commerce Department

FIGURE 7.

Growing Chinese Export Dependence on the US Market

*Percent of total
going to US market*

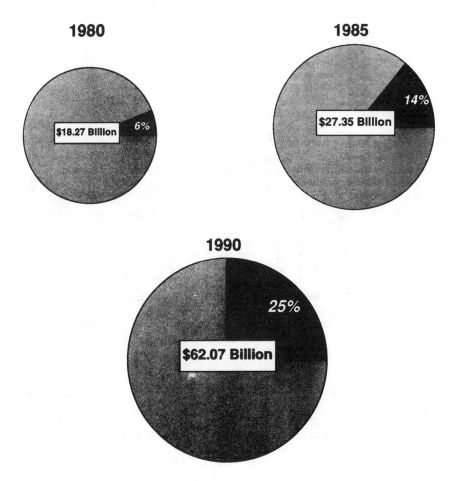

1980

$18.27 Billion   6%

1985

$27.35 Billion   14%

1990

25%

$62.07 Billion

THE BUSINESS CLIMATE IN CHINA: HALF EMPTY OR HALF FULL?

By Martin Weil *

CONTENTS

I. A DECADE OF LIBERALIZATION AND EXPANSION

When Deng Xiaoping took power in 1978, the range of China's economic relations with the outside world was small. China accepted neither foreign debt nor foreign investment. Foreign trade stood at only \$20.6 billion per year,[1] less than that of the island of Taiwan .[2] Only a few foreign companies had permanent representation in China.

All trade was conducted through a handful of foreign trade corporations (FTCs) directly controlled by the central government's Ministry of Foreign Trade (now known as the Ministry of Foreign Economic Relations and Trade, or MOFERT). Import and export volumes were determined by the State Planning Commission's annual plan. Imports were viewed as a residual way to fill in shortages of raw materials for production under the state plan or to provide select plants and equipment that China did not possess. Exports were viewed as a means to generate the cash to pay for imports.

The Chinese use the term "gaige kaifang" (reform and opening to the outside world) to describe the guiding policy of Deng Xiaoping's reign. "Kaifang", meaning "opening up", succinctly defines the progressively greater integration of China's economy with the world economy, and the weakening of the view that foreign trade is merely a residual to a closed domestic economic system. The impact of "kaifang" can be seen from a number of indicators:

---

* US-China Business Council for US-China Joint Economic Committee 1990 Compendium.
[1] State Statistical Bureau of the PRC, China Statistical Yearbook, 1988, (China Statistical Information & Consultancy Center, Beijing & Hong Kong, 1988), p.643.
[2] Republic of China Council for Economic Planning and Development, *Taiwan Statistical Data Book*, Taibei, 1988.

The 16.6 percent per year growth in China's trade from $20.6 billion in 1978 to 111.6 billion in 1989. Foreign trade grew to 28 percent of China's GNP, according to World Bank statistics.[3]

The relaxation of the strictures against foreign borrowing. By the end of 1989, China's debt had ballooned to a total of $44 billion, including approximately $4 billion from the World Bank, $7 billion from foreign governments, and the remainder from commercial banks.[4]

The absorption of $15.5 billion in direct foreign investment. Approximately 22,000 joint ventures or wholly-owned subsidiaries of foreign companies were established in China during the 1980's.[5]

The proliferation of Chinese organizations authorized to engage in direct contact with foreigners. The list expanded to include hundreds of foreign trade corporations under provincial governments and production ministries and thousands of individual enterprises, large and small.

The establishment of thousands of representative offices of foreign companies in China.

The economic integration of large parts of Guangdong Province with Hong Kong and thus with Hong Kong export markets, as Hong Kong companies moved their manufacturing operations in droves to the Pearl River Delta counties. By the end of the decade, coastal Fujian showed signs of becoming to Taiwan what the Pearl River delta had already become to Hong Kong.

The flow of Chinese investment abroad, in part to guarantee the availability of foreign raw materials. Chinese entities acquired significant stakes in North American oil refineries, chemical plants, and timber products facilities, as well as an Australian iron ore mine, and Hong Kong air transport and telephone companies.

HISTORY OF CHANGE

The changes in China's business climate in the 1980s did not follow a detailed master plan, but took place in fits and starts. Many of the most radical developments, such as the rapid growth of export-oriented township and village enterprises, were not even foreseen by the leadership. In retrospect, however, there were several consistent, important trends that can be said to characterize the entire decade: the development of institutions and a legal system to bring China in line with ways of doing business elsewhere in the world; the decentralization of political and economic power; and the steady erosion of ideological taboos against the West. The changes can be divided roughly into the following periods:

1979–1982. Basic concepts of the open policy were formulated, including:

- The promulgation of a Joint Venture Law and tax laws.

---

[3] State Statistical Bureau of the PRC, "Statistics for China's National Socio-Economic Development in 1989", *Beijing Review*, Feb. 26–Mar 4, 1990, supplement p. vi. See also World Bank, China Operations Division, *China: Country Economic Memorandum. Between Plan and Market,* Washington DC, May 1990, p. vii.

[4] World Bank, *China: Country Economic Memorandum,* p. 135.

[5] PRC Ministry of Foreign Economic Relations and Trade statistics cited in "Mofert Stats Underscore Waning Investor Interest in China", *Business China*, Hong Kong, June 25, 1990 pp. 192–193.

- The establishment of Special Economic Zones in Shenzhen (opposite Hong Kong), Zhuhai (opposite Macao), and Shantou in Guangdong Province, as well as Xiamen in Fujian Province. Although these zones developed slowly at first, the principle of more rapid integration of southern coastal areas into the world economy was established.
- The acceptance of foreign debt, and the beginning of the World Bank program in China.
- The decision in principle to allow foreign companies to participate in natural resource development, offshore oil in particular. Japanese and French government oil companies signed oil development contracts with China in 1980, and major American oil companies followed suit in 1987–1988.
- The first hesitant steps towards decentralization of foreign trade authority, with local governments and enterprises allowed for the first time to retain a portion of their foreign exchange earnings (typically at this time, no more than 20 percent), and with the establishment of the first central and local government competitors to the Mofert foreign trade companies.

1984–1986. Starting from the October 1984 Communist Party Central Committee plenary meeting, the pace of "kaifang" picked up considerably. The plenum passed a document that laid out far more explicitly than ever before the desirability of moving towards important features of a market economy, including a certain proportion of privately owned enterprises.[6]

Shortly afterward, the central government announced that 14 coastal cities would be permitted to offer special incentives to foreign investors. These cities were given large central government grants to develop their infrastructure, and rights to approve small foreign investment projects on their own authority.

Levels of local foreign exchange retention from exports were raised to levels of 30–40 percent for many products and localities. Local trading companies were granted expanded authority to compete directly with Beijing as MOFERT freed up hundreds of commodities from the monopoly of the FTCs. Local governments—particularly in Guangdong—began to borrow large volumes of money from foreign banks directly.

The relocation of export-oriented Hong Kong industry into the Pearl River delta region of Guangdong began in earnest during this period, facilitated not only by China's liberalizing domestic policies, but also by the 1984 agreement between China and Britain calling for Hong Kong to revert to mainland control in 1997. By the end of 1986, Hong Kong firms probably employed more people in Guangdong than they did in Hong Kong itself[7]—primarily in so-called "village and township", i.e., quasi-private, enterprises that had not even existed earlier.

Facilitated considerably by the increased local autonomy and by new detailed joint venture implementing regulations, foreign investment aimed at China's domestic market accelerated as well.

---

[6] The plenum communique is reproduced in New China News Ltd., *People's Republic of China Yearbook 1985*, (Hong Kong 1985), pp. 73–86.

[7] Hong Kong Governor David Wilson as reported in Ezra Vogel, *One Step Ahead in China: Guangdong Under Reform*, (Harvard Press, Cambridge, MA) 1989, p. 69.

Large companies such as Otis Elevator, McDermott Babcock and Wilcox, H.J. Heinz, Celanese, American Standard, PPG, Coca Cola, Volkswagen, Peugeot, Philips (Netherlands) and Matsushita all signed joint venture contracts in the 1984–1986 period, a number of them of quite substantial size. Many of these ventures were promised a degree of market access which would have been inconceivable earlier, and many were given foreign exchange convertability guarantees by the Chinese government up front.

1987–1988. The degree of openness peaked as liberal Zhao Ziyang was promoted to the position of Secretary-General of the Communist Party in 1987. Even more forcefully than in 1984, Zhao articulated the concept that coastal China should be linked to the world economy, taking its raw materials from abroad and selling its products on the international market. The export processing economy in Guangdong and, increasingly, Fujian grew ever more rapidly as a result.

In response to perennial foreign investor complaints about the inacessibility of foreign exchange, Zhao's government made the Chinese currency, the renminbi (RMB) partially convertible by setting up over 40 so-called "swap centers" at which domestic currency could exchanged be for foreign exchange controlled by enterprises outside the state plan (including, by definition, almost all enterprises with foreign investment). The price for dollars at these centers was allowed to float by 100 percent or more above the official exchange rate. In 1989, over $8.75 billion was exchanged at the centers.[8]

The swap centers' importance grew as Zhao's government adopted a system of foreign exchange management which greatly increased the percentage of foreign exchange controlled locally outside the plan. Zhao's program allowed local governments and enterprises to retain 80 percent of all foreign exchange earned in excess of 1987 base levels. In the Shenzhen economic zone and other parts of the Pearl River delta, exporters were permitted to keep 100 percent of their foreign exchange earnings.

Local governments in the coastal provinces were permitted in 1988 to approve foreign investment projects valued up to $30 million on their own authority, including wholly foreign-owned manufacturing subsidiaries. Foreign companies desiring a large majority share in Chinese enterprises met far less resistance than they had in earlier years.

For the first time in 1987–1988, foreign companies were given the right to lease land directly in the Special Economic Zones for duration of up to 70 years. Foreign banks obtained their first small operational foothold in the economic zones as well.

II. PROBLEMS IN THE BUSINESS ENVIRONMENT

Despite the ever-increasing openness of the 1980s, few foreign companies perceived China as an easy place to do business. Difficulties arose both from certain deeply ingrained features of the existing bureaucratic command economy that "gaige kaifang" failed

---

[8] China Daily Business Supplement, May 7, 1990, p. 1, reported in US Foreign Broadcast Information Service (FBIS), *China Report*, May 1990, p. 16.

to eradicate, and from unintended side-effects of the reforms themselves. Major problems included:

SHARP FLUCTUATIONS IN MACROECONOMIC GROWTH RATES AND MONEY SUPPLY

Deng Xiaoping's China followed a pattern of boom and bust cycles whose magnitude and frequency exceeded those in developed capitalist countries. Cycles started with a burst of economic activity fueled by a loose money supply and accompanied by a political push for reform and decentralization. The liberated bureaucracies, both at central and local levels, went on spending binges, particularly for new construction projects, which pushed up the rate of growth but brought inflation and tight material supplies in their wake, leading in turn to feverish speculative purchasing by both individuals and insitutions.

Inflation and speculation inevitably generated, however, a strong backlash from central government planners worried about social and political unrest and the erosion of their own powers. Unable to control the economy through exhortation or purely economic levers such as interest rates—local governments underwriting the booms ignored both—the central government resorted to the familiar administrative controls on spending, which were applied with little selectivity. Indiscriminate austerity inevitably produced strong pressures from below for relaxed controls, starting the cycle all over again.

Most foreign corporate activity in 1980s China closely followed the domestic cycles. Not only did a slowdown in domestic economic activity reduce the demand for foreign products; spasmodic expansion tended to draw down China's foreign exchange reserves, while domestic austerity built them up.

The first major downturn of the Deng Xiaoping era took place in 1981–1982. Sharp cuts in government spending in response to a wave of inflation resulted in the suspension of construction projects across China. The majority of foreign companies doing business in China were forced to delay project negotiations for approximately two years.

The next expansionary phase, a major one, coincided with the reformist push of 1984–1985. It was, however, followed by another contraction at the end of 1985, particularly in foreign exchange expenditures, which had ballooned to unsustainable levels as foreign currency control was decentralized. Imports of consumer goods were curtailed abruptly, and a number of newly-established joint ventures experienced severe foreign currency cash flow problems.

But for most foreign companies in China, this contraction proved to be both milder and of shorter duration than in 1981–1982. One reason was the weakened political position of the old central planners, and the growing powers of the provinces. Another was rapid export growth.

By late 1987 the next economic boom—accompanied by the familiar decentralization and reform push—was in full swing, and imports soared 27.9 percent to a level of $55.2 billion in 1988 .[9] But by

---

[9] State Statistical Bureau of the PRC, "Statistics for 1988 Socio-Economic Development," Beijing Review, (Beijing), March 6–13, 1989 Supplement, p. vi.

the end of 1988, retrenchment had set in once again, a political reaction to the unprecedented inflation that the boom had generated. The central government's cutback on the money supply—the single economic lever over which it still had substantial control—had an even more severe impact on the cash flow of most fledgling foreign investment projects than the 1985 contraction.

Retrenchment became a full-scale recession after the Tiananmen massacre of June 4, 1989. The economy squeezed by the cutback in foreign lending and tourism, and the downfall of Zhao Ziyang brought the central planning faction back to its most powerful position since 1981, giving an added bite to the latest austerity policies. Economic growth shrank to zero during the first half of 1990, and China's imports dropped by 18 percent compared to the first half of 1989, the most dramatic drop since 1981.[10]

As a result of these fluctuations, many foreign companies whose presence in China was geared to the domestic market failed to meet the goals laid out during boom periods. While some took better precautions than others to cushion themselves against the impact of a downturn, almost all (with the possible exception of disposable consumer goods companies) were to some extent affected by China's macroeconomic gyrations.

BUREAUCRATIC INTERFERENCE

Ten years of reform did not change the fundamentally bureaucratic nature of China's economy. Not only did foreign business people continue to find the pace of bureaucratic decision-making in most parts of China painfully slow, but they also discovered that political priorities or bureaucratic fiat routinely took precedence over law, and even over the terms of signed contracts. Manipulation of political and personal connections was seen as critical to doing business and solving problems, and corruption became an increasingly common phenomenon.

The pervasive, tangled nature of bureaucratic control left foreign companies vulnerable to restrictions, harassment, and uncertainty on such issues as:

Market access. Strict import controls lay at the core of the pre-1979 system, with foreign exchange bureaucratically allocated by the State Planning Commission to the various ministries and provinces. All import transactions required the approval of one of these agencies. As more and more foreign exchange came to be controlled either by provinces or enterprises during the 1980s, the import control system became more porous. But it by no means disapppeared.

Faced, for example, by a flood of consumer durables imports by speculative local government trading companies, the State Council established a new inter-agency office in 1985 to set national import quotas for these goods and parcel the quotas out among the various buyers. The license system reduced imports of these goods to a relative trickle for the next few years.

---

[10] General Administration of Customs of the PRC, *China's Customs Statistics (Quarterly)*, (Economic Information & Agency, Hong Kong), 1990.3, p.3.

The import approval procedures for many products gave domestic industry an important voice in the process. The Ministry of Chemicals Industry, for example, has sat on an inter-agency consultative committee determining pesticide and herbicide import levels.[11]

The license system restricted not only foreign exporters to China, but also foreign manufacturers in China. Chrysler and Xerox, for example, were forced to operate their respective jeep and photocopier plants in China at a fraction of capacity due to failure to obtain import licenses for an adequate volume of critical parts.

Even when import licenses were not required, some American manufacturers were denied market access in China. The Chinese partner of one American joint venture manufacturing a name-brand consumer product in Shanghai, for example, was ordered by the State Planning Commission to curtail the joint venture's production in late 1988. There were strong suggestions that the action was instigated by the Ministry of Light Industry on behalf of disgruntled domestic manufacturers of the product, and the issue was not resolved until the American company agreed to export much of the additional production.

Another American company making an almost identical product in a Guangzhou joint venture was given the same order by the central agency. Ultimately, however, local authorities ignored it in the interests of keeping the plant running to full capacity, illustrating the increasing divergence between the business climate in North and South China.

Personnel. At the enterprise level, control over personnel was the core of the bureaucracy's power. It is hardly surprising, therefore, that the bureaucracy strongly resisted foreign influence on personnel issues.

Despite regulations to the contrary, Chinese personnel wishing to transfer from state-owned enterprises to joint ventures were often blocked by their old employers (who controlled their all-important personal files and residence cards) from switching. In the same vein, many Chinese joint-venture managers who became too close to foreign partners were abruptly transferred by Chinese partners.

The bureaucratic obsession with control affected wage policies as well. Ironically, on more than one occasion, Chinese joint venture partners or government labor bureaus blocked foreign managers from raising wages to reward productivity, for fear of creating too great a differential between joint venture and domestic enterprise wages.

Taxes and Fees. The extraordinarily wide latitude enjoyed by a host of bureaucratic organs to levy taxes and fees—or exempt foreign companies from them—led to arbitrariness and abuse. One of many examples was the decision in 1989 to revoke the exemption of foreign joint venture feed companies from the Consolidated Industrial and Commercial Tax (CICT, a kind of sales tax) while maintaining the exemption for wholly domestically owned enterprises.

---

[11] Mofert announcement of 1986 cited in American Chamber of Commerce in Hong Kong, "Import Controls in China", *China Business Review*, (National Council for US-China Trade, Washington DC), Jan–Feb 1987, p. 43.

Shift of Bureaucratic Responsibility. Partial reform in the 1980s added to the problem of bureaucracy by blurring the lines of bureaucratic authority. Foreign companies experienced great difficulties determining whether the authority claimed by their negotiating counterparts was real, and if real, how long it would last. Authority either shifted unpredictably back and forth among central and local government, or became fragmented among the various central and local government organs.

Ambiguous lines of bureaucratic authority created particular problems for some foreign banks. In one notable case in 1989–1990, the First National Bank of Chicago attempted to call a guarantee that had been issued by the "Guangdong branch" of a major central government trading company. At the time the loan was made, the Guangdong branch was technically owned by the Beijing head office, but by the time the loan was called, what had been the Guangdong branch was an independent company owned by the Guangdong provincial government. For more than a year and a half, neither Guangdong nor the central government would claim responsibility for the guarantee.[12] Again, the legal system proved unable to even begin to establish systematic principles of responsibility.

A Two-tiered Economy. If bureaucratic interference and macroeconomic fluctuations reflected the persistence of the old command system, the so-called "two-tiered" economy", i.e. the emergence of a quasi-market economy parallel to the command economy, reflected the contradictions of a partially reformed system. Although many foreign companies would not have been able to operate in China at all without the second tier, the tiered system created certain competitive disadvantages for them.

The two-tiered economy was based on the price differentials for materials distributed under the state plan at subsidized prices and those distributed outside the state plan at market prices. These differentials were as great as 300–400 percent in the late 1980s for key industrial raw materials in short supply, such as coal, metals, plastics, etc.

Almost all foreign joint ventures in China, by definition, operated outside the state plan for materials distribution. Their material costs were substantially higher than their competitors within the state plan.

The formation of foreign currency swap centers created a similar two-tiered system for foreign currency, and foreign companies were squeezed on this front as well. When investing their dollars in China, they were required to exchange them for RMB at low official rates. But when converting RMB to repatriate from China, they were forced to convert at the premium swap center rates.

The two-tiered currency system and resulting foreign exchange arbitrage also wreaked havoc on many of the traditional Chinese exporting foreign trade companies (FTCs) and their American customers. The FTCs were required by the central government to trade foreign currency for RMB at official exchange rates. Newly established trading companies in Guangdong, whose swap centers

<hr />

[12] Details of court proceedings on this case are reproduced in "Cases", *China Law and Practice*, (China Law and Practice Ltd., Hong Kong), February 26, 1990.

were the most lively in the country due to the abundance of locally retained foreign exchange, could acquire swap center RMB more cheaply, enabling them to pay a higher RMB procurement price to Chinese export good manufacturers and still sell abroad at a foreign currency price equal to or lower than their FTC competitors.

Lack of Respect for Intellectual Property. The successive publication of trademark, patent, and copyright laws in the reform era marked an important advance in China's recognition of the legitimacy of intellectual property protection. But in practice, there continued to be many violations of intellectual property that disadvantaged foreign companies.

Reports of Chinese attempts to duplicate patented technology without authorization were legion. Indeed, many companies took for granted that such attempts would be made, and that some of their technical trainees came from potential Chinese competitors.

In certain respects, the problems Americans encountered in China were similar to those they encountered in other parts of Asia in the 1970s and 1980s. Unauthorized Chinese infringement of trademarks and copyrights, for example, echoed the experience of many companies in Taiwan and Thailand. Significantly, violations of American company trademarks, particularly for consumer products, took place primarily in the open, freewheeling Southern coastal provinces, the part of China most similar to other developing Asian economies.

But Chinese disregard for intellectual property rights was not always an insurmountable problem. As time passed, China proved increasingly skillful at negotiating legal, legitimate technology transfer in connection with large import projects, although some firms, mindful of Japan's rapid technological advance in the 1960s and 1970s, held back some of their best technology, or insisted on an equity share in any Chinese enterprise using their technology. Some companies succeeded in curtailing local government abuse of their trademarks through appeals to the legal system. Finally, many considered the risk of intellectual property violations worth bearing in order to enter the China market.

"Middle Kingdom Complex". Perhaps the most elusive problem in China's business climate to describe, but one of the most deeply felt by American business people in the 1980s was the cavalier attitude towards their interests of many of their Chinese counterparts. Many sensed a Chinese attitude of superiority or even condescension, a conviction that China was such an important market that the American companies would do anything to enter it, and a willingness to take any action to gain advantage. These tendencies appeared all the more galling in the context of incessant Chinese rhetoric about "mutual benefit" in commercial transactions.

The manifestations of what some foreigners called "the middle kingdom complex" included, for instance, arbitrary violations of contracts under the assumption that the foreign companies needed China more than China needed them. One petroleum equipment supplier, for example, was notified in 1987 that only a 65 percent payment would be made for equipment just shipped, not the 90 percent that the contract and the letter of credit called for. Another characteristic is a tendency to make the resolution of Chinese internal difficulties the responsibility of the foreign party. Numerous

Chinese exporting agencies, for example, simply refused to carry out export commitments to American firms when the domestic Chinese procurement price for the goods in question jumped unexpectedly between the time of contract signing and planned shipment.

Another new tendency is to treat the foreign party to joint ventures more as a resource to be exploited than as a partner. It became a custom, for example, for the Chinese partner to demand salaries for their joint venture managerial personnel commensurate with that of the foreign managers, even though the Chinese managers themselves were not allowed to keep more than a small amount of the money, the rest going to the partner. More significant was the frequent Chinese pressure on foreign partners to make large up-front investments in plant and equipment, regardless of the market prospects for the product.

A final example is the reluctance, or, in some cases, absolute unwillingness of the Chinese authorities to allow foreigners to compete in such services as engineering and design, telecommunications, insurance, transportation and, outside the economic zones, domestic banking.

Some portion of the foreign complaints about Chinese attitudes can be attributed to a lack of cross-cultural understanding, particularly regarding the sanctity of contracts as opposed to personal relationships. Certainly some complaints derive simply from Chinese negotiating skill, and understandable exploitation of China's advantage as the world's largest potential market. Moreover, the behavior of many foreign companies did nothing to disabuse Chinese negotiators of the notion that they would do almost anything to enter the China market.

Many foreign company executives, furthermore, brought their own attitudes of cultural superiority and selfishness to the negotiating table. And there were certainly foreign companies guilty of bad-faith violations of contracts with China. Even when these factors are considered, however, the "middle kingdom complex" still emerged as a salient feature of the China business environment, particularly in the state-run part of China's economy, and an obstacle to the expansion of China's international commerce.

III. Business Environment Prior to June 4, 1989

For corporations, evaluation of a business climate ultimately boils down to whether they are making money, or gaining a market position that will enable them to make money in the future. Judging by this standard, China's business climate in the 1980s presented a very mixed picture.

Many commodities suppliers considered the China business climate favorable simply because of large sales volumes. Most did some business with China prior to the Deng Xiaoping era, but reform, by creating rapid economic growth, greatly increased China's importance to them. Suppliers of wheat, steel, fertilizer, timber, and plastic resins, for all of which China experienced chronic shortages, were outstanding examples of this type of company. World price trends had a much bigger impact on the profitability of these companies' China business than China-specific factors, and China's large purchases themselves tended to support prices.

China was also an important market for certain capital goods of high priority to the Beijing government, such as petroleum, railroad, aviation, telecommunications, power plant, and mining equipment, as well as process control instruments. To be sure, intense international competition eroded the profitability of much of this business. But during the American petroleum industry recession of the mid-1980s, China business kept afloat certain companies, such as the petroleum drill bit manufacturer Hughes Tool (now Baker Hughes).

As China's standard of living increased, it also became a good, though inconsistent, market for consumer electronics such as televisions and refrigerators. Even after the Chinese government clamped down on imports of the finished products, suppliers of components (mostly non-American) for assembly in China continued to do strong business.

Other companies, in contrast, benefitted as much from liberalization of Chinese policies as from growth per se, most notably American retailers of labor-intensive consumer goods such as toys, shoes, apparel, handbags, and even electronic goods. The opening of the southern coastal provinces to foreign investment made China a profitable, indeed critical overseas production platform for makers of these and related items.

Liberalization was also the key to success for a number of American consumer products giants such as Coca Cola and Pepsi Cola, Proctor & Gamble, H.J. Heinz, S. C. Johnson (Johnson Wax), and Squibb, who desired primarily to sell to the Chinese domestic market. For all the bureaucratic obstacles to market access that these manufacturers faced, their ability to establish a manufacturing and sales presence in China—and the consequent steady growth in their market volume—more than made up for the frustrations and even for the low initial profitability.

For a large number, perhaps the majority, of American producer goods firms wishing to penetrate the China market, however, the verdict on the 1980s was more ambiguous. China became a market for some of them, such as the chemical and electronic giants, but hardly a critical one, and often not a terribly profitable one due to the intensity of the competition and the high costs of doing business.

Many such companies established manufacturing operations in China in the second half of the 1980s, and many more were considering doing so at the time of the June 4 massacre. Measured purely in terms of profitability, these joint ventures or wholly owned subsidiaries did not necessarily do badly. Indeed, a survey of 50 of them by the US-China Business Council in early 1989 showed that about half were profitable, at least in local currency.[13] However, the time, effort, and money they spent combatting the various obstacles presented by China's business environment could only be justified by increasing volumes resulting from economic liberaliza-

---

[13] U.S.-China Business Council, *U.S. Investment in China*, Washington DC, 1990, p. 83.

tion and growth. Many, if not most, had not achieved the volumes by 1989 that would completely justify their existence.

For these companies and others that were just entering the market in the late 1980s, China's attraction was not so much its current business climate as the perception that the climate had improved over time and would continue to improve in the future. Although some companies had reached the tentative conclusion by 1989 that the "long term" in China was never going to materialize, optimisim about the future was probably the single most important reason for the generally high level of American corporate interest in China throughout the 1980s.

IV. BUSINESS POST-TIANANMEN

THE DOWNTURN

Confidence in the future has been the main casualty of the killings on June 4, 1989. The political paralysis in April–May 1989, and the turbulence and repression since June 4 have reinforced for western business people just how critical the connection is between politics and economics in China. Most have serious concerns about a political system run by octogenarians with no viable transition mechanism and a disaffected population.

The severe economic recession during the year following June 4 has contributed to business uncertainty about the future. While many corporate China veterans view the recession as just another, albeit an amplified version of the down phase in the China business cycle, the coincidence of political instability with an economic downturn have led many to conclude that a real turnaround in the Chinese economy awaits a transition to a post-Deng leadership. Most still claim to believe in China's long-run growth potential, but their assessment of the next 5–10 years is decidedly more pessimistic than pre-Tiananmen.

Western and Japanese investment in China has fallen off sharply in the year following Tiananmen, a direct reflection of declining confidence in the business environment. According to (probably understated) official Chinese statistics, new foreign investment commitments for the year following Tiananmen trailed commitments for the preceeding year by 21 percent.[14]

Investment statistics do not capture the extent to which June 4 has discouraged companies new to the market, particularly small and medium-sized ones, from initiating projects. The pressures to be in China for prestige reasons have evaporated.

Companies already committed to the market have been affected by a Tiananmen-induced reduction in foreign exchange availability. The U.S. government-led cutback in World Bank lending—which totalled $500 million in new loans June 1989–1990 compared to a pre-Tiananmen projection of $1.5–2 billion—combined with the decline in tourism and the reluctance of many other government and commercial banks to lend when the World Bank was pulling back, was a major factor behind the steep drop in Chinese imports during the 1989–1990 recession.

---

[14] PRC Ministry of Foreign Economic Relations and Trade statistics cited in Xinhua News Agency release of July 23, *FBIS*, July 25 , 1990, p. 36.

Declining foreign exchange cash flow has furthermore created repayments problems for many Chinese foreign exchange borrowers, particularly in the hotel/service sectors catering to foreigners who are no longer flocking to China in such large numbers. Borrowers for Chinese real estate projects have been forced to reschedule billions of dollars of debt (primarily from Japanese banks), and some smaller borrowers have defaulted.

China is thus in a much less favorable position to drive hard bargains with foreign companies and banks. Many foreign governments have curtailed thier concessionary lending to China, and the interest spread on commercial loans to China has risen from less than one-half a percentage point above LIBOR pre-Tiananmen to close to one point above LIBOR. Rising Western government and corporate interest in East Europe following that region's startling transformation increases China's difficulties in attracting cheap funds (particularly German), and the 1990 Middle East crisis may do so as well.

The political tightening of 1989–1990 has also had an impact, particularly for some companies already operating joint ventures in China. Bureaucracies threatened by foreign investment feel more emboldened to interfere in joint venture operations. For example, the U.S.-China Business Council has received numerous reports from member companies of bureaucratic limitations on wages not just for managers, but for workers.

The political repression has taken a particularly strong toll on progressive Chinese managers, who place themselves in danger of political criticism if they take bold reform initiatives. Many students and technicians trained abroad who might serve in China's new managerial class are simply not returning home.

THE SILVER LINING

There have been important exceptions to the pattern of deterioration of China's post-Tiananmen business environment, most notably in southern coastal China. Although the South was not exempted from the cutback in domestic credit for the year following Tiananmen, the export processing economy which has made the region so rich has remained largely intact. Beijing appears to have carried out few, if any, of its early threats to recentralize control of southern foreign exchange, and to do away with the township and village enterprises that have played so important a role in the Southern export drive. The operations of the export processing factories have not been affected by politics.

Indeed, the chief threat to the southern exporting economy has come from the United States in the form of Congressional pressure to abolish China's non-discriminatory tariff treatment, or most favored nation status (MFN), as a signal of disapproval of the Chinese leadership. Without MFN, the tariffs on consumer products shipped from South China to US retailers would rise from an average of about 5–10 percent of value to a level of 50 percent or greater, effectively driving them from the market.[15] As the USA is by

---

[15] U.S. Customs Bureau statistics cited in "Letter from the President", *China Business Review*, U.S.-China Business Council, May–June 1990, p. 7.

far the most important market for these goods, the withdrawal of MFN would thus gut the South China export economy.

Although the Bush Administration appears in late 1990 to have contained the congressional pressure on MFN, the public debate on the subject, combined with the shock of June 4 has led some manufacturers of products such as toys, particularly from Hong Kong, to divert investment away from China to other developing countries to ensure against disruption that might result from removal of MFN or another round of upheaval in China. This diversification is not effecting production in the short run, but might slow the rate of export growth from South China in future years, and will certainly result in a major drop-off in purchases from China in the event of future trouble there.

If American and Hong Kong companies are trying to develop sources other than China, however, Taiwan is moving full force into China despite Tiananmen. Prompted by appreciating Taiwanese currency, rising wage rates, Fujian's proximity and its cultural similarity to Taiwan, Taiwan investors are starting to do in Fujian what Hong Kong investors did in Guangdong in the second half of the 1980s. Unlike Hong Kong, for which Tiananmen was a profound shock, Taiwan, which does not face reabsorption into the mainland political system in 1997, has been able to separate political factors from its evaluation of the China business climate.

Chinese government statistics show that Taiwan companies have committed $1.5 billion dollars of direct investment to China from the beginning of 1988 through the first quarter of 1990.[16] Taiwan shoe manufacturers have moved production lines en masse to Fujian, and manufacturers of other products such as sporting equipment have indicated they might follow. Some of Taiwan's largest companies, including Formosa Plastics Group, are seriously discussing the formation of manufacturing enterprises on the mainland.

In addition to southern export processing, certain other sectors of the Chinese economy appear to have been spared the fallout of Tiananmen, including the petroleum and civil aviation industries. Significantly, both have a substantial foreign exchange income stream (which, in petroleum's case, will likely be increased by the Mideast crisis). Chinese civil aviation and offshore petroleum companies continue to enjoy favorable credit ratings abroad, as does the China International Trust and Investment Corporation (CITIC), a state-run but entrepreneurally-minded merchant bank which easily raised $1 billion in 1990 to buy a share of Hong Kong's telephone company.

TOWARDS THE FUTURE

By the second half of 1990, some foreign companies are starting to see signs of a general improvement in China's business environment. The tight domestic credit policy appears to be easing somewhat, in response to the leadership's alarm about the economic recession. The recentralization rhetoric has subsided and China's in-

---

[16] Ministry of Foreign Economic Relations and Trade statistics cited in *China Market Intelligence*, US-China Business Council, June 1990, p. 5.

quiries for foreign goods are on the increase. Certain companies, such as Amoco Chemical in Jiangsu Province and Westinghouse in Shenzhen, have put the finishing touches on investment plans which had been suspended after the massacre. And the post-Tiananmen international stigma of doing business in China is easing, judging by the resumed flow of high corporate executives to China.

But a rebound from the floor of the second half of 1989 and first-half 1990 by no means signifies a return to the status quo pre-Tiananmen. There remains a powerful sense among foreign business people, as well as Chinese, that there can be no fundamental resolution of the major question marks regarding China's business climate until the political transition from Deng Xiaoping to a new leadership has been completed.

Many of the problems endemic to China's business climate, such as bureaucratic interference in operations, do not appear susceptible to an immediate solution even with political change. But the history of the 1980s suggests that foreign businesspeople perceive that the situation is improving, and that they are willing to bear with considerable difficulties in the China market given its size and potential.

The experience of the reform decade also suggests that there may be increasing divergence in the future between the economic and business climate in southern coastal China that is an integral part of the world economy, and in a northern China that to some extent benefits from the prosperity of South China, but remains a significantly more closed economy and a less inviting place for foreign companies to do business. As in the 1980s, this difference will create both opportunities and complications for foreign companies in China.

CHINA'S POTENTIAL FOR EXPORT-LED GROWTH

By William A. Fischer *

CONTENTS

The success and vitality of China's economic reforms during the early and mid- 1980s generated considerable, even exuberant, optimism among students of economic development. The sheer size of the Chinese market, a sustained period of domestic tranquility, and the strong commitment of the Chinese government toward modernization, growth, and greater involvement in the world economic community, created a buoyant feeling that China was poised for success. Many Western observers began to speak of the inevitability of China joining several of its East Asian neighbors as a newly industrializing country (NIC);[1] a country that was able to overcome the debilitating poverty of underdevelopment and enjoy sufficiently rapid economic growth to allow it to break away from the rest of the "third world." Some authors even saw China approximating, in many dimensions, an *East Asian development model*; a model used to explain the unusual economic success enjoyed by several NICs within the region.

Central to the many explanations that such models offer in an effort to describe the region's growth has been the recognition of export-led growth [2] and relatively open economies as mechanisms for both increasing the availability of foreign exchange (and, hence, foreign technology and management skills) in such societies, and

---

* Dalton L. McMichael, Sr. Professor of Business Administration at the Graduate School of Business Administration, The University of North Carolina at Chapel Hill, and Professor, The International Institute for Management Development, (IMD) Lausanne, Switzerland.

[1] For example, Dwight H. Perkins, *China: Asia's Next Economic Giant?* (Seattle, University of Washington Press, 1986).

[2] Peter L. Berger, "An East Asian Development Model?" in Peter L. Berger and Hsin-Huang Michael Hsiao (eds.), *In Search of An East Asian Development Model* (New Brunswick, NJ, Transaction Books, 1988), p. 5; and John B. Sheehan, *Alternative International Economic Strategies and Their Relevance for China*, World Bank Staff Working Paper No. 759, (Washington, D.C., the World Bank, 1986).

strengthening domestic industrial capabilities through international competitive testing. In China's case, despite strong domestic market protection, the total value of trade, sustained investment, and joint ventures experienced during the 1980s, appeared to be evidence that the nation was well on the way to emulating the success demonstrated by Hong Kong, Singapore, South Korea, Taiwan, and even Japan, despite significant limitations in the capabilities of the Chinese economic system for supporting such growth. It is argued in this paper, however, that such optimism may well have been premature. Significant systemic and infrastructural deficiencies existed throughout China's economic system which, without substantial attention and reform, meant that continued economic growth could not be taken for granted. In addition, the recent retrenchment of key portions of the economic reform program, a significant reduction in managerial autonomy, and a widespread diminution in the attractiveness of China to many potential foreign investors have all further reduced the prospects for exports as an engine of immediate and sustained economic growth.

I. TRADITIONAL EXPORT-LED GROWTH

In almost every case, a significant portion of the initial post-war success of Japan and the East-Asian NICs began with the utilization of low-wage labor to enter world markets.[3] Traditionally nations with abundant labor, working at relatively low wages, have chosen to enter international trade by concentrating on the low-cost production of standardized items in mature markets. Typically such market entrants specialize in bottom-of-the-line, low-fashion-content, items, relying heavily on labor-intensive flow-shop assembly operations, where a high division of labor allows for the capturing of learning economies without the requirement of well-trained or highly participatory labor forces. This, apparently, was what the former secretary-general of the Chinese Communist Party, Zhou Ziyang, had in mind in January 1988, when he spoke of his plans for the development of China's coastal regions:

> Today, our coastal economy has been furnished with an excellent opportunity for development. With the ongoing changes in wage structures around the world, the industrialized nations are reorganizing their industrial structures and shifting labor-intensive production operations to areas offering labor inexpensive labor. China's coastal regions have great potential for benefiting from this movement. They are capable of providing inexpensive labor, a relatively qualified work force, easy access to transportation, and a good infrastructure, coupled with scientific and technological development capabilities. This is all it takes, and if we simply do our work well, we will be able to attract a great deal of foreign investment.[4]

---

[3] In the case of Japan, her postwar exports to the developed world were based on labor-intensive advantages, while her exports to developing countries were based on heavy, capital-intensive products. (G.C. Allen, *The Japanese Economy* (New York, St. Martin's Press, 1981), pp. 162–163.

[4] Zhao Ziyang, Renmin Ribao, January 23, 1988, as quoted in Toshio Watanabe, "Bringing China Out of Its Shell: The Asian NIEs," *JETRO China Newsletter*, No. 87, July–August 1990, p. 2.

The idea is an attractive one. A focus on low-variety, no-fashion, mature products requires little from the manufacturer other than acceptable (but not necessarily *better than acceptable*) quality—an important consideration for those products produced under labor-intensive conditions, where relatively high-quality variances are the norm. Design (to the extent that there is any of significance), distribution, and marketing tend to be the province of buyers from the developed world, who typically then market the products under their own labels, within their own distribution systems. The maturity of the product, and the lack of fashion, ensure that there will be few, if any, surprises in terms of market demand irregularities and, consequently, little if any responsiveness is needed by the factory in the developing country. This is further reinforced to the extent that the production process can be segmented, thus allowing the decoupling of the activities performed in the developing country from vertically dependent preceding and succeeding activities. This reduces the need for integration or infrastructure development on the part of the foreign buyer, and reduces the risk of production disruption due to faulty or inadequate interorganizational linkages.

The logic inherent in the choice of such traditional export-led growth is obvious. The comparative advantage of the developing countries is thought to be their low-wage labor, which is typically unskilled. By employing such labor in a manner that allows it to compete on the basis of price (not quality, responsiveness, or fashion—which essentially means concentrating on the production of standardized, mature products), the developing nation seeks to avoid competition based on technical skills, fashion mastery, geographic proximity, market knowledge, or customer interaction. Such products require little in terms of global integration of a supplier-distributor network and little in terms of organizational agility in responding to national market differences. Instead, they rely on the brute power of the economies of scale inherent in high-volume, low-variety, mass production. Firms in developing countries engaged in this type of trade are selling price, and little else. They qualify to participate in international trade, despite often unsatisfactory quality and unreliable delivery performance, because they are so cheap, and they win orders solely on the basis of this criterion.[5]

In China's case, with a manufacturing base that is characterized by vintage equipment, low labor productivity, unreliable quality, poorly developed supplier-customer relations, information scarcity, excess inventory, obsolete product design, and almost no manufacturing flexibility or responsiveness, a reliance on providing straight forward subcontracting of labor intensive operations makes for a rational approach to entering international commerce. In fact, such a strategy has already had some geographically limited, but nonetheless considerable, success in China, particularly in the coastal regions of Guangdong province. There, close commercial and family ties with Hong Kong producers have resulted in estimates of from 850,000 to 1.7 million Chinese workers employed (in 1988) in for-

---

[5] For a discussion of the importance of *order winners and qualifiers* to manufacturing strategy, see: Terry Hill, *Manufacturing Strategy*, (Homewood, IL, Richard D. Irwin, Inc., 1989).

eign-related manufacturing operations.[6] Similar, but less-developed relationships are emerging among Fujian and Zhejiang and Taiwan, and between the provinces of northeast China and Korea. Yet, despite all this, the long-range prospects for development throughout China are not nearly as optimistic as that experienced along the coast, and it is still not entirely clear that the current export emphasis along the coast will yield the types of results—improved technology and managerial skills—that China needs for the future growth of her own indigenous industrial capabilities.

Alternatives to such traditional low-wage labor-fueled growth, however, are quite difficult for a firm from a developing country, such as China, to master by itself without some form of ongoing relationship with a foreign partner. To compete in international trade without relying on low-wage labor as the key factor of comparative advantage requires the development of some form of market niche that insulates the developing country firm from the competitive strengths (e.g., automated manufacturing, state-of-the-art product design and technology, superior advertising and/or distributional advantages, etc.) of their counterparts from developed countries who are, in this case, defending their home markets. Niche strategies, unlike strategies based solely upon mass-production economies of scale, emphasize some form of particular responsiveness to customer needs, usually either through product design or development or else through a willingness to serve the customer promptly with short production runs, quick delivery, or service. In manufacturing strategy terms, this implies operating in some form of job-shop format and likely maintaining some form of close liaison with the customer (either geographical or informational).

Niche strategies are particularly difficult for the developing country (and especially Chinese) enterprise because they typically require an especially sensitive understanding of the foreign market being served so as to be not only responsive to changing customer desires, but also to be able to anticipate them. This is necessary in those cases where the security of the niche is based primarily upon the niche-holder's ability to "lead" among the market leaders. Such market responsiveness also requires high flexibility in the enterprise's manufacturing process, in order to quickly "gear up" for the production of new or altered products, and high levels of support from the firm's vendors, who must also be able to respond quickly. Needless to say, the quality of such products must be high (to justify the premium that is associated with such strategies), and access to and dependability of distribution systems must also be guaranteed. The difficulties inherent in niche strategies usually suggest that developing countries cannot reliably count on them as export-led growth paths in many industries. Such strategies are effective only if these countries enter into some form of alliance or network with foreign partners, who because of advantages of location, birth, resources, or experience, can navigate the difficulties noted above. In other words, the independent (or even relatively independent) pursuit of niche markets is not likely to be particularly rewarding.

---

[6] Watanabe, ibid.

II. Changes in the Export and Offshore Sourcing Environment

In many of its most important export markets, and particularly in textiles and apparel, China has followed traditional growth paths and concentrated on mass-produced goods. Despite some considerable short-term success in establishing strong export performance of such products, there is real reason for concern over the long-range viability and contribution of such trade. While appearing to follow the experiences of other East Asian NICs in the successful export of low-wage products, there are some significant differences that must be recognized.

First, the world has changed substantially since Japan and the East Asian NICs utilized such price competitiveness to build their growth. The markets of the rich countries in North America and Western Europe, which once welcomed imports from the developing world, are nowhere near as hospitable as they were 20 years ago. Today, rather than struggling to satisfy expanding growth, and hence not being bothered by imports serving the demand that could not otherwise be satisfied, many mature industries in these economies are threatened by low-wage imports and see themselves as being involved in a zero-sum game. Their response, frequently, is to petition for some form of trade barriers in order to resist continued market loss. China, in particular, has been a frequent target for such protectionist action.

Second, the simplicity of the products being produced by the low-wage competitors, and the large volumes involved, have also made such products particularly attractive candidates for automation. This has reached the point in the developed world where in many industries labor as a percentage of cost of goods sold has been reduced to around 10 percent. At such levels, *cheap labor ceases to be an effective comparative advantage* for *entering the most cosmopolitan markets*. It no longer makes sense to produce or assemble overseas, particularly at sites where there are difficulties involved with either operations or living; the economics of cheap labor are no longer as compelling as they once were!

Third, political changes in the world economy have led developing countries to be dissatisfied with commercial relationships that are entirely exploitative. The goal of many, if not most, of these nations today is to acquire enough foreign technology and managerial skills to be able to enter into world markets with some degree of self-assurance and independence. Yet such desires have forced these countries to seriously reexamine the nature of what it is they have to offer in exchange for the technology and skills they need. And this, in turn, often means a reconsideration of the nature of the linkages that exist between their domestic economies and the world market. Traditionally the developing country has offered its low-wage labor resources in such instances in the form of basically selling contract labor and manufacturing capacity to foreign firms that wish to cut costs. These relationships are frequently characterized by foot-loose foreign customers who have no interest in anything by contracting for cheap labor resources. Often there is absolutely no opportunity in the relationship or the production process for learning to take place, or for any sort of skill formation to result from the work performed. In other words, such arrangements do not lead to durable relationships, "partnerships," sharing of technology (actually, the foreign firms in such relationships are only in the developing country for those operations that they have deemed not susceptible to automation, or as a way of forestalling their own need to invest in automation) or management skills, or anything that represents commitment. They are clearly not the *engines of growth* that will rescue the developing economy from its plight.

Increasingly, the developing country must have something more to offer the potential foreign supplier of advanced technology or management skills than merely cheap labor, if the country is to hope for a successful transfer of technology. Principally, it needs some guarantee of intimacy and durability in the transfer relationship. Intimacy is needed to maximize the scope of technologies transferred and to ensure the attention and customization needed in order to guarantee the suitability of what is transferred. Durability is required to guarantee timely responses on the part of the technology supplier to changes in the recipient firm's operating environment, as well as to ensure an ongoing relationship over time so that the transferred technology maintains its currentness. Intimacy and durability, as their biological metaphor suggests, require preparation, commitment, trust, sharing, and occasionally sacrifice on the part of *both* partners. In addition, partners have to believe that they will be enriched by the partnership. For this to happen in an economic context, a number of issues have to be resolved. In China's case, many of these issues are quite formidable.

III. China and the Issues Potentially Constraining Continued Export-Led Growth

China appears to have three major areas that need to be addressed in an effort to establish a solid foundation for future export-led growth. These are its comparative advantage, its manufacturing base, and its managerial resources.

A. CHINA'S COMPARATIVE ADVANTAGE

China's primary comparative advantage is her large domestic market. As has been argued earlier, cheap labor no longer has the attractiveness nor the inducements (for intimate and durable relationships) that would make China an unusually attractive location for foreign economic activity. What China has that no one else has, is the world's potentially largest commercial market. There are, however, a number of significant problems associated with her being able to leverage this market to its full advantage.[7]

Despite its size, China's domestic market is not actually one large market. It is not a nationally integrated market. Rather, it is a market fragmented by infrastructure deficiencies, provincial and regional jealousies, and the immaturity of China's domestic commercial media. Each of these serves to truncate the achievement of economies of scale by Chinese enterprises and to frustrate the

---

[7] William A. Fischer, "China and the Opportunities for Economic Development through Technology Transfer," in Mary Ann Von Glinow (ed.), *The Dialectics of Technology Transfer* (New York, Oxford University Press, forthcoming).

plans of potential foreign investors. Chinese industry, as a result, has not been as strong as it might be,[8] nor have foreign firms been willing to make the sorts of contributions that they might have otherwise been able to make. Without a national market, it has not been possible for China to develop the specialized intermediate producers, or subcontractors, that have been so important for efficient, innovative, and high-quality production in modern economies.[9] To achieve maximum attractiveness, and effectiveness, the domestic market in China must be integrated in a fashion that makes it truly a national market.

To ensure durable and intimate relations with foreign suppliers of technology and managerial skills, the Chinese domestic market must not only be encouraged to pursue export-led growth but it must also be opened to foreign commercial presences. Without intimate and durable economic relations with cosmopolitan foreign partners, China will be consigned to lag behind the rest of the world in technology, management, and the production and distribution of successful, high-value-added exports. It will only be through such relationships that China will be able to attract the knowledge and capital that it needs so badly. However, the only attraction that China holds for such firms is the promise of selling in the domestic Chinese market, in a relatively unfettered manner, and repatriating the resulting profits. This, in turn, means that Chinese industry must be prepared for international competition, something that is quite far removed from the present situation, and that issues such as product design, vendor selection, process technology choice and investment, manpower skills and workload planning, and the like, that have traditionally been the province of bureaus within the industrial structure, must be divested to the discretion of enterprise managers and their foreign associates, in order to assure the manufacturing and technical responsiveness and organizational agility that will be needed to participate in the global market place.

B. CHINA'S MANUFACTURING BASE [10]

The very ability to satisfy most of the day-to-day needs of one-quarter of the world's population in a dependable and reasonably cost-efficient manner makes China a great manufacturing power. Nonetheless, China is far from being well prepared to compete in the global market. Specifically, China's manufacturing base is, in general, quite old and lacking in the quality, efficiency, flexibility, and reliability advantages that are embodied in the newer manufacturing technologies that are increasingly being used in both the developed and developing worlds. A portion of China's industrial productivity problems, both in terms of labor output and in terms of energy efficiency, are related to her aged equipment. Chinese product design skills also are inadequately developed to serve a

---

[8] James C. Abegglen and George Stalk, Jr., provide solid support for the benefits of strengthening domestic industry as a prelude for international competition in *Kaisha*, (Tokyo, Charles E. Tuttle Co., 1981).

[9] Jorge M. Katz, "Technology and Economic Development: An Overview of Research Findings," in Moshe Syrquin and Simon Teitel, (eds.), *Trade, Stability, Technology, and Equity in Latin America* (New York, Academic Press, 1982).

[10] William A. Fischer, "China's Manufacturing Capabilities," Working Paper, Summer 1990.

number of sophisticated, cosmopolitan markets. A major reason for this is the years of estrangement from the world economic and design communities that she suffered. However, the imbalance of demand relative to supply and the persistence of protectionism within the domestic economy have kept many Chinese enterprises from recognizing the role that product design plays as a competitive weapon.

Despite some very obvious successes in improving her manufacturing capabilities, serious deficiencies in some of the more traditional manufacturing areas continue to plague Chinese competitive performance. Quality control, for example, remains a problem despite years of attention from government agencies. Here, problems in sourcing, materials availability, worker and managerial motivation, equipment vintage, distribution, and worker preparation all conspire against dependability in quality manufacturing. Shop floor control and manufacturing information systems also remain relatively underdeveloped within the Chinese economy. Although there are many reasons for this, the problem is more than simply the lack of Management Information System (MIS) hardware. Scarcity of useful information, problems with the operational integrity of the information that is available, no tradition of managerial information, and a work force that is under-informed and not empowered to act on the information that is distributed to them, all limit the flexibility of the Chinese industrial enterprise. One of the results of informational deficiencies is the vast quantities of inventory that are present throughout the Chinese economy. This inventory not only ties up enterprise working capital (and, hence, much of their organizational agility), but it also represents a gross misallocation of resources throughout the economy.

C. CHINA'S MANAGERIAL RESOURCES [11]

Central to the problems facing China's prospects for growing interaction with the global business environment and her ability to sustain and develop export-led growth is the capabilities of her managerial resources. There should be no doubt that China has a sizable cadre of excellent managers. Their performance over the 30 years preceding the economic reforms, and their astonishing successes over the past decade under these reforms, has provided ample witness to the capabilities of Chinese managers. The system that they have worked within, however, has proved to be a considerable burden, and much of their success has been made *despite* the system, rather than because of it.

From a micro-economic perspective, the key policies associated with economic reform have been the decentralization of managerial discretion and the increased autonomy for decision-making. In those situations where decentralization and autonomy have been allowed to occur in a relatively unfettered fashion, the Chinese manager has evolved into capable and competent decision-maker. A particularly vivid illustration of this is the impressive growth of managerial awareness, sophistication, and discipline associated

[11] William A. Fischer, "The State of Chinese Industrial Management," in Nigel Campbell and John Henley (eds.), *Advances in Chinese Industrial Studies: Joint Ventures and Industrial Change in China* (Greenwich, CT, JAI Press, forthcoming).

with the decision to acquire foreign technology that appears to be the direct result of growing managerial accountability within the Chinese economy.[12] Such situations have been too few, however. More typical have been situations characterized by hesitation, ambiguity, and inconsistency in prerogatives allowed to managers. There has also been attitudinal resistance among many government and Party officials to continued reform because of the increased risks and uncertainties associated with competitive economic situations. In these instances, the ability of the Chinese manager to run operations in an efficient, productive, and—from a potential joint-venture partner's perspective—attractive fashion have been severely limited. That such limitations could occur, despite the conscious and sincere attempts by many high-level government officials to rationalize the economic system, shows how strong such obstructions can be.[13]

One of the most unfortunate results of the reexamination and retrenchment of the Chinese reform program has been the recentralization of a number of industries and the restriction of managerial autonomy in many enterprises.[14] Under such circumstances, the vitality of Chinese industry is sapped by administrative control; the flexibility, responsiveness, and innovativeness of Chinese enterprises withers; and accountability is diluted. In the aftermath of such moves backward, the difficulties of dealing with Chinese industrial partners remain significant.[15] By its very nature, the act of rescinding policies that provide the Chinese enterprise manager with greater autonomy serve to reduce the attractiveness and utility of such partnerships to those prospective foreign investors who seek to enter China to bring technology and skills and to create viable partnerships to serve the newly emerging global marketplace. This is particularly true at a time when many foreign investors can also consider Central and Eastern Europe as alternative sites for their operations and investment. In their efforts to "protect" the existing political and economic order, the Chinese government has also moved to perpetuate the country's economic backwardness.

IV. Conclusion

The El Dorado promise of China that has attracted so many foreign suitors in the past has dimmed over the past few years. Difficulties with operations, uncertainties with government policies, the relative attractiveness of producing at home or in other developing country sites, have all served to reduce the allure of China for many foreign firms. China itself suffers from a number of infra-

---

[12] Denis F. Simon and William Fischer, *Technology Transfer to China* (Cambridge, MA, Ballinger, forthcoming).

[13] In a study being conducted by the author in another developing country, a particularly successful owner/manager of a local firm stated that the secret of his success was being able "to forget that I am in the developing world. If I even believe that I am in the developing world, I am lost! I must constantly believe that I am operating in the world market." It is doubtful that such a managerial attitude would be possible in many places in China today.

[14] James Stepanek, "Companies Prepare for Post-Deng Reforms in China," *The Wall Street Journal/Europe*, February 20, 1990, p. 9; Louise do Rosario, "Three Years'Hard Labour," *Far Eastern Economic Review*, November 30, 1989, pp. 68–69; and Louise do Rosario, "Eternal Mandarins," *Far Eastern Economic Review*, November 9, 1989, pp. 33–34.

[15] Oded Shenkar, "International Joint Ventures' Problems in China: Risks and Remedies," *Long Range Planning*, vol. 23, no. 3, pp. 82–90.

structure deficiencies that both make it hard to significantly improve the situation in the immediate term as well as constrain its ability to independently move away from the mass production of standardized items as its prevailing export growth path. The conclusion that can be drawn is that now, more than ever, China needs to sustain its commitment to export-led growth, but also to recognize that such growth will be necessarily different from those historical experiences of other East Asian NICs. In particular, China appears to be in a situation where more widespread and more intimate relationships with foreign firms are essential in order for it to overcome the barriers that exist today for her exports, as well as the impediments of her infrastructure deficiencies.

Central to China's dilemma relating to export-led growth is the realization that low-wage labor is no longer a particularly compelling comparative advantage. Furthermore, China is no longer the only attractive location within the developing world from which to export. China's unique asset, however, is nearly a fifth of the world's population in a relatively untouched market. It is this market potential, rather than cheap labor, that is China's real comparative advantage, and her ticket to advanced technology and managerial skills. How she chooses to utilize this comparative advantage will be a major policy decision for her leaders. It must be made, however, in the face of weak competitive strength among her industrial enterprises and continuing frustration for her managers who seek to exercise their operating responsibilities.

CHINA'S RELATIONS WITH MULTILATERAL ECONOMIC INSTITUTIONS

By William R. Feeney *

CONTENTS

SUMMARY

For more than a decade, China's long-term economic develop-ment strategy has been predicated upon the creation of a viable do-mestic economy using a variety of market incentives and the adop-tion of Ricardo's international trade theory of comparative advan-tage. This development approach utilizes the twin engines of do-mestic production incentives and greatly expanded foreign loans, credits, and investments and international trade within the frame-work of the world capitalist economic system to generate the wealth necessary to build a modern economy. China's current sup-port for the contemporary world economic system stands in sharp contrast to Beijing's earlier system-transforming posture adopted soon after the 1949 Communist Revolution, initially in conjunction with the Soviet Union and later as the self-proclaimed radical leader of the Third world, and to its subsequent system-reforming approach of the early 1970s based upon Third World-oriented New International Economic Order (NIEO) principles.[1]

An integral part of China's integration into the global economic system has been membership and active participation in a variety of multilateral economic institutions (MEIs).[2] Beginning in late 1978, China acknowledged the need for external development as-sistance by shifting from the status of an aid-giver to an aid recipi-

---

* Professor, Department of Political Science, Southern Illinois University at Edwardsville.
[1] See Samuel S. Kim, "Post-Mao China's Develoipment Model in Global Perspective," in Nev-ille Maxwell and Bruce McFarlane, eds. *China's Changed Road to Development* (Oxford: Perga-mon Press, 1984), pp. 214–15.
[2] See my chapters, "Chinese Policy in Multilateral Financial Institutions," in Samuel S. Kim, ed. *China and the World; Chinese Foreign Policy in the Post-Mao Era* (Boulder, Col.: Westview Press, 1984), ch. 11; and "Chinese Policy in Multilateral Economic Institutions," in Samuel S. Kim, ed. *China and the World; New Directions in Chinese Foreign Relations,*, 2nd ed. (Boulder, Col: Westview Press, 1989), ch. 10; and especially Harold K. Jacobson and Michel Oksenberg, *China's Participation in the IMF, the World Bank, and GATT; Toward a Global Economic Order* (Ann Arbor, Mich.: University of Michigan Press, 1990).

ent within the framework of the United Nations Development Program (UNDP). Subsequent policy pronouncements reinterpreted China's long-standing policy of self-reliance to permit direct foreign investment and economic aid, loans, and credit from both bilateral and multilateral sources. As an outgrowth of the Open Door policy adopted in February 1980, China sought and was granted admission into the World Bank Group, or WBG (a collective term for the International Monetary Fund, or IMF; the International Bank for Reconstruction and Development, or IBRD, but commonly called the World Bank; and its affiliated agencies, the International Development Association, or IDA, and the International Finance Corporaiton, or IFC). In 1983 China was granted observer status in the world trading organization, the General Agreement on Tariffs and Trade (GATT). In 1986 China made formal applcation for full GATT membership and joined the Asian Development Bank (ADB).

China has been a MEI participant for a decade, and during that period membership in these organizations has represented both a challenge and an opportunity for Beijing. The absorption of 1.1 billion people into the world and regional economy has not been without its difficulties and problems. On balance, both China and the world have reaped great benefits both from the intangible psychic perspective of linkage and belonging and from the more tangible economic rewards of enhanced prosperity and well-being.

Prior to June 1989 the multidimensional MEI connections which had been forged appear to have laid the groundwork for even further integration of China into the global economic and political system. The June 4, 1989 Tiananmen Square massacre and the subsequent wave of political repression against the democracy movement in China came as a shock of the first magnitude both inside and outside the country and raised serious questions about the permanence and viability of China's participatory role in the global economic system. These events prompted a series of moves by the United States, other G–7 countries, and select MEIs to isolate and penalize China's hard-line leaders. Within two weeks of the crackdown and largely at the behest of the United States, both the World Bank and the Asian Development Bank suspended over $1 billion in loans and credits to China. Bilateral aid programs bankrolled mainly by Japan and the European Community were also placed on hold. And somewhat later the U.S. Congress voted to impose sanctions including the restriction of funds for certain MEI lending to China. Though the UNDP country program in China was not adversely affected, further negotiations on China's GATT membership application were temporarily postponed. Finally, hundreds of foreign firms doing business in China were forced to reevaluate the more uncertain commercial climate and their future economic prospects within a potentially more orthodox Marxist-Leninist political environment.

This chapter focuses upon China's participation in a number of key MEIs since 1979, the nature and consequences of China's relationships with those organizations, the impact of the Tiananmen Square incident on those linkages, and the implications for both China and the global community for the 1990s.

I. CHINA AND THE UNITED NATIONS DEVELOPMENT PROGRAM

China's participation in the UNDP has been the longest of any MEI relationship and began as an adjunct to Beijing's NIEO revisionist orientation soon after the PRC delegation was seated in the United Nations in 1971. In November 1972 China began to take part in UNDP pledging conferences and over the next seven years participated in a number of UNDP supported programs in Asia and Africa. In 1974, China made token contributions in non-convertible renminbi to the organization. In January 1975 China agreed to serve on the UNDP Governing Council, but over the next four years steadfastly refused to accept any UNDP assistance despite its technical eligibility.[3] During this time, China argued that the UNDP approach was ill-conceived and overly limited. Rather than concentrating on technical assistance for Third World countries in the form of pre-investment planning and management, advisory services, fellowships, and demonstration and training, the UNDP role should be expanded across the entire development spectrum in line with the NIEO approach. In November 1978 China unexpectedly shifted gears and sought UNDP assistance, which was approved by the UNDP Governing Council despite displeasure on the part of some Third World states and the Soviet Union and its allies. Much of that concern derived not only from added competition for UNDP aid but also from what later appeared to be artificially deflated and self-serving per capita income statistics used to justify higher aid allotments.

China has done well in its relationship with the UNDP. In 1978 China paid the UN US $27.1 million in regular dues and token contributions and received nothing in UNDP aid. Though the application deadline for the UNDP's second Indicative Planning Figure (IPF-2), or the 1977–81 aid disbursement cycle, had passed, China was able to lobby successfully for a US $15 million grant for the last three years of the cycle (1979–81) which was combined with US $12.5 million from other sources to fund 27 specific projects pending the establishment of China's regular allotment of UNDP resources. In September 1979 the UNDP opened an office in Beijing. Thereafter, China made determined efforts to develop and justify a broad range of technical assistance projects. From IPF-3 (1982–1986), China's First Country Program (CP-1) received some US $66 million (an increase of 340 percent), which was combined with US $15 million in funding from the government and other sources to implement more than 150 projects. IPF-4 (1987–1991) has been even more beneficial to China and increased UNDP assistance to China's Second Country Program (CP-2) (1987–1990) by another 106 percent to US $135.9 million, or an overall total of US $163.1 million to finance over 200 projects. Finally, IPF-5 (1992–1996) tentatively has alloted some US $177.3 million or about 4 percent of its total resources of US $4.476 billion to China. Thus, China's Third Country Program (CP-3), which will run from 1991–1995, will receive about US $140 million, up somewhat compared to the earlier CP-2 level. Cumulatively since 1979, China has received nearly US

---

[3] For a survey of this early relationship, see Samuel S. Kim, *China, the United Nations, and World Order* (Princeton, N.J.: Princeton University Press, 1979), pp. 318–28.

$217 million to fund more than 350 projects, making China the largest single recipient of UNDP resources.

Since 1979 the UNDP/China partnership has grown dramatically from a modest initial program to a large-scale commitment (see Table 1).[4] These resources have helped the world's largest developing country to gain access to some of the most advanced technology and technical expertise, which in turn has made an important contribution to China's modernization program. The UNDP program has promoted dialogue and cooperation between a large number of Chinese national, provincial, and municipal officials, UNDP personnel, and representatives of UN specialized agencies. Indeed, the UN system has contributed over 2000 short-term experts and consultants who have provided instruction, insights, and suggestions in a broad number of areas. Through cost sharing, the UNDP has mobilized additional resources from the PRC government, other governments and international agencies, and private sources. The UNDP has funded such programs as TOKEN (Transfer of Knowledge through Expatriate Nationals), which brings back overseas Chinese specialists for two-to eight-week consultancies, and STAR (Senior Technical Advisers' Recruitment Program) for similar visits by non-Chinese experts. Finally, the UNDP has emphasized specialized training, pre-investment surveys, technology transfer, and highly useful small-scale projects in energy development, agriculture, fishing, forestry, industry, environment, information processing, and rural development.

TABLE 1. UNDP Country Programs in China

Country Program (CP)	No. Projects	Funding (US$M)		
		UNDP	PRC/Other	Total
Ad hoc Initial Program (1978–81)	27	15.0	12.5	27.5
UNDP–CP1 (1982–86)	a 150+	66.0	15.0	81.0
UNDP–CP2 (1986–90)	a 200+	135.9	27.2	163.1
Totals (1978–90)	a 350+	216.9	54.7	271.6
UNDP–CP3 (1991–95)	NA	b 135.0	a 30.0	a 165.0

a UNDP projects do not necessarily conform chronologically to the CP cycle.
b Tentative figures.
   Sources: United Nations Development Program, *UNDP in China*, New York: UNDP, September 1989, pp. 5–6; United Nations Development Programme, *UNDP Advisory Note on the Third Country Programme for the People's Republic of China (1991–1995)*. Beijing, China: UNDP, January 1990, pp. 2, 4.

The events of June 1989 had little perceptible impact on the UNDP/China partnership. Prior to that time, the mid-term CP-2 review which took place in March–April 1988 had resulted in a modest expansion of UNDP activities in China. Not only was a sixth program (economic reform and policy research) with 14 new projects worth US $16 million appended to the five already in place (increased food production and agricultural productivity, increased production of consumer goods and services, energy development and conservation, human resources development, and infrastructure development), but six new agricultural projects valued at US

---

[4] For a survey, see United Nations Development Program, *UNDP in China* (New York: UNDP, September 1989).

$8.6 million were added to the existing agriculture program.[5] The immediate impact of the June upheaval was the evacuation of two-thirds of the 12 UNDP officers and most of the office staff from Beijing and a formal diplomatic note to the PRC government concerning the safety of UNDP personnel. The UNDP office remained open and continued to function, and within two weeks when order was restored the full staff returned. There was also a subsequent review of all UNDP projects in the pipeline. The major rationale was to determine their desirability and feasibility in the light of possible changes in the host government's priorities and altered practical circumstances. As a result one small US$3–400,000 project jointly funded by the UNDP and the Ford Foundation and administered by the World Bank was suspended due to the restructuring of the host institution, but no projects were cancelled.

The major thrust of UNDP activities in China is continuing support for the economic program of the government, which in September 1988 was forced to adopt a far-reaching economic austerity program including greater emphasis on state ownership and control, central planning, and self-reliance. The events of June 1989 forced an even greater reliance on such measures in order to regain control of a volatile political and economic situation. Despite these developments UNDP officials generally believed that the Chinese leadership would continue to adhere to economic reform and the Open Door policy and that the UNDP program would support that commitment. For a time several factors seemed to support this conclusion. First, the core team within the China International Center for Economic and Technical Exchanges (CICETE), which is part of China's Ministry for Foreign Economic Relations and Trade (MOFERT) and responsible for the selection, formulation, and execution of UNDP projects, had not shown any inclination to depart from the existing reform program in preparing China's CP-3. Second, there had been a formal endorsement of China's reform commitment in the UNDP Advisory Note published in January 1990.[6] Finally, all sectors continued to assume as in the past that the UNDP's CP-3 would be closely linked to China's Eighth Five Year Plan which is pledged to reform. However, recent indications seem to suggest that China's future economic reform efforts may be scaled back.[7] Thus, it is possible that those portions of China's UNDP CP-3 which are directly related to or supportive of China's earlier economic reform commitments could be reformulated or downgraded in the future.

II. CHINA AND THE WORLD BANK GROUP

China's relationship with the World Bank Group has also experienced profound changes over time. After the 1949 Communist Revolution and up until its 1971 seating in the UN, China continually disparaged the WBG as "citadels of international capitalism." Beginning in 1979 as part of its new modernization strategy, China

---

[5] United Nations Development Programme, *UNDP Advisory Note on the Third Country Programme for the People's Republic of China (1991–1995).* (Beijing: UNDP, January 1990), p. 4.

[6] See *ibid*, pp. 11, 24.

[7] See Robert Delfs, "Reverse Engines," *Far Eastern Economic Review* (hereafter cited as *FEER*) 149 (September 27, 1990): 12–13.

suspended the usual WBG criticism and called for a restoration of its participation in the WBG. Strenuous efforts were made during 1979–80 which ultimately led to China's formal entry into the International Monetary Fund on April 17, 1980 and the World Bank and its affiliated agencies (IDA and IFC) on May 15, 1980.[8]

An important prerequisite for effective WBG assistance to China was a comprehensive study and analysis of the Chinese economy. In an intensive year-long effort, a 30-member World Bank team launched the most exhaustive study ever undertaken of the Chinese economy and by June 1981 produced a lengthy 3-volume report which examined five priority sectors: human resources (education, health, and population), agriculture, transportation, energy, and industry.[9] A major conclusion was that future Chinese growth would depend mainly upon improved efficiency and resource use and more specifically on medium-and long-term planning; gradual price deregulation of producer but not consumer goods; optimizing and decentralizing investment decisions; skilled labor reallocation; an increase in foreign trade and trade reforms based upon greater freedom for importers, exporters, producers, and consumers, and on cost-benefit analysis of trade options. Special attention was devoted to a number of economic sectors: agriculture, energy (petroleum, coal, electricity/hydropower) and its conservation; transportation; trade expansion; and the export role of raw materials (especially oil and coal), textiles, and other light manufactures. Advanced technology imports and education were deemed critical to China's manufactured exports in the world market. Because projected export earnings, direct investment, and net transfers were considered insufficient to cover import-financing requirements, the report concluded that China would need to borrow foreign funds at a rate commensurate with the desired rate of growth.

This report was soon followed by an extensive analysis of development issues and options and thereafter by a series of focused sector studies which pinpointed specific problem areas, resources, and needs. Accordingly, the World Bank in close collaboration with Chinese officials has been able to develop a thorough array of well-researched studies on the various impediments to China's economic modernization and a lengthy list of recommendations and specific projects designed to surmount these barriers.[10]

China's relationship with the IMF was highly advantageous and useful during the decade of the 1980s. The major functions of the IMF for member states are to facilitate the balanced growth of international trade, promote foreign exchange stability and eliminate exchange restriction, overcome temporary balance of payments problems through the use of general Fund resources, and promote overall international monetary cooperation. On a number of occasions since 1980, China has turned to the IMF for assistance

---

[8] For a survey of this process, see Jacobson and Oksenberg, *China's Participation in the IMF, the World Bank, and GATT*, ch. 3.

[9] See World Bank, *China: Socialist Economic Development*, 3 vols. (Washington, D.C.: IBRD, 1983).

[10] See World Bank, *China: Long-Term Development Issues and Options* (Baltimore and London: The Johns Hopkins University Press, 1985). For a complete listing of World Bank publications on China, see Jacobson and Oksenberg, *China's Participation in the IMF, the World Bank, and GATT*, pp. 176–79.

in dealing with assorted economic problems. In response to domestic economic difficulties and a sharp foreign trade deficit, China made its first IMF drawings from the reserve tranche in December 1980 and January 1981 in the combined amount of SDR 368.1 million (US $478 million) (see Table 2). The following March China received another loan of SDR 309.5 million (US $365 million) from the IMF Trust Fund and utilized its first credit tranche in the amount of SDR 450 million (US $550 million). In return, China pledged to readjust its modernization strategy, eliminate its budget deficit, control the growth of its money supply, lower inflation, and reduce its foreign trade deficit. During its first year of membership China borrowed nearly US $1.4 billion and successfully implemented an economic stabilization program. In May 1983 China announced that it would repay its first credit tranche drawing early, and did so by the end of 1984.

In mid-1984 China's balance of payments position again began to deteriorate, a situation aggravated a year later by a 60 percent surge in imports and lower oil export earnings. In response, China tightened its financial policies and economic management, raised interest rates, and between January 1985 and July 1986 discouraged imports and increased exports by means of a 32 percent decline in the value of the renminbi (including a 15.8 percent devaluation). In November 1986, the IMF approved a 12-month stand-by first credit tranche arrangement for up to SDR 597.7 million (US $717 million) to support these efforts, but a rapid economic turnaround precluded its use.[11] More recently in 1988–89, excessive money supply expansion confronted China with an overheated 11 percent growth rate and escalating double-digit inflation. In September 1988 China responded with an extended 3-year austerity program which ultimately included a further 21.2 percent currency devaluation in December 1989. While Beijing recently has experienced a deteriorating international trade balance, falling foreign exchange reserves (US $19.1 billion as of April 1990), and an escalation of its foreign debt to a projected US $50 billion, thus far China has not needed additional IMF assistance.[12]

The Tiananmen Square incident undoubtedly has aggravated China's earlier economic troubles. While the current Persian Gulf crisis should lead to higher near-term oil export revenues for China, the attendant rise in world interest rates, potentially lower non-petroleum export earnings from a world economic slowdown, increased borrowing costs due to China's recently down-graded credit rating, and the threat of a continued Chinese international trade imbalance and foreign exchange reserves decline could make it increasingly difficult for Beijing to service its foreign debt, which will peak in 1992 at some US $4.2 billion annually.[13] Thus, China could be forced to seek additional IMF assistance in the near term.

China has also enjoyed a highly beneficial relationship with the World Bank and its IDA and IFC affiliates. The primary purpose of the 152-member World Bank (IBRD), the 138-member IDA, and the

---

[11] See Feeney, "Chinese Policy in Multilateral Economic Institutions," pp. 242–44; and Jacobson and Oksenberg, *China's Participation in the IMF, the World Bank, and GATT*, pp. 121–26.
[12] Louise do Rosario, "Foreign Accounting," *FEER*, 145 (July 27, 1990): 56–7; and "A Dictator's Way," *The Economist* (London) 314 (March 24, 1990): 35.
[13] Rosario, "Foreign Accounting," pp. 56–7.

TABLE 2. China's IMF Drawings, 1980–1990

(in millions of SDRS; U.S. Dollar Equivalents in Parentheses)

Date of Inception/Expiration	Source/Amount	Terms
December 1980	Reserve Tranche SDR 218.1 (US $278) ª ..	Interest-free; no service fee; indefinite repayment schedule (repaid)
January 1981	Reserve Tranche SDR 150 (U.S. $200)......	Same as above (repaid)
March 2, 1981/December 31, 1981	First Credit Tranche SDR 450 (U.S. $550).	6.4% interest; 0.5% service fee; 3–5 year repayment (repaid 1984)
March 31, 1981/March 30, 1991..............	IMF Trust Fund SDR 309.5 (U.S. $365)	0.5% interest, 10-year repayment
November 12, 1986/November 11, 1987 ...	First Credit Tranche (standby) SDR 597.7 (*.S. $717).	5.97% interest ᵇ; 0.25% service fee, 3–5 year repayment
Total IMF Drawings 1980–1990: U.S. $2,110..		

ª The SDR (Special Drawing Right) is the composite value of a weighted basket of selected national currencies, the value of which varies over time against individual national currencies. The SDR is an artificial international reserve unit and can be used to settle accounts among central banks. The advantage over individual national currencies is its greater relative stability.
ᵇ Since August 1983, the SDR interest rate has been determined weekly by reference to a combined market interest rate, which is the weighted average of interest rates on specified short-term domestic obligations in the money markets of the same five countries whose currencies are included in the SDR valuation basket.
Sources: Friedrich W. Wu, "External Borrowing and Foreign Aid in Post-Mao China's International Economic Policy: Data and Observations," *Columbia Journal of World Business* 19 (Fall 1984): 57; International Monetary Fund, *Annual Report 1981* (Washington, D.C.: IMF, 1981), pp. 83, 103–104, 120; International Monetary Fund, *Annual Report 1987* (Washington, D.C.: IMF, 1987), pp, 79, 152, 162.

135-member IFC has been to direct large-scale financial resources from the developed to the less developed countries (LDCs) in order to improve LDC living standards. IBRD loans and IDA credits support a wide variety of projects in agriculture and rural development, development finance, education, energy (electric power, oil, gas, coal), industry, population, health, and nutrition, technical assistance, telecommunications, transportation, urban development, and water supply and sewerage.[14] World Bank loan capital is subscribed by its member countries, borrowed on world capital markets, and is also generated by retained earnings and loan repayments. IDA credits are derived mostly from member subscriptions, periodic replenishments by the developed members, and net IBRD earnings transfers. IDA resources have been replenished eight times with the most recent tentative agreement for IDA-9 (1991–1993) in the amount of US $15.5 billion (a 12 percent increase over IDA-8).[15] Finally, the IFC provides equity capital and loans on a smaller scale to aid private and mixed enterprise, especially in Third World members, technical assistance, and investment and management advisory services.

China has been singularly successful in securing World Bank financial assistance in implementing its Open Door modernization policy. Between 1981 and 1990 China has received over US $9.2 billion in loans and credits for some 83 projects, with IBRD loans accounting for US $5.28 billion, or 57.3 percent of the total commitment, and IDA credits contributing nearly US $3.93 billion, or 42.6 percent (see Table 3).

Since 1983 World Bank assistance to China rose each year and peaked in 1988 at nearly US $1.7 billion. In 1989 the US $1.35 billion in lending represents only the first six months of the year and would have been substantially higher in the absence of the suspen-

---

[14] IBRD loans are for 15–20 years and charge current market interest rates; IDA credits are for 50 years (40 years for the poorest LDCs and 35 years under certain conditions) with no interest but a small commitment fee.
[15] The World Bank, *Annual Report 1990* (Washington, D.C.: IBRD, 1990), p. 39.

TABLE 3. World Bank Annual and Cumulative Lending to China, 1981–1990

(US $M)

	IBRD		IDA		Annual Totals		Totals		Cumulative Comparative Numerical Ranking [1]
	No.	Amount	No.	Amount	No.	Amount	No.	Amount	
1981	1	$100.0	0	$100.0	1	$200.0	1	$200.0	70/125
1982	0	—	1	60.0	1	60.0	2	260.0	63/125
1983	5	463.1	1	150.4	6	613.5	8	873.5	28/128
1984	5	616.0	5	423.5	10	1,039.5	18	1,913.0	18/132
1985	7	659.6	5	442.3	12	1,101.9	30	3,014.9	14/136
1986	7	687.0	4	450.0	11	1,137.0	41	4,151.9	11/136
1987	8	867.4	3	556.2	11	1,423.6	52	5,575.5	8/137
1988	10	1,053.7	4	639.9	15	1,693.6	68	7,269.1	6/137
1989	7	833.4	5	515.0	12	1,348.4	78	8,617.5	6/137
1990	0	—	5	590.0	5	590.0	83	9,207.5	6/139
Totals	50	$5,280.0 (57.3%)	33	$3,927.3 (42.6%)	83	$9,207.5 (100.0%)			

[1] China's ranking as a cumulative borrower compared to total WB membership.
Sources: The World Bank, *Annual Report 1981*, pp. 120, 188; *Annual Report 1982*, pp. 118, 184; *Annual Report 1983*, pp. 126, 218; *Annual Report 1984*, pp. 139, 210; *Annual Report 1985*, pp. 145, 166; *Annual Report 1986*, pp. 137, 158; *Annual Report 1987*, pp. 139, 160; *Annual Report 1988*, pp. 131, 152; *Annual Report 1989*, pp. 158, 178; *Annual Report 1990*, pp. 156, 178.

sion of project approvals prompted by the Tianamen Square incident. Though Bank lending was selectively resumed in 1990, the totals were less than one-half of the previous year. As it was, China still retains the ranking of sixth largest combined IBRD/IDA borrower (eleventh largest in the IBRD and third largest in the IDA) (see Table 4). The most important project funding categories have been agriculture and rural development (US $2.38 billion or 25.8 percent), transportation (US $2.154 billion or 23.4 percent), energy (US $1.58 billion or 17.1 percent), and development finance (US $1.1 billion or 11.9 percent) (see Table 5).

TABLE 4. Summary of Cumulative IBRD Loans/IDA Credits to Eleven Largest Borrowers

(As of June 30, 1990) (US $ M)

Country	IBRD Loans			Country	IDA Credits			Country	Combined Lending		
	No.	Amount	% Total		No.	Amount	% Total		No.	Amount	% Total
1. India	134	$18,319.2	10.19	1. India	178	$16,955.7	29.12	1. India	312	$35,274.9	14.40
2. Brazil	185	17,981.6	9.63	2. Bangladesh	126	5,248.6	9.02	2. Brazil	185	17,981.6	7.34
3. Mexico	123	17,363.6	9.30	3. China	33	3,927.3	6.75	3. Mexico	123	17,363.6	7.09
4. Indonesia	147	14,829.4	7.94	4. Pakistan	82	3,237.0	5.56	4. Indonesia	193	15,761.2	6.44
5. Turkey	100	10,165.2	5.45	5. Tanzania	69	1,769.2	3.04	5. Turkey	110	10,343.7	4.22
6. Rep. of Korea	92	7,154.0	3.83	6. Ghana	51	1,448.7	2.49	6. China	83	9,207.5	3.76
7. Philippines	114	6,751.1	3.62	7. Kenya	49	1,397.4	2.40	7. Pakistan	153	7,412.1	3.03
8. Colombia	125	6,533.6	3.50	8. Sudan	47	1,336.9	2.30	8. Rep. of Korea	98	7,264.8	2.97
9. Yugoslavia	89	5,814.7	3.12	9. Sri Lanka	50	1,323.8	2.27	9. Philippines	117	6,873.3	2.81
10. Nigeria	79	5,594.2	3.00	10. Ethiopia	47	1,264.8	2.17	10. Colombia	125	6,553.1	2.68
11. China	50	5,280.2	2.83	11. Uganda	37	1,090.6	1.87	11. Nigeria	83	5,850.6	2.39
Totals [1]	3,176	$186,661.7	100.0		2,005	$58,220.0	100.00		5,181	$244,883.7	100.00

[1] These figures are cumulative totals for all member countries.
Source: The World Bank, *Annual Report 1990* (Washington, D.C.: IBRD, 1990), pp. 178–81.

The immediate effect of the Tiananmen Square incident was the evacuation of much of the staff of the World Bank resident mission in Beijing for about ten days to ensure their personal safety. During that time, World Bank officials, under intense pressure from the international community, deferred discussions on a number of pending loan approvals. On June 26, 1989 a decision was made largely at the urging of the Bush administration to postpone approval for US $780 million in new loans and credits to China.[16] The ramifications of this action were far-reaching and very costly to China. Though on-going projects continued to be implemented and preliminary planning continued for some 44 projects, the approval hiatus ultimately has delayed more than US $7.1 billion in new funding (see Table 6). This action also had a tripwire effect on the third round of Japan's bilateral assistance program for China worth some US $5.8 billion as well as future lending by the Asian Development Bank (see *infra*) and the international banking community.

TABLE 5. World Bank Lending to China by Category, 1980–90

Project Category	No./Percent projects	Loand/Credits (US$M) IBRD	Loand/Credits (US$M) IDA	WB AID Total/Percent
1. Agriculture and Rural Development	23 (27.7%)	$312.3	$2,067.7	$2,380.0 (25.8%)
2. Development Finance Companies	6 (7.2%)	924.6	175.0	1,099.6 (11.9%)
3. Education	9 (10.8%)	145.3	705.9	851.2 (9.2%)
4. Energy	13 (15.7%)	1,578.9	—	1,578.9 (17.1%)
5. Industry	6 (7.2%)	621.1	—	621.1 (6.7%)
6. Population, Health, Nutrition	3 (3.6%)	15.0	202.0	217.0 (2.4%)
7. Technical Assistance	3 (3.6%)	—	50.7	50.7 (0.6%)
8. Transportation	17 (20.5%)	1,638.0	516.0	2,154.0 (23.4%)
9. Urban Development	2 (2.4%)	45.0	130.0	175.0 (1.9%)
10. Water Supply and Sewerage	1 (1.2%)	—	80.0	80.0 (0.9%)
Totals	83 (100.0%)	$5,280.2	$3,927.3	$9,207.5 (100.0%)

Source: The World Bank, *Annual Report 1981*, pp. 122–26; *Annual Report 1982*, pp. 120–24; *Annual Report 1983*, pp. 128–33; *Annual Report 1984*, pp. 142–46; *Annual Report 1985*, pp. 147–52; *Annual Report 1986*, pp. 140–44; *Annual Report 1987*, pp. 141–46; *Annual Report 1988*, pp. 133–38; *Annual Report 1989*, pp. 160–65; *Annual Report 1990*, 158–63.

Following the December 1989 Scowcroft China mission, and the lifting of martial law in Beijing the following month, the Bush administration authorized a partial relaxation of the World Bank lending freeze for so-called basic human needs (BHN) projects. From that time until the Summer of 1990, six IDA projects worth US $654 million have been approved: (1) a US $30 million IDA credit for earthquake relief in Shanxi and Hebei provinces on February 8, 1990; (2) a US $60 million IDA credit for agricultural development in Jiangxi province on February 27, 1990; (3) a US $50 million IDA credit for vocational and technical education on March 27, 1990; (4) a US $300 million IDA credit for a national afforestation project on May 29, 1990; (5) a US $150 million IDA credit for an agricultural development project in Hubei province on June 16, 1990; and (6) a US $64 million IDA credit for the Mid-Yangtze Development project on August 9, 1990.[17]

---

[16] "World Bank on China Aid," *New York Times* (hereafter cited as *NYT*), June 27, 1989, p. 43.

[17] World Bank documents.

World Bank officials led by President Barber Conable have pressed for a full-scale resumption of Bank lending to China on the grounds that under the Bank's Charter, loan decisions should be made on the basis of economic rather than political criteria. While the Bush administration has responded to calls by the U.S. business community for economic normalization by lifting the ban on lending to China by the Export-Import Bank in December 1989 and by extending China's most-favored-nation (MFN) trade status for another year against determined congressional opposition the following May, the White House has been reluctant to support full World Bank normalization for several reasons. First, there is a belief that the prospects for normalization can be used as effective leverage to bolster moderate elements within the Chinese leadership, improve China's human rights performance, and encourage economic liberalization policies. Second, a strong "sustain indignation" school persists in the U.S. Congress which cuts across party and ideological lines and includes substantial numbers of conservative Republicans and three key Democratic congressmen (Rep. Henry B. Gonzalez, Chairman of the House Banking Committee; Rep. David R. Obey, Chairman of the Foreign Operations Appropriation subcommittee, and D.C. delegate Walter E. Fauntroy, Chairman of the banking committee's International Development and Finance Subcommittee).[18] Finally, and most important, the administration was wary of further antagonizing American public opinion so soon after the MFN retention decision. It is likely that the Bush administration will continue its policy of selective BHN-type project approvals, the definition of which can be broadened or narrowed as circumstances warrant until China makes the appropriate human rights and economic liberalization concessions. Such flexibility was apparent in the joint statement issued by the Group of Seven (G-7) industrial countries at the Houston summit in July 1990 which expanded the BHN criterion to include World Bank loans to address environmental concerns.[19] It may also be that a number of conciliatory gestures made by China during the Spring and Summer of 1990 together with Chinese support in the United Nations Security Council for the U.S. position in the Persian Gulf crisis could provide the necessary catalysts to defuse congressional and public opposition and permit normalized World Bank lending by the first half of 1991.

China's relationship with the International Finance Corporation has been far less extensive than with the other WBG agencies.[20] For the first few years of its World Bank participation, China, though technically eligible even as a socialist country, chose not to seek IFC funds for private and mixed enterprises. However, in 1985 China obtained a US $15 million IFC loan to finance the Guangzhou Peugeot Automobile Company, Ltd., a joint French-Chinese motor vehicle production venture. In 1987 the IFC approved two additional China-related investments. The first was a US $5 million loan to the China Bicycles Company, Ltd. to expand production to 1

---

[18] Clyde H. Farnesworth, "China Gets One Loan, but Another Is Put Off," *NYT*, May 30, 1990, pp. Cl, C2. See also Susuma Awanohara, "No More Favours," *FEER*, 148 (June 7, 1990): 56-7.
[19] "The Houston two-step," *FEER* 149 (July 19, 1990): 57.
[20] For a brief survey, see Feeney, "Chinese Policy in Multilateral Economic Institutions," p. 247.

TABLE 6. Proposed World Bank Projects in China

(as of May 15, 1990)

Project Sectors/Title Designations (Project Status) [1]	Project Loan Amount (US $M)		
	IBRD	IDA	Joint
I. Agricultural Projects (5)	$333.0	$260.0	$510.0
II. Education/Training Projects (3)	0.0	345.0	0.0
III. Environment/Pollution Control Projects (3)	270.0	100.0	0.0
IV. Finance Projects (3)	600.0	275.0	0.0
V. Health Projects (1)	0.0	100.0	0.0
VI. Industrial Projects (9)	950.0	0.0	110.0
VII. Power Projects (5)	1,060.0	0.0	87.0
VIII. Ports/Shipping Projects (1)	100.0	0.0	0.0
IX. Railway Projects (1)	350.0	0.0	0.0
X. Technical Assistance Projects (1)	0.0	20.0	0.0
XI. Transportation Projects (5)	350.0	0.0	600.0
XII. Urban Development Projects (5)	0.0	270.0	310.0
XIII. Water Supply Projects (2)	0.0	165.0	0.0
Total Projects (44): US$7,145 million	$4,013.0	$1,535.0	$1,597.0

[1] There are four preliminary stages in the World Bank project cycle prior to formal approval by the Executive Directors of the Bank. These include: I: *Identification* in which the Bank and the prospective government borrower identify specific projects that advance the development process; II: *Preparation* in which the borrower justifies the project and develops feasibility studies; III: *Appraisal* in which the Bank critically reviews all aspects of the project including implementation and evaluation; and IV: *Negotiation* between the Bank and the borrower on the measures needed.
Source: The World Bank, *International Business Opportunities Service; Monthly Operational Summary*, 13 (May 15, 1990), pp. 37–42.

million bicycles annually, 85 percent for export. The second was a US $3 million mixed equity commitment to J.F. China Investment Company Ltd. (CIC) Hong Kong, a project sponsored by the investment company of Jardine Fleming of Hong Kong to finance small- and medium-sized joint ventures in China. In 1988 a fourth IFC loan in the amount of US $15 million went to Shenzhen Crown (China) Electronics Company, Ltd. a joint Sino-Japanese venture to manufacture audio and visual consumer electronic products for export. And in 1989 the IFC made a US $2 million loan to Shenzhen-Chronar Energy Company, Ltd. to establish a plant in Shenzhen, China to manufacture solar energy amorphous silicon photovoltaic panels principally for export.

TABLE 7. IFC Commitments to China (1986–1989)

Enterprise	FY of Commitment	IFC Commitment (US $000)		
		Loans	Equity	Total
1. Guangzhou Peugeot Automobile Co., Ltd.	FY 1986	$15,000	$3,225	$18,225
2. China Bicycles Co., Ltd.	FY 1986	5,000	0	5,000
3. J.F. China Investment Co., Ltd.	FY 1988	3,000	36	3,036
4. Shenzhen Crown (China) Electronics Co., Ltd.	FY 1989	15,000	0	15,000
5. Shenzhen-Chronar Solar Energy Co., Ltd.	FY 1989	2,000	1,000	3,000
Totals		40,000	$4,261	$44,261

Source: International Finance Corporation, *Annual Report 1989* (Washington, D.C.: IFC, 1989), p. 78.

Compared to the magnitude of IBRD/IDA commitments, the US $40 million in IFC loans to China is a relatively minor amount (see Table 7), and formal approval for the small number of projects in the pipeline has also been blocked. The future expansion of the China-IFC partnership once the lending freeze is lifted will depend not only upon a recognition by the former of the utility of the role

of private venture capital in China's economic development and
the linkage between such capital and overall investor confidence,
but especially on China's policy commitment to joint equity ventures and economic liberalization and reform. That linkage could
be strengthened in the short term if China follows up on its April
1990 adherence to the convention which established the Multilateral Investment Guarantee Agency (MIGA), organized in April 1988
as the fourth agency of the World Bank Group. MIGA was designed to encourage and guarantee private investment against various non-commercial risks in the Third World, advise developing
member governments on the design and implementation of policies,
programs and procedures related to foreign investment, and to
sponsor a dialogue between host governments and the international business community on investment issues. Though China has not
yet contracted for any MIGA projects, the staff of the Foreign Investment Advisory Services (FIAS), a joint MIGA-IFC component,
has completed work on a study recommending new approaches to
the problem of foreign-exchange allocation to joint ventures in
China.[21] It is noteworthy from a future economic policy perspective
that China has chosen to join the 58-member body.

Since 1980, China has derived a broad range of benefits from
membership in the World Bank group. These have included: (1) the
preparation and dissemination of a large number of detailed studies of virtually every aspect of the Chinese economy by highly
skilled World Bank and IMF analysts; (2) periodic balance of payments and budgetary deficit assistance through the IMF; (3) the
availability of a large pool of lending capital principally in the
form of IBRD and IFC loans and IDA credits to expand domestic
production and productivity in a broad range of primary and finished products for domestic consumption and foreign trade and to
finance a large number of costly infrastructure projects necessary
for rapid modernization; and (4) an extensive array of IMF and
IBRD-sponsored technical training and educational opportunities in
the form of courses, seminars, colloquia, and symposia in virtually
every aspect of international economic activity for mid-and top-
level career functionaries at staff headquarters in Washington and
the staff missions in Beijing and through the IMF Institute and the
World Bank's Economic Development Institute (EDI). Not only is
China the only country to have its own EDI program, but approximately one-quarter of the EDI budget is devoted to training Chinese officials.[22]

The overall importance of China's relationship with the WBG
cannot be underestimated. Not only have World Bank analyses had
a profound impact upon the economic decisions of the Chinese political leadership, but Bank interaction has prompted the creation
of an extensive government bureaucratic structure to deal specifically with the MEIs. In addition, it has been noted that World
Bank reports have played an important role in the formulation of
China's five year plans, and IBRD and IDA funded projects have
become an integral part of that planning cycle. In the long–run,

---

[21] The World Bank, *Annual Report 1989* (Washington, D.C.: IBRD, 1989), p. 103.
[22] See Jacobson and Oksenberg, *China's Participation in the IMF, the World Bank, and GATT*, pp. 109, 122, 124, 140–43, 146–49, 151-52.

however, it is probably the socialization function of WBG training which will have the most pronounced and enduring impact on the thinking, understanding, and actual future decisions of a large cadre of China's present and future economic and financial bureaucratic elite. One inescapable conclusion is that any significant rupture in that symbiotic relationship would have profoundly negative consequences for China's future economic prospects.

In terms of its relations with other states, China's participation in the WBG has had a variety of consequences. First, though China has long identified with the Third World and has consistently supported the reformist positions of the so-called Group of 24, the LDC lobby in the WBG, Beijing is not a formal member of the group and has not assumed a leading Third World advocacy role within the organization.[23] Second, China's entry into the WBG has had a negative impact on other Third World members who have been faced with much greater competition for limited resources. Though this problem has not developed within the IMF, in a serious economic downturn available resources could become substantially more constrained despite a 50 percent quota increase in June 1990. Far greater competitive resource pressure has occurred in the case of IBRD loans and IDA credits. Not only has China absorbed large amounts of IBRD market interest capital, but China's increasing level of concessionary IDA borrowing has occurred in large part at the expense of such Third World countries as India, Bangladesh, and Pakistan. While there was a tentative decision in early 1989 to allocate fully 60 percent of all IDA credits to China and India in equal amounts, that prospect has been temporarily deferred by the lending freeze, much to the benefit of other Third World recipients.[24] China's future role in the WBG and its claims on Bank resources ultimately will depend upon political decisions made in Beijing and Washington.

III. CHINA AND THE ASIAN DEVELOPMENT BANK

On March 20, 1986 China became the 47th member of the Asian Development Bank (ADB), a relationship that has proved very beneficial for Beijing. To do so, China made a major political concession by agreeing not to press for the expulsion of Taiwan, which had been a founding member of the organization in 1966, and by acceding to separate Taiwan ADB membership under the designation China, Taipei. In departing from its long-standing refusal to accept anything remotely suggestive of a two-China formula in any international organization, China bowed to compelling political reality on two counts.[25] First, the ADB Charter stipulates that a member could be expelled only for loan default. Second, most members including the United States and Japan, which together held just over 27 percent of the votes, opposed Taipei's ouster (new members under the ADB charter had to have a 75 percent majority). Though Taiwan raised strong objections to the arrangement, after a limited boycott of Bank meetings Taiwan's representatives

[23] Feeney, "Chinese Policy in Multilateral Economic Institutions," p. 250.
[24] The World Bank, *Annual Report 1990*, p. 41.
[25] The ADB thus far is the only intergovernmental organization of which both China and Taiwan are members.

did attend the ADB Board of Governors meetings in Manila in April 1988 but registered an objection by covering their country's nameplate with an "Under Protest" sign. In subsequent meetings in Beijing in 1989 and New Delhi in 1990, a more pragmatic business-like approach was apparent.[26]

From 1986 until the Tiananmen Square incident, the ADB provided China with seven loans valued at US $416 million, 22 technical assistance projects in the amount of US $8.42 million; and a US $3 million line of private sector investment equity to the Shanghai SITCO Enterprise Co., Ltd. (see Table 8). Significantly, ADB lending to China had increased each year up to 1989, when China was scheduled to receive some US $500 million in new ADB loans. However, some US $422.5 million in fully negotiated loans for five projects was put on hold as a result of the June 1989 upheavals.[27] As has been true of the World Bank, ADB officials have pressed for a resumption of lending, but unlike the former case the United States thus far has not made exceptions based on BHN criteria. Thus, China's share of 1989 ADB program loans was allocated to other countries, increasing the average loan size by 50 percent. As of mid-1990, there was nearly US $1.3 billion in ADB financing for thirteen China projects in the preapproval or pre-disbursement stage. (see Table 9)

TABLE 8. Asian Development Bank Annual and Cumulative Lending to China, 1986–1989

(US $M)

Year	No. Loans	Amount	No. Technical Assistance Projects	Amount	No. Private Sector Operations	Amount	Total Lending Amount
1986	0	$ 0.0	1	$0.075	0	$0.0	$ 0.075
1987	2	133.3	[a]5	1.402	0	0.0	134.702
1988	4	282.9	[b]5 10	3.359	1	3.0	289.259
1989	1	39.7	[c]5 6	3.585	0	0.0	43.285
Totals	7	455.9	22	8.421	1	3.0	467.321

[a] Two of these projects were financed exclusively by the UNDP in the amount of $750,000.
[b] Five of these projects were funded exlusively by the Japan Special Fund administered through the Bank in the amount of $1.419 million; a sixth project was jointly financed by the Japan Special Fund ($0.412 million) and the UNDP ($0.418 million).
[c] Three of these projects were funded exclusively by the Japan Special Fund in the amount of $3.3 million.
Source: Asian Development Bank, *Loan, Technical Assistance and Private Sector Operations Approvals*, No. 90/105 (May 1990),pp. 1, 20, 52.

The ADB loan shutoff came at a particularly inconvenient time for China. During 1990 negotiations will begin on the sixth cash replenishment for the Asian Development Fund (ADF VI) as well as new funding for the Bank itself in the form of ordinary capital resources, or OCR. To date, neither China nor India has been eligible to draw upon concessionary rate ADF credits. But over the next four years some of the anticipated US $6.5 billion in ADF credits will be made available to both countries.[28] Finally, in August 1989 the ADB set up the Asian Finance and Investment Corporation (AFIC) comparable to the IFC which will co-finance private sector projects with the ADB. China will also lose out on this opportunity should the loan freeze continue for any protracted period of time.

---

[26] See Jonathan Moore, "Pragmatic Diplomacy," *FEER* 144 (April 20, 1989): 26, and Philip Bowring, "Market Developer," *FEER* 148 (May 17, 1990): 71.
[27] Bowring, "Market Developer," p. 71.
[28] *Ibid.*

Again, not until the Bush administration and especially the U.S. Congress give the go-ahead will normal lending be resumed. Regardless of current ADB loan policies, however, the Bank does provide a useful organizational bridge between China and Taiwan to complement the dramatic growth in direct and indirect trade and to facilitate any future reconciliation process.

TABLE 9. Proposed Asian Development Bank Projects in China

Project Sectors	Project Loan Amount (US$M)
I. Agricultural Projects (2) (1–$50m)	$250.0
II. Energy Projects (1)	65.0
III. Industry and Non-Fuel Minerals Projects (4) (3–$305m) *	361.4
IV. Transport and Communications Projects (6) (1–$67.5m)	620.5
Total Projects (13) ª	$1,296.9

* By the end of 1989 loan negotiations had been completed on five projects totaling $422.5 million, but formal approvals were suspended.
ª In addition to new projects, the ADB has proposed spending $9,023,000 for technical assistance related to these and other projects.
Sources: Asian Development Bank, *ADB Business Opportunities, Proposed Projects, Procurement Notices and Contract Awards* 12 (June 1990), pp. 5–7, 28, 46–49; and Asian Development Bank, *Annual Report 1989* (Manila: ADB, 1989), p. 64.

IV. CHINA AND THE GATT

On July 14, 1986 China formally applied to rejoin the General Agreement on Tariffs and and Trade (GATT). The GATT is an international trade regime which encourages its 99 members to trade on the most favorable terms available by developing rules ensuring reciprocity, nondiscrimination, and transparency and by providing an institutional framework for periodic multilateral trade negotiations. China's decision was the latest stage in a lengthy and ambivalent relationship.[29] In April 1948 the Republic of China had been one of the twenty-three original members of the GATT but effectively withdrew in May 1950. Though the PRC government frequently asserted that it alone was the sole legal government of China, implying that China's withdrawal was without effect, Beijing chose not to participate in the GATT, even after its UN seating in 1971. Nevertheless, China monitored GATT activities and remained in indirect contact with GATT officials in Geneva through the United Nations Conference on Trade and Development (UNCTAD).

Between its WBG entry in 1980 and the granting of permanent observer status in November 1984, China increasingly took part in GATT-sponsored meetings and activities. In April 1980 China resumed its seat on the UN Interim Commission for the International Trade Organization (ICITO) which appoints the GATT Secretariat. In July 1981 China which was becoming a major textile exporter was granted observer status at a GATT meeting to renew the Multifibre Arrangement (MFA) which sets rules for the textile

[29] See Robert E. Herzstein, "China and the GATT: Legal and Policy Issues Raised by China's Participation in the General Agreement on Tariffs and Trade," *Law and Policy in International Business* 18 (1986): 371–415; Penelope Hartland-Thunberg, "China's Modernization: A Challenge for the GATT," *Washington Quarterly* 10 (Spring 1987): 81–97; J.E.D. McDonnell, "China's Move to Rejoin the GATT System: An Epic Transition," *World Economy* (London) 10 (September 1987): 331–50; and especially Jacobson and Oksenberg, *China's Participation in the IMF, the World Bank, and GATT*, pp. 62-3; ch. 4; pp. 126–7.

trade. In November 1982 China was granted full observer status at subsequent meetings of the Contracting Parties. In December 1983 China applied for MFA membership and was accepted the next month. Ultimately, with China's Open Door policy in full swing, its foreign trade growing rapidly (some 85 percent with GATT members), the impending start of the Uruguay Round of GATT trade negotiations, and prospects for broader access to foreign markets, China chose to make formal membership application.

GATT membership would entail both benefits and costs for China.[30] On the positive side, China would be able to increase its foreign trade earnings by strengthening its claims to MFN status (lowest prevailing tariff rates) with other GATT members and preferential export market access to the industrialized member states under the Generalized System of Preferences (GSP). China would also belong to a formal organization with rules, procedures, and protections against unfair trade practices, discrimination, and protectionism. Finally, the GATT would also be a valuable source of information and a device to promote and legitimize China's economic policies, provide trade and investment assurances to the international business and banking community, and secure its status in the international trading community.

On the negative side, GATT participation has a number of disadvantages. First, China would need to liberalize its trade policies by reducing tariffs and other trade barriers, decentralizing import and export decision-making and licensing, expanding market access through competitive bidding and limiting import substitution policies. Second, China would be required to end its own trade discrimination practices in the form of direct export subsidies and dumping (the sale of products below market cost), which are chronic problems for non-market centrally planned economies. Third, China would have to end its practices of setting hidden production and trade target levels and regulations, which are considered *nei-bu* (or internal matters), and institute greater transparency in the form of full disclosure of its trade rules and policies, pricing practices, foreign trade organizations' balances, the foreign trade plan, and market and trade data and statistics. Finally, it would have to restructure its current two-tiered exchange rate which is used to subsidize exports and revise the concept of special economic zones to ensure a unified national trade regime. Although China could invoke developing country status under Article XVIII of the GATT and avoid many membership obligations, its overall control and flexibility in managing its economy and foreign trade regime would be diminished.

The initial stage of China's GATT accession process included the receipt in February 1987 of a detailed memorandum from China describing the nature and functioning of its domestic economy and foreign trade regime. A working party was established the following May to examine this document and to draft an accession protocol based upon specific terms negotiated with China. The three-month delay in setting up the working party was due to differences over China's accession status. China contended that it was resum-

[30] Feeney, "Chinese Policy Toward Multilateral Economic Institutions," pp. 255–6; and Jacobson and Oksenberg, *China's Participation in the IMF, the World Bank, and GATT*, pp. 92–4.

ing its GATT membership rather than joining as a new contracting party. In the end the matter was tabled for the negotiating process. In response to China's memorandum, the contracting parties submitted a list of some 300 questions to which the Chinese responded. In February 1988 the working group met for the first time and in a series of subsequent sessions submitted and received answers to over 1200 related questions.[31]

In April 1988 the working party began work on a draft accession protocol to ensure that GATT rules could be applied to China's economy and foreign trade regime. This stage entailed extremely difficult negotiations because of the following obstacles: (1) intensified policy variances from GATT norms due to China's September 1988 austerity program which had expanded central economic controls, slowed domestic reforms, and raised added trade barriers; (2) the question of China's membership application status (resumed or new); (3) China's existing tariff schedule as the basis for negotiation; (4) the granting of developing status to China; and (5) U.S. extension of MFN and GSP treatment to China on an annual rather than a continuing basis.

The Tiananmen Square incident postponed the scheduled July 1989 working group meeting. When the group finally convened in earnest in December, additional questions were raised by a number of contracting parties on the whole range of issues. Since then and especially during the most recent meeting of the working group in September 1990, negotiations have remained unproductive and inconclusive.[32]

A recent GATT-related issue has also become a matter of serious concern for China. The decision of Taiwan on January 1, 1990 to apply for full GATT membership has added an additional complication to the process. Taiwan was granted GATT observer status in 1965 but was ousted after the PRC government was seated in the UN in 1971. Since then, Taiwan has become the world's 13th largest trading entity with total trade for 1989 worth US $118.5 billion and the second largest foreign exchange reserves of US $75 billion. Thus, there was ample justification for Taipei's action. China reacted angrily and accused Taiwan of seeking to secure the recognition of "two Chinas." [33] Despite the precedent of Taiwan's membership in the ADB and two other Asian MEIs (the Pacific Basin Economic Council and the Pacific Economic Cooperation Council), China's major motive was fear of losing face and a post-Tiananmen acceleration of Taiwan's "creeping officiality" in bilateral and multilateral settings.

Prior to the Tiananmen upheaval, China had assumed that once it had joined the GATT, it would sponsor Taiwan for separate membership under Article XXVI, much like Great Britain's 1986 sponsorship of Hong Kong. With China's early GATT membership prospects stalled, Taiwan decided it had little to lose by applying separately, though it sought to finesse the "two Chinas" issue by applying not as the Republic of China but rather under Article III

---

[31] Jacobson and Oksenberg, *China's Participation in the IMF, the World Bank, and GATT*, pp. 94–6.

[32] "GATT Reply to China Bid," *NYT*, September 21, 1990, p. C 17.

[33] Frances Williams and Jonathan Moore, "Who goes first?" *FEER* 147 (February 1, 1990): 36–7.

as "The Customs Territory of Taiwan, Penghu, Kinmen, and Matsu" (the main ROC islands). Taiwan's membership initiative not only preempts the subordinate status implicit in PRC sponsorship, but also raises the possibility of an eventual WBG membership request. For the moment, Taipei's action poses a serious dilemma for the GATT. While there is sufficient support for Taiwan's entry, many GATT members also know that drafting an accession protocol and a tariff schedule for Taiwan will be far easier than for China but that to do so would risk alienating China. In the short run, the issue may serve the interests of the United States most of all, in that calculated delay provides added U.S. leverage against Beijing to press for economic reform and trade liberalization and against Taipei to force concessions to reduce the latter's US $12 billion 1989 trade surplus with Washington. In the long run both China and Taiwan have cast the GATT die, and both will have to make meaningful policy concessions to avoid unacceptable consequences.

For the moment, however, China is in the unenviable position of potentially being frozen out of the GATT picture short of full membership. The upshot of this development will be mounting pressure on the working group and China to make the requisite policy decisions to conclude an acceptable accession protocol and tariff schedule. Failure to do so, especially in the light of rapid prospective GATT membership for the remaining non-member states of Eastern Europe and the extension in May 1990 of observer status to the Soviet Union, would invariably raise serious questions about China's future status in the world trade regime and the extent of its commitment to economic reform and the Open Door policy.

V. CONCLUSIONS

China's MEI affiliations have proved to be extremely beneficial prior to the Tiananmen Square incident. China has garnered billions of dollars in the form of grants, loans, and concessionary rate credits. These funds have been indispensable in accelerating China's modernization by financing an impressive array of infrastructural, developmental, and productive projects, broadening access to advanced technology and expertise, and greatly expanding direct foreign investment and trade, thereby integrating China into the mainstream of the global economic system. MEI membership has also brought China's bureaucratic, technical, and emerging business elites into close personal contact with numerous foreign experts. This interaction has served not only to inform and sensitize China's cadres to the psychological and methodological needs of successful economic development, but also to consolidate general vested bureaucratic career interests among all interested parties. Finally, MEI participation has conferred broad international legitimacy and acceptance upon China's political leadership and its modernization program.

The results for China's economy have been most impressive. In the short span of a decade China's foreign trade has grown from US $29.3 billion in 1979 to US $110.1 billion in 1989, a 376 percent increase, with exports rising from US $13.7 billion to US $51.8 billion, or 378 precent during the same period.[34] At the same time China's exports have soared from 5 percent to 22.2 percent of GNP, a proportion which implies that China's overall prosperity and modernization goals have become inextricably linked to international trade and continued adherence to economic reform, the Open Door policy and MEI participation, and particularly to GATT accession.[35]

However, as one leading scholar has suggested, a number of external developments including the collapse of Communism in Eastern Europe, the rise of an assertive civil society, multiparty politics, and a deteriorating economy in a fragmenting Soviet Union, and a shrinking Communist world movement (North Korea, Vietnam and Cuba) have combined with the trauma of Tiananmen Square to produce profound crises of regime re-legitimation and fundamental national identity as the "People's Republic," and a collapse of the China mystique. And it was this latter mystique which enabled China to claim and extract maximum global resources with minimum responsibilities.[36]

The current Chinese political leadership is well aware of the political and economic stakes in the aftermath of Tiananmen. Accordingly, the regime has adopted a dualistic damage limitation strategy based upon the reassertion of repressive authority and greater centralized control internally, but externally an uncritical approach to developments in Eastern Europe, the Soviet Union, and the MEIs, and carrot and stick leverage against the United States to remove international lending sanctions.[37] For China, the reality is increasing international isolation and loss of influence and status in the global arena. Having eschewed many of the tenets of traditional socialism, much of the Third World is anxious to duplicate China's success but also regards Beijing as a major competitor for foreign investment, product markets, and bilateral and MEI development resources. At the same time China has lost much of the leverage it once enjoyed from U.S.-Soviet Cold War rivalry. To compound China's problem, the political leadership succession questionc has paralyzed any definitive official commitment to economic reform and the Open Door (witness the repeated postponement of the 7th Party plenum).

To be sure, a primary goal of China's current leadership is to bring about the removal of the post-Tiananmen international sanctions. Such action would lead to the unqualified resumption of lending by the MEIs and the industrial democracies and with appropriate Chinese concessions could accelerate the GATT accession process. More important, ending sanctions would help to soften the perception that China is an unstable and unpredictably economic

---

[34] International Monetary Fund, *Direction of Trade Statistics Yearbook 1985.* Washington, D.C.: IMF, 1985, p. 5; and *ibid*., *1990*, p. 5. The official Chinese figure for 1989 foreign trade was US $111.6 billion. See Zhou Ying, "Nation Presses Ahead Despite Sanctions," *Beijing Review* 33 (October 1–7, 1990): 20.

[35] Robert Delfs, "Exit (World Stage Left)," *FEER* 149 (August 23, 1990): 32; and Robert Delfs, "The Long, Long Road Back," *FEER* 149 (August 23, 1990): 40.

[36] Samuel S. Kim, "Chinese Foreign Policy in the Shadows of Tiananmen: The Challenge of Legitimation," unpublished paper presented at the Nineteenth Sino-American Conference on Mainland China on "The Aftermath of the 1989 Crisis," Institute of International Relations, National Chengchi University, Taipei, Taiwan (ROC), June 12–14, 1990, pp. 22, 25, 30–1.

[37] *Ibid.*, pp. 21, 25.

partner and a poor credit risk.[38] To date, the Chinese have had mixed success. The release of Fang Lizhi did lead the United States to relax in part its opposition to so-called BHN World Bank lending. In October 1990 the European Community lifted its economic sanctions against China, and in November Japan agreed to resume its 5-year multi-billion dollar development loan program. Despite conciliatory efforts by the Bush administration, China's hard-line internal policies have persuaded key elements in the U.S. Congress to maintain opposition to further relaxation of MEI lending sanctions and the renewal of China's MFN status.[39]

The current Persian Gulf crisis has afforded China an extraordinary opportunity to achieve its goals of accelerating the removal of sanctions and normalizing its status as a major MEI borrower. With Iraq assuming the enemy spotlight, China has acquired dual leverage with the establishment of diplomatic relations with Saudi Arabia and the power as a permanent member of the UN Security Council to block UN endorsement of U.S. actions in the Gulf. Thus, China is now in an enviable position to extract significant U.S. concessions as the price for its continued support in the Security Council.[40] This strategy option might well dissipate should Iraq back down on Kuwait or if the growth of anti-war opposition in the U.S. Congress and the American public precludes the need for China's assistance. In the meantime, the time is fast approaching when China's leadership succession struggle could well force some resolution of the contradiction between China's internal regime which is committed to traditional socialism, albeit with Chinese characteristics, and the reality of China's pronounced economic linkage with the capitalist global economic system, upon which rests any real hope for achieving Beijing's future modernization goals. In the long term, because China's MEI commitments are an instrinsic and advantageous aspect of its overall modernization strategy, there is a strong likelihood that such ties will be strengthened and expanded in the future, especially once the succession issue is settled.

---

[38] *Ibid.*, p. 22.
[39] During the Summer of 1990 the U.S. House of Representative voted to remove China's MFN status, but Senate inaction prior to adjournament precluded any action.
[40] See Thomas L. Friedman, "Baker Gets Help From China on Gulf," *NYT*, November 7, 1990, p. A8; and Nicholas D. Kristoff, "China Gains in Mideast Crisis But Loses Cold War Benefits," *NYT*, November 11, 1990, pp. 1, 11.

IN SEARCH OF EXCELLENCE IN CHINA'S INDUSTRIAL SECTOR: THE CHINESE ENTERPRISE AND FOREIGN TECHNOLOGY

By Roy F. Grow *

CONTENTS

SUMMARY

The acquisition of foreign technology requires the involvement of several groups: national government authorities, local administrative officials, and enterprise managers must work together for technology transfers to occur. Of the three groups, enterprise managers—the actual end users of new technologies—are the most important. How national policies affect enterprise managers will determine the success or failure of future technology transfer projects.

I. INTRODUCTION

Seeking out and using new technologies requires faith, courage, and vision. New process and product technologies are the lifeblood of most production organizations, but they also present real challenges to those who adopt them. New technologies can change the way an organization processes inputs, alter the way people relate to one another, and rearrange the ways that tasks are accomplished.

Managers in societies around the world have faced the pressures created by the acquisition of new technologies.[1] The famed Toyota just-in-time production system grew out of the insight of Soichiro Toyoda who believed that auto manufacturing could be compared to the operation of an American supermarket. The supermarket required perishable food items to be constantly replenished on

---

* Chairman and Professor, Political Science Department, Carleton College.

[1] See the discussion in Gustav Ranis and Gary Saxonhouse, "Determinants of Technology Choice: the Indian and Japanese Cotton Industries," in Kazushi Ohkawa and Gustav Ranis, *Japan and The Developing Countries* (New York: Basil Blackwell Inc., 1985), pp. 135–154. See also Louis T. Wells, Jr., "Economic Man and Engineering Man" in *Technology Crossing Borders: The Choice, Transfer, and Management of International Technology Flows* (Boston, Harvard Business School Press, 1984), pp. 47–68.

shelves by a well-trained staff that monitored the flow of product; automobile production, Toyoda believed, also could profit from the principle of rapid turnover of parts rather than the wasteful inventory-stockpiling used by many manufacturers.

After the production changes were in place, Eiji Toyoda observed that implementing the American "supermarket vision" made Toyota managers face some difficult choices since it made obsolete many of the skills possessed by office personnel and shop workers in the factory. The new vision changed forever the relationships between Toyota and all of that firm's suppliers and distributors. The flexibility of Toyota's managers in handling these changes made the difference between success and failure.

The Toyota experience illustrates an important point about the acquisition and implementation of foreign technologies. In the Japanese case, it is commonplace to see that country's "economic miracle" in terms of a general national strategy to push structural change by using foreign technologies to move industry along a sharply-inclined learning curve. Such a strategy has, indeed, been responsible for resounding success in many sectors of the Japanese economy.[2]

But in addition to—and often going beyond—the commitment of many Japanese politicians and government administrators to the general process of knowledge acquisition, have been the actions of those Japanese managers, entrepreneurs, and staff and line personnel who actually manned the enterprises and made the decisions about foreign technologies.[3] The "masters of change" in industrial societies, notes Rosabeth Moss Kantor, are most often found in the *functional* economic organizations—the industrial enterprises—that actually implement the new process or product technologies.[4]

Is the enterprise equally important in China's acquisition of foreign technologies? I have sought to answer this question during the course of ten years of work investigating more than 100 Japanese and American firms and almost 250 projects involving technology transfers to China.[5] This same question has been in my mind during several hundred interviews of corporate and government officials who have been closely involved in these projects. (Most of these interviews took place over an extended period of time, and in a number of cases I worked as a consultant for the companies or became involved in the planning process.)

---

[2] Per Sorbom, "The Reception of Western Technology in China and Japan" in Erik Baark and Andrew Jamison (eds.), *Technological Development in China, India, and Japan* (New York: St. Martin's Press, 1986) pp. 35–56; Ronald Dore, *Flexible Rigidities: Industrial Policy and Structural Adjustment in the Japanese Economy 1970–1980* (Stanford: Stanford University Press, 1986) pp. 29–60; Thomas Pepper, Marit E. Janow, and Jimmy W. Wheeler, *The Competition: Dealing With Japan* (New York: Praeger Publishers, 1985) pp. 51–59.

[3] Note the discussion in Chalmers Johnson, "Political Institutions and Economic Performance: The Government-Business Relationship in Japan, South Korea, and Taiwan," in Frederic C. Deyo (ed.), *The Political Economy of the New Asian Industrialism* (Ithaca: Cornell University Press, 1987), pp. 136–164; and the discussion of "new ideas" in Toyohiro Kono, *Strategy and Structure of Japanese Enterprise* (New York: M. E. Sharpe, Inc, 1984), pp. 224–231. Much the same point is made by Daniel Okimoto in *Competitive Edge: The Semiconductor Industry in the U.S. and Japan* (Stanford: Stanford University Press, 1986), pp. 78–133.

[4] Rosabeth Moss Kantor, *The Change Masters: Innovation for Productivity in the American Corporation* (New York: Simon and Schuster, 1983), Chapt. 3. Much the same point is made in Reuven Brenner, *Rivalry: In Business, Science, Among Nations* (New York:Cambridge University Press, 1988).

[5] This research is the basis of my forthcoming book *Competing in China: Japanese and American Businessmen in a New Market.*

What I have found, I believe, is that the actions of the Chinese enterprise (and of the managers of these enterprises) increasingly lies at the heart of the entire Chinese technology acquisition process—especially in cases involving *successful* transfers of technology. It is at the enterprise level that the most important decisions about *specific* technologies—equipment, personnel, work processes—are made. And it is personnel in these enterprises—the managers, chief engineers, shop foremen—who are the key to making work the processes of seeking, accepting, and implementing foreign technologies.[6]

II. THE ROLE OF CHINESE ENTERPRISES IN ACQUIRING FOREIGN TECHNOLOGIES

In the rapidly changing Chinese reality of the 1980s, the decision to acquire foreign technology often begins with small and very specific needs that set in motion a complex and two-tiered process. The first tier in the process involves the national, provincial and local agencies that have the ability to channel the flow of foreign technologies—both hardware and software—across China. These bureaucracies can be thought of as the necessary (but not sufficient) "gateways" through which technology transfers must pass.

The second tier—perhaps even more important than the first—involves the process by which Chinese end users search for, adopt, and then implement, new knowledge. It is these consumers who make many of the most important decisions about technology transfer, and it is in this second tier that we find much of the driving force for technology acquisition.[7]

Chinese enterprises—large state organizations and smaller collective enterprises, technical institutes, and organizations of the distribution system—sit at the nexus of a complex series of information flows and product chains. Take, for example, the recent purchase by a Hospital Association in southern China of CAT scanners. The association, made up of thirteen health delivery organizations, came together specifically to pool their resources for new equipment. For two years, members of this consortium examined brochures, traveled to trade shows, and solicited bids from foreign firms such as Matsushita, Hewlett-Packard, and General Electric.

The Association Board was attracted to equipment from each of these firms. But how to decide what sort of technology was needed and from whom it should be purchased? A number of outside agencies were involved in the discussion of these topics. Several munici-

---

[6] The role of the enterprise on the "supply side" is an equally fascinating story that I have written about elsewhere. It turns out that most of the technology transfers to China—commodities, turnkey projects, scientific processes—have come from corporations, not governments. Especially interesting is the wide variety of factors that shape an American or Japanese firm's decision to transfer a given sort of technology, even within the same industry; the structure of the firm itself, its financial and technological underpinnings, the nature of its organizational and decision-making process, and the pattern of its planning and implementation procedures.

See Roy F. Grow, "Japanese and American Firms in China: Lessons of a New Market," in *Columbia Journal of World Business* (Spring, 1986). See also, Roy F. Grow, *American Firms and the Transfer of Technology to China: How Business People View the Process* (Office of Technology Assessment, Contract No. 633–51550 February, 1987); and Roy F. Grow, "Managing Entry into a New Market: Japanese and American Strategies in China."

[7] Some case-study examples are in Roy F. Grow, "Acquiring Foreign Technology: What Makes the Transfer Process Work?" in Denis Simon and Merle Goldman (eds.) *Science and Technology in Post-Mao China* (Cambridge: Harvard University Press, 1989) Chapt. 13.

pal health agencies were concerned about the kinds of equipment that might be purchased, the training that would be required to run the machinery, and public access to the facilities. Provincial authorities came into the discussion when delivery schedules and financing were debated. And offices in Beijing were notified about the contacts with foreign firms.

Ultimately, the final decision was made by the Association Board, and not by "higher level" authorities. This board weighed the financial and technical information, ranked factors such as reliability and adaptability, and meshed the needs of all thirteen members into a workable proposal. While *approval* of the project had to be discussed with several different agencies, the decision about the *type* of equipment—Matsushita, Hewlett-Packard, or General Electric—was made by the end users themselves.

A similar process occurred when a parts plant in Shenyang needed new die casting technologies.[8] When two foreign firms—one from the United States and the other from Japan—presented proposals for upgrading the factory's heating furnace, the factory head, Manager Xiu, found himself at the center of an intricate negotiation process that included groups both inside and outside the factory. Within the factory, Manager Xiu participated in a series of discussions with workers, engineers, and union heads about the benefits and impact of the new technologies. Outside the factory, he negotiated with upstream suppliers of steel and energy, and downstream purchasers of the factory's output. All were concerned about such things as downtime, quality, and the need for new resources. Manager Xiu also consulted with Beijing ministries such as the Ministry of Metallurgical Industries and the China National Auto Industry Corporation, as well as with his own provincial light industrial bureaus. For the new heating furnace technologies to come to China, all of the groups had to be consulted and most, finally, had to "sign on" to the project.

My examination of several hundred technology transfer projects leads me to believe that Chinese enterprises *that succeed* in acquiring new technologies almost always pass through a process of decision and acquisition consisting of a series of stages. These stages include the following:

Defining the problem. The decision to search for new technologies almost always begins with the definition of a problem—the realization that some piece of equipment or some work-process is not performing adequately or that another enterprise has learned how to do something more effectively. In most cases where foreign technologies are successfully transferred, the problem is first defined by those most immediately involved—the management of the enterprise responsible for the good or service in question.

Searching for solutions. Once the members of an enterprise decide to search for a solution to a problem, there are several sources of support, guidance, and information available to them. The three groups now used most commonly by enterprise managers are administrators in local bureaucracies and agencies who already have familiarity with the unit, managers in other production units

---

[8] Details are in Roy F. Grow, "How Factories Choose Technology," in *China Business Review* (May–June 1987), pp. 35–39.

who have dealt previously with the enterprise, and patrons in municipal and provincial organizations.

Weighing the options. In the *successful* technology transfer projects I have examined, the decisions about *specific* foreign technologies are most often made by the actual end users—the managers, chief engineers, and production specialists who will actually use the new methods. The most sensitive discussions usually occur *within* the Chinese enterprise after the first contacts with a foreign firm have been made. In a series of meetings and seminars, the details of the different possibilities will be made known to various groups who will then voice their concerns. These discussions, wide-ranging at first, will gradually focus on a series of positive and negative consequences that might result from the employment of new technologies. Will job assignments change? Will new skills be required? Will salaries be frozen while the equipment is paid for? Does the technical staff believe that the "mesh" of new and old technologies is acceptable?

The discussions with groups *outside* the enterprise are more complicated. Most enterprises have a web of relationships with upstream suppliers and downstream consumers. Will the new technologies require new inputs such as energy, materials or transportation? Will the new technologies affect products already purchased by other enterprises? How much downtime will be required to install the new equipment? Will prices go up?

Finally, an enterprise almost always consults with a series of local agencies about the impact of the new technologies. Will air and water pollution increase? What will be the new output levels, and what will be the marginal tax rates on this production? Are new workers required? Will there be new work rules? Each of these factors will be discussed—each with a different county, municipal, or provincial agency.

Negotiating the terms. There are several ways to proceed once foreign firms have expressed an interest in a project. "Higher authorities" at the provincial and national levels can handle all of the discussions for an enterprise; a professional negotiating team can be called in to represent all of the players; or the enterprise can handle the negotiation itself.

Negotiations with foreign firms about technology transfers are accompanied by a substantial amount of "baggage," involving more than price, delivery schedules, and mesh. In reality, a Chinese enterprise brings to the negotiation a large number of concerns from all of the different constituencies. Meshing all of these concerns can be delicate and time-consuming work.[9]

Ratifying the decision. Obtaining official imprimatur so that a project may be set in motion is a difficult procedure for outsiders to comprehend. Understanding it means distinguishing between the substantive decisions that have practical consequences and the administrative decisions that result in final approval.

All Chinese enterprises looking for foreign technologies have some sort of relationship to local, provincial, and national agencies and bureaucracies. Some of these agencies are influential and can

---

[9] Roy F. Grow, "Changing the Rules: Debating Price and Contract Regulations in the Northeast," (July, 1988).

have a life or death impact on the proposal under consideration. others are little more than one-room offices with a few file cabinets.

In none of the projects I studied has *one* agency controlled *all* aspects of an enterprise's life. Most often the situation is one in which a number of agencies and organs have a limited influence over some aspect of an enterprise's activities.

In most successful technology transfer projects, it is the actual Chinese end users of the new technologies that determine how well these technologies are accepted. This is not to say that the end user acts alone. Many individuals, offices, and agencies are involved in every stage of the process. But outside involvement comes into play most often during the *ratification* of the choice of a new technology that has been selected by the end user.[10]

III. WHAT MAKES FOR A SUCCESSFUL ENTERPRISE?

Some enterprises are clearly more successful at moving through the different parts of the technology acquisition process than others. Within the same industrial sector, and even among a group of enterprises that are clustered under the same ministerial "umbrella," some enterprises move rapidly and forcefully to acquire foreign technologies while others are more reticent and passive.

In the changing Chinese economic climate of the 1980s, there are certain elements that play an increasingly important role in the pace at which a Chinese enterprise moves through the technology acquisition process. Among the most important in determining the success or failure of the technology transfer process are:[11]

Enterprise size. Bigness, increasingly, gets in the way of technology acquisition. The sheer magnitude of the changes required in large-scale industrial technology transfer projects, for example, brings large state and party entities into play when decisions about change are required. Discussions often become bogged down under the sheer weight of all of the groups that have to be consulted.

In large state enterprises in general, and in many "special" large projects in particular, there is a greater tendency for a "blocking coalition" (to use Mancur Olson's phrase) to act in ways that will, finally, thwart the changes a new technology entails.[12] In the new China, where central allocation is becoming less a fact of life, smaller units now have a better chance of escaping the inertia that often results when large, worried, and contentious groups are threatened with change.

---

[10] See Roy F. Grow, "A Pharmaceutical Deal: How an American Company and a Chinese enterprise adapted to the Changes in China's Pharmaceutical Industry," *China Business Review,* Nov–Dec. 1987, pp. 40–43.

[11] Ultimately, I believe, there must be a set of reciprocal qualities present in both the technology-granting foreign firm and the technology-acquiring Chinese enterprise for the transfer process to work: Particular kinds of foreign firms work best with particular kinds of Chinese enterprise. See Roy F. Grow, *Assessing the Fit Between Foreign Firms and Chinese Enterprises: Comparing Japanese and American Technology Transfers to China* (Second Annual IBEAR Research Conference, USC, April 7, 1988).

I am especially indebted to Bill Fischer and Denis Simon who have helped me think through the problems associated with investigating and demonstrating this reciprocal relationship.

[12] Mancur Olson, "Supply-Side Economics, Industrial Policy, and Rational Ignorance" in Barfield and Schambra (eds.), *The Politics of Industrial Policy,* (Washington, D.C., American Enterprise Institute, 1986) pp. 245–269.

Enterprise autonomy. In the past, having a patron in high places paid off for many industrial enterprises. A patron could look out for an enterprise's interests, nudge the allocation process in the right direction, and push for bureaucratic approval. A patron could also steer technology acquisition projects through all of the important parts of the bureaucratic system.

But nowadays, enterprises that have not tied their carts too closely to one Beijing or provincial horse appear to fare better. Autonomy allows flexibility—the ability to maneuver one's way through the bureaucratic maze when one avenue is blocked.

Enterprise organization. The way that the enterprise itself is put together often influences its ability to acquire foreign technologies. Those firms that most successfully navigate the technology transfer process have some of the following characteristics:

- *They lack deep and immutable divisions.* The scars of the 1960s and 1970s run deep in many enterprises. In many units the "political" and "technical" groups that were antagonistic toward one another in the past now see one another daily in their factory work settings. Technical people—scientists, engineers, accountants—remember their ostracism and expulsion; political people now chafe at the sudden turnaround in their own fortunes and their seeming lack of opportunity for advancement. In enterprises where this bitterness remains deep, the ability to affect the changes required by new technologies is often blocked.

- *They have arenas for discussion.* Fear and tension can run through a work force when new technologies require change in an enterprise. Whose job assignments will be changed? Whose skills will be rendered obsolete? Whose avenue to advancement threatened? Enterprises that move through technology acquisition successfully often develop mechanisms for alleviating these fears. Most of these mechanisms are of the variety well-known to western factory managers: group meetings, retreats, after-hours get-togethers. The importance of these mechanisms is the opportunity they afford for assurances that the fears and tensions associated with change will be taken seriously, and that inputs from the enterprise personnel will be heard.

Enterprise management. The role of the enterprise manager is complex. The best managers try to deal with active and competing needs and desires both within their units and those outside groups whose cooperation is necessary to the unit's work.

Chinese managers who successfully move through the steps of foreign technology acquisition usually demonstrate some combination of the following abilities:

- *They recognize the advantages of change.* The impetus for change in a Chinese unit most frequently originates with some sort of unexpected crisis in the enterprise—the failure of a machine, a new demand for a different sort of production, a serious financial situation, the return from abroad of an employee or local official full of new ideas. Managers successfully acquiring foreign technologies know how to turn necessity to advantage and seize the opportunity when changes are forced on them.

- *They build good relationships with technical subordinates.* While the manager is usually responsible for overall coordination of a project, many Chinese enterprises put a chief engineer in charge of technical decisions. A key variable in the success of foreign technology acquisition projects is the nature of the relationship between the general manager and his chief engineer(s). When managerial and technical perspectives do not mesh, the possibilities of conflict are magnified, and discussion within the enterprise can become fragmented and lack focus. When the manager works easily with technical personnel, the acquisition process proceeds more smoothly, regardless of the "fit" of the new technology.

- *They are sensitive to the needs of major constituencies.* Most Chinese managers seeking to acquire foreign technologies do not exist in a vacuum: upstream suppliers and downstream purchasers are also affected by technological changes. Managers that move most easily through the acquisition and implementation process work closely with all of their constituencies, involving them early on in many of the discussions and negotiations.

- *They maintain multiple lines of communication.* Lines of authority and control have changed dramatically since the late 1970s. As the process of central planning and allocation gives way to a more diffuse system of operation, Chinese enterprise managers face a more fluid decision making process. The most successful managers have a multiplicity of contacts on the local, provincial, and even national levels. Many have built lines of communication with individuals and agencies that in the past would have been out of bounds to them because such lines would have crossed bureaucratic jurisdictional lines.

- *They are entrepreneurial.* Along with the increase in the points of access (both for and to the manager), comes a correspondingly greater amount of time spent looking for a path through the Chinese bureaucratic "maze." Success for managers nowadays necessarily involves the ability to maneuver between and among the different government bureaucracies. Chinese managers who are most effective in acquiring foreign technologies are entrepreneurial types who play multiple points of access and control off against one another and take a certain joy in the process.

IV. CHINESE ENTERPRISES IN THE 1990s

The role of the entrepreneur, noted J. B. Say at the end of the 18th century, is to shift resources from less productive to more productive tasks. The Chinese reforms of the 1980s not only set in motion an energetic drive for new technologies, they also empowered enterprises and their managers to move in new ways—to direct their own and their enterprise's resources more effectively and to use their own creative energies to make the technology acquisition process work.

Will the new role for the enterprise and its managers continue? It is a commonplace in political analysis everywhere to note that public policy is shaped by the interaction of competing forces, and that the fate of a given policy can be quickly turned around by what appears at the time to be a relatively insignificant event or issue.

Now there are several clusters of issues that could affect the Chinese enterprises' role in the technology acquisition process. Some of the most important include the following:

Strains of an inadequate infrastructure. In the mid-1980s almost every analyst—Chinese and foreign alike—argued that important changes in infrastructure would be required if Chinese enterprises were to manage technology acquisition effectively. Some changes were begun: new contract systems, bankruptcy laws, financial institutions, and accounting procedures all came into being.

In 1989 Chinese managers involved in technology acquisition projects argued that these innovations helped them in their projects. Not every manager in every enterprise was affected in a similar manner. But, taken together, most managers argue, the changes (real or promised) in infrastructure created an atmosphere in which innovation became possible and entrepreneurial daring held out the promise of reward.

But many of the Chinese enterprise managers who began to acquire and implement foreign technologies in the mid-1980s now believe that the most important infrastructural changes are still to come. These Chinese managers argue that they still need legislation and support in key areas such as rules governing party personnel in the enterprise, inspection systems for maintaining quality control, guidelines for changing work assignments, and procedures for resolving work grievances.

The continuing lack of managerial skills. Many Chinese enterprises that acquire foreign technologies are very well managed. In these enterprises, there is a depth in important skills, especially of specialized technical expertise areas and of knowledge of interpersonal relations.

But many other skills are in short supply. From the perspective of technology *acquisition,* the most notable need is for negotiation skills that can be used to build relationships *between* Chinese enterprises. When managers do not possess these negotiation skills, the price is inertia: Managers might see a need in their enterprise and find a technology; but they do not know how to handle all of the changing relationships with upstream and downstream constituencies required by the demands of the new technologies.[13]

Negotiating with representatives from foreign firms is an equally difficult skill for Chinese managers to acquire. Most Chinese managers have developed antennae that are reasonably sensitive to the cross-cultural dimension of the negotiation process: They expect a certain "monarchical bearing" on the part of Japanese business people, and they are used to the culinary pickiness of Americans.

---

[13] The most insightful and sensitive work is that of William Fischer. See, for example, his "The Transfer of Managerial Knowledge to China" (Office of Technology Assessment, Contract No. 633–1670.0).

More difficult for Chinese managers is understanding the foreign *context* of their foreign guests' negotiation position. Most Chinese managers have very little understanding about how an American firm operates or how such a firm differs from its Japanese counterpart. Many Chinese negotiation teams miss the subtle nuance in the bargaining process and have real difficulty analyzing the needs of the foreign side.

The unexpected impact of world overcapacity. Most Chinese enterprise managers and officials still have not come to grips with the unexpected appearance of manufacturing and agricultural production overcapacity in the outside world. This "glut" has mixed implications for many Chinese enterprises. On the one hand, the availability of technologies—factories, equipment, expertise—at increasingly lower prices makes possible some good buys for the right Chinese enterprise. On the other hand, Chinese enterprise projects tied to exports will face some very rough times in the years ahead, especially in those sectors where Chinese standards are not yet up to world-class levels.

The arrogance of foreign firms. Many foreign firms—Japanese, American, and European—are involved in the China market in very successful ways: They are participating in solid ventures with Chinese partners, are transferring important knowledge, and are attaining satisfying levels of return. Almost without exception, executives in these foreign firms reconfirm the age-old "when in Rome" lessons of international business: success in China is highly dependent on learning the ways of the host market.

For successful foreign firms, the lessons of the China market are tough but not impossible. They include the need (a) to understand the relationship between the Chinese decision and ratification processes, (b) to recognize the importance of discovering linkages between the enterprise and local and national bureaucracies, (c) to think of the factory manager in terms of his relationship to upstream and downstream constituencies, and (d) to approach Chinese end users in terms of a solution to some troubling problem identified by the end users themselves.

Sadly, many foreign firms have not yet learned these lessons. Instead, they see the China market as irrational, protected, and backward, and think of exploiting it through "quick hits." Many of the foreign firms in this category look past their potential customers' real needs, and look instead at what it, the foreign firm, wants to sell. The results are often unfortunate: Chinese purchasers with equipment that is simply irrelevant to their needs, products that cannot be maintained in the Chinese environment, and promises about performance that cannot be fulfilled.

Every misrepresentation and broken commitment builds warier Chinese enterprise managers and agency officials. The more Chinese managers and officials who are stung by foreign firms, the greater will be the pressure to move away from the promises of the New Open Door.

V. Prospects for the Future

The Chinese enterprise exists in a rapidly changing world: In the late 1980s managerial reforms continued to alter the formal relationship of the enterprise to provincial and national bureaucracies; new sources of funding are still reshaping the basis of formal authority; new rules in the ministerial accounting system are helping enterprises avoid some of the most entangling forms of middle-level bureaucratic control; new bankruptcy laws are challenging fundamental concepts about the relationship of surplus value to the life of a production organization; and the recent banking and accounting regulations are influencing the enterprise's ability to manage retained earnings.

Not every enterprise can adjust to all of these changes. In many cases, resistance to the changes is springing up—both from those in enterprises who find the new demands too great, and from those in state agencies who worry about the increasingly important role that enterprises are playing.

Many Chinese enterprises that seek to acquire new foreign technologies thus find themselves caught between the dynamics of a rapidly changing administrative system and countervailing forces that are pushing for different ways of bringing new technologies to China.

An important part of China's ongoing effort to acquire and assimilate new technologies must be directed at the *primary* agents of change—the Chinese enterprises that will actually use these technologies and the people in the enterprises who will make the technologies work.

CHINESE LAW RELATING TO FOREIGN INVESTMENT AND TRADE: THE DECADE OF REFORM IN RETROSPECT

By James V. Feinerman *

CONTENTS

During the eleven years which have passed since China's historic announcement of its Joint Venture Law (JVL),[1] foreign investors have become very familiar with the existence and the elements of the legal framework for foreign investment in China. At the same time, more than a decade of experience of major foreign corporations in the China market, and the publicity attendant to the serious problems which have arisen from some of this investment and trade, has somewhat lessened the enthusiasm of the international business community to enter and to remain in China.[2] This discussion will focus on the extent to which the emerging legal system of the People's Republic of China (PRC) has succeeded in addressing these difficulties and, where relief has not been forthcoming, on the features of China's laws which are still not conducive to foreign

---

* Associate Professor, Georgetown University Law Center.

[1] Law of the People's Republic of China on Joint Equity Enterprises (adopted July 1, 1979; amended Apr. 4, 1990). The Chinese text and an English translation appear in 1 China Laws for Foreign Business, para. 6-500 at 7,801 (CCH Australia Ltd. ed. 1985).

[2] See e.g., Burns, "Why Investors Are Sour on China," N.Y. Times, June 8, 1986, at C7, col. 1; Burns, "A.M.C.'s Troubles in China," N.Y. Times, April 11, 1986, at D4, col. 1; Schiffman, "AMC Jeep Venture Trying to Get Back on Track After Peking Helps to Ease Currency Squeeze," Asian Wall St. J. Weekly, Aug. 25, 1986, at 4. See also Browning, If Everybody Bought One Shoe (N.Y.: Farrar, Straus & Giroux 1989). Interestingly, most of the negative features were publicized well before the Beijing Massacre of 1989.

investment and trade. Due to the extensive legislative activity of recent years, this treatment will necessarily be selective.[3]

I. DIRECT FOREIGN INVESTMENT

Although a large number of possibilities for investing in China have materialized in recent years, including such sophisticated mechanisms as bank lending, leasing, technology licensing, and compensation trade, the method most publicized by Chinese government authorities has remained direct foreign investment. The chief focus of national and regional legislation, direct foreign investment has grown continuously since the enactment of the JVL until the events of 1989 forced investors to reconsider their China strategies.[4] A combination of primary legislation, secondary implementing regulations and—perhaps most importantly—the precedent of previous foreign investment encouraged such growth. Since the 1979 passage of the JVL, which created the single investment vehicle of a Sino-foreign equity joint venture with the parties owning shares of a newly-created company, additional investment opportunities with different legal features have been developed, including wholly foreign-owned enterprises[5] (WFOE) and cooperative (contractual) joint ventures[6] (CJV) which afford greater flexibility than the equity joint venture (EJV).

Since the Third Plenum of the Eleventh Communist Party Congress in late 1978, China has embarked on an ambitious program of political and economic reform. One of the major elements of this program has been an opening to the outside world, sometimes referred to as China's "Open-Door" or, more simply, "open" policy. In that vein, China promulgated the JVL in July, 1979, to encourage foreign participation in China's modernization program. In furtherance of this program, regulations appeared in 1980 which allowed foreign companies to set up representative offices in China.[7] These provisions represented an extraordinary break with both the rhetoric and the practices of the thirty years immediately following the establishment of the PRC, when China condemned foreign investment in the developing world as exploitation and eliminated all but a few remnants of pre-1949 foreign business in China. The final confirmation of this change was the adoption of an unusual provision in the fourth PRC Constitution, promulgated in 1982, which

---

[3] A recent search of a legal database containing only the most basic Chinese legislation which has been translated into English reveals 216 sets of laws and regulations related to foreign investment and trade. Westlaw, *Chinalaw* Database (West 1990).

[4] Brecher, "The End of Investment's Wonder Years," *The China Business Review*, January-February 1990, at 27–29.

[5] The Law of the People's Republic of China Concerning Enterprises with Sole Foreign Investment (adopted Apr. 11, 1986). The Chinese text and an English translation appear in 1 China Laws for Foreign Business, para. 13–506 at 16,651 (CCH Australia Ltd. ed. 1985).

[6] The Law of the People's Republic of China on Sino-foreign Co-operative Enterprises, (adopted Apr. 13, 1988). The Chinese text and an English translation appear at 1 Chinese Laws for Foreign Business, para. 6–100 at 7,551 (CCH Australia Ltd. ed. 1985).

[7] Interim Regulations of the People's Republic of China Concerning the Control of Resident Offices of Foreign Enterprises (promulgated October 30, 1980). The Chinese text and an English translation appear at 1 Chinese Laws for Foreign Business, para. 7–500, at 9,051 (CCH Australia Ltd. ed. 1985).

reinforced previous legal developments by promising to protect "the lawful rights and interests of foreign investors." [8]

Over the next several years, a surprisingly large body of law was published to implement this policy of encouraging foreign investment. Tax rules, foreign exchange controls, customs regulations and even trademark and patent laws were announced. Implementing regulations to explain and to expand the provisions of the basic laws also appeared, but often only after a considerable period of confusion and uncertainty. For instance, the implementing regulations for the original JVL were promulgated four years after the basic law; [9] WFOE existed for almost three years before they were legally recognized.[10] China asked foreign investors for patience as it accustomed itself to the new rule of law it was promoting in the foreign economic arena, but foreign businesses remained understandably somewhat reluctant to put large sums of money at risk in China without knowing what legal rules would be in force there.

A separate, and generally more favorable legal regime, was created in a number of special economic zones (SEZs) located in the southeastern coastal provinces of Guangdong and Fujian.[11] These SEZs offer lower taxation rates, special customs treatment for the import of raw materials needed in production and for the export of finished goods as well as simplified procedures for establishing 100%-foreign owned enterprises therein. The vast majority of SEZ ventures have been established in the Shenzhen SEZ, just across the border from Hong Kong. An increasing number of ventures have recently begun to appear in the Xiamen SEZ, the special zone closest to Taiwan. Most of the SEZ ventures have been small-scale, low-technology assembly operations attracted by cheaper land and labor costs. Before the recent downturn in the hotel industry, Shenzhen attracted several large hotel projects.

Of the three major forms of direct foreign investment—EJVs, CJVs and WFOEs—the most legislative attention has been paid to the equity joint ventures. For the first several years of their existence, however, foreign business did not seem particularly eager to establish them in China. In part, this hesitation was due to the failure previously mentioned to enact implementing regulations, but flaws in the basic legal form may have also contributed to their lack of attractiveness. Under the original legislation, joint ventures were supposed to be formed as "limited liability companies with the status of Chinese legal persons." [12] Yet, as of this writing, the

[8] The Constitution of the People's Republic of China, art. 18 (adopted Dec. 4, 1982). The article also states that foreign enterprises, other foreign economic organizations and individual foreigners are permitted to invest and to enter into economic co-operation with Chinese enterprises and economic organizations. (Peking: Foreign Languages Press 1983).

[9] Regulations for the Implementation of the Law of the People's Republic of China on Joint Ventures Using Chinese and Foreign Investment (adopted Sept. 20, 1983). The Chinese text and an English translation appear in 1 China Laws for Foreign Business, para. 6–550, at (CCH Australia Ltd. ed. 1985).

[10] See Stein, "Wholly Foreign Owned Ventures in China: A Comparison of 3M China Ltd, Grace China Ltd and the New Foreign Enterprise Law," 4 China Law Reporter 1 (1987). An English translation of the "Law of People's Republic of China on Enterprises Operated Exclusively with Foreign Capital," appears in Foreign Broadcast Information Service (FBIS) *Daily Report: China*, 14 April 1986 at K13–K15; *reprinted in* 4 China Law Reporter 63 (1987).

[11] See Pow and Moser, "Law and Investment in China's Special Investment Areas," in Moser, ed., *Foreign Trade, Investment, and the Law in the People's Republic of China* (Hong Kong: Oxford University Press 2d ed. 1987).

[12] Law of the People's Republic of China on Sino-foreign Joint Equity Enterprises, *supra* note 1, art. 4:A joint venture shall take the form of a limited liability company.

PRC has never adopted a Company Law and, until 1987, did not even have in force a basic Civil Code. As a result, no one knew what the description "limited liability company" or even "legal person" meant under Chinese law.[13] Under the provisions of the original JVL, the management structure required the president to be a PRC national, unanimous board of directors approval for major corporate acts and fixed-term duration of the joint venture. Many foreign investors found the JVL too restrictive, despite the certainty which Chinese government approval lent to this form of foreign investment.

Far more foreign investment in and trade with China has occurred by means of the so-called "contractual" joint venture or CJV. These enterprises also involve joint investments of cash, other property and contributions of technology by foreign and Chinese parties; however, they enjoy greater flexibility. No new, separate legal person is created automatically, and fewer legal restrictions govern the relationship between the co-venturers. Tax rates, under the Foreign Enterprise Income Taxation Law, are higher than for joint ventures, but this has not deterred foreign investors from preferring the contractual form. In contrast to the requirements of the EJV, the sharing of profits is established by the parties' contract rather than on the basis of their respective equity interests.[14]

The WFOE originated in the SEZs, which were the first localities to permit foreigners to establish wholly-foreign-owned enterprises within their boundaries. A United States corporation, Minnesota Mining & Manufacturing (3M) received the first permission to set up a WFOE outside the SEZs, in Shanghai, in 1983. 3M insisted to the Chinese that all of its overseas operations have been conducted on the basis of 100% ownership; China was also very eager for 3M's expertise in adhesives technology.[15] By passing a law formally recognizing WFOEs, China acknowledged officially its previous unofficial policy of permitting entirely foreign-owned enterprises to operate in China. They are also considered to be "legal persons," but—unlike the JVL—no provision in this legislation expressly limits such enterprises' liability. Various restrictions—for example, on the lines of business in which WFOEs may engage—remained to be detailed in subsequent implementing regulations.

II. LEGAL CONCERNS OF FOREIGN INVESTORS

A number of legal issues have become problems common to all these different types of enterprises, regardless of their form. Chinese authorities began to address some of these concerns in the

---

[13] Since January 1, 1987, the General Principles of Civil Law have been in force. "Legal persons" are defined in art. 36; civil liability is described in Chapter 6, arts. 106–141. *See* Jones, ed., *Basic Principles of Civil Law in China* (Armonk: M.E. Sharpe 1989).

[14] Some of this flexibility was eliminated with the enactment of the law authorizing CJVs, *supra* note 6, but the basic distinctions persist. *See* Tao, "New Chinese Law on Cooperative Joint Ventures I—Preliminary Analysis," *International Business Lawyer*, January 1989, at 7.

A number of foreign advisors to international investors have found this law problematic. They complain that local authorities have applied the law rigidly, refusing to allow non-legal-person ventures to be established; that provisions for return of capital to foreign parties are unfortunately vague; and that the imposition of a strict legal form will adversely affect the success that CJVs have heretofore enjoyed. *See* Salbaing and Nee, "New Chinese Law on Cooperative Joint Ventures II—An Editorial Comment," *International Business Lawyer*, January 1989, at 10.

[15] *See* Stein, *supra* note 10.

mid-1980s,[16] but it remains to be seen just how far they will be willing to go to accommodate foreign investors' demands. On the other hand, several high-ranking Chinese officials have indicated that domestic political uncertainty in the aftermath of the events of the spring and summer of 1989 have in no way dampened the PRC's determination to encourage foreign investment.[17] A look at a few of the continuing problems, and recent attempts to remedy some of them with new legislation, may prove instructive.

DISPARATE TAX TREATMENT

Since the early 1980s, it has become difficult to keep count of the number of differing regimes of taxation which have been adopted in China.[18] In addition to China's domestic tax regime, which affects any Chinese legal person, there are now multiple sets of laws for foreigners—EJV taxes, Foreign Enterprise Income Tax, SEZ taxes and a different scheme of reduced taxes for non-SEZ "Economic and Technical Development Zones" in fourteen coastal cities.[19] Each tax regime provides different rates and disparate treatment of such matters as tax holidays, reductions and exemptions for specified businesses and reinvestment, not to mention withholding taxes. As a result, calculating which tax provisions provide any single enterprise or investment possibility the most favorable treatment has become a considerable burden, and expense, for foreign investors. The situation has been little improved by the publication of circulars, notices and other documents by the Ministry of Finance and its General Taxation Bureau intended to clarify these laws and their application. A large number of "secret" (neibu, or "internal") provisions still exist in this area, further complicating matters and raising investor suspicions that such rules are invoked capriciously.[20] A uniform tax system described in detailed, published regulations, fairly enforced, would do much to increase foreign investor confidence.

SALES ON THE DOMESTIC MARKET

Undoubtedly one of the biggest attractions for foreign investment in China is the potential of China's market of one billion consumers. Despite China's announced intention to use foreign investment to increase Chinese export capabilities, foreign companies have continued to view investment in China as a kind of "down payment" against the future, when they hope to tap the huge pool represented by the Chinese population. In many cases, foreign investors have been encouraged by their Chinese counterparts to believe that they would be able to market their products in China almost

---

[16] Provisions of the State Council of the People's Republic of China for the Encouragement of Foreign Investment (promulgated Oct. 11, 1986). An English translation appears in *China Daily*, Nov. 4, 1986, at 2.

[17] *See . e . g.*, "Leadership Vacuum, Continuing Interest in JVs Highlighted at NPC," *Business China*, April 9, 1990, at 49.

[18] Two useful resources which provide background information, an overview of taxation and some guidance as to the application of the laws are Moser and Zee, *China Tax Guide* (Oxford: Oxford University Press 1987) and Easson and Li, *Taxation of Foreign Investment in the People's Republic of China* (Deventer: Kluwer Law and Taxation Publishers 1989).

[19] *See* Pow and Moser, *supra* note 11, particularly, "II. The Fourteen Coastal Cities," at 233–247.

[20] *See , e . g.*, Capener, "An American in Beijing: Perspectives on the Rule of Law in China," 1988 Brigham Young University Law Review 567, at 587.

as soon as in-country production began, as long as they turned out products "urgently needed" in China or which substituted for imports. In the past few years, however, these plans have run into a number of roadblocks. First of all, government approval must be obtained before new products can enter the market. If joint venture products compete with existing Chinese products, approval may not be granted; in some cases approval has been restricted to certain geographical areas. If the product does not replace one already being imported by Chinese state foreign trade companies, payment will most likely be in Chinese currency, which is not convertible. Pricing may be determined by prices fixed for similar products under the central Chinese State Plan.[21]

FOREIGN EXCHANGE

Although Article 75 of the Regulations for the Implementation of the Law of the People's Republic of China on Joint Ventures Using Chinese and Foreign Investment held out the promise that foreign exchange deficiencies experienced by joint ventures selling on the domestic market (presuming such sales were approved) would be remedied by the Chinese government, experience has proven otherwise.[22] In most cases, the Chinese government has simply suggested that the foreign party to the venture defer distribution of its "profits" until the foreign exchange problem can be solved. Of course, such profits can be reinvested inside China, but there are limits on the availability of attractive possibilities.

The prospects for achieving some accommodation of foreign investor concerns with respect to foreign exchange are not good in the short term. The events of the spring and summer of 1989 aggravated an already grim fiscal situation, which encompassed China's worst deficit in ten years, peaking repayment levels on foreign debt and greatly lessened availability of official and private financing from foreign sources.[23] Attempts to remedy previous foreign exchange problems, such as the State Council Regulations Concerning the Balance of Foreign Exchange Income and Expenditure by Sino-Foreign Joint Equity Ventures, have failed to end the chronic imbalances that have plagued foreign enterprises.[24]

Even the creation of local swap centers, where foreign enterprises with surpluses of non-convertible Chinese currency could exchange it with enterprises enjoying a foreign currency surplus, have not eliminated foreign exchange complaints. Beginning with the first such center in the Shenzhen SEZ in 1985, it seemed that a national market for foreign exchange might emerge in China, under the control of the State Administration of Exchange Control.

---

[21] See Zhang, "Improving Conditions for Joint Ventures," Beijing Review, Sept. 1, 1986, at 4; Horsley, "Investing in China in 1985," in Theroux, ed., Legal Aspects of Doing Business with the PRC 1985, 149–150 (New York: Practicing Law Institute 1985).

[22] Article 75 provides: [T]he unbalance [of foreign exchange] shall be solved by the people's government of a relevant province, an autonomous region or a municipality directly under the central government or the department in charge under the State Council from their own foreign exchange reserves....

[23] Okubo, "Financial Difficulties and Prospects for the Future," JETRO China Newsletter, No. 86, at 12 (1990).

[24] Regulations of the State Council Concerning the Balance of Foreign Exchange Income and Expenditure by Sino-Foreign Joint Equity Ventures (promulgated Jan. 15, 1986). The Chinese text and an English translation appear in 1 China Laws for Foreign Business, para. 6–590, at 8,031 (CCH Australia Ltd. ed. 1985).

Yet, clear guidelines for the system were never issued, and full participation remained limited to certain Chinese enterprises and some foreign investors.[25] Most importantly, the general availability of foreign exchange has been subject to wide variation related to central government's management of foreign exchange. The underlying policy, and many of the relevant legal regulations, are unknown, and perhaps unknowable, to foreign investors.[26]

CONTROL

Although it should be theoretically possible for a foreign investor to achieve control over a venture in the PRC by using investment ratios to determine majority voting rights, there has seemed in fact to be little freedom for foreigners to take active control of any Chinese investment. In equity joint ventures, all significant decisions require unanimity. Even the other investment vehicles, which appear to afford greater control, remain subject to a number of restrictions in reality. Hiring labor, marketing product, maintaining access to necessary inputs such as water, electricity or transport all require cooperation from Chinese entities, whether they are venture partners or not. To preserve harmonious relations, a foreign investor will have to consider the wishes of Chinese counterparts, regardless of the nature of legal relationship.

APPROVAL

The approval process in China is maddening not only for foreign investors; domestic enterprises also suffer from what is euphemistically called "bureaucratism." Central government attempts to delegate approval power to lower level authorities have had little effect on the underlying problem. Worst of all, whenever the central government fears even a temporary loss of control over some aspect of China's economy or society, its first impulse is to re-centralize its control over the localities. The domestic austerity program underway since 1988 and the response to political unrest in 1989 once again demonstrated these tendencies.[27] From the preparation of feasibility studies to the granting of final approval, a joint venture proposal or other investment project may languish for several years. A coal-mining joint venture initiated by Occidental Petroleum, finalized in the mid-1980s required six years to gain its approval, and it had the backing of the highest levels of the Chinese state leadership!

LABOR

Although several reforms have been enacted in the administration of China's domestic economy to make workers more efficient and to tie their compensation to their output, many Chinese workers still have the traditional "iron rice bowl" mentality about their

[25] *See* Yowell, "Swap Center System to Expand," *The China Business Review*, September–October 1988, at 10.

[26] Young, "Foreign Exchange Control of Financial Institutions," *East Asian Executive Reports*, February 1988, at 7–13.

[27] *See , e . g.,* Frisbie and Brecher, "What to Watch For: A Guide to China's Current Business Environment," *The China Business Review*, September–October 1989, at 10–11.

work.[28] As a result of this mentality, those who manage Chinese labor—both Chinese and foreign managers—have found it very difficult to discipline workers. Enterprise control of labor has, at least since the Cultural Revolution, been extremely lax. Moreover, recruitment of Chinese workers by foreign enterprises has been tightly controlled by Chinese state agencies. Most significantly, the higher salaries which foreign partners must pay to joint venture workers are not passed through to the workers but are retained by the Chinese venture partners to compensate for "subsidies" for housing, fuel costs, education, medical care and other social welfare benefits normally provided to their employees by Chinese enterprises.

Although the introduction of modern management practices was supposed to have been one of the benefits which foreign investors were meant to introduce into China, it has become clear that, insofar as these involve rewarding diligent and punishing slack workers, there are limits as to what Chinese partners will allow. Despite labor regulations in the SEZs which permit discharge of unsatisfactory workers as a sanction,[29] it seems in practice virtually as impossible to discharge a worker in an SEZ enterprise as it is elsewhere in China. Layoffs have occurred, for example, in Hitachi's joint venture in Fujian province, where 100 workers were determined to be "excess"; the venture was even allowed to fine a few workers who were negligent or insubordinate.[30] Nevertheless, without corresponding reform of employment practices in the Chinese domestic economy, foreign enterprises will continue to find it difficult to enforce a significantly "harsher" regime all by themselves.[31]

A final point of concern in this area for foreign investors has been the extensive rights and powers granted to joint venture trade unions, very little of which seems as of yet to have been exercised. In theory, however, trade union representatives can attend board meetings. Demands of labor, voiced through these organizations, with respect to issues such as wages, welfare benefits and labor discipline are supposed to be "heeded" and "cooperated with." The penalties for failing to heed the demands or not cooperating with the labor unions are unspecified.[32] This vagueness may help to ex-

---

[28] More information about Chinese labor law and the effects of the economic reforms on its recent development can be found in Josephs, *Labor Law in China: Choice and Responsibility* (Salem, New Hampshire: Butterworths Legal Publishers 1990).

[29] *See*, e . g., Regulations on Labour Management in the Xiamen Special Economic Zone, art. 18: The Special Zone enterprise may, according to the seriousness of each case, give necessary punishment and even dismissal to employees who violate the rules and regulations of the enterprise and cause certain consequences.
The Chinese text and an English translation appear in 1 China Laws for Foreign Business, para. 76-506(18), at 89,377 (CCH Australia Ltd. ed. 1985).

[30] Other joint ventures have developed even more creative methods, such as deductions from the salaries of poor producers. *See* "Parker-Hubei JV, Part 3: How the Venture Handles Power, Personnel Issues," *Business China*, June 20, 1988, at 81.

[31] One attempt to distinguish the rights of foreign enterprises from the generally prevailing regime was the "Eight-Point Decision on Personnel Management of Joint Ventures" issued by the Ministry of Labor and the Ministry of Personnel in 1988, emphasizing the autonomy of "foreign investment enterprises" in hiring and firing Chinese personnel. An English translation appears in *China Economic News*, May 30, 1988, at 2–3.

[32] *See* Regulations of the People's Republic of China on Labour Management in Joint Ventures Using Chinese and Foreign Investment (JV Labor Regulations) and Provisions for the Implementation of the Regulations on Labour Management in Joint Ventures Using Chinese

Continued

plain why Japanese investors have conspicuously shunned joint venture investment in China, given a very different tradition of labor-management relations in Japan.

CONTRACTUAL OBLIGATIONS

As many foreign businesses have learned to their chagrin, Chinese conceptions of contract are a good deal more flexible than those shared by most investors from the developed countries of the industrial world. Several highly publicized contractual disputes, including the cancellation of the contracts for the Baoshan Iron & Steel plant in the early 1980s and the AMC/Jeep joint venture disputes in the mid-1980s, have both discouraged additional investment and led existing investors to doubt the security of deals already made.[33] Whether due to their long experience of living under a planned economy or their bitter memories of unequal bargaining with foreigners before 1949, Chinese negotiators believe that every agreement can be reformulated if the circumstances are exigent enough and that foreign parties' insistence on contract observance is yet another example of foreign economic "imperialism."[34] The idea that one's carefully negotiated business agreement might become a platform for political posturing, or that—as was the case with Baoshan and later with the AMC/Jeep joint venture—high level government officials will have to rescue their nationals' investments by direct intervention is deeply disturbing to foreign investors.[35]

In more optimistic times, it was thought that greater familiarity with international commercial practice, as well as the inculcation of basic notions of contract law through the adoption of a Civil Code and economic contracts laws in China, would alleviate these problems with contracts.[36] Subsequent experience has demonstrated some improvement but indicated that many difficulties will prove persistent. Retrenchment of the domestic economy over the past few years and of foreign investment since June 4, 1989 has raised numerous issues related to the continued validity of contracts concluded earlier; the overall expansion of economic activity has ironically loosened the previous tight control of the central government over all foreign investment.

DISPUTE RESOLUTION

Most disputes involving China's foreign economic relations are resolved through non-judicial methods. Foreign investors are not especially keen to proceed in Chinese courts in any event; their rules of procedure are unclear, and the courts are notoriously sub-

---

and Foreign Investment (JV Labor Implementation Provisions). The Chinese text and an English translation of the JV Labor Regulations appear in 1 China Laws for Foreign Business, para. 6–520, at 7,861; the Chinese text and an English translation of the JV Labor Implementation Provisions appear in 1 China Laws for Foreign Business, para. 6–522, at 7,867 (CCH Australia Ltd. ed. 1985).

[33] *See , e . g.,* Sneider, "The Baoshan Debacle: A Study of Sino-Japanese Contract Dispute Settlement," 18 *New York University Journal of International Law and Politics,* No.2, at 541 (1986).

[34] *See* Macneil, "Contract in China: Law, Practice, and Dispute Resolution," 38 *Stanford Law Review,* no. 2, at 303 (1986).

[35] Engholm, *The China Venture: America's Corporate Encounter with the People's Republic of China* (Glenview, IL: Scott, Foresman 1989).

[36] *E . g.,* Hayden, "The Role of Contract Law in Developing the Chinese Legal Culture," 10 *Hastings International & Comparative Law Review* 571 (1987).

ject to political pressures, particularly from the Communist Party. Informal consultation and discussion between the disputants is encouraged by Chinese tradition and practice.[37] Most contracts involving foreigners also provide for some form of international mediation or arbitration, but these clauses themselves can often present a stumbling block for agreement. In the eyes of Chinese negotiators, third-country arbitration is a last resort; they prefer to stipulate friendly negotiation, conciliation and arbitration to take place in China. Foreign investor suggestions that more impartial bodies determine questions regarding investments in China are alternately condemned as an attack on the integrity of Chinese institutions or as an indication of prior intention to breach agreements. Grudgingly, Chinese negotiators have begun to accept third-country arbitration provisions in foreign investment contracts, but little evidence has yet accumulated in the form of outcomes of disputes arising from these contracts to indicate whether China will abide by the decisions of such bodies. Recent reports that China is itself turning to the courts to resolve its disputes with foreign trading companies offer some hope that formal judicial procedures may enjoy a new respectability.[38]

III. RECENT LEGAL REFORMS IN RESPONSE TO FOREIGN CONCERNS

On April 4, 1990, the National People's Congress issued amendments to the basic JVL, the most sweeping changes to this foundational law since its promulgation in 1979. In response to concerns voiced by foreign investors over the years and to the worries about China's continued commitment to foreign investment after the 1989 crackdown, these amendments were intended to heighten confidence and to allay fears. A new paragraph was added to Article 2 stating that the state will not nationalize joint ventures; if special circumstances require the requisitioning of a joint venture, appropriate compensation is to be paid according to legal procedures. Article 6 has been amended to permit a foreigner to be the chairman of the board of a joint venture; previously, the chairman had to be Chinese, although the vice-chairman could be foreign. Other amendments have broadened the terms for enjoyment of tax holidays, permitted the opening of foreign exchange accounts in financial institutions other than the Bank of China and relaxed the limits on duration of joint ventures which had previously stipulated a 50-year maximum.[39]

As was the case during previous attempts to attract foreign investment and to respond to criticism of shortcomings in the prevailing regulatory regime, these amendments seem unlikely to improve China's investment climate dramatically.[40] The general reac-

---

[37] Robinson & Doumar, " 'It is Better to Enter a Tiger's Mouth Than a Court of Law' or Dispute Resolution Alternatives in U.S.-China Trade," 5 *Dickinson Journal of International Law* 247 (1987).

[38] Song, "All Eyes on Swiss Court in Fraud Case," *China Daily*, Business Weekly, Nov. 20, 1989, at 1.

[39] "PRC Amends Joint Venture Law," 2 *Asian Law & Practice*, No. 3, Apr. 16, 1990 at 35.

[40] *E . g.*, Harding, "The Investment Climate in China," *The Brookings Review*, Spring 1987, at 37 (describing the 22 articles designed to encourage foreign investment issued in October, 1986; Harding concluded that even in the articles were interpreted fairly and implemented effectively, they addressed only a fraction of the problems encountered by the foreign business community).

tion of the foreign investor community has been skeptical; these amendments will not really give parties to an EJV significantly greater control over the management of the venture. Many of the provisions merely place the EJV on an equal footing with the other foreign investment enterprises in China, offering the same favorable treatment which CJVs and WFOEs already enjoy.[41] Yet even before the political fallout of the violent suppression of student demonstrators in June, 1989 began to be felt, foreign enthusiasm for investment in China had been waning. Domestic economic belt-tightening, announced in 1988, had adversely affected many joint ventures. Others had long suffered from foreign exchange difficulties, from shortages of raw materials, energy and skilled labor, from arbitrary price controls and restrictions on credit. None of these rather modest adjustments to the JVL addresses these problems. Nor is it likely, given the ambivalence of the top leadership towards foreign investment specifically and the process of economic reform of which it has been part more generally, that fundamental reform of the laws regulating joint ventures will soon occur. Experience at the local level exemplified in regulations formulated recently by the Shanghai Municipal People's Congress parallels that on the national level; some commentators have even argued that these regulations may have created new restrictions on foreign investment and potential sources of interference in the affairs of foreign business enterprises.[42] Despite these adverse reactions, the eagerness of Chinese officials to maintain a certain level of foreign investment should not be underestimated; indeed, the very enactment of new regulations was intended to respond—however unsuccessfully—to foreign investor concerns.

IV. The Regulatory Regime for Foreign Trade

The general trend over the past decade, at least until the last year, has been to shift responsibility for foreign trade to lower levels and to remove the control exercised by the central government Ministry of Foreign Economic Relations and Trade (MOFERT) and the foreign trade corporations (FTCs) which previously monopolized China's foreign commerce. In place of administrative dictates of quotas and production figures, contractual responsibility negotiated by enterprises, trading companies and lower-level governments were instituted in an attempt to move the PRC towards a more market-oriented foreign trade regimen.[43] Enterprises and other producers of goods for export were supposed to be able to choose among trading companies or, in a few instances, even to bypass the bureaucracy and to trade abroad directly.

The 1988 Draft Plan for Restructuring the Foreign Trade System was designed to give significant power to make decisions to enterprises and new trading companies, as well as provincial and local governments, in exchange for their acceptance of new regulatory oversight of their activities. Thus, direct administrative fiat was in-

---

[41] Robertson & Chen, "New Amendments to China's Equity Joint Venture Law: Changes Unlikely to Stimulate Foreign Investment," *East Asian Executive Reports*, April 1990, at 9.

[42] Gelatt, "New Rules for Investors," *The China Business Review*, March–April 1990, at 30.

[43] *See* Ross, "Changing the Foreign Trade System," *The China Business Review*, May–June 1988, at 34.

tended to yield to indirect guidance through legal controls. As had been the case with earlier attempts at reform in 1980 and 1985, however, the managers of China's foreign trade backed away from radical reform. MOFERT and the FTCs, never reconciled to the loss of their prerogatives, used the inevitable disruptions in trade patterns and the complaints of a few foreign buyers about price gouging and other abuses to clamp down on the proliferation of small local trading companies. Concern about the overheating domestic economy led to further restrictions on the foreign trade activities of factories in the hinterland.

Perhaps the greatest worry of Chinese regulators with respect to foreign trade has been the insatiable demand for imports which, left uncontrolled, could drain China of foreign exchange. Particularly with the entry of inexperienced participants into the realm of foreign trade, the dangers of heavy borrowing and shoddy imports were both presented. Central controls have been implemented to address these challenges, but their effectiveness has been limited. Once new avenues were opened up beyond the reach of the central planners, it became very difficult to control the forces unleashed.[44]

Of equal concern to the PRC has been its treatment under the foreign trade laws of other countries, particularly those of the United States. The 1988 Omnibus Trade Bill, which affected U.S. trade relations with almost all of its trading partners, was predicted to have significant effects on U.S.-China trade.[45] Trade relations with the PRC have been affected, but not necessarily as the authors of the trade originally envisioned.

One of the PRC's persistent problems with the United States has been the spate of anti-dumping suits brought by U.S. companies seeking to eliminate competitive low-price imports from the PRC. Under United States trade laws, the Commerce Department may order anti-dumping duties to be imposed on imports of goods sold in the U.S. for "less than fair value." In the case of China, and other non-market economies, this process has involved calculating a fair market value based on prices in a surrogate market-economy country at the same level of economic development to determine values more reliable than those established by a centrally planned, non-market economy.[46] Unfortunately, proposals to rationalize the treatment of non-market economies floated during the drafting of the Omnibus Trade Bill were not incorporated in the final legislation. As a result, China remains subject to the vagaries of U.S. trade policy, and importers remain as little able to predict the likelihood of anti-dumping duties being levied as they were before this legislative overhaul. Worst of all, obvious comparative advantages which the PRC enjoys are largely ignored by the methodology the new law has adopted.[47]

---

[44] See "Peking's About-Face on Trade Reform Leads China in the Wrong Direction," *Business China*, Sept. 11, 1989, at 129.

[45] Cohen, "Omnibus Trade Bill: Potential Effects on U.S.-China Trade," *East Asian Executive Reports*, February 1988, at 7. The bill as finally passed was entitled, "Omnibus Trade and Competitiveness Act of 1988," Pub. L. No. 100–418, pt. 4, Secs. 1371–82, 102 Stat. 1107.

[46] The absurdities resulting from such determinations are legion. See Alford, "When is China Paraguay? An Examination of the Application of the Antidumping and Countervailing Duty Laws of the United States to China and other "Nonmarket Economy" Nations,"61 Southern California Law Review 79 (1987).

[47] Neely, "Nonmarket Economy Import Regulation: From Bad to Worse," 20 Law and Policy in International Business 529 (1989).

Recent controversy over the extension of Most Favored Nation (MFN) status to the PRC has once again highlighted China's peculiar position as a trading partner of the U.S. Although China was granted MFN status in the year following normalization of relations, continued enjoyment of that status was made contingent on an annual review by the President and Congress, an unusual provision stemming from Congressional discomfort at extending MFN to the PRC originally. During the past year, a number of bills have been introduced in Congress to make continuation of China's MFN status contingent upon human rights improvements in the PRC.[48] While the prevailing sentiment seems to support President Bush's decision of May, 1990 to extend China's MFN status for another year, the uncertainty generated by the annual review process further exacerbates the precariousness of U.S.-China trade relations.

V. Conclusion

At this juncture, it is difficult to predict future developments with any assurance. Clearly, the PRC has demonstrated its commitment to the use of legal regulation to encourage foreign investment; without such laws, the current levels of investment would never have been reached. As China has become more familiar with the mechanisms for regulating foreign investment and with modern commercial law, its skill in legislation and enforcement has grown commensurately. Now that devices such as contract have become the norm in domestic economic relations, their use in foreign trade and investment no longer seems exceptional. After a period of experimentation and learning from its mistakes in this area, the PRC seems to have settled upon a clearer, more detailed system of law and regulation relating to foreign trade and investment. The passage of time and the benefit of experience has also provided foreign investors the knowledge necessary to challenge those aspects of Chinese foreign-related law which have disadvantaged foreign trade and investment and to make useful suggestions which will encourage foreign participation in China's economy. Despite some gaps and occasional disappointments, the past decade has seen an encouraging development of legal consciousness with respect to foreign trade and investment in the PRC.

---

[48] *E . g.*, H.R. 4939, 101st Cong., 2d Sess., approved by the House Ways and Means Committee on July 18, 1990.

REFORM AND RETRENCHMENT IN CHINA'S SPECIAL ECONOMIC ZONES

By George T. Crane *

CONTENTS

I. INTRODUCTION/SUMMARY

China's Special Economic Zones (SEZs) encompass all of the complexities and difficulties of the country's reform project. They are leaders in market-oriented economic restructuring and in opening China to the world economy. Taken together, the five SEZs are home to about one-fifth of all foreign investment in China. The Shenzhen SEZ is second only to Shanghai in exports and is vying to establish the PRC's first full-fledged stock market.[1] In the past two years, the Xiamen SEZ has become a major hub of Taiwan-financed joint ventures. Hainan province aspires to the rank of "most special" of SEZs. Even the less well-known zones in Zhuhai and Shantou have made significant strides in economic reform and openness. Yet for all of their accomplishments, SEZs have been vexed by persistent troubles. Infrastructural development has been expensive and inefficient; management has been fraught with charges of corruption; and foreign investment has been periodically disrupted by changing administrative rules and political controversies. In short, SEZs have produced both disappointments and benefits.

Over the past decade, SEZ gains and losses have fallen into a cyclical pattern of development.[2] Boom years have seen remarkable bursts of economic growth, foreign investment, and international trade. Such robust performance has inspired extensions of zone policy to other coastal areas. In 1984, optimistic assessments of SEZ

---

* Department of Political Science, Williams College.
[1] The comparison with Shanghai is made in: *China Today*, 39,6 (June 1990):24.
[2] George T. Crane, *The Political Economy of China's Special Economic Zones* (Armonk, NY: M.E. Sharpe, 1990), chapter 6.

success encouraged the opening of fourteen coastal cities to greater foreign economic participation. Similarly, in early 1985, three larger delta regions were granted SEZ-like preferences. At the other extreme, revelations of costliness and malfeasance have brought on occasional retrenchment. In mid-1985, SEZs were subjected to withering criticism and increasing regulation. Political discord has also hampered zone reform. In 1987, the fall of Communist Party General Secretary Hu Yaobang and the subsequent antibourgeois liberalization campaign sent a chill through the Shenzhen SEZ.

Retrenchment, however, has usually been short-lived. SEZ critics are not unrepentant Maoists longing for a self-reliant, autarkic past. They are technocrats interested in modernizing the country—within certain economic, political, and ideological limits. Their attempts to counter preceived SEZ shortcomings have often contradicted their desire for development. When economic liberalization is constrained, foreign investors reduce their commitments, robbing the zones, and the country as a whole, of the wherewithal for economic modernization. The result is usually a return to liberalizing intiatives, at least until the next local scandal or national crisis. The SEZs are, therefore, both unstable and durable. They are inherently costly and evoke powerful condemnation but cannot be easily restricted or dismantled.

The events of the past three years, 1988–1990, have repeated the cycle of reform and retrenchment in the SEZs. For the first three quarters of 1988, Communist Party General Secretary Zhao Ziyang energetically sponsored coastal development, an effort that lifted the fortunes of the SEZs. The nationwide economic rectification in the fall of 1988 did not spare the zones, however. Infrastructural development was cut, foreign exchange preferences were rescinded, and zonal economic strategy was called into question. The Beijing massacre and fall of Zhao Ziyang in 1989 made matters worse. A number of key SEZ administrators were closely tied to Zhao and his demise weakened the political basis of zone policy. Throughout the summer the future of SEZs was uncertain and foreign investment stagnated. The tide turned in the fall when the reconstituted Beijing leadership endorsed SEZ policy at the Fifth Plenum of the Thirteenth Central Committee. In the first half of 1990, reform was again the priority.

The 1988–1990 period is not exactly the same as previous cycles of reform and retrenchment. The depth of the 1989 political crisis was unprecedented. This, however, did not preclude a reform revival. Perhaps more noteworthy is the introduction of significant levels of investment from Taiwan. In Xiamen, Taiwan is now the single largest "foreign" investor. The increasing presence of Taiwan capital on the mainland may have important implications for the political reconciliation of the PRC and the ROC.

II. Policy and Economic Performance

A. SPECIAL ECONOMIC ZONE POLICY

China's SEZs were instituted in 1979.[3] Shortly after the land-mark Third Plenum of the Eleventh Central Committee meeting in December 1978, the Shekou Industrial District was opened in Guangdong Province. Guangdong officials soon established three "Special Economic Zones" in Shenzhen (which includes the smaller Shekou district), Zhuhai, and Shantou. After some parochial bickering, Fujian province announced plans to establish a fourth SEZ in Xiamen. Hainan Island was not formally identified as an SEZ until 1988.

SEZs are loosely modeled on Export Processing Zones (EPZs) found in other less developed countries. They are specifically delineated areas within which a variety of economic inducements are offered to foreign investors in an effort to turn global opportunities toward national development. Ideally, overseas investors enjoy preferential tax rates, reduced tariffs, flexible labor and wage policies, more modern infrastructure, and less bureaucracy than elsewhere in China. In practice, the SEZ competitive edge has dulled over the years due to recurrent government interventions and the diffusion of reform policies to other coastal areas.

The objectives of China's zone policy are ambiguous.[4] The scope of economic activity is broader than the usual EPZ focus on processing and assembly for export. Agriculture, manufacturing, heavy industry, and infrastructure development are all encouraged and open to foreign investment. The size of the SEZs, especially Shenzhen's 327 square kilometers, also distinguishes them from EPZs, which are often less than 10 square kilometers in area. Nevertheless, the typical EPZ development strategy has been espoused by SEZ administrators. This favors the creation of export-oriented joint ventures and foreign subsidiaries that will provide employment for Chinese workers, managerial experience for Chinese technicians, and markets for Chinese raw materials and inputs. Such an "outward-oriented" strategy contrasts with an "inward-oriented" development plan advocated by some SEZ supporters. This latter approach emphasizes import-substituting production by foreign-funded enterprises. Advanced industrial technology would also be directly transferred through SEZs to the hinterland. Evaluations of SEZ success or failure depend upon which strategy is used as a standard.

By either strategy, SEZs must advance domestic economic restructuring. Successful export promotion and import substitution require improved product quality and productivity. To attain these ends, SEZ administrators have been in the vanguard of institutional reform, reducing party interference in factories, introducing market regulation, and nurturing entrepreneurship. Some of the country's boldest reform experiments are to be found in the SEZs:

---

[3] Excellent analyses of early zone policy are: Victor Falkenheim, "China's Special Economic Zones," in U.S. Congress, Joint Economic Committee, *China's Economy Looks to the Year 2000*, vol. II, (Washington, GPO, 1986), pp.348–370; Suzanne Pepper, "China's Special Economic Zones," *USFI Reports*, 14, 1986.

[4] Crane, 1990, pp. 40–48, 116–122.

public bidding for land rights, commercialization of housing, and stock trading. As in other socialist states, the transition to a market-based economy has created new problems. Inflation and unemployment have, at times, been troublesome. But these are offset by the perceived quality of life in the SEZs. Young and talented Chinese from all over the country, enthusiastic for economic change, long to work in the SEZs.

The actual performance of SEZs reflects their dual character, outward- and inward-oriented. Foreign investment has been drawn into the zones and export industries have been established. In ten years, the five SEZs have attracted a cumulative total of roughly US$ 4.1 billion in *actual* foreign investment and exported over US$ 10 billion worth of products. This is no mean accomplishment in that, before 1979, the SEZ localities were sleepy coastal towns of negligible economic significance. As they turned toward the world, however, SEZs became more closely linked to the national economy. Attracting foreign investment necessitated offering international firms access to the domestic market, a strategy referred to as "exchanging market for technology." [5] Zone-produced goods, many with a very high import content, as well as foreign-made products traded through SEZs, are sold nationwide. SEZs, therefore, have rarely run trade surpluses. Moreover, to maximize linkages between the world market and the domestic economy, Chinese firms from all over the country have been urged to set up operations in SEZs. In Shenzhen, domestic enterprises account for about 40 percent of the gross value of industrial output (GVIO).[6] SEZs thus serve both world market and domestic economy.

B. ECONOMIC PERFORMANCE OF SHENZHEN

Shenzhen is the powerhouse of SEZs. It has the largest economy, the most foreign investment, and the greatest volume of exports (see Table 1).

TABLE 1. Shenzhen SEZ Performance, 1987–1989

Year	GVIO (billion RMB)	Actual Foreign Investment (US $ millions)	Exports (US $ billions)
1987	5.76 (62)	404 (−17)	2.04 (122)
1988	8.88 (54)	444 (10)	1.85 (−9)
1989	11.64 (31)	458 (3)	2.17 (18)

Note: Figures in parentheses are percentage increases over previous year.
Sources: *Far Eastern Economic Review,* March 2, 1989:60; Shenzhen Statistical Bureau, "Shenzhen Vital Statistics Survey, 1989" ["Shenzhenshi 1989 Nian Zhuyao Tongji Shuzi Yilan"].

Shenzhen's economic growth, especially industrial expansion, is extraordinary. Even in "bad" years, such as the 1989 economic contraction, Shenzhen's economy has flourished. High growth rates are due, in part, to the underdevelopment of Shenzhen's economy before 1979. Starting from a very low base, industrialization in the

---

[5] *Ibid.*, pp. 80–81.
[6] Shenzhen Statistical Bureau, "Shenzhen City 1989 Vital Statistics Survey."

1980s is statistically stunning. This is not to suggest that growth is simply a mathematical mirage; it is real, propelled by foreign and domestic investment. Actual foreign investment has exceeded US $400 million annually since 1986, when it reached its peak at US $498 million. Pledged foreign investment is typically higher, climbing to a reported US $1.02 billion in 1985.[7] In some years, less than half of pledged investment has actually been used, an indication of wariness among foreign businessmen. Although actual foreign investment has also flucutated over the years—declining in 1982, 1985, and 1987—a steady inflow of overseas capital has facilitated Shenzhen's growth.

More than three-quarters of Shenzhen's "foreign" investment comes from Hong Kong.[8] The SEZ is adjacent to the British enclave and propinquity facilitates movement of capital across the border. In recent years, Taiwan money has become more visible in Shenzhen. By mid-year 1989, approximately 98 Taiwan-funded joint ventures worth US $148 million in "total investment" were in operation.[9] Large firms from North America, Europe, and Japan, such as Digital Electronic Corporation and Seiko, are to be found in Shenzhen but the vast majority of the more than 2,500 registered foreign-funded businesses are small processing and assembly operations from Hong Kong.[10] Real estate development, particularly housing construction for Shenzhen's burgeoning population, has also been a major attraction for Hong Kong investors.[11]

Investment from domestic Chinese sources is the second pillar of the Shenzhen economy. As mentioned above, Chinese enterprises enter the SEZ to take advantage of the relatively liberal environment. Indigenous firms contribute to joint ventures with foreign partners or they link up with other Chinese companies to do business internationally. Other government agencies and financial institutions have also helped to build Shenzhen. Central government budgetary expenditures, loans from national and provincial banks, and funds from central ministries and provincial offices have all supported capital construction in Shenzhen. Taken together, the various forms of domestic investment have exceeded the total amount of actual foreign investment in most years (see Figure 1).[12]

The relationship between domestic and foreign investment is a sensitive issue for Shenzhen. In 1985, domestic spending toppped US $700 million a year and actual foreign investment fell to under US $200 million. Critics argued that scarce national resources were being wasted, not yielding sufficient levels of foreign investment. In the early years of zone policy such complaints were turned aside

---

[7] This figure may be inflated by pledged debt, see: Crane, 1990, p. 115.

[8] Figures on Hong Kong capital in Shenzhen are often overstated for two reason: some "Hong Kong" investments are actually the work of discreet Taiwan businessmen; and funds from mainland Chinese organizations are sometimes funneled through Hong Kong for investment in Shenzhen.

[9] Zhongguo Xinwen She, July 5, 1989, FBIS, July 7, 1989:37. "Total investment" includes both domestic Chinese and foreign contributions to joint ventures.

[10] Early reports for 1990 suggest a new problem, however. Hong Kong investors, wary of political and economic risks in China, are looking for investment opportunities elsewhere in East Asia. *Far Eastern Economic Review*, September 20, 1990: 92-93.

[11] Total population, including both "temporary" and permanent residents, for Shenzhen municipality in 1989 was 1.9 million an increase of 25 percent over the 1988 number, see: Shenzhen Statistical Bureau, "Shenzhen Vital Statistics Survey, 1989."

[12] Figure 1 is taken from, Crane, 1990: 151.

FIGURE 1.

**A Comparison of Domestic Infrastructural Spending
and Actual Foreign Investment in Shenzhen, 1979–1987.
(U.S.$ million)**

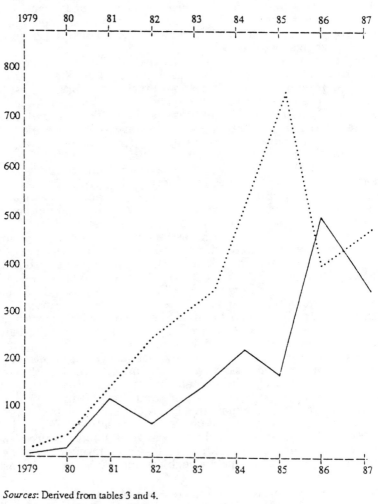

Sources: Derived from tables 3 and 4.

.... = domestic infrastructural spending

_____ = actual foreign investment

with the contention that SEZs needed time to mature fully. Over time, however, the problem has persisted. Vice Premier Tian Jiyun, generally supportive of zone policy, warned in 1989 that

Shenzhen "should not rely on state funds." [13] He thus recalled political, as well as economic, vulnerabilities. It is questionable whether Shenzhen's rapid growth could be sustained without domestic investment. Moreover, competing regional and bureaucratic interests can, and do, argue that the money would be better spent on their pet projects, developing the Pudong zone in Shanghai, for example, or adopting a sectoral industrial policy.

Although domestic investment is double-edged—it both fuels growth and sparks controversy—the resultant economic development has clearly boosted Shenzhen's international trade. Before 1979, its major export was people who slipped across the border to find better lives in Hong Kong. After a decade of investment and growth, Shenzhen now exports upward of US $2 billion of goods annually. A significant portion, over 75 percent, of these products, are manufactures. [14] Export figures must be interpreted with care, however. Goods from other parts of the country are transhipped through Shenzhen and are often reported as SEZ exports. This confounds precise measurement of zone-produced exports, but it does not negate the fact that export-oriented manufacturing has arisen in Shenzhen.

On the other side of the ledger, Shenzhen's imports have usually outstripped exports. In 1984, for example, when exports totaled approximately US $265 million, imports surged to US $807 million. [15] A number of factors contribute to strong import demand. Expensive capital goods must be purchased to build Shenzhen's export base. In addition, the many assembly and processing enterprises in the SEZs are import dependent, relying upon components and materials from overseas suppliers. Consumer goods are also shipped, legally and illegally, through Shenzhen to anxious buyers all over China. Trade deficits are, therefore, the rule for Shenzhen. Official figures suggest that the pattern was reversed in 1988 and 1989 with trade surpluses of US $260 million and $570 million, repectively. These numbers probably under-report imports, however, casting doubt on the achievement of surpluses. [16]

In sum, many of Shenzhen's economic gains are matched by frustrations. Rapid growth comes at a high price in national investment. Exports are borne on a tide of imports. Other facets of zone policy are equally ambiguous. Technology transfer, which is difficult to measure precisely, has occurred, especially through the larger joint ventures, but with few of the dramatic breakthroughs envisioned by optimistic SEZ proponents. The profusion of small processing and assembly enterprises and the appeal of real estate development are not conducive to large-scale technology upgrading. One result, however, may transcend contervailing costs. The entre-

[13] Beijing Radio Report, FBIS, March 27, 1989, p. 23.
[14] Detailed and reliable composition of trade figures are not available. The 75 percent figure is based on a report that 58 percent of GVIO is exported, see: Shenzhen Statistical Bureau, "Shenzhen Vital Statistics Survey, 1989."
[15] People's Daily, December 13, 1985.
[16] Far Eastern Economic Review, March 2, 1989:60 reports 1987 Shenzhen imports as US $2.25 billion. The Shenzhen Statistical Bureau states the 1988 figure as US $1.59 billion. Either one source is inaccurate or Shenzhen's imports dropped by roughly 30 percent in 1988, a year of booming growth in the SEZs and expanding imports natiowide. Since official figures are periodically revised, and sometimes do not count the import content of exported manufactures, a certain skepticism toward the claim of a trade surplus is warranted.

preneurial initiative unleashed in Shenzhen, and throughout the Pearl River Delta, has spawned a multitude of small independent businesses. The productivity and flexiblity of this nascent private sector may be China's best hope for managing successfully the rigors of economic reform.

C. THE XIAMEN, ZHUHAI, SHANTOU, AND HAINAN ZONES

China's other SEZs have generally followed Shenzhen's pattern of development, albeit on smaller scales. After a slow start, Xiamen has become the second most important SEZ. In the past two years, Xiamen's foreign investment and exports have expanded considerably (Table 2).

TABLE 2. Xiamen SEZ Performance, 1987–1989

Year	GVIO (billion RMB)	Planned Foreign Investment (US $ millions)	Exports (US $ billions)
1987	3.174 (47)	58 (111)	304 (44)
1988	n.a.	134 (131)	500 (64)
1989	n.a.	769 (474)	1983 (297)

Note: Figures in parentheses are percentage increases over previous year.
Sources: *Far Eastern Economic Review*, March 2, 1989:60; Xinhua News Service, February 20, 1989, FBIS, February 24, 1989:48; *People's Daily*, January 29, 1990:2, FBIS, February 15, 1990:19.

The reason for Xiamen's recent success is Taiwan capital. In 1988, 80 Taiwan-funded projects were planned for Xiamen. This was a remarkable turn of events as only about 20 Taiwan ventures had been negotiated previously.[17] Taiwan companies signed 138 more agreements in 1989.[18] The year was very good for Xiamen, compared to most other parts of the country, because Taiwan businesses did not retreat in the aftermath of the Beijing massacre.[19] Moreover, future prospects are bright. Formosa Plastics, one of Taiwan's largest multinational corporations, is planning a US multibillion dollar petrochemical plant for Xiamen. If the proposal withstands criticism from the Taiwan government, it would be one of the largest foreign enterprises in China.

The current bull market in Xiamen has not come free of charge. In the past eight years capital construction has totaled 3.7 billion yuan, mostly from Chinese sources.[20] Xiamen has not, however, attracted as much criticism as Shenzhen for "relying on state funds." Perhaps Shenzhen's notoriety has politically shielded the other SEZs. Xiamen's development has also been import-dependent. In 1987, it reported a trade deficit of US $184 million. The absence of reliable import figures for 1988 and 1989 suggests that this trend has yet to be reversed.

The Zhuhai SEZ in Guangdong province has fared less well than Xiamen in the past two years. Situated next to the Portuguese en-

[17] Derived from Xinhua, FBIS, January 4, 1989, p. 78.
[18] Xinhua, FBIS, January 10, 1990, p. 35.
[19] Zhongguo Xinwenshe, FBIS, July 7, 1989, 89–129, p. 37.
[20] *People's Daily*, January 29, 1990:2, FBIS, February 15,1990:19.

clave of Macao, Zhuhai was to be a counterpart to Shenzhen. Although much smaller (15.6 square kilometers), it was originally planned as a "comprehensive" SEZ, open to a wide variety of foreign projects. Real estate development, tourism, processing and assembly enterprises, and some higher technology industrial firms contributed to its economic growth in the early years. 1988 was the high point with industrial production doubling and actual foreign investment tripling (Table 3).

TABLE 3. Zhuhzi SEZ Performance, 1987–1989

Year	GVIO (billion RMB)	Actual Foreign Investment (US $ millions)	Exports (US $ billions)
1987	1.215	69	319
	(80)	(−8)	(122)
1988	2.54	218	421
	(110)	(216)	(32)
1989	2.95	249	350
	(16)	(14)	(−17)

Note: Figures in parentheses are percentage increases over previous year. 1989 numbers are estimates.

Sources: *Far Eastern Economic Review*, [*FEER*] March 2, 1989:60; *People's Daily*, September 11, 1989:4, FBIS, September 20, 1989:43.; *Ming Pao*, January 7, 1990:18, FBIS, January 12, 1990:38; *FEER*, February 8, 1990:38.

The turnabout in 1989 was worse than the official statistics suggest. Although both industrial output and foreign investment apparently grew at relatively modest rates, other sources indicate that nearly 30 percent of the zone's factories were forced to shut down.[21] This casts doubt on whether industrial production could have grown 16 percent. The reasons for Zhuhai's woes were a combination of nationwide economic retrenment begun in the fall of 1988, which curtailed domestic investment, and wariness on the part of foreign businesmen, who scaled back their activities. Zhuhai had neither Xiamen's concentration of Taiwan capital nor Shenzhen's volume of prior foreign investment commitments to carry it through 1989.

The fourth original SEZ, Shantou, trails the other three in trade and investment (Table 4). Its location, further away from Hong Kong than Shenzhen or Zhuhai, is partially responsible for its sluggishness. It also lacks the strong historic ties to Taiwan that have helped Xiamen so much. Shantou's comparatively large GVIO is not an accurate indicator of development in the 1980s; the city had a broader industrial base prior to 1979 than the other SEZs.[22]

Unlike the other SEZs, Shantou's performance in 1988 was not good. Indeed, the success of other zones and coastal cities may have come at Shantou's expense, as indicated by the 58 percent decline in actual foreign investment. The next year was no better. Partial figures show that the number of "projects using foreign funds" fell by almost half in 1989, from 238 in 1988 to 120.[23] The "total invest-

[21] *Far Eastern Economic Review*, February 8, 1990, pp. 38–39.
[22] Shantou Municipal Office, *Handbook on Investment and Tourism in Shantou* (Beijing: Beijing Review, 1986), pp. 22–30.
[23] *Ming Pao*, January 22, 1990, FBIS, January 25, 1990, p. 25.

TABLE 4. Shantou SEZ Performance, 1987–1988

Year	GVIO (billion RMB)	Actual Foreign Investment (US $ millions)	Exports (US $ billions)
1987	4.75	81	279
	(35)	(47)	(−4)
1988	5.47	34	298
	(15)	(−58)	(7)

Note: Figures in parentheses are percentage increases over previous year.
Sources: *Far Eastern Economic Review*, March 2, 1989:60; *People's Daily*, September 11, 1989:4, FBIS, September 20, 1989:43.

ment" of these projects also dropped from US $200 million to US $150 million. Shantou thus remains the least dynamic SEZ.

Hainan island has had mixed fortunes since it officially became a special zone in 1988. Development in the first year was complicated by its simultaneous elevation to provincial administrative status. Basic governing institutions had to be built from scratch. Economically, it had little in the way of modern economic infrastructure. In light of these conditions, Hainan reformers had to devise a novel approach to SEZ development. They decided to lease a large tract of land to foreign investors for a long period of time. Thus 45,000 mu (30km^2) in the Yangpu area of Northwest Hainan would be let for 70 years at a rent of 2000 yuan per mu.[24] The lead investor was a Japanese-based firm, Kumagai Gumi, but overseas Chinese capital was involved as well. The foreign partners were contracted to build modern port facilities, a power plant, and several heavy industrial projects. The area would be managed as a "free port," minimizing economic regulations. To Hainan administrators, Yangpu offered large-scale development with little strain on national resources.

The Yangpu scheme, controversial from the start, ran into serious problems in 1989. Political resentment toward preceived subservience to foreigners and bureaucratic obstacles to effective implementation have cast doubt on the project's viability. Foreign investment from other sources has begun to flow into Hainan. According to incomplete data, Hainan attracted approximately US $350 million in planned foreign investment in 1988.[25] Pledges fell in 1989 by 26 percent to US $280 million.[26] Although the daring Yangpu project is uncertain and economic infrastructure is outmoded, Hainan island is gradually being transformed into an SEZ.

---

[24] *Jingji Ribao*, August 10, 1989, p. 2, FBIS, August 31, 1989, p. 40.

[25] Xinhua, FBIS, December 30, 1988, 88–251, p. 59. A later analysis states 463 contracts signed in 1988 with US $600 million in planned foreign investment, of which US $110 million had actually been utilized, see: Xinhua, FBIS, March 29, 1989, p. 58. The US $600 million seems unlikely, however, since *Far Eastern Economic Review*, August 23, 1990, implies about US $353.

[26] *Far Eastern Economic Review*, August 23, 1990. These numbers contradict an earlier report of 344 new foreign investment enterprises worth US $370 million in planned investment by October of 1989, see: *Wen Wei Po*, January 5, 1990, FBIS, January 23, 1990, 90–015, p. 48.

III. POLITICS

A. THE CYCLE OF SEZ POLITICS

Since their inception, China's SEZs have been buffeted by domestic politics as fluid coalitions of supporters and detractors attempt to, respectively, expand or reduce the scope of zone policy. Opposition has been evident from the start. Bureaucratic, regional, and ideological political forces wary of economic change have warned of a variety of SEZ ills, from foreign exchange imbalances to "Hong Kong-ization." In the early years, SEZ supporters were able to hold skeptics at bay with promises of positive results that would offset most concerns. As time went on, powerful national leaders publicly acclaimed SEZs. Party General Secretary Hu Yaobang energetically backed zone policy in 1983 and Deng Xiaoping offered his praise during a much-heralded trip to Shenzhen, Zhuhai, and Xiamen in 1984. Solid political support reassured foreign investors and engendered domestic budgetary outlays for SEZ development. Expansion of zone policy to other coastal cities and regions followed in 1984 and early 1985. SEZs seemed invincible.

The situation deteriorated rapidly in March 1985, when national and local economic problems animated SEZ critics. Vice-Premier Yao Yilin and Communist party ideologue Hu Qiaomu, openly challenged zone policy. Retrenchment ensued with the reimposition of central government oversight to combat foreign exchange losses, smuggling, and dependence on state funds. The changed political atmosphere caused Deng Xiaoping to back off his previous pro-zone stance; association with an apparent policy failure could have negative political ramifications, even for the paramount leader. Recentralization could not last, however. Increased regulation by more government agencies undermined SEZ comparative advantage in attracting foreign capital. Conservative technocrats, worried that economic modernization might be derailed by declining foreign investment, thus acquiesced in a revival of reform initiatives. By the end of 1986, the ethos of accelerated SEZ development and expansion was ascendant.

The regeneration of reform in 1986 was cut short by the anti-bourgeois liberalization campaign of 1987. Although the economic framework of zone policy was not altered by political events, as was the case in 1985, foreign investors were scared off. Actual foreign investment for 1987 decreased in Shenzhen, Xiamen, and Zhuhai.[27] The pall of political disfavor was lifted by a resurgence of the liberal agenda at the Thirteenth National Party Congress in November 1987.

Following the conclave, newly appointed party General Secretary Zhao Ziyang unequivocally advocated zone expansion during a three-month trip of coastal provinces. Zhao outlined a far-reaching development policy, which would extend liberalization beyond the existing open cities, zones, and deltas, to include virtually all of China's coastal territory.[28] As the year progressed and the propos-

---

[27] *Far Eastern Economic Review*, March 2, 1989:60.
[28] *People's Daily*, January 23, 1988:1; *Beijing Review*, February 8, 1988:14–19.

al was implemented, 288 counties in 10 provinces, encompassing 320,000 square kilometers of land and 160 million people, were given SEZ-like preferences.[29]

Coastal development magnified the significance of SEZs. If the entire coast opened more widely to the world economy, the four original zones would be national models of international economic integration.[30] Ironically, the coastal strategy also robbed SEZs of their specialness. Other areas, especially the townships of the Pearl River Delta, could offer incentives (low-wage labor, tax preferences, cheap land-use fees, etc.) comparable, if not superior to, SEZs. On balance, however, the coastal strategy helped zone policy more than it hurt. Buoyed by the renewed national spirit of economic opening, SEZ administrators redoubled their efforts at reform. In Xiamen, local leaders worked in earnest to attract Taiwan capital.[31] Fujian provincial officials also made a bid for Taiwan-funded enterprises, announcing that several Taiwan investment zones would be established around the province.[32]

Hainan island reflected the liberal tenor of the time. Having been granted provincial status and formally declared an SEZ at the first session of the Seventh National People's Congress in early 1988, Hainan was the most ambitious project of coastal development. The local leadership promised to make their SEZ-province more "special" than other zones. Perhaps the best indication of Hainan's commitment to bold liberalization was its governor: Liang Xiang. As mayor of Shenzhen from 1981 to 1985 Liang had firmly established his reformist credentials; few national figures were as outspoken and energetic in their support of opening China to the world economy. No image better captures the resurgence of zone policy in 1988 than Liang Xiang at the helm of the most special of SEZs.

Revived enthusiasm for SEZs was both a consequence and a cause of national political dynamics. Most important in this regard was the position of Zhao Ziyang. Although he had backed SEZs since 1979, Zhao tended to be circumspect in his support, sensitive to the limits and failings of international opening.[33] His advocacy of coastal development signaled a lessening in his ambivalence. Zhao was now personally linked to the extension of zone policy all along the eastern seaboard. If SEZs or coastal development failed, Zhao's political standing could be endangered. He was thus running a political risk but he may have had little choice. Hu Yaobang's fall in 1987 revealed the strength of ideological conservatives and reform skeptics. To counter these political forces, strong pro-reform constituencies had to be created. Insofar as coastal development gave provincial and local officials a greater stake in the open policy, it widened Zhao's political base. He would be their

[29] Xinhua July 5, 1988, FBIS, July 6, 1988, p. 43.
[30] This point was made in a report by the Economic Structural Reform Research Institute, the Beijing think-tank headed by Chen Yizi. They stressed SEZ contributions to structural reform, especially in furthering the "competitive pluralization of enterprise structure," and the creation of "independent entrepreneurs." See: Shenzhen: Xintizhi Yanjiu (Shenzhen: Zhonggong Shenzhen Shiwei Zhengce Yanjiushi, 1988), chapter 1.
[31] FBIS, June 7, 1988, p. 65.
[32] CEI Database (Beijing) report, FBIS, August 23, 1988, p. 37.
[33] Crane, 1990, pp. 137–138.

benefactor. Political concerns, therefore, may have inspired Zhao's push for SEZ expansion and coastal development.

Zhao's coastal gambit was well played in early 1988. Premier Li Peng promoted Hainan's move to provincial status, suggesting that he was not opposed to SEZ expansion.[34] Although Zhao would later clash with Li over economic strategy, the General Secretary's coastal policy did not diverge widely from the Premier's position. Zhao also enjoyed the apparent support of Deng Xiaoping, who reverted to a pro-zone stance in June.[35] The year was shaping up well for SEZ advocates.

B. THE 1988 RETRENCHMENT

Circumstances changed, however, in September. The nationwide economic retrenchment inaugurated at the Third Plenum of the Thirteen Central Committee spared neither SEZs nor coastal policy. In the wake of the Plenum, the percentage of earned foreign exchange retained in SEZs was reduced from 100 percent to 80 percent.[36] This was especially hurtful because one of the few advantages SEZ administrators had in the keen national competition for overseas investment was their foreign exchange reserves. By one estimate, Shenzhen alone stood to lose US $70 million in foreign exchange that it would now have to remit to Beijing.[37] SEZs were also subject to the recentralization of trade policy and the approval process for foreign investment implemented throughout the country.[38]

Economic retrenchment changed the political context. Criticisms of coastal policy and SEZs were raised by both liberals and conservatives.[39] Zhao Ziyang and others fought back, assuring foreign investors that the coastal policy would be unscathed by retrenchment.[40] In making this argument, however, Zhao began to waver in his support of the SEZs.[41] He characterized zones as "correct and successful" but said that *new* reforms "can become possible only when Shenzhen does not affect the conditions in the interior areas." With this statement, he implicitly accepted the argument that zones did not sufficiently promote inland development. He may have been indicating limits to SEZ development in order to preserve what had already been accomplished there. Alternatively, he may have been willing to countenance restrictions on SEZs so as to deflect criticism away from the larger coastal policy, which was politically more sensitive for him. As further suggested by the dissipation of SEZ preferences, Zhao was possibly sacrificing zones to save the coastal strategy.

Zhao's problems mounted, however, as differences over coastal policy came out into the open at the second session of the Seventh

---

[34] *Ibid.*, pp. 139–140.

[35] *Hong Kong Standard*, August 12, 1988, p. 6, FBIS, August 12, 1988, p. 54.

[36] *Wen Wei Po*, October 15, 1988, p. 2, FBIS, October 19, 1988, pp. 38–39.

[37] *South China Morning Post*, January 4, 1989, FBIS, January 4, 1989, p. 68.

[38] *South China Morning Post*, February 1, 1989, FBIS, February 1, 1989, p. 60; *People's Daily*, March 16, 1989, FBIS, March 23, 1989, p. 64.

[39] For a fuller analysis of the politics of this period see: George T. Crane, "China's Special Economic Zones in 1989: Continuity and Change," *Issues and Studies* (Forthcoming).

[40] FBIS, December 5, 1988, p. 28.

[41] *Wen Wei Po*, February 9, 1989, p. 1, FBIS February 9, 1989, p. 10; *South China Morning Post*, February 10, 1989, p.8, FBIS, February 10, 1989, p. 23.

NPC in March 1989. Premier Li Peng, in his government work report to the NPC, began to move away from his earlier endorsement of Zhao's coastal policy.[42] Li was not looking to return China to the Maoist past; he promised to honor all existing contracts and promote international trade. What he resisted was the threat of trade imbalances and inflation bred of decentralized economic power.

Nor was Li an unregenerate SEZ hater. While no doubt wary of expanding zone reforms to the coastal region as a whole, he was willing to allow SEZs to experiment in new ways. At the NPC meeting it was Li who submitted a controversial plan granting greater legislative autonomy to local Shenzhen authorities.[43] On the other hand, Li would not shield zones from economic rectification as evidenced by the State Council's limitation on SEZ foreign exchange retention. Perhaps he was not worried about the national impact of local Shenzhen legislation because the macroeconomic environment was coming under tigher central control. The overall effect of Li's activities was to deflate the previous celebration of coastal develoment. He did not reject, at this point, coastal strategy or SEZs per se but he did make clear his priority of financial stability.

The opening months of national austerity were thus a trial for SEZs. Revocation of foreign exchange preferences and other reform measures vitiated the zones' uniqueness. A range of criticism, from conservative to liberal, undercut their credibility. Hainan's Yangpu plan was attacked for "selling out to the Japanese." And, to add insult to injury, key central sponsors appeared ready to sacrifice SEZs to save the coastal strategy. As bad as the situation was, however, it worsened after the Beijing massacre.

C. THE IMPACT OF THE BEIJING MASSACRE

The 1989 crisis had two principal effects on zone policy. First, it left SEZ activists politically vulnerable. Many zone officials had close ties to Zhao Ziyang and they were liable to be implicated in the General Secretary's disgrace. Second, as Zhao fell, policies closely associated with him were cast into doubt. Would the coastal strategy continue? If it was undone, what would become of SEZs? Such fundamental political and policy questions dominated the balance of 1989.

Although SEZs were not a focal point of the national student movement, they were involved. The Shekou Industrial Zone in Shenzhen, headed by Yuan Geng, funneled 100,000 yuan to the Beijing protestors, making it one of the leading financiers of the movement.[44] Perhaps this is what Deng Xiaoping had in mind on June 9 when, in a nationally circulated speech to martial law cadres, he castigated SEZs for "obvious inadequacies".[45] Deng equivocated yet again and, in doing so, clouded the future of SEZ reform.

---

[42] See Text of Li's speech in: FBIS, March 21, 1989, pp. 24–25.
[43] FBIS, March 28, 1989, 89–058, p. 9.
[44] *South China Morning Post*, September 15, 1989, FBIS, September 15, 1989, p.8.
[45] *Beijing Review*, number 28, July 10–16, 1989, p. 20.

The more immediate trouble for SEZs was the impending campaign against corruption in Guangdong and Hainan. Southern provinces had their fair share of corruption, but the intensity and scale of the ensuing crusade suggests a political rationale as well. One of the first to be accused was the most prominent: Hainan governor, Liang Xiang. In July, Liang was summoned to Beijing were he remained for several weeks as an investigation into his alleged economic crimes commenced.[46] His close personal ties to Zhao Ziyang and Zhao's sons complicated his case. Finally, in September, Liang was relieved of all his offices by the Central Committee and the State Council. Liu Jianfeng, a Jiang Zemin protege, was named governor of Hainan.

Liang's fall sent a chilling political message to all SEZ admirers. He was among the most senior and well-connected of reformers. His impressive *guanxi* network, which a few weeks earlier insured his political safety, was transformed, virtually overnight, into a reason for his demise. As could be expected, Zhao Ziyang's sons, with whom Liang had worked in both Shenzhen and Hainan, were also charged with economic crimes. These three cases turned the national spotlight on corruption in SEZs. Ultimately, though, all charges against Liang were dropped. He was pushed out of office but not officially convicted of malfeasance.[47] His fame may have saved him. Prosecutors had to limit action against him for fear of scaring off foreign investors. Liang, as a symbol of international openness, was useful even for the conservative Beijing leadership.

Other SEZ leaders felt the glare of official scrutiny. Li Hao, mayor of Shenzhen, was investigated for corruption.[48] The mayor of Zhuhai, Liang Guangda, was formally reprimanded for living in an overly sumptuous residence.[49] The cluster of corruption reports stigmatized the open policy and weakened the political standing of local reformers.[50] In addition, an inquest into Yuan Geng's support of the Beijing students, hampered the administration of the most progressive SEZ enclave, the Shekou Industrial District. The witch-hunt threatened to quash zone policy.

The full extent of the crisis of zone policy was not readily apparent in the summer of 1989. After the Beijing crackdown, official pronouncements asserted that the open policy had not changed and foreign investors were welcome.[51] Ominous silence, however, implied that the entire coastal strategy was being reconsidered. From Zhao Ziyang's fall until October, coastal development was not mentioned by leading policymakers or by the press; it became a nonissue. A long article on open policy in the September 22 edition of *People's Daily*, for example, not only failed to refer to coastal development, but it provided grounds for abandoning it.[52] Deng Xiao-

---

[46] *South China Morning Post*, July 6, 1989, FBIS, July 6, 1989, p. 66. ; *South China Morning Post*, September 4, 1989, FBIS, September 5, 1989, p. 26; The official announcement of his dismissal is made by Xinhua on Spetember 14, 1989, FBIS, Setpember 15, 1989, pp. 7–8.

[47] *South China Morning Post*, January 25, 1990, FBIS, January 30, 1990, p. 37.

[48] *South China Morning Post*, September 15, 1989, FBIS, September 15, 1989, p. 8.

[49] *Wen Wei Po*, November 11, 1989, FBIS, November 20, 1989, p. 49.

[50] In June, 1990, Li Hao lost his position as mayor of Shenzhen, though he remained party secretary.

[51] Xinhua, FBIS, June 15, 1989, p. 35.; *Liaowang* (Overseas Edition), number 27, July 3, 1989, FBIS, July 14, 1989, p. 11.

[52] *People's Daily*, September 22, 1989, p. 1, FBIS, September 22, 1989, p. 11.

ping's public reproach of SEZs was not rebutted. Other hints that the coastal strategy and SEZs were in dire straits were to be found. In August, Lei Yu, vice-mayor of Guangzhou said that international economic policy was shifting from a "regional inclination" to a "sectoral inclination." [53] This pointed to less emphasis on coastal areas in particular and more attention to "strategic industries." [54] Such a sectoral approach was discussed in the rough drafts of the Eighth Five-Year Plan. [55] By moving away from geographical categories, this industrial policy threatened to undermine the integrity of SEZs, which are territorially defined.

D. THE RETURN TO REFORM

Doubts about the status of SEZs and coastal development persisted until the Fifth Plenum of the Thirteenth Central Committee in November. A short but salient passage in the Plenum's primary document acknowlegded SEZs and coastal policy: "The basic policies and measures for SEZs and coastal open areas will remain and will be gradually perfected in the course of practice." [56] Of course, "perfected" was susceptible to interpretations that could work against genuine reform. Nevertheless, the Fifth Plenum changed the policy context; SEZs would remain intact and liberalizing experiments revived.

The change of climate, from disdainful quiet to measured praise, was strikingly captured in a conference on zone policy held February 5–8, 1990. Li Peng, whose split with Zhao over coastal development had boded ill for SEZs, made a surprise appearance and "emphatically" endorsed zone policy. He remarked that SEZ "orientation is correct and the achievements are remarkable." [57] A front page commentary in *People's Daily* on February 9 was even more effusive, praising the "exuberant vitality" and "special superiority" of SEZs. [58] Zone policy was once again out of the political wilderness.

In certain respects, zone policy of 1988–1990 was consistent with past experience. SEZs completed another cylce of an established pattern of political-economc development, moving from expansion to retraction and back to openness. Oscillations in SEZ fortunes lead to two conclusions. First, the political basis of zone policy is unstable, and has been unstable for ten years. SEZs have consistently inspired ideological and economic criticism. When local or national conditions are seen as deteriorating, latent dissatisfaction is mobilized and SEZs confront formidable political threats. Although detractors have not mustered enough influence to close the zones, if they so desire, they have regularly been able to find ammunition for their assaults in the daily workings of SEZs.

Second, the cycles of SEZ political economy further suggest a dilemma for SEZ opponents. To the extent that they are technocrats interested in modernizing the country, skeptics cannot push too

---

[53] *Wen Wei Po*, August 23, 1989, FBIS, Ausgust 28, 1989, p. 67.
[54] *South China Morning Post*, August 25, 1989, FBIS, August 28, 1989, p. 51.
[55] *South China Morning Post*, November 1, 1989, p. 45.
[56] "CPC Central Committee Decision of Further Improving the Economic Environment, Straightening Out the Economic Order and Deepening Reform," FBIS, January 18, 1990, p. 36.
[57] Xinhua, February 9, 1990, FBIS, February 12, 1990, p. 23.
[58] FBIS, February 14, 1990, p. 16.

hard in centralizing and regulating zone administration. If they do, foreign investment, necessary for technocratic modernization, declines. SEZs are, therefore, not easily eradicated.

Two final points need to be made regarding the unique features of the 1988–1989 period. The introduction of considerable amounts of Taiwan capital is a break with the past. Especially in Xiamen, Taiwan investment boosted SEZ performance in 1988 and 1989. This plentiful source of fresh capital could bolster SEZs for some time to come. Second, the political crisis of spring 1989 was unprecendented for SEZs, as it was for all of China. It is, however, difficult to determine the economic impact of the violence on foreign investment in the zones. International businessmen were responding to the problems of austerity, which began before the crackdown, as well as to political repression. By contrast, the political effect of the Beijing massacre was more potent. Zhao Ziyang's fall and the weakening of zone policy repeated the cyclical pattern of SEZ development, establishing a new low point from which SEZs appear to be rising.

HONG KONG AND CHINA IN THE 1990s

By Kerry Dumbaugh *

CONTENTS

INTRODUCTION

The future of Hong Kong-China relations will be influenced by a range of economic, political, and social factors in which Hong Kong, China, and the international community are all important players. These factors include many variables that are neither discrete nor mutually exclusive. When considered together, they make it difficult to offer projections about the nature of future Hong Kong-China relations or the effect that China's resumption of sovereignty will have on Hong Kong. For the most part, however, the determining factors can best be assessed by posing four sets of questions whose answers will be the measures by which future relations will be judged, and the basis on which they depend.

1. What interests does China have in ensuring that Hong Kong's economy continues to thrive in the years leading up to and following 1997, when Great Britain formally cedes control to China?

2. What does China's political situation mean for how its promises on Hong Kong's autonomy will be translated into future actions?

3. As 1997 approaches and British influence wanes, how will Hong Kong's political infrastructure develop to take on the responsibilities of governance, and how will the new government interact with Beijing?

---

* Analyst in Asian Affairs, Congressional Research Service, Library of Congress.

4. How important will the "confidence" factor in Hong Kong be in affecting Hong Kong-China relations?

This paper will attempt to explore these questions by examining China's past attitudes toward and its economic and political stake in Hong Kong, exploring some of the economic, social, and political factors that have influenced Hong Kong's development to date, and analyzing new developments and trends that will be significant in helping to shape future Hong Kong-China relations.

BACKGROUND

Britain originally acquired Hong Kong's land area from China in three segments under the terms of separate treaties: the 1842 Treaty of Nanking, by which Hong Kong Island was ceded in perpetuity; the First Convention of Peking in 1860, by which Kowloon Peninsula and Stonecutters' Island were ceded in perpetuity; and the Second Convention of Peking in 1898, by which the New Territories were leased to Britain for 99 years beginning July 1, 1898. The latter treaty called for the New Territories—90 percent of Hong Kong's land area—to revert to China in 1997. It is under this treaty's terms that the British entered into negotiations with China to determine exactly how and when China would assert its claim to sovereignty.[1] Since the British government believed that those portions of Hong Kong ceded in perpetuity were not viable as an entity separate from the New Territories, the Sino-British Joint Declaration, which was formally signed on December 19, 1984, will formally restore to Chinese sovereignty and administration the entire area now governed by the British.

As the temporary government of an Asian country by virtue of a treaty with China, Great Britain has sought to justify its rule in Hong Kong on ideological or nationalistic grounds. Instead, justification of British governance has been based on performance—legitimized in part by its bureaucratic efficiency and by its willingness to play a restrained role in daily economic and social affairs. Also important has been the government's high level of administrative competence, its appearance of incorruptibility, and its ability to provide economic growth and development.

In the Joint Declaration and separately in various leadership statements, China has given detailed assurances that those elements of Hong Kong's current situation considered essential for its secure economic future—such as local administrative autonomy, convertibility of the Hong Kong dollar, British-style laws and institutions, and recognition of existing land rights—will be maintained for fifty years after 1997. Despite these assurances, Hong Kong residents have always been concerned about the impending takeover. In the post-Tiananmen Square era, many have increased doubts about whether current Chinese leaders have the ability or the will to follow through on the commitments spelled out in the Joint Declaration.

---

[1] For a more complete discussion of Hong Kong's background and the details of the Sino-British negotiations, see Sutter, Robert. "Hong Kong's Future and Its Implications for the United States." *China's Economy Looks Toward the Year 2000.* May 21, 1986. S. Prt. 99–149, v. 2, pp. 371–384. U.S. Congress. Joint Economic Committee. Washington, U.S. Govt. Print. Off.

Economic Factors in Hong Kong-Chinese Relations

China's Stake in Hong Kong

As a British colony, Hong Kong has become a thriving economic entity. Its economic success is partly a matter of geographical accident. Located at the hub of dynamic Pacific Rim economies, close to the China market, and blessed with a spectacular harbor, Hong Kong has had all the natural tools it needs to become an entrepot without other natural resources. An important addition to these endemic features has been the light hand of British administration, under which Hong Kong has enjoyed free port status and a favorable business climate which rewards incentive and nurtures entrepreneurship. Combined with Hong Kong's natural attributes, British administration has helped Hong Kong's indigenous population become among the wealthiest and the most skilled, efficient, and entrepreneurial in the world.[2]

Hong Kong's domestic economy has proven highly attractive to international corporations and investors. In 1989, $72 billion of Hong Kong's imported goods were retained for use within the territory. More than 900 U.S. companies and forty-four U.S. commercial banks have offices in Hong Kong, serving both the domestic and regional markets. Japan has over fifty banks and more than thirty securities firms in the territory. Total U.S. investment in Hong Kong in 1989 was estimated at $7.5 billion, a level surpassed for the first time in 1989 by Japan with an estimated total of $8 billion.[3] Hong Kong has attracted leading retail chains from Japan and Europe, and merchandising offices from major U.S. food and consumer goods manufacturers, all selling to the domestic market.

Measured by western standards of economic and political self-interest, China continues to have an enormous stake in assuring that Hong Kong remains a vibrant economy with the requisite economic freedom and ability to maintain its extensive and flexible international contacts. Hong Kong is currently China's third largest trading partner, and serves as China's major economic conduit to the rest of the world. By 1988, Hong Kong's trade with China had reached $37 billion.[4] The favorable balance of trade the PRC enjoys with Hong Kong provides from 30 to 40 percent of the former's foreign exchange earnings. In addition, 70 percent of external investment in China now comes from Hong Kong, both from indigenous Hong Kong enterprises and from the international community investing in China through Hong Kong.

The PRC also owns sizable percentages of important Hong Kong companies. These include 20 percent of Hong Kong Telephone and 12.5 percent of Cathay Pacific Airways. Chinese-backed banks attract up to 20 percent of total Hong Kong dollar deposits.

Also critical is Hong Kong's regional economic role and its importance as a doorway into the China market. Even absent its planned expansion, Hong Kong's container port is the largest in

---

[2] Hong Kong has the third highest per capita income in Asia, at $12,100 in 1990.
[3] Figures are from the American Consulate General in Hong Kong.
[4] See Dumbaugh, Kerry and Ipson, Michael. *The United States and Hong Kong's Future: Promoting Stability and Growth.* The National Committee on U.S.-China Relations. China Policy Series, No. Three, June 1990. p. 5. All figures in this report are cited in U.S. dollars unless specified otherwise.

the world, handling 4.46 million twenty-foot container units in 1989. In addition, hundreds of companies from Europe, Japan, Korea, Taiwan, Australia, and other countries which operate in Hong Kong sell to China and to other countries and economies in Asia. Daily foreign exchange turnover in April 1989 averaged $49 billion. Hong Kong annually channels billions of dollars in international investment funds and manufacturing work to the PRC from Japanese, American, and European companies.

Hong Kong is also viewed as an asset in promoting China's development. Chinese leaders in the post-Tiananmen era have continued to emphasize the need for modernizing and improving China's own economy, and have reiterated that China's open foreign policy will not change. These economic and foreign policy priorities appear to provide significant incentives for Chinese leaders to exercise restraint in their actions toward Hong Kong.

Despite these incentives for economic restraint, other factors may lead China to take actions which could prove detrimental to Hong Kong's freedom and economic strength. By 1989, China was facing its worst economic slump in a decade, largely due to economic austerity measures launched in 1988. Industrial growth has been weak and productivity has been low. Unemployment has increased, and the profitability of state and entrepreneurial enterprises has suffered. As a result, China's officially announced budget deficit had grown to a record level of $8 billion by the year's end. Should these economic difficulties continue, many are fearful that Chinese leaders may be tempted to divert profits directly from Hong Kong enterprises to bolster sagging national coffers.

Further, China's economically based incentives for restraint toward Hong Kong appear less persuasive when viewed in the context of China's own experience since 1949. The historical record demonstrates that the PRC's communist leadership has often placed ideological and political priorities above those which are economic or pragmatic. Thus some observers have always believed that Beijing's leaders will actively interfere in Hong Kong's economic decisions and manipulate its governing bodies. Others fear that some Chinese authorities intend to honor the country's commitments regarding political and economic autonomy but lack the abilities, experience, or tolerance needed to insulate Hong Kong from the political, economic, and bureaucratic dynamics of Chinese communist government. Some, who perhaps were beginning to have more confidence after a decade of Chinese reform under Deng Xiaoping, point to the Tiananmen Square crackdown as proof that China's communist leaders are unable to provide a consistent and reliable policy environment, whatever their intentions or abilities.

HONG KONG'S SPECIAL CONNECTIONS WITH GUANGDONG PROVINCE

An important element in the last decade of Hong Kong's success, and of significant potential in Hong Kong-China relations, is the substantial link which the territory has developed with South China, particularly in Guangdong Province. Separate entities in the late 1970s, Hong Kong and Guangdong are now economically intertwined. Most of these economic links have occurred after the Sino-British Joint Declaration and in spite of policy shifts and economic downturns in China. Economic alliances and personal connections already have permeated and considerably transformed the Hong Kong-Guangdong relationship, providing mutual benefit.

The Hong Kong-Guangdong border now appears readily permeable. As many as 10,000 commercial vehicles and thousands of business commuters cross the border daily. The two regions have collaborated on major infrastructure projects, including electric power plants, transportation systems, hotels, restaurants, and factories. Many of these projects have involved Hong Kong construction companies and workers. Importantly, many ongoing and completed projects involve continuing Hong Kong management expertise. Hong Kong Polytechnic and other educational facilities have become major training centers for Guangdong personnel, teaching Western business and management practices to Chinese managers. According to one observer, most Guangdong business endeavors are now calculated in Hong Kong dollars rather than the PRC's renminbi.[5]

For its part, Hong Kong's connections to Guangdong have contributed greatly to its own growth. Despite the uncertainties accompanying impending Chinese rule, Hong Kong, constrained both by limited space and a limited and increasingly expensive labor force, has moved decisively to capitalize on the new relationship. A substantial number of Hong Kong's outprocessing centers have been moved to Guangdong Province in the last decade—as much as 18.4 percent of Hong Kong's small and medium industries by 1987, according to one sample survey.[6] In the last eight years, Hong Kong's toy industry has nearly doubled in size, with virtually all of this growth coming from China.[7] By 1988, according to one estimate, Hong Kong manufacturers directly employed two million people in Guangdong.[8]

Guangdong's geographic proximity, virtually limitless labor supply, substantially lower wage rates, and overall lower costs of production have bolstered Hong Kong's international competitive advantage. Hong Kong's special access to Guangdong—and through Guangdong, to China—has increased its attractiveness to foreign businesses anxious to benefit from Hong Kong's export advantages and gain greater access to China's domestic market.

Nor are these benefits one-sided. In the last decade, Guangdong Province, a key success story in China's modernization program, has achieved spectacular growth rates—15.9 percent in 1989, according to one report, a rate which compares favorably with that achieved by Japan in the early 1950s, Taiwan in the late 1950s, and Korea in the early 1960s. Moreover, in achieving this growth rate, Guangdong has had to overcome challenges not faced by these countries. As part of communist China, Guangdong labored under greater economic and political constraints than did these dynamic

---

[5] According to Mark Pratt, former U.S. Consul General in Guangzhou, PRC.

[6] See Sit, Victor F.S. "Industrial out-processing in Hong Kong's new relationship with the Pearl River Delta." *Asian Profile.* v. 17, February 1989, p. 6.

[7] Hong Kong is the world's largest toy exporter, with about half of those exports going to the United States. Hong Kong's toy industry grew from HK$9 billion in 1982 to HK$16 billion by September 1987. Source: Hong Kong Trade Development Council.

[8] This was the estimate of China's Xinhua News Agency, which serves as the de facto Chinese representative in Hong Kong. Cited in Vogel, Ezra. *One Step Ahead in China. Guangdong Under Reform.* Harvard University Press, Cambridge MA, 1989. p. 442.

Asian economies. In addition, the province was not favored with large amounts of foreign aid, and was confronted with an international trading environment decidedly less favorable to the kind of export-driven growth which had contributed to Asian economic success in earlier years. Its proximity to Hong Kong, however, gives Guangdong a special asset. Guangdong has benefited from Hong Kong's high general management skills, well-developed financial and services sectors, and the excellent information network which has enabled Hong Kong to respond rapidly to changing conditions in overseas markets.

The spectacular growth and interconnectedness of the Hong Kong-Guangdong relationship raises important considerations for the future of Hong Kong-China relations, since their ties are an essential element to their decade of growth. Its connections with Hong Kong have given Guangdong the economic advantages to become China's most successful export province (it accounts for 18 percent of national export totals). Likewise, Guangdong's connection with Hong Kong continues to present Beijing with the primary source for the international capital so essential to China's economic modernization goals. This status not only assures Guangdong's continued importance in China's economic reform and modernization programs, but could also increase its growing economic and political influence with—and even autonomy from—Beijing. Thus Guangdong officials could find it in their interests to act as interlocutors in Hong Kong's dialogue with Beijing, augmenting Hong Kong's own voice and perhaps compensating for whatever weaknesses may remain in Hong Kong's indigenous political infrastructure. To an extent, mutual economic self-interest and contacts may even transcend the PRC's political goals and jurisdiction.

But Hong Kong's interdependence with Guangdong also has a darker side. To the extent that they are mutually dependent, each has become more vulnerable to economic and political conditions in the other. Swift economic growth in Guangdong has outstripped the province's infrastructure, power generation capacity, and transportation facilities, thus limiting its current potential for economic growth. Although local officials throughout Guangdong are reported to be planning a number of new infrastructure projects to redress these limitations, such projects may prove ill-founded and wasteful if they are not coordinated at the provincial or even central levels of government. Economic interdependence also means that any tightening of economic restrictions in China which affects Guangdong could have repercussions for Hong Kong's economy, even if not directly aimed at Hong Kong. Continued economic difficulties in China could cut the demand for Guangdong products in China's domestic market, resulting in lower revenues for the province and for Hong Kong investments there. Changes in Guangdong Province's leadership or policies, in its influence with Beijing, or in the level of Western investments there could also adversely affect Hong Kong. Likewise, economic setbacks in Hong Kong could erode its ability to attract the foreign business investment funds so essential to Guangdong's growth, a situation which ultimately could prompt Chinese leaders to reassess the province's role in national economic and modernization plans. Economically, the Hong Kong-

Guangdong connection thus holds both great promise and potential difficulty for future Hong Kong-China relations.

The PRC's credibility in its policy of "one country-two systems" is totally dependent on whether Hong Kong does well, and the consequences for China's economic and political relations with Taiwan and with the world are considerable. If China's dual approach succeeds, if Hong Kong "does well," then not only does China derive economic benefit from its financial stake in Hong Kong, but Taiwan and the international community may be encouraged to foster more rapid and extensive economic ties with other autonomous regions in China. In Taiwan's case, the development of more extensive economic relations could, in time, lead to some mutually acceptable settlement of the "Taiwan question."

CHANGING INTERNATIONAL INVESTMENT PATTERNS

Perhaps the murkiest set of factors in future Hong Kong-China relations involves international economic interests in the region. Hong Kong's extensive economic links with the international community mean that its potential for future growth will depend greatly on continued international willingness to invest. Measures of international investment can be unreliable, making it difficult to draw firm conclusions about the extent of international business confidence in and commitment to Hong Kong based on investment decisions. In addition, international governments and business enterprises undoubtedly will base future investment decisions on their perceptions of other determinants and variables affecting Hong Kong's future, making projections even more problematic.

Estimates over the last few years indicate that major investor countries continued to increase their levels of investment in Hong Kong Kong through 1989. U.S. investment is estimated to have grown from $4.5 billion in 1986 to an estimated $7.1 billion in 1989, while Japan's is estimated to have grown from $4.6 billion to $8 billion during the same period.[9] In the eighteen months since June, 1989, consortia involving major U.S., Japanese, and European concerns have invested in development projects and have successfully bid for contracts to build Hong Kong's cable television network.[10] During the same period, multinational firms, including U.S. companies, have been awarded contracts for pieces of Hong Kong's mammoth airport and port terminal construction projects.[11] U.S. and Japanese concerns also are part of a loan syndicate granting a $1.35 billion loan to Hong Kong International Terminals for the construction of two new container terminals. These huge infrastructure projects, which are in their initial stages, will continue to provide U.S. contractors and other international firms with billions of dollars in investment opportunities.

---

[9] Figures provided by the American Consulate General in Hong Kong.

[10] In July, 1989, the U.S. Citibank corporation took a 10 percent stake in the largest development site ever sold in Hong Kong's Central Business District. U.S West was part of a consortia that has successfully bid for Hong Kong's cable television system—at $700 million, estimated to be the largest in the world.

[11] The U.S. firms of Bechtel and Morgan Stanley are now the project manager and overall financial advisers for the project, respectively. Another U.S. company, Greiner Engineering, in partnership with a Hong Kong company, will produce the new airport's master plan.

Although the current international investment attitude toward Hong Kong itself appears to remain healthy, international investors doubtless have longer-term concerns that will influence investment patterns. The recent growth in Hong Kong investments in Malaysia and Thailand may be due partly to pressure from U.S. and other international customers for diversification of Hong Kong manufacturing capabilities away from locations in China in order to assure reliability of supply. Continuation of such pressure could act as a brake on Hong Kong's economic connections with Guangdong and with the rest of China, and could encourage further diversification by Hong Kong enterprises.

The ability of international business to exert influence over Hong Kong business decisions has the potential for dramatically changing current investment patterns in South China and Hong Kong. Such a change offers opportunities and drawbacks. On the negative side, it could limit Guangdong's profitability and possibly erode its importance in—and thus its influence over—China's ongoing modernization goals. International pressure for diversification of Hong Kong industries could also fuel concerns among Chinese leaders about the "internationalization" of Hong Kong, prompting efforts by Beijing to assert more control over the territory's capital flow and investment decisions. But on the other hand, continued diversification of investments could increase the ability of Hong Kong businesses to weather economic and political climate changes in Beijing.

POLITICAL FACTORS IN FUTURE HONG KONG-CHINA RELATIONS

CHANGING POLITICAL REALITIES IN CHINA

Since the 1989 Tiananmen Square crackdown, most reporting and analysis on conditions in China have been understandably downbeat and generally negative.[12] The reassertion of power by elderly and supposedly retired leaders demonstrated that power in China remains more personal than institution-based, increasing the likelihood of future divisive power struggles as these aged leaders die, and making projections about China's future policies even more problematic. Factional infighting appears to go to the very top of the Chinese leadership. Reformers are seen to be at odds with more conservative-minded leaders like Chen Yun and Yang Shangkun who are judged to be pressing for limits on reform and reversal of key economic and political changes of the last decade. There has been no clear consensus among leaders on many issues and little definable policy vision. The result has been gridlock in Chinese decisionmaking, and a policy process whose future directions and mechanisms remain uncertain.

Chinese leaders now face serious political, economic, and social challenges. At the end of the Long March generation, Chinese authorities are confronted by widespread disaffection with the Communist Party, increasing social pressures for meaningful change in

---

[12] Typical of the bleak projections for China was the most recent CIA annual assessment China's economy. See *The Chinese Economy in 1989 and 1990: Trying to Revive Growth While Maintaining Social Stability.* A report by the Central Intelligence Agency. Presented to the Subcommittee on Technology and National Security of the Joint Economic Committee. June 28, 1990.

the political system, weakened central government authority, and a whole host of increasingly intractable economic troubles. These difficulties come at a time of upheaval in the Soviet Union and Eastern Europe, with world socialism in serious decline, fueling disagreements in Beijing about the viability of China's chosen socialist path. These changing political realities pose new perspectives and challenges for China's resumption of sovereignty over Hong Kong.

Perhaps the most meaningful development within China has been an increase in regional authority at the expense of central governmental authority. With a central government unable to articulate and pursue effective national policies, local and provincial officials—already given increased authority and functions during the reform decade—appear to have gained further power and influence. In 1990, regional power was such that provincial authorities appeared able to influence and help craft important reform provisions in China's new Five-Year plan.[13] In the absence of a renewed consensus in Beijing or the emergence of a strong political center—events seen as unlikely in the near or even medium term—central government authority is likely to continue to weaken while regional authority grows. This being the case, events in Beijing, although politically significant, may be increasingly less important for the daily economic affairs of the rest of the country.

In such a world, Hong Kong's autonomy from Beijing may be more assured, at least by default, than could have been envisioned in 1984 when the Joint Declaration was signed. Guangdong Province, an economic success in China's modernization program, already possesses significant economic and even political autonomy from Beijing. A weak government in Beijing could allow Guangdong to be pulled farther away from central Chinese control and increasingly into Hong Kong's orbit. With this mutual political reinforcement, with extensive economic and personal interconnections, and with revenues economically essential to stated goals of national development, the Hong Kong-Guangdong combination could enjoy influence in Beijing significantly greater than either entity could command separately.

On the negative side, problems may arise from the reform policies which have given coastal regions and Special Economic Zones (SEZs) special benefits and resources. Widening regional financial and infrastructural diversity in China has produced strains which have spawned inter-provincial protectionist measures and conflicts over resources. According to some reports, for example, resources bound for Guangdong, a favored province, have been assessed extra duties at various points en route.[14] In the past, regional tensions have been such that Guangdong officials may be tempted to keep a lower profile in the future to avoid provoking jealousy among other regions and provinces. Weak central government could exacerbate these tensions by diminishing Beijing's ability to be an arbitrator of regional conflicts. Hong Kong, as an economically vital and ad-

---

[13] Provincial influence appeared to be key in Beijing's decisions to retain the contract system which permits provincial government and state enterprises to keep profits exceeding agreed-upon remittances to the central government.

[14] Information provided by Mark Pratt, former U.S. Consul General in Guangzhou, PRC.

vanced entity with strong connections to Guangdong, could easily become a target of such tensions. Moreover, a stronger central government in Beijing headed by more conservative leaders could seek to target Guangdong and other more market-oriented provinces for greater socialist discipline and economic restrictions.

A second potentially negative effect of China's changing political realities concerns the investments of China-backed businesses in Hong Kong. In the mid-1980s, Chinese enterprises began investing in Hong Kong, anxious to capitalize on the territory's wealth and take advantage of the impending resumption of sovereignty. Some ill-founded ventures failed due to lack of accountability for financial and management mistakes, thus hurting Hong Kong enterprises and fostering lack of confidence among investors contemplating ventures with Chinese companies. Although Beijing has responded to these failures by placing restrictions on new Chinese investments in Hong Kong, it remains unclear how effectively a politically and economically weakened central government will be able to exercise control over future investment decisions. Should Chinese enterprises continue to invest in Hong Kong, Beijing may have to muster enough will and revenue to assure their accountability or financial solvency. Absent such assurance and financial backing, Chinese companies could find it more difficult to attract future customers for their Hong Kong ventures.

HONG KONG'S EVOLVING POLITICAL ENVIRONMENT

Hong Kong has never experienced comprehensive democracy, political autonomy, or a decisive power to determine its own political fortunes. Nevertheless, its citizens and business enterprises have enjoyed great personel and economic freedom, and the territory has benefited from being governed by an enlightened western country with assets that the PRC cannot claim. These include a long history of governmental consistency, an extensive international economic and political presence, and a sophisticated industrial and financial base. Yet, this near-century under British administration has been a two-edged sword. On the one hand, it has provided Hong Kong with the luxury to pursue commerce almost exclusive of other concerns, and with spectacular success. But it also has limited the ability of its people to acquire experience and skills they may need in assembling a sufficient political tradition and infrastructure to put "a high degree of autonomy" into practice. Complicating this issue, there is general concern that the influence and effectiveness of a "lame duck" British government in Hong Kong will wane as 1997 approaches. The future of Hong Kong-China political relations will depend in part on Hong Kong's ability to form an indigenous political infrastructure with strong popular backing, first class administrative abilities, and sufficient skill and authority to represent Hong Kong's interests effectively in Beijing.

Hong Kong's political elite continue to be divided in their views about the desirable pace and extent of Hong Kong's political transformation. In particular, there is continuing disagreement over the amount of accommodation that should be reached with Beijing, with some favoring a cautious approach that adjusts more to Beijing's wishes and others pushing for a more assertive approach in an effort to maximize Hong Kong's autonomy. Continued lack of unity could stall Hong Kong's momentum toward establishing a stronger political infrastructure. A further difficulty is the apparent political apathy of the populace-at-large. With some exceptions, Hong Kong's population has remained difficult to mobilize on political issues, raising questions about the extent to which they will be able to contribute to the political process.[15]

These problems have been particularly apparent in the case of Hong Kong's attempts to conduct legislative elections. Hong Kong's new Basic Law, approved in 1990, will serve as the Hong Kong SAR's constitution, and provides for the first direct elections of the Legislative Council (Legco).[16] The Basic Law provides for 18 of the 60 members of Legco to be directly elected in September, 1991.[17] In the wake of the Basic Law's approval, fledgling political parties and groups in Hong Kong have proliferated in preparation for the 1991 elections. None of the new groups has yet attracted sufficient membership or support to seize the political high ground. Although a number have similar platforms and goals, they have not yet merged or united their efforts in an attempt to gain political strength, increasing the likelihood that candidates representing similar constituencies will be running against each other in September.[18] With the political situation in Hong Kong still evolving, the atmosphere for coming elections remains uncertain. Despite the large number of political parties that may field candidates, some Hong Kong officials have expressed concern over whether there will be enough qualified candidates running, to the point where several prominent officials have made public appeals for participation.[19] Even if the transition to an indigenous government is smooth, its ability to govern remains unclear. If government is perceived to be weak, Hong Kong businesses, international investors, and other interest groups in Hong Kong may seek to deal directly with Beijing, bypassing Hong Kong government processes and further undermining governmental authority.

---

[15] Two notable exceptions were the large demonstrations in 1989 after the Tiananmen Square crackdown and a campaign which garnered over one million signatures opposing China's plans to build the Daya Bay nuclear power plant near Hong Kong.

[16] The Basic Law was the work of the Basic Law Drafting Committee (BLDC), comprised of Chinese and Hong Kong members formally tasked with drawing up the political model for post-1997 Hong Kong. The Basic Law was approved by the BLDC on February 16, 1990, and promulgated by the National People's Congress in April, 1990.

[17] This figure is considerably higher than the number directly elected under British administration (zero), but is significantly lower than the number some in Hong Kong supported (as high as 30). Under the Basic Law, the number of directly-elected officials will rise to 20 in 1995, seen as a concession by Beijing, which favored limiting directly-elected members to 18.

[18] Among the new political groups are four judged to be politically liberal—the United Democrats of Hong Kong (UDHK), the Hong Kong Association for Democracy and Peoples' Livelihood (HKADPL), the Meeting Point, and the Hong Kong Affairs Society (HKAS)—and several pro-business organizations considered to be moderate—the Hong Kong Democratic Foundation (HKDF), and the Liberal Democratic Federation (LDF). These groups join existing political organizations such as Reform Club and the Civic Association.

[19] Among those making such appeals have been Hong Kong's Governor, Sir David Wilson, and Lady Lydia Dunn, a senior member of Hong Kong's Executive Council (Exco). For further discussion of the formation of political parties, see *Far Eastern Economic Review.* "Peking's tune." August 23, 1990, p. 22.

OTHER ISSUES

EMIGRATION

Apart from economic and political issues, more elusive indicators in future Hong Kong-China relations show a confidence problem whose severity and direction is difficult to predict. Chief among these problems, and of most concern to Hong Kong, is the increasing emigration rate of skilled personnel. An estimated 62,000 persons emigrated in 1990—a 50 percent increase over 1989—most of these among Hong Kong's most skilled and educated citizens. This creates a number of problems for Hong Kong's future. First, it robs the territory of its primary resource in attracting international business—the highly skilled, talented, and ambitious among its population, or the very people Hong Kong needs to maximize its continued economic vitality. The demographic makeup of emigres appears to have changed since the Tiananmen Square crackdown, shifting from older, wealthier citizens to younger middle-management families with school-age children, who form the core of Hong Kong's skilled work force. Emigration of personnel also deprives Hong Kong of the human resources it needs to assure its traditional highly efficient services sector, such as in the civil service, which has helped make the territory run smoothly.

There appears to be no consensus, either within the Hong Kong government, the Hong Kong business community, or the international community about potential solutions to Hong Kong's emigration worries.[20] Hong Kong managers will undoubtedly have to accept the inevitability of losing personnel, and may consider replacing departing employees by hiring PRC citizens or expatriates and citizens from other countries who have no future citizenship worries. But such measures, while possibly helping to maintain Hong Kong's efficiency and economic vitality, raise other concerns. Replacement of Hong Kong personnel with citizens from other countries may exacerbate Beijing's concerns about the "internationalization" of Hong Kong, particularly since such employees would owe no allegiance to China and would complicate Beijing's authority over them. Replacing emigrating personnel with PRC citizens may exacerbate Hong Kong's sensitivity to a "takeover" by mainlanders who may have little concern for Hong Kong's autonomy.[21]

Informal Hong Kong polls indicate that many foreign and Hong Kong-owned businesses in the territory stand to lose a large percentage of their middle and upper management work force before 1997. Sixty percent in the computer industry was one figure

---

[20] Within the business community, for example, opinion is divided on such basic points as whether Hong Kong employers should help their employees gain foreign residency status or encourage them to stay in Hong Kong in order to assure the territory's economic health. Thus there is no agreement on whether countries such as the United States should provide Hong Kong residents with passports, residency permits, or special delayed-action visas that would provide an option to leave later. Britain's decision to grant right of abode to 50,000 Hong Kong families (estimated to translate into 250,000 people) is controversial for this reason, among others.

[21] In September 1990, the Hong Kong government eased its former restrictions on hiring Chinese nationals. Under the old law, Chinese nationals could be hired by Hong Kong companies either if they were sponsored by a mainland company operating in the territory or by applying for an immigrant visa. The new law permits Chinese nationals who have resided overseas for at least the previous two years to apply directly to private-sector companies for employment.

cited.[22] This could pose challenges for China, which will inherit the consequences of whatever erosion of efficiency and vitality accompanies Hong Kong's loss of skilled personnel. Observers have pointed out that Chinese leaders appear to be unconcerned about keeping talented professionals in Hong Kong. According to some sources, Beijing authorities are reported to have said that those who wanted to leave Hong Kong should do so now—an attitude which has not inspired confidence and which seems to discount the importance of qualified personnel in creating and sustaining a vibrant economy, and exacerbating concerns about the future.[23]

CAPITAL FLIGHT

Related to the emigration question are concerns about capital flight. Since the Hong Kong government does not publish balance of payments figures, measuring capital flows in the territory is an impressionistic undertaking. Nevertheless, some financial reports, such as the Hong Kong and Shanghai Bank's monthly report, suggest that capital outflow is a problem, and that it may have exceeded HK $32 billion in 1990.[24] Hong Kong government officials have admitted that there has been a recent increase in borrowing in Hong Kong dollars for the purposes of financing overseas investments, primarily in Indonesia, Thailand, and Malaysia; in the first quarter of 1990, Hong Kong projects approved by these three countries increased by more than 200 percent over previous rates.[25] At the same time, China's Ministry of Foreign Economic Relations and Trade (MOFERT) reported that the pace of Hong Kong investments in China had slowed. If these projections are correct, it suggests that some Hong Kong companies may be reassessing the costs of doing business in China.

Although the timing of these shifts in investment patterns suggests that the Tiananmen Square crackdown is a significant factor, other related variables may be at work. U.S. imports from Malaysia, Indonesia, and Thailand receive low tariff rates or duty-free status under the U.S. generalized system of preferences schedules (GSP). This favorable tariff treatment is denied to products imported from Hong Kong and China. Moreover, U.S. willingness to continue giving most-favored-nation status (MFN) to products imported from China has remained in doubt since the Tiananmen Square crackdown.[26] Loss of this status would significantly increase the U.S. prices for Hong Kong imports manufactured in China—in some cases, by as much as 90 percent. In addition, some reports have indicated that Hong Kong businesses and international investors may have started to become more cautious about their China

---

[22] This was among the figures cited at a conference in Hong Kong sponsored by the National Committee on U.S.-China Relations on March 29-30, 1990.

[23] See Dumbaugh and Ipson, p. 8.

[24] The Hong Kong and Shanghai Bank recently announced the formation of a holding company which will be incorporated in London. The institution denied that its decision related to concerns for Hong Kong's economic future. The Bank itself will remain in Hong Kong, and the holding company will be managed from Hong Kong.

[25] Jiang, Frank. "Fresh pastures." *Far Eastern Economic Review.* September 20, 1990, p. 92.

[26] MFN status, while higher than the GSP rates given to developing countries, is still considerably lower than non-MFN duty rate schedules. In 1990, the U.S. Congress considered legislation which would have denied or restricted China's MFN status, and may consider such legislation again in 1991.

investments as early as 1988, when Beijing launched its austerity drive and tightened credit.[27] Still another factor may be Hong Kong's increasing shift over the last decade from producing cheap, labor-intensive goods, where China's unlimited labor pool and low costs provide advantages, to producing higher-value technological goods which require a more skilled work force. Although most Hong Kong manufacturing firms are small firms producing labor-intensive goods—companies that should continue to lean on the competitive advantages Guangdong offers—the trends suggest that larger companies with more financial resources and greater mobility will be seeking to diversify their production bases.

IMPLICATIONS AND CONCLUSIONS

The nature of future Hong Kong-China relations will have profound implications for Hong Kong and for Chinese domestic and foreign policy. In the past, Chinese leaders have legitimized their rule primarily on ideological or moralistic grounds. But Hong Kong citizens are likely to judge the legitimacy of Chinese communist rule almost entirely on the basis of performance. And China's "performance" in Hong Kong will be measured largely by how Hong Kong performs throughout the 1990s. In Hong Kong's case, "performance" for the most part means providing an economic environment which continues to foster growth and an effective, incorruptible government capable of delivering efficient services and benefits to the people.

Domestically, China's performance in Hong Kong has far-reaching political implications. In recent years, China's party leaders and government officials have faced increasing public criticism about their administrative abilities, particularly their ability to provide efficient government, pursue effective and consistent policies, and control bureaucratic corruption. At the beginning of the 1990s, the credibility of the Chinese Communist Party has been significantly eroded by the Cultural Revolution and further damaged by the Tiananmen Square crackdown. Events in Europe and the Soviet Union have raised important questions about the very viability of socialism. Hong Kong arguably provides Chinese leaders with opportunities to recapture their lost legitimacy. Some consider that they have an opportunity to demonstrate that socialism and central planning can work side-by-side with capitalism and market mechanisms for mutual benefit. They have an opportunity to demonstrate their tolerance for diverse economic and political systems within a single socialist construct. A poor performance in Hong Kong, however, could further and perhaps irrevocably damage Beijing's mandate to rule under existing socialist theories and leaders.

China's performance in Hong Kong has equally far-reaching foreign policy implications. In the last decade, including the post-Tiananmen Square era, leaders in Beijing have steadfastly maintained that China will continue to "open to the outside world," and will continue to seek the foreign investment so important to China's modernization program. Nevertheless, China's international business contacts have been constrained by limited transportation and

---

[27] Jiang, p. 93.

energy infrastructures, bureaucratic difficulties, and lack of an appropriately skilled work force. In Hong Kong, however, Chinese officials and enterprise managers will be coming into intimate and ongoing daily contact with foreign governments and business enterprises. China can benefit greatly from this vast network of international connections, advanced infrastructure, and highly skilled labor force. On the other hand, the extensive international presence in Hong Kong also provides innumerable opportunities for confrontation between China, other governments, and multinational businesses. A poor performance could adversely affect international views about the abilities of Chinese leaders to govern or about China's own commitments to pursue economic efficiency and progress.

To a great extent, the measure of China's performance in Hong Kong will be burdened by Hong Kong's own past success. Nevertheless, in assessing the future of Hong Kong-China relations, it would appear prudent to avoid extremes, and to remember the wide array of variables that will influence the relationship.

CHINA'S ASIAN TRADE:
OPPORTUNITIES AND DILEMMAS

By John Frankenstein *

CONTENTS

SUMMARY [1]

During the decade of the 1980s, and the Deng reforms, China's trade with Asia grew substantially, surpassing world trade growth trends. China trades more with Asia than with any other region.

---

* John Frankenstein formerly Chinese language officer in the U.S. Foreign Service, and most recently an Associate Professor of International Studies at the American Graduate School of International Management, joined the faculty of the Department of Management Studies at University of Hong Kong in early 1991.

[1] Notes on data sources: Unless otherwise noted, the figures presented here are based on the *Direction of Trade Statistics (DOTS) Yearbooks* (International Monetary Fund, Washington, D.C.) for 1986 and 1989. The 1989 trade figures on China are taken from *Business China*, April 1990. Hong Kong indirect trade figures are taken from the continuing series of Hong Kong government statistics resented in the monthly *China Trade Report (Far Eastern Economic Review*, Hong Kong). Other sources will be noted as appropriate.

There are some important substantive and methodological caveats about the data. DOTS is based on official data reported by governments. These data vary in quality and coverage. For instance, trade data reported by China simply lists the first destination of the commodity

Continued

However, the trade is highly concentrated with Japan and the Newly Industrializing Countries (NICs) of Hong Kong, Taiwan, South Korea and Singapore—all but 10% of China's Asian trade is with this group. Of these countries, Japan and Hong Kong dominate. Japan leads in technology trade. Hong Kong is especially important because of its entrepôt intermediary function; Hong Kong's economy is tightly linked, through trade and investment, with South China's. Trade and investment with Taiwan and South Korea have grown [2] dramatically over the past several years and will continue to expand.

Trade with ASEAN (Association of Southeast Asian Nations) is modest, despite recent Chinese political gains in the region—both ASEAN and China are more concerned with trade with the major capitalist countries than they are with each other. Trade with South Asia is minor because of unpromising economic conditions, political conflict, and inward-looking policies.

China's trade with Asia is likely to take on more importance as the PRC deals with the political fallout of Tiananmen in the West. However, because of different strategies, the gap in economic development is widening between China, which follows habitual Stalinist planning policies, and her major Asian trading partners, which are building up exports and technology. How China deals with the absorption of Hong Kong in 1997 will be crucial to the further development of China's trade and economy.

In 1989 China's exports were valued at $52.5 billion, up 177% from the beginning of the decade, for an annual growth rate of 11.9% China's import growth was even more rapid: in 1980 China's total imports were valued at $18.1 million, reaching $59.1 billion in 1989, an overall increase of 226% between 1980 and 1989 at an average annual rate of 14.1%.

It is important to note that these figures are quoted in current dollars, unadjusted for inflation or exchange rate fluctuations. But one can gain a sense of the size of China's trade on an annual basis. Between 1980 and 1988, the PRC's share of world exports grew by less than 1% annually, going from 1% in 1980 to 1.8% in 1988. For the same period, the industrialized world's share went from 67.7% to 71.6%, Asia's share from 8.1% to 12.6%, and the

---

traded; data reported by the United States counts country of origin. Thus the DOTS China table shows Chinese exports to the United States in 1988 to be U.S. $3.39 billion, but the U.S. table shows imports from China to be U.S. $5.04 billion; the difference lies in transshipments through Hong Kong and elsewhere.

[2] Furthermore, the data do not include trade in services ("invisibles" such as receipts from tourism or labor exports), these figures omit investment flows, are selective in what is counted (arms transfers are often not included) and, of course, leave out data on what economists politely call the "informal economy," which in the Asian case can be rather important.

More specific to the PRC, DOTS follows official accounts and thus omits trade numbers from Taiwan or South Korea, and does not deal with the complex issue of indirect trade via Hong Kong—for these areas the discussion draws from additional sources as noted above and combines them as appropriate with the DOTS data.

It should also be noted that the DOTS figures are in current dollars--while these figures reflect significant growth, for truly comparative purposes one needs to compute a constant dollar value. Fluctuations in the official exchange rate, significant differences between official and "market" (grey or otherwise) exchange rates, varying and officially understated inflation rates, and lack of market pricing for Chinese goods all combine to make that calculation problematic. Adding to the problem, in keeping with international practice, DOTS reports exports on a f.o.b./ f.a.s. basis and reports imports on a c.i.f. basis.

In sum, it must be admitted that there are significant issues of consistency and compatibility. The data are primarily useful to us in providing trends and approximations, the big and the short-term picture.

"Four Dragons" share (Hong Kong, Taiwan, Singapore, and South Korea), which accounted for 4.5% of world exports in 1980, rose to 7.2% in 1988. None of this should be taken to disparage China's trade program, but in any discussion of international commerce, it is useful to have some reference points.

The numbers reflect not only the growth of world trade, but also the superior performance of Asia, particularly the export-oriented Newly Industrializing Countries (NICs) of Asia or "Four Dragons," in that trade. While in the total scheme of world trade China's share is modest, dwarfed by the major industrial powers, its trade growth exceeds that of trade-shy India's by more than a factor of two—the only Third World country outside the NICs with which comparisons are meaningful. In terms of volume, by the end of the decade China ranked with countries such as Spain (in the European context, an NIC) and Switzerland. At the same time we should note—and certainly the leaders in Beijing are not ignorant of this—that the Asian NICs, given their much smaller population and resource bases, are outperforming the People's Republic of China.

I. China's Asian Trade

Given these global and regional numbers, it is not surprising to see that over the same period, Chinese trade with the Asian region expanded both in absolute and relative terms. Taken as a region, China trades more with Asia than with any other area (see table 1).

China's two-way trade with Asia grew 263% between 1980 and 1989 at an annual rate of 15.4% per year, outstripping Chinese trade growth as a whole. As a proportion of total Chinese trade, China-Asia trade went from 45% in 1980 to 55.8% in 1989; indeed, China's Asian trade has consistently exceeded 50% of total trade since 1984. Furthermore, China's Asian trade as a whole from 1980 to 1989 has been in positive balance, easing a cumulative trade deficit of U.S. $44.06 billion. In other words, China's trade with the Asian region makes up a very important part of the overall Chinese trade picture. But that trade is not evenly distributed across the region—quite the contrary, it is highly concentrated and, one might argue, distorted.

II. The Major Players

The economic powerhouses of the region—Japan and the NICs—account for all but about 10% of that trade. Of these trading partners, Japan and Hong Kong are by far the most important, as table 2 shows.

One can get a sense of how these two trading partners have dominated China's trade by observing over the 1982-88 period, during which Japan and Hong Kong together accounted for annual averages of 45% of China's total trade and 86% of China's Asian trade. Certainly one would expect that Japan, for a multiplicity of reasons—sheer economic power, geographic proximity, well-managed business strategies, financial penetration and concessions, etc.—would play a major role in China's foreign economic relations.

Table 1
CHINA'S ASIAN TRADE, 1980-88[a]

Year	Asian Trade (U.S. Millions of current dollars)		Asian Exports	Asian Imports
	Exports	Imports	As % of total	As % of total
1980	10,160	6948	56.0	35.6
1981	12,464	8751	58.0	40.5
1982	12,299	6707	56.2	35.4
1983	12,430	8373	56.3	39.3
1984	14,707	12,176	59.2	46.9
1985	16,995	21,549	62.2	50.7
1986	17,851	20,068	56.9	46.4
1987	23,801	21,148	60.3	48.9
1988	30,703	26,857	64.4	48.5
1989	34,878	27,381	66.5[b]	46.3[b]

a. Cumulative balance + = U.S. $26.34 billion
b. Taiwan and Korea direct trade not included in 1989

JAPAN [3]

Although Sino-Japanese trade was relatively balanced from the mid-1970s to the mid-1980s, Japan began to run massive surpluses in the trade as China relaxed import and foreign exchange controls in 1985. In 1984 the surplus was U.S. $3.1 billion; in 1985, out of U.S.$21.3 billion total trade, the Japanese surplus was $9.1 billion. While Chinese import controls have tightened substantially since 1985, and Japan's positive balance has been cut, Japan still is in the black in the relationship (down to U.S. $3.1 billion in 1988 and U.S. $2.2 billion in 1989).

Japanese skill in the China trade is enhanced by "triple-team-ing" collaboration between trading companies (the sogo shosha), which provide the market penetration; manufacturers, which supply the appropriate goods; and banks, which provide attractive financing. Concessionary loans add to the picture—for instance, in 1990, Japanese banks concluded a $2 billion, 10-year loan with in-

---

[3] The discussion on Japan is drawn from an excellent report on Sino-Japanese economic relations by Todd Thurwacher, an officer in the U.S. Foreign and Commerical Service. See his "Japan in China: The Guangdong Example," *China Business Review*, January–February 1990, pp. 7-17.

TABLE 2
Japan & Hong Kong
Two-Way Trade with China, 1982-89

Year	U.S. $ Millions		·% of total trade		% of Asian Trade	
	Japan	Hong Kong	Japan	Hong Kong	Japan	Hong Kong
1982	8,708	6,495	21.4	15.9	47.7	35.6
1983	10,012	7,507	23.1	17.3	49.6	37.2
1984	13,212	9,416	26.0	18.5	49.9	35.5
1985	11,910	11,910	30.5	17.1	54.8	30.7
1986	17,542	15,348	23.5	20.6	46.2	40.4
1987	16,479	22,201	19.9	26.8	37.3	50.2
1988	19,108	30,244	18.5	29.4	33.7	53.3
1989	18,897	34,458	16.9	30.9	30.4	55.3

terest rates 0.25 percent above LIBOR (London Interbank Offered Rate). Other loans, including one from the Japanese government worth Y810 billion (about U.S. $5 billion) and featuring both low interest and a 10-year grace period, are apparently in the offing.[4]

One outcome of the Japanese strategy is that the majority of Japanese exports are high-valued-added goods; China, on the other hand, exports commodities or low-tech goods, as table 3 shows.

Another outcome of the strategy is that investment has followed the loans and trade. According to Chinese figures, in 1988 Japan provided about one-third of China's total foreign capital utilization (loans plus investment)—$3.3 billion—and about one-sixth of utilized direct foreign investment—$514 billion.[5] Chinese sources, looking at investment pledged or contracted for 1979-89, show Japan as the third largest investor in China after Hong Kong and the United States (see table 4). Toward the end of the decade, Japan surpassed the United States.

Japanese investment is spread across China, but is concentrated in either industrial sites—Shanghai, Beijing-Tainjin—or the Guangzhow economic zones; the industries are, not surprisingly, in those goods in which Japan excels in the Asian market: electronics, (e.g. CRTs), electrical appliances (e.g. refrigerators, washing machines, clock radios), and metals.

---

[4] *Business China*, February 12, 1990, p.17.
[5] *Business China*, February 12, 1990, p.19.

Table 3
Sino-Japanese Trade by Commodity, 1988
(Percent of Value)

Chinese Imports from Japan		Chinese Exports to Japan	
U.S. $11.06 billion		U.S. $8.05 billion	
Machinery	40.8%	Petroleum	38.8%
Iron and Steel	39.7%	Textiles	26.1%
Telecommunications	11.1%	Clothing	17.6%
Vehicles	8.2%	Fruit and Vegetables	9.3%
		Iron and Steel	8.3%

SOURCE: Todd Thurwacher, "Japan in China: The Guangdong Example," *China Business Review*, January-February 1990, pp. 7-17.

8

TABLE 4
Shares of Contracted Foreign Investment in China
Top Five Sources, 1979-89
(U.S. $ billion)

Total	36.79	
Hong Kong and Macao	22.67	61.6%
United States	4.11	11.2%
Japan	3.18	8.7%
Singapore	0.69	1.9%
West Germany	0.59	1.6%

SOURCE: Official Chinese statistics cited in *Business China*, June 25, 1990, p. 193.

HONG KONG

As Table 2 shows, since 1985 Japan has been losing significant market share to Hong Kong. What accounts for this turn of events?

The answer, of course, is to be found in the hundreds of ships that lie at anchor in Victoria Harbor, the crowds of trucks that carry both Chinese and Hong Kong license plates that jam the roads between the territory and Guangdong, the freight cars that shuttle back and forth between Kowloon Station and the mainland and Kaitak's booming airfreight business. In short, Hong Kong has regained its natural and historical role in the political economy of the Pacific as the entrepôt for the China trade.

According to Hong Kong government statistics,[6] Hong Kong's imports from China grew from H.K. $15 billion in 1979 to H.K. $196.7 billion in 1989 (U.S. $1.9 billion to U.S. $25.2 billion at the current rate of exchange of U.S. $ 1=H.K. $7.8), an increase of 1226%. In 1979 about 37% of these imports was reexported; in 1989, 54% were reexports. In other words, there is significant double growth here; the value of Chinese goods reexported from Hong Kong grew by over 1800%.

The same kind of dramatic growth can also be seen in the exports from Hong Kong to China. Hong Kong's domestic exports to China went from H.K. $0.6 billion to H.K. $43 billion over the same period, an increase of well over 7500%. But at the same time, Hong Kong's reexports to China went from H.K. $1.3 billion in 1979 to H.K. $103 billion in 1989, an increase of 7800%. Another way to look at this would be the percentage of total world-wide Hong Kong imports reexported to the PRC: in 1979 the figure was 6.6%; by 1987 it had reached over 32%. In sum, China is the largest market for the territory's reexports. As we might expect, much of this indirect trade originates with or is destined for China's other major trading partners. In 1989, the U.S. took 62% of Hong Kong's China reexports (U.S. $8.46 billion); Japan accounted for 14% (U.S. $1.92 billion). Trade in services—banking, tourism—backs up this trade: in 1989, for instance, about 16 million trips were made from Hong Kong into China (in 1979, 3 million trips were made across the border).

But there is far more to the Hong Kong-China relationship than merchandise trade. Two other aspects are key to the relationship: investment and internal dimension of the reexport trade.

Hong Kong and China are now locked in a entangling web of mutual investments so tight that one might argue that economic union will occur long before 1997, the date for China's political reaccession of the territory. As Hong Kong is the greatest source of direct foreign investment in China, so too China is the leading "overseas investor" in Hong Kong.

Some 70% of direct foreign investment in the PRC comes from Hong Kong; over the decade 1979–1989 almost 22,000 enterprises with a realized capital of U.S. $15.4 billion were approved by the Chinese authorities. Most of these investments are relatively small-scale operations in the Special Economic Zones and Pearl River Delta area of Guangdong province (the home province of most Hong Kong people). They not only are the major source of Hong Kong re-export trade, but also are estimated to employ as many as

---

[6] Hong Kong Government Secretariat, "Notes on Hong Kong-China Economic Relations," Hong Kong, April 1990. All the figures in this section are drawn from this report or are calculations based on them and DOTS.

2 million industrial workers—about twice the number working in industries in the territory.

China also has a very significant presence in Hong Kong, symbolized by the Bank of China building designed by I.M. Pei that dominates the Central district's skyline. According to a study published by the American Chamber of Commerce in Hong Kong in 1988,[7] there are over 360 PRC-related firms in the territory; this is undoubtedly an undercount. While most PRC-related operations have central government connections—the Chinese "flagship" investment vehicle is the China International Trust and Investment Corp. (CITIC) and at least one other firm, Everbright, reports directly to the Chinese State Council of Ministers—virtually every province and municipality in the PRC, with the exception of remote Xinjiang and Tibet—has direct representation in Hong Kong. Overall, China is the leading source of outside funds for investment in Hong Kong; in manufacturing, it ranks third after the United States and Japan.

The exact amounts invested are difficult to estimate—Hong Kong disclosure rules and confidential Chinese business practices obscure ownership and financial details, but *Business Asia* puts the figure at about U.S. $380 million. CITIC's investments, which go beyond manufacturing, are reported to have reached U.S. $1.3 billion. For comparison's sake, it should be noted that U.S. investment in Hong Kong manufacturing totals around U.S. $1.14 billion; Japanese investment equals some U.S. $893 million. China also holds important minority positions in some of the territory's high-profile service industries, including a 12.5% share in Cathay Pacific and 20% of Hong Kong Telecommunications.[8]

Thus it is clear that the economies of Hong Kong and the PRC are closely linked, and may form two legs of a China triad. The third leg of this evolving triad is Taiwan; in a most interesting way, Taiwan's growing relationship with the PRC runs straight through Hong Kong via the territory's indirect trade route.

TAIWAN

There has always been some amount of trade between Taiwan and mainland China. Before the political and economic reforms of Deng Xiaoping on the mainland and Jiang Jingguo on Taiwan this largely unacknowledged trade was restricted to traditional goods such as herbal medicines, and most of it went through Hong Kong. In addition there was some undocumented direct trade—some might call it smuggling—by fishermen and other nautical entrepreneurs across the Taiwan Straits.

But with the reforms on both side of the Straits in the mid-1980s, this trade began to expand, again mostly through Hong Kong. Mainland demand for Taiwan consumer goods and investment grew; funds began to flow to the Chinese special economic zones in Fujian province, directly across from Taiwan and the ancestral

---

[7] American Chamber of Commerce in Hong Kong, *PRC-Related Firms in Hong Kong and Macau*, Hong Kong, 1988.
[8] See Hong Kong Government Industry Department, *Overseas Investment in Hong Kong Manufacturing Industries*, 1989, Hong Kong 1990; Shane Green and Jill McGivering, "Enter the Dragon," *South China Morning Post*, October 6, 1990; "Hong Kong: Statistical Profile," *Business Asia*, April 1990, p. 47.

home of most Taiwanese. A combination of formal moves in the late 1980s facilitated these developments: in 1988 and 1990, Taiwan approved a broad range of PRC goods, from aluminum ingots to sesame seeds, for indirect import to the island; Taiwan business people were allowed to visit the mainland; a semi-official Taiwanese organization was set up in the United States and Hong Kong to ease trade; and on the mainland itself, special incentives for Taiwanese investment were granted by Fujian and Guangdong provinces and by the Special Economic Zones in Xiamen, Zhuhai, and Shantou.[9] Table 5 below indicates the growth in trade via Hong Kong as it also shows the imbalance in the trade in Taiwan's favor.

TABLE 5
Taiwan Trade with PRC via Hong Kong, 1984-1989
(U.S. $ millions)

Trade	1984	1989	1989 as % of 1984
From Taiwan	421.5	2,896.5	587
To Taiwan	128.1	586.9	358
Total	**549.6**	**3,483.5**	**533**

SOURCE: Hong Kong government figures in *China Trade Report*, July 1990, p. 160.

In other words Taiwan's 1989 two-way indirect trade with China through Hong Kong, worth some U.S. $3.48 billion, was greater than the PRC's two-way trade with Singapore (valued at US$3.2 billion). This merchandise trade has perhaps been doubled by Taiwanese tourism on the Mainland.[10]

But there is more to the picture than just trade and tourism. Taiwan has also become a major investor in mainland China; and because the Taipei government bans direct investment, the funds flow through Hong Kong. In 1989, according to Taiwanese sources, out of Taiwan's overseas investments of $3.2 billion, $2 billion went to the mainland, making Taiwan the largest source of foreign investment in China in 1989. Most of these funds have gone to Fujian and Guangdong provinces, and are concentrated in Xiamen, right across the Straits. Indeed, Taiwanese investment in Fujian is so important that some observers have called the province "an industrial park" for Taiwan, and have credited the investment with Fujian's superior economic performance.[11]

---

[9] For a more detailed account and review, see Mitchell A. Silk, "Silent Partners," *China Business Review*, September–October 1990.

[10] "Taiwan: China Trade Explodes," *China Trade Report*, February 1989, p. 4.

[11] Data provided by the Chung Hwa Institute of Economic Research, Taipei, cited in "L'offensive des investisseurs taiwanais," *Le Figaro-Economique*, July 24, 1990, p. VIII. These numbers do not coincide with figures from the PRC Ministry of Foreign Economics Relations and Trade, which puts 1989 investment from Taiwan at U.S. $400 million; the discrepancy, typical of statistics in the China trade, may be due to the difference between amounts pledged and actual investment—see C. Cheng, "Taiwan Money: One Bright Spot," *Far Eastern Economic Review*, August 23, 1990, p. 42. See also Dinah Lee, Taiwan's Dollar Offensive is Gaining Ground in China," *Business Week*, June 11, 1990.

Investment from Taiwan is apt to continue at this startling pace. Taiwan has the largest hard currency reserves of any nation, about U.S. $80 million, and a large current account surplus. As with Hong Kong, the business opportunities and attachments of the mainland combine to provide Taiwan with a good location to which the island's businessmen can spin off their low-wage, low-skill industries as they prepare to compete upscale with Korea and Europe. Indeed, that seems to be the case, since in July 1990 some 600 Taiwan business people met in Beijing to discuss investment opportunities.[12]

SOUTH KOREA

While the growing interdependence of the PRC, Hong Kong, and Taiwan is striking, so too is the increasing competition between "The Chinas" and South Korea. While businesses in Hong Kong and Taiwan tend to be small or medium size family firms, Korean businesses with interests in China tend to be the *chaebols*, or industrial conglomerates. Korea conducts both direct and indirect trade with China, and indeed, there even has been talk of setting up a special economic zone in Shandong, a short boat ride from the Korean peninsula, for Korean investment. There are also reports that the two countries will set up trade offices in their respective capitals.[13]

These trade links are recent but continue to grow, even as China maintains relations with Pyongyang. Before 1985—when Chinese representatives attended an IMF meeting in Seoul—the trade was small and conducted through Hong Kong. But the ice broke that year; if we count both direct and indirect trade, Korea-PRC trade in 1985 totaled about $2 billion, with Korean exports valued at $1.2 billion, and Chinese exports at U.S. $0.8 billion. By 1988, just three years later, direct trade had increased by 150% to $3.65 billion and the total, including indirect trade, had reached $5.7 billion. South Korea, once a minor player in the China trade, by 1988 ranked fifth only behind Hong Kong, Japan, the United States and West Germany.[14]

Thus Korea's trade with China is substantial, greater than Taiwan's (if the island's undocumentable services-related trade is left out). Korean expertise in large-scale industry assures it a continuing role in China's economic evolution. Details are sketchy, but Korean banks are active in Hong Kong, and thus further north, and Korean firms are making investments in China: for instance, Daewoo is reported to have invested in a refrigerator plant in Fujian, and other major *chaebols*—Sunkyong, Samsung, Hyundai,

---

[12] "Red Carpet for Taiwan Money," *International Herald-Tribune*, July 6, 1990. China's relaxed attitude toward the environment may figure here as well. Certainly one of the most publicized nonevents of 1989–90 in the China investment area has been an effort by Formosa Plastics to build a new, U.S.$ 5 billion petrochemical plant in China. The company could not build the plant in Taiwan because of new environmental regulations, and was attempting to locate the new plant in Fujian. While the outcome of the effort remains in doubt, one suspects that other similar efforts will surface in the future. See *Business China*, July 30, 1990, pp. 107–108.

[13] "Mayor of Weihai Welcomes Investment by Korean Firms," *Korea Herald* (Kyodo), April 5, 1988; and James L. Tyson, "China, South Korea Bolster Ties," *Christian Science Monitor*, October 11, 1990.

[14] Ken Yun, "Crossing the Yellow Sea," *China Business Review*, January–February 1989; and "PRC-South Korea Trade Boom Set Back by PRC Political Crisis," *Business China*, June 26, 1989.

and Lucky-Goldstar—likewise are active or at the least considering investments.[15]

III. ASEAN

We have seen that the mainstay of China's Asian trade is with Japan and the NICs. What of China's trade relations with the ASEAN states?

In dollar terms, China's trade with the ASEAN has increased, going from $1.85 billion in 1980 to $6.6 billion in 1989; proportionally, the ASEAN share of the China trade has run to 4–6% of the total, and about 10% of the Asian sector. The annual growth has kept up with China's trade expansion, averaging 15.3% per year.

Of the ASEAN states, only Singapore has an important volume—around $3.2 billion in 1989; only Singapore and Indonesia showed growth in trade above the trend line, so shown in table 6.

TABLE 6
China's Trade with ASEAN
(U.S. $ Millions)

Trading Partner	Total		Growth Rate	% of PRC Asian Trade		% of 1989 Trade
	1980	1989	1980-89	1980	1989	
ASEAN	1,850	6,637	15.3	10.8%	10.6%	5.9%
Singapore	611	3,192	20.2	3.6%	5.1%	2.9%
Thailand	452	1,256	12.0	2.6%	2.0%	1.1%
Indonesia	35	805	41.7	2.0%	1.3%	0.07%
Malaysia	424	1,044	10.5	2.5%	1.7%	0.09%
Philippines	328	340	0.4	1.9%	0.5%	0.03%

NOTE: Brunei's trade with PRC is extremely small, ranging between $4 million and $10 million, much less than 1% and is virtually all Chinese exports.

SOURCE: The numbers in the table are from DOTS; the commentary draws upon the excellent and more detailed article by Clyde D. Stolenberg, "China's Links to Southeast Asia," *China Business Review*, May-June 1990, pp. 33-38.

Singapore's dominance of PRC-ASEAN trade reflects not only Chinese ethnic links but also Singapore's NIC economic capabilities; there are also some investments from Singapore in China, including a hotel in Xiamen, (another example of the strength of provincial sentiments for the motherland), and some joint ventures, including one with China's Satellite Communications Technology

[15] Yun, op. cit., and "South Korea Forges New Links," *China Trade Report*, November 1988.

Corporation, a branch of the Chinese Academy of Sciences. Malaysia's trade record shows high steady growth, essentially consistent with ASEAN's share, but it is small, primarily agricultural commodities. Thailand's economic boom and close relations with China, largely due to the Cambodian crisis, combine to explain Thailand's standing in the PRC trade. Although the numbers suggest a minor decline in the economic relationship, this may just be an exception. In any event, the figures probably do not include China's military assistance and sales to Thailand. Interestingly, there has been some investment from Thailand in the PRC, mostly in processing industries, and China has invested in a small number of enterprises in Thailand, including construction firms and automobile parts factories. To be sure, none of these trade trends are absolutely smooth—for instance, trade with the Philippines hit a low of $188 million in 1983 and a high of 411 in 1985, all reflecting the political turmoil that has hit the island republic.

Certainly the most interesting trend here is that shown by Indonesia, the largest nation in ASEAN. Indonesia has not had diplomatic relations with China since the mid-1960s, when China was involved in a bloody but failed coup attempt that was followed by a massive anti-Chinese program that drew on the Sinophobia of the local Indonesian population. Despite that background, trade in the 1980s grew from year to year. Most of China's imports form Indonesia are in wood and agricultural products; China's exports are light manufactures. But more important, on the political front, Djakarta and Beijing established diplomatic relations in late 1990.

The importance of Indonesian-PRC ties is more than bilateral, however. Because of Indonesia's political weight in ASEAN, the move will have a positive effect on Sino-ASEAN links as a whole. Malaysia may now take a softer attitude toward China; and Singapore, always sensitive to the Chinese factor in the politics of its neighbors, established diplomatic relations with Beijing in October 1990, only after Indonesia made its move. As both the political and economic outlooks improve, PRC-ASEAN links will also solidify. However, in the absence of a truly major industrial base in Southeast Asia, it is unlikely that the ASEAN share of total China trade will exceed general trends. For ASEAN and the PRC alike, it is the major capitalist markets that will remain the most important.

IV. OTHER ASIAN PLAYERS

Two other Asian groups remain to be discussed: the Indian Subcontinent and the Communist countries. Neither group is an important participant in the China trade, and in both cases the change in trade relations has been negative.

Pakistan, not surprisingly, given the country's long-standing political links with China in the Sino-Soviet/Sino-Indian competition, is the PRC's largest trade partner in the region, but over the decade of the 1980s trade volume remained essentially constant or negative, starting at U.S. $312 million in 1980, dipping to U.S. $232 million in 1986, and rising again to U.S. $385 million in 1988 and U.S. $592 million in 1989. In other words, Pakistan's 1988 trade volume with China is just under the PRC-Philippine trade total; in 1989, it was just about equal to PRC-Macao trade throughout (U.S.

$615 million). India's trade over the decade reached a high point of U.S. $271 million in 1989, starting at U.S. $162 million in 1981 and hitting bottom in 1984 at U.S. $62 million. Other trade relations are minor, with only Bangladesh reaching trade volumes of over U.S. $100 million on the strength of Chinese exports in 1982, 1985, 1986, and 1988.

On the whole, the Subcontinent's total share of Chinese trade has declined—from a high of 2.2% in 1981 to a low of 0.8-1% from 1985 on. Pakistan has held about 50% of the area's total trade with China on average over the past decade, and India's share has ranged from 10% to 28% over the same period. Although the absolute numbers remain small, up to 1988, Indian exports to China had gained on Pakistani exports to the PRC; in 1989, however, there was a large jump in Chinese imports from Pakistan as shown in Table 7.

TABLE 7
China's Trade with India and Pakistan, 1981, 1983, 1989
(U.S. $ millions)

Types of Trade	1981		1988		1989	
	India	Pakistan	India	Pakistan	India	Pakistan
Total Two-Way Trade	162	544	247	385	271	592
Total % Subcontinent	17.4	58.4	28.1	43.8	24.9	54.3
Exports % Subcontinent	18.5	48.3	22.3	49.4	23.2	50.5
Imports % Subcontinent	16.4	67.3	46.7	26.4	28.3	62.0
Subcontinent % of total Chinese Trade	2.2		0.9		1.0	

Despite improving political relations with India and continuing friendship with Pakistan and Bangladesh, the economics of the relationships are not promising. Although India certainly has the greatest potential for international trade in South Asia, it has a long way to go—her total trade in 1988 came to U.S. $39.64 billion, about one-third of China's, just a bit more than Malaysia's (U.S. $37.69 billion), and, to look at another large Third World country, much less than Brazil's (U.S. $49.83 billion).

China's trade with Asian communist countries is also small, and is probably dominated by the military sector, which is apt to be unreported in any case. Trade figures with Laos and Kampuchea, if reported at all, barely figure in official statistics (U.S. $21 million total trade with Kampuchea in 1988, U.S. $18 million of which is for imports). Trade with Mongolia reached a high point of U.S. $25 million total in 1987 and 1988; much of this, we suspect, was conducted on a counter-trade basis.

North Korea's trade with China is somewhat more substantial, although as reported across the decade it has declined from a high of U.S. $677 million in 1980 to a low of U.S. $484 million in 1984, and ending at U.S. $562 million in 1989 (according to official figures). This volume is not trivial, but it is far surpassed by South Korea's trade, and falls between China's 1989 trade with Argentina (U.S. $576 million) and Spain (U.S. $498 million). Although it is likely that there is much cross-border and military trade that simply does not show up in the statistics, and it is true that the political relationship between Pyongyang and Beijing still is active, North Korea is simply out of the world economic loop, and thus does not play a very important role.

V. COMMODITIES TRADED

Thus far the discussion has focused on dollar volumes. For another perspective one needs to look at the commodity composition of trade. An important outcome of the Deng reforms has been a shift in China's export goods away from primary commodities toward manufactures—a common development path. The change can be seen by comparing Chinese exports for 1965—admittedly a period of isolation, the year before the Cultural Revolution—with those of 1987 (see Table 8).

TABLE 8
Percentage Structure of Chinese Merchandise Exports,
1965 vs. 1987

Year	Fuels, Minerals, metals	Other Primary Commodities	Machinery, Transport Equipment	Other Manufactured Goods	U.S. $ billion s
1965	6	48	3	43	2.2
1987	14	16	4	66	39.5

SOURCE: The percentages are from *World Development Report*, 1989, World Bank, Washington, D.C., 1989, Table 16, p. 194. The sources for the dollar figures, are from different sources and thus not altogether consistent, 1965 figures from -- *Statistical Yearbook of China 1983*, State Statistical Bureau, Beijing, p. 421; 1987--DOTS (1989).

A more detailed analysis will be difficult for several reasons. First, China exports a variety of commodities, so an analysis may list goods that comprise 3% or less of imports or exports. Second, the way in which trade composition is reported—by Standard International Trade Classification (SITC) categories—may be convenient for customs officials but presents problems for a general analysis. For instance, beverages are classified along with tobacco in the same category (SITC 1), and not in the general food category

(SITC 0, which includes "live animals chiefly for food"). In addition there are two catch-all classifications, SITC 8, "Miscellaneous manufactured articles," and SITC 9, "Commodities not classified elsewhere."

This dilemma is shown by the growth of SITC 9 category goods ("Other") over the decade. In 1980, SITC 9 items comprised only 2% of total Chinese exports (by value); in 1987 the category accounted for 18% of exports. The major shifts that have accompanied this increasing diversity of exported products included a major decline in the value of petroleum exports, which reflected a drop in world oil prices, and a minor drop in food exports. Other categories, including manufactures, remained relatively steady.

Accordingly, one can gain a better understanding of the nature of the Chinese trade by looking at the top dozen items in the trade. Table 9 lists these exports according to Chinese customs statistics for 1987–89.

In other words, if one accepts the estimate that roughly two-thirds of Chinese exports are manufactures of some kind, almost half of those manufactured exports are in textiles (apparel, fabrics, fibers) and less than 5% of manufactured exports are in the higher valued-added areas of telecommunications and sound equipment, metal manufactures, and electrical machinery.

Overall these higher value-added categories, while small, show the greatest growth, far in excess of overall export growth. Since national economies grow through moving up the technological and value-added ladder, the figures indicate not only where China is headed but also why China is so sensitive to international measures affecting textiles and clothing (clothing itself is the next value-added step beyond fibers and fabrics).

Parenthetically it should be noted that the U.S. Arms Control and Disarmament Agency reports that arms made up a varying percentage of Chinese exports between 1980–87, starting at 1.5% of exports in 1980, reaching a peak of 7.2% in 1984 and falling, both in percentage and in value terms, to 2.5% in 1987. China's major customers during the period 1983–87 were Iraq (U.S. $3.3 billion worth of armor, aircraft, missiles and artillery), Iran (U.S. $1.8 billion) and Egypt (U.S. $550 million); in Asia, China sold arms to Thailand (about U.S. $90 million in small arms and substandard armor), Pakistan (U.S. $270 million) and Bangladesh (U.S. $120 million). The hard currency received for these weapons flowed back both to the Chinese military and to the technical industries; the relatively small amounts therefore have an importance. [16]

China's import composition is somewhat less concentrated in value terms, but with one important exception, is concentrated in industrial or intermediate goods, as shown in table 10.

The important exception here is the third item in the list, cereals; because of China's overwhelming concern over and difficulties with food supply, 9% of the PRC's imports went to either cereals for consumption or fertilizer; the jump in petroleum imports (and the corresponding decline in petroleum exports) may be related. But the major point to be drawn from this sea of figures is that

---

[16] Arms Control and Disarmament Agency, *World Military Expenditures and Arms Transfers*, 1988, Tables 3 & 4.

TABLE 9
Top Fifteen Chinese Exports
By Percentage of Total Export Value

Item	1987	1988	1989	1987/89 (% change by value)
Exports in U.S. $ billions (from Chinese customs)	39.44	47.54	52.49	33.1
Textile yarn, fabric	14.7	13.6	13.3	20.8
Clothing	9.5	10.2	11.7	63.5
Petroleum products	10.2	7.1	6.8	-10.5
Miscellaneous manufactures	3.4	3.5	4.3	72.1
Vegetable and fruit	3.3	3.4	3.1	25.8
Textile fibers	3.8	3.5	2.9	2.5
Metal manufactures	2.0	2.1	2.3	51.8
Telecommunications and sound equipment	1.3	1.7	2.2	126.0
Footwear	1.2	1.5	2.1	126.0
Fish, etc.	1.8	2.1	2.0	44.1
Electrical machinery	0.8	1.2	1.6	144.5
Non-metallic mineral manufactures	1.1	1.2	1.5	80.4
Animal feed	1.4	1.8	1.4	37.5
Iron and steel	1.1	2.1	1.4	68.4

SOURCE: Chinese Customs statistics compiled from China Trade Report and Business China, 1988-90.

China presents, in her foreign trade, the picture of a still industrializing nation: high-technology, high-skill goods are imported, and low-to-medium technology and skill products are exported.

Tables 11 and 12 show Asia's importance in trade with China in the top five import and export commodities for 1989.

TABLE 10
Top Fifteen Chinese Imports
By Percentage of Total Import Value
1987-1989

Item	1987	1988	1989	1987-89 % of Change
Imports in U.S. billions (from Chinese Customs)	43.22	55.25	59.14	36.9
Iron and steel	11.1	8.4	9.8	21.1
Specialized machinery	11.5	8.3	9.6	14.0
Cereals	3.9	3.4	5.0	76.7
Textile yarns and fabrics	4.3	4.3	4.8	54.0
Electrical machinery	3.7	4.2	4.1	50.4
General industrial machinery	4.0	3.9	4.0	37.3
Fertilizer	3.2	4.3	4.0	69.0
Textile fibers	2.6	3.5	3.9	102.3
Artificial resins, plastics	3.4	6.4	3.7	50.1
Telecommunications equipment	3.4	3.3	3.0	22.8
Transport equipment	3.4	3.3	3.0	20.2
Petroleum	0.9	1.2	2.5	269.0
Road vehicles	3.0	2.7	2.4	10.5
Organic chemicals	2.3	3.1	2.4	40.8
Power generating equipment	1.3	1.9	2.3	140.7

SOURCE: Chinese Customs statistics compiled from *China Trade Report and Business China*, 1988-90.

VI. OPPORTUNITIES AND DILEMMAS

Opportunities and dilemmas are often the two sides of an issue, and certainly this would seem to apply in the case of China's foreign trade. Two related issues, however, seem to be predominate.

One is China's foreign trade standing relative to her Asian trading partners. Although China's foreign trade has improved in both quantity and quality, she is just keeping pace with the foreign

TABLE 11
Top Chinese Imports
By Country of Origin, 1989
Total Import Value = U.S. $59.14 Billion

Commodity	Value in U.S. $ billions	% of Imports	Nations of Origin	Amount for Each Nation (in U.S. $ billions)	% of Comm.
Iron and Steel (SITC Code 67)	5.80	9.8	Japan	2.84	49
			Germany	0.52	9
			USSR, EC,	0.41	7
			Brazil U.S.,		
			East	0.35	6
			Europe		
Specialized Industrial Machinery (SITC Code 72)	5.68	9.6	Japan	1.14	20
			Germany	0.91	16
			Hong Kong	0.74	13
			U.S.	0.62	11
Grain (SITC Code 4)	2.96	5	U.S.	1.42	48
			Austrailia	0.33	11
			Canada	0.30	10
			Thailand	0.27	9
Textile yarn	2.84	4.8	Hong Kong	1.42	50
			Japan	0.40	14
			EC	0.17	6
Electrical machinery (SITC Code 77)	2.42	4.1	Japan	0.65	27
			Hong Kong	0.51	21
			EC	0.29	12
			U.S.	0.19	8
Totals, top five imports	19.69	33.3			

SOURCE: Calculations based on data from *Business China*, May 14, 1990 and table 8.

trade performance of her smaller NIC neighbors. The key issue here is strategy. Taiwan and Korea, for instance, have not only seized upon a strategy of export-led growth, but have also promoted vigorous internal commercial and technological competition as a prerequisite and continuing condition of that growth. It is true that

TABLE 12
Top Five Chinese Exports
By Country of Destination, 1989
Total Export Value = \$52.49 Billion

Commodity	Value in (U.S. \$ billions)	% of Exports	Nations of Origin	Value (in U.S. billions)	% of Comm.
Textile yarn and fabric (SITC Code 65)	6.98	13.3	Hong Kong	3.42	49
			Japan	0.84	12
			EC	0.77	11
			U.S.	0.49	7
Apparel (SITC Code 84)	6.14	11.7	Hong Kong	1.97	32
			Japan	1.17	19
			U.S.	0.92	15
			EC	0.68	11
Petroleum (SITC Code 33)	3.57	6.8	Japan	1.78	50
			Singapore	0.61	17
			U.S.	0.57	16
			Hong Kong	0.18	5
Miscellaneous manufactures (SITC Code 89)	2.26	4.3	Hong Kong	0.86	38
			EC	0.36	16
			U.S.	0.32	14
			Japan	0.14	6
Vegetables and fruit (SITC Code 05)	1.63	3.1	Japan	0.46	28
			Hong Kong	0.44	27
			EC	0.13	8
			Germany	0.11	7
			U.S.	0.08	5
Totals, Top Five Exports	20.58	39.2			

SOURCE: Calculations based on data from *Business China*, May 28, 1990 and table 7.

these economies reached their take-off stages at the time when not only were the large markets of the capitalist democracies open but when those governments were actively promoting development through such schemes as the Generalized System of Preferences (GSP). But GSP simply provided the framework—the fact is that the NICs jumped on and have remained on the back of the tiger of competitive advantage.

China, on the other hand, persists in following the socialist road at a time when virtually all the traffic on that route, including the

Soviet Union, has taken the emergency exits. Even in the best of times during the decade of reform, the state plan remained the key. Now, after June 1989, the role of the state and the internationally uncompetitive state enterprises are even more important. [17] The issue is not so much planning itself, but rather the nature of that planning—and certainly China's record here has been to suppress the kind of internal competition so vital to international success. Indeed, this is only to be expected, given China's anxieties about competition and foreign-inspired disorder; this is reinforced by or reelected in the PRC's basic trade strategy of technology transfer for import-substitution, a path also now quite abandoned as an avenue to growth.

Several issues arise here. First, China's trade is indeed part of the most dynamic sector of the world trading system, but the strategy being followed may not allow for continued success. To be sure, the inertia of the reforms will keep China playing in the system, but the NICs, not to mention Japan, will ultimately pull away. This trend has not gone unnoticed in China. Fang Lizhi, the noted dissident, has written that because of the "weakness of the state system [that is, the current autocratic regime], the critical trend of the economic distance between mainland China and the developed countries has not been improved. In fact, the distance is increasing. [18]

But still other factors suggest that the distance—and the accompanying political tension—will continue to grow. One doubts that China will settle for simply being the dumping ground for old technologies competitive only because of the low cost of Chinese labor, a hinterland for the more advanced economies of the area. Furthermore, as the kind of foreign loans so necessary for continued upgrading of Chinese industry become harder to get in the post-Tiananmen environment, exports become increasingly important as a source of foreign exchange. But at the same time, protectionism in China's major capitalistic markets is growing and, as a result of China's austerity program, the economy as a whole is slowing. The contradictions facing China's trade are serious.

This economic dilemma, of course, has a larger political context. At the global level, there are the issues of China's perhaps diminished place in the superpower strategic triangle and the potential problems of a looming world recession, issues far beyond our charter here. At the national level, the 1988–89 austerity measures—a reform of the reforms—in China has much to do with the reinforcement of political orthodoxy or "stability," as the Chinese leadership puts it.

One target was the reformist economic decentralization that allowed for growth and development. But the decentralization fostered the reemergence of political regionalism as well, one of the plagues of Chinese history. [19] And thus the twin and stifling Sino-

---

[17] See, for instance, James McGregor, "Beijing Faces Tough Choice between Reform, Political Ideology in Charting Economic Course," *Asian Wall Street Journal Weekly*, October 29, 1990, p. 17.

[18] Fang Lizhi, "Declaration to Support Democratic Reform in Mainland China," December 20, 1988, *World Affairs*, Winter 1989-1990, pp. 135-37.

[19] See, for instnance, Ann Scott Tyson, "Provincial Wars Over Trade Concern Chinese," *Christian Science Monitor*, October 18, 1990.

Leninist orthodoxies of economic and political centralism came to be revised.

Another dilemma/opportunity—closely related to the first—lies in the way in which the PRC handles Hong Kong. In order to understand the Hong Kong dilemma one needs knowledge of the larger Chinese political and economic scene, particularly the importance of personalities and the subordination of economic logic to the political imperative.

Over the past decade, even in the face of the 1997 reaccession of Hong Kong, that nation has become increasingly more important in China's foreign trade picture. Hong Kong's sophisticated infrastructure—physical, financial, communications—is crucial to this achievement. Indeed, a mutual dependency appears to have been established, and it seems logical that China would take genuine steps to assure confidence in the territory.

But the events of June 1989, Chinese maneuvering over the Basic Law that is to govern Hong Kong after 1997, and the specter of centrist economic orthodoxy have combined to introduce doubts. Many of Hong Kong's best and brightest people are emigrating, and recent attempts by the U.K. government to guarantee the right of British abode to a certain number of the Hong Kong public have only been met with Chinese hostility. Accordingly, the immediate psychological outlook for Hong Kong is uncertain—business confidence is down. [20] Would China interfere, to Hong Kong's—and China's—detriment?

On the one hand, Hong Kong's economic importance to China cannot be denied. On the other hand, one should not overlook Hong Kong's political significance. Regaining Hong Kong will, for many Chinese leaders, have a profoundly nationalistic resonance—it will write finis to the Opium War, the conflict which ushered in a century of civil war and humiliation by foreigners.

China's desire to recover the territory and deal with Taiwan may very well have led to the soothing formulation, "One Country, Two Systems"—a slogan that could also be applied to Taiwan. But a certain skepticism must be expressed. Why should we expect a great power to stick to a bilateral agreement without enforcement provisions, particularly when that agreement deals with long-coveted irredenta?

But there are other issues to be raised here as well. To a large degree the course of Chinese history has been an attempt to solve a difficult political problem—how to rule a huge country with a large and fractious population from a single center. The answer, imposed by the First Emperor and pursued by all other Chinese regimes, was One Country, One System—the supremacy of politics. The events of June 1989 show that Chinese tolerance for political heterodoxy—much less political pluralism—remains extremely low.

Furthermore, when other variables in the equation are added—the authoritarian impulse to meddle and to compel conformity, the Chinese habit of seeing politics in all things, and the lack of sophisticated managers to keep Hong Kong running—one can begin to

---

[20] See "Political Uncertainty Hits Optimism," *Asian Business*, April 1990. p. 39.

have a new appreciation for the people standing in lines outside foreign consulates in the territory.

But there is a brighter side. After June 1989, building and investment in the territory continued "without a blip," as a long-time Hong Kong watcher put it. And as another colleague with many years of experience in Hong Kong opined, the political/economic issue is much more likely to result in the "Hongkongization" of South China than in the Communization of Hong Kong. And it certainly is true that south of that age-old dividing line, the Yangtze River, and along the coast, both Hong Kong money and Hong Kong values have had a great impact.

Thus if the nature of the Chinese system does not bode well for Hong Kong, the momentum of change runs in Hong Kong's favor. It is precisely the tension generated by these countervailing currents that sparks the uncertainty in Hong Kong. It may be going too far to say that the future of the China trade depends on the future of Hong Kong, but certainly large parts of those futures overlap.

But Hong Kong's future—and indeed the future of China—is more locked up with issues of personalities than any other factor. Here the key matter will be the outcome of the succession drama that will follow the passing of Deng Xiaoping and other first-generation revolutionaries who, despite their formal retirements, remain the primary power brokers in the system. Political analysis, takes me beyond my charter, but it would appear that the current Li Peng-Yang Shangkun-Zhang Zemin leadership is transitional, dependent on hasty relationships and requirements arising from the Tiananmen events. Furthermore, the time remaining to Hong Kong—six years—is virtually an entire policy cycle in the larger 41-year history of the PRC. Thus one cannot say whether upon the passing of the Old Guard we will see a de facto regionalism with a weak center masquerading as a strong government, military rule, the continuation of a centrist line, or some combination of the three alternatives. Besides, there are some Chinese observers, perhaps reflecting a bit of wishful thinking, who expect acute struggle and maybe even civil war.

But one can say that a peaceful transition—or at the least a transition promising stability—would only enhance trade with the region as a whole. And in the countdown to the reacquisition of Hong Kong there is time for a reassessment of larger trade and economic development strategies to address the dilemmas and opportunities just outlined. The incentives for focused change seem evident; the likelihood of some kind of change seems probable, even if the question of direction remains unresolved. Asia's importance in the China trade is clear. Certainly China's leaders must be aware that in the current global context—the political reaction in the West to Tiananmen, strategic shifts and continuing Asian dynamism in the face of world-wide slowdown—trade with Asia will take on even greater importance for the People's Republic of China.

U.S.-CHINA COMMERCIAL RELATIONS: A DECADE AFTER NORMALIZATION

By Nai-Ruenn Chen *

CONTENTS

SUMMARY

Since the establishment of diplomatic relations between the United States and the People's Republic of China in 1979, a broad range of bilateral economic and commercial ties have gradually developed. U.S. trade with China, driven largely by imports of Chinese goods, has grown rapidly. Investment relations also have expanded significantly, primarily due to large amounts of U.S. investment in China.

Growing U.S.-China commercial relations have been accompanied by a number of trade issues. The main issues relating to U.S. exports to China have focused on U.S. export control policy, U.S. access to the Chinese market, and the protection of U.S. intellectual property rights in China. On the import side, two issues—the textile trade and the application of U.S. import control laws to products from China—have dominated bilateral discussions. The issue of China's growing trade surplus with the U.S. has been complicated by the problem of discrepancies between Chinese and U.S. trade statistics. The business climate in China, in which many foreign companies have found it difficult to operate, has become more restrictive since late 1988 due to the economic recentralization and

---

* International Economist, International Trade Administration, U.S. Department of Commerce. The views expressed in this chapter are those of the writer and do not represent the U.S. Department of Commerce.

increased administrative controls resulting from the austerity policy.

To manage trade issues and facilitate the expansion of commercial relations, the two countries made much progress in the 1980s in developing a general framework for expanded trade largely through government-to-government agreements and consultations. In addition, trade issues were handled through multilateral channels.

This decade-long progress was disrupted by the Tiananmen incident in June 1989. The U.S. government responded to the political events in China by imposing a number of sanctions on important elements in bilateral relations, including those related to trade. At present, many of these elements are still on hold.

In the near term, the U.S.-China commercial relationship is likely to center on issues such as economic sanctions, annual renewal of China's MFN status, the trade imbalance, intellectual property rights, textile trade, and the business environment in China. In the long term, the commercial relationship will be affected by the degree of success that both countries have in resolving these issues, as well as their relations with other trading partners. China's growing economic relations with Hong Kong and Taiwan will especially have a far reaching impact on its trade with the United States. Most fundamentally, however, the long-term commercial relationship between the two countries will be determined by the political environment in China, including the degree of political stability and types of policies pursued by the Chinese leadership.

I. INTRODUCTION

With the establishment of diplomatic relations between the United States and the People's Republic of China in 1979, the two countries began to develop a broad range of economic and commercial ties. U.S. trade with and investment in China, facilitated by government-to-government agreements and consultations, expanded rapidly in the 1980s. The decade-long progress, however, was disrupted by the June 1989 turmoil in Beijing. During the past year, U.S. economic relations with China have been dominated by issues such as sanctions, the debate over the renewal of China's Most-Favored-Nation (MFN) status, and concern about China's retreat from economic reforms. Contrary to the high hopes of a year ago, U.S.-China commercial relations are now clouded by tension and uncertainties.

To assess the future of these relations, the paper begins by looking back at the progress made during the past decade. A recounting of trends in bilateral trade and investment and discussion of the management of major trade issues is followed by a review of the development of government-to-government relations in the decade since 1979, and U.S. economic responses to the political events in China since the Tiananmin incident. Finally, I examine the major factors which will likely shape the course of U.S.-China commercial relations in the 1990s.[1]

---

[1] Information used in this chapter was available as of August 31, 1990.

II. Recent Trends

TRADE

After a twenty-year hiatus, U.S.-China trade resumed in 1972, but remained minimal until 1979, when diplomatic relations were established and China's "open door" policy was initiated. In 1979, bilateral trade totaled $2.3 billion. Ten years later, it reached $17.8 billion. Trade is continuing to grow, and reached $9 billion in the first half of 1990, up 18 percent over the same period in 1989.

U.S. exports to China have fluctuated widely since 1979, largely due to wide variations in Chinese demand for American agricultural products and changes in China's economic, trade, and foreign exchange policies. Political developments since June 1989 have further affected U.S. exports to China. U.S. exports were up 26 percent in the first quarter of 1989 over comparable 1988 levels, 19 percent by mid-year, and only 16 percent at year-end. For 1989 as a whole, U.S. exports to China totaled $5.8 billion. Exports are declining this year, with first six-month export volume estimated at $2.5 billion, down 10.3 percent from the same period last year. In recent years, China has ranked between fifteenth to seventeenth among the largest markets for American products, accounting for about 1.6 percent of total U.S. exports.

The commodity composition of U.S. exports to China has undergone significant changes since 1979. The share of agricultural products in U.S. exports to China was 58 percent in 1979, but declined sharply in the first half of the 1980s to only 2 percent in 1986. Increases in domestic grain production as well as the Chinese government's desire to diversify the sources of foreign grain supplies were largely responsible for this decline. U.S. agricultural exports to China began to recover in 1987, and reached 24 percent of total U.S. exports to China by 1989. The recovery was due to China's failure to meet grain production targets in the last few years. Chinese purchases have been facilitated by the U.S. Export Enhancement Program.

Among U.S. nonagricultural exports to China, machinery and transport equipment shipments have risen most dramatically. These shipments totaled only $229 million in 1979, or 13 percent of U.S. total exports to China, but expanded rapidly in the first half of the 1980s to reach a peak of $1.94 billion in 1985, or 50 percent of the total. This rapid growth was caused by China's demand for these products to support its modernization program, and by the liberalization of U.S. export control policy toward China. Decentralization of China's foreign trade administration was also a contributing factor. U.S. shipments, however, have declined since 1986 largely due to tighter central government control over foreign exchange spending and, more recently, economic retrenchment policies. At $1.91 billion in 1989, machinery and transport equipment still constituted the most important component of U.S. exports to China. The leading exports in this category were aircraft and parts, specialized industrial machinery, power generating equipment, electrical machinery, and office and automatic data processing machines.

Unlike the ups and downs in exports, U.S. import trade with China has grown almost without interruption. U.S. imports from China totaled $592 million in 1979 and, except for a slight dip in 1983, have grown every year at high rates, reaching $12 billion in 1989. Despite the political turmoil in the spring of 1989, import growth accelerated during that year—up 26 percent in the first quarter, 37 percent by mid-year, and 41 percent by the end of the year. This momentum continues to grow, with imports totaling $6.6 billion in the first half of 1990, an increase of 33 percent over January–June 1989 levels. As a result, China now ranks eighth among suppliers to the U.S. with a market share of 2.8 percent.

The commodity composition of U.S. imports from China has changed significantly in recent years. In the early 1980s, U.S. imports from China were dominated by textile and petroleum products. Sales of China's top three export categories—clothing, petroleum, and textiles—accounted for 50–60 percent of China's exports to the United States during 1981–85. Despite the continuing strength of these sales, China's exports have steadily diversified in recent years. In 1989, the same three categories made up only 28 percent of the value of China's exports to the United States. China's exports of light manufactures, telecommunications equipment, and electrical appliances have grown most rapidly. Toys, games, and sporting goods, consumer electronics, footwear, and travel goods are now among China's top export earners in its trade with the United States. The increased diversification of China's exports reflects its competitive strength, which has been bolstered in recent years by the relocation of large numbers of export-oriented processing and assembly plants from Hong Kong and Taiwan to the Chinese mainland.

INVESTMENT

In tandem with increased trade, investment relations between the two countries have grown significantly over the past decade. In response to China's "open door" policies, U.S. firms began to invest in China in 1979. Since then U.S. investment in China has taken a variety of forms—equity joint ventures, contractual joint ventures, wholly-owned subsidiaries, and joint development of offshore oil resources. By the end of 1988, the total amount of investment pledged by U.S. firms had reached $3.3 billion, accounting for 13 percent of total foreign investment in China.

During 1989 U.S. investment in China continued to grow, despite difficulties caused by China's austerity program and mid-year political disturbances. Chinese authorities reported that contracts involving nearly $1 billion in U.S. investment were approved during the year. However, negotiations of most, if not all, of these contracts were initiated before the inception of economic retrenchment in the fall of 1988. U.S. investors' interest has fallen off drastically since Tiananmen. At the end of 1989, U.S. investors had about 950 projects in China, with a total contracted U.S. investment of more than $4 billion and paid-in capital of $1.8 billion.

China is interested in pursuing investments in the United States, although limited foreign exchange availability has prevented the Chinese from undertaking large investment projects. Through

American operations, the Chinese hope to gain access to advanced technology, obtain first-hand experience in modern production and management techniques, and keep abreast of new marketing developments. They may also seek to ensure access to supplies of raw materials for Chinese industry.

As of year-end 1989, the number of Chinese joint ventures in the United States stood at 168, with the amount of capitalization valued at $440 million. Of this total, $370 million has been contributed by the Chinese side. These ventures generally are small in scale and are primarily involved in foreign trade or in production sectors such as electronics manufacturing, machine tools, steel, timber, fishing, and food processing.

III. Main Issues

DIVERGENT OBJECTIVES AND TRADE ISSUES

After a decade of expansion, U.S.-China trade and investment levels remain considerably below their full potential. In 1989, U.S.-China trade constituted only 2.1 percent of U.S. total trade, while U.S. investment in China accounted for only about 1 percent of U.S. investment in Asia. In view of the many complementary aspects of the American and Chinese economies, room for further expansion in trade and investment relations should be substantial. These relations, however, have been restrained by a wide range of issues.

The United States and the PRC have different values, institutions, and expectations. The United States values human rights, democracy, and free enterprise, while China places high priority on socialist ideology, the political principles of the Chinese Communist Party, and a system of public ownership. These basic differences are reflected in different objectives of respective national and foreign policies, which in turn affect both countries' perceptions of their bilateral economic and trade relationship. The impact of these differences on the bilateral relationship has been clearly demonstrated over the past year by the Tiananmen incident and subsequent events.

The United States maintains a basically free trading system. To protect national security, however, the Export Administration Act authorizes the President to impose controls on the export of strategic and high-technology products and technical data originating in the United States. On the import side, U.S. law also provides safeguard measures to protect against unfair trade practices and market disruption from rapidly increasing imports. These American laws run counter to some of the objectives of China's economic modernization and foreign trade policies. For China, the importation of high-technology products is a top national priority. Many of these products, however, are subject to U.S. and multilateral export controls. To pay for imports China needs to generate adequate export earnings. But a number of Chinese export commodities, especially textiles, are subject to import restrictions in the United States.

The United States and China also differ in their expectations of investment. American firms invest abroad primarily to gain access to a foreign market or take advantage of lower production costs.

Their single most important goal is to maximize their profits. In most cases, U.S. firms invest in China in order to establish a foothold that will allow them to penetrate China's domestic market. China turns to foreign capital primarily to supplement domestic financial sources for economic modernization and to obtain greater access to advanced technology, management skills, and international distribution channels. China also seeks to use foreign capital for the purpose of developing its priority sectors, and especially to use foreign capital in ventures which increase China's export competitiveness and introduce advanced technology to China. Profitability, while important to Chinese enterprises participating the joint ventures, may not be an overriding consideration for Chinese policymakers.

The differences between U.S. and Chinese trade and investment policy objectives have been considerably sharpened by recent changes in both economies and in the global marketplace. The chronic trade deficit that the United States suffers has created pressure on Congress and the Administration to support U.S. producers against unfair competition. Moreover, U.S. trade policy also seeks to promote exports by reducing foreign trade barriers and increasing U.S. market access abroad. The Omnibus Trade and Competitiveness Act of 1988 spells out procedures for tackling a number of key issues of concern to American businesses, especially the unfair trade practices used by trading partners and the protection of U.S. intellectual property rights.

Meanwhile, China also has experienced several phases of foreign exchange shortages. In 1984, for example, foreign trade reforms resulted in a sudden reversal of the country's positive trade balance and a rapid decline in its foreign exchange reserves. The situation was aggravated further by losses in export earnings due to a decline in world oil prices. More recently, economic austerity and political turmoil have had a severe impact on external economic relations, resulting in diminishing sources of foreign exchange income. Driven by a desire to maintain a balance in the international payments position, the Chinese government's response to foreign exchange shortages has typically been to restrict imports and promote exports. The effect on U.S.-China trade has been a rapidly growing imbalance for the United States.

Divergent economic objectives have led to trade frictions between the two countries. This section reviews the main issues that have been prominent in the U.S.-China trade relationship over the past decade. These issues are related to U.S. exports, U.S. imports, the balance of trade, and the business climate in China.

U.S. EXPORTS TO CHINA

Bilateral issues pertinent to U.S. exports to China have arisen mostly in two broad areas: the transfer of U.S. technology to China and the access of U.S. products and services to the Chinese domestic market. Related to both areas are also the issues involving the protection of U.S. intellectual property rights in China.

The technology transfer issue centers on U.S. export control policy toward China. One principal incentive for China to normalize relations with the United States in 1979 was its desire to gain greater access to U.S. high-technology products for promoting economic and technological modernization. Prompted by U.S. interest in improving relations with China and mounting pressure from American exporters, the U.S. Government began to liberalize export control policy toward China in May of 1983.[2] It then gradually and significantly enhanced the technical levels of products allowed to be exported to China, and simplified export control procedures. The number of export license approvals increased from about 2,800 in 1983 to 5,700 in 1988, while the value of approved applications rose from $900 million to nearly $3 billion. The United States was close to implementation of a distribution license procedure in June 1989 for China, which would allow multiple shipments under a single license. The procedure has been put on indefinite hold due to Tiananmen.

Prior to June 1989, the U.S. government joined other members of the Coordinating Committee for Multilateral Export Controls (COCOM) to propose further steps to liberalize export controls on high-technology exports to China. The proposal, however, also has been suspended.

Another issue relating to U.S. exports to China has to do with the access of American goods and services to the Chinese market. U.S. firms' entry into the Chinese market is hindered by a complex system of administrative and market controls that China has put in place to keep both exports and imports in line with trade policy and balance-of-payment objectives. The system of administrative controls includes: (1) import bans; (2) import planning; (3) import licensing; (4) import substitution; (5) certificate of approval; (6) import registration; (7) quality licensing; and (8) foreign exchange control.[3] The system of market controls relies on the use of "eco-

---

[2] Shortly after the lifting of the embargo on trade with China in 1971, the United States placed China in country group Y, allowing for sales of nonstrategic goods similar to those allowable for Warsaw Pact countries. In April 1980, more than a year after normalization, China was placed in a separate group of its own, Group P, which was created to maintain the same level of restrictiveness as Group Y, but to allow some differentiation in favor of China. In June 1981, the Reagan Administration announced that for high-technology exports to China there would be "a presumption of approval for products with technical levels twice those previously approved." But this so-called "two-times" policy was not clearly defined, and was difficult to implement. China's complaint about the limits of its "P" status heightened in 1982 and in the spring of 1983, and became a crucial issue in the bilateral relationship.

In May 1983, the Reagan Administration transferred China to country group V, which covered "free world" countries outside of North and South America ranging from NATO allies to India and Yugoslavia. To speed up the processing of license applications, the U.S. Government took additional steps in November 1983 by creating a system of green, yellow, and red "technology zones" to be used in the evaluation of U.S. export license applications for China. "Green zone" applications would be exempt from inter-agency and COCOM review and would be processed with a presumption of approval.

[3] Currently, import bans cover approximately 80 types of consumer goods, raw materials, and production equipment. Under import planning, the government sets limits to the quantity of imports of key commodities.

The system of import licensing began in January 1984 when license requirements were imposed for imports of 26 product categories. Prior to the initiation of retrenchment policies in September 1988, the list had expanded to 53 categories, affecting about one-third of China's imports. Since then China has increased further the use of licensing—the system now covers an estimated 40 to 50 percent of China's imports by value. In recent years, import substitution regulations have been issued restricting the import of a number of products, especially machinery and electronics, for which domestically produced substitutes are available.

Since 1981 certificates of approval from China's automotive industry officials have been required for motor vehicle imports. Beginning in January 1986, this practice has been extended to the import of other foreign products, such as insecticides. Import registration has been introduced for foreign agrochemicals and veterinary drugs, requiring costly tests for quality control and environmental impact prior to importation. Since May 1990, a quality license system has

Continued

nomic levers," such as tariffs, taxation, prices, and exchange rates.[4]

These various administrative and market controls, individually and in combination, have severely restricted access of American goods to the Chinese market. Access to the Chinese services market is even more restrictive. U.S. service industries operating in China generally do not receive the "national" treatment granted Chinese enterprises undertaking service activities in the United States.

Related to both the export control and market access issues is protection of intellectual property—trademarked goods, patented inventions, copyrighted works, and trade secrets. Intellectual property represents a huge investment by U.S. firms in research and development and is the key to their competitiveness at home and abroad. Inadequate protection of foreign intellectual property by the Chinese discourages firms from transferring technology to China, thereby restricting sales.

Under the U.S.-China Agreement on Trade Relations signed in 1979, each country must take steps to protect the patents, trademarks, and copyrights belonging to citizens of the other. Since then China has made significant progress in establishing a regime for the protection of intellectual property. China has adopted a law on trademarks, enacted a patent law, and joined several international organizations and conventions for the protection of intellectual property. Deficiencies, however, remain in several areas.

Of particular concern to U.S. companies is the lack of adequate and effective protection for chemical formulas and copyrighted works, including computer software. The Chinese patent law does not provide product protection for pharmaceuticals and substances produced by means of chemical processes, such as agricultural chemicals. Some U.S. patented products have been produced in China without license for both the domestic and export market. China is in the process of enacting a copyright law. Until the law is promulgated, U.S. publications have no copyright protection in China. Book, tape, and computer software piracy is widespread, resulting in substantial losses in U.S. sales.

In May 1989, both governments negotiated a memorandum of understanding in which China agreed to submit a copyright law to the National People's Congress by the end of that year. The law, which reportedly includes provisions for protection of computer software, has yet to be formally enacted. China also agreed to amend its patent law to extend the term and scope of protection.

---

been adopted, requiring exporters of nine machinery and electronics products to provide product samples and pay for their testing to receive a license.

To obtain foreign exchange, Chinese organizations must comply with a variety of internal regulations and plan guidelines. These regulations and guidelines are generally not available to the public.

[4] Chinese tariffs are relatively high, especially for many industrial items of interest to U.S. exporters. Since June 1985, China has also applied an "import regulatory tax" to selected imports. Imported goods are also subject to the consolidated industrial and commercial tax.

At present, three principal methods are in use to determine the domestic price of imported goods: the agent price, the markup price, and the state-determined price. All of these pricing methods allow considerable leeway for China to raise and lower prices in order to protect its domestic market. China also has progressively devalued the renminbi against major Western currencies to stimulate exports and curb imports. The RMB-to-U.S. dollar exchange rate was approximately 1.7 yuan per U.S. dollar in 1981, and has gradually declined to the current rate of 4.7 yuan per U.S. dollar.

Under the "Special 301" provision of the 1988 Trade Act, China was placed on the "priority watch list" in both 1989 and 1990 due to deficiencies in its intellectual property rights regime. A bilateral working group on intellectual property rights has been established since October 1989 under the auspices of the Joint Commission on Commerce and Trade to meet periodically in Beijing in order to resolve individual company problems.

U.S. IMPORTS FROM CHINA

Two issues affecting U.S. imports from China—the textile trade and the application of U.S. import control laws to products from China—have dominated bilateral discussions over the past decade.

Rapidly rising U.S. imports of Chinese textiles and apparel have become contentious issues in Sino-American trade. In 1979, the year during which diplomatic relations were established, U.S. imports of Chinese textiles and apparel totaled 231.2 million square yard equivalents (SYEs), or 5 percent of total U.S. imports. By 1989, Chinese imports had grown to approximately 2 billion SYEs, accounting for nearly 14 percent of total U.S. imports. In terms of volume, China has become the largest supplier of textiles and apparel to the United States since 1985.

The United States has negotiated three textile agreements with China.[5] The current agreement, signed in February 1988, limits the aggregate growth of China's textile and apparel exports to the United States to about 3.3 percent per year. This rate is calculated on a quantity basis. In value terms, China's exports have been considerably higher than the agreed rate since the Chinese have been able to shift toward exports of higher value-added textile products. The current agreement will expire at the end of 1991.

Although restraints on Chinese textiles are the main source of Chinese displeasure with U.S. restrictions on imports of Chinese goods, China also has complained about U.S. antidumping law and other U.S. trade remedies that have been applied to China. Since 1980, 16 antidumping cases have been filed against Chinese exports to the United States. In 11 cases, Chinese goods were found to have

---

[5] The first agreement, reached in 1980, was applicable to textiles and textile products of cotton, wool, and manmade fibers and provided for specific limitations on eight categories of wearing apparel. The agreement expired at the end of 1982. In the absence of an agreement after four rounds of negotiations, the U.S. Government imposed unilateral controls on 32 textile and apparel categories, beginning in January 1983. In response, China announced that it would stop signing new contracts for delivery of U.S. grain, cotton, and synthetic fibers.

In August 1983, after the seventh round of negotiations, the United States and China signed a new five-year agreement which included specific limits in some 33 product categories and provided for an annual average growth rate of 3.8 percent on U.S. imports of these products alone. China announced at the same time that it would lift its restrictions on imports of U.S. agricultural and fiber products.

As the second textile agreement was approaching expiration, U.S.-China trade relations again became tense. At issue was U.S. imposition of quantitative limits on a number of additional textile categories covered by the new Multifiber Arrangement (MFA) protocol. On August 1, 1986, more than 50 textile-trading nations agreed to the new protocol, which covered a greater range of fibers than previous agreements. The new list extended beyond wool, cotton, cotton blends, and synthetics to ramie, linen, and silk blends, at the insistence of the United States. China, the world's largely producer of ramie, strongly objected to the new restrictions, while the United States continued to exercise its authority under U.S. domestic law to unilaterally control trade in certain new MFA fiber products.

The issue became contentious as the two countries began to negotiate the third textile agreement in early 1987. After several rounds of negotiations, a four-year agreement was signed in February 1988.

been "dumped," or sold at less than fair market value. The dumping margins on these cases ranged from 0.97 to 120.07 percent.

The Chinese, and to some extent U.S. importers, consider the U.S. antidumping law as applied to China unfair and unpredictable.[6] Section 1336 of the 1988 Trade Act required the Department of Commerce to conduct a study of China's market orientation addressing, among other things, the possible need for changes in the U.S. antidumping law applicable to foreign countries, such as China, in transition to a more market-oriented economy. The study, submitted to Congress in August 1989, concludes that "amending this law to provide some form of differential treatment for economies in transition to greater market orientation should not be undertaken until such time that economic reforms have generated meaningful benchmarks for determining whether sales to the United States are made at less than fair value."[7] Section 406 of the Trade Act of 1974 provides a mechanism to prevent or remedy the disruption of the U.S. market by imports from Communist countries.[8] The statute has been applied to China on five occasions. In four of these cases, either the International Trade Commission found no conclusive evidence that imports in question were causing market disruption, or the President declined to take any remedial action against China.[9] Thus Section 406 so far has not been a significant barrier to Chinese exports. To the Chinese, however, the statute is discriminatory because it applies only to imports from non-market economy countries.

In September 1983, the U.S. textile industry's dissatisfaction with the 1983 U.S.-China textile agreement prompted the filing of a countervailing duty case on Chinese textile and apparel imports, which charged that the Chinese benefited unfairly from subsidies conferred by dual exchange rates and other government programs.[10] This was the first attempt ever made to apply the coun-

---

[6] Under the U.S. law, foreign goods are found to be "dumped" if they are sold in the United States at less than fair value, and if such sales consequently cause or threaten material injury to a competing U.S. industry. This determination requires a comparison between the foreign market value of imports (the price at which they are sold in the country of origin), and their sales price in the United States, adjusted for differences in the quality and type of goods and their circumstances of sale. If, however, the economy of the exporting country is "state-controlled," home-market prices may not be regarded as furnishing an acceptable basis for determining the foreign fair market value. In this case, the law provides that foreign market value can be determined by reference to a market-oriented third country whose level of economic development is deemed similar to the country under investigation. To determine fair value in cases involving China, the Department of Commerce has used cost data from "surrogates" in Paraguay, Thailand, Indonesia, India, Sri Lanka, Malaysia, the Philippines, Pakistan, and a few others.

[7] *Study of China's New Market Orientation and U.S. Trade Laws*, U.S. Department of Commerce, August 1989, p.9.

[8] Under Section 406 requirements, three conditions must be satisfied before the International Trade Commission can address the issue of relief. First, imports of the product in question must be increasing rapidly, either in actual terms or relative to domestic production. Second, the domestic industry must have suffered, or be threatened with, material injury or threat of injury. And third, imports must be a significant cause of the material injury or threat of injury. If the ITC determines in favor of the petitioner, the President must make the final determination of what relief, if any, should be granted. The President's discretion under the law is very broad.

[9] In the case of tungsten imports from China, the International Trade Commission voted unanimously that Chinese exports were disrupting the U.S. market. The President decided to provide relief to the domestic industry in the form of an orderly marketing arrangement, which was negotiated in August 1987.

[10] The U.S. law provides that whenever a foreign government subsidizes the production of exportation of an article, the United States may counteract the competitive advantage that the import has in the U.S. market because of the subsidy by levying a countervailing duty equal to the amount of the subsidy.

tervailing duty law to a nonmarket economy country. The case was withdrawn shortly before the White House announcement on December 16, 1983, of additional textile import guidelines designed to moderate the growth of imports.

TRADE IMBALANCE

Traditionally, China has practiced a policy of trying to balance trade bilaterally, and has taken the position that only through expanded exports can it finance increased imports. During periods of rising trade deficits, stringent measures are usually employed both to restrict imports and promote exports. In recent years, the U.S. market especially has been targeted for export growth.

Since 1983 the United States has had a trade deficit with China. The U.S. deficit increased from $71 million in 1983 to $6.2 billion in 1989, the sixth largest bilateral deficit worldwide. The deficit issue has never been thoroughly discussed in bilateral consultations, but, as will be noted later, is likely to become prominent in the future trade agenda.

Closely related to the trade deficit issue is the problem of discrepancies between Chinese and U.S. trade data. Official Chinese trade statistics differ widely from U.S. trade statistics. For 1989, U.S. Department of Commerce statistics show a total of $18 billion in two-way trade, compared to the Chinese Customs Administration's estimate of $12.3 billion. U.S. data disclose a U.S. trade deficit of $6.2 billion with China in 1989, while Chinese customs statistics indicate a Chinese deficit of $3.5 billion in trading with the United States.

Discrepancies in trading partner data are not uncommon, but the gap between Chinese and U.S. statistics has widened significantly since 1981. The gap has increased especially rapidly between U.S. statistics on imports from China and Chinese statistics on exports to the United States—from 27 percent of the U.S. export value in 1981 to 66 percent in 1989. The widening gap is largely the result of rapid growth in re-exports of Chinese goods through Hong Kong. As Hong Kong becomes an increasingly important entrepôt for China, the discrepancy between U.S. and Chinese trade statistics is likely to become even greater.

THE BUSINESS CLIMATE IN CHINA

While the Chinese government has made considerable progress in improving the business environment in China over the past decade, foreign companies continue to encounter many difficult problems. Of particular concern to foreign investors are a lack of access to the domestic market, foreign exchange controls, the inconvertibility of renminbi, difficulties in sourcing materials in China, poor quality control, inadequate infrastructure, and shortages of skilled labor. There also is discontent among foreign investors about weakness of intellectual property rights protection, a lack of transparency of administrative and legal procedures and regulations, inefficient government bureaucracies, and the high cost of doing business in China.

Widespread investor complaints caused the Chinese government to issue "Provisions for the Encouragement of Foreign Investment," in October 1986. The Provisions' 22 articles provide preferential treatment for foreign investment enterprises in general and high-technology and export-oriented enterprises in particular. The investment climate began to improve following the promulgation of the Provisions and other measures taken by the Chinese government.

The recent austerity program and political turmoil dealt foreign investors a severe blow. Economic recentralization and increased administrative controls resulting from the austerity policy made the investment environment much more restrictive. Political events since June 1989 have further shaken foreign investors' confidence, and greatly complicated the task of operating ventures in China.

In addition to investment problems, the number of trade disputes between U.S. companies and Chinese entities has increased over time. These disputes cover a wide range of cases, from nonfulfillment of contractual terms to infringement of trade marks. These are further complicated by a lack of effective mechanisms for dispute resolution. Although third-party arbitration is allowed in some business disputes, China does not recognize a foreign company's right to take the Chinese government to international arbitration.

IV. GOVERNMENTAL RELATIONS

A DECADE OF DEVELOPMENT

In the decade after the establishment of diplomatic relations in 1979, much progress was made in developing a framework for normal commercial relations between the United States and China. This framework was built largely through government-to-government agreements and consultations.

An overall Trade Agreement was concluded in 1979, providing reciprocal nondiscriminatory treatment for each country's products. This was followed by agreements, signed in the early 1980s, in areas such as science and technology cooperation, textiles, grain trade, aviation, nuclear power, maritime relations, taxation, and industrial cooperation.

In addition, three ministerial level joint commissions—the Joint Commission on Science and Technology, the Joint Economic Commission (JEC), the Joint Commission on Commerce and Trade (JCCT) were established. Prior to 1989, these commissions met annually, providing fora for discussing relevant bilateral issues.

The Science and Technology Commission was co-chaired by the Science Advisor to the President on the U.S. side, and the Minister-in-Charge of the State Science and Technology Commission on the Chinese side. The two countries signed 27 agreements on scientific exchange, including the highly successful Dalian Management Program, which introduced Chinese managers and executives to modern management techniques.

The JEC was co-chaired by the U.S. Treasury Secretary and the Chinese Minister of Finance. It focused on financial, banking, taxation, and other macroeconomic issues.

The JCCT was co-chaired by the U.S. Secretary of Commerce and by one of China's Vice Premiers or its Minister of Foreign Economic Relations and Trade. It provided a forum for high-level consideration of bilateral trade issues and served as a vehicle for promoting economic relations. Under JCCT auspices, legal seminars were conducted annually, and executive level trade missions were exchanged in accordance with the U.S.-China Industrial and Technological Cooperation Accord signed in 1984.

Between 1979 and 1989, there were numerous exchanges of visits by high-level government officials. Frequently, trade issues also were discussed during these visits.

In addition to bilateral consultations, commission meetings, and agreements, trade issues were handled through multilateral channels. In the 1980s, China joined the World Bank, the International Monetary Fund, and the Asian Development Bank, adhered to several principal multilateral conventions, and was admitted to the Multilateral Fiber Arrangement. In 1986, China began the process of negotiating full membership in the General Agreement on Tariffs and Trade (GATT). Since then, the U.S. and China have conducted five rounds of bilateral negotiations on the latter's accession to GATT.

THE IMPACT OF TIANANMEN

The decade-long progress in government-to-government commercial relations was disrupted by the Tiananmen incident. The U.S. government responded to the political repression in China by imposing a number of suspensions on important elements in bilateral relations, including those related to trade. In the wake of Tiananmen, the Administration announced on June 5, 1989, and then again on June 20, a series of measures suspending certain bilateral programs. Later in the year, Congress passed several bills containing provisions to legislate some of the existing sanctions announced by the Administration and impose additional ones.

The trade-related programs and activities which have been suspended since Tiananmen as a result of the actions taken by Congress and the Administration are summarized as follows:

- With the exception of the Scowcroft-Eagleburger missions, official exchanges above the assistant secretary level have been stopped.
- Government-to-government sales and commercial exports of weaponry have been halted.
- Consideration of increased liberalization of COCOM restrictions for China has been suspended. In addition, the United States, along with other COCOM members, has postponed implementing a distribution license procedure for China.
- Both the Overseas Private Investment Corporation and the Trade and Development Program have suspended all new activities in China.
- In December 1989 the President made a national interest determination that waived legislative prohibitions on Export-Import Bank activities in China. Since Tiananmen, Exim-bank's financing of U.S. business activities in China has been held at a reduced level. Financial commitments have been approved on a case-by-case basis only where project decisions are

imminent and where U.S. business would lose out in the absence of Eximbank support.

- Since December 1989 when the President waived the restriction on the export of communications satellites to be launched by China for third-party customers, no action has been taken to permit further satellite exports to China.
- No export licenses for crime control and detection instruments have been issued.
- The United States has opposed new loans to China by international financial institutions, except those for projects meeting basic human needs. At the Houston Summit in July, the Group of Seven announced that it agreed to explore further whether there are other World Bank loans that will contribute to the reform of the Chinese economy, especially loans that will address environmental concerns.

This year has seen an intense debate in the United States regarding the extension of China's Most Favored Nation (MFN) status, which allows nondiscriminatory tariff treatment for Chinese exports to the United States, and Export-Import Bank financing for U.S. exports to China. The reciprocal granting of MFN treatment was the main pillar of the U.S.-China Trade Agreement signed in 1979, marking the beginning of the normal commercial relationship between the two countries. Under the Trade Act of 1974, as a nonmarket economy country China's MFN status must be renewed annually by a Presidential determination stipulating that China meets the freedom of emigration requirements set forth in the Jackson-Vanik Amendment, or by a Presidential waiver of these requirements. China received such a waiver in previous years. This year, however, strong pressure emerged from some in Congress to oppose renewal of China's MFN status.

On May 24, the President informed the Congress of his determination to extend the MFN waiver for China for another year. Since then Congress has held a series of hearings. Congressional concern about the human rights situation in China remains high, and legislation placing conditions on MFN extension is still under consideration.

Despite the suspension of high-level governmental exchanges, consultations on commercial matters have continued at the working level. Since October 1989, two embassy-based working groups—one on trade and investment, the other on intellectual property rights—have been established under JCCT auspices. These groups have met periodically in Beijing. In the meetings, U.S. officials from the Department of Commerce and American Embassy in Beijing discussed general concerns of U.S. business with Chinese trade officials, and presented specific individual company problems for resolution by the Chinese.

V. PROSPECTS

Despite the post-Tiananmen disruptions in bilateral commercial relations, the volume of U.S.-China trade continues to grow. This growth, however, is largely driven by U.S. imports. U.S. imports from China in the twelve-month period ending June 1990 rose by 39 percent over July 1988–June 1989 levels, while U.S. exports to

China increased by only 3.4 percent. As a result, the U.S. deficit with China reached $8 billion, compared to $4.4 billion a year earlier.[11]

China had already started an export drive before Tiananmen under the austerity program. This drive has been accelerated in an effort to generate more foreign exchange earnings to make up post-Tiananmen losses in these earnings from nontrade sources such as tourism, foreign direct investment, and external borrowings. Export growth is likely to be fueled further by the establishment of an increasingly large number of labor-intensive export factories in China by Hong Kong and Taiwan investors. Since-many markets have imposed import restrictions on light manufactured products, the lucrative and more accessible market of the United States has become the prime target for China's export promotion efforts.

China will continue to rely on the United States as a major supplier of agricultural commodities, raw materials, aircraft, and other high-technology products. These are the products which China needs to make up for domestic shortfalls and to develop its priority sectors (transport, telecommunications, energy, and raw materials). In other product areas, prospects for U.S. sales will be limited by the generally restrictive import policy that China is presently pursuing, and by the stiff competition from third-country suppliers with government-backed soft loans.

Barring unexpected changes, current trends of rapid growth in imports and sluggishness in exports will likely continue in the next few years. The result will be rapid increases in the U.S. trade deficit with China. At $6.2 billion in 1989, the U.S. deficit with China was the sixth largest bilateral deficit world wide, moving up from the ninth largest in 1988. In the first six months of this year, the U.S. deficit reached $4.1 billion—fourth largest worldwide and 83 percent higher than for the same period of the previous year. If current trends continue, China could rank second or third among the countries with whom the United States has largest trade deficits this year or next. These rapid increases have been of great concern to the United States, and are likely to become a priority issue in the future agenda for bilateral discussions.

Since Tiananmen, U.S. investors' interest in China has dropped precipitously. China's leaders have repeatedly stated that their government's decade-long foreign investment policy remains unchanged. Recently the National People's Congress approved amendments to the joint venture law permitting foreigners to become chairman of the board of a joint venture, eliminating mandatory time limits on contracts for certain types of ventures, and providing protection from nationalization. The new Pudong development project, a 350 square-kilometer area in Shanghai opened to foreign participation, has been pushed forward aggressively. Meanwhile, the open development zones in Guangdong, Fujian, Hainan, Tianjin, and Dalian have continued to expand. Despite these developments, U.S. investment in China is not expected to resume growth soon due to investors' concern over the political future of China.

---

[11] U.S. exports to China totaled $5.4 million during the period July 1988 to June 1989 and $5.6 million during the period July 1989 to June 1990 while U.S. imports from China were estimated at $9.8 million and $13.6 million during the respective periods.

In the absence of substantial growth of new U.S. investment in the next few years, the main issue in U.S.-China investment relations is likely to focus on problems confronted by the existing U.S. investment ventures in China. The current austerity program, accompanied by greater recentralization of economic authority and increased use of administrative methods to manage resource allocation, have created many difficult operational problems for U.S. invested enterprises, including tight credit and more restricted access to production inputs. U.S. investors also may face a growing lack of transparency in economic decision-making and greater red tape on the part of Chinese bureaucracy under pressure to implement the austerity measures. It will be in the best interest of China to see these problems resolved in order to regain the confidence of existing as well as prospective investors.

Beyond the next few years, U.S.-China commercial relations will be affected by a wide range of factors. First of all, these relations will be determined by the degree of success that both countries have in resolving existing issues. Currently, these issues include economic sanctions, intellectual property rights, the trade imbalance, and the business climate in China. Closely related to the last three issues is access to the Chinese market. Negotiations for a new textile agreement could become contentious next year. In the future, annual renewal of the MFN status may no longer be a routine matter as it was in the first decade of the U.S.-China Trade Agreement. The Chinese also may want to press for negotiations of certain multilateral issues, such as China's GATT membership.

U.S.-China commercial relations also will be affected by both countries' relations with other trading partners. The growing importance of the Soviet Union, Eastern Europe, and Pacific Rim countries in the world economic scene may shift U.S. investors' interest away from China. China also may want to expand commercial relations with these countries, thus reducing trade dependency on the United States. China's growing economic relations with Hong Kong and Taiwan are likely to have a far-reaching impact on its trade with the United States.

The impact of China's expanding economic relations with Hong Kong on U.S.-China trade has already been evident in recent years. Hong Kong is becoming an increasingly important entrepôt for China trade—increasing quantities of Chinese products are reexported to the United States through Hong Kong. (Over 35 percent of Hong Kong's total reexports of Chinese-origin products went to the United States last year.) The movement of labor-intensive light manufacturing projects from Hong Kong to China, especially Guangdong Province, has accelerated the growth of China's exports to the United States. In the last few years, U.S. imports of Chinese light manufactures, especially footwear, toys, consumer electronics, furniture, and leather articles have grown sharply, while U.S. imports from Hong Kong of these products have declined. As 1997 approaches, the year when Hong Kong reverts to Chinese administration, economic ties between the two regions are bound to become closer, affecting further the triangular commercial relationship among Hong Kong, China, and the United States.

A similar pattern of these changing relations is emerging among Taiwan, the Chinese mainland, and the United States. Since 1987, economic relations between Taiwan and the PRC have expanded rapidly. Indirect PRC-Taiwan trade grew from nearly $1 billion in 1986 to $3.5 billion in 1989. During the same period, Taiwanese businesses established several hundred investment projects in the PRC with a contracted value of some $1 billion. Many of these projects involved the movement of small-scale, labor-intensive, and export-oriented operations from Taiwan to the mainland. As a result, some of Taiwan's light manufactured exports to the United States, especially footwear, consumer electronics, umbrellas, and leather products, are declining, in contrast to China's growing exports to the United States of these products. The significance of these changes may be seen in the likelihood that the PRC may replace Taiwan very soon as a trading partner with whom the United States has the second largest bilateral trade deficit. Despite Tiananmen, the number of Taiwan's investors going to China is increasing substantially. The impact of the growing economic relationship between the two sides of the Taiwan Strait on U.S.-China trade is likely to become much greater and more complex in the years ahead.

More fundamentally, the U.S.-China commercial relationship in the long term will be determined by the political environment in China, including the degree of political stability and the types of policies pursued by the Chinese leadership. These political and policy factors may have an important bearing on U.S.-China economic and trade relations in two significant ways. First, they will govern China's basic attitude toward the United States, which in turn will affect bilateral economic ties. Second, they will determine the basic policies regarding China's economic system and development strategy. A return to market-oriented economic reforms would facilitate the process of China's integration with the world economy and enhance the prospects for expanded economic relations with other countries, including the United States.

SINO-SOVIET TRADE IN THE 1980s AND 1990s: POLITICS, PRAGMATISM, AND PROFITS

By Sharon E. Ruwart *

CONTENTS

The Sino-Soviet trade relationship today is dramatically different from that of the 1950s, when the Soviet Union accounted for about 50 percent of China's total trade and provided massive amounts of technical and financial assistance to rebuild China's war-ravaged economy. Today, nearly eight years after bilateral trade relations were formally renewed, the amounts exchanged remain small, since both countries are concentrating on developing sources of hard currency and advanced technology, which neither can offer the other.

While at the national level, Sino-Soviet trade ties chiefly serve to symbolize that state-to-state relations are on solid footing, on the local level renewed bilateral trade has had a much greater impact, largely as a result of recent innovations in trade practices. Unlike the 1950–1970s period, when trade was exclusively a government-to-government affair, today a number of provincial and local organizations on both sides are authorized to trade directly across the border, and to establish cooperative projects and joint ventures. As a result, provincial and border trade has increased at a rapid rate, and dozens of joint ventures are operating in the border areas.

Significant problems hamper commercial relations, however, chief among them the inadequately developed financial and transportation infrastructures in both countries. Unless some of the basic problems, such as currency inconvertibility and transport inadequacy, can be solved, Sino-Soviet trade will remain a small-time affair.

---

* Sharon E. Ruwart, a former editor of *The China Business Review*, holds a B.A. in Russian and East European Studies from Yale University.

Aside from the reduced volume of transactions and the localization of commercial links, the major change in Sino-Soviet trade today is how it is affected by the political context in which it takes place. In the 1950s, the USSR was China's Marxist mentor; in the 1960s trade ground to a virtual halt as ideological differences violently split the former socialist comrades. Today, trade has been largely distanced from political disputes. Nevertheless, the contrast between policies in Beijing and Moscow concerning the pace and mechanics of economic and social reform may eventually have an impact on Sino-Soviet trade. The top priority of China's leaders is to preserve social stability, and they fear the pervasive effects of glasnost and perestroika evidenced by the dramatic downfalls of successive East European governments. To help prevent such ideas from infiltrating Chinese society, Beijing would take steps to slow the expansion of commercial contacts on the non-governmental level, particularly on the border.

At this point, however, such concerns are in the background of a commercial relationship that is growing, albeit slowly, and bringing benefits to both sides in the form of needed materials and expertise. For the forseeable future, pragmatism will continue to prevail over politics in trade relations, as both sides prioritize the search for profits.

I. RENEWING TRADE TIES

During the 1950s, the USSR was China's main trading partner, accounting for about half of China's overall imports and exports. Beginning in the early 1960s, however, a variety of ideological, military, and territorial differences cooled the relationship. Soviet technical advisers were recalled, and while the annual government-to-government trade protocols that formed the basis of trade (these do not provide for border trade activities) were signed each year up to 1968, and resumed again in 1970, a number of the later agreements were not completely fulfilled.[1] Though trade never completely ceased, it took nearly twenty years for the political climate to warm up enough to justify resuming a full-fledged trade relationship. With appropriate fanfare and protestations of friendship, the two countries "officially" reopened trade links in 1983.

Since then, trade has grown rapidly. The 1989 bilateral trade agreement totalled $3.1 billion, a 20 percent increase over 1988 ($2.6 billion) and 13 times greater than the 1981 total, according to China's State Statistical Bureau.[2] By 1989, the USSR ranked as China's fifth-largest trading partner, though the totals lagged far behind those of Hong Kong/Macao, Japan, the United States, and Germany, accounting for just three percent of China's overall foreign trade.[3]

Since neither the ruble nor the yuan can be converted to hard currency, Sino-Soviet trade is conducted by barter, with commodities valued in neutral Swiss francs according to world market

---

[1] *Soviet-Chinese Relations*, 1945–1970, O.B. Borisov and B.T. Koloslov. Bloomington: Indiana University Press, 1975, pp. 64–72, 314.

[2] Cited in Hong Kong *Kuang Chiao Ching* in Chinese No. 199, 4/16/89; FBIS–CHI–89–076, 4/21/89, pp. 6–10.

[3] The Journal of Commerce, 5/10/89, p. 4A

prices. The figures in this paper are given in the currency reported by the original source, whether francs, rubles, yuan, or dollars, with some accompanied by estimates of the US dollar value depending on contemporary exchange rates. The appendix lists ruble, yuan, and Swiss franc exchange rates over time.

Despite the rapid expansion of trade volumes, the types of commodities exchanged remain much the same today as in the 1960s. China chiefly exports foodstuffs, light industrial goods, and production materials in exchange for power-plant equipment, steel, and transport machinery. A Xinhua news agency report claimed that during 1981–89, China exported to the USSR 600,000 metric tons of meat, 630,000 tons of fruit, 8,000 tons of filature silk, 970 million Swiss francs' (SFr) worth of nonferrous metals and minerals, SFr3 billion worth of soybeans, corn, and peanuts. China also exported unspecified amounts of light industrial goods. In return, China received from the USSR 7.8 million metric tons of rolled steel and pig iron, 17 million cubic meters of logs and timber, 3.7 tons of urea, SFr2 billion[4] worth of nonferrous and precious metals, 119,000 cars and vehicles, and 57 planes.[5]

As the list indicates, trade fulfills certain complementary needs. The Soviets are strong in production of chemical fertilizer, of which China cannot get enough, and heavy equipment manufacturing, especially power plants. It makes sense for energy-needy China to continue to acquire Soviet technology through barter, especially since the USSR can also help renovate many of the plants built by Soviet engineers in the 1950s. China provides a wide variety of consumer goods ranging from textiles to household appliances, along with many types of fresh and canned food, to the Soviet Far East, which even more than the rest of the USSR suffers from a chronic shortage of many basic consumer commodities.

As in earlier years, the bulk of bilateral trade is conducted on a government-to-government basis. Each year, the two countries' foreign trade ministries sign an agreement setting an aggregate monetary total and outlining approximate amounts of the main commodities to change hands that year. For example, the 1989 "commodities exchange and payment protocol" signed in March 1989 set total trade at $3.1 billion (a 17 percent increase over the 1988 target). China was to export tungsten ore, soybeans, corn, meat and meat by-products, knitwear, thermos flasks, handicrafts, and machinery, in exchange for steel products, nonferrous metals, wood, fertilizer, generators, electric locomotives, cars, airplanes, and refrigerators.[6] The 1990 trade protocol was set at a total of SFr5 billion,[7] and specified Soviet exports of 17 planes, 10 helicopters, and thermal power equipment, among other items.[8]

---

[4] SFr970 million = US$505 million; SFR3 billion = US$1.56 billion; SFr2 billion = US$1.4 billion. Calculated using an average of SFr1.92 : US$1 for the period 1981–89, quoted by the International Monetary Fund (IMF).

[5] Beijing Xinhua Domestic Service in Chinese, 4/19/90; FBIS–CHI–90–078, 4/23/90, pp. 18–19.

[6] Beijing Xinhua in English, 3/3/89; FBIS–CHI–89–041, 3/3/89, p. 11.

[7] SFr5 billion = US$3.1 billion. 1989 exchange rate = SFr1.63 : US$1 (IMF statistics).

[8] Beijing Jingji Ribao in Chinese, 4/21/90, p. 1; FBIS–CHI–90–086, 5/3/90, pp. 3–5.

II. Problems with Purchasing Power

So far, exchanging cement for silk and timber for textiles has worked out more or less to both sides' advantage, especially in terms of meeting local needs in the border areas. The lack of convertible currencies places fundamental constraints on Sino-Soviet trade, however, for two reasons.

First, as both countries strive to make their economies more efficient and market-sensitive by decentralizing planning and trading functions, provincial organizations and even some factories have become responsible for their own profits and losses. Thus they have both greater authority and greater incentive to sell their products to hard-currency purchasers instead of handing them over to the central government to fulfill official trade protocols. As a result, Sino-Soviet trade has actually declined in real terms over the past two years, even as the totals set by annual protocols have increased. For example, 1989 trade fell short of the $3.1 billion target, totalling only $2.4 billion. This was even less than the $2.6 billion in trade actually concluded in 1988.[9]

The second, related, problem is quality. Both countries prefer to save their best products for hard-currency customers. As one Chinese economist at a Beijing research institute noted about barter trade, "We only sell each other things that we can't sell for foreign exchange. They send us low-quality wood, and we send them second-class canned food." [10] With a reputation for shoddy goods, neither country is in a good position to withstand competition for each other's markets—and despite carrying higher price tags, goods from the United States, Japan, and other Asian countries are becoming increasingly popular even in remote regions of both countries.

III. Localizing Trade Links

Despite the problems, there are a number of bright spots in bilateral trade, and one of them is the rapid expansion of commercial links along the 7,500 km Sino-Soviet border. Reliable border trade statistics are virtually impossible to come by given the small size of most border transactions and the fact that most of them take place outside official trade channels, so all figures must be treated with caution. Nevertheless, both sides agree that border trade has been growing even faster than overall trade in this decade. Jingji Ribao asserts, for example,[11] that 1983 border trade totalled SFr16 million and leapt to a total of SFr1.3 billion in 1989.[12] China Economic News describes the 1988 border trade total of $274 million as a 210 percent increase over the 1987 figure.[13]

How does border trade differ from the centrally planned variety? The bulk of the commodities exchanged is locally sourced, and represents many of the same items stipulated in the central protocols:

---

[9] *The Journal of Commerce*, 4/4/90, p. A1.

[10] "China and the Soviet Union Weigh Economic Cooperation Proposals;" supplement to the *Asian Wall Street Journal Weekly*, 5/15/89.

[11] Beijing Jingji Ribao in Chinese, 5/21/90, p. 1.

[12] SFr16 million = US$9.78 million; SFr 1.3 billion = US$790 million. (IMF 1989 exchange rate statistics).

[13] China Economic News in English, 4/17/89, p. 5.

fertilizer, cement, timber, and power station equipment from the Soviets, and garments, light industrial goods, and food—such as soybeans, peanuts, potatoes, apples, and frozen beef—from the Chinese. The amounts exchanged are generally quite small—measured in units and truckloads—and are targeted toward specific local needs. For example, a story recounted by Beijing's Liaowang weekly describes a harried Soviet official from the Amur Oblast border region pleading with the head of the Heihe Trading Co. to send a shipment of 30,000 colored scarves for sale to the local "female comrades" for Women's Day (the scarves were duly procured and reportedly sold out in two days).[14] Chinese border traders also send over wristwatches, brooches, shoes, and hats for the local female comrades, while a large proportion of Heilongjiang's Soviet imports consists of chemical fertilizer for local use.[15]

Several factors are responsible for the rapid increase in border trade, the most obvious of which is geography. Three of China's largest provinces—Heilongjiang, Inner Mongolia, and Xinjiang—border the USSR, along with a tiny section of Jilin. These areas have for centuries traded across the Ussuri and Amur rivers as well as across the long land border to the west. The Soviet regions bordering China include the small Tajikistan, Khirgizia, and Kazakhstan soviet socialist republics to China's west and the enormous and relatively wealthy Russian Soviet Federative Socialist Republic encompassing resource-rich Siberia. Not surprisingly, China's northern provinces have taken the lead in reestablishing trade with the USSR; one story claims that the first "official" transaction was a shipment of Harbin watermelons sent across the Amur in 1983 in exchange for Soviet fertilizer.[16] True or not, the tale accurately prefigures Heilongjiang's leading role in border trade. Nearly 100 towns and other small settlements in Heilongjiang face Soviet counterparts directly across the Amur and Ussuri rivers, making for natural trade links. Vladivostok and Khabarovsk, the only two cities in the entire Soviet Far East with populations of over 500,000, are the principal ports for Sino-Soviet trade, and both are linked by waterways to Heilongjiang's capital city, Harbin.

The most successful trade port in Heilongjiang is Heihe, which faces Blagoveshchensk across the Amur. The two cities are the largest in the region after Khabarovsk, Vladivostok, and Harbin. Blagoveshchensk is connected by a 109-km feeder railway to the main trans-Siberian line across the USSR, which allows imported goods to be transshipped inland. Heihe's 1989 trade with the USSR reportedly totalled SFr150 million,[17] and the volume of traded commodities reached 62,000 tons.[18]

Other major trading ports in Heilongjiang include Suifenhe City, a port city north of Vladivostok along an arm of the Ussuri River (a highway between the two cities opened in March 1990);[19] Tong-

---

[14] Beijing Liaowang in Chinese, No. 21, 5/22/89, pp. 22–24, FBIS–CHI–89–114, 6/15/89, pp. 3–5.

[15] Ibid.

[16] Beijing Liaowang in Chinese No. 21, 5/22/89, pp. 22–24; FBIS–CHI–89–114, 6/15/89, pp.3–4.

[17] SFr150 million = US$91.7 million (IMF 1989 exchange rate statistics).

[18] Hong Kong Zhongguo Tongxun She in Chinese, 3/13/89; FBIS–CHI–89–049, 3/15/89, p.3.

[19] China Economic News in English, 2/15/89, p. 17.

jiang, Fujin, and Jiamusi, all located along the Songhua Jiang, an offshoot of the Amur River with direct access to Khabarovsk; and Mohe, located along the northernmost point of the Amur. Harbin, which was formally reopened to Soviet trade in July 1989—months after regular shipments had actually resumed—is the largest inland water-land transshipment port in northeast China and is connected with seven large Soviet cities via the Amur and Songhua rivers. Sailing time from Harbin to Khabarovsk is approximately five days.[20] A twice-weekly air route between the two cities was also opened in late 1989.[21] At least six other small counties and townships in Western Heilongjiang were opened to Soviet trade in 1989.[22]

As part of a stepped-up export drive, in 1988 Beijing abolished restrictions limiting border trade to small volumes of locally-sourced commodities, and also eased the bureaucratic procedures for transporting goods between provinces. As a result, an ever-increasing percentage of goods exported through China's northern provinces to the USSR comes from further south, such as textiles from Shanghai and electronics from Guangdong. Recognizing the new markets across the border, the southern Chinese provinces have recently begun to develop Soviet trade contacts, attending and hosting trade fairs for Soviet and East European businesspeople and hiring Heilongjiang companies as agents.

Other provincial organizations are cutting out northern middlemen and establishing direct links with the Soviets. In March 1989, for instance, a delegation from Fujian Province held trade talks in Heilongjiang directly with Soviet traders ranging from the Ministry of Chemical Industry to the Vladivostok Fruit and Vegetable Co. They ended up with three barter agreements to exchange Chinese floor tiles, ceramics, filling station equipment, tangerines, and oranges for Soviet plastic agricultural film, gasoline and diesel oil, chemical raw materials, and rolled steel scrap.[23] A Chinese source noted in June 1990 that over 10 large corporations in the Shenzhen Special Economic Zone are doing business directly with the USSR, chiefly exporting electrical goods. The Saige Group, for example, has exported 80,000 tape recorders and 20,000 color TVs. Other Shenzhen companies have sold home electrical appliances, ground satellite receiving systems, mini-computers, clothing, and cars.[24]

IV. A New Export: Manpower

Demonstrating their flexibility in identifying new markets for abundant local resources, local-level Chinese organizations have in the past two years begun contracting out Chinese laborers to work on projects in sparsely populated Siberia. With only 30 million people in the entire vast region, the USSR desperately needs manpower to tap Siberia's wealth of natural resources, including metals and minerals, timber, petroleum, and arable land. In past

[20] Harbin Heilongjiang Provincial Service in Mandarin, 7/10/89; FBIS-CHI-89-132, 7/12/89, p. 8.
[21] Ibid., 9/22/89, FBIS-CHI-89-184, 9/25/89, p. 6.
[22] Hong Kong Zhongguo Tongxun She in Chinese, 4/10/89, FBIS-CHI-89-070, 4/13/89, p. 8.
[23] Fuzhou Fujian Ribao in Chinese, 3/16/89, p. 2; FBIS-CHI-89-058, 3/28/89, p. 3.
[24] Beijing Zhongguo Xinwen She in English, 6/12/90; FBIS-CHI-90-114, 6/15/90, p. 4.

years the USSR has imported laborers from North Korea, Vietnam, Cuba, and East European countries, but China's proximity and abundance of underemployed workers makes it a more attractive source of manpower. In 1988, organizations in the three border provinces began sending laborers as construction workers, lumberjacks, vegetable growers, and railroad repairmen. They are generally paid as much as or more than Soviet workers, and since the ruble is nonconvertible, the Soviet companies often pay in kind. The Harbin company that sent 300 Chinese workers to the Khabarovsk diesel plant in 1989–90, for example, will be paid for their services in diesel engines, which will presumably be sold and the earnings distributed to the workers in Chinese currency.[25] Another typical agreement called for Suifenhe City to send 54 mechanics to a Soviet refrigerator assembly plant. For one year's work each Chinese would receive RMB7,000 (an astronomical sum that should perhaps be read with caution) and a new refrigerator.[26] Inner Mongolia and Xinjiang have sent many small groups of agicultural workers across the border, and Liaoning and Jilin have sent lumbermen to work in the vast Siberian forests. Accurate figures are impossible to establish, but numerous Chinese sources report that up to 10,000 workers were sent to the USSR in 1988, 15,000 in 1989, and up to 20,000 may go in 1990. A central-level Sino-Soviet agricultural cooperation committee has even discussed the idea of sending a veritable army of Chinese workers all the way to the Soviet Ukraine![27]

V. Border Trade Problems

The rapid expansion of border trade has been accompanied by problems reminiscent of those that plagued China's southern and coastal provinces in the wake of a sudden surge in foreign trade in the mid-1980s. While in 1983 only a single organization in northeast China was permitted to trade with the USSR, today roughly 190 organizations throughout the country may do so.[28] In the rush to do business over the border, many organizations contracted to supply goods to the Soviets that ultimately could not be obtained from interior provinces, and many agreements went unfulfilled. Even worse, from the standpoint of Beijing's planners, many of these traders sought a competitive edge by lowering the prices of exports and jacking up the prices of imported goods.[29] As in the southern provinces earlier, Beijing sought to eradicate speculative trade activity, embarking in 1989 on a "rectification" program for organizations trading with the USSR. While few units lost their trading privileges as a result, each was assigned to one of 20 or so trading groups that were allotted loose import and export targets in an effort to keep trade monitored and balanced. In addition, a number of regulations were passed defining acceptable border trade practices.[30]

---

[25] "Peace Along the Ussuri," by Michael Dobbs. *The Washington Post*, 5/9/89, p. A1.
[26] Hong Kong Zhongguo Tongxun She in Chinese, 5/3/89, p. 10.
[27] Bejing Xinhua in English to North America, 9/15/89; FBIS–CHI–89–184, 9/25/89, pp. 6–7.
[28] Beijing Guoji Shangbao in Chinese, 6/24/89, p. 3; FBIS–CHI–89–184, 9/25/89, pp. 6–7.
[29] Ibid.
[30] Ibid.

Another problem with southern precedents is rivalry between the northeastern border provinces and those of these interior. Since 1988, when all provinces were authorized to trade with the USSR, the southern provinces have come to resent the natural advantages of proximity enjoyed by their northern compatriots. Shanghai in particular, which is a major producer of the kinds of light industrial goods in demand in the USSR—and which believes Guangdong's spectacular success in foreign trade has come largely at its expense—resents Heilongjiang's dominant position in border trade. These feelings boiled over during a large East Bloc trade fair held in Harbin in June 1990. After the first four days of the two-week fair, the Northeastern Trading Group consisting of the three border provinces had concluded SFr260 million worth of contracts, with Heilongjiang alone claiming SFr124 million of the total. The East China Trading Group, including Shanghai, Jiangsu, and Zhejiang, had concluded just SFr24 million worth of transactions— Shanghai's total was a mere SFr120,000.[31] Shortly after these figures were announced, Shanghai authorities publicly accused Heilongjiang traders and officials of actively blocking access by other Chinese to the 2,000 Soviet businessmen at the fair. This was hardly consistent, the Shanghainese pointed out, with the official border trade policy of "cooperating with the south to open up the north."[32] The gravity of the situation was emphasized when the Heilongjiang provincial governor made a public apology to Shanghai.[33]

Though Sino-Soviet border trade is probably not in itself significant enough to precipitate protest against central trade policies by disgruntled areas such as Shanghai, it highlights and exacerbates the uneven distribution of foreign trade benefits among Chinese provinces. Chinese authorities recognize that this situation is a potential threat to social stability, but have not yet been devised a way to address it while continuing to promote exports. As a result, organizations on the border may be vulnerable to stricter controls in the future as authorities attempt to keep foreign trade benefits balanced on a national level.

The USSR's internal economic problems have also contributed to border trade frictions in the past year. In 1989, the USSR implemented a licensing system to restrict exports of nearly 200 types of goods, including cement, timber, fuels, metals, and fertilizer. The new system is meant to stabilize the domestic supply of key materials in the face of a dramatic drop in national productivity caused by everything from workers' strikes and transportation bottlenecks to general lack of motivation and enthusiasm for reforms. The Soviet "rectification" drive also reduced the number of organizations authorized to trade abroad from 189 to 26.[34]

According to a Hong Kong source, the tightening measures have had a "severe" effect on 1990 border trade, especially in Heilongjiang. The source notes that because Soviet companies had trouble obtaining licenses for contracted goods, only one-tenth of all 1989

[31] SFr260 million = US$177 million; SFr124 million = US$84.8 million; SFr120,000 = US$82,000. Calculated using June 1990 exchange rate of SFr1.462 : US$1 (IMF).
[32] *Shanghai Jiefang Ribao*, 6/11/90, FBIS–CHI–90–115, 6/14/90, p. 13.
[33] Hong Kong Agence France Presse, 6/15/90, P. 6.
[34] Hong Kong *Zhongguo Tongxun She* in English, 6/20/90; FBIS–CHI–90–120, 6/21/90, p. 5.

Sino-Soviet contracts had been finalized (treat the statistics with caution), and that several million Swiss francs' worth of goods bound for China have been stranded in Soviet ports for lack of licenses. The report goes on to say that the booming port of Heihe reported a Soviet trade deficit of SFr4 million [35] last year, and attributes the shortfall directly to the new licensing system.[36]

In response to the "confusion" on the Soviet side of the border, China's Ministry of Foreign Economic Relations and Trade (MOFERT) began to review the border trade situation in mid-1990, and reportedly plans to reduce the number of companies authorized to trade with the USSR from the current 190 to 26. Mirroring the Soviet move, MOFERT may also institute a permit system for the export of "essential" items.[37]

Another major roadblock to contract fulfillment is the inadequacy of transport links between the two countries. Trade between border settlements thrives in winter, when trucks can be driven across the frozen rivers. But two-thirds of bilateral trade is transported by rail over longer distances, and facilities at the principal northern trading ports have not been renovated since the 1950s. They lack mechanized loading equipment, containerization facilities, and warehouses. Incidents of goods being damaged during shipping or spoiled by weather while sitting on docks and in railyards are all too common. The 6-inch difference in width between Soviet and Chinese rail guages contributes to delays and potential damage, since all goods have to be reloaded onto different railcars upon reaching the border.[38] Water transport links between cities are rapidly expanding, but without concurrent infrastructure improvements in the ports themselves, increasing the number of cargo vessels will only worsen the congestion.

To address these problems, in 1986 the two countries revived the central-level transport working group that met during the 1950s to develop plans for improving links. The centerpiece of the current effort is the construction of a 250-mile railway between Urumqi in Xinjiang and the Soviet border, where it will link up with a major East-West rail route.[39] An agreement on the project was reached in 1988 and work on the railway is proceeding, but even when completed it will only partially alleviate the bottlenecks hampering trade.

The recent changes in the Soviet trade system, along with serious transportation problems, have contributed to a slowdown in border trade growth in 1989–90,[40] and will likely constrain trade for at least several years. This may not be such a bad thing, however. Raising the rate of contract fulfillment by making sure before contracts are signed that appropriate licenses can be obtained and transportation can be arranged will do more to increase the volume of goods actually exchanged than racking up on paper new records for total trade.

---

[35] SFr4 million = US$2.4 million (1989 IMF exchange rate).
[36] Hong Kong *Zhongguo Tongxun She* in English, 6/20/90; FBIS–CHI–90–120, 6/21/90, p. 5.
[37] Ibid.
[38] "Partners in Austerity," by Deborah Diamond-Kim. *The China Business Review*, May–June 1987, pp. 12–20.
[39] Ibid.
[40] Hong Kong *Zhongguo Tongxun She* in English, 6/20/90; FBIS–CHI–90–120, 6/2/90, p. 5.

VI. Expanding Commercial Links

Since the mid-1980s, the Sino-Soviet economic relationship has again expanded to include other forms of cooperation besides trade. It is important to note, however, that these links are a far cry from the close collaboration that characterized the 1950s Sino-Soviet alliance. Rather, they are part of a network of protocols China has established with many trading partners in recent years. These are intended as much to announce and ratify friendly relations as to promote actual economic interchange.

In 1985, the two countries signed a five-year economic and technological cooperation agreement, the first since the 1950s, outlining a joint construction plan for 33 major industrial projects in China. These include renovations of 17 key facilities built by the Soviets in the 1950s.[41] As of 1990, according to a Chinese source, 13 of the 33 projects had been cancelled; negotiations reportedly continue for another eight; while contracts have been signed for the renovation of the remaining 12 projects, all built with Soviet aid: the Harbin Flax Mill (1952), the largest linen mill in China; the Anshan Steelworks in Liaoning, China's largest iron and steel complex (rebuilt with Soviet aid in the 1950s); the Baotou Steelworks in Inner Mongolia (1950s); the Jiamusi Paper Mill (1954-57), China's largest; the Nancha Timber Hydrolysis Mill in Heilongjiang (1957); the Fushun Aluminum Plant in Liaoning (1954); the Jixian Power Plant (details not available); the Luoyang Bearing Plant in Henan, China's largest (1953); the Wuhan No. 3 Blast Furnace and the Wuhan Aluminum Plant (details not available); and transmission lines in two unspecified power plants, one of which is probably the Xi'an Power Rectifier Plant in Shaanxi (1953).[42]

Work has reportedly begun on at least a few of these projects, including the Harbin flax mill,[43] though some of the other contracted renovations may not actually take place. Soviet technology is not all that attractive to China, whose appetite for the state-of-the-art has been whetted by contact with the West. In addition, the vast amounts of time, money, and cooperation needed to complete these ambitious projects may cause them essentially to collapse under their own weight.

The multi-year agreement also calls for developing new projects. As a result, interest in joint power generation projects, an area of cooperation dating back to 1950, was revived in 1988, when the two sides negotiated a Soviet loan to finance the purchase of Soviet power equipment by the Nanjing Government and the Huaneng International Electric Power Generation Co. According to the 1988 agreement, the USSR would be repaid in unspecified countertrade for two sets of generating equipment to be installed in Nanjing.[44]

A similar countertrade deal was also discussed in 1989 involving the import of a nuclear power plant to be installed in two phases on the coast of Liaoning province.[45] In addition, the South China

---

[41] Beijing in Russian to the USSR, 12/29/88; FBIS–CHI–88–002, 1/4/89, p.12.
[42] Author interview with Zhang Deguang, counselor, Embassy of the PRC in Washington, DC; May 1990.
[43] Hong Kong Liaowang Overseas Edition in Chinese No. 19, 5/8/89, pp. 25–26; FBIS–CHI–89–095, 5/18/89, pp. 28–29.
[44] Ibid.
[45] Hong Kong Agence France Presse, 3/14/90; FBIS–CHI–90–070, 3/14/90, p. 3.

Morning Post in April 1989 reported that China was "likely" to import Soviet nuclear technology for the second atomic plant at Daya Bay in Guangdong Province, using similar countertrade arrangements.[46] Finally, a feasibility study was reportedly completed in mid-1989 for a joint hydroelectric plant to be built on the Amur River. The cost of the 2 billion yuan project would be shared equally and would be the biggest Sino-Soviet joint venture to date.[47] The current status of this project is unclear.

Petroleum development has also been added to the list of recent cooperative projects. In 1988–89 a series of talks took place outlining plans for Chinese assistance in developing Soviet petroleum resources on Sakhalin Island. Under discussion are two 600-km oil pipelines and one natural gas pipeline to be built between Sakhalin and Komsomolsk on the Amur. Natural gas might then be exported from Komsomolsk to China. The Chinese hope to send engineers and manual laborers to help build the oil fields and pipelines.[48]

The Soviets, in turn, are offering assistance on at least one Chinese project, a 135-km liquefied coal pipeline planned for Shanxi Province. Both sides reportedly have completed pre-feasibility studies on the 219 million yuan project, and expected to turn in full-scale studies by mid-1990.[49]

As projects continued to be developed under the first agreement, a second one, covering the 1990–2000 period, was signed during Premier Li Peng's April 1990 Moscow visit. The "Outline on Long-Term Cooperation in the Economic, Scientific, and Technical Fields" encourages cooperation in the nonferrous metals, petrochemicals, natural gas, agriculture, transportation, and public health areas (though no projects were specified in the agreement). In addition to this agreement, Li and Soviet Premier Nikolai Ryzhkov signed five other accords further broadening and defining the economic relationship: an agreement calling for the USSR to extend commodity loans (including rails, timber, trucks, and diesel oil) to China to finance the construction of the Xinjiang-Kazakhstan railway (this was a formal ratification of the accord reached in 1988; the terms call for China to repay the loan through exports of food and industrial products); a memorandum on a loan allowing China to import Soviet power equipment and formalizing the intention to build jointly a new nuclear power plant; an agreement to cooperate in the peaceful exploration of space; a consultation accord between the two foreign ministries; and an agreement that China will offer credit toward the Soviet purchase of Chinese consumer goods.[50]

The consumer-goods credit harks back to the 1950s, when the USSR extended to the Chinese numerous credits for the purchase of industrial equipment, agricultural and consumer goods to help rebuild the war-ravaged economy. These agreements were payable in barter trade.[51] The Xinjiang railway agreement formalized by

[46] *South China Morning Post*, 4/3/89, P. 1; FBIS–CHI–89–064, 4/5/89, pp. 39–40.
[47] *Hong Kong Standard*, 4/19/89, p. 7; FBIS–CHI–89–064, 4/15/89, pp. 39–40.
[48] *The Journal of Commerce*, 1/20/89, p. 7B.
[49] Beijing Xinhua in English, 12/21/89; FBIS–CHI–89–245, p. 5.
[50] Beijing Xinhua in Mandarin, 6/25/90; FBIS–CHI–90–124, 6/27/90, pp. 3–5.
[51] Borisov & Koloslov, 1975.

Li Peng in Moscow is an example of this type of arrangement; in fact, it is actually a 20-year-old plan that was shelved during the 1960s turmoil and revived in the mid-1980s as relations warmed.[52] By contrast, the apparent intention is for the new consumer-goods credit to be repaid in cash—not only that, but in hard currency. At a press conference just before his trip to Moscow, Premier Li emphasized that putting Sino-Soviet trade on a hard-currency, cash basis was necessary in order to bring higher quality goods into the exchange, and to give incentives to more local-level organizations to participate in cross-border trade.[53] The new consumer goods credit is apparently meant to pave the way for cash to completely replace barter as of January 1, 1991.

Local resistance to this central directive will likely derail its implementation, however. A few days after the terms of the consumer goods credit were publicized, a senior Heilongjiang party official publicly criticized the Chinese government's position, terming the plan "unworkable" given the shortage of foreign exchange among trading organizations on both sides.[54] In the same article, a MOFERT official agreed that enforcement of this directive would certainly cause trade to decline, at least in the short term. Given publicized local resistance, the absence of follow-up discussions or implementation directives, and Beijing's continuing emphasis on exports, it seems safe to assume that the relationship will continue on a barter basis for the forseeable future.

While the three commercial agreements under the 1990–2000 protocol are already being carried out, the future of cooperation on other long-term industrial projects and in space is less certain. Rather, agreements in these areas serve to "indicate that China and the Soviet Union have earnestly and practically promoted their good-neighborly relations of cooperation based on the five principles of peaceful coexistence." [55] Li's Moscow visit, the first by a Chinese premier in 24 years, provided the perfect occasion to ratify the new relationship, and the agreements served as appropriate vehicles.

Though large joint power and petroleum projects will take years to negotiate and complete, a host of smaller cooperative projects have already been established in the past two years at the provincial and local level. In June 1988, both countries initialled the "Agreement on the Establishment and Development of Trade and Economic Links Between Union Republics, Ministries, Departments, Amalgamations, and Enterprises of the USSR and Provinces, Autonomous Regions and Cities of the PRC," along with the "Agreement on Principles Governing the Establishment and Operation of Soviet-Chinese Joint Ventures." These two documents laid the groundwork for the formation of joint ventures. Two additional agreements signed in July 1990 at the fifth meeting of the Sino-Soviet Trade, Scientific, Economic, and Technological Cooperation Committee also fostered the growth of joint ventures; one accord "protects and encourages investment" in both countries, and the

---

[52] Diamond-Kim, 1987.
[53] Beijing Xinhua in English, 3/31/90; FBIS–CHI–90–065, 4/4/90, p. 5.
[54] *South China Morning Post*, 4/19/90.
[55] Beijing Xinhua in Mandarin, 6/25/90; FBIS–CHI–90–124, 6/27/90, pp. 3–5.

other is a double-taxation treaty. By April 1990, according to MOFERT, the two countries had signed 95 contracts for cooperative projects (including labor services) and 18 joint venture agreements with a total value of $240 million, and held negotiations on up to 300 other projects in a variety of areas. MOFERT estimates that 95 percent of the agreements are concentrated in border areas and managed directly by enterprises.[56]

Virtually all of the ventures are small-scale manufacturing projects and local service enterprises. The scope and terms of the first Sino-Soviet manufacturing joint venture to officially commence operations, in November 1989, typify many of the cooperative agreements. The Tashkent Thermos Flask Factory, established in the USSR, uses Chinese technology and will be jointly run by Xinjiang and the Soviet side for a term of 10 years.[57]

As might be expected, Heilongjiang's Heihe City took an early lead in establishing joint projects with Soviet partners. By May 1989, Heihe had reportedly concluded 49 joint-venture agreements, including a restaurant, factories for making soft drinks, fiber board, washing machines, and plywood, and a color photograph finishing center, all to be set up in Blagoveshchensk. Joint projects in Heihi include a coffee shop and factories making viscose fiberboard and chopsticks. Three processing projects for leather, wood flooring, and wood fiber, were reported in trial operation.[58]

Highlighting the Soviet craving for consumer electronic goods are several reported agreements establishing factories to make radio and video cassette records in the USSR. For example, the Yancheng Radio Plant in Jiangsu Province and Kargan Oblast of the Kazakhstan SSR will jointly construct a radio-cassette recorder plant using Chinese technology and know-how. The entire output, eventually planned for 100,000 units per year, is destined for the Soviet market.[59] Another agreement to produce video cassettes and recorders was reported in June 1990 between China's aerospace ministry, its subsidiary, the Shenzhen Zhonghang Enterprise Group, and the USSR air ministry. This project will also use Chinese equipment and expertise to produce units for the Soviet market. The Chinese side will be repaid in spare parts for use in spaceflights.[60]

An agreement for what was described as "the most technologically advanced joint venture" to date was signed in August 1990 and was set to open in November 1990 in Tyumen, USSR. The 10-year, $3.4 million venture will produce electric typewriters, using Chinese production equipment and parts, with Russian and English alphabets. The Chinese partners are the Beijing Qidi Computer Technique Developing Corp. and the Harbin Foreign Trade Corp.; their Soviet counterparts are the Commercial Center of Tyumen and the Tobolsk Oil & Chemical Co. All output, planned at 20,000–30,000 units per year, will be sold in the USSR and Eastern Europe.[61]

[56] Beijing Xinhua in English, 4/18/90; FBIS–CHI–90–075, 4/18/90, p. 7.
[57] Hong Kong *Zhongguo Tongxun She* in Chinese, 5/15/89; FBIS–CHI–89–094, 5/17/89, pp. 35.
[58] Beijing Xinhua in English, 6/15/89, FBIS–CHI–89–114, 6/15/89. pp. 3–5.
[59] *China Daily*, 5/13/89, p. 2.
[60] Beijing Xinhua Domestic Service in Chinese, 11/13/89; FBIS–CHI–89–022, 11/20/89, p. 9.
[61] Beijing *Zhongguo Tongxun She* in English, 6/12/90; FBIS–CHI–90–114, 6/12/90, p. 4.

Cooperation in agriculture has mainly taken the form of agreements sending Chinese laborers to work on Soviet farms, but in mid-1989 a joint coffee and tea plantation was established in Hainan Province. The 50–50 venture calls for the the Chinese side to grow, harvest, and process the coffee and tea, while the Soviet side will provide equal value of chemical fertilizer, steel products, and farm machinery.[62] Other agreements for joint farming and fish-processing operations have also been discussed.

Labor transfers have also led to more extensive cooperation in the medical field. Many Chinese specialists in traditional medicine have in recent years been sent to hospitals in the Soviet Far East and Central Asian republics for short periods to provide care and to instruct Soviet doctors in some basic techniques, and in February 1990 a ten-year agreement for a jointly-run hospital was signed by the Dalian Foreign Economic and Trade Corp. and an organization in Uzbekistan city of Gulistan. The 1.5 million ruble facility will be built in Gulistan. The Chinese will provide medical instruments and 20 specialists in traditional medicine each year, while the Soviets will provide the buildings and other installations.[63]

Extensive discussions have taken place concerning cooperation in textile production, where the two countries have complementary capabilities and resources. Chinese expertise in processing, particularly of silk and cotton, is far beyond Soviet capabilities, while the Soviets excel in flax and wool manufacture. China lacks sufficient raw materials to fulfill production capacity, while the USSR is the world's second-largest cotton producer and also boasts enormous supplies of wool, flax, chemical fiber pulp, and even some silkworms.[64] Due to inadequate domestic processing capacity, the Soviet market is starving for textile goods of all types. According to a Chinese source, China's textile exports to the USSR totaled $441 million in 1986, or 30 percent of China's total Soviet exports; $250 million in 1988 and about $220 million in 1989.[65] China hopes that joint cooperation will help boost textile exports to the levels of previous years.

So far, the two sides have discussed setting up a large joint venture in Harbin to process Soviet flax into linen for resale back to the USSR. A feasibility study for the venture was completed in mid-1989.[66] Other plans call for a similar project to be set up in Baotou, Inner Mongolia.[67] Another project under consideration is a jointly-built, Chinese-run silk reeling factory to be set up in the USSR.[68] China is also interested in importing Soviet chemical fiber pulp for processing into rayon viscose, to be resold back to the USSR.[69]

Though the textile industry is highly centralized in both countries, some local cooperation has been achieved. For example, Xinjiang's Shihezi Woolen Mill and a mill in Soviet Kazakhstan re-

[62] Beijing Xinhua in English, 6/8/90; FBIS–CHI–90–111, 6/8/90, p. 4.
[63] Hong Kong *Zhongguo Tongxun She* in Chinese, 4/21/89; FBIS–CHI–89–081, 4/28/89, p. 3.
[64] Beijing Xinhua in English, 2/3/90; FBIS–CHI–90–024, 2/5/90, p. 6.
[65] Ibid.; 7/6/89; FBIS–CHI–89–128, 7/6/89, p. 11.
[66] *China Daily*, 3/28/89, p. 3.
[67] Ibid.
[68] Beijing Xinhua in English, 7/6/89.
[69] Ibid.

portedly established a 5,000-spindle mill in Xinjiang in November 1989. The 26 million yuan, 50–50 joint venture will utilize Soviet machinery and raw materials and Chinese labor, know-how, and certain types of equipment. The venture was expected to begin operations in early 1990.[70]

VII. PROBLEMS IN PARTNERSHIP

For the same reasons bilateral trade is destined to play but a tiny role in each country's economic development, joint investment projects are likely to remain limited in scope, especially compared to the level of investment activity of other foreign countries in both China and the USSR. One reason is that it will not take long for each side to acquire from the other the fairly basic technologies and expertise now needed in such areas as consumer goods production. Furthermore, though even the oldest Sino-Soviet joint ventures have been in operation only for a matter of months, it is not difficult to imagine the wide range of operational difficulties they face. In a decade of experience in China, Western investors have drawn upon vast reserves of ingenuity, technology, and management skills to overcome bureaucratic obstacles, inadequate transportation and energy resources, shortages of quality raw materials, and the lack of skills, initiative, and flexibility of workers accustomed to the "iron rice bowl." And despite fairly rapid progress on the part of the Chinese in responding to Western demands and expectations, the chief obstacle to profitable investment—a nonconvertible currency—is no closer to being resolved than it was 10 years ago. Sino-Soviet projects face these same problems twice over, with neither the experience nor the resources other foreign investors can call upon to deal with them. In view of these obstacles, many of the reported joint-venture agreements are unlikely to make it past the paper stage.

Nevertheless, Sino-Soviet cooperation has the potential, like border trade, to play a fairly significant role on the local level in increasing both sides' experience in identifying markets, evaluating partners, assessing the viability and profitability of projects, dealing with cultural and language barriers in the workplace, and coming up with creative ways to solve problems of sourcing materials and repatriating profits—such as taking payment in diesel engines, for instance. Given the small size and local scope of most Sino-Soviet ventures, they represent a low-risk way for each side to experiment with the opportunites and obstacles of international commerce. China's plans to develop the port of Heihe as a major rail entrepôt for the transshipment of goods from Northeast Asia to Europe,[71] along with Soviet plans to exploit Siberian resources, will both be well-served by the increasing commercial connections and business experience gained by both sides in their struggles to conceive and operate viable joint ventures.

---

[70] *China Daily*, 3/28/89.
[71] Beijing Xinhua in English, 11/11/89; FBIS–CHI–89–115, 11/14/89, pp. 15–16.

VIII. China Perceives a New Threat

The long-term prospects for cooperation are not completely positive, however. The upheaval in China in 1989 has fostered among its leaders an alarmist view of the world, and specifically, of the USSR, whose reforms seem to pose a direct threat to China's tenuous economic and social stability. While a threatening impression of the USSR has never been completely absent from Chinese strategic view, the current version took firmer hold among the Chinese leadership in 1989, when Soviet leader Mikhail Gorbachev visited Beijing to formally renew state-to-state ties. What should have been a triumphal occasion for both countries was marred for Chinese leaders when Gorbachev was praised by the demonstrators in Tiananmen Square for reforming Soviet society through glasnost and perestroika. Gorbachev further enraged the leadership by making public remarks that appeared sympathetic to the students' demands. Later that year, the rapid fall of one after another of East Europe's communist regimes sent shock waves through Beijing—the toppling of Romania's Nicolae Ceaucescu, a personal friend of many Chinese leaders, hit particularly hard—and deepened Chinese suspicion of Gorbachev and his apparent willingness to preside over the demise of Communism. In particular, the Soviet government's abolition in February 1990 of the constitutional guarantee of a "leading role" in society for the Communist Party deeply disturbed the Chinese and further highlighted the ideological divide between Beijing and Moscow.

In an effort to understand how the Soviet reform process could have such widespread and dramatic effects, and to evaluate what the implications might be for China, the Chinese Communist Party sent a fact-finding delegation to the USSR in mid-1989. The delegations's analysis, submitted near the end of the year, made three main points that add up to a triple threat for China. First, the sweeping scope and pace of Soviet reforms, and concurrent efforts to reduce the USSR's image as a global military threat, "has captured the imagination of the world." [72] As a result, China's strategic importance to the world has been correspondingly reduced, and its own decade-long reform program has lost significance. Thus the USSR now overshadows China as a favored recipient of international capital and technology. Noting that "The USSR has richer natural resources, a more solid infrastructure, and a higher level of domestic market than China," the delegation's report expresses fears that because of the reforms, the USSR has become irresistibly appealing to the same Western companies whose technology and resources China would like to attract. The report also notes with alarm that Western funds has been "pouring in" to the Soviet Union over the past two years, and that Western companies have rushed to establish joint ventures.

A second potential threat, according to this analysis, is the Soviet plan to develop Siberia's abundant resources. This would have the dual effect of attracting and absorbing even greater amounts of

---

[72] The quotations and summaries of the delegation's analysis in the following pages are all taken from a translation of the report published in three editions of Hong Kong *Tang Tai* in Chinese: No. 13, 2/90. pp. 35–36; FBIS–CHI–90–040, 2/28/90, pp. 7–9; No. 14, 3/90, pp. 17–18; FBIS–CHI–90–045, 3/7/90, pp. 5–7; No. 15, 3/90, pp.20–21; FBIS–CHI–90–0523, 3/16/90, pp. 6–8.

available international assistance, thus reducing the portion available for China, and enhancing the USSR's economic strength, to China's inevitable detriment. Furthermore, as the Soviet economy develops and becomes integrated with the world economy, China will lose market share abroad.

The successful implementation of perestroika and attraction of Western technology and capital leads, in the delegation's analysis, to a third threat: That the Soviet standard of living will dramatically increase relative to China's, thus exacerbating Chinese popular discontent and causing social instability on a scale that could dwarf the Tiananmen Square demonstrations.

The Chinese response to this perceived threat has several parts. First, extensive criticism of the USSR has been made a priority of the official propaganda machine. The CPC's official directive on criticism of Soviet "revisionism," adopted in February 1990—just days after the Soviet government abolished the constitutional guarantee of the Communist Party's "leading role"—stated that all CPC members must be "thoroughly educated" on the "real nature" of Soviet reforms and how they deviate from the "true" path of socialism. Party members are urged, for example, to study theoretical essays on Soviet revisionism dating back to the 1960s, and to focus on such sources of inspiration as the old Lei Feng campaign.[73] Unlike the strident, public polemics of the 1960s, however, this new campaign is intended exclusively for internal consumption. While the leadership views its position as consistent with the policy of "not interfering with other countries' internal affairs," this is a case of making a virtue out of necessity, since public criticism of Soviet reforms would foster the world's image of a progressive, reformist USSR versus a reactionary, regressive China.[74]

In addition to the propaganda campaign, the Chinese are taking certain steps recommended by the fact-finding delegation to counter the USSR's "aggressive behavior." The report lists four types of measures to accomplish this. The first, "To make good use of China's initiatives in its relations with powers and issues of sensitive regions to check Soviet strategy," essentially means that China should try whenever possible to undermine Soviet interests in Asia and prevent its influence from expanding there. One way to do this would be for China to discourage dialogue between North and South Korea, since friendly relations could clear the way for the USSR to expand economic links with South Korea and thus lead to new export markets and assistance in developing Siberian resources. China could also try to hamper the development of Soviet links with Japan and Taiwan, though these can be less directly influenced.[75]

The second recommendation is "to make longer strides in reform and opening up in China, to shift the international community's focus of attention from the USSR. For example, consideration can be given to adopting major action in spheres that the USSR has not touched upon to date, such as ownership." The Chinese will have to move quickly to outpace the USSR, however, since Gorba-

---

[73] Hong Kong *Cheng Ming* in Chinese, No. 150, 4/1/90, pp. 6–8; FBIS–CHI–90, 4/3/90, pp. 6–9.
[74] Hong Kong Agence France Presse, 2/7/90; FBIS–CHI–90–026; 2/7/90, p. 1.
[75] Hong Kong Tang Tai, Ibid.

chev has stepped up the pace of reform, and as of October 1990 was considering permitting private ownership as part of a radical economic restructuring plan.[76]

The third proposal urges that China "lose no time in utilizing international economic resources ... including large-scale foreign loans and attracting direct foreign investment ..."[77] Time is of the essence here, since the USSR's reforms are fast providing a more attractive economic infrastructure to foreign governments and companies alike. China's loss of substantial sums of promised and hoped-for funds in the wake of the Tiananmen massacre increases the sense of urgency.

The fourth recommendation is for China to "grasp the opportunity" presented by Soviet desire to exploit resources in the Far East "to ease China's basic problems of overpopulation and shortage of raw materials. We may consider initialing an accord with the USSR on long-term supply of raw materials, and providing the USSR with labor. ..."[78] Fearing that Soviet development will outpace China's and reduce future Soviet needs for Chinese materials and manpower, China should try to lock in demand for its resources with long-term agreements.

In view of the threat posed by the USSR's economic and political reforms, the delegation sums up by calling for caution in expanding trade and economic links with the USSR. Guangdong companies in particular are advised to slow the pace of ties with Soviet enterprises. The stipulation that the overall trade relationship should develop "naturally," and not at "excessive speed,"[79] is intended both to ensure that the Soviet economy is not becoming stronger at China's expense, and that local contacts do not lead to the spread of glasnost and perestroika-like ideas in Chinese society.

Chinese fears of being imminently outpaced by Soviet economic development seem extremely far-fetched in the late 1980s, as Soviet citizens riot to protest the lack of basic foodstuffs and cigarettes[80] while Chinese enjoy unprecedented access to a wide variety of non-rationed consumer goods even in the midst of a recession. Yet as the denouement of the Tiananmen Square demonstrations harshly revealed, China's current leadership sees itself and its cause embattled on every side—indeed, there is perhaps no surer evidence of paranoia than the conviction that the Soviet economy presents a threat to any other country other than its own. The Chinese have learned many useful lessons in the past ten years of the open door, however, and as time goes by, perhaps they will also come to see that the "threat" of Soviet economic competition is not as great as it may appear today.

IX. PRAGMATISM WILL PREVAIL

Despite their long-term fears over economic competition and social instability, Chinese leaders nevertheless pragmatically per-

---

[76] Ibid.
[77] Ibid.
[78] Ibid.
[79] Ibid.
[80] "1,000 March on Soviet Party Office and Riot Over Food Shortages," *New York Times*, 8/26/90, p. 5.

ceive the various benefits of today's Sino-Soviet trade ties, and will encourage them to expand in a controlled way by means of government-to-government accords, cooperative infrastructure development, and investment in local projects that transfer needed technology and raw materials to China. Despite their continued commitment, in the face of immensely discouraging odds, to structuring a workable society based on Communist principles, the Chinese have nevertheless learned from a decade of doing business with the West—and in particular, from the aftermath of the Tiananmen crisis—to allow for a more flexible relationship between politics and trade. While Western governments condemned the Chinese leadership for the massacre of demonstrators, their companies and financial institutions have continued to seek business in China— and continued to profit. Turning this lesson to China's own advantage, leaders in Beijing realize that sharp political and ideological differences with Gorbachev's government need not affect mutually beneficial commercial ties between the two countries. This new awareness is the chief reason to expect continued slow expansion of the Sino-Soviet economic relationship. It also gives reason to hope that China will continue, in fits and starts, on the path of economic reform that must eventually lead to profound and positive social change as well.

APPENDIX

Date	Swiss franc value	US$ value
1981	1.964	1
1982	2.030	1
1983	2.099	1
1984	2.349	1
1985	2.457	1
1986	1.789	1
1987	1.491	1
1988	1.463	1
1989	1.635	1
1990:		
Jan	1.515	1
Feb	1.487	1
Mar	1.511	1
Apr	1.487	1
May	1.417	1
Jun	1.425	1
Jul	1.393	1

Source: International Monetary Fund

Date	Chinese yuan value	US$ value
1981–85	1.3	1
Dec 1985	3.2	1
Dec 1986	3.7	1
Dec 1989	4.7	1

Source: US-China Business Council

The ruble exchange rate is fixed against a market basket of currencies including the dollar, yen, and deutschemark, and has averaged 1 : US $1.60 in recent years.

Source: PlanEcon, Washington, DC.

○

INDEX